ALL · IN · ONE

CompTIA A+®
Certification

EXAM GUIDE

(Exams 220-1001 & 220-1002)

ABOUT THE AUTHOR

Michael Meyers is the industry's leading authority on CompTIA Core certifications (ITF+, A+, Network+, and Security+). He is the president and founder of Total Seminars, LLC, a major provider of computer and network repair seminars for thousands of organizations throughout the world, and a member of CompTIA.

Mike has written numerous popular textbooks, including the best-selling *Mike Meyers' CompTIA A+® Guide to Managing & Troubleshooting PCs*, *Mike Meyers' CompTIA Network+® Guide to Managing and Troubleshooting Networks*, and *Mike Meyers' CompTIA Security+® Certification Guide*.

About the Contributor

Scott Jernigan wields a mighty red pen as Editor in Chief for Total Seminars. With a Master of Arts degree in Medieval History, Scott feels as much at home in the musty archives of London as he does in the crisp IPS glow of Total Seminars' Houston HQ. After fleeing a purely academic life, he dove headfirst into IT, working as an instructor, editor, and writer.

Scott has written, edited, and contributed to dozens of books on computer literacy, hardware, operating systems, networking, security, and certification, including *Computer Literacy—Your Ticket to IC³ Certification*, and is co-author, with Mike Meyers, of *Mike Meyers' CompTIA Security+ Certification Guide*.

Scott has taught computer classes all over the United States, including stints at the United Nations in New York and the FBI Academy in Quantico. Practicing what he preaches, Scott is a CompTIA A+, CompTIA Network+, and CompTIA Security+ certified technician, a Microsoft Certified Professional, a Microsoft Office User Specialist, and Certiport Internet and Computing Core Certified.

About the Technical Editor

Mark Edward Soper has worked with computers and related technologies for over 30 years, and specializes in technology education through training, writing, and public speaking. He is the author or co-author of 40 books on technology topics ranging from CompTIA A+ certification to Microsoft Windows, networking, and troubleshooting. Mark has also taught these and other topics across the United States.

Mark has CompTIA A+ and Microsoft MOS – Microsoft Excel 2013 certifications, and currently teaches Microsoft Office classes for University of Southern Indiana and IvyTech Community College. Mark blogs at www.markesoper.com.

ALL ▪ IN ▪ ONE

CompTIA A+®

Certification

EXAM GUIDE
Tenth Edition

(Exams 220-1001 & 220-1002)

Mike Meyers

Mc
Graw
Hill
Education

New York   Chicago   San Francisco
Athens   London   Madrid   Mexico City
Milan   New Delhi   Singapore   Sydney   Toronto

Library of Congress Cataloging-in-Publication Data

Names: Meyers, Mike, 1961- author. | Jernigan, Scott, author.
Title: CompTIA A+ certification all-in-one exam guide, (exams 220-1001 &
  220-1002) / Mike Meyers and Scott Jernigan.
Description: Tenth edition. | San Francisco: McGraw Hill Education, [2019]
Identifiers: LCCN 2019007718 | ISBN 9781260454031 (hard cover : alk. paper)
Subjects: LCSH: Microcomputers—Maintenance and repair—Examinations—Study
  guides. | Computer technicians—Certification—Study guides.
Classification: LCC TK7885.54 .M4834 2019 | DDC 621.39/16076—dc23 LC record available at
https://lccn.loc.gov/2019007718

McGraw-Hill Education books are available at special quantity discounts to use as premiums and sales promotions, or for use in corporate training programs. To contact a representative, please visit the Contact Us pages at www.mhprofessional.com.

CompTIA A+® Certification All-in-One Exam Guide, Tenth Edition (Exams 220-1001 & 220-1002)

1 2 3 4 5 6 7 8 9   LWI   23 22 21 20 19

ISBN   978-1-260-45403-1
MHID   1-260-45403-7

Sponsoring Editor	**Technical Editor**	**Production Supervisor**
Tim Green	Mark Edward Soper	James Kussow
Editorial Supervisor	**Copy Editor**	**Composition**
Janet Walden	Bill McManus	Cenveo® Publishing Services
Project Editor	**Proofreader**	**Illustration**
Laura Stone	Richard Camp	Cenveo Publishing Services
Acquisitions Coordinator	**Indexer**	**Art Director, Cover**
Claire Yee	Jack Lewis	Jeff Weeks

To my grandson, William Siegmund Kelly.
Can't wait to build our first system together!

CONTENTS AT A GLANCE

CONTENTS

ACKNOWLEDGMENTS

I'd like to acknowledge the many people who contributed their talents to make this book possible:

To my in-house Editor in Chief, Scott Jernigan: I couldn't have done it without you, amigo. Truthfully, has there ever been a better combo than a wizard and a paladin?

To my Executive Editor, Timothy Green: Thank you for another great book together, Tim! (I admire the new gray hairs, by the way, most likely sprouted because of my finely honed skill for missing deadlines. . . .) In all seriousness, working with you is and has been a true joy.

To Laura Stone, project editor: Laura, thank you, thank you, thank you for abandoning your children to come work with me again! [Readers: Author is joking about the "abandonment" part. Laura is a dedicated and excellent mother. —Ed.] I've enjoyed many editors over the years, but you are the *crème de la crème*. *Santé*!

To Mark Edward Soper, technical editor: Fantastic job, Mark! Very much a pleasure to work with you. The book is much better because of your input and insight.

To Bill McManus, copy editor: Bill, words can't express what an awesome editing job you did on this edition. Your skill continues to amaze me and makes my words so much better. Thank you!

To Michael Smyer, tech guru and photographer: Way to keep me on my toes, Michael, challenging many points big and small. The book is far better because of it, even if I *still don't like losing arguments*. Great photos as well throughout the book, thanks to your genius behind the lens. Cheers!

To Dave Rush, technologist: Love, love, love arguing technology with you, Dave. And your research skills blow me away! Thanks for all the great work in this edition.

To Travis Everett, Internet guru and writer: Great contributions on this edition, Travis, from writing and research to copyedit and page proofing. Looking forward to many more.

To Dudley Lehmer, my partner at Total Seminars: As always, thanks for keeping the ship afloat while I got to play on this book!

To Claire Yee, acquisitions coordinator at McGraw-Hill Education: Always watch out for the quiet voice and polite smile. . . . Who knew that whips cracked in San Francisco could sting so much all the way to Houston? Thanks for shepherding this project through in a timely and relatively painless fashion.

To Janet Walden, editorial supervisor at McGraw-Hill Education: It was a joy to work with you again. I couldn't have asked for a better team. In fact, I asked for the best team and got exactly what I wanted!

To Richard Camp, proofreader: Awesome work!

INTRODUCTION

The field of computing has changed dramatically over the decades since the introduction of the IBM Personal Computer (PC) in 1981, and so has the job of the people who build, maintain, and troubleshoot computers. A *PC tech* for many years serviced IBM-compatible desktop systems running a Microsoft operating system (OS), such as DOS or, later, Windows. All a tech needed to service an early Windows machine was a Phillips-head screwdriver and knowledge of the hardware and OS.

An IBM-compatible PC, circa 1989

The personal computing landscape today includes a zillion devices in all shapes, sizes, and purposes. How many computing devices do you interact with every day? Seriously, count them.

Here's my typical contact in a day. My smartphone alarm clock awakens me in the morning. I use either a Windows or macOS desktop to check the morning news and my e-mail by connecting to other computers over the Internet. Or, if the family is on both systems, I'll retreat to the study with a laptop running Ubuntu Linux to do the same tasks. At the gym, my smart watch keeps track of my exercises and my heart rate. The computer in my car handles navigation and traffic reports for my daily commute. At the office I'm literally surrounded by dozens of computing devices, because everyone has a desktop or laptop computer, a tablet, a smartphone, plus any number of wearable devices.

We're all PCs!

Someone needs to set up, manage, maintain, and troubleshoot all of these devices. Because you're reading this book, I'm guessing that *you* are that someone. You're going to need a lot of knowledge about many systems to be a modern personal computer technician. A modern *PC tech*, therefore, works with many devices running many different systems. Almost everything interconnects as well, and a PC tech makes that connection happen.

NOTE This book uses the term "personal computer" and the initials "PC" generically to refer to any kind of personal computing device. PCs here mean things that techs interact with, can set up, and repair.

This book teaches you everything you need to know to become a great tech. It might seem like a lot of information at first, but I'll show you how each system functions and interacts, so you learn the patterns they all follow. At some point in the process of reading this book and working on computers, it will all click into place. You've got this!

Along the way, you'll pick up credentials that prove your skill to employers and clients. The rest of this chapter explains those credentials and the steps you need to take to gain them.

CompTIA A+ Certification

Nearly every profession has some criteria that you must meet to show your competence and ability to perform at a certain level. Although the way this works varies widely from one profession to another, all of them will at some point make you take an exam or series of exams. Passing these exams proves that you have the necessary skills to work at a certain level in your profession, whether you're an aspiring plumber, teacher, barber, or lawyer.

If you successfully pass these exams, the organization that administers them grants you *certification*. You receive some piece of paper or pin or membership card that you can show to potential clients or employers. This certification gives those potential clients or employers a level of confidence that you can do what you say you can do. Without this certification, either you will not find suitable work in that profession or no one will trust you to do the work.

Modern PC techs attain the *CompTIA A+ certification*, the essential credential that shows competence in the modern field of *information technology (IT)*, a fancy way of saying *computing technology plus all the other stuff needed to connect and support computers.* CompTIA A+ is an industry-wide, vendor-neutral certification program developed and sponsored by the *Computing Technology Industry Association (CompTIA)*. You achieve this certification by taking two computer-based exams consisting of multiple-choice and performance-based questions. The tests cover what technicians should know after 12 months of hands-on work on personal computing devices, either from a job or as a student in the lab. CompTIA A+ certification enjoys wide recognition throughout the computer industry. To date, more than 1,000,000 technicians have become CompTIA A+ certified, making it the most popular of all IT certifications.

Who Is CompTIA?

CompTIA is a nonprofit industry trade association based in Oakbrook Terrace, Illinois. It consists of over 20,000 members in 102 countries. You'll find CompTIA offices in such diverse locales as Amsterdam, Dubai, Johannesburg, Tokyo, and São Paulo.

CompTIA provides a forum for people in these industries to network (as in meeting people), represents the interests of its members to the government, and provides certifications for many aspects of the computer industry. CompTIA sponsors CompTIA A+, CompTIA Network+, CompTIA Security+, and other certifications. CompTIA works hard to watch the IT industry and constantly looks to provide new certifications to meet the ongoing demand from its membership. Check out the CompTIA Web site at www .comptia.org for details on the other certifications you can obtain from CompTIA.

CompTIA began offering CompTIA A+ certification back in 1993. When it debuted, the IT industry largely ignored CompTIA A+ certification. Since that initial stutter, however, the CompTIA A+ certification has grown to become the de facto requirement for entrance into the PC industry. Many companies require CompTIA A+ certification for all of their PC support technicians, and the CompTIA A+ certification is widely recognized both in the United States and internationally.

The Path to Other Certifications

Most IT companies—big and small—see CompTIA A+ certification as the entry point to IT. Where you go next depends on a lot of things, such as your interests and the needs of your organization. Let's look at other CompTIA certifications first and then explore vendor-specific options from Microsoft and Cisco.

CompTIA Core Certifications

CompTIA A+ is part of the CompTIA *Core* certifications. Many techs flow from A+ to the others in the Core before specializing. The Core consists of four certifications:

- CompTIA IT Fundamentals (ITF+)
- CompTIA A+ (1001 is called *Core 1*; 1002 is called *Core 2*)
- CompTIA Network+
- CompTIA Security+

CompTIA calls the A+ exams the Core Series (Core 1 and Core 2) to note the two exams.

CompTIA ITF+ covers essentials of computer literacy, such as everything any modern worker needs to know just to function. That includes information about computing device types, what you can do with computers, how networks work, and basic security. If you're already on CompTIA A+, you don't need to backtrack to ITF+. It's good to recommend for newbies, though, as ITF+ will fill in a lot of gaps for people.

CompTIA Network+ continues the good work you started in the CompTIA A+ networking sections. We live in an interconnected world. Techs need to know networking inside and out to handle jobs at bigger organizations. Getting Network+ certified proves your skills as a network tech, including your understanding of network hardware, infrastructure, installation, and troubleshooting. Network+ is the next logical step after A+.

Similarly, *CompTIA Security+* picks up from the network security sections in both A+ and Network+, taking you much deeper into how to secure networks against attacks and best practices for every security-conscious organization. I recommend taking Security+ after Network+; this rounds out your essential skill set all the way up to enterprise tech.

CompTIA Specialty Certifications

CompTIA offers several tracks to pursue post–Core certifications. These offer either specialization in an IT subfield or unique skills measured. Let me explain the Infrastructure Pathway, Cybersecurity Pathway, and Professional Skills tracks.

NOTE For more information about the CompTIA certification pathway and all its certifications, go here:

https://certification.comptia.org/certifications/which-certification

Moving to the *Infrastructure Pathway* means turning to the machines and operating systems that beat at the heart of enterprise organizations. There are three certifications in this series:

- CompTIA Linux+
- CompTIA Server+
- CompTIA Cloud+

Many organizations rely on Linux-powered servers to accomplish much of the dedicated hardware tasks. The servers and server infrastructure require specialized knowledge. As much of the industry is moving to cloud-based computing, understanding how to take an organization there successfully is increasingly important for IT professionals.

The *Cybersecurity Pathway* goes deep into the Dark Arts of network security—how to protect *against* bad people, not how to be a successful criminal mastermind—with three certifications:

- CySA+
- Pentest+
- CASP+

These certifications show that you know your skills at analyzing a network of any size, can test for vulnerabilities, and can harden the network dramatically. You can leverage all the information learned in the Core certifications, using it as the foundation for becoming a security guru.

The *Professional Skills* series offers three exams, but they're geared to unique skillsets used every day in IT:

- Project+
- Cloud Essentials
- CTT+

Project management is wildly important in managing big IT . . . projects. Project managers use this certification to show their credentials. Cloud Essentials is all about what you—not the IT hero, but the business manager—need to know about cloud computing. CTT+ is for people like me, a certification that shows you know how to teach IT skills to adults.

None of the Professional Skills certifications seem obvious or logical to pursue after the Core certifications, but they're situational. If, for example, you find yourself in a position where getting project management credentials will greatly benefit you and your organization, Project+ makes a lot of sense.

Microsoft Technical Certifications

Microsoft operating systems control a huge portion of all installed networks, and those networks need qualified support people to make them run. Pursuing Microsoft's series of certifications for networking professionals is a natural next step after completing the CompTIA certifications. They offer a whole slew of tracks and exams, ranging from specializations in Windows 10 to numerous *Microsoft Certified Solutions Expert (MCSE)* certifications and beyond. You can find more details on the Microsoft Learning Web site:

www.microsoft.com/learning

Cisco Certification

Cisco routers pretty much run the Internet and most intranets in the world. A *router* is a networking device that controls and directs the flow of information over networks, such as e-mail messages, Web browsing, and so on. Cisco provides multiple levels of IT certification for folks who want to show their skills at handling Cisco products, such as the *Cisco Certified Network Associate (CCNA)*, plus numerous specialty certifications. See the Cisco IT Certification Web site here for more details:

www.cisco.com/web/learning/certifications

CompTIA A+ Objectives

CompTIA splits A+ certification into two exams: *CompTIA A+ 220-1001* and *CompTIA A+ 220-1002*. It's common to refer to these two exams as the "2019" exams, but CompTIA is also now referring to them as Core 1 and Core 2.

Although you may take either of the two exams first, I recommend taking 220-1001 followed by 220-1002. The 220-1001 exam concentrates on understanding terminology and technology, how to do fundamental tasks such as upgrading RAM, and basic network and mobile device support. The 220-1002 exam builds on the first exam, concentrating on operating system support, advanced configuration, and troubleshooting scenarios.

Both of the exams are extremely practical, with little or no interest in theory, aside from troubleshooting. All questions are multiple-choice, simulation, or "click on the right part of the picture" questions. The following is an example of the type of questions you will see on the exams:

Your laser printer is printing blank pages. Which item should you check first?

A. Printer drivers

B. Toner cartridge

C. Printer settings

D. Paper feed

The correct answer is B, the toner cartridge. You can make an argument for any of the others, but common sense (and skill as a PC technician) tells you to check the simplest possibility first.

The 2019 exams use a regular test format in which you answer a set number of questions and are scored based on how many correct answers you give. CompTIA makes changes and tweaks over time, so always check the CompTIA Web site before final preparation for the exams. These exams have no more than 90–100 questions each.

Be aware that CompTIA may add new questions to the exams at any time to keep the content fresh. The subject matter covered by the exams won't change, but new questions may be added periodically at random intervals. This policy puts strong emphasis on understanding concepts and having solid PC-tech knowledge rather than on trying to memorize specific questions and answers that may have been on the tests in the past.

No book or Web resource will have all the "right answers" because those answers change constantly. Luckily for you, however, this book not only teaches you what steps to follow in a particular case, but also explains how to be a knowledgeable tech who understands *why* you're doing those steps. That way, when you encounter a new problem (or test question), you can work out the answer. This will help you pass the exams and function as a master tech.

Windows-Centric

The CompTIA A+ exams cover six different operating systems and many versions within each OS. When you review the objectives a little later in this section, though, you'll see that the majority of content focuses on the Microsoft Windows operating systems you would expect to find on a PC at a workstation or in a home. The exams cover a specific and limited scope of questions on macOS, Linux, Chrome OS, iOS, and Android. You might even get a question on Windows Phone.

Objectives in the exams cover the following operating systems:

- Windows 7 Starter, Windows 7 Home Premium, Windows 7 Professional, Windows 7 Ultimate, Windows 7 Enterprise
- Windows 8, Windows 8 Pro, Windows 8 Enterprise
- Windows 8.1, Windows 8.1 Pro, Windows 8.1 Enterprise
- Windows 10 Home, Windows 10 Pro, Windows 10 Enterprise
- macOS
- Linux
- Chrome OS
- iOS
- Android

Try This!   Recommending an OS

Imagine this scenario. One of your first clients wants to upgrade her computing gear and doesn't know which way to go. It's up to you to make a recommendation. This is a great way to assess your knowledge at the start of your journey into CompTIA A+ certification, so try this!

Open a Web browser on a computer or smartphone and browse to my favorite tech store, Newegg (www.newegg.com). Scan through their computer systems. What operating systems seem to be most common? What can you get from reading reviews of, say, Chrome OS vs. Windows 10? Do they sell any Apple products?

Don't get too wrapped up in this exercise. It's just a way to ease you into the standard research we techs do all the time to stay current. We'll revisit this exercise in later chapters so you can gauge your comfort and knowledge level over time.

Exam 220–1001

The questions on the CompTIA A+ 220-1001 exam fit into one of five domains. The number of questions for each domain is based on the percentages shown in the following table.

Domain (Exam 220-1001)	Percentage
1.0 Mobile Devices	14%
2.0 Networking	20%
3.0 Hardware	27%
4.0 Virtualization and Cloud Computing	12%
5.0 Hardware and Network Troubleshooting	27%

The 220-1001 exam tests your knowledge of computer components, expecting you to be able to identify just about every common device on PCs, including variations within device types. Here's a list:

- Hard drives
- Optical drives
- Solid-state drives (SSDs)
- Motherboards
- Power supplies
- CPUs
- RAM
- Monitors
- Input devices, such as keyboards, mice, and touchscreens
- Video and multimedia cards
- Network and modem cards
- Cables and connectors
- Heat sinks, fans, and liquid cooling systems
- Laptops and mobile devices
- Printers and multifunction devices
- Scanners
- Network switches, cabling, and wireless adapters
- Biometric devices
- Virtualization
- Cloud computing

The 220-1001 exam tests your ability to install, configure, and maintain all the hardware technology involved in a personal computer. You need to be able to install and set up a hard drive, for example, and configure devices in Windows 7, Windows 8, Windows 8.1, and Windows 10. You have to understand device drivers.

The 220-1001 exam tests you on mobile devices. While the smartphone and tablet market covers an impossibly wide array of hardware and software, the 220-1001 exam focuses on Apple iOS and Google Android devices (though you might get a question on Google Chrome OS or Windows Phone). You'll need to know how to interact with the hardware and software.

The 220-1001 exam tests extensively on networking. You need to know how to set up a typical local area network (LAN), for example, understanding cabling standards, network protocols, and Windows configuration.

The 220-1001 exam will quiz you on cloud computing and virtualization technologies. You'll need to know about available cloud services such as online storage and applications only available via the Internet. You'll get asked how to set up and maintain virtual machines in a network environment.

The 220-1001 exam requires you to know a lot about hardware and network troubleshooting. You'll get questions, for example, on how to fix a network failure.

Exam 220-1002

The CompTIA A+ 220-1002 exam covers four domains. This table lists the domains and the percentage of questions dedicated to each domain.

Domain (Exam 220-1002)	Percentage
1.0 Operating Systems	27%
2.0 Security	24%
3.0 Software Troubleshooting	26%
4.0 Operational Procedures	23%

The 220-1002 exam covers the configuration, repair, and troubleshooting of operating systems—primarily Microsoft Windows, but you'll also get questions on Apple macOS, various Linux distributions, and Google Chrome OS. You have to know your way around Windows and understand the tasks involved in updating, upgrading, and installing Windows 7, Windows 8, Windows 8.1, and Windows 10. You need to know the standard diagnostic tools available in Windows so that you can fix problems and work with higher-level techs. Make sure you know Windows; probably a quarter of the questions are going to challenge you on this.

You need to know your way around the Linux and macOS interfaces. Plus, the 220-1002 exam tests you on accessing and properly using various tech tools for running maintenance, backup, and so forth. The exam goes into lots of detail on iOS and Android configuration, such as setting up e-mail and securing the devices. But it's not just mobile devices . . .

In general, security is a big topic on the 220-1002 exam. You need to know quite a bit about computer security, from physical security (door locks to retinal scanners), to knowledge of security threats (malware and viruses), to the ways in which to secure an individual computer. This also includes coverage of how to recycle and dispose of computer gear properly.

You'll also be tested on methods for securing networks. You'll need to know how to access a small office/home office (SOHO) router or wireless access point and configure that device to protect your network.

Additionally, this exam puts a lot of emphasis on operational procedures, such as safety and environmental issues, communication, and professionalism. You need to understand how to avoid hazardous situations. The exam tests your ability to communicate effectively with customers and coworkers. You need to understand professional behavior and demonstrate that you have tact, discretion, and respect for others and their property.

The Path to Certification

You become CompTIA A+ certified, in the simplest sense, by taking and passing two computer-based exams. There are no prerequisites for taking the CompTIA A+ certification exams (although there's an assumption of computer literacy, whether or not you have one of the computer literacy certifications). There is no required training course and no training materials to buy. You *do* have to pay a testing fee for each of the two exams. You pay your testing fees, go to a local testing center, and take the tests. You immediately know whether you have passed or failed. By passing both exams, you become CompTIA A+ certified.

To stay certified, every three years you'll need to either retake the exam or perform sufficient continuing education as specified by CompTIA.

Retaking the exams isn't that hard to understand, but the continuing education requirement is a bit more complex. Instead of trying to explain it all here, please review CompTIA's documentation:

https://certification.comptia.org/continuing-education

Most importantly, if you pursue the continuing education path, you'll need to earn 20 continuing education units (CEUs) each three-year period to renew your CompTIA A+ certification. How do you earn these CEUs? You can participate in industry events and seminars, complete a presentation, participate in IT training, teach a course, or earn another higher-level certification. The number of CEUs that you earn by completing each of these requirements varies, and each requires that you submit documentation to CompTIA for review.

Finding a Testing Center

Pearson VUE administers the CompTIA A+ testing at over 5000 testing centers in 165 countries. You may take the exams at any testing center. You can select the closest training center and schedule your exams right from the comfort of your favorite Web browser by going to the Pearson VUE Web site:

www.vue.com

Alternatively, in the United States and Canada, call Pearson VUE at 877-551-PLUS (7587) to schedule the exams and to locate the nearest testing center. International customers can find a list of Pearson VUE international contact numbers for various regions of the world on their Web site here:

www.pearsonvue.com/comptia/contact/

You must pay for the exam when you call to schedule. Be prepared to sit on hold for a while. Have your Social Security number (or international equivalent) and a credit card ready when you call. Pearson VUE will be glad to invoice you, but you won't be able to take the exam until they receive full payment.

Pearson VUE will accommodate any special needs, although this may limit your selection of testing locations.

Exam Costs

The cost of the exam depends on whether you work for a CompTIA member or not. At this writing, the cost for non-CompTIA members is $219 (U.S.) for each exam. International prices vary, but you can check the CompTIA Web site for international pricing. Of course, the prices are subject to change without notice, so always check the CompTIA Web site for current pricing.

Very few people pay full price for the exam. Virtually every organization that provides CompTIA A+ training and testing also offers discount *vouchers*. You buy a discount voucher and then use the voucher number instead of a credit card when you schedule the exam. Vouchers are sold per exam, so you'll need two vouchers to take the two CompTIA A+ exams. Total Seminars is one place to get discount vouchers. You can call Total Seminars at 800-446-6004 or 281-922-4166, or get vouchers via the Web site: www.totalsem .com. No one should ever pay full price for CompTIA A+ exams.

How to Pass the CompTIA A+ Exams

CompTIA designed the A+ exams to test the knowledge of a technician with only 12 months of experience, so keep it simple! The exams aren't interested in your ability to overclock DDR4 CAS latency in system setup or whether you can explain the differences between Intel and AMD chipsets. Think in terms of practical knowledge and standards. Read this book, do whatever works for you to memorize the key concepts and procedures, take the practice exams on the media accompanying this book, review any topics you miss, and you should pass with no problem.

 NOTE Those of you who just want more knowledge in managing and troubleshooting PCs can follow the same strategy as certification-seekers. Think in practical terms and work with the PC as you go through each chapter.

Some of you may be in or just out of school, so studying for exams is nothing novel. But if you haven't had to study for and take an exam in a while, or if you think maybe you could use some tips, you may find the next section valuable. It lays out a proven strategy for preparing to take and pass the CompTIA A+ exams. Try it. It works.

Obligate Yourself The very first step you should take is to schedule yourself for the exams. Have you ever heard the old adage, "Heat and pressure make diamonds?" Well, if you don't give yourself a little "heat," you'll end up procrastinating and delay taking the exams, possibly forever. Do yourself a favor. Using the following information, determine how much time you'll need to study for the exams, and then call Pearson VUE or visit their Web site and schedule the exams accordingly. Knowing the exams are coming up makes it much easier to put down the game controller and crack open the book. You can schedule an exam as little as a few weeks in advance, but if you schedule an exam and can't take it at the scheduled time, you must reschedule at least a day in advance or you'll lose your money.

Set Aside the Right Amount of Study Time After helping thousands of techs get their CompTIA A+ certification, we at Total Seminars have developed a pretty good feel for the amount of study time needed to pass the CompTIA A+ certification exams. The following table provides an estimate to help you plan how much study time you must commit to the CompTIA A+ certification exams. Keep in mind that these are averages. If you're not a great student or if you're a little on the nervous side, add 10%; if you're a fast learner or have a good bit of computer experience, you may want to reduce the figures.

To use the table, just circle the values that are most accurate for you and add them up to get your estimated total hours of study time.

Tech Task	Amount of Experience			
	None	**Once or Twice**	**Every Now and Then**	**Quite a Bit**
Installing an adapter card	6	4	2	1
Installing and configuring hard drives and SSDs	10	8	6	2
Connecting a computer to the Internet	8	6	4	2
Installing printers and multifunction devices	16	8	4	2
Installing RAM	8	6	4	2
Installing CPUs	8	7	5	3
Repairing printers	6	5	4	3
Repairing boot problems	8	7	7	5
Repairing portable computers	8	6	4	2
Configuring mobile devices	4	3	2	1
Building complete systems	12	10	8	6
Using the command line	8	8	6	4
Installing and optimizing Windows	10	8	6	4
Using Windows 7	6	6	4	2

Tech Task	Amount of Experience			
	None	Once or Twice	Every Now and Then	Quite a Bit
Using Windows 8/8.1	8	6	4	2
Using Windows 10	8	6	4	2
Using Linux	8	6	6	3
Using macOS	8	4	4	2
Configuring NTFS, Users, and Groups	6	4	3	2
Configuring a wireless network	6	5	3	2
Configuring a software firewall	6	4	2	1
Using cloud services	3	2	2	1
Removing malware	4	3	2	0
Using OS diagnostic tools	8	8	6	4
Installing and configuring virtual machines	6	4	2	1

To that value, add hours based on the number of months of direct, professional experience you have had supporting PCs, as shown in the following table.

Months of Direct, Professional Experience	Hours to Add to Your Study Time
0	50
Up to 6	30
6 to 12	10
Over 12	0

A total neophyte often needs roughly 240 hours of study time. An experienced tech shouldn't need more than 60 hours.

Total hours for you to study: _____.

A Strategy for Study   Now that you have a feel for how long it's going to take to prepare for the exams, you're ready to develop a study strategy. I suggest a strategy that has worked for others who've come before you, whether they were experienced techs or total newbies.

This book accommodates the different study agendas of these two groups of students. The first group is experienced techs who already have strong PC experience but need to be sure they're ready to be tested on the specific subjects covered by the CompTIA A+ exams. The second group is those with little or no background in the computer field. These techs can benefit from a more detailed understanding of the history and concepts that underlie modern PC technology, to help them remember the specific subject matter information they must know for the exams. I'll use the shorthand terms Old Techs and New Techs for these two groups. If you're not sure which group you fall into, pick a few chapters and go through some end-of-chapter questions. If you score less than 70%, go the New Tech route.

I have broken most of the chapters into four distinct parts:

- **Historical/Conceptual**   Topics that are not on the CompTIA A+ exams but will help you understand more clearly what is on the CompTIA A+ exams
- **1001**   Topics that clearly fit under the CompTIA A+ 220-1001 exam domains
- **1002**   Topics that clearly fit under the CompTIA A+ 220-1002 exam domains
- **Beyond A+**   More advanced issues that probably will not be on the CompTIA A+ exams—yet

The beginning of each of these parts is clearly marked with a large banner that looks like this:

Historical/Conceptual

Those of you who fall into the Old Tech group may want to skip everything except the 1001 and 1002 parts in each chapter. After reading the sections in those parts, jump immediately to the questions at the end of the chapter. The end-of-chapter questions concentrate on information in the 1001 and 1002 sections. If you run into problems, review the Historical/Conceptual sections in that chapter. Note that you may need to skip back to previous chapters to get the Historical/Conceptual information you need for later chapters.

After going through every chapter as described, Old Techs can move directly to testing their knowledge by using the free practice exams on the media that accompanies the book. Once you start scoring above 90%, you're ready to take the exams. If you're a New Tech—or if you're an Old Tech who wants the full learning experience this book can offer—start by reading the book, *the whole book*, as though you were reading a novel, from page one to the end without skipping around. Because so many computer terms and concepts build on each other, skipping around greatly increases the odds that you will become confused and end up closing the book and firing up your favorite game. Not that I have anything against games, but unfortunately that skill is *not* useful for the CompTIA A+ exams!

Your goal on this first read is to understand concepts, the *whys* behind the *hows*. Having a PC nearby as you read is helpful so you can stop and inspect the PC to see a piece of hardware or how a particular concept manifests in the real world. As you read about hard drives, for example, inspect the cables. Do they look like the ones in the book? Is there a variation? Why? It is imperative that you understand why you are doing something, not just how to do it on one particular system under one specific set of conditions. Neither the exams nor real life as a PC tech will work that way.

If you're reading this book as part of a managing and troubleshooting PCs class rather than a certification-prep course, I highly recommend going the New Tech route, even if you have a decent amount of experience. The book contains a lot of details that can trip you up if you focus only on the test-specific sections of the chapters. Plus, your program might stress historical and conceptual knowledge as well as practical, hands-on skills.

The CompTIA A+ certification exams assume that you have basic user skills. The exams really try to trick you with questions on processes that you may do every day and not think much about. Here's a classic: "To move a file from the C:\DATA folder to the D:\ drive using File Explorer, what key must you hold down while dragging the file?" If you can answer that without going to your keyboard and trying a few likely keys, you're better than most techs! In the real world, you can try a few wrong answers before you hit on the right one, but for the exams, you have to *know* it. Whether Old Tech or New Tech, make sure you are proficient at user-level Windows skills, including the following:

- Recognizing all the components of the standard Windows desktop (Start menu, notification area, etc.)
- Manipulating windows—resizing, moving, and so on
- Creating, deleting, renaming, moving, and copying files and folders within Windows
- Understanding file extensions and their relationship with program associations
- Using common keyboard shortcuts/hotkeys
- Installing, running, and closing a Windows application

When you do your initial read-through, you may be tempted to skip the Historical/Conceptual sections—don't! Understanding the history and technological developments behind today's personal computing devices helps you understand why they work—or don't work—the way they do. Basically, I'm passing on to you the kind of knowledge you might get by apprenticing yourself to an older, experienced PC tech.

After you've completed the first read-through, go through the book again, this time in textbook mode. If you're an Old Tech, start your studying here. Try to cover one chapter at a sitting. Concentrate on the 1001 and 1002 sections. Get a highlighter and mark the phrases and sentences that bring out major points. Be sure you understand how the pictures and illustrations relate to the concepts being discussed.

Once you feel you have a good grasp of the material in the book, you can check your knowledge by using the practice exams included on the media accompanying this book. You can take these in Practice mode or Final mode. In Practice mode, you can use the Assistance window to get a helpful hint for the current questions, use the Reference feature to find the chapter that covers the question, check your answer for the question, and see an explanation of the correct answer. In Final mode, you answer all the questions and receive an exam score at the end, just like the real thing. You can also adjust the number of questions on a Practice or Final mode exam with the Customize option.

Both modes show you an overall grade, expressed as a percentage, as well as a breakdown of how well you did on each exam domain. The Review Questions feature lets you see which questions you missed and what the correct answers are. Use these results to guide further studying. Continue reviewing the topics you miss and taking additional exams until you are consistently scoring in the 90% range. When you get there, you are ready to pass the CompTIA A+ certification exams.

Study Tactics

Perhaps it's been a while since you had to study for a test. Or perhaps it hasn't, but you've done your best since then to block the whole experience from your mind. Either way, savvy test-takers know that certain techniques make studying for tests more efficient and effective.

Here's a trick used by students in law and medical schools who have to memorize reams of information: Write it down. The act of writing something down (not typing, *writing*) in and of itself helps you to remember it, even if you never look at what you wrote again. Try taking separate notes on the material and re-creating diagrams by hand to help solidify the information in your mind.

Another oldie but goodie: Make yourself flash cards with questions and answers on topics you find difficult. A third trick: Take your notes to bed and read them just before you go to sleep. Many people find they really do learn while they sleep!

Contact

If you have any problems, any questions, or if you just want to argue about something, feel free to send an e-mail to the author (michaelm@totalsem.com) or to the editor (scottj@totalsem.com).

For any other information you might need, contact CompTIA directly at their Web site: www.comptia.org.

Safety and Professionalism

In this chapter, you will learn how to
- Present yourself with a proper appearance and professional manner
- Talk to customers in a professional, productive manner
- Discuss the tools of the trade and preparations necessary to deal with problems proactively

I am a "nerd" and I consider the term a compliment. Nerds are smart and like to work with technology—these are the good aspects of nerd-dom. On the other hand, many people think of the term nerd as an insult. Nerds are rarely portrayed in a positive manner in the media, and I think I know why. Nerds generally suffer from some pretty serious social weaknesses. These weaknesses are classics: bad clothing, shyness, and poor communication skills. If you've ever seen an episode of the TV show *The Big Bang Theory*, you know what I'm talking about.

This chapter covers some basic life skills to enable you to enjoy your nerdiness and yet function out in the real world. You'll learn how to act as a professional and how to communicate effectively. After you're well on your way to the beginnings of social graces, we'll discuss some of the hazards (such as static electricity) you may run into in your job and the tools you can use to prevent problems. After all, nerds who cannot stay organized—or who break equipment or themselves—need to learn some tricks to keep everything organized and safe. The chapter finishes with a discussion about troubleshooting. You'll learn the CompTIA A+ troubleshooting methodology, an excellent tool that will serve you well in your studies and career as a tech.

1002

The Professional Tech

A professional tech displays professionalism, which might seem a little trite if it weren't absolutely true. The tech presents a professional appearance and follows a proper ethical code. I call the latter the Traits of a Tech. Let's look at these two areas in more detail.

Appearance

Americans live in a casual society. The problem with casual is that perhaps our society is becoming *too* casual. Customers often equate casual clothing with a casual attitude. You might think you're just fixing somebody's computer, but you're doing much more than that. You are saving precious family photos. You are keeping a small business in operation. This is serious stuff, and nobody wants an unclean, slovenly person doing these important jobs. Look at Figure 1-1. This is our resident illustrator (among other job descriptions), Ford Pierson, casually dressed to hang with his buddies.

Figure 1-1
Casual Ford

I have a question for you. If you ran a small business and your primary file server died, leaving 15 employees with nothing to do, how would you feel about Ford as a tech coming into your office looking like this? I hope your answer would be "not too confident." Every company has some form of dress code for techs. Figure 1-2 shows Ford dressed in a fairly typical example, with a company polo shirt, khaki pants, and dark shoes (trust me on that score). Please also note that both his shirt and his pants are wrinkle free. All techs either know how to iron or know the location of the nearest cleaners.

While we are looking at this model of a man, do you appreciate that his hair is combed and his face is cleanly shaven? It's too bad I can't use scratch-and-sniffs, but if I could, you'd also notice that Professional Ford took a shower, used some deodorant, and brushed his teeth.

I hope that most of the people who read this smile quietly to themselves and say, "Well, of course." The sad truth tells me otherwise. Next time you look at a tech, ask yourself how many of these simple appearance and hygiene issues were missed. Then make a point not to be one of the unkempt techs.

Figure 1-2
Professional Ford

The Traits of a Tech

When I was a Boy Scout in the United States, we learned something called the Boy Scout Law, a list of traits that define the ethics of a Boy Scout. Even though I haven't been active in Boy Scouts for a long time, I still have the Scout Law memorized: "A Scout is trustworthy, loyal, helpful, friendly, courteous, kind, obedient, cheerful, thrifty, brave, clean, and reverent."

My goal here isn't a sales pitch for scouting in any form, but rather to give you an idea of what we are trying to achieve: a list of ethics that will help you be a better technician. The list you are about to see is my own creation, but it does a great job of covering the CompTIA A+ objectives. Let's dive into the traits of a tech: honesty/integrity, dependability/responsibility, and sensitivity.

Honesty/Integrity

Honesty and integrity are not the same thing, but for a tech, they are so closely related that it is best to think of them as one big ethic. *Honesty* means to tell the truth, and *integrity* means doing the right thing.

It's simple to say you have to be honest, but be warned that our industry often makes it difficult. IT technicians get a lot of leeway compared to most starting jobs, making dishonesty tempting. One of the biggest temptations is lying to your boss. A new tech driving around in a van all day may find it convenient to stretch the truth on how long he took for lunch or how far along he is on the next job. Being up front and honest with your boss is pretty obvious and easy to understand.

Being honest with your customers is a lot harder. Don't sell people goods and services they don't need, even if you get a cut of what you sell. Don't lie to your customers about a problem. If you can't explain the problem to them in plain English, don't create techno-babble (see note) and don't be afraid to say, "I don't know." Too many techs seem to think that not knowing exactly what a problem might be reflects poor skill. A skilled tech can say "I don't know, but I know how to figure it out, and I will get you the right answer."

 NOTE *Techno-babble* is the use of (often nonsensical) jargon and technical terms to intimidate and silence a challenge to a technical issue.

A computer tech must bring *integrity* to the job, just like any other service professional. You should treat anything said to you and anything you see as a personal confidence, not to be repeated to customers, coworkers, or bosses. Here's Mike's Rule of Confidentiality: "Unless it's a felony or an imminent physical danger, you didn't see nothin'." You'll learn more about dealing with prohibited content in Chapter 27, "Securing Computers."

There is an exception to this rule. Sometimes you need to separate paying customers from in-house users. A paying customer is someone who doesn't work for your company and is paying for your services. An in-house user is someone who works for the same company you work for and is not directly paying for your services. It's often your job (but not always) to police in-house IT policies. Here's a great example. If you are at a customer's site and you see a sticky note with a password on a user's monitor, you say nothing. If you are in-house and you see the same thing, you probably need to speak to the user about the dangers of exposing passwords.

You have a lot of power when you sit in front of someone's computer. You can readily read private e-mail, discover Web sites surfed, and more. With a click of the Start button, you can know the last five programs the user ran, including Word and Solitaire, and the last few documents the user worked on. Don't do this; you really don't want to know. Plus, if you are caught violating a customer's privacy, you not only will lose credibility and respect, but you could also lose your job. *You need to deal appropriately with customers' confidential and private materials.* This includes files on the computer, items on a physical desktop, and even pages sitting in a printer tray.

Every user's password represents a potential danger spot for techs. We're constantly rebooting computers, accessing protected data, and performing other jobs that require passwords. The rule here is to *avoid learning other folks' passwords at all costs* (see Figure 1-3). If you know a password to access a mission-critical machine and that machine ends up compromised or with data missing, who might be blamed? You, that's who, so avoid learning passwords! If you only need a password once, let the user type it in for you. If you anticipate accessing something multiple times (the more usual situation), ask the user to change the password temporarily.

It's funny, but people assume ownership of things they use at work. John in accounting doesn't call the computer he uses anything but "my PC." The phone on Susie's desk isn't the company phone, it's "Susie's phone." Regardless of the logic or illogic involved with this sense of ownership, a tech needs to respect that feeling. You'll never go wrong if you follow the *Ethic of Reciprocity,* also known as the *Golden Rule*: "Do unto others as you

Figure 1-3
Don't do this!

would have them do unto you." In a tech's life, this can translate as "Treat people's things as you would have other people treat yours." Don't use or touch anything—keyboard, printer, laptop, monitor, mouse, phone, pen, paper, or cube toy—without first asking permission. Follow this rule at all times, even when the customer isn't looking.

Dependability/Responsibility

Dependability and responsibility are another pair of traits that, while they don't mean the same thing, often go together. A dependable person performs agreed-upon actions. A responsible person is answerable for her actions. Again, the freedom of the typical IT person's job makes dependability and responsibility utterly critical.

Dependable techs show up for job appointments and show up on time. Failure to show up for an appointment not only inconveniences the customer, but also can cost your customer a lot of money in lost time and productivity. So, *be on time*.

If you or your company makes an appointment for you, show up. Be there. Don't let simple problems (such as bad traffic) prevent you from showing up on time. Take some time to prepare. Figure out traffic times. Figure out if preceding appointments will cause a problem, and check for traffic. There is a popular old saying in the United States, "Five minutes early is on time, and on time is late." Sometimes events take place that prevent you from being on time. *If late, contact the customer immediately* and give him or her your best estimate of when you will arrive. A simple apology wouldn't hurt, either.

Responsibility is a tricky subject for IT folks. Certainly you should be responsible for your actions, but the stakes are high when critical data and expensive equipment are at risk. Before you work on a computer, always ask the customer if there are up-to-date backups of the data. If there aren't, offer to make backups for the customer, even if this incurs an extra charge for the customer. If the customer chooses not to make a backup, make sure he or she understands, very clearly, the risk to the data on the system you are about to repair.

NOTE Most computer repair companies require a signed Authorization of Work or Work Authorization form to document the company name, billing information, date, scope of work, and that sort of thing. Even if you do your own repairs, these forms can save you from angst and from litigation. You can create your own or do an Internet search for examples.

Sensitivity

Sensitivity is the ability to appreciate another's feeling and emotions. Sensitivity requires observing others closely, taking time to appreciate their feelings, and acting in such a way that makes them feel comfortable. I've rarely felt that technicians I've met were good at sensitivity. The vast majority of nerds I know, including myself, tend to be self-centered and unaware of what's going on around them. Let me give you a few tips I've learned along the way.

Understand that the customer is paying for your time and skills. Also understand that your presence invariably means something is wrong or broken, and few things make users more upset than broken computers. When you are "on the clock," you need to show possibly very upset customers that you are giving their problem your full attention. To do this, you need to avoid distractions. If you get a personal call, let it roll over to voicemail. If you get a work-related call, politely excuse yourself, walk away for privacy, and keep the call brief. Never talk to coworkers while interacting with customers. Never speak badly of a customer; you never know where you'll run into them next.

Last, *be culturally sensitive.* We live in a diverse world of races, religions, etiquettes, and traditions. If a customer's religious holiday conflicts with your work schedule, the customer wins. If the customer wants you to take off your shoes, take them off. If the customer wants you to wear a hat, wear one. *Use appropriate professional titles, when applicable.* If a customer's title is "Doctor," for example, use the title even if you don't recognize the field of medicine. When in doubt, always ask the customer for guidance.

Effective Communication

When you deal with users, managers, and owners who are frustrated and upset because a computer or network is down and they can't work, your job requires you to take on the roles of detective and psychologist. Talking with frazzled and confused people and getting answers to questions about how the personal computing device got into the state it's in takes skill. Communicating clearly and effectively is important.

This section explores techniques for effective communication. It starts with assertive communication and then looks at issues involving respect. We'll examine methods for eliciting useful answers in a timely fashion. The section finishes with a discussion about managing expectations and professional follow-up actions.

Assertive Communication

In many cases, a computer problem results from user error or neglect. As a technician, you must show users the error of their ways without creating anger or conflict. You do this by using assertive communication. *Assertive communication* isn't pushy or bossy, but it's also not the language of a pushover. Assertive communication first requires you to show the other person that you understand and appreciate the importance of his feelings. Use statements such as "I know how frustrating it feels to lose data," or "I understand how infuriating it is when the network goes out and you can't get your job done." Statements like these cool off the situation and let customers know you are on their side. Avoid using the word "you," as it can sound accusatory.

The second part of assertive communication is making sure you state the problem clearly without accusing the user directly. Here's an example: "Help me understand how the network cable keeps getting unplugged during your lunch hour." Last, tell the user what you need to prevent this error in the future. "Please call me whenever you hear that buzzing sound," or "Please check the company's approved software list before installing anything." Always use "I" and "me," and never make judgments. "I can't promise the keyboard will work well if it's always getting dirty" is much better than "Stop eating cookies over the keyboard, you slob!"

Respectful Communication

Generally, IT folks support the people doing a company's main business. You are there to serve their needs and, all things being equal, to do so at their convenience, not yours.

You don't do the user's job, but you should *respect* that job and person as an essential cog in the organization. Communicate with users the way you would like them to communicate with you, were the roles reversed. Again, this follows the Ethic of Reciprocity.

Don't assume the world stops the moment you walk in the door and that you may immediately interrupt a customer's work to do yours. Although most customers are thrilled and motivated to help you the moment you arrive, this may not always be the case. Ask the magic question, "May I start working on the problem now?" Give customers a chance to wrap up, shut down, or do anything else necessary to finish their business and make it safe for you to do yours.

Engage the user with the standard rules of civil conversation. *Actively listen.* Avoid interrupting the customer as he or she describes a problem; *just listen and take notes.* You might hear something that leads to resolving the problem. Rephrase and repeat the problems back to the customer to verify you understand the issue ("So the computer is locking up three times a day?"). Use an even, nonaccusatory tone, and although it's okay to try to explain a problem if the user asks, *never condescend and never argue with a customer.*

Maintain a positive attitude in the face of adversity. Don't get defensive if you can't figure something out quickly and the user starts hassling you. Remember that an angry customer isn't really angry with you—he's just frustrated—so don't take his anger personally. Instead, take it in stride; smile, *project confidence,* and assure him that computer troubleshooting sometimes takes a while.

Avoid distractions that take your focus away from the user and his or her computer problem. Things that break your concentration slow down the troubleshooting process immensely. Plus, customers will feel insulted if you start texting or talking to coworkers while interacting with the customer. You're not being paid to socialize, so turn those cell phones to vibrate. That's why the technogods created voicemail. Avoid personal interruptions or personal calls. Never take any call except one that is potentially urgent. If a call is potentially urgent, explain the urgency to the customer, step away, and deal with the call as quickly as possible.

Also, avoid accessing social media sites while on the job. Checking Facebook or tweeting while your customer waits for his computer to get fixed is rude. And definitely never disclose experiences with customers via social media outlets.

Try This!   Apply the Ethic of Reciprocity

The Ethic of Reciprocity appears in almost every religion on the planet, with versions attributed to Confucius, Jesus, Moses, and Mohammed, among others. Just for practice, try the Ethic of Reciprocity out in nontechnical situations, such as when buying something from the corner store or grocery. Consciously analyze how the clerk behind the counter would want a customer to interact with him or her. Now put yourself in the clerk's shoes. How would you want a customer to communicate with you? Act accordingly!

If you discover that the user caused the problem, either through ignorance or by accident, don't dismiss the customer's problem, but avoid being judgmental or insulting about the cause. We all screw up sometimes, and these kinds of mistakes are your job security. *You get paid because people make mistakes and machines break.* Chances are you'll be back at that workstation six months or a year later, fixing something else. By becoming the user's advocate and go-to person, you create a better work environment. If a mistaken action caused the problem, explain in a positive and supportive way how to do the task correctly, and then have the user go through the process while you are there to reinforce what you said.

Getting Answers

Your job as a tech is to get the computer fixed, and the best way to start that process is to determine what the computer is doing or not doing. You must start by talking to the customer. Allow the customer to explain the problem fully while you record the information.

Although each person is different, most users with a malfunctioning computer or peripheral will be distraught and perhaps defensive about the problem. There are methods for dealing with difficult customers or situations. You need to ask the right questions *and* listen to the customer's answers. Then ask the proper follow-up questions with the goal of *getting answers* that will help you troubleshoot the problem.

Always avoid accusatory questions, because they won't help you in the least (see Figure 1-4). "What did you do?" generally gets a confused or defensive "Nothing" in reply, which doesn't get you closer to solving the problem. First, ask questions that help clarify customer statements. Repeat what you think is the problem after you've listened all the way through the user's story.

Figure 1-4
Never accuse!

Follow up with fact-seeking questions. "When did it last work?" "Has it ever worked in this way?" "Has any software changed recently?" "Has any new hardware been added?" Ask open-ended questions to narrow the scope of the problem ("Which applications are running when the computer locks up?").

By keeping your questions friendly and factual, you show users that you won't accuse them or judge their actions (see Figure 1-5). You also show them that you're there to help them. After the initial tension drops away, you'll often get more information: for instance, a recitation of something the user might have tried or changed. These clues can help lead to a quick resolution of the problem.

Figure 1-5
Keeping it
friendly

Remember that you may know all about computer technology, but the user probably does not. This means a user will often use vague and/or incorrect terms to describe a particular computer component or function. That's just the way it works, so don't bother to correct the user. Wherever possible, use proper language and avoid jargon, acronyms, and slang when applicable. They simply confuse the already upset user and can make you sound like you're talking down to the user. Just ask direct, factual questions in a friendly tone, using simple, non-jargon language to zero in on what the user was trying to accomplish and what happened when things went wrong. Use visual aids when possible. Point at the machine or go to a working computer to have the user show what went wrong or what she did or tried to do.

People do usually want to get a handle on what you are doing—in a simplified way. You don't want to overwhelm them, but don't be afraid to use simple analogies or concepts to give them an idea of what is happening. If you have the time (and the skills), use drawings, equipment, and other visual aids to make technical concepts more clear. If a customer is a closet tech and is really digging for answers—to the point that it's affecting your ability to do your job—compliment her initiative and then direct her to outside training opportunities. Better yet, tell her where she can get a copy of this book!

Beyond basic manners, never assume that just because you are comfortable with friendly or casual behavior, the customer will be too. Even an apparently casual user will expect you to behave with professional decorum. On the flip side, don't allow a user to put you in an awkward or even potentially dangerous or illegal situation. Never do work outside the scope of your assigned duties without the prior approval of your supervisor (when possible in such cases, try to direct users to someone who *can* help them). You are not a babysitter; never volunteer to "watch the kids" while the customer leaves the job site or tolerate a potentially unsafe situation if a customer isn't properly supervising a child. Concentrate on doing your job safely and efficiently, and maintain professional integrity.

Expectations and Follow-up

Users are terrified when their computers and networks go down so hard that they need to call in a professional. Odds are good that they've left critical, or at least important, data on the computer. Odds are equally good they need this computer to work to do their job. When they're ready to lay down money for a professional, they're expecting you to make their system exactly the way it was before it broke. Hopefully you can do exactly that for them, but you also must deal with their expectations and let them know what to expect.

Equally, you should give your customers some follow-up after the job is finished. We've already covered data backups and Authorization of Work forms (and those are very important), but you need to keep the customer's needs in mind. You also want to keep the customer thinking about you, should they need more help in the future. Here are a few items you should consider.

Timeline

If you can give the customer a best guess as to how long the repair will take, you'll be a hero. Don't be afraid to hold off on your time frame prediction until you've diagnosed the machine. If you truly don't have a feel for the time involved, tell the customer that and then tell him or her what you'll need to know before you can make the prediction.

Set and meet expectations and the timeline and communicate status with the customer. Stick to the timeline. If you finish more quickly, great! People love a job that goes faster than predicted. If you're moving past the predicted time frame, contact the customer and tell him or her as soon as possible. Let him or her know what's happened, explain why you need more time, and give the customer a new time frame. The biggest secret here is to keep in communication with the customer on any change in status. People understand delays—they take place in our lives daily. People resent not knowing why a delay is occurring, especially when a precious computer is at stake.

Options

Many times with a computer issue, you can fix the problem and avoid a similar problem in the future in several ways. These options boil down to money. If applicable, offer different repair/replacement options and let the customer decide which route to take.

Route A might replace a faulty component with an upgraded component and a backup in case the new component fails in the future. Route B might replace the faulty device with an upgraded device. Route C might do an even device swap. Provide options and let the customer decide.

Documentation

At the completion of work, provide proper documentation of the services provided. Describe the problem, including the time and day you started work, the solution (again including the time and day the work ended), the number of hours you worked, and a list of all parts you replaced. If the customer owns the replaced parts, offer them to the customer (this is especially true if you replace any storage media). This documentation may or may not include your charges.

Follow-up

Follow up with a customer/user at a later date to verify satisfaction. This can be simple follow-up, usually just a phone call, to confirm that the customer is happy with your work. This gives the customer a chance to detail any special issues that may have arisen, and it also adds that final extra touch that ensures he or she will call you again when encountering a technical problem.

Be Prepared!

Effective communication with your customer enables you to *start* the troubleshooting process, getting details about the problem and clues about things that happened around the same time. To continue troubleshooting, though, you need to be adept at handling computing devices. That starts with knowing how to handle computer components safely and how to use the tools of a tech. You also need a very clear troubleshooting methodology to guide your efforts. Let's look at these issues.

Electrostatic Discharge (ESD)

All computing devices use electricity. As long as the electricity runs properly through the circuits and wires as designed, all is good. There are times when electricity improperly jumps from one place to another in ways that cause damage, an *electromagnetic pulse* (*EMP*). EMP shows up in many ways. Lightning is a form of EMP. Lightning hitting your electrical equipment certainly makes a bad day! Nuclear detonations also create a massive EMP burst (yikes!), but the EMP of most concern to techs is *electrostatic discharge* (*ESD*).

ESD simply means the passage of a static electrical charge from one item to another. Have you ever rubbed a balloon against your shirt, making the balloon stick to you? That's a classic example of static electricity. When that static charge discharges, you may not notice it happening—although on a cool, dry day, I've been shocked so hard by touching a doorknob that I could see a big, blue spark! I've never heard of a human being getting anything worse than a rather nasty shock from ESD, but I can't say the same thing about computers. ESD will destroy the sensitive parts of any computing device, so it is essential that you take steps to avoid ESD when working on a PC or other computing device.

NOTE All computing devices are well protected against ESD on the outside. Unless you take a screwdriver or pry tool and open up a PC or other computing device, you don't need to concern yourself with ESD.

Antistatic Tools

ESD only takes place when two objects that store different amounts (the hip electrical term to use is *potential*) of static electricity come in contact. The secret to avoiding ESD is to keep you and the parts of the computer you touch at the same electrical potential, otherwise known as grounding yourself to the computing device. You can accomplish this by connecting yourself to the computer via a handy little device called an *antistatic wrist strap,* or *ESD strap.* This simple device consists of a wire that connects on one end to an alligator clip and on the other end to a small metal plate that secures to your wrist with an elastic strap. You snap the alligator clip onto any handy metal part of the computer and place the wrist strap on either wrist. Figure 1-6 shows a typical antistatic wrist strap in use.

Figure 1-6
Antistatic wrist
strap in use

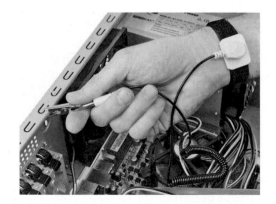

EXAM TIP Static electricity, and therefore the risk of ESD, is much more prevalent in dry, cool environments.

Antistatic wrist straps are standard equipment for anyone working on a computing device, but other tools might also come in handy. One of the big issues when working with a computer occurs if you find yourself pulling out parts from the computer and setting them aside. The moment you take a piece out of the computer, it no longer has contact with the systems and may pick up static from other sources. Techs use antistatic mats to eliminate this risk. An *antistatic mat*—or *ESD mat*—acts as a point of common potential; it's typical to purchase a combination antistatic wrist strap and mat that all connect to keep you, the computer, and any loose components at the same electrical potential (see Figure 1-7).

Figure 1-7
Antistatic wrist
strap and mat
combination

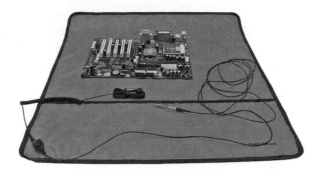

 NOTE Make sure the metal plate on the antistatic wrist strap touches the skin of your wrist. Don't put it on over the sleeve of a long-sleeved shirt.

Antistatic wrist straps and mats use tiny *resistors*—devices that stop or *resist* the flow of electricity—to prevent a static charge from racing through the device. These resistors can fail over time, so it's always a good idea to read the documentation that comes with your antistatic tools to see how to test those small resistors properly.

 EXAM TIP Always put components *in* an antistatic bag, not on the bag.

Any electrical component not in a computer case needs to be stored in an *antistatic bag*, a specially designed bag that sheds whatever static electricity you have when you touch it, thus preventing any damage to components stored within (see Figure 1-8). Almost all components come in an antistatic bag when purchased. Experienced techs never throw these bags away, as you never know when you'll want to pull a part out and place it on a shelf for a while.

Although having an antistatic wrist strap with you at all times would be ideal, the reality is that from time to time you'll find yourself in a situation where you lack the proper antistatic tools. This shouldn't keep you from working on the computer—if you're careful!

Figure 1-8
Antistatic bag

Before working on a computer in such a situation, take a moment to touch the power supply every once in a while as you work—I'll show you where it is in Chapter 2, "The Visible Computer"—to keep yourself at the same electrical potential as the computer. Although this isn't as good as a wrist strap, this *self-grounding* is better than nothing at all.

Use these tools for proper component handling and storage: ESD straps, ESD mats, antistatic bags, and self-grounding.

Try This!   Antistatic Protection Devices

In some circumstances, an antistatic wrist strap could get in the way. Manufacturers have developed some alternatives to the wrist strap, so try this:

1. Take a field trip to a local computer or electronics store.

2. Check out their selection of antistatic devices. Can you find anything other than wrist straps or mats?

3. Do a Web search for "static control products." Can you find anything other than wrist straps or mats?

4. Report what options you can find for protecting your equipment from ESD. Weigh the pros and cons and decide what you would use in various situations.

The last issue when it comes to preventing ESD is that never-ending question—should you work with the computing device plugged in or unplugged? The answer is simple: Do you really want to be physically connected to a computer that is plugged into an electrical outlet? Granted, the chances of electrocution are slim, but why take the risk?

EXAM TIP Always disconnect power before repairing a personal computing device.

Removing the power applies also when working on portable computers. Disconnect both from the wall outlet and remove the battery. With mobile devices such as tablets and smartphones, this creates an issue because the battery is inside the case. Chapter 25, "Care and Feeding of Mobile Devices," covers the special skills needed for working on mobile devices.

Electromagnetic Interference (EMI)

A magnetic field interfering with electronics is *electromagnetic interference* (*EMI*). EMI isn't nearly as dangerous as ESD, but it can cause permanent damage to some components and erase data on some storage devices. You can prevent EMI by keeping magnets away from computer equipment. Certain components are particularly susceptible to EMI, especially storage devices like hard drives.

The biggest problem with EMI is that we often use magnets without even knowing we are doing so. Any device with an electrical motor has a magnet. Many telephones have magnets. Power bricks for laptops and speakers also have magnets. Keep them away!

Radio Frequency Interference (RFI)

Do you ever hear strange noises on your speakers even though you aren't playing any sounds? Do you ever get strange noises on your cell phone? If so, you've probably run into *radio frequency interference* (*RFI*). Many devices emit radio waves:

- Cell phones
- Wireless network cards
- Cordless phones
- Baby monitors
- Microwave ovens

In general, the radio waves that these devices emit are very weak, and almost all electronic devices are shielded to prevent RFI. A few devices, speakers in particular, are susceptible to RFI. RFI will never cause any damage, but it can be incredibly irritating. The best way to prevent RFI is to keep radio-emitting devices as far away as possible from other electronics.

RFI becomes a big problem when two devices share the same frequencies. Cordless phones, baby monitors, and many wireless networks share the same range of frequencies. They sometimes interfere with each other, causing poor signals or even blocking signals completely. These devices need to be tuned to avoid stomping on each other's frequencies. In Chapter 20, "Wireless Networking," you'll see how to tune a wireless network to prevent RFI.

NOTE Computer gear manufacturers package their products in a variety of ways to shield against accidental damage, whether that's physical damage, ESD, EMI, or RFI. The typical pink translucent computer bag is coated with a film that prevents the bag from producing static electricity and mildly protects the contents against physical contact (and thus damage). The two types of metal bags offer shielding against EMI and RFI as well as ESD. These are the silvery bags (such as in Figure 1-8) you'll see hard drives packed in, for example, and the black-and-silver woven bags you'll sometimes see.

Physical Tools

The basic *tech toolkit* consists of a Phillips-head screwdriver and not much else—seriously—but a half-dozen tools round out a fully functional toolkit. Most kits have a star-headed Torx wrench, a nut driver or two, a pair of plastic tweezers, a little grabber tool (the technical term is *parts retriever*), a hemostat, and both Phillips-head and flat-head screwdrivers (see Figure 1-9).

Figure 1-9
Typical
technician toolkit

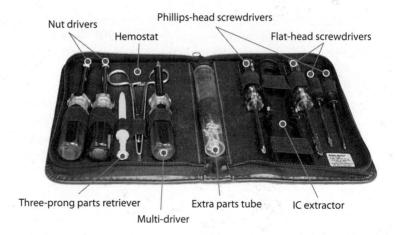

Nut drivers   Hemostat   Phillips-head screwdrivers   Flat-head screwdrivers

Three-prong parts retriever   Extra parts tube   IC extractor   Multi-driver

I'll add a few more tools to this toolkit as the book progresses that you'll want for a not-so-basic toolkit. Those more advanced tools will be introduced as your knowledge grows.

You already own another great tool, the camera in your smartphone or tablet. It's amazing how handy it is to photograph screw locations, cable connections, or other conditions so that you can later retrieve those images when you reinstall something.

A lot of techs throw in an extension magnet to grab hard-to-reach bits that drop into cases (an exception to the "no magnets" rule). Many also add a magnifying glass and a flashlight for those hard-to-read numbers and text on the printed circuit boards (PCBs) that make up a large percentage of devices inside the system unit. Contrary to what you might think, techs rarely need a hammer.

Mobile devices such as tablets and smartphones require more complex kits that include specialized tools, such as prying tools (called *spudgers*—isn't that a great word?). There are many excellent toolkits available for purchase; I recommend the toolkits sold by iFixit (www.ifixit.com) and use one myself (Figure 1-10). These kits are inexpensive and reliable, plus iFixit has hundreds of free videos that walk you through many scenarios using the kits.

Figure 1-10
Author's go-to
iFixit toolkit
(several of the
implements on
the right side are
types of spudger)

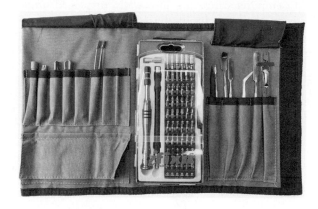

Personal Safety

IT techs live in a dangerous world. We're in constant danger of tripping, hurting our backs, and getting burned by hot components. You also need to keep in mind what you wear (in a safety sense). Let's take a moment to discuss these *personal safety* issues and what to do about them.

CAUTION   When thinking about safety, maintain compliance with government regulations. You may be required to wear certain protective gear or take extra precautions while in the workplace. Make sure you also follow any environmental rules for the disposal of old parts, especially with things like CRT monitors, batteries, and toner cartridges, which may contain hazardous or toxic materials. Check with your employer or your local government's Web site for more information.

If you don't stay organized, hardware technology will take over your life. Figure 1-11 shows a corner of my office, a painful example of cable "kludge."

Figure 1-11
Mike's cable
kludge

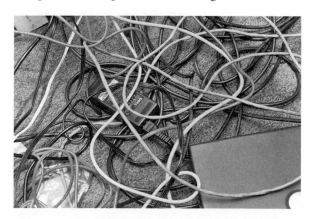

Cable messes such as these are dangerous tripping hazards. While I may allow a mess like this in my home office, all cables in a business environment are carefully tucked away behind computer cases, run into walls, or placed under cable runners. If you see a cable that is an obvious tripping hazard, contact the person in charge of the building to take care of it immediately. The results of ignoring such hazards can be catastrophic (see Figure 1-12). Use proper cable management to avoid these dangers.

Figure 1-12
What a strange,
bad trip it's been.

Another personal safety issue is heavy boxes. Computers, printers, monitors—everything we use—all seem to come to us in heavy boxes. Use proper lifting techniques. Remember never to lift with your back; lift with your legs, and always use a hand truck if available. Pay attention to weight limitations on the devices you use to move anything heavy. You are never paid enough to risk your own health.

You also need to watch out for hot components. It's hard to burn yourself unless you open up a computer, printer, or monitor. First, watch for anything with a cooling fan like the one shown in Figure 1-13. If you see a cooling fan, odds are good that something is hot enough to burn you—such as the metal *cooling fins* below the fan. Also look for labels or stickers warning about hot components. Last, when in doubt, move your hand over components as if you were checking the heat on a stove.

Disconnect a computer from its electrical source before you work on it, if possible. In the rare event where you need to work on a live system, take caution. Provide electrical fire safety equipment in rooms or locations that have a fire risk, such as server rooms. All those electronics and all that juice make a dangerous combination in those rare circumstances in which bad things happen. Keep properly rated (Class C) fire extinguishers handy.

Figure 1-13
Checking for hot
cooling fins

EXAM TIP When you build out a computer space, such as a server closet (the room that has a lot of important computers in it), use standard carpentry safety techniques. Wear an air filter mask when cutting drywall, for example. Wear safety goggles when using power tools.

Finally, remove any jewelry or loose-hanging clothing before working on a computer. If you have long hair, you might consider tying it back in a ponytail. You don't want anything getting caught in a fan or stuck on a component. This can save you and your components a lot of pain.

Troubleshooting Methodology

An effective *troubleshooting methodology* follows a set of steps to diagnose and fix a computer. Troubleshooting methodology includes talking to users to determine how and when the problem took place, determining a cause, testing, verification, and documentation. Techs use a number of good troubleshooting methodologies. Luckily for those taking the CompTIA A+ 220-1001 certification exam, CompTIA clearly defines their vision of troubleshooting methodology:

5.1 Given a scenario, use the best practice methodology to resolve problems

   1. Identify the problem

   - Question the user and identify user changes to computer and perform backups before making changes

   - Inquire regarding environmental or infrastructure changes

   - Review system and application logs

   2. Establish a theory of probable cause (question the obvious)

   - If necessary, conduct external or internal research based on symptoms

3. Test the theory to determine cause

- Once the theory is confirmed, determine the next steps to resolve problem
- If theory is not confirmed re-establish new theory or escalate

4. Establish a plan of action to resolve the problem and implement the solution

5. Verify full system functionality and, if applicable, implement preventive measures

6. Document findings, actions, and outcomes

Identify the Problem

There's a reason you're standing in front of a computer to repair it: something happened that the user of the computer has identified as "not good" and that's why you're here. First, you need to *identify the problem* by talking to the user. Get the user to show you what's not good. Is it an error code? Is something not accessible? Is a device not responding?

Then ask the user that classic tech question (remember your communication skills here!): "Has anything recently changed on the computer that might have made this problem appear?" What you're really saying is: "Have you messed with the computer? Did you install some evil program? Did you shove a USB drive in so hard that you broke the connection?" Of course, you never say these things; simply ask nicely without accusing so the user can help you troubleshoot the problem (see Figure 1-14).

Figure 1-14
Tech asking
nicely

Ask also if any changes have happened in the environment around the workstation. Check for any infrastructure changes that might cause problems. If you can access them, review system and application logs for clues about faulty software.

In most troubleshooting situations, it's important to back up critical files before making changes to a system. To some extent, this is a matter of proper ongoing maintenance, but if some important bit of data disappears and you don't have a backup, you know who the user will blame, don't you? (We cover backup options in detail in Chapter 14, "Maintaining and Optimizing Operating Systems.")

 EXAM TIP The CompTIA A+ certification exams assume that all techs should back up systems *every time* before working on them, even though that's not how it works in the real world.

Establish a Theory of Probable Cause (Question the Obvious)

Now it's time to analyze the issue and come up with a theory as to what is wrong, a *theory of probable cause*. Personally, I prefer the word "guess" at this point because very few errors are so obvious that you'll know what to do. Fall back on your knowledge of the computing process to localize the issue based on the symptoms. Keep your guesses… err…theories…simple. One of the great problems for techs is their desire to overlook the obvious problems in their desire to dig into the system (see Figure 1-15).

Figure 1-15
Ford the Tech misses the obvious.

 NOTE Chapter 2, "The Visible Computer," walks you through the computing process in some detail, showing how all the parts interact to make magic happen. The combination of a solid troubleshooting theory and a fundamental understanding of the computing process is the core knowledge for techs for fixing things.

Research   In many situations, you'll need to access other resources to root out the most probable cause of the problem. If necessary, therefore, you should conduct external or internal research based on the symptoms.

Use the Internet for external research. With the Internet quite literally at the fingertips of anyone with access to a smartphone or tablet, a short search online can result in swift answers to tech problems. If the customer's computer displays an error message, for example, put the whole error message into a search engine.

Internal research means asking other techs on-site for help. It means checking company records regarding a particular machine (for example, checking a problem-tracking database where previous issues have been recorded). This kind of search will reveal any known problems with the machine or with the user's actions.

Outside the Case   Take a moment to look for clues before you open up the case. Most importantly, use all your senses in the process.

What do you see? Is a connector mangled or a plastic part clearly damaged? Even if that connector or part works fine, the physical abuse could provide extra information. If the user can't connect to a network, check the cable. Was something rolled over it that could have broken the thin internal wires? Is that a jelly smear near the jammed optical drive door? (No pun intended, really!) A visual examination of the external computer is important.

When you put your hand on the system unit (that's the case that houses all the computer parts), does it feel hot? Can you feel or hear the vibrations of the fans? If not, that would be a clue to an overheating or overheated computer. Modern computers can run when overly hot, but generally run very sluggishly.

If you spend a moment listening to the computer, you might get some clues to problem sources. A properly running computer doesn't make a lot of sound, just a regular hum from the spinning fans. If you hear clicking or grinding sounds, that's a very bad sign and a very important clue! We'll cover data storage devices—the usual cause of clicking and grinding sounds—in detail in Chapters 8 and 9.

Finally, don't forget your nose. If you smell the unmistakable odor of ozone, you know that's the smell electronic components give off when they cook or are simply running much too hot.

Test the Theory to Determine Cause

Okay, so you've decided on a theory that makes sense. It's time to *test the theory* to see if it fixes the problem. A challenge to fixing a computer is that the theory and the fix pretty much prove themselves at the same time. In many cases, testing your theory does nothing more than verify that something is broken. If that's the case, then replace the broken part.

If your theory doesn't pan out, you should come up with a new theory and test it. (In CompTIA speak, if the theory is not confirmed, you need to re-establish a new theory.) If you verify and the fix lies within your skill set, excellent.

At this point, you need to check in with management to make certain you have permission to make necessary changes. Always consider corporate policies, procedures, and impacts before implementing changes. Having the boss walk in frowning while you're elbows-deep in a machine with the question "Who gave you permission?" can make for a bad day!

If you don't have the skills—or the permissions—to fix the issue, you need to *escalate* the problem.

Escalation is the process your company (or sometimes just you) goes through when you—the person assigned to repair a problem—are not able to get the job done. It's okay to escalate a problem because no one can fix every problem. All companies should have some form of escalation policy. It might mean calling your boss. It might mean filling out and sending some in-house form to another department. Escalation is sometimes a more casual process. You might want to start researching the problem online; you might want to refer to in-house documentation to see if this problem has appeared in the past. (See "Document Findings, Actions, and Outcomes" later in this chapter.) You may want to call a coworker to come check it out (see Figure 1-16).

Figure 1-16
Ford the Tech asks for help from Scott.

Establish a Plan of Action

At this point, you should have a good sense of the problem, including the scope and necessary permissions to do the job. You need to *establish a plan of action* to resolve the problem and implement the solution. Sometimes the plan requires a few steps before you can implement the solution. You might need additional resources such as known good replacement parts. A backup of user data should be part of the plan of action.

Verify and Prevent

Fantastic! Through either your careful work or escalation, you've solved the problem, or so you think. Remember two items here. First, even though *you* think the problem is fixed, you need to verify with the customer/user that it's fixed. Second, try to do something to prevent the problem from happening again in the future, if possible.

Verify Full System Functionality   You need to *verify* full system functionality to make sure the user is happy. Let's say a user can't print. You determine that the Print Spooler service is stalled due to a locked-up laser printer. You reset the printer and the jobs all start printing. Job done, right?

The best way to verify full system functionality is to have the user do whatever she needs to do on the repaired system for a few minutes while you watch. Any minor errors will quickly become apparent, and you might learn some interesting aspects of how the user does her job. Knowing what your users do is critical for good techs to help them do their jobs better (see Figure 1-17).

Figure 1-17
Ford the Tech
sticks around and
watches.

If Applicable, Implement Preventive Measures   A very smart tech once told me, "A truly good support tech's work goal should be to never have to get out of his chair." That's a pretty tall order, but it makes sense to me. Do whatever you can to prevent this problem from repeating. For some problems, there are obvious actions to take, such as making sure anti-malware is installed so a computer doesn't get infected again. Sometimes there's no action to take at all: nothing can prevent a hard drive that decides to die. But you can take one more critical action in almost every case: education. Take advantage of the time with the user to informally train him about the problem. Show him the dangers of malware or tell him that sometimes hard drives just die. The more your users know, the less time you'll spend out of your chair.

Document Findings, Actions, and Outcomes

Based on his famous quote, "Those who cannot remember the past are condemned to repeat it," I think the philosopher George Santayana would have made a great technician. As a tech, the last step of every troubleshooting job should be to *document* your findings, actions, and outcomes. This documentation might be highly formalized in some organizations, or it might just be a few notes you jot down for your own use, but you must document! What was the problem? What did you do to fix it? What worked? What didn't? The best guide to use for documentation is: "What would I have liked to have known about this problem before I walked up to it?" Good documentation is the strongest sign of a good tech (see Figure 1-18).

Figure 1-18
Ford documents
a successful fix.

Documenting problems helps you track the troubleshooting history of a computing device over time, enabling you to make longer-term determinations about retiring it or changing out more parts. If you and fellow techs fix a specific problem with Mary's laptop several times, for example, you might decide to swap out her whole system rather than fix it a fourth time.

Documenting helps fellow techs if they have to follow up on a task you didn't finish or troubleshoot a machine you've worked on previously. The reverse is also true. If you get a call about Frank's computer, for example, and check the records to find other service calls on his computer, you might find that the fix for a particular problem is already documented. This is especially true for user-generated problems. Having documentation of what you did also means you don't have to rely on your memory when your coworker asks what you did to fix the weird problem with Jane's computer a year ago!

Documenting also comes into play when you or a user has an accident onsite. If your colleague Joe drops a monitor on his foot and breaks both the monitor and his foot, for example, you need to fill out an *incident report*, just as you would with any kind of accident: electrical, chemical, or physical. An incident report should detail what happened and where it happened. This helps your supervisors take the appropriate actions quickly and efficiently.

Chapter Review

Questions

1. Which of the following would be most appropriate for the workplace? (Select two.)

   A. Clean, pressed khaki trousers

   B. Clean, wrinkle-free T-shirt

   C. Clean, wrinkle-free polo shirt

   D. Clean, pressed jeans

2. While manning the help desk, you get a call from a distraught user who says she has a blank screen. What would be a useful follow-up question? (Select two.)

   A. Is the computer turned on?

   B. Is the monitor turned on?

   C. Did you reboot?

   D. What did you do?

3. At the very least, what tool should be in every technician's toolkit?

   A. Pliers

   B. Hammer

   C. Straight-slot screwdriver

   D. Phillips-head screwdriver

4. When is it appropriate to yell at a user?

   A. When he screws up the second time

   B. When he interrupts your troubleshooting

   C. When he screws up the fifth time

   D. Never

5. When troubleshooting a software problem on Phoebe's computer and listening to her describe the problem, you get a text from your boss. Which of the following is the most appropriate action for you to take?

   A. Excuse yourself, walk out of the cube, and text your boss.

   B. Pick up Phoebe's phone and dial your boss's number.

   C. Wait until Phoebe finishes her description and then ask to use her phone to call your boss.

   D. Wait until Phoebe finishes her description, run through any simple fixes, and then explain that you need to call your boss on your cell phone.

6. You are at a customer's workstation to install several software and hardware updates, a process that will take a while and require several reboots of the computer. What should you do about the password to the user's account?

A. Require the customer to sit with you throughout the process so she can type in her password each time.

B. Ask the user to write down her password for you to use.

C. Ask the user to change her password temporarily for you to use.

D. Call your supervisor.

7. Which of the following is a good practice after completing a troubleshooting call at someone's office?

A. Follow up with a call within a couple of days to make sure everything is going well with the fixed computer.

B. Make copies of any passwords you used at the site for future reference.

C. Document any particularly important people you met for future reference.

D. Do nothing. Your work is finished there.

8. Which tool helps you avoid accidental static discharge by keeping you at the same electrical potential as the computer on which you're working?

A. Antistatic spray

B. Antistatic bag

C. Antistatic wrist strap

D. Phillips-head screwdriver

9. Once you have ascertained the computer's problem and backed up the critical data, what should you do?

A. Establish a theory of probable cause.

B. Start fixing the machine.

C. Question users more to find out how they caused the problem.

D. Document.

10. What should you do after successfully repairing a machine?

A. Do nothing; your job is done.

B. Admonish the user for causing so much work for the IT department.

C. Document your findings.

D. Lock it down so the user can't cause the same problem again.

Answers

1. **A, C.** Khaki trousers and a polo shirt trump jeans and a T-shirt every time.

2. **A, B.** Go for the simple answer first. When faced with a blank screen, check to see if the computer and the monitor are turned on.

3. **D.** Every tech's toolkit should have a Phillips-head screwdriver, at the very least.

4. **D.** Don't get angry or yell at clients.

5. **D.** Focus on the customer and don't use her things.

6. **C.** In this circumstance, asking for a temporary password is the right answer. Make sure the user changes her password back before you leave the site.

7. **A.** A simple follow-up builds goodwill and trust. This is a very important step to take after completing a job.

8. **C.** An antistatic wrist strap keeps you at the same electrical potential as the computer.

9. **A.** You should establish a theory of probable cause once you have ascertained the problem and backed up data.

10. **C.** At the end of a repair you should always document your findings.

The Visible Computer

In this chapter, you will learn how to
- Describe how computing devices work
- Identify common connectors and devices on typical computer systems
- Discuss features common to operating system software

Charles Babbage didn't set out to change the world. He just wanted to do math without worrying about human error, something all too common in his day. Babbage was a mathematician in the nineteenth century, a time well before anyone thought to create electronic calculators or computers (see Figure 2-1). When he worked on complex math, the best "computers" were people who computed by hand. They solved equations using pen or pencil and paper.

Figure 2-1
Charles Babbage, father of the computer

Babbage thought of making machines that would do calculations mechanically, so the numbers would always be right. Although his ideas were ahead of his time, inventors in the mid-twentieth century picked up the concepts and created huge calculating machines that they called *computers*.

This chapter explores how computing devices work. We'll look first at the computing process, then turn to hardware components common to all devices. The chapter finishes with a discussion about software, exploring commonality among all operating systems and specific functions of application programming. And, there are lots of pictures.

Historical/Conceptual

The Computing Process

In modern terms, a *computer* is an electronic device that can perform calculations. The most common types use special programming languages that people, known as *computer programmers*, have written and compiled to accomplish specific tasks.

When most people hear the word "computer," they picture *general* computing devices, machines that can do all sorts of things. The typical *personal computer* (*PC*) runs the operating system Microsoft Windows and is used for various tasks (see Figure 2-2). You can use it to manage your money and play games, for example, without doing anything special to it, such as adding new hardware.

Figure 2-2
A typical PC

Here are some other general-purpose computing devices:

- Apple Mac
- Apple iPad
- Smartphone
- Laptop (see Figure 2-3)

Figure 2-3
A laptop

Plenty of other devices do *specific* computing jobs, focusing on a single task or set of similar tasks. You probably encounter them all the time. Here's a list of common specific-purpose computers:

- Pocket calculator
- Digital watch
- Digital clock
- Wi-Fi picture frame
- Basic mobile phone
- Xbox One X
- GPS device (Global Positioning System, the device that helps drivers figure out how to get where they need to go)
- Roku
- Point of sale (POS) system (see Figure 2-4)
- Digital camera

Figure 2-4
A point of sale computer in a gasoline pump

This list isn't even close to complete! Plus, there are computers *inside* a zillion other devices. Here are some:

- Modern refrigerators
- Every automobile built since 1995
- Airplanes
- Boats
- Mall lighting systems
- Zambonis
- Home security alarms

You get the idea. Computers help the modern world function.

Modern computer techs need to know how different types of computing devices work so they can support the many devices used by their clients. This diversity is also reflected in the CompTIA A+ exams.

If the list of devices to support seems overwhelming, relax. The secret savior for modern techs is that computing devices function similarly to each other. Once you know what a device should enable a user to do, you'll be able to configure and troubleshoot successfully.

NOTE I picked 1995 as an arbitrary date for when every new car built had a computer. Computers have been used with cars for a long time. Simple computers helped make car factories work better starting in the 1970s, for example. The earliest mass-production car I found that had a central processor chip for added performance was the BMW 3 Series. The 1985–86 BMW 325, for example, can gain a few extra horsepower just from a chip upgrade costing approximately $200.

The Computing Parts

A modern computer consists of three major components:

- Hardware
- Operating system
- Applications

The *hardware* is the physical stuff that you can touch or hold in your hand. With a smartphone, for example, you hold the phone. On a typical personal computer, you touch the keyboard or view images on the monitor.

The *operating system* (*OS*) controls the hardware and enables you to tell the computer what to do. The operating system often appears as a collection of windows and little icons you can click or touch (see Figure 2-5). Collectively these are called the *user interface* (*UI*), which means the software parts with which you can interact. The UI that offers images or icons to select (as opposed to making you type commands) is called a *graphical user interface* (*GUI*).

Applications (or programs) enable you to do specialized tasks on a computer, such as

- Type a letter
- Send a message from your computer in Houston to your friend's computer in Paris
- Wander through imaginary worlds with people all over Earth

Very simple computing devices might have an operating system with only a few features that give you choices. A digital camera, for example, has a menu system that enables you to control things like the quality of the picture taken (see Figure 2-6).

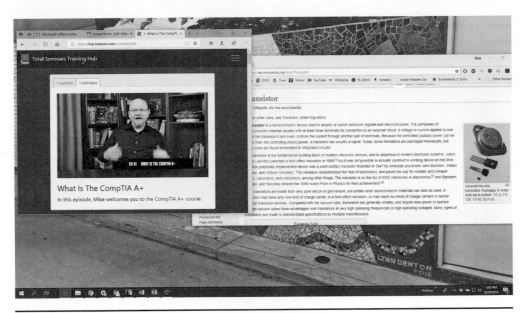

Figure 2-5 The Microsoft Windows 10 operating system

Figure 2-6
Changing
settings on a
digital camera

More complicated devices offer more choices. An Apple iPhone, for example, can do some cool things right out of the box, including make a phone call. But you can visit the Apple online store—the App Store—for programs and download applications (known as apps) to do all sorts of things that Apple didn't include (see Figure 2-7).

Figure 2-7
Monument
Valley II game
from the Apple
App Store

Finally, multipurpose computers like the typical Windows PC or macOS computer offer applications to help you do everything from write a book on CompTIA A+ certification to talk with someone on the other side of the world, with full audio and video (see Figure 2-8).

Figure 2-8
Apple FaceTime
communication

Stages

At the most basic level, computers work through three stages, what's called the *computing process*:

- Input
- Processing
- Output

You start the action by doing something—clicking the mouse, typing on the keyboard, or touching the touch screen. This is *input*. The parts inside the device or case take over at that point as the operating system tells the hardware to do what you've requested. This is *processing*.

In fact, at the heart of every computing device is a *central processing unit* (*CPU*), usually a single, thin wafer of silicon and tiny transistors (see Figure 2-9). The CPU handles the majority of the processing tasks and is, in a way, the "brain" of the computer.

Figure 2-9
An Intel Core i7
CPU on a
motherboard

NOTE Chapter 3, "CPUs," gives a lot more information on CPUs and other processing components.

Once the computer has processed your request, it shows you the result by changing what you see on the display or playing a sound through the speakers. This is *output*. A computer wouldn't be worth much if it couldn't demonstrate that it fulfilled your commands! Figure 2-10 shows the computing process.

Figure 2-10
The computing process

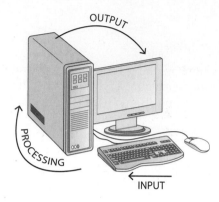

Modern computing devices almost always have two other stages:

- Data storage
- Network connection

Data storage means saving a permanent copy of your work so that you can come back to it later. It works like this. First, you tell the computer to save something. Second, the CPU processes that command and stores the data. Third, the computer shows you something, such as a message saying that the data is stored. Any work that you *don't* save is lost when you turn the computer off or exit the application.

Most computing devices connect to other devices to access other resources. A *network connection* often describes how one computer connects to one or more other computers. And it doesn't just apply to a couple of office computers. Every smartphone, for example, can connect to the Internet and play a video from YouTube (assuming you have a signal from a cell tower and a data plan).

At this point, students often ask me a fundamental question: "Why should I care about the computing process?" The answer to this question defines what makes a good computer technician. Here's my response.

Why the Process Matters to Techs

Because the computing process applies to every computing device, it provides the basis for how every tech builds, upgrades, and repairs such devices. By understanding both the components involved and how they talk to each other, you can work with *any* computing device. It might take a couple minutes to figure out how to communicate with the device via input, for example, but you'll quickly master it because you know how all computing devices work.

Breaking It Down

The whole computer process from start to finish has a lot of steps and pieces that interact. The more you understand about this interaction and these pieces, the better you can troubleshoot when something goes wrong. *This is the core rule to being a great tech.*

Here are nine steps that apply to most computers and computing devices when you want to get something done:

1. Power up. Computers run on electricity.

2. Processing parts prepare for action.

3. You provide input.

4. Processing parts process your command.

5. Processing parts send output information to your output devices.

6. Output devices show or play the results to you.

7. Repeat Steps 3–6 until you're satisfied with the outcome.

8. Save your work.

9. Power down the computer.

We'll come back to these processing steps as we tackle troubleshooting scenarios throughout the book. Keep these steps in mind to answer the essential question a tech should ask when facing a problem: What can it be? Or, in slightly longer fashion: What could cause the problem that stopped this device from functioning properly?

1001

Computing Hardware

Later chapters examine specific computing hardware, such as CPUs and mass storage devices. CompTIA expects competent techs to know what to call every connector, socket, and slot in a variety of computing devices. Rather than describe all of those briefly here, I decided to create a photo walkthrough naming points of interest and the chapters that discuss them.

 EXAM TIP Memorize the names of the components, connectors, and terms discussed and displayed in this section. You'll see them in future chapters, in the real world, and on the CompTIA A+ 1001 exam.

This section serves as a visual introduction to the components and connections. Plus, it should work great as a set of study sheets for memorizing names just before taking the 1001 exam. The images that follow indicate the chapters where you'll find information about a component or connection standard.

System unit or case: the
processing takes place inside
(See Chapter 6, "Motherboards.")

Monitor: visual output
(See Chapter 17, "Display
Technologies.")

Multifunction device, with printer,
scanner, and more: printed output,
scanned input (See Chapter 26,
"Printers and Multifunction Devices.")

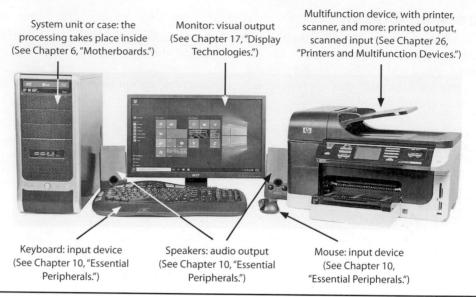

Keyboard: input device
(See Chapter 10, "Essential
Peripherals.")

Speakers: audio output
(See Chapter 10, "Essential
Peripherals.")

Mouse: input device
(See Chapter 10,
"Essential Peripherals.")

Figure 2-11   PC with common peripherals

Figure 2-11 shows a typical PC. The input and output devices should be familiar to most.

NOTE   The computer in Figure 2-11 is technically a *workstation*, meaning a computer you'd use at a desk. This is opposed to a *server*, a computer designed to provide network-available programs or storage. We'll talk about servers when we reach networking, though they're covered more in CompTIA Network+ than in CompTIA A+.

Figure 2-12 shows the back of a PC's system unit, where you'll find the many connection points called ports. Some ports connect to output devices; a couple are exclusively used for input devices. Most (such as the universal serial bus, or USB) handle either type of device.

Figure 2-13 reveals the inside of a PC case, where you'll find the processing and storage devices. Hiding under everything is the motherboard, the component into which everything directly or indirectly connects.

Figure 2-14 shows a clamshell-style laptop, in this case an Apple MacBook Air. The portable nature of the device calls for input and output devices built into the case—some variation from the typical PC displayed earlier, therefore, but all the standard computing component functions apply. Chapter 23, "Portable Computing," goes into a lot of detail about each component displayed here.

Figure 2-15 shows the side of a laptop with three different connection types.

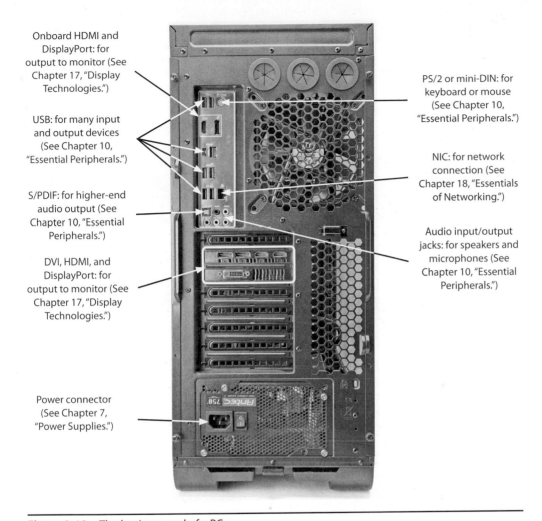

Onboard HDMI and DisplayPort: for output to monitor (See Chapter 17, "Display Technologies.")

USB: for many input and output devices (See Chapter 10, "Essential Peripherals.")

S/PDIF: for higher-end audio output (See Chapter 10, "Essential Peripherals.")

DVI, HDMI, and DisplayPort: for output to monitor (See Chapter 17, "Display Technologies.")

Power connector (See Chapter 7, "Power Supplies.")

PS/2 or mini-DIN: for keyboard or mouse (See Chapter 10, "Essential Peripherals.")

NIC: for network connection (See Chapter 18, "Essentials of Networking.")

Audio input/output jacks: for speakers and microphones (See Chapter 10, "Essential Peripherals.")

Figure 2-12   The business end of a PC

Figure 2-16 shows a tablet computer, an Apple iPad. Note that the screen has a touch interface, which makes it both an input and output device.

We could continue with any number of computing devices in the same picture show, but at this point the uniformity of computing component functions should be clear. They all work similarly, and, as a competent tech, you should be able to support just about any customer device. Let's turn now to a visual feast of software.

SIM   Check out the excellent Chapter 2 Challenge! sim on motherboard matching at http://totalsem.com/100x. It's a cool sim that helps names stick in your head.

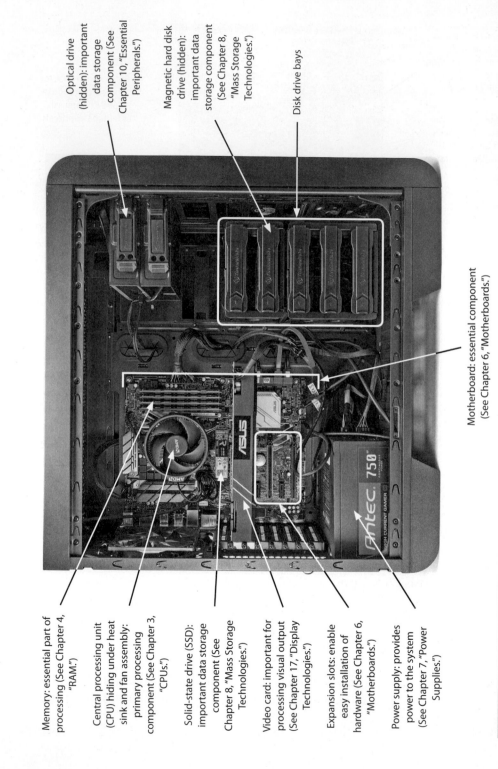

Optical drive (hidden): important data storage component (See Chapter 10, "Essential Peripherals.")

Magnetic hard disk drive (hidden): important data storage component (See Chapter 8, "Mass Storage Technologies.")

Disk drive bays

Motherboard: essential component (See Chapter 6, "Motherboards.")

Memory: essential part of processing (See Chapter 4, "RAM.")

Central processing unit (CPU) hiding under heat sink and fan assembly: primary processing component (See Chapter 3, "CPUs.")

Solid-state drive (SSD): important data storage component (See Chapter 8, "Mass Storage Technologies.")

Video card: important for processing visual output (See Chapter 17, "Display Technologies.")

Expansion slots: enable easy installation of hardware (See Chapter 6, "Motherboards.")

Power supply: provides power to the system (See Chapter 7, "Power Supplies.")

Figure 2-13 Inside the system unit

Figure 2-14
Laptop
(a MacBook Air)

Webcam: visual input device (See Chapter 10, "Essential Peripherals.")

Display: primary visual output device (See Chapter 17, "Display Technologies.")

Keyboard: primary input device (See Chapter 10, "Essential Peripherals.")

Clamshell case: houses the processing components (See Chapter 23, "Portable Computing.")

Touchpad: primary input device (See Chapter 10, "Essential Peripherals.")

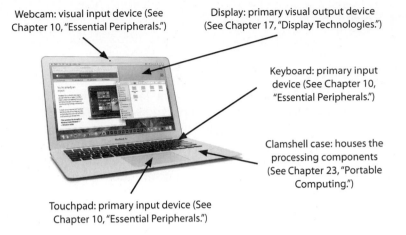

Figure 2-15
Ports on a laptop

USB port: for many input and output devices (See Chapter 10, "Essential Peripherals.")

Secure Digital (SD) card slot: removable data storage port (See Chapter 10, "Essential Peripherals.")

Thunderbolt port: general-purpose input/output connection (See Chapter 10, "Essential Peripherals.")

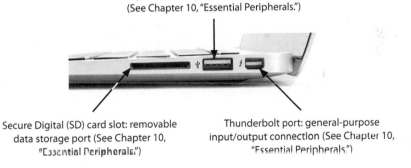

Figure 2-16
Tablet computer

Touchscreen: primary input and output device (See Chapter 24, "Understanding Mobile Devices.")

Home button: input device (See Chapter 24, "Understanding Mobile Devices.")

1002

Computing Software

The CompTIA A+ 1002 exam covers a lot of software, though mostly operating system tools rather than specific applications. The exam explores three workstation operating systems, Microsoft Windows, Apple Macintosh OS, and Linux. The exam covers Windows 7, Windows 8, Windows 8.1, and Windows 10. The current Apple workstation OS is macOS, which is how the book refers to it throughout. The exam covers common Linux features, but not distribution-specific features. The book follows this pattern as well.

 EXAM TIP The exam objectives use "Apple Macintosh OS" and "Mac OS" to refer to Apple's workstation OS. Apple changed the branding from "Mac OS X" to "macOS" in 2016. All these terms refer to the same OS.

In addition to the workstation operating systems, the CompTIA A+ 1002 exam covers four smartphone/tablet operating systems: Microsoft Windows, Google Android, Apple iOS, and Google Chrome OS. Android and iOS utterly dominate the market, with 98%+ market share, which makes including Windows and Chrome OS odd at best.

Common Operating System Functions

All OSs are not created equal, but every OS provides certain functions. Here's a list:

- The OS communicates, or provides a method for other programs to communicate, with the hardware of the PC or device. Operating systems run on specific hardware. For example, if you have a 32-bit CPU, you need to install a 32-bit version of an operating system. With a 64-bit CPU, you need a 64-bit OS (Chapter 3, "Microprocessors," explains 32- vs. 64-bit processors).

- The OS creates a *user interface* (*UI*)—a visual representation of the computer on the monitor that makes sense to the people using the computer.

- The OS enables users to determine the available installed programs and run, use, and shut down the programs of their choice.

- The OS enables users to add, move, and delete the installed programs and data.

- The OS provides a method to secure a system from all sorts of threats, such as data loss or improper access.

All operating systems enable you to use programs, but the formats vary so widely that you can't just install any program on any OS. Programmers have to do extra work to build separate versions of a program that can run on more than one OS. This is one example of what the CompTIA A+ 1002 exam calls *compatibility concerns between operating systems*.

The software your users need can restrict the list of acceptable OS choices, and the OS choice limits available software. This can also affect how well users on multiple operating systems can collaborate!

Another common compatibility concern is whether a specific OS can communicate with a given piece of hardware. A device that works well with one OS may work poorly or not at all with another! One OS may need no extra software to work with a device, while another might need a special program installed in order to control it. Likewise, brand-new hardware may not work well on any OS until the OSs receive updates to support the new hardware.

Almost every chapter in this book explores the interaction of OS and hardware. Chapter 11, "Building a PC," examines adding and removing programs. Many security features show up in multiple chapters, such as Chapter 13, "Users, Groups, and Permissions," and Chapter 27, "Securing Computers." The rest of this chapter, therefore, focuses on the user interface and the file structures.

User Interfaces

This section tours the various operating system *desktop styles/user interfaces*. Like the hardware tours earlier, this section serves a double purpose. First, you need to know the proper names for the various UI features and understand their functions. Second, it serves as a handy quick review section before you take the 1002 exam.

 NOTE Chapter 24, "Understanding Mobile Devices," details the operating systems for mobile devices—iOS, Android, Windows, and Chrome OS.

Windows 7

Figure 2-17 shows the standard interface for Windows 7, a traditional multifunction computer. Windows uses a graphical user interface primarily, so you engage with the mouse or other pointing device and click on elements. The background is called the *Desktop*. The open applications are Internet Explorer—the default browser in Window 7—and a Windows Explorer window showing the Windows 7 default Libraries.

Other visible items are as follows:

- The open applications demonstrate *transparency*, where the edges of the applications show blurred background images. This feature is called *Aero*, or *Aero Glass*.

- Click the *Start button* to get access to applications, tools, files, and folders.

- The *pinned programs* enable you to launch a program with a single left-click.

- The *taskbar* shows running programs.

- The *notification area* shows programs running in the background. Many techs also call it the *system tray*.

Application running
in the foreground

Desktop with a
few icons on it

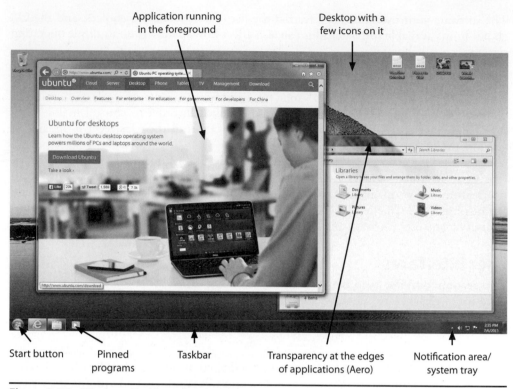

Start button   Pinned   Taskbar   Transparency at the edges   Notification area/
                    programs   of applications (Aero)   system tray

Figure 2-17   Windows 7 with applications open

Interacting with the classic Windows interface for the most part involves using a mouse or touchpad to move the cursor and either left-clicking or right-clicking the icons. Left-clicking selects an item; double left-clicking opens an item. Right-clicking opens a *context menu* from which you can select various options (see Figure 2-18). (Most people refer to a left-click simply as a *click*. This book makes the left/right distinction clear, so you learn how to access tools properly.)

NOTE   The context menu offers options specific to the icon you right-click. Right-clicking a file, for example, gives you a context menu that differs greatly from when you right-click an application.

Windows 8/8.1

Microsoft made significant changes to the Windows interface with the introduction of Windows 8. They borrowed from tablet operating systems, such as Windows Phone, to create a graphical set of *tiles* for full-screen programs, called *apps*. Note that the screen shows *pinned apps*—the default programs and programs selected by the user—and not all the applications installed on the computer.

Figure 2-18 Context menu

The Windows 8 interface, code-named *Metro UI*, works great for touch-enabled devices. The PC becomes in essence a giant tablet. Touch an app to load, drag your finger across the screen to see other apps, and have fun. Figure 2-19 shows the default Windows 8 interface, called the *Start screen*, with various elements called out.

NOTE Microsoft dropped the "Metro UI" moniker just before releasing Windows 8 due to legal concerns, replacing it with "Modern UI." A lot of techs and IT industry pros continue to refer to the unique Windows interface as "Metro."

Windows 8 also features a more classic Desktop, but one with the noticeable absence of a visible Start button (see Figure 2-20). You access this screen by pressing the *Windows logo key* on a standard keyboard.

Start screen

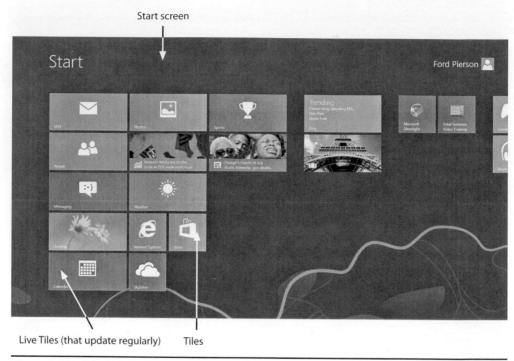

Live Tiles (that update regularly)   Tiles

Figure 2-19   Windows 8 Start screen

Figure 2-20   Windows 8 Desktop

Figure 2-21 Windows 8 Start screen scrolled to the right

Using a keyboard and mouse with Windows 8 bothered a lot of users making the jump from Windows 7. Scrolling with the mouse wheel, for example, scrolls right to left rather than up and down (see Figure 2-21).

Windows 8 took advantage of modern widescreen monitors with the *side-by-side apps* feature. Select an open application and press WINDOWS LOGO KEY + LEFT ARROW and the application will pin to the left half of the monitor. Do the reverse with another application, and it'll pin to the right half of the monitor. With apps like Microsoft Word, where each document opens in a unique window, side-by-side apps make it easy to compare two documents.

NOTE The Windows Store (Windows 7/8.x) or Microsoft Store (Windows 10) enables you to purchase Windows apps directly from Microsoft. The app is called Store when you look at the Windows interface, as you can see in Figure 2-19, among others. Microsoft has updated the Windows Store several times, tying it together with their Xbox gaming system, for example. Finally, the Windows Store is the place to get touch-first apps, meaning programs designed specifically with touchscreen interfaces in mind.

With a series of updates culminating in Windows 8.1, Microsoft brought back features such as the Start button, easy access to a Close button for apps, and the ability to boot directly to the Desktop. Figure 2-22 shows the standard interface for Windows 8.1 with the various elements called out. Note that it's very similar to Windows 7.

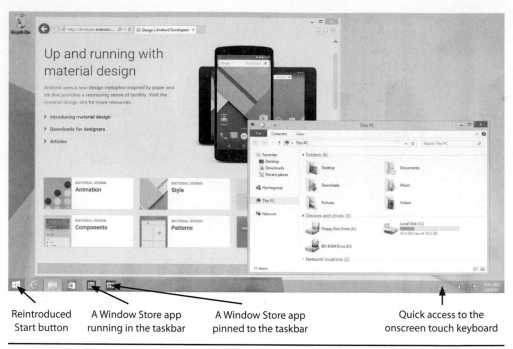

Reintroduced Start button   A Window Store app running in the taskbar   A Window Store app pinned to the taskbar   Quick access to the onscreen touch keyboard

Figure 2-22   Windows 8.1

Windows 8.1 makes it very easy to pin apps to the Start screen. Selecting the arrow at the bottom left brings up the Apps pane where you can sort and select apps and utilities (see Figure 2-23). Right-click an icon to pin it to the Start screen.

Windows 8/8.1 offer lots of hidden interface components that activate when you place the cursor in certain places on the screen. Dropping the cursor to the bottom left corner, for example, activates the Start button (see Figure 2-24) when in the Start screen.

EXAM TIP   The first release of Windows 8 had no visible Start button on the Desktop (except in the Charms bar). Microsoft added it to the Desktop in later patches.

Placing the cursor in the top- or bottom-right corner of the screen reveals the *Charms bar*, a location for tools called *charms*. See the right side of Figure 2-25. Charms include a robust Search tool that enables a search of the computer or even the Internet in one location. There's a Share charm for sharing photos, e-mail messages, and more. We'll revisit the charms later in this chapter when exploring how to access tech tools.

The final version of Windows 8.1 uses the Desktop rather than the Start screen as the default interface. The Start button is visible in the bottom left (see Figure 2-26). You can still access the charms using the cursor and the upper- and lower-right corners of the screen.

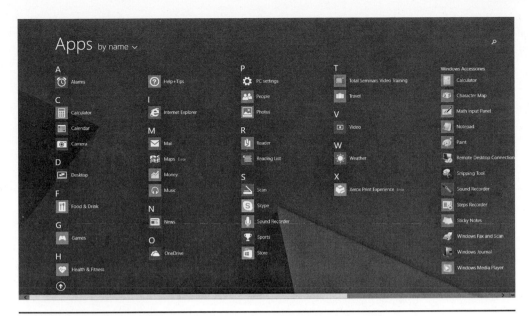

Figure 2-23 Apps sorted by name

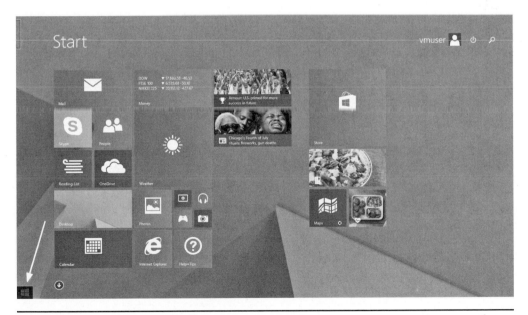

Figure 2-24 Start button magically appears

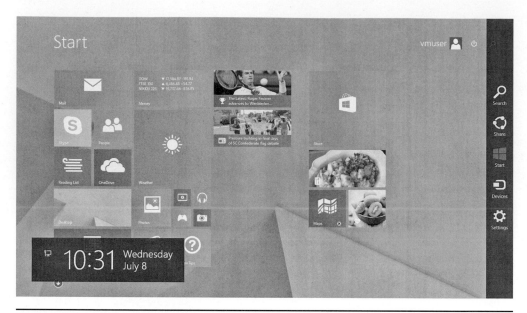

Figure 2-25   Charms accessed by cursor in upper- or lower-right corner

Figure 2-26   Windows 8.1 Desktop

EXAM TIP Windows 8 offers interesting options for the taskbar when used with multiple monitors. The default option duplicates the running and pinned apps on both the main monitor and additional monitor(s). The multimonitor taskbars can also show icons for apps running on a specific monitor. Right-click the taskbar and select Properties to change the taskbar behavior.

Windows 10

With Windows 10, Microsoft created an OS that blends the traditional Windows 7–style Desktop experience with some of the more progressive features of the Windows 8.*x* Metro/Modern UI. Microsoft retained and refined the Start menu and removed many unloved features as well. Microsoft incorporated the essential tools—Search being my go-to feature—into the lower-left corner of the taskbar. Figure 2-27 shows the Windows 10 interface with an active application in the foreground.

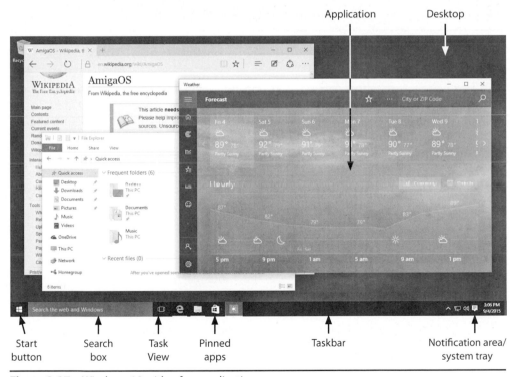

Figure 2-27 Windows 10 with a few applications open

Figure 2-28   Start menu in Windows 10

When you press the WINDOWS LOGO KEY on the keyboard, Windows 10 brings up the Start menu with useful tools and your most used apps on the left and pinned apps on the right (see Figure 2-28). Just like with Windows 8.1, you can click the link helpfully named All apps (bottom left) to open a list of installed applications. Right-click to pin any app to the Start screen.

NOTE   Windows 10 also has a tablet mode that mirrors the full-screen tiled interface of Windows 8/8.1. This mode is very useful in touch-enabled devices.

Click the Windows 10 Task View button to create and manage *multiple Desktops* for grouping your open applications. macOS and Linux each have their own take on this feature, as you'll see in the following sections.

NOTE   Microsoft altered the side-by-side apps feature in Windows 10 in one very cool way. Select the first application you want to pin and press the WINDOWS LOGO KEY + LEFT ARROW or RIGHT ARROW and two things happen. The application pins to the left or right half of the monitor and thumbnails of every other open application pop up on the other side of the screen. Click the thumbnail of whichever application you want to work with and it'll open in that half of the screen.

macOS

The macOS operating system interface offers similar functions to those found on Windows. The background of the main screen is called the *Desktop*. You can access frequently used applications by clicking their icons on the *Dock*, the bar that runs along the bottom of the Desktop by default. Just like with the taskbar pinned apps, you can add and remove apps from the Dock with a right-click. The Dock is more than a set of apps, though. It also shows running applications (like the taskbar in Windows). Figure 2-29 shows a typical macOS interface.

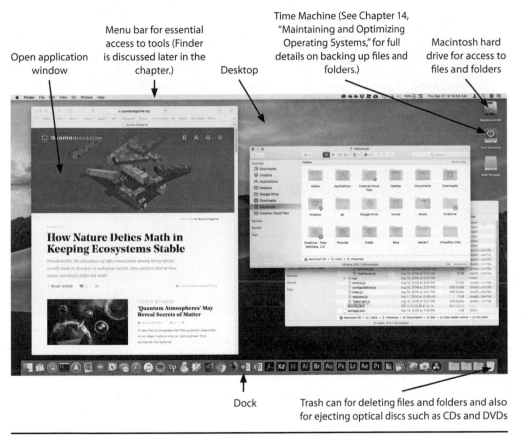

Figure 2-29   macOS

Pressing the Mission Control button on an Apple keyboard (see Figure 2-30) brings up a utility, called *Mission Control*, that enables you to switch between open applications, windows, and more, as shown in Figure 2-31. You can also access Mission Control by pressing and holding the CONTROL/CTRL key and then pressing the UP ARROW key.

Figure 2-30
Mission Control
button on
keyboard

Figure 2-31   Mission Control showing four open apps and nine Desktops

The macOS interface supports *Spaces*—essentially multiple Desktops—that can have different backgrounds and programs, but keep the same Dock. You can optimize your workflow, for example, by putting your primary program full screen on Desktop 1 and putting your e-mail client on Desktop 2 (see Figure 2-32). New messages won't disturb you when working, but you can access the second Desktop easily when you want with Mission Control. On the latest versions of macOS, press and hold the CONTROL key and press the RIGHT ARROW and LEFT ARROW keys to scroll through Spaces.

EXAM TIP   Windows 10 supports multiple Desktops with Task View, but you won't find support for that feature in earlier versions of Windows.

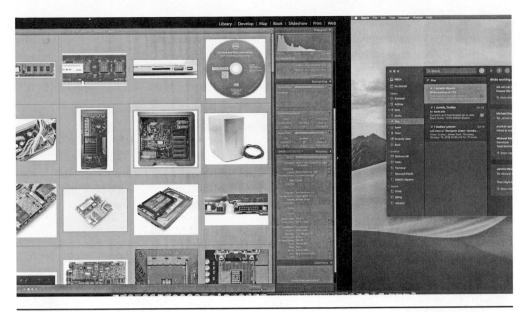

Figure 2-32   Switching between multiple Desktops

Linux

The many different versions or *distributions* (*distros*) of Linux offer a variety of user interfaces, called *desktop environments* (*DEs*). They offer similar functions to those in Windows or macOS. Figure 2-33 shows a popular Linux version—Ubuntu Linux with the GNOME desktop, and notes the various features. Frequently used utilities and applications are locked on the Launcher on the left side of the screen. Most distros give you options for Web browsing, e-mail, accessing files and folders, and so on.

Try This!   Ubuntu Emulator Online

Ubuntu.com has a basic emulator for an older version of Ubuntu Linux that enables you to poke around the desktop to get a sense of its look and feel. Try this! Open the URL http://tour.ubuntu.com/en/ in a Web browser to take the tour. Have fun!

File Structures and Paths

Knowing where to find specific content—files and the folders in which they reside—helps techs help users do their day-to-day tasks more efficiently. Almost every operating system stores files in folders in a tree pattern. The root of the tree is the drive or disc, followed by a folder, subfolder, sub-subfolder, and so on, until you get to the desired file. The drive or disc gets some designation, most usually a *drive letter* like C:. Chapter 9,

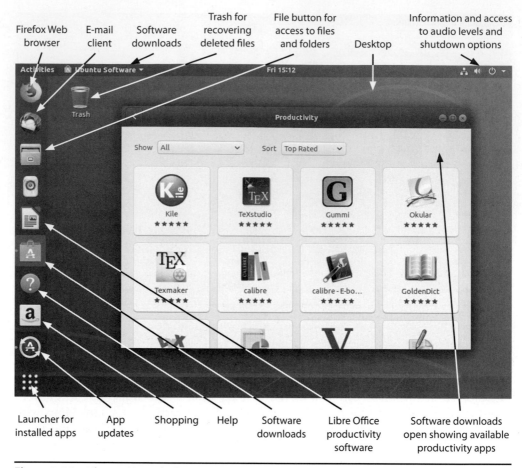

Figure 2-33   Ubuntu Linux desktop environment

"Implementing Mass Storage," goes into gory detail on how modern operating systems implement systems for storing data. This section is more dictated by CompTIA's obsession with requiring examinees to memorize paths.

Windows

Windows has important folders that help organize programs and documents. They sit in the *root directory*—where the operating system is installed—and of course they have variations depending on the version of Windows. The following sections walk through the locations of important folders.

Most users and techs access folders and files in Windows with a tool called *Windows Explorer* in Windows 7 and *File Explorer* in Windows 8/8.1/10—although you can only see that difference in name by right-clicking the Start button or by moving your mouse over the folder icon in the taskbar (see Figure 2-34).

File Explorer

Figure 2-34

Mousing over the
File Explorer icon

The name of the window that opens when you run Windows Explorer or File Explorer generally reflects the current focus of the exploration. Figure 2-35 shows File Explorer displaying the contents of the Documents folder in Windows 10. Note the title of the window is *Documents*. The tool, regardless of the title, is File Explorer.

The default file and folder view in Windows has a couple of notable features that you can see in Figure 2-35. Note the "July 15" file? That X icon says Windows recognizes the file as a Microsoft Excel spreadsheet, which means almost certainly the actual filename is July 15.xlsx. The .xlsx is the *file extension*, hidden by default, that tells the OS which application to use with the file. This pairing of application with file extension is called *file association*.

Note also that Figure 2-35 has the View options displayed—that's the ribbon at the top of the window. To change the default view, make changes here.

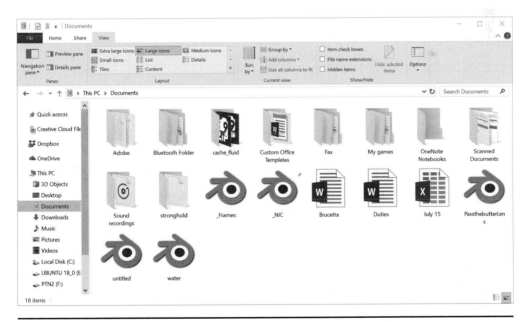

Figure 2-35   File Explorer

EXAM TIP The CompTIA A+ 1002 exam uses slightly older terms to describe the View options, such as *view hidden files* and *hide extensions*. Microsoft changes the wording and placement of things in the View options from version to version. The functions stay the same: show or hide specific elements in a folder.

You can also right-click a file or folder and select Properties to open the Folder Properties—or *Folder Options*, as you'll see on the exam. On the General tab, you can change several aspects of the file or folder. You can make it hidden, for example, or read-only. Context menus unlock many options in Windows features.

The folder structures that follow here use the standard formatting for describing folder structures. This is what you'll see on the 1002 exam and in almost any OS. Windows hides the "\" characters at the beginning to make it prettier. File Explorer might show something like "Local Disk (C:) > Users > Mike." This translates in proper fashion as C:\Users\Mike.

C:\Program Files (All Versions) By default, most programs install some or all of their essential files into a subfolder of the Program Files folder. If you installed a program, it should have its own folder in here. Individual companies decide how to label their sub-folders. Installing Photoshop made by Adobe, for example, creates the Adobe subfolder and then an Adobe Photoshop subfolder within it.

C:\Program Files (x86) The 64-bit editions of Windows create two directory structures for program files. The 64-bit applications go into the C:\Program Files folder, whereas the 32-bit applications go into the C:\Program Files (x86) folder. The separation makes it easy to find the proper version of whatever application you seek.

Personal Documents Modern versions of Windows use subfolders of the C:\Users folder to organize files for each user on a PC. Figure 2-36 shows the default folders for a user named Mike. Let's quickly survey the ones you need to know for the CompTIA A+ exams:

- **C:\Users\Mike\Desktop** This folder stores the files on the user's Desktop. If you delete this folder, you delete all the files placed on the Desktop.
- **C:\Users\Mike\Documents** This is the Documents or My Documents folder for that user. (Only Windows 7 uses My Documents. The others use Documents.)
- **C:\Users\Mike\Downloads** Microsoft's preferred download folder for applications to use. Most applications use this folder, but some do not.
- **C:\Users\Mike\Music** This is the default location for music you download. My guess is that more people have music in iTunes, but that's just me.
- **C:\Users\Mike\Pictures** Pictures is the default location for images imported into the PC, although the Pictures library can (and does) draw from many folder locations.
- **C:\Users\Mike\Videos** Videos is the default location for movies and homebrewed videos imported into a PC.

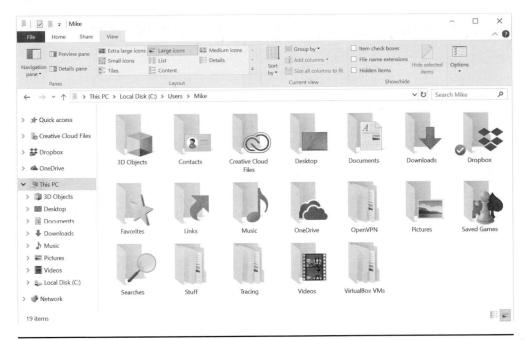

Figure 2-36   File Explorer viewing Mike's folders

macOS

Finder holds the keys to files and folders in macOS. Figure 2-37 shows Finder open to display Mike's Users folder. Note that, although its style differs from the Windows screen shown in Figure 2-36, it has functionally similar folders. These are the default locations for files on the Desktop, in Documents, Downloads, Music, Pictures, and so on. Each user account on the Mac will have a unique Users folder that is inaccessible by other users on that computer.

Linux

Ready to be shocked? Not surprisingly, Linux uses pretty much the same structure for user organization (see Figure 2-38). I guess once something seems logical to enough people, there's no reason to add confusion by changing the structure. The only major difference is the name: Linux uses the Home folder, rather than the Users folder.

The Tech Launch Points

Every OS has two or three areas for tech-specific utilities. This section shows you how to access those areas, primarily so that we don't have to repeat the steps to get to them when accessing them many times throughout the book. Just refer back to this section if you have difficulty remembering how to arrive at a place later on. Also, CompTIA will test your knowledge on how to access these tool locations, with specific steps. Use this section for the last-minute cram before taking the exams.

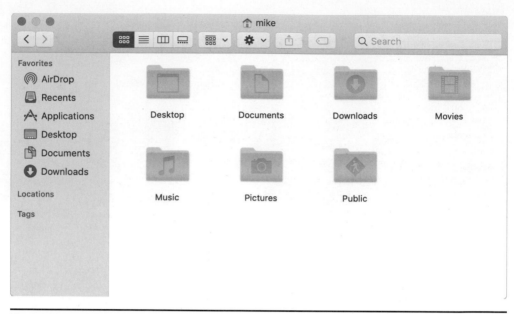

Figure 2-37   Mike's Users directory in Finder

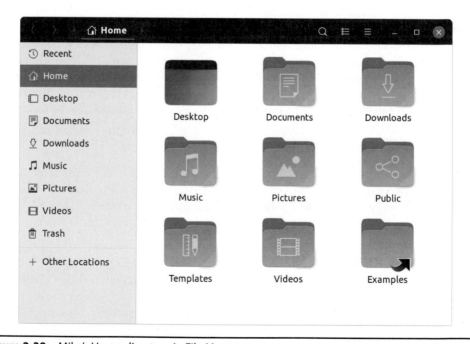

Figure 2-38   Mike's Home directory in File Manager

EXAM TIP The 1002 exam will test you on specific paths to specific tools. Be prepared for several multiple-choice and scenario-based questions on the topic.

Windows 7

Windows 7 has three tech launch points: the Control Panel, System Tools, and the command-line interface. You can get to each launch point in multiple ways.

Control Panel The *Control Panel* handles most of the maintenance, upgrade, and configuration aspects of Windows. As such, the Control Panel is the first set of tools for every tech to explore. You can find the Control Panel by clicking the Start button and choosing Control Panel from the Start menu.

The Control Panel opens in the Control Panel's Category view by default, which displays the icons in groups like Hardware and Sound. See Figure 2-39. This view requires an additional click (and sometimes a guess about which category includes what you need), so many techs use Classic view.

 NOTE The Control Panel enables you to access *Device Manager*, a critically important tool for techs and troubleshooting every device on a PC. With Device Manager, you can examine all of the hardware and drivers in a Windows computer. As you might suspect from that description, every tech spends a lot of time with this tool. You'll work with Device Manager many more times during the course of this book and your career as a PC tech.

Figure 2-39 Windows 7 Control Panel Category view

The CompTIA A+ 1002 exam specifically assumes Classic view with large icons, so you should do what every tech does: switch from Category view to Classic view. In Windows 7, select either Large icons or Small icons from the View by drop-down list for a similar effect. Figure 2-40 shows the Windows 7 Control Panel in Large icons view.

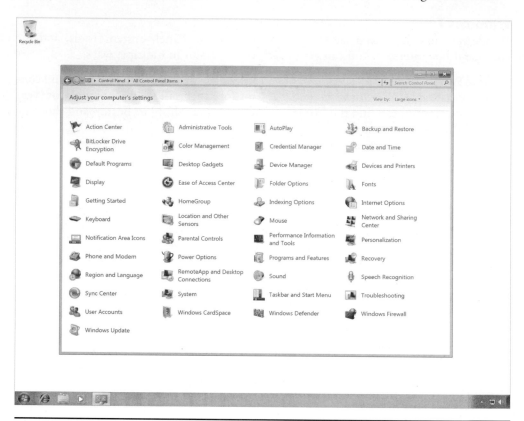

Figure 2-40   Windows 7 Control Panel Large icons view

Many programs, called *applets*, populate the Control Panel. The names and selection of applets vary depending on the version of Windows and whether any installed programs have added applets. But all versions of Windows have applets that enable you to control specific aspects of Windows, such as the appearance, installed applications, and system settings. You will get details on each applet as we put them into use over the course of this book.

System Tools   The Start menu in Windows 7 offers a variety of tech utilities collected in one place: System Tools. In the *System Tools* menu, you'll find commonly accessed tools such as System Information and Disk Defragmenter (see Figure 2-41).

Many techs overlook memorizing how to find the appropriate Windows tool to diagnose problems, but nothing hurts your credibility with a client like fumbling around, clicking on a variety of menus and applets, while mumbling, "I know it's around

Figure 2-41
Windows 7
System Tools
menu options

here somewhere." The CompTIA A+ certification 1002 exam therefore tests you on a variety of paths to appropriate tools.

To access System Tools in Windows 7, go to Start | All Programs | Accessories | System Tools. Each version of Windows shares many of the same tools, but each includes its own utilities as well. Rather than go through every tool here, I'll discuss each in detail during the appropriate scenarios in the book. Here's one example that won't appear again, Character Map.

Ever been using a program only to discover you need to enter a strange character such as the euro character (€) but your word processor doesn't support it? That's when you need the Character Map. It enables you to copy any Unicode character into the Clipboard (see Figure 2-42) and paste it into your document. Unicode has all the special symbols and alphabet characters used in languages throughout the world.

Command Line The Windows *command-line interface* (*CLI*) is a throwback to how Microsoft operating systems worked a long, long time ago when text commands were entered at a command prompt. Figure 2-43 shows the command prompt from DOS, the first operating system commonly used in PCs.

DOS is dead, but the command-line interface is alive and well in every version of Windows. Every good tech knows how to access and use the command-line interface. It is a lifesaver when the graphical part of Windows doesn't work, and it is often faster than

Figure 2-42
Character Map

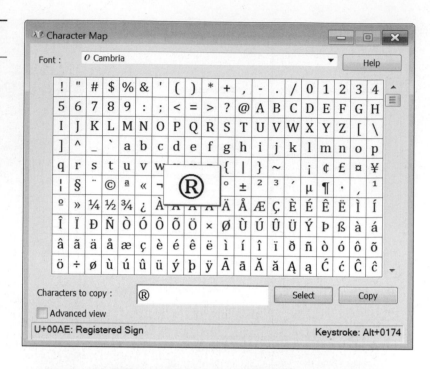

Figure 2-43
DOS command
prompt

```
Volume in drive C is SYSTEM
Volume Serial Number is 3A95-79D2
Directory of C:\

COMMAND  COM        54,645 05-31-94   6:22a
DOS           <DIR>         04-21-09   3:13p
WINDOWS       <DIR>         04-21-09   3:20p
WINA20   386         9,349 05-31-94   6:22a
CONFIG   OLD            71 04-21-09   3:15p
AUTOEXEC OLD            78 04-21-09   3:15p
WIN311        <DIR>         04-21-09   4:20p
CONFIG   SYS            85 04-21-09   3:32p
AUTOEXEC BAT            93 12-22-10   2:31p
GORILLA  BAS        30,702 10-21-09   4:24p
FILE0001 CHK        32,768 02-23-12   5:04p
SHMANSI       <DIR>         04-14-10   2:30p
        12 file(s)       127,791 bytes
                   2,081,423,360 bytes free

C:\>ver

MS-DOS Version 6.22

C:\>_
```

using a mouse if you're skilled at using it. An entire chapter (Chapter 15, "Working with the Command-Line Interface") is devoted to the command line, but let's look at one example of what the command line can do. First, you need to get there. Click the Start button, type **cmd** in the Search text box, and press the ENTER key. Figure 2-44 shows a command prompt in Windows 7.

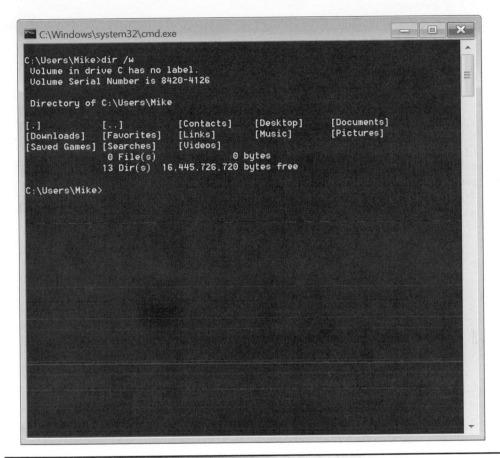

```
C:\Windows\system32\cmd.exe

C:\Users\Mike>dir /w
 Uolume in drive C has no label.
 Uolume Serial Number is 8420-4126

 Directory of C:\Users\Mike

[.]             [..]            [Contacts]      [Desktop]       [Documents]
[Downloads]     [Favorites]     [Links]         [Music]         [Pictures]
[Saved Games]   [Searches]      [Videos]
               0 File(s)                  0 bytes
              13 Dir(s)   16,445,726,720 bytes free

C:\Users\Mike>
```

Figure 2-44 Command prompt in Windows 7

Once at a command prompt, type **dir** and press ENTER. The dir *command-line utility* displays all the files and folders in a specific directory—probably your user folder for this exercise—and displays folder and file names as well as other information. (A *directory* is the same thing as a folder.) The dir command is just one of many command-line tools. You'll learn much more about dir in Chapter 15.

Windows 8/8.1

Windows 8/8.1 have three tech tool starting points, but they differ a little from the big three in Windows 7. The newer versions feature the Control Panel, Administrative Tools, and the command-line interface.

Control Panel The Control Panel in Windows 8/8.1 serves the same function as in previous versions of Windows—the go-to source for tech tools. You can access the Control Panel in several ways:

- Click the down arrow on the lower right of the Start screen and scroll all the way to the right in the list of Apps. In the Windows System category, click Control

Panel (see Figure 2-45). That's the slow way, but you should know it for the exams. You can also start typing **control panel** in the Search field in the Apps list. Control Panel will quickly appear as the best option to select.

- Right-click the Start button and select Control Panel from the menu (see Figure 2-46). You can bring up the same menu by pressing WINDOWS LOGO KEY + X. I call this menu *Tech Essentials* because it gives you very quick access not only to the Control Panel and its collection of tools but also to specific tools that every

Figure 2-45
Selecting Control Panel from the list of Apps

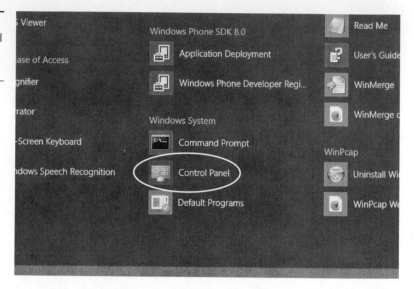

Figure 2-46
Right-clicking the Start button to access Control Panel

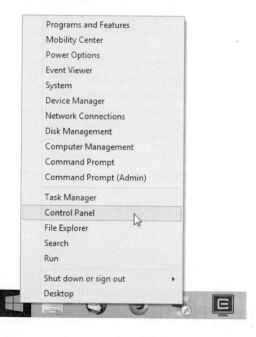

tech relies on heavily, like the Task Manager (for forcing frozen programs to close, among other things).

- In the Start screen, start typing **control panel**; the Control Panel will show up as the top option in the Search charm (see Figure 2-47). Select it to open.

Figure 2-47
Search charm with Control Panel as top option

Administrative Tools   Microsoft beefed up Administrative Tools starting in Windows 8, adding some of the tools found in the System Tools menu in previous versions of Windows. *Administrative Tools* enables you to set up hard drives, manage devices, test system performance, and much more. This is a go-to set of tools for every tech, and one that we will access many times for scenarios in this book.

As with Control Panel, you have several options for accessing Administrative Tools:

- In the Start screen, click the down arrow to open the Apps list. Scroll a little to the right and you'll see the list of Administrative Tools (see Figure 2-48). Select the specific tool you want to open.

- Begin typing **administrative tools** in the Start screen and Administrative Tools will quickly appear as an option in the Search charm (see Figure 2-49). Select it to open.

- Right-click the Start button (or press WINDOWS LOGO KEY + X) and select Control Panel from the context menu. In the Control Panel, select Administrative Tools to open.

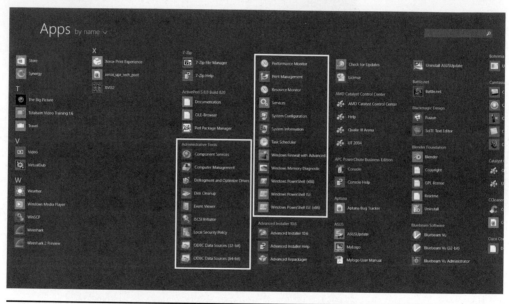

Figure 2-48   Administrative Tools in the Apps list

Command Line   The command-line interface retains its place as a go-to tool for techs. Windows 8/8.1 offer several ways to access it:

- Click the down arrow on the lower right of the Start screen and scroll all the way to the right in the list of Apps. In the Windows System category, click Command Prompt to open the utility. You can also start typing **command prompt** in the Search field in the Apps list. Command Prompt will quickly appear as the best option to select.

- Right-click the Start button (or press WINDOWS LOGO KEY + X) and select Command Prompt from the context menu to open the command-line interface.

- In the Start screen, start typing **cmd** or **command prompt** and Command Prompt will appear in the Search charm. Click on it to open it.

Figure 2-49
Administrative
Tools option in
the Search charm

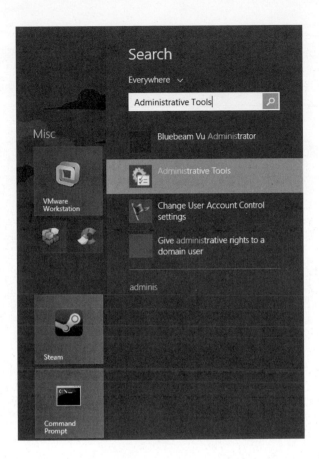

Windows 10

Windows 10 keeps the Control Panel and command-line interfaces seen in earlier versions of Windows, but focuses on an expanded Settings app for day-to-day administration. A vastly more powerful command-line interface, called Windows PowerShell, is also available, offering a much deeper set of command-line utilities as well as support for power scripting. Check out Chapter 15 to see more on PowerShell (see Figure 2-50).

 NOTE Windows PowerShell has been around for a while, predating Windows 7, but PowerShell has gone through six major updates, making the Windows 10 PowerShell much more powerful than the original versions. Windows 10 puts PowerShell as the default command-line interface when you right-click the Start button, though you can get to the older command line (cmd.exe) by typing **cmd** or **command** in the *Type here to search* field on the taskbar.

Control Panel   To get to the Control Panel, click the Start button, start typing **control panel**, and select Control Panel from the Search results.

Figure 2-50   PowerShell in Windows 10

Settings   *Settings* in Windows 10 combines many otherwise disparate utilities, apps, and tools traditionally spread out all over your computer into one fairly unified, handy Windows app (see Figure 2-51). Since the Settings app was introduced in Windows 8, it has taken over more and more tasks from the Control Panel. Expect Settings to grow as Windows 10 matures.

To access the Setting app, press the WINDOWS LOGO KEY to access the Start menu. Select Settings from the lower left to open the tool (see Figure 2-52).

macOS

macOS has two key launch points for techs: the System Preferences app and the Utilities folder. You can access both quickly.

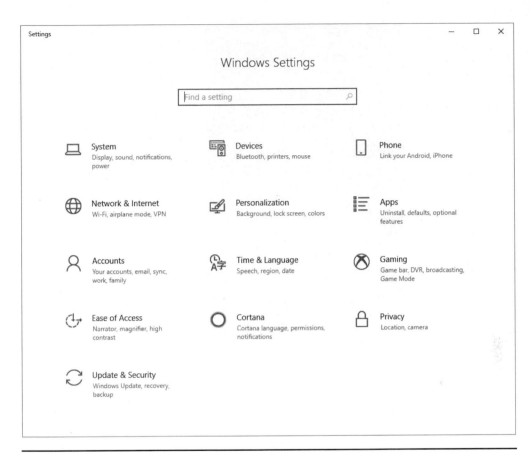

Figure 2-51 Windows Settings app

System Preferences To access *System Preferences*, click the Apple icon (top-left corner of screen). Select System Preferences from the permanent Apple menu to open the app (see Figure 2-53). From System Preferences you have access to almost all settings you will need to administer a macOS system.

Utilities Folder The second launch point is the *Utilities* folder, located neatly in the Applications folder. Because of its importance, Apple provides a quick shortcut to access it. With the Finder in focus, click Go on the menu bar and select Utilities (see Figure 2-54). Alternatively, use the hot-key combination: COMMAND-SHIFT-U. This gives you access to the tools you need to perform services on a Mac beyond what's included in System Preferences, including Activity Monitor and Terminal. The latter is the command-line interface for macOS, a very powerful tool for techs that we explore in detail in Chapter 15.

Figure 2-52
Accessing
Settings in
Windows 10
(note PowerShell
as default
command line)

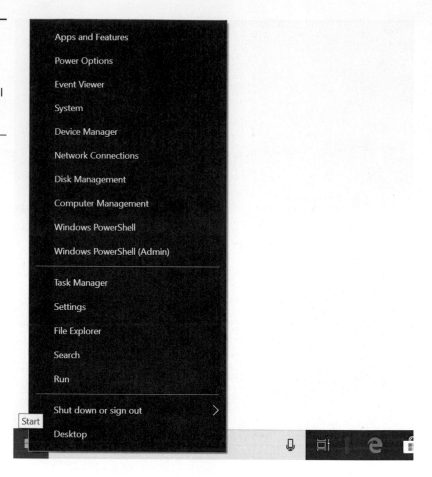

Figure 2-53
Accessing System
Preferences

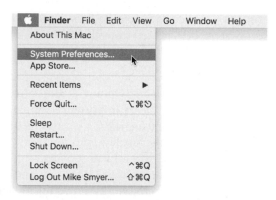

Figure 2-54
Accessing the
Utilities folder

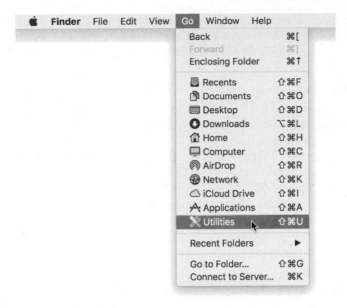

Linux

An essential tool in Linux for techs is the command line, called Terminal. You can get there in most distros by pressing CTRL-ALT-T. (See Chapter 15 for a lot of details about essential Linux commands.)

Other launch points vary from distro to distro. Here are the locations of the launch points for common desktop environments.

GNOME 3   The first launch point in a GNOME 3 DE is the All Settings application. To access All Settings, click the down arrow icon on the far right of the menu bar and select the wrench and screwdriver icon (see Figure 2-55).

Figure 2-55
Accessing All
Settings

For other system utilities such as System Monitor or Terminal, click the Activities button on the far left of the menu bar. From here you can search for the utility from the box at the top. This will open a menu showing all installed applications, and within this list is a folder for Utilities.

KDE Plasma Desktop   "Choice!" could be the unofficial motto of Linux, and when you are working on a KDE-based distro, you are certainly spoiled for choices. The downside to this abundance is that the configuration utilities can vary among the different KDE-based distros.

The one thing that is the same in all the KDE-based distros is that everything you need to work on the system is accessible from the *Kickoff* menu on the far left of the Panel (see Figure 2-56). The Kickoff menu looks and works a lot like the Start menu in Windows 7, so it should be relatively easy to navigate. Once in the Kickoff menu, you can search for a needed utility or select the Applications tab at the bottom. From here, most distros have a Utilities or System menu that holds all the key system configuration and maintenance applications.

Figure 2-56   KDE Kickoff menu

Chapter Review

Questions

1. Which version of Windows introduced the Metro UI?

    A. Windows 7

    B. Windows 8

    C. Windows 8.1

    D. Windows 10

2. Which Windows 8 feature did Microsoft not include in Windows 10?

    A. Metro/Modern UI

    B. Start button

    C. Control Panel

    D. Charms bar

3. What macOS feature is essentially multiple Desktops?

    A. Charms

    B. Desktop

    C. Mission Control

    D. Spaces

4. What KDE feature is essentially the Start button?

    A. Metro UI

    B. Kickoff

    C. Terminal

    D. GNOME 3

5. The user Mike has downloaded files with his Web browser. Where will they be stored by default?

    A. C:\Downloads

    B. C:\Mike\Desktop\Downloads

    C. C:\Users\Mike\Downloads

    D. C:\Users\Mike\Desktop\Downloads

6. 32-bit programs are installed into which folder by default in a 64-bit edition of Windows?

   A. C:\Program Files

   B. C:\Program Files (x32)

   C. C:\Program Files\Wins\Old

   D. C:\Program Files (x86)

7. Which macOS feature is functionally equivalent to Windows File Explorer?

   A. Finder

   B. Dock

   C. Quartz

   D. File Manager

8. Which of the following paths would open Administrative Tools in Windows 8.1?

   A. Right-click the taskbar and select Administrative Tools from the context menu.

   B. Right-click the Start button and select Administrative Tools from the context menu.

   C. Right-click anywhere on the Desktop and select Administrative Tools from the context menu.

   D. Press the WINDOWS KEY-L combination to open Administrative Tools.

9. What feature of macOS is the equivalent of the command-line interface in Windows?

   A. Dock

   B. Spaces

   C. Terminal

   D. Unity

10. What Windows app in Windows 10 combines many utilities into a unified tool?

   A. Settings

   B. Control

   C. Command Center

   D. Control Center

Answers

1. **B.** Microsoft introduced Metro UI with Windows 8.

2. **D.** Microsoft did not include the Charms bar in Windows 10. Bye!

3. **D.** *Spaces* is the term Apple uses for multiple Desktops in macOS.

4. **B.** Kickoff functions like a Start button for KDE desktops.

5. **C.** The default download location in Windows is C:\Users\<user name>\Downloads.

6. **D.** By default, 32-bit applications install into the C:\Program Files (x86) folder.

7. **A.** Finder is the equivalent of File Explorer.

8. **B.** To open Administrative Tools, right-click the Start button and select Administrative Tools. Easy!

9. **C.** Terminal is the equivalent of the Windows command-line interface.

10. **A.** The Settings app in Windows 10 offers many utilities in a unified interface.

CPUs

In this chapter, you will learn how to
- Identify the core components of a CPU
- Describe the relationship of CPUs with memory
- Explain the varieties of modern CPUs
- Select and install a CPU
- Troubleshoot CPUs

The *central processing unit* (*CPU*), also called the *microprocessor*, is a single silicon-based electronic chip that makes your computer...well, a computer. Desktop computers, laptops, smartphones, even tiny computers in a smartwatch or a washing machine have a CPU. A CPU invariably hides on the motherboard below a heat sink and often a fan assembly as well. CPU makers name their microprocessors in a fashion similar to the automobile industry: CPUs get a make and a model, such as Intel Core i9, Qualcomm Snapdragon 835, or AMD Ryzen 7. But what's happening inside the CPU to make it able to do the amazing things asked of it every time you step up to the keyboard?

This chapter delves into microprocessors in detail. We'll first discuss how processors work and the components that enable them to interact with the rest of the computer. The second section describes how CPUs work with memory. The third section takes you on a tour of modern CPUs. The fourth section gets into practical work, selecting and installing CPUs. The final section covers troubleshooting CPUs in detail.

EXAM TIP CompTIA only uses the term *CPU*, not *microprocessor*. Expect to see CPU on the 1001 exam.

Historical/Conceptual

CPU Core Components

Although the computer might seem to act quite intelligently, comparing the CPU to a human brain hugely overstates its capabilities. A CPU functions more like a very powerful calculator than like a brain—but, oh, what a calculator! Today's CPUs add, subtract, multiply, divide, and move billions of numbers per second. Processing that much information so quickly makes any CPU look intelligent. It's simply the speed of the CPU, rather than actual intelligence, that enables computers to perform feats such as accessing the Internet, playing visually stunning games, or editing photos.

A good technician needs to understand some basic CPU functions to support computing devices, so let's start with an analysis of how the CPU works. If you wanted to teach someone how an automobile engine works, you would use a relatively simple example engine, right? The same principle applies here. Let's begin our study of the CPU with the granddaddy of all PC CPUs: the Intel 8088, invented in the late 1970s. This CPU defined the idea of the modern microprocessor and contains the same basic parts used in the most advanced CPUs today.

The Man in the Box

Begin by visualizing the CPU as a man in a box (see Figure 3-1). This is one clever guy. He can perform virtually any mathematical function, manipulate data, and give answers *very quickly*.

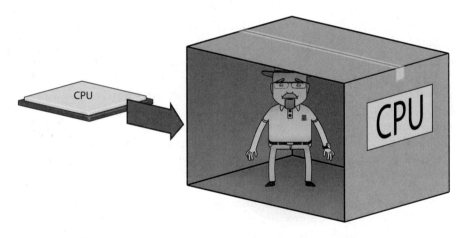

Figure 3-1   Imagine the CPU as a man in a box.

This guy is potentially very useful to us, but there's a catch—he lives in a tiny, closed box. Before he can work with us, we must come up with a way to exchange information with him (see Figure 3-2).

Imagine that we install a set of 16 light bulbs, 8 inside his box and 8 outside his box. Each of the 8 light bulbs inside the box connects to one of the 8 bulbs outside the box to form a pair. Each pair of light bulbs is always either on or off. You can control the 8 pairs of bulbs by using a set of 8 switches outside the box, and the Man in the Box can also control them by using an identical set of 8 switches inside the box. This light-bulb communication device is called the *external data bus* (*EDB*).

Figure 3-2   How do we talk with the Man in the Box?

Figure 3-3 shows a cutaway view of the external data bus. When either you or the Man in the Box flips a switch on, *both* light bulbs go on, and the switch on the other side is also flipped to the on position. If you or the Man in the Box turns a switch off, the light bulbs on both sides are turned off, along with the other switch for that pair.

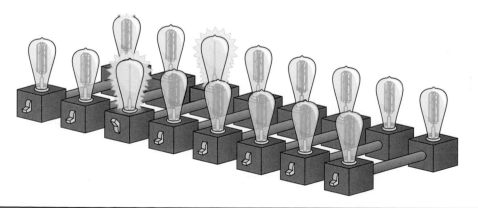

Figure 3-3   Cutaway of the external data bus—note that one light bulb pair is on.

Can you see how this works? By creating on/off patterns with the light bulbs that represent different pieces of data or commands, you can send that information to the Man in the Box, and he can send information back in the same way—*assuming that you agree ahead of time on what the different patterns of lights mean.* To accomplish this, you need some sort of codebook that assigns meanings to the many patterns of lights that the EDB might display. Keep this thought in mind while we push the analogy a bit more.

Before going any further, make sure you're clear on the fact that this is an analogy, not reality. There really is an EDB, but you won't see any light bulbs or switches on the CPU. You can, however, see little wires sticking out of many CPUs (see Figure 3-4). If you apply voltage to one of these wires, you in essence flip the switch. Get the idea? So, if that wire had voltage and if a tiny light bulb were attached to the wire, that light bulb would glow, would it not? By the same token, if the wire had no power, the light bulb would not glow. That is why the switch-and-light-bulb analogy may help you picture these little wires constantly flashing on and off.

Figure 3-4
Close-up of
the underside
of a CPU

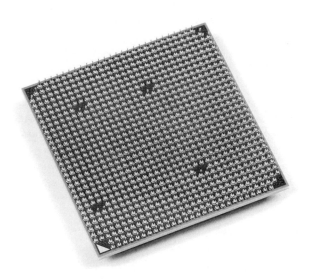

Now that the EDB enables you to communicate with the Man in the Box, you need to see how it works by placing voltages on the wires. This brings up a naming problem. It's a hassle to say something like "on-off-on-off-on-on-off-off" when talking about which wires have voltage. Rather than saying that one of the EDB wires is on or off, use the number 1 to represent on and the number 0 to represent off (see Figure 3-5). That way, instead of describing the state of the lights as "on-off-on-off-on-on-off-off," I can instead describe them by writing "10101100."

In computers, wires repeatedly turn on and off. As a result, we can use this "1 and 0" or *binary* system to describe the state of these wires at any given moment. (See, and you just thought computer geeks spoke in binary to confuse normal people. Ha!) There's much more to binary numbering in computing, but this is a great place to start.

Figure 3-5   Here "1" means on, "0" means off.

Registers

The Man in the Box provides good insight into the workspace inside a CPU. The EDB gives you a way to communicate with the Man in the Box so you can give him work to do. But to do this work, he needs a worktable; in fact, he needs at least four worktables. Each of these four worktables has 16 light bulbs. These light bulbs are not in pairs; they're just 16 light bulbs lined up straight across the table. Each light bulb is controlled by a single switch, operated only by the Man in the Box. By creating on/off patterns like the ones on the EDB, the Man in the Box can use these four sets of light bulbs to work math problems. In a real computer, these worktables are called *registers* (see Figure 3-6) and store internal commands and data.

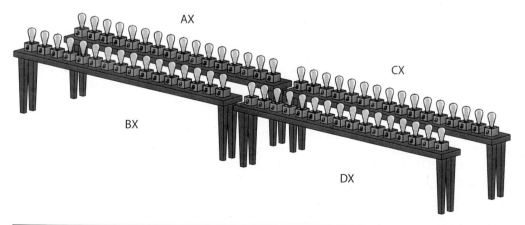

Figure 3-6   The four general-purpose registers

Registers provide the Man in the Box with a workplace for the problems you give him. All CPUs contain a large number of registers, but for the moment let's concentrate on the four most common ones: the *general-purpose registers*. Intel named them AX, BX, CX, and DX.

> **NOTE** The 8088 was the first CPU to use the four AX–DX general-purpose registers, and they still exist in even the latest CPUs. (But they have a lot more light bulbs!) In 32-bit processors, the registers add an E for extended, so EAX, EBX, and so on. The 64-bit registers get an R (I don't know why), thus RAX, RBX, and so on.

Great! We're just about ready to put the Man in the Box to work, but before you close the lid on the box, you must give the Man one more tool. Remember the codebook I mentioned earlier? Let's make one to enable us to communicate with him. Figure 3-7 shows the codebook we'll use. We'll give one copy to him and make a second for us.

Figure 3-7
CPU codebook

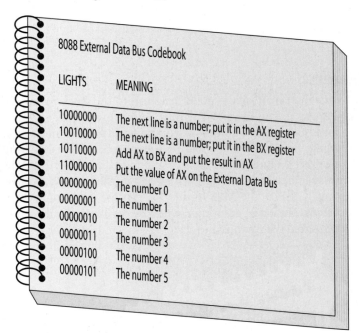

In this codebook, for example, 10000111 means *Move the number 7 into the AX register.* These commands are called the microprocessor's *machine language.* The commands listed in the figure are not actual commands; as you've probably guessed, I've simplified dramatically. The Intel 8088 CPU actually used commands very similar to these, plus a few hundred others.

Here are some examples of real machine language for the Intel 8088:

10111010	The next line of code is a number. Put that number into the DX register.
01000001	Add 1 to the number already in the CX register.
00111100	Compare the value in the AX register with the next line of code.

By placing machine language commands—called *lines of code*—onto the EDB one at a time, you can instruct the Man in the Box to do specific tasks. All of the machine language commands that the CPU understands make up the CPU's *instruction set*.

So here is the CPU so far: the Man in the Box can communicate with the outside world via the EDB; he has four registers he can use to work on the problems you give him; and he has a codebook—the instruction set—so he can understand the different patterns (machine language commands) on the EDB (see Figure 3-8).

Figure 3-8 The CPU so far

Clock

Okay, so you're ready to put the Man in the Box to work. You can send the first command by lighting up wires on the EDB. How does he know when you've finished setting up the wires and it's time to act?

Imagine there's a bell inside the box activated by a button on the outside of the box. Each time you press the button to sound the bell, the Man in the Box reads the next set of lights on the EDB. Of course, a real computer doesn't use a bell. The bell on a real CPU is a special wire called the *clock wire* (most diagrams label the clock wire CLK).

A charge on the CLK wire tells the CPU that another piece of information is waiting to be processed (see Figure 3-9).

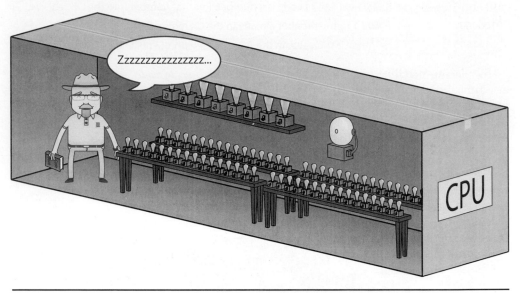

Figure 3-9   The CPU does nothing until activated by the clock.

For the CPU to process a command placed on the EDB, a certain minimum voltage must be applied to the CLK wire. A single charge to the CLK wire is called a *clock cycle*. Actually, the CPU requires at least two clock cycles to act on a command, and usually more. In fact, a CPU may require hundreds of clock cycles to process some commands (see Figure 3-10).

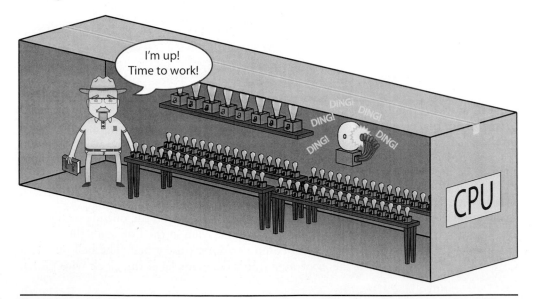

Figure 3-10   The CPU often needs more than one clock cycle to get a result.

The maximum number of clock cycles that a CPU can handle in a given period of time is referred to as its *clock speed*. The clock speed is the fastest speed at which a CPU can operate, determined by the CPU manufacturer. The Intel 8088 processor had a clock speed of 4.77 MHz (4.77 million cycles per second), extremely slow by modern standards, but still a pretty big number compared to using a pencil and paper. High-end CPUs today run at speeds in excess of 5 GHz (5 billion cycles per second). You'll see these "hertz" terms a lot in this chapter, so here's what they mean:

1 hertz (1 Hz) = 1 cycle per second

1 megahertz (1 MHz) = 1 million cycles per second

1 gigahertz (1 GHz) = 1 billion cycles per second

A CPU's clock speed is its *maximum* speed, not the speed at which it *must* run. A CPU can run at any speed, as long as that speed does not exceed its clock speed. Many CPU models have the clock speed printed clearly (see Figure 3-11). Other models might have a cryptic code.

Figure 3-11
Clock speed
printed on a CPU
(3.30GHZ)

The *system crystal* determines the speed at which a CPU and the rest of the PC operate. The system crystal is usually a quartz oscillator, very similar to the one in a wristwatch, soldered to the motherboard (see Figure 3-12).

 NOTE CPU makers sell the exact make and model of CPU at a number of different speeds. All of these CPUs come off of the same assembly lines, so why do they have different speeds? Every CPU comes with subtle differences—flaws, really—in the silicon that makes one CPU run faster than another. The speed difference comes from testing each CPU to see what speed it can handle.

Figure 3-12
One of many
types of system
crystals

The quartz oscillator sends out an electric pulse at a certain speed, many millions of times per second. This signal goes first to a clock chip that adjusts the pulse, usually increasing the pulse sent by the crystal by some large multiple. (The folks who make motherboards could connect the crystal directly to the CPU's clock wire, but then if you wanted to replace your CPU with a CPU with a different clock speed, you'd need to replace the crystal too.) As long as the computer is turned on, the quartz oscillator, through the clock chip, fires a charge on the CLK wire, in essence pushing the system along.

Visualize the system crystal as a metronome for the CPU. The quartz oscillator repeatedly fires a charge on the CLK wire, setting the beat, if you will, for the CPU's activities. If the system crystal sets a beat slower than the CPU's clock speed, the CPU will work just fine, though at the slower speed of the system crystal. If the system crystal forces the CPU to run faster than its clock speed, it can overheat and stop working. Before you install a CPU into a system, you must make sure that the crystal and clock chip send out the correct clock pulse for that particular CPU. In the old days, this required very careful adjustments. With today's systems, the motherboard talks to the CPU. The CPU tells the motherboard the clock speed it needs, and the clock chip automatically adjusts for the CPU, making this process now invisible.

NOTE Aggressive users sometimes intentionally overclock CPUs by telling the clock chip to multiply the pulse faster than the CPU's designed speed. They do this to make slower (cheaper) CPUs run faster and to get more performance in demanding programs. See the "Overclocking" section later in this chapter.

Back to the External Data Bus

One more reality check. We've been talking about tables with racks of light bulbs, but of course real CPU registers don't use light bulbs to represent on/1 and off/0. Registers are tiny storage areas on the CPU made up of microscopic semiconductor circuits that hold charges. It's just easier to imagine a light bulb lit up to represent a circuit holding a charge; when the light bulb is off, there is no charge.

Figure 3-13 is a diagram of an 8088 CPU, showing the wires that comprise the external data bus and the single clock wire. Because the registers are inside the CPU, you can't see them in this figure.

Figure 3-13

Diagram of an Intel 8088 showing the external data bus and clock wires

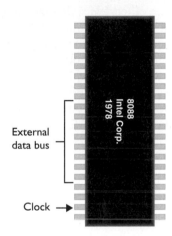

Now that you have learned what components are involved in the process, try the following simple exercise to see how the process works. In this example, you tell the CPU to add 2 + 3. To do this, you must send a series of commands to the CPU; the CPU will act on each command, eventually giving you an answer. Refer to the codebook in Figure 3-7 to translate the instructions you're giving the Man in the Box into binary commands.

Did you try it? Here's how it works:

1. Place 10000000 on the external data bus (EDB).

2. Place 00000010 on the EDB.

3. Place 10010000 on the EDB.

4. Place 00000011 on the EDB.

5. Place 10110000 on the EDB.

6. Place 11000000 on the EDB.

When you finish step 6, the value on the EDB will be 00000101, the decimal number 5 written in binary.

Congrats! You just added 2 + 3 by using individual commands from the codebook. This set of commands is known as a *program*, which is a series of commands sent to a CPU in a specific order for the CPU to perform work. Each discrete setting of the EDB is a line of code. This program, therefore, has six lines of code.

Memory

Now that you've seen how the CPU executes program code, let's work backward in the process for a moment and think about how the program code gets to the external data bus. The program itself is stored on the hard drive. In theory, you could build a computer that sends data from the hard drive directly to the CPU, but there's a problem—the hard drive is too slow. Even the ancient 8088, with its clock speed of 4.77 MHz, could conceivably process several million lines of code every second. Modern CPUs crank out billions of lines every second. Hard drives simply can't give the data to the CPU at a fast enough speed.

Computers need some other device that takes copies of programs from the hard drive and then sends them, one line at a time, to the CPU quickly enough to keep up with its demands. Because each line of code is nothing more than a pattern of eight ones and zeros, any device that can store ones and zeros eight-across will do. Devices that in any way hold ones and zeros that the CPU accesses are known generically as *memory*.

Many types of devices store ones and zeros perfectly well—technically even a piece of paper counts as memory—but computers need memory that does more than just store groups of eight ones and zeros. Consider this pretend program:

1. Put 2 in the AX register.
2. Put 5 in the BX register.
3. If AX is greater than BX, run line 4; otherwise, go to line 6.
4. Add 1 to the value in AX.
5. Go back to line 1.
6. Put the value of AX on the EDB.

This program has an IF statement, also called a *branch* by CPU makers. The CPU needs a way to address each line of this memory—a way for the CPU to say to the memory, "Give me the next line of code" or "Give me line 6." Addressing memory takes care of another problem: the memory must store not only programs but also the result of the programs. If the CPU adds 2 + 3 and gets 5, the memory needs to store that 5 in such a way that other programs may later read that 5, or possibly even store that 5 on a hard drive. By addressing each line of memory, other programs will know where to find the data.

Memory and RAM

Memory must store not only programs, but also data. The CPU needs to be able to read and write to this storage medium. Additionally, this system must enable the CPU to jump to *any* line of stored code as easily as to any other line of code. All of this must be done at or at least near the clock speed of the CPU. Fortunately, this magical device has existed for many years: *random access memory (RAM)*. Chapter 4, "RAM," develops the concept in detail, so for now let's look at RAM as an electronic spreadsheet, like one you can generate in Microsoft Excel (see Figure 3-14). Each cell in this spreadsheet can store

Figure 3-14
RAM as a
spreadsheet

1	0	0	0	0	0	1	1
0	1	0	0	0	0	0	0
0	0	0	0	1	1	0	1
0	1	0	1	0	0	0	0
0	0	0	0	0	0	0	1
0	1	0	1	1	0	1	0
0	0	1	1	1	1	0	0
0	0	0	0	1	0	0	1
1	1	1	0	0	0	0	0
0	0	1	0	1	1	1	0
1	0	0	0	0	0	0	0
1	0	1	0	1	0	1	0

only a one or a zero. Each cell is called a *bit*. Each row in the spreadsheet is 8 bits across to match the EDB of the 8088. Each row of 8 bits is called a *byte*. In PCs, RAM transfers and stores data to and from the CPU in byte-sized chunks. RAM is therefore arranged in byte-sized rows. Here are the terms used to talk about quantities of bits:

- Any individual 1 or 0 = a bit
- 4 bits – a nibble
- 8 bits = a byte
- 16 bits = a word
- 32 bits = a double word
- 64 bits = a paragraph or quad word

The number of bytes of RAM varies from PC to PC. In earlier PCs, from around 1980 to 1990, the typical system would have only a few hundred thousand bytes of RAM. Today's systems often have billions of bytes of RAM.

Let's stop here for a quick reality check. Electronically, RAM looks like a spreadsheet, but real RAM is made of groups of semiconductor chips soldered onto small cards that snap into your computer (see Figure 3-15). In Chapter 4, you'll see how these groups of chips actually make themselves look like a spreadsheet. For now, don't worry about real RAM and just stick with the spreadsheet idea.

Figure 3-15
Typical RAM

The CPU accesses any one row of RAM as easily and as fast as any other row, which explains the "random access" part of RAM. Not only is RAM randomly accessible, it's also fast. By storing programs on RAM, the CPU can access and run them very quickly. RAM also stores any data that the CPU actively uses.

Computers use *dynamic RAM* (*DRAM*) for the main system memory. DRAM needs both a constant electrical charge and a periodic refresh of the circuits; otherwise, it loses data—that's what makes it dynamic rather than static in content. The refresh can cause some delays, because the CPU has to wait for the refresh to happen, but modern CPU manufacturers have clever ways to get by this issue, as you'll see when you read about modern processor technology later in this chapter.

Don't confuse RAM with mass storage devices such as hard drives and flash drives. You use hard drives and flash drives to store programs and data permanently. Chapters 8 through 10 discuss permanent storage in intimate detail.

Address Bus

So far, the entire PC consists of only a CPU and RAM. But the CPU and the RAM need some connection so they can talk to each other. To do so, extend the external data bus from the CPU so it can talk to the RAM (see Figure 3-16).

Figure 3-16
Extending the EDB

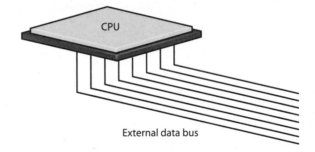

External data bus

Wait a minute. This is not a matter of just plugging the RAM into the EDB wires! RAM is a spreadsheet with thousands and thousands of discrete rows, and you need to look at the contents of only one row of the spreadsheet at a time, right? So how do you connect the RAM to the EDB in such a way that the CPU can see any one given row but still give the CPU the capability to look at *any* row in RAM?

We need some type of chip between the RAM and the CPU to make the connection. The CPU needs to be able to say which row of RAM it wants, and the chip should handle the mechanics of retrieving that row of data from the RAM and putting it on the EDB. This chip comes with many names, but for right now just call it the *memory controller chip* (*MCC*).

The MCC contains special circuitry so it can grab the contents of any line of RAM and place that data or command on the EDB. This in turn enables the CPU to act on that code (see Figure 3-17).

Once the MCC is in place to grab any discrete byte of RAM, the CPU needs to be able to tell the MCC which line of code it needs. The CPU therefore gains a second set

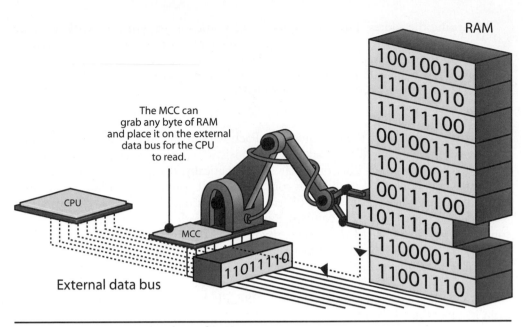

Figure 3-17 The MCC grabs a byte of RAM.

of wires, called the *address bus*, with which it can communicate with the MCC. Different CPUs have different numbers of wires (which, you will soon see, is very significant). The 8088 had 20 wires in its address bus (see Figure 3-18).

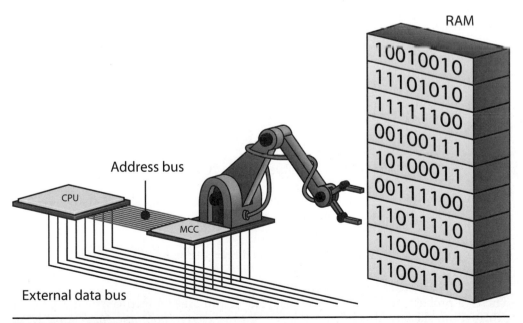

Figure 3-18 Address bus

By turning the address bus wires on and off in different patterns, the CPU tells the MCC which line of RAM it wants at any given moment. Every different pattern of ones and zeros on these 20 wires points to one byte of RAM. There are two big questions here. First, how many different patterns of on-and-off wires can exist with 20 wires? And second, which pattern goes to which row of RAM?

How Many Patterns?

Mathematics can answer the first question. Each wire in the address bus exists in only one of two states: on or off. If the address bus consisted of only one wire, that wire would at any given moment be either on or off. Mathematically, that gives you (pull out your old pre-algebra books) $2^1 = 2$ different combinations. If you have two address bus wires, the address bus wires create $2^2 = 4$ different combinations. If you have 20 wires, you would have 2^{20} (or 1,048,576) combinations. Because each pattern points to one line of code and each line of RAM is one byte, if you know the number of wires in the CPU's address bus, you know the maximum amount of RAM that a particular CPU can handle.

Because the 8088 had a 20-wire address bus, the most RAM it could handle was 2^{20} or 1,048,576 bytes. The 8088, therefore, had an *address space* of 1,048,576 bytes. This is not to say that every computer with an 8088 CPU had 1,048,576 bytes of RAM. Far from it! The original IBM PC only had a measly 65,536 bytes—but that was considered plenty back in the Dark Ages of Computing in the early 1980s.

Okay, so you know that the 8088 had 20 address wires and a total address space of 1,048,576 bytes. Although this is accurate, no one uses such an exact term to discuss the address space of the 8088. Instead you say that the 8088 had one *megabyte* (1 MB) of address space.

What's a "mega"? Well, let's get some terminology down. Dealing with computers means constantly dealing with the number of patterns a set of wires can handle. Certain powers of 2 have names used a lot in computing. The following list explains.

1 kilo = 2^{10} = 1024 (abbreviated as "K")

1 kilobyte = 1024 bytes (abbreviated as "KB")

1 mega = 2^{20} = 1,048,576 (abbreviated as "M")

1 megabyte = 1,048,576 bytes (abbreviated as "MB")

1 giga = 2^{30} = 1,073,741,824 (abbreviated as "G")

1 gigabyte = 1,073,741,824 bytes (abbreviated as "GB")

1 tera = 2^{40} = 1,099,511,627,776 (abbreviated as "T")

1 terabyte = 1,099,511,627,776 bytes (abbreviated as "TB")

Metric System and Computer Memory

There's a problem with that list you just read. If you asked a metric system expert for explanation, she would say that a *kilo* is equal to exactly *1000*, not *1024*! Am I lying to you?

Well, yes, I am, but not out of malice. I'm just the messenger of yet another weird aspect to computing. Here's what happened, a long time ago.

In the early days of computing there arose a need to talk about large values, but the words hadn't been invented. In one case, the memory address folks were trying to describe permutations. They used values based on powers of two as just described. No one had ever invented terms for 1024 or 1,048,576, so they used kilo and mega, as 1000 was close enough to 1024 and 1,000,000 was close enough to 1,048,576.

In the meantime, computer people measuring quantities such as CPU speeds and hard drive capacities didn't count with powers of two. They just needed regular 1000 for kilo and 1,000,000 for mega.

From the early 1980s until around 1990, nobody cared about this weird thing where one word could mean two values. Everything was fine until the math nerds and the attorneys started making trouble. To fix this, in 1998 the International Electrotechnical Committee (IEC) invented special prefixes for binary values I call the *ibis* (pronounced *eee-bees*).

1 kibi = 2^{10} = 1024 (abbreviated as "Ki")

1 mebi = 2^{20} = 1,048,576 (abbreviated as "Mi")

1 gibi = 2^{30} = 1,073,741,824 (abbreviated as "Gi")

1 tebi – 2^{40} – 1,099,511,627,776 (abbreviated as "Ti")

To follow this revised naming convention, you should say, "the 8088 processor could address one mebibyte (MiB) of memory." The problem is that *no one* but math nerds use these ibis. If you buy RAM, the manufacturers use the term gigabyte even though technically they should use gibibyte. Welcome to the weird world of counting in IT. Let's get back to memory.

 NOTE The jury is still out on correct pronunciation of the ibis. You will find ardent supporters of "keebeebyte" and equally passionate supporters of "kehbeebyte." It doesn't really matter, because the rest of us just say "kilobyte."

Which Pattern Goes to Which Row?

The second question is a little harder: "Which pattern goes to which row of RAM?" To understand this, let's take a moment to discuss binary counting. In binary, only two numbers exist, 0 and 1, which makes binary a handy way to work with wires that turn on and off. Let's try to count in binary: 0, 1…what's next? It's not 2—you can only use zeros and ones. The next number after 1 is 10! Now let's count in binary to 1000: 0, 1, 10, 11, 100, 101, 110, 111, 1000. Try counting to 10000. Don't worry; it hardly takes any time at all.

Super; you now count in binary as well as any math professor. Let's add to the concept. Stop thinking about binary for just a moment and think about good old base 10 (regular numbers). If you have the number 365, can you put zeros in front of the 365, like this: 000365? Sure you can—it doesn't change the value at all. The same thing is true in binary. Putting zeros in front of a value doesn't change a thing! Let's count again to 1000 in binary. In this case, add enough zeros to make 20 places:

00000000000000000000

00000000000000000001

00000000000000000010

00000000000000000011

00000000000000000100

00000000000000000101

00000000000000000110

00000000000000000111

00000000000000001000

Hey, wouldn't this be a great way to represent each line of RAM on the address bus? The CPU identifies the first byte of RAM on the address bus with 00000000000000000000. The CPU identifies the last RAM row with 11111111111111111111. When the CPU turns off all the address bus wires, it wants the first line of RAM; when it turns on all the wires, it wants the 1,048,576th line of RAM. Obviously, the address bus also addresses all the rows of RAM in between. So, by lighting up different patterns of ones and zeros on the address bus, the CPU can access any row of RAM it needs.

 NOTE Bits and bytes are abbreviated differently. Bits get a lowercase b, whereas bytes get a capital B. So for example, 4 Kb is 4 kilobits, but 4 KB is 4 kilobytes. The big-B little-b standard applies all the way up the food chain, so 2 Mb = 2 megabits; 2 MB = 2 megabytes; 4 Gb = 4 gigabits; 4 GB = 4 gigabytes; and so on.

1001

Modern CPUs

CPU manufacturers have achieved stunning progress with microprocessors since the days of the Intel 8088, and the rate of change doesn't show any signs of slowing. At the core, though, today's CPUs function similarly to the processors of your forefathers. The *arithmetic logic unit (ALU)*—that's the Man in the Box—still crunches numbers many millions of times per second. CPUs rely on memory to feed them lines of programming as quickly as possible.

This section brings the CPU into the present. We'll first look at models you can buy today, and then we'll turn to essential improvements in technology you should understand.

Developers

When IBM awarded Intel the contract to provide the CPUs for its new IBM PC back in 1980, it established for Intel a virtual monopoly on all PC CPUs. The other home-computer CPU makers of the time faded away: MOS Technology, Zilog, Motorola—no one could compete directly with Intel. Over time, other competitors have risen to challenge Intel's market-segment share dominance. A company called Advanced Micro Devices (AMD) began to make clones of Intel CPUs, creating an interesting and rather cutthroat competition with Intel that lasts to this day.

NOTE The ever-growing selection of mobile devices, such as the Apple iPhone and iPad and most Android devices, use a CPU architecture developed by ARM Holdings, called *ARM*. ARM-based processors use a simpler, more energy-efficient design, the reduced instruction set computing (RISC) architecture. They can't match the raw power of the Intel and AMD complex instruction set computing (CISC) chips, but the savings in cost and battery life make ARM-based processors ideal for mobile devices. (Note that the clear distinction between RISC and CISC processors has blurred. Each design today borrows features of the other design to increase efficiency.)

ARM Holdings designs ARM CPUs, but doesn't manufacture them. Many other companies—most notably, Qualcomm—license the design and manufacture their own versions. See Chapter 24, "Understanding Mobile Devices."

Intel

Intel Corporation thoroughly dominates the personal computer market with its CPUs and motherboard support chips. At nearly every step in the evolution of the PC, Intel has led the way with technological advances and surprising flexibility for such a huge corporation. Intel CPUs—and more specifically, their instruction sets—define the personal computer. Intel currently produces a dozen or so models of CPU for both desktop and portable computers. Most of Intel's desktop and laptop processors are sold under the Core, Pentium, and Celeron brands. Their high-end server chips are called Xeon.

AMD

AMD makes superb CPUs for the PC market and provides competition that keeps Intel on its toes. Like Intel, AMD doesn't just make CPUs, but their CPU business is certainly the part that the public notices. AMD has made CPUs that clone the function of Intel CPUs. If Intel invented the CPU used in the original IBM PC, how could AMD make clone CPUs without getting sued? Chipmakers have a habit of exchanging technologies through cross-license agreements. Way back in 1976, AMD and Intel signed just such an agreement, giving AMD the right to copy certain types of CPUs.

The trouble started with the Intel 8088. Intel needed AMD's help to supply enough CPUs to satisfy IBM's demands. But after a few years, Intel had grown tremendously and no longer wanted AMD to make CPUs. AMD said, "Too bad. See this agreement you signed?" Throughout the 1980s and into the 1990s, AMD made pin-for-pin identical CPUs that matched the Intel lines of CPUs (see Figure 3-19). You could yank an Intel CPU out of a system and snap in an AMD CPU—no problem!

Figure 3-19
Electronically identical Intel and AMD 486 CPUs from the early 1990s

In January 1995, after many years of legal wrangling, Intel and AMD settled and decided to end the licensing agreements. As a result of this settlement, AMD chips are no longer compatible with sockets or motherboards made for Intel CPUs—even though in some cases the chips look similar. Today, if you want to use an AMD CPU, you must purchase a motherboard designed for AMD CPUs. If you want to use an Intel CPU, you must purchase a motherboard designed for Intel CPUs. You have a choice: Intel or AMD.

Model Names

Intel and AMD differentiate product lines by using different product names, and these names have changed over the years. For a long time, Intel used *Pentium* for its flagship model, just adding model numbers to show successive generations—Pentium, Pentium II, Pentium III, and so on. AMD used the *Athlon* brand in a similar fashion.

Most discussions on PC CPUs focus on four end-product lines: desktop PC, budget PC, portable PC, and server computers. Table 3-1 displays many of the current product lines and names.

Market	Intel	AMD
Enthusiast	Core i7/i9	Ryzen, Ryzen Threadripper
Mainstream desktop	Core i7/i5/i3	A-Series Pro, Ryzen
Budget desktop	Pentium, Celeron	A-Series, FX
Portable/Mobile	Core i7/i5/i3 (mobile), Mobile Celeron	Ryzen, A-Series
Server	Xeon	Opteron, EPYC
Workstation	Xeon	Ryzen PRO, Ryzen Threadripper

Table 3-1   Current Intel and AMD Product Lines and Names

Microarchitecture

Intel and AMD continually develop faster, smarter, and generally more capable CPUs. In general, each company comes up with a major new design, called a *microarchitecture*, about every three years. They try to minimize the number of model names in use, however, most likely for marketing purposes. This means that they release CPUs labeled as the same model, but the CPUs inside can be very different from earlier versions of that model. Both companies use *code names* to keep track of different variations within models (see Figure 3-20). As a tech, you need to know both the models and code names to be able to make proper recommendations for your clients. One example illustrates the need: the Intel Core i7.

Figure 3-20

Same branding, but different capabilities

Intel released the first Core i7 in the summer of 2008. By spring of 2012, the original microarchitecture—code named Nehalem—had gone through five variations, none of which worked on motherboards designed for one of the other variations. Plus, in 2011, Intel introduced the Sandy Bridge version of the Core i7 that eventually had two desktop versions and a mobile version, all of which used still other sockets. Just about every year since then has seen a new Core i7 based on improved architectures with different code names such as Ivy Bridge, Haswell, Broadwell, and so on. (And I'm simplifying the variations here.)

NOTE The processor number helps a lot when comparing processors once you decode the meanings. We need to cover more about modern processors before introducing processor numbers. Look for more information in the upcoming section, "Deciphering Processor Numbers."

At this point, a lot of new techs throw their hands in the air. How do you keep up? How do you know which CPU will give your customer the best value for his or her money and provide the right computing firepower for his or her needs? Simply put, you need to research efficiently.

Your first stop should be the manufacturers' Web sites. Both companies put out a lot of information on their products.

- www.intel.com
- www.amd.com

You can also find many high-quality tech Web sites devoted to reporting on the latest CPUs. When a client needs an upgrade, surf the Web for recent articles and make comparisons. Because you'll understand the underlying technology from your CompTIA A+ studies, you'll be able to follow the conversations with confidence. Here's a list of some of the sites I use:

- http://arstechnica.com
- www.anandtech.com
- www.tomshardware.com
- www.bit-tech.net

Finally, you can find great, exhaustive articles on all things tech at Wikipedia:

- www.wikipedia.org

 NOTE Wikipedia is a user-generated, self-regulated resource. I've found it to be accurate on technical issues the majority of the time, but you should always check other references as well. Nicely, most article authors on the site provide their sources through footnotes. You can often use the Wikipedia articles as jumping-off points for deeper searches.

Desktop Versus Mobile

Mobile devices, such as portable computers, have needs that differ from those of desktop computers, notably the need to consume as little electricity as possible. This helps in two ways: extending battery charge and creating less heat.

Both Intel and AMD have engineers devoted to making excellent mobile versions of their CPUs that sport advanced energy-saving features (see Figure 3-21). These mobile CPUs consume much less power than their desktop counterparts. They also run in very low power mode and scale up automatically if the user demands more power from the CPU. If you're surfing the Web at an airport terminal, the CPU doesn't draw too much power. When you switch to playing an action game, the CPU kicks into gear. Saving energy by making the CPU run more slowly when demand is light is generically called *throttling*.

Figure 3-21
Desktop vs.
mobile, fight!

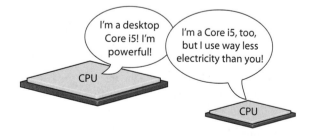

Unfortunately this picture gets more complicated when you throw in heat. Because most portable and mobile computing devices are very compact, they can't dissipate heat as quickly as a well-cooled desktop system. Mobile CPUs can scale up to handle demanding tasks, but they'll start accumulating heat quickly. As this heat nears levels that could damage the CPU, it will engage in *thermal throttling* to protect itself. A system trying to do demanding work with only a fraction of its full power available may grind to a halt!

NOTE The industry describes how much heat a busy CPU generates with a figure (measured in watts) called its *thermal design power* (*TDP*). The TDP can give you a rough idea of how much energy a CPU draws and what kind of cooling it will need. It can also help you select more efficient CPUs.

TDP has been trending down over time (especially in recent years), but it may help to have a sense of what these values look like in the real world. The CPUs in a smartphone or tablet typically have a TDP from 2 to 15 watts, laptop CPUs range from 7 to 65 watts, and desktop CPUs tend to range from 50 to 140 watts.

Many of the technologies developed for mobile processors migrate back into their more power-hungry desktop siblings. That's a bonus for the planet (and maybe your power bill).

Technology

Although microprocessors today still serve the same function as the venerable 8088—crunching numbers—they do so far more efficiently. Engineers have altered, enhanced, and improved CPUs in a number of ways. This section looks at eight features:

- Clock multipliers
- 64-bit processing
- Virtualization support
- Parallel execution
- Multicore processing
- Integrated memory controller (IMC)
- Integrated graphics processing unit (GPU)
- Security

Clock Multipliers

All modern CPUs run at some multiple of the system clock speed. The system bus on my Ryzen 7 machine, for example, runs at 100 MHz. The clock multiplier goes up to ×32 at full load to support the 3.2 GHz maximum speed. Originally, CPUs ran at the speed of the bus, but engineers early on realized the CPU was the only thing doing any work much of the time. If the engineers could speed up just the internal operations of the CPU and not anything else, they could speed up the whole computing process. Figure 3-22 shows a nifty program called CPU-Z displaying my CPU details. Note that all I'm doing is typing at the moment, so the CPU has dropped the clock multiplier down to ×15.5 and the CPU core speed is only 1546 MHz.

Figure 3-22

CPU-Z showing the clock speed, multiplier, and bus speed of a Ryzen 7 processor hardly breaking a sweat

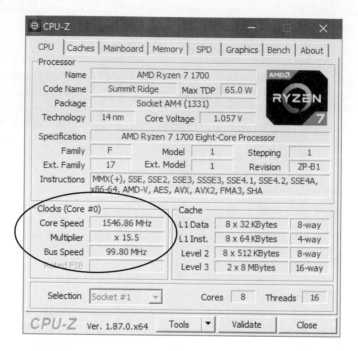

Try This!   CPU-Z

Imagine a scenario where you're dumped into an office full of unfamiliar PCs. There's no documentation about the systems at all, so your boss tells you to get cracking and find out as much as possible about each PC ASAP. Try this! Download a copy of the very popular and free CPU-Z utility from www.cpuid.com. CPU-Z gives you every piece of information you'll ever want to know about a CPU. Copy it to a thumb drive, then insert it into a bunch of different computers. (Ask permission, of course!) What kinds of processors do you find in your neighbors' computers? What can you tell about the different capabilities?

The clock speed and the multiplier on early clock-multiplying systems had to be manually configured via jumpers or dual in-line package (DIP) switches on the motherboard (see Figure 3-23). Today's CPUs report to the motherboard through a function called CPUID (CPU identifier), and the speed and multiplier are set automatically. (You can manually override this automatic setup on many motherboards. See "Overclocking," later in this chapter, for details.)

Figure 3-23
DIP switches on
a motherboard

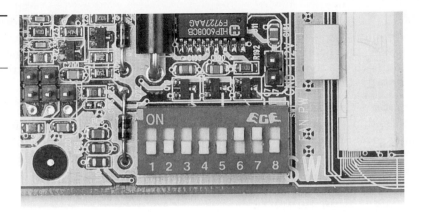

64-Bit Processing

Over successive generations of microprocessors, engineers have upgraded many physical features of CPUs. The EDB gradually increased in size, from 8- to 16- to 32- to 64-bits wide. The address bus similarly jumped, going from 20- to 24- to 32-bits wide (where it stayed for a decade).

The technological features changed as well. Engineers added new and improved registers, for example, that used fancy names like multimedia extensions (MMX) and Streaming SIMD Extensions (SSE). A mighty shift started several years ago and continues to evolve: the move to 64-bit computing.

Most new CPUs support *64-bit processing*, meaning they can run a compatible 64-bit operating system, such as Windows 10, and 64-bit applications. They also support 32-bit processing for 32-bit operating systems, such as some Linux distributions, and 32-bit applications. The general-purpose registers also make the move up to 64-bit. The primary benefit to moving to 64-bit computing is that modern systems can support much more than the 4 GB of memory supported with 32-bit processing.

With a 64-bit address bus, CPUs can address 2^{64} bytes of memory, or more precisely, 18,446,744,073,709,551,616 bytes of memory—that's a lot of RAM! This number is so big that gigabytes and terabytes are no longer convenient, so we now go to an exabyte (2^{60}), abbreviated *EB*. A 64-bit address bus can address 16 EB of RAM.

In practical terms, 64-bit computing greatly enhances the performance of programs that work with large files, such as video editing applications. You'll see a profound improvement moving from 4 GB to 8 GB or 16 GB of RAM with such programs.

EXAM TIP   The primary benefit of 64-bit computing is to support more than 4 GB of memory, the limit with 32-bit processing.

x86   CPUs from the early days can be lumped together as *x86* CPUs, because they used an instruction set that built upon the earliest Intel CPU architecture. The Intel Core 2 Duo, for example, could run a program written for an ancient 80386 processor that was in fashion in the early 1990s.

x64 When the 64-bit CPUs went mainstream, marketing folks needed some way to mark applications, operating systems, and so on such that consumers could quickly tell the difference between something compatible with their system or something not compatible. Since you generally cannot return software after you open it, this is a big deal. The marketing folks went with *x64*, and that created a mess.

x86-64 The earlier 32-bit stuff had been marketed as *x86*, not *x32*, so now we have *x86* (old, 32-bit stuff) versus *x64* (new, 64-bit stuff). It's not pretty, but do you get the difference? To make matters even worse, however, *x64* processors quite happily handle *x86* code and are, by definition, *x86* processors too! It's common to marry the two terms and describe current 64-bit CPUs as *x86-64* processors.

Virtualization Support

Intel and AMD have built in support for running more than one operating system at a time, a process called *virtualization*. Virtualization is very cool and gets its own chapter later in the book (Chapter 22), so I'll skip the details here. The key issue from a CPU standpoint is that virtualization used to work entirely through software. Programmers had to write a ton of code to enable a CPU—that was designed to run one OS at a time—to run more than one OS at the same time. Think about the issues involved. How does the memory get allocated, for example, or how does the CPU know which OS to update when you type something or click an icon? With hardware-based virtualization support, CPUs took a lot of the burden off the programmers and made virtualization a whole lot easier.

 EXAM TIP The CompTIA A+ 1001 objectives refer to virtualization support as the *virtual technology* CPU feature.

Parallel Execution

Modern CPUs can process multiple commands and parts of commands in parallel, known as *parallel execution*. Early processors had to do everything in a strict, linear fashion. The CPUs accomplish this parallelism through multiple pipelines, dedicated cache, and the capability to work with multiple threads or programs at one time. To understand the mighty leap in efficiency gained from parallel execution, you need insight into the processing stages.

Pipelining To get a command from the data bus, do the calculation, and then send the answer back out onto the data bus, a CPU takes at least four steps (each of these steps is called a *stage*):

1. **Fetch** Get the data from the EDB.
2. **Decode** Figure out what type of command needs to be executed.
3. **Execute** Perform the calculation.
4. **Write** Send the data back onto the EDB.

Smart, discrete circuits inside the CPU handle each of these stages. In early CPUs, when a command was placed on the data bus, each stage did its job and the CPU handed back the answer before starting the next command, requiring at least four clock cycles to process a command. In every clock cycle, three of the four circuits sat idle. Today, the circuits are organized in a conveyer-belt fashion called a *pipeline*. With pipelining, each stage does its job with each clock-cycle pulse, creating a much more efficient process. The CPU has multiple circuits doing multiple jobs, so let's add pipelining to the Man in the Box analogy. Now, it's *Men* in the Box (see Figure 3-24)!

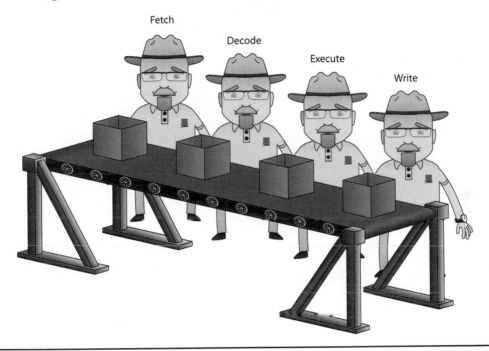

Figure 3-24   Simple pipeline

Pipelines keep every stage of the processor busy on every click of the clock, making a CPU run more efficiently without increasing the clock speed. Note that at this point, the CPU has four stages: fetch, decode, execute, and write—a four-stage pipeline. No CPU ever made has fewer than four stages, but advancements in caching (see "Cache," next) have increased the number of stages over the years. Current CPU pipelines contain many more stages, up to 20 in some cases.

Pipelining isn't perfect. Sometimes a stage hits a complex command that requires more than one clock cycle, forcing the pipeline to stop. Your CPU tries to avoid these stops, or *pipeline stalls*. The decode stage tends to cause the most pipeline stalls; certain commands are complex and therefore harder to decode than other commands. Current processors use multiple decode stages to reduce the chance of pipeline stalls due to complex decoding.

The inside of the CPU is composed of multiple chunks of circuitry to handle the many types of calculations your PC needs to do. For example, one part, the *arithmetic logic unit* (*ALU*) (*or integer unit*), handles integer math: basic math for numbers with no decimal point. A perfect example of integer math is 2 + 3 = 5. The typical CPU spends most of its work doing integer math. CPUs also have special circuitry to handle complex numbers, called the *floating point unit* (*FPU*). With a single pipeline, only the ALU or the FPU worked at any execution stage. Worse yet, floating point calculation often took many, many clock cycles to execute, forcing the CPU to stall the pipeline until the FPU finished executing the complex command (see Figure 3-25). Current CPUs offer multiple pipelines to keep the processing going (see Figure 3-26).

Figure 3-25   Bored integer unit

Cache   When you send a program to the CPU, you run lots of little programs all at the same time. Okay, let's be fair here: *you* didn't run all these little programs—you just started your Web browser or some other program. The moment you double-clicked that icon, Windows started sending many programs to the CPU. Each of these programs breaks down into some number of little pieces, called *threads*, and data. Each thread is a series of instructions designed to do a particular job with the data.

Modern CPUs don't execute instructions sequentially—first doing step 1, then step 2, and so on—but rather process all kinds of instructions. Most applications have certain instructions and data that get reused, sometimes many times.

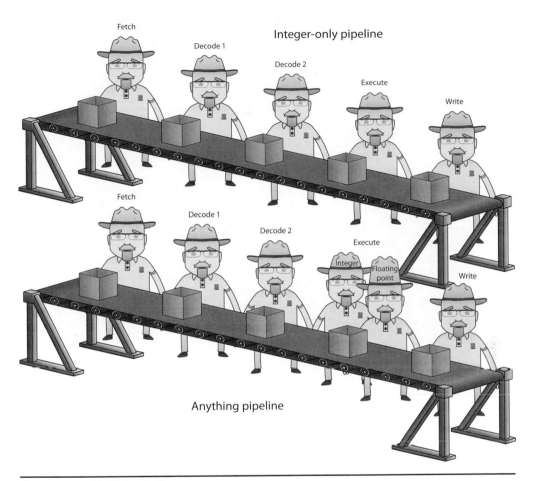

Figure 3-26 Multiple pipelines

Pipelining CPUs work fantastically well as long as the pipelines stay filled with instructions. Because the CPU runs faster than the RAM can supply it with code, you'll always get pipeline stalls—called *wait states*—because the RAM can't keep up with the CPU. To reduce wait states, CPUs come with built-in, very high-speed RAM called *static RAM (SRAM)*. This SRAM preloads as many instructions as possible and keeps copies of already run instructions and data in case the CPU needs to work on them again (see Figure 3-27). SRAM used in this fashion is called a *cache*.

The SRAM cache inside the early CPUs was tiny, only about 16 KB, but it improved performance tremendously. In fact, it helped so much that many motherboard makers began adding a cache directly to the motherboards. These caches were much larger, usually around 128 to 512 KB. When the CPU looked for a line of code, it first went to the built-in cache; if the code wasn't there, the CPU went to the cache on the motherboard. The cache on the CPU was called the *L1 cache* because it was the one the CPU first tried

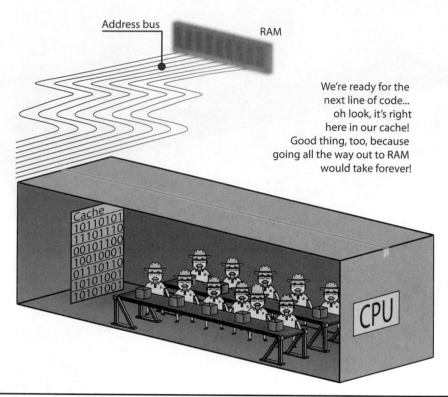

Figure 3-27   SRAM cache

to use. The cache on the motherboard was called the *L2 cache*, not because it was on the motherboard, but because it was the second cache the CPU checked.

Eventually, engineers took this cache concept even further and added the L2 cache onto the CPU package. Many modern CPUs include three caches: an L1, an L2, and an *L3 cache* (see Figure 3-28).

The L2 cache on the early CPUs that had L2 cache included on the CPU package ran at a slower clock speed than the L1 cache. The L1 cache was in the CPU and thus ran at the speed of the CPU. The L2 cache connected to the CPU via a tiny set of wires on the CPU package. The first L2 caches ran at half the speed of the CPU.

The inclusion of the L2 cache on the chip gave rise to some new terms to describe the connections between the CPU, MCC, RAM, and L2 cache. The address bus and external data bus (connecting the CPU, MCC, and RAM) were lumped into a single term called the *frontside bus*, and the connection between the CPU and the L2 cache became known as the *backside bus* (see Figure 3-29). (These terms don't apply well to current computers,

Figure 3-28
CPU-Z displaying
the cache
information
for a Ryzen 7
processor

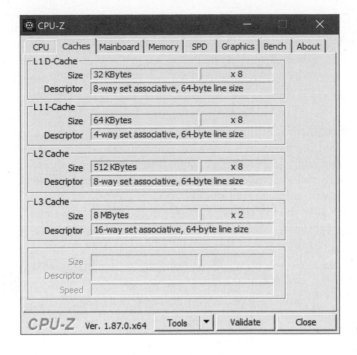

so they have fallen out of use. See the "Integrated Memory Controller" section later in this chapter.)

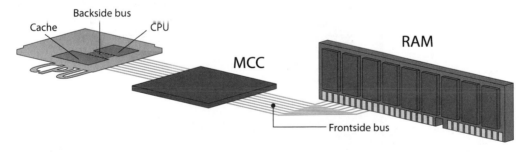

Figure 3-29   Frontside and backside buses

NOTE   To keep up with faster processors, motherboard manufacturers began to double and even quadruple the throughput of the frontside bus. Techs sometimes refer to these as *double-pumped* and *quad-pumped* frontside buses.

EXAM TIP Typically, the CompTIA A+ exams expect you to know that L1 cache will be the smallest and fastest cache; L2 will be bigger and slower than L1; and L3 will be the biggest and slowest cache. (This is not completely true anymore, with L1 and L2 running the same speed in many CPUs, but it is how it will appear on the exams.)

Multithreading At the peak of the single-CPU 32-bit computing days, Intel released a CPU called the Pentium 4 that took parallelism to the next step with Hyper-Threading. *Hyper-Threading* enabled the Pentium 4 to run multiple threads at the same time, what's generically called *simultaneous multithreading*, effectively turning the CPU into two CPUs on one chip—with a catch.

Figure 3-30 shows the Task Manager in an ancient Windows XP computer on a system running a Hyper-Threaded Pentium 4. Note how the CPU box is broken into two groups—Windows thinks this one CPU is two CPUs.

Figure 3-30
Windows Task Manager with the Performance tab displayed for a system running a Hyper-Threaded Pentium 4

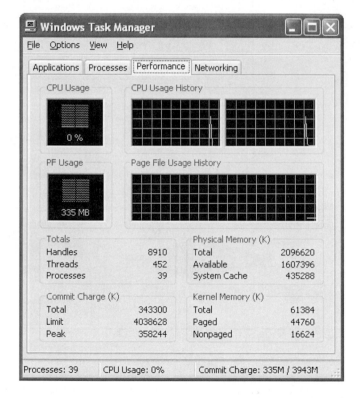

Multithreading enhances a CPU's efficiency but with a couple of limitations. First, the operating system and the application must be designed to take advantage of the feature. Second, although the CPU simulates the actions of a second processor, it doesn't double the processing power because the main execution resources are not duplicated.

Multicore Processing

Microarchitecture hit a plateau back in 2002 when CPU clock speeds hit a practical limit of roughly 4 GHz, motivating the CPU makers to find new ways to get more processing power for CPUs. Although Intel and AMD had different opinions about 64-bit CPUs, both decided at virtually the same time to move beyond the *single-core* CPU and combine two CPUs (or *cores*) into a single chip, creating a *dual-core* architecture. A dual-core CPU has two execution units—two sets of pipelines—but the two sets of pipelines share caches and RAM. A single-core CPU has only one set of everything.

Today, multicore CPUs—with four, six, or eight cores—are common. Higher-end CPUs have up to 32 cores! With each generation of multicore CPU, both Intel and AMD have tinkered with the mixture of how to allocate the cache among the cores. Figure 3-31 shows another screenshot of CPU-Z, this time displaying the cache breakdown of a Haswell-based Core i7.

Figure 3-31

CPU-Z showing the cache details of a Haswell Core i7

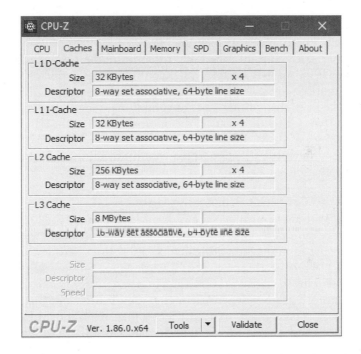

Figure 3-31 reveals specific details about how this Intel CPU works with cache. The Core i7 has L1, L2, and L3 caches of 32 KB, 256 KB, and 8 MB, respectively. (The L1 cache divides into 32 KB to handle data—the *D-Cache*—and another 32 KB for instructions—the *I-Cache*.) Each core has dedicated L1 and L2 caches. (You can tell this by the ×4 to the right of the capacity listing.) All six cores share the giant L3 cache. That pool of memory enables the cores to communicate and work together without having to access the radically slower main system RAM as much.

CPU manufacturers engineered the cores in multicore CPUs to divide up work independently of the OS, known as *multicore processing*. This differs from Hyper-Threading, where the OS and applications must be written specifically to handle the multiple threads. Note that even with multicore processors, applications must be modified or optimized for this parallelism to have a huge impact on performance.

Because one great technology advancement isn't enough, both Intel and AMD make multicore CPUs that incorporate Hyper-Threading as well. The Intel Core i9-7960X, for example, sports 16 cores, Hyper-Threading, 16 MB of L2 cache and 22 MB of L3 cache, and Turbo Boost to crank the clock speed over 4 GHz when the system needs it. I get shivers just thinking about it!

 SIM This is a great time to head over to the Chapter 3 Show! and Click! sims to see how to download and use the CPU-Z utility. Check out "What is CPU-Z?" here: http://totalsem.com/100x.

Integrated Memory Controller

All current microprocessors have an *integrated memory controller* (*IMC*), moved from the motherboard chip into the CPU to optimize the flow of information into and out from the CPU. An IMC enables faster control over things like the large L3 cache shared among multiple cores.

Just like in so many other areas of computing, manufacturers implement a variety of IMCs in their CPUs. In practice, this means that different CPUs handle different types and capacities of RAM. I'll save the details on those RAM variations for Chapter 4. For now, add "different RAM support" to your list of things to look at when making a CPU recommendation for a client.

Integrated Graphics Processing Unit

As you'll read about in much more detail in Chapter 17, "Display Technologies," the video processing portion of the computer—made up of the parts that put a changing image on the monitor—traditionally has a discrete microprocessor that differs in both function and architecture from the CPUs designed for general-purpose computing. The generic term for the video processor is a *graphics processing unit* (*GPU*). I'll spare you the details until we get to video in Chapter 17, but it turns out that graphics processors can handle certain tasks much more efficiently than the standard CPU. Integrating a GPU into the CPU enhances the overall performance of the computer while at the same time reducing energy use, size, and cost. With the proliferation of mobile devices and portable computers today, all these benefits have obvious merit.

Both Intel and AMD produce CPUs with integrated GPUs. For many years, the quality of the GPU performance with demanding graphical programs like games made the choice between the two easy. The *Intel HD Graphics* and *Intel Iris Pro Graphics* integrated into many Core i3/i5/i7 processors pale in comparison with the AMD *accelerated processing unit* (*APU*), such as the AMD A10. AMD bought one of the two dedicated GPU manufacturers—ATI—years ago and used their technology for microprocessors with integrated CPU and GPU. (The Xbox One and PlayStation 4 gaming systems, for example, use AMD APUs.) Intel is slowly closing the gap.

Security

All modern processors employ the *NX bit* technology that enables the CPU to protect certain sections of memory. This feature, coupled with implementation by the operating system, stops malicious attacks from getting to essential operating system files. Microsoft calls the feature Data Execution Prevention (DEP), turned on by default in every OS (see Figure 3-32).

Figure 3-32
DEP in
Windows 10

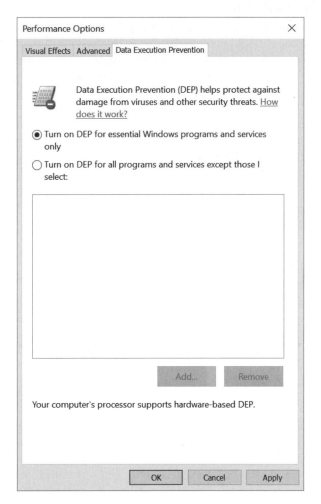

Everybody calls the NX bit technology something different (but you don't need to memorize any of this for the exams):

- **Intel** XD bit (eXecute Disable)
- **AMD** Enhanced Virus Protection
- **ARM** XN (eXecute Never)

Selecting and Installing CPUs

Now that you know how CPUs work, it's time to get practical. This last section discusses selecting the proper CPU, installing several types of processors, and troubleshooting the few problems techs face with CPUs.

Selecting a CPU

When selecting a CPU, you need to make certain you get one that the motherboard can accommodate. Or, if you're buying a motherboard along with the CPU, then get the right CPU for the intended purpose. Chapter 11, "Building a PC," discusses computer roles and helps you select the proper components for each role. You need to have a lot more knowledge of all the pieces around the CPU to get the full picture, so we'll wait until then to discuss the "why" of specific processors. Instead, this section assumes you're placing a new CPU in an already-acquired motherboard. You need to address two key points in selecting a CPU that will work. First, does the motherboard support Intel CPUs or AMD CPUs? Second, what socket does the motherboard have?

To find answers to both those questions, you have two sources: the motherboard book or manual and the manufacturer's Web site. Figure 3-33 shows a manual for an ASUS motherboard open to reveal the supported processors and the socket type.

Figure 3-33
Supported
processors and
socket type

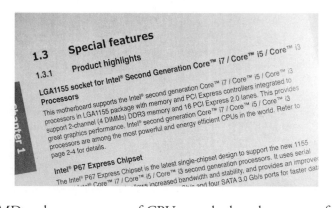

Just as Intel and AMD make many types of CPUs, motherboards are manufactured with various different types of sockets. There have been hundreds of sockets developed over the years. Table 3-2 charts a few of the more popular ones in production today. CompTIA has traditionally tested on both the socket number/name and the alternative name, in the case of Intel sockets. I've included the most recent socket names and alternative names here.

EXAM TIP The CompTIA A+ 1001 objectives do not list any specific processor sockets, but previous versions frequently included questions about them. Hopefully you won't run into one of these questions, but it's not a bad idea to know the sockets just in case. Beyond the exam, just make sure that you understand that every CPU has a specific socket into which it fits and make sure a client's motherboard has the socket that works with a suggested CPU.

Socket	Alternative Name	Platform	CPU
LGA 1150	H3	Intel	Core i3/i5/i7, Pentium, Celeron, Xeon
LGA 1151	H4	Intel	Core i3/i5/i7, Pentium, Celeron, Xeon
LGA 2011	R or R3	Intel	Core i7, Core i7 Extreme Edition, Xeon
LGA 2066	R4	Intel	Core i5/i7/i9, Xeon
FM2+	n/a	AMD	A-Series
AM3+	n/a	AMD	FX, Opteron
AM4	n/a	AMD	Ryzen, A-Series
TR4	n/a	AMD	Ryzen Threadripper

Table 3-2   Common Sockets

Deciphering Processor Numbers

Intel and AMD use different processor numbering schemes that help you compare multiple CPUs with similar names, such as Core i5. AMD and Intel both have fairly similar numbering schemes. Here's the scoop on both.

Intel processor numbers follow a very clear pattern. An Intel Core i7 7500 U processor, for example, maps out like this:

- Intel Core = brand
- i7 = brand modifier
- 7 = generation
- 500 = SKU numbers
- U = alpha suffix (U indicates that it's a desktop processor using ultra-low power)

Contrast the previous processor with an Intel Core i7 8650 U, where the numbers map like this:

- Intel Core = brand
- i7 = brand modifier
- 8 = generation
- 650 = SKU numbers
- U = alpha suffix (U indicates that it's a desktop processor using ultra-low power)

AMD processor nomenclature is similar. Here's the breakdown for an AMD Ryzen 7 2700X:

- AMD Ryzen = brand
- 7 = market segment

- 2 = generation
- 7 = performance level
- 00 = model number
- X = power suffix (X indicates high-performance)

Try This!   Processor Research

Both Intel and AMD maintain accessible Web sites with exhaustive information about their recent CPUs. All three Web sites listed here provide details you can use for client support and for recommendations when dealing with specific sockets for upgrades. Try this! Put one or more of the following links into a Web browser and explore the CPUs. Then tuck the URLs into your tech toolkit for later reference when needed.

- https://ark.intel.com
- https://www.amd.com/en/products/processors-desktop
- https://www.amd.com/en/products/processors-laptop

Installation Issues

When installing a CPU, you need to use caution with the tiny pins on the CPU or the socket. Plus, you must make certain that the power supply can supply enough electricity for the processor to function along with all the other components on the computer. Third, you must provide adequate cooling. Finally, you can decide whether to leave the CPU at stock settings or overclock it.

Socket Types

When installing a CPU, you need to exercise caution not to bend any of the tiny pins. The location of the pins differs between Intel and AMD. With Intel-based motherboards, the sockets have hundreds of tiny pins that line up with contacts on the bottom of the CPU (see Figure 3-34). Intel CPUs use a *land grid array* (*LGA*) package for socketed CPUs, where the underside of the CPU has hundreds of contact points that line up with the socket pins.

AMD CPUs have the pins (see Figure 3-35); the sockets have holes. The pins on the AMD *pin grid array* (*PGA*) CPUs align with the holes in the sockets.

All CPUs and sockets are keyed so you can't (easily) insert them incorrectly. Look at the underside of the CPU on the left side of Figure 3-36. Note that the pins do not make a perfect square, because a few are missing. Now look at the top of the CPU on the right in Figure 3-36. See the little mark at the corner? The socket also has tiny markings so you can line the CPU up properly with the socket.

Figure 3-34
Intel-based
socket with pins

In both socket styles, you release the retaining mechanism by pushing the little lever down slightly and then away from the socket (see Figure 3-37). You next raise the arm fully, and then move the retaining bracket (see Figure 3-38).

Align the processor with the socket and gently drop the processor into place. If it doesn't go in easily, check the orientation and try again. These sockets are generically called *zero insertion force (ZIF) sockets*, which means you never have to use any force at all.

Figure 3-35
AMD-based
socket without
pins

Figure 3-36
Underside and
top of a CPU

Cooling

CPUs work very hard and thus require power to function. In electrical terms, CPUs consume *wattage* or *watts*, a unit of electrical power, just like a 100-watt light bulb consumes power whenever it's on. (See Chapter 7, "Power Supplies," for more details about electricity.) Have you ever touched a light bulb after it's been on for a while? Ouch! CPUs heat up, too.

Figure 3-37
Moving the
release arm

Figure 3-38
Fully opened
socket

To increase the capability of the CPUs to handle complex code, CPU manufacturers have added a lot of microscopic transistors over the years. The more transistors the CPU has, the more power they need and thus the hotter they get. CPUs don't tolerate heat well, and modern processors need active cooling solutions just to function at all. Almost every CPU uses a combination of a heat sink and fan assembly to wick heat away from the CPU.

EXAM TIP A heat sink by itself (no fan) on a chip provides *passive cooling*. A heat sink and fan combination provides *active cooling*. You'll sometimes hear the latter described as an *active heat sink*.

A *heat sink* is a copper or other metal device designed to dissipate heat from whatever it touches. Figure 3-39 shows the standard Intel heat sink and fan. Here are some cooling options:

- **OEM CPU coolers** Original equipment manufacturer (OEM) heat-sink and fan assemblies are included with most Intel and AMD retail-boxed CPUs. OEM in this case means that Intel makes the heat-sink/fan assemblies. Rather confusingly, you'll see the term "OEM CPUs" used to mean CPUs you buy in bulk or not in the retail packaging. These are still made by Intel or AMD and are functionally identical to the retail versions. They don't come bundled with CPU coolers. Crazy, isn't it? OEM CPU coolers have one big advantage: you know absolutely they will work with your CPU.

Figure 3-39
Intel stock heat-sink and fan assembly

- **Specialized CPU coolers** Many companies sell third-party heat-sink and fan assemblies for a variety of CPUs. These usually exceed the OEM heat sinks in the amount of heat they dissipate. These CPU coolers invariably come with eye-catching designs to look really cool inside your system (see Figure 3-40)—some are even lighted.

Figure 3-40
Cool retail heat sink

The last choice is the most impressive of all: liquid cooling! *Liquid cooling* works by running some liquid—usually water—through a metal block that sits on top of your CPU, absorbing heat. The liquid gets heated by the block, runs out of the block and into something that cools the liquid, and is then pumped through the block again. Any liquid-cooling system consists of three main parts:

- A hollow metal block that sits on the CPU
- A pump to move the liquid around
- Some device to cool the liquid

And of course, you need plenty of hosing to hook them all together. Figure 3-41 shows a typical liquid-cooled CPU.

Figure 3-41
Liquid-cooled
CPU

Several companies sell liquid-based cooling systems. Although they look impressive and certainly cool your CPU, unless you're overclocking or want a silent system, a good fan will more than suffice.

EXAM TIP In some instances, you can create a system that has no fan for the CPU, what's called *fanless cooling*. Aside from mobile devices (like an Apple iPad) that have no fans, the term can be very misleading. The Xeon CPUs powering the servers in my office, for example, only have heat sinks with no fans. On the other hand, they have ducts directly to the case fans, which serve the same function as an active CPU fan. So, go figure.

See also the "Beyond A+" section at the end of this chapter for interesting passive cooling developments.

Once you have a heat-sink and fan assembly sorted out, you need to connect it to the motherboard. To determine the orientation of the heat-sink and fan assembly, check the power cable from the fan. Make sure it can easily reach the three- or four-wire standout on the motherboard (see Figure 3-42). If it can't, rotate the heat sink until it can. (Check the motherboard manual if you have trouble locating the CPU fan power standout.)

Figure 3-42
CPU fan power standout on motherboard

Next, before inserting the heat sink, you need to add a small amount of *thermal paste* (also called *thermal compound*, *heat dope*, or *nasty silver goo*). Many heat sinks come with some thermal paste already on them; the thermal paste on these pre-doped heat sinks is covered by a small square of tape—take the tape off before you snap it to the CPU. If you need to put thermal paste on from a tube, know that you need to use only a tiny amount of this compound (see Figure 3-43). Spread it on as thinly, completely, and evenly as you can. Unlike so many other things in life, you *can* have too much thermal paste!

Figure 3-43
Applying thermal paste

You secure heat sinks in various ways, depending on the manufacturer. Stock Intel heat sinks have four plungers that you simply push until they click into place in corresponding holes in the motherboard. AMD stock heat sinks generally have a bracket that you secure to two points on the outside of the CPU socket and a latch that you swivel to lock it down (see Figure 3-44).

Figure 3-44
AMD stock heat-sink and fan assembly

Finally, you can secure many aftermarket heat-sink and fan assemblies by screwing them down from the underside of the motherboard (see Figure 3-45). You have to remove the motherboard from the case or install the heat sink before you put the motherboard in the case.

Figure 3-45
Heat-sink and
fan assembly
mounted to
motherboard
with screws

For the final step, plug the fan power connector into the motherboard standout. It won't work if you don't!

Overclocking

For the CPU to work, the motherboard speed, multiplier, and voltage must be set properly. In most modern systems, the motherboard uses the CPUID functions to set these options automatically. Some motherboards enable you to adjust these settings manually by moving a jumper, changing a CMOS setting, or using software; many enthusiasts deliberately change these settings to enhance performance.

NOTE Chapter 5, "Firmware," goes into gory detail about the system setup utility and the area in which it stores important data (called *CMOS*), but invariably students want to experiment at this point, so I'll give you some information now. You can access the system setup utility by pressing some key as the computer starts up. This is during the text phase, well before it ever says anything about starting Windows. Most systems require you to press the DELETE key, but read the screen for details. Just be careful once you get into the system setup utility not to change anything you don't understand. And read Chapter 5!

Starting way back in the days of the Intel 80486 CPU, people intentionally ran their systems at clock speeds higher than the CPU was rated, a process called *overclocking*, and it worked. Well, *sometimes* the systems worked, and sometimes they didn't. Intel and AMD have a reason for marking a CPU at a specific clock speed—that's the highest speed they guarantee will work.

Before I say anything else, I must warn you that intentional overclocking of a CPU immediately voids most warranties. Overclocking has been known to destroy CPUs. Overclocking might make your system unstable and prone to *system lockups*, *reboots*, and *unexpected shutdowns.* I neither applaud nor decry the practice of overclocking. My goal here is simply to inform you of the practice. You make your own decisions. If a client wants to overclock, explain the potential consequences.

CPU makers do not encourage overclocking. Why would you pay more for a faster processor when you can take a cheaper, slower CPU and just make it run faster? Bowing to enthusiast market pressure, however, both Intel and AMD make utilities that help you overclock their respective CPUs.

- **Intel Extreme Tuning Utility (Intel XTU)** Don't skip the additional Performance Tuning Protection Plan if you go this route.

- **AMD Overdrive Utility** No extra warranty is provided here; you're on your own.

Most people make a couple of adjustments to overclock successfully. First, through jumpers, CMOS settings, or software configuration, you would increase the bus speed for the system. Second, you often have to increase the voltage going into the CPU by just a little to provide stability. You do that by changing a jumper or CMOS setting (see Figure 3-46).

Figure 3-46 Manually overriding CPU settings in the system setup utility

Overriding the defaults can completely lock up your system, to the point where even removing and reinstalling the CPU doesn't bring the motherboard back to life. (There's also a slight risk of toasting the processor, although all modern processors have circuitry that shuts them down quickly before they overheat.) Most motherboards have a jumper setting or a button called *CMOS clear* or *CLRTC* (see Figure 3-47) that makes the CMOS go back to default settings. Before you try overclocking on a modern system, find the CMOS-clear jumper or button and make sure you know how to use it! Hint: Look in the motherboard manual.

Figure 3-47
CMOS-clear
jumper

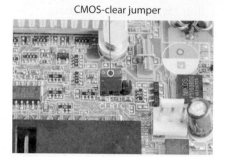

CMOS-clear jumper

To clear the CMOS, turn off the PC. Then locate one of those tiny little plastic pieces (officially called a *shunt*) and place it over the two jumper wires for a moment. Next, restart the PC and immediately go into CMOS and restore the settings you need.

Troubleshooting CPUs

Troubleshooting CPU issues falls into two categories: overheating and catastrophic failures, with overheating being far more common than the latter. Once a CPU is installed properly and functioning, it rarely causes problems. The only exception is when you ask a CPU to do too much too quickly. Then you'll get a sluggish PC. The Intel Atom processor in my vintage netbook, for example, does a great job at surfing the Web, working on e-mail, and writing stellar chapters in your favorite textbook. But if you try to play a game more advanced than *Half-Life* (the original, circa 1998), the machine stutters and complains and refuses to play nice.

The vast majority of problems with CPUs come from faulty installation or environmental issues that cause overheating. Very rarely will you get a catastrophic failure, but we'll look at the signs of that, too.

Symptoms of Overheating

Failure to install a CPU properly results in either nothing—that is, you push the power button and nothing at all happens—or a system lock-up in a short period of time. Because of the nature of ZIF sockets, you're almost guaranteed that the issue isn't the CPU itself, but rather the installation of the heat-sink and fan assembly. Here's a checklist of possible problems that you need to address when faced with a CPU installation problem:

1. Too much thermal paste can impede the flow of heat from the CPU to the heat sink and cause the CPU to heat up rapidly. All modern CPUs have built-in fail-safes that tell them to shut down before getting damaged by heat.

2. Not enough thermal paste or thermal paste spread unevenly can cause the CPU to heat up and consequently shut itself down.

3. Failure to connect the fan power to the motherboard can cause the CPU to heat up and shut itself down.

The fan and heat-sink installation failures can be tricky the first few times you encounter them. You might see the text from the system setup. You might even get into an installation of Windows before the crash happens. The key is that as soon as you put the CPU under load—that is, make it work for a living—it heats up beyond where the faulty heat-sink connection can dissipate the heat and then shuts down.

With a system that's been running fine for a while, environmental factors can cause problems. An air conditioning failure in my office last summer, deep in the heart of very hot Texas, for example, caused machines throughout the office to run poorly. Some even shut down entirely. (At that point it was time to close the doors and send the staff to the beach, but that's another story.) A client called the other day to complain about his computer continuously rebooting and running slowly. When I arrived on the scene, I found a house with seven cats. Opening up his computer case revealed the hairy truth: the CPU fan was so clogged with cat hair that it barely spun at all! A quick cleaning with a computer vacuum and a can of compressed air and he was a happily computing client.

The CPU needs adequate ventilation. The CPU fan is essential, of course, but the inside of the case also needs to get hot air out through one or more exhaust fans and cool air in through the front vent. If the intake vent is clogged or the exhaust fans stop working or are blocked somehow, the inside of the case can heat up and overwhelm the CPU cooling devices. This will result in a system running slowly or spontaneously rebooting.

Catastrophic Failure

You'll know when a catastrophic error occurs. The PC will suddenly get a Blue Screen of Death (BSoD), what's technically called a Windows Stop error (see Figure 3-48). On macOS, by comparison, you might get a spinning pinwheel that doesn't stop or a kernel panic (i.e., automatic restart). (CompTIA calls the BSoD and pinwheel *proprietary crash screens* and adds a space in the latter, so *pin wheel*.)

Or the entire computer will simply stop and go black, perhaps accompanied by a loud pop. The acrid smell of burnt electronics or ozone will grace your nasal passages.

Figure 3-48
Blue Screen
of Death

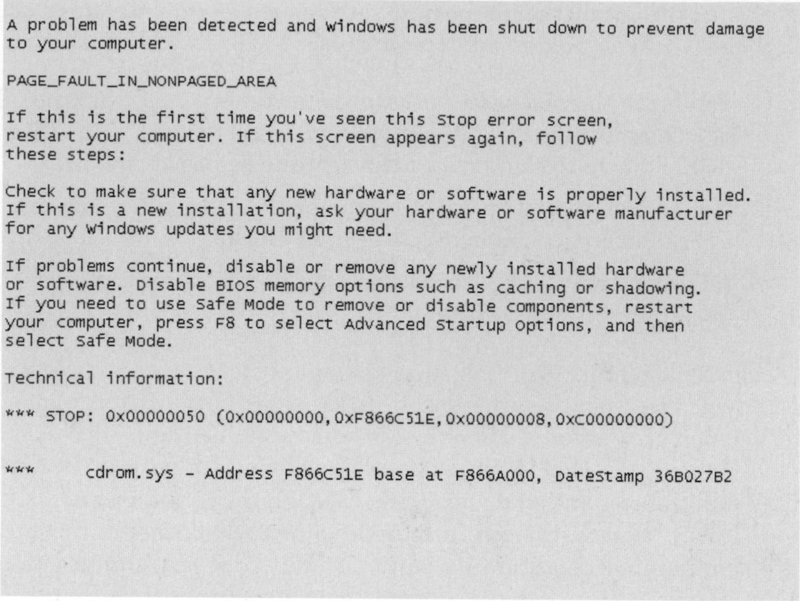

```
A problem has been detected and windows has been shut down to prevent damage
to your computer.

PAGE_FAULT_IN_NONPAGED_AREA

If this is the first time you've seen this Stop error screen,
restart your computer. If this screen appears again, follow
these steps:

Check to make sure that any new hardware or software is properly installed.
If this is a new installation, ask your hardware or software manufacturer
for any windows updates you might need.

If problems continue, disable or remove any newly installed hardware
or software. Disable BIOS memory options such as caching or shadowing.
If you need to use Safe Mode to remove or disable components, restart
your computer, press F8 to select Advanced Startup Options, and then
select Safe Mode.

Technical information:

*** STOP: 0x00000050 (0x00000000,0xF866C51E,0x00000008,0xC00000000)


***      cdrom.sys - Address F866C51E base at F866A000, Datestamp 36B027B2
```

You might even see trails of smoke coming out of the case. You might not know immediately that the CPU has smoked, but follow your nose. Seriously. Sniff the inside of the case until you find the strongest smell. If it's the CPU, that's bad news. Whatever electrical short hit it probably caused damage to the motherboard too, and you're looking at a long day of replacement and rebuilding.

Beyond A+

Intel Core M

The Intel Core M runs cool and sips juice for incredibly long battery life in mobile devices. The official TDP is just 4.5 watts—compared to a mobile version of a Core i7 that demands 57 watts. The trade-off Intel makes with the Core M is in raw processing power. It's a little less powerful than a mobile Core i3—enough to get the job done, but not enough to run a serious game or other demanding application. On the other hand, the incredibly low electricity use means manufacturers can skip the fan and make super-skinny devices.

Chapter Review

Questions

1. What do registers provide for the CPU?

    A. Registers determine the clock speed.

    B. The CPU uses registers for temporary storage of internal commands and data.

    C. Registers enable the CPU to address RAM.

    D. Registers enable the CPU to control the address bus.

2. What function does the external data bus have in the PC?

    A. The external data bus determines the clock speed for the CPU.

    B. The CPU uses the external data bus to address RAM.

    C. The external data bus provides a channel for the flow of data and commands between the CPU and RAM.

    D. The CPU uses the external data bus to access registers.

3. What is the function of the address bus in the PC?

    A. The address bus enables the CPU to communicate with the memory controller chip.

    B. The address bus enables the memory controller chip to communicate with the RAM.

    C. The address bus provides a channel for the flow of data and commands between the CPU and RAM.

    D. The address bus enables the CPU to access registers.

4. Which of the following terms are measures of CPU speed?

    A. Megahertz and gigahertz

    B. Megabytes and gigabytes

    C. Megahertz and gigabytes

    D. Frontside bus, backside bus

5. Which CPU feature enables the microprocessor to support running multiple operating systems at the same time?

    A. Clock multiplying

    B. Caching

    C. Pipelining

    D. Virtualization support

6. Into which socket could you place an Intel Core i5?

   A. Socket LGA 2011

   B. Socket LGA 1151

   C. Socket C

   D. Socket AM3+

7. Which feature enables a single-core CPU to function like two CPUs?

   A. Hyper-Threading

   B. SpeedStep

   C. Virtualization

   D. x64

8. What steps do you need to take to install a Core i3 CPU into an FM2+ motherboard?

   A. Lift the ZIF socket arm; place the CPU according to the orientation markings; snap on the heat-sink and fan assembly.

   B. Lift the ZIF socket arm; place the CPU according to the orientation markings; add a dash of thermal paste; snap on the heat-sink and fan assembly.

   C. Lift the ZIF socket arm; place the CPU according to the orientation markings; snap on the heat-sink and fan assembly; plug in the fan.

   D. Take all of the steps you want to take because it's not going to work.

9. A client calls to complain that his computer starts up, but crashes when Windows starts to load. After a brief set of questions, you find out that his nephew upgraded his RAM for him over the weekend and couldn't get the computer to work right afterward. What could be the problem?

   A. Thermal paste degradation

   B. Disconnected CPU fan

   C. Bad CPU cache

   D. There's nothing wrong. It usually takes a couple of days for RAM to acclimate to the new system.

10. Darren has installed a new CPU in a client's computer, but nothing happens when he pushes the power button on the case. The LED on the motherboard is lit up, so he knows the system has power. What could the problem be?

    A. He forgot to disconnect the CPU fan.

    B. He forgot to apply thermal paste between the CPU and the heat-sink and fan assembly.

    C. He used an AMD CPU in an Intel motherboard.

    D. He used an Intel CPU in an AMD motherboard.

Answers

1. **B.** The CPU uses registers for temporary storage of internal commands and data.

2. **C.** The external data bus provides a channel for the flow of data and commands between the CPU and RAM.

3. **A.** The address bus enables the CPU to communicate with the memory controller chip.

4. **A.** The terms megahertz (MHz) and gigahertz (GHz) describe how many million or billion (respectively) cycles per second a CPU can run.

5. **D.** Intel and AMD CPUs come with virtualization support, enabling more efficient implementation of virtual machines.

6. **B.** You'll find Core i5 processors in several socket types, notably LGA 1150 and LGA 1151.

7. **A.** Intel loves its Hyper-Threading, where a single-core CPU can function like a dual-core CPU as long as it has operating system support.

8. **D.** Intel and AMD processors are not compatible at all.

9. **B.** Most likely, the nephew disconnected the CPU fan to get at the RAM slots and simply forgot to plug it back in.

10. **B.** The best answer here is that he forgot the thermal paste, though you can also make an argument for a disconnected fan.

4

RAM

In this chapter, you will learn how to
- Identify the different types of DRAM packaging
- Explain the varieties of RAM
- Select and install RAM
- Perform basic RAM troubleshooting

Whenever people come up to me and start professing their computer savvy, I ask them a few questions to see how much they really know. In case you and I ever meet and you decide you want to "talk tech" with me, I'll tell you my first two questions now so you'll be ready. Both involve *random access memory* (*RAM*), the working memory for the CPU.

1. "How much RAM is in your computer?"

2. "What is RAM and why is it so important that every PC has enough?"

Can you answer either of these questions? Don't fret if you can't—you'll know how to answer both before you finish this chapter. Let's start by reviewing what you know about RAM thus far.

When not in use, programs and data are held in a mass storage device such as a solid-state drive (SSD), USB thumb drive, optical drive, or some other device that can hold data while the computer is off. When you load a program in Windows, your PC copies the program from the mass storage device to RAM and then runs it (see Figure 4-1).

You saw in Chapter 3, "CPUs," that the CPU uses *dynamic random access memory* (*DRAM*) as RAM for all PCs. Just like CPUs, DRAM has gone through evolutionary changes over the years, resulting in improved DRAM technologies such as SDRAM, RDRAM, and DDR RAM. This chapter starts by explaining how DRAM works, and then discusses the types of DRAM used over the past several years and how they improve on the original DRAM. The third section, "Working with RAM," goes into the details of finding and installing RAM. The chapter finishes with troubleshooting RAM problems.

Figure 4-1
Mass storage holds programs, but programs need to run in RAM.

Historical/Conceptual

Understanding DRAM

As discussed in Chapter 3, DRAM functions like an electronic spreadsheet, with numbered rows containing cells and each cell holding a one or a zero. Now let's look at what's physically happening. Each spreadsheet cell is a special type of semiconductor that can hold a single bit—one or zero—by using microscopic capacitors and transistors. DRAM makers put these semiconductors into chips that can hold a certain number of bits. The bits inside the chips are organized in a rectangular fashion, using rows and columns.

Each chip has a limit on the number of lines of code it can contain. Think of each line of code as one of the rows on the electronic spreadsheet; one chip might be able to store a million rows of code while another chip might be able to store over a billion lines. Each chip also has a limit on the width of the lines of code it can handle. One chip might handle 8-bit-wide data while another might handle 16-bit-wide data. Techs describe chips by bits rather than bytes, so they refer to *×8* and *×16*, respectively. Just as you could describe a spreadsheet by the number of rows and columns—John's accounting spreadsheet is huge, 48 rows × 12 columns—memory makers describe RAM chips the same way. An individual DRAM chip that holds 1,048,576 rows and 8 columns, for example, would be a *1M×8* chip, with "M" as shorthand for "mega," just like in megabytes (2^{20} bytes). It is difficult if not impossible to tell the size of a DRAM chip just by looking at it—only the DRAM makers know the meaning of the tiny numbers on the chips (see Figure 4-2), although sometimes you can make a good guess.

Figure 4-2
What do these numbers mean?

NOTE Serious RAM enthusiasts can enjoy chip specifics available at memory-maker Web sites. Check out the charts at Micron, for example:

www.micron.com/products/dram/ddr4-sdram/part-catalog

Organizing DRAM

Because of its low cost, high speed, and capability to contain a lot of data in a relatively small package, DRAM has been the standard RAM used in all computers—not just PCs—since the mid-1970s. DRAM can be found in just about everything, from automobiles to automatic bread makers.

The PC has very specific requirements for DRAM. The original 8088 processor had an 8-bit frontside bus. Commands given to an 8088 processor were in discrete 8-bit chunks. You needed RAM that could store data in 8-bit (1-byte) chunks, so that each time the CPU asked for a line of code, the *memory controller chip* (*MCC*) could put an 8-bit chunk on the data bus. This optimized the flow of data into (and out from) the CPU. Although today's DRAM chips may have widths greater than 1 bit, all DRAM chips back then were 1 bit wide, meaning only sizes such as 64 K × 1 or 256 K × 1 existed—always 1 bit wide. So how was 1-bit-wide DRAM turned into 8-bit-wide memory? The solution was quite simple: just take eight 1-bit-wide chips and use the MCC to organize them electronically to be eight wide (see Figure 4-3).

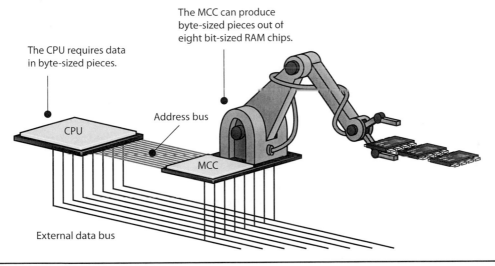

Figure 4-3 The MCC accessing data on RAM soldered onto the motherboard

Practical DRAM

Okay, before you learn more about DRAM, I need to clarify a critical point. When you first saw the 8088's machine language in Chapter 3, all the examples in the "codebook" were exactly 1-byte commands. Figure 4-4 shows the codebook again—see how all the commands are 1 byte?

Figure 4-4
Codebook again

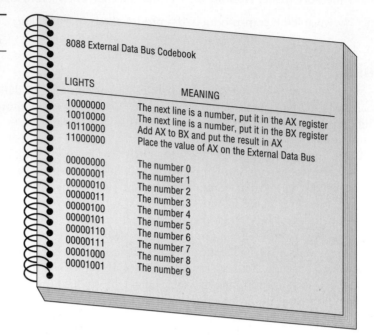

8088 External Data Bus Codebook

LIGHTS
        MEANING

10000000 The next line is a number, put it in the AX register
10010000 The next line is a number, put it in the BX register
10110000 Add AX to BX and put the result in AX
11000000 Place the value of AX on the External Data Bus

00000000 The number 0
00000001 The number 1
00000010 The number 2
00000011 The number 3
00000100 The number 4
00000101 The number 5
00000110 The number 6
00000111 The number 7
00001000 The number 8
00001001 The number 9

Well, the reality is slightly different. Most of the 8088 machine language commands are 1 byte, but more-complex commands need 2 bytes. For example, the following command tells the CPU to move 163 bytes "up the RAM spreadsheet" and run whatever command is there. Cool, eh?

1110100110100011

The problem here is that the command is 2 bytes wide, not 1 byte. So how did the 8088 handle this? Simple—it just took the command 1 byte at a time. It took twice as long to handle the command because the MCC had to go to RAM twice, but it worked.

So if some of the commands are more than 1 byte wide, why didn't Intel make the 8088 with a 16-bit frontside bus? Wouldn't that have been better? Well, Intel did. Intel invented a CPU called the 8086. The 8086 predates the 8088 and was absolutely identical to the 8088 except for one small detail: it had a 16-bit frontside bus. IBM could have used the 8086 instead of the 8088 and used 2-byte-wide RAM instead of 1-byte-wide RAM. Of course, they would have needed to invent an MCC that could handle that kind of RAM (see Figure 4-5).

Why did Intel sell the 8088 to IBM instead of the 8086? There were two reasons. Nobody had invented an affordable MCC or RAM that handled 2 bytes at a time. Sure, chips had been invented, but they were *expensive*, and IBM didn't think anyone would want to pay $12,000 for a personal computer. So IBM bought the Intel 8088, not the Intel 8086, and all our RAM came in bytes. But as you might imagine, it didn't stay that way for long.

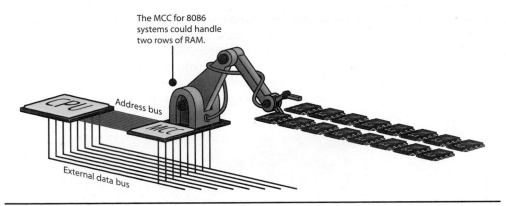

The MCC for 8086 systems could handle two rows of RAM.

Address bus

External data bus

Figure 4-5   Pumped-up 8086 MCC at work

DRAM Sticks

As CPU data bus sizes increased, so too did the need for RAM wide enough to fill the bus. The Intel 80386 CPU, for example, had a 32-bit data bus and thus the need for 32-bit-wide DRAM. Imagine having to line up 32 one-bit-wide DRAM chips on a motherboard. Talk about a waste of space! Figure 4-6 shows motherboard RAM run amuck.

Figure 4-6   That's a lot of real estate used by RAM chips!

DRAM manufacturers responded by creating wider DRAM chips, such as ×4, ×8, and ×16, and putting multiples of them on a small circuit board called a *stick* or *module*. Figure 4-7 shows an early stick, called a *single inline memory module* (*SIMM*), with eight DRAM chips. To add RAM to a modern machine, you need to get the right stick or sticks for the particular motherboard. Your motherboard manual tells you precisely what sort of module you need and how much RAM you can install.

Figure 4-7
A 72-pin SIMM

Modern CPUs are a lot smarter than the old Intel 8088. Their machine languages have some commands that are up to 64 bits (8 bytes) wide. They also have at least a 64-bit frontside bus that can handle more than just 8 bits. They don't want RAM to give them a puny 8 bits at a time! To optimize the flow of data into and out of the CPU, the modern MCC provides at least 64 bits of data every time the CPU requests information from RAM.

Try This!   Dealing with Old RAM

Often in the PC world, old technology and ways of doing things are reimplemented with some newer technology. A tech who knows these ancient ways will have extra opportunities. Many thousands of companies—including hospitals, auto repair places, and more—use very old proprietary applications that keep track of medical records, inventory, and so on. If you're called to work on one of these ancient systems, you need to know how to work with old parts, so try this.

Obtain an old computer. Ask your uncle, cousin, or Great Aunt Edna if they have a PC collecting dust in a closet that you can use. Failing that, go to a secondhand store or market and buy one for a few dollars.

Open up the system and check out the RAM. Remove the RAM from the motherboard and then replace it to familiarize yourself with the internals. You never know when some critical system will go down and need repair immediately—and you're the one to do it!

Modern DRAM sticks come in 32-bit- and 64-bit-wide data form factors with a varying number of chips. Many techs describe these memory modules by their width, so we call them *×32* and *×64*. Note that this number does *not* describe the width of the individual DRAM chips on the module. When you read or hear about *by whatever* memory, you need to know whether that person is talking about the DRAM width or the module width. When the CPU needs certain bytes of data, it requests those bytes via the address bus. The CPU does not know the physical location of the RAM that stores that data, nor the physical makeup of the RAM—such as how many DRAM chips work together to provide the 64-bit-wide memory rows. The MCC keeps track of this and just gives the CPU whichever bytes it requests (see Figure 4-8).

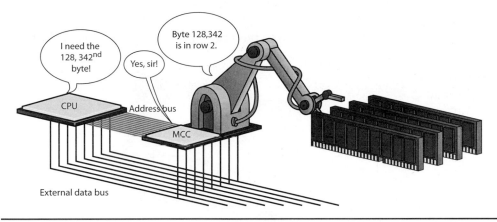

Figure 4-8 The MCC knows the real location of the DRAM.

Consumer RAM

If modern DRAM modules come in sizes much wider than a byte, why do people still use the word "byte" to describe how much DRAM they have? Convention. Habit. Rather than using a label that describes the electronic structure of RAM, common usage describes the *total capacity of RAM on a stick in bytes*. John has a single 8-GB stick of RAM on his motherboard, for example, and Sally has two 4-GB sticks. Both systems have a total of 8 GB of system RAM. That's what your clients care about. Having enough RAM makes their systems snappy and stable; not enough RAM means their systems run poorly. As a tech, you need to know more, of course, to pick the right RAM for many different types of computers.

Types of RAM

Development of newer, wider, and faster CPUs and MCCs motivates DRAM manufacturers to invent new DRAM technologies that deliver enough data at a single pop to optimize the flow of data into and out of the CPU.

SDRAM

Most modern systems use some form of *synchronous DRAM* (*SDRAM*). SDRAM is still DRAM, but it is *synchronous*—tied to the system clock, just like the CPU and MCC, so the MCC knows when data is ready to be grabbed from SDRAM. This results in little wasted time.

SDRAM made its debut in 1996 on a stick called a *dual inline memory module* (*DIMM*). The early SDRAM DIMMs came in a wide variety of pin sizes. The most common pin sizes found on desktops were the 168-pin variety. Laptop DIMMs came in 68-pin, 144-pin (see Figure 4-9), or 172-pin *micro-DIMM* packages; and the 72-pin, 144-pin, or 200-pin *small-outline DIMM* (*SO-DIMM*) form factors (see Figure 4-10). With the exception of the 32-bit 72-pin SO-DIMM, all these DIMM varieties delivered 64-bit-wide data to match the 64-bit data bus of every CPU since the original Pentium.

Figure 4-9
144-pin micro-DIMM (photo courtesy of Micron Technology, Inc.)

Figure 4-10
A (168-pin) DIMM above a (144-pin) SO-DIMM

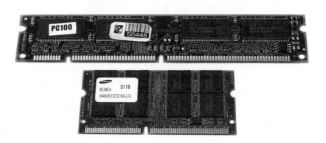

 EXAM TIP Some manufacturers (and CompTIA) drop the hyphen: *SODIMM*. You might see the RAM package spelled as SO-DIMM, SODIMM, or even SoDIMM.

To take advantage of SDRAM, you needed a PC designed to use SDRAM. If you had a system with slots for 168-pin DIMMs, for example, your system used SDRAM. A DIMM in any one of the DIMM slots could fill the 64-bit bus, so each slot was called a *bank*. You could install one, two, or more sticks and the system would work. Note that on laptops that used the 72-pin SO-DIMM, you needed to install two sticks of RAM to make a full bank, because each stick only provided half the bus width.

SDRAM was tied to the system clock, so its clock speed matched the frontside bus. Five clock speeds were commonly used on the early SDRAM systems: 66, 75, 83, 100, and 133 MHz. The RAM speed had to match or exceed the system speed, or the computer would be unstable or wouldn't work at all. These speeds were prefixed with a "PC" in the front, based on a standard forwarded by Intel, so SDRAM speeds were PC66 through PC133. For a Pentium III computer with a 100-MHz frontside bus, you needed to buy SDRAM DIMMs rated to handle it, such as PC100 or PC133.

RDRAM

When Intel was developing the Pentium 4, they knew that regular SDRAM just wasn't going to be fast enough to handle the quad-pumped 400-MHz frontside bus. Intel announced plans to replace SDRAM with a very fast, new type of RAM developed by Rambus, Inc., called *Rambus DRAM*, or simply *RDRAM* (see Figure 4-11). Hailed by Intel as the next great leap in DRAM technology, RDRAM could handle speeds up to 800 MHz, which gave Intel plenty of room to improve the Pentium 4.

Figure 4-11
RDRAM

RDRAM was greatly anticipated by the industry for years, but industry support for RDRAM proved less than enthusiastic due to significant delays in development and a price many times that of SDRAM. Despite this grudging support, almost all major PC makers sold systems that used RDRAM—for a while. From a tech's standpoint, RDRAM shared almost all of the characteristics of SDRAM. A stick of RDRAM was called a *RIMM*. In this case, however, the letters didn't actually stand for anything; they just rhymed: SIMMs, DIMMs, and RIMMs, get it?

NOTE The 400-MHz frontside bus speed wasn't achieved by making the system clock faster—it was done by making CPUs and MCCs capable of sending 64 bits of data two or four times for every clock cycle, effectively doubling or quadrupling the system bus speed.

1001

DDR SDRAM

AMD and many major system and memory makers threw their support behind an alternative to RDRAM, *double data rate SDRAM* (*DDR SDRAM*). DDR SDRAM basically copied Rambus, doubling the throughput of SDRAM by making two processes for every clock cycle. This synchronized (pardon the pun) nicely with the Athlon and later

AMD processors' double-pumped frontside bus. DDR SDRAM could not run as fast as RDRAM—although relatively low frontside bus speeds made that a moot point—but cost only slightly more than regular SDRAM.

DDR SDRAM for desktops comes in 184-pin DIMMs. These DIMMs match 168-pin DIMMs in physical size but not in pin compatibility (see Figure 4-12). The slots for the two types of RAM appear similar as well but have different guide notches, so you can't insert either type of RAM into the other's slot. DDR SDRAM for laptops comes in either 200-pin SO-DIMMs or 172-pin micro-DIMMs (see Figure 4-13).

Figure 4-12
DDR SDRAM

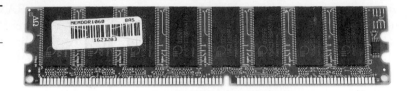

Figure 4-13
172-pin DDR SDRAM micro-DIMM (photo courtesy of Kingston/Joint Harvest)

NOTE Most techs drop some or all of the SDRAM part of DDR SDRAM when engaged in normal geekspeak. You'll hear the memory referred to as DDR, DDR RAM, and the weird hybrid, DDRAM.

DDR sticks use a rather interesting naming convention based on the number of bytes per second of data throughput the RAM can handle. To determine the bytes per second, take the MHz speed and multiply by 8 bytes (the width of all DDR SDRAM sticks). So 400 MHz multiplied by 8 is 3200 megabytes per second (MBps). Put the abbreviation "PC" in the front to make the new term: PC3200. Many techs also use the naming convention used for the individual DDR chips; for example, *DDR400* refers to a 400-MHz DDR SDRAM chip running on a 200-MHz clock.

Even though the term DDR*xxx* is really just for individual DDR chips and the term PC*xxxx* is for DDR sticks, this tradition of two names for every speed of RAM is a bit of a challenge because you'll often hear both terms used interchangeably. Table 4-1 shows all the speeds for DDR—not all of these are commonly used.

Clock Speed	DDR Speed Rating	PC Speed Rating
100 MHz	DDR-200	PC-1600
133 MHz	DDR-266	PC-2100
166 MHz	DDR-333	PC-2700
200 MHz	DDR-400	PC-3200
217 MHz	DDR-433	PC-3500
233 MHz	DDR-466	PC-3700
250 MHz	DDR-500	PC-4000
275 MHz	DDR-550	PC-4400
300 MHz	DDR-600	PC-4800

Table 4-1   DDR Speeds

Following the lead of AMD and other manufacturers, the PC industry adopted DDR SDRAM as the standard system RAM. In the summer of 2003, Intel relented and stopped producing motherboards and memory controllers that required RDRAM.

One thing is sure about PC technologies: any good idea that can be copied will be copied. One of Rambus' best concepts was the *dual-channel architecture*—using two sticks of RDRAM together to increase throughput. Manufacturers have released motherboards with MCCs that support dual-channel architecture using DDR SDRAM. Dual-channel DDR motherboards use regular DDR sticks, although manufacturers often sell RAM in matched pairs, branding them as dual-channel RAM.

Dual-channel DDR requires two identical sticks of DDR and they must snap into two paired slots. Many motherboards offer four slots (see Figure 4-14).

Figure 4-14
A motherboard showing four RAM slots. By populating the same-colored slots with identical RAM, you can run in dual-channel mode.

SIM I've got a great Chapter 4 Challenge! sim on calculating RAM speeds at http://totalsem.com/100x. Check it out right now!

DDR2

DDR2 is DDR RAM with some improvements in its electrical characteristics, enabling it to run even faster than DDR while using less power. The big speed increase from DDR2 comes by clock doubling the input/output circuits on the chips. This does not speed up the core RAM—the part that holds the data—but speeding up the input/output and adding special buffers (sort of like a cache) makes DDR2 run much faster than regular DDR. DDR2 uses a 240-pin DIMM that's not compatible with DDR (see Figure 4-15). Likewise, the DDR2 200-pin SO-DIMM is incompatible with the DDR SO-DIMM. You'll find motherboards running both single-channel and dual-channel DDR2.

Figure 4-15
240-pin DDR2
DIMM

NOTE DDR2 RAM sticks will not fit into DDR sockets, nor are they electronically compatible.

Table 4-2 shows some of the common DDR2 speeds.

Core RAM Clock Speed	DDR I/O Speed	DDR2 Speed Rating	PC Speed Rating
100 MHz	200 MHz	DDR2-400	PC2-3200
133 MHz	266 MHz	DDR2-533	PC2-4200
166 MHz	333 MHz	DDR2-667	PC2-5300
200 MHz	400 MHz	DDR2-800	PC2-6400
266 MHz	533 MHz	DDR2-1066	PC2-8500

Table 4-2 DDR2 Speeds

DDR3

DDR3 boasts higher speeds, more efficient architecture, and around 30 percent lower power consumption than DDR2 RAM. Just like its predecessor, DDR3 uses a 240-pin DIMM, albeit one that is slotted differently to make it difficult for users to install the wrong RAM in their system without using a hammer (see Figure 4-16). DDR3 SO-DIMMs for portable computers have 204 pins. Neither fits into a DDR2 socket.

Figure 4-16
DDR2 DIMM on
top of a DDR3
DIMM

—— DDR2
—— DDR3

EXAM TIP The 220-1001 exam loves to test you on pin counts with RAM! It will challenge your knowledge of the various RAM types, including DDR2, DDR3, and DDR4. Make sure you know their individual characteristics and differences. DDR3 DIMMs have 240 pins, for example, and DDR3 SO-DIMMs have 204 pins.

DDR3 doubles the buffer of DDR2 from 4 bits to 8 bits, giving it a huge boost in bandwidth over older RAM. Not only that, but some DDR3 (and later) modules also include a feature called *XMP*, or *Extreme Memory Profile*, that enables power users to overclock their RAM easily, boosting their already fast memory. DDR3 modules also use higher-density memory chips, up to 16-GB DDR3 modules. AMD's version of XMP is called *AMP*, for *AMD Memory Profile*.

NOTE Do not confuse DDR*x* with GDDR*x*; the latter is a type of memory used solely in video cards (e.g., GDDR5). See Chapter 17, "Display Technologies," for the scoop on video-specific types of memory.

Some motherboards that support DDR3 also support features called *triple-channel architecture* or *quad-channel architecture*, which work a lot like dual-channel, but with three or four sticks of RAM instead of two. More recently, Intel and AMD systems have switched back to dual-channel, although there's plenty of systems out there using triple- or quad-channel memory.

EXAM TIP Be sure you are familiar with single-, dual-, triple-, and quad-channel memory architectures.

Table 4-3 shows common DDR3 speeds. Note how DDR3 I/O speeds are quadruple the clock speeds, whereas DDR2 I/O speeds are only double the clock. This speed increase is due to the increased buffer size, which enables DDR3 to grab twice as much data every clock cycle as DDR2 can.

Core RAM Clock Speed	DDR I/O Speed	DDR3 Speed Rating	PC Speed Rating
100 MHz	400 MHz	DDR3-800	PC3-6400
133 MHz	533 MHz	DDR3-1066	PC3-8500
166 MHz	667 MHz	DDR3-1333	PC3-10667
200 MHz	800 MHz	DDR3-1600	PC3-12800
233 MHz	933 MHz	DDR3-1866	PC3-14900
266 MHz	1066 MHz	DDR3-2133	PC3-17000
300 MHz	1200 MHz	DDR3-2400	PC3-19200

Table 4-3 DDR3 Speeds

DDR3L/DDR3U

Memory manufacturers offer a low-voltage version of DDR3, most commonly labeled *DDR3L*, that provides substantial cost savings when used in massive RAM applications. (Think big data centers, like the ones that power Google.) DDR3L runs at 1.35 volts (V), compared to the 1.5 V or 1.65 V of regular DDR3, providing cost savings up to 15 percent—that adds up fast! The ultra-low-voltage version of DDR3, *DDR3U*, runs at a miserly 1.25 V.

Lower voltage means less heat generated. In a server farm or data center, that can reduce the air conditioning bill by a lot. That's a good thing.

The DIMM is slot-compatible with DDR3, although not necessarily a drama-free replacement on older motherboards. A motherboard pushing 1.5 V to the RAM slots and RAM only capable of running at 1.35 V would not result in happiness.

For best results, check the manual that came with the motherboard in question or check the manufacturer's Web site for support. Also, many RAM manufacturers produce RAM modules capable of running at 1.35 V or 1.5 V; those will work in any motherboard that supports DDR3. Some modules can handle the full gamut, from 1.25 V to 1.65 V.

DDR4

DDR4 arrived on the scene in late 2014 with much fanfare and slow adoption, although it's the mainstream memory now. DDR4 offers higher density and lower voltages than DDR3, and can handle faster data transfer rates. In theory, manufacturers could create DDR4 DIMMs up to 512 GB. DIMMS running DDR4 top out at 64 GB, compared to the 16 GB max of DDR3, but run at only 1.2 V. (There's a performance version that runs at 1.35 V and a low-voltage version at 1.05 V too.)

 NOTE By the time you read this, the 64-GB limit on DDR4 might have been eclipsed. Check www.newegg.com for the latest.

DDR4 uses a 288-pin DIMM, so they are not backwardly compatible with DDR3 slots. DDR4 SO-DIMMs have 260 pins that are not compatible with DDR3 204-pin SO-DIMM slots. Some motherboard manufacturers have released boards that offer support for both DDR3 and DDR4, by providing both slot types.

With DDR4, most techs have switched from bit rate to megatransfers per second (MT/s), a way to describe the number of data transfer operations happening at any given second. For DDR4, the number is pretty huge. Table 4-4 shows *some* DDR4 speeds and labels.

Clock Speed	Bandwidth	DDR4 Speed Rating	PC Speed Rating
200 MHz	1600 MT/s	DDR4-1600	PC4-12800
266 MHz	2133 MT/s	DDR4-2133	PC4-17000
300 MHz	2400 MT/s	DDR4-2400	PC4-19200
400 MHz	3200 MT/s	DDR4-3200	PC4-25600
... Skipping a whole bunch here in the middle ...			
563 MHz	4500 MT/s	DDR4-4500	PC4-36000
575 MHz	4600 MT/s	DDR4-4600	PC4-36800
588 MHz	4700 MT/s	DDR4-4700	PC4-37600

Table 4-4   Standard DDR4 Varieties

EXAM TIP   The CompTIA A+ 1001 exam covers DDR2, DDR3, and DDR4. You won't find DDR, DDR3L, or DDR3U on the exam.

RAM Variations

Within each class of RAM, you'll find variations in packaging, speed, quality, and the capability to handle data with more or fewer errors. Higher-end systems often need higher-end RAM, so knowing these variations is of crucial importance to techs.

Double-Sided DIMMs

Every type of RAM stick comes in one of two types: *single-sided RAM* and *double-sided RAM*. As their name implies, single-sided sticks have chips on only one side of the stick. Double-sided sticks have chips on both sides (see Figure 4-17). Double-sided sticks are basically two sticks of RAM soldered onto one board. There's nothing wrong with double-sided RAM sticks other than the fact that some motherboards either can't use them or can only use them in certain ways—for example, only if you use a single stick and it goes into a certain slot.

Latency

Different RAM responds to electrical signals at varying rates. When the memory controller starts to grab a line of memory, for example, a slight delay occurs; think of it as the RAM getting off the couch. After the RAM sends out the requested line of memory,

Figure 4-17
Double-sided
DDR SDRAM

there's another slight delay before the memory controller can ask for another line—the RAM sat back down. The delay in RAM's response time is called its *latency*, but shorthand like CL17 or CL19 uses initials for the technical name: *column array strobe (CAS) latency*.

If both have the same speed rating, RAM with a lower latency—such as CL17—is slightly faster than RAM with a higher latency—such as CL19—because it responds more quickly. The CL refers to clock cycle delays. The 17 means that the memory delays 17 clock cycles before delivering the requested data; the 19 means a 19-cycle delay. Because it's measured in clock cycles, CL is relative to the clock speed of the RAM—a 19-cycle delay takes up more real-world time at a lower clock speed than it will at a higher clock speed.

Back when DDR2 and DDR3 were the latest and greatest, these latency numbers were a big deal. Gamers and other PC enthusiasts paid a handsome premium for lower-latency RAM. When DDR4 debuted, its relatively high CL numbers made enthusiasts question the memory companies, afraid it would be too slow. In real-world tests, DDR4's higher clock speeds result in latencies in line with the older DDR3. It's still worth looking at latency when you go memory shopping, but it's a lot less important than it used to be.

NOTE Latency numbers reflect how many clicks of the system clock it takes before the RAM responds. If you speed up the system clock—say, from 200 MHz to 266 MHz—the same stick of RAM might take an extra click before it can respond. When you take RAM out of an older system and put it into a newer one, you might get a seemingly dead PC, even though the RAM fits in the DIMM slot. Many motherboards enable you to adjust the RAM timings manually. If yours does so, try raising the latency to give the slower RAM time to respond. See Chapter 5, "Firmware," to learn how to make these adjustments (and how to recover if you make a mistake).

From a tech's standpoint, you need to get the proper RAM for the system you're working on. If you put a high-latency stick in a motherboard set up for a low-latency stick, you'll get an unstable or completely dead PC. Check the motherboard manual or RAM manufacturer's Web site and get the quickest RAM the motherboard can handle, and you should be fine.

Parity and ECC

Given the high speeds and phenomenal amount of data moved by the typical DRAM chip, a RAM chip might occasionally give bad data to the memory controller. This doesn't necessarily mean that the RAM has gone bad. It could be a hiccup caused by some unknown event that makes a good DRAM chip say a bit is a zero when it's really a one. In most cases you won't even notice when such a rare event happens. In some environments, however, even these rare events are intolerable. A bank server handling thousands of online transactions per second, for example, can't risk even the smallest error. These important computers need a more robust, fault-resistant RAM.

The first type of error-detecting RAM was known as parity RAM (see Figure 4-18). Compared with non-parity RAM, *parity RAM* stored an extra bit of data (called the parity bit) that the MCC used to verify whether the data was correct. Parity wasn't perfect. It wouldn't always detect an error, and if the MCC did find an error, it couldn't correct the error. For years, parity was the only available way to tell if the RAM made a mistake.

Figure 4-18
Ancient parity
RAM stick

Today's PCs that need to watch for RAM errors use a special type of RAM called *error correction code RAM (ECC RAM)*. ECC is a major advance in error checking on DRAM. ECC detects and corrects any time a single bit is flipped, on-the-fly. It can detect but *not correct* a double-bit error. The checking and fixing come at a price, however, as ECC RAM is always slower than non-ECC RAM.

ECC DRAM comes in every DIMM package type and can lead to some odd-sounding numbers. You can find DDR2, DDR3 (Figure 4-19), or DDR4 RAM sticks, for example, that come in 240-pin, *72*-bit versions. Similarly, you'll see 200-pin, 72-bit SO-DIMM format. The extra 8 bits beyond the 64-bit data stream are for the ECC.

Figure 4-19
Stick of ECC
DDR3 with
9 memory chips

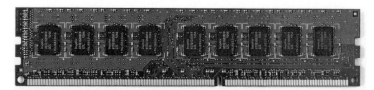

You might be tempted to say, "Gee, maybe I want to try this ECC RAM." Well, don't! To take advantage of ECC RAM, you need a motherboard designed to support ECC. Only expensive motherboards for high-end systems use ECC. The special-use-only nature of ECC makes it fairly rare in desktop systems. Plenty of techs with years of experience have never even seen ECC RAM.

 NOTE Some memory manufacturers call the technology *error checking and correction* (*ECC*). Don't be thrown off if you see the phrase—it's the same thing, just a different marketing slant for error correction code.

Registered and Buffered Memory

When shopping for memory, especially for ECC memory, you are bound to come across the terms *registered RAM* or *buffered RAM*. Either term refers to a small register installed on some memory modules to act as a buffer between the DIMM and the memory controller. This little extra bit of circuitry helps compensate for electrical problems that crop up in systems with lots of memory modules, such as servers.

The key thing to remember is that a motherboard will use either buffered or *unbuffered RAM* (that's typical consumer RAM), not both. If you insert the wrong module in a system you are upgrading, the worst that will happen is a blank screen and a lot of head scratching.

Working with RAM

Whenever people come up to me and ask what single hardware upgrade they can do to improve their system performance, I always tell them the same thing—add more RAM. Adding more RAM can improve overall system performance, processing speed, and stability—if you get it right. Botching the job can cause dramatic system instability, such as frequent, random crashes and reboots. Every tech needs to know how to install and upgrade system RAM of all types.

To get the desired results from a RAM upgrade, you must first determine if insufficient RAM is the cause of system problems. Second, you need to pick the proper RAM for the system. Finally, you must use good installation practices. Always store RAM sticks in anti-static packaging whenever they're not in use, and use strict ESD handling procedures. Like many other pieces of the PC, RAM is *very* sensitive to ESD and other technician abuse (see Figure 4-20).

Do You Need More RAM?

Two symptoms point to the need for more RAM in a PC: general system sluggishness and excessive hard drive accessing. If programs take forever to load and running programs seem to stall and move more slowly than you would like, the problem could stem from insufficient RAM.

Figure 4-20
Don't do this!
Grabbing the
contacts is a bad
idea!

A friend with an older Windows system complained that her PC seemed snappy when she first got it but now takes a long time to do the things she wants to do with it, such as photograph retouching in Adobe Photoshop. Over the years, new applications and updates to her existing operating system and applications piled up until her system, with only 2 GB of RAM, was woefully insufficient for her tasks—she kept maxing out the RAM and thus the system slowed to a crawl. I replaced her single 2-GB stick with a pair of 4-GB sticks and suddenly she had the speedy workstation she desired.

Excessive hard drive activity when you move between programs points to a need for more RAM. Every computer has the capability to make a portion of your hard drive look like RAM in case you run out of real RAM.

Virtual Memory

Computers use a portion of the hard drive (or solid-state drive) as an extension of system RAM called *virtual memory*. The operating system uses part of the available drive space to save a *page file* or *swap file*. When a computer starts running out of real RAM because you've loaded too many programs, the system swaps less-used programs from RAM to the page file, opening more space for programs currently active. All versions of Windows, macOS, and Linux use virtual memory. Let's use a typical Windows PC as an example of how paging works.

EXAM TIP   The default and recommended page-file size in Windows is 1.5 times the amount of installed RAM on your computer.

Let's assume you have a PC with 4 GB of RAM. Figure 4-21 shows the system RAM as a thermometer with gradients from 0 to 4 GB. As programs load, they take up RAM, and as more and more programs are loaded (labeled A, B, and C in the figure), more RAM is used.

Figure 4-21
A RAM thermometer showing that more programs take more RAM

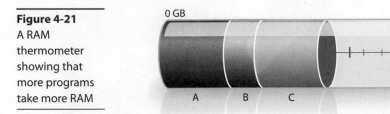

At a certain point, you won't have enough RAM to run any more programs (see Figure 4-22). Sure, you could close one or more programs to make room for yet another one, but you can't keep all of the programs running simultaneously. This is where virtual memory comes into play.

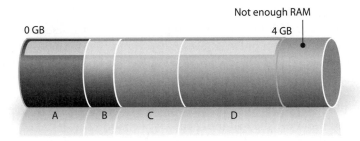

Figure 4-22   Not enough RAM to load program D

Windows' virtual memory starts by creating a page file that resides somewhere on your hard drive. The page file works like a temporary storage box. Windows removes running programs temporarily from RAM into the page file so other programs can load and run. If you have enough RAM to run all your programs, Windows does not need to use the page file—Windows brings the page file into play only when insufficient RAM is available to run all open programs.

 NOTE   Virtual memory is a fully automated process and does not require any user intervention. This is true of virtual memory in Windows, macOS, and Linux.

To load, Program D needs a certain amount of free RAM. Clearly, this requires unloading some other program (or programs) from RAM without actually closing any programs.

Windows looks at all running programs—in this case A, B, and C—and decides which program is the least used. That program is then cut out of or swapped from RAM and copied into the page file. In this case, Windows has chosen Program B (see Figure 4-23). Unloading Program B from RAM provides enough RAM to load Program D (see Figure 4-24).

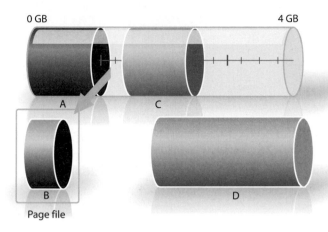

Figure 4-23   Program B being unloaded from memory

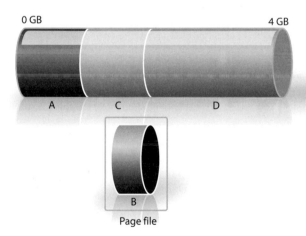

Figure 4-24   Program B stored in the page file, making room for Program D

It is important to understand that none of this activity is visible on the screen. Program B's window is still visible, along with those of all the other running programs. Nothing tells the user that Program B is no longer in RAM (see Figure 4-25).

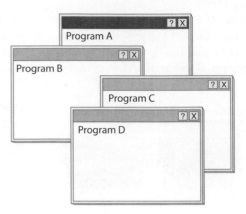

Figure 4-25
You can't tell whether a program is swapped or not.

So what happens if you click on Program B's window to bring it to the front? The program can't actually run from the page file; it must be loaded back into RAM. First, Windows decides which program must be removed from RAM, and this time Windows chooses Program C (see Figure 4-26). Then it loads Program B into RAM (see Figure 4-27).

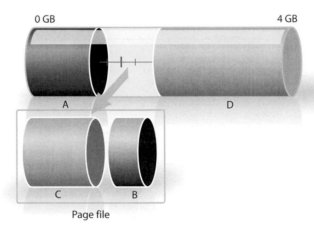

Figure 4-26   Program C is swapped to the page file.

Swapping programs to and from the page file and RAM takes time. Although no visual clues suggest that a swap is taking place, the machine slows down quite noticeably as Windows performs the swaps. Page files are a crucial aspect of Windows operation.

Windows handles page files automatically, but occasionally you'll run into problems and need to change the size of the page file or delete it and let Windows re-create it automatically. The page file is pagefile.sys. You can often find it in the root directory of the C: drive, but again, that can be changed. Wherever it is, the page file is a hidden system file, which means in practice that you'll have to play with your folder-viewing options to see it.

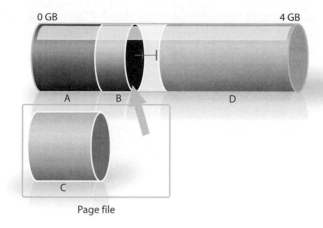

Page file

Figure 4-27 Program B is swapped back into RAM.

If Windows needs to access the page file too frequently, you will notice the hard drive access LED going crazy as Windows rushes to move programs between RAM and the page file in a process called *disk thrashing*. Windows uses the page file all the time, but excessive disk thrashing suggests that you need more RAM.

System RAM Recommendations

Microsoft sets very low the minimum RAM requirements listed for the various Windows operating systems to get the maximum number of users to upgrade or convert, and that's fine. Microsoft recommends a minimum system requirement of 1 GB of RAM for 32-bit versions of Windows and 2 GB of RAM for 64-bit versions. This applies to any version of Windows. I think that results in dreadfully sluggish computers. Here are my recommendations:

- **32-bit Windows**   2 GB to get by; 4 GB for best results
- **64-bit Windows**   4 GB to get by; 8 GB for a solid machine; 16+ GB for any machine doing serious, processor-intensive work.

The latest versions of macOS require a minimum of 2 GB of RAM. Like Windows, however, the 64-bit-only OS does much better with a lot more RAM. I would go with 4 GB at a minimum, 8 GB for good performance, and more for peak performance.

NOTE   Beware sealed systems! Almost all smartphones and tablets are sealed. Today many desktop and laptop systems—in the past easily upgraded by a good tech—are sealed, making upgrades impossible. If you get a sealed system, don't scrimp on the RAM at the time of purchase!

Linux RAM requirements and recommendations depend entirely on which distribution (distro) is being used. The mainstream distros, like Ubuntu, have requirements similar to Windows and macOS. But many distros get by on very minimal system requirements.

Determining Current RAM Capacity

Before you go get RAM, you obviously need to know how much RAM you currently have in your PC. Windows displays this amount in the System Control Panel applet (see Figure 4-28). You can also access the screen with the WINDOWS-PAUSE/BREAK keystroke combination on standard keyboards.

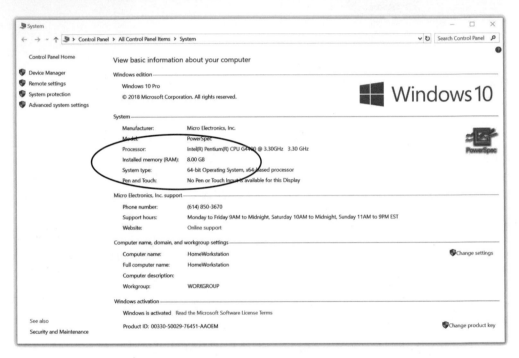

Figure 4-28 Mike's Windows 10 system only has 8 GB of RAM.

Windows also includes the handy Performance tab in the Task Manager (as shown in Figure 4-29). The Performance tab includes a lot of information about the amount of RAM being used by your PC. Access the Task Manager by pressing CTRL-SHIFT-ESC and selecting the Performance tab.

ReadyBoost

Traditional (spinning) hard drives for virtual memory offer slow performance. High-speed flash drives offer much better virtual memory performance. Windows offers a feature called *ReadyBoost* that enables you to use flash media devices—removable USB thumb drives or memory cards—as super-fast, dedicated virtual memory. The performance gain

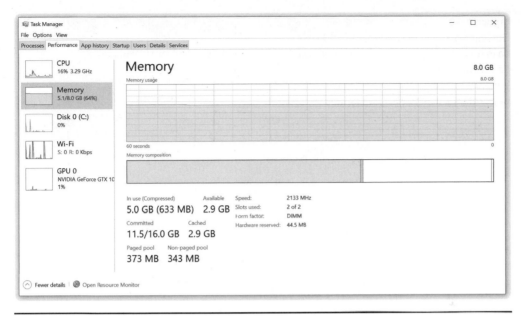

Figure 4-29   Performance tab in Windows 10 Task Manager

over using only a traditional hard drive for virtual memory can be significant with Ready-Boost because read/write access times on flash memory blow away hard drive read/write access times.

Plug a ReadyBoost-approved device into a USB port or built-in flash memory card reader slot. Right-click the device in Computer and select Properties. Click the Ready-Boost tab and select the radio button next to either *Dedicate this device to ReadyBoost* or *Use this device* (see Figure 4-30). Click Apply to enhance your system's performance.

NOTE   ReadyBoost isn't for every system. A modern system running SSDs won't see much benefit with ReadyBoost. Also, adding more RAM will always give a system a far better boost in performance than messing with ReadyBoost. Add RAM and blow off ReadyBoost. Just remember ReadyBoost for the exams.

Getting the Right RAM

To do the perfect RAM upgrade, determine the optimum capacity of RAM to install and then get the right RAM for the motherboard. Your first two stops toward these goals are the inside of the case and your motherboard manual. Open the case to see how many sticks of RAM you have installed currently and how many free slots you have open.

Check the motherboard book or RAM manufacturer's Web site to determine the total capacity of RAM the system can handle and what specific technology works with your system.

Figure 4-30
Dedicating a
flash drive to
ReadyBoost to
enhance system
performance

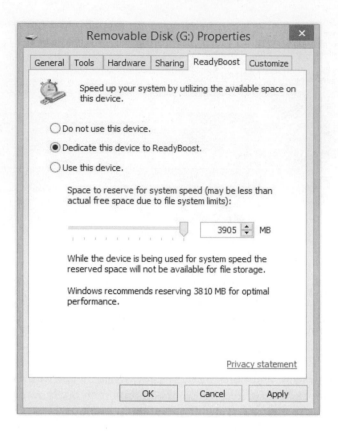

You can't put DDR4 into a system that can only handle DDR3 SDRAM, after all, and it won't do you much good to install a pair of 4-GB DIMMs when your system tops out at 4 GB. Figure 4-31 shows the RAM limits for an ASUS-brand motherboard.

Figure 4-31
The motherboard
book shows how
much RAM the
motherboard will
handle.

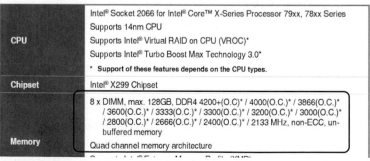

ROG RAMPAGE VI EXTREME specifications summary

CPU	Intel® Socket 2066 for Intel® Core™ X-Series Processor 79xx, 78xx Series Supports 14nm CPU Supports Intel® Virtual RAID on CPU (VROC)* Supports Intel® Turbo Boost Max Technology 3.0* * Support of these features depends on the CPU types.
Chipset	Intel® X299 Chipset
Memory	8 x DIMM, max. 128GB, DDR4 4200+(O.C)* / 4000(O.C.)* / 3866(O.C)* / 3600(O.C.)* / 3333(O.C.)* / 3300(O.C.)* / 3200(O.C.)* / 3000(O.C.)* / 2800(O.C.)* / 2666(O.C.)* / 2400(O.C.)* / 2133 MHz, non-ECC, un- buffered memory Quad channel memory architecture

NOTE The freeware CPU-Z program tells you the total number of slots on your motherboard, the number of slots used, and the exact type of RAM in each slot—very handy. CPU-Z not only determines the latency of your RAM but also lists the latency at a variety of motherboard speeds. The media accompanying this book has a copy of CPU-Z, so check it out or download it from www.cpuid.com.

Mix and Match at Your Peril

All motherboards can handle different capacities of RAM. If you have three slots, you may put a 2-GB stick in one and a 4-GB stick in the other with a high chance of success. To ensure maximum stability in a system, however, shoot for as close as you can get to uniformity of RAM. Choose RAM sticks that match in technology, capacity, speed, and latency (CL).

Mixing Speeds

With so many different DRAM speeds available, you may often find yourself tempted to mix speeds of DRAM in the same system. Although you may get away with mixing speeds on a system, the safest, easiest rule to follow is to use the speed of DRAM specified in the motherboard book, and make sure that every piece of DRAM runs at that speed. In a worst-case scenario, mixing DRAM speeds can cause the system to lock up every few seconds or every few minutes. You might also get some data corruption. Mixing speeds sometimes works fine, but don't do your tax return on a machine with mixed DRAM speeds until the system has proven to be stable for a few days. The important thing to note here is that you won't break anything, other than possibly data, by experimenting.

Okay, I have mentioned enough disclaimers. Modern motherboards provide some flexibility regarding RAM speeds and mixing. First, you can use RAM that is faster than the motherboard specifies. For example, if the system needs PC 19200 DDR4, you may put in PC-25600 DDR4 and it should work fine. Faster DRAM is not going to make the system run any faster, however, so don't look for any system improvement.

Second, you can sometimes get away with putting one speed of DRAM in one bank and another speed in another bank, as long as all the speeds are as fast as or faster than the speed specified by the motherboard. Don't bother trying to put different-speed DRAM sticks in the same bank with a motherboard that uses dual-channel DDR.

Installing DIMMs

Installing DRAM is so easy that it's one of the very few jobs I recommend to non-techie folks. First, attach an anti-static wrist strap or touch some bare metal on the power supply to ground yourself and avoid ESD. Then swing the side tabs on the RAM slots down from the upright position. Pick up a stick of RAM—don't touch those contacts—and line up the notch or notches with the raised portion(s) of the DIMM socket (see Figure 4-32). A good hard push down is usually all you need to ensure a solid connection. Make sure that the DIMM snaps into position to show it is completely seated. Also, notice that the one or two side tabs move in to reflect a tight connection.

Figure 4-32
Inserting a DIMM

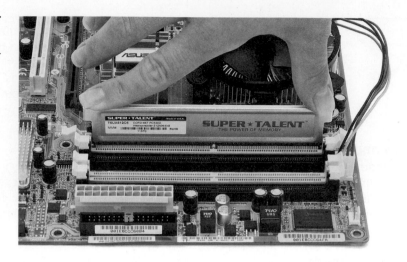

Your motherboard should detect and automatically set up any DIMM you install, assuming you have the right RAM for the system, using a technology called *serial presence detect* (*SPD*). RAM makers add a handy chip to modern sticks called the SPD chip (see Figure 4-33). The SPD chip stores all the information about your DRAM, including size, speed, ECC or non-ECC, registered or unregistered, and other more technical bits of information.

Figure 4-33
SPD chip on
a stick

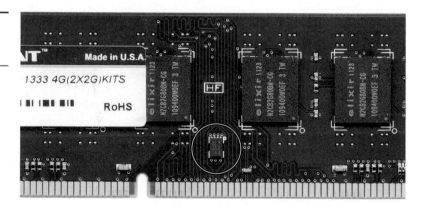

When a PC boots, it queries the SPD chip so that the MCC knows how much RAM is on the stick, how fast it runs, and other information. Any program can query the SPD chip. Take a look at Figure 4-34 with the results of the popular CPU-Z program showing RAM information from the SPD chip.

Figure 4-34
CPU-Z showing
RAM information

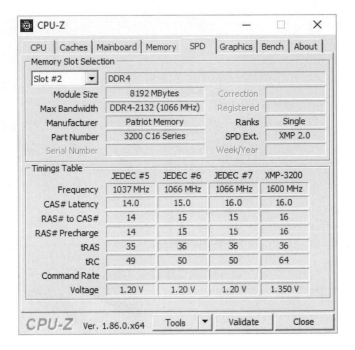

All new systems count on SPD to set the RAM timings properly for your system when it boots. If you add a RAM stick with a bad SPD chip, you'll get a POST error message and the system will not boot. You can't fix a broken SPD chip; you just buy a new stick of RAM.

Installing SO-DIMMs in Laptops

It wasn't that long ago that adding RAM to a laptop was either impossible or required you to send the system back to the manufacturer. Long ago, laptop makers used expensive, proprietary, custom-made RAM packages that were hard to handle. Wide acceptance of SO-DIMMs solved these problems for a time—until ultra-thin laptops started turning up with soldered-on RAM. Most larger laptops still provide relatively convenient access to their SO-DIMMs, making it easy to add or replace RAM.

Access to RAM usually requires removing a panel or lifting up the keyboard—the procedure varies among laptop manufacturers. Figure 4-35 shows a typical laptop RAM access panel. You can slide the panel off to reveal the SO-DIMMs. Slide the pins into position and snap the SO-DIMM down into the retaining clips (see Figure 4-36).

Before doing any work on a laptop, turn the system off, disconnect it from the AC wall socket, and remove all batteries. Use an anti-static wrist strap because laptops are far more susceptible to ESD than desktop PCs.

Figure 4-35
A RAM access
panel on a laptop

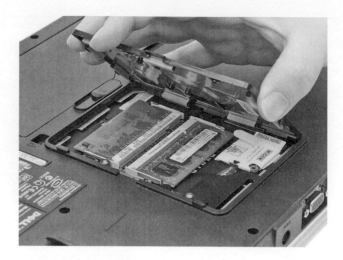

Figure 4-36
Snapping in
a SO-DIMM

Troubleshooting RAM

"Memory" errors show up in a variety of ways on modern systems, including system lockups, page faults, and other error screens. These errors can indicate bad RAM but often point to something completely unrelated. This is especially true with intermittent problems. Techs need to recognize these errors and determine which part of the system caused the memory error. Then they need to follow up with various testing methods.

System lockups and page faults (they often go hand in hand) in Windows can indicate a problem with RAM. A system lockup is when the computer stops functioning.

A *page fault* is a milder error that can be caused by memory issues but not necessarily system RAM problems. Certainly page faults *look* like RAM issues because Windows generates frightening error messages filled with long strings of hexadecimal digits, such as "KRNL386 caused a page fault at 03F2:25A003BC." Just because the error message contains a memory address, however, does not mean that you have a problem with your RAM. Write down the address. If it repeats in later error messages, you probably have a bad RAM stick. If Windows displays different memory locations, you need to look elsewhere for the culprit.

Every once in a while, something potentially catastrophic happens within the PC, some little electron hits the big red panic button, and the operating system has to shut down certain functions before it can save data. This panic button inside the PC is called a *non-maskable interrupt* (*NMI*), more simply defined as an interruption the CPU cannot ignore. An NMI manifests as a *proprietary crash screen*. In Windows 7, for example, the crash screen is what techs call the *Blue Screen of Death* (*BSoD*)—a bright blue screen with a scary-sounding error message on it (see Figure 4-37).

Figure 4-37
Blue Screen of
Death

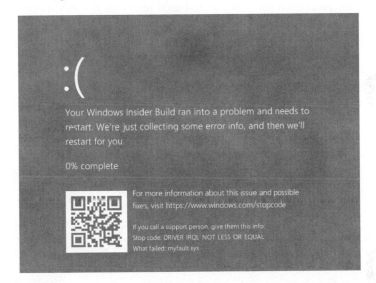

Windows 8/8.1/10 display a blue screen with a sad face and the words to the effect of Windows has a problem. Restart the machine. A macOS machine might display a spinning rainbow wheel sometimes called the *Spinning Pinwheel of Death* (*SPoD*) or, more likely, will simply reboot.

NOTE   The CompTIA A+ objectives refer to the SPoD as the *pin wheel of death*.

Bad RAM sometimes triggers an NMI, although often the culprit lies with buggy programming or clashing code. The BSoD/SPoD varies across Windows versions and operating systems, and it would require a much lengthier tome than this one to cover all the variations. Suffice it to say that RAM *could* be the problem when that delightful blue screen or pinwheel appears.

Finally, intermittent memory errors can come from a variety of sources, including a dying power supply, electrical interference, buggy applications, buggy hardware, and so on. These errors show up as lockups, general protection faults, and page faults, but they never have the same address or happen with the same applications. I always check the power supply first.

Once you discover that you may have a RAM problem, you have a couple of options. First, several companies manufacture hardware RAM-testing devices. Second, you can use the method I use—*replace and pray*. Open the system case and replace each stick, one at a time, with a known good replacement stick. (You have one of those lying around, don't you?) This method, although potentially time-consuming, certainly works. With PC prices as low as they are now, you could simply replace the whole system for less than the price of a dedicated RAM tester.

Third, you could run a software-based tester on the RAM. Because you have to load a software tester into the memory it's about to scan, there's always a small chance that simply starting the software RAM tester might cause an error. Still, you can find some pretty good free ones out there. Windows 7 and later include the *Windows Memory Diagnostic* tool, which can automatically scan your computer's RAM when you encounter a problem. If you're using another OS, my favorite tool is the open source Memtest86+ (memtest.org). The Memtest86+ software exhaustively checks your RAM and reports bad RAM when it finds it (see Figure 4-38).

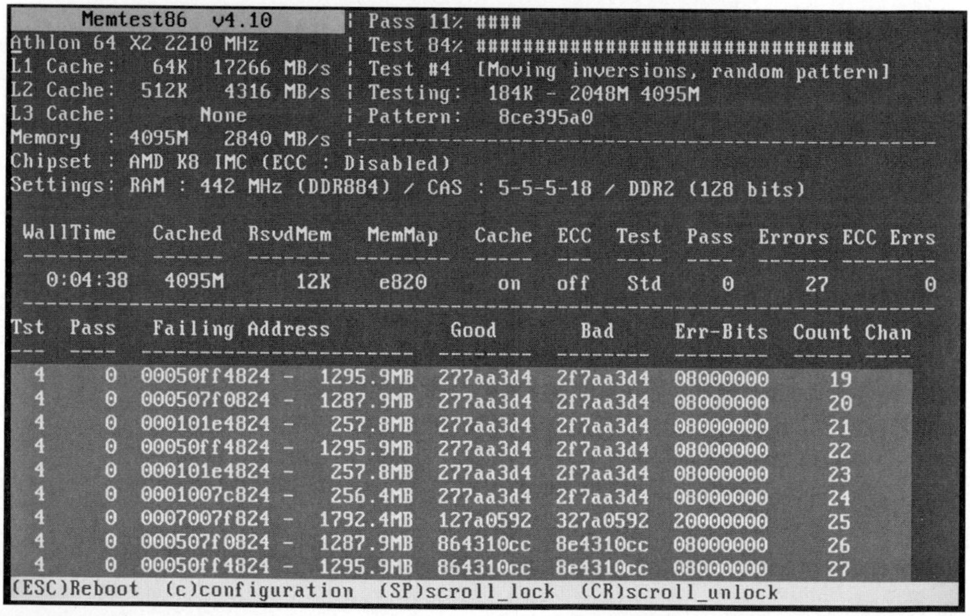

Figure 4-38   Memtest86+ detecting failing RAM

NOTE A *general protection fault* (*GPF*) is an error that can cause an application to crash. Often GPFs are caused by programs stepping on each other's toes. Chapter 16, "Troubleshooting Operating Systems," goes into more detail on GPFs and other Windows errors.

Chapter Review

Questions

1. Steve adds a second 8-GB 288-pin DIMM to his PC, which should bring the total RAM in the system up to 16 GB. The PC has an Intel Core i7 4-GHz processor and four 288-pin DIMM slots on the motherboard. When he turns on the PC, however, only 8 GB of RAM shows up in Windows Settings app. Which of the following is most likely to be the problem?

   A. Steve failed to seat the RAM properly.

   B. Steve put DDR4 in a DDR3 slot.

   C. The CPU cannot handle 16 GB of RAM.

   D. The motherboard can use only one RAM slot at a time.

2. Scott wants to add 8 GB of PC3-12800 DDR3 to an aging but still useful desktop system. The system has a 200-MHz motherboard and currently has 4 GB of non-ECC DDR3 RAM in the system. What else does he need to know before installing?

   A. What speed of RAM he needs

   B. What type of RAM he needs

   C. How many pins the RAM has

   D. If the system can handle that much RAM.

3. What is the primary reason that DDR4 RAM is faster than DDR3 RAM?

   A. The core speed of the DDR4 RAM chips is faster.

   B. The input/output speed of the DDR4 RAM is faster.

   C. DDR3 RAM is dual-channel and DDR4 RAM is quad-channel.

   D. DDR3 RAM uses 240-pin DIMMs and DDR4 uses 288-pin DIMMs.

4. What is the term for the delay in the RAM's response to a request from the MCC?

   A. Variance

   B. MCC gap

   C. Latency

   D. Fetch interval

5. How does an NMI manifest on a Windows system?

   A. Blue Screen of Death.

   B. Spinning Pinwheel of Death.

   C. Interrupt of death.

   D. NMIs only happen on macOS systems.

6. Silas has an AMD-based motherboard with two sticks of DDR3 RAM installed in two of the three RAM slots, for a total of 8 GB of system memory. When he runs CPU-Z to test the system, he notices that the software claims he's running single-channel memory. What could be the problem? (Select the best answer.)

   A. His motherboard only supports single-channel memory.

   B. His motherboard only supports dual-channel memory with DDR2 RAM, not DDR3.

   C. He needs to install a third RAM stick to enable dual-channel memory.

   D. He needs to move one of the installed sticks to a different slot to activate dual-channel memory.

7. Which of the following Control Panel applets will display the amount of RAM in your PC?

   A. System

   B. Devices and Printers

   C. Device Manager

   D. Action Center

8. What is the best way to determine the total capacity and specific type of RAM your system can handle?

   A. Check the motherboard book.

   B. Open the case and inspect the RAM.

   C. Check the Device Manager.

   D. Check the System utility in the Control Panel.

9. Gregor installed a third stick of known good RAM into his Core i7 system, bringing the total amount of RAM up to 12 GB. Within a few days, though, he started having random lockups and reboots, especially when doing memory-intensive tasks such as gaming. What is most likely the problem?

   A. Gregor installed DDR2 RAM into a DDR3 system.

   B. Gregor installed DDR3 RAM into a DDR4 system.

   C. Gregor installed RAM that didn't match the speed or quality of the RAM in the system.

   D. Gregor installed RAM that exceeded the speed of the RAM in the system.

10. Cindy installs a second stick of DDR4 RAM into her Core i5 system, bringing the total system memory up to 16 GB. Within a short period of time, though, she begins experiencing Blue Screens of Death. What could the problem be?

    A. She installed faulty RAM.

    B. The motherboard could only handle 12 GB of RAM.

    C. The motherboard needed dual-channel RAM.

    D. There is no problem. Windows always does this initially, but gets better after crashing a few times.

Answers

1. **A.** Steve failed to seat the RAM properly.

2. **D.** Scott needs to know if the system can handle that much RAM.

3. **B.** The input/output speed of DDR4 RAM is faster than that of DDR3 RAM (although the latency is higher).

4. **C.** Latency is the term for the delay in the RAM's response to a request from the MCC.

5. **A.** A non-maskable interrupt on a Windows system often results in the Blue Screen of Death.

6. **D.** Motherboards can be tricky and require you to install RAM in the proper slots to enable dual-channel memory access. In this case, Silas should move one of the installed sticks to a different slot to activate dual-channel memory. (And he should check the motherboard manual for the proper slots.)

7. **A.** You can use the System applet to see how much RAM is currently in your PC.

8. **A.** The best way to determine the total capacity and specific type of RAM your system can handle is to check the motherboard book.

9. **C.** Most likely, Gregor installed RAM that didn't match the speed or quality of the RAM in the system.

10. **A.** If you have no problems with a system and then experience problems after installing something new, chances are the something new is at fault.

Firmware

In this chapter, you will learn how to
- Explain the function of BIOS
- Distinguish among various CMOS setup utility options
- Describe option ROM and device drivers
- Troubleshoot the power-on self test (POST)
- Maintain BIOS and CMOS properly

In Chapter 3, "CPUs," you saw how the address bus and data bus connect RAM to the CPU via the memory controller to run programs and transfer data. Assuming you apply power in the right places, you don't need anything else to make a simple computer. The only problem with such a simple computer is that it would bore you to death—there's no way to do anything with it! A PC needs devices such as keyboards and mice to provide input, and output devices such as monitors and speakers to communicate the current state of the running programs to you. A computer also needs permanent storage devices, such as solid-state drives, to store programs and data when you turn off the computer.

This chapter discusses in detail the software that controls a PC at its core. We'll start with a couple of sections on why and how it all works, and then we'll look at hardware and self-testing circuits. The chapter finishes with the finer points of maintaining this essential programming and hardware.

1001

We Need to Talk

For a keyboard or a monitor or a hard drive to work with a CPU, they must communicate via some kind of physical connection. More than that, these peripherals (usually) can't connect directly to the CPU. This communication requires a controller, a chip that connects the device to the CPU (see Figure 5-1).

Getting the CPU to communicate with a controller starts with some kind of interconnection—a communication bus (that means *wires*) that enables the CPU to send

Figure 5-1
A controller
chip acts as an
interface

commands to and from devices. To make this connection, let's extend the data bus and the address bus throughout the motherboard, connecting all of the computer's controllers to the CPU (see Figure 5-2).

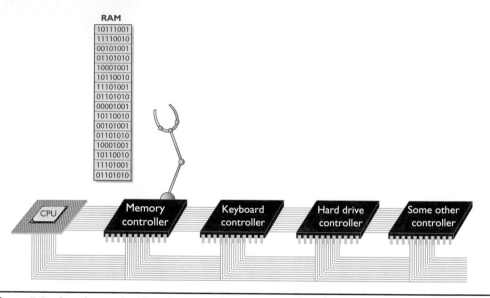

Figure 5-2   Data bus and address bus extended

Early motherboards were covered in controller chips. Figure 5-3 shows a very early motherboard, absolutely covered in controller chips (as well as many other chips).

Over time, chip manufacturers began to combine multiple controllers into specifically designed *chipsets*. Early chipsets such as the Intel 430VX shown in Figure 5-4 consisted of two paired chips called the *northbridge* and *southbridge*.

Chipsets were in pairs for many years, roughly from 1990 to around 2010. Today's CPUs have controllers built in, such as the memory and display controllers. Almost all chipsets are now a single chip—Intel's name for this chip is *Platform Controller Hub* (*PCH*). Figure 5-5 shows a motherboard with both the CPU and the PCH visible. AMD (and most of the tech industry) refers to the chip as the chipset.

 NOTE   All but the lowest-powered chipsets require cooling fins or fans. Also, even though chipsets are often single-chip solutions, it's common tech speak to say "chipset" (even though "set" implies more than one chip).

Figure 5-3
Early motherboard, loaded with chips

Figure 5-4
Ancient 430VX chipset showing northbridge and southbridge

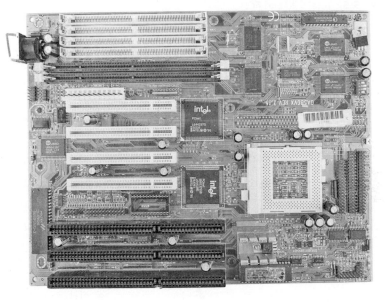

The chipset extends the data bus to every device on the PC. The CPU uses the data bus to move data to and from all the devices of the PC. Data constantly flows on the data bus among the CPU, chipset, RAM, and other devices on the PC (see Figure 5-6).

Figure 5-5 Intel CPU and PCH

It's not too hard to swallow the concept that the CPU uses the address bus to talk to the devices, but how does it know what to *say* to them? How does it know all of the patterns of ones and zeros to place on the address bus to tell the hard drive it needs to send a file? Let's look at the interaction between the keyboard and CPU for insight into this process.

Figure 5-6
Everything
connecting

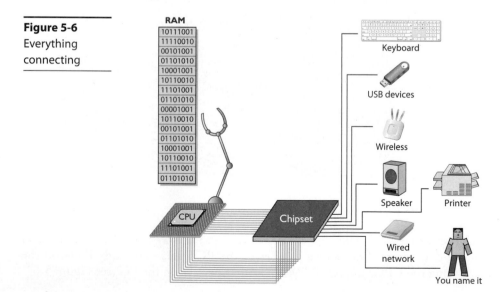

Talking to the Keyboard

The keyboard provides a great example of how the buses and support programming help the CPU get the job done. In early computers, the keyboard connected to the data bus via a special chip known as the *keyboard controller*. Don't bother looking for this chip on your motherboard—the chipset handles keyboard controller functions. The way the keyboard controller—or technically, the keyboard controller *circuitry*—works with the CPU, however, has changed only a small amount in the past decades, making it a perfect tool to illustrate how the CPU talks to a device.

NOTE Techs commonly talk about various functions of the chipset as if those functions were still handled by discrete chips. You'll hear about memory controllers, keyboard controllers, mouse controllers, USB controllers, and so on, even though they're all just circuits on the CPU or chipset.

The keyboard controller was one of the last single-function chips to be absorbed into the chipset. Figure 5-7 shows a typical keyboard controller from those days. Electronically, it looked like Figure 5-8.

Figure 5-7
A keyboard chip on an older motherboard

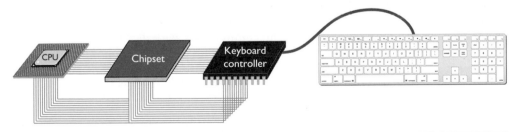

Figure 5-8   Electronic view of the keyboard controller

Every time you press a key on your keyboard, a scanning chip in the keyboard notices which key you pressed. Then the scanner sends a coded pattern of ones and zeros—called the *scan code*—to the keyboard controller. Every key on your keyboard has a unique scan code. The keyboard controller stores the scan code in its own register. Does it surprise you that the lowly keyboard controller has a register similar to a CPU? Lots of chips have registers—not just CPUs (see Figure 5-9).

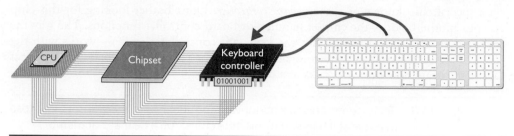

Figure 5-9   Scan code stored in keyboard controller's register

How does the CPU get the scan code out of the keyboard controller? While we're at it, how does the CPU tell the keyboard to change the typematic buffer rate (when you hold down a key and the letter repeats) or to turn the number lock LED on and off, to mention just a few other jobs the keyboard needs to do for the system? The point is that the keyboard controller must be able to respond to multiple commands, not just one.

The keyboard controller accepts commands exactly as you saw the CPU accept commands in Chapter 3. Remember when you added 2 to 3 with the 8088? You had to use specific commands from the 8088's codebook to tell the CPU to do the addition and then place the answer on the external data bus. The keyboard controller has its own codebook—much simpler than any CPU's codebook, but conceptually the same. If the CPU wants to know what key was last pressed on the keyboard, the CPU needs to know the command (or series of commands) that orders the keyboard controller to put the scan code of the letter on the external data bus so the CPU can read it.

BIOS

The CPU doesn't magically or otherwise automatically know how to talk with any device; it needs some sort of support programming loaded into memory that teaches it about a particular device. This programming is called *basic input/output services* (*BIOS*). The programs dedicated to enabling the CPU to communicate with devices are called *services* (or device drivers, as you'll see later in the chapter). This goes well beyond the keyboard, by the way. In fact, *every* device on the computer needs BIOS! But let's continue with the keyboard for now.

Bringing BIOS to the PC

A talented programmer could write BIOS for a keyboard if the programmer knew the keyboard's codebook; keyboards are pretty simple devices. This begs the question: Where would this support programming be stored? Programming could be incorporated into the operating system. Storing programming to talk to the hardware of your PC in the operating system is great—all operating systems have built-in code that knows how to talk to your keyboard, your mouse, and just about every piece of hardware you may put into your PC.

That's fine once the operating system's up and running, but what about a brand-new stack of parts you're about to assemble into a new PC? When a new system is being built, it has no operating system. The CPU must have access to BIOS for the most important hardware on your PC: not only the keyboard, but also the monitor, mass storage drives, optical drives, USB ports, and RAM. This code can't be stored on a hard drive or optical disc—these important devices need to be ready at any time the CPU calls them, even before installing a mass storage device or an operating system.

The perfect place to store the support programming is on the motherboard. That settles one issue, but another looms: What storage medium should the motherboard use? DRAM won't work, because all of the data would be erased every time you turned off the computer. You need some type of permanent program storage device that does not depend on other peripherals to work. And you need that storage device to sit on the motherboard.

ROM

Motherboards store the keyboard controller support programming, among other programs, on a special type of device called a *read-only memory* (*ROM*) chip. A ROM chip stores programs, *services*, exactly like RAM. ROM differs from RAM in two important ways. First, ROM chips are *nonvolatile*, meaning that the information stored on ROM isn't erased when the computer is turned off. Second, traditional ROM chips are read-only, meaning that once you store a program on one, you can't change it.

Motherboards use a type of ROM called *flash ROM*, the same stuff that stores your data in your smartphone or SSD. That is why we call updating the BIOS firmware, "flashing the BIOS," which we will cover later in this chapter. Figure 5-10 shows a typical flash ROM chip on a motherboard.

Figure 5-10
Typical flash ROM

Every motherboard has a flash ROM chip, called the *system ROM* chip because it contains code that enables your CPU to talk to the basic hardware of your PC (see Figure 5-11). As alluded to earlier, the system ROM holds BIOS for more than just the keyboard controller. It also stores programs for communicating with hard drives, optical drives, display devices, USB ports, and other basic devices on your motherboard.

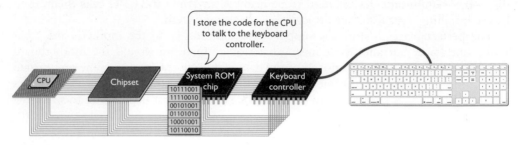

Figure 5-11 Function of the flash ROM chip

To talk to all of that hardware requires hundreds of little services (2 to 30 lines of code each). These hundreds of little programs stored on the system ROM chip on the motherboard are called, collectively, the *system BIOS* (see Figure 5-12). Techs call programs stored on ROM chips of any sort *firmware*. You will commonly hear techs today refer to the *system firmware*—what CompTIA (and this book) calls system BIOS.

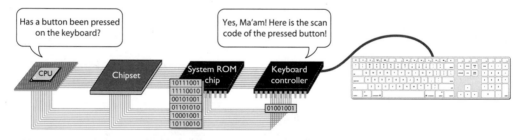

Figure 5-12 CPU running BIOS service

 EXAM TIP Programs stored on ROM chips—flash or any other kind of ROM chip—are known collectively as *firmware*, as opposed to programs stored on dynamic media, which are collectively called *software*.

System BIOS Support

Every system BIOS has two types of hardware to support. First, the system BIOS supports all of the hardware that never changes, such as the keyboard. Another example of hardware that never changes is the PC speaker (the tiny one that beeps at you, not the ones that play music). The system ROM chip stores the BIOS for these and other devices that never change.

Second, the system BIOS supports all of the hardware that might change from time to time. This includes RAM (you can add RAM) and hard drives (you can replace your hard disk drive [HDD] with a larger drive or a solid-state drive [SSD] or add a second drive of either type). The system ROM chip stores the *BIOS* for these devices, but the system needs another place to store information about the specific *details* of a piece of hardware. This enables the system to differentiate between a Western Digital Blue 4-TB HDD and a Samsung 860 EVO 2-TB SSD, and yet still support both drives right out of the box.

UEFI

Modern systems use firmware programming called the *Unified Extensible Firmware Inter-face* (*UEFI*). Here are a few advantages of UEFI over the original BIOS in PCs:

- UEFI supports booting to partitions larger than 2.2 TB.
- UEFI firmware is native 32- or 64-bit; this lets the manufacturers include lots of features for setup and diagnoses.
- UEFI handles all boot-loading duties; no more jumping from boot sector to boot sector.
- UEFI is portable to other chip types, not just 16-bit x86.

All current systems use UEFI. Many also provide legacy support for BIOS services in case you feel some retro gaming is in order. But a zillion older systems use the older BIOS. Most techs continue to call the support software BIOS, even though technically the terms differ. There's no standardization on how to pronounce UEFI, by the way. Microsoft initializes it: "U-E-F-I." Others say "you-fee" or "you-fie." For a job interview, stick with initializing it. You can't go wrong that way.

CMOS and RTC

Because the BIOS firmware is stored in ROM, and ROM is *read only*, it needs a place to store all its settings so they don't have to be re-entered every time you boot your computer. That place is a tiny bit of RAM hooked up to a small battery to keep it working with the PC off. We call this memory the *complementary metal-oxide semiconductor* (*CMOS*) chip (Figure 5-13). In addition to storing all the various BIOS settings, the CMOS also handles the system's *real-time clock* (*RTC*) so you don't have to keep setting the time on every boot.

The standalone CMOS chip has long since been incorporated into the main chipset. The information stored in CMOS is necessary for the PC to function.

If the data stored in CMOS about a piece of hardware (or about its fancier features) is different from the specs of the actual hardware, the computer cannot access that piece of hardware (or use its fancier features). It is crucial that this information be correct. If you change any of the previously mentioned hardware, you must update CMOS to reflect those changes. You need to know, therefore, how to change the data in CMOS.

Figure 5-13
Old-style CMOS

EXAM TIP All the details of UEFI and CMOS that you're going to spend many hours memorizing for the 1001 exam only apply to PCs and Linux machines. Apple computers have EFI and CMOS, but Apple designs their systems from the ground up as unified systems. Apple has done all the work for you and you simply use the macOS machine.

Every PC ships with a program built into the system ROM called the *system setup utility* that enables you to access and modify CMOS data. On a completely new system, with no operating system installed, you'll see something like Figure 5-14. After the OS is installed, these screens effectively disappear. I'll show you how to access them in a little bit.

NOTE The terms *CMOS setup program*, *CMOS*, and *system setup utility* are functionally interchangeable today. You'll even hear the program referred to as the *BIOS setup utility*, UEFI/BIOS setup, or UEFI firmware settings.

Typical System Setup Utility

Every BIOS/UEFI maker's system setup utility looks a little different, but don't let that confuse you. They all contain basically the same settings; you just have to be comfortable poking around the different interfaces. To avoid doing something foolish, *do not save anything* unless you are sure you have it set correctly.

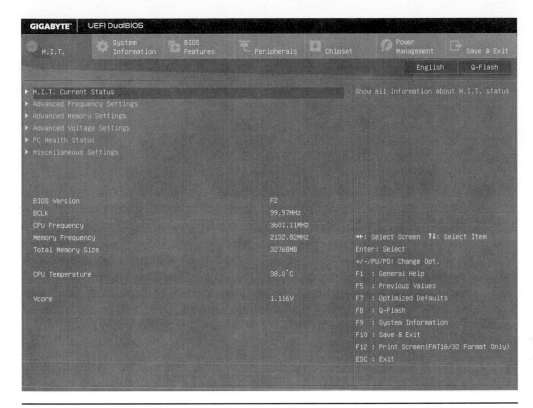

Figure 5-14 Gigabyte system setup utility

Several years ago, BIOS/UEFI manufacturers in the consumer space migrated to graphical system setup utilities that enable you to use a mouse. You'll still find plenty of examples in the field of the classic text-only system setup utilities. You need to know both, so this section will show you both styles. We'll run through a graphical version first, then skim through an older text-only version.

Graphical UEFI System Setup Utility

Figure 5-15 shows a typical, simple graphical setup screen. This system setup utility has two modes: EZ and Advanced. You can't do much in this first EZ Mode screen except view information about installed components, select one of three preset System Performance optimization options, and change the boot priority.

Click the option to go into Advanced Mode and you'll get a much more versatile utility (see Figure 5-16) for changing the interface configurations. The Main tab offers some

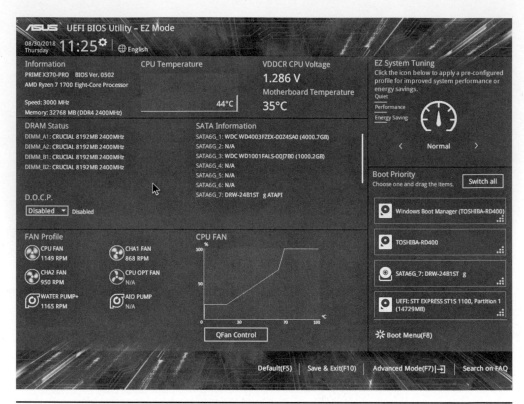

Figure 5-15   ASUS UEFI system setup utility

BIOS component information, such as surface details on amount of RAM and speed of CPU, plus a couple of options to modify the language and date and time. (Some utilities will show information about installed hard drives and optical drives; this UEFI firmware presents that information elsewhere.)

The Main tab also enables you to configure modest *BIOS security* by setting an administrator or user password. (The default for the pictured UEFI BIOS is Access Level: Administrator. Click the Security option to change access information. UEFI setup screens differ somewhat, but you'll find similar options in all of them.)

An *administrator password* locks or unlocks access to the system setup utility. A *user password* locks or unlocks the computer booting to an operating system. Set a BIOS/ UEFI password when you encounter a scenario like installing computer kiosks at a

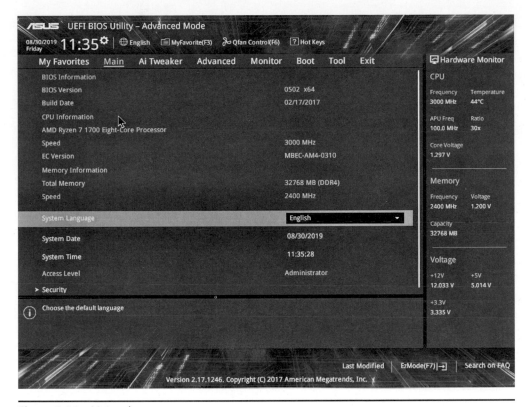

Figure 5-16 Main tab

convention or installing systems in a public library. A BIOS/UEFI password stops casual miscreants from messing with your accessible systems.

Things get far more interesting in the other tabs. Selecting the Ai Tweaker tab, for example, enables you to delve into the Dark Arts of overclocking both the CPU and RAM (see Figure 5-17). You can change the clock multiplier, clock speeds, voltages, and more here. This is a great place to go to fry a new CPU!

The Advanced tab (see Figure 5-18) gives component information about CPUs, hard drives and optical drives, and all the built-in components, such as USB ports. In this tab, as you drill down to each subcategory, you can configure drive settings, enable and disable devices, and more.

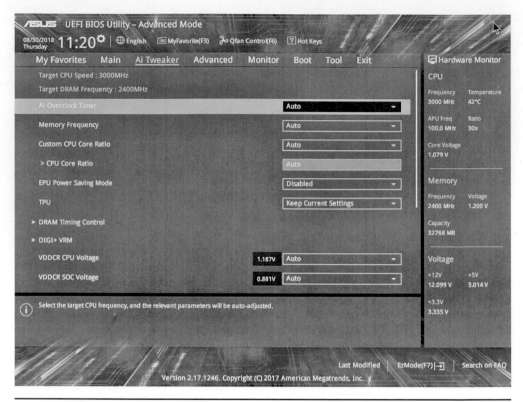

Figure 5-17 Ai Tweaker tab

The Monitor tab (see Figure 5-19) shows monitoring . ormation for CPU and motherboard temperatures, fan speeds, and voltages. You can modify the behavior of the chassis fans here too. All of this monitoring information is considered some of the *built-in diagnostics* for both the motherboard and the full system.

NOTE Some systems refer to the Monitor display as PC Health.

The Boot tab (see Figure 5-20) enables you to adjust boot settings. You can select devices to boot by priority, setting the *boot sequence* used by the motherboard. (See "The Boot Process" later in this chapter for more information.) You can determine how the system will react/inform if booting fails, and more.

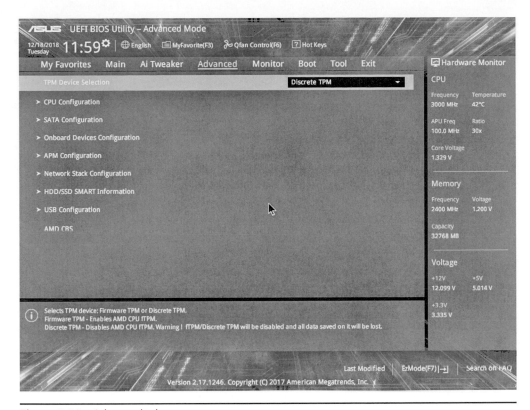

Figure 5-18   Advanced tab

The Tool tab (see Figure 5-21) has a couple of very important features. The EZ Flash 3 utility enables you to update the motherboard firmware. See the "Flashing the ROM" section later in this chapter for more details. The Tool tab also shows RAM information. That's the SPD option (for *serial presence detect*) you should recognize from Chapter 4, "RAM."

Text-Based UEFI Intel-Based Setup Utility

In this second walkthrough, we'll switch to a UEFI motherboard on an Intel-based portable computer. As we go through the screens, pay attention to the options listed on each. I'll call out features that the graphical AMD-based UEFI didn't have.

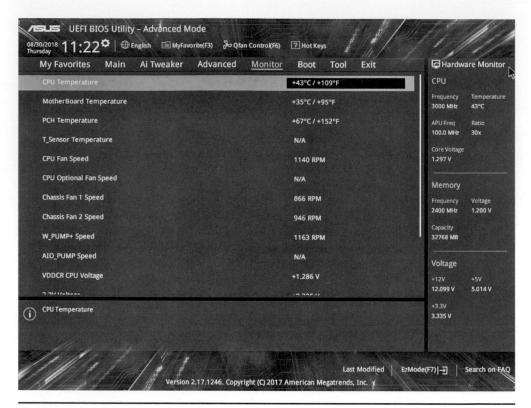

Figure 5-19   Monitor tab

The Information tab (see Figure 5-22) offers straightforward information about the CPU and RAM amount, and cryptic information about the hard drive. Other tabs do more.

The Configuration tab (see Figure 5-23) shows a number of built-in devices that you configure or enable/disable here. Because this is a portable, it has an option to turn on/off wireless networking capabilities.

There are two interesting options here that are covered in detail in other chapters but warrant a brief discussion now. The Intel Virtual Technology option enables or disables *virtualization support* for virtual machines.

A *virtual machine* is a powerful type of program that enables you to run a second (or third or fourth), software-based machine inside your physical PC. It re-creates the motherboard, hard drives, RAM, network adapters, and more, and is just as powerful as a real PC. To run these virtual machines, however, you'll need a very powerful PC—you are trying to run multiple PCs at the same time, after all.

To support this, CPU manufacturers have added *hardware-assisted virtualization.* Intel calls their version Intel Virtualization Technology (Intel VT for short), and AMD

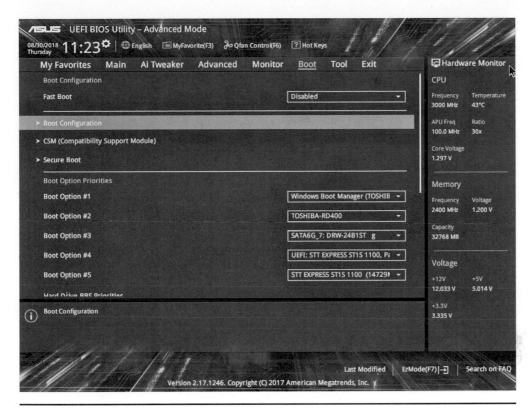

Figure 5-20 Boot tab

calls theirs AMD Virtualization (AMD-V) technology. This technology helps the virtual machines use your hardware more efficiently and is controlled by the BIOS. This feature is disabled by default in BIOS, so if your virtual machine requires hardware-assisted virtualization, you'll need to enable it here.

 NOTE Chapter 22, "Virtualization," covers virtual machines in gory detail. Stay tuned!

This particular laptop has built-in graphics courtesy of the Intel Core i7 processor, plus it has a dedicated add-on video card for gaming. The Graphic Device option, set here to Discrete, means to use the dedicated video card when possible. This uses more electricity than the graphics support using only the processor, but it makes for way better gaming!

Figure 5-21   Tool tab

Figure 5-22

Information tab

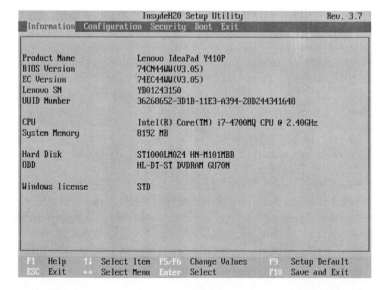

Figure 5-23
Configuration
tab

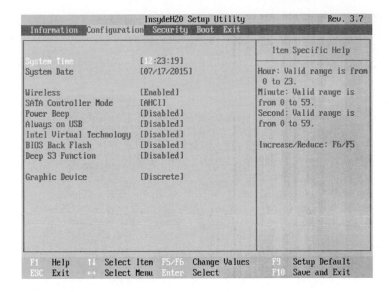

NOTE   Chapter 17, "Display Technologies," goes into video options (and gaming) in modern systems.

The Security tab (see Figure 5-24) offers a lot more options for configuring BIOS security than found on the Main tab of the AMD-based system. You see the Administrator Password and User Password options, but there's also an option to set a couple of different hard drive passwords.

Figure 5-24
Security tab

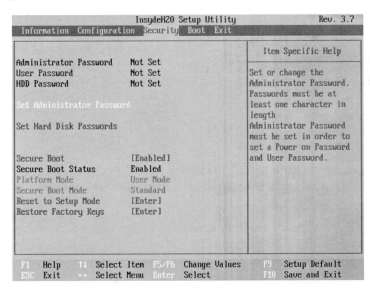

The *Secure Boot* feature you can see on the Security tab is a UEFI protocol that secures the boot process by requiring properly signed software. This includes boot software and software that supports specific, essential components. (See "Device Drivers" a little later in this chapter.) Secure Boot requires an Intel CPU, a UEFI BIOS, and an operating system designed for it, such as Windows.

NOTE Secure Boot is an example of a tool that uses *drive encryption*. Various types of encryption—essentially scrambling the information to make it inaccessible to bad guys—secure all sorts of processes and data in modern computing. We'll hit the subject in several places later in the book. Chapter 9, "Implementing Mass Storage," discusses drive encryption specifically in more detail.

The Boot tab (see Figure 5-25) enables you to set *boot options* to determine which bootable device gets priority. Here is where you provide support for booting to a USB device as well. It looks a little different from the graphical example presented earlier. See "The Boot Process" later in this chapter for more explanation.

Figure 5-25
Boot tab

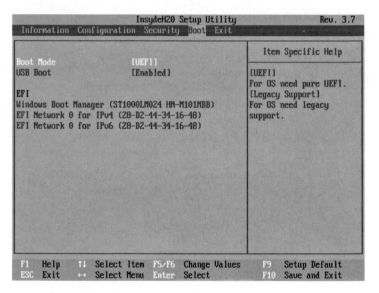

Other BIOS Security Settings

Motherboard manufacturers, BIOS/UEFI writers, and programmers have implemented all kinds of security features over the years. This section mentions a couple you might run into on various motherboards (or on a certain exam in your near future).

Chassis Intrusion Detection/Notification

Many motherboards support the *chassis intrusion detection/notification* feature provided by the computer case, or chassis. Compatible cases contain a switch that trips when someone opens the case. With motherboard support and a proper connection between the motherboard and the case, the CMOS logs whether the case has been opened and, if it has, posts a notification to the screen on the subsequent boot. How cool is that?

LoJack

Some PC manufacturers include *LoJack* security features in their firmware—this way, if your PC is stolen, you can track its location, install a keylogger, or even remotely shut down your computer.

Trusted Platform Module

The *Trusted Platform Module* (*TPM*) acts as a secure cryptoprocessor, which is to say that it is a hardware platform for the acceleration of cryptographic functions and the secure storage of associated information. The specification for the TPM is published by the Trusted Computing Group, an organization whose corporate members include Intel, Microsoft, AMD, IBM, Lenovo, Dell, Hewlett-Packard, and many others.

The TPM can be a small circuit board plugged into the motherboard, or it can be built directly into the chipset. The CMOS setup program usually contains settings that can turn the TPM on or off and enable or disable it.

TPMs can be used in a wide array of cryptographic operations, but one of the most common uses of TPMs is hard disk encryption. For example, the *BitLocker Drive Encryption* feature of Microsoft Windows can be accelerated by a TPM, which is more secure because the encryption key is stored in the tamper-resistant TPM hardware rather than on an external flash drive. Other possible uses of TPMs include digital rights management (DRM), network access control, application execution control, and password protection.

 EXAM TIP BIOS security-related options can include TPM, passwords, Secure Boot, intrusion detection/notification, and drive encryption.

Exiting and Saving Settings

Of course, all system setup utilities provide some method to Save, Exit Saving Changes, or Exit Discarding Changes (see Figure 5-26). Use these as needed for your situation. Exit Discarding Changes is particularly nice for those folks who want to poke around the CMOS setup utility but don't want to mess anything up. Use it!

The CMOS setup utility would meet all the needs of a modern system for BIOS if manufacturers would just stop creating new devices. That's not going to happen, of course, so let's turn now to devices that need to have BIOS loaded from elsewhere.

Figure 5-26

Exit options

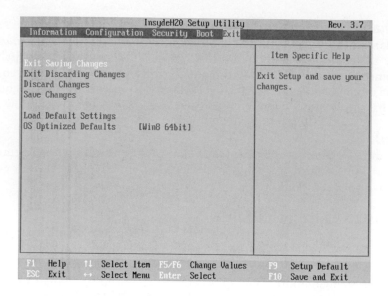

NOTE People serious about tweaking UEFI settings for maximum performance (overclocking) or minimum energy use (underclocking) can use a feature in some system setup utilities to save customized settings. Various utilities call them presets or profiles—essentially it's a "save these settings as" option. If something isn't quite right with the changes, go back into setup, make some changes, and try again. If you're done fiddling for the day and want to play with a stable machine, pick the profile you created that is the stable machine. See "Care and Feeding of BIOS/UEFI and CMOS" later in this chapter for the ultimate undo features.

Option ROM and Device Drivers

Every piece of hardware in your computer needs some kind of programming that tells the CPU how to talk to that device. When IBM invented the PC decades ago, they couldn't possibly have included all of the necessary BIOS routines for every conceivable piece of hardware on the system ROM chip. How could they? Most of the devices in use today didn't exist on the first PCs. When programmers wrote the first BIOS, for example, network cards, mice, and sound cards did not exist. Early PC designers at IBM understood that they could not anticipate every new type of hardware, so they gave us a few ways to add programming other than on the BIOS. I call this *BYOB*—Bring Your Own BIOS. You can BYOB in two ways: option ROM and device drivers. Let's look at both.

Option ROM

The first way to BYOB is to put the BIOS on the hardware device itself. Look at the card displayed in Figure 5-27. This is a serial ATA RAID hard drive controller—basically just a card that lets you add more hard drives to a PC. The chip in the center with the wires coming out the sides is a flash ROM that stores BIOS for the card. The system BIOS does not have a clue about how to talk to this card, but that's okay, because this card brings its own BIOS on what's called an *option ROM* chip.

Figure 5-27
Option ROM

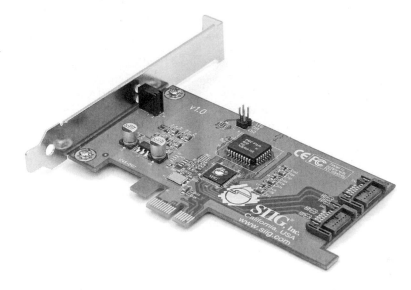

Most BIOS that come on option ROMs tell you that they exist by displaying information when you boot the system. Figure 5-28 shows a typical example of an option ROM advertising itself.

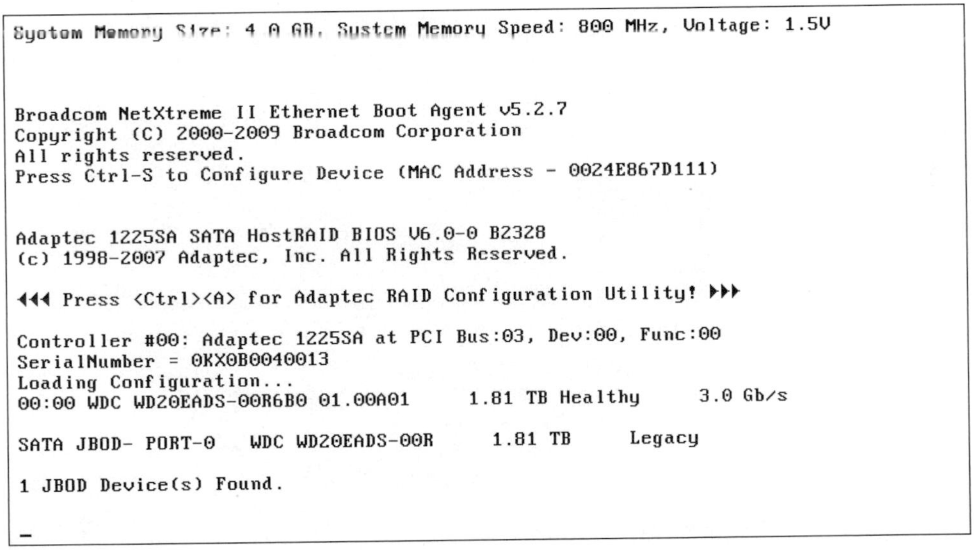

```
System Memory Size: 4.0 GB, System Memory Speed: 800 MHz, Voltage: 1.5V


Broadcom NetXtreme II Ethernet Boot Agent v5.2.7
Copyright (C) 2000-2009 Broadcom Corporation
All rights reserved.
Press Ctrl-S to Configure Device (MAC Address - 0024E867D111)


Adaptec 1225SA SATA HostRAID BIOS V6.0-0 B2328
(c) 1998-2007 Adaptec, Inc. All Rights Reserved.

◄◄◄ Press <Ctrl><A> for Adaptec RAID Configuration Utility! ►►►

Controller #00: Adaptec 1225SA at PCI Bus:03, Dev:00, Func:00
SerialNumber = 0KX0B0040013
Loading Configuration...
00:00 WDC WD20EADS-00R6B0 01.00A01      1.81 TB Healthy      3.0 Gb/s

SATA JBOD- PORT-0   WDC WD20EADS-00R    1.81 TB     Legacy

1 JBOD Device(s) Found.

_
```

Figure 5-28   Option ROM at boot

In the early days of the PC, you could find all sorts of devices with BIOS on option ROMs. Today, option ROMs have mostly been replaced by more flexible software methods (more on device driver software in the next section), with one major exception: video cards. Every video card made today contains its own BIOS. Option ROMs work well but are hard to upgrade. For this reason, most hardware relies on software for BYOB.

Device Drivers

A *device driver* is a file stored on the PC's hard drive that contains all of the commands necessary to talk to whatever device it was written to support. All operating systems employ a method of loading these device drivers into RAM every time the system boots. They know which device drivers to install by reading a file (or files) that lists which device drivers the system needs to load at boot time. All operating systems are designed to look at this list early on in the boot process and copy the listed files into RAM, thereby giving the CPU (and the OS) the capability to communicate with the hardware supported by the device driver.

Device drivers come with the device when you buy it. When you buy almost any device for your computer, that new sound card or monitor or whatever usually comes with some kind of media, often an optical disc, that holds all of the necessary device drivers (and usually a bunch of extra goodies—see Figure 5-29).

Figure 5-29

Installation disc for monitor

In many cases you may not want to use installation media and just let the OS handle things. All operating systems use online tools to detect and automatically install device drivers. You might want to add or remove device drivers manually at times. Windows stores device drivers (and a lot more) in a database called the Registry, which we'll talk about in detail in Chapter 12, "Windows Under the Hood." Techs rarely deal directly with the Registry, but rather indirectly through the Device Manager utility (mentioned in Chapter 2, "The Visible Computer"). You'll see plenty more about Device Manager throughout this book.

BIOS, BIOS, Everywhere!

As you should now understand, every piece of hardware on a system must have an accompanying program that provides the CPU with the code necessary to communicate with that particular device. This code may reside on the system ROM on the motherboard, on ROM on a card, or in a device driver file on the hard drive loaded into RAM at boot. BIOS is everywhere on your system, and you need to deal with it occasionally.

Power-On Self Test (POST)

BIOS isn't the only program on system ROM. When the computer is turned on or reset, it initiates a special program, also stored on the system ROM chip, called the *power-on self test* (*POST*). The POST program checks out the system every time the computer boots. To perform this check, the POST sends out a command that says to all of the devices, "Check yourselves out!" All of the standard devices in the computer then run their own built-in diagnostic—the POST doesn't specify what they must check. The quality of the diagnostic is up to the people who made that particular device.

Let's consider the POST for a moment. Suppose some device—let's say it's the keyboard controller chip—runs its diagnostic and determines that it is not working properly. What can the POST do about it? Only one thing really: tell the human in front of the PC! So how does the computer tell the human? PCs convey POST information to you in two ways: beep codes and text messages.

Before and During the Video Test: The Beep Codes

The computer tests the most basic parts of the computer first, up to and including the video card. In early PCs, you'd hear a series of beeps—called *beep codes* or *POST beep codes*—if anything went wrong. By using beep codes before and during the video test, the computer could communicate with you. (If a POST error occurs before the video is available, obviously the error must manifest itself as beeps, because nothing can display on the screen.) The meaning of the beep code you'd hear varied among different BIOS manufacturers. You could find the beep codes for a specific motherboard in its motherboard manual.

 NOTE CompTIA refers to beep codes as *POST code beeps*.

Most modern PCs have only two beep codes: one for bad or missing video (one long beep followed by two or three short beeps), and one for bad or missing RAM (a single beep that repeats indefinitely).

 CAUTION You'll find lots of online documentation about beep codes, but it's usually badly outdated.

You'll hear three other beep sequences on most PCs (although they're not officially beep codes). At the end of a successful POST, the PC produces one or two short beeps, simply to inform you that all is well. Most systems make a rather strange noise when the RAM is missing or very seriously damaged. Unlike traditional beep codes, this code repeats until you shut off the system. Finally, your speaker might make beeps for reasons that aren't POST or boot related. One of the more common is a series of short beeps after the system's been running for a while. That's a CPU alarm telling you the CPU is approaching its high heat limit.

Text Errors

After the video has tested okay, any POST errors display on the screen as text errors. If you get a text error, the problem is usually, but not always, self-explanatory (see Figure 5-30). Text errors are far more useful than beep codes, because you can simply read the screen to determine the bad device.

Figure 5-30
POST text error messages

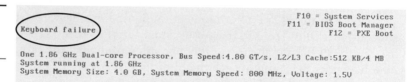

```
                                                      F10 = System Services
                                                      F11 = BIOS Boot Manager
  Keyboard failure                                          F12 = PXE Boot

  One 1.86 GHz Dual-core Processor, Bus Speed:4.80 GT/s, L2/L3 Cache:512 KB/4 MB
  System running at 1.86 GHz
  System Memory Size: 4.0 GB, System Memory Speed: 800 MHz, Voltage: 1.5V
```

POST Cards

Beep codes, numeric codes, and text error codes, although helpful, can sometimes be misleading. Worse than that, an inoperative device can sometimes disrupt the POST, forcing the machine into an endless loop. This causes the PC to act dead—no beeps and nothing on the screen. In this case, you need a device, called a *POST card*, to monitor the POST and identify which piece of hardware is causing the trouble.

POST cards are simple cards that snap into expansion slots on your system. A small, two-character light-emitting diode (LED) readout on the card indicates which device the POST is currently testing (see Figure 5-31).

POST cards used to be essential tools for techs, but today I use them only when I have a "dead" PC to determine at which level it's dead. If the POST card shows no reading, I know the problem is before the POST and must be related to the power, the CPU, the RAM, or the motherboard. If the board posts, then I know to look at more issues, such as the drives and so on.

Figure 5-31
POST card in
action

The Boot Process

All PCs need a process to begin their operations. Once you feed power to the PC, the tight interrelation of hardware, firmware, and software enables the PC to start itself, to "pull itself up by the bootstraps" or boot itself.

When you first power on the PC, the power supply circuitry tests for proper voltage and then sends a signal down a special wire called the *power good* wire to awaken the CPU. The moment the power good wire wakes it up, every Intel and clone CPU immediately sends a built-in memory address via its address bus. This special address is the same on every Intel and clone CPU, from the oldest 8086 to the most recent microprocessor. This address is the first line of the POST program on the system ROM! That's how the system starts the POST. After the POST has finished, there must be a way for the computer to find the programs on the hard drive to start the operating system. What happens next differs between the old BIOS way and the UEFI way.

In the older BIOS environment, the POST passes control to the last BIOS function: the bootstrap loader. The *bootstrap loader* is little more than a few dozen lines of BIOS code tacked to the end of the POST program. Its job is to find the operating system. The bootstrap loader reads CMOS information to tell it where to look first for an operating system. Your PC's CMOS setup utility has an option that you configure to tell the bootstrap loader which devices to check for an operating system and in which order—that's the *boot sequence* (see Figure 5-32).

Figure 5-32
CMOS boot
sequence

▶ Hard Disk Book Priority	[Press Enter]
First Boot Device	[CDROM]
Second Boot Device	[Hard Disk]
Third Boot Device	[CDROM]

Almost all storage devices—hard disk drives, solid-state drives, CDs, DVDs, and USB thumb drives—can be configured to boot an operating system by setting aside a specific location called the *boot sector*. If the device is bootable, its boot sector contains special programming designed to tell the system where to locate the operating system. Any device with a functional operating system is called a *bootable disk* or a *system disk*. If the bootstrap loader locates a good boot sector, it passes control to the operating system and removes itself from memory. If it doesn't, it goes to the next device in the boot sequence you set in the CMOS setup utility. The boot sequence is an important tool for techs because you can set it to load in special bootable devices so you can run utilities to maintain PCs without using the primary operating system.

In UEFI systems, the POST hands control of the boot process to the Boot Manager, which checks the boot configuration, and then loads the operating system boot loader directly (see Figure 5-33). There's no need for scanning for a boot sector or any of that. UEFI firmware stores the boot manager and boot configuration.

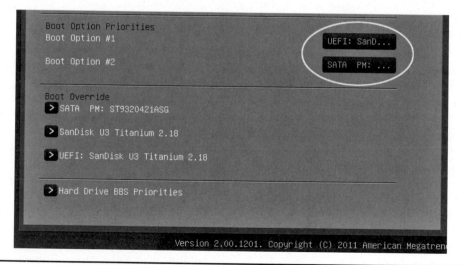

Figure 5-33   UEFI Boot Mode with Boot Manager options displayed

NOTE   If you put an old-style BIOS bootable disk in a UEFI system, the system will most likely drop into BIOS compatibility mode and boot just like the old days. See Chapter 9 for more on drive structures.

Some BIOS include a feature that enables a PC to use a *preboot execution environment* (*PXE*). A PXE enables you to boot a PC without any local storage by retrieving an OS from a server over a network. You'll see more on PXE when we talk about installing Windows in Chapter 11, "Building a PC."

Care and Feeding of BIOS/UEFI and CMOS

BIOS and CMOS are areas in your PC that you don't go to very often. BIOS itself is invisible. The only real clue you have that it even exists is the POST. The CMOS setup utility, on the other hand, is very visible if you start it. Most CMOS setup utilities today work acceptably well without ever being touched. You're an aspiring tech, however, and all self-respecting techs start up the CMOS setup utility and make changes. That's when most CMOS setup utility problems take place.

If you mess with the CMOS setup utility, remember to make only as many changes at one time as you can remember. Document the original settings and the changes on a piece of paper or take a photo so you can put things back if necessary. Don't make changes unless you know what they mean! It's easy to screw up a computer fairly seriously by playing with CMOS settings you don't understand.

Default/Optimized Settings

Every CMOS setup utility has a couple of reset options, commonly called Load Default Settings and OS Optimized Defaults (see Figure 5-34). These options keep you from having to memorize all of those weird settings you'll never touch. Default or Fail-Safe sets everything to very simple settings—you might occasionally use this setting when very low-level problems such as freeze-ups occur and you've checked more obvious areas first. Optimized sets the CMOS to the best possible speed/stability for the system. You would use this option after you've tampered with the CMOS too much and need to put it back like it was!

Figure 5-34
Options for
resetting CMOS

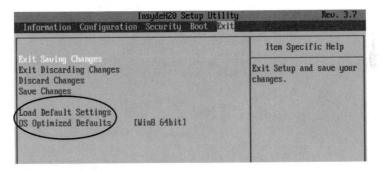

Clearing CMOS RTC RAM

You read about the process for clearing system settings back in Chapter 3, but the process is worth repeating here. When you mess up a setting (by overclocking too much or disabling something that should have remained enabled—or vice versa) that renders the computer dead, you can reset the CMOS RTC RAM back to factory defaults and start over.

Almost every motherboard has a dedicated set of wires called *CLRTC* or something similar (see Figure 5-35).

Figure 5-35
CMOS RTC clear
wires

 NOTE Many techs use older language to describe the reset CMOS RTC RAM, simply *CMOS clear*, describing both the process and the motherboard option.

Turn off and unplug the computer, then open the case to access the motherboard. Find the CMOS RTC clear wires. Move the shunt (the little plastic and metal jumper thing) from wires 1 and 2 to wires 2 and 3 (see Figure 5-36). Wait for 10 seconds and then move the shunt back to the default position. Plug in and boot the system.

Figure 5-36
Changing shunt
location to clear
CMOS RAM

NOTE Manufacturers of enthusiast boards designed for easy overclocking experimentation know you're going to screw up during the overclocking process. You'll often find a dedicated clear CMOS button hardwired to the motherboard. Now that's service!

If that doesn't work or if you get one of the truly odd motherboards without CLRTC jumpers, power down the system and unplug. Pry out the little coin battery (see below) and wait for several seconds. Reinstall and reboot.

Losing CMOS RTC Settings

As mentioned before, your CMOS RAM needs a continuous trickle charge to keep the internal clock running and remember its settings. Motherboards use some type of battery, usually a 3-volt Lithium coin battery, to give the CMOS RAM the charge it needs when the computer is turned off (see Figure 5-37). This is called the *CMOS battery*. Typical systems use a *CR2032* battery. (What does your system use?)

Figure 5-37
A CMOS battery

If some mishap suddenly erases the information on the CMOS RAM, the computer might not boot or you'll get nasty-looking errors at boot. Any PC will boot to factory defaults if the CMOS clears, so the chances of not booting are slim—but you'll still get errors at boot. Here are a few examples of errors that point to a lost CMOS information scenario:

- CMOS configuration mismatch
- CMOS date/time not set

- BIOS time and settings reset
- No boot device available
- CMOS battery state low

Here are some of the more common reasons for losing CMOS data:

- Pulling and inserting cards
- Touching the motherboard
- Dropping something on the motherboard
- Dirt on the motherboard
- Faulty power supplies
- Electrical surges

If you run into any of these scenarios, or if the clock in Windows resets itself to January 1st every time you reboot the system, the battery on the motherboard is losing its charge and needs to be replaced. To replace the battery, use a screwdriver to pry the battery's catch gently back. The battery should pop up for easy removal. Before you install the new battery, double-check that it has the same voltage and amperage as the old battery. To retain your CMOS settings while replacing the battery, simply leave your PC plugged into an AC outlet. The 5-volt soft power on all modern motherboards provides enough electricity to keep the CMOS charged and the data secure. Of course, I know you're going to be *extremely* careful about ESD while prying up the battery from a live system!

Flashing the ROM

Flash ROM chips can be reprogrammed to update their contents. With flash ROM, when you need to update your system BIOS to add support for a new technology, you can simply run a small command-line program, combined with an update file, and voilà, you have a new, updated BIOS! This is called a *firmware update*. Different BIOS makers use slightly different processes for *flashing the BIOS*, but, in general, you insert a removable disk of some sort (usually a USB thumb drive) containing an updated BIOS file and use the updating utility in CMOS setup.

Some motherboard makers provide Windows-based flash ROM update utilities that check the Internet for updates and download them for you to install. Most of these utilities also enable you to back up your current BIOS so you can return to it if the updated version causes trouble. Without a good backup, you could end up throwing away your motherboard if a flash BIOS update goes wrong, so you should always make one.

Finally, a lot of motherboards these days have system setup utilities that can connect directly to the Internet and access updates that way. Figure 5-38 shows one such update utility.

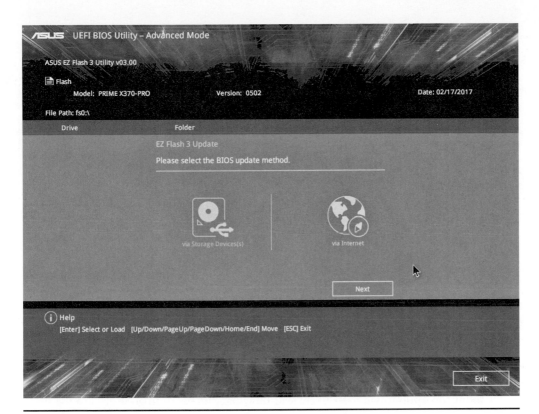

Figure 5-38 ROM-updating program for an ASUS motherboard

NOTE A failed BIOS/UEFI update—where something goes wrong during the process—can *brick* a computer or device. The failure turns a computing device into a brick, useless for anything but a paperweight.

Just a word of caution to complete the BIOS update section. Don't update your BIOS unless you have some compelling reason to do so. As the old saying goes, "If it ain't broke, don't fix it!"

EXAM TIP While techs usually talk about "flashing the BIOS," the CompTIA A+ exams refer to this process also as "firmware updates."

Chapter Review

Questions

1. What does BIOS provide for the computer? (Choose the best answer.)

    A. BIOS provides the physical interface for various devices such as USB and FireWire ports.

    B. BIOS provides the programming that enables the CPU to communicate with other hardware.

    C. BIOS provides memory space for applications to load into from the hard drive.

    D. BIOS provides memory space for applications to load into from the main system RAM.

2. What is the correct boot sequence for an older BIOS-based PC?

    A. CPU, POST, power good, boot loader, operating system

    B. POST, power good, CPU, boot loader, operating system

    C. Power good, boot loader, CPU, POST, operating system

    D. Power good, CPU, POST, boot loader, operating system

3. Jill decided to add a second hard drive to her computer. She thinks she has it physically installed correctly, but it doesn't show up in Windows. Which of the following options will most likely lead Jill where she needs to go to resolve the issue?

    A. Reboot the computer and press the F key on the keyboard twice. This signals that the computer has two hard disk drives.

    B. Reboot the computer and watch for instructions to enter the CMOS setup utility (for example, a message may say to press the DELETE key). Do what it says to go into CMOS setup.

    C. In Windows, press the DELETE key twice to enter the CMOS setup utility.

    D. In Windows, go to Start | Run and type **hard drive**. Click OK to open the Hard Drive Setup Wizard.

4. Henry bought a new card for capturing television on his computer. When he finished going through the packaging, though, he found no driver disc, only an application disc for setting up the TV capture software. After installing the card and software, it all works flawlessly. What's the most likely explanation?

    A. The device doesn't need BIOS, so there's no need for a driver disc.

    B. The device has an option ROM that loads BIOS, so there's no need for a driver disc.

    C. Windows supports TV capture cards out of the box, so there's no need for a driver disc.

    D. The manufacturer made a mistake and didn't include everything needed to set up the device.

5. Which of the following most accurately describes the relationship between BIOS and hardware?

   A. All hardware needs BIOS.

   B. All hardware that attaches to the motherboard via ribbon cables needs BIOS.

   C. All hardware built into the motherboard needs BIOS.

   D. Some hardware devices need BIOS.

6. After a sudden power outage, Samson's PC rebooted, but nothing appeared on the screen. The PC just beeps at him, over and over and over. What's most likely the problem?

   A. The power outage toasted his RAM.

   B. The power outage toasted his video card.

   C. The power outage toasted his hard drive.

   D. The power outage toasted his CPU.

7. Davos finds that a disgruntled former employee decided to sabotage her computer when she left by putting a password in CMOS that stops the computer from booting. What can Davos do to solve this problem?

   A. Davos should boot the computer while holding the left SHIFT key. This will clear the CMOS information.

   B. Davos should try various combinations of the former employee's name. The vast majority of people use their name or initials for CMOS passwords.

   C. Davos should find the CLRTC jumper on the motherboard. Then he can boot the computer with a shunt on the jumper to clear the CMOS information.

   D. Davos should find a replacement motherboard. Unless he knows the CMOS password, there's nothing he can do.

8. Richard over in the sales department went wild in CMOS and made a bunch of changes that he thought would optimize his PC. Now most of his PC doesn't work. The computer powers up, but he can only get to CMOS, not into Windows. Which of the following tech call answers would most likely get him up and running again?

   A. Reboot the computer about three times. That'll clear the CMOS and get you up and running.

   B. Open up the computer and find the CLRTC jumper. Remove a shunt from somewhere on the motherboard and put it on the CLRTC jumper. Reboot and then put the shunt back where you got it. Reboot, and you should be up and running in no time.

   C. Boot into the CMOS setup program and then find the option to load a plug-and-play operating system. Make sure it's set to On. Save and exit CMOS; boot normally into Windows. You should be up and running in no time.

   D. Boot into the CMOS setup program and then find the option to load OS Optimized Defaults. Save and exit CMOS; boot normally into Windows. You should be up and running in no time.

9. Jill boots an older Pentium system that has been the cause of several user complaints at the office. The system powers up and starts to run through POST, but then stops. The screen displays a "CMOS configuration mismatch" error. Of the following list, what is the most likely cause of this error?

A. Dying CMOS battery

B. Bad CPU

C. Bad RAM

D. Corrupt system BIOS

10. Where does Windows store device drivers?

A. Computer

B. Hardware

C. Registry

D. Drivers and Settings

Answers

1. **B.** BIOS provides the programming that enables the CPU to communicate with other hardware.

2. **D.** Here's the correct boot sequence for a BIOS-based PC: power good, CPU, POST, boot loader, operating system.

3. **B.** Jill should reboot the computer and watch for instructions to enter the CMOS setup utility (for example, a message may say to press the DELETE key). She should do what it says to go into CMOS setup.

4. **B.** Most likely the device has an option ROM, because it works.

5. **A.** All hardware needs BIOS!

6. **A.** The long repeating beep and a dead PC most likely indicate a problem with RAM.

7. **C.** Davos should find the CLRTC jumper on the motherboard and then boot the computer with a shunt on the jumper to clear the CMOS information.

8. **D.** Please don't hand Richard a screwdriver! Having him load Optimized Default settings will most likely do the trick.

9. **A.** The CMOS battery is likely dying.

10. **C.** Windows stores device drivers in the Registry.

Motherboards

In this chapter, you will learn how to
- Explain how motherboards work
- Recognize modern expansion buses
- Upgrade and install motherboards
- Troubleshoot motherboard problems

The *motherboard* provides the foundation for the personal computer. Every piece of hardware, from the CPU to the lowliest expansion card, directly or indirectly plugs into the motherboard. The motherboard contains the wires—called *traces*—that make up the buses of the system. It holds the vast majority of the ports used by the peripherals, and it distributes the power from the power supply (see Figure 6-1). Without the motherboard, you literally have no PC.

Figure 6-1
Traces visible beneath the CPU socket on a motherboard

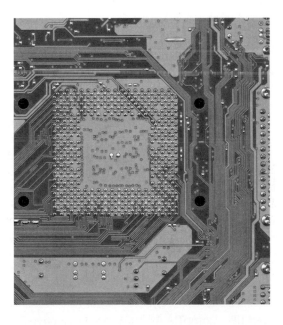

This chapter starts with an explanation of how motherboards work, identifying various types or form factors of motherboards, including distinguishing features. The second section examines expansion capabilities on motherboards, specifically the types of expansion slots you'll run into in the wild and how to install expansion cards. The third section goes through the pragmatic steps of upgrading and installing motherboards. The chapter finishes with techniques for troubleshooting motherboard problems.

Layers of the PCB

Modern motherboards are layered *printed circuit boards* (*PCBs*), copper etched onto a nonconductive material and then coated with some sort of epoxy for strength. The layers mask some of their complexity. You can see some of the traces on the board, but every motherboard is four or more layers thick. The layers contain a veritable highway of wires, carrying data and commands back and forth between the CPU, RAM, and peripherals. The layered structure enables multiple wires to send data without their signals interfering with each other. The layered approach allows the manufacturer to add complexity and additional components to the board without extending the overall length and width of the board. Shorter traces also allow signals to travel faster than they would if the wires were longer, as would be necessary if motherboards did not use layers. The multiple layers also add strength to the board itself, so it doesn't bend easily.

Historical/Conceptual

How Motherboards Work

Three variable and interrelated characteristics define modern motherboards: form factor, chipset, and components. The *form factor* determines the physical size of the motherboard as well as the general location of components and ports. The *chipset* defines the type of processor and RAM the motherboard requires and determines to a degree the built-in devices the motherboard supports, including the expansion slots. Finally, the built-in components determine the core functionality of the system.

Almost all chipsets used in desktops and laptops are made by either Intel or AMD. It's fitting that the two biggest CPU manufacturers for Windows-, macOS-, and Linux-based computers would also produce the essential supporting chipsets.

Any good tech should be able to make a recommendation to a client about a particular motherboard simply by perusing the specs. Because the motherboard determines function, expansion, and stability for the whole PC, it's essential that you know your motherboards!

 EXAM TIP CompTIA A+ 1001 exam objective 3.5 focuses specifically on motherboards you find in classical Windows and Linux-based desktop PCs. This style of motherboard enables techs to do things such as update components. Thus, this chapter uses the term "PC" pretty much throughout.

Form Factors

Motherboard form factors are industry-standardized shapes and layouts that enable motherboards to work with cases and power supplies. A single form factor applies to all three components. All motherboards come in a basic rectangular or square shape but vary in overall size and in the layout of built-in components (see Figure 6-2). You need to install a motherboard in a case designed to fit it, so the ports and slot openings on the back fit correctly.

Figure 6-2
Typical
motherboard

The power supply and the motherboard need matching connectors, and different form factors define different connections. Given that the term "form factor" applies to the case, motherboard, and power supply—the three parts of the PC most responsible for moving air around inside the PC—the form factor also defines how the air moves around in the case.

To perform motherboard upgrades and provide knowledgeable recommendations to clients, techs need to know their form factors. The PC industry has adopted—and dropped—a number of form factors over the years with such names as AT, ATX, and ITX. Let's start with the granddaddy of all PC form factors, AT.

NOTE   In case your curiosity has run rampant, yes, the form factor initials stand for words. AT was Advanced Technology; ATX stands for Advanced Technology Extended; and ITX stands for Information Technology Extended. No one used or uses the full terms. Stick with the initials.

AT Form Factor

The *AT* form factor (see Figure 6-3), invented by IBM in the early 1980s, was the predominant form factor for motherboards through the mid-1990s. AT is now obsolete.

Figure 6-3
AT-style
motherboard

The AT motherboard had a few size variations (see Figure 6-4), ranging from large to very large. The original AT motherboard was huge, around 12 inches wide by 13 inches deep. PC technology was new and needed lots of space for the various chips necessary to run the components of the PC.

Figure 6-4
AT motherboard
(bottom)
and Baby AT
motherboard
(top)

The single greatest problem with AT motherboards was the lack of external ports. When PCs were first invented, the only devices plugged into the average PC were a monitor and a keyboard. That's what the AT was designed to handle—the only dedicated connector on an AT motherboard was the keyboard port (see Figure 6-5).

Figure 6-5
Keyboard
connector on
the back of an AT
motherboard

Over the years, the number of devices plugged into the back of the PC has grown tremendously. Your average PC today has a keyboard, a mouse, a printer, some speakers, a monitor, and—if your system's like mine—four to six USB devices connected to it at any given time. These added components created a demand for a new type of form factor, one with more dedicated connectors for more devices. Many attempts were made to create a new standard form factor. Invariably, these new form factors integrated dedicated connectors for at least the mouse and printer, and many even added connectors for video, sound, and phone lines.

1001

ATX Form Factor

There continued to be a tremendous demand for a new form factor, one that had more standard connectors and also was flexible enough for possible changes in technology. This demand led to the creation of the ATX form factor in 1995 (see Figure 6-6). ATX got off to a slow start, but by around 1998, ATX overtook AT to become the most common form factor, a distinction it holds over 20 years later.

ATX is distinct from AT in the lack of an AT keyboard port, replaced with a rear panel that has all necessary ports built in. Note the mini-DIN (PS/2) keyboard and mouse ports at the left of Figure 6-7, standard features on some ATX boards. You recall those from Chapter 2, "The Visible Computer," right?

The ATX form factor includes many improvements over AT. The position of the power supply creates better air movement. The CPU and RAM are placed to provide easier access, and the rearrangement of components prevents long expansion cards from colliding with the CPU or northbridge. Other improvements, such as placing the RAM closer to the northbridge and CPU than on AT boards, offer users enhanced performance as well. The shorter the wires, the easier to shield them and make them capable of handling double or quadruple the clock speed of the motherboard. Figure 6-8 shows AT and ATX motherboards—note the radical differences in placement of internal connections.

ATX motherboards come in three variations to accommodate different types of cases. So far, you've seen the full-sized ATX form factor, which is 12 by 9.6 inches.

The *microATX* motherboard (see Figure 6-9) floats in at a svelte 9.6 by 9.6 inches (usually), or about 30 percent smaller than standard ATX, yet uses the standard ATX connections.

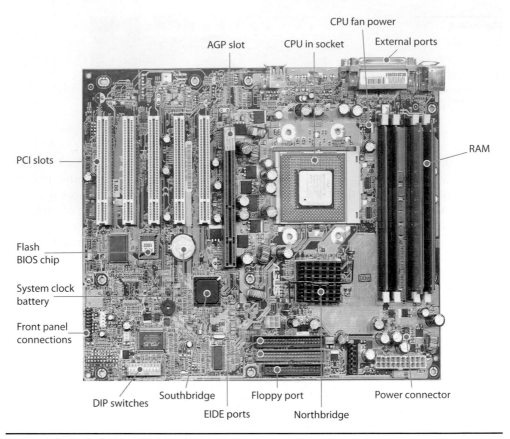

CPU fan power

AGP slot CPU in socket External ports

PCI slots

RAM

Flash
BIOS chip

System clock
battery

Front panel
connections

DIP switches Southbridge Floppy port Power connector

EIDE ports Northbridge

Figure 6-6 Early ATX motherboard

Figure 6-7
ATX ports

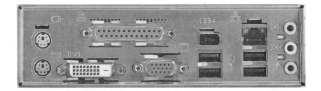

Figure 6-8
AT (left) and
ATX (right)
motherboards
for quick visual
comparison

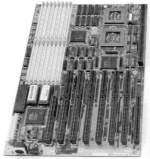

Figure 6-9
A microATX
motherboard

A microATX motherboard fits into a standard ATX case or in the much smaller micro-ATX cases. Note that not all microATX motherboards have the same physical size. You'll sometimes see microATX motherboards referred to with the Greek symbol for micro, as in *μATX*.

EXAM TIP The CompTIA A+ 1001 objectives refer to microATX oddly as *mATX*. Don't be thrown off by the letter *m*. It just means *micro* here.

In 1999, Intel created a variant of the microATX called the FlexATX. *FlexATX* motherboards have maximum dimensions of just 9 by 7.5 inches, which makes them the smallest motherboards in the ATX standard. FlexATX is pretty much gone now.

ITX

VIA Technologies started the process to create a small form factor (SFF) motherboard, the *ITX*. The ITX itself wasn't a success, but VIA in turn created smaller form factors that today populate the SFF market, specifically Mini-ITX.

Mini-ITX is a miniscule 6.7 by 6.7 inches (see Figure 6-10) and competes head to head with the virtually identical microATX.

Figure 6-10
Mini-ITX

One of the great benefits of these SFF motherboards is the tiny amount of power needed to support them. ITX power supplies are quite small compared to a typical power supply. Lower power usage produces less heat, thus enabling passive cooling on many SFF systems. The lack of fan noise makes them ideal for media center PCs.

 EXAM TIP CompTIA lists ITX as a motherboard form factor. Straight ITX doesn't exist in the real world, but Mini-ITX is quite common. The CompTIA A+ 1001 objectives also refer to Mini-ITX as *mITX*.

Proprietary Form Factors

Several major PC makers in the past made motherboards that worked only with their cases. These *proprietary* motherboards enabled these companies to create systems that stood out from the generic ones and, not coincidentally, pushed you to get service and upgrades from their authorized dealers. Some of the features you'll see in proprietary systems are *riser cards*—part of a motherboard separate from the main one but connected by a cable of some sort—and unique power connections. Riser cards on some proprietary systems plug into a unique socket or slot on the motherboard. These are also called *daughter boards*. Proprietary motherboards used to be common on full-sized systems; these days you'll see them in niche systems, like very small cubes and such.

Try This!   Motherboard Varieties

Motherboards come in a wide variety of form factors. Go to your local computer store and check out what is on display. Note the different features offered by ATX, microATX, and Mini-ITX motherboards.

1. ATX is common, but does the store stock Mini-ITX or proprietary motherboards?

2. Did the clerk use tech slang and call the motherboards "mobos"? (It's what most of us call them outside of formal textbooks, after all!)

Chipset

You learned in the previous chapter that every motherboard has a chipset, one or more discrete integrated circuit chips that support the CPU's interfacing to all the other devices on the motherboard. The chipset determines the type of processor the motherboard accepts, the type and capacity of RAM, and the sort of internal and external devices that the motherboard supports. Chipsets vary in features, performance, and stability, so they factor hugely in the purchase or recommendation of a particular motherboard. Good techs know their chipsets!

Because the chipset facilitates communication between the CPU and other devices in the system, its component chips are relatively centrally located on the motherboard (see Figure 6-11). As you'll recall from Chapter 5, "Firmware," chipsets were originally composed of two primary chips: the northbridge and the southbridge.

Figure 6-11
Chipset hidden under cooling fins on modern motherboards

The northbridge chip handled RAM, while the southbridge handled some expansion devices and mass storage drives, such as hard drives. Some motherboard manufacturers added (or still add) a third chip called the *Super I/O chip* to handle these chores, especially in dealing with legacy devices. Figure 6-12 shows a typical Super I/O chip.

Figure 6-12
Super I/O
chip on ASUS
motherboard

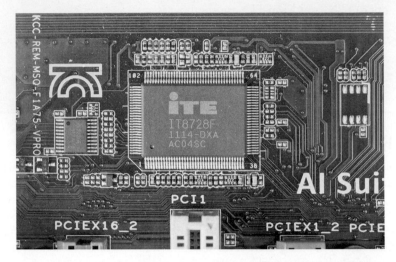

Today, other chips have absorbed many of the functions of the classic chipset. The CPU handles the memory controller features the northbridge used to do. The primary expansion bus communication (see "Expansion Bus" later in this chapter) goes through the CPU as well, something the southbridge handled back in the day. Most techs refer to the remaining support chips on the motherboard as the chipset, although the terms northbridge and southbridge are dead.

The system ROM chip provides part of the BIOS for the chipset, but only at a bare-bones, generic level. The chipset still needs support for the rest of the things it can do. So how do expansion devices get BIOS? From software drivers, of course, and the same holds true for modern chipsets. You have to load the proper drivers for the specific OS to support all of the features of today's chipsets. Without software drivers, you'll never create a stable, fully functional PC. Most motherboards ship with an optical disc with drivers, support programs, and extra-special goodies such as antivirus software (see Figure 6-13).

Different chipsets offer support for a lot of different hardware options, including type of memory slot (DDR3 or DDR4), number and version of USB ports, various mass storage devices, integrated network connections, video support, and so on. Figure 6-14 shows a schematic with typical chipset chores for an Intel Z390 chipset.

Good techs need to know the hot chipsets in detail. The chipset defines almost every motherboard feature short of the CPU itself. Techs love to discuss chipsets and expect a fellow tech to know the differences between one chipset and another. You also need to be able to recommend a motherboard that suits a client's needs. Chapter 11, "Building a PC," covers choosing components and building PCs for specific purposes, such as video editing and gaming. One of the most important choices you'll make in building a custom rig is selecting a chipset.

Figure 6-13

Driver disc
for ASUS
motherboard

Standard Components

Every motherboard provides a socket (or two) for a CPU and slots for RAM. I already covered the variety of both sockets (in Chapter 3, "CPUs") and slot types (in Chapter 4, "RAM"), so I won't rehash them here. You'll also find ports to support standard mass storage devices, such as hard drives and solid-state drives (covered in more detail in Chapter 8, "Mass Storage Technologies").

Additional Components

The connections and capabilities of a motherboard sometimes differ from those of the chipset the motherboard uses. This disparity happens for a couple of reasons. First, a particular chipset may support eight USB ports, but to keep costs down, the manufacturer might include only four ports. Second, a motherboard maker may choose to install extra features—ones not supported by the chipset—by adding additional chips. A common example is a motherboard that supports an old serial port. Other technologies you might find are built-in sound, hard drive RAID controllers, network cards, and more. Some motherboards have added convenience features, such as case fan power connectors and running lights so you can see what you're working on.

USB

All chipsets support USB, but it seems no two motherboards offer the same port arrangement. My motherboard supports eight USB ports, for example, but if you look on the back of the motherboard, you'll only see four USB ports (see Figure 6-15).

Most motherboards have sockets—*internal USB connectors*—to plug in dongles for additional external ports. These dongle connectors are standardized, so many cases have

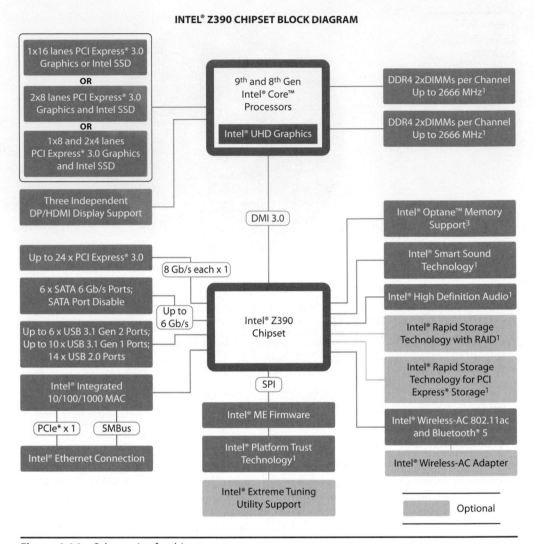

INTEL® Z390 CHIPSET BLOCK DIAGRAM

Figure 6-14 Schematic of a chipset

built-in front USB ports that have dongles attached (see Figure 6-16). This is very handy for USB devices you might want to plug and unplug frequently, such as thumb drives or digital cameras.

Sound

Most motherboards come with onboard sound support. As with USB, a lot of motherboards have a port for connecting to audio jacks on the front of the case, another example (like USB) of *front panel connectors*. These enable you to plug headphones or microphones into the front rather than the rear of the case, a very convenient feature. These

Figure 6-15
USB connectors
showing on back
of PC

Figure 6-16
Front USB
connections

connectors are identical to the ones used on sound cards, so we'll save more discussion for Chapter 10, "Essential Peripherals."

Networking

Most desktop motherboards come with one RJ-45 jack for attaching a network cable. The networking support is built into the chipset or comes as an additional chip soldered to the motherboard. Chapter 18, "Essentials of Networking," covers the physical aspects of networking in detail.

Video

Many motherboards sport one or more video ports for attaching a display. These vary a lot, from the older VGA ports to newer HDMI ports. Chapter 17, "Display Technologies," discusses video in depth, so we'll save further discussion until then.

RAID

RAID stands for *redundant array of independent* (or *inexpensive*) *disks* and is very common on motherboards. There are many types of RAID, such as *mirroring* (the process of using two drives to hold the same data, which is good for safety, because if one drive dies, the other still has all of the data) or *striping* (making two drives act as one drive by spreading data across them, which is good for speed). RAID is a very cool but complex topic that's discussed in detail in Chapter 8.

Case Fan Support

Every motherboard has a CPU fan power connector, as you'll recall from Chapter 3, usually a four-wire connector that supports three-wire fans too. Some motherboards offer one or more fan power connectors for case fans. These are almost always only three-wire connectors. The case fans plugged into the motherboard can be monitored and controlled in Windows, unlike case fans connected only to the power supply, so they add a nice feature.

Expansion Bus

Expansion slots have been part of the PC from the very beginning. Way back then, IBM created the PC with an eye to the future; the original IBM PC had slots built into the motherboard—called *expansion slots*—for adding expansion cards and thus new functions to the PC. The slots and accompanying wires and support chips on the first PC and on the latest and greatest PC are called the *expansion bus*.

Structure and Function of the Expansion Bus

As you've learned, every device in the computer—whether soldered to the motherboard or snapped into a socket—connects to the external data bus and the address bus. The expansion slots are no exception. They connect to the rest of the PC through the chipset. Exactly *where* on the chipset varies depending on the system. On newer systems, the expansion slots connect to the CPU (see Figure 6-17) because modern CPUs contain a lot of controller features that used to be in the chipset. In older systems, the expansion slots connect directly to the chipset (see Figure 6-18). Finally, many systems have more than one type of expansion bus, with slots of one type connecting to the CPU and slots of another type connecting to the chipset (see Figure 6-19).

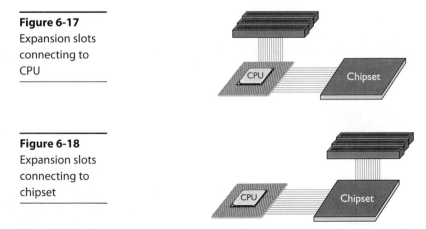

Figure 6-17
Expansion slots connecting to CPU

Figure 6-18
Expansion slots connecting to chipset

The chipset provides an extension of the address bus and data bus to the expansion slots, and thus to any expansion cards in those slots. If you plug a hard drive controller card into an expansion slot, it functions just as if it were built into the motherboard,

Figure 6-19
Expansion slots connecting to both CPU and chipset

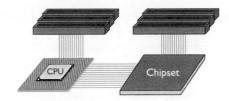

albeit with one big difference: speed. As you'll recall from Chapter 3, the system crystal—the clock—pushes the CPU. The system crystal provides a critical function for the entire PC, acting like a drill sergeant calling a cadence, setting the pace of activity in the computer. Every device soldered to the motherboard is designed to run at the speed of the system crystal. A 200-MHz motherboard, for example, has its chipset chips all timed by a 200-MHz crystal (see Figure 6-20).

Figure 6-20
The system crystal sets the speed.

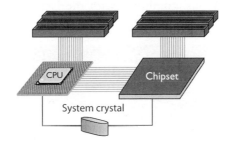

Clock crystals aren't just for CPUs and chipsets. Pretty much every chip in your computer has a CLK wire and needs to be pushed by a clock chip, including the chips on your expansion cards. Suppose you buy a device that did not come with your computer—say, a sound card. The chips on the sound card need to be pushed by a CLK signal from a crystal. If PCs were designed to use the system crystal to push that sound card, sound card manufacturers would need to make sound cards for every possible motherboard speed. You would have to buy a 100-MHz sound card for a 100-MHz system or a 200-MHz sound card for a 200-MHz system.

That would be ridiculous, and IBM knew it when they designed the PC. They had to make an extension to the external data bus that *ran at its own standardized speed*. You would use this part of the external data bus to snap new devices into the PC. IBM achieved this goal by adding a different crystal, called the *expansion bus crystal*, which controlled the part of the external data bus connected to the expansion slots (see Figure 6-21).

Figure 6-21
Function of system and expansion bus crystals

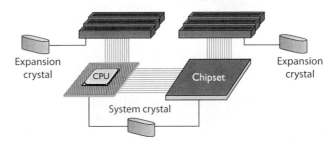

The expansion slots run at a much slower speed than the frontside bus. The chipset acts as the divider between the two buses, compensating for the speed difference with wait states and special buffering (storage) areas. No matter how fast the motherboard runs, the expansion slots run at a standard speed. In the original IBM PC, that speed was about 14.318 MHz ÷ 2, or about 7.16 MHz. Luckily, modern expansion buses run much faster! Let's start with the oldest of the modern expansion slots, PCI.

PCI

Intel introduced the *Peripheral Component Interconnect* (*PCI*) bus architecture (see Figure 6-22) in the early 1990s, and the PC expansion bus was never again the same. Intel made many smart moves with PCI, not the least of which was releasing PCI to the public domain to make PCI very attractive to manufacturers. PCI provided a wider, faster, more flexible alternative than any previous expansion bus. The exceptional technology of the new bus, combined with the lack of a price tag, made manufacturers quickly drop older buses and adopt PCI.

Figure 6-22
PCI expansion
bus slots

PCI really shook up the PC world with its capabilities. The original PCI bus was 32 bits wide and ran at 33 MHz, which was superb, but these features were expected and not earth-shattering. The coolness of PCI came from its capability to coexist with other expansion buses. When PCI first came out, you could buy a motherboard with both PCI and older slots. This was important because users could keep their old expansion cards and slowly migrate to PCI. Equally impressive was that PCI devices were (and still are) self-configuring, a feature that led to the industry standard that became known as plug and play (PnP). Finally, PCI had a powerful burst-mode feature that enabled very efficient data transfers.

Mini-PCI

PCI made it into laptops in the specialty *Mini-PCI* format (see Figure 6-23). Mini-PCI was designed to use low power and to lie flat—both good features for a laptop expansion slot. Mini-PCI, like full-sized PCI, is only on older computers.

Figure 6-23
Tiny card in Mini-PCI slot. See the contacts at the bottom of the picture?

PCI Express

PCI Express (*PCIe*) is still PCI, but it uses a point-to-point *serial* connection instead of PCI's shared *parallel* communication. Consider a single 32-bit chunk of data moving from a device to the CPU. In PCI parallel communication, 32 wires each carry one bit of that chunk of data. In serial communication, only one wire carries those 32 bits. You'd think that 32 wires are better than one, correct?

First of all, PCIe doesn't share the bus. A PCIe device has its own direct connection (a point-to-point connection) to the CPU, so it does not wait for other devices. Plus, when you start going really fast (think gigabits per second), getting all 32 bits of data to go from one device to another at the same time is difficult, because some bits get there slightly faster than others. That means you need some serious, high-speed checking of the data when it arrives to verify that it's all there and in good shape. Serial data doesn't have this problem, as all of the bits arrive one after the other in a single stream. When data is really going fast, a single point-to-point serial connection is faster than a shared 32-wire parallel connection.

And boy howdy, is PCIe ever fast! A PCIe connection uses one wire for sending and one for receiving. Each of these pairs of wires between a PCIe controller and a device is called a *lane*. Each direction of a lane runs at 2.5 gigatransfers per second (GTps) with PCIe 1.*x*, 5 GTps with PCIe 2.*x*, 8 GTps with PCIe 3.*x*, and a whopping 16 GTps with

PCIe 4.0! Better yet, each point-to-point connection can use 1, 2, 4, 8, 12, or 16 lanes to achieve a maximum theoretical bandwidth of up to 256 GTps. The *transfer rate* describes the number of operations happening per second. With serial communication, you almost get a one-to-one correlation between transfer rate and binary data rate. The effective data rate drops a little bit because of the *encoding scheme*—the way the data is broken down and reassembled—but full-duplex data throughput can go up to a whopping 32 GBps on a ×16 connection.

EXAM TIP   You need to know the various motherboard expansion slots for the CompTIA 220-1001 exam, especially PCI and PCIe.

The most common PCIe slot is the 16-lane (×16) version most often used for video cards, as shown in Figure 6-24. The first versions of PCIe motherboards used a combination of a single PCIe ×16 slot and a number of standard PCI slots. (Remember, PCI is designed to work with other expansion slots, even other types of PCI.) There is also a popular small form factor version of PCI Express for laptop computers called *PCI Express Mini Card*, or *Mini-PCIe*, which Chapter 23, "Portable Computing," covers in detail.

Figure 6-24
PCIe ×16 slot (center) with PCI slots (top and bottom)

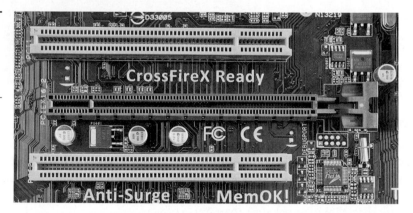

The bandwidth generated by a ×16 slot is far more than anything other than a video card would need, so most PCIe motherboards also contain slots with fewer lanes. Currently ×1 is the most common general-purpose PCIe slot (see Figure 6-25). You'll also see ×4 slots on some motherboards.

Figure 6-25
PCIe ×1 slot (top)

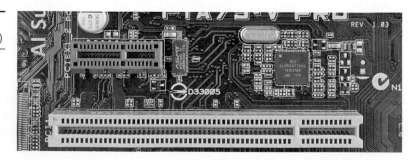

NOTE When you talk about the lanes, such as ×1 or ×16, use "by" rather than "ex" for the multiplication mark. So "by 1" and "by 16" are the correct pronunciations.

Try This! Shopping Trip

So, what's the latest PCIe motherboard out there? Get online or go to your local computer store and research higher-end motherboards. What combinations of PCIe slots can you find on a single motherboard? Which motherboard has the most ×16 lanes? Why? Jot them down and compare your findings with your classmates' findings.

Installing Expansion Cards

Installing an expansion card successfully—another one of those bread-and-butter tasks for the PC tech—requires at least four steps. First, you need to know that the card works with your system and your operating system. Second, you have to insert the card in an expansion slot properly and without damaging the card or the motherboard. Third, you need to provide drivers for the operating system—*proper* drivers for the *specific* OS. Fourth, you should always verify that the card functions properly before you walk away from the PC.

 EXAM TIP The four steps involved in installing expansion cards apply to all types of expansion cards. The CompTIA A+ exams will ask you about cards ranging from common—sound, video, and networking—to other specific cards for USB, Thunderbolt, and modem connections. They'll ask about wireless and cellular networking cards, storage cards, TV tuner cards, video capture cards, riser cards, and more, all of which we'll cover in their proper chapters in this book. You install any of them using the same four steps: knowledge, physical installation, device drivers, and verification.

Step 1: Knowledge

Learn about the device you plan to install—preferably before you purchase it! Does the device work with your system and operating system? Does it have drivers for your operating system? If you use a recent version of Windows, the answer to these questions is almost always "yes." If you're attempting to install an old device or if you're trying to install a very unique device in a less-common operating system such as Linux, these questions become important. A lot of older hardware simply won't work with new versions of Windows, especially Windows 10. Check the device's documentation and check the device manufacturer's Web site to verify that you have the correct drivers. While you're checking, make sure you have the latest version of the driver; most devices get driver updates more often than the weather changes in Texas.

Step 2: Physical Installation

To install an expansion card successfully, you need to take steps to avoid damaging the card, the motherboard, or both. This means knowing how to handle a card and avoiding electrostatic discharge (ESD) or any other electrical issue. You also need to place the card firmly and completely into an available expansion slot.

Optimally, a card should always be in one of two places: in a computer or in an anti-static bag. When inserting or removing a card, be careful to hold the card only by its edges. Do not hold the card by the slot connectors or touch any components on the board (see Figure 6-26).

Figure 6-26
Where to handle
a card

If possible, use an anti-static wrist strap properly attached to the PC, as noted in Chapter 1, "Safety and Professionalism." If you don't have a wrist strap, you can use the tech way of avoiding ESD by touching the power supply after you remove the expansion card from its anti-static bag. This puts you, the card, and the PC at the same electrical potential and thus minimizes the risk of ESD.

Modern systems have a trickle of voltage on the motherboard at all times when the computer is plugged into a power outlet. Chapter 7, "Power Supplies," covers power for the PC and how to deal with it in detail, but here's the short version: *Always unplug the PC before inserting an expansion card!* Failure to do so can destroy the card, the motherboard, or both. It's not worth the risk.

Never insert or remove a card at an extreme angle. This may damage the card. A slight angle is acceptable and even necessary when removing a card. Always secure the card to the case with a connection screw or other retaining mechanism. This keeps the card from slipping out and potentially shorting against other cards. Also, many cards use the screw connection to ground the card to the case (see Figure 6-27).

Figure 6-27
Always secure all
cards properly.

Many technicians have been told to clean the slot connectors if a particular card is not working. This is almost never necessary after a card is installed and, if done improperly, can cause damage. You should clean slot connectors only if you have a card that's been on the shelf for a while and the contacts are obviously dull.

Never use a pencil eraser for this purpose. Pencil erasers can leave behind bits of residue that wedge between the card and slot, preventing contact and causing the card to fail. Grab a can of electronic contact cleaning solution and use it instead. Electronic contact cleaning solution is designed for exactly this purpose, cleans contacts nicely, and doesn't leave any residue. You can find electronic contact cleaning solution at any electronics store or online, of course.

A fully inserted expansion card sits flush against the back of the PC case—assuming the motherboard is mounted properly, of course—with no gap between the mounting bracket on the card and the screw hole on the case. If the card is properly seated, no contacts are exposed above the slot. Figure 6-28 shows a properly seated (meaning fitted snugly in the slot) expansion card.

Step 3: Device Drivers

You know from Chapter 5, "Firmware," that all devices, whether built into the motherboard or added along the way, require BIOS. For almost all expansion cards, that BIOS comes in the form of *device drivers*—software support programs—loaded automatically by the operating system or manually from an optical disc provided by the card manufacturer.

Figure 6-28
Properly seated expansion card; note the tight fit between case and mounting bracket and the evenness of the card in the slot.

Installing device drivers is fairly straightforward. You should use the correct drivers—kind of obvious, but you'd be surprised how many techs mess this up—and, if you're upgrading, you might have to unload current drivers before loading new drivers. Finally, if you have a problem, you may need to uninstall the drivers you just loaded or roll back to earlier, more stable drivers.

Getting the Correct Drivers   To be sure you have the best possible driver you can get for your device, you should always check the manufacturer's Web site. The drivers that come with a device may work well, but odds are good that you'll find a newer and better driver on the Web site. How do you know that the drivers on the Web site are newer? First, take the easy route: look on the disc. Often the version is printed right on the optical media. If it's not printed there, you're going to have to load the disc in your optical drive and poke around. Many driver discs have an AutoRun screen that advertises the version. If nothing is on the pop-up screen, look for a Readme file (see Figure 6-29).

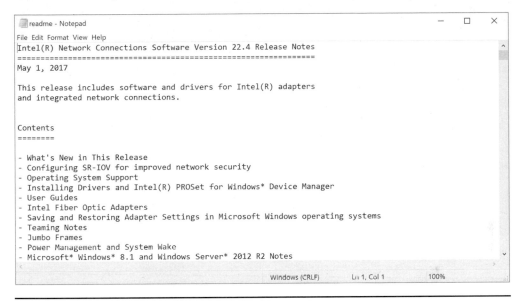

Figure 6-29 Part of a Readme file showing the driver version

Driver or Device? In almost all cases, you should install the device driver after you install the device. Without the device installed, the driver installation will not see the device and will give an error screen. The only exceptions to this rule are USB devices—with these you should always install the driver first. (The other excellent external connection, Thunderbolt, works great however you install drivers when you're in macOS. With Windows? It totally depends on the hardware manufacturer. Read the documentation.)

Removing the Old Drivers Some cards—and this is especially true with video cards—require you to remove old drivers of the same type before you install the new device. To do this, you must first locate the driver in Device Manager. Right-click the device driver you want to uninstall and select Uninstall device (see Figure 6-30).

Unsigned Drivers Microsoft truly wants your computer to work, so they provide an excellent and rigorous testing program for hardware manufacturers called the *Windows Hardware Certification Program*. The drivers get a digital signature that says Microsoft tested them and found all was well.

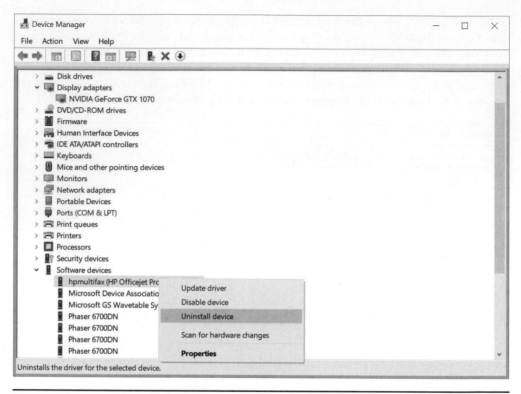

Figure 6-30 Uninstalling a device

The last of the 32-bit versions of Windows had support for *unsigned drivers*, essentially drivers that had not gone through the Windows Certification Program (as it was called then), so their software did not get a digital signature from Microsoft. Windows would bring up a scary-looking screen (see Figure 6-31) that warned against the driver. Although you might see unsigned drivers on the CompTIA A+ 1001 exam, you'll rarely see them on any modern Windows machine.

Installing the New Driver   You have two ways to install a new driver in Windows. The first option is to let Windows detect the new hardware and find the proper device driver. The second method is to install the drivers manually by downloading them from the manufacturer or using the installation disc. Most installation media give clear options so you can choose what you want to install (see Figure 6-32).

Driver Rollback   All versions of Windows offer the nifty feature of rolling back to previous drivers after an installation or driver upgrade. If you decide to live on the edge and install beta drivers for your video card, for example, and your system becomes frightfully unstable, you can revert to the drivers that worked before. (Not that I've ever had

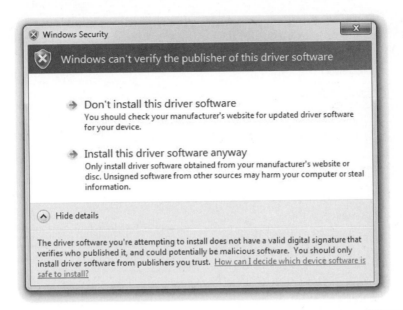

Figure 6-31 Unsigned driver warning

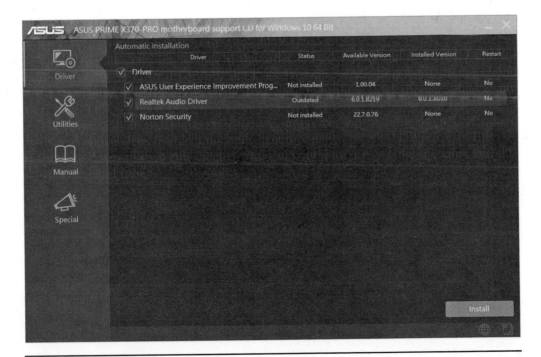

Figure 6-32 Installation menu

to use that feature, of course.) To access the rollback feature, simply open Device Manager and access the properties for the device you want to adjust. On the Driver tab (see Figure 6-33), you'll find the Roll Back Driver button.

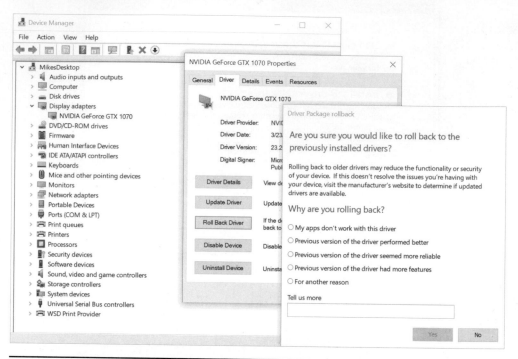

Figure 6-33 Driver rollback feature

NOTE To install drivers in a Windows computer, you need to have the proper permission. I'm not talking about asking somebody if you're allowed to install the device. Permissions are granted in Windows to enable people to do certain things, such as add a printer to a local computer or install software, or to stop people from being able to do such tasks. Specifically, you need administrative permissions to install drivers. See Chapter 13, "Users, Groups, and Permissions," for more on permissions.

Step 4: Verify

As a last step in the installation process, inspect the results of the installation and verify that the device works properly. Immediately after installing, you should open Device Manager and verify that Windows sees the device (see Figure 6-34). Assuming that

Device Manager shows the device working properly, your next check is to put the device to work by making it do whatever it is supposed to do. If you installed a printer, print something; if you installed a scanner, scan something. If it works, you're finished!

Figure 6-34
Device Manager shows the device working properly.

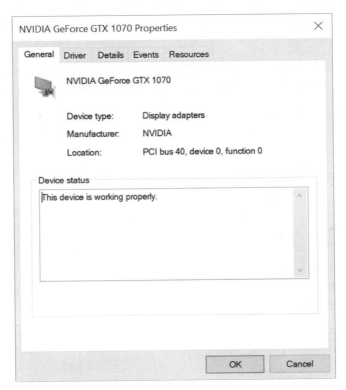

NOTE Many PC enthusiasts try to squeeze every bit of performance out of their PC components, much as auto enthusiasts tinker with engine tunings to get a little extra horsepower out of their engines. Expansion card manufacturers love enthusiasts, who often act as free testers for their unpolished drivers, known as beta drivers. Beta drivers are fine for the most part, but they can sometimes cause amazing system instability—never a good thing! If you use beta drivers, make sure you know how to uninstall or roll back to previous drivers.

Troubleshooting Expansion Cards

A properly installed expansion card rarely makes trouble; it's the botched installations that produce headaches. Chances are high that you'll have to troubleshoot an expansion card installation at some point, usually from an installation you botched personally.

The first sign of an improperly installed card usually shows up the moment you first try to get that card to do whatever it's supposed to do, and it doesn't do it. When this happens, your primary troubleshooting process is a reinstallation—after checking in with Device Manager.

Other chapters in this book cover specific hardware troubleshooting. For example, troubleshooting video cards is covered in Chapter 17. Use this section to help you decide what to look for and how to deal with the problem.

Device Manager provides the first diagnostic and troubleshooting tool in Windows. After you install a new device, Device Manager gives you many clues if something has gone wrong.

Occasionally, Device Manager may not even show the new device. If that happens, verify that you inserted the device properly and, if needed, that the device has power. Run the Add Hardware Wizard and see if Windows recognizes the device (see Figure 6-35). In Windows, you run the program by clicking Start and typing the name of the executable in the Search bar: **hdwwiz.exe**.

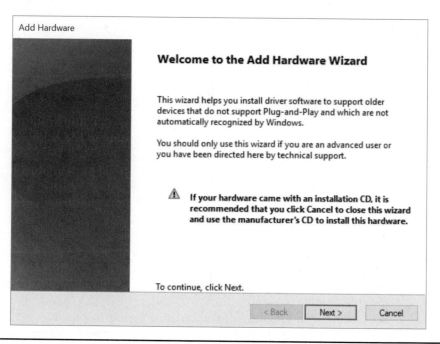

Figure 6-35   Running Add Hardware Wizard in Windows 10

If Device Manager doesn't recognize the device at this point, you have one of two problems: either the device is physically damaged and you must replace it, or the device is an onboard device, not a card, and is turned off in CMOS.

Device Manager rarely completely fails to see a device. More commonly, device problems manifest themselves in Device Manager via error icons:

- A black "!" on a triangle indicates that a device is missing (see Figure 6-36), that Windows does not recognize a device, or that there's a device driver problem. A device may still work even while producing this error.

- A black downward-pointing arrow on a white field indicates a disabled device. This usually points to a device that's been manually turned off, or a damaged device. A device producing this error will not work.

Figure 6-36
An "!" in Device Manager, indicating a problem with the selected device

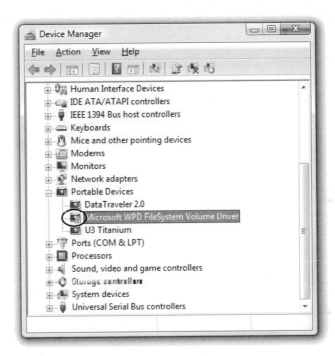

The "!" symbol is the most common error symbol and usually the easiest to fix. First, double-check the device's connections. Second, try reinstalling the driver with the Update Driver button. To get to the Update Driver button, right-click the desired device in Device Manager and select *Update driver* to open the updating wizard (see Figure 6-37).

If you get a downward-pointing arrow, first check that the device isn't disabled. Right-click the device and select Enable. If that doesn't work (it often does not), try rolling back the driver (if you updated the driver) or uninstalling (if it's a new install). Shut the system down and make triple-sure you have the card physically installed. Then redo the entire driver installation procedure, making sure you have the most current driver for that device. If none of these procedures works, return the card—it's almost certainly bad.

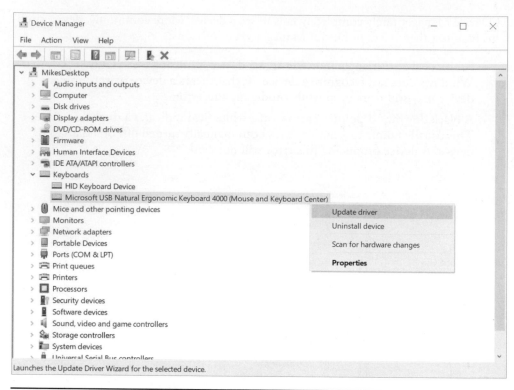

Figure 6-37   Updating the driver

Upgrading and Installing Motherboards

To most techs, the concept of adding or replacing a motherboard can be extremely intimidating. It really shouldn't be; motherboard installation is a common and necessary part of PC repair. It is inexpensive and easy, although it can sometimes be a little tedious and messy because of the large number of parts involved. This section covers the process of installation and replacement and shows you some of the tricks that make this necessary process easy to handle.

Choosing the Motherboard and Case

Choosing a motherboard and case can prove quite a challenge for any tech, whether newly minted or a seasoned veteran. You first have to figure out the type of motherboard you want, such as AMD- or Intel-based. Then you need to think about the form factor, which of course influences the type of case you'll need. Third, how rich in features is the motherboard and how tough is it to configure? You have to read the motherboard manual to find out. Finally, you need to select the case that matches your space needs, budget, and form factor. Now look at each step in a little more detail.

EXAM TIP Being able to select and install a motherboard appropriate for a client or customer is something every CompTIA A+ technician should know.

Try This! Building a Recommendation

Family, friends, and potential clients often solicit the advice of a tech when they're thinking about upgrading their PC. This solicitation puts you on the spot to make not just any old recommendation, but one that works with the needs and budget of the potential upgrader. To handle this scenario successfully, you need to manage expectations and ask the right questions, so try this!

What does the upgrader want to do that compels him or her to upgrade? Write it down! Some of the common motivations for upgrading are to play that hot new game or to take advantage of new technology. What's the minimum system needed to run tomorrow's action games? What do you need to make multimedia sing? Does the motherboard need to have SuperSpeed USB 3.0 or SuperSpeed+ USB 3.1 built in to accommodate digital video or some other special purpose?

How much of the current system does the upgrader want to save? Upgrading a motherboard can very quickly turn into a complete system rebuild. What form factor is the old case? If it's a microATX case, that constrains the motherboards you can use with it to microATX. If the desired motherboard is a full-sized ATX board, you'll need to get a new case. Does the new motherboard possess the same type of CPU socket as the old motherboard? If not, that's a sure sign you'll need to upgrade the CPU as well.

What about RAM? If the old motherboard was using DDR3 SDRAM, and the new motherboard requires DDR4, you'll need to replace the RAM. If you need to upgrade the memory, it is best to know how many channels the new RAM interface supports, because performance is best when all channels are populated.

Once you've gathered information on motivation and assessed the current PC of the upgrader, it's time to get down to business: field trip time! This is a great excuse to get to the computer store and check out the latest motherboards and gadgets. Don't forget to jot down notes and prices while you're there. By the end of the field trip, you should have the information to give the upgrader an honest assessment of what an upgrade will entail, at least in monetary terms. Be honest—in other words, don't just tell upgraders what you think they want to hear—and you won't get in trouble.

First, determine what motherboard you need. What CPU are you using? Will the motherboard work with that CPU? Because most of us buy the CPU and the motherboard at the same time, make the seller guarantee that the CPU will work with the motherboard. How much RAM do you intend to install? Are extra RAM sockets available for future upgrades?

NOTE Chapter 11, "Building a PC," covers items needed for specialized PCs.

A number of excellent motherboard manufacturers currently exist. Some of the more popular brands are ASUS, BIOSTAR, GIGABYTE, Intel, and MSI. Your supplier may also have some lesser-known but perfectly acceptable brands of motherboards. As long as the supplier has an easy return policy, it's fine to try one of these.

Second, make sure you're getting a form factor that works with your case. Don't try to put a regular ATX motherboard into a microATX case!

Third, all motherboards come with a technical manual, better known as the *motherboard book* (see Figure 6-38). You must have this book! This book is your primary source for all of the critical information about the motherboard. If you set up CPU or RAM timings incorrectly in CMOS, for example, and you have a dead PC, where would you find the CMOS-clear jumper? Where do you plug in the speaker? Even if you let someone else install the motherboard, insist on the motherboard book; you will need it.

Figure 6-38
Motherboard box
and book

NOTE If you have a motherboard with no manual, you can usually find a copy of the manual in Adobe Acrobat (.PDF) format online at the manufacturer's Web site. Make sure you match the revision number of the motherboard as well as the model number.

It's a good idea to grab and print a copy to keep with the motherboard. I often tape a copy (either hard copy, burned onto a disc, or copied to a USB drive) of the manual in the case where I installed the motherboard. A good spot is in an unused drive bay. Just don't cover any vents!

Fourth, pick your case carefully. Cases come in many sizes: slimline, desktop, mini-tower, mid-tower, tower, and cube. You can also get specialized cases, such as tiny cases for entertainment systems or ones that fit the same format as a stereo receiver or DVD player. The latter case is called a home theater PC (HTPC). See Figure 6-39.

Figure 6-39
An HTPC

Slimline and desktop models generally sit on the desk, beneath the monitor. The various tower cases usually occupy a bit of floor space next to the desk. The mini-tower and mid-tower cases are the most popular choices. Make sure you get a case that fits your motherboard—most microATX cases are too small for a regular ATX motherboard. Cube cases generally require a specific motherboard, so be prepared to buy both pieces at the same time. A quick test-fit before you buy saves a lot of return trips to the supplier.

Better cases offer tool-free component installation, so you don't have to screw down cards or drives. They just snap into place. You'll still need a trusty screwdriver to secure the motherboard, though. No installation is completely tool-free yet.

Power supplies sometimes come with the case. Watch out for "really good deal" cases because that invariably points to a cheap or missing power supply. You also need to verify that the power supply has sufficient wattage. This issue is handled in Chapter 7.

Installing the Motherboard

If you're replacing a motherboard, first remove the old motherboard. Begin by removing all of the cards. Also remove anything else that might impede removal or installation of the motherboard, such as a hard drive. Keep track of your screws—the best idea is to return the screws to their mounting holes temporarily, at least until you can reinstall the parts. Sometimes you even have to remove the power supply temporarily to enable access to the motherboard.

 EXAM TIP The CompTIA A+ exams may test you on the basics of installing a motherboard, so you need to know this section.

Unscrew the motherboard. *It will not simply lift out.* The motherboard mounts to the case via small connectors called *standoffs* that screw into the bottom of the case (see Figure 6-40). Screws then go into the standoffs to hold the motherboard in place. Be sure to place the standoffs properly before installing the new motherboard.

Figure 6-40
Standoff in a
case, ready for
the motherboard

 CAUTION Watch out for ESD here! Remember that it's very easy to damage or destroy a CPU and RAM with a little electrostatic discharge. It's also fairly easy to damage the motherboard with ESD. Always wear your anti-static wrist strap.

When you insert the new motherboard, do not assume that you will put the screws and standoffs in the same place as they were in your old motherboard. When it comes to the placement of screws and standoffs, only one rule applies: anywhere it fits. Do not be afraid to be a little tough here! Installing motherboards can be a wiggling, twisting, knuckle-scraping process.

 CAUTION Pay attention to the location of the standoffs if you're swapping a motherboard. If you leave a screw-type standoff beneath a spot on the motherboard where you can't add a screw and then apply power to the motherboard, you run the risk of frying the motherboard.

The next part of motherboard installation is connecting the LEDs, buttons, and front-mounted ports on the front of the box. This is sometimes easier to do before you install the motherboard fully in the case. You can trace the wire leads from the front of the case to the appropriate standoffs on the motherboard. These usually include the following:

- Soft power button
- Reset button

- Speaker
- Hard drive activity light
- Power light
- USB
- Sound
- Thunderbolt

These wires have specific pin connections to the motherboard. Although you can refer to the motherboard book for their location, usually a quick inspection of the motherboard will suffice for an experienced tech (see Figure 6-41).

Figure 6-41
Motherboard
wire connections
labeled on the
motherboard

You need to follow a few rules when installing these wires. First, the lights are LEDs, not light bulbs; they have a positive side and a negative side. If they don't work one way, turn the connector around and try the other. Second, when in doubt, guess. Incorrect installation only results in the device not working; it won't damage the computer. Refer to the motherboard book for the correct installation. The third and last rule is that, with the exception of the soft power switch on an ATX system, you do not need any of these wires for the computer to run.

No hard-and-fast rule exists for determining the function of each wire. Often the function of each wire is printed on the connector (see Figure 6-42). If not, track each wire to the LED or switch to determine its function.

Figure 6-42
Sample of case
wires

 NOTE   A lot of techs install the CPU, CPU fan, and RAM into the motherboard before installing the motherboard into the case. This helps in several ways, especially with a new system. First, you want to make certain that the CPU and RAM work well with the motherboard and with each other—without that, you have no hope of setting up a stable system. Second, installing these components first prevents the phenomenon of *flexing* the motherboard. Some cases don't provide quite enough support for the motherboard, and pushing in RAM can make the board bend. Third, attaching a CPU fan can be a bear of a task, one that's considerably easier to do on a table top than within the confines of a case. A lot of third-party CPU fan and heat-sink assemblies mount on brackets on the bottom of the motherboard, requiring installation before placement in the case.

Finally, install the motherboard into the case fully and secure it with the appropriate screws. Once you get the motherboard mounted in the case, with the CPU and RAM properly installed, it's time to insert the power connections and test it. A POST card can be helpful with the system test because you won't have to add the speaker, a video card, monitor, and keyboard to verify that the system is booting. If you have a POST card, start the system, and watch to see if the POST takes place—you should see a number of POST codes before the POST stops. If you don't have a POST card, install a keyboard, speaker, video card, and monitor. Boot the system and see if the BIOS information shows up on the screen. If it does, you're probably okay. If it doesn't, it's time to refer to the motherboard book to see where you made a mistake.

EXAM TIP Very old motherboards used to require techs to set jumpers to determine the bus speed for the motherboard. This enabled these motherboards to accommodate CPUs that needed a 100-MHz bus, for example, and other CPUs that needed a 66-MHz bus. The CompTIA A+ exams might refer to these kinds of manual adjustments needed for installation.

Setting these jumpers incorrectly resulted in bizarre behavior. First, if you set the bus speed too high, many CPUs wouldn't even try to power up. If you set the speed too low, you wouldn't get optimal use out of the CPU. The motherboard manuals had extensive charts for settings for the CPUs supported.

Modern motherboards autodetect CPU and RAM settings and adjust accordingly, so these errors only happen when you intentionally overclock or underclock a CPU through the CMOS setup utility.

If you get no power at all, check to make sure you plugged in all the necessary power connectors. If you get power to fans but get nothing on the screen, you could have several problems. The CPU, RAM, or video card might not be connected to the motherboard properly. The only way to determine the problems is to test. Check the easy connections first (RAM and video) before removing and reseating the CPU. Also, see Chapter 7 for more on power issues.

SIM Check out the Chapter 6 Challenge! sim, "Label Motherboard," over at http://totalsem.com/100x. It'll help you remember all the motherboard components in case you get a performance-based challenge on the CompTIA A+ 1001 exam.

Troubleshooting Motherboards

Motherboards fail. Not often, but motherboards and motherboard components can die from many causes: time, dust, cat hair, or simply slight manufacturing defects made worse by the millions of amps of current sluicing through the motherboard traces. Installing cards, electrostatic discharge, flexing the motherboard one time too many when swapping out RAM or drives—any of these factors can cause a motherboard to fail. The motherboard is a hard-working, often abused component of the PC. Unfortunately for the common tech, troubleshooting a motherboard problem can be difficult and time-consuming. Let's wrap up this chapter with a look at symptoms of a failing motherboard, techniques for troubleshooting, and the options you have when you discover a motherboard problem.

Symptoms

Motherboard failures commonly fall into three types: catastrophic, component, and ethereal. With a *catastrophic failure*, the computer just won't boot. It might have been working just fine; you hear a pop—*a loud noise*—followed by the acrid smell of ozone;

and then a dead computer. Use your nose to lead you to a popped capacitor or other motherboard component. Check the power and hard drive activity *indicator lights* on the front of the PC. Assuming they worked before, having them completely flat points to power supply failure or motherboard failure.

 EXAM TIP For several years in the mid-2000s, suppliers of capacitors—devices that store and release energy, essentially smoothing the power on motherboards and other PCBs—released some seriously bad ones. Millions of these incorrectly formulated capacitors made it into computers and failed at high rates. The failure led to dead PCs, but the culprit was obviously the bulging capacitors, what you'll see on the 1001 exam as *distended capacitors*.

This sort of problem happens to brand-new systems because of manufacturing defects—often called a *burn-in failure*—and to any system that gets a shock of ESD. Burn-in failure is uncommon and usually happens in the first 30 days of use. Swap out the motherboard for a replacement and you should be fine. If you accidentally zap your motherboard when inserting a card or moving wires around, be chagrined. Change your daring ways and wear an anti-static wrist strap!

Component failure happens rarely and appears as flaky connections between a device and motherboard, or as intermittent problems. A hard drive plugged into a faulty controller on the motherboard, for example, might show up in CMOS autodetect but be inaccessible in Windows. Another example is a USB port that worked fine for months until a big storm took out the external modem hooked to it, and now it doesn't work, even with a replacement modem.

The most difficult of the three types of symptoms to diagnose are those I call *ethereal* symptoms. Stuff just doesn't work all of the time. The PC reboots itself. You get a Blue Screen of Death (BSoD) in the midst of heavy computing, such as right before you smack the villain and rescue the damsel. What can cause such symptoms? If you answered any of the following, you win the prize:

- Faulty component
- Buggy device driver
- Buggy application software
- Slight corruption of the operating system
- Power supply problems

Err…you get the picture.

What a nightmare scenario to troubleshoot! The Way of the Tech knows paths through such perils, though, so let's turn to troubleshooting techniques now.

Techniques

Troubleshooting a potential motherboard failure requires time, patience, and organization. Some problems will certainly be quicker to solve than others. If the hard drive doesn't work as expected, as in the previous example, check the settings on the drive. Try a different drive. Try the same drive with a different motherboard to verify that it's a good drive. Like every other troubleshooting technique, what you're trying to do with motherboard testing is to isolate the problem by eliminating potential causes.

Use a modern POST card with a good diagnostic screen. You'll find cards that plug into both PCI and PCIe slots, for example, and even USB-based POST cards that enable quick diagnostic tests on portable computers. See Figure 6-43.

Figure 6-43   USB POST card (left) and PCI POST card (right)

This three-part system—check, replace, verify good component—works for both simple and more complicated motherboard problems. You can even apply the same technique to ethereal-type problems that might be anything, but you should add one more verb: *document*. Take notes on the individual components you test so you don't repeat efforts or waste time. Plus, taking notes can lead to the establishment of patterns. Being able to re-create a system crash by performing certain actions in a specific order can often lead you to the root of the problem. Document your actions. Motherboard testing is time-consuming enough without adding inefficiency.

Options

Once you determine that the motherboard has problems, you have several options for fixing the three types of failures. If you have a catastrophic failure, you must replace the motherboard. Even if it works somewhat, don't mess around. The motherboard should provide bedrock stability for the system. If it's even remotely buggy or problematic, get rid of it!

CAUTION   If you've lost components because of ESD or a power surge, you would most likely be better off replacing the motherboard. The damage you can't see can definitely sneak up to bite you and create system instability.

If you have a component failure, you can often replace the component with an add-on card that will be as good as or better than the failed device. Adaptec, for example, makes fine cards that can replace the built-in SATA ports on the motherboard (see Figure 6-44).

Figure 6-44
Adaptec PCIe
SATA card

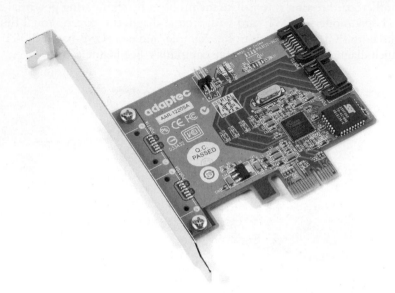

If your component failure is more a technology issue than physical damage, you can try upgrading the BIOS on the motherboard. As you'll recall from Chapter 5, every motherboard comes with a small set of code that enables the CPU to communicate properly with the devices built into the motherboard. You can quite readily upgrade this programming by *flashing the BIOS*: running a small command-line program to write a new BIOS in the flash ROM chip. Refer to Chapter 5 for the details on flashing.

NOTE Flashing the BIOS for a motherboard can fix a lot of system stability problems and provide better implementation of built-in technology. What it cannot do for your system is improve the hardware. If AMD comes out with a new, improved, lower-voltage A-Series CPU, for example, and your motherboard cannot scale down the voltage properly, you cannot use that CPU—even if it fits in your motherboard's Socket AM4. No amount of BIOS flashing can change the hardware built into your motherboard.

Finally, if you have an ethereal, ghost-in-the-machine type of problem that you have finally determined to be motherboard related, you have only a couple of options for fixing the problem. You can flash the BIOS in a desperate attempt to correct whatever it is, which sometimes does work and is less expensive than the other option, which is replacing the motherboard.

Chapter Review

Questions

1. Which of the following statements about the expansion bus is true?

   A. The expansion bus runs at the speed of the system clock.

   B. The expansion bus crystal sets the speed for the expansion bus.

   C. The CPU communicates with RAM via the expansion bus.

   D. The frontside bus is another name for the expansion bus.

2. What does a black down arrow next to a device in Device Manager indicate?

   A. A compatible driver has been installed that may not provide all of the functions for the device.

   B. The device is missing, or Windows cannot recognize it.

   C. The system resources have been assigned manually.

   D. The device has been disabled.

3. Which variation of the PCI bus was specifically designed for laptops?

   A. PCI-X

   B. PCIe

   C. Mini-PCI

   D. AGP

4. Which of the following form factors dominates the PC industry?

   A. AT

   B. ATX

   C. ITX

   D. BTX

5. Amanda bought a new system that, right in the middle of an important presentation, gave her a Blue Screen of Death. Now her system won't boot at all, not even to CMOS. After extensive troubleshooting, she determined that the motherboard was at fault and replaced it. Now the system runs fine. What was the most likely cause of the problem?

   A. Burn-in failure

   B. Electrostatic discharge

   C. Component failure

   D. Power supply failure

6. Martin bought a new motherboard to replace his older ATX motherboard. As he left the shop, the tech on duty called after him, "Check your standoffs!" What could the tech have meant?

   A. Standoffs are the connectors on the motherboard for the front panel buttons, such as the on/off switch and reset button.

   B. Standoffs are the metal edges on some cases that aren't rolled.

   C. Standoffs are the metal connectors that attach the motherboard to the case.

   D. Standoffs are the dongles that enable a motherboard to support more than four USB ports.

7. Solon has a very buggy computer that keeps locking up at odd moments and rebooting spontaneously. He suspects the motherboard. How should he test it?

   A. Check settings and verify good components.

   B. Verify good components and document all testing.

   C. Replace the motherboard first to see if the problems disappear.

   D. Check settings, verify good components, replace components, and document all testing.

8. When Jane proudly displayed her new motherboard, the senior tech scratched his beard and asked, "What kind of northbridge does it have?" What could he possibly be asking about?

   A. The PCI slot

   B. The PCIe slot

   C. The chipset

   D. The USB controller

9. What companies dominate the chipset market? (Select ˈo.)

   A. AMD

   B. Intel

   C. NVIDIA

   D. SiS

10. If Windows recognizes a device, where will it appear?

   A. Device Manager

   B. C:\Windows\System32\Devices

   C. Desktop

   D. Safely remove hardware applet

Answers

1. **B.** A separate expansion bus crystal enables the expansion bus to run at a different speed than the frontside bus.

2. **D.** The device has been disabled.

3. **C.** The Mini-PCI format conserved space and power, which made it an ideal card type for use in laptops.

4. **B.** Almost all modern motherboards follow the ATX form factor.

5. **A.** Although all of the answers are plausible, the best answer here is that her system suffered burn-in failure.

6. **C.** Standoffs are the metal connectors that attach the motherboard to the case.

7. **D.** Solon needs to check settings, verify good components, replace components, and document all testing.

8. **C.** The tech is using older terminology to refer to the chips—the chipset—that help the CPU communicate with devices.

9. **A, B.** AMD and Intel produce the vast majority of the chipsets used in personal computers.

10. **A.** Windows displays recognized devices in Device Manager.

Power Supplies

In this chapter, you will learn how to

- Explain the basics of electricity
- Describe the details of powering the PC
- Install and maintain power supplies
- Explain power supply troubleshooting and fire safety

Computers need electricity to run. Where this electricity comes from depends on the device. Mobile devices use batteries (covered in great detail in Chapter 23, "Portable Computing"). Desktop computers need a special box—the *power supply unit* (*PSU*)—that takes electricity from the wall socket and transforms it into electricity your computer can use. Figure 7-1 shows a typical power supply.

Figure 7-1
Power supply about to be mounted inside a system unit

As simple as this appears on the surface, power supply issues are of critical importance for techs. Problems with power can create system instability, crashes, and data loss—all things most computer users would rather avoid! Good techs therefore know an awful lot about powering the PC, from understanding the basic principles of electricity to knowing the many variations of PC power supplies. Plus, you need to know how to recognize power problems and implement the proper solutions. Too many techs fall into the "just plug it in" camp and never learn how to deal with power, much to their clients' unhappiness.

EXAM TIP Some questions on the CompTIA A+ 220-1001 certification exam refer to a power supply as a *PSU*, for *power supply unit*. A power supply also falls into the category of *field replaceable unit* (*FRU*), which refers to the typical parts a tech should carry, such as RAM and a hard drive.

Historical/Conceptual

Understanding Electricity

Electricity is a flow of negatively charged particles, called electrons, through matter. All matter enables the flow of electrons to some extent. This flow of electrons is very similar to the flow of water through pipes; so similar that the best way to learn about electricity is by comparing it to how water flows through pipes. So let's talk about water for a moment.

Water comes from the ground, through wells, aquifers, rivers, and so forth. In a typical city, water comes to you through pipes from the water supply company that took it from the ground. What do you pay for when you pay your water bill each month? You pay for the water you use, certainly, but built into the price of the water you use is the surety that when you turn the spigot, water will flow at a more or less constant rate. The water sits in the pipes under pressure from the water company, waiting for you to turn the spigot.

Electricity works essentially the same way as water. Electric companies gather or generate electricity and then push it to your house under pressure through wires. Just like water, the electricity sits in the wires, waiting for you to plug something into the wall socket, at which time it'll flow at a more or less constant rate. You plug a lamp into an electrical outlet and flip the switch, electricity flows, and you have light. You pay for reliability, electrical pressure, and electricity used.

The pressure of the electrons in the wire is called *voltage* and is measured in units called *volts* (*V*). See Figure 7-2.

Figure 7-2
Electrical voltage
as water pressure

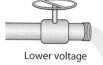

Lower voltage

Higher voltage

The amount of electrons moving past a certain point on a wire is called the *current* (or *amperage*), which is measured in units called *amperes* (*amps* or *A*). See Figure 7-3.

Figure 7-3
Electrical
amperage as
amount of water
flowing

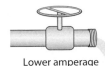

Lower amperage   Higher amperage

The amps and volts needed so that a particular device will function is expressed as how much *wattage* (*watts* or *W*) that device needs. The correlation between the three is very simple math: V × A = W. You'll learn more about wattage a little later in this chapter.

Wires of all sorts—whether copper, tin, gold, or platinum—have a slight *resistance* to the flow of electrons, just as water pipes have a slight amount of friction that resists the flow of water. Resistance to the flow of electrons is measured in *ohms* (Ω).

- Pressure = voltage (V)
- Volume flowing = amperes (A)
- Work = wattage (W)
- Resistance = ohms (Ω)

A particular thickness of wire only handles so much current at a time. If you push too much through, the wire will overheat and break, much as an overloaded water pipe will burst. To make sure you use the right wire for the right job, all electrical wires have an amperage rating, such as 20 amps. If you try to push 30 amps through a 20-amp wire, the wire will break, and electrons will seek a way to return into the ground. Not a good thing, especially if the path back to ground is through you!

Circuit breakers and ground wires provide the basic protection from accidental overflow. A circuit breaker is a heat-sensitive or electromagnetically operated electrical switch rated for a specified amperage. If you push too much amperage through the circuit breaker, the wiring inside detects the increase in heat or current and automatically opens, stopping the flow of electricity before the wiring overheats and breaks. You reset the circuit breaker to reestablish the circuit, and electricity flows once more through the wires. A ground wire provides a path of least resistance for electrons to flow back to ground in case of an accidental overflow.

Many years ago, your home and building electrical supply used fuses instead of circuit breakers. Fuses are small devices with a tiny filament designed to break if subjected to too much current. Unfortunately, fuses had to be replaced every time they blew, making circuit breakers much more convenient. Even though you no longer see fuses in a building's electrical circuits, many electrical devices—such as a PC's power supply—often still use fuses for their own internal protection. Once blown, these fuses are not replaceable by users or technicians without special training and tools.

EXAM TIP An electrical outlet must have a ground wire to be suitable for PC use.

Electricity comes in two flavors: *direct current* (*DC*), in which the electrons flow in one direction around a continuous circuit, and *alternating current* (*AC*), in which the flow of electrons alternates direction back and forth in a circuit (see Figure 7-4). Most electronic devices use DC power, but all power companies supply AC power because AC travels long distances much more efficiently than DC.

Figure 7-4
Diagrams
showing DC and
AC flow

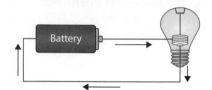

Direct current (DC)
• Constant power in one direction
• Best for electronics

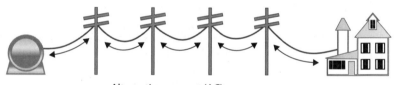

Alternating current (AC)
• Power alternates back and forth
• Best for long distance

1001

Powering the PC

Your PC uses DC voltage, so some conversion process must take place before the PC can use AC power from the power company. The power supply in a computer converts high-voltage AC power from the wall socket to low-voltage DC. The first step in powering the PC, therefore, is to get and maintain a good supply of AC power. Second, you need a power supply to convert AC to the proper voltage and amperage of DC power for the motherboard and peripherals. Finally, you need to control the byproduct of electricity use—namely, heat. Let's look at the specifics of powering the PC.

Supplying AC

Every PC power supply must have standard AC power from the power company, supplied steadily rather than in fits and spurts, and protection against accidental blurps in the supply. The power supply connects to the power cord (and thus to an electrical outlet) via a standard *IEC-320* connector. In the United States, standard AC comes in somewhere between 110 and 120 V, often written as ~115 VAC (volts of alternating current). Most of the rest of the world uses 220–240 VAC, so power supplies are available with *dual-voltage options*, making them compatible with either standard. Power supplies with voltage-selection switches are referred to as fixed-input. Power supplies that you do not have to manually switch for different voltages are known as auto-switching. Figure 7-5 shows the back of a power supply. Note the three components, from top to bottom: the hard on/off switch, the 115/230 switch, and the IEC-320 connector.

Figure 7-5
Back of fixed-input power supply, showing typical switches and power connection

Although the higher voltage differs among the many countries that use it, the CompTIA A+ 1001 exam objectives refer to it only as *220V*, not the range (220–240 VAC) that this chapter uses. That's what they mean, though.

 CAUTION Flipping the voltage-selection switch on the back of a power supply can wreak all kinds of havoc on a PC. Moving the switch to ~230 V in the United States makes for a great practical joke (as long as the PC is off when you do it)—the PC might try to boot up but probably won't get far. You don't risk damaging anything by running at half the AC the power supply is expecting. In countries that run ~230 standard, on the other hand, firing up the PC with this switch set to ~115 can cause the power supply to die a horrid, smoking death. Watch that switch!

Before plugging any critical components into an AC outlet, take a moment to test the outlet first by using a multimeter or a device designed exclusively to test outlets. Failure to test AC outlets properly can result in inoperable or destroyed equipment, as well as possible electrocution. The IEC-320 plug has three holes, called hot, neutral, and ground. These names describe the function of the wires that connect to them behind the wall plate. The hot wire carries electrical voltage, much like a pipe that delivers water. The neutral wire carries no voltage, but instead acts like a water drain, completing the circuit by returning electricity to the local source, normally a breaker panel. The ground wire makes it possible for excess electricity to return safely to the ground, such as in a short-circuit condition.

When testing AC power, you want to check for three things: that the hot outputs approximately 115 V (or whatever the proper voltage is for your part of the world), that the neutral connects to ground (0 V output), and that the ground connects to ground (again, 0 V). Figure 7-6 shows the voltages at an outlet. You can use a *multimeter*—often also referred to as a *volt-ohm meter* (*VOM*) or *digital multimeter* (*DMM*)—to measure a number of aspects of electrical current. A multimeter consists of two probes, an analog or digital meter, and a dial to set the type of test you want to perform. Refer to Figure 7-7 to become familiar with the components of the multimeter.

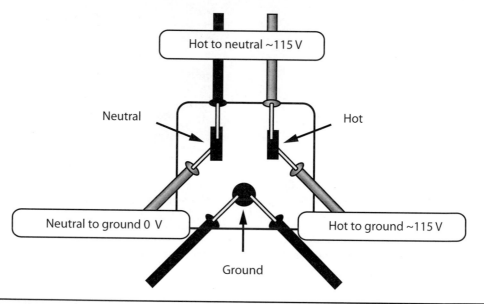

Figure 7-6   Outlet voltages

Note that some multimeters use symbols rather than letters to describe AC and DC settings. For example, the *V* with the solid line above a dashed line in Figure 7-8 refers to direct current. The *V~* stands for alternating current.

Figure 7-7
Author's ancient but reliable digital multimeter

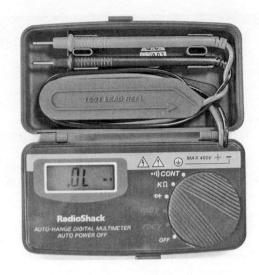

Most multimeters offer at least four types of electrical tests: continuity, resistance, AC voltage (VAC), and DC voltage (VDC). Continuity tests whether electrons can flow from one end of a wire to the other end. If so, you have continuity; if not, you don't. You can use this setting to determine if a fuse is good or to check for breaks in wires. If your multimeter doesn't have a continuity tester (many cheaper multimeters do not), you can use the resistance tester. A broken wire or fuse will show infinite resistance, while a good wire or fuse will show no resistance. Testing AC and DC voltages is a matter of making sure the measured voltage is what it should be.

Figure 7-8
Multimeter featuring DC and AC symbols

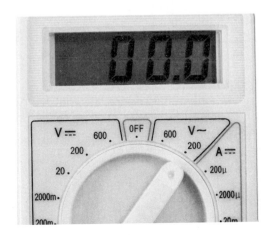

Try This!   Using a Multimeter to Test AC Outlets

Every competent technician knows how to use a multimeter, so if you haven't used one in the past, get hold of one and work through this scenario. Your boss tasks you with checking the existing electrical outlets in a new satellite location for the company. Caution: During this exercise, do *not* physically touch any of the metal parts of the probes or sockets!

First you need to set up the meter for measuring AC. Follow these steps:

1. Move the selector switch to the AC V (usually red). If multiple settings are available, put it into the first scale higher than 120 V (usually 200 V). *Autorange* meters set their own range; they don't need any selection except AC V.

2. Place the black lead in the common (–) hole. If the black lead is permanently attached, ignore this step.

3. Place the red lead in the V-Ohm-A (+) hole. If the red lead is permanently attached, ignore this step.

Once you have the meter set up for AC, go through the process of testing the various wires on an AC socket. Just don't put your fingers on the metal parts of the leads when you stick them into the socket! Follow these steps:

1. Put either lead in hot, the other in neutral. You should read 110 to 120 V AC.

2. Put either lead in hot, the other in ground. You should read 110 to 120 V AC.

3. Put either lead in neutral, the other in ground. You should read 0 V AC.

If any of these readings is different from what is described here, it's time to call an electrician.

Using Special Equipment to Test AC Voltage

A number of good AC-only testing devices are available. With these devices, you can test all voltages for an AC outlet by simply inserting them into the outlet. Be sure to test all of the outlets the computer system uses: power supply, external devices, and monitor. Although convenient, these devices aren't as accurate as a multimeter. My favorite tester is a seemingly simple tool available from a number of manufacturers (see Figure 7-9). This handy device provides three light-emitting diodes (LEDs) that describe everything that can go wrong with a plug.

AC Adapters

Many computing devices use an AC adapter rather than an internal power supply. Even though it sits outside a device, an AC adapter converts AC current to DC, just like a

Figure 7-9
Circuit tester

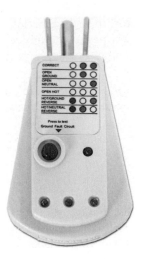

power supply. Unlike internal power supplies, AC adapters are rarely interchangeable. Although manufacturers of different devices often use the same kind of plug on the end of the AC adapter cable, these adapters are not necessarily interchangeable. In other words, just because you can plug an AC adapter from your friend's laptop into your laptop does not mean it's going to work.

You need to make sure that three things match before you plug an AC adapter into a device: voltage, amperage, and polarity. If either the voltage or amperage output is too low, the device won't run. If the polarity is reversed, it won't work, just like putting a battery in a flashlight backward. If either the voltage or amperage— especially the former—is too high, on the other hand, you can very quickly toast your device. Don't do it! Always check the voltage, amperage, and polarity of a replacement AC adapter before you plug it into a device.

1002

Equipment Grounding

Computer equipment safety starts with proper grounding. The ground wire functions as an emergency outlet for excess current in case of any short or malfunction of a device. Don't assume that a convenient three-prong outlet has proper grounding, especially in older buildings. Use a multimeter to check that ground wire.

Protecting the PC from Spikes and Sags in AC Power

If all power companies could supply electricity in smooth, continuous flows with no dips or spikes in pressure, the next two sections of this chapter would be irrelevant. Unfortunately, no matter how clean the AC supply appears to a multimeter, the truth is that voltage from the power company tends to drop well below (sag) and shoot far above (surge or spike) the standard 115 V (in the United States). These sags and spikes usually don't affect lamps and refrigerators in such scenarios, but they can keep your PC from running or can even destroy a PC or peripheral device. Two essential devices handle spikes and sags in the supply of AC: surge suppressors and uninterruptible power supplies.

 EXAM TIP Large sags in electricity are also known as *brownouts*. When the power cuts out completely, it's called a *blackout*.

Surge Suppressors Surges or spikes are far more dangerous than sags. Even a strong sag only shuts off or reboots your PC; any surge can harm your computer, and a strong surge destroys components. Given the seriousness of surges, every PC should use a *surge suppressor* device that absorbs the extra voltage from a surge to protect the PC. The power supply does a good job of surge suppression and can handle many of the smaller surges that take place fairly often. But the power supply takes a lot of damage from this and will eventually fail. To protect your power supply, a dedicated surge suppressor works between the power supply and the outlet to protect the system from power surges (see Figure 7-10).

Figure 7-10
Surge suppressor

Most people tend to spend a lot of money on their PC and for some reason suddenly get cheap on the surge suppressor. Don't do that! Make sure your surge suppressor has the Underwriters Laboratories UL 1449 for 330-V rating to ensure substantial protection for your system. Underwriters Laboratories (www.ul.com) is a U.S.-based, not-for-profit, widely recognized industry testing laboratory whose testing standards are very important to the consumer electronics industry. Additionally, check the joules rating before buying a new surge suppressor. A *joule* is a unit of electrical energy. How much energy a surge suppressor can handle before it fails is described in joules. Most authorities agree that your surge suppressor should rate at a minimum of 2000 joules—and the more joules, the better the protection. My surge suppressor rates at 3500 joules.

While you're protecting your system, don't forget that surges also come from telephone and cable connections. If you use a modem, DSL, or cable modem, make sure to get a surge suppressor that includes support for these types of connections. Many manufacturers make surge suppressors with telephone line protection (see Figure 7-11).

 CAUTION No surge suppressor in the world can handle the ultimate surge, the electrical discharge of a lightning strike. If your electrical system takes such a hit, you can kiss your PC and any other electronic devices goodbye if they were plugged in at the time. Always unplug electronics during electrical storms!

Figure 7-11

Surge suppressor with cable and telephone line protection

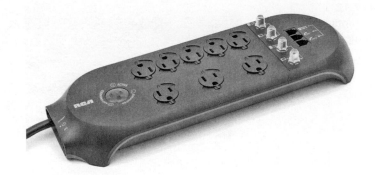

No surge suppressor works forever. Make sure your surge suppressor has a test/reset button so you'll know when the device has—as we say in the business—turned into an extension cord. If your system takes a hit and you have a surge suppressor, call the company! Many companies provide cash guarantees against system failure due to surges, but only if you follow their guidelines.

NOTE Surge suppression isn't just about joules. Surge suppressors are also rated in clamping voltage, in which an overvoltage condition is "clamped" to a more manageable voltage for a certain amount of time. Good consumer suppressors can clamp 600 volts down to 180 volts or less for at least 50 microseconds and can do so on either the hot line or neutral line.

If you want really great surge suppression, you need to move up to *power conditioning*. Your power lines take in all kinds of strange signals that have no business being in there, such as electromagnetic interference (EMI) and radio frequency interference (RFI). Most of the time, this line noise is so minimal it's not worth addressing, but occasionally events (such as lightning) generate enough line noise to cause weird things to happen to your PC (keyboard lockups, messed-up data). All better surge suppressors add power conditioning to filter out EMI and RFI.

UPS An *uninterruptible power supply* (*UPS*) protects your computer (and, more importantly, your data) in the event of a power sag or power outage. Figure 7-12 shows a typical UPS. A UPS essentially contains a big battery that provides AC power to your computer regardless of the power coming from the AC outlet.

All uninterruptible power supplies are measured in both watts (the true amount of power they supply in the event of a power outage) and in *volt-amps* (*VA*). Volt-amps is the amount of power the UPS could supply if the devices took power from the UPS in a perfect way. Your UPS provides perfect AC power, moving current smoothly back and forth 60 times a second (or 50 in other parts of the world). Power supplies, monitors, and other devices, however, may not take all of the power the UPS has to offer at every point as the AC power moves back and forth, resulting in inefficiencies. If your devices took all of the power the UPS offered at every point as the power moved back and forth, VA would equal watts.

Figure 7-12
Uninterruptible
power supply

EXAM TIP   You'll want to be familiar with the technology and use of surge suppressors and battery backup systems (UPSs) for the CompTIA A+ 220-1002 exam.

If the UPS makers knew ahead of time exactly what devices you planned to plug into their UPS, they could tell you the exact watts, but different devices have different efficiencies, forcing the UPS makers to go by what they can offer (VAs), not what your devices will take (watts). The watts value they give is a guess, and it's never as high as the VAs. The VA rating is always higher than the watt rating.

Because you have no way to calculate the exact efficiency of every device you'll plug into the UPS, go with the wattage rating. You add up the total wattage of every component in your PC and buy a UPS with a higher wattage. You'll spend a lot of time and mental energy figuring precisely how much wattage your computer, monitor, drives, and so on require to get the proper UPS for your system. But you're still not finished! Remember that the UPS is a battery with a limited amount of power, so you then need to figure out how long you want the UPS to run when you lose power.

NOTE   There are two main types of UPS: online, where devices are constantly powered through the UPS's battery, and standby, where devices connected to the UPS receive battery power only when the AC sags below ~80–90 V. Another type of UPS is called line-interactive, which is similar to a standby UPS but has special circuitry to handle moderate AC sags and surges without the need to switch to battery power.

The quicker and far better method to use for determining the UPS you need is to go to any of the major surge suppressor/UPS makers' Web sites and use their handy power calculators. My personal favorite is on the APC by Schneider Electric (formerly known as American Power Conversion Corporation) Web site: www.apc.com (type **UPS selector** in the search field). APC makes great surge suppressors and UPSs, and the company's online calculator will show you the true wattage you need—and teach you about whatever new thing is happening in power at the same time.

Try This!   Shopping for a UPS

When it comes to getting a UPS for yourself or a client, nothing quite cuts through the hype and marketing terms like a trip to the local computer store to see for yourself. You need excuses to go to the computer store, so here's a valid one for you.

1. Go to your local computer store—or visit an online computer site if no stores are nearby—and find out what's available.

2. Answer this question: How can you tell the difference between an online UPS and a standby UPS?

Every UPS also has surge suppression and power conditioning, so look for the joule and UL 1449 ratings. Also look for replacement battery costs—some UPS replacement batteries are very expensive. Last, look for a UPS with a USB or Ethernet (RJ-45) connection. These handy UPSs come with monitoring and maintenance software (see Figure 7-13) that tells you the status of your system and the amount of battery power available, logs power events, and provides other handy options.

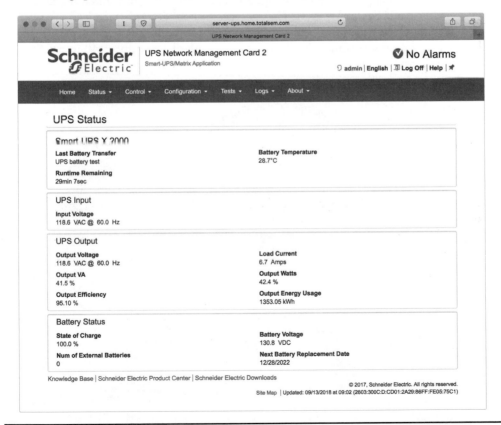

Figure 7-13   UPS management application

Table 7-1 gives you a quick look at the low end and the very high end of UPS products.

Brand	Model	Outlets Protected	Backup Time	Price	Type
APC	BE425M	3 @ 120 V	3 min @ 200 W, 10 min @ 100 W	$49.99	Standby
APC	Pro BR 1000MS	4 @ 120 V	4 min @ 600 W, 64 min @ 100 W	$184.99	Standby
CyberPower	CPS1500AVR	6 @ 120 V	18 min @ 950 W, 6 min @ 475 W	$379.99	Line-interactive

Table 7-1 Typical UPS Devices

1001

Supplying DC

After you've ensured the supply of good AC electricity for the PC, the power supply unit takes over, converting public utility voltage AC (115/120 V in the United States, 230 V in many other countries) into several DC voltages (notably, 3.3, 5.0, and 12.0 V) usable by the delicate interior components. Power supplies come in a large number of shapes and sizes, but the most common size by far is the standard 150 mm × 140 mm × 86 mm desktop PSU shown in Figure 7-14.

Figure 7-14
Desktop PSU

EXAM TIP   The CompTIA A+ objectives list "Output 5.5V vs. 12V." I'm pretty sure it's a typo because power supplies offer 3.3-, 5-, and 12-VDC. Assume the "5.5V" means power to the electronics.

The PC uses the 12-V current to power motors on devices such as hard drives and optical drives, and it uses the 3.3- and 5-V current for support of onboard electronics. Manufacturers may use these voltages any way they wish, however, and may deviate from these assumptions. Power supplies also come with standard connectors for the motherboard and interior devices.

Power to the Motherboard

Modern motherboards use a 20- or 24-pin *P1 power connector*. Some motherboards may require special 4-, 6-, or 8-pin connectors to supply extra power (see Figure 7-15). We'll talk about each of these connectors in the form factor standards discussion later in this chapter.

Figure 7-15
Motherboard
power
connectors

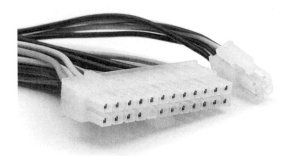

Power to Peripherals: Molex, Mini, and SATA

Many devices inside the PC require power. These include hard drives, solid-state drives, optical drives, and fans. The typical PC power supply has at least three types of connectors that plug into peripherals: Molex, mini, and SATA. (Higher-end video cards get their own connector(s) as well, covered a little later in this chapter.)

Molex Connectors   The *Molex connector* supplies 5-V and 12-V current for fans and older drives (see Figure 7-16). The Molex connector has notches, called *chamfers*, that guide its installation. The tricky part is that Molex connectors require a firm push to plug in properly, and a strong person can defeat the chamfers, plugging a Molex in upside down. Not a good thing. *Always* check for proper orientation before you push it in!

Mini Connectors   A few power supplies still support the *mini connector* or *Berg connector* (see Figure 7-17). The mini supplies 5 V and 12 V to peripherals. Originally adopted as the standard connector on 3.5-inch floppy disk drives, you'll still see the occasional device needing this connector.

Figure 7-16
Molex connector

Figure 7-17
Mini connector

Try This!   Testing DC

A common practice for techs troubleshooting a system is to test the DC voltages coming out of the power supply. Even with good AC, a bad power supply can fail to transform AC to DC at voltages needed by the motherboard and peripherals. The best way to learn how to perform this common technique is to try it yourself, so grab your trusty multimeter and walk through the following steps on a powered-up PC with the side cover removed. Note that you must have P1 connected to the motherboard and the system must be running (you don't have to be in Windows or Linux, of course).

1. Switch your multimeter to DC, somewhere around 20 V DC if you need to make that choice. Make sure your leads are plugged into the multimeter properly: red to hot, black to ground. The key to testing DC is that which lead you touch to which wire matters. Red goes to hot wires of all colors; black *always* goes to ground.

2. Plug the red lead into the red wire socket of a free Molex connector and plug the black lead into one of the two black wire sockets. You should get a reading of ~5 V. What do you have?

3. Now move the red lead to the yellow socket. What voltage do you get?

4. Testing the P1 connector is a little more complicated. You push the red and black leads into the top of P1, sliding in alongside the wires until you bottom out. Leave the black lead in one of the black wire ground sockets. Move the red lead through all of the colored wire sockets. What voltages do you find?

CAUTION As with any power connector, plugging a mini connector into a device the wrong way will almost certainly destroy the device. Check twice before you plug one in!

SATA Power Connectors Serial ATA (SATA) drives need a 15-pin *SATA power connector* (see Figure 7-18). The larger pin count supports the SATA hot-swappable feature and 3.3-, 5-, and 12-V devices. The 3.3-V pins are not used in any current iteration of SATA drives and are reserved for possible future use. All three generations of SATA use the same power connectors. SATA power connectors are L shaped, making it almost impossible to insert one incorrectly into a SATA drive. No other device on a computer uses the SATA power connector. For more information about SATA drives, see Chapter 8, "Mass Storage Technologies."

Figure 7-18
SATA power
connector

Splitters and Adapters You may occasionally find yourself without enough connectors to power all of the devices inside your PC. In this case, you can purchase splitters to create more connections (see Figure 7-19). You might also run into the phenomenon of

Figure 7-19
Molex splitter

needing a SATA connector but having only a spare Molex. Because the voltages on the wires are the same, a simple adapter will take care of the problem nicely.

ATX

The original ATX power supplies had two distinguishing physical features: the motherboard power connector and soft power. Motherboard power came from a single cable with a 20-pin P1 motherboard power connector. ATX power supplies also had at least two other cables, each populated with two or more Molex or mini connectors for peripheral power.

When plugged in, ATX systems have 5 V running to the motherboard. They're always "on," even when powered down. The power switch you press to power up the PC isn't a true power switch like the light switch on the wall in your bedroom. The power switch on an ATX system simply tells the computer whether it has been pressed. The BIOS or operating system takes over from there and handles the chore of turning the PC on or off. This is called *soft power*.

Using soft power instead of a physical switch has a number of important benefits. Soft power prevents a user from turning off a system before the operating system has been shut down. It enables the PC to use power-saving modes that put the system to sleep and then wake it up when you press a key, move a mouse, or receive an e-mail (or other network traffic). (See Chapter 23, "Portable Computing," for more details on sleep mode.)

All of the most important settings for ATX soft power reside in CMOS setup. Boot into CMOS and look for a Power Management section. Take a look at the Power Button Function option in Figure 7-20. This determines the function of the on/off switch. You may set this switch to turn off the computer, or you may set it to the more common *4-second delay*.

Figure 7-20
Soft power
setting in CMOS

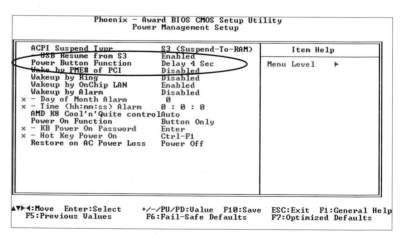

ATX did a great job supplying power for more than a decade, but over time more powerful CPUs, multiple CPUs, video cards, and other components began to need more current than the original ATX provided. This motivated the industry to introduce a number of updates to the ATX power standards: ATX12V 1.3, EPS12V, multiple rails, ATX12V 2.0, other form factors, and active PFC.

ATX12V 1.3 The first widespread update to the ATX standard, ATX12V 1.3, came out in 2003. This introduced a 4-pin motherboard power connector, unofficially but commonly called the *P4 power connector*, that provides more 12-V power to assist the 20/24-pin P1 motherboard power connector. Any power supply that provides a P4 connector is called an ATX12V power supply. The term "ATX" was dropped from the ATX power standard, so if you want to get really nerdy you can say—accurately—that there's no such thing as an ATX power supply. All power supplies—assuming they have a P4 connector—are ATX12V or one of the later standards.

EXAM TIP SATA also supports a slimline connector that has a 6-pin power segment and a micro connector that has a 9-pin power segment.

The ATX12V 1.3 standard also introduced a 6-pin auxiliary connector—commonly called an *AUX* connector—to supply increased 3.3- and 5-V current to the motherboard (see Figure 7-21). This connector was based on the motherboard power connector from the precursor of ATX, called *AT*.

Figure 7-21
Auxiliary power
connector

The introduction of these two extra power connectors caused the industry some teething problems. In particular, motherboards using AMD CPUs tended to need the AUX connector, while motherboards using Intel CPUs needed only the P4. As a result, many power supplies came with only a P4 or only an AUX connector to save money. The biggest problem with the ATX12V standard was the lack of enforcement—it made a lot of recommendations but few requirements, giving PSU makers too much choice (such as choosing or not choosing to add AUX and P4 connectors) that weren't fixed until later versions.

EPS12V Server motherboards are thirsty for power, and sometimes ATX12V 1.3 just didn't cut it. An industry group called the Server System Infrastructure (SSI) developed a non-ATX standard motherboard and power supply called EPS12V. An EPS12V power supply came with a 24-pin main motherboard power connector that resembled a 20-pin ATX connector, but it offered more current and thus more stability for motherboards. It also came with an AUX connector, an ATX12V P4 connector, and a unique

8-pin connector. That's a lot of connectors! EPS12V power supplies were not interchangeable with ATX12V power supplies.

EPS12V may not have seen much life beyond servers, but it introduced a number of power features, some of which eventually became part of the ATX12V standard. The most important issue was something called *rails*.

Rails   Generally, all of the PC's power comes from a single transformer that takes the AC current from a wall socket and converts it into DC current that is split into three primary DC voltage rails: 12 V, 5 V, and 3.3 V. Groups of wires run from each of these voltage rails to the various connectors.

Each rail has a maximum amount of power it can supply. Normal computer use rarely approaches this ceiling, but powerful computers with advanced processors and graphics cards require more power than some rails can provide. In the past, 12-V rails only supplied about 18 amps, which wasn't enough to power all that high-end equipment.

The most popular solution was to include multiple 12-V rails in the power supply. This worked fine, but you needed to make sure that you weren't drawing all of your power from the same 12-V rail. The key circuitry that monitors the amount of amperage going through each rail, called the over-current protection (OCP), will shut down the power supply if the current goes beyond its cap. In a *single-rail system*, a single OCP circuit monitors all the pathways. In a *multi-rail system*, each pathway gets its own OCP circuit.

When first implemented, multi-rail power supplies didn't do a great job balancing the circuitry, so enthusiasts still ran into problems with systems shutting down under heavy load. This has been fixed since 2008 or so, so any multi-rail PSU you buy today can handle whatever you throw at it.

Today's power supply manufacturers produce single- and multi-rail, high-amperage PSUs. You can find power supplies now with 12-V rails pushing 70 amps or more!

ATX12V 2.0   The ATX12V 2.0 standard incorporated many of the good ideas of EPS12V, starting with the 24-pin connector. This 24-pin motherboard power connector is backward compatible with the older 20-pin connector, so users don't have to buy a new motherboard if they use an ATX12V 2.0 power supply. ATX12V 2.0 requires two 12-V rails for any power supply rated higher than 230 W. ATX12V 2.0 dropped the AUX connector and requires SATA hard drive connectors.

Many ATX12V 2.0 power supplies have a convertible *24-to-20-pin motherboard adapter*. These are handy if you want to make a nice "clean" connection, because many 20-pin connectors have interfaces that prevent plugging in a 24-pin connector. You'll also see many 24-pin connectors constructed in such a way that you can slide off the extra four pins. Figure 7-22 shows 20-pin and 24-pin connectors; Figure 7-23 shows a convertible adapter. Although they look similar, those extra four pins won't replace the P4 connector. They are incompatible!

Many modern ATX motherboards feature an 8-pin CPU power connector like the one found in the EPS12V standard to help support high-end CPUs that demand a lot of power. This connector is referred to by several names, including EPS12V, EATX12V, and ATX12V 2x4. One half of this connector will be pin compatible with the P4 power

Figure 7-22
20- and 24-pin
connectors

Figure 7-23
Convertible
motherboard
power connector

connector, and the other half may be under a protective cap. Be sure to check the motherboard installation manuals for recommendations on when to use the full 8 pins. For backward compatibility, some power supplies provide an 8-pin power connector that can split into two 4-pin sets, one of which is the P4 connector.

Another notable connector is the auxiliary PCI Express (PCIe) power connector. Figure 7-24 shows the 6-pin PCIe power connector. Some motherboards add a Molex socket for PCIe, and some cards come with a Molex socket as well. Higher-end video cards have one or two sockets that require specific *6-pin or 8-pin PCIe power connectors*. The 8-pin PCIe connector should not be confused with the EPS12V connector, as they are not compatible. Some PCIe devices with the 8-pin connector will accept a 6-pin PCIe power connection instead, but this may put limits on their performance. Often you'll find that 8-pin PCIe power cables have two pins at the end that you can detach for easy compatibility with 6-pin devices.

Figure 7-24
PCI Express 6-pin
power connector

 SIM Check out the Chapter 7 Challenge! sim, "ID PSU Connector," over at http://totalsem.com/100x. It'll help you identify and memorize the standard power supply connectors.

Niche-Market Power Supply Form Factors The demand for smaller and quieter PCs led to the development of a number of niche-market power supply form factors. All use standard ATX connectors but differ in size and shape from standard ATX power supplies.

Here are some of the more common specialty power supply types:

- **Mini-ITX** and **microATX** Smaller power supply form factors designed specifically for mini-ITX and microATX cases, respectively

- **TFX12V** A small power supply form factor optimized for low-profile ATX systems

- **SFX12V** A small power supply form factor optimized for systems using FlexATX motherboards (see Figure 7-25)

 NOTE You'll commonly find niche-market power supplies bundled with computer cases (and often motherboards as well). These form factors are rarely sold alone.

Active PFC Visualize the AC current coming from the power company as water in a pipe, smoothly moving back and forth, 50 or 60 times each second. A PC's power supply, simply due to the process of changing this AC current into DC current, is like a

Figure 7-25

SFX power
supply

person sucking on a straw on the end of this pipe. It takes gulps only when the current is fully pushing or pulling at the top and bottom of each cycle and creating an electrical phenomena—sort of a back pressure—that's called *harmonics* in the power industry. These harmonics create the humming sound you hear from electrical components. Over time, harmonics damage electrical equipment, causing serious problems with the power supply and other electrical devices on the circuit. Once you put a few thousand PCs with power supplies in the same local area, harmonics can even damage the electrical power supplier's equipment!

Good PC power supplies come with *active power factor correction* (*active PFC*), extra circuitry that smooths out power coming from the wall before passing it to the main power supply circuits. This smoothing process eliminates any harmonics (see Figure 7-26). Never buy a power supply that does not have active PFC—all power supplies with active PFC will announce it on the box.

Wattage Requirements

Every device in a PC requires a certain wattage to function. A typical hard drive draws about 15 W of power when accessed, for example, whereas a quad-core Intel i7-4790K draws a whopping 151 W at peak usage. The total wattage of all devices combined is the minimum you need the power supply to provide.

When selecting a power supply for a system, in other words, make sure the power supply provides enough wattage to run the number of devices in the system. Also, the power supply needs to be able to support all the *types* of devices to be powered in the system. I updated the video card in a system the other day, for example, from a card that required a single 6-wire power cable to one that required two 8-wire power cables (see Figure 7-27). The power supply clearly had to have the latter capability.

If the power supply cannot produce the wattage a system needs, that PC won't work properly or at all. Because most devices in the PC require maximum wattage when first starting, the most common result of insufficient wattage is a paperweight that looks like

Figure 7-26
Power supply
advertising
active PFC

Figure 7-26 Power supply advertising active PFC

a PC. This can lead to some embarrassing moments. You might plug in a new hard drive for a client, push the power button on the case, and nothing happens—a dead PC! Eek! You can quickly determine if insufficient wattage is the problem. Unplug the drive and power up the system. If the system boots up, the power supply is a likely suspect. The only fix for this problem is to replace the power supply with one that provides more wattage (or leave the new drive out—a less-than-ideal solution).

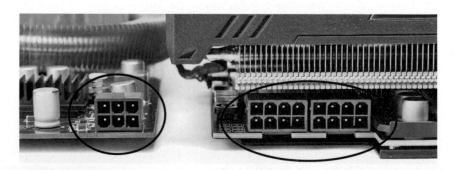

Figure 7-27   Big jump in power requirements!

NOTE An undersized power supply may not necessarily result in a complete paperweight. Some graphics cards that are dependent on additional rail power from a PSU may continue to operate but will do so at reduced frame rates. That means your games won't play well, but the computer will function in other capacities. See Chapter 17, "Display Technologies," for the scoop on power-hungry video cards.

No power supply can turn 100 percent of the AC power coming from the power company into DC current, so all power supplies provide less power to the system than the wattage that they draw from the wall. The difference is lost in heat generation. The amount of this differential is advertised on the box. ATX12V 2.0 standards require a power supply to be at least 70 percent efficient, but many power supplies operate with better than 80 percent efficiency.

Power supplies are typically graded for their efficiency under a voluntary standards program called *80 Plus*. Under 80 Plus, power supplies are rated from 80 percent to 94 percent efficiency for a given load and badged with "metal labels" such as Bronze (85 percent), Gold (90 percent), or Titanium (94 percent) levels. These levels are achieved within a narrow range of watts provided, while lower levels of efficiency are achieved at higher and lower power draw. Power and efficiency curves are usually provided in the power supply documentation. More efficiency can tell you how many watts the system draws to supply sufficient power to the PC in actual use. The added efficiency means the power supply wastes less power, saving you money.

EXAM TIP The CompTIA A+ 1001 exam does not require you to figure precise wattage needs for a particular system. When building a PC for a client, however, you do need to know this stuff!

One common argument these days is that people buy power supplies that provide far more wattage than a system needs and therefore waste power. This is untrue. A power supply provides only the amount of power your system needs. If you put a 1500-W power supply into a system that needs only 250 W, that big power supply will put out only 250 W to the system. So buying an efficient, higher-wattage power supply gives you two benefits. First, running a power supply at less than 100 percent load helps it live longer. Second, you'll have plenty of extra power when adding new components.

Don't cut the specifications too tightly for power supplies. All power supplies produce less wattage over time, simply because of wear and tear on the internal components. If you build a system that runs with only a few watts of extra power available from the power supply initially, that system will most likely start causing problems within a year or less. Do yourself or your clients a favor and get a power supply that has more wattage than you need.

As a general recommendation for a new system, use at least a 500-W power supply. This is a common wattage and gives you plenty of extra power for booting as well as for whatever other components you might add to the system in the future.

> **Try This!   Calculating Power Needs**
>
> The Internet has some great tools to help you determine power needs for specific computer systems. As noted earlier in the chapter, I recently upgraded from a decent video card to a high-end gaming card (and added another solid-state drive for more storage), and needed to determine whether I needed to upgrade the power supply for a stable system. You will find yourself in similar situations as a tech, so try this!
>
> Open a Web browser and check out the OuterVision Power Supply Calculator here:
>
> https://outervision.com/power-supply-calculator
>
> Put in the details on your desired systems and let their amazing tool do the math for you. Note the calculator puts in efficiency information and even makes a recommended purchase for you (and not from OuterVision). It's a very slick, very convenient tool. Bookmark it!

Installing and Maintaining Power Supplies

Although installing and maintaining power supplies takes a little less math than selecting the proper power supply for a system, they remain essential skills for any tech. Installing takes but a moment, and maintaining is almost as simple. Let's take a look.

Installing

The typical power supply connects to the PC with four standard computer screws, mounted in the back of the case (see Figure 7-28). Unscrew the four screws and the power supply lifts out easily (see Figure 7-29). Insert a new power supply that fits the case and attach it by using the same four screws.

Handling ATX power supplies requires special consideration. Understand that an ATX power supply *never turns off.* As long as that power supply stays connected to a power outlet, the power supply will continue to supply 5 V to the motherboard. Always unplug an ATX system before you do any work! For years, techs bickered about the merits of leaving a PC plugged in or unplugged when servicing it. ATX settled this issue forever. Many ATX power supplies provide a real on/off switch on the back of the PSU (see Figure 7-30). If you really need the system shut down with no power to the motherboard, use this switch.

When working on an ATX system, you may find using the power button inconvenient because you're not using a case or you haven't bothered to plug the power button's leads into the motherboard. That means there is no power button. One trick when in that situation is to use a metal key or a screwdriver to contact the two wires to start and stop the system (see Figure 7-31).

Figure 7-28
Mounting screws
for power supply

Figure 7-29
Removing power
supply from
system unit

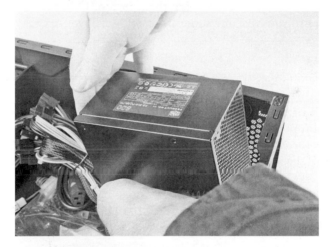

Figure 7-30
On/off switch for
an ATX system

Figure 7-31
Shorting the soft
on/off jumpers

Your first task after acquiring a new power supply is simply making sure it works. Insert the motherboard power connectors before starting the system. If you have video cards with power connectors, plug them in too. Other connectors such as hard drives can wait until you have one successful boot—or if you're cocky, just plug everything in!

Cooling

Heat and computers are not the best of friends. Cooling is therefore a vital consideration when building a computer. Electricity equals heat. Computers, being electrical devices, generate heat as they operate, and too much heat can seriously damage a computer's internal components.

The *power supply fan* provides the basic cooling for the PC (see Figure 7-32). It not only cools the voltage regulator circuits *within* the power supply but also provides a

Figure 7-32
Power supply fan

constant flow of outside air throughout the interior of the computer case. A dead power supply fan can rapidly cause tremendous problems, even equipment failure. If you ever turn on a computer and it boots just fine but you notice that it seems unusually quiet, check to see if the power supply fan has died. If it has, quickly turn off the PC and replace the power supply.

Some power supplies come with a built-in sensor to help regulate the airflow. If the system gets too hot, the power supply fan spins faster (see Figure 7-33).

Figure 7-33
3-wire fan sensor
connector

Case fans are large, square fans that snap into special brackets on the case or screw directly to the case, providing extra cooling for key components (see Figure 7-34). Most cases come with a case fan, and no modern computer should really be without one or two.

Figure 7-34
Case fan

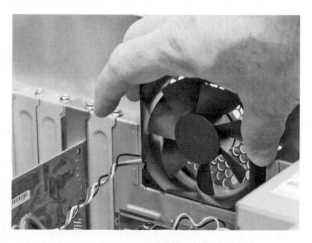

The single biggest issue related to case fans is where to plug them in. Case fans may come with standard Molex connectors, which are easy to plug in, or they may come with special three-pronged power connectors that need to connect to the mother-board. You can get adapters to plug three-pronged connectors into Molex connectors or vice versa.

Maintaining Airflow

A computer is an enclosed system, and computer cases help the fans keep things cool: everything is inside a box. Although many tech types like to run their systems with the side panel of the case open for easy access to the components, in the end they are cheat-ing themselves. Why? A closed case enables the fans to create airflow. This airflow sub-stantially cools off interior components. When the side of the case is open, you ruin the airflow of the system, and you lose a lot of cooling efficiency.

An important point to remember when implementing good airflow inside your com-puter case is that hot air rises. Warm air always rises above cold air, and you can use this principle to your advantage in keeping your computer cool.

In the typical layout of case fans for a computer case, an intake fan is located near the bottom of the front bezel of the case. This fan draws cool air in from outside the case and blows it over the components inside the case. Near the top and rear of the case (usually near the power supply), you'll usually find an exhaust fan. This fan works the opposite of the intake fan: it takes the warm air from inside the case and sends it to the outside.

Another important part of maintaining proper airflow inside the case is ensuring that *slot covers* are covering all empty expansion bays (see Figure 7-35). To maintain good airflow inside your case, you shouldn't provide too many opportunities for air to escape. Slot covers not only assist in maintaining a steady airflow; they also help keep dust and smoke out of your case.

Figure 7-35
Slot covers

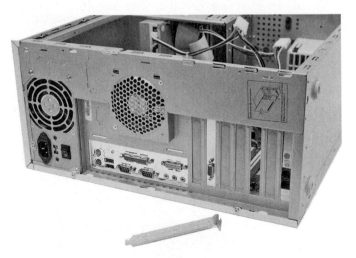

 EXAM TIP Missing slot covers can cause the PC to overheat!

Reducing Fan Noise

Fans generate noise. In an effort to ensure proper cooling, many techs put several high-speed fans into a case, making the PC sound like a jet engine. You can reduce fan noise by using manually adjustable fans, larger fans, or specialty "quiet" fans. Many motherboards enable you to control fans through software.

Manually adjustable fans have a little knob you can turn to speed up or slow down the fan (see Figure 7-36). This kind of fan can reduce some of the noise, but you run the risk of slowing down the fan too much and thus letting the interior of the case heat up. A better solution is to get quieter fans.

Figure 7-36

Manual fan
adjustment
device

Knob for adjusting fan speed

Larger fans that spin more slowly are another way to reduce noise while maintaining good airflow. Fans sizes are measured in millimeters (mm) or centimeters (cm). Traditionally, the industry used 80-mm power supply and cooling fans, but today you'll find 100-mm, 120-mm, and even larger fans in power supplies and cases.

Many companies manufacture and sell higher-end low-noise fans. The fans have better bearings than run of the mill fans, so they cost a little more, but they're definitely worth it. They market these fans as "quiet" or "silencer" or other similar adjectives. If you run into a PC that sounds like a jet, try swapping out the case fans for a low-decibel fan from Cooler Master or NZXT. Just check the decibel rating to decide which one to get. Lower, of course, is better. Also, note that the type of bearing makes a difference. Sleeve-bearing fans get a lot louder as they age; ball-bearing fans don't. The price difference is minimal, so go with ball-bearing fans every time.

Because the temperature inside a PC changes depending on the load put on the PC, the best solution for noise reduction combines a good set of fans with temperature sensors to speed up or slow down the fans automatically. A PC at rest uses less than half of the power of a PC running a video-intensive computer game and therefore makes a lot less heat. Virtually all modern systems support three fans through three 3-pin fan connectors on the motherboard. The CPU fan uses one of these connectors, and the other two are for system fans or the power supply fan.

Most CMOS setup utilities provide a little control over fans plugged into the motherboard. Figure 7-37 shows typical CMOS settings for the fans. Note that you can't use CMOS settings to tell the fans when to turn on or off—only to set off an alarm if they reach a certain temperature or fall below a certain speed.

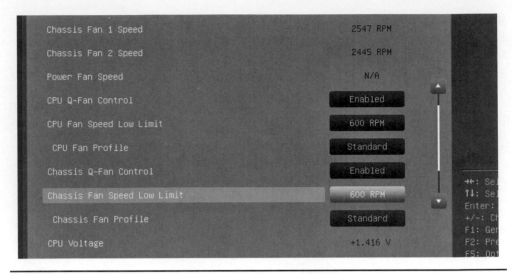

Figure 7-37 CMOS fan options

Software is the best way to control your fans. Some motherboards come with system-monitoring software that enables you to set the temperature at which you want the fans to turn on and off. If no program came with your motherboard, and the manufacturer's Web site doesn't offer one for download, try the freeware SpeedFan utility (see Figure 7-38).

Figure 7-38

SpeedFan

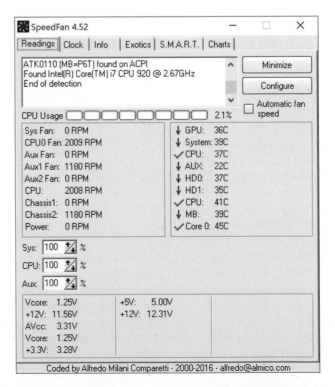

Written by Alfredo Milani Comparetti, SpeedFan monitors voltages, fan speeds, and temperatures in computers with hardware monitor chips. SpeedFan can even access S.M.A.R.T. information (see Chapter 8) for hard disks that support this feature and show hard disk temperatures, too. You can find SpeedFan at www.almico.com/speedfan.php.

 NOTE When shopping for fans, remember your metric system: 80 mm = 8 cm; 120 mm = 12 cm; 200 mm = 20 cm. You'll find fans marketed both ways.

Even if you don't want to mess with your fans, always make a point to turn on your temperature alarms in CMOS. If the system gets too hot, an alarm will warn you. There's no way to know if a fan dies other than to have an alarm.

 CAUTION SpeedFan is a powerful tool that does far more than work with fans. Don't tweak any settings you don't understand!

Troubleshooting Power Supplies

Power supplies fail in two ways: sudden death and slowly over time. When they die suddenly, the computer will not start and the fan in the power supply will not turn. In this case, verify that electricity is getting to the power supply before you do anything. Avoid the embarrassment of trying to repair a power supply when the only problem is a bad outlet or an extension cord that is not plugged in. Assuming that the system has electricity, the best way to verify that a power supply is working or not working is to use a multimeter to check the voltages coming out of the power supply (see Figure 7-39).

Figure 7-39
Testing one of the 5-V DC connections

Do not panic if your power supply puts out slightly more or less voltage than its nominal value. The voltages supplied by most PC power supplies can safely vary by as much as ±10 percent of their stated values. This means that the 12.0-V line can vary from roughly 10.8 to 13.2 V without exceeding the tolerance of the various systems in the PC. The 5.0- and 3.3-V lines offer similar tolerances.

Be sure to test every connection on the power supply—that means every connection on your main power as well as every Molex and mini. Because all voltages are between −20 and +20 VDC, simply set the multimeter to the 20-V DC setting for everything. If the power supply fails to provide power, dispose of it properly and get a new one—even if you're a component expert and a whiz with a soldering iron. Don't waste your time or your company's time; the price of new power supplies makes replacement the obvious way to go.

No Motherboard

Power supplies will not start unless they're connected to a motherboard, so what do you do if you don't have a motherboard you trust to test? First, try an ATX tester. Many companies make these devices. Look for one that supports both 20- and 24-pin motherboard connectors as well as all of the other connectors on your power supply. Figure 7-40 shows a power supply tester.

Figure 7-40
ATX power
supply tester

 NOTE Many CMOS utilities and software programs monitor voltage, saving you the hassle of using a multimeter. Of course, you have to have enough functionality to get into the CMOS utilities!

Switches

Broken power switches form an occasional source of problems for power supplies that fail to start. The power switch is behind the on/off button on every PC. It is usually secured to the front cover or inside front frame on your PC, making it a rather challenging part to access. To test, try shorting the soft power jumpers as described earlier. A key or screwdriver will do the trick.

 EXAM TIP Be sure you are familiar with power-testing tools such as multimeters and power supply testers.

When Power Supplies Die Slowly

If all power supplies died suddenly, this would be a much shorter chapter. Unfortunately, the majority of PC problems occur when power supplies die slowly over time. This means that one of the internal electronics of the power supply has begun to fail. The failures are *always* intermittent and tend to cause some of the most difficult to diagnose problems in PC repair. The secret to discovering that a power supply is dying lies in one word: intermittent. Whenever you experience intermittent problems, your first guess should be that the power supply is bad. Here are some other clues you may hear from users:

- "Whenever I start my computer in the morning, it starts to boot, and then locks up. If I press CTRL-ALT-DEL two or three times, it will boot up fine."

- "Sometimes when I start my PC, I get an error code. If I reboot, it goes away. Sometimes I get different errors."

- "My computer will run fine for an hour or so. Then it locks up, sometimes once or twice an hour."

- "It takes a couple of tries—plugging and unplugging—with a new USB device before my system recognizes it."

Sometimes something bad happens and sometimes it does not. That's the clue for replacing the power supply. And don't bother with the multimeter; the voltages will show up within tolerances, but only *once in a while* they will spike and sag (far more quickly than your multimeter can measure) and cause these intermittent errors. When in doubt, change the power supply. Power supplies break in computers more often than any other part of the PC except components with moving parts. You might choose to keep extra power supplies on hand for swapping and testing.

Fuses and Fire

Inside every power supply resides a simple fuse. If your power supply simply pops and stops working, you might be tempted to go inside the power supply and check the fuse. This is not a good idea. First off, the capacitors in most power supplies carry high-voltage charges that can hurt a lot if you touch them. Second, fuses blow for a reason. If a power supply is malfunctioning inside, you want that fuse to blow because the alternative is much less desirable.

Failure to respect the power of electricity will eventually result in the most catastrophic of all situations: an electrical fire. Don't think it can't happen to you! Keep a fire extinguisher handy. Every computer workbench needs a fire extinguisher, but make sure you have the right one. The fire prevention industry has divided fire extinguishers into five fire classes:

- **Class A** Ordinary free-burning combustible, such as wood or paper
- **Class B** Flammable liquids, such as gasoline, solvents, or paint
- **Class C** Live electrical equipment
- **Class D** Combustible metals such as titanium or magnesium
- **Class K** Cooking oils, trans-fats, or fats

As you might expect, you should use only a Class C fire extinguisher on a burning computing device. All fire extinguishers are required to have their type labeled prominently on them. Many fire extinguishers are multiclass in that they can handle more than one type of fire. The most common fire extinguisher is type ABC—it works on all common types of fires, though it can leave residue on computing equipment.

 EXAM TIP   If your power supply is smoking or you smell something burning inside of it, stop using it now. Replace it with a new power supply.

Beyond A+

Power supplies provide essential services for the PC, creating DC out of AC and cooling the system, but that utilitarian role does not stop the power supply from being an enthusiast's plaything. Plus, servers and high-end workstations have somewhat different needs than more typical systems, so naturally they need a boost in power. Let's take a look Beyond A+ at these issues.

Modular Power Supplies

It's getting more and more popular to make PCs look good on both the inside and the outside. Unused power cables dangling around inside PCs creates a not-so-pretty picture and can impede airflow. To help stylish people, manufacturers created power supplies with modular cables (see Figure 7-41).

Modular cables are pretty cool, because you add only the lines you need for your system. On the other hand, some techs claim that modular cables hurt efficiency because the modular connectors add resistance to the lines. You make the choice: Is a slight reduction in efficiency worth a clean look?

Figure 7-41
Modular-cable
power supply

Temperature and Efficiency

Watch out for power supplies that list their operating temperature at 25° C—about room temperature. A power supply that provides 500 W at 25° C will supply substantially less in warmer temperatures, and the inside of your PC is usually 15° C (59° F) warmer than the outside air. Sadly, many power supply makers—even those who make good power supplies—fudge this fact.

Chapter Review

Questions

1. What is the proper voltage for a U.S. electrical outlet?

   A. 120 V

   B. 60 V

   C. 0 V

   D. −120 V

2. What voltages does an ATX12V P1 connector provide for the motherboard?

   A. 3.3 V, 5 V

   B. 3.3 V, 12 V

   C. 5 V, 12 V

   D. 3.3 V, 5 V, 12 V

3. What sort of power connector do better video cards require?

   A. Molex

   B. Mini

   C. PCIe

   D. SATA

4. Joachim ordered a new power supply but was surprised when it arrived because it had an extra 4-wire connector. What is that connector?

   A. P2 connector for plugging in auxiliary components

   B. P3 connector for plugging in case fans

   C. P4 connector for plugging into modern motherboards

   D. Aux connector for plugging into a secondary power supply

5. What should you keep in mind when testing DC connectors?

   A. DC has polarity. The red lead should always touch the hot wire; the black lead should touch a ground wire.

   B. DC has polarity. The red lead should always touch the ground wire; the black lead should always touch the hot wire.

   C. DC has no polarity, so you can touch the red lead to either hot or ground.

   D. DC has no polarity, so you can touch the black lead to either hot or neutral but not ground.

6. What voltages should the two hot wires on a Molex connector read?

   A. Red = 3.3 V; Yellow = 5 V

   B. Red = 5 V; Yellow = 12 V

   C. Red = 12 V; Yellow = 5 V

   D. Red = 5 V; Yellow = 3.3 V

7. Why is it a good idea to ensure that the slot covers on your computer case are all covered?

   A. To maintain good airflow inside your case.

   B. To help keep dust and smoke out of your case.

   C. Both A and B are correct reasons.

   D. Trick question! Leaving a slot uncovered doesn't hurt anything.

8. A PC's power supply provides DC power in what standard configuration?

   A. Two primary voltage rails, 12 volts and 5 volts, and an auxiliary 3.3-volt connector

   B. Three primary voltage rails, one each for 12-volt, 5-volt, and 3.3-volt connectors

    C. One primary DC voltage rail for 12-volt, 5-volt, and 3.3-volt connectors

    D. One voltage rail with a 12-volt connector for the motherboard, a second voltage rail with a 12-volt connector for the CPU, and a third voltage rail for the 5-volt and 3.3-volt connectors

9. What feature of ATX systems prevents a user from turning off a system before the operating system has been shut down?

    A. Motherboard power connector

    B. CMOS setup

    C. Sleep mode

    D. Soft power

10. How many pins does a SATA power connector have?

    A. 6

    B. 9

    C. 12

    D. 15

Answers

1. A. U.S. outlets run at 120 V.

2. D. An ATX12V power supply P1 connector provides 3.3, 5, and 12 volts to the motherboard.

3. C. Better video cards require one or two 6- or 8-pin PCIe connectors.

4. C. The P4 connector goes into the motherboard to support more power-hungry chips.

5. A. DC has polarity. The red lead should always touch the hot wire; the black lead should touch a ground wire.

6. B. A Molex connector's red wires should be at 5 volts; the yellow wire should be at 12 volts.

7. C. Both A and B are correct reasons. Keeping the slots covered helps keep a good airflow in your case and keeps the dust and smoke away from all those sensitive internal components.

8. B. The standard PC power supply configuration has three primary voltage rails, one each for 12-volt, 5-volt, and 3.3-volt connectors.

9. D. The soft power feature of ATX systems prevents a user from turning off a system before the operating system has been shut down.

10. D. SATA power connectors have 15 pins.

Mass Storage Technologies

In this chapter, you will learn how to
- Explain how hard drives work
- Identify mass storage interface connections
- Describe how to protect data with RAID
- Describe hard drive installation

Of all the hardware on a PC, none gets more attention—or gives more anguish—than mass storage drives. There's a good reason for this: if a drive breaks, you lose data. As you probably know, when data goes, you have to redo work, restore from a backup, or worse, just kiss the data goodbye. It's good to worry about data, because that data runs the office, maintains the payrolls, and stores the e-mail.

This chapter focuses on how drives work, beginning with the internal layout and organization of drives. You'll look at the different types of drives used today and how they interface with the PC. The chapter covers how more than one drive may work with other drives to provide data safety and improve speed through a feature called RAID. The chapter wraps up with an extensive discussion on how to install drives properly into a system. Let's get started.

NOTE Chapter 9, "Implementing Mass Storage," continues the hard drive discussion by adding in the operating systems, showing you how to prepare drives to receive data, and teaching you how to maintain and upgrade drives in modern operating systems.

Historical/Conceptual

How Hard Drives Work

Hard drives come in two major types: the traditional type with moving parts; and a newer, more expensive technology with no moving parts. Let's look at both.

Magnetic Hard Drives

A traditional *hard disk drive* (*HDD*) is composed of individual disks, or *platters*, with read/write heads on actuator arms controlled by a servo motor—all contained in a sealed case that prevents contamination by outside air (see Figure 8-1).

Figure 8-1
An enclosed HDD (top) and an opened HDD (bottom)

The aluminum platters are coated with a magnetic medium. Two tiny read/write heads service each platter, one to read the top of the platter and the other to read the bottom of the platter (see Figure 8-2). Each head has a bit-sized *transducer* to read or write to each spot on the drive. Many folks refer to traditional HDDs as *magnetic hard drives*, *rotational drives*, or sometimes *platter-based hard drives*.

Figure 8-2
Read/write heads on actuator arms

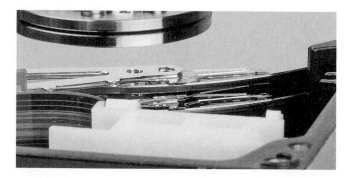

1001

Spindle (or Rotational) Speed

Hard drives run at a set *spindle speed*, with the spinning platters measured in *revolutions per minute* (*RPM*). Older drives ran at a speed of 3600 RPM, and drives are sold with speeds up to 15,000 RPM. The faster the spindle speed, the faster the drive stores and retrieves data. By far the two most common speeds are 5400 and 7200 RPM. Higher performance drives (which are also far less common) run at 10,000 and 15,000 RPM.

Faster drives generally equate to better performance, but they also generate more noise and heat. Excess heat cuts the life of hard drives dramatically. A rise of 5 degrees (Celsius) may reduce the life expectancy of a hard drive by as much as two years. So even if replacing an old pair of 5400-RPM drives with a shiny new pair of 15,000-RPM drives doesn't generate enough heat to crash the entire system, it may severely put your storage investment at risk of a short life cycle.

You can deal with the warmth of these very fast drives by adding drive bay fans between the drives or migrating to a more spacious case. Most enthusiasts end up doing both. *Drive bay fans* sit at the front of a bay and blow air across the drive. They range in price from $10 to $100 (USD) and can lower the temperature of your drives dramatically. Some cases come with a bay fan built in (see Figure 8-3).

Figure 8-3
Bay fan

Airflow in a case can make or break your system stability, especially when you add new drives that increase the ambient temperature. Hot systems get flaky and lock up at odd moments. Many things can impede the airflow—jumbled-up ribbon cables (used by older storage systems, USB headers, and other attachments), drives squished together in a tiny case, fans clogged by dust or animal hair, and so on.

Technicians need to be aware of the dangers when adding a new hard drive to an older system. Get into the habit of tying off non-aerodynamic cables, adding front fans to cases when systems lock up intermittently, and making sure any fans run well. Finally, if a client wants a new drive for a system in a tiny minitower with only the power supply fan to cool it off, be gentle, but definitely steer the client to one of the slower drives!

Form Factors

Magnetic hard drives are manufactured in two standardized form factors, 2.5-inch and 3.5-inch (see Figure 8-4). A desktop system can use either form factor size; most laptops use the 2.5-inch form factor.

Figure 8-4
2.5-inch drive stacked on top of a 3.5-inch drive

The form factor only defines size. The connections and the storage technology inside these drives can vary.

Solid-State Drives

Booting up a computer takes time in part because a traditional hard drive needs to spin up before the read/write heads can retrieve data off the drive and load it into RAM. All of the moving metal parts of a platter-based hard drive use a lot of power, create a lot of heat, take up space, wear down over time, and take a lot of nanoseconds to get things done. A *solid-state drive* (*SSD*) addresses all of these issues nicely.

In technical terms, solid-state technology and devices are based on the combination of semiconductors and transistors used to create electrical components with no moving parts. That's a mouthful! In simple terms, SSDs use flash memory chips to store data instead of all those pesky metal spinning parts used in platter-based hard drives (see Figure 8-5).

Figure 8-5
A solid-state
drive

Solid-state technology is commonly used in desktop and laptop hard drives, memory cards, cameras, USB thumb drives, and other handheld devices.

SSDs for personal computers come in one of three form factors: the 2.5-inch form factor previously mentioned and two flat form factors called *mSATA* and *M.2* (see Figure 8-6). mSATA and M.2 drives connect to specific mSATA or M.2 slots on motherboards (see Figure 8-7). Many current motherboards offer two or more M.2 slots.

Figure 8-6
M.2 SSD

Figure 8-7
M.2 SSD installed
in motherboard

EXAM TIP Although you can still buy mSATA cards as we go to print, the technology is definitely on its way out for both laptop and desktop computers, replaced by M.2. The latter standard is half the physical size and offers substantially better performance. The M.2 form factor is incorrectly referred to as M2 (with no dot) in CompTIA A+ 1001 exam objective 3.4.

M.2 slots come in a variety, keyed for different sorts of mass storage uses. The keys have a letter associated. M.2 slots that use Key B, Key M, or Keys B+M support mass storage devices, for example, like in Figure 8-7. Other slots like Key A and Key E are used in wireless networking devices. The specifics of the keys are beyond the current A+ exam, but M.2 looks like it's here to stay, so you need to be aware of the variations.

SSDs use nonvolatile flash memory such as *NAND* that retains data when power is turned off or disconnected. (See Chapter 10, "Essential Peripherals," for the scoop on flash memory technology.)

Cost

SSDs cost more than HDDs. Less expensive SSDs typically implement less reliable *multi-level cell* (*MLC*) memory technology in place of the more efficient *single-level cell* (*SLC*) technology to cut costs. The most popular type of memory technology in SSDs is *3D NAND*, a form of MLC that stacks cells vertically, providing increased density and capacity.

Solid-state drives operate internally by writing data in a scattershot fashion to high-speed flash memory cells in accordance with the rules contained in the internal SSD controller. That process is hidden from the operating system by presenting an electronic façade to the OS that makes the SSD appear to be a traditional magnetic hard drive.

Performance Variables

There are three big performance metrics to weigh when you buy an SSD: how fast it can read or write long sequences of data stored in the same part of the drive, how fast it can read or write small chunks of data scattered randomly around the drive, and how quickly it responds to a single request. The value of each metric varies depending on what kind of work the drive will do. Before we dive into how you should weigh each metric, let's look at how the storage industry measures the sequential read/write performance, random read/write performance, and latency of individual SSDs.

Sequential Read/Write Performance A common measure of a storage device's top speed is its *throughput*, or the rates at which it can read and write long sequences of data. We usually express a device's *sequential read* and *sequential write* throughput in megabytes per second (MBps). Most drives read a little faster than they write.

For context, traditional hard drives generally have sequential read/write speeds that top out at 200 MBps; SATA SSDs can hit 600 MBps; and NVMe SSDs roll at 2500 MBps or faster. These numbers are useful if you know your drives will frequently read and write huge files, but very few real-world systems do.

Random Read/Write Performance   Because real-world drives rarely get to read and write huge files all day, we also look at a drive's *random read*, *random write*, and *mixed random* performance. Basically, we measure how many times per second a device can read or write small, fixed-size chunks of data at random locations on the drive.

The labels for these measurements often reflect the size of the data chunk (usually 4 KB), so you may see them called *4K Read*, *4K Random Write*, *4K Mixed*, and so on. These measurements are all typically expressed as a number of *input/output operations per second* (*IOPS*), but you may also see them expressed in MBps. For context, traditional hard drives typically clock in at fewer than 150 IOPS, whereas the latest NVMe SSDs boast *hundreds of thousands* of IOPS.

Latency   It's also useful to look at a drive's *response time*, *access time*, or *latency*, which measures how quickly it responds to a single request. Latency is usually expressed in milliseconds (ms) or microseconds (μs). Low-latency storage is critical for high-performance file and database servers, but the latency of most modern drives is fine for general use. For context, traditional hard drives often have latencies under 20 ms, whereas SSDs commonly clock in well under 1 ms.

A lot of factors determine which combination of performance and price makes sense for a specific situation. A typical machine, for example, doesn't put a huge demand on the SSD. Users boot up the computer and then open an application or two and work. The quality of the SSD matters for boot-up time and application load, but the machine will rarely break a sweat after that. A workstation for high-end video editing, on the other hand, may read and write massive files for hours on end. A large file server may need to read and write thousands of tiny files a minute.

In practical terms, you can get by with a cheaper, lower-performing SSD in a general-use computer, but need to spend more for a higher performing SSD in demanding circumstances. When it comes to picking exactly which high-performance SSD, the throughput, IOPs, and latency metrics help you avoid overpaying for performance characteristics that don't matter for your use.

Hybrid Hard Drives

Windows supports *hybrid hard drives* (*HHDs*), drives that combine flash memory and spinning platters to provide fast and reliable storage. (HHDs are also known as *SSHDs*.) The small SSD in these drives enables them to store the most accessed data in the flash memory to, for example, slash boot times and, because the platters don't have to spin as much, extend the battery life for portable computers.

Apple computers can use a *Fusion Drive*, which offers the same concept as a hybrid hard drive. The Fusion Drive separates the hard drive and SSD; macOS does all the work about deciding what should go in the SSD.

Connecting Mass Storage

Setting up communication between a CPU and a mass storage drive requires two main items. First, there must be standardized physical connections between the CPU, the drive controller, and the physical drive. These connections must send data between these devices as quickly as possible while still retaining good security (see Figure 8-8).

Figure 8-8
Standardized physical connections are essential.

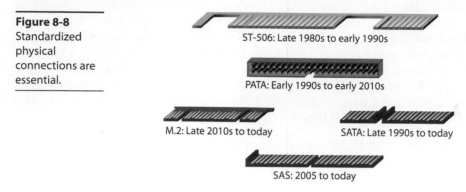

ST-506: Late 1980s to early 1990s

PATA: Early 1990s to early 2010s

M.2: Late 2010s to today   SATA: Late 1990s to today

SAS: 2005 to today

Secondly, the CPU needs to use a standardized protocol, sort of like a special language, so it knows how to speak to the mass storage device to read and write data to the device (see Figure 8-9).

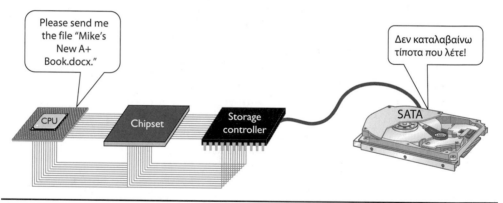

Figure 8-9   We need a common language!

In most cases, the standards bodies that define both the physical connections as well as the language used for communications are the same organization. For the last 25+ years, the Storage Networking Industry Association's Small Form Factor (SFF) committee has defined mass storage standards, the most important to CompTIA A+ techs being *ATA/ATAPI*.

NOTE   Check out www.snia.org for a good source for mass storage standards.

The *advanced technology attachment* (*ATA*) standards started with version 1 way back in 1990, going through ATA/ATAPI version 7. Let's make it even easier, because only two versions of this standard have interest to techs: PATA and SATA. *Parallel ATA* (*PATA*) was introduced with ATA/ATAPI version 1. *Serial ATA* (*SATA*) was introduced with ATA/ATAPI version 7. Let's look at both standards.

NOTE ATA hard drives are often referred to as *integrated drive electronics* (*IDE*) drives. The term IDE refers to any hard drive with a built-in controller. All hard drives are technically IDE drives, although we only use the term IDE when discussing PATA drives. Many techs today use IDE only to refer to the older PATA standard.

PATA

PATA drives are easily recognized by their data and power connections. PATA drives used unique 40-pin ribbon cables. These ribbon cables usually plugged directly into a system's motherboard. Note that the exam will call these *IDE cables*. Figure 8-10 provides an example of a typical connection. All PATA drives used a standard Molex power connector (see Figure 8-11).

Figure 8-10
PATA cable
plugged into a
motherboard

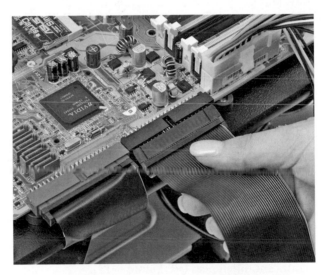

Figure 8-11
Molex connector

NOTE   The last ATA/ATAPI standard that addressed PATA provided support for very large hard drives (144 petabytes [PB], more than 144 million gigabytes) at speeds up to 133 megabytes per second (MBps). A single PATA ribbon cable could connect up to two PATA drives—including hard drives, optical drives, and tape drives—to a single ATA controller. You set jumpers on the drives to make one master and the other slave. (See the discussion on installation in the "Installing Drives" section later in this chapter for the full scoop.)

As a technology standard, ATA went through seven major revisions, each adding power, speed, and/or capacity to storage system capabilities. I could add 15 pages discussing the changes, but they're not particularly relevant for modern techs. There is one feature added back then that we still use today, though, called *S.M.A.R.T.*

ATA/ATAPI version 3 introduced *Self-Monitoring, Analysis, and Reporting Technology* (*S.M.A.R.T.*), an internal drive program that tracks errors and error conditions within the drive. This information is stored in nonvolatile memory on the drive and can be examined externally with S.M.A.R.T. reader software. There are generic S.M.A.R.T. reading programs, and every drive manufacturer has software to get at the vendor-specific information being tracked. Regular usage of S.M.A.R.T. software will help you create a baseline of hard drive functionality to predict potential drive failures.

SATA

For all its longevity as the mass storage interface of choice for the PC, parallel ATA had problems. First, the flat ribbon cables impeded airflow and could be a pain to insert properly. Second, the cables had a limited length, only 18 inches. Third, you couldn't hot-swap PATA drives. You had to shut the computer down completely before installing or replacing a drive. Finally, the technology had simply reached the limits of what it could do in terms of throughput. It was time to revamp both the connection and the language for ATA/ATAPI drives.

Serial ATA addressed these issues. SATA creates a point-to-point connection between the SATA device—magnetic hard drives, solid-state drives, optical media drives—and the SATA controller, the *host bus adapter* (*HBA*). At a glance, SATA devices look identical to PATA devices. Take a closer look at the cable and power connectors, however, and you'll see significant differences (see Figure 8-12).

Figure 8-12
SATA hard disk power (left) and data (right) cables

Because SATA devices send data serially instead of in parallel, the SATA interface needs far fewer physical wires—only 7 connectors instead of the 40 typical of PATA—resulting in much thinner cabling. Thinner cabling means better cable control and better airflow through the PC case, resulting in better cooling.

Further, the maximum SATA-device cable length is more than twice that of a PATA cable—about 40 inches (1 meter) instead of 18 inches. This facilitates drive installation in larger cases.

EXAM TIP The CompTIA A+ 1001 exam objectives refer to the 40-pin PATA ribbon cable as an *IDE cable*. They're the same thing, so don't miss this one on the exam!

SATA did away with the two drives per cable of PATA. Each drive connects to one port. Further, there's no maximum number of drives—many motherboards today support up to eight SATA drives (see Figure 8-13). Want more? Snap in a SATA HBA and load 'em up!

Figure 8-13
SATA cable plugged into typical motherboard (note the other available socket)

The biggest news about SATA is in data throughput. As the name implies, SATA devices transfer data in serial bursts instead of parallel, as PATA devices do. Typically, you might not think of serial devices as being faster than parallel, but in this case, a SATA device's single stream of data moves much faster than the multiple streams of data coming from a parallel ATA device—theoretically, up to 30 times faster. SATA drives come in three common SATA-specific varieties: *1.5 Gbps*, *3 Gbps*, and *6 Gbps*, which have a maximum throughput of 150 MBps, 300 MBps, and 600 MBps, respectively. It should be noted that if a system has an (external) eSATA port (discussed next), it will operate at the same revision and speed as the internal SATA ports.

NOTE Number-savvy readers might have noticed a discrepancy between the names and throughput of SATA drives. After all, SATA 1.0's 1.5-Gbps throughput translates to 192 MBps, a lot higher than the advertised speed of a "mere" 150 MBps. The encoding scheme used on SATA drives takes about 20 percent of the transferred bytes as overhead, leaving 80 percent for pure bandwidth.

SATA 2.0's 3-Gbps drive created all kinds of problems because the committee working on the specifications was called the SATA II committee, and marketers picked up on the SATA II name. As a result, you'll find many hard drives labeled "SATA II" rather than 3 Gbps.

The SATA committee now goes by the name SATA-IO. In keeping with tradition, when SATA II speed doubled from 3 Gbps to 6 Gbps, two names were attached: SATA III and SATA 6 Gbps.

Connecting a mass storage device to a fully functioning and powered-up computer can result in disaster. The outcome may be as simple as the component not being recognized or as dire as a destroyed component or computer. Enter the era of the hot-swappable device. Hot-swapping entails two elements, the first being the capacity to plug a device into the computer without harming either. The second is that once the device is safely attached, it will be automatically recognized and become a fully functional component of the system. SATA handles hot-swapping just fine in modern systems (see "AHCI" later in the chapter for more details).

SATA Express (*SATAe*) or *SATA 3.2* ties capable drives directly into the PCI Express bus on motherboards. SATAe drops both the SATA link and transport layers, embracing the full performance of PCIe. The lack of overhead greatly enhances the speed of SATA throughput, with each lane of PCIe 3.0 capable of handling up to 8 Gbps of data throughput. A drive grabbing two lanes, therefore, could move a whopping 16 Gbps through the bus. Without the overhead of earlier SATA versions, this translates as 2000 MBps!

SATAe has unique connectors (see Figure 8-14) but provides full backward compatibility with earlier versions of SATA. Note that the center and left portions of the port look just like regular SATA ports? They function that way too, so you can plug two regular SATA drives into a SATAe socket. Feel free to upgrade your motherboard! Oh yeah, did I forget to mention that? You'll need a motherboard with SATAe support to take advantage of these superfast versions of SATA drives.

Figure 8-14
SATAe connector

EXAM TIP Each SATA variety is named for the revision to the SATA specification that introduced it, with the exception of SATAe:

- SATA 1.0: 1.5 Gbps/150 MBps
- SATA 2.0: 3 Gbps/300 MBps
- SATA 3.0: 6 Gbps/600 MBps
- SATA 3.2: up to 16 Gbps/2000 MBps, also known as SATAe

SATA's ease of use has made it the choice for desktop system storage. Most hard drives sold today are SATA drives.

NOTE The SATA 3.3 (2016) revision increased supported drive sizes, among other things. The throughput speed of the interface did not increase.

eSATA and Other External Drives

External SATA (*eSATA*) extended the SATA bus to external devices, as the name would imply. The eSATA drives used connectors that looked similar to internal SATA connectors, but were keyed differently so you couldn't mistake one for the other. Figure 8-15 shows an eSATA connector on the back of a motherboard.

Figure 8-15
eSATA connector

External SATA used shielded cable in lengths up to 2 meters outside the PC and was hot-swappable. eSATA extended the SATA bus at full speed, mildly faster than the fastest USB connection when it was introduced.

eSATA withered when USB 3.0 hit the market and quickly disappeared. You'll only find it today on very old systems and drive enclosures, and on the CompTIA A+ exam.

EXAM TIP   The CompTIA A+ 1001 exam objectives mention *eSATA cards*, as in expansion cards you add to a system that doesn't have the connectors. You can certainly buy these today to support older, external mass storage enclosures.

Current *external enclosures* (the name used to describe the casing of external HDDs and SSDs) use the USB (3.0, 3.1, or C-type) ports or Thunderbolt ports for connecting external hard drives. Chapter 10 goes into the differences among these types of ports in detail. The drives inside the enclosures are standard SATA HDDs or SSDs.

EXAM TIP   Know your cable lengths:

- PATA: 18 inches

- SATA: 1 meter

- eSATA: 2 meters

Refining Mass Storage Communication

The original ATA standard defined a very specific series of commands for the CPU to communicate with the drive controller. The current drive command sets are AHCI and NVMe. The SCSI command set is still around as well, though primarily in the server market.

AHCI

Current versions of Windows support the *Advanced Host Controller Interface* (*AHCI*), an efficient way to work with SATA HBAs. Using AHCI unlocks some of the advanced features of SATA, such as native command queuing and hot-swapping.

Native command queuing (*NCQ*) is a disk-optimization feature for SATA drives. It takes advantage of the SATA interface to achieve faster read and write speeds that are simply impossible with the old PATA drives. Also, while SATA supports hot-swapping ability, the motherboard and the operating system must also support this.

AHCI mode is enabled at the CMOS level (see "BIOS Support: Configuring CMOS and Installing Drivers" later in this chapter) and generally needs to be enabled before you install the operating system. Enabling it after installation will cause Windows to Blue Screen. How nice.

Successfully Switching SATA Modes Without Reinstalling

You can attempt to switch to AHCI mode in Windows without reinstalling. This scenario might occur if a client has accidentally installed Windows in Legacy/IDE mode, for example, and finds that the new SSD he purchased requires AHCI mode to perform well.

First, back up everything before attempting the switch. Second, you need to run through some steps in Windows before you change the BIOS/UEFI settings.

Windows 7 and 8/8.1 require manual changes to the Registry (the database that handles everything in Windows, covered in Chapter 12, "Windows Under the Hood"). Windows 10 uses an elevated command prompt exercise with the bcdedit command. (The command line is covered in Chapter 15, "Working with the Command-Line Interface.")

A quick Google search for "switch from ide to ahci windows" will reveal several excellent walkthroughs of the process for Windows 7/8/8.1 and Windows 10. Back everything up first!

When you plug a SATA drive into a running Windows computer that does not have AHCI enabled, the drive doesn't appear automatically. With AHCI mode enabled, the drive should appear in Computer immediately, just what you'd expect from a hot-swappable device.

NVMe

AHCI was designed for spinning SATA drives to optimize read performance as well as to effect hot-swappability. As a configuration setting, it works for many SSDs as well, but it's not optimal. That's because for an SSD to work with the operating system, the SSD has to include some circuitry that the OS can see that makes the SSD appear to be a traditional spinning drive. Once a read or write operation is commenced, the virtual drive circuits pass the operation through a translator in the SSD that maps the true inner guts of the SSD.

The *Non-Volatile Memory Express* (*NVMe*) specification supports a communication connection between the operating system and the SSD directly through a PCIe bus lane, reducing latency and taking full advantage of the wicked-fast speeds of high-end SSDs (see Figure 8-16). NVMe SSDs come in a couple of formats, such as an add-on expansion card, though most commonly in M.2 format. NVMe drives are more expensive than other SSDs, but offer much higher speeds. NVMe drives use SATAe.

SCSI

SATA drives dominate the personal computer market, but another drive technology, called the *small computer system interface* (*SCSI*), rules the roost in the server market. SCSI has been around since the early days of HDDs and has evolved over the years from a parallel to a wider parallel to—and this should be obvious by now—a couple of super-fast serial interfaces. SCSI devices—parallel and serial—use a standard SCSI command set, meaning you can have systems with both old and new devices connected and they can communicate with no problem. SCSI drives used a variety of ribbon cables, depending on the version.

Serial Attached SCSI (*SAS*) hard drives provide fast and robust storage for servers and storage arrays today. The latest SAS interface, SAS-3, provides speeds of up to 12 Gbps. SAS controllers also support SATA drives, which is cool and offers a lot of flexibility for techs, especially in smaller server situations. SAS implementations offer literally more

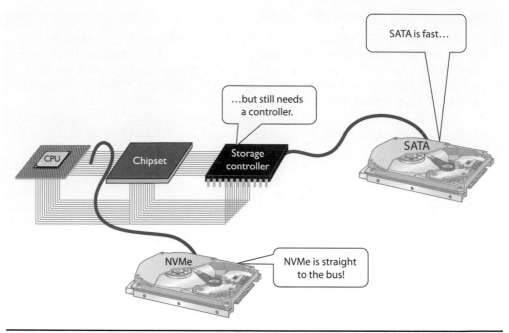

Figure 8-16 NVMe enables direct-to-the-bus communication.

than a dozen different connector types. Most look like slightly chunkier versions of a SATA connector.

The CompTIA A+ certification includes SCSI, but surely that only means SAS. If you want to make the move to server tech, though, you'll definitely need to know about SCSI. The SCSI Trade Association (STA) Web site provides a good starting point: www .scsita.org.

Protecting Data with RAID

Ask experienced techs "What is the most expensive part of a PC?" and they'll all answer in the same way: "It's the data." You can replace any single part of your PC for a few hundred dollars at most, but if you lose critical data—well, let's just say I know of two small companies that went out of business just because they lost a hard drive full of data.

Data is king; data is your PC's *raison d'être*. Losing data is a bad thing, so you need some method to prevent data loss. Of course, you can do backups, but if a hard drive dies, you have to shut down the computer, reinstall a new hard drive, reinstall the operating system, and then restore the backup. There's nothing wrong with this as long as you can afford the time and cost of shutting down the system.

A better solution, though, would save your data if a hard drive died and enable you to continue working throughout the process. This is possible if you stop relying on a single hard drive and instead use two or more drives to store your data. Sounds good, but how do you do this? Well, you could install some fancy hard drive controller that reads and writes data to two hard drives simultaneously (see Figure 8-17). The data on each drive would always be identical. One drive would be the primary drive and the other drive, called the *mirror* drive, would not be used unless the primary drive failed. This process of reading and writing data at the same time to two drives is called *disk mirroring*.

Figure 8-17
Mirrored drives

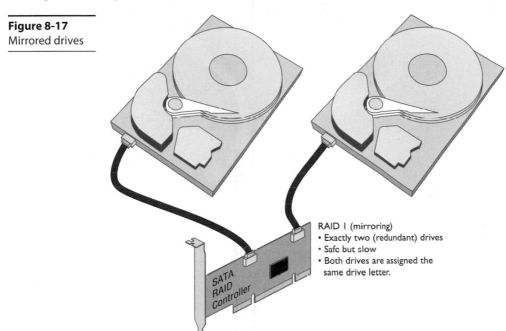

RAID 1 (mirroring)
• Exactly two (redundant) drives
• Safe but slow
• Both drives are assigned the same drive letter.

SATA RAID Controller

If you really want to make data safe, you can use a separate controller for each drive. With two drives, each on a separate controller, the system will continue to operate even if the primary drive's controller stops working. This super-drive mirroring technique is called *disk duplexing* (see Figure 8-18). Disk duplexing is also marginally faster than disk mirroring because one controller does not write each piece of data twice.

Even though duplexing is faster than mirroring, they both are slower than the classic one-drive, one-controller setup. You can use multiple drives to increase your hard drive access speed. *Disk striping* (without parity) means spreading the data among multiple (at least two) drives. Disk striping by itself provides no redundancy. If you save a small Microsoft Word file, for example, the file is split into multiple pieces; half of the pieces go on one drive and half on the other (see Figure 8-19).

The one and only advantage of disk striping is speed—it is a fast way to read and write to hard drives. But if either drive fails, *all* data is lost. You should not do disk striping—unless you're willing to increase the risk of losing data to increase the speed at which your hard drives store and retrieve data.

Figure 8-18
Duplexing drives

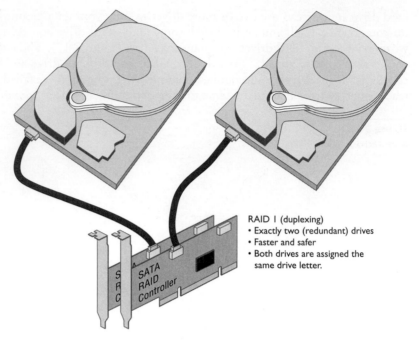

RAID 1 (duplexing)
• Exactly two (redundant) drives
• Faster and safer
• Both drives are assigned the
  same drive letter.

Figure 8-19
Disk striping

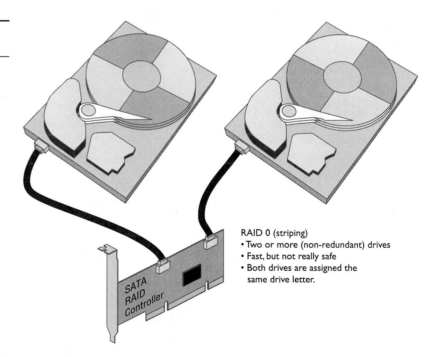

RAID 0 (striping)
• Two or more (non-redundant) drives
• Fast, but not really safe
• Both drives are assigned the
  same drive letter.

NOTE In practice (as opposed to benchmarking) you won't experience any performance difference between mirroring and striping.

Disk striping with parity, in contrast, protects data by adding extra information, called *parity data*, that can be used to rebuild data if one of the drives fails. Disk striping with parity requires at least three drives, but it is common to use more than three. Disk striping with parity combines the best of disk mirroring and plain disk striping. It protects data and is quite fast. The majority of network servers use a type of disk striping with parity.

NOTE There is actually a term for a storage system composed of multiple independent disks of various sizes, *JBOD*, which stands for *just a bunch of disks* (or *drives*). Many drive controllers support JBOD.

RAID

A couple of sharp guys in Berkeley back in the 1980s organized many of the techniques for using multiple drives for data protection and increasing speeds as the *redundant array of independent* (or *inexpensive*) *disks* (*RAID*). An *array* describes two or more drives working as a unit. They outlined several forms or "levels" of RAID that have since been numbered 0 through 6 (plus a couple of special implementations). Only a few of these RAID types are in use today: 0, 1, 5, 6, 10, and 0+1.

- *RAID 0*—**Disk Striping** Disk striping requires at least two drives. It does not provide redundancy to data. If any one drive fails, all data is lost. I've heard this called *scary RAID* for that very reason.

- *RAID 1*—**Disk Mirroring/Duplexing** RAID 1 arrays require at least two hard drives, although they also work with any even number of drives. RAID 1 is the ultimate in safety, but you lose storage space because the data is duplicated; you need two 2-TB drives to store 2 TB of data.

- *RAID 5*—**Disk Striping with Distributed Parity** Instead of dedicated data and parity drives, RAID 5 distributes data and parity information evenly across all drives. This is the fastest way to provide data redundancy. RAID 5 requires at least three drives. RAID 5 arrays effectively use one drive's worth of space for parity. If, for example, you have three 2-TB drives, your total storage capacity is 4 TB. If you have four 2-TB drives, your total capacity is 6 TB.

NOTE RAID 5 sounds great on paper and will seem great on your CompTIA A+ exam, but it's out of favor today. The failure rate of drives combined with the huge capacity (and rebuilding times) mean most RAID implementations shy away from the "lose only one drive" RAID 5.

- *RAID 6*—**Disk Striping with Extra Parity**   If you lose a hard drive in a RAID 5 array, your data is at great risk until you replace the bad hard drive and rebuild the array. RAID 6 is RAID 5 with extra parity information. RAID 6 needs at least four drives, but in exchange you can lose up to two drives at the same time.

- *RAID 10*—**Nested, Striped Mirrors**   RAID levels have been combined to achieve multiple benefits, including speed, capacity, and reliability, but these benefits must be purchased at a cost, and that cost is efficiency. Take for instance RAID 10, also called RAID 1+0 and sometimes a "stripe of mirrors." Requiring a minimum of four drives, a pair of drives is configured as a mirror, and then the same is done to another pair to achieve a pair of RAID 1 arrays. The arrays look like single drives to the operating system or RAID controller. So now, with two drives, we can block stripe across the two mirrored pairs (RAID 0). Cool, huh? We get the speed of striping and the reliability of mirroring at the cost of installing two bytes of storage for every byte of data saved. Need more space? Add another mirrored pair to the striped arrays!

- *RAID 0+1*—**Nested, Mirrored Stripes**   Like RAID 10, RAID 0+1 (or a "mirror of stripes") is a nested set of arrays that works in opposite configuration from RAID 10. It takes a minimum of four drives to implement RAID 0+1. Start with two RAID 0 striped arrays, then mirror the two arrays to each other. Which is better: the RAID 10 or the RAID 0+1? Why not do a bit of research and decide for yourself?

 EXAM TIP   In preparation for the CompTIA A+ 220-1001 exam, you'll want to be familiar with RAID levels 0, 1, 5, and 10. Know the minimum number of drives in a given level array, and how many failures a given array can withstand and remain functional.

RAID Level	Minimum Drives	Number of Functional Failures
RAID 0	2	0
RAID 1	2	1
RAID 5	3	1
RAID 6	4	2
RAID 10	4	Up to 2

Implementing RAID

RAID levels describe different methods of providing data redundancy or enhancing the speed of data throughput to and from groups of hard drives. They do not say *how* to implement these methods. Literally thousands of methods can be used to set up RAID. The method you use depends largely on the level of RAID you desire, the operating system you use, and the thickness of your wallet.

The obvious starting place for RAID is to connect at least two hard drives in some fashion to create a RAID array. Specialized RAID controller cards support RAID arrays of up to 15 drives—plenty to support even the most complex RAID needs. Dedicated storage boxes with built-in RAID make implementing a RAID solution simple for external storage and backups.

Once you have hard drives, the next question is whether to use hardware or software to control the array. Let's look at both options.

Software Versus Hardware

All RAID implementations break down into either software or hardware methods. Software is often used when price takes priority over performance. Hardware is used when you need speed along with data redundancy. Software RAID does not require special controllers; you can use the regular SATA controllers to make a software RAID array. But you do need "smart" software. The most common software implementation of RAID is the built-in RAID software that comes with Windows. The Disk Management program in Windows Server versions can configure drives for RAID 0, 1, or 5, and it works with PATA or SATA (see Figure 8-20). Windows 7/8/8.1/10 Disk Management can do RAID 0 and 1.

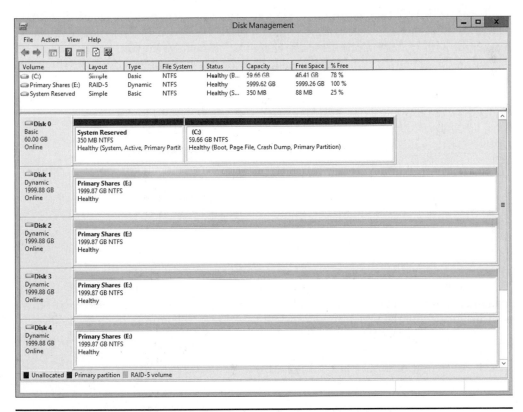

Figure 8-20 Disk Management tool of Computer Management in Windows Server

NOTE Chapter 9, "Implementing Mass Storage," discusses RAID solutions implemented in Windows.

Windows Disk Management is not the only software RAID game in town. A number of third-party software programs work with Windows or other operating systems.

Software RAID means the operating system is in charge of all RAID functions. It works for small RAID solutions but tends to overwork your operating system easily, creating slowdowns. When you *really* need to keep going, when you need RAID that doesn't even let the users know a problem has occurred, hardware RAID is the answer.

NOTE See Chapter 9 for a thorough discussion of *Storage Spaces*, a software RAID implementation available in Windows 8/8.1/10.

Hardware RAID centers on an *intelligent* controller that handles all of the RAID functions (see Figure 8-21). Unlike regular PATA/SATA controllers, these controllers have chips with their own processor and memory. This allows the card or dedicated box, instead of the operating system, to handle all of the work of implementing RAID.

Figure 8-21
Serial ATA RAID
controller

Most traditional RAID setups in the real world are hardware-based. Almost all of the many hardware RAID solutions provide *hot-swapping*—the ability to replace a bad drive without disturbing the operating system. Hot-swapping is common in hardware RAID.

Hardware-based RAID is invisible to the operating system and is configured in several ways, depending on the specific chips involved. Most RAID systems have a special configuration utility in Flash ROM that you access after CMOS but before the

Figure 8-22
RAID
configuration
utility

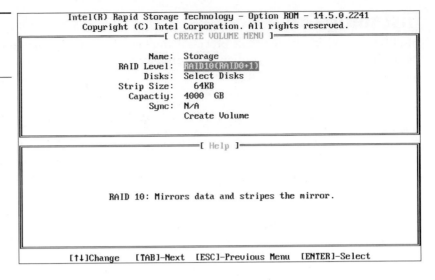

```
        Intel(R) Rapid Storage Technology - Option ROM - 14.5.0.2241
             Copyright (C) Intel Corporation. All rights reserved.
        ════════════════════[ CREATE VOLUME MENU ]════════════════════

                        Name:  Storage
                  RAID Level:  RAID10(RAID0+1)
                       Disks:  Select Disks
                  Strip Size:  64KB
                    Capactiy:  4000  GB
                        Sync:  N/A
                               Create Volume

        ═════════════════════════[ Help ]═════════════════════════



              RAID 10: Mirrors data and stripes the mirror.




        [↑↓]Change    [TAB]-Next   [ESC]-Previous Menu   [ENTER]-Select
```

OS loads. Figure 8-22 shows a typical firmware program used to configure a hardware RAID solution.

SIM   Check out the Chapter 8 Challenge! sim, "Storage Solution," to examine best RAID practices at http://totalsem.com/100x.

Dedicated RAID Boxes

Many people add a dedicated RAID box to add both more storage and a place to back up files. These devices take two or more drives and connect via one of the ports on a computer, such as USB or Thunderbolt (on modern systems) or FireWire or eSATA (on older systems). (See Chapter 10 for details on USB and FireWire.) Figure 8-23 shows an external RAID box (also called an *enclosure*). This model is typical, offering three options for the two drives inside: no RAID, RAID 0, or RAID 1.

Figure 8-23
Western Digital
RAID enclosure

Installing Drives

Installing a drive is a fairly simple process if you take the time to make sure you have the right drive for your system, configure the drive and system setup properly, and do a few quick tests to see if it's running properly. Since PATA and SATA have different cabling requirements, we'll look at each separately.

 EXAM TIP Don't let the length of explanation about installation throw you during CompTIA A+ 1001 exam prep. PATA installation is much more complicated than SATA installation, so we've devoted more ink to the process here. SATA is what you will most likely see in the field and on the exam.

Choosing Your Drive

First, decide where you're going to put the drive. If you have a new motherboard, just slip the drive into the M.2 socket and secure it with the tiny screw. If you plan to install a 3.5-inch HDD or 2.5-inch SSD, then you need to go old school. Look for an open SATA connection. Is it part of a dedicated RAID controller? Many motherboards with built-in RAID controllers have a CMOS setting that enables you to turn the RAID controller on or off (see Figure 8-24).

Figure 8-24
Settings for RAID in CMOS

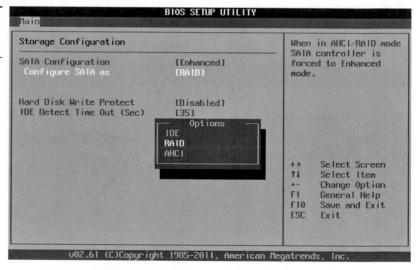

Second, make sure you have room for the drive in the case. Where will you place it? Do you have a spare power connector? Will the data and power cables reach the drive? A quick test fit is always a good idea.

Try This! Managing Heat with Multiple Drives

Adding three or more fast magnetic hard drives into a cramped PC case can be a recipe for disaster to the unwary tech. While the heat generated may not threaten the fabric of the time-space continuum, heat reduces the life expectancy of drives and computers. You have to manage the heat inside a RAID-enabled system because such systems usually have more than the typical quantity of drives found in desktop computers. The easiest way to do this is to add fans.

Open up the PC case and look for built-in places to mount fans. How many case fans do you have installed now? What size are they? What sizes can you use? (Most cases use 80-mm fans, but 120-mm and even larger fans are common as well.) Jot down the fan locations of the case and take a trip to the local PC store or online retailer to check out the fans.

Before you get all fan-happy and grab the biggest and baddest fans to throw in your case, don't forget to think about the added noise level. Try to achieve a compromise between keeping your case cool enough and avoiding early deafness.

PATA Drive Installation

Sorry, but CompTIA still has PATA (IDE) drives obliquely listed as a competency, so let's go through installation of these ancient drives quickly. PATA drives have jumpers on the drive that must be set properly. If you have only one hard drive, set the drive's jumpers to master or standalone. If you have two drives, set one to master and the other to slave. Or set both to cable select. See Figure 8-25 for a close-up of a PATA hard drive, showing the jumpers.

Figure 8-25
Master/slave jumpers on a PATA drive

Some drives don't label the jumpers *master* and *slave*. So how do you know how to set them properly? The easiest way is to read the front of the drive; you'll find a diagram on the housing that explains how to set the jumpers properly. Figure 8-26 shows the label of one of these drives, so you can see how to set the drive to master, slave, or cable select.

Figure 8-26
Drive label
showing
master/slave
settings

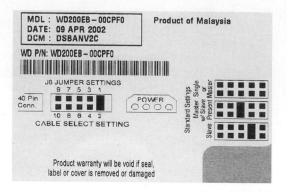

Hard drive cables have a colored stripe that corresponds to the number-one pin—called *pin 1*—on the connector. You need to make certain that pin 1 on the controller is on the same wire as pin 1 on the hard drive. Failing to plug in the drive properly will also prevent the PC from recognizing the drive. If you incorrectly set the master/slave jumpers or cable to the hard drives, you won't break anything; it just won't work.

Older motherboards have dedicated PATA ports built in, so you connect PATA cables directly to the motherboard. Newer motherboards do not have such ports, so to connect a PATA drive requires a special add-on PATA controller expansion card.

Finally, you need to plug a Molex connector from the power supply into the drive. All PATA drives use a Molex connector. Okay, that's it—no more PATA discussion!

 EXAM TIP The CompTIA A+ 1001 objectives list PATA motherboard ports as *IDE connectors*. Don't get thrown off by the different terminology!

Cabling SATA Drives

Installing SATA hard disk drives is much easier than installing PATA devices because there are no jumper settings to worry about at all, as SATA supports only a single device per controller channel. Simply connect the power and plug in the controller cable as shown in Figure 8-27—the OS automatically detects the drive and it's ready to go. The keying on SATA controller and power cables makes it impossible to install either incorrectly.

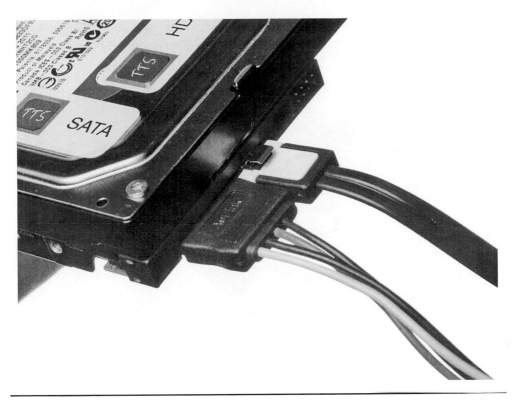

Figure 8-27   Properly connected SATA cable

> **NOTE**   Some older SATA drives have jumpers, but they are used to configure SATA version/speed (1.5, 3.0) or power management. The rule of one drive for one controller applies to these drives, just like more typical jumperless SATA drives.

Every modern motherboard has two or more SATA ports (or *SATA connectors*) built in, like you saw in pictures in Chapter 6, "Motherboards." The ports are labeled (SATA 1 to however many are included). Typically, you install the primary drive into SATA 1, the next into SATA 2, and so on. With non-booting SATA drives, such as in M.2 motherboards, it doesn't matter which port you connect the drive to.

Connecting Solid-State Drives

SATA SSDs possess the same connectors as magnetic SATA drives, so you install an SSD as you would any SATA drive. SATA SSDs usually come in 2.5-inch laptop sizes. Just as with earlier hard drive types, you either connect SSDs correctly and they work, or you forget to plug in the power cable and they don't.

M.2 and mSATA drives slip into their slot on the motherboard or add-on card, then either clip in place or secure with a tiny screw (see Figure 8-28). Both standards are keyed, so you can't install them incorrectly.

Figure 8-28
mSATA SSD
secured on
motherboard

Keep in mind the following considerations before installing or replacing an existing HDD with an SSD:

- Do you have the appropriate drivers and firmware for the SSD? Newer Windows versions will load the most currently implemented SSD drivers. As always, check the manufacturer's specifications as well.

- Do you have everything important backed up? Good!

BIOS Support: Configuring CMOS and Installing Drivers

Every device in your PC needs BIOS support, whether it's traditional BIOS or UEFI. Hard drive controllers are no exception. Motherboards provide support for the SATA hard drive controllers via the system BIOS, but they require configuration in CMOS for the specific hard drives attached.

In the old days, you had to fire up CMOS and manually enter hard drive information whenever you installed a new drive. Today, this process is automated.

Configuring Controllers

As a first step in configuring controllers, make certain they're enabled. Most controllers remain active, ready to automatically detect new drives, but you can disable them. Scan through your CMOS settings to locate the controller on/off options (see Figure 8-29 for typical settings). This is also the time to check whether the onboard RAID controllers work in both RAID and non-RAID settings.

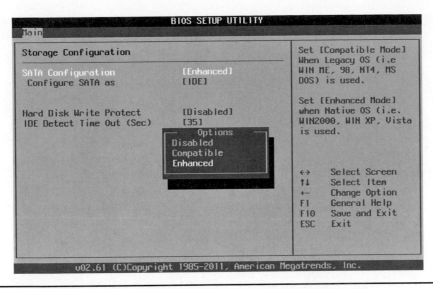

Figure 8-29 Typical controller settings in CMOS

Autodetection

If the controllers are enabled and the drive is properly connected, the drive should appear in CMOS through a process called *autodetection*. Autodetection is a powerful and handy feature that takes almost all the work out of configuring hard drives. Motherboards use a numbering system to determine how drives are listed—and every motherboard uses its own numbering system! One common numbering method uses the term *channels* for each controller. The first boot device is channel 1, the second is channel 2, and so on. So instead of names of drives, you see numbers. Look at Figure 8-30.

Whew! Lots of hard drives! This motherboard supports six SATA connections. Each connection has a number, with an M.2 SSD on SATA 0, hard drives on SATA 1 and SATA 2, and the optical drive on SATA 3. Each was autodetected and configured by the BIOS without any input from me. Oh, to live in the future!

Boot Order

If you want your computer to run, it's going to need an operating system to boot. You assign *boot order* priority to drives and devices in CMOS.

Figure 8-31 shows a typical boot-order screen, with a first, second, and third boot option. Many users like to boot first from the optical drive and then from a hard drive. This enables them to put in a bootable optical disc if they're having problems with the system. Of course, you can set it to boot first from your hard drive and then go into CMOS and change it when you need to—it's your choice.

Most modern CMOS setup utilities include a second screen for determining the boot order of your hard drives. You might want to set up a boot order that goes optical drive, followed by hard drive, and then USB thumb drive, but what if you have more than one

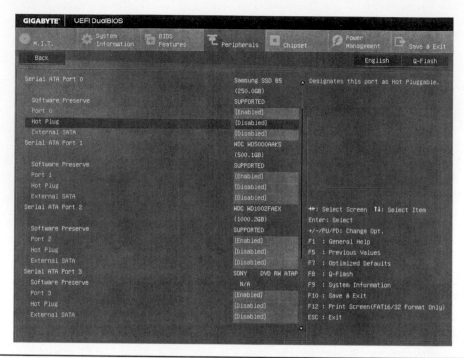

Figure 8-30   Standard CMOS features

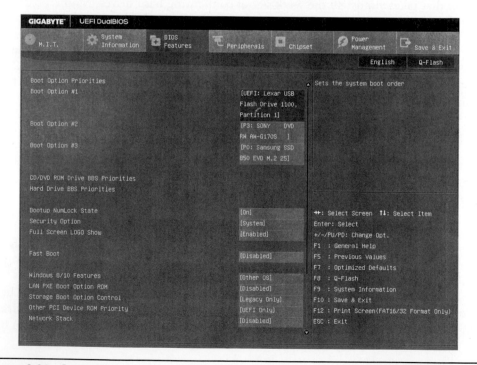

Figure 8-31   Boot order

hard drive? This screen enables you to set which hard drive goes first. If you have a different operating system on each hard drive, this can be very helpful.

Enabling AHCI

On motherboards that support AHCI, you implement it in CMOS. You'll generally have up to three options/modes/HBA configurations: IDE/SATA or compatibility mode, AHCI, or RAID. Don't install modern operating systems in compatibility mode; it's included with some motherboards to support ancient (Windows XP) or odd (some Linux distros, perhaps?) operating systems. AHCI works best for current HDDs and SSDs, so make sure the HBA configuration is set to AHCI.

Troubleshooting Hard Drive Installation

The best friend a tech has when it comes to troubleshooting hard drive installation is the autodetection feature of the CMOS setup utility. When a drive doesn't work, the most obvious question, especially during installation, is "Did I plug it in correctly? Or did I plug both data and power in correctly?" With autodetection, the answer is simple: If the system doesn't see the drive, something is wrong with the hardware configuration. Either a device has physically failed or, more likely, you didn't give the hard drive power, plugged a cable in improperly, or messed up some other connectivity issue. To troubleshoot hard drives, simply work your way through each step to figure out what went wrong.

Make sure the BIOS recognizes the hard drive. Use the CMOS setup program to check. Check the physical connections, then run through these issues in CMOS. Is the controller enabled? Similarly, can the motherboard support the type of drive you're installing? If not, you have a couple of options. You may be able to flash the BIOS with an upgraded BIOS from the manufacturer or get a hard drive controller that goes into an expansion slot.

Chapter Review

Questions

1. Which of the following is a common spindle speed for an HDD?
    A. 5200
    B. 7200
    C. 9200
    D. Not applicable. HDDs have no moving parts.
2. Which form factor connects directly to a dedicated motherboard socket?
    A. 2.5-inch SSD
    B. 3.5-inch SSD
    C. M.2 SSD
    D. eSATA SSD

3. How many PATA hard drives can you have on a system with two PATA hard drive controllers?

   A. 1

   B. 2

   C. 3

   D. 4

4. How do you differentiate two PATA drives on the same cable?

   A. The flat ribbon cable has a seven-wire twist that determines which is which.

   B. You set jumpers on the individual drives to determine which is master and which is slave.

   C. The PATA controller determines the hierarchy.

   D. Both drives are considered equal.

5. What happens if you cable a PATA hard drive incorrectly?

   A. You can destroy that hard drive.

   B. The data will be erased, but the hard drive will be okay.

   C. The system will not be able to communicate with that hard drive.

   D. The drive installs in compatibility mode.

6. What is the maximum cable length of an internal SATA device?

   A. 2 meters

   B. 12 inches

   C. 18 inches

   D. 1 meter

7. What is the maximum number of SATA drives you can have on a system?

   A. One master, one slave

   B. Two, with no master/slave distinction

   C. Eight

   D. There is no maximum other than the limitations of your motherboard/host card.

8. Which SATA version offers the least overhead (and thus best performance)?

   A. AHCI

   B. SATA 2.0

   C. PATA 3.0

   D. SATAe

9. Which standard supports magnetic SATA drives most efficiently?

   A. AHCI

   B. CMOS

   C. SATA-IO

   D. SATA 3.2

10. Which RAID standard requires at least four drives?

   A. RAID 1

   B. RAID 4

   C. RAID 5

   D. RAID 10

Answers

1. **B.** Common spindle speeds on magnetic hard drives are 5400, 7200, 10,000, and 15,000 RPM.

2. **C.** The M.2 (and mSATA) SSD has a dedicated motherboard socket.

3. **D.** Each controller supports two drives.

4. **B.** PATA drives use master/slave jumpers to differentiate between the two drives.

5. **C.** Nothing will be damaged or lost—there just won't be any communication.

6. **D.** The maximum cable length of an internal SATA device is 1 meter.

7. **D.** There is no maximum number of SATA drives you can have on a system beyond the limits imposed by the number of ports on your motherboard/host card.

8. **D.** SATA Express (SATAe) uses the PCIe bus and has none of the traditional SATA overhead.

9. **A.** The AHCI standard supports magnetic SATA drives efficiently.

10. **D.** RAID 10 requires at least four drives.

Implementing Mass Storage

In this chapter, you will learn how to
- Explain the partitions available in Windows
- Discuss hard drive formatting options
- Partition and format hard drives
- Maintain and troubleshoot hard drives

From the standpoint of your PC, a freshly installed hard drive is nothing more than a huge pile of unorganized storage space. Sure, CMOS recognizes it as a drive—always a step in the right direction—but your operating system is clueless without more information. Your operating system must organize that storage so you can use the drive to store data. This chapter covers that process.

 NOTE This chapter uses the term "hard drive" as a generic term that covers all the drive types you learned about in Chapter 8, "Mass Storage Technologies." Once you get into Windows, the operating system doesn't particularly care if the drive is a magnetic hard disk drive (HDD) or a solid-state drive (SSD). The tools and steps for preparing the drives for data are the same.

Historical/Conceptual

After you've successfully installed a hard drive, you must perform two more steps to translate a drive's raw media into something the system can use: partitioning and formatting. *Partitioning* is the process of electronically subdividing a physical drive into one or more units called *partitions*. After partitioning, you must *format* the drive. Formatting installs a *file system* onto the drive that organizes each partition in such a way that the operating system can store files and folders on the drive. Several types of file systems are used by Windows. This chapter will go through them after covering partitioning.

The process of partitioning and formatting a drive is one of the few areas remaining on the software side of PC assembly that requires you to perform a series of fairly complex manual steps. The CompTIA A+ 220-1002 exam tests your knowledge of *what* these processes do to make the drive work, as well as the steps needed to partition and format hard drives in Windows.

This chapter continues the exploration of hard drive installation by explaining the concepts of partitioning and formatting, and then going through the process of partitioning and formatting hard drives. The chapter wraps with a discussion on hard drive maintenance and troubleshooting issues, the scope of which includes all the operating systems covered on the current exams.

Hard Drive Partitions

Before a magnetic disk drive leaves the factory, it is magnetically preset with millions (hundreds of millions on really big drives) of storage areas known as *sectors*. Older hard drives had 512-byte sectors; modern drives use 4096-byte *Advanced Format* (*AF*) sectors. Figure 9-1 shows a close-up of a few sectors on a typical HDD.

Figure 9-1
Sectors on
an HDD

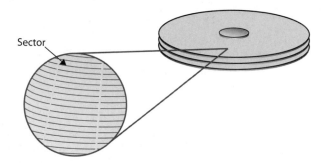

Solid-state drives come from the factory with each NAND chip storing millions (hundreds of millions on really big drives) of 4096-byte storage areas known as *pages*. A group of pages are combined into a *block*. The size of a block varies, but 128 pages per block isn't uncommon. Figure 9-2 shows a simplified concept of how this looks.

The CPU and operating system never talk to these internal structures. Instead, the controller on the HDD or SSD uses *logical block addressing* (*LBA*) to present all these storage chunks as nothing more than a number that starts at LBA0 and goes until every sector or page has an LBA number (see Figure 9-3). These LBA chunks are also called *blocks*.

LBA makes addressing any form of mass storage easy, and that's how the operating system interacts with the mass storage, via blocks. The operating system presents to the user files and folders, not LBA addresses. We must organize mass storage in a way that enables us to store and retrieve files, create folders, etc. The first step to doing this is partitioning.

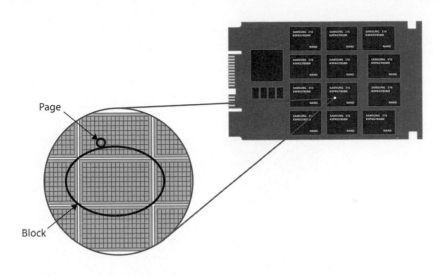

Figure 9-2 SSD pages and blocks

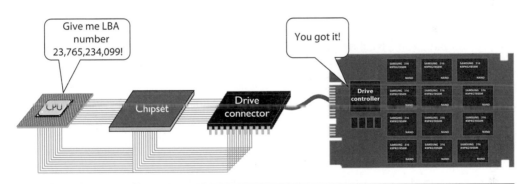

Figure 9-3 LBA in action

If you think of a hard drive as an empty building filled with many rooms (the blocks), partitioning is what organizes the rooms into something bigger (like suites or companies) and gives each bigger entity a name (see Figure 9-4). Partitioning takes a single physical drive and electronically organizes it into one or more . . . partitions. With that analogy, think of partitions as collections of rooms in the building. Partitions provide tremendous flexibility in hard drive organization. With partitions, you can organize a drive to suit your personal taste.

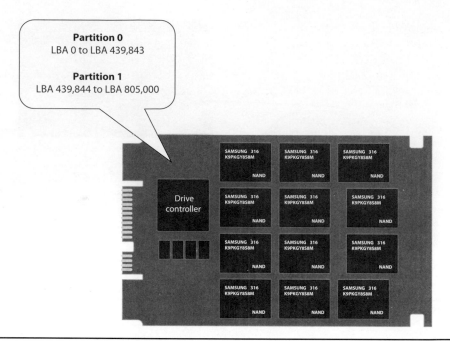

Figure 9-4 Partitions on an SSD

You can partition a hard drive to store more than one operating system: store one OS in one partition and create additional partitions for another OS. Granted, most people use only one OS, but if you want the option to boot to either Windows or Linux, partitions are the key.

1002

Windows supports three different partitioning methods: the older master boot record (MBR) partitioning scheme, Windows' proprietary dynamic storage partitioning scheme, and the GUID partition table (GPT). (I'll cover all three of these in their respective sections, following this introduction.) Microsoft calls a hard drive that uses either the MBR partitioning scheme or the GPT partitioning scheme a *basic disk* and calls a drive that uses the dynamic storage partitioning scheme a *dynamic disk*.

 EXAM TIP You might see the terms *basic partition* and *dynamic partition* on the CompTIA A+ 1002 exam. These mean, logically, volumes partitioned as basic disks or dynamic disks, respectively.

A single Windows system with three hard drives may have one of the drives partitioned with MBR, another with GPT, and the third set up as a dynamic disk, and the system will run perfectly well. The bottom line? You get to learn about three totally different types of partitioning. I'll also cover a few other partition types, such as hidden partitions, and tell you when you can and should make your partitions.

Master Boot Record

The first sector of an MBR hard drive contains the *master boot record* (*MBR*), code that informs the system about installed operating systems. To clarify, hard drives that use the MBR partitioning scheme have a tiny bit of data that is also called the "master boot record." While your computer boots up, BIOS looks at the first sector of your hard drive for instructions. At this point, it doesn't matter which OS you use or how many partitions you have. Without this bit of code, your OS will never load.

NOTE Techs often refer to MBR-partitioned drives as "MBR drives." The same holds true for GPT-partitioned drives, which many techs refer to as "GPT drives."

The master boot record also contains the *partition table*, which describes the number and size of partitions on the disk (see Figure 9-5). MBR partition tables support up to four partitions—the partition table is large enough to store entries for only four partitions. The instructions in the master boot record use this table to determine which partition contains the active operating system.

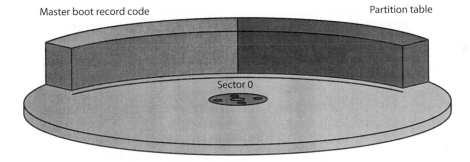

Figure 9-5 The master boot record

After the MBR locates the appropriate partition, the *partition boot sector* loads the OS on that partition. The partition boot sector stores information important to its partition, such as the location of the OS boot files (see Figure 9-6).

Figure 9-6
Using the master boot record to boot an OS

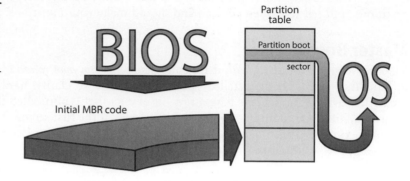

EXAM TIP   Only one master boot record and one partition table within that master boot record exist per MBR disk. Each partition has a partition boot sector.

MBR partition tables support two types of partitions: primary partitions and extended partitions. *Primary partitions* are designed to support bootable operating systems. *Extended partitions* are not bootable. A single MBR disk may have up to four primary partitions or up to three primary partitions and one extended partition.

Primary Partitions and Multiple Operating Systems

Primary partitions are usually assigned drive letters and appear in Windows Explorer/File Explorer (once you format them). The first lettered primary partition in Windows is always C:. After that, you can label the partitions D: through Z:.

NOTE   Partitions don't always get drive letters. Windows creates a small primary partition named "System Reserved" for essential Windows boot files. See also the section "Mounting Partitions as Folders," later in this chapter, for details.

In a related topic, the first primary Windows partition is called "C:" because early PCs had one or two floppy drives installed and they got the "A:" and "B:" labels.

Only primary partitions can boot operating systems. On an MBR disk, you can easily install four different operating systems, each on its own primary partition, and boot to your choice each time you fire up the computer.

Every primary partition on a single drive has a special setting stored in the partition table called *active* that determines the *active partition*. During boot-up, the BIOS/POST reads the MBR to find the active partition and boots the operating system on that partition. Only one partition can be active at a time because you can run only one OS at a time (see Figure 9-7).

Figure 9-7
The active partition containing Windows

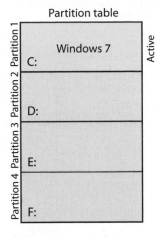

Partition table

Partition 1 / Partition 2 / Partition 3 / Partition 4

C: Windows 7 — Active

D:

E:

F:

To control multiboot setups, many people use a free Linux-based boot manager called Grand Unified Bootloader (GRUB), shown in Figure 9-8, although some people prefer Partition Commander by Avanquest Software to set up the partitions. When the computer boots, the boot manager software yanks control from the MBR and asks which OS you want to boot. Once a partition is set as active, the partition boot sector loads the operating system.

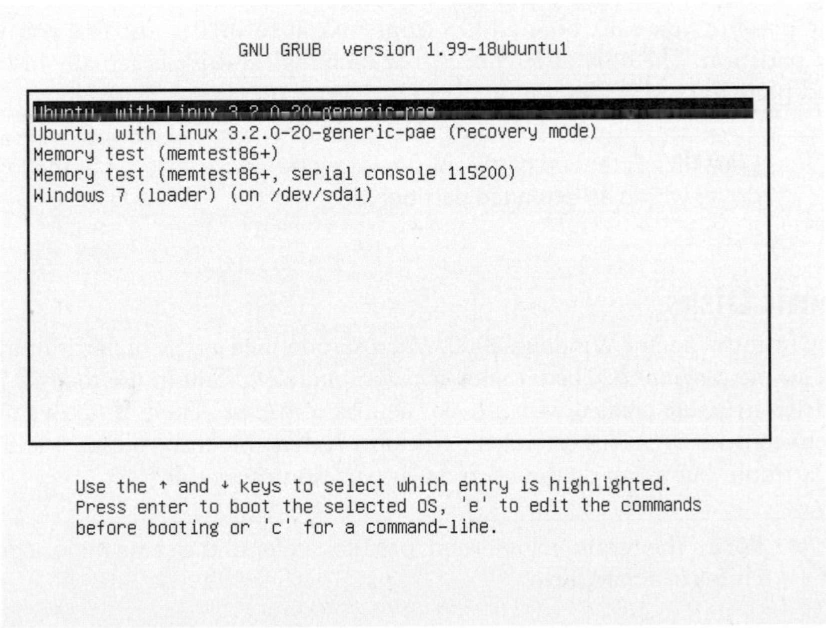

```
              GNU GRUB   version 1.99-18ubuntu1

Ubuntu, with Linux 3.2.0-20-generic-pae
Ubuntu, with Linux 3.2.0-20-generic-pae (recovery mode)
Memory test (memtest86+)
Memory test (memtest86+, serial console 115200)
Windows 7 (loader) (on /dev/sda1)




      Use the ↑ and ↓ keys to select which entry is highlighted.
      Press enter to boot the selected OS, 'e' to edit the commands
      before booting or 'c' for a command-line.
```

Figure 9-8   GRUB in action

Extended Partitions

With a four-partition limit, an MBR disk would be limited to only four drive letters if using only primary partitions. An extended partition overcomes this limit. An extended partition can contain multiple *logical drives*, each of which can get a drive letter (see Figure 9-9).

Figure 9-9

An extended partition containing multiple logical drives

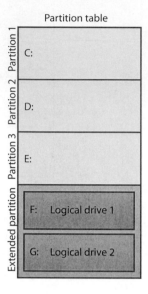

A logical drive works like a primary partition—it usually gets a drive letter such as D: or E:—but you can't boot an OS from it. You format it just like you would a primary partition. The only difference is that each logical drive is actually in the same extended partition.

 EXAM TIP Extended partitions do not receive drive letters, but the logical drives within an extended partition do.

Dynamic Disks

With the introduction of Windows 2000, Microsoft defined a type of partitioning called *dynamic storage partitioning*, better known as *dynamic disks*. Still in use today, Microsoft calls a drive structure created with a dynamic disk a *volume*. There is no dynamic disk equivalent to primary versus extended partitions. A dynamic disk volume is still technically a partition, but it can do things a regular partition cannot do.

 NOTE The terms "volume" and "partition" refer to the same thing: a defined chunk of a hard drive.

First off, when you turn a hard drive into a dynamic disk, you can create as many volumes on it as you want. You're not limited to four partitions.

Second, you can create—in software—new drive structures that you can't do with MBR drives. Specifically, you can implement RAID, span volumes over multiple drives, and extend volumes on one or more drives. Table 9-1 shows you which version of Windows supports which volume type.

Volume	Windows 7	Windows 8/8.1/10	Windows Server
Simple	X	X	X
Spanned	X	X	X
Striped	X	X	X
Mirrored	X	X	X
RAID 5			X

Table 9-1 Dynamic Disk Compatibility

 EXAM TIP Only the lower-end editions of Windows 7 don't support dynamic disks. Every version and edition you'll run into these days supports dynamic disks.

Simple volumes work a lot like primary partitions. If you have a hard drive and you want to make half of it E: and the other half F:, for example, you create two volumes on a dynamic disk. That's it.

Spanned volumes use unallocated space on multiple drives to create a single volume. Spanned volumes are a bit risky: if any of the spanned drives fails, the entire volume is lost.

Striped volumes are RAID 0 volumes. You may take any two unallocated spaces on two separate hard drives and stripe them. But again, if either drive fails, you lose all of your data.

Mirrored volumes are RAID 1 volumes. You may take any two unallocated spaces on two separate hard drives and mirror them. If one of the two mirrored drives fails, the other keeps running.

RAID 5 volumes, as the name implies, are for RAID 5 arrays. A RAID 5 volume requires three or more dynamic disks with equal-sized unallocated spaces.

 NOTE Windows 8 and later can use a software RAID system called Storage Spaces that's distinct from dynamic disks. See the appropriately named section of this chapter for the scoop.

GUID Partition Table

MBR partitioning came out a long time ago, in an age where 32-MB hard drives were thought to be larger than you would ever need. While it's lasted a long time as the partitioning standard for bootable drives, there's a newer kid in town with the power to outshine the aging partitioning scheme and assume all the functions of the older partition style.

The *GUID partition table* (*GPT*) partitioning scheme shares a lot with the MBR partitioning scheme, but most of the MBR scheme's limitations have been fixed. Here are the big improvements:

- While MBR drives are limited to four partitions, a GPT drive can have an almost unlimited number of primary partitions. Microsoft has limited Windows to 128 partitions.

- MBR partitions can be no larger than 2.2 TB, but GPT partitions have no such restrictions. Well, there is a maximum size limit, but it's so large, we measure it in zettabytes. A zettabyte, by the way, is roughly a billion terabytes.

On paper, a GPT drive looks a lot like an MBR drive, except it's arranged by LBA instead of sectors (see Figure 9-10). LBA 0, for instance, is the *protective MBR*. This is a re-creation of the master boot record from MBR drives so that disk utilities know it is a GPT drive and don't mistakenly overwrite any partition data.

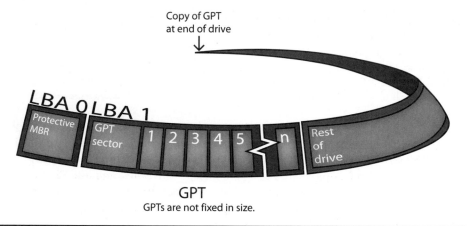

Figure 9-10 GUID partition table

Instead of the old master boot record and partition table, GPT drives use a GPT header and partition entry array. Both are located at the beginning and end of the drive so there is a protected backup copy. The partitions on a GPT drive go between the primary and backup headers and arrays, as shown in Figure 9-10.

You can configure the 64-bit versions of modern Windows to boot from GPT only if you use a UEFI motherboard. In other words, if you're trying to install Windows 10 on an ancient motherboard, you're stuck with MBR. The same is true of macOS. Most Linux distributions can boot from GPT partitions with older BIOS or UEFI firmware.

NOTE Okay, if GPT stands for GUID partition table, I guess we had better see what GUID stands for, eh? A *globally unique identifier* (*GUID*) provides a reference number for an object or process that has an almost impossibly small chance of duplication. The number is, therefore, *unique* to a specific object or process.

Other Partition Types

The partition types supported by Windows are not the only partition types you may encounter; other types exist. One of the most common is called the *hidden partition*. A hidden partition is really just a primary partition that is hidden from your operating system. Only special BIOS tools may access a hidden partition. Hidden partitions are used by some PC makers to hide a backup copy of an installed OS that you can use to restore your system if you accidentally trash it—by, for example, learning about partitions and using a partitioning program incorrectly.

EXAM TIP CompTIA refers to a hidden partition that contains a restorable copy of an installed OS as a *factory recovery partition*.

A *swap partition* is another special type of partition, but swap partitions are found only on Linux and UNIX systems. A swap partition's only job is to act like RAM when your system needs more RAM than you have installed. Windows has a similar function with a *page file* that uses a special file instead of a partition, as you'll recall from Chapter 4, "RAM."

When to Partition

Partitioning is not a common task for an already setup system. The two most common situations likely to require partitioning are when you install an OS on a new system, and when you add an additional drive to an existing system. When you install a new OS, the installation program asks you how you would like to partition the drive. When you add a new hard drive to an existing system, every OS has a built-in tool to help you partition it.

Each version of Windows offers a different tool for partitioning hard drives. For more than 20 years, through the days of DOS and early Windows (up to Windows Me), we used a command-line program called *FDISK* to partition drives. Figure 9-11 shows the FDISK program. Modern versions of Windows use a graphical partitioning program called *Disk Management*, shown in Figure 9-12. You'll find it in Computer Management in Administrative Tools. (Windows has an advanced command-line disk management tool as well, called *diskpart*, discussed in detail in Chapter 16, "Troubleshooting Operating Systems.")

Figure 9-11
FDISK

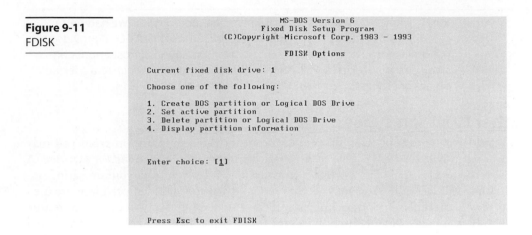

```
                          MS-DOS Version 6
                      Fixed Disk Setup Program
                 (C)Copyright Microsoft Corp. 1983 - 1993

                          FDISK Options

Current fixed disk drive: 1

Choose one of the following:

1. Create DOS partition or Logical DOS Drive
2. Set active partition
3. Delete partition or Logical DOS Drive
4. Display partition information


Enter choice: [1]




Press Esc to exit FDISK
```

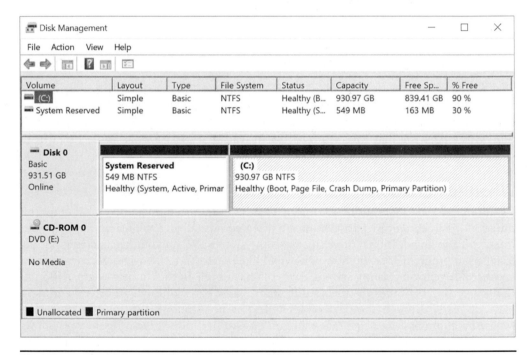

Figure 9-12 Windows 10 Disk Management tool in Computer Management

Linux uses several tools for partitioning. The oldest is called *fdisk*—yes, the same name as the DOS/Windows tool (though case-sensitive). That's where the similarities end, however, as Linux fdisk has a totally different command set. Even though every copy of Linux comes with the Linux fdisk, it's rarely used because so many better partitioning tools are available. One of the newer Linux partitioning tools is called GParted. See the "Beyond A+" section for more discussion on third-party partitioning tools.

In the early days of PCs, you couldn't change a partition's size or type (other than by erasing it) once you'd made it with any Microsoft tools. A few third-party tools, led by PartitionMagic, gave techs the tools to resize partitions without losing the data the partitions held. Current Microsoft tools have more. Windows enables you to resize partitions nondestructively by shrinking or expanding existing partitions with available free space.

 SIM Check out the excellent Chapter 9 Show! and Click! simulations, both titled "Resizing a Partition," at the Total Seminars Training Hub: http://totalsem.com/100x. These give you a quick shot at addressing probable simulation questions on the 1002 exam.

Partition Naming Problems

So far, you've learned that MBR and GPT disks use partitions and dynamic disks use volumes. Unfortunately, when you create a new partition or volume in current versions of Windows (8, 8.1, 10), the tool (Disk Management) only shows that you're about to create a volume. See Figure 9-13.

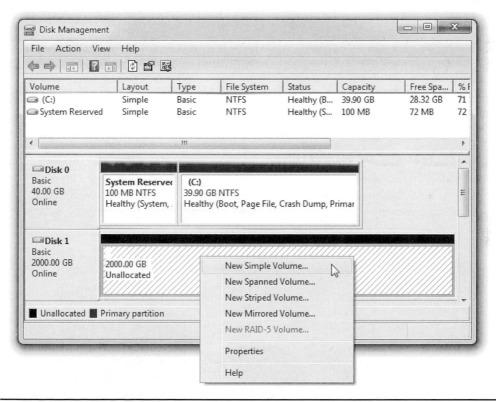

Figure 9-13 Note that the context menu only mentions volumes, not partitions.

Even though the context menu says "volumes," you create partitions on basic disks. Figure 9-14 shows Disk Management in Windows 8.1 with a basic disk with four partitions. The first three (from left to right) are primary partitions. The two structures on the right are a logical drive and some blank, unpartitioned "Free space" in an extended partition.

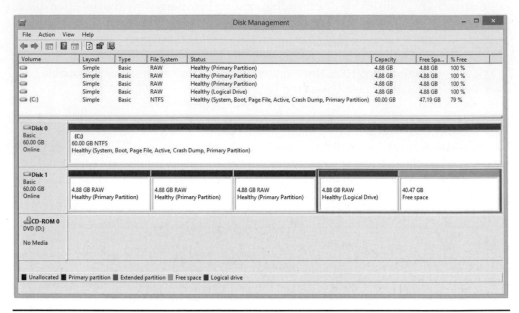

Figure 9-14 Drive with four partitions displayed in Disk Management

Hard Drive Formatting

Once you've partitioned a hard drive, that partition is nothing more than a large number of blocks. Your operating system needs to store files, files with names like VacationMemories.mp4 or chrome.exe. We need to organize those blocks (see Figure 9-15).

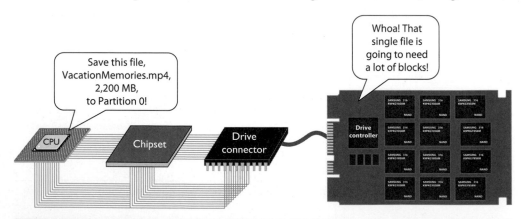

Figure 9-15 Big files require many blocks.

Formatting, the process of making a partition into something that stores files, does two things. First, it creates a file system—an organization of all the blocks contained in that partition, enabling file storage and retrieval. Second, formatting creates a root directory in the file system to enable the partition to store folders. You must format every partition/volume so they can hold and retrieve data.

Every operating system has its own file systems. For the Apple folks, macOS uses a couple of file systems called APFS and HFS+. Linux users have lots to choose from; most use ext4 but you will see others with names like BTRFS, XFS, ZFS, etc. Windows has file systems with names like NTFS, FAT32, and exFAT. Let's first understand what a file system does (using Windows as an example), and then we will discuss the differences.

 NOTE Different operating systems may or may not be able to read other operating systems' file systems. For example, most Linux systems easily read Windows' NTFS.

File Systems in Windows

Every version of Windows comes with a built-in formatting utility with which to create one or more file systems on a partition or volume. The versions of Windows in current use support three Microsoft file systems: FAT32, NTFS, and exFAT (for removable media). All Windows file systems organize blocks of data into groups called *clusters*. The size of each cluster varies according to the file system and the size of the partition. Windows uses clusters to overcome some of the limitations in addressing inherent to each file system. (I'll add charts with each file system to show how the clusters scale.)

FAT32

The base storage area for hard drives is a block; each block stores up to 4096 bytes of data. In a small partition, each cluster is made up of one block. If a file is larger than 4096 bytes, it will use as many clusters as needed to store the file. The OS needs a method to fill one cluster, find another that's unused, and fill it, continuing to fill clusters until the file is completely stored. Once the OS stores a file, it must remember which cluster holds the file, so it can be retrieved later. If an OS stores a file smaller than 4096 bytes, the rest of the cluster goes to waste. We accept this waste because most files are far larger than 4096 bytes.

MS-DOS version 2.1 first supported hard drives using a data structure and indexing system to keep track of stored data on the hard drive, and Microsoft called this structure the *file allocation table* (*FAT*). Think of the FAT as nothing more than a card catalog that keeps track of which clusters store the various parts of a file. The official jargon term for a FAT is *data structure*, but it is more like a two-column spreadsheet.

The left column (see Figure 9-16) gives each cluster a hexadecimal number from 00000000 to FFFFFFFF. Each hexadecimal character represents four binary numbers or 4 bits. Eight hex characters, therefore, represent 32 bits. If you do the math (232), you'll find that there are over four billion clusters that can be tracked or indexed.

Figure 9-16

32-bit FAT

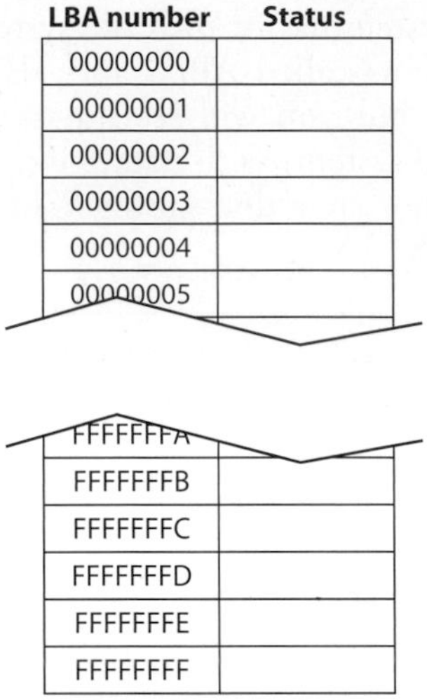

LBA number	Status
00000000	
00000001	
00000002	
00000003	
00000004	
00000005	

LBA number	Status
FFFFFFFA	
FFFFFFFB	
FFFFFFFC	
FFFFFFFD	
FFFFFFFE	
FFFFFFFF	

NOTE Hexadecimal characters cover the decimal numbers 0–15, numbering from 0–9 and then A–F; each character reflects the state of four binary characters. You add them up to make the number. So, 0000 in binary shows zero numbers and the hex number is 0. When you go up numerically in binary to 0001, this represents the number 1 in decimal and also in hex. The key to hex is when you reach the number 10. In binary, this looks like this: 1010. But because hex sticks with a single digit, it's represented as A. B translates as 11 in decimal or 1011 in binary, and so on.

We call this type of FAT a *32-bit FAT* or *FAT32*. And it's not just hard drives and SSDs that have FATs. Many USB flash drives use FAT32.

The right column of the FAT contains information on the status of clusters. All hard drives, even brand-new drives fresh from the factory, contain faulty blocks that cannot store data because of imperfections in the construction of the drives. The OS must locate these bad blocks, mark them as unusable, and then prevent any files from being written to them. This mapping of bad blocks is one of the functions of *high-level formatting*. After the format program creates the FAT, it marches through every block of the entire partition, writing and attempting to read from each block sequentially. If it finds a bad block, it places a special status code (0000FFF7) in the block's FAT location, indicating that the cluster is unavailable for use. Formatting also marks the good blocks with code 00000000 (see Figure 9-17).

Figure 9-17
Bad blocks
marked

LBA number	Status	
00000000	00000000	
00000001	00000000	
00000002	00000000	
00000003	00000000	
00000004	0000FFF7	Bad block
00000005	00000000	

FFFFFFFA		
FFFFFFFB	00000000	
FFFFFFFC	0000FFF7	Bad block
FFFFFFFD	00000000	
FFFFFFFE	00000000	
FFFFFFFF	00000000	

 NOTE *High-level formatting*, as noted, creates the FAT and then creates a blank root directory. This process is known in Microsoft speak as a *quick format*. At your option, you can cause the format utility to test every sector to mark out the unusable ones in the FAT. This is called a *full format*.

FAT32 in Action

Suppose you have a system with a drive using FAT32. When an application such as Microsoft Word tells the OS to save a file, Windows starts at the beginning of the FAT, looking for the first space marked "open for use" (00000000), and begins to write to that cluster. If the entire file fits within that one cluster, Windows places the code *0000FFFF* (last cluster) into the cluster's status area in the FAT. That's called the *end-of-file marker*. Windows then goes to the folder storing the file and adds the filename and the cluster's number to the folder list. If the file requires more than one cluster, Windows searches for the next open cluster and places the number of the next cluster in the status area, filling and adding clusters until the entire file is saved. The last cluster then receives the end-of-file marker (0000FFFF).

Let's run through an example of this process, starting by selecting an arbitrary part of the FAT: from 03213ABB to 03213AC7. Assume you want to save a file called mom.txt. Before saving the file, the FAT looks like Figure 9-18.

Figure 9-18
The initial FAT

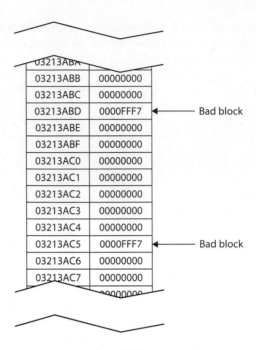

Windows finds the first open cluster, 03213ABB, and fills it. But the entire mom.txt file won't fit into that cluster. Needing more space, the OS goes through the FAT to find the next open cluster. It finds cluster 03213ABC. Before filling 03213ABC, the value *03213ABC* is placed in 03213ABB's status. Even after filling two clusters, more of the mom.txt file remains, so Windows must find one more cluster. The 03213ABD cluster has been marked 0000FFF7 (bad block), so Windows skips over 03213ABD, finding 03213ABE.

Before filling 03213ABE, Windows enters the value *03213ABE* in 03213ABC's status. Windows does not completely fill 03213ABE, signifying that the entire mom.txt file has been stored. Windows enters the value *0000FFFF* in 03213ABE's status, indicating the end of file (see Figure 9-19).

After saving all of the clusters, Windows locates the file's folder (yes, folders also are stored on blocks, but they get a different set of blocks, somewhere else on the disk) and records the filename, size, date/time, and starting cluster, like this:

```
mom.txt      13234 05-19-19 2:04p 03213ABB
```

If a program requests that file, the process is reversed. Windows locates the folder containing the file to determine the starting cluster and then pulls a piece of the file from each cluster until it sees the end-of-file cluster. Windows then hands the reassembled file to the requesting application.

Clearly, without the FAT, Windows cannot locate files. FAT32 automatically makes two copies of the FAT. One FAT backs up the other to provide special utilities a way to recover a FAT that gets corrupted—a painfully common occurrence.

Figure 9-19
End of file
reached

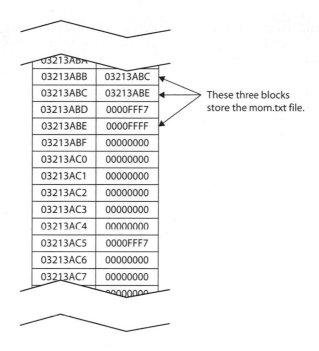

These three blocks
store the mom.txt file.

Cluster Sizes in FAT32

Cluster sizes scale according to the file system. FAT32 offers 4-KB cluster sizes up to a partition size of 2 GB, which matches the size of a 4-KB block. Larger partitions require clusters with more blocks, thus reducing somewhat the efficiency of that drive. Table 9-2 shows the scaling effect in FAT32.

Table 9-2
FAT32 Cluster
Sizes

Drive Size	Cluster Size
512 MB to 1023 MB	4 KB
1024 MB to 2 GB	4 KB
2 GB to 8 GB	4 KB
8 GB to 16 GB	8 KB
16 GB to 32 GB	16 KB
>32 GB	32 KB

FAT32 is still very much commonly used today, though not for operating system partitions. Rather, you'll see it on smaller (< 32-GB) flash-media USB drives.

Fragmentation

Continuing with the example, let's use Microsoft Word to save two more files: a letter called Important Document 31.docx and a letter named System Storage.docx. The Important

Document 31.docx file takes the next three clusters—03213ABF, 03213AC0, and 03213AC1—and System Storage.docx takes two clusters—03213AC2 and 03213AC3 (see Figure 9-20).

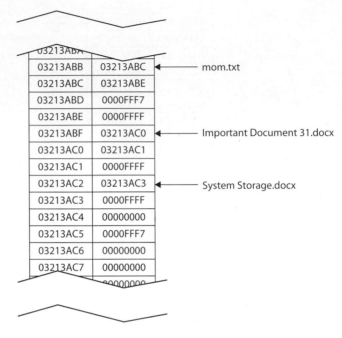

Figure 9-20
Three files saved

Assuming these files are all in the same folder, the file information looks like this:

```
mom.txt                         13234    05-19-20 2:04p 03213ABB
Important Document 31.docx       9276    05-19-20 2:07p 03213ABF
System Storage.docx             5434    05-19-20 2:10p 03213AC2
```

Now suppose you erase mom.txt. Windows does not delete the block entries in the FAT for mom.txt when it erases the file. Windows only alters the information in the folder, simply changing the first letter of mom.txt to the lowercase Greek letter σ (sigma), as shown next. This causes the file to "disappear" as far as the OS knows. It won't show up, for example, in Windows Explorer, even though the data still resides on the hard drive for the moment.

```
σom.txt                         13234    05-19-20 2:04p 03213ABB
```

Note that under normal circumstances, Windows does not actually delete files when you press the delete key. Instead, Windows moves the file listing (but not the actual blocks) to a special hidden directory that you can access via the Recycle Bin. The files themselves are not actually deleted until you empty the Recycle Bin.

Because the data for mom.txt is intact, you could use some program to change the σ back into another letter and thus get the document back. A number of third-party undelete tools are available. Figure 9-21 shows one such program at work. Just remember that if you want to use an undelete tool, you must use it quickly. The space allocated to your deleted file may soon be overwritten by a new file.

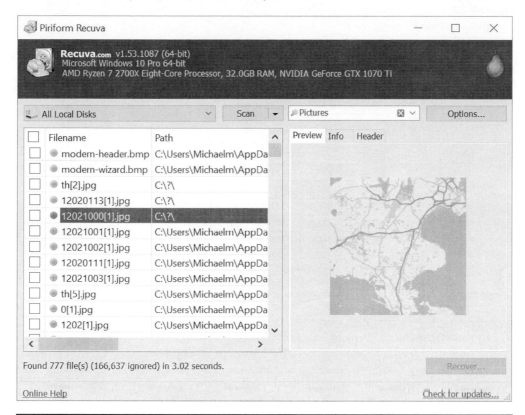

Figure 9-21   Piriform Recuva in action

 EXAM TIP   CompTIA may ask you how to recover a deleted file. If the file is still in the Recycle Bin, simply browse to the Recycle Bin, right-click the deleted file, and select Restore. If the file was deleted and bypassed the Recycle Bin or for any other reason is no longer there, Microsoft offers no utility that can recover or restore the file. You must resort to one of the third-party utilities that are available.

Let's say you just emptied your Recycle Bin. You now save one more file, Taxrec.xls, a big spreadsheet that will take six clusters, into the same folder that once held mom.txt. As Windows writes the file to the drive, it overwrites the space that mom.txt used, but it needs three more clusters. The next three available clusters are 03213AC4, 03213AC6 (skipping cluster 03213AC5, which is marked bad), and 03213AC7 (see Figure 9-22).

Figure 9-22
The taxrec.xls file, fragmented

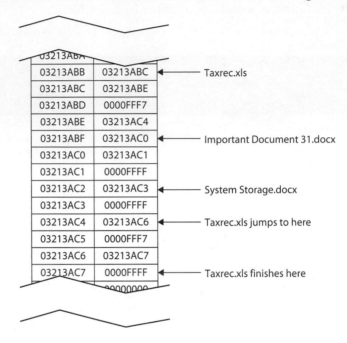

03213ABA	
03213ABB	03213ABC	◄—— Taxrec.xls
03213ABC	03213ABE	
03213ABD	0000FFF7	
03213ABE	03213AC4	
03213ABF	03213AC0	◄—— Important Document 31.docx
03213AC0	03213AC1	
03213AC1	0000FFFF	
03213AC2	03213AC3	◄—— System Storage.docx
03213AC3	0000FFFF	
03213AC4	03213AC6	◄—— Taxrec.xls jumps to here
03213AC5	0000FFF7	
03213AC6	03213AC7	
03213AC7	0000FFFF	◄—— Taxrec.xls finishes here
	00000000	

Notice that taxrec.xls is in two pieces, thus *fragmented. Fragmentation* takes place all of the time on FAT32 systems. Although the system easily negotiates a tiny fragmented file split into only two parts, excess fragmentation slows down the system during hard drive reads and writes. This example is fragmented into two pieces; in the real world, a file might fragment into hundreds of pieces, forcing the read/write heads to travel all over the hard drive to retrieve a single file. You can dramatically improve the speed at which the hard drive reads and writes files by eliminating this fragmentation.

Windows comes with a program called Disk Defragmenter (Windows 7) or Optimize Drives (Windows 8/8.1/10) that can rearrange the files into neat contiguous chunks (see Figure 9-23). Windows does this automatically by default. Defragmentation is crucial for ensuring the top performance of a mechanical hard drive. The "Maintaining and Troubleshooting Hard Drives" section of this chapter gives the details on working with the various defragmenting tools in Windows.

SSDs also have fragmentation of a sort, but the nature of an SSD means almost any page is as easily accessed as any other. In the first-generation SSDs, once data was written into a memory cell, it stayed there until the drive was full. Even if the cell contained file contents from a "deleted" file, the cell was not immediately erased or overwritten, because the SSD controller had no way to know the cell's contents were deleted as far as the OS was concerned.

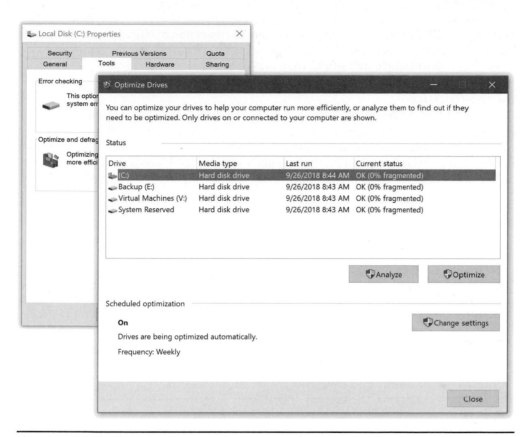

Figure 9-23   Windows 10 Optimize Drives

Because SSD memory cells have a finite number of times that they can be written to before wearing out, the first generation of SSDs waited until all the cells of an SSD were filled before erasing and reusing a previously written cell.

Modern SSDs have a feature called *trim* that enables the OS to issue commands to clean up and reuse deleted areas. This happens automatically, so there's no reason at all to defragment any SSD.

NTFS

The Windows format of choice these days is the *New Technology File System* (*NTFS*). NTFS came out a long time ago with the first version of Windows NT, thus the name. Over the years, NTFS has undergone several improvements. NTFS uses clusters of blocks and file allocation tables, but in a much more complex and powerful way compared to FAT32. NTFS offers six major improvements and refinements: redundancy, security, compression, encryption, disk quotas, and cluster sizing.

TIP If you have a geeky interest in what version of NTFS you are running, open a Command Prompt as an administrator and type this command: **fsutil fsinfo ntfsinfo c:**. Then press ENTER.

NTFS Structure

NTFS utilizes an enhanced file allocation table called the *master file table* (*MFT*). An NTFS partition keeps a backup copy of the most critical parts of the MFT in the middle of the disk, reducing the chance that a serious drive error can wipe out both the MFT and the MFT copy. Whenever you defragment an NTFS partition, you'll see a small, immovable chunk somewhere on the drive, often near the front; that's the MFT (see Figure 9-24).

Figure 9-24 The NTFS MFT appears in a defragmenter program as the highlighted red blocks (although those are hard to see in black and white printing!).

Security

NTFS views individual files and folders as objects and provides security for those objects through a feature called the *Access Control List* (*ACL*). Future chapters go into this in much more detail.

NOTE Microsoft has never released the exact workings of NTFS to the public.

Compression

NTFS enables you to compress individual files and folders to save space on a hard drive. Compression makes access time to the data slower because the OS must uncompress files every time you use them, but in a space-limited environment, sometimes that's what you have to do. Windows Explorer/File Explorer displays filenames for compressed files in blue.

 NOTE Sometimes compression makes access faster. In cases where the CPU can decompress faster than the storage system can give it bytes, compressing the files means that the disk will have fewer bytes to send and the CPU can just rip right through them, expanding them into memory.

Encryption

One of the big draws with NTFS is file encryption, the black art of making files unreadable to anybody who doesn't have the right key. You can encrypt a single file, a folder, or a folder full of files. Microsoft calls the encryption utility in NTFS the *encrypting file system* (*EFS*), but it's simply an aspect of NTFS, not a standalone file system. You'll learn more about encryption when you read Chapter 13, "Users, Groups, and Permissions."

Disk Quotas

NTFS supports *disk quotas*, enabling administrators to set limits on drive space usage for users. To set quotas, you must log on as an Administrator, right-click the hard drive name, and select Properties. In the Drive Properties dialog box, select the Quota tab and make changes. Figure 9-25 shows configured quotas for a hard drive. Although rarely used on single-user systems, setting disk quotas on multi-user systems prevents any individual user from monopolizing your hard disk space.

Figure 9-25

Hard drive quotas in Windows 10

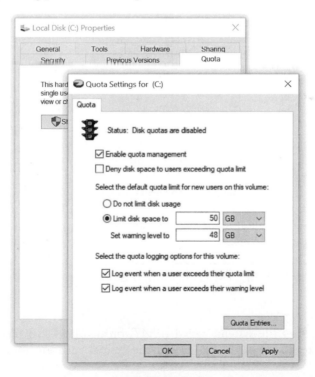

Cluster Sizes

NTFS uses clusters, much like FAT32. The numbers equate to block size until you get to very large partitions. Table 9-3 shows the default cluster sizes for NTFS.

	Drive Size	Cluster Size
Table 9-3 NTFS Cluster Sizes	7 MB to 16 TB	4 KB
	16 to 32 TB	8 KB
	32 to 64 TB	32 KB
	64 to 128 TB	64 KB
	128 to 256 TB	128 KB

By default, NTFS supports partitions up to ~16 TB on a dynamic disk (though only up to 2 TB on a basic disk). By tweaking the cluster sizes, you can get NTFS to support partitions up to 16 exabytes, or 18,446,744,073,709,551,616 bytes! That might support any and all upcoming hard drive capacities for the next 100 years or so.

EXAM TIP NTFS supports partitions up to 16 TB by default.

With so many file systems, how do you know which one to use? In the case of internal hard drives, you should use the most feature-rich system your OS supports. For all modern versions of Windows, use NTFS. External hard drives and flash drives still often use FAT32 because NTFS features such as the ACL and encryption can make access difficult when you move the drive between systems, but with that exception, NTFS is your best choice on a Windows-based system.

exFAT

Everyone loves USB flash drives. Their ease of use and convenience make them indispensable for those of us who enjoy sharing a program, some photos, or a playlist. But people today want to share more than just a few small files, and they can do so with larger flash drives. As flash drives grow bigger in capacity, however, the file system becomes a problem.

The file system we have used for years on flash drives, FAT32, does not work on drives larger than 2 TB. Worse, FAT32 limits *file* size to 4 GB. Because there is frequent need to physically transport many files that are often larger than 4 GB, Microsoft developed a replacement for FAT32.

EXAM TIP FAT32 only supports drives up to 2 TB and files up to 4 GB.

The newer file system, called *exFAT*, breaks the 4-GB file-size barrier, supporting files up to 16 exabytes (EB) and a theoretical partition limit of 64 zettabytes (ZB).

Microsoft recommends a partition size of up to 512 TB on today's larger USB flash drives, which should be enough for a while. The exFAT file system extends FAT32 from 32-bit cluster entries to 64-bit cluster entries in the file table. Like FAT32, on the other hand, exFAT still lacks all of NTFS's extra features such as permissions, compression, and encryption.

NOTE An exabyte is 2^{60} bytes; a zettabyte is 2^{70} bytes. For comparison, a terabyte is 2^{40} bytes. Remember from your binary practice that each superscript number doubles the overall number, so $2^{41} = 2$ TB, $2^{42} = 4$ TB, and so on. That means a zettabyte is really, really big!

File Systems in macOS

As this book goes to print, Apple is in the middle of changing out the file systems used on Macs. The classic file system for Macs is *Hierarchical File System Plus* (*HFS+*). While still required for Time Machine drives, all new Macs (and existing systems upgrading macOS) come with the *Apple File System* (*APFS*) by default. Like Windows and Linux, macOS can read and write to several different file systems such as FAT32 and exFAT, though only read NTFS.

File Systems in Linux

Most Linux distributions use a file system known as the *Fourth Extended File System* (*ext4*) by default. Some older distros use one of its predecessors, such as *ext2* or *ext3*. The ext4 file system supports volumes up to 1 exabyte (EB) with file sizes up to 16 TB and is backwardly compatible with ext2 and ext3. In other words, you can mount an ext3 volume as an ext4 volume with no problems. You don't need to know the details of ext3 or ext4, just that they are Linux file systems and that ext4 supports volumes up to 1 EB with file sizes up to 16 TB.

NOTE Linux file system capabilities exceed those of both macOS and Windows, being able to read and write to NTFS, FAT32, exFAT, HFS+, and ext4. Sweet!

Many Linux distributions, especially at the enterprise level (big data centers), use ZFS file system or its newer cousin, BTRFS (pronounced, "butter eff ess"). Both offer powerful copy and disk management features that go well beyond the scope of CompTIA A+. For more information on ZFS and most likely the file system wave of the future, even in Windows, start with the Wikipedia article and follow the links to the sources.

The Partitioning, Formatting, and Pooling Process

Now that you understand the concepts of partitioning and formatting, let's go through the process of setting up an installed hard drive by using different partitioning and formatting tools. At the end of the section, we'll look at the process of creating a storage pool by creating a virtual disk. If you have access to a system, try following along with these descriptions. Don't make any changes to a drive you want to keep, because both partitioning and formatting are destructive processes. The pooling process is also destructive. You cannot follow the procedure in that discussion unless you have a few drives to erase.

Bootable Media

Imagine you've built a brand-new PC. The hard drive has no OS, so you need to boot up something to set up that hard drive. Any software that can boot up a system is by definition an operating system. You need an optical disc or USB flash drive with a bootable OS installed. Any removable media that has a bootable OS is generically called a *boot device* or *boot disc*. Your system boots off of the boot device, which then loads some kind of OS that enables you to partition, format, and install an OS on your new hard drive. Boot devices come from many sources. All Windows OS installation media are boot devices (see Figure 9-26), as are Linux installation media.

Figure 9-26   Windows 10 bootable media

Boot devices may also be a medium that has an image of an installation disc. These images are usually stored as a file with a name that has an extension of ".iso." Image files may be on a traditional boot device, such as a disc or flash drive, but they can come from anyplace, such as on a network drive.

Every boot device has partitioning tools and a way to format a new partition. A hard drive must have a partition and has to be formatted to support an OS installation.

Partitioning and Formatting with the Installation Media

When you boot up Windows installation media and the installation program detects a hard drive that is not yet partitioned, it prompts you through a sequence of steps to partition and format the hard drive. Chapter 11, "Building a PC," covers the entire installation process, but we'll jump ahead and dive into the partitioning part of the installation here to see how this is done.

The process of partitioning and formatting when installing Windows is straightforward. You'll go through a couple of installation screens (see Figure 9-27) where you select things such as language and get prompted for a product key and acceptance of the license agreement. Eventually you'll get to the *Where do you want to install Windows?* dialog box (see Figure 9-28).

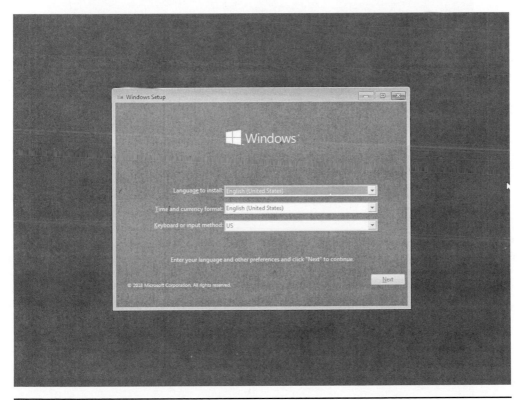

Figure 9-27   Starting the Windows 10 installation

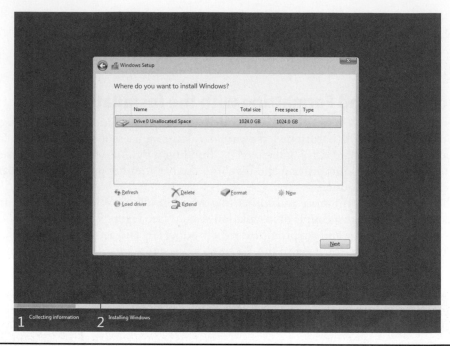

Figure 9-28   Where do you want to install Windows?

Click Next to do the most common partitioning and formatting action: creating a single C: partition, making it active, and formatting it as NTFS. Note that Windows creates two partitions, a System Reserved partition and the C: partition. This is normal, the way the system was designed to work. Figure 9-29 shows a typical Windows installation in Disk Management.

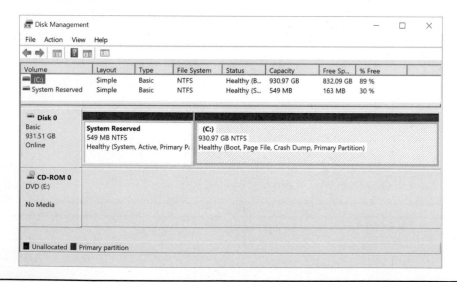

Figure 9-29   Disk Management showing the default partitions in Windows 10

If you want to do any custom partitioning or delete existing partitions, select one of the options. To create a new partition, click the New button. Type in an amount in megabytes that you want to use for a new partition, then click Apply. In Windows 10, you will get a notice that Windows might create additional partitions for system files. When you click OK, Windows will create the System Reserved partition as well as the partition you specified (see Figure 9-30). Any leftover drive space will be listed as Unallocated Space.

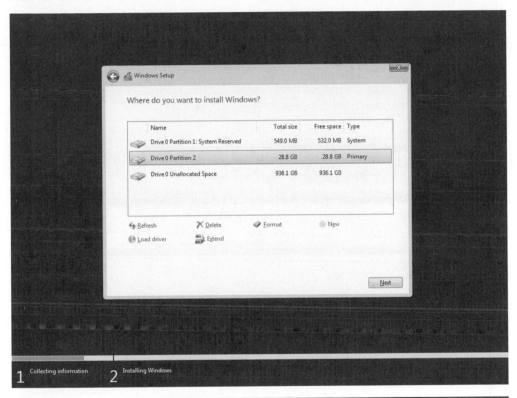

Figure 9-30   New partition with System Reserved partition and Unallocated Space

Once you create a new partition, click the Format button. The installer won't ask you what file system to use. Newer Windows versions can read FAT32 drives, but they won't install to such a partition by default.

The example here has a 1-TB drive with a 29-GB partition and 936 GB of unallocated space. If you've gone through this process and have changed your mind, now wanting to make the partition use the full terabyte, what do you have to do? You can simply click the Extend button and then apply the rest of the unallocated space to the currently formatted partition. The Extend function enables you to tack unpartitioned space onto an already partitioned drive with the click of the mouse.

Disk Management

The Disk Management utility is the primary graphical tool for partitioning and formatting drives after installation. Figure 9-31 shows the tool in Windows 7; Microsoft has not updated the interface in subsequent versions of Windows. You can use Disk Management to do just about everything you need to do to a hard drive or solid-state drive in one handy tool, including initialization, creating volumes, using dynamic disks, extending drives, and more. You can find Disk Management in the Control Panel Administrative Tools applet, or just type **disk management** in the Search bar and open it directly.

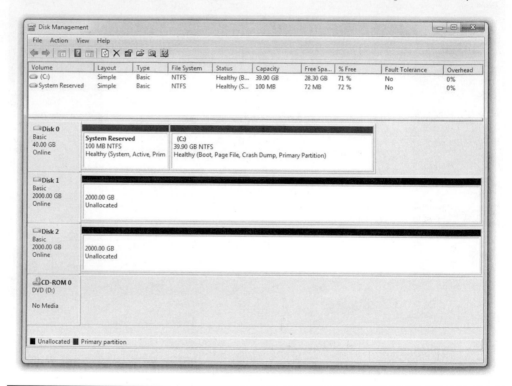

Figure 9-31 Disk Management

 NOTE Windows offers a command-line tool for managing mass storage: *diskpart*, the successor to FDISK. It's incredibly powerful and useful (and dangerous without adequate knowledge). The book discusses diskpart in Chapter 16, "Troubleshooting Operating Systems."

Disk Initialization

Every hard drive in a Windows system has special information placed onto the drive through a process called *disk initialization*. (CompTIA refers to this as *initializing* a disk.) This initialization information includes identifiers that say, "this drive belongs in this system" and other information that defines what this hard drive does in the system. If the hard drive is part of a software RAID array, for example, its RAID information is stored in the initialization. If it's part of a spanned volume, this is also stored there.

All new drives must be initialized before you can use them. When you install an extra hard drive into a Windows system and start Disk Management, it notices the new drive and starts the Hard Drive Initialization Wizard. If you don't let the wizard run, the drive will be listed as unknown (see Figure 9-32).

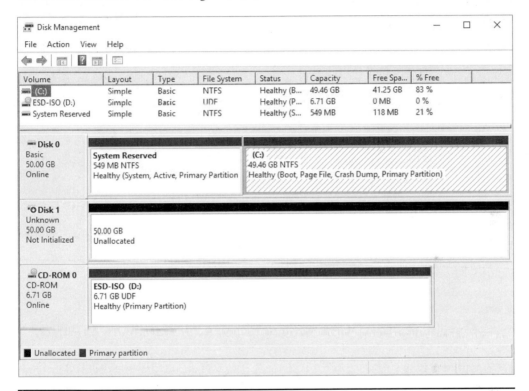

Figure 9-32   Unknown drive in Disk Management

To initialize a disk, right-click the disk icon and select Initialize. You will get the option to select MBR or GPT as a partition style (see Figure 9-33). Once a disk is initialized, you can see the status of the drive—a handy tool for troubleshooting.

Disk Management enables you to view the *drive status* of every mass storage device in your system. Hopefully, you'll mostly see each drive listed as Healthy, meaning that nothing is happening to it and things are going along swimmingly. You're also already familiar with the Unallocated and Active statuses, but here are a few more to be familiar with for the CompTIA A+ exams and real life as a tech:

- **Foreign drive**   You see this when you move a dynamic disk from one computer to another.

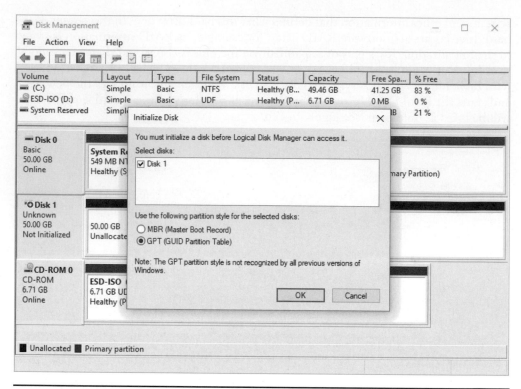

Figure 9-33 Initializing a drive

- **Formatting**   As you might have guessed, you see this when you're formatting a drive.
- **Failed**   Pray you never see this status, because it means that the disk is damaged or corrupt and you've probably lost some data.
- **Online**   This is what you see if a disk is healthy and communicating properly with the computer.
- **Offline**   The disk is either corrupted or having communication problems.

A newly installed drive is always set as a basic disk. There's nothing wrong with using basic disks, other than that you miss out on some handy features.

Creating Partitions and Volumes in Disk Management

To create partitions or volumes, right-click the unallocated part of the drive and select New Simple Volume. Disk Management runs the New Simple Volume Wizard. You'll go straight to the sizing screen (see Figure 9-34).

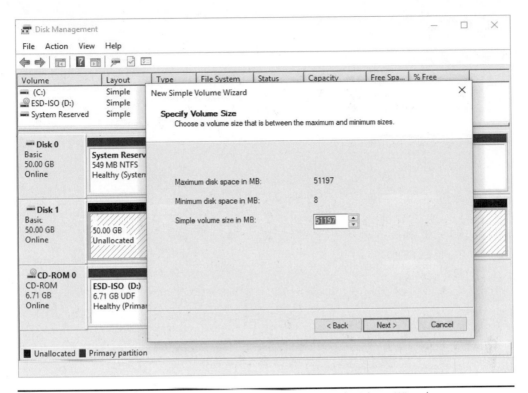

Figure 9-34 Specifying the simple volume size in the New Simple Volume Wizard

Specify a volume size and click Next. The wizard will ask if you want to assign a drive letter to the volume, mount it as a folder to an existing volume, or do neither (see Figure 9-35). In almost all cases, you'll want to give simple volumes a drive letter.

NOTE Disk Management does *not* enable you to specify whether you want a primary or extended partition when you create a volume on MBR drives. The first three volumes you create will be primary partitions. Every volume thereafter will be a logical drive in an extended partition. The command-line tool, diskpart, offers options not available in Disk Management. Check out Chapter 16 for more details.

The last screen of the New Simple Volume Wizard asks for the type of format you want to use for this partition (see Figure 9-36). If your partition is 32 GB or less, you can make the drive FAT32 or NTFS. Windows requires NTFS on any partition greater than 32 GB. Although FAT32 supports partitions up to 2 TB, Microsoft wants you to use NTFS on larger partitions and creates this limit. With today's multi-terabyte drives, there's no good reason to use anything other than NTFS in Windows. In addition to the

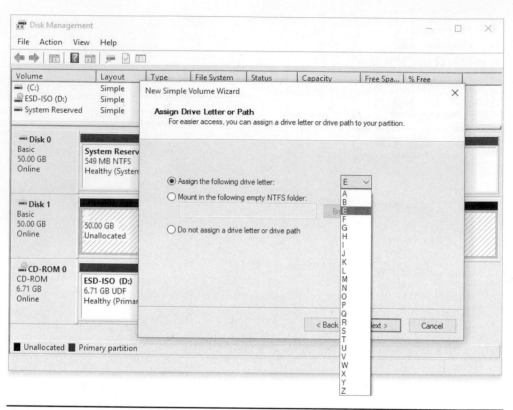

Figure 9-35   Assigning a drive letter to a volume

file system selection, you are offered a checkbox to perform a quick format or a full format. A quick format does not test the blocks as part of the format process, while the full format option does. (See "Formatting a Partition" later in this chapter for more details.)

You have a few more tasks to complete at this screen. You can add a volume label if you want. You can also choose the size of your clusters (Allocation unit size). You can sure speed up the format if you select the Perform a quick format checkbox. This will format your drive without checking every block. It's fast and a bit risky, but new hard drives almost always come from the factory in perfect shape—so you must decide whether to use it or not.

 EXAM TIP   Know the differences between a quick format versus a full format for the exam.

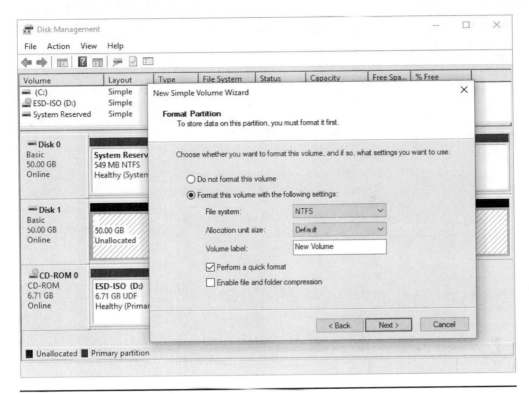

Figure 9-36 Choosing a file system type

Last, if you chose NTFS, you may enable file and folder compression. If you select this option, you'll be able to right-click on any file or folder on this partition and compress it. To compress a file or folder, choose the one you want to compress, right-click, and select Properties. Then click the Advanced button and turn compression on (see Figure 9-37). Compression is handy for opening up space on a hard drive that's filling up.

Dynamic Disks

You create dynamic disks from basic disks in Disk Management. Once you convert a drive from a basic disk to a dynamic disk, primary and extended partitions no longer exist; dynamic disks are divided into volumes instead of partitions. Because current versions of Windows call partitions *volumes*, the change to dynamic disk isn't obvious at all.

 EXAM TIP When you move a dynamic disk from one computer to another, it shows up in Disk Management as a foreign drive. You can import a foreign drive into the new system by right-clicking the disk icon and selecting Import Foreign Disks.

Figure 9-37
Turning on
compression

To convert a basic disk to dynamic, just right-click the drive icon and select Convert to Dynamic Disk (see Figure 9-38). The process is very quick and safe, although the reverse is not true. The conversion from dynamic disk to basic disk first requires you to delete all volumes off the hard drive.

Once you've converted the disk, you can make one of the five types of volumes on a dynamic disk: simple, spanned, striped, mirrored, or RAID 5. You'll next learn how to implement the three most common volume types. The final step involves assigning a drive letter or mounting the volume as a folder.

Simple Volumes   A simple volume acts just like a primary partition. If you have only one dynamic disk in a system, it can have only a simple volume. It's important to note here that a simple volume may act like a traditional primary partition, but it is very different because you cannot install an operating system on it.

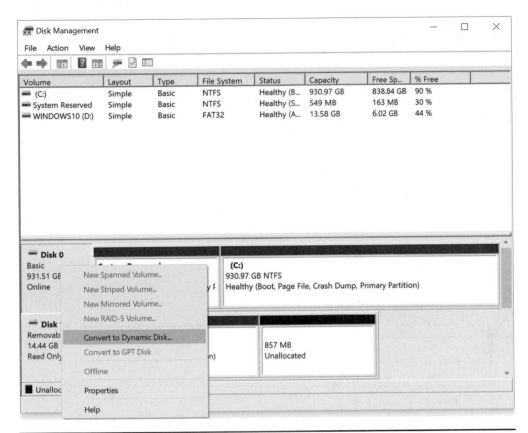

Figure 9-38 Converting to a dynamic disk

In Disk Management, right-click on any unallocated space on the dynamic disk and choose New Simple Volume to run the New Simple Volume Wizard (see Figure 9-39). You'll see a series of screens that prompt you on size and file system, and then you're finished. Figure 9-40 shows Disk Management with three simple volumes.

Spanning Volumes You can extend the size of a simple volume to any unallocated space on a dynamic disk. You can also extend the volume to grab extra space on completely different dynamic disks, creating a spanned volume. This capability is very helpful if you manage an older system that needs a little more space, but you don't have time or inclination to upgrade. To extend or span, simply right-click the volume you want to make bigger, and choose Extend Volume from the options (see Figure 9-41). This opens the Extend Volume Wizard, which prompts you for the location of free space on a dynamic disk and the increased volume size you want to assign (see Figure 9-42). If you have multiple drives, you can span the volume just as easily to one of those drives.

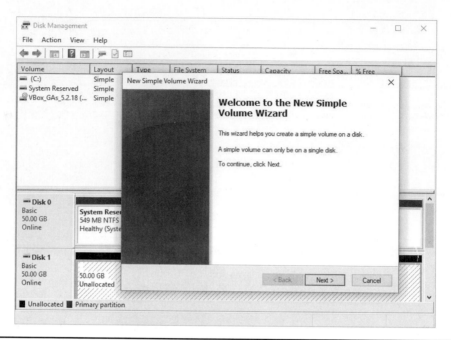

Figure 9-39   Starting the New Simple Volume Wizard

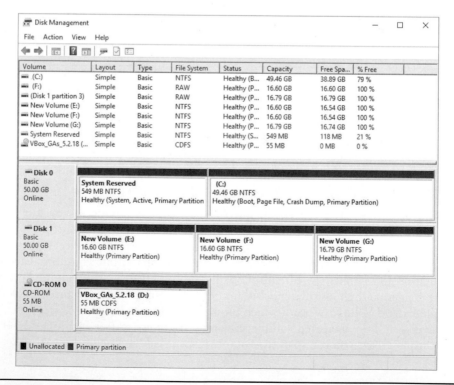

Figure 9-40   Simple volumes

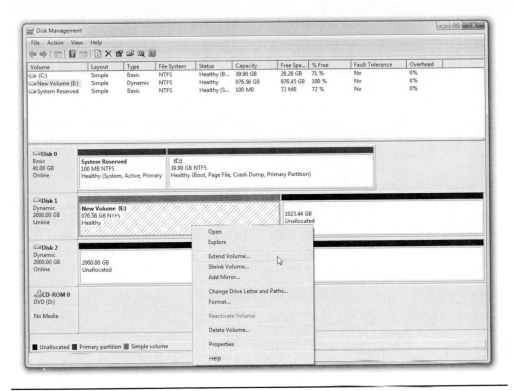

Figure 9-41 Selecting the Extend Volume option (Windows 7)

Figure 9-42
The Extend
Volume Wizard
(Windows 7)

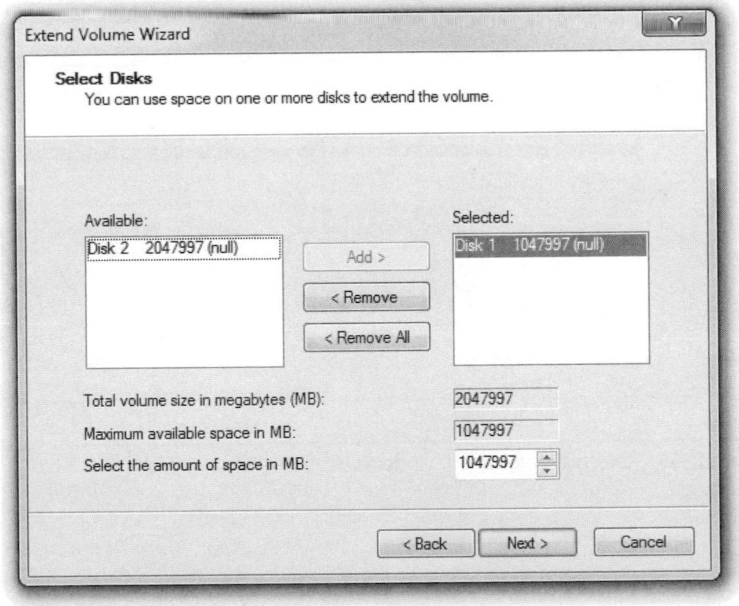

The capability to extend and span volumes makes dynamic disks worth their weight in gold. If you start running out of space on a volume, you can simply add another physical hard drive to the system and span the volume to the new drive. This keeps your drive letters consistent and unchanging so your programs don't get confused, yet enables you to expand drive space when needed.

CAUTION Once you convert a drive to dynamic, you cannot revert it to a basic disk without losing all the data on that drive. Be prepared to back up all data before you convert.

You can extend or span any simple volume on a dynamic disk, not just the "one on the end" in the Disk Management console. You simply select the volume to expand and the total volume increase you want. Figure 9-43 shows a simple 488.28-GB volume named Extended that has been enlarged an extra 1316.40 GB in a portion of the hard drive, skipping the 195.31-GB section of unallocated space contiguous to it. This created an 1804.68-GB volume. Windows has no problem skipping areas on a drive.

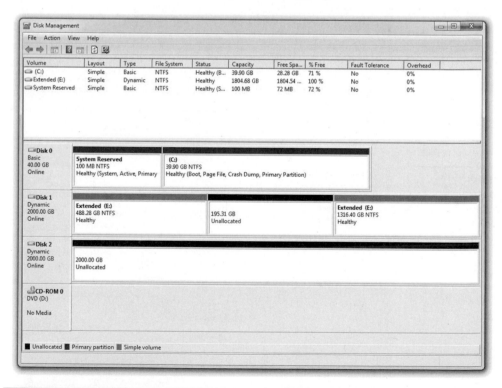

Figure 9-43 Extended volume (Windows 7)

> ## Extending Hard Drives in Windows
>
> You can extend and shrink volumes in current versions of Windows without using dynamic disks. You can shrink any volume with available free space (though you can't shrink the volume by the whole amount of free space, based on the location of unmovable sectors such as the MBR), and you can expand volumes with unallocated space on the drive.
>
> To shrink a volume, right-click on it and select Shrink Volume. Disk Management will calculate how much you can shrink it, and then you can choose up to that amount.
>
> Extending volumes is equally straightforward. To extend, right-click and select Extend Volume.
>
> Note that CompTIA refers to the processes as *extending partitions* and, in an odd pairing of grammar, *shrink partitions*.

Striped Volumes   If you have two or more dynamic disks in a PC, Disk Management enables you to combine them into a striped volume. Although Disk Management doesn't use the term, you know this as a RAID 0 array. A striped volume spreads out blocks of each file across multiple disks. Using two or more drives in a group called a *stripe set*, striping writes data first to a certain number of clusters on one drive, then to a certain number of clusters on the next drive, and so on. It speeds up data throughput because the system has to wait a much shorter time for a drive to read or write data. The drawback of striping is that if any single drive in the stripe set fails, all the data in the stripe set is lost.

To create a striped volume, right-click on any unused space on a drive, choose New Volume, and then choose Striped. The wizard asks for the other drives you want to add to the stripe, and you need to select two unallocated spaces on other dynamic disks. Select the other unallocated spaces and go through the remaining screens on sizing and formatting until you've created a new striped volume (see Figure 9-44). The two stripes in Figure 9-44 appear to have different sizes, but if you look closely you'll see they are both 1000 GB. All stripes must be the same size on each drive.

Mirrored Volumes   Windows 7 and later Professional, Enterprise, and Ultimate editions can create a *mirror set* with two drives for data redundancy. You know mirrors from Chapter 8 as RAID 1. To create a mirror, right-click on unallocated space on a drive and select New Mirrored Volume (see Figure 9-45). This runs the New Mirrored Volume Wizard. Click Next to continue. Select an available disk in the Available box and click the Add button to move it to the Selected box (see Figure 9-46). Click Next to get to the by-now-familiar Assign Drive Letter or Path dialog box and select what is appropriate for the PC.

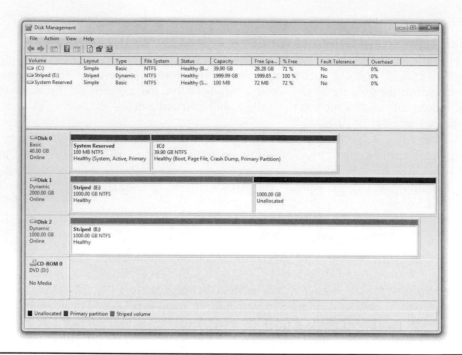

Figure 9-44   Two striped drives (Windows 7)

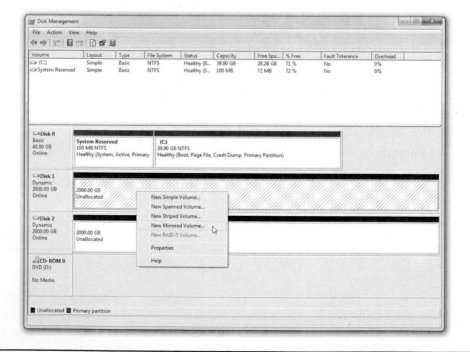

Figure 9-45   Selecting a new mirror (Windows 7)

Figure 9-46
Selecting drives
for the array
(Windows 7)

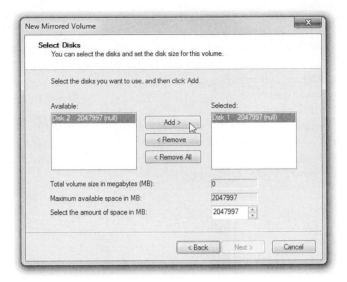

Other Levels of RAID   Disk Management enables you to create a RAID 5 array that uses three or more disks to create a robust solution for storage. This applies to all the Professional editions of Windows. Unfortunately for users of those operating systems, you can only make the array on a Windows Server machine that you access remotely across a network. (Starting with the Professional and Enterprise editions of Windows 8, Microsoft includes Storage Spaces, an alternative way to do software pseudo-RAID in the form of pooling; one option closely resembles RAID 5. See the "Storage Spaces" section later in the chapter for more details.)

Disk Management cannot do any nested RAID arrays. So if you want RAID 0+1 or RAID 1+0 (RAID 10), you need to use hardware RAID.

Mounting Partitions as Folders

While partitions and volumes can be assigned a drive letter, D: through Z:, they can also be mounted as a folder on another drive, also known as a *mount point*. This enables you to use your existing folders to store more data than can fit on a single drive or partition/volume (see Figure 9-47).

Figure 9-47
Mounting a drive
as a folder

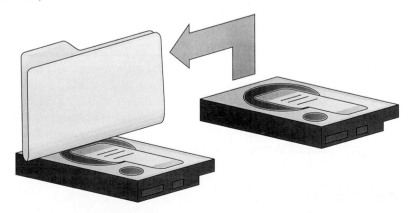

Imagine you use your Documents folder on a Windows machine to store your digital photos. As your collection grows, you realize your current 500-GB hard drive is running out of space. You're willing to buy another hard drive, but you have a great organizational structure in your existing Documents folder and you don't want to lose that. You don't have to move everything to the new hard drive, either.

After you install the new hard drive, you can *mount* the primary partition (or logical drive) as a folder within the existing Documents folder on your C: drive (for example, C:\Users\Mike\My Photos). At this point the drive doesn't have a letter (though you could add one later, if you wanted). To use the new drive, just drop your files into the My Photos folder. They'll be stored on the second hard drive, not the original 500-GB drive (see Figure 9-48). Amazing!

Figure 9-48
Adding photos to the mounted folder stores them on the second hard drive.

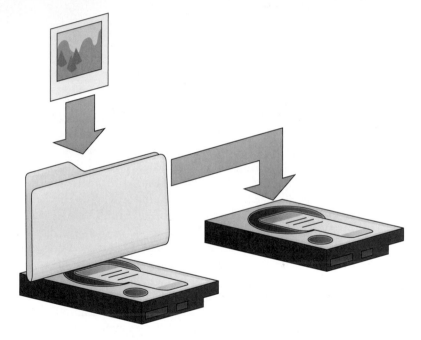

To create a mount point, right-click on an unallocated section of a drive and choose New Simple Volume. This opens the appropriately named wizard. In the second screen, you can select a mount point rather than a drive letter (see Figure 9-49). Browse to a blank folder on an NTFS-formatted drive or create a new folder and you're in business.

EXAM TIP The CompTIA A+ 1002 exam objectives mention "splitting" partitions. To be clear, you never actually split a partition. If you want to turn one partition into two, you need to remove the existing partition and create two new ones, or shrink the existing partition and add a new one to the unallocated space. If you see the term on the exam, know that this is what CompTIA means.

Figure 9-49
Choosing
to create a
mounted volume
(Windows 7)

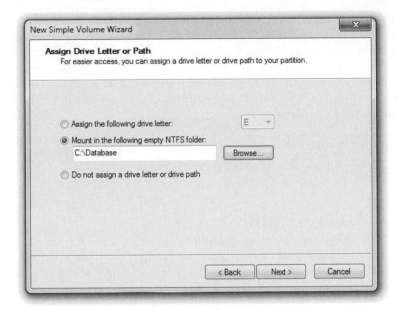

Try This!   Working with Dynamic Drives and Mount Points
Play with Disk Management to experience the simplicity and elegance of the utility.
Get a couple of spare drives and install them into a Windows PC. Open the Disk
Management console and try the following setup options:

1. Make a mirror set.

2. Make a stripe set.

3. Make them into a single volume spanned between both drives.

4. Make a single volume that takes up a portion of one drive, and then extend
   that volume onto another portion of that drive. Finally, span that volume to
   the other hard drive as well.

5. Create a volume of some sort—you decide—and then mount that volume to
   a folder on the C: drive.

You'll need to format the volumes after you create them so you can see how they
manifest in Windows Explorer/File Explorer. Also, you'll need to delete volumes to
create a new setup. To delete a volume, right-click on the volume and choose Delete
Volume. It's almost too easy.

Assigning/Changing Drive Letters and Paths

Disk Management enables you to modify the drive letter, path, or mount point on currently installed mass storage devices. Right-click a drive and select Change Drive Letter and Paths. You can assign a desired drive letter to an optical drive—say, from D: to Z:, for example. Or, you can change a hard drive from D: to a non-letter-named mount point so it shows up in Windows Explorer/File Explorer as a subfolder. You have a ton of flexibility with Disk Management.

EXAM TIP Disk Management is the go-to tool in Windows when adding drives or adding arrays to a system.

Formatting a Partition

You can format any Windows partition/volume in Windows Explorer/File Explorer. Just right-click on the drive name and choose Format. You'll see a dialog box that asks for the type of file system you want to use, the cluster size, and a volume label (see Figure 9-50). You can also do a quick format or compress the volume. The Quick Format option tells Windows not to test the blocks and is a handy option when you're in a hurry—and feeling lucky.

Figure 9-50
Format New
Volume
dialog box

Disk Management is today's preferred formatting tool for Windows. When you create a new partition or volume, the wizard also asks you what type of format you want to use. Always use NTFS unless you're that rare and strange person who wants to dual-boot some ancient version of Windows.

All OS installation media partition and format as part of the OS installation. Windows simply prompts you to partition and then format the drive. Read the screens and you'll do great.

Storage Spaces

With Windows 8 and later versions of the OS, you can group one or more physical drives of any size into a single *storage pool*. These drives can be internal HDD or SSD or external storage connected via USB. It's pretty sweet. *Storage Spaces* functions like a RAID management tool, except it goes well beyond the typical tool. Here's the scoop.

First off, to run the tool, get to the Start screen and type **storage spaces**. Storage Spaces will show up in the Search. Click on it to run the program. The opening screen gives you pretty much a single option, to *Create a new pool and storage space* (see Figure 9-51). Click that option.

Figure 9-51   Storage Spaces opening window (Windows 8.1)

Storage Spaces will show you the available installed and formatted physical drives and give you a warning that proceeding will erase the drives (see Figure 9-52). Select the drives you want to include in the pool and click the Create pool button.

Once you've created a pool, you need to select what Microsoft calls the *resiliency mechanism*, which essentially means providing one or more layers of redundancy so you can lose a hard drive or two and not lose any data. Sounds a lot like RAID, doesn't it? Figure 9-53 shows the Create a storage space window with a *Two-way mirror* storage layout. Here's where Storage Spaces gets pretty much cooler than any RAID management tool.

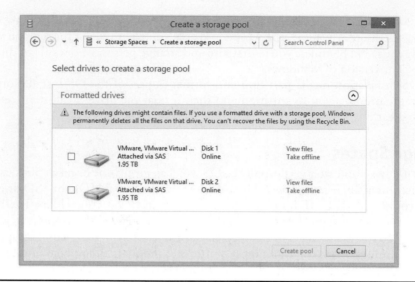

Figure 9-52   Formatted drives revealed (Windows 8.1)

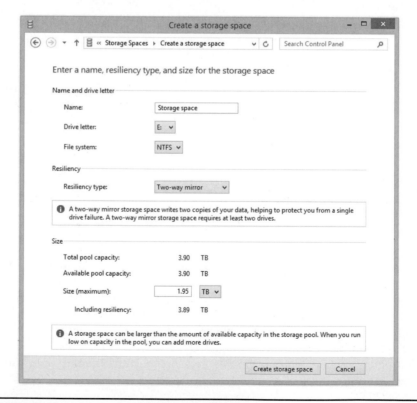

Figure 9-53   Ready to create the storage space (Windows 8.1)

Storage Spaces offers three different types of storage spaces:

- **Simple spaces** are just pooled storage, like JBOD, that has multiple drives of whatever capacity added together to form a single virtual drive. Simple spaces provide no resiliency, so if a drive fails, the data goes away. These are good for temporary storage, scratch files, and the like.

- **Mirror spaces** keep more than one copy of the data, like in a RAID mirror array, so you can lose one or more drives and still save your data. The number of drives in the array determines which mirror options you have. A two-way mirror requires at least two drives; a three-way mirror requires five or more. Mirror spaces work like RAID 1 or RAID 10, providing excellent redundancy and resiliency, and robust performance.

- **Parity spaces** add another layer of resiliency to the array, similar to how a RAID 5 or RAID 6 provides redundancy. The added resiliency comes with both an upside and a downside. The good thing about parity spaces is that they are more space efficient than two-way mirroring. In two-way mirroring, for every 10 GB of data to be stored, 20 GB of storage must be installed. With parity spaces, for every 10 GB of stored data, only 15 GB of storage needs to be installed. The downside is that the performance overhead to manage parity spaces can have a significant impact on overall performance. Microsoft recommends using parity spaces for big files that don't change a lot, like your movie collection. You can lose one drive and recover in a three-drive parity space. It takes a seven-drive parity space (at minimum) to enable you to recover from a two-drive loss.

When a disk fails in a space, Storage Spaces sends a warning through the standard Windows Action Center messaging. You can open Storage Spaces to reveal the failed drive and replace the drive readily.

 EXAM TIP A storage pool is a collection of physical drives that enables you to flexibly add and expand capacity. Storage spaces are virtual drives that are created from storage pool free space. Storage spaces have resiliency and fixed provisioning.

Storage Spaces enables you to do one more very cool action: future-proof your storage needs. The *thin provisioning feature* means you can create a space with more capacity than your current physical drives provide. You might have a storage pool composed of two 2-TB drives and one 3-TB drive, laid out as a two-way mirror. Rather than limit your new space to a 3-TB capacity, you can assign whatever capacity you want, such as 12 TB, because you know your movie collection will grow. When you start to reach the capacity of the physical drives in the pool, Storage Spaces will tell you and enable you to add more physical capacity at that time. Thin provisioning means you don't have to redo an array or space when you reach the limits of current hardware.

NOTE SSDs work great with some space types and not others. With a simple two-way or three-way mirror, go for it. You'll add some speed and lots of resiliency. With parity spaces, on the other hand, the nature of how SSDs function inside might cause premature failure. It's best to use HDDs with parity spaces.

Maintaining and Troubleshooting Hard Drives

Hard drives are complex mechanical and electrical devices. With platters spinning at thousands of rotations per minute, they also generate heat and vibration. All of these factors make hard drives susceptible to failure. In this section, you will learn some basic maintenance tasks that will keep your hard drives healthy, and for those inevitable instances when a hard drive fails, you will also learn what you can do to repair them.

NOTE The "Maintaining and Troubleshooting Hard Drives" section applies primarily to HDDs, not SSDs. The few parts that apply to the latter have been salted into the discussion.

Pay attention to the terminology used both on the CompTIA A+ exam and in the field. Current storage for drives focuses on blocks and logical block addressing. A block is one step above the physical layout of the drive, which gives a lot of flexibility in the media. Microsoft continues to use the term cluster to refer to locations in their file allocation tables. With NTFS, a cluster and a block are pretty much the same thing, a 4-KB chunk of a drive (until you get partitions larger than 16 TB). The official term for a cluster is an allocation unit. You'll see all three terms used interchangeably in the field.

Maintenance

Hard drive maintenance can be broken down into two distinct functions: checking the disk occasionally for failed blocks, and keeping data organized on the drive so it can be accessed quickly.

Error Checking

Individual blocks on hard drives sometimes go bad. There's nothing you can do to prevent this from happening, so it's important that you check occasionally for bad blocks on drives. The tools used to perform this checking are generically called error-checking utilities, although the term for an older Microsoft tool—*chkdsk* (pronounced "check-disk")—is often used. Chkdsk is a command-line utility. Microsoft called the graphical tool Error-checking in Windows 7. Windows 8 and later drop the hyphen, so *Error checking* is the current name. macOS uses the *Disk Utility*. Linux offers a command-line tool called *fsck*. Whatever the name of the utility, each does the same job: when the tool finds bad blocks, it puts the electronic equivalent of orange cones (placing 0000FFF7 in the FAT/MFT) around them so the system won't try to place data in those bad blocks.

EXAM TIP The CompTIA A+ exam objectives mention chkdsk specifically, but not Error checking. Even without the shout out in the objectives, expect a question on disk maintenance that refers to Error checking.

Most error-checking tools do far more than just check for bad blocks. They go through all the drive's filenames, looking for invalid names and attempting to fix them. They look for blocks that have no filenames associated with them (we call these *lost chains*) and erase them or save them as files for your review. From time to time, the underlying links between parent and child folders are lost, so a good error-checking tool checks every parent and child folder. With a folder such as C:\Test\Data, for example, they make sure that the Data folder is properly associated with its parent folder, C:\Test, and that C:\Test is properly associated with its child folder, C:\Test\Data.

To access Error checking on a Windows system, open Windows Explorer/File Explorer, right-click on the drive you want to check, and choose Properties to open the drive's Properties dialog box (see Figure 9-54). Select the Tools tab and click the Check or Check now button.

Figure 9-54

The Tools tab in the Properties dialog box

In macOS, you'll find Disk Utility in the Utilities folder. When open, you'll get one or two options, such as Verify Disk or both Verify Disk and Repair Disk. Figure 9-55 shows the options available for a non-startup disk. Verify Disk checks for errors; Repair Disk fixes those errors. You can verify but not fix the startup disk from within macOS. If Disk

Utility finds errors on the startup disk, reboot the system and press APPLE KEY-R until the Recovery partition loads. You can fix the startup disk from there.

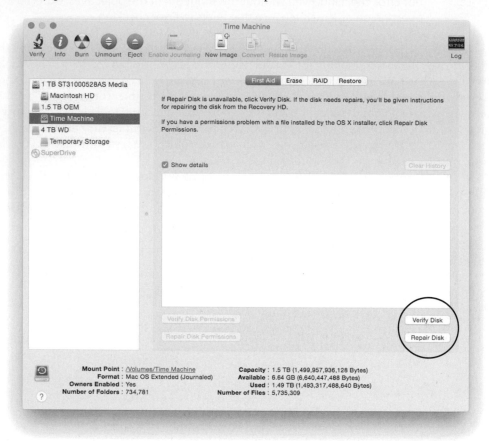

Figure 9-55   Disk Utility options

Now that you know how to run Error checking, your next question should be, "How often do I run it?" A reasonable maintenance plan would include running it about once a week. Error checking is fast and it's a great tool for keeping your system in top shape. The same is true for Disk Utility. Many Linux distributions run fsck periodically, automatically, so you don't have to do anything at all.

Defragmentation

You read about fragmentation earlier in this chapter. Fragmentation of blocks increases your drive access times dramatically. It's a good idea to *defragment*—or *defrag*—your drives as part of monthly maintenance. You access the defrag tool Optimize Drives the same way you access Error checking—right-click a drive in Windows Explorer/File

Explorer and choose Properties—except you click the Optimize or Defragment now button on the Tools tab to open Optimize Drives (see Figure 9-56).

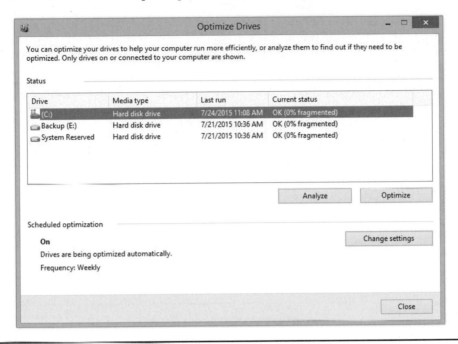

Figure 9-56   Optimize Drives, the defragmenting tool in Windows

Defragmentation is not interesting to watch. Schedule disk defragmentation to run late at night. You should defragment your drives about once a month, although you could run Optimize Drives every week, and if you run it every night, it takes only a few minutes. The longer you go between defrags, the longer it takes. In Windows 7 and later, Microsoft has made defragging even easier by automatically defragging HDDs once a week. You can adjust the schedule or even turn it off altogether, but remember that if you don't run Optimize Drives, your system will run slower. If you don't run Error checking, you may lose data.

NOTE   If you manage a system with a solid-state drive, you don't have to defrag your drive. In fact, you should *never* defrag an SSD, because it can shorten its lifetime. Windows will not defragment SSDs automatically.

Disk Cleanup

Did you know that the average hard drive is full of trash? Not the junk you intentionally put in your hard drive such as the 23,000 e-mail messages that you refuse to delete from your e-mail program. This kind of trash is all the files that you never see that Windows keeps for you. Here are a few examples:

- **Files in the Recycle Bin**   When you delete a file, it isn't really deleted. It's placed in the Recycle Bin in case you decide you need the file later. I just checked my Recycle Bin and found around 3 GB worth of files (see Figure 9-57). That's a lot of trash!

- **Temporary Internet files**   When you go to a Web site, Windows keeps copies of the graphics and other items so the page will load more quickly the next time you access it. (Modern browsers handle this automatically.)

- **Downloaded program files**   Your system always keeps a copy of any applets it downloads. You can see these in the Internet Options applet by clicking the Settings button under the Browsing history label. Click the View objects button on the Temporary Internet Files and History Settings dialog box. You'll generally find only a few tiny files here.

- **Temporary files**   Many applications create temporary files that are supposed to be deleted when the application is closed. For one reason or another, these temporary files sometimes aren't deleted. The location of these files varies with the version of Windows, but they always reside in a folder called "Temp."

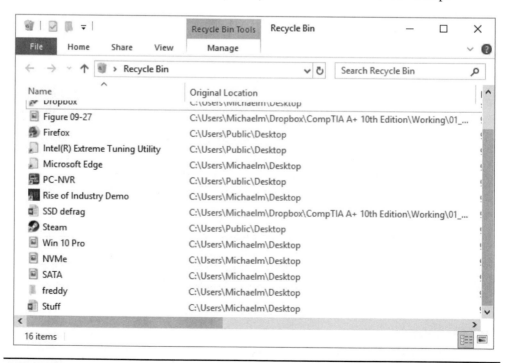

Figure 9-57   Mike's Recycle Bin

Every hard drive eventually becomes filled with lots of unnecessary trash. All versions of Windows tend to act erratically when the drives run out of unused space. Fortunately, all versions of Windows have a powerful tool called *Disk Cleanup* (see Figure 9-58). You can access Disk Cleanup in Windows by clicking the Start button and typing "disk cleanup." Click it to run the program.

Figure 9-58
Disk Cleanup

Disk Cleanup gets rid of the four types of files just described (and a few others). Run Disk Cleanup once a month or so to keep plenty of space available on your hard drive.

NOTE macOS and Linux do not have a tool equivalent to Disk Cleanup. That said, there are third-party utilities such as BleachBit for Linux that can perform similar operations as Windows Disk Cleanup.

1001

Troubleshooting Hard Drive Implementation

There's no scarier computer problem than an error that points to trouble with a hard drive. This section looks at some of the more common problems that occur with hard drives and how to fix them. These issues fall into four broad categories: installation errors, data corruption, dying hard drives, and RAID issues.

Installation Errors

Installing a drive and getting to the point where it can hold data requires four distinct steps: connectivity, system setup, partitioning, and formatting. If you make a mistake at any point on any of these steps, the drive won't work. The beauty of this is that if you make an error, you can walk back through each step and check for problems. The "Troubleshooting Hard Drive Installation" section in Chapter 8 covered physical connections and system setup, so this section concentrates on the latter two issues.

Partitioning   Partitioning errors generally fall into two groups: failing to partition at all, and making the wrong size or type of partition. You'll recognize the former type of error the first time you open Windows Explorer/File Explorer after installing a drive. If you forgot to partition it, the drive won't even show up in Windows Explorer/File Explorer, only in Disk Management. If you made the partition too small, that'll become painfully obvious when you start filling it up with files.

The fix for partitioning errors is simply to open Disk Management and do the partitioning correctly. Just right-click and select Extend Volume to correct the mistake. Remember that deleting any volume will permanently delete any data on that drive.

Formatting   Failing to format a drive makes the drive unable to hold data. Accessing the drive in Windows results in a drive "is not accessible" error, and from a C:\> prompt, you'll get an "Invalid media type" error. Format the drive unless you're certain that the drive has a format already. Corrupted files can create the invalid media error. Check the upcoming "Data Corruption" section for the fix.

Most of the time, formatting is a slow, boring process. But sometimes the drive makes "bad sounds" and you start seeing errors like the one shown in Figure 9-59 at the top of the screen. Remember, an *allocation unit* is another term for a block or cluster.

| **Figure 9-59** <br> The "Trying <br> to recover <br> lost allocation <br> unit" error | ```
A:\>format C:/s

WARNING:  ALL DATA ON NON-REMOVABLE DISK
DRIVE C:  WILL BE LOST!
Proceed with Format  (Y/N)?y

Formatting  30709.65M

Trying to recover lost allocation unit 37,925
``` |

The drive has run across a bad cluster and is trying to fix it. For years, I've told techs that seeing this error a few times doesn't mean anything; every drive comes with a few bad spots. This is no longer true. Modern drives hide a significant number of extra blocks that they use to replace bad blocks automatically. If a new drive gets a lot of "Trying to
```

recover lost allocation unit" errors, you can bet that the drive is dying and needs to be replaced. Get the hard drive maker's diagnostic tool to be sure. Bad clusters are reported by S.M.A.R.T. (introduced in Chapter 8), one of several S.M.A.R.T. errors possible.

Mental Reinstallation   Focus on the fact that all of these errors share a common thread—you just installed a drive! Installation errors don't show up on a system that has been running correctly for three weeks; they show up the moment you try to do something with the drive you just installed. If a newly installed drive fails to work, do a "mental reinstallation." Does the drive show up in the UEFI or traditional BIOS setup screens? No? Then recheck the data and power cables. If it does show up, did you remember to partition and format the drive? Did it need to be set to active? These are commonsense questions that come to mind as you march through your mental reinstallation. Even if you've installed thousands of drives over the years, you'll be amazed at how often you do things such as forget to plug in power to a drive. Do the mental reinstallation—it really works!

Data Corruption

All hard drives occasionally get corrupted data in individual blocks. Power surges, accidental shutdowns, corrupted installation media, and viruses, along with hundreds of other problems, can cause this corruption. In most cases, this type of error shows up while Windows is running. Figure 9-60 shows a classic example.

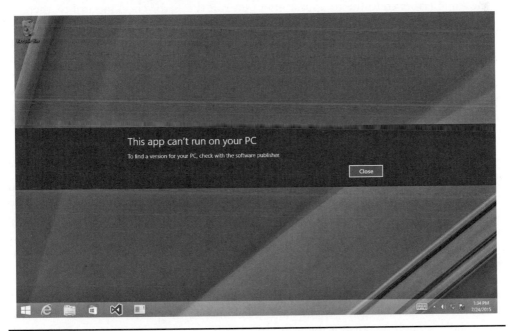

Figure 9-60   A corrupted data error

You may also see Windows error messages saying one of the following:

- "The following file is missing or corrupt"
- "The download location information is damaged"
- "Unable to load file"
- "… is not a valid Win32 application"
- "Bootmgr is missing…Press Ctrl+Alt+Del to restart"
- "Your PC ran into a problem…This problem caused your PC to restart"
- "This app can't run on your PC"

If core boot files become corrupted, you may see text errors at boot, such as the following:

- "Error loading operating system"
- "An error occurred while attempting to read the boot configuration data"

The first fix for any of these problems is to run the Error checking utility. Error checking will go through and mark bad blocks and, hopefully, move your data to a good block. If the same errors continue to appear after you run the Error checking utility, there's a chance that the drive has too many bad blocks and may need to be recycled.

Almost all drives today take advantage of built-in *error correction code* (*ECC*) that constantly checks the drive for bad blocks. If the ECC detects a bad block, it marks the block as bad in the drive's internal error map. Don't confuse this error map with a FAT. The partitioning program creates the FAT. The drive's internal error map was created at the factory on reserved drive heads and is invisible to the system. If the ECC finds a bad block, you will get a corrupted data error as the computer attempts to read the bad block. Disk-checking utilities fix this problem most of the time.

Dying Hard Drive

Physical problems are rare, thankfully, but they are devastating when they happen. If a hard drive is truly damaged physically, there is nothing that you or any service technician can do to fix it. Fortunately, hard drives are designed to take a phenomenal amount of punishment without failing. Physical problems manifest themselves in several ways: you start getting read/write failures, the drive works properly but makes a lot of noise, or the drive seems to disappear. You might get a failure to boot after experiencing any of these events.

Windows will give you error messages with read/write failures. Good hard drives don't fail to read or write. Only dying ones have these problems.

All mechanical hard drives make noise—the hum as the platters spin and the occasional slight scratching noise as the read/write heads access sectors are normal. However, if your drive begins to make any of the following sounds, it is about to die:

- Continuous high-pitched squeal
- A loud clicking noise, a short pause, and then another series of clicks
- Continuous grinding or rumbling

Back up your critical data and replace the drive. Windows comes a with a decent backup utility, but don't be afraid to research third-party options if it doesn't meet your needs. The cloud backup services are particularly nice options because they provide off-site protection in addition to backing up your data.

 NOTE Most hard drives have a three-year warranty. Before you throw away a dead drive, check the hard drive maker's Web site or call them to see if the drive is still under warranty. Ask for a return material authorization (RMA). You'll be amazed how many times you get a newer, and sometimes larger, hard drive for free. It never hurts to check!

You'll know when a drive simply dies. If it's the drive that contains your operating system, the system will lock up. When you try to restart the computer, you'll see this error message or something similar to it:

```
No Boot Device Present
```

If it's a second drive, it will simply stop showing up in Windows Explorer/File Explorer. The first thing to do in either case is to access the system setup program and see if autodetect sees the drive. If it does, you do not have a physical problem with the drive. If autodetect fails, shut off the system and remove the data cable, but leave the power cable attached. Restart the system and listen to the drive. If the drive spins up, you know it is getting good power. This is usually a clue that the drive is probably good. In that case, you need to look for more mundane problems such as an unplugged data cord or jumpers incorrectly set (PATA only). If the drive doesn't spin up, try another power connector. If it still doesn't spin up and you've triple-checked the jumpers and data cable, you have a problem with the onboard electronics, and the drive is dead.

If the drive is an SSD, the troubleshooting process is similar: either the power or motherboard controller is bad, a power or data cable has failed, or the drive electronics are dead. Start with the power cable, changing it for a known good one. Then try a known good data cable using the original motherboard connection. Next, try a different motherboard connector. Still haven't got it? It's likely a bad drive, but you should confirm so by testing it in another known good computer to see if it is detected by UEFI/BIOS and then by Windows Disk Management.

 NOTE If you ever lose a hard drive that contains absolutely critical information, you can turn to a company that specializes in hard drive data recovery. The job will be expensive—prices usually start around $1000 (USD)—but when you have to have the data, such companies are your only hope. Do a Web search for "data recovery" or check the Yellow Pages for companies in this line of business.

Troubleshooting RAID

For the most part, drive problems in a RAID array are identical to those seen on individual drives. There are a couple of errors unique to RAID, however, that need their own separate discussion.

Drive Not Recognized   If you're using hardware RAID and the configuration firmware doesn't recognize one of the drives, first check to make sure the drives are powered and that they are connected to the proper connections. This is especially true of motherboards with onboard RAID that require you to use only certain special RAID connectors.

RAID Stops Working   When one of the drives in a RAID array fails, several things can happen depending on the type of array and the RAID controller. With RAID 0, the effect is dramatic. Many enthusiasts use RAID 0 for their OS drive to make it snappier. If you're running such a rig that then loses a drive, you'll most likely get a critical stop error that manifests as some sort of proprietary crash screen. Windows will show a *Blue Screen of Death* (*BSoD*), for example. On reboot, the computer will fail to boot or you'll get a message such as *OS not found*. You lose all your data because there's no redundancy on a stripe set. You may see error messages before the crash related to read/write failures. On macOS machines, a failing drive or array may result in the *Spinning Pinwheel of Death* (*SPoD*). If there are no other systemic problems such as low RAM or low disk space, it's time to break out RAID- or disk-diagnostic tools such as S.M.A.R.T. reader software.

All the other levels of RAID tend to do nothing extraordinary when one drive in the array fails. When you reboot the system, that's when the RAID controller (if hardware) or Windows (if you've used the built-in tools) will squeal and tell you that a drive has failed.

Often, the failure of a drive will cause access to the contents of the drive to slow to a crawl, and that *slow performance* is your clue to check Device Manager or the RAID controller firmware. Some drive failures will cause the computer to crash. Others will show no effects until you get the error messages at reboot.

Regardless of the reason a RAID stops working or the effects, the fix is simple. Replace the failed drive and let the RAID rebuild itself. Life is good. If you need to know the reason for the failure, trying running S.M.A.R.T. reader software on the failed drive. If the drive electronics have some functionality, you may get results.

RAID Not Found   The CompTIA A+ 220-1001 exam objectives use the term "RAID not found," which doesn't really exist as an error but instead implies a series of errors where an existing RAID array suddenly fails to appear. The problem with these errors is that they vary greatly depending on the make and model of hardware RAID or (heaven forbid) if you used software RAID.

A properly functioning hardware RAID array will always show up in the configuration utility. If an existing array stops working and you enter the configuration utility only to find the array is gone, you have big trouble. This points to either dead drives or faulty controllers. In either case they must be replaced.

If the array is gone but you can still see the drives, then the controller may have broken the array on its own. This is a rare action that some controllers take to try to save data. You should at least try to rebuild the array using whatever tools the controllers provide.

Beyond A+

Modern hard drives have many other features that are worth knowing about but that rarely impact beginning techs. A couple of the more interesting ones are spindle speed and third-party hard drive tools. If you have a burning desire to dive into hard drives in all their glory, you need not go any farther than the StorageReview.com, an excellent site dedicated to HDDs and SSDs, and more advanced storage devices such as storage area networks (SANs) and network attached storage (NAS) devices.

Third-Party Partition Tools

Disk Management is a good tool, but it's still limited for some situations. Some really great third-party tools on the market can give you incredible flexibility and power to structure and restructure your hard drive storage to meet your changing needs. They each have interesting unique features, but in general they enable you to create, change, and delete partitions on a hard drive *without* destroying any of the programs or data stored there. Slick! These programs aren't covered on the CompTIA A+ exams, but all PC techs use at least one of them, so let's explore two of the most well-known examples: Avanquest Partition Commander Professional and the open source Linux tool GParted.

Avanquest offers a variety of related products, one of which is the very useful Partition Commander. It supports all versions of Windows and enables you to play with your partitions without destroying your data. Among its niftier features are the capability to convert a dynamic disk to a basic disk nondestructively (which you can't do with the Microsoft-supplied Windows tools), to defrag the master file table on an NTFS partition, and to move unused space from one partition to another on the same physical drive, automatically resizing the partitions based on the amount of space you tell it to move. Figure 9-61 shows the Partition Commander dialog box for moving unused space between partitions.

Figure 9-61
Partition
Commander

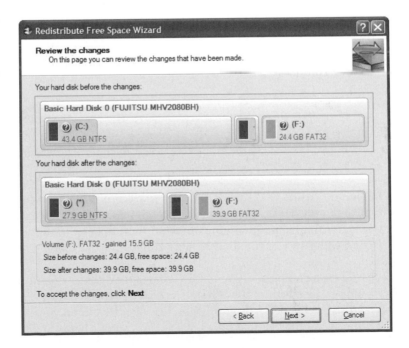

The only problem with Partition Commander is that it costs money. There's nothing wrong with spending money on a good product, but if you can find something that does the job for free, why not try it? If you think like I do, check out the GNOME Partition Editor, better known as *GParted*. You can find it at https://gparted.org.

GParted is an incredibly powerful partition editor and does almost everything the for-pay partition editors do, but it's free. In fact, you might already have a copy lying around in the form of an Ubuntu desktop live CD. If you look closely at Figure 9-62, you'll notice that it uses strange names for the partitions, such as sda1 or hda2. These are Linux conventions and are well documented in GParted's Help screens. Take a little time and you'll love GParted too.

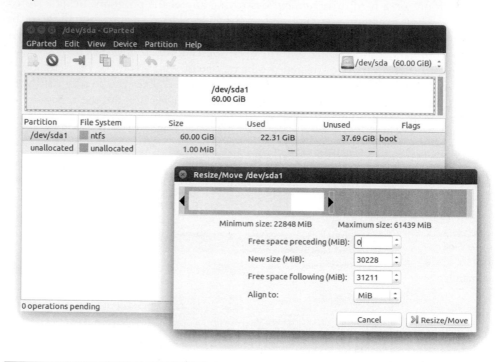

Figure 9-62 GParted in action

The one downside to GParted is that it is a Linux program—because no Windows version exists, you need Linux to run it. So how do you run Linux on a Windows system without actually installing Linux on your hard drive? The answer is easy—the folks at GParted will give you the tools to burn a live CD that boots Linux so you can run GParted.

A *live CD* is a complete OS on a CD. Understand this is not an installation CD like your Windows installation disc. The OS is already installed on the CD. You boot from the live CD and the OS loads into RAM, just like the OS on your hard drive loads into RAM at boot. As the live CD boots, it recognizes your hardware and loads the proper drivers into RAM so everything works. You get everything you'd expect from an OS with one big exception: a live CD does not touch your hard drive. Of course, you may run programs (such as GParted) that work on your hard drive, which makes live CDs popular with PC techs, because you can toss them into a cranky system and run utilities.

NOTE You can install the GPartedLive tool on a USB flash-media drive as well as on CD-R. The installation takes a few more steps, but gives you the advantage of having a bootable version of Linux with powerful partitioning tools in a robust and compact package. Check the GParted pages at SourceForge for specific instructions: https://gparted.sourceforge.io/livecd.php.

The truly intrepid might want to consider using The Ultimate Boot CD (UBCD), basically a huge pile of useful freeware utilities compiled by frustrated technician Ben Burrows, who couldn't find a boot disk when he needed one. His Web site is www.ultimatebootcd.com. The UBCD has more than 100 different tools, all placed on a single live CD. It has all of the low-level diagnostic tools for all of the hard drive makers, four or five different partitioning tools, S.M.A.R.T. viewers, hard drive wiping utilities, and hard drive cloning tools (nice for when you want to replace a hard drive with a larger one). Little documentation is provided, however, and many of the tools require experience way beyond the scope of the CompTIA A+ exams. I will tell you that I have a copy and I use it.

Chapter Review

Questions

1. Which is the most complete list of file systems Windows can use?

    A. FAT32, NTFS

    B. FAT32, exFAT, NTFS

    C. FAT32

    D. NTFS

2. Which of the following correctly identifies the four possible entries in a file allocation table?

    A. Filename, date, time, size

    B. Number of the starting cluster, number of the ending cluster, number of used clusters, number of available clusters

    C. An end-of-file marker, a bad-block marker, code indicating the cluster is available, the number of the cluster where the next part of the file is stored

    D. Filename, folder location, starting cluster number, ending cluster number

3. What program does Microsoft include with Windows to partition and format a drive?

   A. Format

   B. Disk Management console

   C. Disk Administrator console

   D. System Commander

4. What does NTFS use to provide security for individual files and folders?

   A. Dynamic disks

   B. ECC

   C. Access Control List

   D. MFT

5. Jaime wishes to check her hard drive for errors. What tool should she use in Windows 8.1?

   A. FDISK

   B. Format

   C. Disk Management

   D. Error checking

6. To make your files unreadable by others, what should you use?

   A. Clustering

   B. Compression

   C. Disk quotas

   D. Encryption

7. How can you effectively expand the capacity of an NTFS drive?

   A. Create an extended partition to extend the capacity.

   B. Install a second drive and mount it to a folder on the original smaller NTFS drive.

   C. Convert the drive to a dynamic disk and create a mirrored set.

   D. Format the drive with the Quick Format option.

8. Which configuration requires three same-sized volumes?

   A. RAID 5

   B. Mirrored set

   C. Spanned volume

   D. Striped volume

9. Which of the following partitioning schemes enable the creation of more than four partitions or volumes on a single hard drive? (Select two.)

   A. MBR

   B. GPT

   C. Dynamic disk

   D. MFT

10. Which storage option in Windows 8 or later offers the best mix of resiliency and performance with two drives?

    A. Simple space

    B. Two-way mirror space

    C. Three-way mirror space

    D. Parity space

Answers

1. **B.** Modern versions of Windows can use FAT32, and NTFS for hard drives, and exFAT for removable flash-media drives.

2. **C.** The four possible entries in a file allocation table are an end-of-file marker, a bad-block marker, code indicating the cluster is available, and the number of the cluster where the next part of the file is stored.

3. **B.** Windows uses the Disk Management console to partition and format a drive.

4. **C.** Because NTFS views individual files and folders as objects, it can provide security for those objects through an Access Control List.

5. **D.** Error checking is used to check a drive for errors.

6. **D.** To make your files unreadable by others, use encryption.

7. **B.** You can effectively expand the capacity of an NTFS drive by installing a second drive and mounting it to a folder on the original smaller NTFS drive.

8. **A.** RAID 5 requires three same-sized volumes.

9. **B, C.** Both GPT and dynamic disk partitioning schemes enable the creation of more than four partitions or volumes on a single hard drive.

10. **B.** A two-way mirror space efficiently and effectively uses two drives for resilience and performance. A simple space offers no resiliency; the other options require three or more drives.

Essential Peripherals

In this chapter, you will learn how to

- Explain how to support multipurpose connectors
- Identify and install standard peripherals on a computer
- Identify and install standard storage devices (that aren't SSDs or HDDs) and their media

Modern computing devices sport a variety of peripherals—stuff you plug into the system unit—that extend and enhance their capabilities. This chapter looks at common ports first, then turns to a laundry list of standard peripherals. The chapter finishes with a discussion of various mass storage devices, such as flash drives and the fading but not yet gone optical disc technologies.

NOTE This chapter does *not* cover ports or devices used for standalone monitors, such as the typical computer desktop display. That's such a big and important topic that it gets its own chapter! Chapter 17, "Display Technologies," covers monitors and their ports in detail.

1001

Supporting Common Ports

Whenever you're dealing with a device that isn't playing nice, you need to remember that you're never dealing with just a device. You're dealing with a device *and* the port to which it is connected. Before you start troubleshooting the device, you need to look at the issues and technologies of some of the more common input/output (I/O) ports and see what needs to be done to keep them running well.

Serial Ports

Techs at times have to support or service older gear, such as installed point-of-sale systems or networking components soldiering on in the background. Many of these old devices connect to computers using *serial connections*, which use the Recommended Standard 232 (RS-232), introduced way back in 1960. A *serial port* manifests as a 9-pin, D-shell male socket, called a *DB-9* or an *RS-232*. You won't find serial ports on anything made in the last decade, but CompTIA thinks they're important enough to include in the A+ 1001 objectives. Figure 10-1 shows a serial connector on a cable and a DB-9 port.

Figure 10-1
DB-9 connector
and port

 EXAM TIP   You don't need to know how serial ports work to get through the CompTIA A+ 1001 exam. Just remember the names of the ports and connectors, DB-9 and RS-232.

USB Ports

Universal serial bus (*USB*) connects almost every type of peripheral one might consider today. Most folks have used USB ports and USB devices, but let's go beyond the user level and approach USB as techs.

Understanding USB

The core of USB is the *USB host controller*, an integrated circuit normally built into the chipset. The host controller acts as the interface between the system and every USB device that connects to it. Connected to the host controller is a *USB root hub*, the part of the host controller that makes the physical connection to the USB ports. Every USB root hub is a bus, similar in many ways to an expansion bus. Figure 10-2 shows one possible diagram of the relationship between the host controller, root hub, and USB ports.

Figure 10-2
Host controller,
root hub, and
USB ports in a
typical system

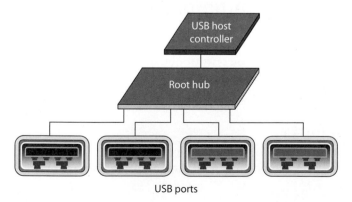

USB ports

A single host controller supports up to 127 USB devices, though real-life circumstances create sharper limits. Even if a host controller supports a certain number of USB ports, there's no guarantee that the motherboard maker will supply that many ports. To give a common example, the AMD X370 chipset supports 16 USB ports, but only a few motherboard makers supply that many USB ports.

A USB host controller is the boss, the master, of any device (the slave) that plugs into that host controller. The host controller sends commands and provides power to USB devices. The host controller is *upstream*, controlling devices connected *downstream* to it (see Figure 10-3). The host controller is shared by every device plugged into it, so speed and power are reduced with each new device.

Figure 10-3
Host controller
and USB mouse
showing
upstream/
downstream

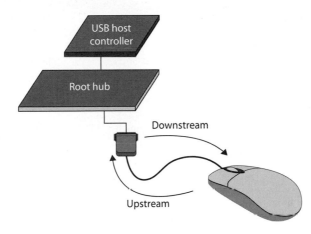

USB Standards and Compatibility

The USB standard has gone through several revisions:

- USB 1.1 was the first widely adopted standard and defined two speeds: *Low-Speed USB*, running at a maximum of 1.5 Mbps (plenty for keyboards and mice), and *Full-Speed USB*, running at up to 12 Mbps.

- The USB 2.0 standard introduced *Hi-Speed USB* running at 480 Mbps.

- USB 3.0 is capable of speeds of up to 5 Gbps—ten times faster than USB 2.0. USB 3.0 is marketed as *SuperSpeed USB*. It's also referred to as *USB 3.1 Gen 1*, though *not* on the CompTIA A+ exams.

- USB 3.1 can handle speeds up to 10 Gbps. It's marketed as *SuperSpeed USB 10 Gbps* or *USB 3.1 Gen 2*.

NOTE Each standard defines more than just the speed. Because they were incorporated into the newer standard, many Low-Speed and Full-Speed USB devices are also USB 2.0 devices.

If you think all of those names and numbers are confusing, you're right. Table 10-1 provides a quick reference to help you sort it all out.

Name	Standard	Maximum Speed	Common Usage
Low-Speed USB	USB 1.1	1.5 Mbps	Keyboards, mice
Full-Speed USB	USB 1.1	12 Mbps	Headphones, Bluetooth devices
Hi-Speed USB	USB 2.0	480 Mbps	Webcams, card scanners, older wireless adapters, older flash-media drives
SuperSpeed USB	USB 3.0	5 Gbps	Flash-media drives, external storage, cameras, current wireless adapters
SuperSpeed USB 10 Gbps	USB 3.1	10 Gbps	Flash-media drives, external storage, networking

Table 10-1 USB Standards

USB 2.0 is fully backward compatible with USB 1.1 devices, while USB 3.0/3.1 is backward compatible with USB 2.0 devices. Older devices won't run any faster than they used to, however. To take advantage of the fastest USB speeds, you must connect a USB device to a USB port at least as fast as the device. Backward compatibility may enable you to use a faster USB device with a slower port, but a quick bit of math tells you how much time you're sacrificing when you're transferring a 2-GB file at 480 Mbps instead of 10 Gbps!

EXAM TIP The *USB Implementers Forum* (*USB-IF*) does not officially use "Low-Speed" and "Full-Speed" to describe 1.5-Mbps and 12-Mbps devices, calling both simply "USB 1.1." The CompTIA A+ certification exams, though, traditionally refer to the marketplace-standard nomenclature used here.

Most people want to take advantage of these amazing speeds, but what do you do if your motherboard doesn't have built-in SuperSpeed USB ports? One option is to add an adapter card like the one shown in Figure 10-4. CompTIA refers to these cards (at any version) as *USB expansion cards*.

Figure 10-4
USB expansion
card

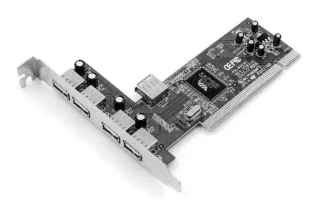

Motherboards capable of both USB 1.1 and USB 2.0 usually share the available USB ports (see Figure 10-5). For every USB port on your computer, a Low-Speed or Full-Speed device uses the USB 1.1 host controller, whereas a Hi-Speed device uses the USB 2.0 host controller.

Figure 10-5
Shared USB ports
for 1.1 and 2

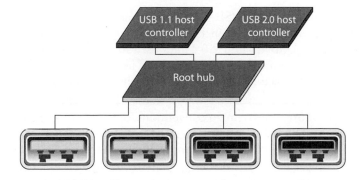

USB 3.0 and 3.1, on the other hand, are different enough from USB 2.0 that they typically use separate host controllers. You can plug older USB devices into a USB 3.0 or 3.1 port, as noted, but they will run at the slower speeds. The only ports that work at 10 Gbps are the USB 3.1 ports (see Figure 10-6).

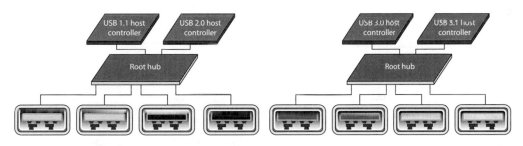

Figure 10-6   Shared USB ports for all speeds of USB

USB Cables and Connectors

When USB 1.1 was introduced, the standard defined two types of connectors: USB A and USB B. USB A connectors plug upstream toward the host controller (which is why you see them on the PC) and USB B connectors plug downstream into USB devices.

The A and B plugs come in sizes: "standard" USB A/USB B, mini USB A/mini USB B, and micro USB A/micro USB B (see Figure 10-7). The mini and micro USB A connectors were basically ignored; most devices come hard wired. The mini USB B and micro USB B connect smaller devices such as cameras and smartphones.

Figure 10-7
USB type A and B
connectors

Type-A   Type-B   Mini-B   Micro-B   Micro-B 3.0

The introduction of USB 3.0 required an upgraded USB A connector and new Micro-B (see last connector in Figure 10-7) connectors, capable of handling the much greater speeds. USB 1.1 and 2.0 cables used four-pin connectors, while USB 3.0/3.1 A and B ports and connectors use nine pins. The USB 3 A connector looks exactly like the older USB A connectors, sneaking the new pins into the same old USB A connector.

NOTE   The naming conventions for the various USB plugs and ports have changed over time. The most recent specification calls the original full-sized A and B connectors *Standard-A* and *Standard-B*. Most people in the industry call them *Type-A* and *Type-B* (refer to Figure 10-7). You'll also most commonly see the mini and micro versions of the connectors as *Mini-A*, *Mini-B*, *Micro-A*, *Micro-B*, and *Micro-B 3.0*.

The CompTIA A+ 1001 exam objectives get even muddier, using the nonstandard terms *Mini-USB* and *Micro-USB*. I can only assume they mean USB Mini-B and USB Micro-B.

The USB industry introduced color schemes to identify the different port types (see Figure 10-8). Table 10-2 lists the colors and the standards.

Figure 10-8
USB 3.0 ports
(left) and USB 3.1
ports (center)

Table 10-2
USB Connector
Colors

USB Standard	Port Color
USB 1.1	White
USB 2.0	Black
USB 3.0	Blue
USB 3.1	Teal

NOTE It's not uncommon to see laptops with red, orange, or yellow USB A ports. These are "always on" ports to charge other devices even if the laptop is turned off. There is no standard to these colors.

The keyed USB Standard-A connector has proven remarkably difficult to insert. The long-running joke on it, for example, is that it takes three tries to insert a plug: up position, down position, and then, finally, the superposition (which is the up position when you try it again).

The USB-IF standards body released the universal *USB Type-C* plug and port to address the problem with A and to unify the connector types. USB Type-C replaces both A and B plugs of all sizes.

EXAM TIP The naming conventions for USB Type-C connectors are all over the place, just like with A and B connectors. A lot of industry folks shorten and hyphenate the connector to *USB-C*. That's also how you'll see it on the CompTIA A+ 1001 exam.

USB Type-C uses 24 pins, can be inserted in either orientation, fully supports USB 3.1, and even supports other busses such as Thunderbolt (see "Thunderbolt Ports" later in this chapter). USB Type-C is quickly replacing Micro-USB as the dominant USB connection for devices (see Figure 10-9).

Figure 10-9
USB Type-C
connector

NOTE In general, your connection will operate at the speed of the slowest device involved. If you have a USB 2.0 device connected to a USB 3.*x* port on your PC, it will operate at USB 2.0 speeds.

Cable length is an important limitation to keep in mind with USB. USB 1.1 and USB 2.0 specifications allow for a maximum cable length of 5 meters. Although most USB devices never get near this maximum, some devices, such as digital cameras, can come with cables at or near the maximum 5-meter cable length. The USB 3.*x* standards don't define a maximum cable length. Because USB is a two-way (bidirectional) connection, as the cable grows longer, even a standard, well-shielded, 20-gauge, twisted-pair USB cable begins to suffer from electrical interference. To avoid these problems, I stick to cables that are no more than about 2 meters long, except in special circumstances. My staff photographer, for example, has a 4.5-meter cable between his camera (at the photo station) and his Mac. It works just fine in the studio.

EXAM TIP Numerous manufacturers make USB A to B adapters of various sorts. These enable you to use an all A cable, for example, to connect a printer to a PC.

USB Hubs

Each USB host controller supports up to 127 USB devices, but as mentioned earlier, most motherboard makers provide only six to eight real USB ports. So what do you do when you need to add more USB devices than the motherboard provides ports? You can add more host controllers (in the form of internal cards), or you can use a USB hub. A *USB hub* is a device that extends a single USB connection to two or more USB ports, almost always directly from one of the USB ports connected to the root hub. Figure 10-10 shows a typical USB hub. USB hubs are often embedded into peripherals. The monitor in Figure 10-11 comes with a built-in USB hub—very handy!

Figure 10-10
USB hub

Figure 10-11
Monitor with
built-in USB hub

Hubs also come in powered and bus-powered versions. If you choose to use a general-purpose USB hub like the one shown in Figure 10-10, try to find a powered one, as too many devices on a single USB root hub will increase power usage and decrease the bus speed. All the devices share the same bus.

USB Configuration

The biggest troubleshooting challenge you encounter with USB is a direct result of its widespread adoption and ease of use. Pretty much every modern PC comes with multiple

USB ports, and anyone can easily pick up a cool new USB device at the local computer store. The problems arise when all of this USB installation activity gets out of control, with too many devices using the wrong types of ports or pulling too much power. Happily, by following a few easy steps, you can avoid or eliminate these issues.

Windows, Linux, and macOS include many built-in drivers for USB devices. You can count on the OSs to recognize keyboards, mice, and other basic devices with their built-in drivers. Just be aware that if your new mouse or keyboard has some extra buttons, the default USB drivers might not support them. To be sure I'm not missing any added functionality, I always install the driver that comes with the device or an updated one downloaded from the manufacturer's Web site.

The last and toughest issue is power. A mismatch between available and required power for USB devices results in scary error codes and can result in nonfunctioning or malfunctioning USB devices. If you're pulling too much power, you must disconnect devices off that root hub until the error goes away. Install an add-in USB expansion card if you need to use more devices than your current USB hub supports.

There's one more problem with USB power: sometimes USB devices go to sleep and won't wake up. Actually, the system is telling them to sleep to save power. You should suspect this problem if you try to access a USB device that was working earlier but that suddenly no longer appears in Device Manager. To fix this, head to Device Manager to inspect the hub's Properties, then open the Power Management tab and uncheck the *Allow the computer to turn off this device to save power* checkbox, as shown in Figure 10-12.

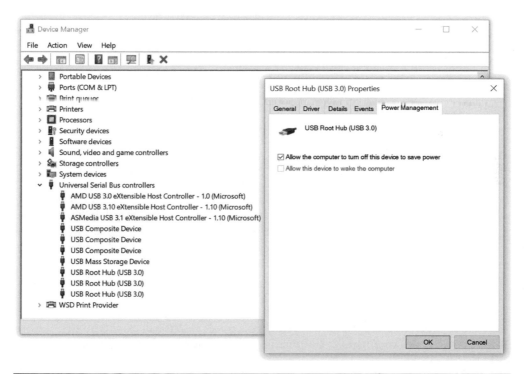

Figure 10-12 Power Management tab

SIM   Check out the Chapter 10 Challenge! sim, "USB Speeds," to prepare for questions on the CompTIA A+ 1001 exam. You'll find it here: http://totalsem .com/100x.

FireWire Ports

At first glance, *FireWire*, also known as IEEE 1394, looks and acts much like USB. FireWire has all the features of USB, but it uses different connectors and is actually the older of the two technologies. FireWire has a variety of port and cable types (see Figure 10-13) to accommodate full-size devices, such as external hard drives, and smaller devices, such as camcorders. Like USB, FireWire went through a few iterations over its lifetime. The first standard was *IEEE 1394a* running at 400 Mbps; later it was upgraded to 800 Mbps with the introduction of *IEEE 1394b*. You'll find some FireWire devices still in the field, although they're becoming more rare. FireWire enjoyed a brief day in the sun, primarily in Apple devices, but has been supplanted by Thunderbolt.

Figure 10-13
FireWire 800
port and cable
above a FireWire
400 port

Thunderbolt Ports

Intel and Apple developed *Thunderbolt* ports as a high-speed alternative to existing technologies such as USB and FireWire, tapping the PCI Express bus for up to six external peripherals (Thunderbolt functions alongside USB these days.) PC developers have adopted the technology and you will find it standard on many laptop and desktop systems these days. If you have a custom-built PC, assuming your motherboard is Thunderbolt-ready, you can readily upgrade by purchasing PCIe *Thunderbolt cards*. Thunderbolt supports video (up to a single 4K video monitor—see Chapter 17) and audio signals. It handles data storage devices just fine, too.

Thunderbolt 1 and Thunderbolt 2 connect computing devices with a Mini Display-Port (mDP) connector. Thunderbolt 3 uses a USB Type-C connector. Thunderbolt can use copper or fiber cabling. With copper, Thunderbolt chains can extend up to 3 meters. With fiber, on the other hand, a Thunderbolt chain can extend up to 60 meters.

Even though both USB and Thunderbolt use the same USB Type-C connector, they are not compatible, prompting manufacturers to mark their ports with clear logos (see Figure 10-14).

Figure 10-14
Thunderbolt and
USB logos

Thunderbolt   USB 3.1

And did I mention that Thunderbolt offers amazing bandwidth? Thunderbolt 1 runs full duplex at 10 Gbps, so it compares to USB 3.1. Thunderbolt 2 combines internal data channels, enabling throughput at up to 20 Gbps. Thunderbolt 3 offers throughput up to 40 Gbps at half the power consumption of Thunderbolt 2. Nice!

EXAM TIP   Know the characteristics and purposes of USB and Thunderbolt connection interfaces for the exams.

General Port Issues

No matter what type of port you use, if it's not working, you should always check out a few issues. First of all, make sure you can tell a port problem from a device problem. Your best bet here is to try a second "known good" device in the same port to see if that device works. If it does *not*, you can assume the port is the problem. It's not a bad idea to reverse this and plug the device into a known good port.

If you're pretty sure the port's not working, you can check three things: First, make sure the port is turned on. Almost any I/O port on a motherboard can be turned off in system setup. Reboot the system and find the device and see if the port's been turned off. You can also use Windows Device Manager to enable or disable most ports. Figure 10-15 shows a disabled USB controller in Device Manager; you'll see a small down-pointing arrow in Windows. To enable the port, right-click the device's icon and choose Enable.

Ports need drivers just as devices need drivers. All operating systems have excellent built-in drivers for all common ports, so if you fail to see an active port (and you know the port is enabled in system setup), you can bet the port itself has a physical problem.

Try This!   Expansion Opportunities
Manufacturers constantly update and produce expansion cards and peripherals to give consumers the latest technology, so try this! Check your system for USB, FireWire, or Thunderbolt ports. What does it have? Then go to an online retailer such as www.newegg.com and search for upgrades. Can you get a PCIe USB 3.1 card with Type-C ports? What about an add-on Thunderbolt card? As a related search, check the availability of powered and unpowered USB hubs. What variations can you get?

Figure 10-15
Disabled USB
controller in
Device Manager
in Windows 10

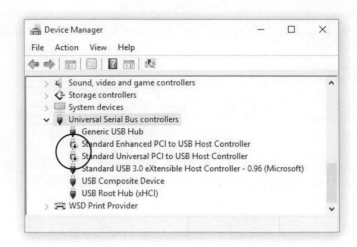

Common Peripherals

Peripherals enhance the capabilities of computing devices. Common peripherals include keyboards and mice, but there are many more. The CompTIA A+ 220-1001 exam explores a lot of peripherals. Here's a list for this chapter:

- Keyboards
- Pointing devices
  - Mouse
  - Touchpad
- Biometric devices
- Smart card readers
- Barcode scanners/QR scanners
- Touch screens
- KVM switches
- Game controllers and joysticks
- Digitizers
- Multimedia devices
  - Digital cameras
  - Webcams
  - Sound processors, speakers, and microphones

You probably don't use all of these "common" devices every day, so I'll cover each of them in detail. (Later chapters explore other common peripherals, such as video capture cards, TV tuners, printers, and scanners.)

Keyboards

The *keyboard* is both the oldest and still the primary way you input data into a PC. All modern operating systems come with perfectly good drivers for any keyboard, although some fancier keyboards may come with specialized features (screens, lights, programmable keys) that require special drivers to operate properly.

Modern keyboards connect via USB port, whether wired or wireless. In the last few years there's been a resurgence of the ancient, but fast PS/2 port. Figure 10-16 shows a combination mouse/keyboard PS/2 port on a modern motherboard.

Figure 10-16
Combination mouse/ keyboard PS/2 port (circular connector, top left)

NOTE Wireless keyboards remove the cable between you and the PC. Make sure to keep a complete set of spare batteries around.

There's not much to do to configure a standard keyboard. The only configuration tool you might need in Windows is the Keyboard Control Panel applet. This tool enables you to change the repeat delay (the amount of time you must hold down a key before the keyboard starts repeating the character), the repeat rate (how quickly the character is repeated after the repeat delay), and the default cursor blink rate. Figure 10-17 shows the default Windows Keyboard Properties dialog box. Some keyboard makers provide drivers that add extra tabs.

Windows and Linux share the same standard QWERTY keyboards, including the ctrl and alt *modifier keys* that enable you to do certain keyboard shortcuts. (Press CTRL-Z to undo an action, for example.) Windows-specific keyboards also come with the WINDOWS LOGO modifier key. Apple keyboards have three modifier keys: CONTROL, OPTION, and COMMAND. The first two correspond to CTRL and ALT; the COMMAND key is the macOS special modifier key. You can use Windows keyboards with macOS, but you need to go into the Keyboard preferences in System Preferences to map the modifier keys properly (see Figure 10-18).

Keyboards might be easy to install, but they do fail occasionally. Given their location—right in front of you—the three issues that cause the most keyboard problems stem from spills, physical damage, and dirt.

Figure 10-17
Keyboard Control
Panel applet

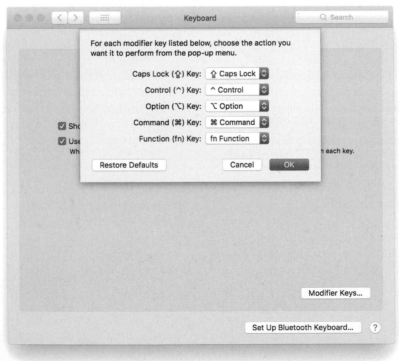

Figure 10-18   Keyboard options in macOS System Preferences

Spilling a soda onto your keyboard can make for a really bad day. If you're quick and unplug the keyboard from the PC before the liquid hits the electrical components, you might be able to save the keyboard. It'll take some cleaning, though. More often than not, you'll get a sticky, ill-performing keyboard that is not worth the hassle—just replace it!

Other common physical damage comes from dropping objects onto the keyboard, such as a heavy book (like the one in your hands). This can have bad results! Most keyboards are pretty resilient, though, and can bounce back from the hit.

Clean grime off the keys by using a cloth dampened with a little water, or if the water alone doesn't do the job, use a bit of isopropyl alcohol on a cloth (see Figure 10-19).

Figure 10-19
Cleaning keys

Dirty keys might be unsightly, but dirt under the keys might cause the keyboard to stop working completely. When your keys start to stick, grab a bottle of compressed air and shoot some air under the keys. Do this outside or over a trash can—you'll be amazed how much junk gets caught under the keys!

The bottom line when it comes to stuck keys is that the keyboard's probably useless with the stuck key, so you might as well try to clean it. Worse comes to worst, you can always buy another keyboard.

Pointing Devices

Have you ever tried to use Windows or macOS without a mouse or other device to move the cursor? It's not fun, but it can be done. All techs eventually learn the navigation hot keys for those times when mice fail, but all in all we do love our mice. There are two common pointing devices, mice and touchpads. A *mouse* moves the cursor as you move the mouse; a *touchpad* moves the cursor as you move your fingers over its surface.

In macOS, Apple definitely ups the ante for touchpads, including those on Apple laptops and the Magic Trackpad, with *Multi-Touch gestures*. With two fingers together, for example, you can scroll up and down on a page by moving your fingers up and down. Have a bunch of Windows open and want to access your desktop? Spread your thumb and three middle fingers apart on the touchpad. See something interesting on a Web page or PDF? Double-tap with two fingers to zoom in; then double-tap again to zoom out. The list of possible combinations goes on and on. Check here for the scoop: https://support.apple.com/en-us/HT204895.

In Windows, you can adjust your mouse or touchpad settings through the Mouse Control Panel applet or Settings app. Figure 10-20 shows the Windows 10 Settings app and Control Panel applet. macOS has both Mouse and Trackpad applets in System Preferences.

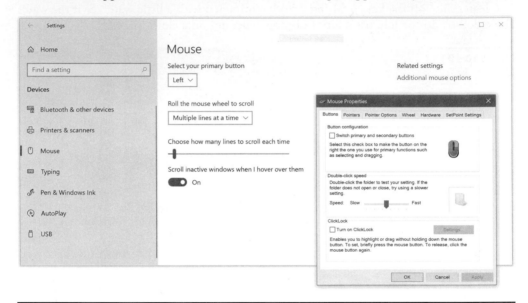

Figure 10-20 Mouse Settings and Control Panel applet

Modern pointing devices require little maintenance and almost never need cleaning, as the optics that make them work are never in contact with the grimy outside world. On the rare occasion where an *optical mouse* begins to act erratically, try using a cloth or damp cotton swab to clean out any bits of dirt that may be blocking the optics (see Figure 10-21).

Figure 10-21
Cleaning an
optical mouse

407

Biometric Devices

Biometric devices scan and remember unique aspects of various body parts, such as your iris, face, head image, or fingerprint, using some form of sensing device. This information is used as a key to prevent unauthorized people from accessing whatever the biometric device is securing. Both macOS and Windows 10 have built-in support for using biometrics like fingerprint scanners (see Figure 10-22) and facial recognition to secure user accounts. Windows uses Windows Hello to manage biometric authentication; in Figure 10-23, I'm training my system to recognize my face using a Windows Hello–compatible infrared camera.

Figure 10-22
Laptop with built-in fingerprint scanner

Figure 10-23
Training Windows Hello facial recognition

Keep looking directly at your camera.

Biometric security is very common with smartphones. Both Apple and Android vendors support fingerprint scanners for phones that have that feature. This replaces password/pin security. Figure 10-24 shows the Android fingerprint scanner learning a new fingerprint. When asked by Android or an application, you simply press your finger against the fingerprint scanner. It confirms your identity (assuming your fingerprint matches), and then special software that comes with the scanner supplies your credentials.

Figure 10-24
Fingerprint
scanner on an
Android phone

Biometric devices are also used for recognition. Recognition is different from security in that the biometric device doesn't care who you are; it just wants to know what you're doing. The best example of this is voice recognition. Voice recognition programs convert human voice input into commands or text. Apple, Microsoft, and Google use voice recognition in many forms, including Siri in iOS and Cortana in Windows 10 (both can respond to input for searching and other functions). Google uses voice recognition in its flagship office productivity app, Google Docs, so students can speak in addition to type.

No matter what biometric device you use, you use the same steps to make it work:

1. Install the device.

2. Register your identity with the device by following the setup routine to register your unique fingerprints, retina, face, etc.

3. Configure software to tell the device what to do when it recognizes your scanned identity.

Smart Card Readers

Many enterprise-level businesses use a smart-card system to enable employees to access company resources and display proper credentials so they have proper levels of access too. A *smart card reader* comes in many forms, from small devices that can attach to a laptop computer (see Figure 10-25) to a panel next to a secure door. The smart card reader scans the chip embedded in such devices as ID badges to enhance access and security.

Figure 10-25
Smart card
reader

Barcode/QR Scanners

Barcode scanners read standard *Universal Product Code* (*UPC*) barcodes or *Quick Response* (*QR*) codes (see Figure 10-26), primarily to track inventory. Scanners enable easy updating of inventory databases stored on computing devices.

Figure 10-26
UPC code (left)
and QR code
(right)

7 23456 93472 3

Two types of barcode scanners are commonly found with personal computers: pen scanners and hand scanners. Pen scanners look like an ink pen and must be swiped across the barcode. Hand scanners are held in front of the UPC code while a button is pressed to scan (see Figure 10-27). All barcode scanners emit a tone to let you know the scan was successful.

Figure 10-27
Barcode hand
scanner

Barcode scanners use USB ports or go wireless. No configuration is usually necessary, other than making sure that the particular barcode scanner works with whatever database or point-of-sale software you use.

Touch Screens

A *touch screen* is a monitor with some type of sensing device across its face that detects the location and duration of contact, usually by a finger or stylus. All touch screens then supply this contact information to the PC as though it were a click event from a mouse. Touch screens are used in situations for which conventional mouse/keyboard input is either impossible or impractical.

- Smartphones
- Smart watches
- Fitness monitors
- Information kiosks
- Point-of-sale systems
- Tablets
- E-readers

Touch screens can be separated into two groups: built-in screens like the ones in smartphones, and standalone touch screen monitors like those in many point-of-sale systems. From a technician's standpoint, you can think of a standalone touch screen as a monitor with a built-in mouse. These touch screens have a separate USB port for the "mouse" part of the device, along with drivers you install just as you would for any USB mouse.

Windows includes a Control Panel applet for configuring the touch screens on Tablet PCs, such as the Microsoft Surface. Windows also has Tablet mode Settings for standard touch-screen-enabled computers, such as many laptops (see Figure 10-28). You can use these applets to adjust how you interact with the touch screen just as you would with the Mouse or Keyboard applets. The applets enable you to configure what happens when you tap, double-tap, use gestures called "flicks," and more.

KVM Switches

A *keyboard, video, mouse (KVM) switch* is a hardware device that most commonly enables multiple computers to be viewed and controlled by a single mouse, keyboard, and screen. Some KVM switches reverse that capability, enabling a single computer to be controlled by multiple keyboards, mice, or other devices. KVM switches are especially useful in data centers where multiple servers are rack mounted, space is limited, and power is a concern. An administrator can use a single KVM switch to control multiple server systems from a single keyboard, mouse, and monitor.

There are many brands and types of KVM switches. Some enable you to connect to only two systems, and some support hundreds. Some even come with audio output jacks to support speakers. Typical KVM switches come with two or more sets of wires that are used for input devices such as PS/2 or USB mice and video output (see Figure 10-29).

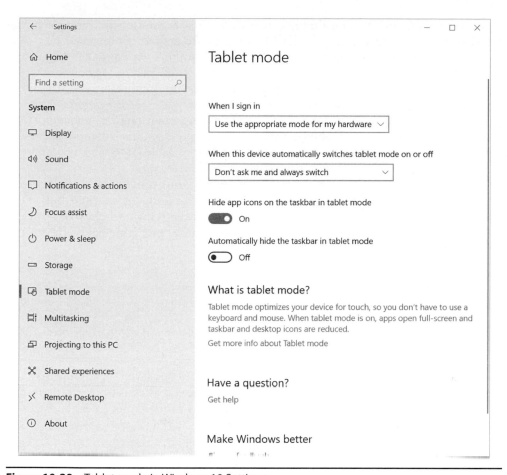

Figure 10-28 Tablet mode in Windows 10 Settings

Figure 10-29
A typical KVM
switch

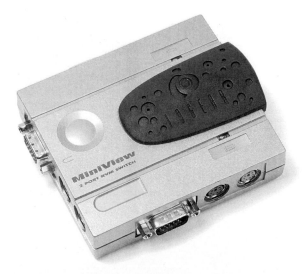

To use a KVM switch, you simply connect a keyboard, mouse, and monitor to the KVM switch and then connect the KVM switch to the desired computers. Once connected and properly configured, assigned keyboard hotkeys—a combination of keys typically assigned by the KVM switch manufacturer—enable you to toggle between the computers connected to the KVM switch. In most cases, you simply tap the SCROLL LOCK key twice to switch between sessions.

Installing a KVM switch is not difficult; the most important point to remember is to connect the individual sets of cables between the KVM ports and each computer one at a time, keeping track of which keyboard, mouse, and video cable go to which computers. (I highly recommend labeling and using twist or zip ties.)

If you get the connections wrong, the KVM switch won't function as desired. If you connect a mouse and keyboard wires to the correct KVM port, for example, but attach the same computer's video cable to a different port on the KVM switch, you won't get the correct video when you try to switch to that computer. The same holds true for the mouse and keyboard cables. Don't cross the cables!

Game Controllers and Joysticks

Whether you're racing through tight turns at top speeds or flying a state-of-the-art jet fighter, having the right controller for the job is important for an enjoyable gaming experience. Two peripherals are commonly used for controlling PC games, game controllers and joysticks.

Some PC games, especially those that were designed to be played on consoles like the Microsoft Xbox One or Sony PlayStation 4, are best enjoyed when using a game controller. A *game controller* has an array of buttons and triggers to affect movement and actions on the screen (see Figure 10-30).

Figure 10-30
An Xbox
controller

Over the past decade, flight simulator programs have declined in popularity, and so have *joysticks* (see Figure 10-31). Once a required component of a gamer's arsenal, you only need joysticks now if you are a *serious* flight simulator fan. Most modern games are controlled by game controller or mouse and keyboard.

Figure 10-31
A joystick

Game controllers and joysticks have used plenty of connectors over the years, including the eponymous joystick connector. These days, they all connect to computers via USB or wireless connections. Depending on the complexity of the controller, you may need to install drivers to get a game controller or joystick working.

You'll need to configure a game controller or joystick to make sure all the buttons and controls work properly. In Windows, go to the Devices and Printers applet. Depending on your game controller or joystick, you'll be able to configure the buttons, sticks, triggers, and more (see Figure 10-32). You can calibrate the analog sticks so they accurately register your movements. You can even adjust the amount of vibration used by the controller's force feedback (if available). Force feedback adds vibration or resistance to the controller to mirror what's happening in the game.

NOTE You might also need to configure your controller from within the game you want to play. Most games are set to use keyboard and mouse controls by default. You'll need to play around with the settings to enable your game controller.

Once you've set up your controller, you should be ready to take to the skies, or the streets, or wherever else you go to game.

Digitizers

PCs and Macs provide powerful and flexible tools for visual artists to render and share their creative ideas. Given the number of applications dedicated to producing various visual styles—including painting, sketching, animation, and more—digital art stands

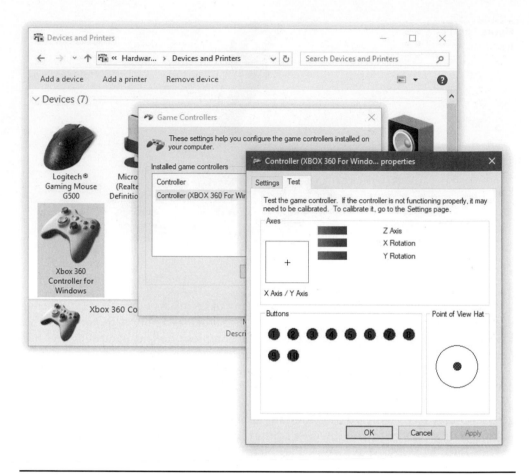

Figure 10-32 Game controller properties

toe-to-toe with its more traditional counterpart. It's only reasonable that a category of hardware would appear to help users take advantage of these tools.

A *digitizer* (otherwise known as a *pen tablet*) enables users to paint, ink, pencil, or otherwise draw on a computer (see Figure 10-33). Now, don't get carried away and start taking watercolors to your monitor. The digitizer receives input using a special surface. When a user presses against the surface, usually with a stylus, the surface transforms (or digitizes) the analog movements into digital information. The drawing application receives the information from the digitizer and turns it into an image onscreen (see Figure 10-34). If you draw a line on the digitizer, for example, that line should appear onscreen.

Figure 10-33
A type of
digitizer known
as the Wacom
pen tablet

Figure 10-34
Drawing with
a digitizer

NOTE   Not all digitizers are designed for digital art. Some are used for
handwriting, technical drawings, writing complex characters, or even as a
replacement pointing device.

Most digitizers connect via a USB or wireless connection. You'll need to install drivers
before you connect the device, although they should be included in the box. The digitizer
should also include a configuration utility. Here you can adjust the pressure sensitivity
of the stylus, configure buttons on the tablet, and set the portion of the screen to which
the tablet can draw.

People interact with simple digitizer technology a lot in the form of *signature pads*, devices that enable you to sign your name and have that signature converted to digital. Every time you sign a credit card pad, for example, you use a signature pad.

EXAM TIP The CompTIA A+ 1001 exam might ask about signature pads as peripherals that plug into a PC. These devices exist (and plug in via USB), primarily to help with electronic signing of forms, but they've been replaced in many cases by tablets such as Apple iPads for face-to-face commerce.

Multimedia Devices and Formats

Multimedia devices like digital cameras and webcams enable sharing of photographs and video chats with friends and family around the world. Almost all mobile devices come with some capability to produce and record multimedia.

Digital Cameras

Digital cameras capture every moment of life today and are essential tools for everything from note taking to capturing your child's first steps. Because digital cameras seem to be integrated with every new gadget, I need to clarify that this section will be talking about dedicated cameras. Because these digital cameras interface with computers, CompTIA A+ certified techs need to know the basics.

Storage Media   Digital cameras save pictures and videos onto some type of *removable storage media*. The most common removable storage media used in modern digital cameras is the Secure Digital (SD) card (see Figure 10-35), but there are others you might run across as you get into professional cameras. (For details about removable storage media, see the discussion in the "Storage Devices" section later in this chapter.)

Figure 10-35
Secure Digital
card

Connection   Digital cameras either plug directly into a USB port (see Figure 10-36) or connect to a Wi-Fi network. Another common option is to connect the camera's storage media to the computer, using one of the many digital media readers available.

Figure 10-36
USB connection
port on camera

You can find readers designed specifically for SD cards, as well as other types. Plenty of readers can handle multiple media formats. Many computers come with a decent built-in SD card reader (see Figure 10-37).

Figure 10-37
Digital media
reader built into
computer

Webcams

Cameras in or on computer monitors, often called *webcams* because their most common use is for Internet video communication, enable people to interact over networks with both voice and video. Webcams range greatly in quality and price.

Webcams vary in both image and sound capture quality. Because webcams are mostly used for video chat, they tend to be marketed similar to other video cameras using terms like 720p, HD, and 4K. The most common dedicated webcams today provide 1080p HD resolution experience, with cameras integrated into laptops often being 720p.

 NOTE Unfamiliar with terms such as 1080p? Pixels? All is covered in Chapter 17.

Figure 10-38 shows two of my editors chatting via webcam using Skype software.

Figure 10-38
Video chatting
by webcam
with Skype

Most people who use online video also want a *microphone*. Many webcams come with microphones, or you can use a standalone device. Those who do a lot of video chatting may prefer to get a good-quality headset with which to speak and listen.

Sound Components

Virtually every computing device today comes with four critical components for capturing and outputting sound: a sound device built into the motherboard or a dedicated sound card, speakers, microphone, and recording/playback software. This section explores each component. But let's start with how *digital* devices—computers—deal with *analog* input/output—sound waves.

Analog to Digital (and Vice Versa) Sound Computers capture (record) sound waves in electronic format through a process called *sampling*. In its simplest sense, sampling means capturing the state or quality of a particular sound wave a set number of times each second. The sampling rate is measured in units of thousands of cycles per second, or kilohertz (KHz). The more often a sound is sampled, the better the reproduction of that sound. Most sounds in computing are recorded with a sampling rate ranging from 11 KHz (very low quality, like an ancient telephone) to 192 KHz (ultra-high quality, better than the human ear).

NOTE Every modern motherboard comes with sound-processing capabilities built in. Techs refer to built-in sound as either built-in sound or a *sound card*, even when there's no expansion card for sound. People use dedicated sound card expansion cards for specific tasks, such as turning a computer into a recording studio device. For typical use, the built-in sound suffices for most users.

Sounds vary according to their loudness (*amplitude*), how high or low their tone (*frequency*), and the qualities that differentiate the same note played on different instruments (*timbre*). All the characteristics of a particular sound wave—amplitude, frequency, timbre—need to be recorded and translated into ones and zeros to reproduce that sound accurately within the computer and out to your speakers.

The number of characteristics of a particular sound captured during sampling is measured by the *bit depth* of the sample. The greater the bit depth used to capture a sample, the more characteristics of that sound can be stored and thus re-created. An 8-bit sample of a Slash guitar solo, for example, captures 2^8 (256) characteristics of that sound per sample. It would sound like a cheap recording of a recording, perhaps a little flat and thin. A 16-bit sample, in contrast, captures 2^{16} (65,536) different characteristics of his solo and reproduces all the fuzzy overtones and feedback that gives Slash his unique sound.

The last aspect of sound capture is the number of tracks of sound you capture. Most commonly, you can capture either a single track (*monaural*) or two tracks (*stereo*). More advanced captures record many more sound tracks, but that's a topic for a more advanced sound capture discussion.

The combination of sampling frequency and bit depth determines how faithfully a digital version of a sound captures what your ear would hear. A sound capture is considered *CD quality* when recorded at 44.1 KHz, with 16-bit depth and in stereo. Most recording programs let you set these values before you begin recording. Figure 10-39 shows the configuration settings for Audacity, a free and powerful sound recording and editing tool.

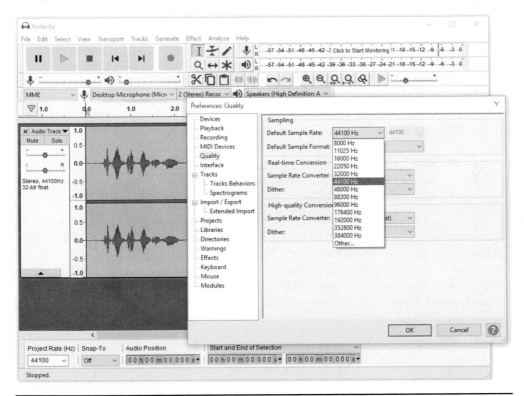

Figure 10-39   Audacity's quality settings

Recorded Sound Formats   Audio files have numerous file formats, both uncompressed and compressed. The granddaddy of all sound formats is *pulse code modulation* (*PCM*). PCM was developed in the 1960s to carry telephone calls over the first digital lines. With just a few minor changes to allow for use in PCs, the PCM format is still alive and well, although it's better known as the *WAV* format in the PC world. WAV files are great for storing faithfully recorded sounds and music, but they do so at a price. WAV files can be large, especially when sampled at high frequency and depth. A 4-minute song at 44.1 KHz and 16-bit stereo, for example, weighs in at a whopping 40-plus MB.

What's interesting about sound quality is that the human ear cannot perceive anywhere near the subtle variations of sound recorded at 44.1 KHz and 16-bit stereo. Clever programmers have written algorithms to store full-quality WAV files as compressed files, discarding unnecessary audio qualities of that file. These algorithms—really nothing more than a series of instructions in code—are called compressor/decompressor programs or, more simply, *codecs*. You've most likely encountered the Fraunhoffer MPEG-1 Layer 3 codec, more often called by its file extension, *MP3*. The most common format these days is *Advanced Audio Encoding* (*AAC*), the format used for YouTube, Apple iPhone and iPad, and more.

Streaming media is a broadcast of data that is played on your computer and immediately discarded. Streaming media is incredibly popular and has spawned an entire industry of Internet radio stations and music services.

MIDI   Every sound card (built in or add-on) can produce sounds in addition to playing prerecorded sound files. Sounds cards come with a second processor designed to interpret standardized *musical instrument digital interface* (*MIDI*) files. It's important to note that a MIDI file is not an independent music file like a WAV file. A WAV file sounds more or less the same on many different personal computing devices. A MIDI file is a text file that takes advantage of the sound-processing hardware to enable the computing device to produce sound. Programmers use these small files to tell the sound card which notes to play; how long, how loud, which instruments to use, and so forth. Think of a MIDI file as a piece of electronic sheet music, with the instruments built into your sound card.

 NOTE   MIDI files typically have the file extension .MID in Windows. This harkens back to the ancient three-character file extension limitation of Microsoft's first OS, DOS.

The beauty of MIDI files is that they're tiny in comparison to equivalent WAV files. The first movement of Beethoven's Fifth Symphony, for example, weighs in at a whopping 78 MB as a high-quality WAV file. The same seven-minute song as a MIDI file, in contrast, slips in at a svelte 60 KB. MIDI is hardware dependent, meaning the capabilities and quality of the individual sound processor make all the difference in the world on the sound produced.

Speaker Support   You'd be hard pressed to find a motherboard without built-in sound (see Figure 10-40). Every motherboard at the very least supports two speakers or a pair of headphones, but most motherboards support five or more speakers in discrete channels. These multiple speakers provide surround sound—popular not only for games but also for those who enjoy watching movies on their personal computers. The motherboard shown in Figure 10-40, for example, has outputs for many speakers.

Figure 10-40
A motherboard with multiple speaker connections

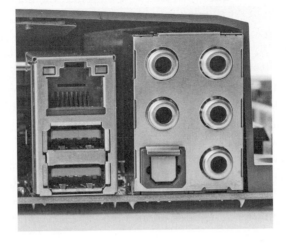

Another popular speaker addition is a subwoofer. A *subwoofer* provides the amazing low-frequency sounds that give an extra dimension to your movies, music, and games. Almost all modern systems support both surround sound and a subwoofer and advertise this with a nomenclature such as Dolby Digital or DTS. The nomenclature for multiple speakers follows a simple format: the number of speakers plus the subwoofer. A *2.1* system, for example, has two satellites and a sub (Figure 10-41). A *5.1* system has five satellites and a sub.

Figure 10-41
A 2.1 speaker set

Jacks Virtually every system comes with at least three connections, called *jacks* when used with sound: one for a stereo speaker system, one for a microphone, and one for a secondary input called line in. If you look at the back of a motherboard with built-in sound, you'll invariably see at least these three connections. On most systems, the main stereo speaker jack is green, the line in jack is blue, and the microphone jack is pink. You'll often find plenty of other connectors as well. Refer back to Figure 10-40.

Here's a list of some of the standard audio jacks:

- **Main speaker out**   Just what it sounds like, the main speaker output is where you plug in the standard speaker connector.
- **Line out**   Some systems will have a separate line out jack that is often used to connect to an external device such as a CD or MP3 player. This enables you to output sounds from your computer.
- **Line in**   The line in port connects to an external device such as a CD or MP3 player to enable you to import sounds into your computer.
- **Rear out**   The rear out jack connects to the rear speakers for surround sound audio output.
- **Analog/digital out**   The multifunction analog/digital out jack acts as a special digital connection to external digital devices or digital speaker systems, and it also acts as the analog connection to center and subwoofer channels.
- **Microphone**   The microphone port connects to an external microphone for voice input.

Many sound processors also come with a special *Sony/Philips Digital Interface* (*S/PDIF* or *SPDIF*) connector that enables you to connect your sound card directly to a 5.1 speaker system or receiver (see Figure 10-42). Using a single S/PDIF instead of a tangle of separate wires for each speaker greatly simplifies your sound setup. S/PDIF connections come in two types, optical and coaxial. The optical variety looks like a square with a small door (at right in Figure 10-42). The coaxial is a standard RCA connector (at left), the same type used to connect a CD player to your stereo. It doesn't matter which one you use; just make sure you have an open spot on your receiver or speakers.

Figure 10-42
S/PDIF
connectors

Configure speakers and speaker settings with the Sound applet/preferences. (Go to the Control Panel in Windows; System Preferences in macOS.)

NOTE   Both HDMI and DisplayPort are capable of carrying audio to, say, a TV or stereo receiver. This is very handy, as you only need one cable for audio and video, making everything nice and tidy. If you have a video card that can send audio over HDMI/DisplayPort, its ports will be listed as playback devices along with your traditional speaker and S/PDIF ports in the Windows Settings/Sound dialog (Windows 10) and Sound applet (all versions) in the Control Panel.

Microphones   Speakers are great for listening to music, but what if you're a musician looking to record your own music? You'll need to plug a *microphone* into your sound card if you want to input audio into your computer (see Figure 10-43). A microphone records sound by detecting vibrations and turning them into an electronic signal. Microphones are most commonly used for recording voices, though you can easily record any other sounds.

Figure 10-43
A standard
microphone

NOTE   You can also buy microphones that connect via USB instead of the microphone port.

Headsets   If you want to listen to music without disturbing others or if you want to enjoy voice communication while gaming (see Figure 10-44), you'll probably want a headset. Headsets come with or without a microphone and use the same connectors as speakers and microphones. Headsets without microphones more commonly use 1/8-inch RCA jacks, while headsets with microphones more commonly use USB—although there are many exceptions to that rule.

Figure 10-44
Headsets are
great for gaming.

Many systems have moved to dedicated USB audio boxes for recording or listening. Figure 10-45 shows a recording box, the Focusrite Scarlett 2 (left), and a Schiit *digital-to-analog converter* (*DAC*) for listening to music.

Figure 10-45
Scarlett recording box and Schiit DAC

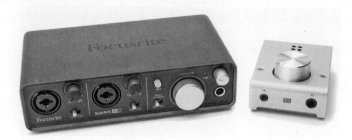

Video Formats

Video files can be massive, so let's take a moment to see how video files are stored. With an audio file, as discussed earlier, this is a simple process. You pick a format such as AAC and save the file. Video is far more complicated.

A video is two or more separate tracks—moving picture and audio—that each go through a compression algorithm (codec). Otherwise, the resulting files would be huge, even for short videos. The compressed tracks then get wrapped up into a *container file*, what's often called a *wrapper*. When you receive a file saved in a standard wrapper, such as .MOV for a QuickTime Movie file, you have no way to know for certain which codecs were used to compress the video or audio tracks inside that container file (see Figure 10-46).

Figure 10-46
A standard container file holds multiple tracks, each encoded separately.

Codecs   Video files use standard audio codecs for the audio tracks, such as WAV or MP3, but vary wildly in the type of video codecs used. Just as with audio codecs, video codecs take a video stream and compress it by using various algorithms. Here are some of the standard video codecs:

- MPEG-2 Part 2, used for DVDs, broadcast TV
- H.264, used for everything from smartphone video and streaming video to Blu-ray movies

- H.265, half the size of h.264 at the same quality, used to support 4k video
- VP9, Google's competitor to h.265, used in places like Android devices and YouTube

Wrappers   When both the video and audio streams of your video file are compressed, the file is placed into some sort of container file or wrapper. The key thing to note here is that the wrapper file doesn't necessarily specify how the video or audio tracks were encoded. You can look at two seemingly identical movie files—for example, both saved with the .MP4 file extension—and find that one will play audio and video just fine in Windows Media Player, but the other one might play only the audio and not the video because Media Player lacks the specific codec needed to decode the video stream. Here are some of the more common video wrappers you might run across:

- AVI, a container file for Windows (not used much these days)
- MOV, the standard format for Apple QuickTime
- MP4, probably the most common format these days, used for h.264 and h.265 video

Storage Devices

Removable media refers to any type of mass storage device that you may use in one system and then physically remove from that system and use in another. Today's highly internetworked computers have reduced the need for removable media as a method of sharing programs and data, but removable media has so many other uses that it's still going strong. Removable media is the perfect tool for software distribution, data archiving, and system backup.

This section of the chapter covers the most common types of removable media used today. For the sake of organization, the removable media types are broken down into these groups:

- **Flash memory**   From USB thumb drives to flash memory cards
- **Optical discs**   Any shiny disc technology, from CD-ROMs to DVDs and Blu-ray Discs

We can add external drives to this mix, meaning any hard drive, SSD, or optical drive that connects to a PC via an external cable. These drives manifest just like an internal drive, as you studied in Chapter 8, "Mass Storage Technologies," and Chapter 9, "Implementing Mass Storage," so there's nothing special to discuss here.

Flash Memory

Flash memory, the same flash memory that replaced ROM chips for system BIOS, found another home in personal computing devices in the form of removable mass storage devices. Flash memory comes in two families: USB thumb drives and memory cards.

USB thumb drives are flash devices that have a standard USB connector. "Memory card" is a generic term for a number of tiny cards used in cameras, smartphones, and other devices. Both of these families can manifest themselves as drives in modern OSs, but they usually perform different jobs. USB thumb drives have replaced virtually all other rewritable removable media as the way people transfer files or keep copies of important programs. My thumb drives (yes, I have two on me at all times) keep backups of my current work, important photos, and a stack of utilities I need to fix computers. Memory cards are very small and make a great way to store data on cameras and smartphones and then transfer that data to your computer.

Thumb Drives

Moving data between computers has historically been a pain, but USB flash memory drives, also known as thumb drives, jump drives, and flash drives, make the process much easier (see Figure 10-47). For a low price, you can get a 64-GB thumb drive that holds a ton of data.

Figure 10-47
Thumb drives

The smallest thumb drives are slightly larger than an adult thumbnail; others are larger and more rounded. The drives are hot-swappable in all modern operating systems. You simply plug one into any USB port and it appears in File Explorer or on the Desktop as a removable storage device. After you plug the drive into a USB port, you can copy or move data to or from the drive and then unplug the unit and take it with you. You can read, write, and delete files directly from the drive. Because these are USB devices, they don't need an external power source. The nonvolatile flash memory is solid-state, so it's shock resistant and is supposed to retain data safely for a decade.

Current systems enable you to boot to a thumb drive, replacing the traditional CDs and DVDs with fast flash drives. Most of the classic bootable-utility-CD makers have created USB versions that seek out your thumb drive and add an operating system with the utilities you wish to use.

NOTE Change the boot order in system setup when you want to boot from a USB flash drive. If you use the wrong boot order, the BIOS will ignore the thumb drive and go straight to the hard drive or SSD.

Flash Cards

Flash cards are the way people store data on small appliances. Memory cards come in several formats, so let's start by making sure you know the more common ones.

CompactFlash *CompactFlash (CF)* is the oldest, most complex, and physically largest of all removable flash media cards (see Figure 10-48). CF cards come in two sizes: CF I (3.3 mm thick) and CF II (5 mm thick). CF II cards are too thick to fit into CF I slots.

Figure 10-48
CF card

Secure Digital *Secure Digital (SD)* cards, as mentioned earlier, are common. About the size of a small postage stamp, you'll see SD cards in just about any type of device that uses flash media.

SD cards come in two smaller forms called *mini Secure Digital (miniSD)* cards and *micro Secure Digital (microSD)* cards. Today the miniSD format has fallen out of use, but microSD cards are extremely popular in Android-based phones that let you add storage and other small devices where its small size is an advantage. Figure 10-49 shows the three forms of SD cards.

Figure 10-49
SD, miniSD, and
microSD cards

 EXAM TIP The CompTIA A+ 1001 objectives refer to miniSD and microSD cards as *Mini-SD* and *Micro-SD cards*. Don't get thrown off by the naming differences.

SD cards come in three storage capacities. *Standard SD* cards store from 4 MB to 4 GB, *Secure Digital High Capacity* (*SDHC*) cards store 4 GB to 32 GB, and *Secure Digital Extended Capacity* (*SDXC*) cards have a storage capacity of 32 GB to 2 TB. Early SD card readers and devices cannot read the SDHC or SDXC cards, though the latter standards provide backward compatibility.

When it comes to figuring out how fast a given SD card is, things start to get complicated. Card speeds matter when it comes to intensive uses like high-quality video and high-resolution or high-speed photography.

To try and make it easy for users to pick a card that will be fast enough for their use, the people behind the SD cards have created a number of standards to communicate performance. These standards roughly break down into three different generations. The first-generation cards use the *speed class* (2, 4, 6, and 10) ratings to indicate the card's minimum MB/s write speed; a Class 10 card should write at a minimum of 10 MB/s.

The second generation of speed ratings coincided with the introduction of the new *Ultra High Speed* (*UHS*) bus. These cards use the *UHS Speed Class* standard; Class U1 cards should both read and write at a minimum of 10 MB/s, while U3 cards should read and write at a minimum of 30 MB/s.

The third generation of performance standards is the *Video Speed Class*. These standards are designed to support the newest video standards such as 4k and even 8K. The slowest class is V6, supporting 6 MB/s, but it goes all the way up to V90, which guaranties 90 MB/s write speed. If this wasn't confusing enough, modern cards often sport indicators for more than one (if not all) of these speed rating systems.

But wait, there's more! The speed classes we've looked at guarantee that a card can continuously write at the indicated rate or higher. Ratings like this are critical for figuring out whether a card can keep up with a device like a video camera. But these days, SD cards are just as likely to be used in a smartphone as they are in a camera. That's where the *Application Performance Class* ratings come in. This standard has two classes, A1 and A2. They both support a minimum of 10 MB/s sustained write. Where they differ is how many *input/output operations per second* (*IOPS*) the card can do. The A1 class can sustain 1500 IOPS while reading and 500 IOPS while writing. The A2 class can keep up with at least 4000 IOPS while reading and 2000 IOPS while writing. These performance characteristics don't matter much when a card is writing video, but they make all the difference when multiple smartphone apps are using it.

Beyond these ratings, SD cards often have a maximum read-speed (in MB/s) printed on the card or packaging. This practice started years ago with cards oriented toward professionals, but has become relatively common on cards of any quality. If you're wondering why the maximum write speed isn't also on the card, that's a great question; while it isn't printed on any card we've seen yet, product listings for high-performance SD cards typically mention the maximum write speed.

Because there's a wide variety of SD cards available with different qualities, two cards of the same capacity can vary wildly in price and performance. It's important to evaluate each card's properties to avoid wasting money on performance you don't need, or thinking you got a great deal on a massive card only to find it can't keep up with your brand-new professional video camera.

xD-Picture Card The proprietary *Extreme Digital* (*xD*) *Picture Cards* (see Figure 10-50) were about half the size of an SD card. They were used in Olympus and Fujifilm digital cameras. The xD-Picture Cards came in three flavors: original, Standard (Type M), and Hi-Speed (Type H). Fuji and Olympus have moved on to using SD cards in their cameras; you'll see xD cards only on the CompTIA A+ exams.

Figure 10-50
xD-Picture Card

 EXAM TIP Some high-end cameras (notably, Nikon) use a card format called *XQD*, which offers very high-speed transfers and capacities of 2+ TB. This format is *not* on the exam and shouldn't be confused with the older, slower xD-Picture Card format that you will find on the exam. XQD is being replaced by *CFexpress* (also not on the exam) that uses NVMe rather than PCI Express for even faster transfers and lower latency.

Card Readers Whichever type of flash memory you use, your computer must have a *card reader* to access the data on the card directly. A number of inexpensive USB card readers are available today (see Figure 10-51), and many computers and home printers come with built-in SD readers—handy to have when you want to pull the photos from your camera for editing or quickly print a photo.

Figure 10-51
USB card reader

Whichever type of flash memory you have, understand that it acts exactly like any other mass storage drive. If you wish, you can format a memory card or copy, paste, and rename files.

Optical Media

Optical disc is the generic term for shiny, 12-centimeter-wide discs. The drives that support them are called *optical drives*. This section examines optical discs, finishing with the details about installing optical drives. Optical drives are dying or dead, replaced by flash media and streaming Internet feeds. You'll see them on legacy computers and the CompTIA A+ exams. Memorize the contents of this section for the exams, then just let optical media go.

CD, DVD, and Blu-ray Disc drives and discs come in a variety of flavors and formats. *CD* stands for *compact disc*, a medium that was originally designed before Ronald Reagan won the presidency as a replacement for vinyl records. The *digital versatile disc* (*DVD*) first eliminated VHS cassette tapes from the commercial home movie market, and grew into a contender for backups and high-capacity storage. *Blu-ray Disc* (*BD*) became the only high-definition and 4K, high-capacity optical format.

Going beyond those big three household names, the term "optical disc" refers to technologies such as CD-ROM, CD-R, CD-RW, DVD, DVD+RW, BD-R, BD-RE, and so on. Each of these technologies will be discussed in detail in this chapter—for now, understand that although "optical disc" describes a variety of exciting formats, they all basically boil down to the same physical object: that little shiny disc.

CD-Media

The best way to understand optical disc technologies is to sort out the many varieties available, starting with the first: the compact disc. All you're about to read is relevant and fair game for the CompTIA A+ certification exams.

CDs store data by using microscopic pits burned into a glass master CD with a powerful laser. Expensive machines create plastic copies of the glass master that are then coated with a reflective metallic coating. CDs store data on one side of the disc only. The CD drive reads the pits and the non-pitted areas (lands) and converts the pattern into ones and zeros.

CD Formats   The first CDs were designed for playing music and organized the music in a special format called *CD-Digital Audio* (*CDDA*), which we usually just call CD-audio. CD-audio divides the CD's data into variable-length tracks; on music CDs, each song gets one track. CD-audio is an excellent way to store music, but it lacks advanced error checking, file support, or directory structure, making it a terrible way to store data. For this reason, The Powers That Be created a special method for storing data on a CD, called—are you ready—*CD-ROM*. The CD-ROM format divides the CD into fixed sectors, each holding 2353 bytes.

At first glance you might think, "Why don't CD-ROMs just use a FAT or an NTFS format like hard drives?" Well, first of all, they could. There's no law of physics that prevented the CD-ROM world from adopting any file system. The problem is that the CD makers did not want CD-ROM to be tied to Microsoft's or Apple's or anyone else's file format. In addition, they wanted non-PC devices to read CDs, so they invented their own file system just for CD-ROMs called *ISO-9660*. This format is sometimes referred to by the more generic term, *CD File System* (*CDFS*). The vast majority of data CD-ROMs today use this format.

CD-ROM Speeds   The first CD-ROM drives processed data at roughly 150,000 bytes per second (150 KBps), copying the speed from the original CD-audio format. Although this speed is excellent for listening to music, the CD-ROM industry quickly recognized that installing programs or transferring files from a CD-ROM at 150 KBps was the electronic equivalent of watching paint dry. Since the day the first CD-ROM drives for PCs hit the market, there has been a desire to speed them up to increase their data throughput. Each increase in speed is measured in multiples of the original 150-KBps drives and given an × to show speed relative to the first (1×) drives. Here's a list of the common CD-ROM speeds, including most of the early speeds that are no longer produced:

1× 150 KBps	24× 3600 KBps
2× 300 KBps	36× 5400 KBps
4× 600 KBps	48× 7200 KBps
16× 2400 KBps	72× 10,800 KBps

CD-R   Making CD-ROMs requires specialized, expensive equipment and substantial expertise, so a relatively small number of CD-ROM production companies do it. Yet, since the day the first CD-ROMs came to market, demand was high for a way that ordinary PC users could make their own CDs. The CD industry made a number of attempts to create a technology that would let users record, or *burn*, their own CDs.

In the mid-1990s, the CD industry introduced the *CD-recordable* (*CD-R*) standard, which enables affordable CD-R drives, often referred to as *CD burners*, to add data to special CD-R discs. Any CD-ROM drive can then read the data stored on the CD-R, and all CD-R drives can read regular CD-ROMs. CD-R discs come in two varieties: a 74-minute disc that holds approximately 650 MB, and an 80-minute variety that holds approximately 700 MB (see Figure 10-52). A CD-R burner must be specifically designed to support the longer, 80-minute CD-R format, but most drives you'll encounter can do this.

Figure 10-52
A CD-R disc,
with its capacity
clearly labeled

CD-R discs function similarly to regular CD-ROMs, although the chemicals used to make them produce a brightly colored recording side on almost all CD-R discs. CD-ROM discs, in contrast, have a silver data side. CD-R technology records data by using organic dyes embedded into the disc. CD-R burners have a second burn laser, roughly ten times as powerful as the read laser, that heats the organic dye. This causes a change in the reflectivity of the surface, creating the functional equivalent of a CD-ROM's pits.

CD-R drives have two speeds that matter: the record speed and the read speed, both expressed as multiples of the 150-KBps speed of the original CD-ROM drives. The record speed, which is listed first, is always equal to or slower than the read speed. For example, a CD-R drive with a specification of 8×24× would burn at 8× and read at 24×.

CD-RW   Just as CD-R drives could both burn CD-R discs and read CD-ROMs, a newer type of drive called *CD-rewritable (CD-RW)* took over the burning market from CD-R drives. Although this drive has its own type of CD-RW discs, it also can burn to CD-R discs, which are much cheaper.

CD-RW technology enables you not only to burn a disc, but to *burn over* existing data on a CD-RW disc. The CD-RW format essentially takes CD-media to the functional equivalent of a 650-MB flash-media drive. Once again, CD-RW discs look exactly like CD-ROM discs with the exception of a colored bottom side. Figure 10-53 shows all three formats.

Figure 10-53
CD-ROM, CD-R, and CD-RW discs

A CD-RW drive works by using a laser to heat an amorphous (noncrystalline) substance that, when cooled, slowly becomes crystalline. The crystalline areas are reflective, whereas the amorphous areas are not. Because both CD-R and CD-RW drives require a powerful laser, making a drive that could burn CD-Rs and CD-RWs was a simple process, and plain CD-R drives disappeared almost overnight. Why buy a CD-R drive when a comparably priced CD-RW drive could burn both CD-R and CD-RW discs?

CD-RW drive specs have three multiplier values. The first shows the CD-R write speed, the second shows the CD-RW rewrite speed, and the third shows the read speed. Write, rewrite, and read speeds vary tremendously among the various brands of CD-RW drives; here are just a few representative samples: 8×4×32×, 12×10×32×, and 48×24×48×.

Windows and CD-Media   Virtually all optical drives use the same interface as your mass storage drives. You just plug in the drive and, assuming you didn't make any physical installation mistakes, the drive appears in Windows (see Figure 10-54).

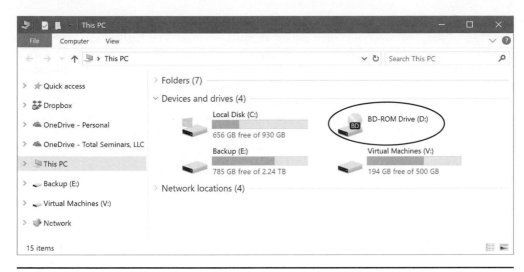

Figure 10-54 Optical drive in Windows

DVD-Media

For years, the video industry tried to create an optical-media replacement for videotape. The DVD was developed by a large consortium of electronics and entertainment firms during the early 1990s and released as digital *video* discs in 1995. The transformation of DVD to a data storage medium required a name change to digital *versatile* discs. You'll still hear both terms used. The industry also uses the term *DVD-video* to distinguish the movie format from the data formats. With the exception of the DVD logo stamped on all commercial DVDs (see Figure 10-55), DVDs look exactly like CD-media discs, but that's pretty much where the similarities end.

Figure 10-55
Typical
DVD-video

The single best word to describe DVD is *capacity*. The lowest capacity DVD holds 4.37 GB of data, or two hours of standard-definition video. The highest capacity DVD versions store roughly 16 GB of data, or more than eight hours of video. DVD uses a number of technologies, but three are most important. First, DVD uses smaller pits than CD-media, and packs them much more densely. Second, DVD comes in both *single-sided* (*SS*) and *double-sided* (*DS*) formats. As the name implies, a DS disc holds twice the data of an SS disc, but it also requires you to flip the disc to read the other side. Third, DVDs come in *single-layer* (*SL*) and *dual-layer* (*DL*) formats. DL formats use two pitted layers on each side, each with a slightly different reflectivity index. Table 10-3 shows the common DVD capacities.

DVD Version	Capacity
DVD-5 (12 cm, SS/SL)	4.37 GB, more than two hours of video
DVD-9 (12 cm, SS/DL)	7.95 GB, about four hours of video
DVD-10 (12 cm, DS/SL)	8.74 GB, about four and a half hours of video
DVD-18 (12 cm, DS/DL)	15.90 GB, more than eight hours of video

Table 10-3 DVD Versions/Capacities

DVD-ROM   *DVD-ROM* is the DVD equivalent of the standard CD-ROM data format except that it's capable of storing up to almost 16 GB of data. Almost all DVD-ROM drives also fully support DVD-video, as well as most CD-ROM formats. Most DVD drives sold with PCs are DVD-ROM drives.

Recordable DVD   The IT industry has no fewer than *three* distinct standards of recordable DVD-media: DVD-R, DVD-RW, and DVD-RW DL. DVD-R discs work like CD-Rs. You can write to them but not erase or alter what's written. *DVD-RW* discs can be written and rewritten, just like CD-RW discs. DVD-RW DL can be written to on two layers, doubling the capacity. Most DVD drives can read all formats.

EXAM TIP   The CompTIA A+ 1001 objectives mention *DVD-RW DL* as a common recordable disc type. The specification has been out for several years, but the media is not around. Rewritable Blu-ray Discs have eclipsed DVD discs.

EXAM TIP   Apple stopped including optical drives on both desktop and portable systems a long time ago. Because optical media enjoys some popularity, Apple gave macOS machines *Remote Disc*, the capability to read optical media from an optical drive in another system.

Blu-ray Disc Media

Blu-ray Disc is the last generation in optical disc formatting and storage technology (see Figure 10-56). Because of its near-perfect audio and video quality; mass acceptance by industry-leading computer, electronics, game, music, retail, and motion picture companies; and huge storage capacities of up to 25 GB (single-layer disc), 50 GB (dual-layer disc), and 100 GB (BDXL), Blu-ray Disc technology enjoyed wild popularity until flash memory prices dropped in the 2010s to basically kill off all optical media.

Figure 10-56
Standard
Blu-ray Disc

NOTE   If you own an Xbox One or PlayStation 3 or later, you already have a Blu-ray Disc player. That's the optical format the game system uses.

BD-ROM   *BD-ROM (read only)* is the Blu-ray Disc equivalent of the standard DVD-ROM data format except, as noted earlier, it can store much more data and produces superior audio and video results. Almost all BD-ROM drives are fully backward compatible and support DVD-video as well as most CD-ROM formats. If you want to display the best possible movie picture quality on your HDTV, you should get a Blu-ray Disc player and use Blu-ray Discs in place of DVDs. Most new computer systems don't come standard with optical drives installed. You can often custom-order a system with a Blu-ray Disc drive or you can simply connect one yourself. Figure 10-57 shows a Blu-ray Disc drive.

Figure 10-57
A combination
CD/DVD/Blu-ray
Disc drive

BD-R and BD-RE Blu-ray Discs come in two writable formats, *BD-R* (*recordable*) and *BD-RE* (*rewritable*). You can write to a BD-R disc one time. You can write to and erase a BD-RE disc several times. There are also BD-R and BD-RE versions of mini Blu-ray Discs.

Installing Optical Drives

From ten feet away, optical drives of all flavors look absolutely identical. Figure 10-58 shows a CD-RW drive, a DVD drive, and a BD-R drive. Can you tell them apart just by a glance? In case you were wondering, the CD-RW drive is on the bottom, the DVD drive is next, and finally the BD-R drive is on the top. If you look closely at an optical drive, you will normally see its function either stamped on the front of the case or printed on a label somewhere less obvious (see Figure 10-59).

Figure 10-58
CD-RW, DVD, and BD-R drives

Figure 10-59
Label on optical drive indicating its type

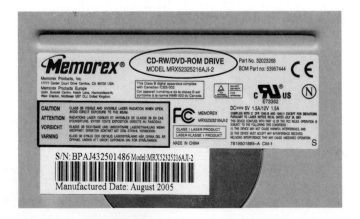

Most internal optical drives use SATA. External optical drives often use USB or Thunderbolt connections. Plug them in and go.

Chapter Review

Questions

1. Jason put in a recommendation that the company upgrade the SD cards used in the company smartphones from 32 GB SDHC A1 to 128 GB SDXC A2. What does A2 signify?

   A. A2 cards offer much greater capacity than A1 cards.

   B. A2 cards offer much faster sustained write speeds than A1 cards.

   C. A2 cards cost a lot less than A1 cards and offer similar performance.

   D. A2 cards sustain faster IOPS than A1 cards.

2. What happens to bus speed and power usage when you plug multiple devices into a USB hub?

   A. The bus speed stays constant, but power usage increases.

   B. The bus speed increases because each device brings a little burst; power usage increases.

   C. The bus speed decreases because all devices share the same total bandwidth; power usage increases.

   D. The bus speed decreases because all devices share the same total bandwidth; power usage decreases.

3. Which port type offers the fastest transfer speed?

   A. IEEE 1394a

   B. SuperSpeed USB

   C. Full-Speed USB

   D. Hi-Speed USB

4. You take a tech call from a user who complains that she gets an error message, "Hub power exceeded," when she plugs her new thumb drive into her USB keyboard's external USB port. Worse, the device won't work. What's most likely the problem?

   A. Her USB port is defective.

   B. She has a defective thumb drive.

   C. She plugged a Hi-Speed device into a Full-Speed port.

   D. She plugged one too many devices into the USB hub.

5. What is the fastest speed that Hi-Speed USB 2.0 can go?

   A. 12 Mbps

   B. 120 Mbps

   C. 400 Mbps

   D. 480 Mbps

6. What is the maximum cable length for USB 2.0?

   A. 1.2 meters

   B. 1.2 yards

   C. 5 meters

   D. 5 feet

7. How many speakers are in a 5.1 setup?

   A. Five speakers plus a subwoofer

   B. Six speakers plus a subwoofer

   C. Seven speakers plus a subwoofer

   D. Eight speakers plus a subwoofer

8. What type of file is a MIDI file?

   A. Audio

   B. Binary

   C. MP3

   D. Text

9. Which optical disc type offers the most capacity writing and rewriting data files?

   A. DVD-R

   B. DVD+RW DL

   C. BD-RE

   D. BD-RW

10. Jack downloaded a video shared by a friend, ourfamilyholiday.avi. When he opens it in his media player software, he hears sound but gets no picture. What's the most likely problem and solution?

    A. His media player software doesn't support AVI files. He needs to install a new media player.

    B. His computer is a Mac; he needs to play the file on a Windows system.

    C. His computer lacks the proper video codec. He needs to update the codecs installed on his computer.

    D. The video is corrupt. His friend needs to share it with him again.

Answers

1. **D.** A1 and A2 Application Performance Class ratings refer to the IOPS rating of the card, with A2 cards offering better performance than A1. This matters for smartphones with multiple apps running. SDHC and SDXC refer to the capacity of a card's storage.

2. **C.** The bus speed decreases because all devices share the same total bandwidth; power usage increases.

3. **B.** SuperSpeed USB easily spanks the competition here.

4. **D.** Just like the error message said, the thumb drive drew too much power for the hub to handle.

5. **D.** Hi-Speed USB 2.0 has a theoretical maximum of 480 Mbps.

6. **C.** USB has a maximum cable length of 5 meters.

7. **A.** A 5.1 setup has five speakers and one subwoofer.

8. **D.** A MIDI file is a text file.

9. **C.** BD-RE offers the highest rewritable capacity of the discs mentioned here.

10. **C.** Most likely, Jack's system lacks the video codec needed for the video portion of the file. He needs to update the codecs on his machine.

Building a PC

In this chapter, you will learn how to
- Research and spec out specialized PCs
- Install and upgrade Windows
- Describe Windows post-installation best practices

Techs build computers. We fix them too, of course, but very little beats the chance to show off our knowledge, research skill, and technical savvy like creating excellent custom PCs for clients.

This chapter puts together a lot of what you know about hardware from the previous ten chapters and layers on the essential component that makes Windows PCs so excellent: Windows. Let's start with customized PCs for specialized jobs, then turn to installing and upgrading Windows. The final section covers post-installation tasks.

1001

Specialized PCs

People need computers to get work done. The type of system a person needs depends on what types of tasks he or she needs to perform with it and how the IT department has configured the organization's network. This section explores what you should consider when creating specialized computers, including hardware and software compatibility, upgradability, and end-of-life issues. We'll examine seven custom PC configurations to give you ideas about variations and what kind of scenarios you might encounter as a tech.

Prerequisites to Building

In a typical scenario for building a custom PC, a customer has a specific need, such as a machine for editing video and audio files to make movies. The customer will have a budget and a software package in mind to get the job done. Common choices for movie production, for example, are Adobe Premier and Adobe After Effects—both part of the Adobe Creative Suite that the customer can license via a monthly fee. Let's look at issues around new hardware versus upgrading existing hardware.

New Hardware Builds

If the customer wants all-new hardware, then your path is straightforward. Consider Johan, who has a small business and wants to add two new specialized machines: a storage system for general-purpose file storage and a media system for the lounge. Follow the recommendations in this chapter: research the hardware compatibility and operating system compatibility for the software the customer needs.

To recommend an edition of Windows, you need to weigh its features against the customer's needs. Microsoft releases three editions anyone can purchase, which you can think of in terms of how their features address *corporate versus personal needs*. Home is the least expensive, Pro costs more, and Enterprise costs the most. The Home version of Windows 10 can certainly handle any kind of *media center* activity, so it would be perfect for Johan's lounge machine. Definitely go 64-bit for the additional RAM capacity.

If the business uses a *Windows Domain/Active Directory* for controlling network access and user accounts, then your recommendation would need to be for the Pro or Enterprise edition. (See Chapter 19, "Local Area Networking," for the details on network organization options such as workgroups and domains.) These editions enable domain access, whereas the Home version does not. Furthermore, the Pro and Enterprise editions offer much better control over files and folders with *BitLocker* and the *Encrypting File System* (*EFS*), two options for encrypting drives and data. (You'll learn a lot about both file protection technologies in Chapter 13, "Users, Groups, and Permissions.") Finally, if Johan's office is part of a larger network connecting many offices over a wide area, the Enterprise edition offers a refined method for distributing applications to many locations, called *BranchCache*.

 EXAM TIP   Expect a question or two on the CompTIA A+ 1002 exam that asks you to compare features of Windows versions and editions. You got an overview about the versions way back in Chapter 2, "The Visible Computer." The section here adds some detail, but you should come back to these comparisons after you read about networking later in the book. Mark your notes to come back and reflect on objective 1.2 of the 1002 exam.

Upgrade Builds

Wrinkles can slip in when customers want to leverage hardware they already own. Here's a typical scenario for an upgrade plan with potential problems. Maria has a small business and wants to produce some videos to promote her products. She has a Windows 8.1 Dell workstation that cost her a lot a few years ago. It has a first-generation Intel Core i7 processor, 4 GB of DDR3 RAM, and a 500-GB hard drive. You know (or will, when you read the section "Audio/Video Editing Workstation," later in this chapter) that you'll need to increase the RAM and mass storage to make the system work well as an A/V workstation. Now you have a whole host of questions to answer before you do any upgrading.

What are the *hardware prerequisites/hardware compatibility issues* with the application software (Creative Suite, in this case)? How much RAM will the software need? How much RAM can the existing system handle? Can you still purchase DDR3 RAM that works with the system? What size and how many drives will work in the case; does the motherboard support those drives?

What are the *application compatibility issues* with the system? Can a first-generation Intel Core i7 handle the current versions of the applications? If not, can you upgrade the CPU without spending a fortune? (CPUs for older sockets tend to cost more than CPUs for current sockets; it's just supply and demand.)

What are the *operating system compatibility issues* between the OS and the application software? Can you run the latest Adobe Creative Suite in Windows 8.1? If not, what is the *upgrade path* to put Windows 10 on the system? What about the customer's OS *user interface* preferences? What if Maria prefers the Windows 8.1 *desktop style* over the Windows 10 user interface? How do you resolve such an unusual situation?

Finally, are there any *vendor-specific limitations* regarding the Dell components and the operating system? How close is the system to its *end-of-life* date (when the manufacturer no longer supports the hardware)? Does the manufacturer have update limitations on the OS, such as certain custom features that work in Windows 8.1 by design, but not in Windows 10? You must address these kinds of *compatibility concerns between the operating systems* before you can make a recommendation for the customer.

Custom PCs for Specific Jobs

The CompTIA A+ 1001 exam defines seven specific custom PC configurations: standard thick clients, thin clients, virtualization workstations, gaming PCs, graphic/CAD/CAM design workstations, audio/video editing workstations, and network attached storage devices. Let's go through each of these custom builds and see what each needs.

Standard Thick Clients

A *thick client* runs a modern operating system and general productivity applications to accomplish the vast majority of tasks needed by office and home users (see Figure 11-1). When most folks hear the term "PC," the thick client comes to mind. Thick clients are the quiet workhorses of modern computing.

Figure 11-1
A typical thick client

The thick part of thick client doesn't necessarily refer to the physical thickness of the computer case or system unit that houses everything. It means more what the computer can do if the computer isn't connected to any type of network.

A thick client has everything it needs to do its work without a network connection. The hard drive is bootable with an operating system. The computer has a set of desktop applications. You can write letters. You can run a spreadsheet, play a game, or edit a video. Granted, at some point you might need to send an e-mail message, upload a document, or play an online game; but in general you can do most of your work without a network connection.

The key to a good thick client is sufficient hardware to support the operating system and applications typical of an office or home-office environment. All operating systems define minimum hardware requirements. Table 11-1 shows the minimum hardware requirements for Windows 10.

Component	Minimum Hardware Requirements
CPU	1 gigahertz (GHz) or faster 32-bit (x86) or 64-bit (x64)
Memory	1 gigabyte (GB) RAM (32-bit) or 2 GB RAM (64-bit)
Hard drive	16 GB available hard drive space (32-bit) or 20 GB (64-bit)
Graphics	DirectX 9 graphics device with WDDM driver
Network	Internet access

Table 11-1   Minimum Hardware Requirements for Windows 10

These are minimum requirements, not optimal requirements. The numbers are laughably low. In the industry we say, "It might be enough to *walk* Windows, but it won't be enough to *run* Windows!" (We nerds find this very funny.) Instead we look for recommended hardware requirements. Operating systems don't always publish recommended requirements, so Table 11-2 presents my recommended hardware for a typical Windows 10 thick client.

Component	Mike's Recommended Hardware Requirements
	32-bit is obsolete! Everything is 64-bit!
CPU	2 GHz or faster
Memory	8 GB RAM
Hard drive	500 GB available drive space (HDD or SSD)
Graphics	DirectX 10 graphics device with WDDM driver
Network	50 megabits per second (Mbps) download speed Internet access

Table 11-2   Author's Recommended Hardware for Windows 10

A standard thick client should meet or exceed the recommended hardware specifications for the operating system and offer typical desktop applications, such as office productivity and network applications (like a Web browser and an e-mail client).

Ubuntu Linux does a great job clarifying both minimum and recommended hardware requirements, as shown in Figure 11-2.

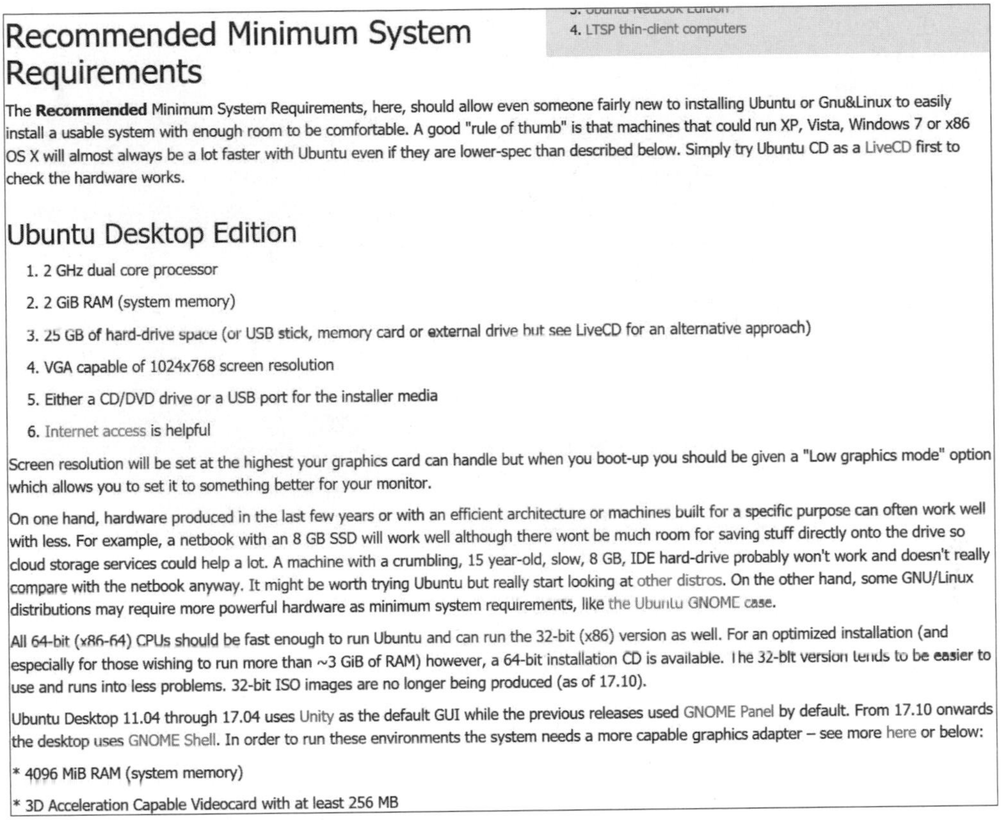

3. Ubuntu Netbook Edition
4. LTSP thin-client computers

Recommended Minimum System Requirements

The **Recommended** Minimum System Requirements, here, should allow even someone fairly new to installing Ubuntu or Gnu&Linux to easily install a usable system with enough room to be comfortable. A good "rule of thumb" is that machines that could run XP, Vista, Windows 7 or x86 OS X will almost always be a lot faster with Ubuntu even if they are lower-spec than described below. Simply try Ubuntu CD as a LiveCD first to check the hardware works.

Ubuntu Desktop Edition

1. 2 GHz dual core processor

2. 2 GiB RAM (system memory)

3. 25 GB of hard-drive space (or USB stick, memory card or external drive but see LiveCD for an alternative approach)

4. VGA capable of 1024x768 screen resolution

5. Either a CD/DVD drive or a USB port for the installer media

6. Internet access is helpful

Screen resolution will be set at the highest your graphics card can handle but when you boot-up you should be given a "Low graphics mode" option which allows you to set it to something better for your monitor.

On one hand, hardware produced in the last few years or with an efficient architecture or machines built for a specific purpose can often work well with less. For example, a netbook with an 8 GB SSD will work well although there wont be much room for saving stuff directly onto the drive so cloud storage services could help a lot. A machine with a crumbling, 15 year-old, slow, 8 GB, IDE hard-drive probably won't work and doesn't really compare with the netbook anyway. It might be worth trying Ubuntu but really start looking at other distros. On the other hand, some GNU/Linux distributions may require more powerful hardware as minimum system requirements, like the Ubuntu GNOME case.

All 64-bit (x86-64) CPUs should be fast enough to run Ubuntu and can run the 32-bit (x86) version as well. For an optimized installation (and especially for those wishing to run more than ~3 GiB of RAM) however, a 64-bit installation CD is available. The 32-bit version tends to be easier to use and runs into less problems. 32-bit ISO images are no longer being produced (as of 17.10).

Ubuntu Desktop 11.04 through 17.04 uses Unity as the default GUI while the previous releases used GNOME Panel by default. From 17.10 onwards the desktop uses GNOME Shell. In order to run these environments the system needs a more capable graphics adapter – see more here or below:

* 4096 MiB RAM (system memory)

* 3D Acceleration Capable Videocard with at least 256 MB

Figure 11-2   Ubuntu desktop hardware requirements (from ubuntu.com)

To wrap, a standard thick client:

- Is a complete system that has its own operating system and desktop applications
- Does not need a network connection to run
- Meets recommended requirements for its operating system

Thin Clients

A *thin client* is a system designed to outsource much of its work. Thin clients usually rely on resources from powerful servers, so they may not have hard drives, for example, or store any data. Thin clients often serve as single-purpose systems, like point-of-sale machines (cash registers). Another common example today is office workstations where applications are stored on servers. A thin client might look like a thick client, but it requires fewer resources, thus making it cheaper and easier to deploy. Centralized storage of data also enables a lot more control on behalf of the administrators. Figure 11-3 shows a typical thin client.

Figure 11-3
Thin client in an office

Because the classic thin client relies on *network connectivity* and access to servers over those networks, we'll revisit them when we get to networking in Chapters 18–21.

To wrap, a thin client:

- Stores only basic applications; may be a single-purpose system
- Needs a network connection to run; may need a network connection to boot
- Meets minimum hardware requirements for its operating system

Virtualization Workstation

Virtualization is a powerful technology that enables you to run more than one operating system at the same time on a single computer. With virtualized servers, you can consolidate multiple, power-hungry machines into one box, saving floor space, electricity, and a lot of running around. With *virtualization workstations*, virtualization is most often used to run a second OS within the OS installed on the computer's hard drive (see Figure 11-4).

For good performance on a virtualization workstation, install lots and lots of RAM. Each virtualization workstation needs enough memory to run the native operating system, the guest operating system, and any applications running in either OS, so RAM is the

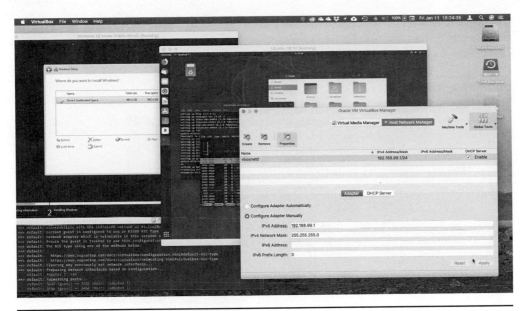

Figure 11-4 Two virtual machines running on my macOS system

most important thing in virtualization. A powerful 64-bit CPU with many cores also helps virtual machines run smoothly. Many desktop computers can run virtual machines, but if you want the best possible performance, you want lots of RAM and a good CPU.

EXAM TIP You'll need lots of RAM—think *maximum RAM*—and a fast CPU with many cores to get great performance out of a virtualization workstation.

To wrap, a virtualization workstation:

- Needs very large amounts of RAM—often the maximum the system can accept
- Needs a fast CPU with as many cores as the systems—and your wallet—allow

Chapter 22, "Virtualization," discusses virtual machines in great detail. We'll take the opportunity there to flesh out the discussion of virtualization workstations.

Gaming PC

Computer gaming is one of the most process-intensive operations you can do with a PC. As an aspiring PC tech, you probably took your first apprehensive steps into the dark underbelly of PCs with a game: *Fortnite, Minecraft, Grand Theft Auto, Borderlands 2, World of Warcraft* . . . you've played at least one of them. While casual gamers can get by with a standard desktop PC (like the thick client you read about earlier), those who take their gaming seriously want a powerful *gaming PC* ready to pump out the latest games (see Figure 11-5).

Figure 11-5
Author's gaming rig, ready to shame you (Steam account name: desweds)

The name of the game with a gaming rig is a higher-end graphics card. A gamer goes through a game's graphics settings and sets everything to the max. And since games aren't all about how good they look, you'll also want a good sound card and headphones. (Okay—you also need a good game, but one thing at a time.)

A high-end graphics card with a powerful *graphics processing unit* (*GPU*) is important, but it's not the only upgrade you need to make your games play well. You'll need a fast, multicore processor, more than thick client RAM (at least 16+ GB), and a high-definition sound card to provide optimal positional audio.

EXAM TIP Standalone sound cards are pretty much irrelevant in today's systems. You'll see the "requirement" for one only on the CompTIA A+ exams.

We haven't covered the GPUs yet; you'll get all the details in Chapter 17, "Display Technologies." The rest of the pieces should make a lot of sense at this point. Remember the high-end CPUs from Chapter 3? Crank them up and throw on some high-end cooling, like a purpose-built *water-cooling rig*, to give a gaming system the foundation for greatness.

To wrap, a gaming PC needs:

- Multicore processor
- High-end cooling (maybe liquid)
- High-end video/specialized GPU
- High-definition sound card

Graphics/CAD/CAM Design Workstation

Professional photographers and graphic designers generally work with pretty hefty files, so at its core, a *graphics workstation* requires a fast, multicore CPU, maximum RAM, and serious storage space. Because designers work visually, add to that mix the need for high-end video components. Finally, throw in specialized software to make it all work. Professional photographers use Adobe Photoshop and Adobe Lightroom. Graphics engineers have a few other options, but they fall into *computer-aided design* (*CAD*) and *computer-aided manufacturing* (*CAM*) categories.

 NOTE CAD/CAM software programs enable engineers to create and build components in an industrial setting.

Graphics designers need to have the clearest view possible of their images and image editing software. Whether you're editing a wedding shoot in Lightroom or drafting mechanical components in SolidWorks, you need to make sure you can see what you're working on! Because of this, a primary need for a graphics workstation is a large, high-quality monitor. A $200 LCD panel from Best Buy won't help you here—you need to make sure that the colors you see on the screen are as accurate as possible.

Chapter 17 covers all the various high-end video components, such as In-Plane Switching (IPS) monitors and multi-thousand-dollar graphics workstation video cards. We'll reopen the discussion on graphics workstations in that chapter.

To wrap, a graphics/CAD/CAM design workstation needs:

- Multicore processor
- High-end video/specialized GPU
- Very large amounts of RAM, often the maximum the system can accept
- Robust storage

Audio/Video Editing Workstation

When George Lucas made the first *Star Wars* movie, he used camera tricks, miniature models, and stop-motion animation to create the illusion of massive spaceships and robots battling it out in a galaxy far, far away. Twenty years later, he filmed the *Star Wars* prequels in front of massive green screens and used *computer-generated imagery* (*CGI*) to transform the bland sets into exotic planets and space stations. I won't get into an argument about which approach produced better movies, but the fact remains that the act of creating films has changed. It's not just films, either—computers have changed the way we create all types of media, including movies, television shows, photography, music, and more.

If you want to get involved in this creative revolution, you're going to need a powerful computer. Workstations for creative professionals are customized for the type of media they create.

Audio Editing Workstations

The requirements for *audio editing workstations* are very similar to those for graphics workstations—a fast, multicore CPU, gobs of RAM, and a large monitor. Plus, you need lots of fast storage. Add to that the need for a high-quality audio interface.

An *audio interface* is a box that you hook up to a PC with inputs that enable you to connect professional microphones and instruments. Functionally, an audio interface is just a really high-end sound card, though it usually connects to your computer via USB rather than plugging into the motherboard. Audio interfaces range in size from an interface you can fit in your hand to one that will take up most of your desk. A more expensive interface includes more inputs and produces higher-quality sound, though you'll also need some expensive speakers to hear the difference.

Just like with graphics workstations, audio editing workstations frequently make use of specialized input devices. These devices, referred to as *control surfaces*, mimic the look and feel of older, analog mixing consoles. They have a large number of programmable inputs that make controlling the software much faster and more accurate than with just a mouse and keyboard. These control surfaces range in size from small desktop units, all the way up to room-filling behemoths that are used in recording studios. Some of these boards also contain an audio interface.

Video Editing Workstations

Video editing workstations combine the requirements of a graphics workstation and an audio editing workstation. Video editors often use two or more color-calibrated monitors so they can view the video stream they're working on with one monitor and see their video editor open on the other, making dual monitors very useful; if used to produce high-resolution 4K video, a monitor supporting this resolution is also essential. Video editing workstations require a very powerful CPU paired with as much RAM as possible, since video editing is a far more intensive process than graphics or audio editing. Lots of high-speed storage is also required since video projects eat terabytes for breakfast. Many video editing workstations have multiple hard drives set up in a RAID array for added storage capacity and enhanced read/write speed.

Video editing workstations, like CAD/CAM workstations, benefit enormously from a professional-level graphics card. This is almost as important as the fast CPU and piles of RAM; you won't see a video editing workstation without one.

Because video editing workstations are frequently used as audio editing workstations, too, you will often find video editing workstations with the same audio interfaces and control surfaces as you'd see on an audio editing workstation. There are also video interfaces that enable editors to connect to various cameras. Additionally, many video editors use custom keyboards that have special labels and controls for popular video editing software.

 EXAM TIP The CompTIA A+ 1001 objectives use the term *audio/video editing workstation*, combining both types into a single thing. These machines often do double duty, so that's cool, and keep that in mind for the exam. In practice, you'll find dedicated audio editing workstations and dedicated video editing workstations, as well as the combined units.

To wrap, an audio/video editing workstation needs:

- Specialized audio and video card
- Large, fast storage
- Very large amounts of RAM, often the maximum the system can accept
- Dual monitors (or more)

Network Attached Storage Devices

How many computing devices are in your house right now? If you're like me, the answer is "a lot." Between multiple smartphones, streaming media boxes, game consoles, tablets, and various computers, you might shock yourself with the count.

As more and more computing devices move into the home environment, there's a need for a centralized storage space, a *network attached storage (NAS) device* to dish out files and folders on demand—a place for all your media to stream to multiple devices. This NAS has very specialized needs that take it beyond the typical thick client.

A NAS supplies three discrete functions: media streaming, file sharing, and print sharing. Media streaming can use specialized software, but just like file and print sharing, it works fine through the default tools in Windows and macOS. The NAS has to have a very fast network connection and gobs of storage. Plus, that storage needs to be fault tolerant. Losing your video collection because of a hard drive crash would make for a very bad day.

Software

Any modern operating system enables you to share files and folders through standard sharing features. The same is true of sharing a printer. To turn a PC into a print server, get to the printer's Properties dialog box—either through Settings or via the Control Panel—and then check the Share this printer checkbox on the Sharing tab (see Figure 11-6).

You can easily turn a Windows PC into a media streaming server. Click in the Search field in the Taskbar, type **streaming**, and press the ENTER key to open the Network and Sharing Center/Media streaming options screen (see Figure 11-7).

After turning on media streaming, you can choose to share your streams with other systems that are sharing (see Figure 11-8). By default, Windows wants to share everything, though you can customize what's shared in case you have young children and don't want them to have access to inappropriate content.

Finally, both Windows Media Player and iTunes have a feature to share media files on a local network. Figure 11-9 shows iTunes sharing via the Bonjour protocol.

Hardware

Hardware needs on a NAS apply primarily to the network speed and hard drive redundancy, at least according the CompTIA objectives. If you have a very active server, you should also pay attention to the amount of RAM it has and the speed of the CPU. Beefing both up above the standard thick client can help if you start getting some lag.

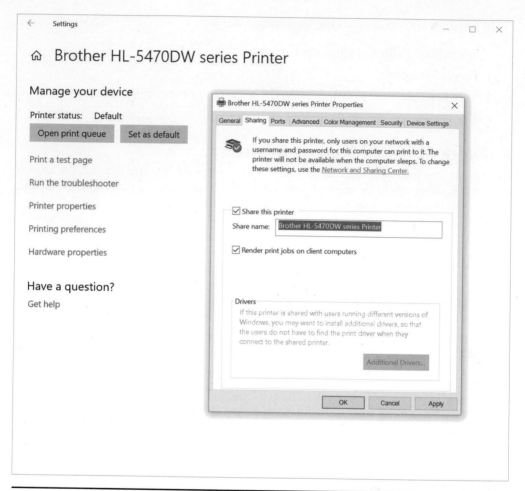

Figure 11-6 Sharing a printer in Windows 10

For the network, a wired Gigabit Ethernet NIC should be standard issue. Although it sounds cool to go wireless, you should limit the use of wireless to the single connection between the wireless access point and the client. The home server should connect via Ethernet to minimize any lag or dropped frames.

A file server's hard drives do the heavy and sustained lifting for the PC, so you should not stint on them. At a minimum, get two drives of identical size that have as much capacity as you can afford. Plus, because you need fault tolerance on the data, you simply must use a RAID 1 configuration at a minimum (and thus the need to get two identical drives). If your budget can afford it and your motherboard supports it, get four identical drives and run in RAID 10.

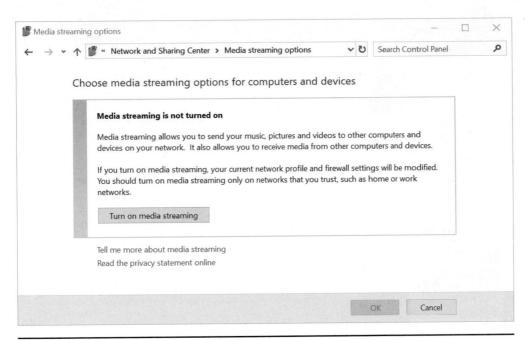

Figure 11-7 Media streaming turned off

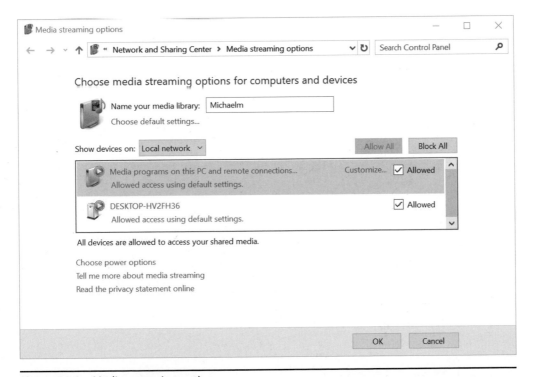

Figure 11-8 Media streaming options

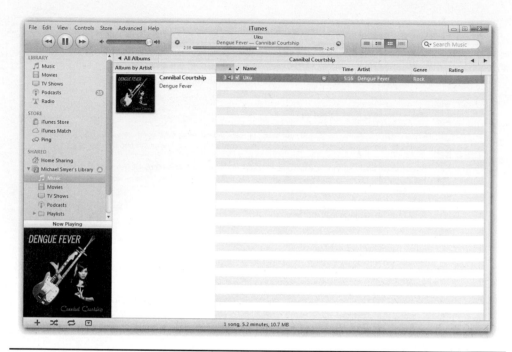

Figure 11-9 Streaming with iTunes

You'll recall from Chapter 9, "Implementing Mass Storage," that Windows 8/8.1/10 offer *Storage Spaces* and storage pools where you can toss in any number of drives and create an array. If you do this sensibly, like putting three 4-TB drives into a pool and creating a single Storage Space, you're essentially creating a RAID 5 array.

To wrap, NAS storage needs:

- File sharing
- Media streaming
- RAID array
- Gigabit NIC

 SIM   Check out the excellent Challenge! sim "Build More Thick Clients" in the Chapter 11 section of the online TotalSims here: http://totalsem.com/100x. It will help reinforce different needs for different system types.

1002

Installing and Upgrading Windows

Once you have the hardware lined up for whichever specialized PC you want to build, it's time to install an operating system. For most computers, you'll want to install a version of Windows—and the appropriate edition within each version. This section looks at media selection, types of installation, then the installation and upgrade process. It completes with a discussion on troubleshooting installations.

NOTE This section explores the installation details for *thick clients*, the typical Windows standalone systems. Installation of *thin clients* means plugging a machine into a network, booting, and doing minimal configuration. The main action happens on the network server. Thin clients require much more extensive discussion of networking, covered in Chapters 18 through 21. Some thin client implementations use virtual machines that run on the remote machine, so we'll take a closer look at thin clients in Chapter 22, "Virtualization."

Media Sources

At its most basic, a Windows installation has two steps. First, boot the system from the OS installation media. Second, answer the installation wizard's initial queries and let it do its thing. At the end of the 10- to 40-minute process, you'll be looking at a Welcome screen (see Figure 11-10) and be ready to begin your love affair with the PC.

EXAM TIP Successful installation results in a properly formatted boot drive with the correct partitions/formats.

Windows offers a surprising number of *boot methods*, giving you many options to get the process started. The most common way to start—historically at least—is to insert a Windows installation DVD, change the boot order in the system setup utility, and power up the system.

EXAM TIP The CompTIA A+ 1002 objectives list *CD* as a viable Windows boot method, but that's not the case since Windows Vista, the predecessor to Windows 7. If you see it as an option on the exam, though, read the question very carefully.

Alternatively, you can boot to a storage device inserted into a USB port. That includes flash drives, external hard drives, or external solid-state drives. Any number of *external/ hot-swappable drives* will do the job. Microsoft will even sell you a Windows 10 installation thumb drive (see Figure 11-11).

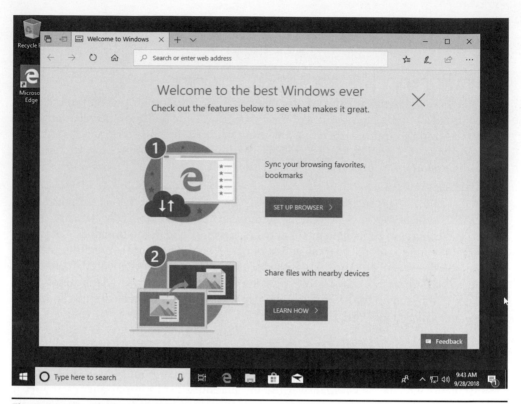

Figure 11-10 Windows 10 Welcome screen

NOTE Microsoft has shifted with the times. The primary way to install Windows 10 is downloading an ISO image and writing that image to some bootable media. With the Windows Media Creation Tool (a quick download from Microsoft), you can easily make that bootable media a DVD or USB flash drive.

Don't feel like plugging something into the computer? No problem. You can access Windows installation files over a network. See "Installing Windows over a Network," a little later in this chapter, for details.

Finally, many system builders add a small, hidden partition to the primary hard drive containing an image of the factory-fresh version of Windows. In the event of a corrupted or very messy instance of Windows, you can reboot, access this *recovery partition*, and reinstall Windows. Chapter 16, "Troubleshooting Operating Systems," covers recovery partitions and other forms of restoration in some detail.

EXAM TIP The CompTIA A+ 220-1002 exam objectives offer "internal hard drive (partition)" as a viable boot method for installing Windows. My best guess is that they mean the hidden recovery partition.

Figure 11-11   Windows flash installation media

Types of Installation

You can install Windows in several ways. A *clean installation* of an OS involves installing it onto an empty hard drive or completely replacing an existing installation. An *upgrade installation* means installing an OS on top of an earlier installed version, thus inheriting all previous hardware and software settings. You can combine versions of Windows by creating a *multiboot installation*. Let's look at all the options.

Clean Installation

A clean installation means your installation ignores a previous installation of Windows, wiping out the old version as the new version of Windows installs. A clean installation is also performed on a new system with a completely blank mass storage drive. The advantage of doing a clean installation is that you don't carry problems from the old OS over to the new one. The disadvantage is that you need to back up and then restore all your data, reinstall all your applications, and reconfigure the desktop and each application to the user's preferences. You typically perform a clean installation by setting CMOS to boot from the optical drive or USB before the hard drive or SSD. You then boot off a Windows installation disc/drive, and Windows gives you the opportunity to partition and format the hard drive or SSD during the installation process.

NOTE The CompTIA A+ 1002 objectives mention *refresh/restore* as an appropriate method of installing Windows, and in some scenarios this is true. Both refresh and restore install some or all of an operating system as an attempt to fix an OS that's not functioning properly. We'll cover System Restore in detail in Chapter 14, "Maintaining and Optimizing Operating Systems," and tackle Refresh your PC when we hit troubleshooting in Chapter 16.

Upgrade Installation

For decades, if you wanted to take advantage of a new version of some operating system, you had to grab (usually purchase) the new version and go through a process called an upgrade installation. You might find yourself in a situation where you need to upgrade an older version of Windows to Windows 10, so let's talk about an upgrade installation.

In an upgrade installation, the new OS installs into the same folders as the old OS, or in tech speak, the new installs *on top of* the old. The new OS replaces the old OS, but retains data and applications and also inherits all of the personal settings (such as font styles, desktop themes, and so on). The best part is that you don't have to reinstall your favorite programs. Figure 11-12 shows the start of the Windows 10 installation, asking if you want an upgrade installation.

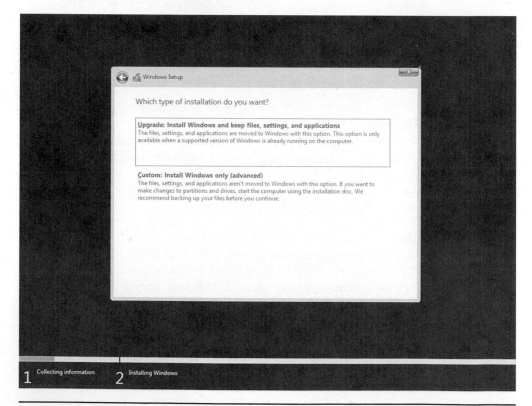

Figure 11-12 Windows installation

EXAM TIP Microsoft often uses the term *in-place upgrade* to define an upgrade installation, so you might see it on the CompTIA A+ 1002 exam. On the other hand, Microsoft documentation also uses the term for a completely different process, called a *repair installation*, so read whatever questions you get on the exam carefully for context. For repair installations, see Chapter 16.

Before you begin an upgrade of Windows, *always* back up all user data files! You can use the backup tools in Windows or a third-party tool, but don't skip this step.

To begin the upgrade of Windows, you should run the appropriate program from the optical disc or USB drive. This usually means inserting a Windows installation disc/disk into your system while your old OS is running, which autostarts the installation program. The installation program will ask you whether you want to perform an upgrade or a new installation; if you select new installation, the program will remove the existing OS before installing the new one.

NOTE Before starting an OS upgrade, make sure you have shut down all other open applications.

Multiboot Installation

A third option that you need to be aware of is the dual-boot or multiboot installation. This means your system has more than one Windows installation and you may choose which installation to use when you boot your computer. Every time your computer boots, you'll get a menu asking you which version of Windows you wish to boot (see Figure 11-13).

You'll recall from Chapter 9 that Windows enables you to shrink the C: partition, so if you want to dual boot but have only a single drive, you can make it happen even if Windows is already installed and the C: partition takes up the full drive. Use Disk Management to shrink the volume and create another partition in the newly unallocated space. Install another copy of Windows to the new partition.

Apple makes an excellent tool called Boot Camp that enables you to install Windows on an Apple machine. Once you run through the Windows installation, Boot Camp enables you to decide when you start up the computer each time whether you want to run macOS or Windows. Choose Boot Camp if you have some Windows-only program (cough . . . "game" . . . cough) that you simply must run on your Mac.

You can also multiboot Windows and Linux. The Linux installers add this multiboot capability by default. Just note that the reverse is not true. You need to install Windows *first*, then install Linux.

NOTE When configuring a computer for multibooting, there are two basic rules: first, you must format the system partition in a file system that is common to all installed operating systems; and second, you must install the operating systems in order from oldest to newest (or from Windows to other).

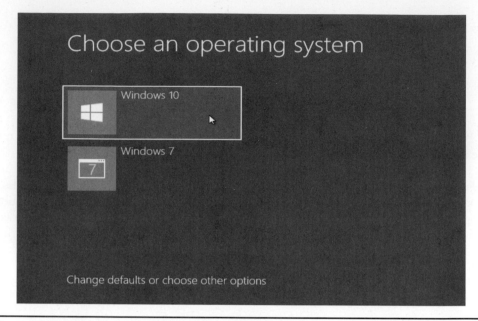

Figure 11-13   End result of multiboot installation

Other Installation Methods

In medium to large organizations, more advanced installation methods are often employed, especially when many computers need to be configured identically. A common method is to place the source files in a shared directory on a network server. Then, whenever a tech needs to install a new OS, he or she can boot up the computer, connect to the source location on the network, and start the installation from there. This is called generically a *remote network installation* (see Figure 11-14). This method alone has many

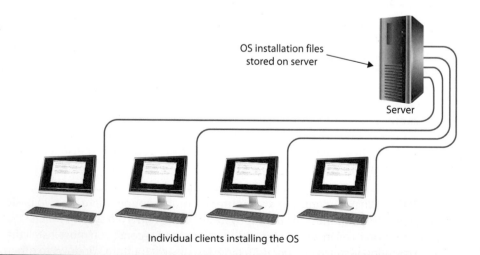

Figure 11-14   Remote network installation

variations and can be automated with special scripts that automatically select the options and components needed. The scripts can even install extra applications at the end of the OS installation, all without user intervention once the installation has been started. This type of installation is called an *unattended installation*.

Another type of installation that is very popular for re-creating standard configurations is an *image deployment* (Figure 11-15). An image is a complete copy of a hard drive volume on which an operating system and any desired application software programs have been preinstalled. Images can be stored on servers, optical discs, or flash-media drives, in which case the tech runs special software on the computer that copies the image onto the local hard drive or SSD. Images can also be stored on special network servers, in which case the tech connects to the image server by using special software that copies the image from the server to the local HDD or SSD. A leader in this technology for many years was Norton Ghost, which was available from Symantec. Symantec now offers Symantec Ghost Solution Suite. Other similar programs are Clonezilla and Acronis True Image.

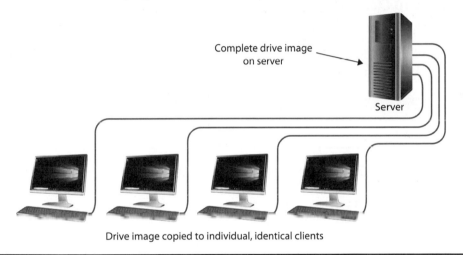

Complete drive image on server

Server

Drive image copied to individual, identical clients

Figure 11-15   Image deployment over a network

EXAM TIP   Although not covered in detail on the CompTIA A+ exams, Microsoft bundles the *Deployment Image Servicing and Management* (*dism.exe*) command-line tool with Windows 10 to enable image deployment. Check the TechNet Web site or the PowerShell help files for more information. Look for dism as a tool for installation on the CompTIA A+ 1002 exam.

The OS Installation Process

At the most basic level, installing any operating system follows a standard set of steps. You turn on the computer, insert an operating system disc/disk into the optical drive or USB port, or access the media some other way, and follow the installation wizard until you have everything completed. Along the way, you'll accept the *End User License*

Agreement (*EULA*)—the terms and conditions for using the OS—and enter the product key that says you're not a pirate. The product key is invariably located on the installation disc's case or USB packaging. Ah, but there is a devil in the details!

First of all, the CompTIA A+ 1002 objectives list the following Windows versions: Windows 7, Windows 8, Windows 8.1, and Windows 10. I am confident that CompTIA is only interested in an upgrade installation from one of these older Windows versions to Windows 10. If you want to upgrade Windows 7 to Windows 8.1 . . . good luck.

Second, you need to decide on a clean install, an upgrade install, or a multiboot install. Review the steps covered earlier in this chapter to make your decision. The following is an example of a clean installation of Windows.

Third, Windows isn't the only operating system out there. Even though the following example uses Windows, keep in mind that both macOS and all Linux desktop distributions share similar installation steps.

Windows 10 Clean Installation Process

Start by booting your computer from some sort of Windows 10 installation media. When you've booted into the installer, the first screen you see asks you if you want 32-bit or 64-bit Windows. Since almost all CPUs support 64-bit, select that option (see Figure 11-16). If you're wrong, don't worry. The installation will fail and you'll just try again.

```
                        Windows Boot Manager

 Choose an operating system to start, or press TAB to select a tool:
 (Use the arrow keys to highlight your choice, then press ENTER.)

        Windows 10 Setup (64-bit)                                    >
        Windows 10 Setup (32-bit)




 To specify an advanced option for this choice, press F8.




 Tools:

        Windows Memory Diagnostic




 ENTER=Choose                     TAB=Menu                     ESC=Cancel
```

Figure 11-16 Windows 64-bit or 32-bit selection screen

EXAM TIP Early in the installation process, if you're installing Windows onto drives connected via a RAID controller, you'll be prompted to press F6 to *load alternative third-party drivers if necessary*. Nothing happens immediately when you respond to this request. You'll be prompted later in the process to insert a driver disc.

Your next screen asks for language, time and currency, and keyboard settings, as shown in Figure 11-17. These are sometimes called *regional settings*. Click Next to proceed.

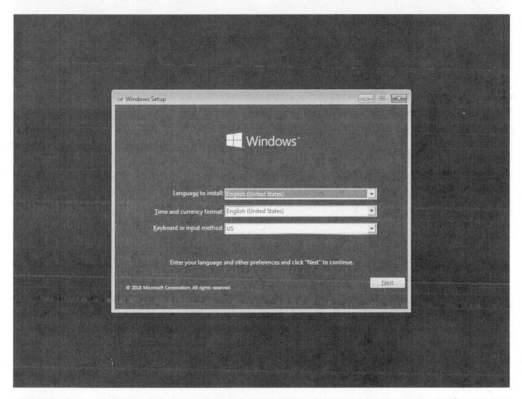

Figure 11-17 Windows regional settings

EXAM TIP The CompTIA A+ 1002 1.3 objectives refer to the regional settings step as *Time/date/region/language setup*.

The next screen starts the installation process, but note the lower-left corner. This screen also enables techs to start the installation disc's repair tools (see Figure 11-18). You'll learn more about those tools in Chapter 16, but for now all you need to know is that you click where it says *Repair your computer* to use the repair tools. Because you're just installing Windows in this chapter, click Install now.

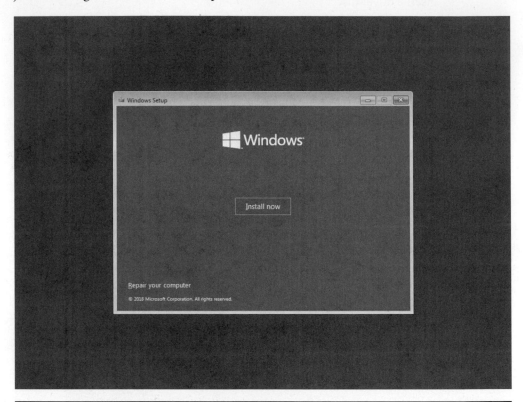

Figure 11-18   The Windows setup welcome screen

The next screen prompts you to enter your product key before you do anything else, as you can see in Figure 11-19. The product key comes with the installation media. You should never lose it.

Every Windows installation disc/disk contains all of the available editions within a version. The product key not only verifies the legitimacy of your purchase; it also tells the installer which edition you purchased.

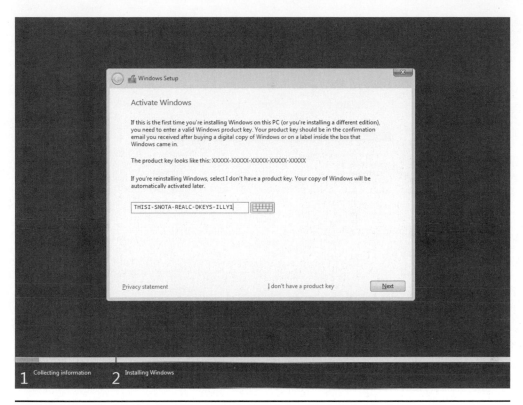

Figure 11-19 The Windows product key screen

If you click the *I don't have a product key* link (or leave the product key blank and click the Next button in versions before Windows 10), you will be taken to a screen asking you which version of Windows you would like to install (see Figure 11-20). Lest you start to think that you've discovered a way to install Windows without paying for it, you should know that doing this simply installs a 30-day trial of the operating system. After 30 days, you will no longer be able to boot to the desktop without entering a valid product key that matches the edition of Windows you installed. After the product key screen, you'll find Microsoft's EULA, shown in Figure 11-21.

On the next page, you get to decide whether you'd like to do an upgrade installation or a clean installation. (Windows calls the clean installation a *Custom* installation, as you can see in Figure 11-22.) This option enables customization of various items, such as partitions.

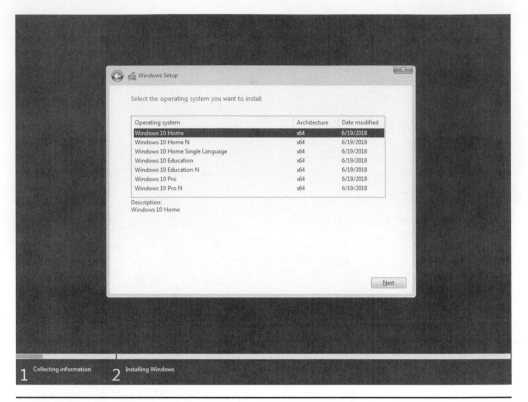

Figure 11-20 Choosing the edition of Windows you want to install

Figure 11-23 shows how you can partition hard drives and choose a destination partition for Windows. From this screen, you can click the New link [or Drive options (advanced) link in pre–Windows 10 versions] to display a variety of partitioning options.

Once you've partitioned drives and selected a destination partition for install Windows, the installation process takes over, copying files, expanding files, installing features, and just generally doing lots of computerish things. This can take a while, so if you need to get a snack or read *War and Peace*, do it during this part of the installation.

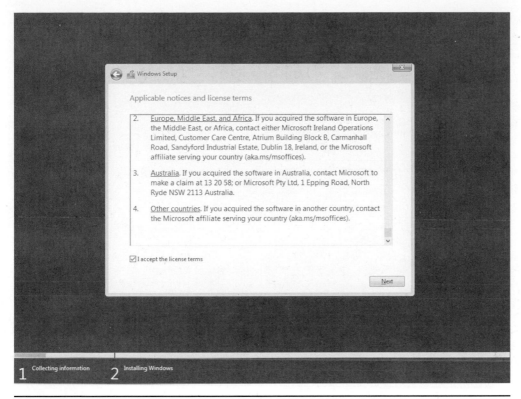

Figure 11-21 The Windows EULA

NOTE It doesn't take *that* long to install Windows. Windows 10 is far snappier than its predecessors, especially on an SSD.

When Windows has finished unpacking and installing itself, it lights up the oh-so-irritating Cortana to help you finish up the installation. Figure 11-24 shows where you configure a system to work in a workgroup (personal use) or in an organization. Note that the latter option does *not* join the computer to a classic Windows Active Directory domain, but it is useful if the company uses subscription services like Microsoft Office 365.

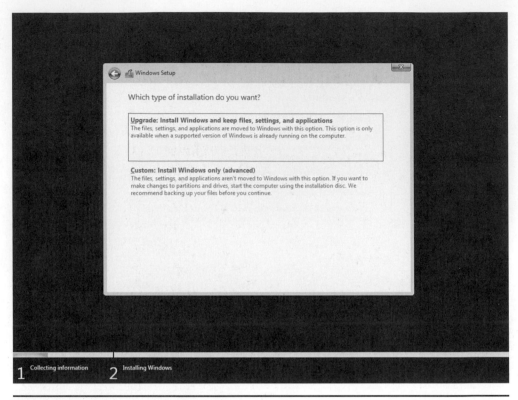

Figure 11-22 Choose your installation type.

 EXAM TIP Expect a question on *Workgroup vs. Domain setup* on the CompTIA A+ 1002 exam. Choosing the *Personal* option in Figure 11-24 puts you squarely in a workgroup. Installing a computer in a classic Windows Active Directory domain requires a lot of steps on behalf of the domain administrator. The computer needs to be joined to the domain. A user needs a domain account set up. Windows Active Directory domains accentuate security; they require more aggressive setup.

With a classic domain, setup usually requires creating a local administrator account that, after rebooting at the end, you use to join the computer to the domain. At that point, you can log off and log back on with a verified domain account. Then the user will have appropriate access to domain resources.

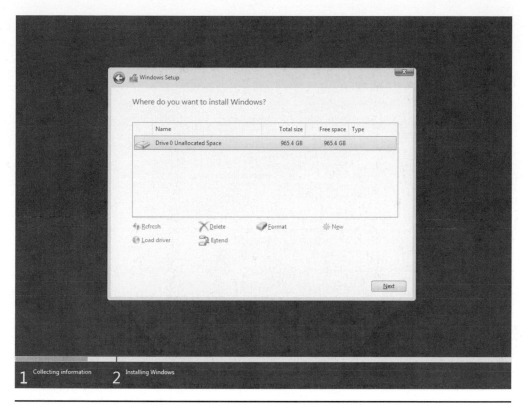

Figure 11-23 The partitioning screen

This following screen (Figure 11-25) asks you to set up a user name and password for your main user account. All operating systems require the creation of this account. Cortana asks you to choose a user name and tries to get you to open a Microsoft account if you don't already have one. I skip the Microsoft account and simply create a regular local account on the computer. My editors use Microsoft accounts. Choose which works best for you.

Microsoft and Apple are big on users logging in with accounts tied not to the PC, but to Microsoft and Apple. These accounts provide some amount of convenience and are acceptable for home users, but any organization larger than the smallest mom-and-pop shops will skip these and use more traditional accounts. Your author recommends you do the same.

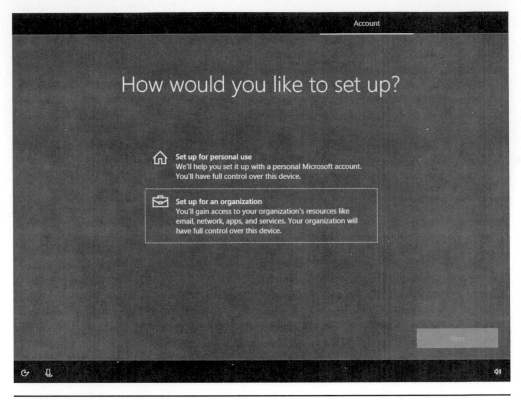

Figure 11-24 Choosing personal or organization

 EXAM TIP Look for a question on the CompTIA A+ *1001* exam on installing desktop computers, specifically with *account setup/settings*. You have four basic options on current machines—local user account, global account, organizational account, or domain account.

Microsoft also adds another installation feature at this point, privacy settings (see Figure 11-26). Turning everything off on this screen still doesn't prevent Microsoft from taking some amount of information.

 NOTE Activation is mandatory, but you can skip this step during installation. You have 30 days in which to activate the product, during which time it works normally. If you don't activate it within that time frame, the OS will be labeled as not genuine and you won't receive updates. Don't worry about forgetting, though, because once it's installed, Windows frequently reminds you to activate it with a balloon message over the tray area of the taskbar. The messages even tell you how many days you have left.

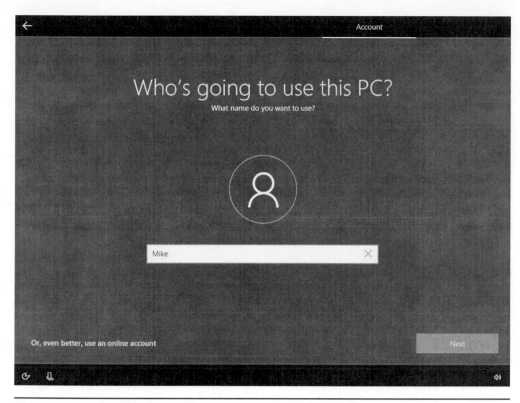

Figure 11-25 Choosing a user name

Once you're past that screen, Windows gets to work on the installation (see Figure 11-27) and warns you that it may take some time. Awfully polite for a piece of software, don't you think?

Installing Windows over a Network

Techs working for big corporations can end up installing Windows a lot. When you have a hundred PCs to take care of and Microsoft launches a new update of Windows, you don't want to have to walk from cubicle to cubicle with an installation disc, running one install after the other. You already know about automated installations, but network installations take this one step further.

Imagine another scenario. You're still a tech for a large company, but your boss has decided that every new PC will use an image with a predetermined set of applications and configurations. You need to put the image on every workstation, but most of them don't have optical drives. Network installation saves the day again!

The phrase "network installation" can involve many different tools depending on which version of Windows you use. Most importantly, the machines that receive the

Figure 11-26   Choosing privacy settings for your device

Figure 11-27
Okay, Windows,
thanks for the
warning

installations (the clients) need to be connected to a server. That server might be another copy of Windows 7, 8, 8.1, or 10; or it might be a fully fledged server running Windows Server. The serving PC needs to host an image, which can either be the default installation of Windows or a custom image, often created by the network administrator.

All of the server-side issues should be handled by a network administrator—setting up a server to deploy Windows installations and images goes beyond what the CompTIA A+ exams cover.

On the client side, you'll need to use the *Preboot Execution Environment* (*PXE*). PXE uses multiple protocols such as IP, DHCP, and DNS to enable your computer to boot from a network location. That means the PC needs no installation disc or USB drive. Just plug your computer into the network and go! Okay, it's a little more complicated than that.

To enable PXE, you'll need to enter system setup; in CompTIA speak, you need to configure the *BIOS* (*on board NIC*) for PXE boot. Find the screen that configures your NIC (see Figure 11-28). If there is a PXE setting there, enable it. You'll also need to change the boot order so that the PC boots from a network location first.

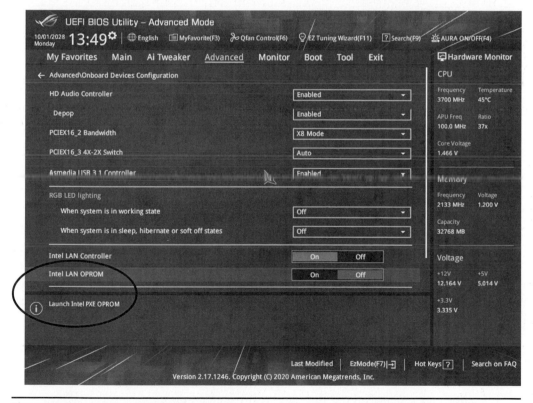

Figure 11-28   Setting up PXE in system setup

NOTE Most, but not all, NICs support PXE. To boot from a network location without PXE, you can create boot media that forces your PC to boot from a mapped network location.

When you reboot the PC, you'll see the familiar first screens of the boot process. At some point, you should also see an instruction to "Press F12 for network boot." (It's almost always F12.) The PC will attempt to find a server on the network to which it can connect. When it does, you'll be asked to press F12 again to continue booting from the network, as you can see in Figure 11-29.

Figure 11-29
Network boot

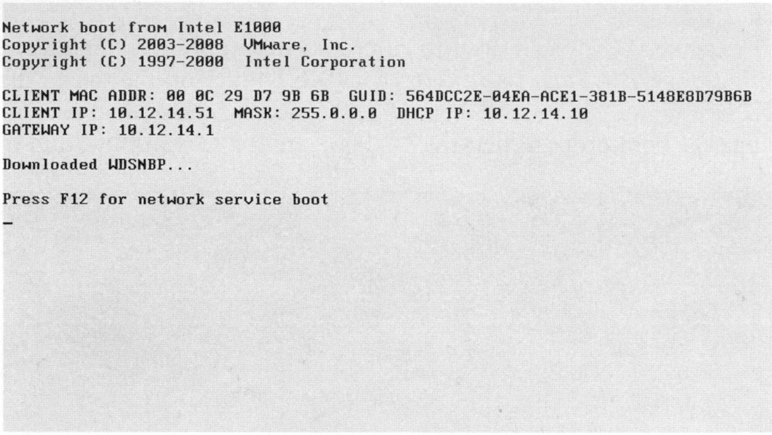

```
Network boot from Intel E1000
Copyright (C) 2003-2008  VMware, Inc.
Copyright (C) 1997-2000   Intel Corporation

CLIENT MAC ADDR: 00 0C 29 D7 9B 6B  GUID: 564DCC2E-04EA-ACE1-381B-5148E8D79B6B
CLIENT IP: 10.12.14.51  MASK: 255.0.0.0  DHCP IP: 10.12.14.10
GATEWAY IP: 10.12.14.1

Downloaded WDSNBP...

Press F12 for network service boot
_
```

Depending on how many images are prepared on the server, you'll either be taken directly to the Windows installation screen or be asked to pick from multiple images. Pick the option you need, and everything else should proceed as if you were installing Windows from the local optical drive.

Installing macOS over a Network

NetBoot is Apple's tool for network installation and imaging. It enables you to do some amazing installation types for macOS over a network. With this tool, you can boot a bunch of identical macOS machines remotely—so they have the look and feel you want. Any user-generated content on them simply goes away when you reboot the machines. This is a great tool for a classroom or conference.

Secondly, you can load identical images on multiple Macs, installing macOS on the hard drives of many remote systems. This is great when you're rolling out a new corporate default build, for example, at the enterprise level.

Finally, you can use NetBoot to push specific applications to many computers at once. This is huge for product rollout throughout any organization.

Troubleshooting Installation Problems

The term "installation problem" is rather deceptive. The installation process itself almost never fails. Usually, something else fails during the process that is generally interpreted as an "install failure." Let's look at some typical installation problems and how to correct them.

Media Errors

If you're going to have a problem with a Windows installation, have a media error, like a scratched DVD or a corrupted USB drive. It's always better to have the error right off the bat as opposed to when the installation is nearly complete.

RAID Array Not Detected   If Windows fails to detect a RAID array during installation, this could be caused by Windows not having the proper driver for the hard drive or RAID controller. If the hard drives show up properly in the RAID controller setup utility, then it's almost certainly a driver issue. Get the driver disc from the manufacturer and run setup again. Press F6 when prompted very early in the Windows installation process. Nothing happens right away when you push F6, but later in the process you'll be prompted to install drivers.

No Boot Device Present When Booting Off the Windows Installation Disc   Either the installation media is bad or the system setup is not set to look at that installation media first. Access the system setup utility as discussed in Chapter 5, "Firmware."

Graphical Mode Errors

Once the graphical part of the installation begins, errors can come from a number of sources, such as hardware or driver problems. Failure to detect hardware properly by any version of Windows Setup can be avoided by simply researching compatibility beforehand. Or, if you decided to skip that step, you might be lucky and only have a hardware detection error involving a noncritical hardware device. You can troubleshoot this problem at your leisure. In a sense, you are handing in your homework late, checking out compatibility and finding a proper driver after Windows is installed.

Every Windows installation depends on Windows Setup properly detecting the computer type (motherboard and BIOS stuff, in particular) and installing the correct hardware support. Microsoft designed Windows to run on several hardware platforms using a layer of software tailored specifically for the hardware, called the *hardware abstraction layer* (*HAL*).

Lockups During Installation

Lockups are one of the most challenging problems that can take place during installation, because they don't give you a clue as to what's causing the problem. Here are a few things to check if you get a lockup during installation.

Disc, Drive, or Image Errors   Bad media can mess up an installation during the installation process (as well as at the beginning, as you read earlier). Bad optical discs, optical drives, or hard drives may cause lockups. Similarly, faults on a USB-based drive can stop an installation in its tracks. Finally, problems with a downloaded ISO image—also part of the media—can cause lockups. Check each media component. Check the optical disc for scratches or dirt, and clean it up or replace it. Try a known-good disc in the drive. If you get the same error, you may need to replace the drive or perhaps the ISO.

Log Files   Windows versions before Windows 10 generate a number of special text files called *log files* that track the progress of certain processes. Windows creates different log files for different purposes. The Windows installation process creates about 20 log files, organized by installation phase. Each phase creates a setuperr.log file to track any errors during that phase of the installation. Windows 10 creates a setup.etl file (among others) in the %WINDIR%/Panther folder that you can open with Event Viewer.

Try This!   Locating Windows Setup Log Files

1. If you are using a pre–Windows 10 version, go to the following Microsoft Web site: https://technet.microsoft.com/en-us/library/Hh824819.aspx. For Windows 10, check out https://docs.microsoft.com/en-us/windows-hardware/manufacture/desktop/windows-setup-log-files-and-event-logs.

2. Identify the specific log file locations and descriptions.

3. Using Windows Explorer or File Explorer on your PC, navigate to the specific log file locations and see if you can find your setup log files.

Who knows, you may be on your way to becoming a Microsoft log file reader!

Windows stores these log files in the Windows directory (the location in which the OS is installed). These operating systems have powerful recovery options, so the chances of ever actually having to read a log file, understand it, and then get something fixed because of that understanding are pretty small. What makes log files handy is when you call Microsoft or a hardware manufacturer. They *love* to read these files, and they actually have people who understand them. Don't worry about trying to understand log files for the CompTIA A+ exams; just make sure you know the names of the log files and their location. Leave the details to the übergeeks.

 EXAM TIP   Expect a question or two about setup log files generated during upgrades on the CompTIA 1001 or 1002 exam. You might expect questions on the 1002 exam dealing with scenarios where Windows chokes on a dated driver or network setting and fails to load. The log files will readily show such problems, which you can correct by updating everything before you try upgrading to Windows 10.

The question you might see on the 1001 exam relates to hardware, specifically to system setup configuration problems. The CompTIA A+ 1001 5.3 objective tosses log entries and error messages under problems with essential hardware, such as motherboards and RAM. If you get such an error in the log file, try resetting the system setup to default settings. That has worked for a lot of people.

Post-Installation Tasks

You might think that's enough work for one day, but your task list has a few more things. They include updating the OS with patches and service packs, upgrading drivers, restoring user data files, and migrating and retiring systems.

Patches, Service Packs, and Updates

Someone once described an airliner as consisting of millions of parts flying in close formation. I think that's also a good description for an operating system. And we can even carry that analogy further by thinking about all of the maintenance required to keep an airliner safely flying. Like an airliner, the parts (programming code) of your OS were created by different people, and some parts may even have been contracted out. Although each component is tested as much as possible, and the assembled OS is also tested, it's not possible to test for every possible combination of events. Sometimes a piece is simply found to be defective. The fix for such a problem is a corrective program called a *patch*.

In the past, Microsoft provided patches for individual problems. They also accumulated patches up to some sort of critical mass and then bundled them together as a *service pack*, but Windows 7 was the last version to get one. Today, Windows simply sends individual updates to your system via the Internet.

Immediately after installing Windows, Windows should install the latest updates on the computer. The easiest way to accomplish this task it to turn on *Windows Update*. Chapter 14, "Maintaining and Optimizing Operating Systems," covers this process more thoroughly.

Upgrading Drivers

During installation, you may decide to go with the default drivers that come with Windows and then upgrade them to the latest drivers after the fact. This is a good strategy because installation is a complicated task that you can simplify by installing old but adequate drivers. Maybe those newest drivers are just a week old—waiting until after the Windows installation to install new drivers gives you a usable driver to go back to if the new driver turns out to be a lemon.

Restoring User Data Files (If Applicable)

Remember when you backed up the user data files before your upgrade installation? You don't? Well, check again, because now is the time to restore that data. Your method of restoring depends on how you backed up the files in the first place. If you used a third-party backup program, you need to install it before you can restore those files, but if you used Backup and Restore, you are in luck, because they are installed by default. If you did something simpler, such as copying to optical discs, USB or other external drive, or a network location, all you have to do is copy the files back to the local hard drive. Good luck!

 NOTE Backup and Restore is called Backup and Restore (Windows 7) in Windows 10.

Install Essential Software

The final step in the installation process is to install the software that makes the computer work the way you or your client wants. If you install software that requires a license key, have it ready. Similarly, if you install subscription software such as Microsoft Office 365, make sure you have accurate user names and passwords available. Don't forget to install Steam and download essential leisure applications!

 EXAM TIP Look for a question on the CompTIA A+ 1002 exam that addresses the final steps in the installation process—*driver installation, software [installation], and Windows update.*

Migrating and Retiring Systems

Seasons change and so does the state of the art in computing. At a certain point in a computer's life, you'll need to retire an old system. This means you must move the data and users to a new system or at least a new hard drive—a process called *migration*—and then safely dispose of the old system. Microsoft offers a few tools to accomplish this task, and because it's important to know about them for the CompTIA A+ exams (not to mention for your next new computer purchase), I'm going to go over them.

User State Migration Tool

If you're the sort of computer user who demands maximum functionality and power from your operating system, you'll probably want to use the *User State Migration Tool* (*USMT*). The USMT's primary use is in businesses because it has to be run in a Windows Server Active Directory domain. If you need to migrate many users, the USMT is the tool. If you only need to migrate a few, Windows Easy Transfer, described next, is the way to go.

 NOTE USMT is extremely handy for large-scale Windows operating system deployments. Microsoft provides a detailed overview that includes the benefits and limitations of USMT. Take a look here: https://docs.microsoft .com/en-us/windows/deployment/usmt/usmt-overview.

Windows Easy Transfer

Windows Easy Transfer enables you to migrate user data and personalizations quickly. In Windows 7, it is located in the System Tools subfolder of the Accessories folder in the Programs menu. To locate it in Windows 8/8.1, open the Start screen, type **Windows Easy Transfer**, and then click on Windows Easy Transfer from the results. Unfortunately, it is not available in Windows 10.

The first screen of Windows Easy Transfer simply gives you information about the process, so there's not really much to do there. When you click Next, you're taken to a screen that asks if you want to start a new transfer or continue an old one (see Figure 11-30). If you've already set up your old computer to transfer the files, select the latter option; if you haven't, select the former.

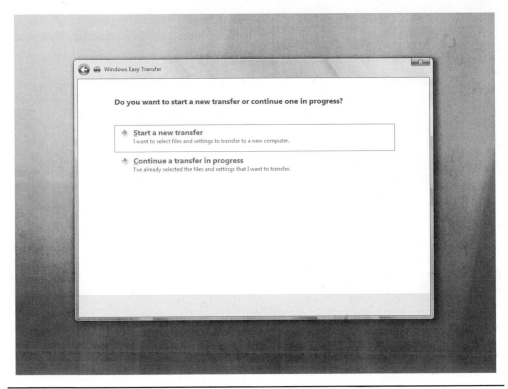

Figure 11-30   Start a new transfer or continue one?

If you choose to start a new transfer, select whether you're using your new or old computer and then follow the prompts.

Migration Practices

When talking about migration or retirement in terms of security, you need to answer one question: What do you do with the old system or drive?

All but the most vanilla new installations have sensitive data on them, even if it's simply e-mail messages or notes-to-self that would cause embarrassment if discovered. Most PCs, especially in a work environment, contain a lot of sensitive data. You can't just format C: and hand over the drive.

Follow three principles when migrating or retiring a computer. First, migrate your users and data information in a secure environment. Until you get passwords properly in place and test the security of the new system, you can't consider that system secure. Second, remove data remnants from hard drives that you store or give to charity. Third, recycle the older equipment; don't throw it in the trash. PC recyclers go through a process of deconstructing hardware, breaking system units, keyboards, printers, and even monitors into their basic plastics, metals, and glass for reuse.

The easiest way for someone to compromise or access sensitive data is to simply walk up and take it when you're not looking. This is especially true when you are in the process of copying information to a new, unprotected system. Don't set a copy to run while you go out to lunch, but rather be there to supervise and remove any remnant data that might still reside on any mass storage devices, especially hard drives.

Data Destruction

You might think that, as easy as it seems to be to lose data, you could readily get rid of data if you tried. That's definitely not the case with magnetic media such as hard drives. When you delete something in Windows, or even empty the Recycle Bin, the "deleted" data remains on your storage device until new data overwrites it, or replaces it. (This "deleted" data is also what you see as free space in Windows.) This can be a big security hole when you dispose of a drive.

Cleaning a drive completely is very difficult. You can either physically destroy the hard drive or *sanitize* it using a software utility. Physical destruction isn't complicated—you bust up the drive into tiny little bits or melt it. Tools to accomplish this include drive shredders, drills, hammers, electromagnets, and degaussing tools (which reduce or remove the magnetic fields that store data on HDDs). Incineration pretty much clears all data. Keep in mind that, as hard drives advance and pack more data into smaller spaces, you'll need to break the hard drive into smaller pieces to prevent anyone from recovering your data.

EXAM TIP Professional hard drive disposal services will guarantee they have truly, thoroughly destroyed drives by issuing a *certificate of destruction*. This certificate brings peace of mind, among other things, that precious data won't slip into unwanted hands.

Sanitizing your drive means the hard drive will still function once the data has been destroyed. There are several more or less effective ways to do this. The CompTIA A+ exams want you to know the difference between a standard format and a *low-level format*. You already learned about standard formatting back in Chapter 9, so how is low-level formatting different? With older drives (pre-1990s), low-level formatting would create the physical marks on the disk surface so that the drive knew where to store data; in the process, it erased the data from the drive. This was initially done at the factory, but utilities existed to repeat this operation later. As drives became more complex, hard drive manufacturers disabled the ability to perform low-level formats outside the factory.

Today, the term "low-level formatting" is often used to describe a *zero-fill* or *overwrite* operation. This process returns the drive to a state as close to like-new as possible by writing zeros to every location on the drive.

You can also use a *drive wiping* utility to erase any old, deleted data that hasn't been overwritten yet. Simply put, this overwrites the free space on your drive with junk data that makes the original data harder to recover. Piriform's CCleaner is a data-sanitizing utility that can erase your Web browsing history, erase your recent activity in Windows (such as what programs you ran), and even scrub your hard drive's free space to make deleted files unrecoverable (see Figure 11-31).

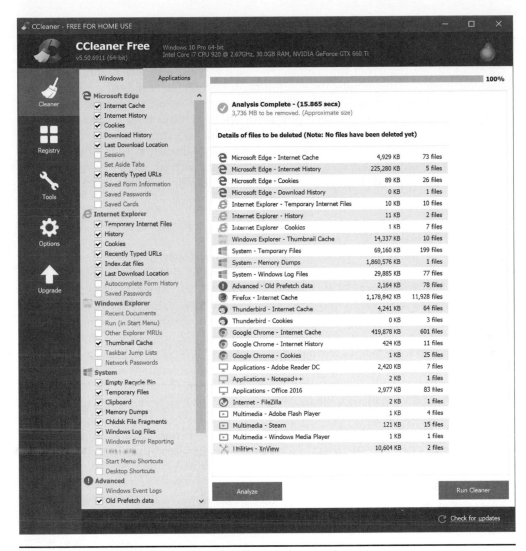

Figure 11-31 Piriform's CCleaner showing files to be removed

Recycle

An important and relatively easy way to be an environmentally conscious computer user is to follow *recycle or repurpose best practices*. Recycling products such as paper and printer cartridges not only keeps them out of overcrowded landfills but also ensures that the more toxic products are disposed of in the right way. Safely disposing of hardware containing hazardous materials, such as computer monitors, protects both people and the environment.

Anyone who's ever tried to sell a computer more than three or four years old learns a hard lesson: they're not worth much, if anything at all. It's a real temptation to take that old computer and just toss it in the garbage, but never do that!

First of all, many parts of your computer—such as your computer monitor—contain hazardous materials that pollute the environment. Luckily, thousands of companies now specialize in computer recycling and will gladly accept your old computer. If you have enough computers, they might even pick them up. If you can't find a recycler, call your local municipality's waste authority to see where to drop off your system.

An even better alternative for your old computer is donation. Many organizations actively look for old computers to refurbish and to donate to schools and other organizations. Just keep in mind that the computer can be too old—not even a school wants a computer more than five or six years old.

No Installation Is Perfect

Even when the installation seems smooth, issues may slowly surface, especially in the case of upgrades. Be prepared to reinstall applications or deal with new functions that were absent in the previous OS. If things really fall apart, you can go back to the previous OS. Or, if you have an OEM computer (one built by, for example, Dell or HP instead of by you), your computer likely came with a special recovery partition on its hard drive, a recovery disc, or a recovery USB flash drive; you can use any of these to restore your operating system to its factory settings. You usually invoke a system recovery by pressing a certain key during boot-up—usually F10 or F11—and then following a set of prompts.

The procedures I've laid out in this chapter may seem like a lot of work—how bad could it be to grab installation media, fling a copy of Windows onto a system, and, as the saying goes, let the chips fall where they may? Plenty bad, is how bad. Not only is understanding these procedures important for the CompTIA A+ certification exams, but these procedures can also save your, ah, hide once you're a working PC tech and tasked to install the latest version of Windows 10 on the boss's new computer!

Beyond A+

Privacy Concerns with Windows 10

All of the positives of Windows 10 are countered by Microsoft's unprecedented and questionable use of what many consider private data. One of the most controversial questions is why Windows 10 seemingly requires you to log in using a Microsoft (Hotmail or Outlook) account. Savvy techs discovered that logging in with a Microsoft account enables Windows to grab a disturbing amount of personal information, including data such as your Wi-Fi passwords. Security-conscious users should consider creating and using an old-style local user account. Be warned that not using a Microsoft account disables the Microsoft Cortana voice command feature.

There are a number of privacy issues beyond the Microsoft account issue. Here's a list of features you should consider turning off. Most of these features may be shut down using the Privacy utility in the Settings app.

- **Let apps use my advertising ID for experiences across apps**   This gives Microsoft the right to create, use, and share a unique advertising ID that will at the very least create custom advertising on Web sites.

- **Send Microsoft information about how I write to help us improve typing and writing in the future**   Microsoft doesn't clearly state the purpose of this option, but suffice it to say they may capture all of your keystrokes. Scary!

- **Let websites provide locally relevant content by accessing my language list**   Why does Microsoft need to access language settings given that a Web site can easily tell your default language? Unless you go between multiple languages, it's a good idea to turn this off.

- **Location**   Location services enable Microsoft to track your location unless this setting is disabled.

- **Getting to know you**   This happy-sounding feature tracks a large amount of information about you such as your contacts, calendar events, speech, handwriting, and more. Turn it off.

The bottom line is this: Windows 10 is easy to use and full of features. You can tighten up privacy settings if you so desire.

Chapter Review

Questions

1. What is a thin client?

    A. A computer with a 32-bit-wide address bus

    B. A portable computer

    C. A system designed to handle only very basic applications with the minimum hardware required by the operating system

    D. A computer in a narrow, small form-factor case

2. What functions does a network attached storage PC provide? (Select three.)

    A. Media streaming

    B. File sharing

    C. Web hosting

    D. Print sharing

3. Cindy's client wants a new graphics workstation. The client's small business has ten current workstations connected in a Windows domain, and the client wants the new graphics workstation to be part of that domain. What edition of Windows 10 should Cindy install on the new computer to accomplish this goal and provide the best value?

    A. Windows 10 Starter Edition

    B. Windows 10 Home

    C. Windows 10 Pro

    D. Windows 10 Enterprise

4. What is the most important component for building a virtualization workstation?

    A. CPU

    B. Power supply

    C. RAM

    D. Large monitor

5. What tool enables installing Windows over a network?

    A. Windows DVD.

    B. NetBoot.

    C. PXE.

    D. Windows can't be installed over a network.

6. When you install an operating system alongside an existing operating system, what do you create?

    A. A clean installation

    B. An upgrade installation

    C. A multiboot installation

    D. A network installation

7. If you do not complete the activation process for Windows, what will happen to your computer?

    A. Nothing. Activation is optional.

    B. The computer will work fine for 30 days and then Windows will be disabled.

    C. Microsoft will not know how to contact you to provide upgrade information.

    D. It will work if you check the "I promise to pay for Windows later" box.

8. If Windows locks up during the installation, what should you do?

    A. Press CTRL-ALT-DEL to restart the installation process.

    B. Push the Reset button to restart the installation process.

    C. Press the ESC key to cancel the installation process.

    D. Unplug the computer and restart the installation process.

9. Which term describes a combination of many updates and fixes in Windows?

    A. Hot fix

    B. Hot pack

    C. Service pack

    D. Service release

10. You've just replaced Jane's Windows 7 PC with a new Windows 10 machine. What post-installation tool should you run to make the transition as painless as possible for her?

    A. Windows Activation

    B. Repair installation

    C. Windows Easy Transfer

    D. User State Migration Tool

Answers

1. C. Thin clients rely on servers to perform anything beyond the most basic computing tasks.

2. A, B, D. NAS devices share files, stream media, and share printers.

3. C. Windows 10 Pro offers the best choice here. The Enterprise edition would also work, but it costs more and adds features the client doesn't need.

4. C. Every virtual machine you run consumes a large share of RAM, so the more RAM you have, the more VMs you can run.

5. C. The Preboot Execution Environment, or PXE, enables installation of Windows over a network.

6. C. An OS added to an existing OS creates a multiboot system.

7. B. If you do not complete the activation process for Windows 7, the computer will work fine for 30 days and then Windows will be disabled.

8. D. If Windows locks up during the installation, you should unplug the computer and restart the installation process.

9. C. A service pack is a combination of many updates and fixes in Windows.

10. C. Run the Windows Easy Transfer tool to move all her Windows 7 personal files and familiar settings, like her desktop, to the new Windows 10 computer.

Windows Under the Hood

In this chapter, you will learn how to
- Work with the Registry
- Understand and observe the Windows boot process
- Manage processes, services, and threads
- Explore Windows tools for programmers

Windows is powerful, easy to use, surprisingly idiot proof, backwardly compatible, and robust. A large part of Windows' power is hidden—*under the hood*—in programs and processes that Microsoft doesn't want normal users to see. For the record, I think hiding anything normal users don't need is a smart idea. Technicians, on the other hand, need to not only understand these processes and programs, but also know how to use, configure, and fix them when needed. This chapter explores the Registry; boot process components; processes, services, and threads; and Windows tools that are useful to programmers.

1002

Registry

The *Registry* is a huge database, part of every installed Windows system, that stores everything about a PC, including information on all the hardware, network information, user preferences, file types, passwords, desktop color . . . virtually everything you might find in Windows. Almost any form of configuration you do to a Windows system involves editing the Registry. The Registry is critically important; your system will not boot into Windows without it.

Every version of Windows stores the numerous Registry files (called *hives*) in the \%SystemRoot%\System32\config folder and each user account folder. Fortunately, you rarely have to access these files directly. Instead, you can use a set of relatively tech-friendly applications to edit the Registry.

Surprisingly, the CompTIA A+ 1002 exam does not have an objective covering the Windows Registry. Every competent tech should, however, understand the basic components of the Registry, know how to edit the Registry manually, and know the best way to locate a particular Registry setting. CompTIA, include this objective!

Accessing the Registry

Even though the Registry is important, you rarely access the Registry directly. Instead, when you use Windows' Settings or Control Panel (or just about any other utility), you are editing the Registry. There are some situations where a tech might need to access the Registry directly.

Before you look in the Registry, let's look at how you access the Registry directly by using the *Registry Editor*, so you can open the Registry on your machine and compare what you see to the examples in this chapter. The go-to command to open the Registry Editor is *regedit*. To open the Registry Editor, enter **regedit** in the Start | Search bar. This will also run from the command line.

Registry Components

The Registry is organized in a tree structure similar to the folders on the file system. Once you open the Registry Editor in Windows, you will see five main subgroups, or *root keys*:

- HKEY_CLASSES_ROOT
- HKEY_CURRENT_USER
- HKEY_LOCAL_MACHINE
- HKEY_USERS
- HKEY_CURRENT_CONFIG

Try opening one of these root keys by clicking the plus sign to its left; note that more subkeys are listed underneath. A subkey also can have other subkeys, or *values*. Values define aspects of the subkey. Figure 12-1 shows an example of a subkey with some values. Notice that the Registry Editor shows only keys—root keys and subkeys—on the left and values on the right. Each of the root keys has a specific function, so let's take a look at them individually.

HKEY_CLASSES_ROOT

Historically, the HKEY_CLASSES_ROOT root key defined the standard **class objects** used by Windows. A *class object* is a named group of functions that defines what you can do with the object it represents. Pretty much everything that has to do with files on the system is defined by a class object. The Registry, for example, uses two class objects to define the JPG image file. One object is located at HKEY_CLASSES_ROOT\.jpg and one at HKEY_CURRENT_USER\Software\Classes\.jpg that covers user-specific associations for JPG files.

This root key combines class objects from \Software\Classes under both HKEY_CURRENT_USER and HKEY_LOCAL_MACHINE to provide backward compatibility for older applications.

HKEY_CURRENT_USER and HKEY_USERS

Windows is designed to support more than one user on the same system, storing personalized information such as desktop colors, screensavers, and the contents of the desktop

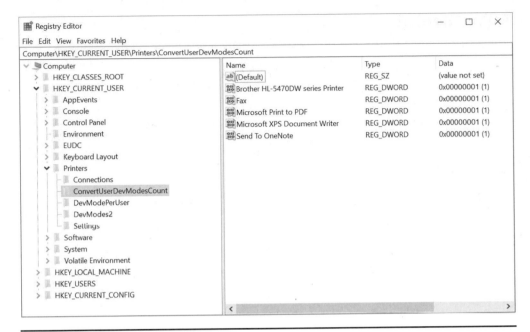

Figure 12-1 Typical Registry root keys, subkeys, and values

for every user that has an account on the system. HKEY_CURRENT_USER stores the current user settings, and HKEY_USERS stores all of the personalized information for each user. While you certainly can change items such as the screensaver here, the better way is to right-click on the desktop and select Personalize.

HKEY_LOCAL_MACHINE
The HKEY_LOCAL_MACHINE root key contains all the data for a system's non-user-specific configurations. This encompasses every device and every program in your computer.

HKEY_CURRENT_CONFIG
If the values in HKEY_LOCAL_MACHINE have more than one option, such as two different monitors, this root key defines which one is currently being used. Because most people have only one type of monitor and similar equipment, this area is almost never touched.

 SIM Check out the excellent trio of sims on "Registry Files Location" in the Chapter 12 section of the online TotalSims here: http://totalsem.com/100x. The combination of Type!, Show!, and Click! sims will prepare you for any scenario-based question on the Windows Registry.

Talkin' Registry

When describing a Registry setting, we use a simple nomenclature. For example, I once moved my copy of *World of Warcraft* from my C: drive to my D: drive and had problems when the program started. I went online to www.blizzard.com (home of Blizzard Entertainment, the folks who make *World of Warcraft*) and contacted the support staff, who gave me instructions to access the Registry and make this change:

> "Go to HKLM\SOFTWARE\Blizzard Entertainment\World of Warcraft and change the GamePath object and the InstallPath object to reflect the new drive letter of your new WoW location."

To do so, I opened the Registry Editor. Using this nomenclature, I was able to find the location of these Registry settings. Figure 12-2 shows this location. Compare this image to the path described in the instructions from Blizzard. Note that HKEY_LOCAL_MACHINE is abbreviated as HKLM.

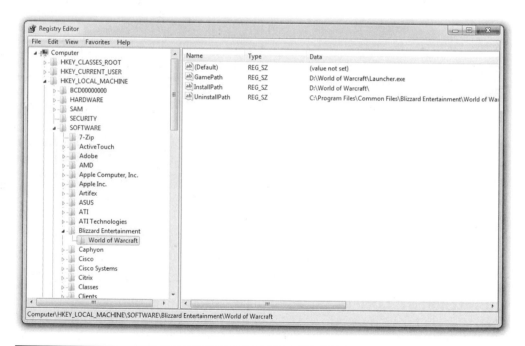

Figure 12-2   Editing the Registry to move *World of Warcraft* to a new drive

To describe the location of a specific Registry value, like where the Blizzard tech told me to go, requires a little bit of repetition. To wit, in the previous example, World of Warcraft is a subkey to Blizzard Entertainment, which is in turn a subkey to the root key HKLM. The World of Warcraft subkey has four values. All keys have the (Default) value, so in this case the World of Warcraft subkey offers three functional values.

Values must have a defined type of data they store:

- **String value**   These are the most flexible type of value and are very common. You can put any form of data in these.
- **Binary value**   These values store nothing more than long strings of ones and zeros.
- **DWORD value**   These values are like Binary values but are limited to exactly 32 bits.
- **QWORD value**   These values are like Binary values but are limited to exactly 64 bits.

There are other types of values, but these four are used for most Registry entries.

Manual Registry Edits

There's little motivation for you to go into the Registry and make manual edits unless you've done some research that tells you to do so. When you do find yourself using the Registry Editor to access the Registry, you risk breaking things in Windows: applications might not start, utilities might not work, or worst of all, your computer might not boot. To prevent these problems, always make a backup of the Registry before you change anything. Once the backup is in a safe place (I like to use a thumb drive, personally), reboot the system to see if the changes you made had the desired result. If it worked, great. If not, you'll need to restore the old Registry settings using your backup. Let's watch this in action.

One of the more common manual Registry edits is to delete autostarting programs. I want to prevent a program installed by my Logitech GamePanel keyboard and mouse from autostarting. The most common place for making this change is here:

HKLM\SOFTWARE\Microsoft\Windows\CurrentVersion\Run

Opening the Registry Editor and going to this subkey, you'll see something like Figure 12-3.

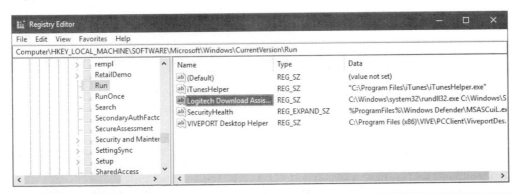

Figure 12-3   Mike's Run subkey

Before I delete these keys, I'm going to save a copy of my Registry. The Registry Editor's Export feature enables you to save either the full Registry or only a single root key or subkey (with all subkeys and values under it). Select Run from the left pane and then click File | Export. Save the subkey as a Registration file with the extension .reg. Be sure to put that file somewhere you'll remember. Should you need to restore that key, use the File | Import command, or just right-click on the icon as shown in Figure 12-4 and click Merge.

Figure 12-4
Merging keys
from a backup
file

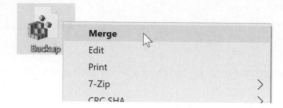

Command-Line Registry Editing Tools

Windows includes a couple of command-line tools to edit the Registry (plus a lot more in PowerShell). The two that you might need on occasion are reg and regsvr32.

NOTE If the command-line interface is new to you, you might want to flag this section and skip it for now, then return to it after reading about the command line and how it works in Chapter 15, "Working with the Command-Line Interface."

The *reg* command is a full Registry editing tool. You can view Registry keys and values, import and export some or all of a Registry, and even compare two different versions of a Registry. The tool is so powerful that it has multiple levels of help so you can tailor a command to accomplish very tight Registry edits. For example, typing **reg /?** brings up a list of 12 specific operations that you can search for help on, such as reg query /? and reg add /?.

The *regsvr32* command, in contrast with reg, can modify the Registry in only one way, adding (or *registering*) dynamic link library (DLL) files as command components in the Registry. By default, if you run regsvr32 in a 64-bit version of Windows, the 64-bit version runs. This can cause problems if you're trying to add a 32-bit DLL to the Registry. To accomplish the latter, run the regsvr32.exe file in the %SystemRoot%Syswow64 folder.

On the very off chance you'll ever need to run reg or regsvr32 (either version), refer to Chapter 15 for how to use the command-line interface effectively.

The Boot Process

The Windows installation creates a number of specific files and folders that the OS needs to run. Some of these files and folders are directly on the root of the C: drive; others can be elsewhere. The best way to remember the locations of these files and folders and to know their importance to the OS is by looking at how they interact to boot the system.

Current Windows versions support both BIOS and UEFI boot processes. The very first thing that happens when you power on a system with Windows is that either the BIOS or the UEFI starts up. The difference between BIOS and UEFI systems is in what happens next.

- In a BIOS-based system, the BIOS uses its boot order to scan a hard drive for a master boot record (MBR). The MBR holds a small bit of file system boot code that scans the partition table for the system partition and then loads its boot sector. The boot sector in turn contains code that does nothing but point the boot process toward a file called *bootmgr* (pronounced *boot manager*, or "boot mugger" if you're trying to make nerds laugh), the Windows Boot Manager. In short, the BIOS looks for the MBR, which finds the boot code to launch the OS.

- In a UEFI system, on the other hand, neither the MBR/GUID partition table (GPT) nor the file system boot code is run, and UEFI simply loads bootmgr directly.

 NOTE Windows keeps bootmgr in the special System Reserved partition you learned about in Chapter 9, "Implementing Mass Storage." If you are using a UEFI system, the helpfully named EFI system partition contains a special version of bootmgr called bootmgr.efi.

When bootmgr starts, it reads data from a *Boot Configuration Data* (*BCD*) file that contains information about the various operating systems installed on the system as well as instructions for how to actually load (bootstrap) them. Once an operating system is selected (or immediately if only one is present), bootmgr loads a program called winload .exe, which readies your system to load the operating system kernel (called ntoskrnl.exe) itself rather like the way you clean up your house before Aunt Edna comes to visit. It does this by loading into memory the hardware abstraction layer, the system Registry, and the drivers for any boot devices before the operating system itself takes over.

 NOTE If you work with Windows long enough, you may encounter an error message saying that Windows cannot boot because bootmgr is missing. This message is generated when the boot sector code is unable to locate bootmgr, which can be caused by file system corruption, a botched installation, or viruses.

Once the operating system process takes over, it loads up all of the various processes and systems that comprise Windows, the Windows logo comes up, and you're happily computing, completely oblivious to all of the complex electronic communication that just took place inside your computer.

Applications, Processes, and Services

Back in Chapter 3, "CPUs," you learned that CPUs run *threads*—bits of programs that are fed into the CPU. Let's see how all of this looks from Windows' point of view.

NOTE I'm simplifying things a little for the purposes of the CompTIA A+ 220-1002 exam, but know that applications, processes, and services can get a lot more complicated.

In Windows, programs are executable files waiting on a mass storage device. When you start a program, Windows loads it into RAM as a process. Once there, the CPU reads the process and the process tells the CPU which chunks of code to run. Dealing with processes in their many forms is a big part of understanding what's happening "under the hood."

Windows is a multitasking operating system, running lots of processes simultaneously. Many of these processes appear in a window (or full screen) when you open them and end when you close that window. These processes are called *applications*.

There's an entire class of processes that, due to the nature of their job, don't require a window of any form. These processes run invisibly in the background, providing a large number of necessary support roles. Collectively, these are called *services*. Let's look at applications, processes, and services, and the tools we use to control them.

Task Manager

Microsoft offers the Windows *Task Manager* as the one-stop-shop for anything you need to do with applications, processes, and services (see Figure 12-5). The Microsoft development team significantly redesigned Task Manager for Windows 8. We'll look at the tool in Windows 7 first, then examine the Task Manager in Windows 8/8.1/10.

Figure 12-5
Task Manager in
Windows 7

Task Manager in Windows 7

The quickest way to open the Task Manager is to press CTRL-SHIFT-ESC. There are two other ways to open the Task Manager that you might see on the CompTIA A+ exams: go to Start | Search, type **taskmgr**, and press ENTER; or press CTRL-ALT-DELETE and select Task Manager.

Applications The *Applications* tab shows all the running applications on your system. If you're having trouble getting an application to close normally, this is the place to go. To force an application to shut down, select the naughty application and click End Task, or right-click on the application and select End Task from the context menu. Be careful when using this feature! There is no "Are you sure?" prompt, and it's easy to accidently close the wrong application.

There are two other handy buttons on the Applications tab:

- Switch To enables you to bring any program to the front (very handy when you have a large number of applications running).
- New Task enables you to run programs if you know the executable. Click New Task, type **cmd**, and press ENTER, for example, to open the command-line interface.

Because applications are processes, they are also listed in the Processes tab. Right-click on an application and select Go To Process to open the Processes tab and see which process (or processes) is running the application.

Processes If you really want to tap the power of the Task Manager, you need to click the *Processes* tab (see Figure 12-6). Since everything is a process, and the Processes tab shows you every running process, this is the one place that enables you to see everything running on your computer.

All processes have certain common features that you should recognize:

- A process is named after its executable file, which usually ends in .exe but can also end with other extensions.
- All processes have a user name to identify who started the process. A process started by Windows has the user name System.
- All processes have a process identifier (PID). To identify a process, you use the PID, not the process name. The Task Manager doesn't show the PID by default. Click View | Select Columns and select the PID (Process Identifier) checkbox to see the PIDs (see Figure 12-7).

The Task Manager provides important information about processes. It shows the amount of CPU time (percentage) and the amount of RAM (in kilobytes) the process is using. Most processes also provide a description to help you understand what the process is doing, although you'll probably need to scroll right to see this information (see Figure 12-8).

Figure 12-6
Processes tab in Windows 7

Figure 12-7
Processes tab showing the PID column in Windows 7

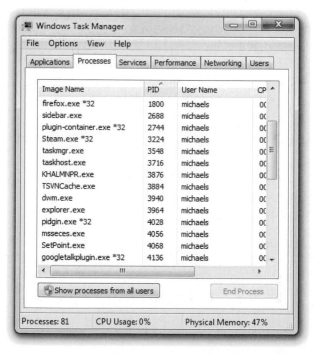

Figure 12-8

Processes tab with more details in Windows 7

You'll notice that almost all of the processes have the same user name. By default, the Task Manager shows only processes associated with the current user. Click *Show processes from all users* to see every process on the system (see Figure 12-9). Note that some of the processes show a user name of Local Service or Network Service. As you might imagine, those are services!

Now that you understand the basics, let's watch the Task Manager do its magic with processes. If you select a process and click the *End Process* button, you'll get a chance to confirm your intent to end it. If the process is an application, that application will close.

Closing processes is important, but to take it even further, you need to select a process and right-click on it to see a number of options. If you select a process that's an application (the name of the process is a strong clue—winword.exe is Microsoft Word), you see something like Figure 12-10.

Try This!   Closing Applications

Start up Notepad and then start up the Task Manager. In the Task Manager, right-click on the Notepad application and select Go To Process. It takes you to the process. Right-click and select End Process to close the application.

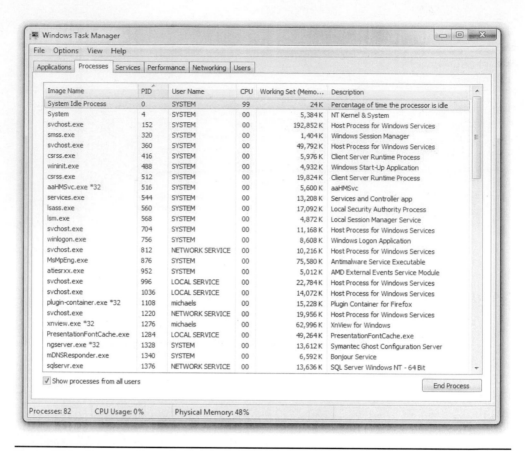

Figure 12-9   Processes from all users in Windows 7

Open File Location takes you to wherever the file is located. This is extremely helpful when you're looking at a mysterious process and are trying to find out what it's doing on your computer.

You already know what End Process does. End Process Tree is extremely important but also complex, so let's save that for later.

Debug is grayed out, unless you're running a Windows debugger program—see the explanation of dump files below.

In Windows 7, UAC Virtualization gives older programs that weren't written to avoid accessing protected folders a way to do so by making a fake protected folder. In most cases, Windows handles this automatically, but there are rare cases where you'll need to set this manually. Again, you won't do this on your own—you'll be on the phone with the tech support for some software company and they'll tell you how to use UAC Virtualization.

Figure 12-10
Processes detail
on right-click

Dump files show the status of the program at the moment you click Create Dump File. Developers use special debugging utilities to read dump files to analyze problems with programs. The only time you'd ever use this option is if you're having problems with a program and the support people ask you to make a dump file.

Set Priority gives you the ability to devote more or less processor time to a process (see Figure 12-11). This is very handy when you have a process that is slowing down your machine or if you have a process that is running too slowly and you want to speed it up.

Messing with priorities can get complicated quickly. Maybe it's best to think about priority as a bit like the VIP lines most amusement parks have these days. Having a VIP pass doesn't make the rides any faster—nor does it help you get back in line any quicker—it just changes how many people you have to wait behind to ride again. But what happens to everyone else if there are so many people in the VIP line that the non-VIP queue almost never moves?

Imagine you need to render out some video on your system, but when you start the job, you find out it'll take six hours. As soon as the job starts, your music starts skipping and jumping along. The video renders might be more important in the grand scheme of things, but you won't be able to get anything else done with your music stuttering along. The best idea here is to increase the priority of a single process you need to run normally, such as your audio player, or reduce the priority of a single process that isn't as time sensitive, such as the video renderer, without touching any other priorities. It may be better

Figure 12-11
Process priority

to have your system spend eight hours rendering a video while you use it for other work than to have your system rendered unusable for six.

NOTE   Setting any single process to Realtime priority will often bring the entire system to a crawl as no other process gets much CPU time—avoid Realtime priority.

Set Affinity enables you to specify which CPU cores a process can run on (see Figure 12-12). You probably won't need to touch affinity; the most likely reason you would need to do so is a situation in which you have some processes (perhaps older programs that are not well designed for multicore systems) that need to be separated from others.

The Properties option isn't too exciting. It's the same as if you were to right-click on the executable file and select Properties in Windows Explorer (Windows 7). Finally, the Go to Service(s) option will move you to the Services tab of the Task Manager, showing you any and all services associated with the process. Depending on the process, it could use no services or multiple services. This is a great tool for those "Program won't start because associated services aren't running" situations. Figure 12-13 shows what happens when you use Go to Service(s) for a process called LSASS.EXE.

Figure 12-12
Turning off
affinity to the
first two cores

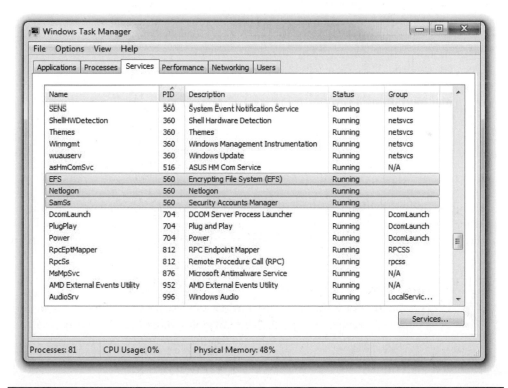

Figure 12-13 Services associated with the LSASS.EXE process

Let's get back to the End Process Tree option. It's very common for a single process to be dependent on other processes (or for a process to start other processes). This creates a tree of dependencies. Sadly, the Task Manager doesn't give you any clue as to what processes depend on other processes, but it still gives you the option to *End Process Tree*, which ends not only the process, but any process it depends on. At first glance, this is scary since it's very common for many processes to depend on one important process. Microsoft makes this less scary, as it will not let you kill a process tree for the most important system processes.

Even so, it would be nice to actually *see* what processes you're about to kill, wouldn't it? That's when the popular (and free) Process Explorer, written by Mark Russinovitch, is your go-to tool (see Figure 12-14).

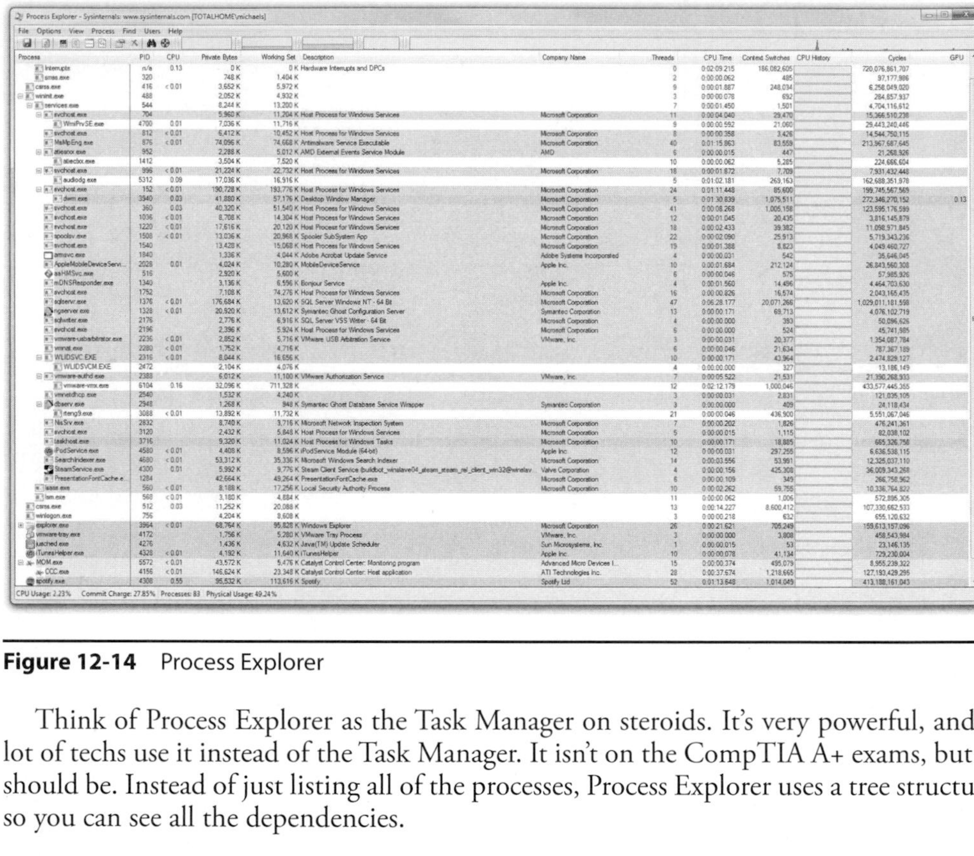

Figure 12-14 Process Explorer

Think of Process Explorer as the Task Manager on steroids. It's very powerful, and a lot of techs use it instead of the Task Manager. It isn't on the CompTIA A+ exams, but it should be. Instead of just listing all of the processes, Process Explorer uses a tree structure so you can see all the dependencies.

NOTE Process Explorer does so much more than just show a tree structure. Download a copy and play with it. You'll see why it's so popular. You can find a copy with a quick Google search or by going directly to the Sysinternals Web site: https://docs.microsoft.com/en-us/sysinternals/downloads/process-explorer.

Services   You can use the *Services* tab in the Task Manager to work with services directly (see Figure 12-15). Here, you can stop or start services, and you can go to the associated process.

Figure 12-15
Services tab in
Task Manager

The best way to see services in action is to use the Services Control Panel applet. To open it, click the Services button at the bottom of the Services tab in the Task Manager or open Services in Administrative Tools. Figure 12-16 shows the Services applet running in Windows 7.

 EXAM TIP   You can open the Services applet from the Start | Search bar. Type **services.msc** and press ENTER.

Look closely at Figure 12-16. Each line in this applet is an individual service. Services don't have their own window, so you use the Services applet to start, stop, and configure them. You can see if a service is running by reading the Status column. To configure a service, right-click on the service name. The context menu enables you to start, stop, pause, resume, or restart any service. Click Properties to see a dialog box similar to the one shown in Figure 12-17.

Of the four tabs you see in the Properties dialog box, General and Recovery are by far the most used. The General tab provides the name of the service, describes the service, and enables you to stop, start, pause, or resume the service. You can also define how the service starts: Manual (return here to start it), Automatic (starts at beginning of

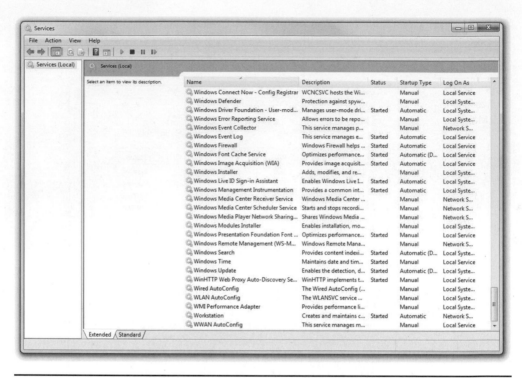

Figure 12-16   Services applet

Figure 12-17
Service
Properties dialog
box

Windows boot), Disabled (prevents the service from starting in any fashion), or Automatic (delayed start), which starts the service at boot but only after pretty much everything else has started.

 EXAM TIP   You can start any service at a command prompt by typing **net start <*service name*>**. Likewise, you can stop a running service by typing **net stop <*service name*>**.

Performance   For optimization purposes, the Task Manager is a great tool for investigating how hard your RAM and CPU are working at any given moment and why. Click the *Performance* tab to reveal a handy screen with the most commonly used information: CPU usage, available physical memory, size of the disk cache, and other details about memory and processes. Figure 12-18 shows a system with an eight-core processor, which is why you see eight graphs under CPU Usage History. A system with a single-core processor would have a single graph.

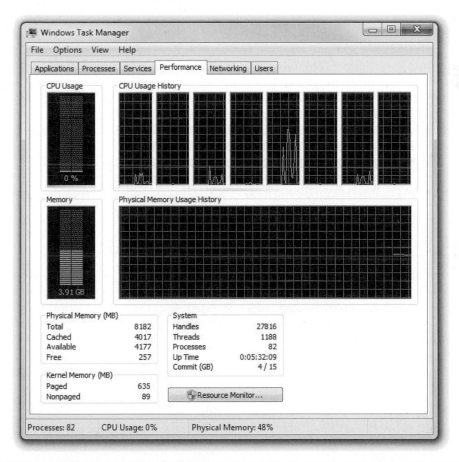

Figure 12-18   Task Manager Performance tab

Not only does the Task Manager tell you how much CPU and RAM usage is taking place, it also tells you what program is using those resources. Let's say your system is running slowly. You open the Task Manager and see that your CPU usage is at 100 percent. You then click the Processes tab to see all the processes running on your system. Click the CPU column heading to sort all processes by CPU usage to see who's hogging the CPU (see Figure 12-19). If necessary, shut down the program or change its priority to fix the issue.

Figure 12-19
CPU usage

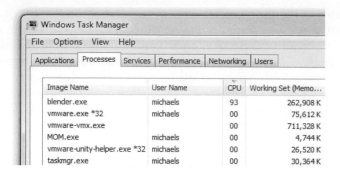

Networking and Users   The other two tabs in the Task Manager, Networking and Users, enable you to see network use at a glance and see which users' accounts are currently logged on to the local machine. The *Networking* tab is a good first spot to look if you think the computer is running slowly on the network. If there's little activity displayed, then it's not traffic from your computer that's causing the slowdown, so you need to look elsewhere. Chapter 19, "Local Area Networking," covers network troubleshooting in a lot more detail, so we'll leave the Networking tab alone for now.

If you have the proper permissions, the *Users* tab enables you to log off any user (even yours), freeing system resources (including files locked for editing) for other users. Be careful! Logging a user off closes his or her applications and discards any unsaved changes in the process.

Task Manager in Windows 8/8.1/10

Now that you know a little about the Task Manager in the days before Windows 8, let's look at how the significant update it received has shuffled things around and improved its usefulness. The latest Task Manager has a new *Fewer details* view (see Figure 12-20) with a dead-simple interface for seeing and terminating running programs. For some users, this is all they'll ever need—and as a tech you need to be aware that not all users will be looking at the *More details* view by default when they open the Task Manager. Once you click More details, the Task Manager will start to look much more familiar, but don't let that trick you—a lot has changed. Let's take a moment to go over the biggest changes.

EXAM TIP   While you can still open the Task Manager by pressing CTRL-SHIFT-ESC, you can also right-click Start and select Task Manager from the context menu.

Figure 12-20
Fewer details
view in Windows
10 Task Manager

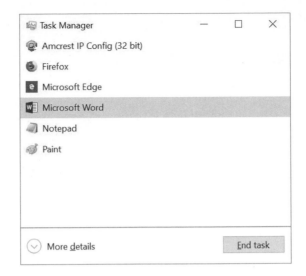

The new Task Manager no longer opens on the simple Applications tab; instead it opens on a much-changed Processes tab. While the Performance, Services, and Users tabs all still exist, the Networking tab has been merged into the Performance tab (along with other new data). Finally, the Task Manager gains three new tabs: App history, Startup, and Details. There are also some huge usability improvements in this update, like the ability to simply right-click column headers (well, on most of the tabs) to select which columns are enabled, and a Search online option any time you right-click a process or service. Let's look at each tab.

Processes You might've noticed that the Fewer details view previously discussed looks a lot like a pared-down version of the older Task Manager Applications tab. The rest of the former Applications tab is best thought of as having been merged with Processes. In detailed mode, you might also notice that Processes is now broken down into three sections: Apps, Background processes, and Windows processes (see Figure 12-21).

NOTE The three categories on the Processes tab—Apps, Background processes, and Windows processes—only appear when you sort the tab by Name (the default view). Otherwise the Task Manager just shows a list of processes running.

Beyond these changes to reorganize the Processes tab, there's also a philosophical shift in what the Processes tab is trying to communicate. Before Windows 8, the Processes tab listed the executable, user, CPU/memory use, and a description of the process (these values have moved to the Details tab, which we'll discuss in a moment). Now by default the Processes tab lists a process description, its status, and its resource use, including CPU, Memory, Disk I/O, and Network I/O. If you expand the Task Manager to the right,

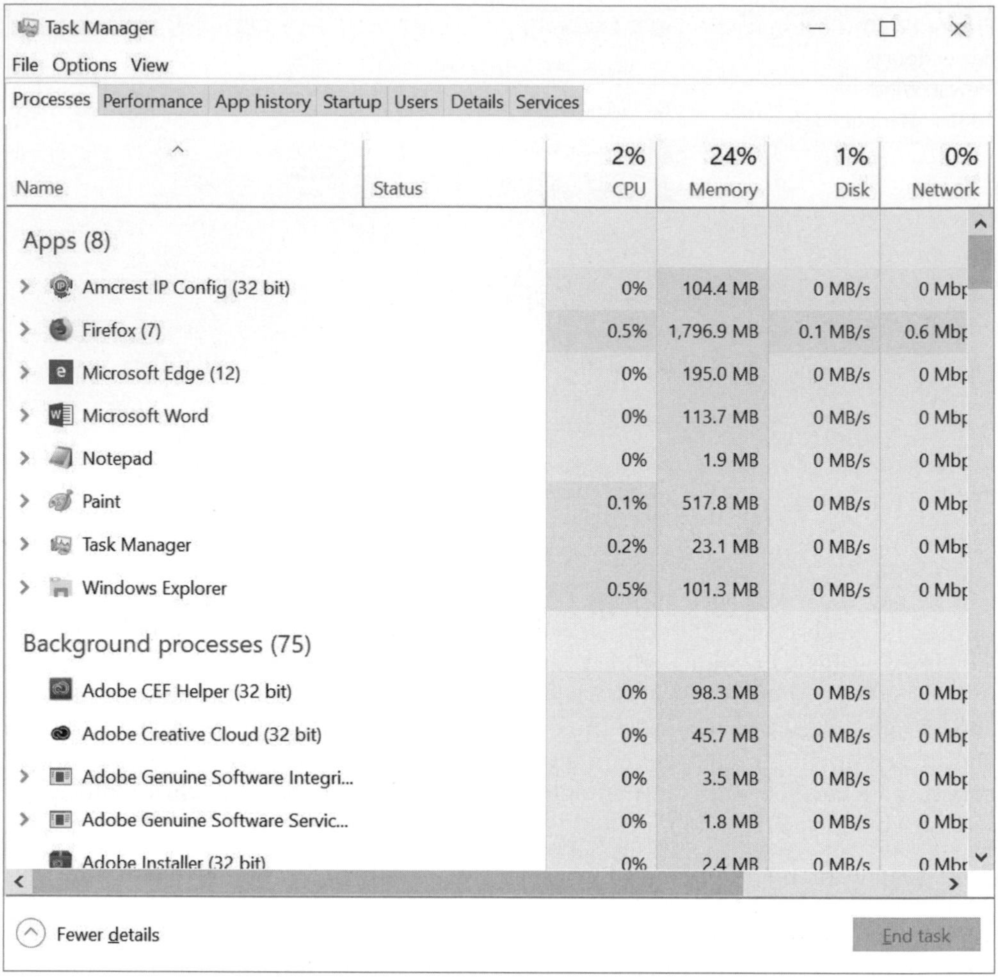

Figure 12-21 Processes tab in detailed Windows 10 Task Manager

you'll see four more columns (see Figure 12-22): GPU and GPU engine (which track how much the graphics engine is being used and in what way), then Power usage and Power usage trend (which track how much power each process is using). These resource values are color-coded to make problems easy to spot, and you can change the enabled columns by right-clicking a column header.

The Task Manager does a good job of showing multiple instances of the same application, as shown in Figure 12-23. Much like the information given has changed, the context menu (again, see Figure 12-23) has a different focus. Most of the advanced options (End Process Tree, UAC Virtualization, Set Priority, Set Affinity, Go to Service[s]) have also moved to the context menu of the Details tab, and are replaced by simpler ones.

Task Manager									

File Options View

Processes Performance App history Startup Users Details Services

		53%	76%	23%	7%	3%			
Name	Status	CPU	Memory	Disk	Network	GPU	GPU engine	Power usage	Power usage trend
Apps (5)									
> Adobe Photoshop CC 2019 (11)		0.1%	911.1 MB	0 MB/s	0 Mbps	0%	GPU 0 - 3D	Very low	Very low
> Firefox (5)		17.5%	564.4 MB	0.2 MB/s	0.5 Mbps	1.8%	GPU 0 - 3D	Very high	Very low
> Task Manager		0.7%	25.2 MB	0 MB/s	0 Mbps	0%		Very low	Low
> Ubuntu (5)		0.1%	6.3 MB	0 MB/s	0 Mbps	0%		Very low	Very low
> VMware Workstation (32 bit)		0%	53.3 MB	0 MB/s	0 Mbps	0%		Very low	Very low
Background processes (82)									
> Adobe Acrobat Update Service (...		0%	0.1 MB	0 MB/s	0 Mbps	0%		Very low	Very low
Adobe CEP HTML Engine		0%	36.1 MB	0 MB/s	0 Mbps	0%		Very low	Very low
Adobe CEP HTML Engine		0%	13.2 MB	0 MB/s	0 Mbps	0%		Very low	Very low
> Adobe Genuine Software Integr...		0%	1.2 MB	0 MB/s	0 Mbps	0%		Very low	Very low
> Adobe Update Service (32 bit)		0%	0.3 MB	0 MB/s	0 Mbps	0%		Very low	Very low
> Antimalware Service Executable		0.5%	141.6 MB	0.1 MB/s	0 Mbps	0%		Very low	Very low
Application Frame Host		0%	6.8 MB	0 MB/s	0 Mbps	0%		Very low	Very low
AppVShNotify		0%	0.4 MB	0 MB/s	0 Mbps	0%		Very low	Very low
apt		0.2%	0.7 MB	0.1 MB/s	0 Mbps	0%		Very low	
bash		0%	0.1 MB	0 MB/s	0 Mbps	0%		Very low	Very low
> Bonjour Service		0%	1.3 MB	0 MB/s	0 Mbps	0%		Very low	Very low
C++ application development f...		0%	0.4 MB	0 MB/s	0 Mbps	0%		Very low	Very low

Fewer details | End task

Figure 12-22   Processes showing GPU, GPU engine, Power usage, and Power usage trend. Note how Firefox's power usage stands out.

To close a process, right-click on it and select End task. Note that this option differs from the Windows 7 option. The End Process and End Process Tree options in Windows 8/8.1/10 are in Resource Monitor (discussed a little later in this chapter.)

Performance   The spirit of the Performance tab (see Figure 12-24) is intact from the earlier Task Manager, and the update made it both easier on the eyes and quite a bit better at its job. The Networking tab has been folded in with Performance, and Disk I/O has been added as well. The result is that there's now one simple place to view all of your major performance metrics—CPU, memory, disk, network, and GPU (added in Windows 10)—at once.

 NOTE   The Performance tab provides a graph of overall CPU utilization by default. You can right-click on the graph and choose Change graph to | Logical processors to see each processor's graph.

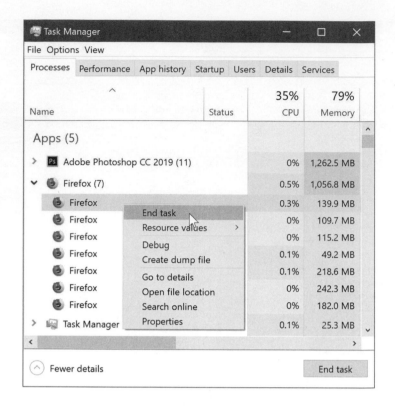

Figure 12-23 Processes tab with multiple instances and context menu

App history When it comes to identifying resource-hungry programs, the resource consumption of a program right this second is often less important than its usage over time. The new Task Manager has an *App history* tab (see Figure 12-25) that collects recent statistics on CPU time and network usage. If you look at the list when you first click on this tab, you'll notice it's not showing history for all processes; you can click Options and select *Show history for all processes* to see a more comprehensive list. Above the list is a sentence stating when the current data began, and a chance to clear the current data by clicking Delete usage history.

Startup If you've used Windows for very long, you've almost inevitably had an undesired program open every time you load Windows. You might've been content to just close it every time, or uninstall the application altogether, but you also could've used the Startup tab in a utility called *msconfig* to specify programs you didn't want to load

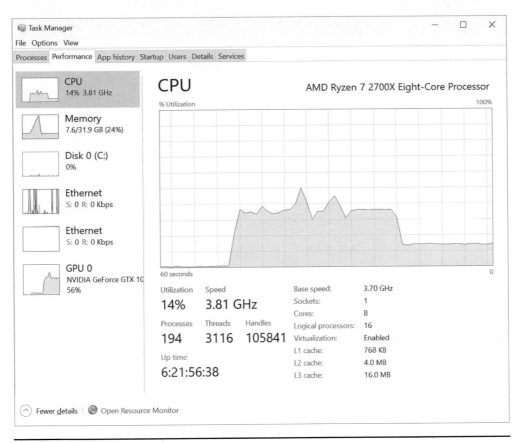

Figure 12-24 Performance tab in Windows 10 Task Manager

with Windows. Starting with Windows 8, Microsoft included the *Startup* tab (see Figure 12-26) in the Task Manager, enabling you to identify and disable rogue startup programs in the same place. It even has a Startup impact column that will help you identify which programs slow down your boot the most.

Users The Users tab (see Figure 12-27) allows most of the same basic functionality it used to—a place to see, disconnect, or log off connected users—but it also shows the programs running under a user's account and clearly indicates the associated resource use. This makes it easier to diagnose a system that is sluggish due to resources tied up by other logged-in users.

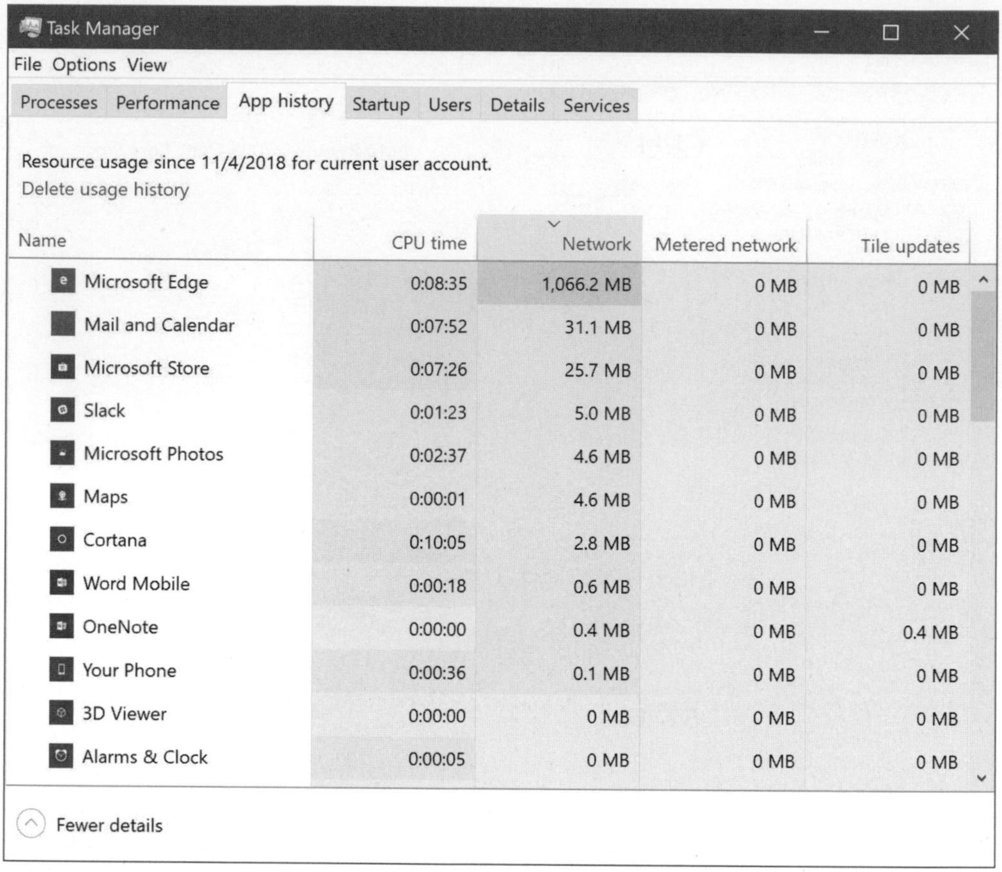

Figure 12-25 App history tab in Windows 10 Task Manager. Note Microsoft Edge's heavy use of Network resources.

Details As previously noted, the *Details* tab (see Figure 12-28) inherited most of the functionality removed from the old Processes tab. It lists processes by executable name, and includes their PID, status, the user running them, CPU/memory use, and a description. If you right-click any column header and choose Select columns, you can enable or disable a dizzying array of columns containing information about each running process. The context menu also introduces a debugging option called *Analyze wait chain* for identifying why a program is frozen.

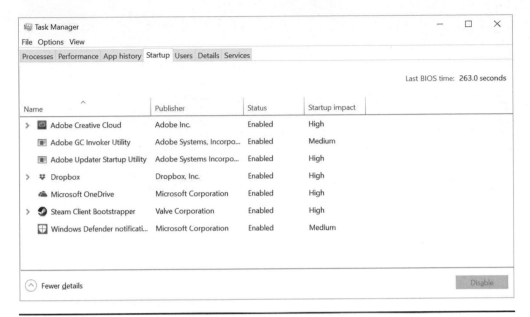

Figure 12-26   Startup tab in Windows 10 Task Manager

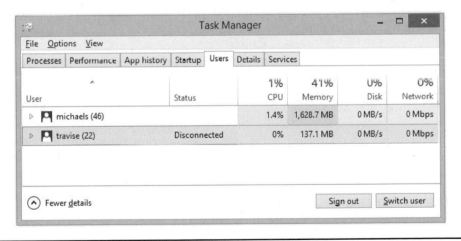

Figure 12-27   Users tab in Windows 8 Task Manager

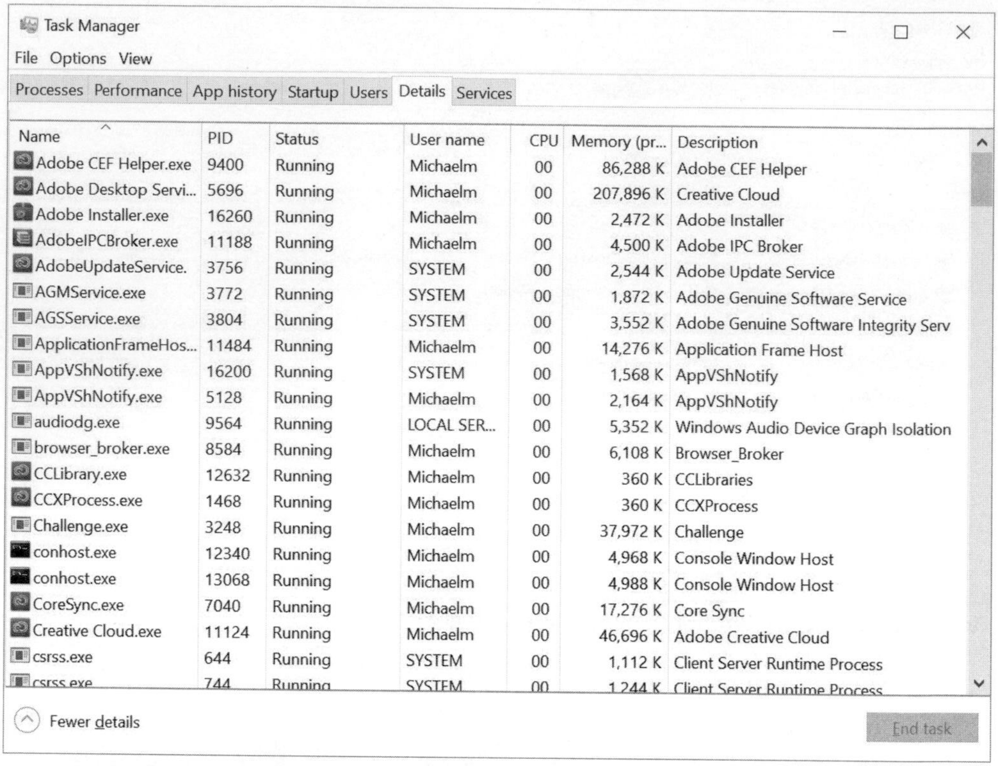

Figure 12-28 Details tab in Windows 10 Task Manager

Services The Services tab in Windows 10 (see Figure 12-29) itself is virtually unchanged from previous versions of the Task Manager, aside from a cosmetic update; the same columns appear in the same order. Still, if you right-click on a service, there are a few nice usability tweaks, including the *Search online* option for investigating unknown services, and an option to restart a service with a single click (instead of only stopping it, and then starting it).

The tasklist and taskkill Commands

The two command-line utilities *tasklist* and *taskkill* enable you to work with tasks, similarly to what you can do with the Task Manager. Here is a scenario I ran into recently: I was looking at the log files from a server that was having some security problems, and I attempted to open one of the logs in Notepad. What I failed to notice was the size of the file, 300 MB! A bit bigger than Notepad was designed to handle, and this caused Notepad to promptly freeze. Because I was already in the command line, I decided to take advantage of a couple of useful commands to quickly kill my frozen Notepad.

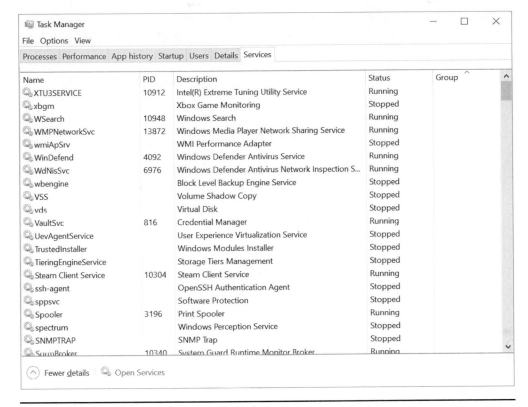

Figure 12-29   Services tab in Windows 10 Task Manager

The first command I used was tasklist, which enables you to view running processes on a local or remote system. Open up a command prompt and type **tasklist**. The following is a partial example of the output:

```
C:\Users\mike>tasklist

Image Name                     PID Session Name        Session#    Mem Usage
========================= ======== ================ =========== ============
System Idle Process              0 Services                   0         24 K
System                           4 Services                   0        940 K
smss.exe                       268 Services                   0        340 K
csrss.exe                      372 Services                   0      2,388 K
wininit.exe                    444 Services                   0        968 K
csrss.exe                      452 Console                    1      9,788 K
winlogon.exe                   500 Console                    1      2,420 K
services.exe                   544 Services                   0      4,536 K
svchost.exe                    756 Services                   0      4,320 K
atiesrxx.exe                   904 Services                   0        824 K
notepad.exe                   3932 Console                    1    584,868 K
```

Once I found Notepad's PID, I was ready to kill it with the taskkill command. See the memory-hungry notepad.exe in the preceding tasklist output? You can kill the process using either the name or the PID. I'm using Notepad's PID in this example along with the force flag (/f) to make sure Windows actually closes Notepad, instead of just asking it nicely. This is necessary when dealing with frozen apps like my logjammed Notepad.

```
C:\>taskkill /f /pid 3932
SUCCESS: The process "notepad.exe" with PID 3932 has been terminated.
```

 EXAM TIP You can use the *kill* command in the Windows PowerShell command-line environment to stop a running process. Kill is actually an alias for the Stop-Process cmdlet, although you don't need to know that for the exam. See Chapter 15 for a more in-depth discussion of working with the command line and PowerShell.

Resource Monitor

The Task Manager should always be the first choice for quick checks on system usage, but there are times where you might need more detail and more control. In these cases, it's time to use Resource Monitor. Think of *Resource Monitor* as a super Task Manager with all the same features, plus many more (see Figure 12-30). You can access Resource Monitor from the Performance tab in Task Manager, from the Control Panel under Administrative tools, or just by typing **resource monitor** in the *Type here to search* field.

Resource Monitor starts on the Overview tab. This is handy, and the graphs on the right are pretty, but the work is done in one of the four other tabs: CPU, Memory, Disk, and Network.

Resource Monitor organizes everything by PID (process ID) number. Using PIDs can facilitate diagnosis of problems, because tracking a four-digit number is much easier than remembering a text string.

Beyond that, each tab brings subtle but interesting features you don't see in the Task Manager:

- **CPU** Enables you to start or suspend any process without killing it
- **Memory** Breaks down memory into specific types
- **Disk** Breaks disk activity down by PID
- **Network** Shows network activity by PID, open connections, much more

Resource Monitor enables you to close running applications and all associated programs with the End Process and End Process Tree context menu options. It makes sense to put the options here, so you can look specifically at programs jamming CPU usage, for example, or network utilization.

In general, if you want a quick overview of what's happening on your system, use the Task Manager. When you need to get down to the details of what process is using what resource and then close a buggy process, go to Resource Monitor.

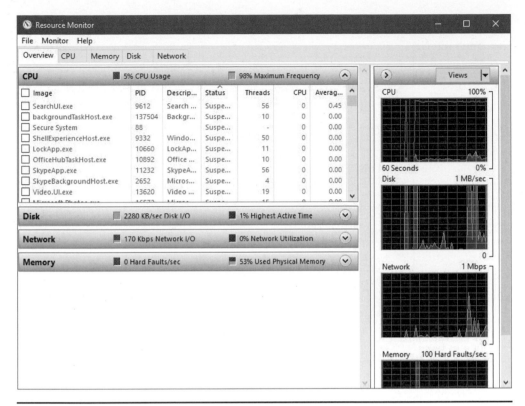

Figure 12-30 Resource Monitor

Performance Tools

The Task Manager and Resource Monitor are great at identifying current problems, but what about problems that happen when you're not around? What about problems that happen over time? For example, what if your system is always running at a CPU utilization of 60 percent—is that good or bad? Windows comes with tools to log resource usage so you can track metrics such as CPU and RAM usage over time. In Windows a good tech turns to *Performance Monitor* as the primary tool for tracking system resources over time.

You can find Performance Monitor in the Administrative Tools applet in Control Panel. You can also open the tool by going to Start | Search, typing **perfmon.msc**, and pressing ENTER. Performance Monitor opens to a screen that displays some text about Performance Monitor and a System Summary (see Figure 12-31). Little is done on this screen.

Click the Performance Monitor icon on the left side to start the real-time tracking tool. All versions of Windows have had this tool in one form or another. In most cases

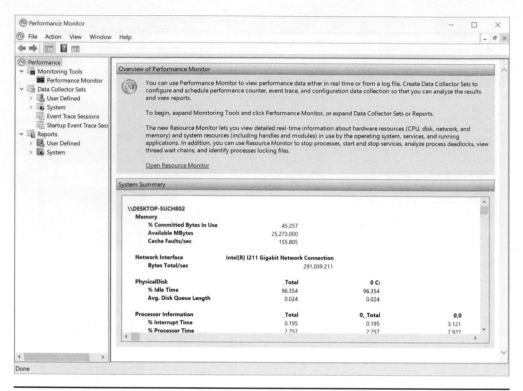

Figure 12-31 Initial Performance Monitor screen in Windows 10

it is easily replaced with Resource Monitor. It's rather boring when you first select it (see Figure 12-32). If you want very detailed, specific tracking, then you might still find a good reason to use this tool. That requires an understanding of objects and counters.

Objects and Counters

Two tool types define the usefulness of Performance Monitor: object and counter. An *object* is a system component that is given a set of characteristics and can be managed by the operating system as a single entity. A *counter* tracks specific information about an object. The Processor object counter %Processor Time, for example, tracks the percentage of elapsed time the processor uses to execute a non-idle thread. Many counters can be associated with an object.

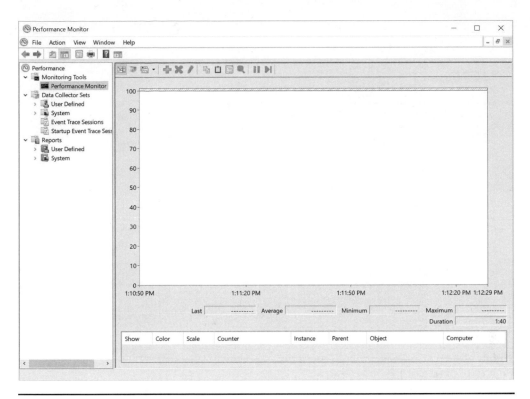

Figure 12-32 Blank Performance Monitor

Working with the Tools

Performance Monitor gathers real-time data on objects such as memory, physical disk, processor, and network, and displays this data as a graph (line graph), histogram (bar graph), or simple report. When you first open it, Performance Monitor shows data in graph form. The data displayed is from the set of counters listed below the chart. If you want to add counters, click the Add button (the one that looks like a plus sign) or press CTRL-I to open the Add Counters dialog box. Select one of the many different objects you can monitor. (Click the Performance object drop-down list to see the options in Windows versions before 10.) The Add Counters dialog box includes a helpful feature: you can select a counter and click the Show description checkbox (or Explain button prior to Windows 10) to learn about the counter, as shown in Figure 12-33. Try that now.

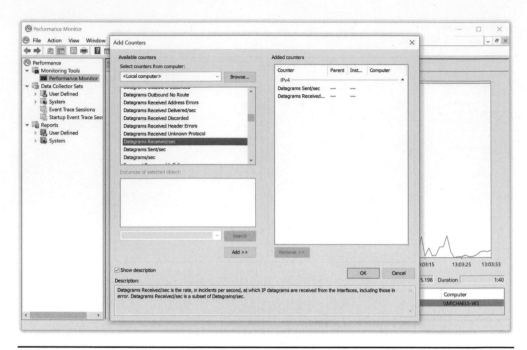

Figure 12-33   Add Counters dialog box with descriptions enabled

Data Collector Sets

To track data long term, use the *Data Collector Sets*, groups of counters you can use to make reports. You can make your own Data Collector Sets (User Defined), or you can just grab one of the predefined system sets. Once you start a Data Collector Set, you can use the Reports option to see the results (see Figure 12-34). Data Collector Sets not only enable you to choose counter objects to track, but also enable you to schedule when you want them to run.

 EXAM TIP   The CompTIA A+ 1002 exam won't ask too many detailed questions on Performance Monitor. That doesn't mean you should ignore this tool. Make sure you understand that this tool enables you to inspect anything happening on a system to help diagnose problems.

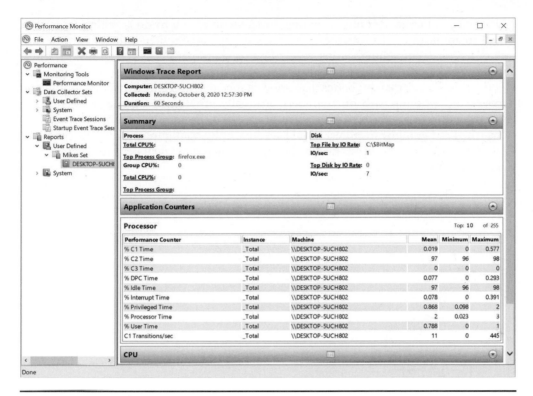

Figure 12-34 Sample report

Tools for Programmers

Microsoft provides an assortment of tools in Windows that go well beyond what techs typically need. The CompTIA A+ 1002 exam includes two such programmer-specific tools to deal with some low-level functionality in Windows that affects how a lot of applications are programmed. Read on to find out more about the Component Services and ODBC Data Source Administrator applets, both found in Administrative Tools.

Component Services

To understand all that *Component Services* can do would require a huge amount of information—far greater than the scope of CompTIA's A+ exams. Simply put, as long as Windows has existed, Microsoft has come up with many tools (with names like COM, DCOM, and COM+) to enable programmers to share data objects (an element of programs) between applications on a single computer. Over time, this sharing was extended so that you could share objects between computers on a network.

In almost all cases, this object sharing doesn't require you to do anything more than install an application that uses these features. Component Services is there for those very rare times when something's either wrong or a programmer needs you to make manual changes (see Figure 12-35). If you have a company that buys custom applications or creates them in-house, there's a better than good chance that you'll be firing up Component Services and working with programmers, manually installing programs, and tweaking those programs to get them to work the way you wish. Professional, third-party applications (the kind you buy in stores) should automatically configure any of these programs during the installation process, making it extremely rare that you'll need to go into Component Services.

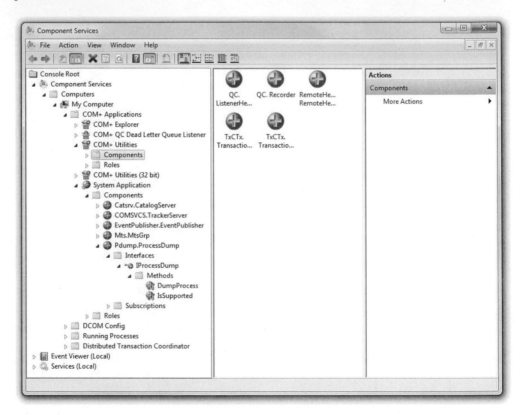

Figure 12-35 Component Services in Windows 7

Data Sources

One of the oldest and most common motivations to make networks is the idea of a number of computers accessing one or more shared databases. These computers might not all be running the same operating system, nor will they always use the same application to access those databases. That's where Open Database Connectivity (ODBC) really shines.

ODBC is a coding standard that enables programmers to write databases and the applications that use them in a way that they can query ODBC on how to locate and access a database without any concern about what application or operating system is used.

Microsoft's tool to configure ODBC is called *ODBC Data Source Administrator* (see Figure 12-36). ODBC Data Source Administrator enables you to create and manage entries called Data Source Names (DSNs) that point ODBC to a database. DSNs are used by ODBC-aware applications to query ODBC to find their databases. Keep in mind that you'll rarely go into Data Source Administrator unless you're making your own shared databases.

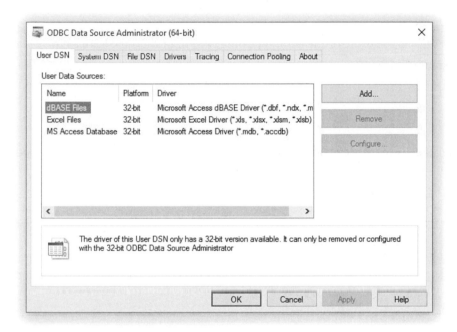

Figure 12-36 ODBC Data Source Administrator in Windows 8.1

The 64-bit versions of Windows offer both a 64-bit and a 32-bit version of the ODBC tool. The 64-bit tool is used on 64-bit databases and the 32-bit tool is used on 32-bit databases.

We'll talk a lot more about sharing resources over networks when we get to networking in depth in Chapter 19.

Chapter Review

Questions

1. What is the name of the program that boots Windows?

   A. NTFS

   B. msconfig

   C. bootmgr

   D. Registry

2. What is the name of the command-line version of the Task Manager?

   A. taskman

   B. tasklist

   C. taskkill

   D. tasks

3. When using Performance Monitor, which settings are defined to track resource usage? (Select two.)

   A. Processes

   B. Objects

   C. Counters

   D. Values

4. Which of the following are organized inside the Registry's root keys? (Select two.)

   A. Subkeys

   B. Subfolders

   C. Values

   D. Objects

5. Which of the following root keys contains the data for a system's non-user-specific configurations?

   A. HKEY_LOCAL_MACHINE

   B. HKEY_USERS

   C. HKEY_CURRENT_USER

   D. HKEY_CLASSES_ROOT

6. Which of the following statements about booting Windows is true?

   A. BIOS does not use bootmgr.

   B. UEFI looks for the MBR, which finds the boot code that launches bootmgr.

   C. BIOS looks for the MBR, which finds the boot code that launches bootmgr.

   D. UEFI does not use bootmgr.

7. How do you open the Registry Editor from the command prompt?

   A. regedit

   B. reg

   C. regeditor

   D. rgstry

8. Sven calls the Help Desk to complain that a certain program (I won't name names here) has locked up. In such a scenario, which tool should you use to force the program to quit and how do you open the tool?

   A. Task Manager; press CTRL-SHIFT-ESC to open

   B. Task Manager; press CTRL-T-M to open

   C. Performance Monitor; open in Administrative Tools

   D. Performance Monitor; press CTRL-P-M to open

9. What tool enables you to track resource usage by PID, rather than a text string, for easier problem diagnosis?

   A. Performance Monitor

   B. PID Monitor

   C. Resource Monitor

   D. Task Manager

10. Which option in Windows 7 enables you to quickly close a potentially problem program and all the code that might be running along with it?

   A. CTRL-ALT-DELETE

   B. CTRL-ALT-ESC

   C. Task Manager | right-click process and select End Process

   D. Task Manager | right-click process and select End Process Tree

Answers

1. **C.** On Windows machines, bootmgr is used to boot the operating system.

2. **B.** The tasklist command opens the command-line version of the Task Manager.

3. **B, C.** To track resource usage in Performance Monitor, you need to configure objects and counters.

4. **A, C.** The Registry's root keys are further organized into subkeys and values.

5. **A.** The system's non-user-specific configurations are stored in the HKEY_LOCAL_MACHINE root key of the Registry.

6. **C.** When booting Windows, the BIOS looks for the MBR, which finds the boot code to launch the OS.

7. A. From the command prompt, you use regedit to open the Registry Editor.

8. A. The Task Manager is the tool you need to use to force a program to close in Windows. The easiest way to access the tool is to press CTRL-SHIFT-ESC simultaneously.

9. C. Resource Monitor organizes everything by PID (process ID) number. Using PIDs often can facilitate diagnosis of problems, because tracking a four-digit number is much easier than remembering a text string.

10. D. The Windows 7 Task Manager featured the End Process Tree option to close a program and all associated programs running with it. You'll find the option on the Details tab in Windows 8/8.1/10.

Users, Groups, and Permissions

In this chapter, you will learn how to

- Create and administer Windows users and groups
- Define and use NTFS permissions for authorization
- Share a Windows computer securely
- Secure PCs with policies and User Account Control

Your computer's mass storage is filled with files that need protection. You might have personal Word documents, spreadsheets, photos, and videos that you do not want others to access. You have critical files, such as the operating system itself, that cannot be accidentally deleted. You have browser histories and download folders full of files that you want and need. So how are these protected from others, even others who may use the same computer from time to time? The answer is user accounts, groups, and permissions.

Through the combination of user accounts and groups and NTFS permissions, Windows provides incredibly powerful file and folder security. This user/group/NTFS combination scales from a single computer up to a network of computers spanning the world.

When learning about users, groups, and NTFS permissions, it's helpful to know how NTFS works on a single PC with multiple users logging on and off during the day. To that end, this chapter focuses on Windows security from the point of view of a single, or *standalone*, machine. Chapter 19, "Local Area Networking," takes over where this chapter stops and will revisit these topics in more detail and show you how the same tools scale up to help you protect a computer in a networked environment.

This chapter begins by examining user accounts, passwords, and groups, then turns to the high level of granular security afforded by NTFS. The third section describes methods for sharing and accessing shared content. The chapter wraps with a look under the hood at security policies and User Account Control.

1002

Authentication with Users and Groups

Security begins with a *user account*, a unique combination of a user name and an associated password, stored in a database on your computer, that grants the user access to the system. Although we normally assign a user account to a human user, user accounts are also assigned to everything that runs programs on your computer. For example, every Windows system has a SYSTEM account that Windows uses when it runs programs. Two mechanisms enable user account security: authentication and authorization.

Authentication is the process of identifying and granting access to some user, usually a person, who is trying to access a system. In Windows, authentication is most commonly handled by a password-protected user account. The process of logging into a system is where the user types in an active user name and password.

 NOTE Authentication is the process of giving a user access to a system. Authorization determines what an authenticated user can do to a system.

Once a user authenticates, he or she needs *authorization*: the process that defines what resources an authenticated user may access and what he or she may do with those resources. Authorization for Windows' files and folders is controlled by the NTFS file system, which assigns permissions to users and groups. These permissions define exactly what users may do to a resource on the system. Let's start authentication with an overview of user accounts, passwords, and groups, then look at configuring users and groups in Windows.

 NOTE This chapter uses Windows as an example of user accounts, passwords, and groups, but understand that all operating systems—without exception—use user accounts, passwords, and groups.

User Accounts

Every user account has a user name and a password. A user name is a text string that identifies the user account assigned to a system. Three examples of possible user names are "Mike1" or "john.smith" or "some.person@hotmail.com." Associated with every user name is a password: a unique key known only by the system and the person using that user name. This user name and password are encrypted on the system—and only those with a user name and password are allowed access to the system via the login process.

Every Windows system stores the user accounts as an encrypted database of user names and passwords. Windows calls each record in this database a *local user account* (see Figure 13-1).

Figure 13-1
Local user
accounts are
stored on the
system.

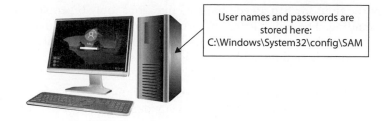

User names and passwords are
stored here:
C:\Windows\System32\config\SAM

User accounts in our always-on Internet environment get complicated quickly. On Chrome OS, the only way to get the full experience is by logging in with a Google account. The opposite is true on Linux, where local user accounts (tied to a specific computer and user) rule. Windows and macOS split the difference, supporting traditional local user accounts as well as the ability to log in with your Microsoft or Apple account, respectively.

You can set up a local machine connected to the Internet to connect to a global account. That global account functions like a local account but adds the benefit of synchronizing some of your stuff with the global account settings. My custom desktop picture at home, for example, matches the desktop picture on my laptop computer. I've logged in to both machines with my Microsoft account.

NOTE *Global user account* is my term. Each company uses specific naming for its accounts, such as a Microsoft account, Apple ID, or Gmail account. Still, you get the idea, right?

Creating a user account (local or global) not only adds a user name to a database, it also generates several folders on a computer. In Windows, for example, each user account gets unique personal folders, such as Documents, Desktop, Pictures, Music, and more. By default, only a person logged in as a specific user can access the personal folders for that user account. So, the next step is to secure that local user account.

Passwords

Passwords help secure user accounts. Protect your passwords. Never give out passwords over the phone. If someone learns your user name and password, he or she can log on to your computer. Even if the user account has only limited permissions—perhaps it can only read files, not edit them—you still have a security breach.

Make your users choose good passwords. I once attended a security seminar, and the speaker had everyone stand up. She then began to ask questions about our passwords—if we responded yes to the question, we were to sit down. She began to ask questions like these:

"Do you use the name of your spouse as a password?"

"Do you use your pet's name?"

By the time she had asked about 15 questions, only 6 people out of some 300 were still standing. The reality is that most of us choose passwords that are amazingly easy to hack. Make sure users have a *strong password*: at least eight characters in length, including letters, numbers, and nonalphanumeric symbols.

NOTE For the latest password recommendations, check out the National Institute of Technology and Standards (NIST) Special Publication 800-63B, *Digital Identity Guidelines*.

Using non-alphanumeric characters makes any password much more difficult to crack, for two reasons. First, adding non-alphanumeric characters forces the hacker to consider many more possible characters than just letters and numbers. Second, most password crackers use a combination of common words and numbers to hack passwords.

Because non-alphanumeric characters don't fit into common words or numbers, a character such as an exclamation point defeats these common-word hacks. Not all systems allow you to use characters such as @, $, %, or \, however, so you need to experiment.

CompTIA also recommends that you should have users change passwords at regular intervals; this can be enforced with a *password expiration* policy that forces users to select a new password periodically. Although this concept sounds good on paper, it is a hard policy to maintain in the real world. For starters, users tend to forget passwords when they change a lot. This can lead to an even bigger security problem because users start writing passwords down.

NOTE Every secure organization sets up various security policies and procedures to ensure that security is maintained. Windows has various mechanisms to implement such things as requiring a strong password, for example. Chapter 27, "Securing Computers," goes into detail about setting up Local Policies and Group Policy.

If your organization forces you to change passwords often, one way to remember the password is to use a numbering system. I worked at a company that required me to change my password at the beginning of each month, so I did something very simple. I took a root password—let's say it was "m3y3rs5"—and simply added a number to the end representing the current month. So, when June rolled around, for example, I would change my password to "m3y3rs56." It worked pretty well.

CAUTION Blank passwords or passwords that are easily visible on a sticky note provide no security. Always insist on non-blank passwords, and do not let anyone leave a password sitting out in the open.

Windows requires you to create a password hint or password questions for your local accounts. In Windows 10 this clue appears after your first logon attempt fails under the reset password option (see Figure 13-2).

Figure 13-2
Password hint on
the Windows 10
logon screen

Groups

A *group* is a container that holds user accounts and defines the capabilities of its members. A single account can be a member of multiple groups. Groups are an efficient way of managing multiple users, especially when you are dealing with a whole network of accounts. Standalone computers rely on groups too, though Windows obscures this a little, especially with Home edition users.

Groups make Windows administration much easier in two ways. First, you can assign a certain level of access for a file or folder to a group instead of to just a single user account. You can make a group called Accounting, for example, and put all user accounts for the accounting department in that group. If a person quits, you don't need to worry about assigning all the proper access levels when you create a new account for his or her replacement. After you make an account for the new person, just add her account to the appropriate access group! Second, Windows provides numerous built-in groups with various access levels already predetermined.

While all versions and editions of Windows come with many of these built-in groups, Windows Home editions handle these very differently than more advanced editions. For starters, make sure you are aware of the following groups for the exam:

- **Administrators**   Any account that is a member of the *Administrators group* has complete administrator privileges. Administrator privileges grant complete control over a machine. It is common for the primary user of a Windows system to have her account in the Administrators group.

  When you create the Jane user account, in other words, and make Jane an administrator, you place the Jane account in the Administrators group. Because the Administrators group has all power over a system, Jane has all power over the system.

 EXAM TIP   Note that the default administrator account is Administrator. You should use this default only if no other administrators can log on. Best practice is to make a complex password for Administrator; write it down, and put it in a safe for emergency use. *Change the default admin user account/password* to reflect one or more of the user accounts added to the Administrators group.

- **Power Users**   Members of the *Power Users group* are almost as powerful as members of the Administrators group, but they cannot install new devices or access other users' files or folders unless the files or folders specifically provide them access.

- **Users**   Members of the *Users group* cannot edit the Registry or access critical system files. They can create groups but can manage only those they create. Members of the Users group are called *standard users*.

  If you change the Jane account from administrator to standard user, you specifically take the Jane account out of the Administrators group and place it into the Users group. Nothing happens with her personal files or folders, but what the Jane account can do on the computer changes rather dramatically.

- **Guests**   The *Guests group* enables someone who does not have an account on the system to log on by using a guest account. You might use this feature at a party, for example, to provide casual Internet access to guests, or at a library terminal. Most often, the guest account remains disabled.

Standard User and Elevated Privileges

The typical scenario with Windows machines will have a single primary user account—a standard user—and a local administrator account for doing important tasks like installing or uninstalling apps, updating software, and so on. When you're logged in as a standard user and need to do something that requires an administrator account, you have a couple of options. You could log out and log back in as an administrator, but that's clunky. Windows gives you a way to open and run utilities with the context menu of a right-click, called *Run as administrator*, or generically, *using elevated privileges*. The mechanism that will pop when you want to do something beyond your user account level is called UAC. See the "Beyond Sharing Resources" section at the end of this chapter for the gory details.

Configuring Users and Groups in Windows

Windows comes with many tools to help you create, modify, and delete users and groups. Every version of Windows includes at least two user and group management tools; let's focus on the simplest, *Local Users and Groups* (see Figure 13-3). You can access Local Users and Groups in two ways:

- Select Control Panel | Administrative Tools | Computer Management | Local Users and Groups.

- Type **lusrmgr.msc** in the search field in the taskbar and press ENTER.

For reasons that will be described shortly, Windows 10 Home edition does not have Local Users and Groups.

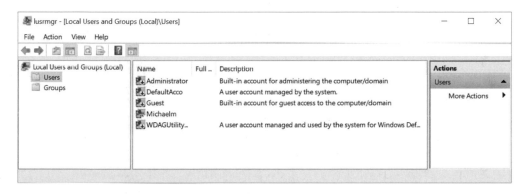

Figure 13-3   Local Users and Groups in Windows 10

Local Users and Groups has two folders: Users and Groups. By default, the Users folder should already be selected. If not, click on the Users folder now. Note the existing user accounts shown in Figure 13-3. Do you see Administrator? Do you see Michaelm? Do you see Guest? Note the down arrow on the Guest account (and others) to show that they are disabled.

Create a new user (JimT) by right-clicking on the whitespace below the existing users and selecting New User from the context menu. You then add the information to create the new account as shown in Figure 13-4.

By default, all new user accounts are automatically added to the Users group. Click on the Groups folder to see the many default groups. Figure 13-5 shows the default groups in Windows 10. Do you see Users, Power Users, Guests, and Administrators?

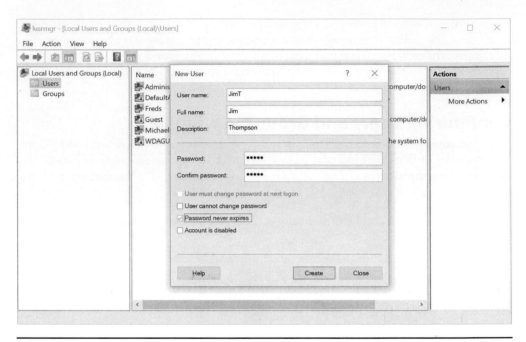

Figure 13-4   Creating a new user account called JimT

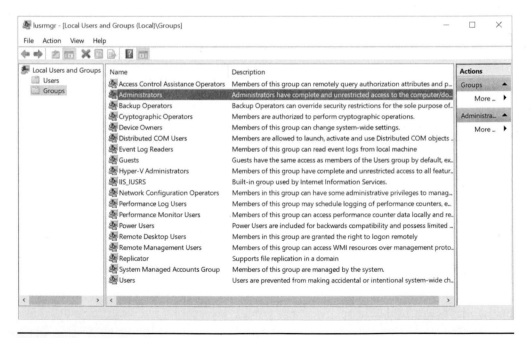

Figure 13-5   Default groups

Let's add the JimT account to the Administrators group. Double-click on the Administrators group and select Add. You may then enter JimT into the Select Users dialog box (see Figure 13-6), then click OK.

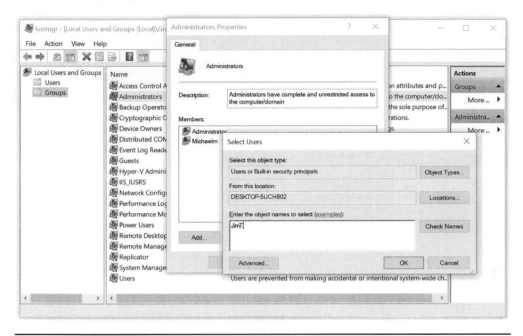

Figure 13-6   Adding JimT to the Administrators group

You're not limited to the default Windows groups. Here are the steps to create a group called *Morning*. Click on the Groups folder, right-click on any whitespace on the right under the existing groups and select New Group, then fill out the name of the new group (and add an optional description) (see Figure 13-7). You can add members to this group.

NOTE   To create and manage users, you must run Local Users and Groups as an administrator. The easiest way to do this is to open a command prompt with elevated privileges and then type **lusrmgr.msc** (and press ENTER). See Chapter 15, "Working with the Command-Line Interface," for the scoop on running commands from the command-line interface.

Local Users and Groups is a perfectly fine tool for dealing with local users and groups on a single Windows system. Microsoft offers other tools as well; the names change with the versions. Let's take a look.

Managing Users in Windows 7

Windows 7 offers a utility called the *User Accounts* applet in the Control Panel. To create a user account, open the User Accounts applet and select *Manage another account* to see something like Figure 13-8.

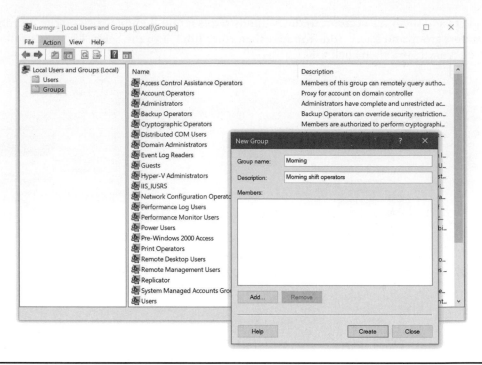

Figure 13-7 Creating the Morning group

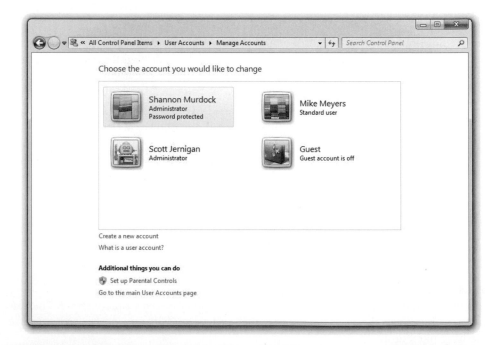

Figure 13-8 Manage Accounts

Click *Create a new account* to see your options for making a new account (see Figure 13-9). Note that this applet only enables you to make administrator accounts (in the Administrators group) or standard users (in the Users group).

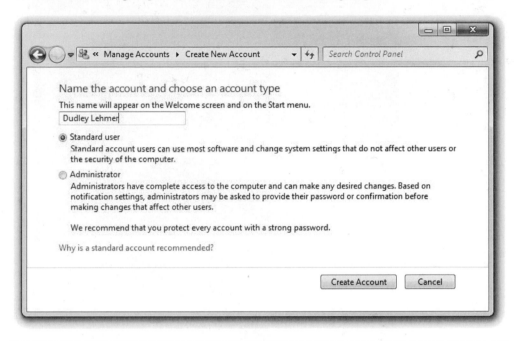

Figure 13-9 Adding a new user

Managing Users in Windows 8/8.1

Starting with Windows 8, Microsoft shifted the focus of user accounts from local accounts to Internet-wide Microsoft accounts. Windows 8 debuted the Settings charm (see Figure 13-10). Select *Change PC settings* from the initial charm screen to open PC settings (see Figure 13-11) and get access to the *Accounts* option. Note that the User Accounts applet in Control Panel enables you to make changes to local user accounts, and gives you access to the Settings charm when you opt to add a new account.

When you set up a Windows 8/8.1 PC, you are aggressively prompted to dump the local user account and instead log on with a Microsoft global account or create one at that time. In fact, Windows makes it very challenging to create a regular old local user account. Although the language of the sign-up option for the new account suggests a Microsoft-sponsored e-mail address (like user@hotmail.com), any valid e-mail address will serve as a Microsoft account. You could opt to create a local user account instead and that functions like any local account on previous versions. But if you opt for a global Microsoft account, you'll synchronize photos, files, and Desktop settings (like the background picture and colors).

Figure 13-10
Settings charm

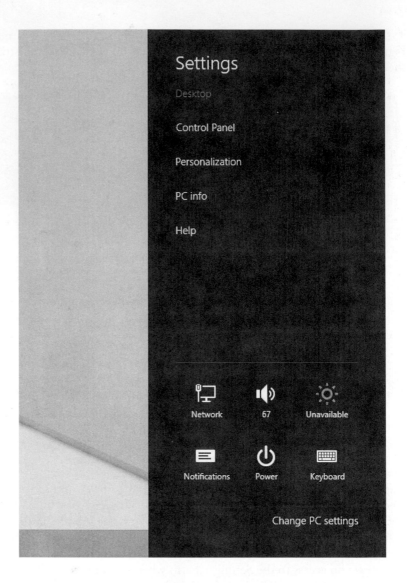

Once you have a valid user account set up and have a functioning system, the Accounts area of the Settings app enables you to sign out, sign in, modify your profile picture, and so on. Figure 13-12 shows a typical Accounts default screen.

To create a new account, click the *Other accounts* option. This opens the Manage other accounts page (see Figure 13-13). From this page you can modify the status or group of any current local user account. Click the + symbol next to *Add an account* to get started.

On the *How will this person sign in?* screen (see Figure 13-14), you'll see options to use a valid Microsoft account, get a Microsoft account, add a child's account, or create a local account only. The *Add a child's account* option creates an account with parental controls enabled.

Figure 13-11 PC settings

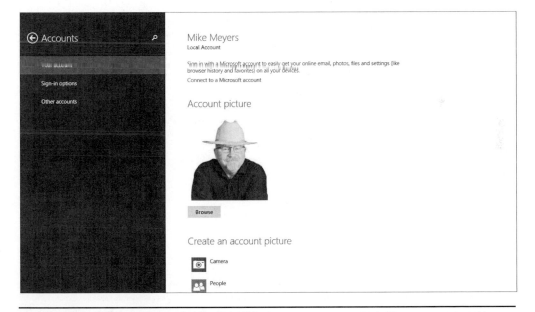

Figure 13-12 Accounts screen in Windows 8.1

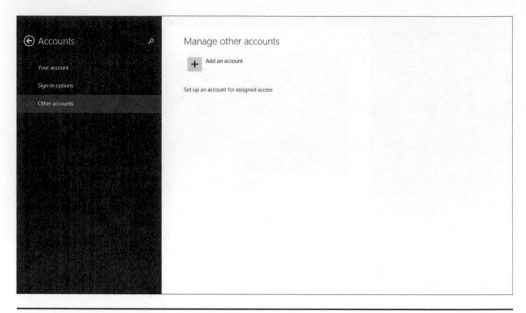

Figure 13-13   Manage other accounts

Figure 13-14   Options for a new account

Once you've opted to do either a global or local account, Windows creates that account on the local machine. This process takes a while; Windows creates all the folder structures and updates the local profile. Eventually, you'll have a new account ready to roll (see Figure 13-15).

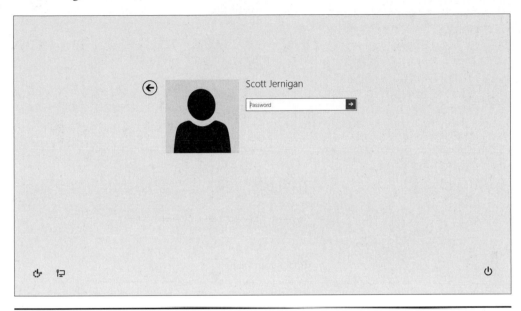

Figure 13-15   Shiny new account

Managing Users in Windows 10

Windows 10 suffers from the legacy of Microsoft's many attempts to make alternatives to Local Users and Groups, leaving three different tools to deal with user account and group management. First, Windows 10 greatly updated the Accounts app and moved it to Settings (see Figure 13-16).

The Accounts app is more for configuring your personal account than adding users or moving an account into a group. You can work with other users, however, by moving to the *Family & other people* menu option and selecting *Add someone else to this PC* (see Figure 13-17). Good luck creating a local user account though, because Microsoft hides this ability, pressuring you to use or create a Microsoft global account.

The User Accounts control panel utility in Windows 10 (Figure 13-18) is handy for making more technical changes to your account. Here you can change (but not create) your group memberships as well as make simple changes to your account and other accounts (like changing passwords). You need to be a member of the Administrators group to make these changes.

If you're not using the Windows 10 Home edition, Local Users and Groups is still the best way to go if you're comfortable with the power of the tools (and don't try to do something dangerous such as deleting the administrator account).

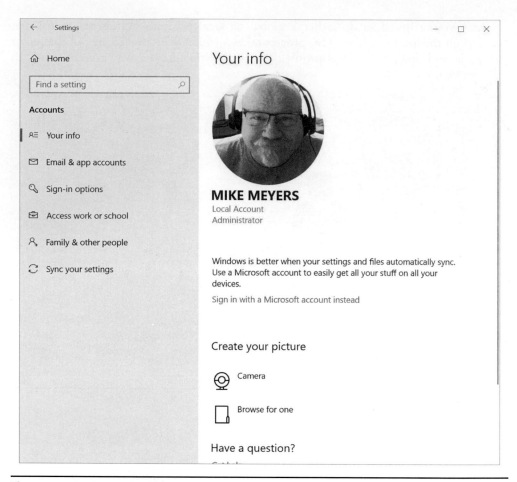

Figure 13-16 Accounts app home

 NOTE Windows 10 Home users need to use Accounts in Settings or User Accounts in Control Panel.

Whew! All this hubbub with local user accounts and groups is designed to only do one thing: get a user logged on to a Windows system. But once a user is logged on, it's time to see what they can do to the data. That's where authorization with NTFS kicks in.

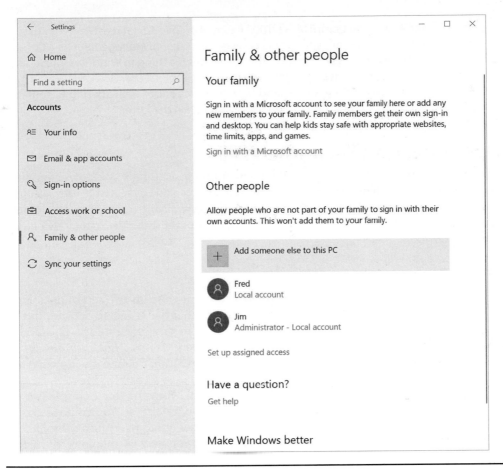

Figure 13-17 Family & other people

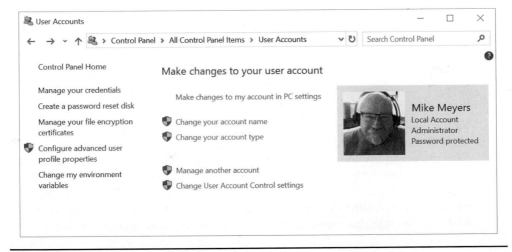

Figure 13-18 User Accounts in Windows 10

EXAM TIP The CompTIA A+ 1002 exam objective 1.5 (at least in the initial release—your mileage may vary) lists *User Account Management* as a Control Panel applet in Windows. This has *never* been a thing in Windows. Most likely, the objectives conflate two separate applets: *User Accounts*—which we just covered in detail—and *User Account Control*. See "Sharing Resources Securely" later in this chapter for the scoop on the latter.

Authorization Through NTFS

User accounts and passwords provide the foundation for securing a Windows computer, enabling users to authenticate to log on to a PC. After you've created a user account, you need to determine what the user can do with the available resources (files, folders, applications, and so on). This *authorization* process uses the NT File System (NTFS) as the primary tool.

NTFS Permissions

Every file and folder on an NTFS partition has a list that contains two sets of data. First, the list details every user and group that has access to that file or folder. Second, the list specifies the *level* of access that each user or group has to that file or folder. The level of access is defined by a set of restrictions called NTFS permissions. *NTFS permissions* are rulesets, connected to every folder and file in your system, that define exactly what any account or group can or cannot do to the file or folder.

NTFS permissions are quite detailed and powerful. You can, for example, set up NTFS permissions for a user account to edit a file but not delete it. You could also configure NTFS permissions to enable any member of a user group to create a subfolder for a folder. You can even configure a folder so that one group may be able to read the files but not delete them, modify them, or even see them in Windows Explorer.

NTFS file and folder permissions are powerful and complicated. Entire books have been written just on NTFS permissions. Fortunately, the CompTIA A+ 220-1002 exam tests your understanding of only a few basic concepts of NTFS permissions: Ownership, Take Ownership permission, Change permission, folder permissions, and file permissions.

- **Ownership**   When you create a new file or folder on an NTFS partition, you become the *owner* of that file or folder. This is called *ownership*. Owners can do anything they want to the files or folders they own, including changing the permissions to prevent anybody, even administrators, from accessing them.

- **Take Ownership permission**   With the *Take Ownership* permission, anyone with the permission can seize control of a file or folder. Administrator accounts have Take Ownership permission for everything. Note the difference here between owning a file and accessing a file. If you own a file, you can prevent anyone from accessing that file. An administrator whom you have blocked, however, can take that ownership away from you and *then* access that file!

- **Change permission** Another important permission for all NTFS files and folders is the *Change* permission. An account with this permission can give or take away permissions for other accounts.

- **Folder permissions** *Folder permissions* define what a user may do to a folder. One example might be "List folder contents," which gives the permission to see what's in the folder.

- **File permissions** *File permissions* define what a user may do to an individual file. One example might be "Read and Execute," which gives a user account the permission to run an executable program.

The primary way to set NTFS permissions is through the Security tab under the Properties of a folder or file (see Figure 13-19). The Security tab contains two main areas. The top area shows the list of accounts that have permissions for that resource. The lower area shows exactly what permissions have been assigned to the selected account.

Figure 13-19
The Security tab
enables you to
set permissions.

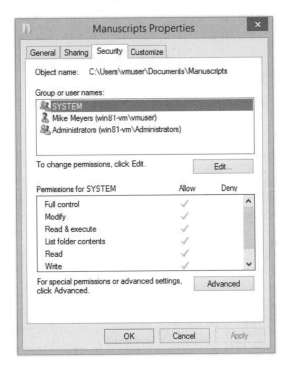

You add or remove NTFS permissions by first selecting the user or group you wish to change and then clicking Edit to open a Permissions dialog box. To add an NTFS permission, select the Allow checkbox next to the NTFS permission you want to add. You remove an NTFS permission by deselecting the Allow checkbox next to the NTFS permission you want to remove. The Deny checkbox is not used very often and has a very different job—see the next section, "Inheritance."

Here are the standard NTFS permissions for a folder:

- **Full Control**   Enables you to do anything you want
- **Modify**   Enables you to read, write, and delete both files and subfolders
- **Read & Execute**   Enables you to see the contents of the folder and any subfolders as well as run any executable programs or associations in that folder
- **List Folder Contents**   Enables you to see the contents of the folder and any subfolders
- **Read**   Enables you to view a folder's contents and open any file in the folder
- **Write**   Enables you to write to files and create new files and folders

NTFS file permissions are quite similar to folder permissions, with the main difference being the Special Permissions option, which I'll talk about a bit later in the chapter.

- **Full Control**   Enables you to do anything you want to the file
- **Modify**   Enables you to read, write, and delete the file
- **Read & Execute**   Enables you to open and run the file
- **Read**   Enables you to open the file
- **Write**   Enables you to open and write to the file

Here are a few important points about NTFS permissions:

- You may see the NTFS permissions on a folder or file by accessing the file's or folder's Properties dialog box and opening the Security tab.
- NTFS permissions are assigned both to user accounts and groups, although it's considered a best practice to assign permissions to groups and then add user accounts to groups instead of adding permissions directly to individual user accounts.
- Permissions are cumulative. If you have Full Control on a folder and only Read permission on a file in the folder, you get Full Control permission on the file.
- Whoever creates a folder or a file has complete control over that folder or file. This is ownership.
- If an administrator wants to access a folder or file they do not have permission to access, they may go through the Take Ownership process.

Take some time to think about these permissions. Why would Microsoft create them? Think of scenarios where you might want to give a group Modify permission. Also, you can assign more than one permission. In many situations, administrators give users both the Read and Write permissions to files or folders.

Inheritance

Inheritance determines which NTFS permissions any newly introduced files or subfolders contained in a folder receive. Techs should understand how inheritance works (see Figure 13-20).

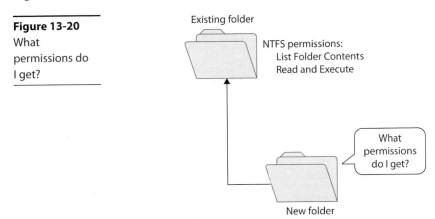

Figure 13-20
What permissions do I get?

The base rule of Windows inheritance is that any new files or folders placed into a folder automatically get all the NTFS permissions of the parent folder. So if, for example, you have Read and Execute access to a folder and someone else copies a file to that folder, you will automatically get Read and Execute permissions (see Figure 13-21).

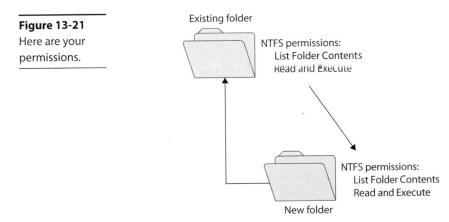

Figure 13-21
Here are your permissions.

All versions of Windows have inheritance turned on by default, which most of the time is a good idea. If you access a folder's Properties dialog box, click on the Security tab, and then click the Advanced button, you'll see a little checkbox that says *Include inheritable permissions from this object's parent.* If you wanted to turn off inheritance, you would just uncheck this box. Don't do that. Inheritance is good. Inheritance is expected.

NOTE The Deny checkbox always overrides the NTFS inheritance.

If you look closely at Figure 13-22, you'll see that there are several grayed-out NTFS Allow permissions. That's how Windows tells you that the permissions here are inherited. Grayed-out checkboxes can't be changed, so what do you do if you need to make a change here?

Figure 13-22
Inherited permissions

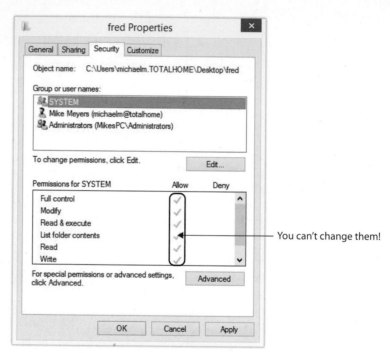

You can't change them!

In rare situations you may want to turn off inheritance for a specific folder or file. Instead of shutting down inheritance completely, use the Deny checkbox. Clicking the Deny checkbox for an NTFS permission (see Figure 13-23) tells Windows to overrule inheritance and stop that NTFS permission.

Permission Propagation

Permission propagation determines what NTFS permissions are applied to files that are moved or copied into a new folder. Be careful here! You might be tempted to think, given you've just learned about inheritance, that any new files/folders copied or moved into a folder would just inherit the folder's NTFS permissions. This is not always true, and CompTIA wants to make sure you know it. It depends on two issues: whether the data

Figure 13-23
Special
permissions

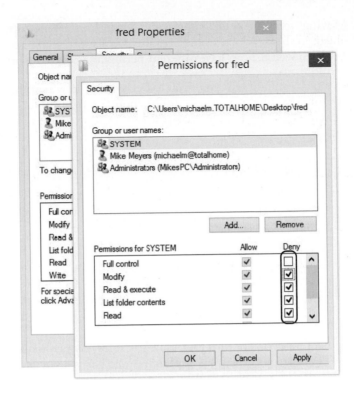

is being copied or moved, and whether the data is coming from the same volume or a different one. So, we need to consider four situations:

- Copying data within one NTFS-based volume
- Moving data within one NTFS-based volume
- Copying data between two NTFS-based volumes
- Moving data between two NTFS-based volumes

Let's look at a list of four things techs need to know to see what happens when you copy or move an object, such as a file or folder.

1. Copying within a volume creates two copies of the object. The copy of the object in the new location *inherits* the permissions from that new location. The new copy can have different permissions than the original.

2. Moving within a volume creates one copy of the object. That object *retains* its permissions, unchanged.

3. Copying from one NTFS volume to another creates two copies of the object. The copy of the object in the new location *inherits* the permissions from that new location. The new copy can have different permissions than the original.

4. Moving from one NTFS volume to another creates one copy of the object. The object in the new location *inherits* the permissions from that new location. The newly moved file can have different permissions than the original.

From a tech's standpoint, you need to be aware of how permissions can change when you move or copy files. If you're in doubt about a sensitive file, check it before you sign off to a client. Table 13-1 summarizes the results of moving and copying between NTFS volumes.

	Same Volume	Different Volume
Move	Keeps original permissions	Inherits new permissions
Copy	Inherits new permissions	Inherits new permissions

Table 13-1　Permission Propagation

 EXAM TIP　Current versions of Windows refer to sections of an HDD or SSD as *volumes*, as you'll recall from Chapter 9. Earlier versions—and many techs and exams in your near future—refer to such groupings as *partitions*. Be prepared for either term.

Any object that you put on a FAT partition loses any permissions because FAT doesn't support NTFS permissions. This applies in most current scenarios involving FAT32- or exFAT-partitioned mass storage devices, such as the ubiquitous thumb drives that all of us use for quick copying and moving of files from device to device.

Techs and Permissions

You must have local administrative privileges to do almost anything on a Windows machine, such as install updates, change drivers, and install applications; most administrators hate giving out administrative permissions (for obvious reasons). If an administrator does give you administrative permission for a PC and something goes wrong with that system while you're working on it, you immediately become the primary suspect!

If you're working on a Windows system administered by someone else, make sure he or she understands what you are doing and how long you think it will take. Have the administrator create a new temporary account for you that's a member of the Administrators group. Never ask for the password to a permanent administrator account! That way, you won't be blamed if anything goes wrong on that system: "Well, I told Janet the password when she installed the new hard drive . . . maybe she did it!" When you have fixed the system, *make sure the administrator deletes the account you used.*

Permissions in Linux and macOS

While the CompTIA A+ 1002 exam concentrates hard on Windows users, groups, and permissions, this is a good time to consider that Linux and macOS also have their own concepts pertaining to users, groups, and permissions. Let's take a short jaunt into Linux and macOS users, groups, and permissions. We'll look at the chmod and chown commands because they are listed as objectives for the CompTIA A+ 1002 exam.

 NOTE Understanding this section requires some understanding of the Linux command line. You may need to refer to Chapter 15, "Working with the Command-Line Interface," to practice some of the commands shown here.

Just as in Windows, every file and folder on a Linux or macOS system has permissions. You can easily see this if you go to a Linux terminal and type this command: ls -l. This shows a detailed list of all the files and folders in a location. Chapter 15 discusses the ls command in a lot more detail, but this is enough for our present discussion.

```
drwxrwxr-x 2 mikemeyers mi6     4096 Oct  2 18:35 agent_bios
-rw-rw-r-- 1 mikemeyers mi6    34405 Oct  2 18:39 datafile
-rwxrwxrwx 1 mikemeyers mi6     7624 Oct  2 18:39 honeypot
-rw-rw-r-- 1 mikemeyers users    299 Oct  2 18:36 launch_codes
-rw-rw-r-- 1 mikemeyers mi6      905 Oct  2 18:36 passwords.txt
```

Let's zero in on one line of this output:

```
-rwxrwxrwx 1 mikemeyers mi6     7624 Oct  2 18:39 honeypot
```

First, ignore almost everything: The 1 is about links that programmers care about; mikemeyers is the owner and mi6 is the group. The file size is 7624; the date and time are next. The file name is honeypot.

Now note the string -rwxrwxrwx. Each of those letters represents a permission for this file. Ignore the dash at the beginning. That is used to tell us if this listing is a file, directory, or shortcut. What we have left are three groups of rwx. The three groups, in order, stand for:

- **Owner** Permissions for the owner of this file or folder
- **Group** Permissions for members of the group for this file or folder
- **Everyone** Permissions for anyone for this file or folder

The letters r, w, and x represent the following permissions:

- **r** Read the contents of a file
- **w** Write or modify a file or folder
- **x** Execute a file or list the folder contents

Figure 13-24 shows the relationships.

Figure 13-24
Linux file
permissions

Let's look at another example:

```
-rw-rw-r-- 1 mikemeyers users   299 Oct  2 18:36 launch_codes
```

- This file is called launch codes. The owner of this file is me. This file is in the users group.
- The owner, mikemeyers, has read and write privileges (rw-).
- The group, users, has read and write privileges (rw-).
- No one has execute permissions (x) because this is just a text file, not a script or program.
- Everyone can read the launch codes (r--). We should probably fix that.

chown Command

The *chown* command enables you to change the owner and the group with which a file or folder is associated. The chown command uses the following syntax:

```
chown <new owner> filename
```

To change the group, use the following syntax:

```
chown <owner>:<group> filename
```

So, to change the owner of launch_codes to sally, type

```
chown sally launch_codes
```

To change the group to mi6, type

```
chown sally:mi6 launch_codes
```

If you retype the ls -l command, you would see the following output:

```
-rw-rw-r-- 1 sally mi6    299 Oct  2 18:36 launch_codes
```

Be aware that the chown command needs superuser privileges (sudo or su). Refer to Chapter 15 for details.

chmod Command

The *chmod* command is used to change permissions. Sadly, it uses a somewhat nonintuitive addition system that works as follows:

```
r: 4
w: 2
x: 1
```

For example, we can interpret the permissions on

```
-rw-rw-r-- 1 mikemeyers mi6    299 Oct  2 18:36 launch_codes
```

as follows:

- Owner's permissions are 6: 4+2 (rw-)
- Group's permissions are 6: 4+2 (rw-)
- Everyone's permissions are 4: 4 (r--)

The chmod command uses the following syntax to make permission changes:

```
chmod <permissions> <filename>
```

Using this nomenclature, we can make any permission change desired using only three numbers. The current permissions can be represented by 664. To keep the launch codes out of the wrong hands, just change the 4 to a 0: 660. To make the change, use the chmod command as follows:

```
chmod 660 launch_codes
```

To give everyone complete control, give everyone read + write + execute. 4 + 2 + 1 = 7. So, use the command as follows:

```
chmod 777 launch_codes
```

 NOTE The *most common* syntax for the chmod command uses 3 digits, from 0 to 7, but the command technically supports 4 digits (and even an entirely different *symbolic* syntax). Run the command **man chmod** for more detail.

Sharing Resources Securely

By using NTFS, Windows makes private the folders and files in a specific user's personal folders (Documents, Music, Pictures, and so on). In other words, only the user who created those documents can access those documents. Members of the Administrators group can override this behavior, but members of the Users group (standard users) cannot. To make resources available to multiple users on a shared Windows machine requires you to take extra steps and actively share.

Here's a scenario. The Snyder family has a computer in the media room that acts as a media server. It has accounts for each family member. The family could be smart and run something that makes sharing music easy, like iTunes, but they stuck with Media Player. Each user needs access to the shared collection of MP3 files.

Windows 7 makes sharing with everyone very simple through the public libraries for Documents, Music, Pictures, and Videos. Open Windows Explorer and click the down arrow next to one of the public libraries folders; for example, click the down arrow next to Music to see My Music and Public Music (see Figure 13-25). Every user can access anything saved in the Public Music folder. All of these public library folders are stored in the Public folder, C:\Users\Public.

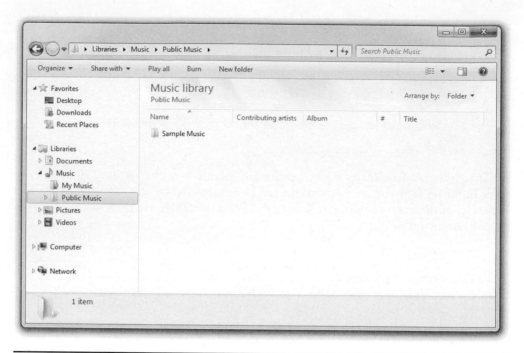

Figure 13-25 Music library

NOTE Sharing gets more interesting and complicated when you put a computer into a network setting. We'll cover network sharing and accessing of shared resources in depth in Chapter 18, "Essentials of Networking."

Windows 8/8.1/10 versions have the same public libraries as Windows 7, but they are not visible by default. Right-click on some whitespace in the navigation section (left side) of File Explorer and select Show libraries (see Figure 13-26). The public library folders show up just fine.

So, the next obvious question follows: how do you share non-library folders with one or more users on a single computer? The next sections walk through the details.

Sharing Folders and Files

The primary way to share resources on a single computer is to give users or groups NTFS permissions to specific folders and files. This process requires you to a right-click on a file or folder, select Properties, and head over to the *Security tab*. You'll notice the Security tab has two sections. The top section is a list of users and groups that currently have NTFS permissions to that folder, and the bottom section is a list of NTFS permissions for the currently selected users and groups (see Figure 13-27).

Figure 13-26
Selecting Show
libraries in File
Explorer

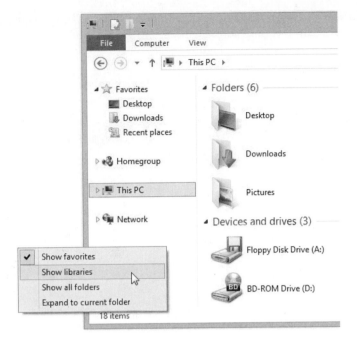

Figure 13-27
Folder Security
tab

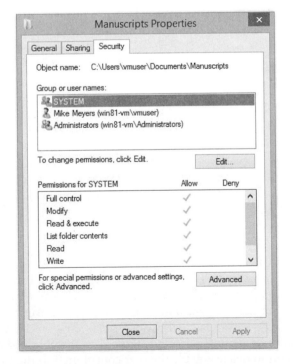

To add a new user or group, click the Edit button. In the Permissions dialog box that opens, you can not only add new users and groups but also remove them and edit existing NTFS permissions (see Figure 13-28).

Figure 13-28
Permissions
dialog box

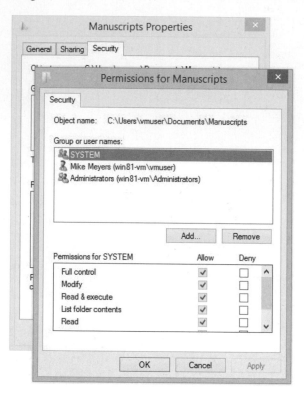

 NOTE The Sharing tab you can see in Figure 13-27 accesses the Sharing Wizard, discussed shortly. It's about network shares rather than NTFS sharing.

While the method just shown works for all versions of Windows, it's a tad old fashioned. Windows provides the *Sharing Wizard* that's less powerful but easier to use. To use this method, pick anything you want to share (even a single file) in Windows Explorer/File Explorer. Then simply right-click on it and select Share with (Windows 7/8/8.1) or Give access to (Windows 10) | Specific people. In Windows 7/8/8.1, selecting Share with | Specific people opens the File Sharing dialog box, shown in Figure 13-29, where you can select specific user accounts from a drop-down list.

Once you select a user account, you can then choose what permission level to give to that user. Note that your account is listed as Owner. You have two choices for permissions to give to others: Read and Read/Write (see Figure 13-30). *Read* simply means the user has read-only permissions. *Read/Write* gives the user read and write permissions and the permission to delete any file the user contributed to the folder.

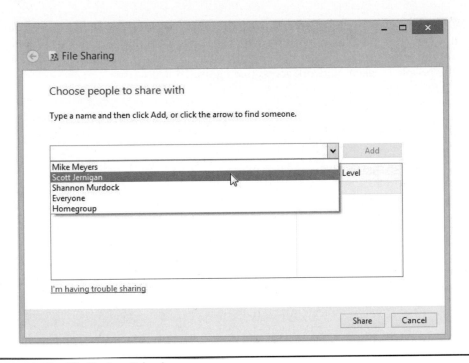

Figure 13-29 File Sharing dialog box

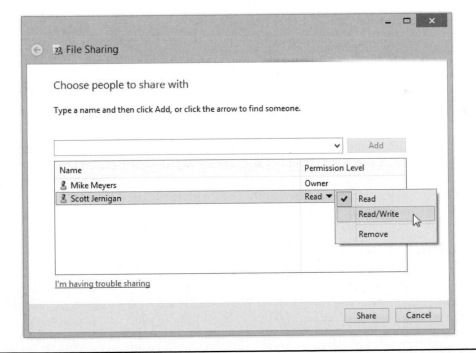

Figure 13-30 Permissions options

With Windows 10, Microsoft blurred the lines between the classic share-among-multiple-users-on-one-machine and network sharing. Note that the sharing with people follows the same process, but the dialog box that opens after selecting Give access to | Specific people is called Network access (see Figure 13-31).

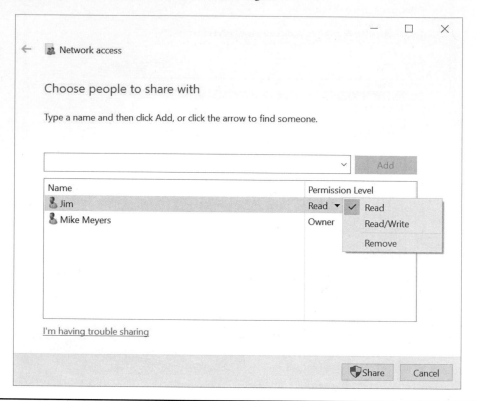

Figure 13-31   Network access dialog box in Windows 10

 NOTE   If the computer in question is on a Windows domain, the File Sharing (Windows 7/8/8.1) and Network access (Windows 10) dialog boxes let you search the network for user accounts in the domain. This makes it easy to share throughout the network. See Chapter 19, "Local Area Networking," to learn about Windows domains.

Locating Shared Folders

Before you walk away from a computer, you should check for any unnecessary or unknown (to you) shared folders on the hard drives. This enables you to make the computer as secure as possible for the user. When you look in Windows Explorer/File Explorer, shared folders don't just jump out at you, especially if they're buried deep within the file system. A shared C: drive is obvious, but a shared folder all the way down in D:\temp\backup\Simon\secret share would not be obvious, especially if none of the parent folders were shared.

Windows comes with a handy tool for locating all the shared folders on a computer, regardless of where they reside on the drives. The Computer Management console in the Administrative Tools has a Shared Folders option under System Tools. Under Shared Folders are three options: Shares, Sessions, and Open Files. Select Shares to reveal all the shared folders (see Figure 13-32).

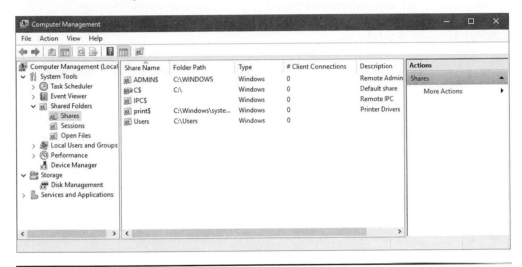

Figure 13-32 Shared Folders tool in Computer Management

You can double-click on any share to open the Properties dialog box for that folder. At that point, you can make changes to the share—such as users and permissions—just as you would from any other sharing dialog box.

Administrative Shares

A close look at the screenshot in Figure 13-32 might have left some of you with raised eyebrows and quizzical looks. What kind of share is ADMIN$ or C$?

Every version of Windows since Windows NT comes with several default shares, notably all hard drives—not optical drives or removable devices, such as thumb drives—plus the %system-root% folder (usually C:\Windows) and a couple of others, depending on the system. These *administrative shares* give local administrators administrative access to these resources, whether they log on locally or remotely. (In contrast, shares added manually are called *local shares*.)

Administrative shares are odd ducks. You cannot change the default permissions on them. You can delete them, but Windows will re-create them automatically every time you reboot. They're hidden, so they don't appear when you browse a machine over the network, though you can map them by name. Keep the administrator password safe, and these default shares won't affect the overall security of the computer.

Protecting Data with Encryption

The scrambling of data through *encryption* techniques provides the only true way to secure your data from access by any other user. Administrators can use the Take Ownership permission to seize any file or folder on a computer, even those you don't actively share. Thus, you need to implement other security measures for that data that needs to be ultra secure. Depending on the version of Windows, you have between zero and three encryptions tools: Windows Home editions have basically no security features. Advanced editions of Windows add a system that can encrypt files and folders called Encrypting File System. Finally, the most advanced editions feature drive encryption through BitLocker.

Encrypting File System

The professional editions of Windows offer a feature called the *Encrypting File System* (*EFS*), an encryption scheme that any user can use to encrypt individual files or folders on a computer.

To encrypt a file or folder takes seconds. You right-click on the file or folder you want to encrypt and select Properties. In the Properties dialog box for that object, select the General tab and click the Advanced button (see Figure 13-33) to open the Advanced Attributes dialog box. Click the checkbox next to *Encrypt contents to secure data* (see Figure 13-34). Click OK to close the Advanced Attributes dialog box and then click OK again on the Properties dialog box, and you've locked that file or folder from any user account aside from your own.

Figure 13-33
Click the
Advanced button
on the General
tab.

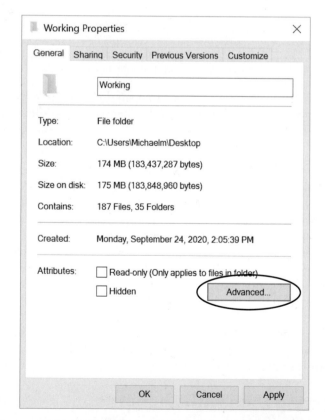

Figure 13-34
Selecting
encryption

As long as you maintain the integrity of your password, any data you encrypt by using EFS is secure from prying. That security comes at a potential price, though, and your password is the key. The Windows security database stores the password (securely, not plain text, so no worries there), but that means access to your encrypted files is based on that specific installation of Windows. If you lose your password or an administrator resets your password, you're locked out of your encrypted files permanently. There's no recovery. Also, if the computer dies and you try to retrieve your data by installing the hard drive in another system, you're likewise out of luck. Even if you have an identical user name on the new system, the security ID that defines that user account will differ from what you had on the old system.

NOTE If you use EFS, you simply must have a valid password reset disk in the event of some horrible catastrophe.

And one last caveat. If you copy an encrypted file to a drive formatted as anything but NTFS, you'll get a prompt saying that the copied file will not be encrypted. If you copy to a drive with NTFS, the encryption stays. The encrypted file—even if on a removable disk—will only be readable on your system with your login.

BitLocker Drive Encryption

Windows Ultimate and Enterprise editions and Windows 8/8.1/10 Pro offer full drive encryption through *BitLocker Drive Encryption*. BitLocker encrypts the whole drive, including every user's files, so it's not dependent on any one account. The beauty of BitLocker is that if your hard drive is stolen, such as in the case of a stolen portable computer, all the data on the hard drive is safe. The thief can't get access, even if you have a user on that system who failed to secure his or her data through EFS.

BitLocker requires a special Trusted Platform Module (TPM) chip on the motherboard to function. The TPM chip (which we looked at earlier, in Chapter 5, "Firmware") validates on boot that the computer has not changed—that you still have the same operating system installed, for example, and that the computer wasn't hacked by some malevolent program. The TPM also works in cases where you move the BitLocker drive from one system to another.

NOTE   As of Windows 10 BitLocker can use a USB flash drive to store its recovery key if you don't have a TPM chip. While this is better than nothing, you do sacrifice some of the security that a TPM chip provides.

If you have a legitimate BitLocker failure (rather than a theft) because of tampering or moving the drive to another system, you need to have a properly created and accessible recovery key or recovery password. The key or password is generally created at the time you enable BitLocker and should be kept somewhere secure, such as a printed copy in a safe or a file on a network server accessible only to administrators.

To enable BitLocker, double-click the BitLocker Drive Encryption icon in the Classic Control Panel, or select Security in Control Panel Home view and then click Turn on BitLocker (see Figure 13-35).

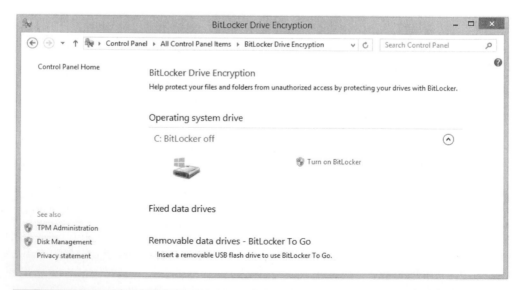

Figure 13-35   Enabling BitLocker Drive Encryption

BitLocker To Go enables you to apply BitLocker encryption to removable drives, like USB-based flash drives. Although it shares a name, BitLocker To Go applies encryption and password protection, but doesn't require a TPM chip. Still, every little bit counts when it comes to securing data.

Beyond Sharing Resources

As you've just seen, users and groups are powerful tools for authenticating users to systems as well as authorizing NTFS permissions, but that's not where their power ends. There are two more areas where we use users and groups to go beyond logging on to a system or sharing folders and files: security policies and User Account Control. Let's discuss security policies first and then cover User Account Control.

Security Policies

Security policies are rules applied to users and groups to do, well, just about everything *but* NTFS permissions. Would you like to configure your system so that the Accounting group can only log on between 9 A.M. and 5 P.M.? There's a security policy for that. How about forcing anyone who logs on to your system to use a password that's at least eight characters long? There's a security policy for that as well. Windows provides thousands of preset security policies that you may use simply by turning them on in a utility called *Local Security Policy*.

All versions of Windows have the Local Security Policy utility. You may access this tool through Control Panel | Administrative Tools | Local Security Policy, but all of us cool kids just open a command line and run **secpol.msc**. However you choose to access this tool, it will look something like Figure 13-36.

EXAM TIP Local security policies are incredibly powerful—so powerful that one could make a career out of understanding all they can do. We're covering just enough on the Local Security Policy editor to cover the few basic questions you can expect on the CompTIA A+ 220-1002 exam.

Local Security Policy has a number of containers that help organize the many types of policies on a typical system. Under each container are subcontainers or preset policies. As an example, let's set a local security policy that causes user passwords to expire every 30 days—better known as account password expiration or password age. To do this, open the Account Policies container and then open the Password Policy subcontainer.

Look at the Maximum password age setting. On almost all versions of Windows, your local user accounts passwords expire after 42 days. You can easily change this to 30 days just by double-clicking on Maximum password age and adjusting the setting in the Properties dialog box, as shown in Figure 13-37. You can also set the value to 0 and the password will never expire.

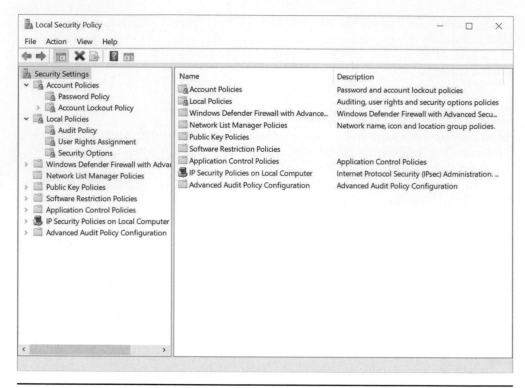

Figure 13-36   Local Security Policy utility

User Account Control

Microsoft implemented a feature in Windows called *User Account Control* (*UAC*) starting with Vista to stop unauthorized changes to Windows. These potential changes can come from installing applications or malicious software, among other things. You'd think consumers would applaud such a feature, right?

When picking the poster child for the "327 Reasons We Hated Vista" list, I'll bet most folks put Vista's UAC at the very top. Vista's UAC manifested as a pop-up dialog box that seemed to appear every time you tried to do *anything* on a Vista system (see Figure 13-38).

It's too bad that UAC got such a bad rap. Not only is UAC an important security update for all versions of Windows, both macOS and Linux/UNIX have an equivalent feature. Figure 13-39 shows the equivalent feature on a Mac.

If every other major operating system uses something like UAC, why was Microsoft slammed so hard when they unveiled UAC in Windows Vista? The reason was simple: Windows users are spoiled rotten, and until UAC came along, the vast majority of users had no idea how risky their computing behavior was.

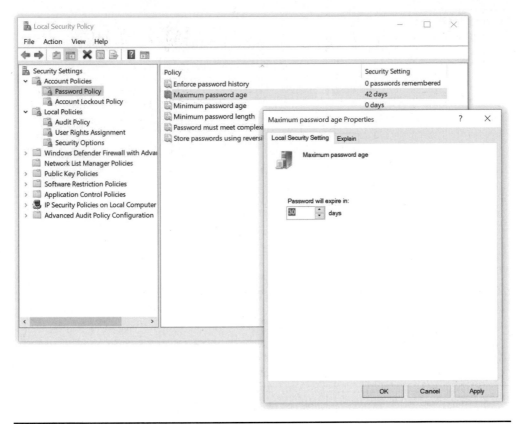

Figure 13-37 Editing Maximum password age in Local Security Policy

The problem started years ago when Microsoft created NTFS. NTFS uses robust user accounts and enables fine control over how users access files and folders—but at a cost: NTFS in its pure form is somewhat complicated.

Figure 13-38
UAC in action.
Arrgh!

Figure 13-39
UAC equivalent
on a Mac

User accounts have always been a bit of a challenge. The only account that can truly do *anything* on a Windows system is the administrator. Sure, you can configure a system with groups and assign NTFS permissions to those groups—and this is commonly done on large networks with a full-time IT staff—but what about small offices and home networks? These users almost never have the skill sets to deal with the complexities of users and groups, which often results in systems where the user accounts are all assigned administrator privileges by default—and that's when it gets dangerous (see Figure 13-40).

Figure 13-40
The danger of
administrator
privileges in the
wrong hands!

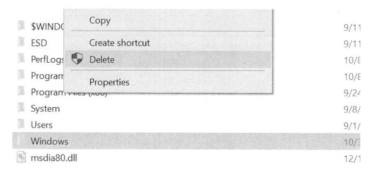

User Account Control enables users to know when they are about to do something that has serious consequences. Here are some examples of common actions that require administrator privileges:

- Installing and uninstalling applications
- Installing a driver for a device (e.g., a digital camera driver)
- Installing Windows Updates
- Adjusting Windows Firewall settings

- Changing a user's account type
- Browsing to another user's directory

Before Vista, Microsoft invented the idea of the Power Users group to give users almost all the power of an administrator account (to handle most of the situations just described) without actually giving users the full power of the account. Assigning a user to the Power Users group still required someone who knew how to do this, however, so most folks at the small office/home level simply ignored the Power Users group (see Figure 13-41).

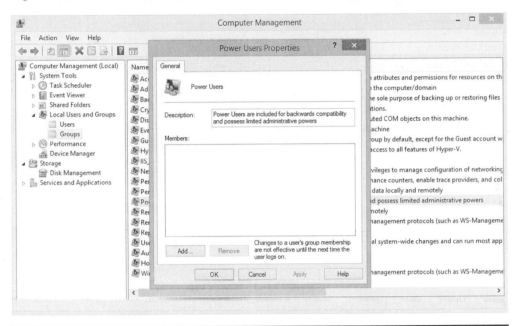

Figure 13-41   Power Users group—almost never used at the small office/home level

Clearly, Microsoft needed a better method to prevent people from running programs that they should not run. If users have the correct privileges, however—or the ability to "escalate" their privileges to that of an administrator—then they should be able to do what they need to do as simply as possible. Microsoft needed to make the following changes:

- The idea of using an administrator account for daily use needed to go away.
- Any level of account should be able to do anything as easily as possible.
- If a regular account wants to do something that requires administrator privileges, the user of the regular account will need to enter the administrator password.
- If a user with administrator privileges wants to run something that requires administrator privileges, the user will not have to reenter his or her password, but the user will have to respond to an "Are you sure?"–type dialog box so he or she appreciates the gravity of the action—thus, the infamous UAC dialog box.

NOTE Both Linux and macOS have a UAC command-line function called *sudo*. Check it out in Chapter 15.

How UAC Works

UAC works for both standard user accounts and administrator accounts. If a standard user attempts to do something that requires administrator privileges, he or she sees a UAC dialog box that prompts for the administrator password (see Figure 13-42).

Figure 13-42
Prompting for
an administrator
password in
Windows 10

NOTE The official name for the UAC dialog box is the "UAC consent prompt."

If a user with administrator privileges attempts to do something that requires administrator privileges, a simpler UAC dialog box appears, like the one shown in Figure 13-43.

UAC uses small shield icons to warn you ahead of time that it will prompt you before certain tasks, as shown in Figure 13-44. Microsoft updated this somewhat redundant feature in subsequent versions of Windows after Vista, as you'll soon see.

UAC gives users running a program an opportunity to consider their actions before they move forward. It's a good thing, but spoiled Windows users aren't accustomed to something that makes them consider their actions. As a result, one of the first things everyone learned how to do when Vista came out was to turn off UAC. While it's all but impossible to truly shut down UAC, reducing the impact of UAC is easy.

Figure 13-43
Classic UAC
prompt

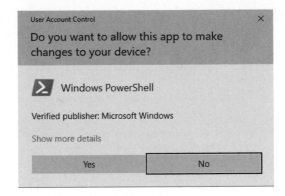

Figure 13-44 Shield icons in User Accounts

UAC in Modern Windows

Microsoft may be a huge company, but it still knows how to react when its customers speak out about features they don't like. Windows 7 unveiled a more refined, less "in-your-face" UAC that makes the feature much easier to use. This is the version of UAC used in all later versions of Windows as well.

A More Granular UAC

Microsoft did some research on why UAC drove users nuts, concluding that the problem wasn't UAC itself but the "I'm constantly in your face or you can turn me off and you get no help at all" aspect. To make UAC less aggressive, Microsoft introduced four UAC levels. To see these levels, start typing **user account control** in the search field and select the option to Change User Account Control settings to open the Control Panel app (see Figure 13-45). This is Windows 10. You can also go to the User Accounts applet in Control Panel and select Change User Account Control settings, as shown in Figure 13-46. When you select this option, you see the dialog box in Figure 13-45. (This option applies to Windows 7/8/8.1/10.)

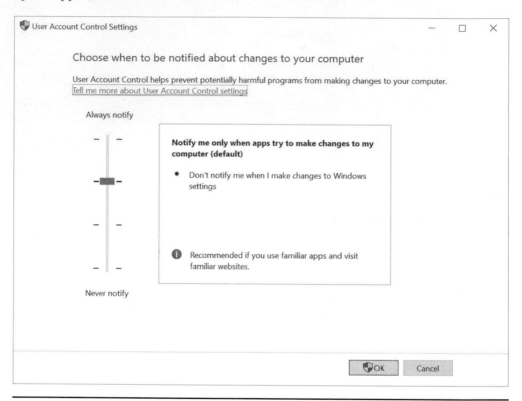

Figure 13-45 Four levels of UAC

Figure 13-46 Change User Account Control settings option in Windows 7

In Figure 13-45, you can see a slider with four levels. The top level (Always notify) means you want UAC to work exactly as it does in Vista, displaying the aggressive consent form every time you do anything that typically requires administrator access. The bottom option (Never notify) turns off UAC. The two levels in the middle are new and are very similar. Both do the following:

- Don't notify me when I make changes to Windows settings.
- Notify me only when apps/programs try to make changes to my computer.

The only difference is in *how* they show the change. The second-from-top level will display the typical consent form, but only when apps/programs try to make changes. The third-from-top level displays a consent form, but where the normal consent form dims your desktop and doesn't allow you to do anything but address the form, this consent form just pops up like a normal dialog box.

 EXAM TIP Make sure you know what each of the four UAC levels does.

Program Changes Versus Changes I Make

So, what's the difference between a program making a change and you making a change? Look at Figure 13-47. In this case, Windows 7 is set to the second-from-top option. A program (the very safe and, judging by the color of the banner, verified) Adobe Download Manager is attempting to install a feature into Internet Explorer. Because this is a program trying to make changes, the UAC consent form appears and darkens the desktop. If you lower the UAC to the third-from-top option, you still see a consent form, but now it acts like a typical dialog box.

Figure 13-47
Darkened UAC

EXAM TIP The default behavior for UAC in Windows is the second-from-top option, which results in a screen similar to Figure 13-47.

A program such as the Adobe program described earlier is very different from a feature *you* want to change. Notice the shields, as shown in earlier figures.

Each of these options isn't a program—each is merely a feature built into Windows. Those shields tell you that clicking the feature next to a shield will require administrator privileges. If you were to pick the Vista-strength UAC option, you'd get a UAC consent prompt when you click one of those features. If you set UAC to any of the three lower settings, however, you'd go straight to that feature without *any* form of UAC consent prompt. Of course, this isn't true if you don't have administrator privileges. If you're a standard user, you'll still be prompted for a password, just as in Vista.

Overall, the improvements to UAC in Windows 7 and later show that it has a place on everyone's computer. UAC might cause an occasional surprise or irritation, but that one more "Are you sure?" could mean the difference between safe and unsafe computing.

Chapter Review

Questions

1. Which tool or mechanism defines what resources a user may access and what he or she may do with those resources?

   A. Authentication through user accounts and passwords

   B. Authorization through user accounts and passwords

   C. Authentication through NTFS

   D. Authorization through NTFS

2. Which is the best password for the user Joy, who has a pet named Fido and a birth date of January 8, 1982?

   A. joy1982

   B. joylovesfido

   C. 1982cutie

   D. oddvr88*

3. How can you encrypt an entire drive, including files and folders belonging to other users?

   A. EFS

   B. User Account Control

   C. Administrative Shares

   D. BitLocker

4. What feature in Windows 7 opens a consent prompt for standard users to enter administrator credentials to accomplish various tasks reserved for the latter group?

    A. User Access Command

    B. User Access Control

    C. User Account Command

    D. User Account Control

5. Which permission enables an administrator to change the ownership of a file without knowing the user account password for that file?

    A. Change permission

    B. Change Ownership permission

    C. Ownership permission

    D. Take Ownership permission

6. You copy a file from a folder on a hard drive formatted as NTFS, with permissions set to Read for everyone, to a USB thumb drive formatted as FAT32. What effective permissions does the copy of the file have?

    A. Read-only for everyone.

    B. Full Control for everyone.

    C. None.

    D. You can't copy a file from an NTFS drive to a FAT32 drive.

7. Which of the following commands is used to change file permissions in Linux?

    A. chmod

    B. chown

    C. users

    D. pwn

8. Which tool in Windows 8.1 enables you to create a new user account based on a global Microsoft account?

    A. User Accounts in Control Panel

    B. Users and Groups in Control Panel

    C. Settings charm

    D. Users charm

9. Which option enables you to share files easily among multiple users on a single Windows system?

    A. Place the files in the Public libraries.

    B. Place the files in the Public Shares.

    C. Place the files in the EFS folders.

    D. You cannot. Windows locks down sharing on a single system.

10. Which of the following file systems enables you to encrypt files, thus making them unviewable by any account but your own?

    A. EFS

    B. FAT

    C. FAT32

    D. OSR

Answers

1. **D.** Authorization through NTFS defines resources a user may access and what he or she can do with those resources.

2. **D.** Of the choices listed, oddvr88* would be the best password; it has a non-alphanumeric character, which makes it more difficult for a hacker to crack.

3. **D.** BitLocker Drive Encryption enables you to encrypt an entire drive, including files and folders belonging to other users.

4. **D.** The User Account Control feature in Windows 7 provides a consent prompt for standard users to enter administrator credentials to accomplish various tasks normally reserved for the Administrators group.

5. **D.** The Take Ownership permission enables an administrator to change the ownership of a file without knowing the user account password for that file.

6. **C.** The key here is that you are copying from an NTFS hard drive to a FAT32 USB drive. Copying from an NTFS-based partition to a FAT- or exFAT-based partition creates two copies of the object; the copy of the object in the new location has no effective permissions at all.

7. **A.** The chmod command enables you to change file permissions in Linux.

8. **C.** The Settings charm in Windows 8.1 enables you to create a new user account based on a global Microsoft account.

9. **A.** The Public libraries make it easy to share files among multiple users of a single system.

10. **A.** The Encrypting File System (EFS) enables you to encrypt files, making them unviewable by any account but your own.

Maintaining and Optimizing Operating Systems

In this chapter, you will learn how to
- Perform operating system maintenance tasks
- Optimize operating systems
- Prepare for problems

Every computer running a modern operating system (OS) requires both occasional optimization to keep the system running snappily and ongoing maintenance to make sure nothing goes wrong. Microsoft, Apple, and the many Linux developers use decades of experience with operating systems to search for ways to make the tasks of maintaining and optimizing surprisingly easy and very automatic, but there's still plenty to do to keep things humming along.

This chapter covers maintenance and optimization, so let's make sure you know what these two terms mean. *Maintenance* means jobs you do from time to time to keep the OS running well, such as running mass storage drive utilities. CompTIA sees *optimization* as changes you make to a system to make it better—a good example is adding RAM. This chapter covers the standard maintenance and optimization activities performed on Windows, macOS, and Linux, and the tools techs use to perform them.

Even the best maintained, most perfectly optimized computer is going to run into trouble. Hard drives crash, naïve coworkers delete files, and those super great new video card drivers sometimes fail. The secret isn't to try to avoid trouble, because trouble will find you, but rather to make sure you're ready to deal with problems when they arise. This is one area that very few users do well, and it's our job as techs to make recovery from trouble as painless as possible. OS developers give us plenty of tools to prepare for problems—we just need to make sure we use them.

NOTE This chapter covers maintenance and optimization techniques for all the operating systems currently on the CompTIA A+ exams. But, like the exams and the reality of market share, Windows features a lot more than macOS or Linux.

1002

Maintaining Operating Systems

Operating systems need patching; mass storage devices must be kept organized and running well. Registries and temporary files need the occasional cleaning. In the past many of these jobs were handled manually. Today, operating systems handle many if not most of these jobs automatically. This section looks at the most common maintenance jobs techs do on systems. It finishes with a discussion on making customized tools for maintaining Windows.

Patch Management

There's no such thing as a perfect operating system. First, all operating system makers come up with new or improved features. Second, bad actors discover weaknesses and generate malware to take advantage of those weaknesses. The process of keeping software updated in a safe and timely fashion is known as *patch management*. From the moment Microsoft releases a new version of Windows, malware attacks, code errors, new hardware, new features, and many other issues compel Microsoft to provide updates, known more generically as *patches*, to the operating system. Patch management isn't only for Windows. Both macOS and Linux require patch management, and I'll cover those needs as well.

Windows Patch Management

Microsoft's primary distribution tool for handling patch management is a Settings tool or Control Panel applet called *Windows Update*. In its two-decade+ history, Windows Update has gone through many iterations; fortunately CompTIA cares only that you know how it works on Windows 7 and newer.

In Windows 7, Windows Update separates fixes into distinct types: updates and service packs. *Updates* in Windows 7 are individual fixes that come out fairly often, on the order of once a week or so. Individual updates are usually fairly small, rarely more than a few megabytes. A *service pack* is a large bundle of updates plus anything else Microsoft might choose to add. Service packs are invariably large (hundreds of megabytes) and are often packaged with Windows, as shown in Figure 14-1.

With Windows 8 Microsoft ditched the service pack terminology and uses only updates to indicate changes. Microsoft did release one big update that could be construed as a service pack, called 8.1. It was only available through the then new app store that was added in Windows 8.

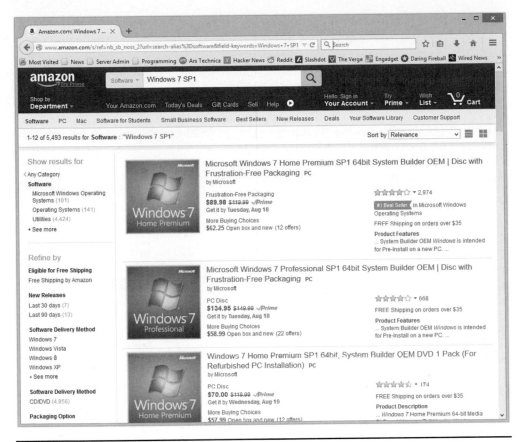

Figure 14-1   Windows 7 with Service Pack 1 (#1 Best Seller   back in the day)

EXAM TIP   You might be asked about installing updates on the CompTIA A+ exams. Pay attention to the steps listed here.

Windows Update checks your system, grabs the updates, and patches your system automatically. Even if you don't want to allow Windows Update to run automatically, it'll nag you about updates until you patch your system (and you really should). Microsoft provides Windows Update for all versions of Windows.

Windows Update can run automatically, so you'll probably see new updates to install every time you open the applet. Windows 7 divides updates into three common types:

- **Important**   These updates address security or stability issues and are the most critical. You can configure Windows Update to install these updates automatically.

- **Recommended**   A recommended update is an added feature or enhancement that is not critical. You can configure Windows Update to install these updates automatically.

- **Optional**   These include device drivers, language packs, and other nonessential updates. You must install these updates manually.

EXAM TIP   Windows Update only updates the OS and drivers. It never touches the firmware—BIOS or UEFI—of your computer.

Figure 14-2 shows you what Windows Update looks like in Windows 7. Note that the Important update is Windows 7 Service Pack 1.

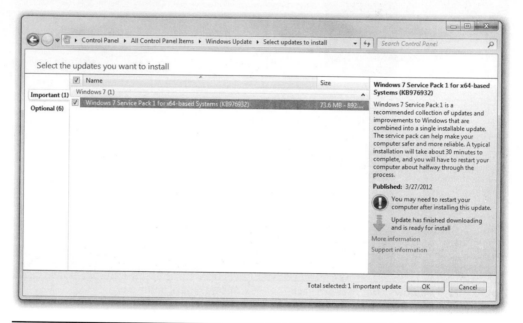

Figure 14-2   Windows Update in Windows 7

NOTE   All Windows 10 updates download and install automatically by default and you cannot selectively choose individual updates to download.

Installing an update is as easy as selecting the updates you want to install and clicking OK. If you don't want to install a specific update, and don't want to look at it every time you open Windows Update, you can hide it. To hide an update, right-click the update you wish to hide and select Hide update (see Figure 14-3).

Windows Update got a fresh coat of paint in Windows 8 with the PC settings app. The PC settings app is a touch-friendly alternative to the traditional tiny-buttoned Control Panel applet, but gives you access to the same options as the Control Panel applet (see Figure 14-4).

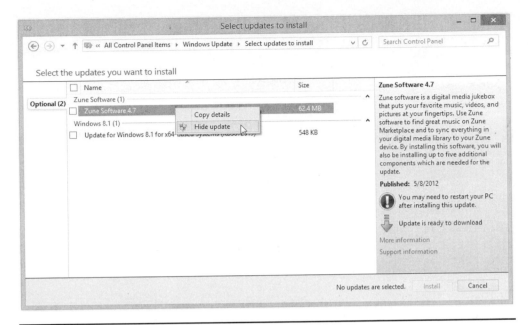

Figure 14-3 Hiding an update

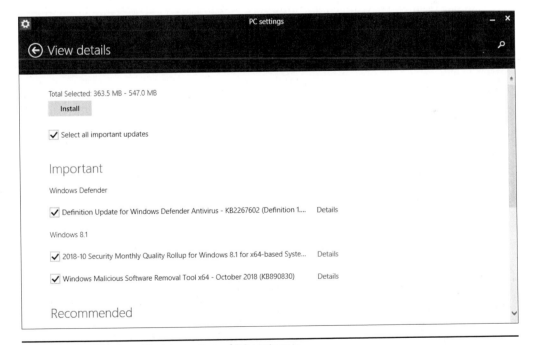

Figure 14-4 Windows Update section of PC settings

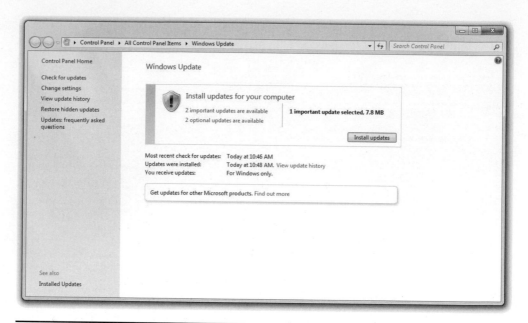

Figure 14-5   Windows 7 Windows Update Control Panel applet

Fortunately, the PC settings app didn't replace the Windows Update Control Panel applet. Figure 14-5 shows the Windows 7 Windows Update; compare with the Windows 8.1 Windows Update in Figure 14-6. Note the strong similarity.

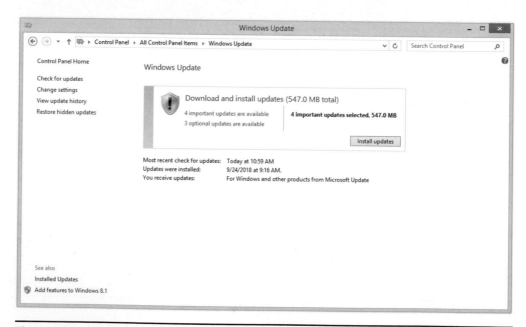

Figure 14-6   Windows 8.1 Windows Update Control Panel applet

You can review installed updates by clicking View update history. To remove an update requires using the Program and Features Control Panel applet. Click View installed updates on the left to get to the *Uninstall an update* screen (see Figure 14-7).

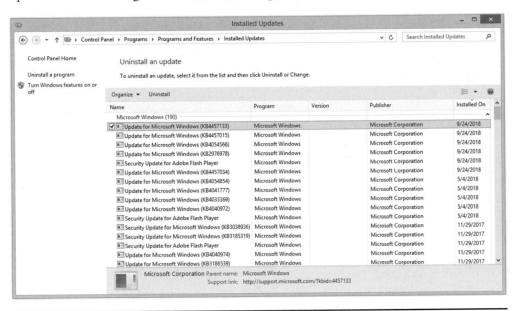

Figure 14-7 Windows 8.1 Uninstall an update

While Windows 8's changes to Windows Update were primarily cosmetic, Windows 10 introduced major structural changes to Windows Update. Windows 10 does not have a Windows Update Control Panel applet. If you want to make changes to Windows updates, you must go to Settings | Windows Update (see Figure 14-8). Note that two items are missing.

First, individual users can't turn off updates, part of the *Windows as a service* model that Microsoft uses with Windows 10. A user may only pause updates for up to 35 days, but cannot skip or hide updates. Users do not completely lack control though; you can set Active hours to tell Windows when it can reboot to install the latest updates.

Second, Windows 10 did away with critical, recommended, and optional updates and replaced them with quality and feature updates. *Quality updates* are the classic patches that you know and love, with one twist: they are now cumulative. Each update includes all the changes from all previous quality updates. This cuts down on the update, reboot, update again drudgery of installing Windows from scratch.

Feature updates are a whole new beast. These "updates" are really new versions of Windows and they are released twice a year in the spring and fall. Here is a rundown of key points you need to know about feature updates.

- They are a reinstall of Windows.
- They are named by year and month, such as 1703, 1709, 1803, and 1809; and they have marketing names, like *Creators update* or *October 2018 update*.

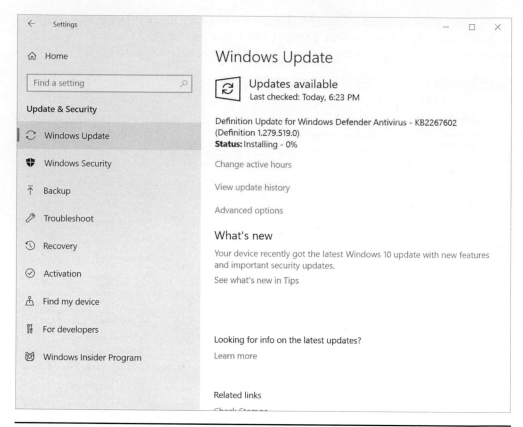

Figure 14-8   Windows 10 Windows Update

- They are controlled by what channel you are on: Insiders, Semi-Annual Channel (Targeted), Semi-Annual Channel, or Long-Term Servicing Branch. The LTSB is only available in the Enterprise license.

Although users cannot prevent Windows updates, users may uninstall some non-system updates using Programs and Features | View installed updates in the Control Panel, just as in Windows 7 and Windows 8/8.1.

Patch Management in macOS and Linux

Like Windows, both macOS and Linux take an automated approach to patching and alert you when software needs updating. With macOS 10.13, for example, you access updates through the *App Store* pane in System Preferences (see Figure 14-9). Most desktop-focused Linux distros have a GUI updating tool like the Software Updater in Ubuntu (see Figure 14-10).

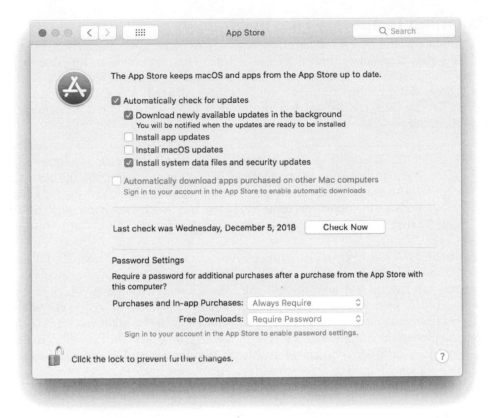

Figure 14-9   App Store update options

Figure 14-10   Software Updater in Ubuntu Linux

Managing Temporary Files in Windows

You should run the *Disk Cleanup* utility regularly to make sure you've cleared out the junk files that accumulate from daily use. All that late-night Web surfing doesn't just use up time; it also uses up disk space, leaving behind hundreds of temporary Internet files. Those, and other bits and pieces (such as those "deleted" files still hanging around in your Recycle Bin), can add up to a lot of wasted drive space if you don't periodically clean them out.

NOTE   The latest versions of Windows 10 use a feature called *Storage sense* to manage files. You can use it instead of Disk Cleanup, although the older tool is also available. You'll only see Disk Cleanup on the CompTIA A+ 1002 exam because the objectives came out before the switch to Storage sense. Storage sense intelligently removes unnecessary files for you.

Access an HDD or SSD in File Explorer, right-click, and select Properties. Click the Disk Cleanup button on the General tab to run it. The application first calculates the space you can free up and then displays the Disk Cleanup dialog box, which tells you how much disk space it can free up—the total amount possible as well as the amount you'll get from each category of files it checks. Windows will also ask if you want to clean up all the files on the computer or just your files. In Figure 14-11, the list of files to delete has a couple of categories checked; also listed is the amount of disk space to be gained by allowing Disk Cleanup to delete these files. As you select and deselect choices, watch this value change.

Figure 14-11
Disk Cleanup
dialog box

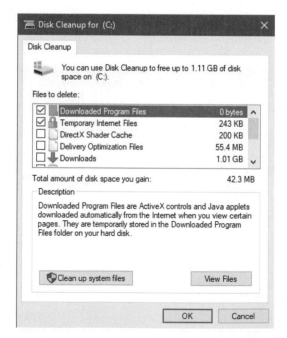

If you scroll down through the list, you will see a choice to compress old files. What do you know—Disk Cleanup does more than just delete files! In fact, this file compression trick is where Disk Cleanup really, uh, cleans up. This is one of the few choices where you will gain the most space. The other big heavyweight category is Temporary Internet Files, which Disk Cleanup will delete. Try Disk Cleanup on a computer that gets hours of Internet use every day and you'll be pleased with the results.

NOTE Just because you can get back disk space does not mean that using Disk Cleanup is a free lunch. Cleaning many of these options, like the selected-by-default Image Thumbnails, can cause your computer to run a little slow until Windows rebuilds those caches.

Registry Maintenance

The Registry is a huge database that Windows updates every time you add a new application or hardware or make changes to existing applications or hardware. As a result, the Registry tends to be clogged with entries that are no longer valid. These usually don't cause any problems directly, but they can slow down your system. Interestingly, Microsoft does not provide a utility to clean up the Registry. To clean your Registry, you need to turn to a third-party utility. Quite a few Registry cleaner programs are out there, but my favorite is the freeware CCleaner by Piriform (see Figure 14-12). You can download the latest copy at www.piriform.com/ccleaner/. (Pay attention when downloading and installing not to add extra programs, just get the free version—unless you want tech support from Piriform; then by all means support the company with some cash.)

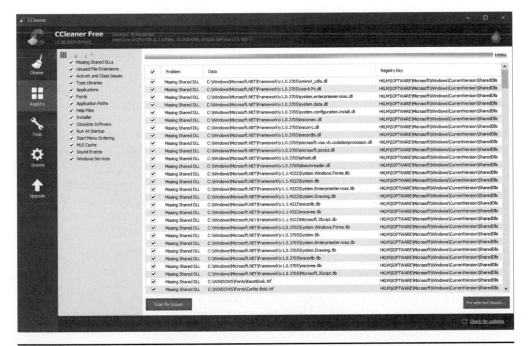

Figure 14-12 CCleaner Registry Cleaner

Before you start cleaning your Registry with wild abandon, keep in mind that all Registry cleaners are risky in that they may delete something you want in the Registry. Because Microsoft makes changes to the Registry for every version of Windows, make sure your utility supports the Windows version you're running. This is especially true for any 64-bit version of Windows!

 NOTE CCleaner also helps clean all of the most common Web browsers and a number of popular applications.

Disk Maintenance Utilities

Every modern OS has one or more utilities designed to maintain hard disk drives (HDDs) and solid-state drives (SSDs), though Windows requires a little more manual action than macOS or Linux. Let's look at all three.

 EXAM TIP Performance-based exam questions will likely test your knowledge of the various OS-related tools listed in the CompTIA objectives and in this chapter. Given a scenario, be sure you know what tool to use, where to find it, and how to achieve the desired result.

Error Checking and Disk Defragmentation in Windows

Keeping drives healthy and happy is a key task for every tech. Error checking and Disk Defragmenter, discussed way back in Chapter 9, "Implementing Mass Storage," are the key Windows maintenance tools used to accomplish this task.

When you can't find a software reason (and there are many possible ones) for a problem such as a system freezing on shutdown, the problem might be the actual physical mass storage drive. You can test the drive with *Error checking*. You can run Error checking by using the *chkdsk* command from an elevated command prompt. Alternatively, you can run Error checking through the GUI by opening Computer, Explorer, or File Explorer (depending on the OS), right-clicking on the drive you want to check, selecting Properties, and then clicking the Tools tab. Click *Check now* (in Windows 7) or *Check* (in Windows 8 forward) to have Error checking scan the drive for problems with the file system and repair them if possible (see Figure 14-13).

Disk Defragmenter (in Windows 7) or Optimize Drives (in Windows 8 forward) keeps hard drives running efficiently by reorganizing files scattered into pieces on your hard drive into tight, linear complete files (see Figure 14-14). Long ago Disk Defragmenter was a manual process. Today, current versions of Windows run Disk Defragmenter/Optimize Drives automatically by default on HDDs. You can access Optimize Drives by right-clicking on a drive and selecting Properties | Tools tab | and either Defragment now or Optimize Drives.

Error checking and Disk Defragmenter/Optimize Drives are such critical maintenance features that you really should have them run automatically. Let's glance at macOS and Linux tools, then look at scheduling.

Figure 14-13
Error checking in
Windows 10

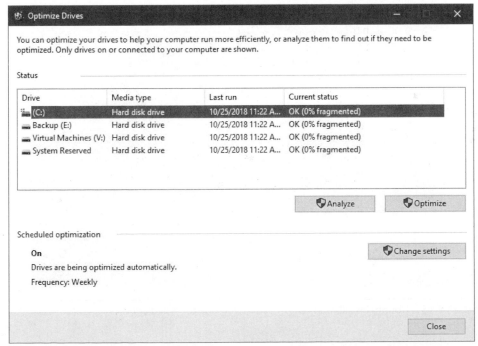

Figure 14-14   Optimize Drives in Windows 10

NOTE SSDs are optimized completely differently than HDDs. Luckily, all operating systems know this and handle drive optimization for each type of mass storage automatically.

Disk Utility in macOS

macOS handles disk maintenance chores automatically, just like Windows. If you need to error check your disk, macOS includes the *Disk Utility*, Apple's disk maintenance utility/tool that combines error checking with partitioning and other disk management tasks. To check a disk for problems, select the disk and click the First Aid button.

Linux Options

Just about every Linux distro offers one or more disk maintenance utilities, plus you can download a ton of really good applications for free. The best option for most techs is to use the diagnostic tool on the installation media. Reboot with the installation media in the drive. In some installation discs/flash media, you'll see a little keyboard icon that, when you press ENTER, shows you options to try, install, check disk for defects, test memory, and more (see Figure 14-15). Another option is to download the everything-but-the-kitchen-sink utility package, Ultimate Boot CD. Get it here: www.ultimatebootcd.com.

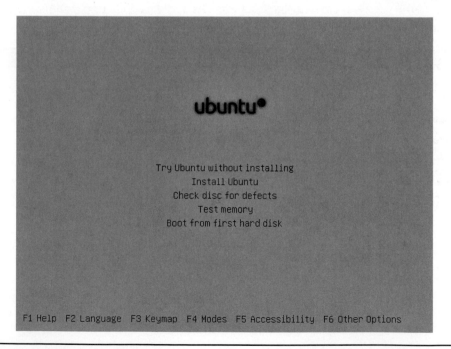

Figure 14-15 Ubuntu installation options, including one for disk diagnosis

Scheduling Maintenance

Maintenance only works properly when you do it at regular intervals. Depending on the version of Windows installed, for example, you can schedule maintenance jobs to run automatically. The CompTIA A+ 220-1002 exam objectives define two areas for you to consider for scheduled maintenance: backups and disk maintenance.

Windows Task Scheduler

Current versions of Windows use a single Administrative Tool, *Task Scheduler*, to schedule maintenance. You can choose an executable program and define when you want that program to run. The key to running scheduled maintenance is to know the names of the executable programs and any special switches you may need to enter.

Task Scheduler divides tasks into triggers, actions, and conditions. *Triggers* are actions or schedules that start a program. *Actions* are steps that define both the program to run and how it is to run. *Conditions* are extra criteria that must be met for the program to run. (Is the system idle? Is it connected to the Internet?) Figure 14-16 shows the Conditions tab for Disk Defragmenter. To create a basic task, all you need to do is name it, set how often it should run, and decide what it should do.

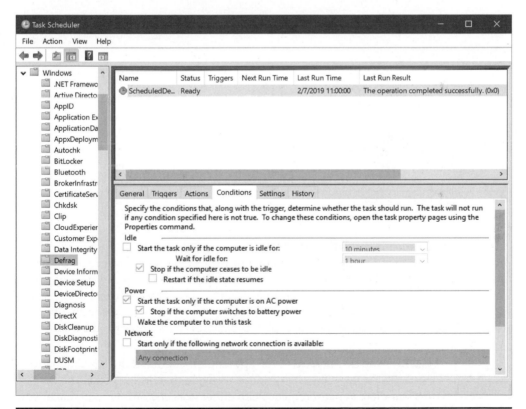

Figure 14-16   Conditions tab in Windows 10 Task Scheduler

Many Windows utilities include built-in scheduling options. Here's the twist, though: they're still using Task Scheduler, although Windows blocks users from editing many of these built-in scheduled programs. If you want to modify the automated defragmentation from within Disk Defragmenter, for example, you can open up Task Scheduler and see it listed as a scheduled task; but to change it you must use the dialog box from the Optimize Drives feature (Figure 14-17).

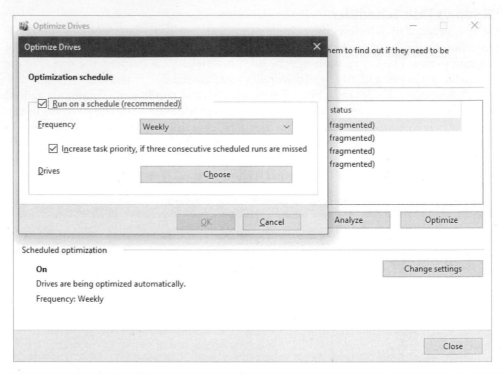

Figure 14-17   Optimize Drives scheduler

macOS and Linux: launchd and cron

macOS and most Linux distributions use one of two scripting tools to run all sorts of tasks automatically in the background. Apple developed *launchd* for automation; most Linux distros use the more universal and older *cron*. Although you can create custom launchd and cron jobs, the details on making custom scripts go way beyond CompTIA A+, so I'll leave them out here. Just remember the names of the tools for the exam.

 EXAM TIP   You do *not* have to run any kind of scheduled drive maintenance on macOS. (In fact, Disk Utility doesn't provide that option at all.) The OS runs scans late at night regularly and either fixes any problems or makes you aware of them when you next access the Mac.

Scheduling Backups in Windows

Backing up critical files is an important part of maintaining any operating system. Every operating system comes with some form of backup utility to copy important files to extra hard drives, thumb drives, over the network, or to the cloud.

The backup utility in Windows varies depending on your version of the OS: in Windows 7, it's called Backup and Restore; Windows 8/8.1/10 use a tool called File History (Windows 10 retains Backup and Restore for restore only). You'll learn more about each of these tools later in the chapter, but for right now, since we're discussing scheduling, let's talk about scheduling backups of your data, something necessary in Windows 7 and handy in later versions of Windows.

All backup tools have two important steps. First, you choose which files to back up. Second, you choose when these backups take place using some form of scheduling. Windows 10's File History applet includes a scheduler, too. Near the end of the Set up backup wizard, after you've turned on File History and selected a backup medium, you click on Advanced Settings to set when and how often you want Windows to create the backup (see Figure 14-18). It's that easy.

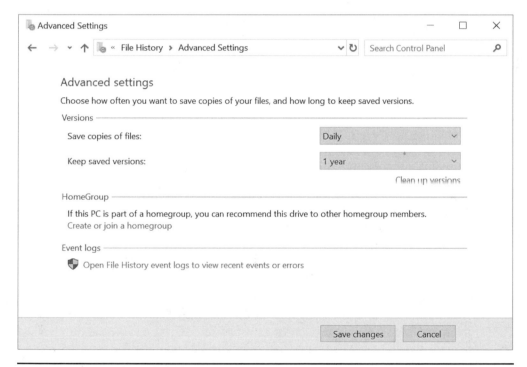

Figure 14-18 File History scheduling

How often should you back up your files on the older versions of Windows? If you create new documents, download music, and take lots of digital photos, you'll want to back up your files hourly. If you're a casual, Internet-browsing, Solitaire-playing PC user, you're probably safe making a new backup once a day.

Controlling Autostarting Software

A lot of software loads when you boot up any computing device, such as small programs that provide support for the various functions of the operating system. These small programs are called *services*. As you add applications and peripherals to a system, more software loads automatically at startup. Most of the time these autostarting programs are welcome—you want that latest peripheral to work, right? Sometimes, though, autostarting programs cause problems and need to be stopped, either temporarily or from loading at all.

Every OS gives you the capability to stop autostarting applications, processes, and services. Windows has two tools, System Configuration and Task Manager. Apple discourages startup programs, but each user account will have certain login items that load. To manage those, use the Users & Groups pane in System Preferences. In Linux, check the Startup Applications folder for automatic programs.

System Configuration

Techs use the *System Configuration utility* (also known by its executable name, *msconfig*) in Windows 7 to edit and troubleshoot operating system and program startup processes and services. From Windows 8 on, you can make these changes from the Task Manager.

To start the System Configuration utility, go the Start | Search bar, enter **msconfig**, and click OK or press ENTER. The program runs after you provide the necessary credentials, depending on the User Account Control (UAC) setup.

The System Configuration utility offers a number of handy features, distributed across the following tabs:

- **General** Select the type of startup you would like to use for the next boot (see Figure 14-19). You can perform a normal startup with all device drivers and services launching normally, a diagnostic startup with only basic devices and services, or a selective startup where you choose whether to load system services, startup items, or use original boot configuration.

- **Boot** This tab contains advanced boot features. Here you can see every copy of Windows you have installed, set a default OS, or delete an OS from the boot menu. You can set up a safe boot, or adjust advanced options like the number of cores or amount of memory to use. Selecting Safe boot, by the way, will force Windows to start in Safe mode on every reboot until you deselect it. *Safe mode* loads minimal, generic, trusted drivers and is used for troubleshooting purposes. It's better to use the F8 key to get into Safe mode (Windows 7 only), but see Chapter 16, "Troubleshooting Operating Systems," for troubleshooting issues.

Figure 14-19   Windows 7 System Configuration utility

- **Services**   This tab is similar to the Services tab in the Task Manager. You can enable or disable any or all services running on your PC.

- **Startup**   This tab enables you to toggle on or off any startup programs (programs that load when you launch Windows). This is perhaps the most useful tab, especially if Windows is slow to load on your PC.

- **Tools**   This tab lists many of the tools and utilities available in Windows, including Event Viewer, Performance Monitor, Command Prompt, and so on. There's nothing here that you can't find elsewhere in Windows, but it's a handy list all the same.

NOTE   Windows 10 has the System Configuration utility, but the Startup tab redirects you to the Task Manager.

Task Manager

Microsoft placed the Startup applications and services in the *Task Manager* (press CTRL-SHIFT-ESC) in Windows 8/8.1/10. You can readily see the status (enabled or disabled) of each application and a handy guide to the startup impact that program has (see Figure 14-20). As you might imagine, programs that require syncing of a lot of files across the Internet will have a higher impact than applications that just load local files.

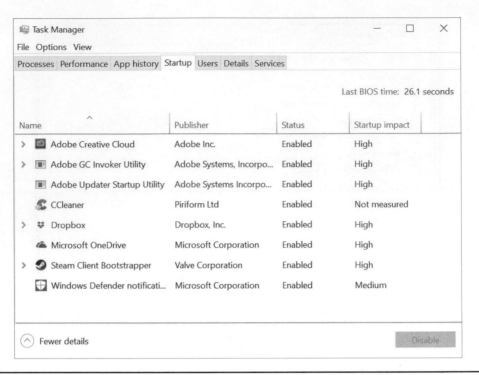

Figure 14-20   Startup tab in Task Manager

To enable or disable an application, right-click and select one of those options. When you reboot the system next, the behavior of the application will be changed according to your previous action.

SIM   Nervous about using the Task Manager? Check out the excellent Chapter 14 Click! sim, "Manage Tasks with Task Manager," at http://totalsem .com/100x. You'll get a very nice walkthrough with no risk to your system.

Users & Groups in macOS

In the Users & Groups pane of System Preferences, you can readily select or deselect any application that might load with specific user accounts (see Figure 14-21). There's not a lot more to say about the process, so I'll throw in some filler words for fun. macOS is easy to use and maintain because Apple exercises extreme control over the platform.

NOTE   You know the importance of users and groups in Windows from Chapter 13, "Users, Groups, and Permissions."

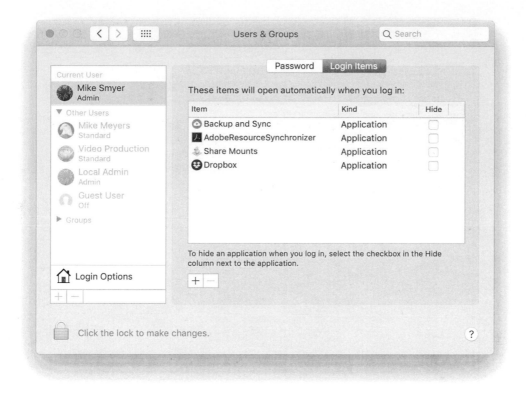

Figure 14-21   Login Items in Users & Groups pane

Startup Applications Preferences in Ubuntu Linux

With Ubuntu Linux, you can access the Startup Applications Preferences dialog box by clicking the Search button (top left of screen, on the Unity bar) and starting to type **startup**. When the Startup Applications icon appears, click it. From there, you deselect the check box next to a program you don't want to start at boot and you're done (see Figure 14-22).

Handy Windows Administration Tools

Microsoft includes a couple of handy tools in each version of Windows. This section explores System Information and the MMC.

System Information

Windows comes with a built-in utility known as the *System Information tool* (see Figure 14-23) that collects information about hardware resources, components, and the software environment. When it finishes doing that, it provides a tidy little report, enabling you to troubleshoot and diagnose any issues and conflicts. As with many other

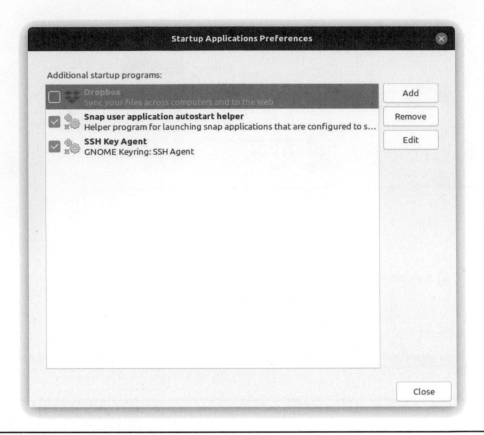

Figure 14-22 Disabling an autostarting program in Startup Applications Preferences

tools, you can access this tool from the Start | Search bar; simply enter **msinfo32**. The CompTIA A+ exams also refer to System Information by its executable, *msinfo32*.

Note that you can use System Information to gather information about remote computers by selecting View | Remote Computer and then entering the remote computer's network machine name. Under Tools, you even get quick access to System Restore and the DirectX Diagnostic Tool, a tool for checking your video card that Chapter 17, "Display Technologies," discusses.

Microsoft Management Console

The *Microsoft Management Console* (*MMC*) is a shell program in Windows that holds individual utilities called *snap-ins*, designed for administration and troubleshooting. The apps in Administrative Tools are preconfigured MMCs, for example. You can also create customized MMCs for your task needs.

To start an MMC, select Start | Search bar in Windows 7 or start typing from the Start screen in Windows 8 or later. Type **mmc** and press ENTER to get a blank MMC. Blank MMCs aren't much to look at (see Figure 14-24).

Figure 14-23 System Information

You make a blank MMC console useful by adding snap-ins, which include most of the utilities you use in Windows. Even Device Manager is a snap-in. You can add as many snap-ins as you like, and you have many to choose from.

To add the Device Manager snap-in in the blank MMC, for example, select File | Add/Remove Snap-ins. In the Add or Remove Snap-ins dialog box, you will see a list of available snap-ins (see Figure 14-25). Select Device Manager in the list; click the Add

Figure 14-24 Blank MMC

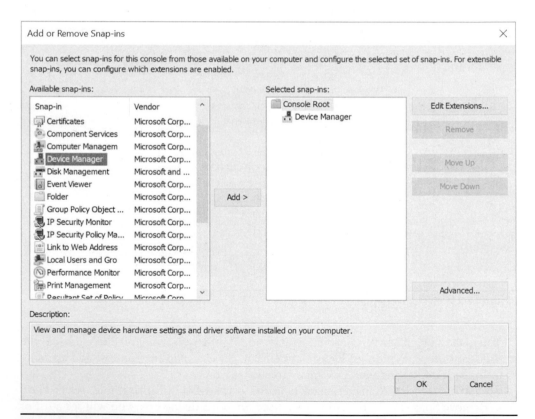

Figure 14-25 Available snap-ins

button to open a Device Manager dialog box that prompts you to choose the local PC or a remote PC for the snap-in to work with. Choose Local computer for this exercise, and click the Finish button. Click the Close button to close the Add Standalone Snap-in dialog box, and then click OK to close the Add or Remove Snap-ins dialog box.

You should see Device Manager listed in the console. Click it. Hey, that looks kind of familiar, doesn't it (see Figure 14-26)?

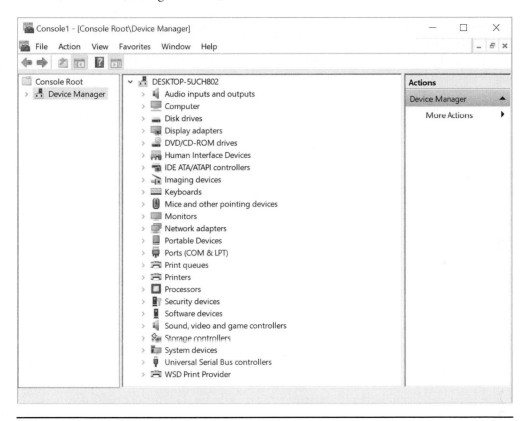

Figure 14-26   Device Manager as a snap-in

Once you've added the snap-ins you want, just save the console under any name, anywhere you want. I'll save this console as Device Manager, for example, and drop it on my desktop (see Figure 14-27). I'm now just a double-click away from Device Manager.

Figure 14-27
The Device
Manager
shortcut on the
desktop

Device
Manager

Optimizing Operating Systems

Maintenance means keeping the performance of an OS from degrading with time and use. Of course, you don't just want to keep trouble at bay—you want to make your systems better, stronger, faster! Anything you do that makes Windows better than it was before, such as adding a piece of software or hardware to make something run better, is an *optimization*.

Installing and Removing Software

Optimizing by installing and removing software is part of the normal life of any computing device. Each time you add or remove software, you make changes and decisions that can affect the system beyond whatever the program does, so it pays to know how to do it right.

Installation Concepts

Installing software in any OS requires consideration of several issues. First, what are the system requirements? Does the target computer have sufficient drive space for the app? Does it have enough RAM to run the program well? (Think back on Chapter 11, "Building a PC," and systems designed for video processing for a typical scenario where you'd need to beef up the RAM to support the software.) Does the version of OS running on the system match the OS requirements for compatibility with the application?

The methods for installing software have morphed over the years. For a long time, most software was distributed on some sort of removable media, such as a floppy disk (from my youth) to an optical disc, such as a CD-ROM or DVD-ROM. These days, most application software comes from the Internet, so a network download is the process.

The user account trying to install the software has to have administrative or root privileges. The installing person could also run the installation process with elevated privileges, assuming he or she knows the admin/root password.

Finally, whenever installing applications, think about the security considerations. How will this app affect overall system security? What does an Internet search on the app reveal as far as potential exploits currently in use? What is the impact on the computer? Is it more vulnerable to attacks? Assuming the computer is attached to a local area network, what kind of potential impact could installing this software have on the network?

It sounds like a lot of questions when you just want to install an application to get some work done or play a game. These questions—and answers—can make the difference between a happy, functional computer/network and one really bad day. Keep these questions in mind when installing applications.

Installing Software in Windows

If you can't download or access an application over the Internet, it'll probably come on an optical disc. Windows supports *Autorun*, a feature that enables the operating system to look for and read a special file called—wait for it—autorun.inf. Immediately after a removable media device (optical disc or thumb drive) is inserted into your computer, whatever program is listed in autorun.inf runs automatically. Most applications distributed on removable media have an autorun file that calls up the installation program (see Figure 14-28). Closely related is *AutoPlay*, which pops up a little dialog box when removable media is inserted into the computer. The options the dialog box provide are based on what Windows finds on the drive, including starting the Autorun application.

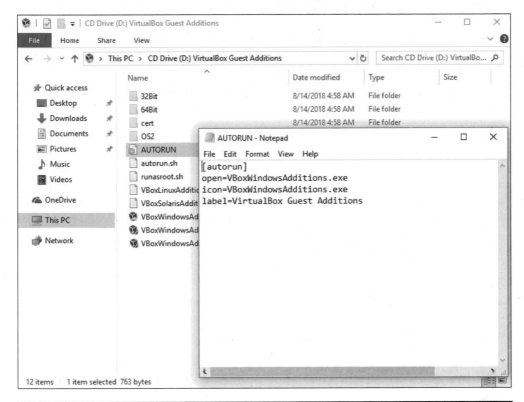

Figure 14-28   Autorun.inf file open in Notepad

To start an installation manually, double-click on the disc icon in Explorer or File Explorer. All OSs will scan the disc or other removable media for an executable file and run it.

The UAC in Windows complicates the installation process a bit. You will most likely be prompted by UAC when installing an application, giving you time to review what is happening to your system in case you did not intend to install the program. If you are using an administrator account, you can simply click Yes or Continue and finish the installation (see Figure 14-29).

Should you be logged in with a less privileged account, you will need to enter a user name and password of an account with administrative privileges. Some installers have trouble letting UAC know that they need more privileges and simply fail no matter what account you are logged in with. In those cases, it is best to right-click the installer icon and select Run as administrator to give the installer the access it expects from the start.

Figure 14-29
Installation UAC

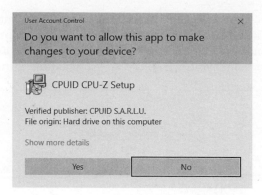

Assuming all is well, you typically must accept the terms of a software license before you can install an application. These steps are not optional; the installation simply won't proceed until you accept all terms the software manufacturer requires (see Figure 14-30). You may also be asked to make several decisions during the installation process. For example, you may be asked where you would like to install the program and if you would like certain optional components installed. It is best to accept the suggested settings unless you have a very specific reason for changing the defaults.

Figure 14-30
Accepting
software terms

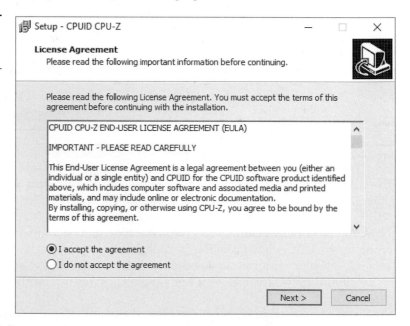

Every copy of Windows 10 also comes with the Microsoft Store. Microsoft tests Store applications to assure they're malware-free and safe for use (see Figure 14-31). The Microsoft Store represents only a small percentage of application installations; most people prefer to use more traditional methods of software installation for Windows systems.

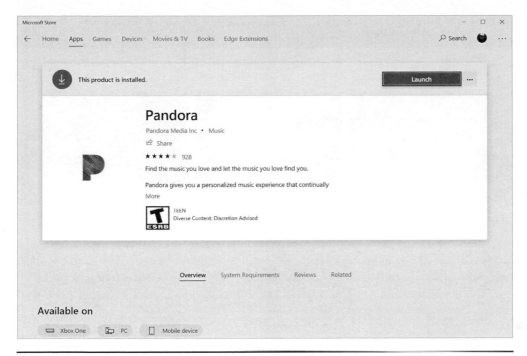

Figure 14-31   Microsoft Store

Installing Software in macOS

You have a couple of options for installing software in macOS. One method involves the Mac App Store, which you can get to via the Apple menu. Installing via the App Store is just like installing an app on your phone. You click a button, and the app installs (see Figure 14-32). Alternatively, you can download installation programs, often .dmg files, that you open by double-clicking on them. Inside you find either the app itself, which you just drag to the Applications folder, or an installer, which walks you through a wizard to install the program.

Installing Software in Linux

Linux distros differ in the process of installing applications (*packages* in Linux parlance). Many distros such as Ubuntu have a "store" similar to the Microsoft Store or the Mac App Store (see Figure 14-33). Another way is to download a package file, double-click it, and select Install from the options.

But the most common way to install new apps is through a built-in package manager like Ubuntu's Advanced Package Tool (APT). You can use it via the apt-get or apt command from the Terminal. (See Chapter 15, "Working with the Command-Line Interface," for more on the Terminal interface.) As an interesting side note, Ubuntu's "store" actually uses apt underneath its GUI.

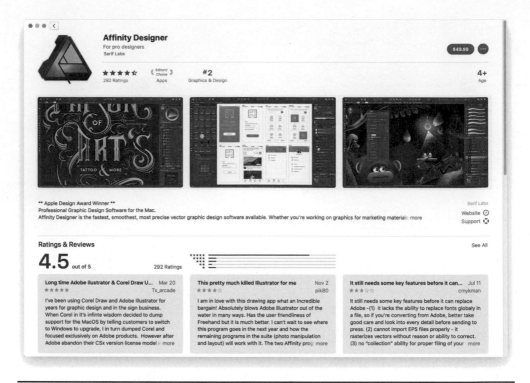

Figure 14-32 Affinity Designer offered on the Mac App Store in macOS

 EXAM TIP Windows, macOS, and Linux require you to type in root or admin credentials when you install many applications. Many times, you'll get prompted a few more times for credentials before the installation completes.

Removing Software

Each installed program takes up space on a computer's hard drive, and programs that you no longer need waste space that could be used for other purposes. Removing unnecessary programs is an important piece of optimization.

You remove a program from a Windows PC in much the same manner as you install it. That is, you use the application's own uninstall program, when possible. You normally find the uninstall program listed in the application's folder in the Start menu, as shown in Figure 14-34.

If an uninstall program is not available, use the *Programs and Features* applet in Control Panel (see Figure 14-35) or *Apps & features* in Settings (Windows 10) to remove the software. You select the program you want to remove and click the Uninstall/Change button or Change/Remove button. Windows displays a message warning you that the program will be permanently removed from your PC. If you're certain you want to continue, click Yes.

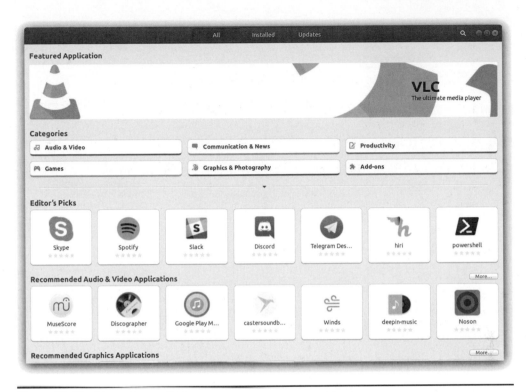

Figure 14-33   Linux store options

Figure 14-34
Uninstall me!

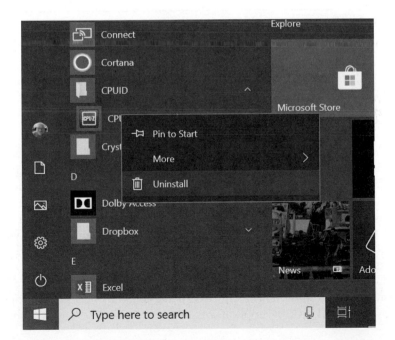

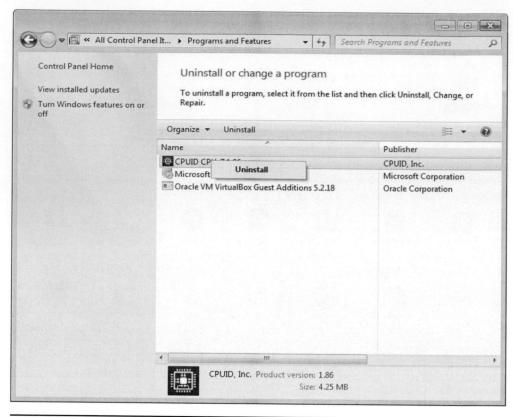

Figure 14-35   Programs and Features applet

NOTE   The Uninstall/Change and Change/Remove buttons change depending on the program. Not all programs can be changed.

You may then see a message telling you that a shared file that appears to no longer be in use is about to be deleted, and asking your approval. Generally speaking, it's safe to delete such files. If you do not delete them, they will likely be orphaned and remain unused on your hard disk forever. In some cases, clicking the Uninstall/Change or Change/Remove button starts the application's install program (the one you couldn't find before) so you can modify the installed features. This is a function of the program you're attempting to remove. The end result should be the removal of the application and all of its pieces and parts, including files and Registry entries.

Uninstalling applications in macOS varies based on how they were installed. Mac App Store apps are removed very similarly to apps on your phone. First, open the Launchpad app from the Dock or Applications folder (it looks like a rocket ship), then click and hold on any app icon until all the icons start to wiggle. An × in a circle will appear on the upper left of any app that can be removed (see Figure 14-36). Click the × to remove the app. If you accidentally remove an app you wanted, you can re-download it from the Mac App Store.

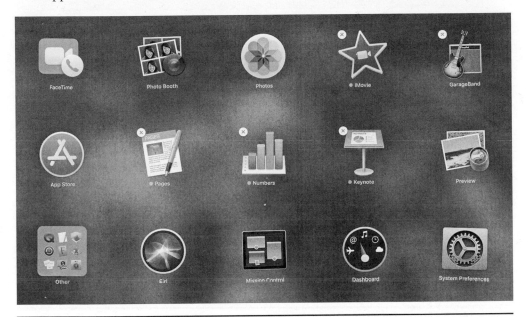

Figure 14-36 Uninstalling App Store–purchased applications using the Launchpad app

For all other macOS apps, removing them comes down to two options. Drag the app to the Trash or run the uninstaller if the app came with one. Of the two, the first option of just deleting the app is the most common, with a dedicated uninstaller only being available for some of the larger (and often cross-platform) apps like Photoshop. Be aware that deleting an app can leave behind various files on the system, most often a few user preference files and other customizations in the user's Library folder.

Removing software in mainstream Linux distros is just as easy as installing it. Open the software manager, find the app, and then click Remove (see Figure 14-37). The underlying package manager, which we'll work with directly in Chapter 15, will handle all the deleting and cleanup for you.

Adding or Removing Windows Components/Features

When you installed Windows, it included certain features by default. It installed Notepad, network support, and games on your computer. You can remove these Windows components from your system if you like, and add other components as well.

Open the Programs and Features applet in the Control Panel, and then click the *Turn Windows features on or off* option on the Tasks list. Click Yes or Continue if prompted by UAC and you will be presented with the Windows Features dialog box (see Figure 14-38). To toggle a feature on or off, simply click its checkbox.

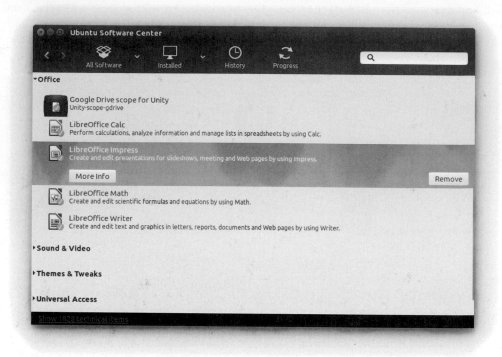

Figure 14-37   Removing an application in Ubuntu Linux

Figure 14-38
Windows
Features dialog
box

Installing and Optimizing a Device

The processes for optimizing hardware in Windows are absolutely identical between the versions, even down to the troubleshooting utilities, and are very similar to the steps for installing a new device. The installation process is covered in every chapter of this book that deals with one type of device or another. You should also recall the optimization and troubleshooting processes you read about specifically way back in Chapter 6, "Motherboards." (Refer to that chapter to refresh your memory if any of the following steps don't seem crystal clear.) So, these are the important steps/action items:

- Update the drivers, usually from the manufacturer's Web site.
- Verify that the device works properly.
- If the drivers prove buggy, use the driver rollback feature to restore the older drivers.
- Never run beta drivers.

Updating Drivers in macOS

macOS will notify you about available *system updates* that contain driver updates for built-in components. Make a quick trip to the App Store to get updates installed (see Figure 14-39). If the system has third-party devices, like a Wacom tablet, you will need to manually check and update any drivers for those devices.

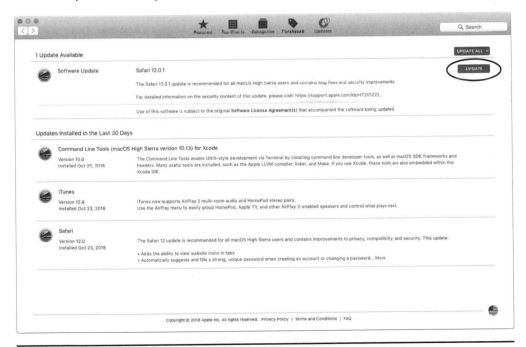

Figure 14-39   App Store showing an available update

EXAM TIP Unlike Windows Update, the macOS system updates will update drivers and the firmware of the Apple computer, if necessary. Apple is a hardware company, after all.

Updating Drivers in Linux

Most Linux distros regularly check for updates and will signal any new updates. Download and install the updates using the Software Updater.

Device Manager

You've worked with *Device Manager* in other chapters when installing and troubleshooting devices; it's also the tool to use when optimizing device drivers. Right-click on a device in Device Manager to display the context menu. From here you can update or uninstall the driver, disable the device, scan for hardware changes, or display the Properties dialog box. When you open the Properties dialog box, you'll see several tabs that vary according to the specific device. Most have General, Driver, Details, and Resources. The tab that matters most for optimization is the Driver tab.

The Driver tab has buttons labeled Driver Details, Update Driver, Roll Back Driver, Uninstall, and Disable. Most of these you'll recall from Chapter 6. Driver Details lists the driver files and their locations on disk.

Adding a New Device

Windows should automatically detect any new device you install in your system. If Windows does not detect a newly connected device, use the *Add a device* option in the Devices and Printers applet in Windows to get the device recognized and drivers installed (see Figure 14-40).

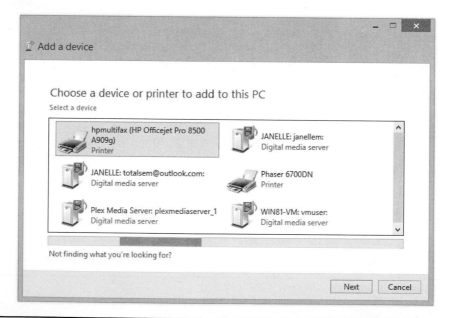

Figure 14-40 Adding a device in Windows 8.1

Performance Options

One optimization you can perform on all Windows versions is setting Performance Options. *Performance Options* are used to configure CPU, RAM, and virtual memory (page file) settings. To access these options right-click Computer or This PC and select Properties, and then click the Advanced system settings link in the Tasks list. On the Advanced tab, click the Settings button in the Performance section.

The Performance Options dialog box has three tabs: Visual Effects, Advanced, and Data Execution Prevention (see Figure 14-41). The Visual Effects tab enables you to

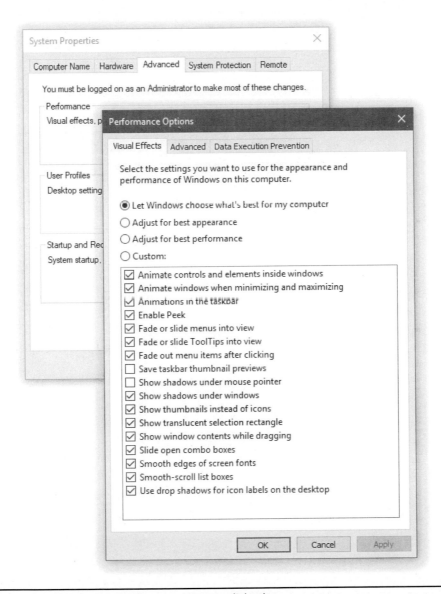

Figure 14-41   Windows 10 Performance Options dialog box

adjust visual effects that impact performance, such as animations, thumbnails, and transparencies. Try clicking the top three choices in turn and watch the list of settings. Notice the tiny difference between the first two choices (*Let Windows choose what's best for my computer* and *Adjust for best appearance*). The third choice, *Adjust for best performance*, turns off all visual effects, and the fourth option is an invitation to make your own adjustments.

If you're on a computer that barely supports Windows, turning off visual effects can make a huge difference in the responsiveness of the computer. For the most part, though, just leave these settings alone.

The Advanced tab, shown in Figure 14-42, has two sections: Processor scheduling and Virtual memory. Under the Processor scheduling section, you can choose to adjust for

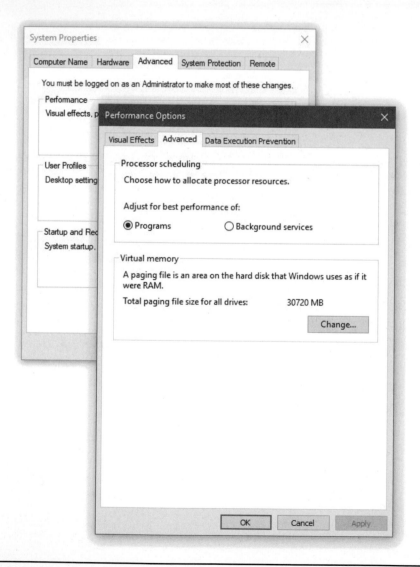

Figure 14-42   Advanced tab of Performance Options dialog box

best performance of either Programs or Background services. The Virtual memory section of this tab enables you to modify the size and location of the page file.

Data Execution Prevention (*DEP*) works in the background to stop viruses and other malware from taking over programs loaded in system memory. It doesn't prevent viruses from being installed on your computer, but makes them less effective. By default, DEP is only enabled for critical operating system files in RAM, but the Data Execution Prevention tab enables you to have DEP turned on for all running programs. It works, but you might take a performance hit or find that some applications crash with it enabled for all programs. Like other options in Performance Options, leaving the default DEP settings is the best option most of the time.

Preparing for Problems

Techs need to prepare for problems. You must have critical system files and data backed up and tools in place for the inevitable glitches. Every modern operating system has options for backing up data and, as you might imagine, they all offer different features. Windows offers System Restore to recover from problems, too. Let's take a look.

Backing Up Personal Data

The most important data on your computer is the personal data: your documents, e-mail messages and contacts, Web favorites, photographs, and other files. To handle backing up personal data, every version of Windows comes with some form of backup utility. macOS and Linux of course have backup tools as well.

Backup and Restore for Windows 7

Microsoft includes the automated and simple *Backup and Restore* Control Panel applet in Windows 7. The process begins by asking where you want to save your backup (see Figure 14-43).

Windows then asks you what you want to back up. As you can see in Figure 14.44, there are two choices: *Let Windows choose* (*recommended*) and *Let me choose*.

If you select *Let Windows choose* (*recommended*), you'll back up each user's personal data, but Windows 7 doesn't stop there. Assuming you have enough space in your backup location, Windows 7 will automatically add a system image that includes the entire Windows operating system, every installed program, all device drivers, and even the Registry.

Selecting *Let me choose* is equally interesting. Windows 7 enables you to pick individual users' files to back up (see Figure 14-45). This can be a handy situation when you store important files outside of the folders the *Let Windows choose* option covers.

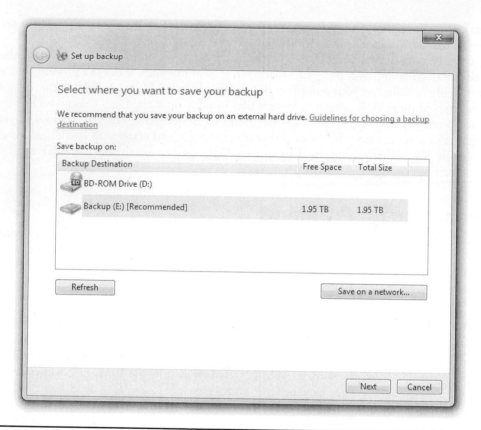

Figure 14-43 Backup options in Windows 7

By selecting a user, you can choose libraries or the user's personal folders to back up, as shown in Figure 14-46. Also note the checkbox that gives you the option to make a system image, just as if you selected the *Let Windows choose (recommended)* option.

Once you complete the wizard, Windows starts backing up your files. While the backup runs, you can monitor its progress with an exciting and handy progress bar (see Figure 14-47). If you can't handle that much excitement, you can close the backup window while the OS backs up files. The process can take a long time, many hours with a modern system with a large hard drive.

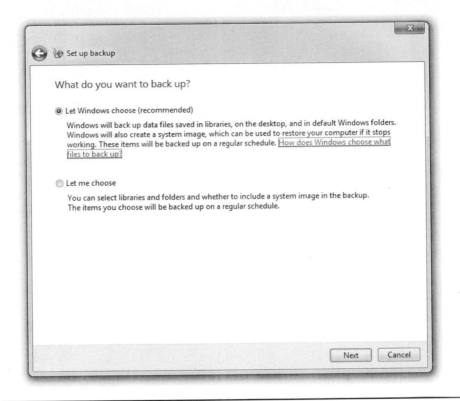

Figure 14-44 What do you want to back up?

  NOTE You can also choose to create just a system image in Windows 7. From the Backup and Restore applet, select Create a system image.

File History in Windows 8/8.1/10

Microsoft introduced the robust *File History* Control Panel applet in Windows 8 that enables aggressive backup of personal files and folders (see Figure 14-48). File History requires a second drive and is not enabled by default. You can use any type of HDD or SSD as the second drive, internal or external. (You could choose to back up to a second partition on the same drive, I suppose, but what would be the point?) Enable File History and start backing up your Libraries, Desktop, Contacts, and Favorites right now.

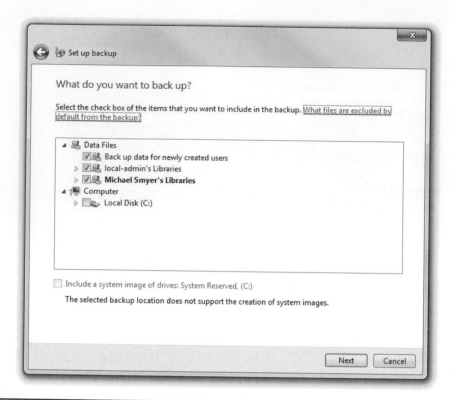

Figure 14-45   Backup showing a list of users

Note that File History won't back up all your personal files unless you either add them to the default Libraries or create custom Libraries. Also, File History does not replace full system backups at all. Microsoft recommends that you use third-party backup software if you want to do full system backups of Windows 8 or newer.

 NOTE   Windows 8/8.1 lacked a backup utility other than File History. Windows 10 brought back the Windows 7 Backup and Restore utility to allow you to restore older backups created with it. In fact, it's even called "Backup and Restore (Windows 7)" in the Windows 10 Control Panel.

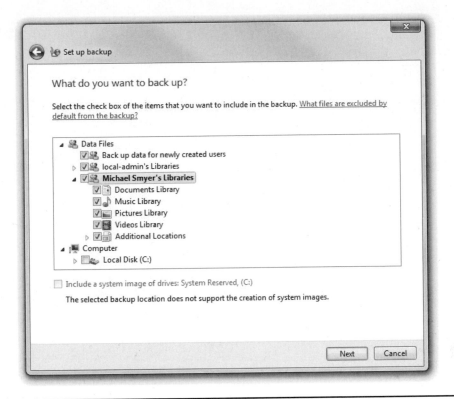

Figure 14-46 Showing some of a single user's libraries/folders

Time Machine in macOS

macOS provides the excellent *Time Machine* to create full system backups (see Figure 14-49). These backups are called *local snapshots*. Time Machine enables you to recover some or all files in the event of a crash; it also enables you to *restore* deleted files and recover previous versions of files. Time Machine requires an external HDD or SSD, or you can use a shared network drive. Find Time Machine in System Preferences.

Backups in Linux

Different Linux distros offer different tools for backing up files, folders, and drives. Ubuntu Linux uses Déjà Dup, although it goes by the name *Backups* in System Settings (see Figure 14-50). Déjà Dup will happily back up your files to wherever you tell it, such as an external drive, network share, or even a folder on your main hard drive (not

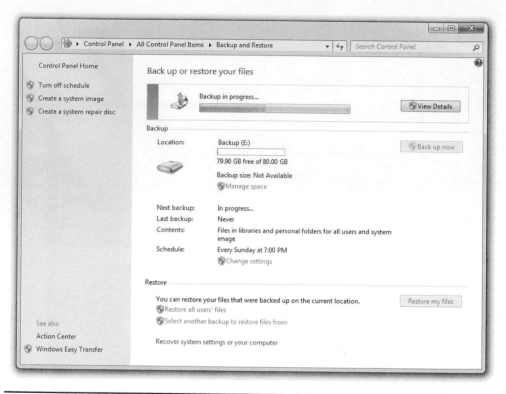

Figure 14-47 Backup in progress . . .

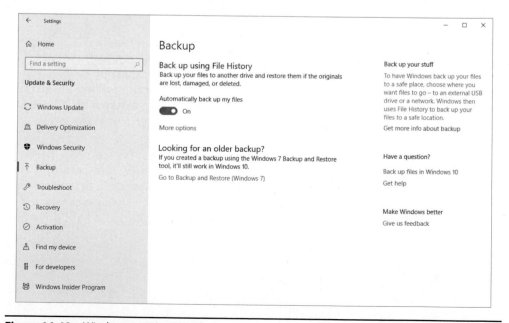

Figure 14-48 Windows 10 File History

Figure 14-49 Time Machine

recommended if you care about your files!). Déjà Dup backs up a user's Home folder by default; that's where most users store all personal documents. Déjà Dup will store files and versions of files permanently, as long as the storage location has sufficient space.

System Restore in Windows

Every technician has war stories about the user who likes to add the latest gadget and cool software to his computer. Then he's amazed when things go very, very wrong: the system locks up, refuses to boot, or simply acts weird. This guy also can't remember what he added or when. All he knows is that you should be able to fix it—fast.

The *System Restore* tool enables you to create a *restore point*, a *snapshot* of a computer's configuration at a specific point in time. If the computer later crashes or has a corrupted OS, you can restore the system to its previous state, specifically *restoring system files and folders*.

When System Restore is turned on, it makes a number of restore points automatically. To make your own restore point, right-click Computer or This PC and select Properties, and then click the System protection link in the Tasks list. On the System Protection tab, click the Create button to open the dialog box shown in Figure 14-51. Name your restore point appropriately and then click Create.

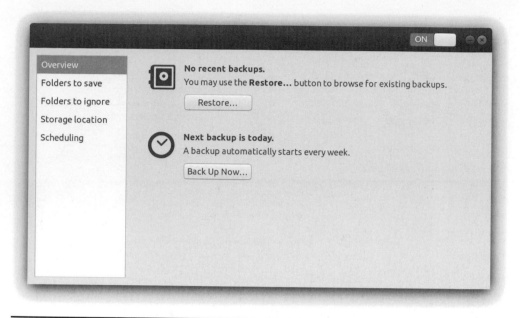

Figure 14-50   Backups under System Settings in Ubuntu

NOTE   System Restore in Windows 10 is disabled by default. If you find yourself needing to roll back a Windows 10 machine, don't expect to find any restore points. In this case, you may need to look at using Windows 10's Reset this PC feature, which we will talk about in Chapter 16, "Troubleshooting Operating Systems."

If you click the System Restore button on the System Protection tab, you might be surprised at how many restore points have already been made for you automatically (see Figure 14-52).

The System Restore tool creates some of the restore points automatically, including every time you install new software. Thus, if installation of a program causes your computer to malfunction, simply restore the system to a time point prior to that installation, and the computer should work again.

During the restore process, only settings and programs are changed. No data is lost. Your computer includes all programs and settings as of the restore date. This feature is absolutely invaluable for overworked techs. A simple restore fixes many

Figure 14-51
Creating a
manual restore
point in Windows

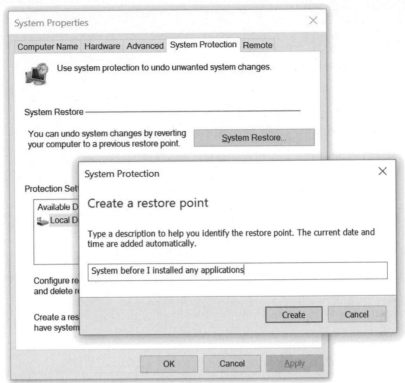

user-generated problems. To restore to a previous time point, start the System Restore Wizard in System Tools.

You don't have to count on the automatic creation of restore points. You can open System Restore at any time and simply select *Create a restore point*. Consider doing this before making changes that might not trigger an automatic restore point, such as directly editing the Registry.

System Restore is turned on by default (except in Windows 10) and uses some mass storage space to save information on restore points. To turn System Restore on or off or change the space usage, right-click Computer or This PC and select Properties, and then click the System protection link in the Tasks list. Return to the System Protection tab and click the Configure button to change System Restore configuration settings (see Figure 14-53).

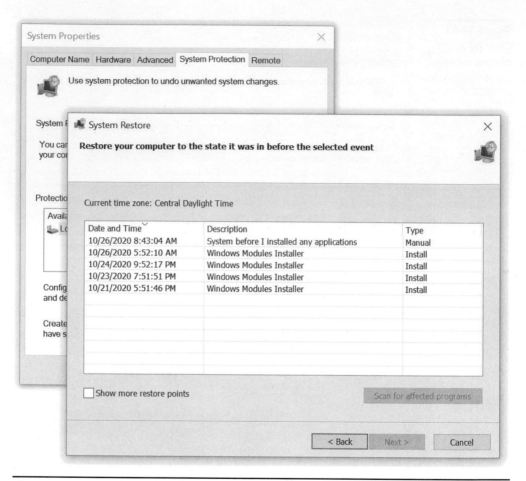

Figure 14-52   Restore points in Windows

NOTE   Windows 7 Restore Settings options differ from the Windows 10 options shown in Figure 14-53. The three options are *Restore system settings and previous versions of files*, *Only restore previous versions of files*, and *Turn off system protection*. The text introducing the options also differs. The functions are similar, however, so if you find yourself dealing with Windows 7 backups, you should be golden.

Figure 14-53
System Restore
settings and Disk
Space Usage
options

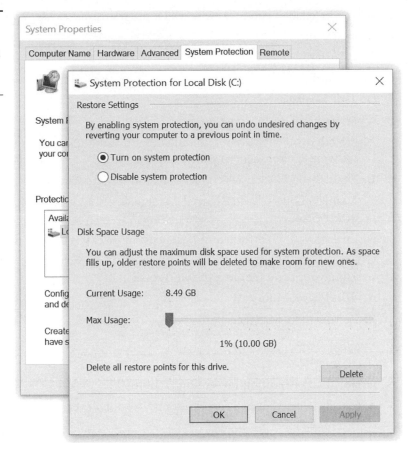

Chapter Review

Questions

1. What tool enables you to modify which programs start when Windows 7 starts?

   A. msstartup

   B. msinfo32

   C. msconfig

   D. ipconfig

2. What tool enables you to modify which programs start when Windows 10 starts?

   A. msstartup

   B. msinfo32

   C. msconfig

   D. Task Manager

3. What does System Information do?

   A. Provides you with a report about the hardware resources, components, and software environment in your computer

   B. Enables you to select which programs and services start when Windows boots up

   C. Enables you to schedule hard drive defragmentation, chkdsk scans, and other computer tasks

   D. Enables you to perform automatic custom backups of your files and settings

4. What tool enables you to correct a corrupted Windows operating system by reverting your computer to a previous state?

   A. Windows Restore

   B. Restore State Manager

   C. Time Machine

   D. System Restore

5. What is Data Execution Prevention (DEP)?

   A. A technology that prevents viruses from taking over programs loaded in system memory

   B. A technology that enables you to set permissions for different users on your computer

   C. A technology that prevents programs from being installed on your computer

   D. A technology that prevents files from being written to your hard drive

6. If you install a driver on your system and it causes problems, which tool can you use to roll back to a previous driver?

   A. Driver Manager

   B. msconfig

   C. Device Manager

   D. System Info

7. Which tool enables you to test and repair a mass storage device in Windows?

   A. Disk Defragmenter

   B. Disk Utility

   C. Error checking

   D. Error utility

8. Joan recently bought a new game controller and used the Add a device wizard to install it, but it still won't work. What should she do next? (Select two.)

   A. Check the manufacturer's Web site for updated drivers.

   B. Run the Driver Rollback tool to return the PC to a functioning state.

   C. Use a restore point in System Restore to return the PC to a functioning state.

   D. Run Windows Update to search for new drivers.

9. What tool is used in macOS to perform full system backups?

   A. AppleBack

   B. Users and Groups

   C. Time Machine

   D. System Preferences Backup

10. What feature included in Windows 8, 8.1, and 10 allows you to back up your important files and folders regularly?

    A. System Configuration

    B. Backup and Restore

    C. AutoPlay

    D. File History

Answers

1. **C.** The System Configuration utility (msconfig) enables you to select the programs and services that start with Windows 7.

2. **D.** The Task Manager enables you to modify the applications and services that start with Windows 10.

3. **A.** System Information gives you a wide variety of information about your system.

4. **D.** Using System Restore, you can restore your computer to a previous restore point.

5. **A.** Data Execution Prevention prevents viruses from taking control of programs loaded into memory.

6. **C.** The Roll Back Driver option in Device Manager is a great tool for fixing driver problems.

7. **C.** Windows uses Error checking for testing and repairing mass storage devices, such as HDDs and SSDs.

8. **A, D.** Joan should check both the manufacturer's Web site and Windows Update for the latest drivers.

9. **C.** macOS uses Time Machine to perform full system backups.

10. **D.** File History is an awesome backup tool included with Windows 8, 8.1, and 10. It enables you to perform backups of important files and folders regularly.

Working with the Command-Line Interface

In this chapter, you will learn how to
- Explain the operation of the command-line interface
- Describe fundamental commands
- Explain file manipulation
- Describe additional useful Windows commands
- Describe additional helpful macOS and Linux commands
- Explain scripting languages and platforms

Whenever I teach a class of new techs and we get to the section on working with the command line, I'm invariably met with a chorus of moans and a barrage of questions and statements like "Why do we need to learn this old stuff?" and "Is this ritualistic hazing appropriate in an IT class?"

For techs who master the interface, the command line provides a powerful, quick, and flexible tool for working on a computer. Learning that interface and understanding how to make it work is not only useful, but also necessary for all techs who want to go beyond baby-tech status. You simply cannot work on modern computers without knowing the command line! I'm not the only one who thinks this way. The CompTIA A+ 220-1002 certification exam tests you on a variety of command-line commands, both in Windows and Linux, for doing everything from renaming a file to rebuilding a system file.

If you're interested in moving beyond Windows and into other operating systems such as Linux, you'll find that pretty much all of the serious work is done at a command prompt. Even macOS supports a command prompt.

The command prompt is popular for many reasons. Let's consider three for this chapter. First, if you know what you're doing, you can do most jobs more quickly by typing a text command than by clicking through a graphical user interface (GUI). Second, a *command-line interface (CLI)* doesn't take much operating system firepower, so it's the natural choice for jobs where you don't need or don't want a full-blown GUI for an OS. Third, text commands are easily added to scripts, enabling you to perform complex tasks automatically.

So, are you sold on the idea of the command prompt? Good! This chapter gives you a tour of the Windows and macOS and Linux command-line interfaces, explaining how they work and what's happening behind the scenes. You'll learn the concepts and master essential commands. You'll work with files and folders and learn about scripting. It's all fun! A good tactic for absorbing the material in this chapter is to try out each command as it's presented.

NOTE If you're using a Windows system, this is a great opportunity to jump ahead to Chapter 22, "Virtualization," and try some virtualization. Consider loading up a virtual machine and installing Linux so you can practice. Check out and install my favorite virtualization tool, Oracle VirtualBox at www .virtualbox.org, and then download an ISO file from www.ubuntu.com.

1002

Deciphering the Command-Line Interface

So, how does a command-line interface work? It's a little like having a Facebook Messenger conversation with your computer. The computer tells you it's ready to receive commands by displaying a specific set of characters called a *prompt*. Here's an example of a generic prompt:

```
>: Want to play a game?
>: _
```

You type a command and press ENTER to send it:

```
>: Want to play a game?
>: What kind of game?
>: _
```

The computer executes the command and, when finished, displays a new prompt, often along with some information about what it did:

```
>: Want to play a game?
>: What kind of game?
>: A very fun game...
>: _
```

Once you get a new prompt, it means the computer is ready for your next instruction. Running commands from the command line is similar to clicking on icons in the operating system's GUI. The results are basically the same: you tell the computer to do something and it responds.

Try This!   Opening Windows GUI Programs from the Command Prompt

Keep in mind as you go through this chapter that the command line is just another tool for communicating with the operating system. Windows responds whether you click or type and sometimes does both, so try this! At a command prompt, type **notepad** and press ENTER. What happens? The graphical program Notepad opens up, just as if you'd double-clicked on its icon. Here's another: type **explorer** and press ENTER. Voilà! Windows Explorer or File Explorer loads. Windows just responds.

Shells

The command prompt, like a GUI, is just another way to interface with a computer. The command line interprets input and sends it to the OS in a form the OS understands, and then shows the results. The tool that interprets input is called the *command-line interpreter*, also known as the *shell*. The default Windows shell is *Command*. On macOS and on most Linux distros, the default shell is called *bash*.

While most operating systems have only one GUI, that's not the case with the shell. Every operating system has the ability to interface with different types of shells. On macOS and Linux, it's easy to use popular shells with names like Z shell (zsh), Korn shell (ksh), and C shell (csh). In Windows you can use PowerShell instead of Command. It's a standard rite of nerd passage to start experimenting with these alternative shells.

 NOTE   When you open a command prompt, you start a shell. The shell acts as the command-line interpreter. Both Windows and Linux give you a choice of shells. Different shells come with different capabilities. Choose the right shell for the job you're doing.

Accessing the Command-Line Interface in Windows

You access the command-line interface in Windows by starting the shell program Command. We touched on accessing the CLI in Chapter 2, "The Visible Computer," but let's develop this procedure more here.

A common way to access the command-line interface is through the Start menu or the Start screen's Search bar. Type **cmd** from the Start screen. The Search option will appear with the full command (see Figure 15-1). Press ENTER.

A command prompt window pops up on your screen with a black background and white text—welcome to the Windows command-line interface (see Figure 15-2). To close the CLI, you can either click the Close box in the upper-right corner, as on any other window, or simply type **exit** and press ENTER.

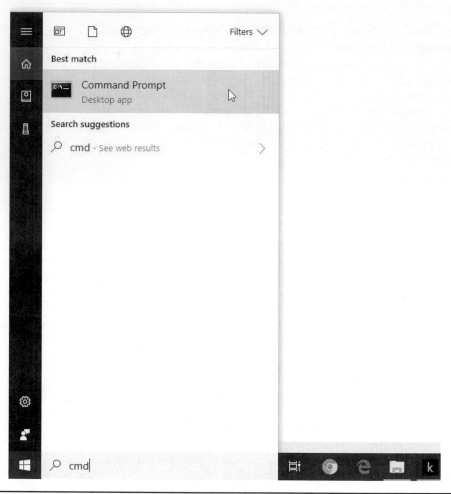

Figure 15-1   Starting the command prompt in Windows 10

If you attempt to enter at the Windows command prompt a command that requires elevated or administrative privileges, you receive a UAC "Windows needs your permission to continue" dialog box. (You learned about UAC in Chapter 13, "Users, Groups, and Permissions.") You can also manually run a command with elevated privileges by right-clicking on a command-prompt shortcut and then selecting *Run as administrator.* If Windows prompts for the administrator password or credentials, enter whatever is needed.

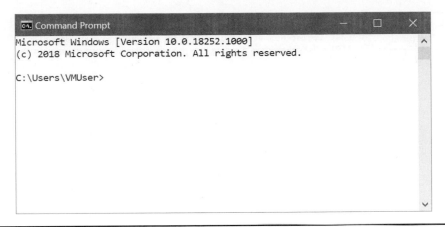

Figure 15-2   The Windows 8.1 command-line interface

 NOTE   You can create a shortcut to a Windows command prompt with elevated privileges by right-clicking on the desktop and selecting New | Shortcut. For the location of the item, type **cmd** and click Next. Type **cmd** to name the shortcut, and click Finish. The shortcut appears on the Desktop. Next, right-click the shortcut and select the Advanced button. In the Advanced Properties dialog box, check the *Run as administrator* box and click OK. You have now created a Windows command-prompt shortcut that will always run with administrative privileges. (Note that these are the steps for Windows 10. You can do the same thing in Windows 7/8/8.1, but the screens vary a little.)

Accessing the Command-Line Interface in macOS and Linux

The command line in macOS and the command line in Linux function virtually identically. This isn't too surprising given that both macOS and Linux are based on UNIX. The terminal emulator in macOS has a specific name, *Terminal*. The many distros of Linux use different emulators, such as Konsole Terminal and GNOME Terminal. To make things easy, we'll use the command-line interface in Ubuntu Linux, conveniently also *Terminal*.

To open Terminal in macOS, either launch the Terminal app from the Utilities folder (located in the Applications folder) or activate Spotlight (COMMAND-SPACEBAR), type **terminal**, and press ENTER to bring up the macOS Terminal (see Figure 15-3).

 EXAM TIP   *Spotlight* (or Spot Light, as the A+ objectives list it) is a phenomenal search tool in macOS. It indexes your drive(s), not just for file names, but for content. That means you can search for specific files, of course, plus all sorts of other things, like apps, e-mail messages, music, contacts, and even flight information! Try it!

Figure 15-3

macOS Terminal

The way to open a terminal emulator in Linux varies depending on the Linux distribution (distro) you use. Generally, every desktop-focused Linux distro has some form of finder or search function on the desktop that works similarly to the search tools in macOS and Windows. Find this tool and then type **terminal** and press ENTER to start the program. This brings up the terminal window, as shown in Figure 15-4.

Figure 15-4

Linux Terminal

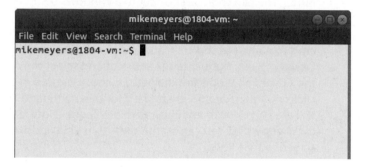

Both macOS and Linux enable you to run the command line with advanced privileges, called *super user* or *root privileges*. Two commands do the trick: *su* and *sudo*. Even though the macOS and Linux advanced privileges function is equivalent to the elevated privileges in Windows, they handle this elevation differently. First, open Terminal. Whenever you need to run a command as root, type **sudo** followed by the desired command. The system will prompt for a password and then run the command.

If the system doesn't have sudo, it should have its older cousin *su*. With su, you typically type **su** at the prompt and press ENTER; you will then be prompted for the root password. Once you have successfully entered the password, the prompt will change (usually changing the character at the end from a $ to a #) and every command you enter from then on will be executed as root. When you finish working as root, type **exit** and press ENTER. Terminal won't close like before, but you will return to a normal prompt. You can see how the prompt changes in the following example:

```
mike@server:~$ su
Password:_
root@server:/home/mike# exit
mike@server:~$
```

EXAM TIP Many Linux systems disable the root account for safety, rendering the su command inoperable. The sudo command enables users to do root things without having the root password.

The Command Prompt

Regardless of what shell you use, the command prompt always *focuses* on a specific folder, the *working directory*, usually indicated by the prompt. The OS executes commands in the specified folder unless otherwise directed. Here's an example of focus. In Windows, if you see a prompt that looks like the following line, you know that the focus is on the root directory of the C: drive:

```
C:\>
```

In macOS and Linux the prompt is subtly different, but functionally the same. First, macOS and Linux systems don't use the Windows drive lettering concept, as all forms of storage are simply mounted as folders. Second, Linux prompts show the currently logged-on user and system as well as the current directory. Third, macOS and Linux use a forward slash (/) instead of a backslash (\). This prompt shows user mike is on the "server" system and is in the home directory:

```
mike@server:/home$
```

In Windows, if you see a prompt that looks like Figure 15-5, you know that the focus is on the \Diploma\APLUS\ folder of the C: drive. The trick to using a command line is first to focus the prompt on the drive and folder where you want to work.

Figure 15-5
Command prompt indicating focus on the C:\ Diploma\APLUS\ folder

Closing the Terminal

Closing a command prompt is easy and is done the same way in Windows, macOS, and Linux. At the prompt just type **exit**. The terminal window will disappear.

```
mike@server:/home$ exit
```

File Formats and Filenames

The command line requires precision. That means you need to type commands, filenames, and switches accurately. Otherwise you get errors or no results at all. What you type (or typo) can have tremendous impact when working in the command-line interface. Here's the scoop.

All operating systems manifest each program and piece of data as individual files. All files are stored in mass storage devices in binary format, but every program has a unique method of binary organization, called a *file format*. One program cannot read another program's files unless it can convert the other program's file format into its file format.

Each file has a name, which is stored with the file on the drive. Names are broken down into two parts: the filename and the *extension*. In the early days of PCs, Microsoft used a file system that dictated the filename could be no longer than eight characters. The extension, which was optional, could be up to three characters long. The filename and extension are separated by a period, or *dot*. Here's an example of an old-style filename:

```
thisfile.txt
```

The "8.3" format does not apply to modern operating systems. Here are some examples of acceptable filenames:

fred.exe	Myfirstattempt.aes	file1.longextension
driver3.h	Janet likes long file names.doc	Noextension

Whether you're running Windows, macOS, or Linux, the filename extension is very important because it tells the operating system what type of program uses this data. This is called the file's *association*. For example, Microsoft Word is associated with any file that has the extension .docx or .doc. PowerPoint uses .pptx or .ppt. Graphics file extensions, in contrast, often reflect the graphics standard used to render the image, such as .gif for CompuServe's Graphics Interchange Format or .jpg for the JPEG (Joint Photographic Experts Group) format. Figure 15-6 shows the file association for a PowerPoint .pptx file.

NOTE Every operating system has some method to change file associations. If you want to open Microsoft Office .docx files in LibreOffice instead of Word, there is always a way to do this.

Changing the extension of a data file does not affect the format of its contents, but without the proper extension, your operating system won't know which program uses it. Figure 15-7 shows a folder with two identical image files. The one on the right shows a thumbnail because Windows recognizes this as a JPEG image; the one on the left shows a generic icon because I deleted the extension. Windows' GUI doesn't show file extensions by default, but macOS and most Linux distros do.

The filename and extension matter when working in the command-line interface because you need to know what type of file you're accessing when you type a command. Typing certain filenames, for example, causes the OS to run an application or run a series of commands to do *stuff*. Check out "Running a Program in Windows" later in this chapter for the details on *executable files*.

Figure 15-6
File association in
File Properties

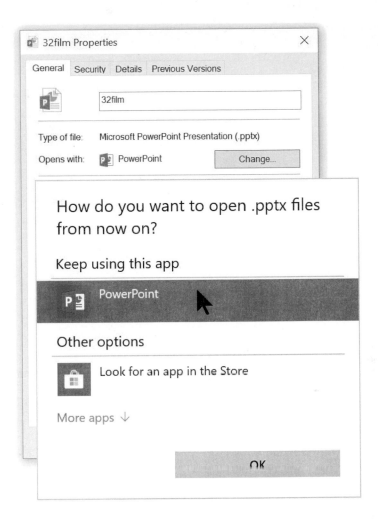

Drives and Folders

When working from the command line, you need to be able to focus the prompt at the specific drive and folder that contains the files or programs with which you want to work. This can be a little more complicated than it seems.

Before we get too deep here, let's review what you studied in Chapter 9, "Implementing Mass Storage." Windows assigns drive letters to each hard drive partition (except the system partition) and to every recognized form of mass storage. Hard drive partitions usually start with the letter C:. Optical drives by default get the next available drive letter after the last hard drive partition. On top of that, you can mount a hard drive as a volume in another drive.

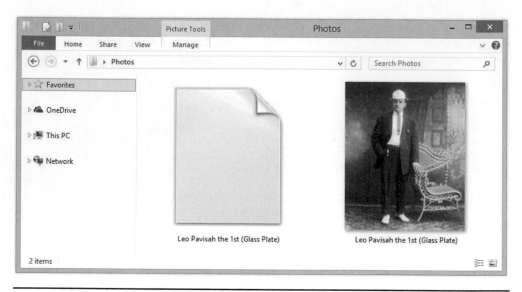

Figure 15-7   What kind of file is the one on the left?

macOS and Linux don't use drive letters. Instead, the boot partition is defined as the root drive, shown as just a slash: /. All other storage—partitions, optical discs, thumb drives, and so on—must go through a process called *mounting* to enable the OS to treat them as folders. These folders are most often mounted to a single folder off the root drive called /mount or /media in Linux and /Volumes in macOS.

Whatever the names of the drives, all operating systems use a hierarchical directory tree to organize the contents of these drives. All files are put into groups called *folders*, although you'll often hear techs use the interchangeable term *directory*. Any file not in a folder *within* the tree—that is, any file in the folder at the root of the directory tree—is said to be in the *root directory*. A folder inside another folder is called a *subfolder*. Any folder can have multiple subfolders. Two or more files with the same name can exist in different folders on a PC, but two files in the same folder cannot have the same name. In the same way, no two subfolders under the same folder can have the same name, but two subfolders under different folders can have the same name.

NOTE   It helps to visualize a directory tree as upside down, because in geekspeak, the trunk, or root directory, is described as "above" the folders that divide it, and those subfolders "below" root are spoken of as being "above" the other subfolders inside them. For example, "The file is in the Adobe folder under Program Files."

When describing a drive in Windows, you use its letter and a colon. For example, the hard drive would be represented by C:. To describe the root directory, put a backslash (\)

after the C:, as in C:\. To describe a particular directory, add the name of the directory. For example, if a PC has a directory in the root directory called Test, it is C:\Test. Subdirectories in a directory are displayed by adding backslashes and names. If the Test directory has a subdirectory called System, it is shown like this: C:\Test\System. This naming convention provides for a complete description of the location and name of any file. If the C:\Test\System directory includes a file called test2.txt, it is C:\Test\System\test2.txt.

The exact location of a file is called its *path*. The path for the test2.txt file is C:\Test\System. Here are some examples of possible Windows paths:

```
C:\Program Files
C:\Users\mike\Desktop
F:\FRUSCH3\CLEAR
D:\
```

macOS and Linux also use paths. Folder names are separated by a forward slash (/), however, instead of the backslash used by Windows. Also, Windows and macOS are not case sensitive, while Linux is. For example, in Linux it's perfectly acceptable to have two folders called "Mike" and "mike" inside the same folder. Windows does not allow this. Here are some examples of macOS and Linux paths:

```
/usr/local/bin
/Applications/Utilities
/home/mike/Desktop
/
```

macOS and Linux prompts show your folder location a bit differently than Windows. Generally, your default prompt is pointing at the /home/<username>/ folder. By default, however, macOS and Linux do not show that path. They only show a tilde, ~, as follows:

```
mike@server:~$
```

The ~ is really just a shorthand for your users folder; in this case it means you are in /home/mike. Yes, a little confusing, but welcome to UNIX! macOS and Linux provide a handy utility, *pwd*, that tells you exactly where you are if you're unsure:

```
mike@server:~$ pwd
/home/mike
```

 EXAM TIP The CompTIA A+ objectives want you to know the difference between the pwd versus passwd commands. You've seen the pwd command; later in this chapter we'll cover passwd.

In more precise terms, pwd will show you the working directory. The output includes the full path.

Here are a few items to remember about folder names and filenames:

- Folders and files may have spaces in their names.
- The only disallowed characters in Windows are the following eleven:
  * " / \ [ ] : ; | = ,

- In macOS and Linux the only disallowed character is a forward slash: /
- Files aren't required to have extensions, but in most cases the OS won't know the file association type without an extension.

Mastering Fundamental Commands

It's time to try using the command line, but before you begin, a note of warning is in order: the command-line interface is picky and unforgiving. It will do what you *say*, not what you *mean*, so it always pays to double-check that those are one and the same before you press ENTER and commit the command. One careless keystroke can result in the loss of crucial data, with no warning and no going back. In this section, you'll explore the structure of commands and then play with basic commands to navigate and manipulate your OS's folder structure.

 EXAM TIP The CompTIA A+ 1002 exam objectives question your knowledge of when to use specific commands in Windows, macOS, and Linux. The objectives start with "Given a scenario, use [specific OS tools.]" That's absolutely appropriate. Techs need to know when to use a specific tool, especially when it comes to the command-line interface.

This chapter assumes that you recognize when to use commands in an obvious scenario and doesn't hammer you with the word "scenario." When would you use a command to delete a file? The obvious scenario is, "when you want to delete a file." When a tool requires a more elaborate explanation, the chapter gives it.

Expect questions on the exam that couch command-line actions in scenario language.

Structure: Syntax and Switches

All commands in every command-line interface use a similar structure and execute in the same way. You type the name of the command, followed by the target of that command and any modifications of that command that you want to apply. You can call up a modification by using an extra letter or number, called a *switch* or *option*, which may follow either the command or the target, depending on the command. The proper way to write a command is called its *syntax*. The key with commands is that you can't spell anything incorrectly or use a \ when the syntax calls for a /. The command line is almost completely inflexible, so you have to learn the correct syntax for each command.

```
[command] [target (if any)] [switches]
```

or

```
[command] [switches] [target (if any)]
```

How do you know what switches are allowed? How do you know whether the switches come before or after the target? If you want to find out the syntax and switches used by a particular command, in Windows type the command followed by **/?** to get help:

```
[command name] /?
```

In macOS or Linux, type the command **man** (manual) followed by the command you're interested in:

```
man [command name]
```

When you are done reading the manual, press the Q key to quit back to the prompt.

Viewing Directory Contents: dir and ls

The Windows *dir* command and the macOS and Linux *ls* command show you the contents of the working directory. If you're like most techs, you'll use dir or ls more often than any other command at the command prompt. When you open a command-line window in Windows, it opens focused on your user folder. You will know this because the prompt looks like C:\Users*User name*>. By typing **dir** and then pressing the ENTER key (remember that you must always press ENTER to execute a command from the command line), you will see something like this:

```
C:\Users>dir
 Volume in drive C has no label.
 Volume Serial Number is 98F4-E484

 Directory of C:\Users

07/16/2020  10:52 AM    <DIR>          .
07/16/2020  10:52 AM    <DIR>          ..
12/20/2019  06:59 PM    <DIR>          DefaultAppPool
08/14/2021  10:42 AM    <DIR>          Mike
07/16/2020  02:07 AM    <DIR>          Public
               0 File(s)              0 bytes
               5 Dir(s)  295,888,113,664 bytes free
C:\Users>
```

The default prompts in Linux don't show the full path, but on my Ubuntu Linux system, typing ls shows the following in the mike user's Home folder:

```
mike@server:~$ ls
Desktop     Downloads  Public     Videos
Documents   photo.jpg  timmy.doc
mike@server:~$
```

If you are following along on a PC, remember that different computers contain different folders, files, and programs, so you will absolutely see something different from what's shown in the previous example. If a lot of text scrolls quickly down the screen in Windows, try typing **dir /p** (pause). Don't forget to press ENTER. The dir /p command is a lifesaver when you're looking for something in a large directory. Just press SPACEBAR to display the next screen.

In macOS and Linux, you can get the same result as dir /p by typing **ls | more**. The | symbol is called a *pipe*. You are telling the OS to take the output of ls and, instead of sending it directly to the screen, "pipe" or send it through the second command, *more*. The pipe command works in all three operating systems and is incredibly powerful. You'll see lots more of the pipe command later in this chapter.

 NOTE Some commands give you the same result whether you include spaces or not. Typing *dir/p* and *dir /p*, for example, provide the same output. Some commands, however, *require* spaces between the command and switches. In general, get into the habit of putting spaces between your command and switches and you won't run into problems.

dir Command

When you type a simple **dir** command, you will see that some of the entries look like this:

```
09/04/2021   05:51 PM            63,664 photo.jpg
```

All of these entries are files. The dir command lists the creation date, creation time, file size in bytes, filename, and extension.

Any entries that look like this are folders:

```
12/31/2021  10:18 AM     <DIR>          Windows
```

The dir command lists the creation date, creation time, *<DIR>* to tell you it is a folder, and the folder name.

Now type the **dir /w** command. Note that the dir /w command shows only the filenames, but they are arranged in four or five columns across your screen. Finally, type **dir /?** to see the screen shown in Figure 15-8, which lists all possible switches for the command.

ls Command

The ls command, like most UNIX commands, is very powerful and contains over 50 different switches. For now let's just cover one of the more important ones: –l.

Using **ls** with the **–l** switch, which stands for long listing, gives detailed information about all the files:

```
$ ls -l
-rw-rw-r-- 0 mike 2313443 Jun 13 15:27 photo.jpg
```

We'll discuss this output in more detail as we continue through the chapter.

Windows help screens sometimes seem a little cryptic and macOS and Linux help screens are often impossibly hard to read. Still, they're useful when you're not too familiar with a command or you can't figure out how to get a command to do what you need. Even though I have many commands memorized, I still refer to these help screens; you should use them as well. If you're really lost, type **help** at the command prompt for a list of commands you may type.

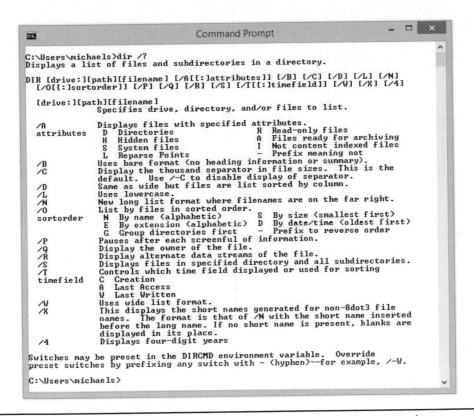

```
                    Command Prompt                          _  □  ×

C:\Users\michaels>dir /?
Displays a list of files and subdirectories in a directory.

DIR [drive:][path][filename] [/A[[:]attributes]] [/B] [/C] [/D] [/L] [/N]
  [/O[[:]sortorder]] [/P] [/Q] [/R] [/S] [/T[[:]timefield]] [/W] [/X] [/4]

  [drive:][path][filename]
              Specifies drive, directory, and/or files to list.

  /A          Displays files with specified attributes.
  attributes   D  Directories               R  Read-only files
               H  Hidden files              A  Files ready for archiving
               S  System files              I  Not content indexed files
               L  Reparse Points            -  Prefix meaning not
  /B          Uses bare format (no heading information or summary).
  /C          Display the thousand separator in file sizes.  This is the
              default.  Use /-C to disable display of separator.
  /D          Same as wide but files are list sorted by column.
  /L          Uses lowercase.
  /N          New long list format where filenames are on the far right.
  /O          List by files in sorted order.
  sortorder    N  By name (alphabetic)       S  By size (smallest first)
               E  By extension (alphabetic)  D  By date/time (oldest first)
               G  Group directories first    -  Prefix to reverse order
  /P          Pauses after each screenful of information.
  /Q          Display the owner of the file.
  /R          Display alternate data streams of the file.
  /S          Displays files in specified directory and all subdirectories.
  /T          Controls which time field displayed or used for sorting
  timefield    C  Creation
               A  Last Access
               W  Last Written
  /W          Uses wide list format.
  /X          This displays the short names generated for non-8dot3 file
              names.  The format is that of /N with the short name inserted
              before the long name. If no short name is present, blanks are
              displayed in its place.
  /4          Displays four-digit years

Switches may be preset in the DIRCMD environment variable.  Override
preset switches by prefixing any switch with - (hyphen)--for example, /-W.

C:\Users\michaels>
```

Figure 15-8   Typing **dir /?** in Windows lists all possible switches for the dir command.

NOTE   Extra text typed after a command to modify its operation, such as /w or /p after dir, is called a switch. Almost all switches can be used simultaneously to modify a command. For example, try typing **ls –a –l –h** in macOS or Linux.

With many commands, you can run multiple switches together. With the aforementioned ls, for example, ls –alh works just fine, with all three switches applied.

Changing Directory Focus: The cd Command

The *cd* command works in every operating system, although there are differences between Windows and macOS and Linux. You can use the cd command to change the focus of the command prompt to a different directory. To use the cd command, type **cd** followed by the name of the directory on which you want the prompt to focus. For example, in Windows, to go to the Obiwan directory in the root directory, you type **cd \obiwan** and then press ENTER. If the system has an Obiwan directory there, the prompt changes focus to that directory and appears as C:\Obiwan>. If no Obiwan directory exists or if you accidentally type something like **obiwam**, you get the error "The system cannot find the path specified." If only I had a dollar for every time I've seen those errors! I usually get them because I've typed too fast. If you get this error, check what you typed and try again.

Errors Are Good!

Consider errors in general for a moment—not just command-prompt errors such as "Invalid directory," but any error, including errors in the GUI. Many new computer users freeze in horror when they see an error message. Do not fear error messages. Error messages are good! Love them. Worship them. They will save you.

Seriously, think how confusing it would be if the computer didn't tell you when you messed up. Error messages tell you what you did wrong so you can fix it. You absolutely cannot hurt your PC in any way by typing the dir or cd command incorrectly. Take advantage of this knowledge and experiment. Intentionally make mistakes to familiarize yourself with the error messages. Have fun and learn from errors!

To return to the root directory, type **cd ** and press ENTER. You can use the cd command to point the prompt to any directory. For example, typing **cd obiwan\my\hope** from a C:\ prompt would change it to C:\Obiwan\my\hope>—assuming, of course, that your system *has* a directory called C:\Obiwan\my\hope.

Once the prompt has changed, type **dir** again. You should see a different list of files and directories. Every directory holds different files and subdirectories, so when you point the prompt to different directories, the dir command shows you different contents.

Changing directory focus in macOS and Linux is similar to doing so in Windows, but you use a / instead of a \. Using the same example just shown for Windows, from the root directory you type **cd /obiwan**. To go to the /Obiwan/my/hope directory you type **cd /obiwan/my/hope**.

 NOTE On a Linux system it is considered bad manners to create files and folders in the root (/) directory. In fact, you need "root" permissions to do such a thing. This is because of Linux's history as a multi-user system; it was important to include restrictions so that users couldn't break the underlying OS on which everyone depended.

In the previous examples we have been using what are known as *absolute paths*, meaning we have been typing out the entire path of a directory destination. This might work OK for an ancient DOS system from the '80s, but it's way too much work to move around in today's deeply nested directory trees.

That's where relative paths come in handy; instead of starting the path with a \, you can just type the name of the directory. For example, you could go to the C:\Obiwan directory from the root directory simply by typing **cd obiwan** at the C:\> prompt. You can then move one level at a time, like this:

```
C:\>cd Obiwan
C:\Obiwan>cd my
C:\Obiwan\my>cd hope
```

Or, you can jump multiple directory levels in one step, like this:

```
C:\>cd Obiwan\my\hope
C:\Obiwan\my\hope>
```

These tricks also work for macOS and Linux, but of course you always use a forward slash instead of a backslash as needed:

```
mike@server:~$ cd Obiwan
mike@server:~/Obiwan$
```

A final trick: if you want to go *up* a single directory level, you can type cd followed immediately by *two periods* or a *space and two periods*. So, for example, if you're in the C:\Obiwan\my directory and you want to move up to the C:\Obiwan directory, you can simply type **cd ..** and you'll be there:

```
C:\Obiwan\my>cd ..
C:\Obiwan>
```

Take some time to move the prompt focus around the directories of your PC, using the cd and dir commands. Use dir to find a directory, and then use cd to move the focus to that directory. Remember, cd \ (or cd / in macOS and Linux) always gets you back to the root directory.

 EXAM TIP Look for the **..** option or switch with the dir and other commands on the CompTIA A+ 1002 exam. It moves the focus up one level when navigating from the command line.

Moving Between Drives

Windows and macOS and Linux have very different techniques for moving between drives, given that Windows uses drive letters while macOS and Linux do not. Let's start with Windows and then we'll take a look at macOS and Linux.

Moving Between Drives in Windows

The cd command is *not* used to move between Windows' drive letters. To get the prompt to point to another drive ("point" is command-line geekspeak for "switch its focus"), just type the drive letter and a colon. If the prompt points at the C:\Users\mike directory and you want to see what is on the USB thumb drive (E:), just type **e:** and the prompt will point to the USB drive. You'll see the following on the screen:

```
C:\Users\mike>e:
E:\>
```

To return to the C: drive, just type **c:** and you'll see the following:

```
E:\>c:
C:\Users\mike>
```

Note that you return to the same directory you left. Just for fun, try typing in a drive letter that you know doesn't exist. For example, I know that my system doesn't have a W: drive. If I type in a nonexistent drive on a Windows system, I get the following error:

```
The system cannot find the drive specified.
```

Try inserting an optical disc or a thumb drive and entering its drive letter to point to its drive. Type **dir** to see the contents of the optical disc. Type **cd** to move the focus to any folders on the optical disc. Now return focus to the C: drive.

Using the dir, cd, and drive letter commands, you can access any folder on any storage device on your system. Make sure you can use these commands comfortably to navigate inside your computer.

Moving Between Drives in macOS and Linux

So if macOS and Linux don't use drive letters, how do you access your other drive partitions, optical media, thumb drives, and so on? Well, all media is mounted as a folder, but the location of those folders is going to vary by the OS. In macOS, you need to look in the /Volumes folder. In Ubuntu Linux, you need to look in the /mnt folder for drives and the /media/<user name> folder for removable media. In other Linux distributions, well, you're going to have to explore—good thing you know how to use the cd and ls commands, eh? The following commands show my optical drive and a thumb drive in an Ubuntu Linux system:

```
mike@server:/media/mike$ ls -l
drwx------ 3 mike mike 4096 Dec 31  1969 THUMBDRIVE
dr-xr-xr-x 6 mike mike 2048 May 13 10:15 Age of Empires
mike@server:/media/mike$
```

Making Directories: The md/mkdir Command

Now that you have learned how to navigate in a command-prompt world, it's time to start making stuff, beginning with a new directory.

To make a directory, use the *md* command in Windows. Alternatively, you can use the *mkdir* command, which works in all operating systems and is identical to md. In Windows, to create a directory called practice under your user's folder, for example, open a new Command Prompt window or **cd** to your users folder at \Users\<your username>. You should see the prompt

```
C:Users\mike>_
```

Now that the prompt points to the C:\Users\mike directory, type **md practice** to create the directory:

```
C:\Users\mike>md practice
```

Once you press ENTER, Windows executes the command, but it won't volunteer any information about what it did. You must use the **dir** command to see that you have, in fact, created a new directory. Note that the practice directory in this example is not listed last, as you might expect.

```
C:\>dir
 Volume in Drive C is
 Volume Serial Number is 1734-3234
Directory of C:\Users\mike
08/21/2021  03:58 PM    <DIR>          .
08/21/2021  03:58 PM    <DIR>          ..
08/21/2021  09:55 AM    <DIR>          Desktop
07/15/2021  08:25 AM    <DIR>          Documents
08/20/2021  09:16 AM    <DIR>          Downloads
07/15/2021  08:25 AM    <DIR>          Favorites
07/15/2021  08:25 AM    <DIR>          Music
07/15/2021  08:25 AM    <DIR>          Pictures
08/21/2021  03:58 PM    <DIR>          practice
07/15/2021  08:25 AM    <DIR>          Videos
                1 File(s)            240 bytes
               10 Dir(s)  216,876,089,344 bytes free
```

What about distinguishing between uppercase and lowercase? Windows displays both in file and folder names but rarely makes any distinction with commands—which is a nice way to say that Windows doesn't support case. For clarity, try using the **md** command to make a folder called Practice (note the uppercase) and see what happens. This also happens in the graphical Windows. Go to your desktop and try to make two folders, one called files and the other called FILES, and see what Windows tells you.

To create a files subdirectory in the practice directory, first use the **cd** command to point the prompt to the practice directory:

```
C:Users\mike>cd practice
C:Users\mike\practice>_
```

 NOTE Make sure that the prompt points to the directory in which you want to make the new subdirectory before you execute the md command.

Then run the **md** command to make the files directory:

```
md files
```

When you're finished, type **dir** to see the new files subdirectory. Just for fun, try the process again and add a games directory under the practice directory. Type **dir** to verify success.

Creating folders in macOS and Linux is again identical, but you must use the mkdir command. Here is the same example just given but done on my Ubuntu system:

```
mike@server:~$ mkdir practice
```

You can see the results by running the **ls** command:

```
mike@server:~$ls
practice
```

Don't forget that Linux is case sensitive. Check out the results of these three different folders, all different capitalizations of "files":

```
mike@server:~/practice$ ls
files  Files  FILES
mike@server:~/practice$
```

Removing Directories: The rd/rmdir Command

Removing subdirectories works exactly like making them. First, get to the directory that contains the subdirectory you want to delete, and then execute either the *rmdir* or *rd* command. Both of these commands are functionally identical, but where they work is important. The rmdir command works equally well in Windows, macOS, and Linux, but the rd command only works in Windows.

So, with that in mind, let's get rid of some folders. It's actually quite simple. In this example, let's use Linux as an example to delete the files subdirectory in our ~/practice directory (remember ~ means your home directory). First, get to where the files subdirectory is located—~/practice—by typing **cd practice** (make sure you're in your home directory first). Then type **rmdir files**. If you received no response, you probably did it right! Type **ls** to check that the files subdirectory is gone. Windows works exactly the same, although we tend to use the rd command more often, simply because it's faster to type.

The rmdir/rd command alone will not delete a directory if the directory contains files or subdirectories. If you want to delete a directory that contains files or subdirectories, you must first empty that directory. However, Windows folks can use the rd command followed by the /s switch to delete a directory as well as all files and subdirectories. The rd command followed by the /s switch is handy but dangerous, because it's easy to delete more than you want. There is no Recycle Bin when deleting from the command line, so when deleting, always follow the maxim "Check twice and delete once."

Let's delete the practice and games directories with rd followed by the /s switch. Because the practice directory is in your home directory, point to it with **cd \Users\<*your username*>**. Now execute the command **rd practice /s**. In a rare display of mercy, Windows responds with the following:

```
C:\Users\mike>rd practice /s
practice, Are you sure (Y/N)?
```

Press the Y key and both C:\Users\mike\practice and C:\Users\mike\practice\games are eliminated.

 EXAM TIP   Make sure you know how to use md, mkdir, rd, rmdir, rm, and cd for the CompTIA A+ 220-1002 exam.

Want to remove a folder and all of its contents in Linux? No problem, but we don't use rmdir. Instead we turn to the very handy rm command. (More on rm a little later in the chapter—see "Deleting Files.") With the same scenario just presented, type the **rm** command with the **–r** switch as shown:

```
mike@server:~$ rm -r practice
```

Try This!   Working with Directories

PC techs should be comfortable creating and deleting directories. To get some practice, try this!

1. Create a new directory in your home directory by using the make directory command (md). At the command prompt from your home directory, make a directory called Jedi:

   ```
   C:\Users\padawan>md Jedi
   ```

2. As usual, the prompt tells you nothing; it just presents a fresh prompt. Do a dir (that is, type the **dir** command) to see your new directory. Windows creates the new directory wherever it is pointing when you issue the command, whether or not that's where you meant to put it. To demonstrate, point the prompt to your new directory by using the cd command:

   ```
   C:\Users\padawan>cd jedi
   ```

3. Now use the make directory command again to create a directory called Yoda:

   ```
   C:\Users\padawan\Jedi>md Yoda
   ```

   Do a **dir** again, and you should see that your Jedi directory now contains a Yoda directory.

4. Type **cd ..** to go up one level and return to your home directory so you can delete your new directories by using the remove directory command (rd):

   ```
   C:Users\padawan>rd /s jedi
   ```

   Yet again showing mercy, Windows responds with the following:

   ```
   jedi, Are you sure <Y/N>?
   ```

5. Press Y to eliminate both Jedi and Jedi\Yoda.

6. Using a macOS or Linux system, repeat this entire process using the mkdir, cd, and rm commands.

Running a Program in Windows

To run a program from the Windows command line, simply change the prompt focus to the folder where the program is located, type the name of the program, and then press ENTER. Try this safe example. Go to the C:\Windows\System32 folder—the exact name of this folder is pretty standard on all Windows systems, but your mileage may vary. Type **dir /p** to see the files one page at a time. You should see a file called mmc.exe (see Figure 15-9).

```
Command Prompt                                                    —    □    ×
04/11/2020  06:34 PM            79,360 MitigationConfiguration.dll          ^
04/11/2020  06:34 PM           243,200 miutils.dll
04/28/2020  09:01 AM           256,000 MixedReality.Broker.dll
04/12/2020  04:20 AM            79,360 MixedRealityCapture.Broker.dll
04/12/2020  04:20 AM           641,536 MixedRealityCapture.Pipeline.dll
09/03/2020  04:04 AM    <DIR>          mk-MK
09/03/2020  04:04 AM    <DIR>          ml-IN
04/11/2020  06:34 PM           673,088 mlang.dat
04/11/2020  06:34 PM           242,688 mlang.dll
04/11/2020  06:34 PM         1,859,584 mmc.exe
04/11/2020  06:34 PM             3,186 mmc.exe.config
04/11/2020  06:34 PM           340,480 mmcbase.dll
04/11/2020  06:34 PM            63,488 mmci.dll
04/11/2020  06:34 PM            15,360 mmcico.dll
04/11/2020  06:34 PM         2,901,504 mmcndmgr.dll
04/11/2020  06:34 PM           127,488 mmcshext.dll
04/11/2020  06:34 PM           469,576 MMDevAPI.dll
04/11/2020  06:34 PM         2,126,848 mmgaclient.dll
04/11/2020  06:34 PM           155,136 mmgaproxystub.dll               v
```

Figure 15-9 The mmc.exe program listed in the System32 folder

All files with extensions .exe and .com are programs, so mmc.exe is a program. Remember MMC from the previous chapter? To run the mmc.exe program, just type the filename, in this case **mmc**, and press ENTER (see Figure 15-10). Note that you do not have to type the .exe extension, although you can. Congratulations! You have just run another application from the command line.

NOTE Windows includes a lot of command-line tools for specific jobs such as starting and stopping services, viewing computers on a network, converting hard drive file systems, and more. This book discusses these task-specific tools in the chapters that reflect their task. Chapter 19, "Local Area Networking," goes into detail on the versatile and powerful net command, for example.

Running a Program in macOS and Linux

As much as I like to tell folks how similar the macOS, Linux, and Windows command lines are, they are very different in some areas, one of which is how you run executable programs from the command line. For starters, macOS and Linux executable programs don't rely on any kind of extension such as .exe in Windows. Instead, any file, whether it's compiled code or a text file, can be given the property of executable, as shown in Figure 15-11.

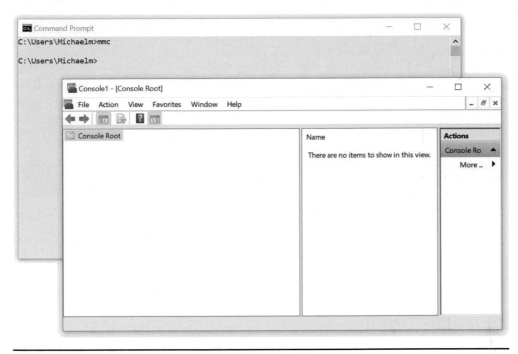

Figure 15-10 Running mmc in Windows

Figure 15-11
Showing file
properties in
Ubuntu

So it's really up to the person using the program to verify they are even using a program. One does not just start programs haphazardly in macOS or Linux. You make a point to know your executable before you run it.

macOS and Linux help you in the command line when it comes to executables. First of all, macOS and almost all versions of Linux come with color-coded command lines, as shown in Figure 15-12. In this particular version the executable files are colored green (though that's a little tough to see in black and white print!). The lone su command has a unique color code to show that any user can run that program.

```
                    mike@mike-VirtualBox: /bin

File  Edit  View  Search  Terminal  Help
chmod           journalctl      ntfs-3g.probe   setupcon             whiptail
chown           kbd_mode        ntfscat         sh                   ypdomainname
chvt            kill            ntfscluster     sh.distrib           zcat
cp              kmod            ntfscmp         sleep                zcmp
cpio            less            ntfsfallocate   ss                   zdiff
dash            lessecho        ntfsfix         static-sh            zegrep
date            lessfile        ntfsinfo        stty                 zfgrep
dd              lesskey         ntfsls          su                   zforce
df              lesspipe        ntfsmove        sync                 zgrep
dir             ln              ntfsrecover     systemctl            zless
dmesg           loadkeys        ntfssecaudit    systemd              zmore
dnsdomainname   login           ntfstruncate    systemd-ask-password znew
domainname      loginctl        ntfsusermap     systemd-escape
dumpkeys        lowntfs-3g      ntfswipe        systemd-hwdb
echo            ls              open            systemd-inhibit
mike@mike-VirtualBox:/bin$
```

Figure 15-12 Color-coded files in Ubuntu

macOS and Linux have two very different types of executable file types: built-in and executables. Built-in programs are like the ones you see in Figure 15-12. You just worked with three built-in programs: ls, mkdir, and rm. To run a built-in program you just type it in as you have already done many times in this chapter.

Executable programs are programs that are, well, not built in. If you download a program from somewhere (and Linux people do this a lot), you first unzip the program and then run the program. But there's one problem. If you try to run it, Linux can't find it, even though it is in the exact folder you are running it from! Interestingly, this is by design. When you run a program from a Linux command line, Linux first looks through a series of folders called the *path* (not to be confused with the other type of path discussed earlier). You can see the path by typing the command **echo $PATH**:

```
mike@server:~/$ echo $PATH
/usr/local/sbin:/usr/local/bin:/usr/sbin:/usr/bin:/sbin:/bin:/usr/games:/usr/local/games
```

NOTE Downloading and running command-line programs is not a macOS thing.

To make Linux run the executable, you need to add a period and a slash (**./**, commonly called "dot-slash") in front of the executable to make it run:

```
mike@server:~/$ ./runme
```

Working with Files

This section deals with basic file manipulation. You will learn how to look at, copy, move, rename, and delete files. The examples in this section are based on a C: root directory with the following files and directories:

```
C:\>dir
 Volume in drive C has no label.
 Volume Serial Number is 4C62-1572

 Directory of C:\

05/26/2021  11:37 PM                 0 AILog.txt
05/29/2021  05:33 PM             5,776 aoedoppl.txt
05/29/2021  05:33 PM             2,238 aoeWVlog.txt
07/12/2021  10:38 AM    <DIR>          books
07/15/2021  02:45 PM             1,708 CtDrvStp.log
06/04/2021  10:22 PM    <DIR>          Impressions Games
09/11/2021  11:32 AM    <DIR>          NVIDIA
01/03/2021  01:12 PM    <DIR>          pers-drv
09/14/2021  11:11 AM    <DIR>          Program Files
09/12/2021  08:32 PM                21 statusclient.log
07/31/2021  10:40 PM               153 systemscandata.txt
03/13/2021  09:54 AM         1,111,040 t3h0
04/21/2021  04:19 PM    <DIR>          temp
01/10/2021  07:07 PM    <DIR>          WebCam
12/31/2021  10:18 AM    <DIR>          WINDOWS
01/03/2021  09:06 AM    <DIR>          WUTemp
               6 File(s)     1,120,936 bytes
               9 Dir(s)  94,630,002,688 bytes free
```

Because you probably don't have a PC with these files and directories, follow the examples but use what's on your drive. In other words, create your own folders and copy files to them from various folders currently on your system.

Using Wildcards to Locate Files

Visualize having 273 files in one directory. A few of these files have the extension .docx, but most do not. You are looking only for files with the .docx extension. Wouldn't it be nice to be able to type the dir command in such a way that only the .docx files come up? You can do this by using wildcards.

A *wildcard* is one of two special characters—asterisk (*) and question mark (?)—that you can use in place of all or part of a filename, often so that a command-line command will act on more than one file at a time. Wildcards work with all command-line commands that take filenames. A great example is the dir command. When you execute a plain dir command, it finds and displays all the files and folders in the specified directory; however, you can also narrow its search by adding a filename. For example, if you type the command **dir ailog.txt** while in your root (C:\) directory, you get the following result:

```
C:\>dir ailog.txt
 Volume in drive C has no label.
 Volume Serial Number is 4C62-1572
 Directory of C:\
05/26/2021  11:37 PM                      0 AILog.txt
                   1 File(s)              0 bytes
                   0 Dir(s)   94,630,195,200 bytes free
```

If you just want to confirm the presence of a particular file in a particular place, this is very convenient. But suppose you want to see all files with the extension .txt. In that case, you use the * wildcard, like this: **dir *.txt**. A good way to think of the * wildcard is "I don't care." Replace the part of the filename that you don't care about with an asterisk (*). The result of dir *.txt would look like this:

```
 Volume in drive C has no label.
 Volume Serial Number is 4C62-1572

 Directory of C:\

05/26/2021  11:37 PM                      0 AILog.txt
05/29/2021  05:33 PM                  5,776 aoedoppl.txt
05/29/2021  05:33 PM                  2,238 aoeWVlog.txt
07/31/2021  10:40 PM                    153 systemscandata.txt
                   4 File(s)          8,167 bytes
                   0 Dir(s)   94,630,002,688 bytes free
```

Wildcards also substitute for parts of filenames. This dir command will find every file that starts with the letter *a*:

```
C:\>dir a*.*
 Volume in drive C has no label.
 Volume Serial Number is 4C62-1572

 Directory of C:\

05/26/2021  11:37 PM                      0 AILog.txt
05/29/2021  05:33 PM                  5,776 aoedoppl.txt
05/29/2021  05:33 PM                  2,238 aoeWVlog.txt
                   3 File(s)          8,014 bytes
                   0 Dir(s)   94,629,675,008 bytes free
```

Wildcards in macOS and Linux work basically the same as in Windows. Head over to the /bin directory on a typical Linux system (it's so full of files) and try using a wildcard with the ls command. Let's find everything that starts with the letter *s* by using the command **ls s* –l**:

```
mike@server:/bin$ ls s* -l
-rwxr-xr-x 1 root root 73352 Feb 13  2021 sed
-rwxr-xr-x 1 root root 36232 May 23  2021 setfacl
-rwxr-xr-x 1 root root 39896 Feb 18  2021 setfont
-rwxr-xr-x 1 root root 12052 Jan 29  2021 setupcon
lrwxrwxrwx 1 root root     4 Jun 29 13:06 sh -> dash
```

```
lrwxrwxrwx 1 root root     4 Jun 29 13:06 sh.distrib -> dash
-rwxr-xr-x 1 root root 31296 Jan 13  2021 sleep
-rwxr-xr-x 1 root root 76624 Feb 17  2021 ss
lrwxrwxrwx 1 root root     7 Jun 29 13:06 static-sh -> busybox
-rwxr-xr-x 1 root root 68256 Jan 13  2021 stty
-rwsr-xr-x 1 root root 36936 Feb 16  2021 su
-rwxr-xr-x 1 root root 27200 Jan 13  2021 sync
```

We've used wildcards only with the dir and ls commands in the previous examples, but virtually every command that deals with files and folders will take wildcards. Let's examine some more commands and see how they use wildcards.

 SIM   Check out the four "Wildcard" sims in the Chapter 15 section of http://totalsem.com/100x. The two Type! sims plus the Show! and the Click! will prepare you for any number of performance-based questions CompTIA throws at you in the 1002 exam.

Deleting Files

To delete files, you use the *del* (or *erase*) command in Windows and the *rm* command in macOS and Linux. Deleting files is simple—maybe too simple. As I said before, deleting a file in your GUI gives you the luxury of retrieving deleted files from the Recycle Bin on those "Oops, I didn't mean to delete that" occasions everyone encounters at one time or another. The command line, however, shows no such mercy to the careless user. It has no function equivalent to the Recycle Bin or Trash. Once you have erased a file, you can recover it only by using special recovery utilities (maybe . . . but don't bet on it). Again, the rule here is to *check twice and delete once*.

To delete a single file in Windows, type the **del** command followed by the name of the file to delete. To delete the file reportdraft1.docx, for example, type this:

```
del reportdraft1.docx
```

In macOS and Linux, do the same thing but type **rm** in place of del, like this:

```
rm reportdraft1.docx
```

Although nothing appears on the screen to confirm it, the file is now gone. To confirm that the reportdraft1.docx file is no longer listed, use the **dir** or **ls** command.

You can use wildcards with the del and rm commands to delete multiple files. For example, to delete all files with the extension .txt in a folder, you can type this in macOS/Linux:

```
rm *.txt
```

You can place the wildcard anywhere in the name. For example, to delete all files with the filename "config" in a Windows directory, type **del config.***. To delete all of the files in a directory, you can use this dangerous but useful *.* wildcard (often pronounced "star-dot-star"):

```
del *.*
```

This is one of the few command-line commands that elicits a response—but only in Windows. Upon receiving the del *.* command, Windows responds with "Are you sure? (Y/N)," to which you respond with a *Y* or *N*. Pressing Y erases every file in the directory, so again, use *.* with care!

With Windows, we only use del to delete files; it will not remove directories. Use rd to delete directories. In macOS and Linux, you can use the rm command to delete both files and folders. Here's an example of the rm command using the –r switch to delete the folder Jedi as well as all of its contents:

```
rm -r Jedi
```

The Windows rd command comes with a switch, /s, which makes it act identically to the rm –r command:

```
rd /s Jedi
```

Clearly it can be very dangerous to use the rm and rd commands with these switches. Use them carefully.

 NOTE If you spend any time reading about macOS or Linux Terminal commands online, you might see jokes involving the sudo rm –rf / command. It tells the system to delete every file and folder on the computer's hard drive! The sudo portion means run this as root, rm means to delete, –r means to go into every folder, f means to use force (in other words, delete it no matter what), and finally the / points it at the root of the drive!

Copying and Moving Files

Being able to copy and move files in a command line is crucial to all technicians. Because of its finicky nature and many options, the copy command is also rather painful to learn, especially if you're used to dragging icons in Windows, macOS, or Linux. The following tried-and-true, five-step process makes it easier, but the real secret is to get in front of a prompt and just copy and move files around until you're comfortable. Keep in mind that the only difference between copying and moving is whether the original is left behind (*copy*) or not (*move*). Once you've learned the copy command, you've also learned the move command! In macOS and Linux, the copy command is *cp* and the move command is *mv*. Otherwise, use the same syntax.

Mike's Five-Step copy/move Process

I've been teaching folks how to copy and move files for years by using this handy process. Keep in mind that hundreds of variations on this process exist. As you become more confident with these commands, try doing a copy /? or move /? in Windows and man cp or man mv in macOS and Linux at any handy prompt to see the real power of the commands. But first, follow this process step by step:

1. Point the command prompt to the directory containing the file(s) you want to copy or move.

2. Type **copy** or **move** (Windows) or **cp** or **mv** (macOS and Linux) and a space.

3. Type the *name(s)* of the file(s) to be copied/moved (with or without wildcards) and a space.

4. Type the *path* of the new location for the file(s).

5. Press ENTER.

Let's try an example using Windows. The directory Jedi (in my \Users folder) contains the file notes.txt. Copy this file to a USB thumb drive (E:).

1. Type **cd Jedi** to point the command prompt to the Jedi directory.

```
C:\Users\mike>cd Jedi
```

2. Type **copy** and a space.

```
C:\Users\mike\Jedi>copy
```

3. Type **notes.txt** and a space.

```
C:\Users\mike\Jedi>copy notes.txt
```

4. Type **e:**.

```
C:\Users\mike\Jedi>copy notes.txt e:\
```

5. Press ENTER.

The entire command and response would look like this:

```
C:\Users\mike\Jedi>copy notes.txt e:\
1 file(s) copied
```

If you point the command prompt to the E: drive and type **dir**, the notes.txt file will be visible. Let's try another example, this time in macOS and Linux. Suppose 100 files are in the ~/Jedi directory, 30 of which have the .odf extension, and suppose you want to move those files to ~/Screenplays/sw2020. Follow these steps:

1. Type **cd Screenplays/sw2020** to get the command prompt to the correct folder.

```
mike@server:~$ cd Screenplays/sw2020
```

2. Type **mv** and a space.

```
mike@server:~/Screenplays/sw2020$ mv_
```

3. Type ***.odf** and a space.

```
mike@server:~/Screenplays/sw2020$ mv_*.odf_
```

4. Type **~/Jedi**.

```
mike@server:~/Screenplays/sw2020$ mv_*.odf_~/Jedi
```

5. Press ENTER.

```
mike@server:~/Screenplays/sw2020$
```

macOS and Linux don't give you any feedback at all unless you use special switches. You can check to see if they all made it with **ls**.

Pruning and Grafting Folder Trees

There's a number of situations where you find yourself wanting to grab a folder, complete with all of the subfolders and any files that might be anywhere in any of the folders, and copy or move the whole "pile" in one command. We call this process *pruning and grafting* and it's one of the places where the command line really shines in comparison to GUI file manipulation. Done properly, command-line pruning and grafting is faster and gives you much finer control of the process.

In Windows, the standard copy and move commands can work only in one directory at a time, making them a poor choice for copying or moving files in multiple directories. To help with these multi-directory jobs, Microsoft added the *xcopy* command. (Note that there is no xmove, only xcopy.) We'll also look at robocopy, cp, and mv.

xcopy

The xcopy command functions similarly to copy, but xcopy has extra switches that give it the power to work with multiple directories. Here's how it does that. Let's say I have a directory called Logs in the root of my C: drive. The Logs directory has three subdirectories: Jan, Feb, and Mar. All of these directories, including the Logs directory, contain about 50 files. If I wanted to copy all of these files to my E: drive in one command, I would use xcopy in the following manner:

```
xcopy c:\Logs e:\Logs /s
```

Because xcopy works on directories, you don't have to use filenames as you would in copy, although xcopy certainly accepts filenames and wildcards. The /s switch, the most commonly used of all the many switches that come with xcopy, tells xcopy to copy all subdirectories except for empty ones. The /e switch tells xcopy to copy empty subdirectories. When you have a lot of copying to do over many directories, xcopy is the tool to use.

robocopy

Microsoft introduced the *robocopy* command—short for Robust File Copy—many years ago as an add-on tool for Windows Server to enable techs to manage files and folders more quickly and efficiently than with xcopy or copy. The robocopy command is powerful indeed, enabling you to, for example, copy the files and folders from one computer to another across a network, fully replicating the structure on the destination system *and* deleting anything on that system that wasn't part of the copy. It can do this with a simple command.

The robocopy syntax does not resemble xcopy, so if you're going to use the tool, you need to unlearn a few things. Here's the basic syntax:

```
robocopy [source] [destination] [options]
```

Here's an example of the command in action. The following command would copy all files and subfolders from a local machine's D:\testserver\website folder to a shared folder on the remote server \\liveserver\website.

```
robocopy d:\testserver\website \\liveserver\website /mir
```

The /mir switch, for mirror, tells robocopy to copy everything from the source and make the destination mirror it. That means robocopy will also delete anything in the destination that doesn't match the source folders and files.

If that were it, robocopy would be powerful, but that's not even the tip of the iceberg. The robocopy command can copy encrypted files. It enables an administrator to copy files even if the administrator account is expressly denied access to those files. It will also resume copying after an interruption, and do so at the spot it stopped. For the full syntax, type the following:

```
robocopy /?
```

Their power and utility make the del, copy/move, xcopy, and robocopy commands indispensable for a PC technician, but that same power and utility can cause disaster. Only a trained Jedi, with The Force as his ally . . . well, wrong book, but the principle remains: Beware of the quick and easy keystroke, for it may spell your doom. Think twice and execute the command once. The data you save may be yours!

EXAM TIP Know xcopy and robocopy for the CompTIA A+ 220-1002 exam.

cp and mv (again!)

If you really want to see some powerful commands, let's head over to Linux. Unlike Windows, you can both move and copy folders and their contents, using the same cp and mv commands we saw earlier for regular copying and moving. Let's say we have a folder called /home/mike/Backups. The Backups folder has ten subfolders and hundreds of files. I want to save a copy of these files to a folder called /mnt/storage. To do this I only need to run cp with the –R (recursive) switch (note that the ~ in my prompt shows that I'm in the home folder):

```
mike@server:~$ cp -R Backups /mnt/storage
```

If I want to move all of that to storage instead of copy, I use the mv command. Interestingly, the mv command doesn't even need a special switch—just run the program, pointing at the folder of interest and giving it a destination:

```
mike@server:~$ mv Desktop/Backups /mnt/storage
```

Assorted Windows Commands

As a proficient IT technician in the field, you need to be familiar with a whole slew of command-line tools and other important utilities. The CompTIA A+ 220-1002 exam focuses in on several of them, and although many have been discussed in detail in previous chapters, it is extremely important that you understand and practice with chkdsk, format, hostname, gpupdate, gpresult, sfc, and shutdown.

chkdsk (/f /r)

The *chkdsk* (checkdisk) command scans, detects, and repairs file system issues and errors. You can run the chkdsk utility from a command prompt with the switches /f and /r. The /f switch attempts to fix file system–related errors, while the /r switch attempts to locate and repair bad sectors. To run successfully, chkdsk needs direct access to a drive. In other words, the drive needs to be "unlocked." For example, if you run chkdsk /f /r and chkdsk does not consider your drive unlocked, you will receive a "cannot lock current drive" message, meaning that another process has the drive locked and is preventing chkdsk from locking the drive itself. After this, chkdsk presents you with the option to run it the next time the system restarts (see Figure 15-13).

Figure 15-13

The chkdsk /f /r utility and switches on a locked drive

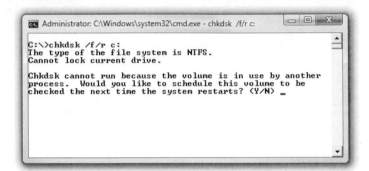

format

After the previous chapters, you should have an expert-level knowledge of (or, at the very least, a passing familiarity with) formatting and partitioning hard drives. Formatting, you may remember, is the process of writing a new file system to a volume (or partition, if you're old school) so it can hold an operating system or data. We have already discussed the various built-in Windows utilities available to provide the formatting of drives, and you no doubt know that many third-party formatting tools are out there. In this chapter, you just need to become familiar with the format command and its switches.

The *format* command, you may have guessed, enables you to format volumes from the command line. Figure 15-14 shows an example of the format command in action. Note the complex switches that let me specify what file system to use, which volume, that I want compression, etc. The very best way to familiarize yourself with the format command and its available switches is simply to enter **format /?** from the command prompt.

The CompTIA A+ 220-1002 exam focuses on both GUI and command-line operating system formatting utilities and options, so you should familiarize yourself with the format command and its switches by practicing them on a test system you are literally not afraid to wipe out. Besides, you never know what antiques CompTIA may dust off.

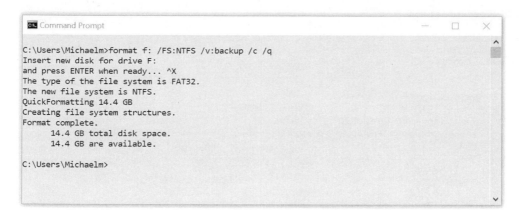

Figure 15-14 The format command in action

hostname

The *hostname* command is the most straightforward of all command-line commands. If you type **hostname** at the command prompt, it will display the name of your computer, also known as the hostname. When I type **hostname**, for example, it displays "MikesPC." (The hostname command doesn't appear in the 1002 exam objectives, but it's very useful to know.)

gpupdate

Group policies define various security settings for Windows systems, such as password complexity, logon attempts, and permissions for users to install software. Group policies can apply to a standalone system or to systems on a domain. It takes time for a group policy change to propagate throughout a domain, but you can force a workstation to update to new policies by running *gpupdate* on the workstation.

gpresult

If you need a quick overview of all security policies applied to a single user or computer, the *gpresult* tool is for you. You can run gpresult for any user or computer on your network (assuming you have a valid username and password) and you can ask for detailed or summary information. This command shows the summary results for user michaelm on the local computer:

```
C:\>gpresult /USER michaelm /R

Microsoft (R) Windows (R) Operating System Group Policy Result tool v2.0
c 2018 Microsoft Corporation. All rights reserved.
Created on 8/20/2020 at 1:54:20 PM
RSOP data for TOTALBOGUS\michaelm on MIKEPC : Logging Mode
---------------------------------------------------------
```

```
OS Configuration:            Member Workstation
OS Version:                  6.3.9600
Site Name:                   N/A
Roaming Profile:             N/A
Local Profile:               C:\Users\michaelm
Connected over a slow link?: No

USER SETTINGS
--------------
    CN=michaelm,CN=Users,DC=totalbogus
    Last time Group Policy was applied: 8/20/2020 at 1:39:10 PM
    Group Policy was applied from:      dc1.totalbogus
    Group Policy slow link threshold:   500 kbps
    Domain Name:                        TOTALBOGUS
    Domain Type:                        Windows 2008 or later

    Applied Group Policy Objects
    ----------------------------
        Default Domain Policy
    The following GPOs were not applied because they were filtered out
    -------------------------------------------------------------------
        Local Group Policy
         Filtering:  Not Applied (Empty)
    The user is a part of the following security groups
    ----------------------------------------------------
        Domain Users
        Everyone
```

sfc

The Windows *sfc* (*System File Checker*) command scans, detects, and restores important Windows system files, folders, and paths. Techs often turn to sfc when Windows isn't quite working correctly and use it to find and fix critical Windows system files that have become corrupt. If you run sfc and it finds issues, it attempts to replace corrupted or missing files from cached DLLs (backups of those system files) located in the Windows\System32\Dllcache\ directory. Without getting very deep into the mad science involved, just know that you can use sfc to correct corruption. To run sfc from a command prompt, enter **sfc /scannow**. To familiarize yourself with sfc's switches, enter **sfc /?** (see Figure 15-15).

shutdown

The *shutdown* command enables you to do exactly that to a local or remote computer—namely, shut it down (or reboot it). The cool part of the tool is that you can use a number of switches to control and report the shutdown. A network administrator could use this tool to restart a computer remotely, for example, like this:

```
shutdown /r /m \\devserver
```

The /r switch tells shutdown to have the computer reboot rather than just shut down. If you want to see the full syntax for shutdown, type the following:

```
shutdown /?
```

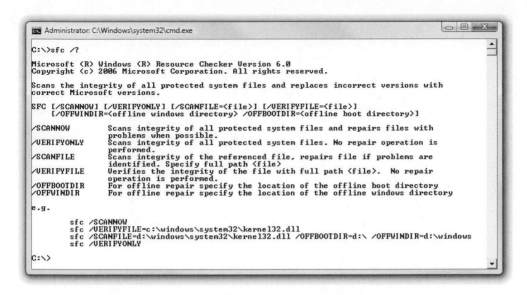

Figure 15-15 Checking sfc options with sfc /? at a command prompt

Using Special Keys in Windows

You might find yourself repeatedly typing the same commands, or at least very similar commands, when working at a prompt. Microsoft has provided a number of ways to access previously typed commands. Type the **dir** command at a command prompt. When you get back to a prompt, press F1, and the letter *d* appears. Press F1 again. Now the letter *i* appears after the *d*. Do you see what is happening? The F1 key brings back the previous command one letter at a time. Pressing F3 brings back the entire command at once. Now try running these three commands:

```
dir /w
hostname
md Skywalker
```

Now press the UP ARROW key. Keep pressing it till you see your original dir command—it's a history of all your old commands. Now use the RIGHT ARROW key to add /w to the end of your dir command. Windows command history is very handy.

NOTE macOS and Linux shells come with their own sets of special keys, many of which match those in Windows. Actually, Windows copied many of the handier keys, like the history feature, from the UNIX world. macOS and Linux take the command history one step further and remember it even if you close the terminal or reboot the machine—useful if you accidentally closed the terminal. macOS and Linux shells don't use the function keys as Windows does but instead have many hotkeys that use the CTRL key. For example, you can search your history with the CTRL-R keystroke. This can pay for itself if you have been working with a long, complex command one day and need to use it again two weeks from now!

PowerShell

Microsoft's *PowerShell* is a powerful replacement for the traditional Windows Command shell. PowerShell enables you to do all the typical command-line activities, such as dir, cd, md, and so on, but brings a series of vastly more powerful tools called *cmdlets* that enable you to accomplish some amazing tasks. Figure 15-16 shows two commands that do the same thing by default, show the contents of a directory: dir and Get-ChildItem.

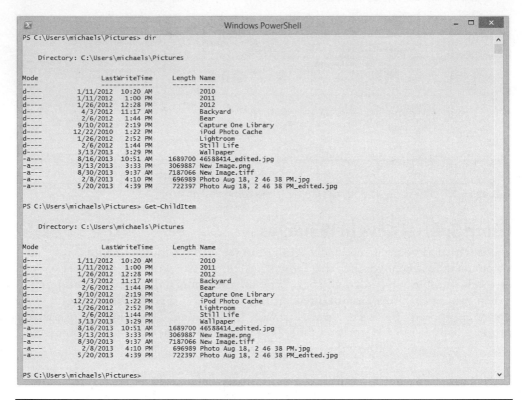

Figure 15-16 Simple commands in PowerShell

With dir, you know you can search for items in a directory, such as "find all the JPEG files in a folder" with this command:

```
dir *.jpg
```

PowerShell lets you dial it all the way to 11, though, with a few more characters on a search string. The following command will find all the JPEG files in the current directory, plus all the mentions of .jpg files in any document format, such as Word, Power-Point, and Acrobat:

```
Get-ChildItem . -Include *.jpg -Recurse -Force
```

Just in case you want to know what each piece of that string in the cmdlet means, here's the scoop: Get-ChildItem is the main command. The dot (.) indicates the current directory, while –Include tells the command to fetch the file type indicated next, in this case *.jpg. –Recurse means go into every subdirectory, and –Force retrieves hidden and system files too. It's like dir on steroids!

This is just scratching the surface with what you can do with PowerShell. If you want to give it a try yourself, simply type **powershell** in the Search bar and press ENTER. Good luck!

Assorted macOS and Linux Commands

macOS and Linux have a massive number of built-in command-line utilities and probably hundreds of thousands of easily accessed and installed third-party tools that work amazingly well. In fact, one of the most interesting challenges to Terminal is that for almost any job, there is more than one tool for the job (see the vi command, later). What you are going to see here are the commands listed by the CompTIA A+ objectives—you could spend the rest of your life learning all of the Terminal commands!

 NOTE The first and second commands below are ifconfig and iwconfig, very network-specific Terminal commands. If you don't have a good grasp on networking yet, skip these commands until after you read Chapters 18 through 21. Then come back to them.

ifconfig

The *ifconfig* command enables you to view and change the settings for your network connections. Running **ifconfig** shows the following output (yours will certainly be different):

```
mike@server:~$ ifconfig
eth0      Link encap:Ethernet  HWaddr 08:00:27:c1:1f:5a
          inet addr:10.0.2.15  Bcast:10.0.2.255  Mask:255.255.255.0
          inet6 addr: fe80::a00:27ff:fec1:1f5a/64 Scope:Link
          UP BROADCAST RUNNING MULTICAST  MTU:1500  Metric:1
          RX packets:27 errors:0 dropped:0 overruns:0 frame:0
          TX packets:96 errors:0 dropped:0 overruns:0 carrier:0
          collisions:0 txqueuelen:1000
          RX bytes:3604 (3.6 KB)  TX bytes:12254 (12.2 KB)

lo        Link encap:Local Loopback
          inet addr:127.0.0.1  Mask:255.0.0.0
          inet6 addr: ::1/128 Scope:Host
          UP LOOPBACK RUNNING  MTU:65536  Metric:1
          RX packets:166 errors:0 dropped:0 overruns:0 frame:0
          TX packets:166 errors:0 dropped:0 overruns:0 carrier:0
          collisions:0 txqueuelen:0
          RX bytes:11849 (11.8 KB)  TX bytes:11849 (11.8 KB)
```

macOS and Linux use special terms to define your network connections:

- eth0, eth1, en0, en1, and so on: wired Ethernet NICs
- wlan0, wlan1, and so on: wireless 802.11 NICs
- lo: loopback

You can disable a NIC using the following:

```
mike@server:~$ ifconfig eth0 down
```

NOTE While CompTIA wants you to be familiar with ifconfig, it is considered to be *deprecated* (i.e., not the preferred tool to use) for Linux (it's still the only game in town on macOS). Its replacement is called simply ip, and it can do everything ifconfig does and more. If you want to learn more, try reading its manual page by typing **man ip** in your terminal.

You can also temporarily change any IP setting with ifconfig. This command will set the IP address of a wireless NIC to 192.168.4.15 until the computer is rebooted:

```
mike@server:~$ sudo ifconfig wlan0 192.168.4.15
```

NOTE Windows has a command similar to ifconfig and ip called ipconfig. Rather than a just a passing mention here, ipconfig shows up in all its networking power in Chapter 19.

iwconfig

The ifconfig command is a powerful tool, but when you need to know about (and to change) your wireless settings, you need *iwconfig*. Typing **iwconfig** by itself gives you all the wireless details about your wireless NICs:

```
mike@server:~$ iwconfig
 eth0    no wireless extensions

 wlan0   IEEE 802.11abg  ESSID:"TOTALHQ"
         Mode:Managed  Frequency:2.427 GHz  Access Point: 00:0A:13:93:2F:07
         Bit Rate=48 Mb/s  Tx-Power=20 dBm  Sensitivity=8/0
         Retry limit:7  RTS thr:off  Fragment thr:off
         Link Quality=91/100  Signal level=-39 dBm  Noise level=-87 dBm
         Rx invalid nwid:0  Rx invalid crypt:860  Rx invalid frag:0
         Tx excessive retries:0  Invalid misc:39  Missed beacon:8

 lo      no wireless extensions.
```

To change the SSID for wlan0 to AnotherSSID, you would type

```
mike@server:~$ sudo iwconfig wlan0 essid "AnotherSSID"
```

Note that you don't use iwconfig to view base IP information. That's ifconfig's job.

ps

If you want to see the processes running on your system, you need the *ps* command. The ps command is a very old command and is designed to provide detailed and customizable information about the processes running on your system. This deep history shows up even on the most basic use of ps, as it has two totally different types of switch sets! Anyway, let's look at one of the most common examples of ps, the ps aux command. The aux command is actually three switches: a = processes for all users, u = show process owner, x = process not attached to a terminal.

```
mike@server:~$ ps aux
USER         PID %CPU %MEM     VSZ    RSS TTY      STAT START   TIME COMMand
root           1  0.0  0.2   33968   4416 ?        Ss   11:08   0:00 /sbin/init
```

Note that I'm skipping a lot of lines right here between the beginning and the end of the displayed results of the ps aux command.

```
root        2188  0.0  0.0       0      0 ?        S    11:08   0:04 [kworker/0:2]
mike        2195  0.0  0.6  385292  13836 ?        Sl   11:08   0:00 zeitgeist-datah
mike        2200  0.0  0.3  283340   7352 ?        Sl   11:08   0:00 /usr/bin/zeitge
mike        2207  0.0  0.8  325764  16832 ?        Sl   11:08   0:00 /usr/lib/x86_64
mike        2215  0.0  0.0   11416    836 ?        S    11:08   0:00 /bin/cat
mike        2218  0.0  1.5  574732  30908 ?        Sl   11:08   0:03 gnome-terminal
mike        2225  0.0  0.0   14828   1916 ?        S    11:09   0:00 gnome-pty-helpe
mike        2226  0.0  0.2   26820   5244 pts/10   Ss   11:09   0:00 bash
mike        2267  0.0  1.0  571544  20856 ?        Sl   11:09   0:00 update-notifier
mike        2290  0.0  0.3  459824   7216 ?        Sl   11:10   0:00 /usr/lib/x86_64
mike        2524  0.0  0.2  145804   5652 ?        Sl   14:12   0:00 /usr/lib/libreo
mike        2543  0.0  5.5 1140216 114080 ?        Sl   14:12   0:00 /usr/lib/libreo
root        2570  0.0  0.0       0      0 ?        S    14:19   0:00 [kworker/u2:1]
root        2577  0.0  0.0       0      0 ?        S    14:29   0:00 [kworker/u2:0]
root        2578  0.0  0.0       0      0 ?        S    14:34   0:00 [kworker/u2:2]
mike        2579  0.0  0.1   22648   2568 pts/10   R+   14:34   0:00 ps aux
mike@server:~$
```

One of the big problems with ps aux is the enormous output. There's a number of ways to make dealing with this output easier. One way is to use ps | less. The less tool makes it easy to scroll up and down through the output. Remember the | more tool we used earlier in this chapter? Well, "less" is "more." Humor! Get it? I'll see myself out. . . . But seriously, less and more will both work for this task; the difference between the two are details for power users and programmers.

Let's discuss the output of the ps aux command:

- USER: Who is running this process
- PID: The process ID number assigned to the process
- %CPU: What percentage of CPU power this process is using
- %MEM: What percentage of memory this process is using
- VSZ: Total paged memory in kilobytes
- RSS: Total physical memory in kilobytes

- TTY: The terminal that is taking the process's output
- STAT: S = waiting, R = running, l = multithreaded, + = foreground process
- START: When the process was started
- TIME: Length of time process has been running
- COMMAND: Name of the executable that created this process

One of the many reasons we run ps is to determine the PID for a process we want to kill. To kill a particular process, we use the kill command (functionally identical to the Windows taskkill command). The following command will stop the process with the PID 2218:

```
mike@server:~$ kill 2218
```

There's more fun to be had with the ps command output, but we will save that for the grep command next.

grep

The *grep* command enables you to search through text files or command output to find specific information or to filter out unneeded information. Let's look at just two of the countless potential ways we use the powerful grep.

Finding a specific process is easy using grep with the ps command. Let's say I have a LibreOffice document that I need to kill. I have no idea what the PID is, but I can use grep with ps to find it. I know the command uses the word "libre," so I type

```
mike@server:~$ ps aux | grep libre
mike      2524  0.0  0.2 145804  5652 ?        Sl   14:12   0:00 /usr/lib/
libreoffice/program/oosplash --writer
mike      2543  0.0  5.5 1140216 114080 ?      Sl   14:12   0:01 /usr/lib/
libreoffice/program/soffice.bin --writer --splash-pipe=5
```

So I see there are two processes from LibreOffice: 2524 and 2543. Cool! The grep command can find any string of text and show you the line it was in. Let's do it again, this time using ifconfig. Let's say you want to know if any of your NICs is using 192.168.4.15. You can use **ifconfig** and **grep** together:

```
mike@server:~$ ifconfig | grep 192.168.4.15
inet addr:192.168.4.15  Bcast:10.0.2.255  Mask:255.255.255.0
collisions:0 txqueuelen:1000
```

Note that grep shows us a line from the ifconfig output indicating that something is using that IP address.

Again, this is only a light overview of grep; it is one of the most powerful tools in Linux. If you need to look in anything to find a string of text, grep is the go-to tool.

apt-get/APT

The first ten years of Linux was interesting from the standpoint of installing programs on a computer. Linux was always a nerdy operating system used primarily by programmers and server administrators; most of the big commercial software companies didn't write applications for Linux. If you needed an application, you dug around the Internet looking for a program, downloaded the code, and tried to compile it on your system, only to find that it depended on yet more code that you had to find, then manually set up configuration files . . . ugh! It wasn't a pretty process, certainly compared to the relative ease of installing Windows or Mac programs.

Over the years many improvements have been made to the availability, acquisition, and installation of Linux programs, culminating in a number of different tools called *package managers* that give you the ability to download and fully install and update software from a single command.

Different Linux distributions use different package management systems. For Debian Linux–based distributions (like Ubuntu and Mint), we use APT, the *advanced packaging tool*. For Red Hat–based systems, we use *Red Hat Package Manager* (*RPM*). There are other package management systems available, of course, but APT and RPM currently dominate the field. The CompTIA A+ objectives only list *apt-get*, the command-line tool for APT. This fact tells us a lot about where CompTIA is looking when it comes to what Linux distro they want you to know: Ubuntu!

 TIP For some reason, the Red Hat Package Manager today is called the RPM Package Manager. It's silly and redundant, like ATM machine, but don't be surprised if that's what you hear in the field.

The apt-get command is wonderfully simple to use, assuming you know the name of the program you wish to install. Many Linux users aren't big fans of the old fashioned vi text editor, for example, and prefer to use the substantially better vim text editor. To download and install the latter program, start by typing the following:

```
mike@server:~$ sudo apt-get update
```

Have APT update its *package index*, the list of all the available packages (software). You can technically skip this step, but you might end up installing an old version or, if the package is new enough, not finding it. Once APT's index has been updated, type this next:

```
mike@server:~$ sudo apt-get install vim
```

That's it! Vim will now be installed and ready to use. Got vim already installed but want the newest version? No problem! Just use **apt-get** again:

```
mike@server:~$ sudo apt-get upgrade vim
```

The only downside to apt-get is that you need to know the name of the package you want to install. While there are command-line tools that help (apt-cache), many people prefer to use the graphical search tool their Linux distro provides, such as the Ubuntu Software Center.

As useful as APT is for fetching and installing single applications, that's not where its real power lies. These package managers can manage *all* the software (minus the stuff you compiled yourself) on the system and are the tool that you use to keep the whole system up to date, just as Windows Update handles much of the software on Windows. All that it takes to upgrade all the packages on your system is to type

```
mike@server:~$ sudo apt-get update
mike@server:~$ sudo apt-get upgrade
```

If apt-get finds any out-of-date packages, it will let you know which ones and ask you to confirm the upgrade, then away it goes to download and update your system. Keeping your system up to date in this way is critical to close any security vulnerabilities that might be lurking on your system.

vi

You will sometimes need to edit raw text files in macOS and Linux, and *vi* is the default text editor, built-in to macOS and most distros of Linux. Figuring out how to edit a file (or even just exit) with vi in some ways is a rite of passage. Only after your have mastered vi's non-intuitive and perhaps even downright weird interface can you truly start to think of yourself as a UNIX Terminal Jedi master. Well, maybe not a Jedi master, but the fact that vi is almost always available will make you want to know how to use it. Let's get started with vi by creating a new text file called "fred":

```
mike@server:~$ vi fred
```

You'll now be in the vi text editor, staring at a blank file as shown in Figure 15-17.

The vi editor uses a non-intuitive "mode" concept where the editor is always in either *insert mode* or *command mode*. Insert mode allows you to insert and edit text. Command mode allows you to give commands such as cut, paste, delete line or characters, and save the file. By default you are in command mode, so press the I key to go into insert mode. Enter a few lines of text, such as shown in Figure 15-18, press ENTER at the end of each line, and use the BACKSPACE key if you make an error. None of the other keys you're used to working with in any other text editor (such as Windows Notepad) work here! Press the ESC key to leave insert mode and return to command mode.

To save your new file and quit vi, type **ZZ** (note the uppercase) and press ENTER. To edit an existing file, just type **vi** followed by the name of the file you wish to edit. If you wanted to edit the fred file, for example, you would type

```
mike@server:~$ vi fred
```

Figure 15-17
vi open

The biggest trick to vi is making sure you know which mode you are in and how to swap between the two modes. Press ESC to get into command mode and press I to get into insert mode. Be ready to make lots of mistakes the first few times you use vi!

Figure 15-18
vi with text

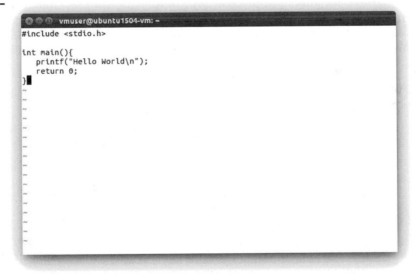

The vi command set is archaic, but it is powerful if you take the time to learn it. Here is a list of a few command mode keys that you'll find helpful:

Key	Function
h	Move cursor one character to left
j	Move cursor one line down
k	Move cursor one line up
l	Move cursor one character to right
w	Move cursor one word to right
b	Move cursor one word to left
0	Move cursor to beginning of line
$	Move cursor to end of line
i	Insert to left of current cursor position
r	Change current character
dd	Delete current line
D	Delete portion of current line to right of the cursor
x	Delete current character
:w	Save file
:q!	Quit vi, do not save
ZZ	Save file and quit vi

Granted, it's important to know how to use vi, but most Linux people quickly find themselves going to one of the hundreds of alternatives. Check out one of the terminal-based editors such as vim, joe, or emacs, or one of the graphical editors such as gedit or gVim.

dd

The *dd* command is primarily used to create an exact, bit-by-bit image of any form of block storage, meaning mass storage devices such as hard drive volumes, thumb drives, and optical media. In its most simple form, the dd command is just

```
$ dd if=<source block device> of=<destination image file location>
```

There's no way to show you all the possible uses for dd, so I'll just show three of the typical places I use it. Let's start with something simple: copying a hard drive.

Be careful here! The dd command name is sometimes said jokingly to stand for "Disk Destroyer." This powerful tool will wreak havoc on your data if not used correctly. There are a number of issues that I'm not covering here that could greatly affect the success of running the dd command. While all of the following commands are valid, simply running them on your systems without understanding these subtleties can wipe drives. You have been warned!

Copying a Hard Drive

Let's say you have a hard drive (sda) you want to copy onto another hard drive (sdb). In this case we will say they are exactly the same size. The following command will copy the entire sda drive, partition table, file systems . . . everything to the sdb drive:

```
dd if=/dev/sda of=/dev/sdb
```

Backing Up a Thumb Drive

Let's say you have thumb drive full of important files you really want to back up. Using dd as follows, you can copy the entire USB drive and make an image file (I chose to call it thumbBackup.bak) and place that image file on your Desktop:

```
dd if=/dev/sdc of=/home/mike/Desktop/thumbBackup.bak
```

Wiping a Disk

I have a drive (sdb) that I want to totally wipe. The dd command can take input from anywhere, but in this case I'll use Linux's random number generator, /dev/urandom, to write a stream of random bits completely over the entire drive. It's not a perfect wipe, but it will stop all but the most sophisticated tools.

```
dd if=/dev/urandom of=/dev/sdb
```

shutdown

Same as in Windows, you can shut down or restart the system from a terminal using the *shutdown* command. Run the command as follows:

```
shutdown <options> <time>
```

By far the most common time is *now*. To shut the system down immediately, type this:

```
shutdown now
```

To restart the system, run **shutdown** with the **–r** option:

```
shutdown -r now
```

passwd

The *passwd* command enables you to change your password or, if logged in as root (the super user), any user's password. To change your own password, type the following:

```
mike@server:~$ passwd
changing password for mike
(current) UNIX password:
Enter new UNIX password:
Retype new UNIX password
Passwd: password updated successfully
```

Scripting

Up until now, we've entered commands into the command prompt one by one. Most of the time all you need is to enter one or two commands, but sometimes you will find yourself repeating the same series of commands over and over. When you find yourself in this situation, it might be a good idea to write a *script* to run that series of commands. A *script* is a small program used to help automate computing tasks.

In fact, you can make a super simple *shell script* by copying a few shell commands to a new file and saving it. Wait, *shell script* and *shell command*? When you work at the command line in Windows, you're working at the Command shell. Every time you type a Windows command at a prompt, you're using a shell command. You've been working with shell commands this whole chapter!

Each command shell has its own *shell scripting language*, so the appropriate file extension will depend on which shell you're using. Imagine you have an application (importantapp.exe) that requires a weekly maintenance restart, where you run the following commands:

```
kill /IM importantapp.exe /P gudpwd1      (shut down the application)
cd \Program files\importantapp\Data        (Go to a specific location)
del *.tmp                                   (delete the temporary files)
copy config.bak config.txt /Y              (overwrite last week's config file
                                            with a copy of the backup)
importantapp.exe                           (start the
                                            application)
```

Typing these commands one after the other every week is tedious, and you may mistype or misremember them. Instead, you can put them in a text file—using Notepad, for example—and save that text file with a file extension—like wklyrestart.bat in this case—so the OS knows it's a shell script.

You can run the wklyrestart.bat script from the Command shell, the prompt. You wrote the script in a separate program, Notepad. Running the script automates the shell, in effect telling the Command shell to do a sequence of actions. Got it?

High-end techs use scripts all the time to automate a zillion tasks. My office is relatively small, but has a lot of computers doing tasks all the time. My sysad (systems administrator), Michael, as part of his morning routine, checks the status of every one of those computers, looking for errors, proper functioning, and so forth. That's a lot of stuff. If he had to go to each machine—even over the network—and check the status, it would take him all day. Michael created a script that automates this task. He sits at his Mac with his morning coffee, opens Terminal, and runs a few scripts that check all the machines and gives him detailed reports. Sweet!

Let's make the script process very clear here. You can *run* scripts from a prompt, but you *create scripts in a text editor*. Notepad is a simple text editor that comes with Windows. You learned about vi and vim earlier in the chapter—text editors often used in Linux. The wklyrestart.bat script we just made used a very limited *scripting language* called *batch file*, with the extension, .bat. But scripts aren't limited to such simple shell commands and batch files. High-end techs can use a bunch of different text editors to create awesome scripts in many different languages.

Script Types and Languages

Scripting is a kind of *programming*; a scripting language is a type of *programming language* optimized for writing scripts. As with any kind of programming, there are many different scripting languages designed for a variety of purposes. The CompTIA A+ objectives expect you to be able to identify the file types for six different scripting languages.

Table 15-1 shows common languages and their file extensions.

Language	File Extension	Description
Batch File	.bat	Batch files are the shell scripting language for the old-school Command shell on Windows and DOS (yes, that DOS).
PowerShell	.ps1	PowerShell is a shell scripting language written from the ground up for automating modern Windows systems. Replaces batch files in almost all situations.
UNIX shell script	.sh	By convention, the first line of a UNIX shell script file specifies which shell should execute the script (and thus, which shell scripting language it is written in). These files often have a .sh file extension, but it is not necessary.
Python	.py	Python is a flexible programming language with simple syntax that makes it well suited for writing both simple scripts and large applications.
JavaScript	.js	JavaScript is a browser scripting language developed back in the 1990s to enhance Web pages, but these days you can find it in command-line programs, extensions for many desktop applications, and much more.
Visual Basic Script	.vbs	Visual Basic Script is a legacy scripting language for Windows and other Microsoft applications. Slowly being replaced by other languages like PowerShell.

Table 15-1 Common Languages and Their File Extensions

 NOTE The first three scripting languages in Table 15-1 are *shell* scripting languages, but the other three are more general scripting languages. In a shell scripting language, any normal command you would type at the prompt is a valid part of the language. This is not true in the more general scripting languages (but they have many other useful features).

Anatomy of a Script

At their core, programming languages can tell a computer to do something to some piece of data. You've solved math problems, so you are already halfway to understanding this. In a simple math problem like 3 + 4, you have two numbers, and a symbol that tells you what operation to perform. In this case, addition.

To do this math problem, you need to know the rules. You learned the rules of arithmetic back in grade school, right? In arithmetic, each of these numbers is a *value*; the rules tell you to add two numbers when you see the + sign.

But what if the equation looked a little different? What would you do if it was 3 + cow? That doesn't make sense! Cow isn't a number, it's a word for a large, grass-eating bovine. You and I know this, but a C and a 3 are both just characters to the computer. How does it know that it can't add them?

Data Types

To be able to treat numbers and words differently, computers need a new concept—data types. A data type is a defined category, like *number* or *word*. In many programming languages, these rules dictate important details, such as you can't add the number 3 and the word cow because the two values have different data types. The number 3 is an *integer* (i.e., a whole number) data type, and cow (i.e., a word) is what programmers call a *string* data type. Here's where it gets a little more complicated, but stick with me and it'll become more clear!

A way to think of a string is as a *sequence of characters*, like c – o – w. Most programming languages require that you identify a string with 'single' or "double" quotes, so 'cow' or "cow" in this example. While only some characters are valid integers, all characters can be valid in a string. Every programming language dictates actions that the computer can perform on strings (like joining two strings together, breaking one string into pieces, checking how many characters are in a string, and so on). While arithmetic dictates that you can't add 3 + cow (probably because it would upset the cow), you can combine "brown " + "cow" and create a "brown cow" (and have a happier cow).

Here's the next cool concept. Numbers are characters too, just like words. Numbers, therefore, can show up in strings—and programming languages have to treat number characters differently when quoted or not quoted. A programming language determines what to do with a telephone number without quotes and with quotes, for example, like these:

```
281-922-4166
"281-922-4166"
```

In the first case, a computer wouldn't have any choice but to compute the result of `281 minus 922 minus 4166`, which results in –4807 (an integer data type). In the second case, a computer would keep intact a string containing the phone number to my office. Yes, our refrigerator is running.

Variables

As soon as the computer thinks it's done with this value (whether it's –4807 or "281-922-4166"), it will forget it. If you need to use it more than once, you have to tell the computer to save it. Most programming languages tell the computer to remember the value by *naming* it; we call these named values *variables*. My office phone number is saved as the variable phone_number:

```
phone_number = "281-922-4166"
```

A variable in a scripting or programming language is a named value or thing. The CompTIA A+ objectives refer to a variable as a basic script *construct*, meaning, I think, *concept*.

Conditionals and Basic Loops

Once you move beyond the most basic shell scripts—those that are just a list of commands—you often need to control when and how different commands run. Not surprisingly, more sophisticated scripting languages and programming languages give you excellent tools, called *control constructs*, to control commands.

 NOTE I've included some scripting examples in this section. Each one uses the *Python* language. If you try to copy them into a script file for another language, they may not work!

The most basic control constructs are *conditionals*. *Conditionals* enable you to specify code that should run only when some condition is (or is not) met. Most languages have *keywords*, such as an "if" statement. The "if" statement specifies a condition, and what code to run if the condition is met. Here's a simple example:

```
animal = "cow"
if animal == "cat":
    print("meow")
```

Here's what each line means:

1. The *animal* variable holds a string called "cow".

2. The if statement checks to see if the animal variable contains a value of "cat".

3. If that's the case, the computer will print the word "meow" to the command prompt. If not, then nothing will happen.

In this case, the script would never print "meow" because the condition *was not met*.

Conditionals are a critical building block for most scripts and programs. One of the main reasons to write a script in the first place is because you need to do something many times. In programming, a good way to accomplish this is with a loop. Basic *loops* are another kind of conditional, but tell the computer to run the code over and over *until the condition is* (or *is not*) *met*. Depending on the language, you'll usually see loops indicated with keywords like *for* and *while*. Here's an example:

```
cows = 0
while cows < 4:
    print("moo")
    cows = cows + 1
```

This loop will run until the number of cows *is* 4, so it will print "moo" four times—one for each cow. Because the cows variable has an integer value, we can do math with it. Each time the loop runs, it prints "moo" once, and adds one to the number of cows.

 EXAM TIP Different languages have different control structures. Most of them have at least a few. This section looked at two—if statements and loops—but the CompTIA A+ objectives only expect you to identify *basic loops*.

Comments

Scripting and programming languages usually have a way to insert special text—called a *comment*—that helps anyone reading the script later (including the writer, a few months on!) understand what's going on. The computer ignores this text, as it's only for the humans. Leaving comments is a really good idea, even if you don't expect anyone else to ever read your script. Comments are a great way to describe the problem a script exists to solve. You should also use them to describe how, when, and where to use the script.

Each language has its own comment syntax, though *most* languages share two common formats. Three of the languages (PowerShell, Python, and UNIX shell) that you should be able to identify for the CompTIA A+ objectives use a single format, which begins a comment with the # symbol. The comment symbol can start a line or follow statements on the same line. Let's take a look:

```
# This script makes all of the cows moo.
# Be careful with this power.
cows = 0 # start with no cows
while cows < 4: # only 4 cows allowed to moo :(
    print("moo") # moo, cow, moo
    cows = cows + 1 # add one cow
```

The comments in this example describe the goal of the script—make all the cows moo—and caution the user of the script. They note that the script starts with no cows and limits the total number of cows to four; and so on.

The other three languages are all a little different, so they'll be easy to tell apart. JavaScript:

```
// This is a single-line comment in JavaScript
/* This is a multiline comment
in JavaScript */
```

Batch file:

```
REM This is the older way to comment in Batch files
:: But many newer scripts use this format.
```

Visual Basic Script:

```
' Visual Basic Script's comments start with a single quote.
```

Comments are absolutely essential in scripting and programming for humans who need to work on scripts and programs. Nothing's worse than trying to remember how many cows will moo a year after you write the script!

Environment Variables

Any system you access has important values stored in variables that make up what we call the *environment* of a running program. Some of these values are set systemwide, but these values can also be set by the user, the script/program, or even the shell it is running in. These values, which we call *environment variables*, tell running programs all sorts of things, like what the current directory or user is, or where to store temporary files. Figure 15-19 shows the default environment variables for program run under the scottj user account.

We also use environment variables to configure scripts because they make it easy for many different users to customize how the same script will behave on a given system without having to edit the script itself. Here's an example of Windows Command shell environment variables in a batch file (note that *REM* here means *comment*):

```
@echo off
REM prints the name of the currently logged-in account
echo You are logged in as %username%
REM prints the currently logged-in user's main folder
echo Your home directory is %homepath%
```

The text surrounded by percent signs (for example, %username%) is an environment variable in batch that will change depending on the user running the script. If I run the script, it'll say "Mike" all over the place. If my editor runs it, it'll spam "Scott."

Linux and macOS have a set of environmental variables that are similar to those in Windows, but they look a bit different. Here is the same script as above but written for a macOS system:

```
#!/bin/bash
# Prints the name of the currently logged-in account
echo You are logged in as $USER
# Prints the currently logged-in user's main folder
echo Your home directory is $HOME
```

Every high-end tech relies on scripting to accomplish many mundane tasks quickly and efficiently. Scripts give you power over the machine. The CompTIA A+ 1002 exam tests you on the few scripting concepts covered in this chapter, but the magic of scripting might just sweep you away. See you on the other side!

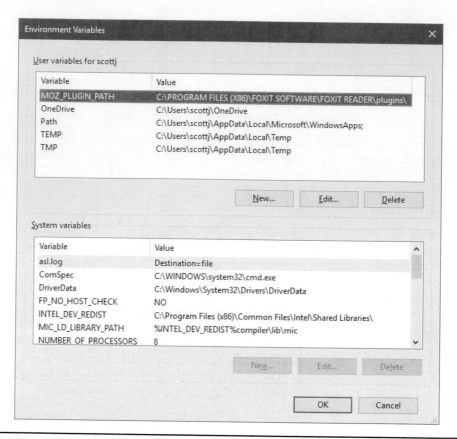

Figure 15-19   Environment variables in Windows 10

Chapter Review

Questions

1. Which of the following is an illegal character in a Linux filename?

   A. * (asterisk)

   B. . (dot)

   C. / (forward slash)

   D. _ (underscore)

2. Which command pauses after displaying a screen's worth of directory contents? (Choose two.)

   A. dir p

   B. ls | more

   C. ls –p

   D. dir /p

3. Which of the following commands will delete all the files in a directory in Linux?

   A. del *.*

   B. del all

   C. rm *

   D. rm all

4. Which command do you use to determine your exact folder location (path) in Linux?

   A. dir

   B. path

   C. pwd

   D. prompt

5. Which Windows command is functionally equivalent to the Linux ls command?

   A. dir

   B. command

   C. copy

   D. dd

6. What do you type before a Linux command to access help for that command?

   A. help

   B. ?

   C. man

   D. /?

7. Which of the following Linux commands will show detailed information about the contents of a folder?

   A. ls –l

   B. ls –e

   C. ls –h

   D. ls –k

8. What command, identical in both Windows and Linux, will tell you the name of the computer?

   A. hosts | grep

   B. whoami

   C. hostname

   D. net name

9. Of the following, which best describes the function of the Windows gpresult command?

   A. Lists all recently updated group policies

   B. Lists the group policies applied to a user

   C. Lists all changes to a user's group policies since the last refresh

   D. Lists any and all conflicting group policies

10. How do you run a command at the Windows command prompt with administrative privileges?

   A. Enter an elevated username and password at the command prompt.

   B. Right-click a command-prompt shortcut and then select Run as PowerUser.

   C. Right-click a command-prompt shortcut and then select Run as administrator.

   D. The cmd command only runs with administrator privileges.

Answers

1. **C.** Any of these characters are acceptable in a Linux filename except the forward slash (/), which is used exclusively as a path separator.

2. **B, D.** The ls | more and dir /p commands in Linux and Windows, respectively, pause a long listing at the end of the page.

3. **C.** Type **rm** * and press ENTER to delete all files in a directory in Linux.

4. **C.** The pwd command enables you to determine the current folder location in Linux.

5. **A.** The Windows dir command accomplishes a similar function to the Linux ls command.

6. **C.** Access the help for a Linux command by typing **man [command name]**.

7. **A.** Type **ls –l** and press ENTER to see detailed information about a folder in Linux.

8. **C.** Type **hostname** and press ENTER to discover the hostname for just about any computer.

9. **B.** The gpresult command in Windows lists group policies applied to a user.

10. **C.** To run a command at the Windows command prompt with administrative privileges, you would right-click a command-prompt shortcut and then select Run as administrator.

Troubleshooting Operating Systems

In this chapter, you will learn how to
- Troubleshoot boot problems
- Troubleshoot GUI problems
- Troubleshoot application problems

This chapter looks at operating system problems from the ground up. It starts with catastrophic failure—a personal computer that won't boot—and then discusses ways to get past that problem. The next section covers the causes and workarounds when the GUI fails to load. Once you can access the GUI, the many diagnostic and troubleshooting tools that you've spent so much time learning about come to your fingertips. The chapter finishes with a discussion on application problems.

The CompTIA A+ 1002 exam focuses primarily on troubleshooting in Windows, so the basic structure of this chapter follows that example. We'll look first at various issues through the prism of a PC tech working on modern Windows versions, then, when applicable, discuss the symptom, tools, and techniques in macOS and Linux.

macOS and Linux systems have the same problems you'll find in Windows, such as hardware failure, system and driver flaws, and buggy applications. The differences among the three OS families when troubleshooting are stark.

A ton of companies manufacture hardware and write software for Windows. The resulting *heterogeneous ecosystem* (that is, a lot of variety) of Windows greatly expands on the number of possibilities for what could be causing problems in any system.

Because Apple has always strictly controlled the hardware and drivers used with macOS, hardware flaws are easier to diagnose. The same can be said with macOS and application problems. macOS has a more *homogeneous ecosystem* (that is, not a lot of variety) than Windows. Aside from upgrading RAM, most macOS machines get few hardware updates and thus dodge problems that dog Windows machines. Likewise, Apple provides a lot of excellent productivity software with the basic macOS system, so most users have little incentive to add much additional software. This avoids problems too.

Linux production machines—generally servers—often lack the excess complexity of Windows or macOS systems and just work solidly. When you switch to the enthusiast or dabbler systems that most of us use, on the other hand, they have all kinds of problems.

That's because the most common of those systems use random spare parts from old Windows machines. You get what you pay for, I suppose.

The chapter intertwines the common problems in the operating systems with the tools and common solutions listed in 1002 objectives 1.5, 1.6, and 3.1. Let's dive into troubleshooting now.

1002

Failure to Boot

When a computer fails to boot, you need to determine whether the problem relates to hardware or software. You'll recall from Chapter 9, "Implementing Mass Storage," that drives need proper connectivity and power, and that CMOS must be configured correctly. If not, you'll get an error like the one in Figure 16-1. We'll look more closely at these sorts of scenarios in the first part of this section as a refresher.

Figure 16-1
If you see this screen, the problem is with hardware. Windows hasn't even started trying to boot.

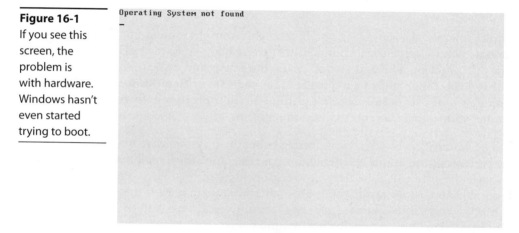

```
Operating System not found
_
```

But after the drive powers on and the POST completes successfully, the computer tries to boot to an OS. Failure at *this* point gives you an entirely different set of errors, such as *BOOTMGR is missing* (see Figure 16-2). You need a totally different set of tools from the ones used to troubleshoot hardware or CMOS issues.

Failure to Boot: Hardware or Configuration

Most failed-boot scenarios require you to determine where the fault occurred: with the hardware and configuration, or in Windows. This is a pretty straightforward problem. Imagine that a user calls and says "My PC won't boot" or "My computer is dead." At this

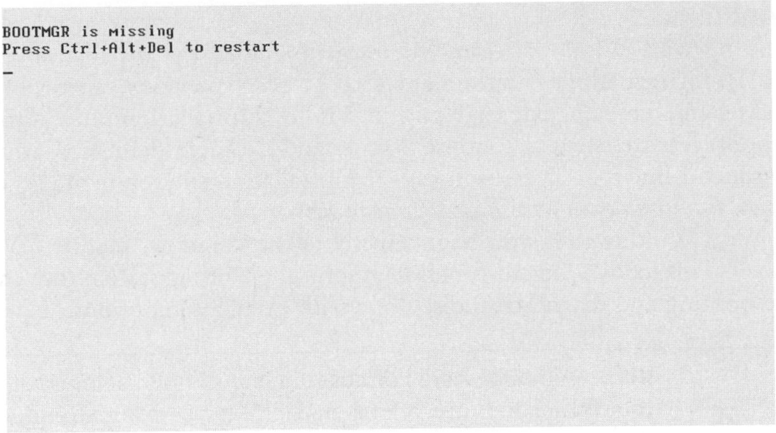

Figure 16-2
Scary error

```
BOOTMGR is missing
Press Ctrl+Alt+Del to restart
_
```

point, your best tools are knowledge of the boot process and asking lots of questions. Here are some I use regularly:

"What displays on the screen—if anything—after you press the power button on the case?"

"What do you hear—if anything—after you press the power button on the case?"

"Is the PC plugged in?"

"Do you smell anything weird?"

Hardware problems can give you a blank screen on boot-up, so you follow the tried-and-true troubleshooting methodology for hardware. Make sure everything is plugged in and turned on. If the PC is new, as in less than 30 days old, you know it might have suffered a *burn-in failure*, a rare problem that can affect any new electronics device. If the customer smells something, one of the components might have fried. Try replacing with known good devices: RAM, power supply, CPU, hard drive, motherboard.

If the user says that the screen says "No boot device detected" and the system worked fine before, it *could* mean something as simple as the computer has attempted to boot to an incorrect device, such as to something other than the primary hard drive. This scenario happens all the time. Someone plugs a thumb drive into a USB port and the CMOS is configured to boot to removable media before hard drives—boom! "No boot device detected" error. The first few times it happened to me, I nearly took my machine apart before experiencing that head-slapping moment. I removed the thumb drive and then watched Windows boot normally.

Failure to Boot: Windows

Two critical boot files risk corruption in Windows, bootmgr and bcd, both of which you can fix with one tool, bcdedit. You can use this tool in the Windows Recovery Environment.

WinPE

Starting with Windows Vista, Microsoft upgraded the installation environment from the 16-bit text mode environment used in every previous version of Windows to 32- and 64-bit. This upgrade enabled the Windows installation process to go graphical and support features such as a mouse pointer and clickable elements, rather than relying on command-line tools. Microsoft calls the installation environment the *Windows Preinstallation Environment* (*WinPE* or *Windows PE*).

With Windows PE, you boot directly to the Windows media (DVD or flash-media drive). This loads a limited-function graphical operating system that contains both troubleshooting and diagnostic tools, along with installation options.

 NOTE   Although here I discuss only how WinPE helps boot repair, know that WinPE goes much further. WinPE can assist unattended installations, network installations, and even booting diskless workstations on a network.

When you access Windows PE and opt for the troubleshooting and repair features, you open a special set of tools called the *Windows Recovery Environment* (*WinRE or Windows RE*). The terms can get a little confusing because of the similarity of letters, so mark this: Windows RE is the repair tools that run within Windows PE. WinPE powers WinRE. Got it? Let's tackle WinRE.

 EXAM TIP   Microsoft also refers to the Windows Recovery Environment as the *System Recovery Options menu*.

Enter Windows RE

WinRE includes an impressive, powerful set of both automated and manual utilities that collectively diagnoses and fixes all but the most serious of Windows boot problems. Although WinRE does all the hard work for you, you still need to know how to access and use it. When faced with a failure-to-boot scenario in modern versions of Windows, WinRE is one of your primary tools.

Getting to Windows RE

In Windows 7, you can access WinRE in three ways. First, you can boot from the Windows installation media and select Repair. Second, you can use the Repair Your Computer option on the Advanced Boot Options (F8) menu (see Figure 16-3). Third, you can create a system repair disc or system image before you have problems. Go to Control Panel | Backup and Restore and select *Create a system repair disc* or select *Create a system image*.

Windows 8/8.1/10 do not have the F8 Advanced Boot Options by default, nor a Backup and Restore applet. Instead, you create a recovery drive on a 16 GB+ USB flash drive by accessing the Recovery applet in Control Panel (see Figure 16-4). (Advanced Boot Options is still there, mind you, but Microsoft removed the easy access of the F8 key.) Boot to the recovery drive to access WinRE. (You can get to WinRE in several ways once you have access to the Windows Desktop, but this section assumes you can't get there yet.)

Figure 16-3
Selecting Repair
Your Computer
in the Windows 7
Advanced Boot
Options menu

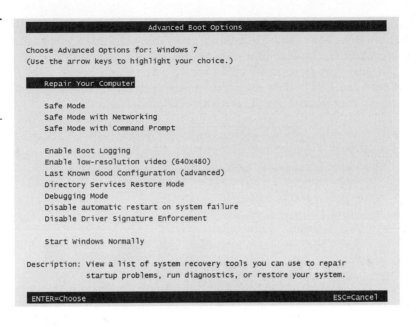

```
                        Advanced Boot Options

Choose Advanced Options for: Windows 7
(Use the arrow keys to highlight your choice.)

    Repair Your Computer

    Safe Mode
    Safe Mode with Networking
    Safe Mode with Command Prompt

    Enable Boot Logging
    Enable low-resolution video (640x480)
    Last Known Good Configuration (advanced)
    Directory Services Restore Mode
    Debugging Mode
    Disable automatic restart on system failure
    Disable Driver Signature Enforcement

    Start Windows Normally

Description: View a list of system recovery tools you can use to repair
            startup problems, run diagnostics, or restore your system.

ENTER=Choose                                            ESC=Cancel
```

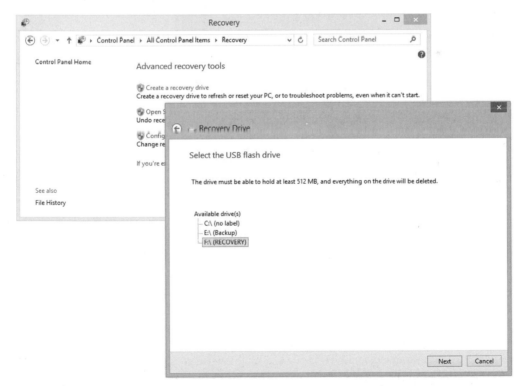

Figure 16-4   Making a recovery drive in Windows 8.1

You can also create Windows installation media in Windows 10 by downloading it directly from Microsoft and making a bootable USB drive. Here's the URL as we go to print: www.microsoft.com/en-us/software-download/windows10.

Alternatively, search the Web for the *Windows media creation tool*. This will get you to the current page. Insert a thumb drive and click the *Download tool now* link to create a bootable thumb drive that'll take you to WinPE (Figure 16-5).

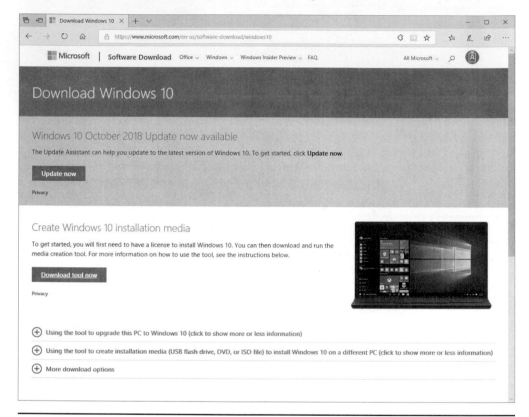

Figure 16-5   Download Windows 10 page

Although any of these methods works fine, I recommend that you access WinRE from the Windows installation media or the dedicated recovery drive for three reasons:

- The hard drive can be so messed up that you won't make it to the Advanced Boot Options menu.

- Accessing WinRE using the Repair Your Computer option in the Advanced Boot Options menu requires a local administrator password.

- Using a bootable disc/USB flash drive enables you to avoid any malware that might be on the system.

Using Windows RE

The look and feel of Windows RE differ a lot between Windows 7 and Windows 8/8.1/10, although you'll find similar options in both. Windows 7 WinRE has a simple interface (see Figure 16-6) with five options:

- Startup Repair
- System Restore
- System Image Recovery
- Windows Memory Diagnostic
- Command Prompt

Figure 16-6
Recovery Environment main screen in Windows 7

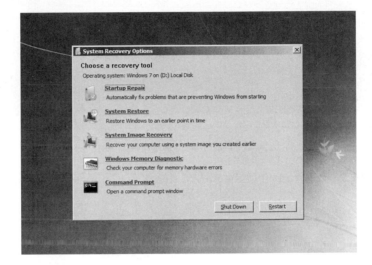

Windows 8/8.1/10 WinRE offers fewer choices initially and varies a bit from version to version, but you'll find all the troubleshooting options with a little clicking around. In Windows 10 1809, the main menu starts (see Figure 16-7) with a few options:

- Continue
- Use a device
- Troubleshoot
- Turn off your PC

Click the Troubleshoot option to see a couple more options, although Windows 10 differs from earlier versions. Windows 8.1, for example, offers three choices:

- Refresh your PC
- Reset your PC
- Advanced options

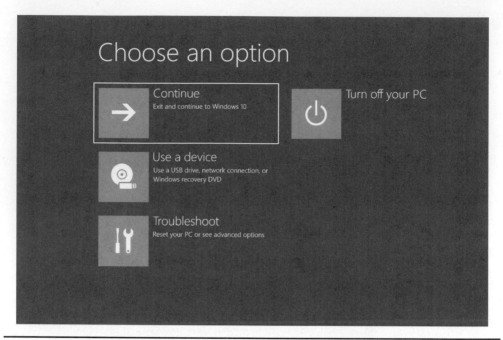

Figure 16-7   Recovery Environment main screen in Windows 10

Windows 10 combines the Refresh and Reset options into a single button, Reset this PC (see Figure 16-8).

Understanding Refresh and Reset is critically important for troubleshooting and rebuilding a Windows 8/8.1/10 PC. We'll discuss these options in a moment.

Clicking the Advanced options reveals another menu (see Figure 16-9) that shows a lot of the same options you see in the Windows 7 System Recovery Options menu:

- System Restore
- Uninstall Updates
- System Image Recovery
- Startup Repair
- Command Prompt
- UEFI Firmware Settings (available if your motherboard uses UEFI rather than classic BIOS)

Let's look at the details of these Windows RE options. We'll use the Windows 7 menu order and then tackle the two extra Windows 10 options, Uninstall Updates and UEFI Firmware Settings. The section ends with the Refresh and Reset options.

EXAM TIP   Make sure you know how to access the Windows Recovery Environment and what each of the available tools does.

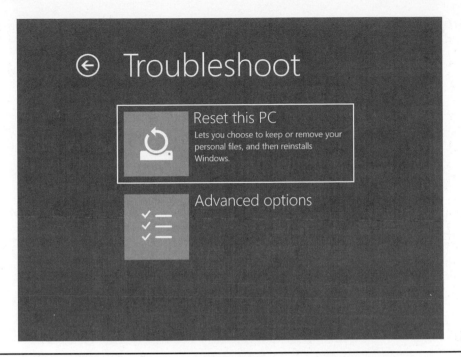

Figure 16-8   WinRE Troubleshoot screen in Windows 10

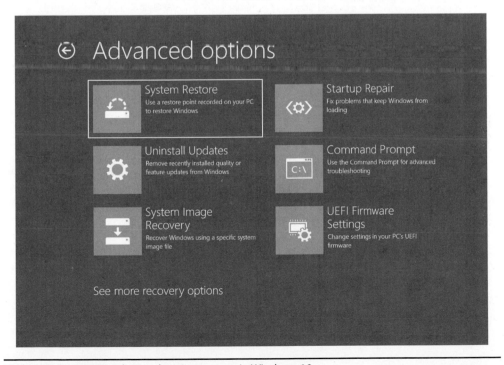

Figure 16-9   WinRE Advanced options screen in Windows 10

Startup Repair   The *Startup Repair* utility serves as a one-stop, do-it-all option (see Figure 16-10). When run, it performs a number of repairs, including:

- Repairs a corrupted Registry by accessing the backup copy on your hard drive
- Restores critical boot files
- Restores critical system and driver files
- Rolls back any non-working drivers
- Rolls back updates
- Runs chkdsk
- Runs a memory test to check your RAM

Figure 16-10
Startup Repair
for Windows 7 in
action

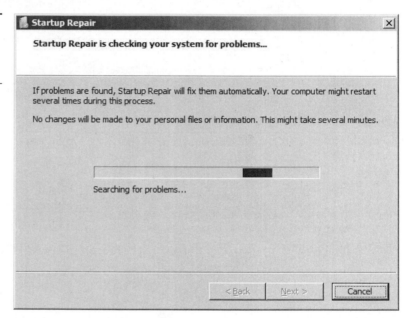

Startup Repair fixes almost any Windows boot problem. In fact, if you have a system with one hard drive containing a single partition with Windows 7 installed, you'd have trouble finding something Startup Repair *couldn't* fix. Upon completion, Startup Repair shows the screen shown in Figure 16-11.

Note the link in Figure 16-11 that says *View diagnostic and repair details*. This opens a text file called srttrail.txt that lists exactly what the program found, what it fixed, and what it failed to do. It may look cryptic, but you can type anything you find into

Figure 16-11
Startup Repair
complete; no
problems found.

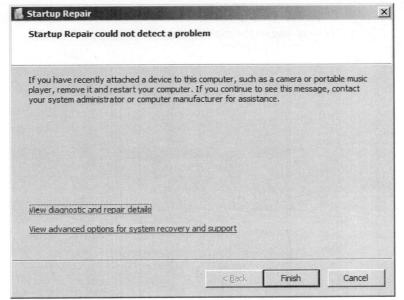

Google for more information. I've reproduced only the beginning of the (very long)
srttrail.txt file here:

```
Startup Repair diagnosis and repair log
---------------------------
Last successful boot time: 9/14/2019 2:37:43 AM (GMT)
Number of repair attempts: 6

Session details
---------------------------
System Disk = \Device\Harddisk0
Windows directory = C:\Windows
AutoChk Run = 0
Number of root causes = 1

Test Performed:
---------------------------
Name: Check for updates
Result: Completed successfully. Error code =  0x0
Time taken = 32 ms

Test Performed:
---------------------------
Name: System disk test
Result: Completed successfully. Error code =  0x0
Time taken = 0 ms
```

NOTE The *View advanced options for system recovery and support* link simply returns you to the main screen.

Startup Repair starts automatically if your system detects a boot problem. If you power up a Windows system and see the screen shown in Figure 16-12, Windows has detected a problem in the startup process.

Figure 16-12
Windows Error
Recovery

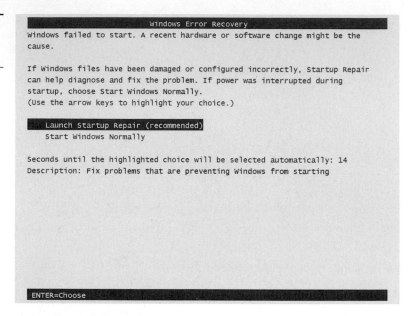

Although powerful, a tool like Startup Repair doesn't cover everything. You may have specific needs that require more finesse than a single, do-it-all approach. In many cases, you've already discovered the problem and simply want to make a single fix. You might want to perform a system restoration or check the memory. For this, we'll need to explore the other options available in WinRE.

 EXAM TIP If you have trouble booting your computer, you should try Startup Repair first. This includes if you're in a scenario with a *slow bootup*, not just no bootup.

System Restore *System Restore* does the same job here it has done since Microsoft first introduced it in Windows Me, enabling you to go back to a time when your computer worked properly. Placing this option in Windows RE gives those of us who make many *restore points*—snapshots of a system at a given point of time—a quick and handy way to return systems to a previous state (see Figure 16-13).

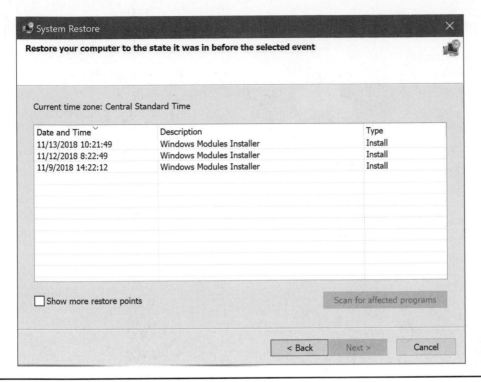

Figure 16-13 System Restore list of restore points

NOTE As we discussed back in Chapter 14, "Maintaining and Optimizing Operating Systems," Windows 10 disables System Restore by default. So, if you are attempting to fix a Windows 10 machine by rolling back with System Restore, there is a good chance you will find that there are no snapshots available.

EXAM TIP macOS offers a powerful tool for application problems called Force Quit. Press the OPTION-COMMAND-ESC keyboard combination to access the Force Quit menu. It'll show you every running application.

System Image Recovery Use the System Image Recovery tool to restore a system after a catastrophe. This is a great tool if you manage a set of uniform systems, typical in many workplaces. Keep a default image on hand, including OS settings, network settings, and applications, and you can quickly reimage a borked computer to get clients up and running. You can keep a simpler image as well, one that reloads the OS for further customization.

If you have the drive containing the system image plugged in when you first run the wizard, it should detect your latest backup and present you with the dialog box shown in

Figure 16-14
Selecting a
system image in
Windows 7

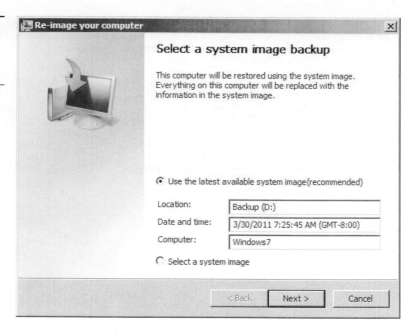

Figure 16-14. If it doesn't list a system image or it lists the wrong one, you can select an image from another date on the same disk or even a remote network share.

After you select the image you want to restore, the utility presents you with a few more options, as shown in Figure 16-15. Most importantly, you can choose to format and repartition disks. With this option selected, the utility wipes out the existing partitions

Figure 16-15
Additional
restore options

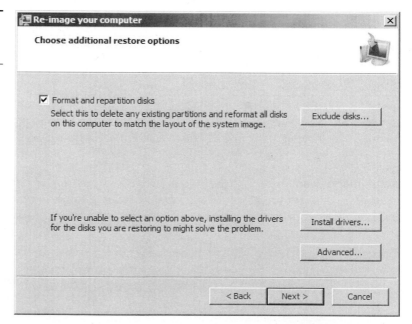

Figure 16-16
Confirming your
settings

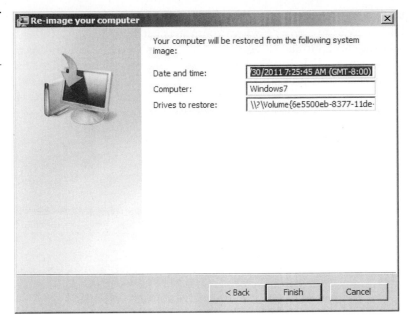

and data on all disks so the restored system will get the same partitions that the backed-up system had.

After you click Finish on the confirmation screen (see Figure 16-16), which also contains a final warning, the restore process begins (see Figure 16-17). The utility removes the old system data and then copies the backed-up system image to the hard drive(s). Once the process completes, your system reboots and should start up again with all of your data and programs just where you left them when you last backed up.

For image recovery in Windows 10, macOS, and Linux, you need to turn to third-party tools. I like Acronis True Image for both Windows and macOS, and Clonezilla for Linux.

Figure 16-17
Restoring your
computer

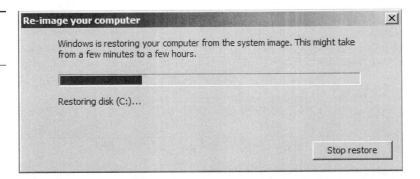

Windows Memory Diagnostic Bad RAM causes huge problems for any operating system, creating scenarios where computers get Blue Screens of Death (BSoDs), system lockups, and continuous reboots. In Windows 7, the Windows Recovery Environment enables you to click the Windows Memory Diagnostic link from the main WinRE screen. When clicked, it prompts you to *Restart now and check for problems (recommended)* or *Check for problems the next time I start my computer* (see Figure 16-18). It doesn't really matter which option you choose, but if you think you need to test the system's RAM, that probably means you should do it now.

Figure 16-18
Windows
Memory
Diagnostic
screen

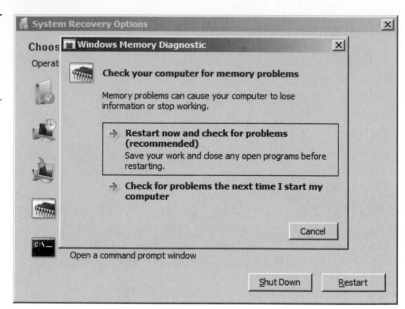

 EXAM TIP You can access the Windows Memory Diagnostic Tool in Windows 8/8.1/10 from the Control Panel or by typing its name in the Search box. It does not show up as an option in WinRE in those versions of Windows. The steps once you restart are similar.

Once you restart, your system immediately starts running the Windows Memory Diagnostic Tool, as shown in Figure 16-19. While the program runs, you can press F1 to see options (see Figure 16-20).

The tool lists three important Test Mix options at the top of the screen: Basic, Standard, and Extended. *Basic* runs quickly (about one minute) but performs only light testing. *Standard*, the default choice, takes a few minutes and tests more aggressively. *Extended* takes hours (you should let it run overnight), but it will very aggressively test your RAM.

 NOTE You can also find Windows Memory Diagnostic in the Control Panel under Administrative Tools, or start it from an administrative command prompt using the mdsched command.

Figure 16-19
Windows
Memory
Diagnostic Tool
running

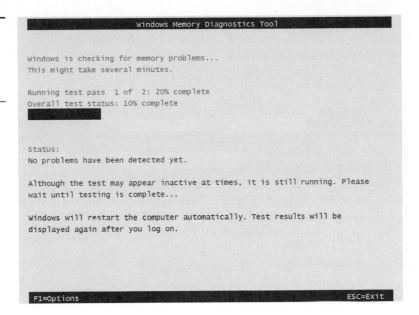

This tool includes two other options: Cache and Pass Count. The *Cache* option enables you to set whether the tests use the CPU's built-in cache as well as override the default cache settings for each test type. Simply leave Cache set at Default and never touch it. *Pass Count* sets the number of times each set of tests will run. This option defaults to 2.

Figure 16-20
Windows
Memory
Diagnostic Tool
options

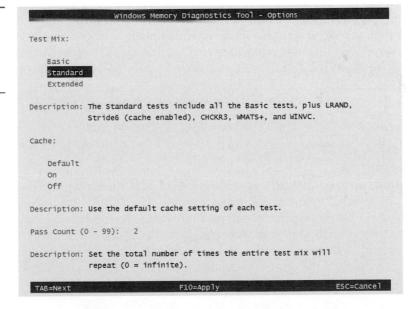

After the tool runs, your computer reboots normally. In Windows 10 you will get a notification with the results; if you missed it, you can open Event Viewer to see the results as well (see Figure 16-21).

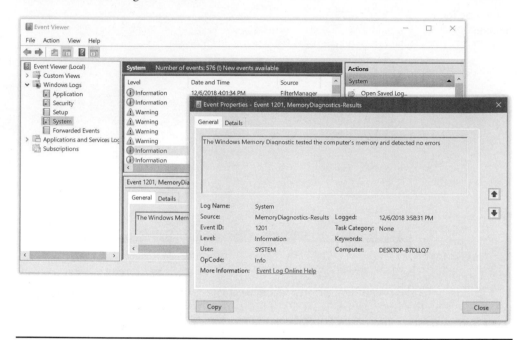

Figure 16-21   Event Viewer results

Sadly, I've had rather poor results with the Windows Memory Diagnostic Tool. We keep lots of bad RAM around the labs here at Total Seminars, and, when put to the test, we were unable to get this tool do anything other than give us a BSoD or lock up the system. We still turn to tried-and-tested tools such as the free Memtest86+ when we're worried about bad RAM.

NOTE   You can find out more about Memtest86+ at www.memtest.org.

Command Prompt and bootrec   The last, most interesting, and easily nerdiest option in the WinRE menu is Command Prompt. The WinRE command prompt is a true 32- or 64-bit prompt that functions similarly to the regular cmd.exe shell in Windows. WinRE's command prompt, however, includes an important utility (bootrec) that you can't find in the regular command prompt. The WinRE command prompt also lacks a large number of the command-prompt tools you'd have in a regular Windows command prompt (though all the important ones remain). Let's begin by looking at the bootrec command. After that, we'll look at some other utilities that the WinRE command prompt offers.

NOTE The Startup Repair tool runs many of these command-prompt utilities automatically. You need to use the WinRE command prompt only for unique situations where the Startup Repair tool fails.

It's important for you to understand that the CompTIA A+ exams do not expect you to know everything about all these command-prompt utilities. The CompTIA A+ exams expect that you do know these things, however:

- Which utilities are available and their names
- How to access these utilities (WinRE in particular)
- What these utilities basically do
- Some of the basic switches used for these utilities
- With higher-level support, that you can fix computers using these tools (being led by a specialist tech over the phone, for example)

With that attitude in mind, let's take a look at probably the most important command to use in WinRE's command prompt, bootrec.

The *bootrec* command is a Windows Recovery Environment troubleshooting and repair tool that repairs the master boot record, boot sector, or BCD store. It replaced the old fixboot and fixmbr Recovery Console commands (a Windows XP tool) and adds two more repair features:

- **bootrec /fixboot**   Rebuilds the boot sector for the active system partition
- **bootrec /fixmbr**   Rebuilds the master boot record for the system partition
- **bootrec /scanos**   Looks for Windows installations not currently in the BCD store and shows you the results without doing anything
- **bootrec /rebuildmbr**   Looks for Windows installations not currently in the BCD store and gives you the choice to add them to the BCD store

NOTE Boot configuration data (BCD) files contain information about operating systems installed on a computer. In Microsoft speak, that information is called a store or BCD store.

You use a tool called *bcdedit* to see how Windows boots. Running bcdedit by itself (without switches) shows the boot options. The following boot information comes from a system with a single copy of Windows installed. Note there are two sections: the

Windows Boot Manager section describes the location of bootmgr, and the *Windows Boot Loader* section describes the location of the winload.exe file.

```
Windows Boot Manager
--------------------
identifier              {bootmgr}
device                  partition=\Device\HarddiskVolume1
description             Windows Boot Manager
locale                  en-US
inherit                 {globalsettings}
default                 {current}
resumeobject            {d4539c9b-481a-11df-a981-a17cb98be35c}
displayorder            {current}
toolsdisplayorder       {memdiag}
timeout                 30

Windows Boot Loader
-------------------
identifier              {current}
device                  partition=C:
path                    \Windows\system32\winload.exe
description             Windows 7
locale                  en-US
inherit                 {bootloadersettings}
recoverysequence        {d4539c9d-481a-11df-a981-a17cb98be35c}
recoveryenabled         Yes
osdevice                partition=C:
systemroot              \Windows
resumeobject            {d4539c9b-481a-11df-a981-a17cb98be35c}
nx                      OptIn
```

To make changes to the BCD store, you need to use switches:

- **bcdedit /export <filename>** exports a copy of the BCD store to a file. This is a very good idea whenever you use bcdedit!

- **bcdedit /import <filename>** imports a copy of the BCD store back into the store.

If you look carefully at the previous bcdedit output, you'll notice that each section has an identifier such as {bootmgr} or {current}. You can use these identifiers to make changes to the BCD store using the /set switch. Here's an example:

```
BCDEDIT /SET {current} path \BackupWindows\system32\winload.exe
```

This changes the path of the {current} identifier to point to an alternative winload.exe.

The bcdedit command supports multiple OSs. Notice how this BCD store has three identifiers: {bootmgr}, {current}, and {ntldr}. The ntldr identifier points to a very old operating system, most likely Windows XP. It means this computer can boot to a legacy OS as well as Windows 7.

```
Windows Boot Manager
--------------------
identifier              {bootmgr}
device                  partition=D:
description             Windows Boot Manager
locale                  en-US
inherit                 {globalsettings}
```

```
default                    {current}
resumeobject               {60b80a52-8267-11e0-ad8a-bdb414c1bf84}
displayorder               {ntldr}
                           {current}
toolsdisplayorder          {memdiag}
timeout                    30

Windows Legacy OS Loader
-----------------------
identifier                 {ntldr}
device                     partition=D:
path                       \ntldr
description                Earlier Version of Windows

Windows Boot Loader
-------------------
identifier                 {current}
device                     partition=C:
path                       \Windows\system32\winload.exe
description                Windows 7
locale                     en-US
inherit                    {bootloadersettings}
recoverysequence           {60b80a54-8267-11e0-ad8a-bdb414c1bf84}
recoveryenabled            Yes
osdevice                   partition=C:
systemroot                 \Windows
resumeobject               {60b80a52-8267-11e0-ad8a-bdb414c1bf84}
nx                         OptIn
```

A BCD store like this will cause the menu shown in Figure 16-22 to pop up at boot.

Figure 16-22
bootmgr
showing
available versions
of Windows

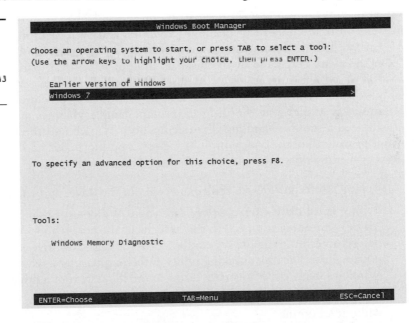

You can use bcdedit to update the boot order options. If you have a multiboot system like the one above, for example, and you find that you need to reboot a lot to troubleshoot an application in one of the non-Windows 10 OSs installed, you can change the boot order to default to the older OS. Once you've finished debugging, use bcdedit to change the default boot order to Windows 10.

The command prompt also includes *diskpart*, a fully featured partitioning tool. This tool lacks many of the safety features built into Disk Management (covered in Chapters 8 and 9), so proceed with caution. You can, for example, delete any partition of any type at any time. Starting diskpart opens a special command prompt as shown here:

```
C:\Windows\system32>diskpart
Microsoft DiskPart version 10.0.17134.345
Copyright (C) Microsoft Corporation.
On computer: MIKESPC
DISKPART>
```

You can list volumes (or partitions on basic disks):

```
DISKPART> list volume
  Volume ###  Ltr  Label       Fs     Type       Size     Status     Info
  ----------  ---  --------    -----  --------   -------   ---------  -------
  Volume 0    D                       DVD-ROM        0 B   No Media
  Volume 1    C    New Volume  NTFS   Partition  1397 GB   Healthy    System

DISKPART>
```

Select a volume to manipulate (you may also select an entire drive):

```
DISKPART> select volume 1
Volume 1 is the selected volume.
DISKPART>
```

You can run commands at the diskpart prompt to add, change, or delete volumes and partitions on drives, mount or dismount volumes, and even manipulate software-level RAID arrays. Use the **format** command to format a newly created volume.

Run the **clean** command at the diskpart prompt to wipe all partition and volume information off the currently selected disk. This tool handles nasty corruptions that simply won't let Windows boot and serves as my last-ditch step before I toss a drive.

Commands available at the diskpart prompt handle volumes and partitions, but you still need a tool for handling file systems. Both WinRE and the regular command prompt provide all of the typical utilities such as copy, move, del, and format. One tool, however—fsutil—does a few more interesting jobs:

- Typing **fsinfo** provides a detailed query about the drives and volumes.
- Typing **fsutil dirty** *<drive name>* tells you if Windows considers the drive to be "dirty"—meaning you need to run autochk at the next reboot. When Windows detects an error in the file system for a drive, it flags that drive as a *dirty drive* or *dirty volume*. The disk checking utility autochk runs after a reboot and before Windows loads and will correct errors in the file system of a drive.
- Typing **fsutil repair initiate** *<drive letter>* runs a basic version of chkdsk without rebooting.

Uninstall Updates Use the Uninstall Updates option in the very odd chance that Microsoft pushes out an update that breaks things in your system. It's happened in the past, exceedingly infrequently, so Microsoft includes this option just in case. You'll likely never need to use it.

UEFI Firmware Settings   Getting into system settings in UEFI-based motherboards can be a challenge. Although pressing the Delete key repeatedly works sometimes, the opportunity flashes by very quickly. The UEFI Firmware Settings option enables you to access the system setup utility when you restart your computer via the Recovery option in Settings. Use this option when you're tweaking things like CPU or RAM timings, or want to change the boot order for some reason.

Refresh and Reset   Windows 8/8.1 has two options, one to Refresh and the other to Reset the PC from the Troubleshoot screen. Windows 10 offers those same options, although they're named differently and you'll find them under *Reset this PC*:

- *Refresh* in Windows 8/8.1 equates to *Keep my files* in Windows 10.
- *Reset* in Windows 8/8.1 equates to *Remove everything* in Windows 10.

The outcome from these two options is dramatically different.

The Windows RE option to Refresh your PC in Windows 8/8.1 or Keep my files in Windows 10 rebuilds Windows, but preserves all user files and settings and any applications purchased from the Windows Store. Note well: Refresh/Keep my files *deletes every other application on your system*.

The Reset your PC/Remove everything option nukes your system—all apps, programs, user files, user settings—and presents a fresh installation of Windows. Use Reset/Remove as the last resort when troubleshooting a PC. And back up your data first.

Failure to Boot: Linux

Linux offers two common boot managers: GRUB and LILO. Everyone uses GRUB these days; LILO is older and simpler and doesn't support UEFI BIOS systems.

If GRUB gets corrupted or deleted, Linux won't start and you'll get a "Missing GRUB" error message at boot. (Similarly, on older systems you'd get a "Missing LILO" error message.)

You have a couple of options to fix this problem. For GRUB2-based systems, boot to the OS media disc/flash-media drive and let it "install" into memory. In other words, don't install it to the hard drive. From there, you can access the Terminal and run the **sudo grub-install** command (along with the location of the boot drive) to repair.

Failure to Start Normally

Assuming that Windows gets past the boot part of the startup, it continues to load the graphical Windows OS. You will see the Windows startup image on the screen, hiding everything until Windows gets to the Login screen (see Figure 16-23). Once you log in, you'll get the Windows Desktop or the Start screen, depending on which version of Windows you have.

Several issues can create a scenario where Windows fails to start normally. Windows can hang because of buggy device drivers or Registry problems. Even autoloading

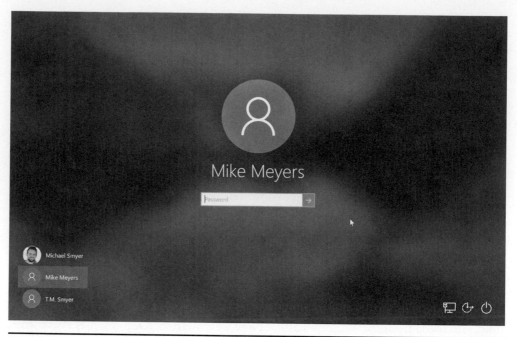

Figure 16-23 Login screen

programs can cause Windows to hang on load. A corrupted user profile can also block normal login. The first step in troubleshooting these sorts of scenarios is to use one of the Advanced Startup Options (covered later in the chapter) to try to get past the hang spot and into Windows.

EXAM TIP The first step in a scenario where Windows fails to start normally is to *reboot the computer*. It's the simplest option, so try it!

Device Drivers

Device driver problems that stop Windows from loading look pretty sad. Figure 16-24 shows a Windows *Stop error*, better known as the *Blue Screen of Death* (*BSoD*). The BSoD only appears when something causes an error from which Windows cannot recover. The BSoD is not limited to device driver problems, but device drivers are one of the reasons you'll see the BSoD.

Whenever faced with a scenario where you get a BSoD, read what it says. Windows BSoDs tell you the name of the file that caused the problem and usually suggest a recommended action. Once in a while these are helpful.

BSoD problems due to device drivers almost always take place immediately after you've installed a new device and rebooted. Take out the device and reboot. If Windows

Figure 16-24
BSoD in
Windows 10

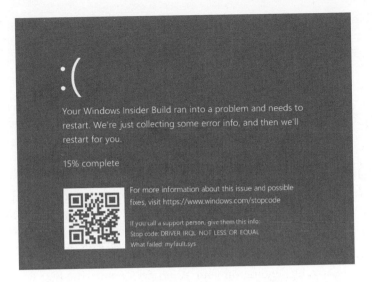

loads properly, head over to the manufacturer's Web site. A new device producing this type of problem is a serious issue that should have been caught before the device was released. In many cases, the manufacturer will have updated drivers available for download or will recommend a replacement device.

Buggy video drivers can result in a *black screen* in Windows, rather than a blue screen. Usually the screen will have information, just like the BSoD, so you get a clue about the next step to take to resolve the issue.

EXAM TIP Malware can cause Windows to fail to start normally or make it appear to be missing. One nasty malware running around recently, for example, caused what appeared to be a BSoD warning of imminent hard drive controller failure. Even after getting rid of the malware, Windows appeared devoid of any graphical elements at all: no Start button, icons, or files even in Computer. That's because the malware had changed the attributes of every file and folder on the hard drive to hidden! See Chapter 27, "Securing Computers," for recovery techniques for malware-attacked computers.

The second indication of a device problem that shows up during the final part of startup is a freeze-up: the Windows startup screen just stays there and you never get a chance to log on. If this happens, try one of the Advanced Startup Options, covered following the Registry.

Device drivers can trip up Linux systems too, causing their own form of BSoD, called a *kernel panic*. The fix follows along the same lines as for Windows—go to the manufacturer's Web site and find updated drivers or *kernel modules* (code that gets inserted directly into the kernel).

Note that failing hardware can create kernel panic in macOS and Linux and bring the system down. Kernel panic in macOS is demonstrated by a black or gray screen of death and is, I assure you, a terrifying moment to experience.

 EXAM TIP The Spinning Pinwheel of Death (SPoD) that you see on macOS systems indicates an unresponsive system. These often get lumped into the same discussion as BSoDs and kernel panic, but the SPoD is not nearly as bad.

Registry

The Registry files load every time the computer boots. Windows does a pretty good job of protecting your Registry files from corruption, but from time to time something may slip by Windows and it will attempt to load a bad Registry. These errors may show up as BSoDs that say "Registry File Failure" or text errors that say "Windows could not start." Whatever the case, when you run into these sorts of scenarios, you need to restore a good Registry copy. Depending on your Windows version, the best way to do this is the Last Known Good Configuration boot option (see the upcoming section). If that fails, you can restore an earlier version of the Registry through Windows RE.

Windows 8.1 and prior (and early versions of Windows 10) keep a regular backup of the Registry handy in case you need to overwrite a corrupted Registry. By default, the task runs every 10 days, so that's as far back as you would lose if you replaced the current Registry with the automatically backed-up files. Of course, it would be better if you kept regular backups too, but at least the damage would be limited. You can find the backed-up Registry files in \Windows\System32\config\RegBack (see Figure 16-25).

Name	Date modified	Type	Size
DEFAULT	12/6/2018 12:38 PM	File	236 KB
SAM	12/6/2018 12:38 PM	File	32 KB
SECURITY	12/6/2018 12:38 PM	File	24 KB
SOFTWARE	12/6/2018 12:38 PM	File	72,560 KB
SYSTEM	12/6/2018 12:38 PM	File	9,340 KB

Figure 16-25 The backed-up Registry files located in the RegBack folder

To replace the Registry, boot to the Windows media to access Windows RE and get to the Command Prompt shell. Run the **reg** command to get to a reg prompt. From there, you have numerous commands to deal with the Registry. The simplest is probably the *copy* command. You know the location of the backed-up Registry files. Just copy the files to the location of the main Registry files—up one level in the tree under the \config folder.

Advanced Startup Options

If Windows fails to start up normally, you have a couple of options depending on the version of the OS. In Windows 7, press F5 at boot-up to boot directly to Safe Mode. Or, you can use the Windows *Advanced Boot Options/Advanced Startup Options* menu to discover the cause. To get to this menu, restart the computer and press F8 after the POST messages but before the Windows logo screen appears.

In Windows 8 and later, you can get to the Advanced Startup Options by hard rebooting the computer each time it hangs or starts to load Windows. Windows will eventually figure out that it has a problem and will run a diagnostic. If the computer fails the test, you'll be offered Advanced options. Check here for the steps and screenshots from Microsoft:

> https://support.microsoft.com/en-us/help/12376/windows-10-start-your-pc-in-safe-mode

Safe Mode

Safe Mode starts up Windows but loads only very basic, non-vendor-specific drivers for mouse, 800 × 600 (7) or 1024 × 768 (8/8.1/10) resolution monitor, keyboard, mass storage, and system services (see Figure 16-26).

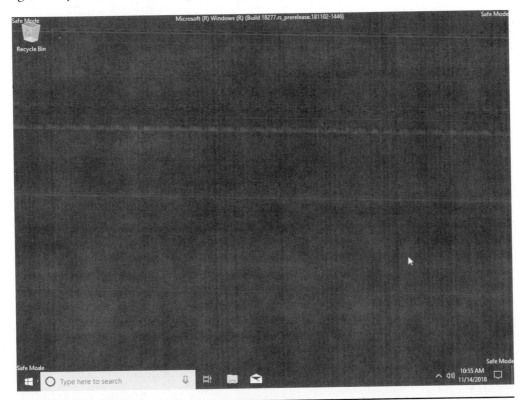

Figure 16-26 Safe Mode

Once in Safe Mode, you can use tools such as Device Manager to locate and correct the source of the problem. When you use Device Manager in Safe Mode, you can access the properties for all the devices, even those that are not working in Safe Mode. The status displayed for the device is the status for a normal startup. Even the network card will show as enabled. You can disable any suspect device or perform other tasks, such as removing or updating drivers. If a problem with a device driver is preventing the operating system from starting normally, check Device Manager for warning icons that indicate an unknown device.

There is no safety or repair feature in any version of Windows that makes the OS boot to Safe Mode automatically. In most cases, Windows automatically booting to Safe Mode indicates that someone has set the System Configuration utility to force Windows to do so. Type **msconfig** at the Start | Search box and press ENTER to open the System Configuration utility, and then click the Boot tab and deselect the Safe boot checkbox (see Figure 16-27).

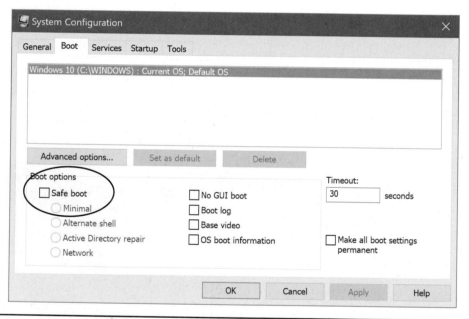

Figure 16-27   Uncheck Safe boot.

Safe Mode with Networking

This mode is identical to plain Safe Mode except that you get network support. I use this mode to test for a problem with network drivers. If Windows won't start up normally but does start up in Safe Mode, I reboot into Safe Mode with Networking. If it fails to start up with Networking, the problem is a network driver. I reboot back to Safe Mode, open Device Manager, and start disabling network components, beginning with the network adapter.

Safe Mode with Command Prompt

When you start Windows in this mode, rather than loading the GUI Desktop, it loads the command prompt (cmd.exe) as the shell to the operating system after you log on. From here you can run any of the commands you learned about in Chapter 15, "Working with the Command-Line Interface," plus a lot of utilities as well. Error checking runs fine as chkdsk, for example. Disk Defragmenter probably runs even faster when you type **defrag** followed by a drive letter at the command prompt than it does from the graphical version of the tool.

 EXAM TIP   Look for a question on the CompTIA A+ 1002 exam about defragmenting a hard disk drive (HDD) as a common solution to Windows OS problems. You can readily defrag an HDD from the command prompt in Safe Mode.

Safe Mode with Command Prompt is a handy option to remember if the Desktop does not display at all, which, after you have eliminated video drivers, can be caused by corruption of the explorer.exe program. From the command prompt, you can delete the corrupted version of explorer.exe and copy in an undamaged version. This requires knowing the command-line commands for navigating the directory structure, as well as knowing the location of the file you are replacing. Although Explorer is not loaded, you can load other GUI tools that don't depend on Explorer. All you have to do is enter the correct command. For instance, to load Event Viewer, type **eventvwr.msc** at the command line and press ENTER.

Enable Boot Logging

Selecting the Enable boot logging option starts Windows normally and creates a log file of the drivers as they load into memory. The file is named Ntbtlog.txt and is saved in the %SystemRoot% folder. If the startup failed because of a bad driver, the last entry in this file may be the driver the OS was initializing when it failed.

Reboot and go into the WinRE. Use the tools there to read the boot log and disable or enable problematic devices or services.

Enable Low-Resolution Video

Selecting the Enable low-resolution video option starts Windows normally, but only loads a default video driver. If this mode works, it may mean you have a bad driver, or it may mean you are using the correct video driver but it is configured incorrectly (perhaps with the wrong refresh rate and/or resolution). After successfully starting in this mode, open the Display applet and change the settings.

Last Known Good Configuration

When Windows' startup fails immediately after installing a new driver but before you have logged on again, try the *Last Known Good Configuration* option. This option applies specifically to new device drivers that cause failures on reboot.

Directory Services Restore Mode

The title says it all here; this option only applies to Active Directory domain controllers, and only Windows Server versions can be domain controllers. I have no idea why Microsoft includes this option. If you choose it, you simply boot into Safe Mode.

Debugging Mode

If you select this choice, Windows starts in kernel debug mode. It's a super-techie thing to do, and I doubt that even über techs do debug mode anymore. To do this, you have to connect the computer you are debugging to another computer via a serial connection, and as Windows starts up, a debug of the kernel is sent to the second computer, which must also be running a debugger program.

Disable Automatic Restart on System Failure

Sometimes a BSoD will appear at startup, causing your computer to spontaneously reboot. That's all well and good, but if it happens too quickly, you might not be able to read the BSoD to see what caused the problem. Selecting *Disable automatic restart on system failure* from the Advanced Boot Options menu stops the computer from rebooting on Stop errors. This gives you the opportunity to write down the error and hopefully find a fix.

Disable Driver Signature Enforcement

Windows requires that all very low-level drivers (kernel drivers) must have a Microsoft driver signature. If you are using an older driver to connect to your hard drive controller or some other low-level feature, you must use this option to get Windows to load the driver. Hopefully you will always check your motherboard and hard drives for Windows compatibility and never have to use this option.

Start Windows Normally

This choice will simply start Windows normally, without rebooting. You already rebooted to get to this menu. Select this if you changed your mind about using any of the other exotic choices.

Reboot

This choice will actually do a soft reboot of the computer.

Return to OS Choices Menu

On computers with multiple operating systems, you get an OS Choices menu to select which OS to load. If you load Windows 7 and press F8 to get the Advanced Boot Options menu, you'll see this option. Choosing it returns you to the OS Choices menu, from which you can select the operating system to load.

Rebuild Windows Profiles

Each user account on a Windows machine has an associated *profile* that records settings such as Desktop preferences—like background and color—shortcuts, and other icons.

A corrupted profile can block a user from logging in and getting access to his or her stuff. Corrupted profiles can also manifest as very slow profile load times. Anti-malware software can sometimes corrupt a profile, as can upgrading from one version of Windows to another. You have two options to rebuild a profile, several direct Registry edits or creating a new user account and copying the old profile settings to the new account.

The Registry edits are a little complex, so here are the steps. The first step is to get into Safe Mode.

If you can access the sign-in screen but can't log in, the easiest way to get to Safe Mode is to hold the SHIFT key and then click Power | Restart. Your computer will reboot, and you'll get the Choose an option screen, as described earlier. Get to the Startup Settings screen and click Restart. This brings you to the Startup Settings screen where you can select Safe Mode.

Once in Safe Mode, access an elevated command prompt. (Type **cmd** in the Search field, right-click the Command Prompt option, and select Run as administrator.) Type **regedit** and press ENTER to open the Registry Editor. Navigate to this string to get to Figure 16-28:

```
HKEY_LOCAL_MACHINE\SOFTWARE\Microsoft\Windows NT\CurrentVersion\ProfileList
```

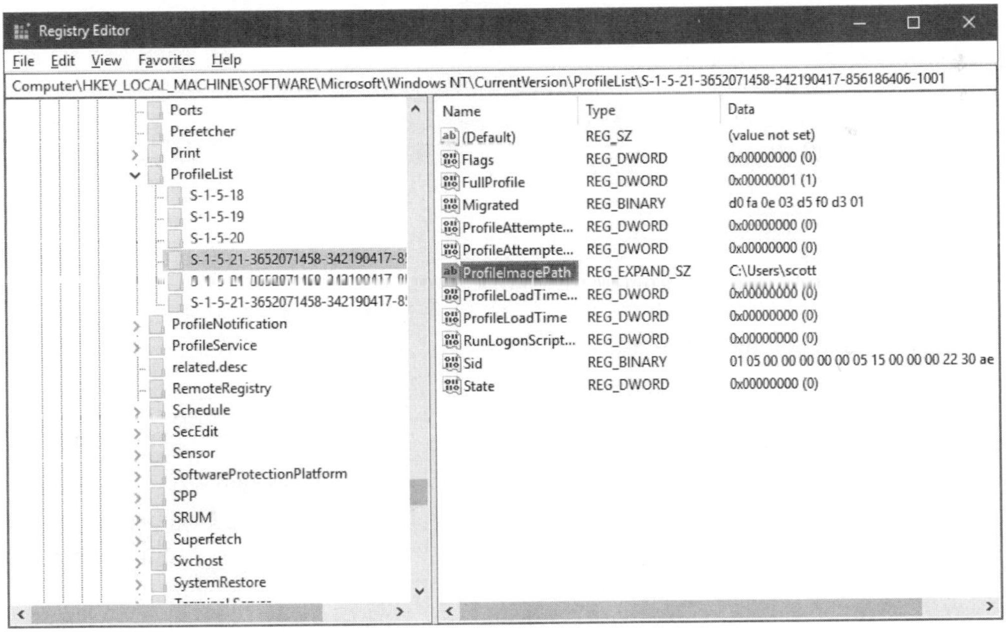

Figure 16-28   ProfileList in Registry

Click the ProfileList arrow on the left to see a set of entries that start with S-1-5. Select the one that matches the messed-up profile. Figure 16-28 shows a user named Scott (which you can barely make out in the ProfileImagePath on the right pane. On the right pane, double-click the State entry and set the value to 0 (see Figure 16-29).

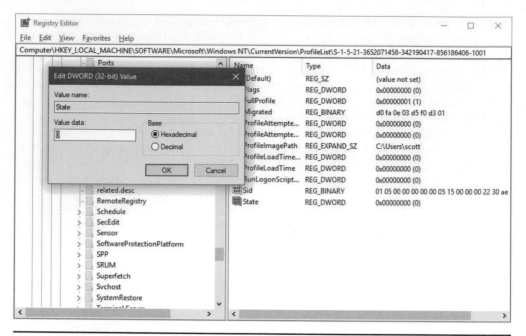

Figure 16-29 Setting the State to 0

Here's the last step. If you have an option for RefCount on the right, double-click it and set the value to 0. If you don't have that entry, create it: Edit | New | DWORD (32-bit) Value. Close the Registry Editor and reboot the computer. That profile should work.

If the profile doesn't work, then the next option is to create a new user account and essentially duplicate the earlier profile. Boot back into Safe Mode and open an elevated command prompt. You need an administrator account to create a new user, so that's what you're about to access. To activate the super-secret-hidden local administrator account, type the *net user* command and press ENTER:

```
net user administrator /active:yes
```

Reboot the computer and log in as the local administrator you just activated. Create a new user account: Settings | Accounts | Family & other people | Add someone else to this PC (see Figure 16-30). Give the account a unique name. Go to the Users folder of the corrupted account and copy all the contents to the new account's Users folder, but do it one folder at a time to avoid getting any of the corrupted hidden files copied.

When you reboot the computer, you should be able to log on to the newly created account and access all the old/corrupt accounts files. Once *verified*, log back on as administrator, delete the corrupted account, and rename the new account to the same as the old account.

Both processes for recovering a corrupted user profile are clunky, but they work. Expect to see a question or two on this topic on the 1002 exam.

Figure 16-30
Creating a new
user account in
Windows 10

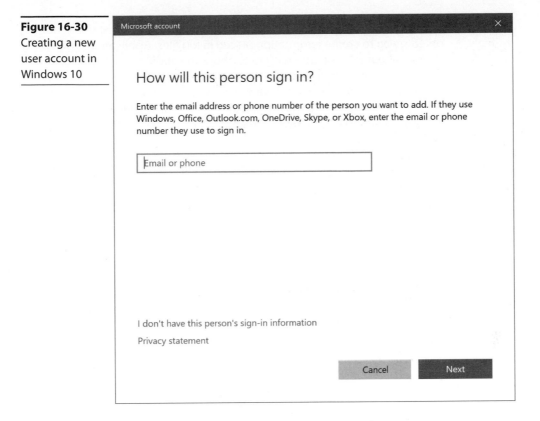

Microsoft account   ✕

How will this person sign in?

Enter the email address or phone number of the person you want to add. If they use
Windows, Office, Outlook.com, OneDrive, Skype, or Xbox, enter the email or phone
number they use to sign in.

Email or phone

I don't have this person's sign-in information

Privacy statement

Cancel   Next

Troubleshooting Tools

Once you're able to load into Windows, whether through Safe Mode or one of the other
options, the whole gamut of Windows tools is available for you. In the previous scenario
where a bad device driver caused the startup problems, for example, you can open Device
Manager and begin troubleshooting just as you've learned in previous chapters. If you
suspect some service or Registry issue caused the problem, head on over to Event Viewer
and see what sort of logon events have happened recently. Let's go there first.

Event Viewer

When you get to the Desktop, one of the first tools you should use is Event Viewer to
see what's causing the problems on your computer. *Event Viewer* is Windows' default
tattletale program, spilling the beans about a number of interesting happenings on the
system. With a little tweaking, Event Viewer turns into a virtual recording of anything
you might ever want to know about on your system.

EXAM TIP UNIX systems (like macOS and various Linux distros) use a tool called *syslog* to create information placed in log files. Applications use syslog to write about issues happening to or about the application. Syslog also works over networks, so you can imagine how useful that is! syslog is not a program, like Event Viewer. Programs use syslog to write events. You'll find the log files at /var/log in most Linux distros. Note that there is third-party support for syslog in Windows, so it's not limited to UNIX-based systems.

Keep in mind that Event Viewer is a powerful tool for more than just troubleshooting Windows—it's a powerful tool for security as well, as you'll see in Chapter 27. But for now let's examine Event Viewer to see what we can do with this amazing utility.

Opening Event Viewer (Control Panel | Administrative Tools | Event Viewer) shows you the default interface (see Figure 16-31).

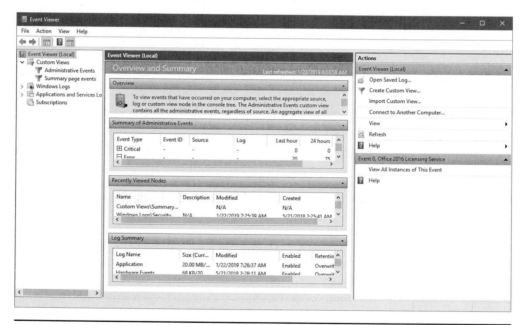

Figure 16-31 Windows 10 Event Viewer default screen

Note the four main bars in the center pane: Overview, Summary of Administrative Events, Recently Viewed Nodes, and Log Summary. Pay special attention to the Summary of Administrative Events. It breaks down the events into different levels: Critical, Error, Warning, Information, Audit Success, and Audit Failure. Figure 16-32 shows a typical Summary with the Warning Events opened. You can then click any event to see a dialog box describing the event in detail. Microsoft refers to these as *Views*. (I toggled the Action pane off so you can see more of the center pane.)

Windows Event Viewer still includes the classic logs (Application, Security, and System) but leans heavily on Views to show you the contents of the logs. Views filter existing

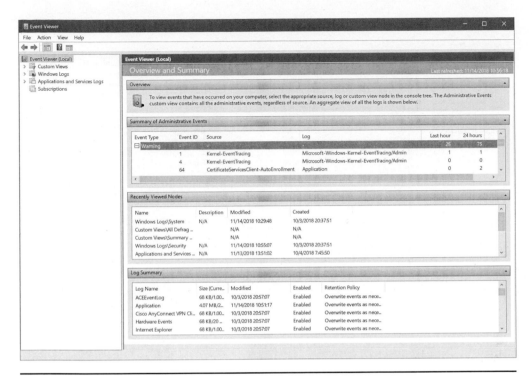

Figure 16-32   Warning Events open

log files, making them great for custom reports using beginning/end times, levels of errors, and more. You can use the built-in Views or easily create custom Views, as shown in Figure 16-33.

NOTE   By default, Event Viewer stores logs as .evtx files in the C:\Windows\ System32\winevt\Logs folder.

You record all data to logs. Logs in Windows have limitations, such as a maximum size, a location, and a behavior for when they get too big (such as overwrite the log or make an error). Figure 16-34 shows a typical Log Properties dialog box in Windows 10. Note that only users with Administrator privileges can make changes to log files in Event Viewer.

EXAM TIP   If you run into a scenario where a device has failed and this created problems with Windows' startup, you would turn to the primary Windows tool for hardware issues: Device Manager. We've covered Device Manager in chapters specific to hardware, so there's no need to go into it yet again here.

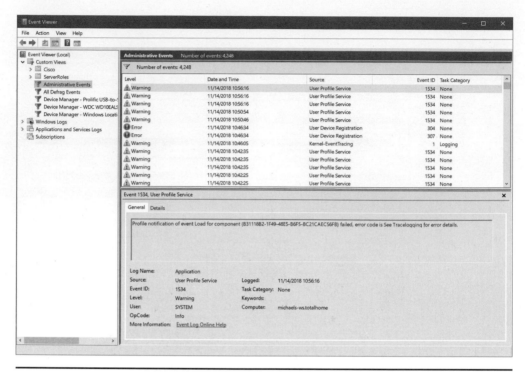

Figure 16-33 Created custom Views

Autoloading Programs

Windows loves to autoload programs so they start at boot. Most of the time this is an incredibly handy option, used by every Windows PC in existence. The problem with autoloading programs is that when one of them starts behaving badly, you need to shut off that program! Use the System Configuration utility in Windows 7 or the Task Manager in Windows 8/8.1/10 to temporarily stop programs from autoloading. If you want to make the program stop forever, go into the program and find a load on startup option (see Figure 16-35).

 EXAM TIP You can disable Windows services/applications from Control Panel | Programs and Features. There's an option on the left to Turn Windows features on or off. You can always enable a service or application later from the same menu.

Services

Windows loads many services as it starts. In a scenario where a critical service fails to start, Windows tells you at this point with an error message. The important word here is *critical*. Windows will not report *all* service failures at this point. If a service that is less

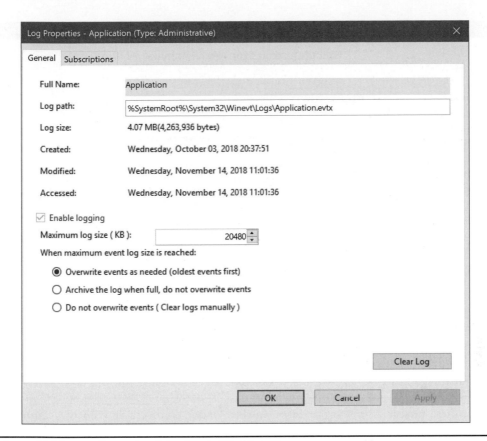

Figure 16-34 Log Properties dialog box in Windows 10

than critical to Windows doesn't start, the OS usually waits until you try to use a program that needs that service before it prompts you with an error message (see Figure 16-36).

To work with your system's services, go to the Control Panel | Administrative Tools | Services and verify that the service you need is running. If not, restart the service. Also notice that each service has a Startup Type—Automatic, Manual, or Disabled—that defines when it starts. It's very common to find that a service has been set to Manual when it needs to be set to Automatic so that it starts when Windows boots (see Figure 16-37).

Task Manager and Command-Line Options

As we discussed in Chapter 12, "Windows Under the Hood," the *Task Manager* is a great place to go to shut down errant processes that won't otherwise close properly. You can quickly close a program that is hogging CPU resources, for example, by right-clicking the program under the Processes tab and selecting End Process. The Task Manager enables you to see all processes and services currently running or to close an application that has stopped working. You remember how to get to it, right? Press CTRL-SHIFT-ESC to

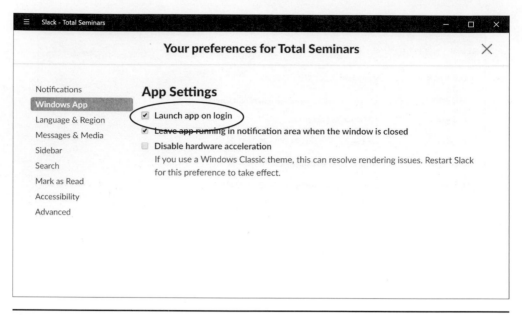

Figure 16-35 Typical load on startup option

open it directly or CTRL-ALT-DELETE to get to a list of action items, one of which opens the Task Manager.

If you're unable to get to the Task Manager or are comfortable with the command line, you can get to a command prompt (like in the Windows Recovery Environment) and type the command **tasklist** to find the names and process IDs of all the running processes. You can then run **taskkill** to end any process either by filename or by process ID. As with the Task Manager, look back to Chapter 12 for more details on managing processes from the command line. If you're in the Windows PowerShell, the commands are **tasklist** and **kill**.

Figure 16-36
Service error

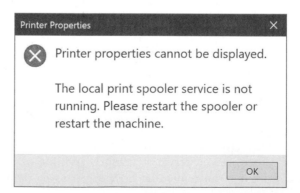

Figure 16-37
Autostarting a service

 EXAM TIP The *kill* command at the Bash or Terminal shell enables you to terminate running programs in Linux or macOS, just like the tools in Command or PowerShell. Expect to see it on the CompTIA A+ 1002 exam.

System Files

Windows lives on dynamic link library (DLL) files. Almost every program used by Windows—and certainly all of the important ones—call to DLL files to do most of the heavy lifting that makes Windows work.

Windows protects all of the critical DLL files very carefully, but once in a while you may get an error saying Windows can't load a particular DLL. Although rare, the core system files that make up Windows itself may become corrupted, preventing Windows from starting properly. You usually see something like "Error loading XXXX.DLL," or sometimes a program you need simply won't start when you double-click its icon. In these cases, the tool you need is the *System File Checker* (*sfc*) that you learned about in Chapter 15. Use it to check and replace a number of critical files, including the ever-important DLL cache.

System Restore

System Restore is the final step in recovering from a major Windows meltdown. Earlier in the chapter, you learned that you can use System Restore from the Windows Recovery Environment, but don't forget that you can also use restore points from within Windows. Follow the process explained in Chapter 14. Windows Restore can also help if you fix a computer that seems sluggish or has slow performance. Some systems bog down over time with poorly written applications added and such. Restoring to an earlier time can add pep to an ailing PC with little pain to the user or the tech.

 EXAM TIP   If you can get into Windows but the OS is buggy, sluggish, or just plain wrong, you have yet another option for fixing the problems. A *repair installation* starts from within Windows, where you run the Windows setup.exe file from the OS media (DVD, thumb drive, etc.) and essentially reinstall Windows. One of the options you have in the process is to keep or delete personal files and apps. Opt to keep everything and the Windows installation routine will overwrite all the system files and drivers and check for updates (assuming the computer is connected to the Internet).

Disable Secure Boot in UEFI settings and any third-party anti-malware software you have before you begin. It's also always a good idea to back up your data files before you start. If things go badly for some reason, you want your data safe.

More Control Panel Tools

The Control Panel offers several other tools that techs need to troubleshoot a variety of issues. The two composite applets are Troubleshooting and Security and Maintenance/Action Center.

Troubleshooting

The *Troubleshooting* applet offers a selection of common solutions to both hardware and application problems (Figure 16-38). The default window offers four categories of help—Programs, Hardware and Sound, Network and Internet, and System and Security—plus a Search box when you have a problem and feel lucky. (Windows 7 has a fifth category, Appearance and Personalization, to troubleshoot display-related problems.) I'll let you explore the tool on your own (and return to it in other sections of the book), but here are a few highlights.

If you're having printing issues, click the Use a printer option under Hardware and Sound. This opens a Printer troubleshooting wizard (see Figure 16-39).

Follow the process by clicking Next and reading the screens. The troubleshooter looks at spooler problems, checks drivers, and so on. Chapter 26, "Printers and Multifunction Devices," goes into a lot more detail on printers and printer troubleshooting, but the Troubleshooting applet is a good starting spot.

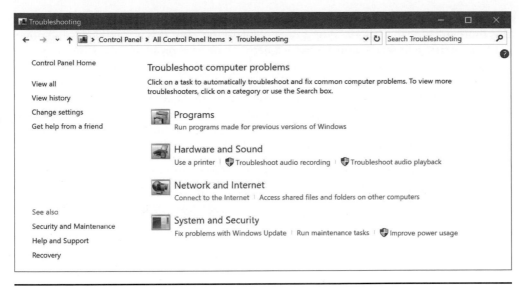

Figure 16-38 Troubleshooting applet

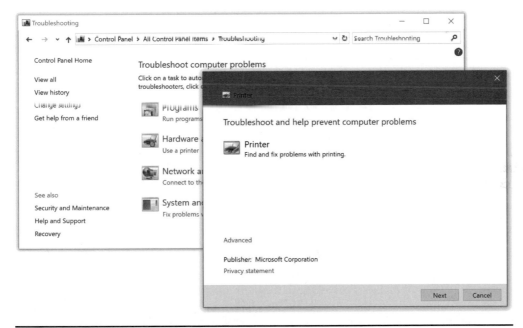

Figure 16-39 Printer troubleshooting wizard in the Troubleshooting applet

Use the Network and Internet options to update network settings quickly. We'll cover this more fully in Chapter 19, "Local Area Networking," but this is a good starting point if you experience limited connectivity to a network or have problems accessing resources over a network.

If you run into problems with Windows Update, a scenario such as a device stops working after patch Tuesday, click Fix problems with Windows Update in the System and Security section. This opens a Windows Update troubleshooting wizard (see Figure 16-40). Just like with Printers, click Next and pay attention to the screens. Click Apply this fix or Skip this fix once the wizard checks for pending updates.

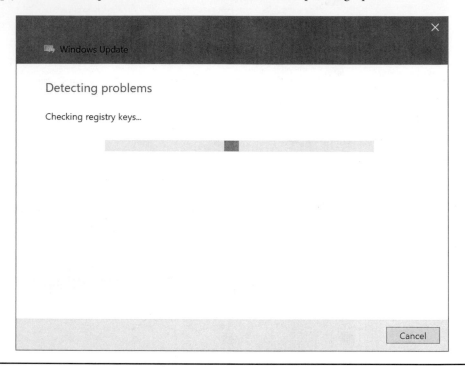

Figure 16-40   Windows Update troubleshooting wizard in action

Security and Maintenance/Action Center

Security and Maintenance in Windows 10 and the *Action Center* in Windows 7/8/8.1 provide a one-page aggregation of event messages, warnings, and maintenance messages that, for many techs, might quickly replace Event Viewer as the first place to look for problems. The tool makes it easy to scan a system quickly (see Figure 16-41).

Security and Maintenance/Action Center only compiles the information, taking data from well-known utilities such as Event Viewer, Windows Update, Windows Firewall, and UAC and placing it into an easy-to-read format. If you wish, you can tell Security and Maintenance/Action Center where to look for information by selecting *Change Security and Maintenance settings* (see Figure 16-42) or *Change Action Center settings*.

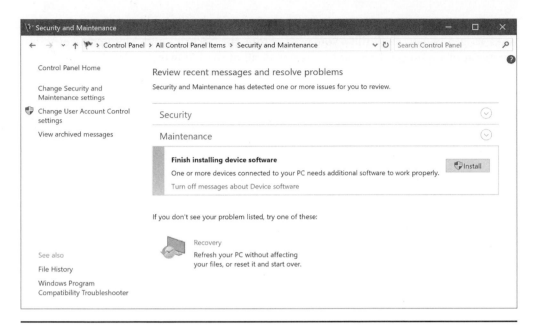

Figure 16-41 Security and Maintenance

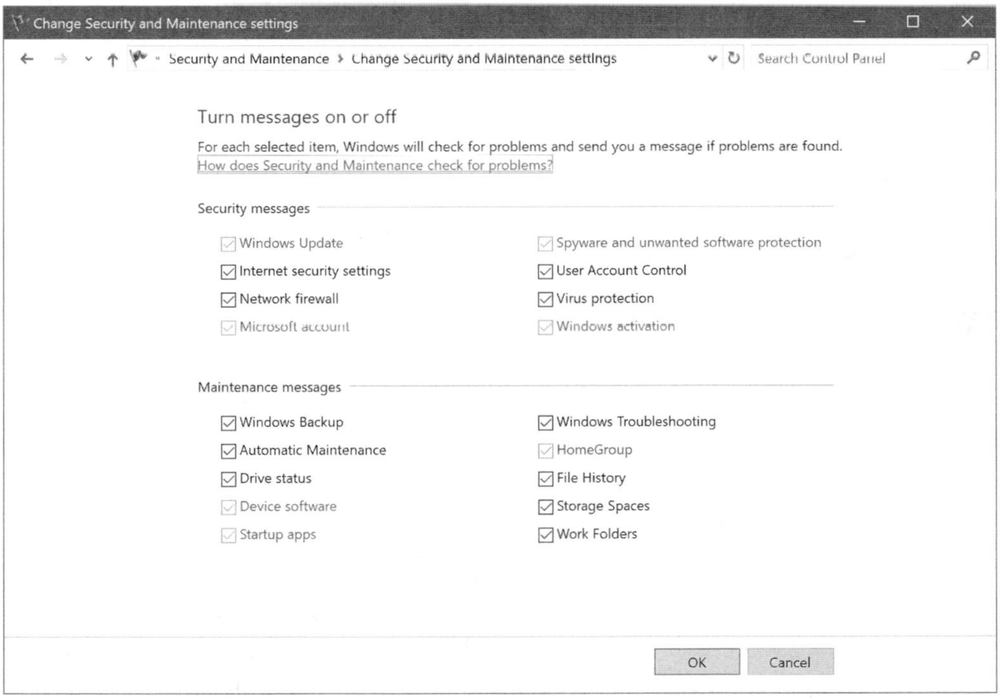

Figure 16-42 Change Security and Maintenance settings

If you see a problem, Security and Maintenance/Action Center includes plenty of links to get you to the utility you need. From the Security and Maintenance/Action Center applet, you get direct links to some or all of the following tools:

- UAC settings
- Backup and Restore
- Windows Update
- Troubleshooting Wizard
- System Restore
- Recovery

Although Security and Maintenance/Action Center does little more than reproduce information from other utilities, it makes finding problems quick and easy. Combined with quick links to most of the utilities you'll need, Security and Maintenance/Action Center should become your base of operations when something goes wrong on your Windows PC.

Try This!   Security and Maintenance

If you haven't had a chance to explore Security and Maintenance in Windows 10, now's the time, so try this! Open the app in Control Panel or directly by typing Secur. . . in the Search field and selecting the shortcut that pops up. Are Windows Firewall and Windows Defender active? Do you have any messages under Maintenance that need addressing? What behavior can you change when you select *Change Security and Maintenance settings*? Finally, while you're at the app, click on the File History related app (lower left corner) and segue into exploring that tool, too.

Application Problems

Programmers want to write applications that work well, enable you to accomplish a specific task, and be good enough to earn your money. But PCs are complicated and programmers can't get it right every time with every combination of hardware and software.

Application problems show up in several ways. The typical scenario has the application failing to install or uninstall. Operating system version issues can cause compatibility problems. Another typical scenario is where an application tries to access a file and that file is either missing or won't open. The least common problems come from sloppy or poorly written code that causes the application or the operating system to crash. Finally, corrupted applications can corrupt data too, but Windows has tools for recovering previous versions of files and folders.

EXAM TIP Every once in a while you'll get an application that reports an error if the clock settings in Windows don't match. This can cause the application not to run. Likewise, if a computer has a failing battery and is offline for a while, the BIOS time and settings will be off. You'll get a brief "error" noting the change when you connect that computer to a network timeserver. This is both a hardware issue (failing battery) and an application issue. When the Windows clock resets, so do the BIOS time and settings.

Application Installation Problems

Almost all Windows programs come with some form of handy installer. When you insert the disc or USB drive, Windows knows to look for a text file called autorun.inf that tells it which file to run off the disc or USB drive, usually setup.exe. If you download the application, you'll need to double-click its icon to start the installation. Either way, you run the installer and the program runs. It almost couldn't be simpler.

 EXAM TIP The fact that Windows looks for the autorun.inf file by default when you insert a disc or USB drive creates a security issue. Someone could put a malicious program on some form of media and write an autorun.inf file to point to the malware. Insert the media and boom! There goes your clean PC. Of course, if someone has access to your computer and is fully logged on with administrator privileges, then you've already lost everything, with or without a media-borne program, so this "big" security issue is pretty much not an issue at all. Nevertheless, you should know that to turn off this behavior in Windows requires opening the Registry Editor and changing up to six different settings.

A well-behaved program should always make itself easy to uninstall as well. In most cases, you should see an uninstallation option in the program's Start menu area; and in all cases (unless you have an application with a badly configured installer), the application should appear in either the Programs and Features applet in the Control Panel or Apps & features in Settings (see Figure 16-43).

 NOTE Remember that you need local administrator privileges to install applications in all versions of Windows.

Programs that fail to install usually aren't to blame in and of themselves. In most cases, a problem with Windows prevents them from installing, most notably the lack of some other program that the application needs so it can operate. One of the best examples of this is the popular Microsoft .NET Framework. .NET is an extension to the Windows operating system that includes support for a number of features, particularly powerful interface tools and flexible database access. If a program is written to take advantage of

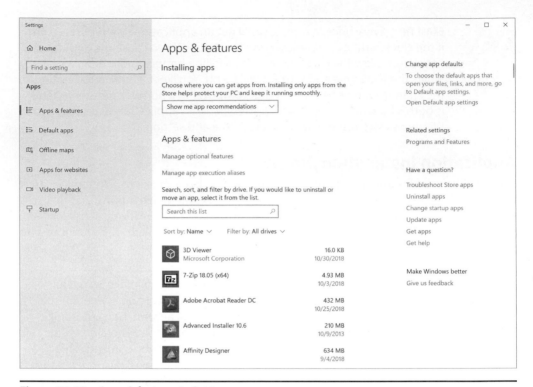

Figure 16-43   Apps & features in Settings

.NET, .NET must itself be installed. In most cases, if .NET is missing, the application should try to install it at the same time it is installed, but you can't count on this. If .NET is missing or if the version of .NET you are using is too old (there have been a number of .NET versions since it came out in 2002), you can get some of the most indecipherable errors in the history of Windows applications.

Figure 16-44 shows one such example in Windows 7 where the VMware vSphere Client fails due to the wrong .NET version. Too bad the error doesn't give you any clues!

These types of errors invariably require you to go online and do Web searches, using the application name and the error. No matter how bad the error, someone else has already suffered from the same problem. The trick is to find out what they did to get around it.

Problems with Uninstalling

The single biggest problem with uninstalling is that people try to uninstall without administrator privileges. If you try to uninstall and get an error, log back on as an administrator and you should be fine. Don't forget you can right-click most uninstallation menu options on the Programs menu and select *Run as administrator* to switch to administrator privileges (see Figure 16-45).

Figure 16-44
.NET error

Compatibility

Most applications are written with the most recent version of Windows in mind, but as Windows versions change over time, older programs have difficulty running in more recent Windows versions. In some cases, such as the jump from Windows 7 to Windows 8, the changes are generally minor enough to cause few if any compatibility problems. In other cases—say, a program written back when Windows XP reigned supreme—the underpinnings of the OS differ enough that you have to perform certain

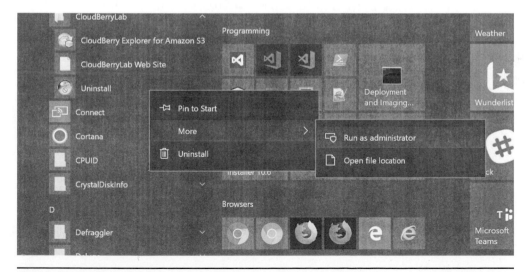

Figure 16-45   Selecting Run as administrator from the context menu

steps to ensure that the older programs run. Windows provides various different forms of *compatibility modes* to support older applications.

Windows handles compatibility using the aptly named Compatibility tab (see Figure 16-46) in every executable program's Properties dialog box (right-click the executable file and click Properties). Select the version of Windows you want Windows to emulate and click OK; in many cases that is all you need to do to make that older program work (see Figure 16-47).

Figure 16-46

Windows 8.1 Compatibility tab

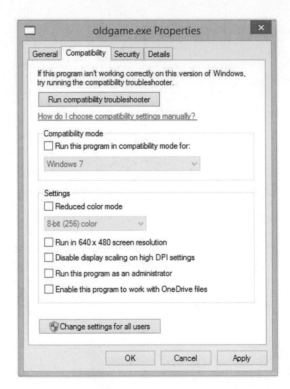

You can also set other settings on the Compatibility tab, such as some of the following located under Settings in the various versions of Windows:

- **Reduced color mode**   Many old Windows programs were designed to run in 256 colors. Later versions of Windows that support more colors can confuse these older programs.

- **Run in 640 × 480 screen resolution**   A few (badly written) older programs assume the screen to be at 640 × 480 resolution. This setting enables them to work.

- **Disable desktop composition (Windows 7)**   Disables all display features such as Aero. More advanced Windows display features often bog down older programs.

Figure 16-47
Compatibility
mode options in
Windows 8.1

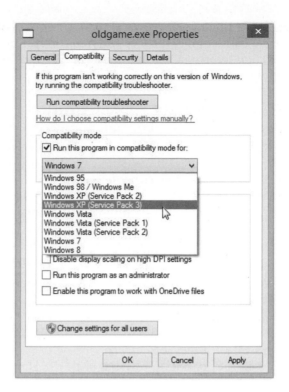

- **Disable display scaling on high DPI settings**   Turns off automatic resizing of a program's windows if you're using any high DPI (dots per inch) font. This was added because many programs with large fonts would look bizarre if resized.

- **Run this program as an administrator**   As stated, enables you to run the program as an administrator. If this option isn't available, log on as an administrator to see it.

- **Enable this program to work with OneDrive files (Windows 8/8.1/10)**   This option provides networking support for older applications that might not understand the cloud aspects of file storage.

- **Change settings for all users**   Clicking this button applies compatibility changes made to a program to every user account on the machine. Otherwise, the settings are only for the current user.

NOTE   In April 2014 Microsoft stopped providing technical support for Windows XP, including the Windows XP Mode VM. This means that Windows XP Mode no longer gets security patches; use with caution!

The secret to using compatibility mode isn't much of a secret at all: if the program doesn't run, try a compatibility mode. If you want to be really careful, do a Web search on your application before you try to run it. Compatibility mode is a handy tool to get older applications running.

Missing File or Incorrect File Version

An application may rely on other files, in particular DLL files. Sometimes the application installer will bring specially formatted versions of common DLL or other files to Windows, overwriting the previous versions. Later applications might look for the earlier version of the DLL and fail when it's not found.

You'll experience this sort of scenario with error messages such as "missing DLL" or "cannot open file *xyz*." The easiest fix is to first try to reinstall the program, and check for any special instructions about versions of support files. Barring that, the usual second step for either issue is to perform an Internet search for the missing DLL or file that fails to open, along with the name of the program you're trying to use.

Unresponsive Apps

For a variety of reasons, some default apps in Windows and some bought from the Microsoft Store will stop working. A code update in Windows, for example, might change some critical file for an app.

You have a couple of options for dealing with this sort of scenario. First, go to the Store and select *Get Updates* for the problematic app or apps (see Figure 16-48). (You'll

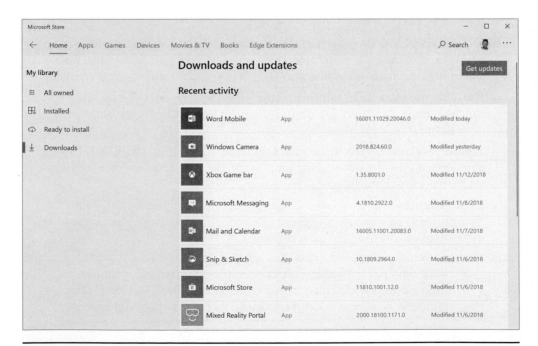

Figure 16-48   Searching for updates in the Microsoft Store

find the option when you click the three horizontal dots in the top right of the screen and select Downloads and updates.) Second, look for options to repair the application. Microsoft Edge, for example, has options to repair and reset the app.

To repair Microsoft Edge, open Settings | Apps | Apps & features and scroll down to Microsoft Edge. Click the Advanced options link to access the window shown in Figure 16-49. *Repair* tries to fix the program, but leaves all your personal data and configurations intact. *Reset* nukes any customizations you've made and restores Edge to its factory defaults. Choose Repair first; then, if that doesn't work, Reset the app.

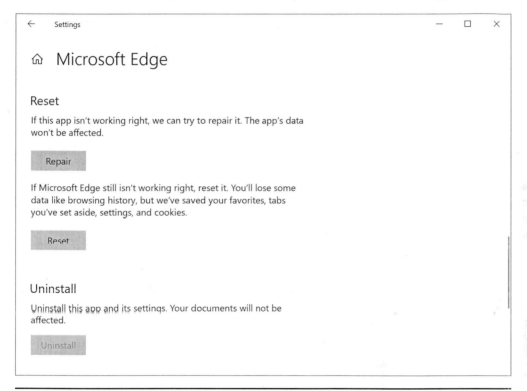

Figure 16-49 Repair and Reset options in Apps & features for Microsoft Edge

Application Crashes

Occasionally, an application gets released that isn't ready for prime time and the error-prone code causes the application to crash or even causes the operating system to crash. I've seen this most often with games rushed to market near the winter holidays. The results of this rushed code can be pretty spectacular. You're right in the middle of a thrilling fight with the bad guy and then what happens? A crash to desktop (CTD).

Poorly written or buggy programs can have awful effects on you and your clients. Some of the scenarios caused by such programs are the computer locking up or unexpectedly shutting down. The system might spontaneously shut down and restart. That kind of improper shutdown can cause problems, especially to open files and folders.

The problem here is that all this crashing can be caused by hardware and driver problems, not just application problems. You've got to keep in mind all of these things as you approach troubleshooting a crash.

Here's a typical scenario where you need to troubleshoot broadly first. If you're playing a graphically intensive game that happens to be huge and takes up a lot of RAM, what could the problem be if the screen locks up and Windows locks up too? It could be that the program ran a routine that clashed with some other application or used a Windows feature improperly. It could be that the video card was marginal and failed when taxed too much. It could be that the system accessed a section of RAM that had gone bad.

In that same scenario, though, where the game runs but degrades the overall performance of Windows, what could cause that problem? That points more squarely at the application side of things rather than the hardware or drivers, especially if the computer successfully runs other programs. The bottom line with crash issues is to keep an open mind and not rule out anything without testing it first.

Volume Shadow Copy Service and System Protection

One of the big headaches to a failure with an application isn't so much the application itself but any data it may have corrupted. Sure, a good backup or a restore point might save you, but these can be a hassle. Unless the data was specifically saved (in the backup), there's a chance you don't have a backup in the first place. Windows comes to your rescue with a feature called System Protection.

This amazing feature is powered by Volume Shadow Copy Service (VSS). VSS enables the operating system to make backups of any file, even one that is in use. Windows uses VSS for its *System Protection* feature, enabling you to access previous versions of any data file or folder. Try right-clicking any data file and selecting Restore previous versions, which opens the file's Properties dialog box with the Previous Versions tab displayed, as shown in Figure 16-50.

 NOTE For some unknown reason, Microsoft removed the Previous Versions tab for local volumes in Windows 8/8.1 and then added it back for Windows 10. If you need to restore a single file in Windows 8/8.1, you can set up and use the File History applet in Control Panel that you read about in Chapter 14. Just make sure you set it up before you need it!

If any of the following criteria are met, you will have at least one previous version in the list:

- The file or folder was backed up using the backup program.
- You created a restore point.
- The file or folder was changed.

Figure 16-50
Previous Versions
tab

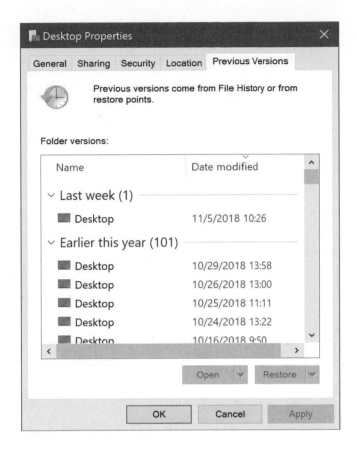

You must make sure System Protection is enabled as well. Go to the System Protection tab in the System Properties dialog box (see Figure 16-51) to see if the feature is enabled (it should be running by default).

NOTE Keep in mind that System Protection doesn't have to be only for recovery of corrupted data files caused by bad applications. It's also a great tool to recover previous versions of files that users accidently overwrite.
The System Protection tab also enables you to load a restore point and to create restore points manually, very handy features.

System Protection falls in the category generically called *file recovery software*, and does an outstanding job. You can also get many third-party utilities that accomplish general file recovery. I've used Recuva from Piriform many times, for example, to get "deleted" data off hard drives and solid-state drives (like thumb drives).

Figure 16-51
System
Protection tab

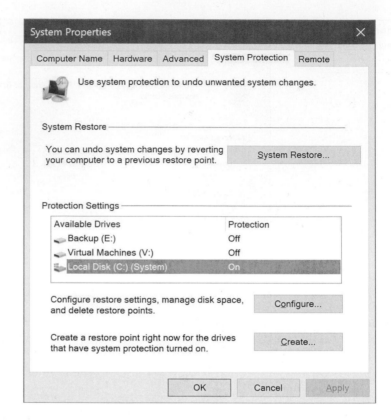

Chapter Review

Questions

1. Which utility is useful in identifying a program that is hogging the processor?

    A. Task Manager

    B. Device Manager

    C. Action Center

    D. System Information

2. Which Windows utility uses points in time that enable you to return your system to a previous date and state?

    A. System Configuration utility

    B. Snapshot Manager

    C. System Restore

    D. GRUB or LILO

3. Scott's Windows 10 computer isn't performing as well as it once did. What option can he use to reset his system without deleting any personal files or changing any settings?

   A. Keep my files

   B. Remove everything

   C. Advanced options/System Restore

   D. System Refresh

4. What can device drivers and failing hardware in macOS and Linux cause?

   A. Spinning windmill

   B. Blue Screen of Death (BSoD)

   C. Kernel panic

   D. Terminal emulation

5. Which of the following points to a hardware or CMOS problem rather than an OS problem with a PC that won't boot?

   A. A black screen with the error message "invalid boot disk"

   B. A black screen with the error message "NTLDR Bad or Missing"

   C. A black screen with the error message "Missing BOOT.INI"

   D. A black screen with the error message "Invalid BCD"

6. John's computer has an error that says bootmgr is corrupted. What tool can he use to fix this problem?

   A. bcdedit

   B. chkdsk

   C. diskpart

   D. regedit

7. What does Microsoft call the 32- or 64-bit installation environment in Windows?

   A. WinEE

   B. WinPE

   C. WinRE

   D. WinVM

8. Jane suspects a bad RAM stick is causing Windows to fail to boot. What default Windows tool can she use to check the RAM?

   A. MEMMAKER

   B. Memtest86+

   C. Windows RAM Diagnostic Tool

   D. Windows Memory Diagnostic Tool

9. Which of the following commands will repair a damaged master boot record in a Windows 10 PC?

   A. bootrec /fixboot

   B. bootrec /fixmbr

   C. fixboot

   D. fixmbr

10. Which feature in Windows 7 and Windows 10 enables you to right-click a file or folder and restore previous versions of that file or folder?

   A. System Recovery Options

   B. System Protection

   C. File History

   D. Undelete

Answers

1. **A.** Task Manager will identify very quickly a program that is hogging the processor.

2. **C.** System Restore uses *restore points*—snapshots of a system at a given point of time—a quick and handy way to return your system to a previous state.

3. **A.** Keep my files in Windows 10 rebuilds Windows, but preserves all user files and settings. Remove everything removes all apps, programs, user files, user settings—and presents a fresh installation of Windows.

4. **C.** Device drivers and failing hardware can trip up macOS and Linux and create kernel panic, which can bring the system down.

5. **A.** A black screen with an "invalid boot disk" error message points to a hardware or CMOS problem with a PC that won't boot.

6. **A.** The bcdedit program can fix a corrupted bootmgr.

7. **B.** Microsoft calls the 32- or 64-bit installation environment in Windows the Windows Preinstallation Environment, or WinPE.

8. **D.** Jane should use the Windows Memory Diagnostic Tool to scan her RAM.

9. **B.** Run bootrec /fixmbr in the Windows RE to repair a damaged master boot record in a Windows 10 PC.

10. **B.** The System Protection feature in Windows 7 and Windows 10 enables you to right-click a file or folder and restore previous versions of that file or folder.

Display Technologies

In this chapter, you will learn how to
- Explain how video displays work
- Select the proper video card
- Install and configure video
- Troubleshoot basic video problems

The term *video* encompasses a complex interaction among numerous parts of personal computing devices, all designed to put a picture on the screen. The *monitor* or *video display* shows you what's going on with your programs and operating system. It's the primary output device for most computing devices. The video card or *display adapter* handles all the communication between the CPU and the monitor or display (see Figure 17-1). The operating system needs to know how to handle communication between the CPU and the display adapter, which requires drivers specific for each card and proper setup within the operating system. Finally, each application needs to be able to interact with the rest of the video system. The components specific to video fall into the category of *display technologies*. This chapter explores all four types of components, finishing with a section on troubleshooting display issues.

Figure 17-1
Typical monitor
and video card

Video Displays

Video displays for computing devices come in three varieties: flat-panel monitors, projectors, and virtual reality headsets. Almost every modern personal computer uses an LCD monitor, and there's a pair of similar display panels mounted inside serious virtual reality headsets. You'll find projectors in boardrooms and classrooms, splashing a picture onto a screen. This section explores the technology variations in video displays and describes the connection options.

 EXAM TIP PCs and Macs originally used a display called a *CRT*, very heavy, bulky units. CRTs are long gone, but show up in one CompTIA 1002 exam objective on toxic waste disposal. CRTs had toxic materials inside, so we used licensed recycling services when disposing of them, rather than tossing them into landfills with other solid waste. Don't miss that question on the exam.

LCD Monitors

Almost every computing device today uses a *liquid crystal display* (*LCD*) panel as the primary visual output component. LCDs vary a lot, as you might imagine, considering the amazing variety of computing devices out there. This section explores how LCDs work in the Historical/Conceptual area, and then examines features that differentiate them.

Historical/Conceptual

How LCDs Work

The secret to understanding the most common type of LCD panels is to understand the concept of the polarity of light. Anyone who played with a prism in sixth grade or has looked at a rainbow knows that light travels in waves (no quantum mechanics here, please!), and the wavelength of the light determines the color. What you might not appreciate is the fact that light waves emanate from a light source in three dimensions. It's impossible to draw a clear diagram of three-dimensional waves, so instead, let's use an analogy. To visualize this, think of light emanating from a flashlight. Now think of the light emanating from that flashlight as though someone was shaking a jump rope. This is not a rhythmic shaking, back and forth or up and down; it's more as if a person went crazy and was shaking the jump rope all over the place—up, down, left, right—constantly changing the speed.

That's how light really acts. Well, I guess we could take the analogy one step further by saying the person has an infinite number of arms, each holding a jump rope shooting out in every direction to show the three-dimensionality of light waves, but (a) I can't draw that and (b) one jump rope will suffice to explain the typical LCD panels. The varying speeds create wavelengths, from very short to very long. When light comes into your eyes at many different wavelengths, you see white light. If the light came in only one wavelength, you would see only that color. Light flowing through a polarized filter (like sunglasses) is like putting a picket fence between you and the people shaking the ropes. You see all of the wavelengths, but only the waves of similar orientation. You would still see all of the colors, just fewer of them because you only see the waves of the same orientation, making the image darker. That's why many sunglasses use polarizing filters.

Now, what would happen if you added another picket fence but put the slats in a horizontal direction? This would effectively cancel out all of the waves. This is what happens when two polarizing filters are combined at a 90-degree angle—no light passes through.

Now, what would happen if you added a third fence between the two fences with the slats at a 45-degree angle? Well, it would sort of "twist" some of the shakes in the rope so that the waves could then get through. The same thing is true with the polarizing filters. The third filter twists some of the light so that it gets through. If you're really feeling scientific, go to any educational supply store and pick up three polarizing filters for about US$3 each and try it. It works.

Liquid crystals take advantage of the property of polarization. Liquid crystals are composed of a specially formulated liquid full of long, thin crystals that always want to orient themselves in the same direction, as shown in Figure 17-2. This substance acts exactly like a liquid polarized filter. If you poured a thin film of this stuff between two sheets of glass, you'd get a darn good pair of sunglasses.

Figure 17-2

Waves of similar orientation

Imagine cutting extremely fine grooves on one side of one of those sheets of glass. When you place this liquid in contact with a finely grooved surface, the molecules naturally line up with the grooves in the surface (see Figure 17-3).

Figure 17-3
Liquid crystal
molecules
tend to line up
together.

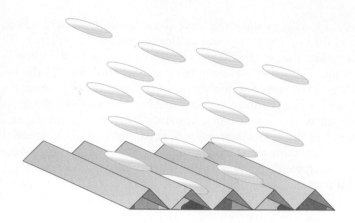

If you place another finely grooved surface, with the grooves at a 90-degree orientation to the other surface, opposite of the first one, the molecules in contact with that side will attempt to line up with it. The molecules in between, in trying to line up with both sides, will immediately line up in a nice twist (see Figure 17-4). If two perpendicular polarizing filters are then placed on either side of the liquid crystal, the liquid crystal will twist the light and enable it to pass (see Figure 17-5).

Figure 17-4
Liquid crystal
molecules
twisting

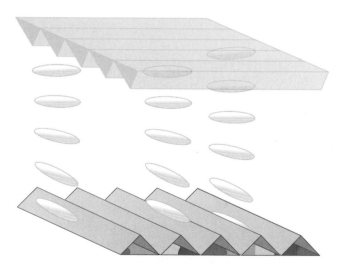

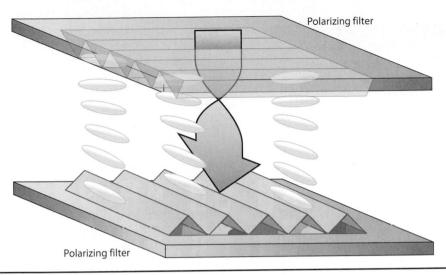

Figure 17-5 No charge, enabling light to pass

If you expose the liquid crystal to an electrical potential, however, the crystals will change their orientation to match the direction of the electrical field. The twist goes away and no light passes through (see Figure 17-6).

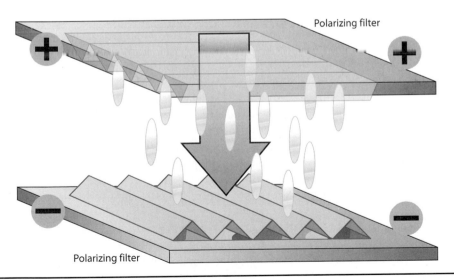

Figure 17-6 Electrical charge, no light is able to pass

1001

A color LCD screen is composed of a large number of tiny liquid crystal molecules (called *sub-pixels*) arranged in rows and columns between polarizing filters. A translucent sheet above the sub-pixels is colored red, green, or blue. Each tiny distinct group of three sub-pixels—one red, one green, and one blue—forms a physical *pixel*, as shown in Figure 17-7.

Figure 17-7
LCD pixels

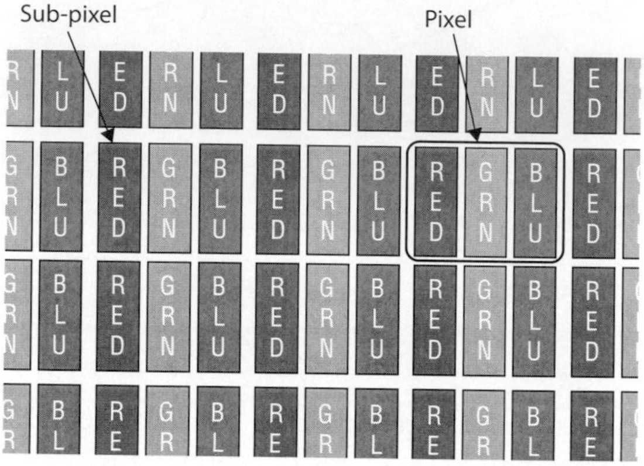

Once all of the pixels are laid out, how do you charge the right spots to make an image? Early LCDs didn't use rectangular pixels. Instead, images were composed of different-shaped elements, each electrically separate from the others. To create an image, each area was charged at the same time. Figure 17-8 shows the number zero, a display made possible by charging six areas to make an ellipse of sorts. This process, called *static charging*, is still quite popular in more basic numeric displays such as calculators.

The static method would not work in PCs due to its inherent inflexibility. Instead, early LCD screens used a matrix of wires (see Figure 17-9). The vertical wires, the Y wires, ran to every sub-pixel in the column. The horizontal wires, the X wires, ran along an entire row of sub-pixels. There had to be a charge on both the X wires and the Y wires to make enough voltage to light a single sub-pixel.

If you wanted color, you had to have three matrices. The three matrices intersected very close together. Above the intersections, the glass was covered with tiny red, green, and blue dots. Varying the amount of voltage on the wires made different levels of red, green, and blue, creating colors (see Figure 17-10). This technology was called *passive matrix*.

Current LCD monitors use some form of *thin film transistor* (*TFT*) or *active matrix* technology (see Figure 17-11). To refine the X and Y wires, one or more tiny transistors control each color dot, providing faster picture display, crisp definition, and much tighter color control than earlier technologies could provide.

Figure 17-8
Single character
for static LCD
numeric display

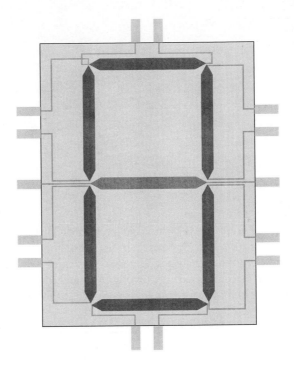

Figure 17-9
An LCD matrix of
wires

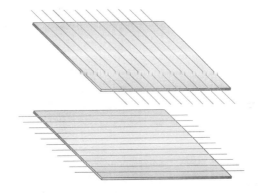

Figure 17-10
Passive matrix
display

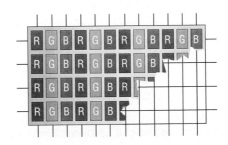

Figure 17-11
Active matrix
display

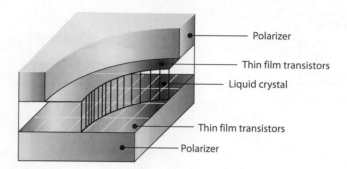

LCD Components

The typical LCD monitor is composed of two or three main components: the LCD panel, the backlight(s), and the inverters (in older models). The *LCD panel* creates the image, the *backlights* illuminate the image so you can see it, and the *inverters* send power to backlights that need alternating current (AC) electricity. Figure 17-12 shows a typical layout for the internal components of an older LCD monitor.

Figure 17-12
LCD components

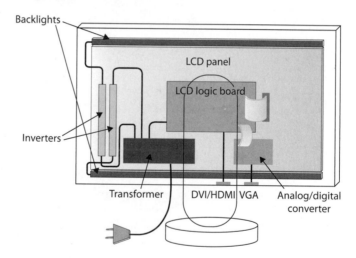

LCD Panel Technologies   LCD panel manufacturers use a lot of variation in things like the orientation of the liquid crystal molecules within the glass substrates and the underlying electronics to try to create displays that respond quickly to user demands and show accurate color and details. The three most common panel types today are *twisted nematic* (*TN*), *in-plane switching* (*IPS*), and *vertical alignment* (*VA*). As a general rule, TN panels are the fastest but offer adequate color; IPS panels display beautiful color; and VA panels fall somewhere in between the two in terms of responsiveness and color accuracy. To understand the variations—which you need to do—requires a lot of discussion in how they reproduce specific monitor features. After backlights, we'll discuss the feature variations and then come back at the end to compare the three main panel technologies.

NOTE Samsung offers a proprietary version of IPS called *Plane to Line Switching* (*PLS*). They claim it's better, naturally, though it functions very similarly to IPS and can be considered an IPS variation.

Backlights Backlights light up the panel, as mentioned, but vary according to the technology used and the implementation of the lighting. Current LCDs use *light-emitting diode* (*LED*) technology for backlights; previous generations used CCFL technology (more on that in a moment). These modern monitors are marketed as *LED displays* to differentiate them from the older CCFL panels. LEDs took over from CCFLs because the former uses DC electricity, just like the logic boards and panels in LCDs, consume much less electricity, and give off no heat. LEDs enable super thin screens like you see on almost every computing device today, from smartphones to tablets to desktop monitors. Figure 17-13 shows an illustration of a typical modern LCD; note the inverters missing from the previous figure.

Figure 17-13
Modern LCD
internals

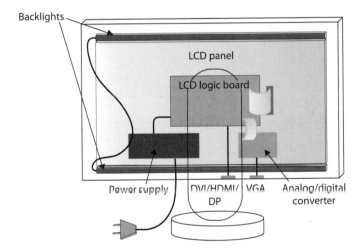

The LCD illustrated in Figure 17-13 has two backlights: one at the top and one at the bottom. That's a typical implementation for backlights, called *edge LED backlighting*. The drawback is that you can sometimes see that the edges are a little brighter than the center.

Direct LED backlighting puts a bank of LEDs behind the panel, providing better uniformity of image. The technology is more expensive, of course, and uses more electricity than edge LED backlighting, but it's becoming more common on higher-end LCD televisions and filtering into computer monitors as well.

Early LCDs used *cold cathode fluorescent lamp* (*CCFL*) technology, popular for its low power use, even brightness, and long life. Figure 17-14 shows a CCFL from an LCD panel. CCFLs needed high frequency AC electricity and so required the use of an inverter to convert the DC from the monitor's power supply. This resulted in panels noticeably thicker than what you'll see today. You will find CCFL-backlit monitors in use still, but

Figure 17-14
CCFL backlight

it's advisable to replace them when any of the internal parts die, rather than try to fix them. (Modern monitors are superior in every way.)

LCD Variations

LCDs vary in a lot of different ways and competent techs need to know this stuff so you can help your customers find the right monitor for their needs. To keep this section focused, we'll look at the variations you'll see on the 1001 exam (like resolution and color depth). The exam falls well short of modern display variations, so I've added information about the many ways manufacturers are trying to get a display to show what the human eye can see in the Beyond A+ section of this chapter. The monitor is the primary output for most computing devices; getting it right is arguably more important than any other part of the computer. That said, let's hit these variations here:

- Resolution
- Brightness
- Viewing angle
- Response rate
- Refresh rate
- Contrast ratio
- Color depth

Resolution A *resolution*, such as 2560 × 1440, describes the number of pixels on a display (in this case, 2560 pixels across, and 1440 pixels down). LCD monitors are designed to run at a single *native resolution*. You simply cannot run an LCD monitor at a resolution higher than the native resolution, and running it at a *lower* than native resolution severely degrades the image quality. The LCD has to use an edge-blurring technique called *interpolation* to soften the jagged corners of the pixels when running at lower than native resolution, which simply does not look as good. The bottom line? Always set the LCD at native resolution!

NOTE Two LCD panels that have the same physical size may have different native resolutions.

The native resolutions of monitors have names (or technically, *initialisms*) that you'll see in advertisements and branding. These *video modes* range from the ancient 640 × 480 resolution (*VGA*) to the 1366 × 768 resolution (*WXGA*) found on many inexpensive 15-inch laptops. The typical 1920 × 1080 monitors have two names: *FHD* (for full high definition) and *1080p*. I've included a table in the Beyond A+ section to fulfill your curiosity. The only one you'll see on the exam is in troubleshooting, and that's *VGA mode* (see the discussion later in the chapter).

The number of pixels arranged on the screen define the *aspect ratio* of the picture, such as 16:9 or 21:9 (see Figure 17-15). A typical widescreen monitor running at 1920 × 1080 is an example of 16:9 aspect ratio. A video workstation monitor running at 3440 × 1440 is an example of 21:9. You can change the aspect ratio of many monitors in the operating system tools, such as Display in Windows, but the quality of picture will degrade.

Figure 17-15

Various aspect ratios compared

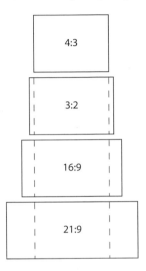

Modern computing devices use different aspect ratios. Many smartphones stick to 16:9, but a lot of newer Android and iPhone models have gone wider with aspect ratios like 18:9 and 19.5:9. Most Apple iPads, in contrast, have a 4:3 aspect ratio screen; the Microsoft Surface laptop uses a 3:2 screen.

PPI

The combination of the resolution and physical size of a display determines the *pixels per inch* (*PPI*) of a panel. The higher the PPI, the finer the picture a monitor can produce. That means, in practical terms, that a smaller, high-resolution monitor will look substantially better than a much larger monitor running at the same resolution. A 24-inch 1080p monitor, for example, looks good at just under 100 PPI. A 32-inch 1080p monitor looks kind of grainy, because its PPI is sub-70.

This PPI number is part of what makes a MacBook Pro laptop so visually stunning. The 15.4-inch screen has a resolution of 2880 × 1800, which puts it at 220 pixels per inch. That's sweet! Modern smartphones have outrageous PPI levels, which again is why they look so much better than a typical desktop monitor.

Brightness   The strength of an LCD monitor's backlights determines the brightness of the monitor. The brightness is measured in *nits*. LCD panels vary from 100 nits on the low end to over 1000 nits or more on the high end. Average LCD panels are around 300 nits, which most monitor authorities consider excellent brightness.

NOTE   One nit equals one candela/m². One candela is roughly equal to the amount of light created by a candle.

Viewing Angle   LCD panels have a limited *viewing angle*, meaning the screen fades out when viewed from the side (or any angle not dead center). TN panels have a fairly narrow viewing angle or (*viewing cone*), as little as 70 degrees from the center line. Manufacturers and consumers jumped on IPS technology not just for the awesome color, but because the viewing angle is much wider than TN panels. Figure 17-16 illustrates the differences. Note the viewing angle when shopping for a monitor. Wider is better for typical users. Narrow works when you want to limit what anyone but the user can see on the monitor.

Figure 17-16
Narrow versus wide viewing angles

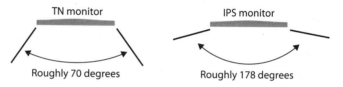

Try This!   Test the Viewing Angle of LCDs

Take a trip to your local computer store to look at LCD displays. Don't get distracted looking at all the latest graphics cards, CPUs, motherboards, and RAM—well, actually, it's okay to look at those things. Just don't forget to look at monitors!

Stand about two feet in front of an LCD display. Look directly at the image on the screen and consider the image quality, screen brightness, and color. Take a small step to your right. Compare the image you see now to the image you saw previously. Continue taking small steps to the right until you are no longer able to discern the image on the display. You've reached the edge of the viewing angle for that LCD.

Do this test with a few different monitors. Do smaller LCDs, such as 20-inch displays, have smaller viewing angles? Do larger displays have better viewing angles? You might also want to test the vertical viewing angles of some monitors. Try to find a monitor that is on your eye level; then look at it from above and below—does it have a large viewing range vertically? There's also a curved LCD monitor variant not discussed in this chapter, but worth looking at. What kind of viewing angle do they have?

Response Rate   An LCD panel's *response rate* is the amount of time it takes for all of the sub-pixels on the panel to change from one state to another. Manufacturers measure LCD response rates in milliseconds (ms), with lower being better. There are two ways manufacturers measure this change. One is *black-to-white (BtW)*: how long it takes the pixels to go from pure black to pure white and back again. The other is *gray-to-gray (GtG)*: how long it takes the pixels to go from one gray state to another.

The GtG time will always be faster than the BtW time. A typical modern LCD has an *advertised* response rate of around 5 ms. The manufacturer will almost always advertise the GtG response time. I found an LG display that listed both times: 5-ms GtG and 14-ms BtW. You might find older displays in use with BtW response times over 20 ms—this is slow enough that you might notice image smearing if you try to watch a movie or play a fast-paced game.

Refresh Rate   The *refresh rate* for an LCD monitor refers to how often a screen can change or update completely. Think of the refresh rate as a metronome or timer and you'll be closer to how it works in an LCD. For most computing issues, 60 Hz is fine and that's been the standard for the industry. Humans see things that change as infrequently as 24 times per second—the standard for motion pictures at the cinema—as motion, not a series of flickering pictures. To be able to change almost three times faster makes the movement smoother with less lag, important in applications such as fast-moving games. Common higher-end monitors today, though, go well beyond, offering refresh rates of 144, 165, and 240 Hz.

NOTE   Higher-end video cards can push well beyond the limits of even the best monitor refresh rates. See the discussion on "Adaptive Sync" later in this chapter for the scoop.

Contrast Ratio   Old CRT monitors lingered in a few professions for a long time because early LCDs just couldn't produce the color saturation or richness of contrast of a CRT. It was not unusual, even in the late 2000s, to walk into a design studio and see a few working CRTs.

LCD technology continues to improve every year, and manufacturers today can produce panels that rival the old CRT technology. A good *contrast ratio*—the difference between the darkest and lightest spots that the monitor can display—is 450:1, although a quick trip to a computer store will reveal LCDs with lower levels (250:1) and higher levels (1000:1).

LCD monitor manufacturers market a *dynamic contrast ratio* number for their monitors, which measures the difference between a full-on, all-white screen, and a full-off, or all-black screen. This yields a much higher number than the standard contrast ratio. My Samsung panels have a 1000:1 contrast ratio, for example, but a 20,000:1 dynamic contrast ratio. Sounds awesome, right? In general, the dynamic contrast ratio doesn't affect viewing on computer monitors. Focus on the standard contrast ratio when making decisions on LCD screens.

Color Depth LCD panels vary in the amount of colors they can display, the *color depth*. This is reflected in the bit-depth of the panel. Very old TN monitors, for example, used a 6-bit panel. That meant that each color channel—red, green, and blue—had 64 (2^6) color variations. Most monitors today use an 8-bit panel, with 256 (2^8) colors per channel. This translates in marketing as 24-bit color, meaning the monitor can display 16.7 million color variations. At the higher end, manufacturers have 10-bit panels that display 1024 (2^{10}) color variations per channel, providing over 1 billion color variations. This jump in color variation becomes very apparent when you do a lot of photo editing or video color grading.

Comparing LCDs

At this point, you have a lot of information to sort when comparing LCDs to purchase for yourself or a client. Size and native resolution, of course, should take top consideration. The panel technology—TN vs. IPS vs. VA—and backlight—edge LCD vs. full LCD—can impact the overall quality of the display as well as the price. Because the monitor is both the primary visual interactive component on a computer and the component most likely to stick with you the longest, these decisions matter.

For the exam, also keep in mind the resolution, brightness, refresh rate, and color depth. Most modern monitors have acceptable specifications on those items.

The vast majority of users will go with an IPS panel with an edge LCD backlight. You'll have amazing color and viewing angle. Size and resolution will be determined by your budget and space considerations. TN panels occupy two spots in the buying spectrum. The *least* expensive monitors are TN. Gaming monitors also sport TN panels, however, because no other technology can currently beat TN for responsiveness. Gaming monitors are among the *most* expensive displays you can buy in the consumer space. TN therefore resides at both the low and high end of things.

Projectors

Projectors generate an image in one device and then use light to throw (or project) it onto a screen or some other object. You'll mostly encounter *front-view* projectors, which shoot an image out the front and count on you to place a screen in front at the proper distance. Front-view projectors connected to PCs running Microsoft PowerPoint have been the cornerstone of every meeting almost everywhere since the Clinton administration (see Figure 17-17). This section deals exclusively with front-view projectors that connect to PCs.

Figure 17-17
Front-view
projector
(photo courtesy
of Dell Inc.)

Projector Technologies

The first generation of projectors used CRTs. Each color used a separate CRT that projected the image onto a screen (see Figure 17-18). CRT projectors created beautiful images but were expensive, large, and very heavy, and have for the most part been abandoned for more recent technologies.

Figure 17-18
CRT projector

Given that light shines through an LCD panel, LCD projectors are a natural fit for front projection. LCD projectors are light and very inexpensive compared to CRTs but lack the image quality (see Figure 17-19).

Figure 17-19
LCD projector
(photo courtesy
of ViewSonic)

The proprietary *Digital Light Processing* (*DLP*) technology from Texas Instruments uses a single processor and an array of tiny mirrors to project a front-view image. The technology differs substantially from LCD. DLP projectors offer a softer image than LCD, but that's not necessarily a bad thing, especially with HD content, like movies. DLP projectors use more electricity but aren't as heavy as LCD projectors. Choose your projector wisely!

All projectors share the same issues as their equivalent-technology monitors. LCD projectors have a specific native resolution, for example. In addition, you need to understand three concepts specific to projectors: lumens, throw, and lamps.

Lumens

The brightness of a projector is measured in lumens. A *lumen* is the amount of light given off by a light source from a certain angle that is perceived by the human eye. The greater the lumen rating of a projector, the brighter the projector will be. The best lumen rating depends on the size of the room and the amount of light in the room. There's no single answer for "the right lumen rating" for a projector, but use this as a rough guide: If you use a projector in a small, darkened room, 1000 to 1500 lumens will work well. If you use a projector in a mid-sized room with typical lighting, you'll need at least 2000 lumens. Projectors for large rooms have ratings over 10,000 lumens and are very expensive.

Throw

A projector's *throw* is the size of the image at a certain distance from the screen. All projectors have a recommended minimum and maximum throw distance that you need to take into consideration. A typical throw would be expressed as follows, always in terms of the distance required to project a 100-inch diagonal screen. A standard-throw projector needs to be 11 to 12 feet away from the projection surface. A short-throw projector can display the same 100-inch image from 4 feet away. An ultra-short-throw projector can accomplish the image from a mere 15 inches away, although the price for such a lens makes the price go way up. Figure 17-20 illustrates the different throw distances.

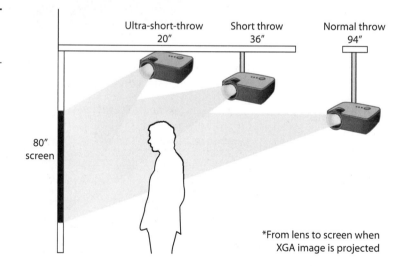

Figure 17-20
Projector throw variations

Lamps

The bane of every projector is the lamp. *Lamps* work hard in your projector, as they must generate a tremendous amount of light. As a result, they generate quite a bit of heat, and all projectors come with a fan to keep the lamp from overheating. When you turn off a projector, the fan continues to run until the lamp is fully cooled. Lamps are also expensive, usually in the range of a few hundred dollars (U.S.), which comes as a nasty shock to someone who's not prepared for that price when the lamp dies!

The majority of projectors use one of three lamp technologies: metal halide, LED, or lasers. Metal halide has been the standard for many years. These lamps produce a tremendous amount of lumens in a small form factor. The drawbacks are excessive heat and fan noise, an average life span of ~3000 hours, and the expense to replace them.

LED-based projectors use red, green, and blue LEDs to provide light. LEDs don't heat up, so fans are smaller and quieter. LED projectors used to cost more than metal halide ones, but that price difference has narrowed considerably. They don't offer nearly as much lumens, though, so typically require a much darker room. On the other hand, LED lamps have lifespans of 20,000+ hours.

Laser-based projectors come in a variety, from white lasers hitting color wheels to colored lasers doing all the work. Laser projectors produce vibrant, high-contrast images and very little heat; lamps can last 30,000+ hours. Laser-based projectors are currently more expensive than competing technologies, but the price is coming down.

VR Headsets

Virtual reality (VR) headsets create an immersive experience by mounting two high-resolution screens into a headset that blocks external visual sensory input (see Figure 17-21). They enable the wearer to enter into a 360-degree space that makes it feel like he or she has been transported to another place and time. There aren't many households or organizations using VR yet, but modern VR headsets offer a glimpse of a possible future direction for computing technologies.

Figure 17-21
HTC Vive Pro headset, viewed from the inside

Coupled with a very high-end system, VR can transport the viewer into another space entirely. Google Earth VR, for example, enables you to walk the streets of Paris from the comfort of your couch in Chattanooga, scale Mt. Everest while tanning in Southern California, or hang out with astronauts aboard the International Space Station without leaving the planet. And that's just the tip of the iceberg.

VR is very much still in the enthusiast realm, but the technology has made great strides in the past few years, especially with the refinement of tiny displays. Current VR headsets use *organic light-emitting diode (OLED)* technology (or active matrix OLED [AMOLED] with added transistors) to power the tiny, high-resolution stereo panels.

OLED differs from LCD in a couple of ways. First, OLED screens use organic compounds between the glass layers that light up when given an electrical charge. This means they require no backlight at all, making them perfect for ultra-thin, energy-efficient displays. Also, with no backlight, OLED pixels can turn off completely, enabling pure black and thus phenomenal contrast compared with LCD panels.

OLED has found three niches so far: high-end televisions, small mobile devices, such as smart watches and some smartphones, and VR headsets.

NOTE   See the "MicroLED" discussion in Beyond A+ for a look at a potential competitor to OLED and possibly LCD. We'll also revisit OLED in Chapter 24, "Understanding Mobile Devices."

Common Monitor Features

All monitors share characteristics that you need to know for purchase, installation, maintenance, and troubleshooting. They vary in connection types, on-screen controls for adjustments, mounting brackets, and additional features such as built-in USB hubs, webcams, speakers, and microphones.

Connections

Monitors connect to computers via one of six connectors:

- VGA
- DVI
- HDMI
- DisplayPort
- Thunderbolt
- HDBaseT

VGA   Many monitors for Windows PCs use a 15-pin, three-row, D-type connector (see Figure 17-22) and a power plug. The connector has a *lot* of names, including *D-shell* and *D-subminiature*, but most people simply call it the *VGA connector*. VGA is the oldest and least-capable monitor connection type.

Figure 17-22
A VGA connector

DVI A lot of LCDs connect via the *digital visual interface* (*DVI*) standard. DVI is actually three different connectors that look very much alike: DVI-D is for digital, DVI-A is for analog (for backward compatibility if the monitor maker so desires), and the DVI-A/D or DVI-I (interchangeable) accepts either a DVI-D or DVI-A. DVI-D and DVI-A are keyed so that they will not connect.

DVI-D and DVI-I connectors come in two varieties, single-link and dual-link. *Single-link DVI* has a maximum bandwidth of 165 MHz, which, translated into practical terms, limits the maximum resolution of a monitor to 1920 × 1080 at 60 Hz or 1280 × 1024 at 85 Hz. *Dual-link DVI* uses more pins to double throughput and thus grant higher resolutions (see Figure 17-23). With dual-link DVI, you can have displays up to 2048 × 1536 at 60 Hz.

Figure 17-23
Dual-link DVI-I
connector

HDMI Many LCDs, projectors, and VR headsets connect to a computer via the *High Definition Multimedia Interface* (*HDMI*) connector, which carries both HD video and audio signals (see Figure 17-24). HDMI can handle just about any resolution monitor and not skip a beat. HDMI enables laptop computers to connect to high-end projectors, for example, and create brilliant multimedia presentations. A lot of smaller devices have *Mini-HDMI* ports, so require a cable with a Mini-HDMI connector on one end and a full-sized HDMI connector on the other. Works just fine!

Figure 17-24
HDMI port on a
monitor

DisplayPort and Thunderbolt Some monitors use either *DisplayPort* (*DP*) or *Thunderbolt* to connect to computers. Both support full-HD video and audio.

I've lumped them together here for a reason. Full-sized DP connections are common these days, like with my Dell monitors (see Figure 17-25). These connect to full-sized DP ports on display adapters, as you would expect.

Figure 17-25
DisplayPort
connection on
monitor

Thunderbolt 1 and Thunderbolt 2, which you'll recall from Chapter 10, "Essential Peripherals," adopted the same connector type that's used for the small version of DisplayPort, called *Mini DisplayPort* (*mDP*). Thunderbolt 3 uses the USB Type-C connector. Fair warning: you'll find monitors that connect mDP-to-mDP without using Thunderbolt 1 or 2, and many USB Type-C connectors and cables lack Thunderbolt 3 support. Look for the little symbols next to the ports to determine which technology should connect the display to the computer (see Figure 17-26).

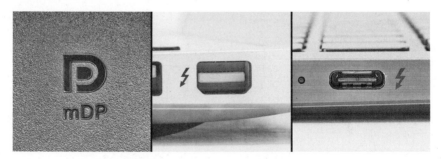

Figure 17-26   Plain mDP (left), Thunderbolt 2 mDP (center), Thunderbolt 3 USB Type-C (right)

HDBaseT   Some projectors use a connection technology called *HDBaseT* that enables long-range connectivity for uncompressed HD video and audio over Cat 5a or Cat 6 network cables (see Figure 17-27). We haven't talked yet about network cabling (we'll get to it in Chapter 19, "Local Area Networking"), but keep this technology in mind. In practical terms, it means you can connect a projector in a conference room via runs of up to 100 meters. The projector needs HDBaseT technology for this to work, or you can use an HDBaseT receiver to convert to something your projector can use. HDBaseT isn't on the CompTIA A+ 1001 exam, but you might encounter it in the real world.

Figure 17-27
HDBaseT port on a projector

Adapters   You will most likely find yourself in a situation where you have a monitor that accepts one type of video connector and an adapter card that has different output options. In such a case, you have a couple of solutions. The CompTIA A+ 1001 exam assumes you'll use a small adapter device, like the *DVI-to-VGA adapter* in Figure 17-28. Another common adapter is *DVI-to-HDMI*. Apple and other manufacturers have added Thunderbolt to their ultra-thin portables, so adapter developers have added *Thunderbolt-to-DVI* and *Thunderbolt-to-HDMI* adapters, too.

Figure 17-28
DVI-to-VGA adapter

Alternatively, you can readily pick up cables with different end connectors. Figure 17-29 shows a typical DVI-to-HDMI cable. Many new devices only have Type-C connectors for output (like plain USB Type-C or Thunderbolt-enabled USB Type-C). If the display doesn't have a matching port, you might have to use a USB Type-C-to-mDP or USB Type-C-to-HDMI cable to make that connection.

Figure 17-29
DVI-to-HDMI
cable

Adjustments

Most adjustments to the monitor take place at installation, but for now, let's just make sure you know what they are and where they are located. Clearly, all monitors have an On/Off button or switch. Also, see if you can locate the Brightness and Contrast buttons. Beyond that, most monitors (at least the only ones you should buy) have an *onscreen display* (*OSD*) menu, enabling a number of adjustments. Every monitor maker provides a different way to access these menus, but they all provide two main functions: physical screen adjustment (bigger, smaller, move to the left, right, up, down, and others) and color adjustment. The color adjustment enables you to adjust the red, green, and blue levels to provide the best color tones. All these settings are a matter of personal taste. Make sure the person who will use the computer understands how to adjust these settings (see Figure 17-30).

Figure 17-30
Typical OSD
menu controls

VESA Mounts

Almost every monitor these days has a standardized bracket option for mounting the monitor on the wall or on a special stand called a *VESA mount*. Figure 17-31 shows the bracket option on a monitor. Figure 17-32 shows a stand for mounting two monitors side-by-side. VESA mounts vary as you scale up on LCD panels, so big televisions will have a larger mounting bracket than a typical 24-inch computer monitor.

Figure 17-31
VESA mounting
option on
monitor

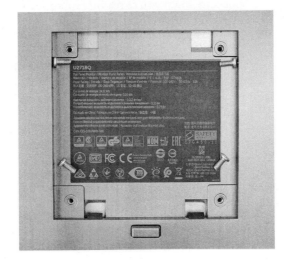

Figure 17-32
Dual-monitor
stand that uses
VESA mounts

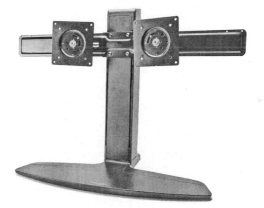

NOTE The VESA mount standards have a couple of official names. You'll see them in literature as the *Flat Display Mounting Interface* (*FDMI*) and the *VESA Mounting Interface Standard* (*MIS*). Curved panels do not have VESA mount options.

Add-on Features

Some monitor manufacturers add extra features to their products, such as USB hubs, speakers, webcams, and microphones. These manifest (for techs) as a USB Type-B port on the monitor to connect a cable to a USB Type-A port on the computer, just like any other USB peripheral. If you buy a new monitor *today*, it might have a USB Type-C port to run a cable to a USB Type-C port on a computer; the standard will change between print time of this book and when you're reading it. Figure 17-33 shows USB ports on the side of a monitor—it's a very handy feature!

Figure 17-33
USB ports on monitor

Display Adapters

The display adapter, or video card, handles the video chores within computing devices, processing information from the CPU and sending it to the display. The display adapter is a complex set of devices. A graphics processor of some type processes data from the CPU and outputs commands to the display. Like any other processor, the graphics processor needs RAM. The graphics processor needs fast connectivity between it, the CPU, and system RAM. The display adapter must have a connection compatible with the monitor.

Traditionally, and still quite commonly in Windows PCs, the display adapter was an expansion card that plugged into the motherboard (see Figure 17-34). Although many new systems have the display adapter circuitry built into the CPU and motherboard, most techs still call it the video card, so we'll start there. This section looks at five aspects that define a video card: motherboard slot, graphics processor, video memory, integrated GPUs, and connections.

Motherboard Slot

Techs will encounter four ways that display adapters connect to a motherboard. The oldest connector type, PCI, is used today only for an additional card to support extra

Figure 17-34
Typical video
card

monitors on older systems. Slightly newer, but still quite old in computer terms, is AGP. Every current discrete video card plugs into the PCIe slot on a motherboard. Finally, many motherboards have the display adapter built-in. I'll discuss integrated graphics after talking about graphics processors and memory types, at which point the topic will make more sense. For now, let's look at PCI, AGP, and PCIe.

PCI

Using more color depth slows down video functions. Data moving from the video card to the display has to go through the video card's memory chips and the expansion bus, and this can happen only so quickly. The *peripheral component interconnect* (*PCI*) slots used in almost all systems for many years are limited to 32-bit transfers at roughly 33 MHz, yielding a maximum bandwidth of 132 MBps. This sounds like a lot until you start using higher resolutions, high color depths, and higher refresh rates (which mattered in the CRT days). Plus, almost every system had more than one PCI device, each requiring part of that bandwidth. The PCI bus simply cannot handle the video needs of any current systems.

AGP

Intel answered the desire for more video bandwidth than PCI provided with the *Accelerated Graphics Port* (*AGP*). AGP was a single, special port, similar to a PCI slot, dedicated to video. No motherboard had two AGP slots; in fact, no current motherboard even has an AGP slot, so you'll only encounter these on ancient systems. Figure 17-35 shows an early-generation AGP slot.

PCIe

The *PCI Express* (*PCIe*) interface was developed to replace PCI and, in the process, replace AGP. PCIe was a natural fit for video because it is incredibly fast. All PCIe video cards use the PCIe ×16 connector (see Figure 17-36). PCIe replaced AGP as the primary video interface almost overnight.

Figure 17-35
AGP

Figure 17-36
PCIe video card
connected in
PCIe slot

Graphics Processor

The graphics processor handles the heavy lifting of taking commands from the CPU and translating them into coordinates and color information that the monitor understands and displays. Most techs today refer to the device that processes video as a *graphics processing unit* (*GPU*).

Video card discussion, at least among techs, almost always revolves around the graphics processor the video card uses and the amount of RAM onboard. A typical video card might be called an MSI GeForce GTX 1080ti 11-GB 384-bit GDDR5X PCI Express 3.0, so let's break that down. MSI is the manufacturer of the video card; GeForce GTX 1080ti is the graphics processor; 11-GB 384-bit GDDR5X describes the dedicated video RAM and the connection between the video RAM and the graphics processor; and PCI Express 3.0 describes the motherboard expansion slot the card requires.

NOTE Many video cards come with a digital anti-theft technology called *High-bandwidth Digital Content Protection* (*HDCP*). HDCP stops audio and video copying between high-speed connections, such as HDMI, DisplayPort, and DVI. The technology also stops playback of HDCP-encrypted content on devices designed to circumvent the system.

Many companies make the hundreds of different video cards on the market, but only three companies produce the vast majority of graphics processors found on video cards: NVIDIA, AMD, and Intel. NVIDIA and AMD make and sell graphics processors to third-party manufacturers who then design, build, and sell video cards under their own branding. Intel made its own line of cards, but now concentrates on graphics processors built into motherboards. Figure 17-37 shows an NVIDIA GeForce GTX 570 on a board made by EVGA.

Figure 17-37
NVIDIA GeForce
GTX 570

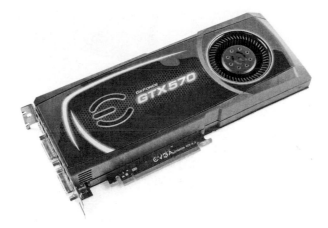

Your choice of graphics processor is your single most important decision in buying a video card. Low-end graphics processors usually work fine for the run-of-the-mill user who wants to write letters or run a Web browser. High-end graphics processors are designed to support the beautiful 3-D games that are so popular today, and they provide excellent video playback for high-definition video. We'll look at 3-D issues a little later in this chapter.

Video Memory

Video memory is crucial to the operation of a PC. It is probably the hardest-working set of electronics on the PC. Video RAM constantly updates to reflect every change that takes place on the screen. When you're working with heavy-duty applications (such as games), video memory can prove to be a serious bottleneck in three ways: data through-put speed, access speed, and simple capacity.

Manufacturers have overcome these bottlenecks by upping the width of the bus between the video RAM and video processor; using specialized, super-fast RAM; and adding more and more total RAM.

First, manufacturers reorganized the video display memory on cards to use a wider bus, giving them more memory bandwidth. Because the system bus is limited to 32 or 64 bits, this would not be of much benefit if video display cards weren't really coprocessor boards. Most of the graphics rendering and processing is handled on the card by the video processor chip rather than by the CPU. The main system simply provides the input data to the processor on the video card. Because the memory bus on the video card can be many times wider than the standard 64-bit pathway, data can be manipulated and then sent to the monitor much more quickly (see Figure 17-38).

Figure 17-38
Wide path
between video
processor and
video RAM

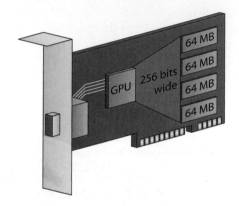

Specialized types of video RAM have been developed for graphics cards, and many offer substantial improvements in video speeds. The single most important feature that separates DRAM from video RAM is that video RAM can read and write data at the same time. Table 17-1 lists common video memory technologies, but keep in mind that you may run into graphics cards (particularly budget cards) using any recent generation of DDR RAM.

Acronym	Name	Purpose
DDR3	Double Data Rate SDRAM version 3	Used on budget graphics cards and common on laptop video cards
GDDR3	Graphics Double Data Rate, version 3	Similar to DDR3 but runs at faster speeds; different cooling requirements
GDDR4	Graphics Double Data Rate, version 4	Upgrade of GDDR3; faster clock
GDDR5	Graphics Double Data Rate, version 5	Successor to GDDR4; double the input/ output rate of GDDR4
GDDR5X	Graphics Double Data Rate, version 5X	Successor to GDDR5
GDDR6	Graphics Double Data Rate, version 6	Successor to GDDR5X
HBM	High Bandwidth Memory	Competitor to GDDR5
HBM2	High Bandwidth Memory version 2	Successor to HBM; competitor to GDDR6

Table 17-1 Video RAM Technologies

The majority of video cards, especially once you get into gaming-oriented cards, sport recent generations of specialized video RAM such as *GDDR5* or GDDR5X. That said, *DDR3* is still the most popular memory on low-end, non-gaming cards. *High Bandwidth Memory version 2 (HBM2)* offers a very different style of memory from DDR or GDDR by using stacked DRAM connected via super-wide buses. GDDR has a 32-bit bus width; HBM sports a 1024-bit bus. The fight is unfolding as this book goes to press and you won't see HBM or HBM2 on the CompTIA 1001 exam, but you'll want to know about it by the time you read this book.

Finally, many advanced 3-D video cards come with huge amounts of video RAM. It's very common to see cards with 1, 2, 3, or 4 GB of RAM! (As this book goes to press, you can drop a lot of money and get a card with 8–24 GB of video RAM.) Why so much? Even with PCI Express, accessing data in system RAM always takes a lot longer than accessing data stored in local RAM on the video card. The huge amount of video RAM enables game developers to optimize their games and store more essential data on the local video RAM.

Integrated GPUs

Some motherboards have *integrated GPUs,* and quite a few can support a CPU with an integrated GPU. The motherboard GPU can be a separate chip attached to the motherboard or can be built into the Northbridge chip. When a motherboard has its own GPU, we often say it has *onboard video* (an *onboard* video card). Onboard video isn't very powerful, but it's fairly common in laptops because it saves a lot of space and power.

AMD and NVIDIA both make integrated GPU chips, and Intel has long integrated the Intel Graphics Media Accelerator (GMA) into its chipsets. Some of AMD's Fusion processors, for example, have a CPU/GPU combination that rivals any CPU/discrete graphics card combination, though only at a level seen in portable computers. They're good enough for casual gaming and even some medium-duty games. Intel's graphics support is geared to desktop performance, not gaming at all. NVIDIA's Tegra line is focused on gaming (Nintendo Switch) and automotive entertainment systems.

With an integrated GPU, the CPU circuitry is getting pretty crowded. A single AMD *Accelerated Processing Unit (APU)* chip, for example, integrates two to four CPU cores, a memory controller that supports DDR4 for system memory, cache memory, and a GPU that can handle advanced 3-D graphics. Wow! One of the best parts of all this integration is that the chip requires far less electricity than comparable discrete components.

Connector Types and Associated Cables

You can find a variety of connector types on video cards, plus variations within those types. CompTIA also makes a distinction between the names of the ports on the cards and the cables associated with them, though most techs will refer to the connectors and cables by multiple names interchangeably. Here's the scoop.

Display adapters offer one of six connectors, corresponding to the connection points on the monitors discussed earlier in the chapter:

- VGA
- DVI

- HDMI (including Mini- and Micro- variants)
- DisplayPort (including full and Mini DP variants)
- Thunderbolt (including mDP Thunderbolt 1 and 2 ports, and USB Type-C Thunderbolt 3 ports)

You can also find video cards (especially older ones) with any of a huge number of connector types for interfacing with other media devices such as camcorders, projectors, television sets, and so on. The video card shown in Figure 17-39 has three connectors: VGA, DVI-I, and a once-common S-video connector. In the days before HDMI, an S-video connector like this was a great (okay . . . *decent*) way to connect your computer to a TV.

Figure 17-39
Video card connectors: VGA, S-video, and DVI-I

The video card in Figure 17-40, in contrast, offers five connectors: DVI, HDMI, DP (×3). And yes, in case you were wondering, the card can drive five monitors simultaneously.

Figure 17-40
Video card connectors: DVI, HDMI, DisplayPort

Installing and Configuring Video

Once you've decided on the features and price for your new video card and monitor, you need to install them into your system. As long as you have the right connection to your video card, installing a monitor is straightforward. The challenge comes when installing the video card.

NOTE The installation steps in this section apply to Windows PCs and Linux computers. None of Apple's current macOS systems enable you to upgrade the internal display adapter, but you can still configure it or attach an *external GPU*. (See the Beyond A+ section, "eGPUs," for more details.)

During the physical installation of a video card, watch out for three possible issues: long cards, the proximity of the nearest expansion card, and the presence of power connectors. Some high-end video cards simply won't fit in certain cases or will block access to needed motherboard connectors such as the SATA sockets. There's no clean fix for such a problem—you simply have to change at least one of the components (video card, motherboard, or case). Because high-end video cards run very hot, you don't want them sitting right next to another card; make sure the fan on the video card has plenty of ventilation space. A good practice is to leave the slot next to the video card empty to allow better airflow (see Figure 17-41).

Figure 17-41

Installing a video card

Many high-end video cards come as double-wide cards with built-in air vents, so you don't have any choice but to take up double the space. Mid-range to high-end video cards typically require at least one additional PCIe power connector because they use more power than the PCIe slot can provide. Make sure that your power supply can provide adequate power, and confirm that it has open PCIe power connectors.

Try This!   Install a Video Card

You know how to install an expansion card from your reading in earlier chapters. Installing a video card is pretty much the same, so try this:

1. Refer to Chapter 6, "Motherboards," for the steps on installing a new card and Chapter 7, "Power Supplies," for a visual on video power connectors.

2. Plug the monitor cable into the video card port on the back of the PC and power up the system. If your PC seems dead after you install a video card, or if the screen is blank but you hear fans whirring and the internal speaker sounding off *long-short-short-short*, your video card likely did not get properly seated. Unplug the PC and try again.

Once you've properly installed the video card and connected it to the monitor, you've fought half the battle for making the video process work properly. You're ready to tackle the drivers and tweak the operating system, so let's go!

Software

Configuring your video software is usually a two-step process. First you need to load drivers for the video card. Then you need to open Display Settings and Personalization Settings (Window 10) or open the Display and Personalization applets (Windows 7/8/8.1) to make your adjustments. Let's explore how to make the video card and monitor work in Windows, then look briefly at display options in macOS and Linux.

Drivers

Just like any other piece of hardware, a video card needs drivers to function. Display adapter drivers install pretty much the same way as all the other drivers we've discussed thus far: Windows has the driver already; insert the installation media that came with the card; or download the latest driver from the Internet.

Video card makers are constantly updating their drivers. Odds are good that any video card more than a few months old has at least one driver update. If possible, check the manufacturer's Web site and use the driver located there if there is one. If the Web site doesn't offer a driver, it's usually best to use the installation media. Always avoid using the built-in Windows driver as it tends to be the most dated.

We'll explore driver issues in more detail after we discuss the Display Settings/Display applet and the Personalization Settings/Personalization applet. Like so many things about video, you can't fully understand one topic without understanding at least one other!

1002

Using Display and Personalization

With the driver installed, you're ready to configure your display settings. The Display Settings or Display applet and Personalization Settings or Personalization applet provide convenient, central locations for all of your display settings, including resolution, refresh rate, driver information, and color depth.

Display Settings/Display Applet The *Display Settings* in Windows 10 and the *Display applet* in previous versions of Windows enable adjusting most display options. Open Display Settings by clicking Start | Settings | System. You can open the Display applet in the Control Panel in Windows 7/8/8.1. This section focuses on the Windows 10 tool. The two versions are visually different, but you can find similar options in both.

Figure 17-42 shows the default initial Display Settings screen (on a triple-monitor system). Each monitor attached to the system gets a number, and you can drag and drop them to change the location. Figure 17-43 shows a different system with two monitors stacked vertically.

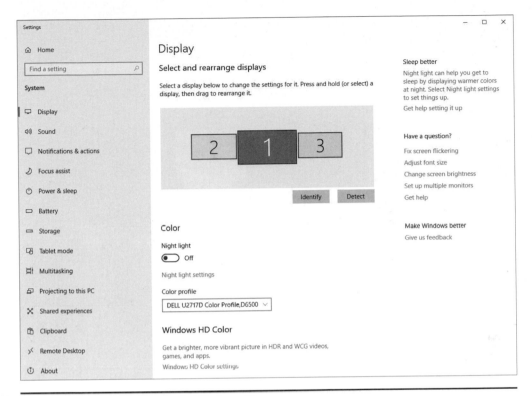

Figure 17-42 Display Settings in Windows 10

The two options under Color are Night light and Color profile. The *Night light* setting enabled reduces eye strain for those of us who tend to work or play after dark. You can set it to change the screen automatically during the evening, reducing the blue in the default screen, turning the "white" into a vaguely pale orange color. This isn't on the exam, but it's a helpful feature. *Color profile* enables you to select a *profile*—a set of parameters specific to a monitor—to get the precise color on screen that you'll see in print (assuming the print device is calibrated for proper color as well). The Color profile in Figure 17-43 is grayed out because Windows set up the profiles automatically. Check the Color Management applet in Control Panel to adjust further (see Figure 17-44).

Scrolling down in Display Settings reveals more advanced options (see Figure 17-45). You can change the scale of text, icons, and more with a drop-down menu. This helps with high-resolution monitors and people who need things a little bigger to navigate the screen options. Changing scaling is preferable to changing resolution, because the interface remains at the default (and best) resolution.

In some scenarios, you'll need to adjust the resolution or orientation of the monitor. The drop-down Resolution menu enables you to change the resolution (to match

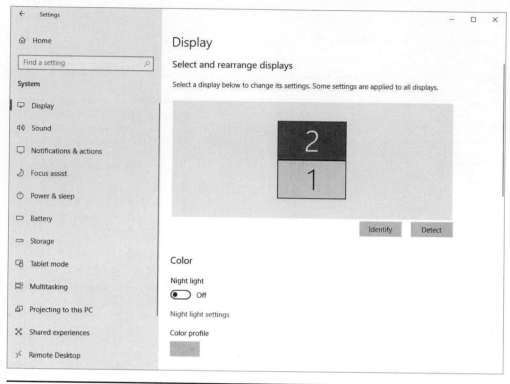

Figure 17-43   Vertically stacked monitors in Display Settings

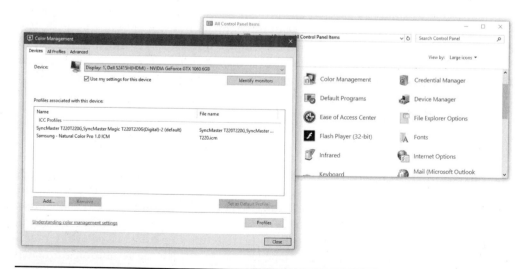

Figure 17-44   Color Management applet in Control Panel

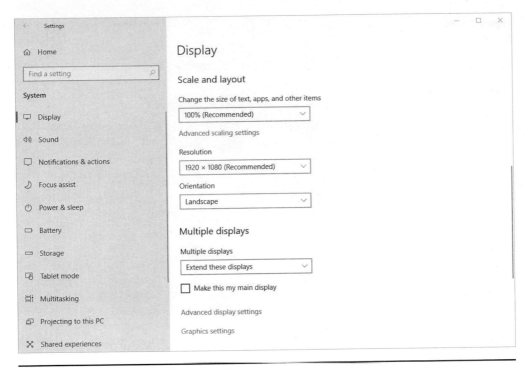

Figure 17-45 More Display Settings options

a projector, for example, so the presentation you see on the monitor looks the same as your audience will see). The Orientation option enables you to change from the default Landscape mode to Portrait mode if you have a monitor that swivels (see Figure 17-46).

The Multiple displays option gives you control over what shows on the second (or more) screen. The default is *Extend these displays*, which gives you more desktop space for workflow. Figure 17-47 shows my editor with extended displays. You can also duplicate the main display, so the same image shows on all connected monitors, or blank one or the other monitor.

NOTE You can readily add additional displays to a system. In years past, you would add a second video card to the system and plug the second monitor into it, then go to the Display applet to extend the displays. Most mid-range and better video cards you can buy today have more than one port, often of different types. Get a cable that matches and plug in for better computing.

Click the *Advanced display settings* option for specific information about the monitor(s) connected. Figure 17-48 shows the settings for a pair of Dell monitors. Note the screen shows the resolution, refresh rate, and bit depth of the panels (as well as color format and color space, which we'll discuss in Beyond A+).

Figure 17-46
Monitor in
portrait mode

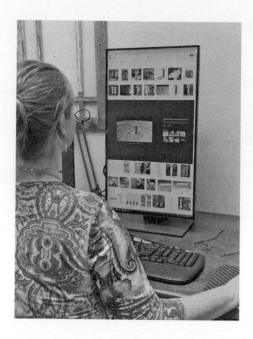

This screen also enables you to open the general Properties for the display adapter and monitor by clicking *Display adapter properties* (see Figure 17-49). The Adapter tab shows information about the adapter, such as GPU and RAM. Clicking the Properties button will open a dialog box to update or roll back the driver. See "Working with Drivers" later in this chapter for more information.

Figure 17-50 shows the Windows 8.1 Display applet. It has most of the same options as Display Settings, just arranged differently.

Figure 17-47
My editor hard at
work with dual
monitors

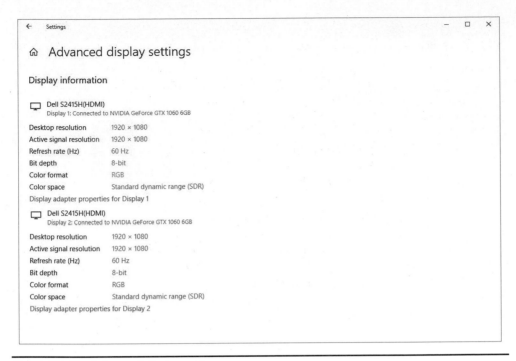

Figure 17-48   Advanced display settings

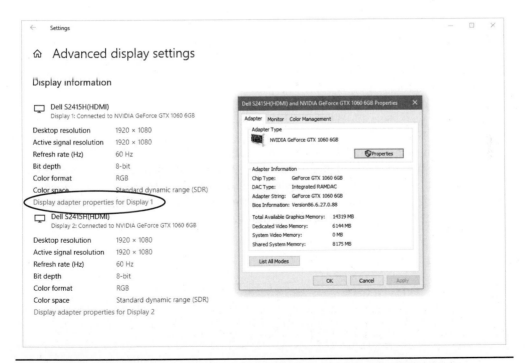

Figure 17-49   Properties dialog box with Adapter, Monitor, and Color Management tabs

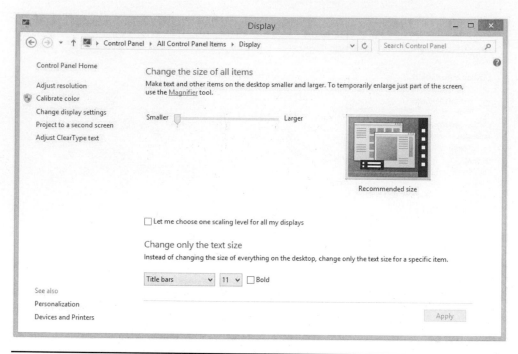

Figure 17-50 Display applet in Windows 8.1

Personalization Settings/Personalization Applet

Personalization-branded tools handle user preferences, such as background picture, colors of various interface elements, and that sort of thing. Figure 17-51 shows the *Personalization Settings* default screen. The changes you can make are pretty obvious: make your background a solid color and pick a picture; you can use one of the images that come with Windows or choose your own. (The current background you can see is a photograph of wall art in Philadelphia that I took last summer.)

The list on the left gives you many more options for tweaking the look and feel of Windows, such as customizing a theme (the overall look and feel), changing the default font, and adjusting the Start menu and Taskbar. The Related Settings at the bottom can help people who have trouble with the default interface, with *High contrast settings*. The *Sync your settings* option enables you to synchronize multiple Windows machines that you log on to with your Microsoft global account. These are all enabled by default (see Figure 17-52).

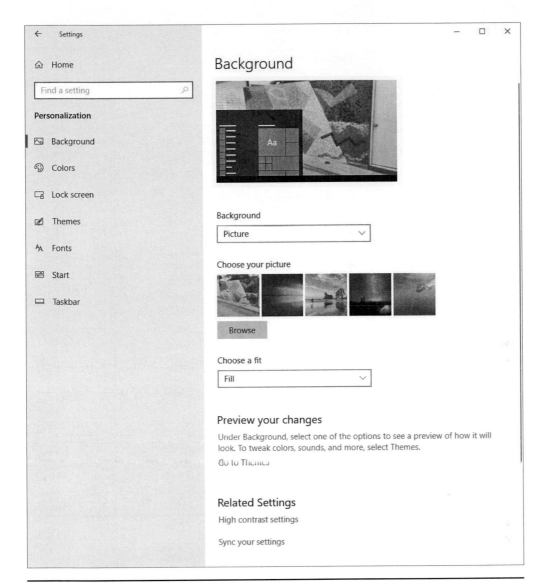

Figure 17-51 Personalization Settings

Figure 17-53 shows the *Personalization applet* in Windows 8.1. You have pretty much the same options as the Personalization Settings in Windows 10, just arranged differently.

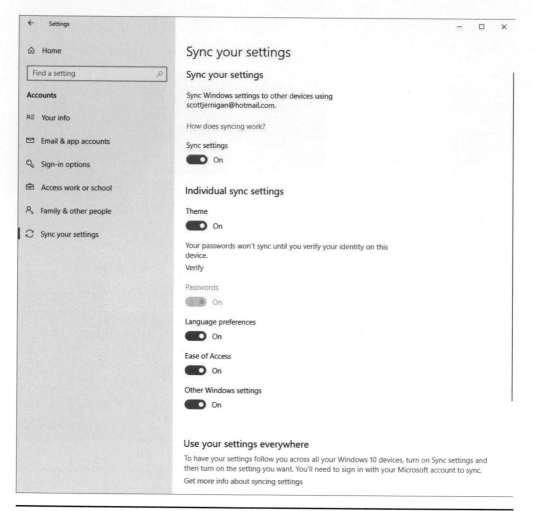

Figure 17-52   Sync your settings options

Display Options in macOS and Linux

macOS and most modern Linux distros offer clear options for changing display settings. To no one's surprise, you'll find the options in macOS in System Preferences (see Figure 17-54). General enables you to change color schemes. You can change the Desktop background in Desktop & Screen Saver.

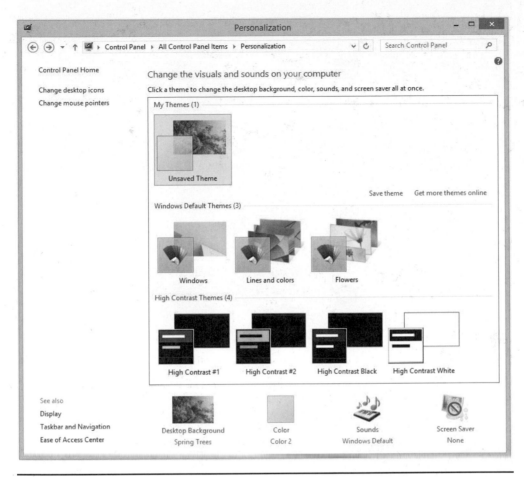

Figure 17-53   Personalization applet in Windows 8.1

Click the Dock option to access a place that can be used to change the user experience a lot (see Figure 17-55). The Dock resides by default along the bottom of the screen. You can make the icons tiny and less distracting. You can move the Dock to the right or left. You can change the default animation behavior for mouseovers.

Different Linux distros put the display options in various places, but you'll commonly find one or more utilities in the System Settings. Figure 17-56 shows the Settings app in Ubuntu, for example, where you can alter most of your system settings, including the background, theme, and Launcher icon size.

All the things you can modify in Windows, you can modify in Linux. You just might have to do a little hunting.

Figure 17-54   System Preferences in macOS

Working with Drivers

Now that you know the locations of the primary video tools within the operating system, it's time to learn about fine-tuning your video. You need to know how to work with video drivers from within Settings (or in the Display applet), including how to update them, roll back updates, and uninstall them.

When you update the drivers for a card, you have a choice of uninstalling the outdated drivers and then installing new drivers—which makes the process the same as for installing a new card—or you can let Windows flex some digital muscle and install the new ones right over the older drivers.

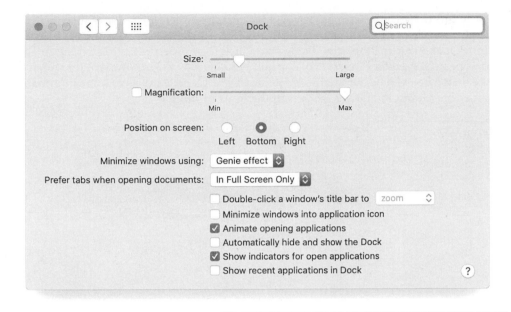

Figure 17-55 Dock options

Figure 17-56 Changing the wallpaper in Ubuntu's Settings app

To get to the adapter settings, as you'll recall from earlier, open the Display Settings, click *Advanced display settings*, and click the *Display adapter properties* link to open the Monitor and Adapter Properties dialog box. Click the Properties button on the Adapter tab to open the Adapter Properties dialog box (see Figure 17-57). (Note that the "Adapter" in the dialog box will be the specific video card.) The General tab gives some information about the card, but the Driver tab gets to the heart of things.

Figure 17-57
Adapter
Properties dialog
box with Driver
tab selected

To update drivers, click the Update Driver button. Windows will give you the option of searching for updated drivers on both your computer and the Internet or just on your computer (see Figure 17-58). The former option these days is pretty magical, as long as the computer is connected to the Internet, of course.

Previous versions of Windows require you to open the Display applet in Control Panel. Drill down the same way to get to the Adapter Properties dialog box and select the Driver tab, just like in Windows 10. You'll get the same options for viewing driver details, updating drivers, and more.

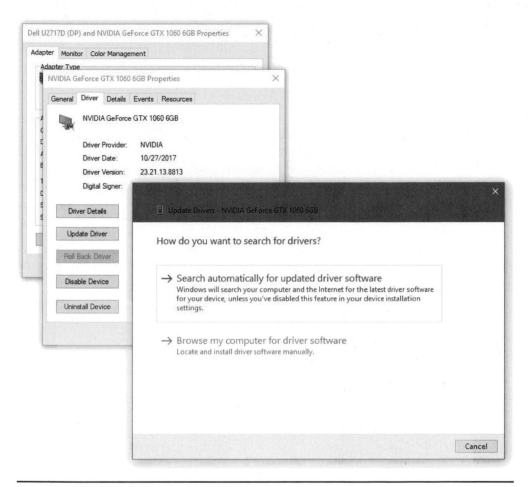

Figure 17-58   Windows looking for driver updates

Historical/Conceptual

3-D Graphics

No other area in computing reflects the amazing acceleration of technological improvements more than *3-D graphics*—in particular, 3-D gaming—which attempts to create images with the same depth and texture as objects seen in the real world. We are spectators to an amazing world where software and hardware race to produce new levels of realism and complexity displayed on the computer screen. Powered by the wallets of tens of millions of PC gamers always demanding more and better, the video industry constantly introduces new video cards and new software titles that make today's games so incredibly realistic and fun.

Although gaming certainly leads the PC industry in 3-D technologies, many other PC applications—such as *Computer Aided Design* (*CAD*) programs—quickly snatch up these technologies, making 3-D useful for much more than games. In this section, we'll add to the many bits and pieces of 3-D video encountered over previous chapters in the book and build an understanding of the function and configuration of 3-D graphics.

Before the early 1990s, PCs did not mix well with 3-D graphics. Certainly, many 3-D applications existed, primarily 3-D design programs such as AutoCAD and Intergraph, but these applications would often run only on expensive, specialized hardware—not so great for casual users.

The big change took place in 1992 when a small company called id Software created a new game called *Wolfenstein 3D* (see Figure 17-59). They launched an entirely new genre of games, now called *first-person shooters* (*FPSs*), in which the player looks out into a 3-D world, interacting with walls, doors, and other items, and shoots whatever bad guys the game provides.

Figure 17-59 Wolfenstein 3D

Wolfenstein 3D shook the PC gaming world to its foundations. That this innovative format came from an upstart little company made *Wolfenstein 3D* and id Software into overnight sensations. Even though their game was demanding on hardware, they gambled that enough people could run it to make it a success. The gamble paid off for

John Carmack and John Romero, the creators of id Software, making them the fathers of 3-D gaming.

Early 3-D games used fixed 2-D images called *sprites* to create the 3-D world. A sprite is nothing more than a bitmapped graphic. These early first-person shooters would calculate the position of an object from the player's perspective and place a sprite to represent the object. Any single object had only a fixed number of sprites—if you walked around an object, you noticed an obvious jerk as the game replaced the current sprite with a new one to represent the new position. Figure 17-60 shows different sprites for the same bad guy in *Wolfenstein 3D*. Sprites weren't pretty, but they worked without seriously taxing the 486s and early Pentiums of the time.

Figure 17-60
Each figure had a limited number of sprites.

The second generation of 3-D games began to replace sprites with true 3-D objects, which are drastically more complex than sprites. A true 3-D object is composed of a group of points called *vertices*. Each vertex has a defined X, Y, and Z position in a 3-D world. Figure 17-61 shows the vertices for a video game character in a 3-D world.

Figure 17-61
Vertices for a video game warrior

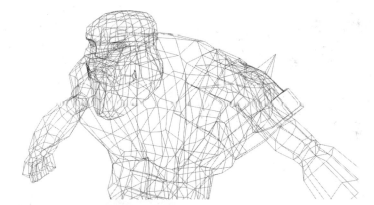

The computer must track all the vertices of all the objects in the 3-D world, including the ones you cannot currently see. Keep in mind that objects may be motionless in the 3-D world (a wall, for example), may have animation (such as a door opening and closing), or may be moving (like bad monsters trying to spray you with evil alien goo). This calculation process is called *transformation* and, as you might imagine, is extremely taxing to most CPUs. Intel and AMD's SIMD (SSE, etc.) processor extensions help to calculate these transformations faster.

Once the CPU has determined the positions of all vertices, the system begins to fill in the 3-D object. The process begins by drawing lines (the 3-D term is *edges*) between vertices to construct the 3-D object from many triangles. Why triangles? Well, mainly by consensus of game developers. Any shape works, but triangles make the most sense from a mathematical standpoint. I could go into more depth here, but that would require talking about trigonometry, and I'm gambling you'd rather not read such a detailed description! All 3-D games use triangles to connect vertices. The 3-D process then groups triangles into various shapes called *polygons*. Figure 17-62 shows the same model as Figure 17-61, now displaying all of the connected vertices to create a large number of polygons.

Figure 17-62
Connected
vertices forming
polygons on a
3-D character

Originally, the CPU handled these calculations to create triangles. With the introduction of the GeForce 256 in 1999, this transform process was moved from the CPU to the video card, greatly accelerating 3-D performance.

The last step in second-generation games was texturing. Every 3-D game stores a number of image files called *textures*. The program wraps textures around an object to give it a surface. Textures work well to provide dramatic detail without using a lot of triangles. A single object may take one texture or many textures, applied to single triangles or groups of triangles (polygons). Figure 17-63 shows the finished character.

Figure 17-63
Video game
warrior with
textures added

True 3-D objects immediately created the need for massively powerful video cards and much wider data buses. Intel's primary motivation for creating AGP was to provide a big enough pipe for massive data pumping between the video card and the CPU. Intel gave AGP the ability to read system RAM to support textures. If it weren't for 3-D games, AGP (and probably even PCIe) would almost certainly not exist.

3-D Video Cards

No CPU of the mid-1990s could ever hope to handle the massive processes required to render 3-D worlds. Keep in mind that to create realistic movement, the 3-D world must refresh at least 24 times per second. That means that this entire process, from transformation to texturing, must repeat once every 1/24th of a second! Furthermore, although the game re-creates each screen, it must also keep score, track the positions of all the objects in the game, provide some type of intelligence to the bad guys, and so on. Something had to happen to take the workload off the CPU. The answer came from video cards.

Video cards were developed with smart onboard GPUs. The GPU helped the CPU by taking over some, and eventually all, of the 3-D rendering duties. These video cards not only have GPUs but also have massive amounts of RAM to store textures.

But a problem exists with this setup: How do we talk to these cards? This is done by means of a device driver, of course, but wouldn't it be great if we could create standard commands to speed up the process? The best thing to do would be to create a standardized set of instructions that any 3-D program could send to a video card to do all the basic work, such as "make a cone" or "lay texture 237 on the cone you just made."

The video card instructions standards manifested themselves into a series of *application programming interfaces* (*APIs*). In essence, an API is a library of commands that people who make 3-D games must use in their programs. Programs use these APIs to issue generic commands that the device drivers for many different video cards will understand. The device drivers for each card translate the API commands into instructions the hardware on that card will understand, and then send these instructions down to the graphics hardware.

Several APIs have been developed over the years, with two clear winners among all of them: OpenGL and DirectX. The *OpenGL* standard was developed for UNIX systems but has since been *ported*, or made compatible with a wide variety of computer systems, including Windows and Apple computers. As the demand for 3-D video grew increasingly strong, Microsoft decided to throw its hat into the 3-D graphics ring with its own API, called DirectX. We look at DirectX in depth in the next section.

 NOTE Two other standards are making inroads these days. The open source folks have started to embrace *Vulcan*. Apple is pushing its in-house *Metal API*.

Although they might accomplish the same task (for instance, translating instructions and passing them on to the video driver), every API handles things just a little bit differently. In some 3-D games, the OpenGL standard might produce more precise images with less CPU overhead than the DirectX standard. In general, however, you won't notice a large difference between the images produced by OpenGL and those produced by DirectX.

1002

DirectX and Video Cards

In the old days, many applications communicated directly with much of the PC hardware and, as a result, could crash your computer if not written well enough. Microsoft tried to fix this problem by placing all hardware under the control of Windows, but programmers balked because Windows added too much work for the video process and slowed everything down. For the most demanding programs, such as games, only direct access to hardware would work.

This need to "get around Windows" motivated Microsoft to unveil a new set of protocols called *DirectX*. Programmers use DirectX to take control of certain pieces of hardware and to talk directly to that hardware; it provides the speed necessary to play the advanced games so popular today. The primary impetus for DirectX was to build a series of products to enable Windows to run 3-D games. That's not to say that you couldn't run 3-D games in Windows *before* DirectX; rather, it's just that Microsoft wasn't involved in the API rat race at the time and wanted to be. Microsoft's goal in developing DirectX was to create a 100-percent-stable environment, with direct hardware access, for running 3-D applications and games within Windows.

Microsoft regularly updates DirectX. The latest games require the latest version of DirectX. Windows updates automatically, so you don't have to do anything. But if you want to look at the DirectX version installed on a computer (because you'll see this on the 1002 exam), use the *DirectX Diagnostic Tool* (*dxdiag*) (see Figure 17-64). In Windows 10, type **dxdiag** in the *Type here to search* box. Press ENTER to run the program. The System tab gives the version of DirectX. The system pictured in Figure 17-64 runs DirectX 12.

EXAM TIP The CompTIA A+ 1002 exam refers to the DirectX Diagnostic Tool as *DxDiag*.

Trying to decide what video card to buy gives me the shakes—too many options! One good way to narrow down your buying decision is to see what GPU is hot at the moment. I make a point to check out these Web sites whenever I'm getting ready to buy, so I can see what everyone says is best.

- www.arstechnica.com
- www.hardocp.com
- www.tomshardware.com
- www.anandtech.com

SIM Check out the excellent "DxDiag" Show! and Click! simulations over in the Chapter 17 section of the hub: totalsem.com/100x. These will get you prepared for any performance-based questions CompTIA might throw at you.

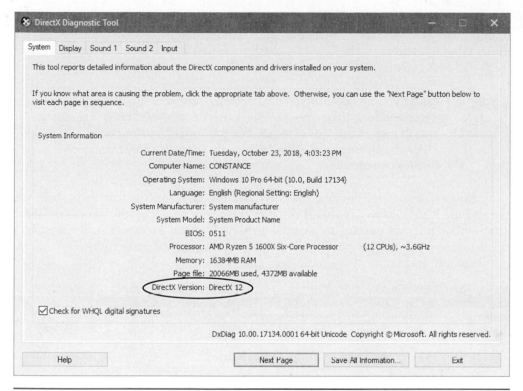

Figure 17-64   The DirectX Diagnostic Tool

Troubleshooting Video

People tend to notice when their monitors stop showing the Windows desktop, making video problems an urgent issue for technicians. Users might temporarily ignore a bad printer or other device, but will holler like crazy when the screen doesn't look the way they expect. To fix video problems quickly, the best place to start is to divide video problems into two groups: video cards/drivers, and monitors.

Troubleshooting Video Cards and Drivers

Video cards rarely go bad, so the majority of video card/driver problems are bad or incompatible drivers or incorrect settings. Always make sure you have the correct driver installed. If you're using an incompatible driver, you might get a Blue Screen of Death (BSoD) as soon as Windows starts to load. A system with a suddenly corrupted driver usually doesn't act up until the next reboot. If you reboot a system with a corrupted driver, Windows will do one of the following: go into *SVGA mode*, blank the monitor (*no image on screen*), lock up, or display a garbled screen with weird patterns, incorrect color patterns, or a distorted image. You might get oversized images and icons. You might even see a 3-D image with amazingly distorted geometry.

Whatever the output, reboot into Safe mode and roll back or delete the driver. Keep in mind that more advanced video cards tend to show their drivers as installed programs under Programs and Features, so always check there first before you try deleting a driver by using Device Manager. Download the latest driver and reinstall.

 EXAM TIP The CompTIA A+ 1002 objectives mention that buggy drivers can cause Windows to go into *VGA mode*, that's 640 × 480. This was certainly true in ancient versions of the OS, but the current versions will go 800 × 600 (*SVGA mode*). Be prepared for "VGA mode" to be the only correct-ish answer on an exam question.

Video cards are pretty durable, but they have two components that do go bad: the fan and the RAM. Lucky for you, if either of these goes out, it tends to show the same error—bizarre screen outputs followed shortly by a screen lockup. Usually Windows keeps running; you may see your mouse pointer moving around and windows refreshing, but the screen turns into a huge mess (see Figure 17-65).

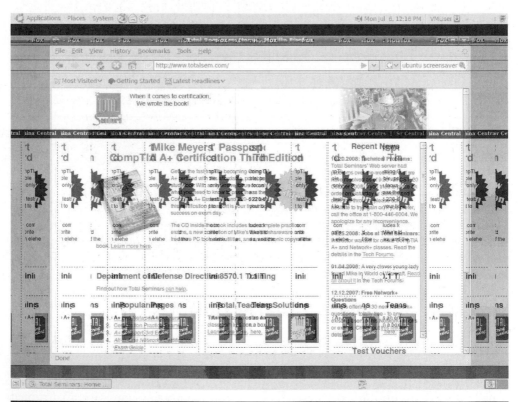

Figure 17-65   Serious video problem

Bad drivers sometimes also make this error, so always first try going into Safe mode to see if the problem suddenly clears up. If it does, you do not have a problem with the video card!

 EXAM TIP The CompTIA A+ 1001 objectives mention *multiple failed jobs in logs* as a potential symptom of video or display issues. If you have recurring graphics trouble and the other troubleshooting steps here don't help, it's not a bad idea to check system logs (i.e., Event Viewer) for any clues to what's going on. On the exam, keep an eye out for questions that combine logs and display issues.

Excessive heat inside the case, even with the video card fan running at full blast, can create some interesting effects. The computer could simply shut down due to overheating (CompTIA calls this an *overheat shutdown*). You'll recognize this possible cause because the computer will come back up in a minute or two, but then shut down again as you use it hard and it heats up again. Sometimes the screen will show bizarre artifacts or start distorting. Check your case fans and make sure nothing is too close to the video card. You might need to take the whole system outside to blow out dust from its filters, vents, and fans.

Troubleshooting Monitors

Because of the inherent dangers of the high-frequency and high-voltage power required by monitors, and because proper adjustment requires specialized training, this section concentrates on giving a support person the information necessary to decide whether a trouble ticket is warranted. Virtually no monitor manufacturers make schematics of their monitors available to the public, because of liability issues regarding possible electrocution. To simplify troubleshooting, look at the process as three separate parts: common monitor problems, external adjustments, and internal adjustments.

Common Monitor Problems

Although I'm not super comfortable diving into the guts of a monitor, you can fix a substantial percentage of monitor problems yourself. The following list describes the most common monitor problems and tells you what to do—even when that means sending it to someone else.

- For problems with ghosting, streaking, and/or fuzzy vertical edges, check the cable connections and the cable itself. These problems rarely apply to monitors; more commonly, they point to the video card.

- If one color is missing, check cables for breaks or bent pins. Check the front controls for that color. If the color adjustment is already maxed out, the monitor will require internal service.

- As monitors age, they lose brightness. If the brightness control is turned all the way up and the picture seems dim, the monitor will require internal adjustment. This is a good argument for power-management functions. Use the power switch or the power-management options in Windows to turn off the monitor after a certain amount of time.

- An LCD monitor may have bad pixels. A bad pixel is any single pixel that does not react the way it should. A pixel that never lights up is a *dead pixel*, a pixel that is stuck on pure white is a *lit pixel*, and a pixel on a certain color is a *stuck pixel*. If you discover a bad pixel on a monitor under warranty, the best course of action is to contact the manufacturer. If the monitor isn't under warranty, you can try to revive the pixel using techniques discussed online, learn to live with the bad pixels, or replace the monitor. All LCD panel makers allow a certain number of bad pixels, even on a brand-new LCD monitor! You need to check the warranty for your monitor and see how many they allow before you may return the monitor.

- If an LCD monitor cracks, it is not repairable and must be replaced.

- A flickering image with an LCD usually points to either a very inexpensive panel with too much light bleed from the backlight or a dying CCFL backlight. LEDs don't flicker, so you won't see this issue with those types of LCDs. Replace the backlight if necessary (according to the exam). Just replace the monitor with a modern one (Mike's advice).

- A dim image, especially on only the top or bottom half of the screen, points to a dead or dying backlight.

- If the LCD goes dark but you can still barely see the image under bright lights, you lost either the backlight or the inverter. In many cases, especially with super-thin panels, you'll replace the entire panel and backlight as a unit.

- If your LCD makes a distinct hissing noise, an inverter is about to fail. You can replace the inverter if needed.

- If an image displayed for a long time (common with OS interface elements) leaves a shadow or impression, you're seeing image *persistence*. Most persistence problems these days are temporary and should go away if you turn the display off for at least as long as it was on. If it doesn't go away, you may be witnessing permanent *burn-in*. Early generations of each new display technology tend to struggle with burn-in, so it's a good idea to protect them with time-tested solutions: configure the OS to turn off idle displays or protect them with an animated screen saver.

Be careful if you open an LCD to work on the inside. The inverter can bite you in several ways. First, it's powered by a high-voltage electrical circuit that can give you a nasty shock. Worse, the inverter will retain a charge for a few minutes after you unplug it, so unplug and wait for a bit. Second, inverters get very hot and present a very real danger of burning you at a touch. Again, wait for a while after you unplug it to try to replace it. Finally, if you shock an inverter, you might irreparably damage it. Use proper ESD-avoidance techniques.

Bottom line on fixing LCD monitors? You can find companies that sell replacement parts for LCDs, but repairing an LCD is difficult, and there are folks who will do it for you faster and cheaper than you can. Search for a specialty LCD repair company. Hundreds of these companies exist all over the world.

Dealing with High-Resolution Monitors

High-resolution monitors offer beautiful visuals, but can make screen elements—buttons, menus, stuff for navigating operating systems and applications—too small for some viewers. If you recall from earlier in the chapter, LCD monitors have a default resolution; the picture will degrade if you set the resolution lower than the default. But, that's what a lot of people do, because it makes the screen elements bigger and thus useable. That's not the solution!

The best way to deal with the scenario of tiny screen elements is through the Display Settings/Display applet. Every version of Windows enables you to change the size of screen elements directly, making the screen elements appear larger (or smaller). The resolution doesn't change; only the size of the screen elements change. Open Display Settings/Display applet. Figure 17-66 shows the drop-down options in Windows 10. Note that changing the size of text, apps, and other items from 100 percent to 125 or 200 percent is a simple selection.

Figure 17-66
Changing the size of text, apps, and other items in Windows 10

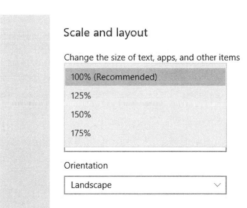

Scale and layout

Change the size of text, apps, and other items

100% (Recommended)

125%

150%

175%

Orientation

Landscape

Try This!   Scaling the UI
Most of you have access to a Windows computer, so try this! Open Display Settings/ Display applet and experiment with the element size settings. This is something you absolutely need to understand to help users with high-resolution monitors.

Cleaning Monitors

Cleaning monitors is easy. Always use antistatic monitor wipes or at least a general anti-static cloth. Microfiber cloth works great. Some LCD monitors may require special cleaning equipment. Never use window cleaners that contain ammonia or any liquid because getting liquid into the monitor may create a shocking experience! Many commercial cleaning solutions will also melt older LCD screens, which is never a good thing.

NOTE Video cards can handle multiple monitors that differ from one another in size or resolution, but this can create problems. Connecting a 4:3 aspect ratio projector to a widescreen laptop for a presentation when you're mirroring the displays, for example, can create a pretty bizarre misalignment in layout. Using monitors with different orientation—landscape and portrait—can also produce undesirable effects. Try variations before your presentations!

Also, Windows enables you to designate which monitor is right or left or top or bottom. Making an alignment error here can cause problems when extending a display. You might drag the cursor to the right side of the left monitor, for example, and hit a wall because the "right" monitor is supposed to be on the left. These kinds of issues require a trip to the Display Settings/ Display applet.

Privacy with Multiple Monitors

Adding a second or third monitor to your setup can have a couple of downsides. The added viewing area can increase the potential for glare or reflection from other objects, making optimal monitor placement difficult. The extra visual real estate and viewing angles also make it easy for even casual passersby to see what you're doing or browsing or whatever.

Monitor peripheral vendors address these problems with privacy screens. The screens fit over and slightly around the LCD panels. They stop wide-angle viewing of the screen and also drop the glare caused by external object reflection.

Troubleshooting Projectors

Many of the concepts for troubleshooting traditional monitors also apply when you need to troubleshoot a projector, but there are also a few special points to keep in mind.

- Projector lamps can produce a *lot* of heat. If you can, let a projector cool off before you work on it. After you turn it off, the fan will run for a while to cool the lamp. If that isn't an option, be very careful where you touch to avoid burning yourself.

- Projector lamps have a relatively short life (usually a few thousand hours) compared to most other display components. They're expensive, but otherwise simple to replace. Keep a spare lamp on hand; not only will you be ready to save the day when one burns out before a big executive meeting, but a spare lamp will help you rule out lamp issues when troubleshooting a projector.

- Speaking of replacement parts, keep some spare batteries around for the remote. Most projectors are mounted in a hard-to-reach location. If the projector won't respond, try swapping out the remote's batteries before you break out a ladder to reach the projector's physical buttons.

- Projectors have a fan to cool off the lamp. If the fan goes out or the filter gets clogged, the lamp could overheat. The screen may suddenly go black if it goes into an overheat shutdown. Trying to turn the projector immediately back on to troubleshoot the issue may not work at all. If it does, it certainly won't help the main problem.

- Like any display that goes unused for long enough, a projector might go into sleep mode. They'll usually wake up if you use the computer or press the right button on the remote. If the projector is clearly running but there's no image on screen, you may have to reboot it.

- Some projectors compose a full-color image from multiple LCDs. If the image has incorrect color patterns such as a strong tint, one or more of these panels may have failed. If you have strange or flickering color on a DLP projector, you could be dealing with a failing color wheel assembly.

Above all else, don't get *too* focused on the fact that you're dealing with a projector when you have to troubleshoot one. It's easy to jump straight to projector-specific solutions and miss simple problems like a poorly connected cable, or a laptop that isn't configured to extend or mirror its display to the projector.

Beyond A+

Additional Display Topics

Display technologies play such a huge role in modern computing that it's hard to believe people used computers for years without anything like a modern display. The rapid growth and development of computing technology is nowhere more visible than in the ever-growing selection of super-thin, curved, astonishingly clear, ultra-wide, blazing-fast, efficient, jaw-droppingly huge displays.

The pace of change in display technologies is so fast that it's hard to keep up, but some of these new bells and whistles cost an arm and a leg. A good tech needs to keep up with these developments in order to pick out displays with features that are meaningful to their users, and avoid blowing the budget on features they could live without. With that in mind, let's look at a few display topics that you won't find on this edition of the exam, but you're bound to run into in the real world: microLED displays, High Dynamic Range, adaptive sync, video display modes, and external GPUs.

MicroLED

Although not yet ready for prime time (or mass production), *microLED* (*μLED*) monitors form pixels using groups of microscopic LEDs. MicroLED displays perform better than traditional LCD panels, offering better energy efficiency, brightness, contrast, and response times. As we go to print, several companies have scores of engineers working on the technology, including heavyweights such as Sony, Samsung, and Apple. There's no definite timeline on the technology, but expect to see it sooner rather than later.

High Dynamic Range

The typical human eye can see an astonishing variety of colors, luminance (aka brightness), and contrast. Scientists interested in what people see have defined this visual variety into graphs known technically as *chromaticity diagrams* or, more commonly, *color spaces* (see Figure 17-67).

Figure 17-67
Example of a
chromaticity
diagram

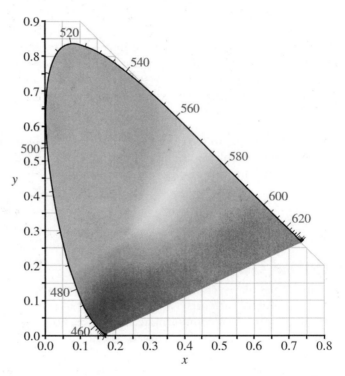

Computers only display a fraction of what people can see and thus use more limited color spaces. Matching color spaces among devices provides some consistency in color output. Several standards define the color space for the IT industry. *sRGB* has long been the standard of how displays show images.

The *dynamic range* a monitor displays reflects the amount of detail possible in the picture between pure white and pure black. Have you watched the sunrise or sunset, with the phenomenal difference in brightness between the vibrant sunlit clouds and deep shadows around the trees? That's dynamic range.

The standard 8-bit panel uses *Standard Dynamic Range* (*SDR*), and that's good enough for almost every computing need, from movies to games to productivity applications. Good enough, that is, until you see a big monitor with a 10-bit panel running *High Dynamic Range* (*HDR*) and your jaw drops in shock. The visible details, textures, and shading make for a very different computing experience.

 NOTE I'd love to show you a comparison between SDR and HDR, but it's impossible in print. Go to your local computer store and ask for a demo.

Adaptive Sync

When a graphics card is working hard, the number of frames it can generate in any given second fluctuates wildly. When the display and graphics card are out of sync, different parts of the screen may show different frames. This jarring effect is called *tearing*, and the people who make graphics cards and displays have been working on this problem for years.

An early approach to this problem, vertical sync (V-sync), avoids tearing by using a fixed refresh cycle—at the expense of higher latency. *Adaptive sync* addressed this trade-off by enabling a display to synchronize its refresh rate with the graphics card's refresh rate. Nvidia developed proprietary adaptive sync technology it calls *G-Sync*, and in response, AMD developed a royalty-free adaptive sync technology called *FreeSync*. Both technologies are entering their second generations with HDR support: FreeSync 2 and G-Sync HDR.

These technologies are a big improvement for gaming, but there's a downside: minimal cross-compatibility. To take advantage of adaptive sync, your graphics card and monitor either both need to support FreeSync or both need to support G-Sync (although Nvidia has very recently announced support for a handful of FreeSync monitors). If you want adaptive sync, research the compatibility of your components carefully!

Video Modes

Running a display at its native resolution is essential for a good computing experience, but the quality of your experience will also depend to some extent on how well the video card, operating system, applications, multimedia files, and Web sites you use support that resolution. These resolutions are also known as *video modes* or *display modes*, and each one has a shorthand name.

Memorizing every possible resolution isn't the best use of your time (there are a *ton* of resolutions out there), but it is a good idea to be familiar with the ones you're most likely to buy, see in the real world, or field questions about. Table 17-2 shows some common display modes. Note that this leaves out mobile devices.

eGPUs

Manufacturers have taken advantage of the blistering throughput of the latest USB and Thunderbolt busses to create *external graphics processing units (eGPUs)*, standalone boxes

Table 17-2 Typical Display Modes	Video Mode	Resolution	Aspect Ratio	Typical Device
	VGA	640 × 480	4:3	Ancient monitors
	SVGA	800 × 600	4:3	Ancient monitors
	HDTV 720p	1280 × 720	16:9	Lowest resolution that can be called HDTV
	HDTV 1080p	1920 × 1080	16:9	Full HDTV resolution
	WUXGA	1920 × 1200	16:10	Older widescreen monitors
	WQHD (2K)	2560 × 1440	16:9	Widescreen displays
	4K Ultra HD	3840 × 2160	16:9	Televisions, excellent monitors
	5K	5120 × 2880	16:9	Excellent monitors
	8K Ultra HD	7680 × 4320	16:9	Televisions

with video cards for video processing and gaming. eGPUs enable you to edit 4K on the go and then play graphics-intensive games on portable computers, such as ultrabooks and MacBook Pros. The portables stay thin and light, unlike dedicated gaming portables. Plus, if you want to edit or game but need an ultra-portable computer, you don't need to shell out for a dedicated video production or gaming machine in addition.

Different video and peripheral companies, such as Gigabyte, Alienware, and ASUS, offer several styles of eGPU. The Gigabyte AORUS Gaming Box comes with a power supply, a high-end Gigabyte-branded NVIDIA gaming card, a circuit board, and an enclosure with HDMI, DP, and DVI for video out. Plus the enclosure has four USB ports. Connectivity to the portable comes via Thunderbolt.

The Alienware Graphics Amplifier, in contrast, is an enclosure specifically for Alienware notebooks. It doesn't come with a graphics card, but offers a circuit board with a PCIe slot for inserting your GPU of choice. Connectivity to the portable comes via a proprietary Alienware connector. The ASUS ROG XG Station 2 offers a similar case to the Alienware, but without the proprietary stuff.

The difference between fully featured and do-it-yourself (DIY) builds is reflected in the prices. The Gigabyte rolls in at $600; the Alienware at only $200. (ASUS really loves its enclosure design, apparently. It sells for over $500 without a video card. Yikes!)

Chapter Review

Questions

1. What do we call the time it takes for all of the sub-pixels on the panel to change from one state to another?

   A. Refresh rate

   B. Redraw rate

   C. Response rate

   D. Vertical refresh rate

2. What provides the illumination for LCD monitors?

   A. Backlights

   B. Inverter

   C. Lamp

   D. LCD panel

3. Dudley wants to connect his new MacBook Pro to an LCD monitor that has a Digital Visual Interface. What type of adapter should he use?

   A. BNC-to-DVI

   B. DisplayPort-to-HDMI

   C. Mini-HDMI-to-VGA

   D. Thunderbolt-to-DVI

4. How do you measure brightness of a projector?

   A. Lumens

   B. Pixels

   C. LEDs

   D. CCFLs

5. What is 1080p resolution?

   A. 1024 × 768

   B. 1280 × 1024

   C. 1680 × 1050

   D. 1920 × 1080

6. What is the processor on a video card called?

   A. CPU

   B. GPU

   C. GDDR

   D. MPU

7. What Microsoft API supports 3-D graphics?

   A. Active Desktop

   B. DirectX

   C. Glide

   D. OpenGL

8. Which two kinds of backlight might you find in LCD monitors?

   A. CCFL and LED

   B. CCFL and LCD

   C. CCFL and AC

   D. HDMI and DisplayPort

9. A company executive calls complaining that the conference room projector suddenly cut off in the middle of her presentation to the board. What could be the problem? (Select two).

   A. The power cord wiggled loose.

   B. The lamp went out.

   C. The projector went to sleep because she forgot to configure her OS to extend the desktop to the projector.

   D. The projector overheated and shut down because the fan stopped working or its filter is clogged.

10. A client calls complaining that his aging LCD monitor is flickering. What is most likely the problem?

   A. The refresh rate is set too high.

   B. The refresh rate is set too low.

   C. The CCFL backlight is failing.

   D. The LED backlight is failing.

Answers

1. **C.** The amount of time it takes for all of the sub-pixels on the panel to go from pure black to pure white and back again is called the response rate.

2. **A.** The backlights provide the illumination for the LCD panel.

3. **D.** Dudley should use a Thunderbolt-to-DVI adapter to connect his new MacBook Pro to the LCD monitor.

4. **A.** The brightness of a projector is measured in lumens.

5. **D.** 1080p resolution is 1920 × 1080.

6. **B.** You'll typically see video card processors referred to as GPUs.

7. **B.** Microsoft makes the DirectX API to support 3-D programs.

8. **A.** Current LCD monitors use one of two competing backlight technologies, CCFL and LED.

9. **B, D.** Projector lamps only last a few thousand hours, so they may go out regularly in a busy conference room. If the projector overheats due to a dead fan or clogged filter, it will shut down to protect itself.

10. **C.** LCD monitors have a fixed refresh rate, so the most likely cause here is that the CCFL backlight is failing. LED backlights don't flicker.

Essentials of Networking

In this chapter, you will learn how to
- Describe the basic roles of various networked computers
- Discuss network technologies and Ethernet
- Describe a typical Ethernet implementation

It's hard to find a computer that's not connected to a network. Whether you're talking about a workstation that's part of a large enterprise network or discussing that smartphone in your pocket, every computer has some form of network connection. CompTIA includes a lot of networking coverage in the CompTIA A+ exams.

This chapter dives into networks in detail, especially the underlying hardware and technologies that make up the bulk of networks in today's homes and businesses. The discussion starts by examining the roles computers play in networking, helping you associate specific names with devices and services you've undoubtedly used many times already. The second portion, and the heart of the chapter, focuses on the now-standard network technology used in most networks, regardless of operating system. The final section examines how this network technology looks in a normal workplace.

1001

Roles Hosts Play in Networks

Take a moment to think about what you do on a network. Most of us, when asked, would say, "surf the Internet," or "watch YouTube videos," or maybe "print to the printer downstairs." These are all good reasons to use a network, but what ties them together? In each of these situations, you use your computer (the *local host*) to access "stuff" stored on a *remote host* (not your local computer). A *host* is any computing device connected to a network. So what do remote computers have that you might want (see Figure 18-1)?

Figure 18-1   Accessing remote computers

NOTE   Terminology shifts as soon as computing devices network together. Because a computing device can take many forms, not just a PC or workstation, we need a term to define networked devices. A *host* is any computing device connected to a network. A *local host*, therefore, refers to what's in front of you, like your macOS workstation. A *remote host* refers to some other computing device on the network or reachable beyond the network (more on those later).

Each networked host fulfills a certain *role*. A remote computer called a *Web server* stores the files that make up a Web site. The Web server uses server programs to store and share the data. So the role of the Web server is to provide access to Web sites. Two popular Web server programs are Apache HTTP Server and Microsoft Internet Information Services (IIS). When you access a Web site, your *Web browser* (likely Internet Explorer, Mozilla Firefox, Google Chrome, or Microsoft Edge) asks the Web server to share the Web page files and then displays them (see Figure 18-2). Because your computer asks for the Web page, we call it the *client*. That's the role of the local host in this example. The remote computer that serves the Web site is a *server*.

NOTE   Any computer that's running a sharing program is by definition a server.

But what about YouTube? YouTube also uses Web servers, but these Web servers connect to massive video databases. Like a normal Web server, these remote computers share the videos with your client device, but they use special software capable of sending video fast enough that you can watch it without waiting (see Figure 18-3).

Figure 18-2
Accessing a Web
page

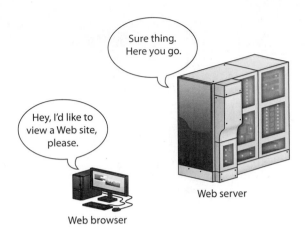

But we don't need the Internet to share stuff. Figure 18-4 shows a small home network with each computer running Windows. One of the computers on the network has a printer connected via a USB port. This computer has enabled a printer-sharing program built into Windows so that the other computers on the network can use the printer. That computer, therefore, takes on the role of a *print server*.

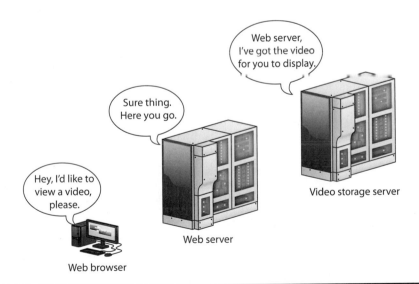

Figure 18-3 Accessing a YouTube page

Figure 18-4
Sharing a printer
in Windows

No matter how big the network, we use networks to share and access stuff. This stuff might be Web pages, videos, printers, folders, e-mail messages, music . . . what you can share and access is limited only by your ability to find a server program capable of sharing it and a client program that can access it.

Each type of server gets a label that defines its role. A networked host that enables you to access a bunch of files and folders is called a *file server*. The networked host you use to access e-mail messages? It's called a *mail server*. Truth in advertising!

NOTE Along with common modern servers, you'll find a lot of *legacy* and *embedded systems* performing very specific, non-modern tasks. A factory producing a widget, for example, might use a proprietary controller that works over a network. Even though technically obsolete, that network unit isn't broken, so why replace it?

Network people call anything that one computer might share with another a *resource*. The goal of networking, therefore, is to connect computers so that they can share resources or access other shared resources.

To share and access resources, a network must have the following:

1. Something that defines and standardizes the design and operation of cabling, network cards, and the interconnection of multiple computers

2. An addressing method that enables clients to find servers and enables servers to send data to clients, no matter the size of the network

3. Some method of sharing resources and accessing those shared resources

Let's look now at the first of these network needs and discuss current industry standards.

Historical/Conceptual

Networking Technologies

When the first network designers sat down at a café to figure out how to get two or more computers to share data and peripherals, they had to write a lot of notes on little white napkins to answer even the most basic questions. The first question was: *How?* It's easy to say, "Well, just run a wire between them!" But that doesn't tell us how the wire works or how the computers connect to the wire. Here are some more big-picture questions:

- How will each computer be identified?

- If two or more computers want to talk at the same time, how do you ensure that all conversations are understood?

- What kind of wire? What gauge? How many wires in the cable? Which wires do what? How long can the cable be? What type of connectors?

Clearly, making a modern network entails a lot more than just stringing up some cable! As you saw a bit earlier, most networks have one or more client machines, devices that request information or services, and a server, the machine that hosts and shares the data. Both clients and servers need *network interface controllers (NICs)* that define or label the machine on the network. A NIC also breaks files into smaller data units to send across the network and reassembles the units it receives into whole files. You also need some medium for delivering the data units between two or more devices—most often this is a wire that can carry electrical pulses; sometimes it's radio waves or other wireless methods. Finally, a computer's operating system has to be able to communicate with its own networking hardware and with other machines on the network. Figure 18-5 shows a typical network layout.

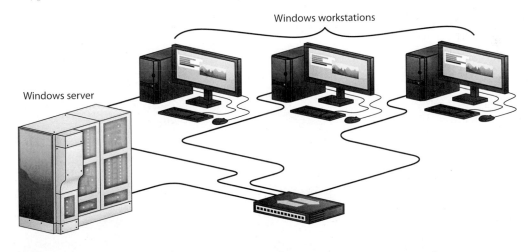

Figure 18-5   A typical network

EXAM TIP Not too many years ago, every NIC came on an expansion card that you added to a motherboard. Most techs called that card a *network interface card,* or *NIC.* Now that every motherboard has the networking feature built in, the acronym has shifted to network interface *controller.* You're likely to see only the term *NIC* on the exams, although the objectives this go-around call them *network interface cards.*

1001

Frames and NICs

Data is moved from one device to another in discrete chunks called *frames*. NICs create and process frames.

NOTE You'll sometimes hear the word *packet* used instead of frames—this is incorrect. Packets are included within a frame. You'll find more information about packets in Chapter 19, "Local Area Networking."

Every NIC in the world has a built-in identifier, an address unique to that network card, called a *media access control (MAC) address*. A MAC address is a *binary number*, meaning it's a string of ones and zeros. Each one or zero is called a *bit*.

The MAC address is 48 bits long, providing more than 281 *trillion* MAC addresses, so there are plenty of MAC addresses to go around. Because people have trouble keeping track of that many ones and zeros, we need another way to display the addresses. *Hexadecimal* is shorthand for representing strings of ones and zeros. One hex character is used to represent four binary characters. Here's the key:

$$0000 = 0$$
$$0001 = 1$$
$$0010 = 2$$
$$0011 = 3$$
$$0100 = 4$$
$$0101 = 5$$
$$0110 = 6$$
$$0111 = 7$$
$$1000 = 8$$
$$1001 = 9$$
$$1010 = A$$
$$1011 = B$$
$$1100 = C$$

$$1101 = D$$
$$1110 = E$$
$$1111 = F$$

So, MAC addresses may be binary, but we represent them by using 12 hexadecimal characters. These MAC addresses are burned into every NIC, and some NIC makers print the MAC address on the card. Figure 18-6 shows the System Information utility description of a NIC, with the MAC address highlighted.

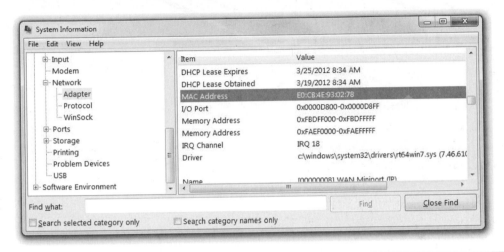

Figure 18-6 MAC address

NOTE Even though MAC addresses are embedded into the NIC, some NICs allow you to change the MAC address on the NIC. This is rarely done.

Hey! I thought we were talking about frames! Well, we are, but you needed to understand MAC addresses to understand frames.

The many varieties of frame share common features (see Figure 18-7). First, frames contain the MAC address of the network card to which the data is being sent. Second, they have the MAC address of the network card that sent the data. Third is the data itself (at this point, we have no idea what the data is—certain software handles that question), which can vary in size depending on the type of frame. Finally, the frame must contain some type of data check to verify that the data was received in good order. Most frames use a clever mathematical algorithm called a *cyclic redundancy check (CRC)*.

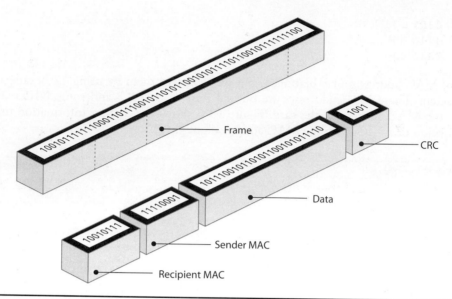

Figure 18-7 Generic frame

Try This! MAC Address Search

Every personal computing device has a MAC address assigned to each network connection type it offers. Any number of troubleshooting scenarios will have you scrambling to find a device's MAC address, so try this!

You have many ways to discover the MAC address(es) in Windows, macOS, and Linux. The simplest is through the command-line interface. Here's a method in Windows. At the prompt, type **ipconfig /all** and press ENTER. You'll find the MAC address listed as the "Physical Address" under the Ethernet adapter Local Area Connection category.

Which command do you think would work at the Terminal in macOS and Linux? How do you figure out which switch to use? (Refresh your memory of commands in Chapter 15, "Working with the Command-Line Interface.")

This discussion of frames raises a question: How big is a frame? Or more specifically, how much data do you put into each frame? How do you ensure that the receiving system understands the *way* the data was broken down by the sending machine and can thus put the pieces back together? The hard part of answering these questions is that they encompass so many items. When the first networks were created, *everything* from the frames to the connectors to the type of cable had to be invented from scratch.

To make a successful network, you need the sending and receiving devices to use the same network technology. Over the years, many hardware protocols came and went, but today only one hardware protocol dominates the modern computing landscape: *Ethernet*. Ethernet was developed for wired networking, but even wireless networks use Ethernet as the basis for their signals. If you want to understanding networking, you need to understand Ethernet.

Ethernet

A consortium of companies, including Digital Equipment Corporation, Intel, and Xerox, invented the first network in the mid-1970s. More than just create a network, they wrote a series of standards that defined everything necessary to get data from one computer to another. This series of standards was called *Ethernet*. Over the years, Ethernet has gone through hundreds of distinct improvements in areas such as speed, signaling, and cabling. We call these improvements *Ethernet flavors*.

Through all the improvements in Ethernet, the Ethernet frame hasn't changed in over 25 years. This is very important: you can have any combination of hardware devices and cabling using different Ethernet flavors on a single Ethernet network and, in most cases, the hosts will be able to communicate just fine.

Most modern Ethernet networks employ one of three speeds: *10BaseT*, *100BaseT*, or *1000BaseT*. As the numbers in the names suggest, *10BaseT* networks run at 10 Mbps, *100BaseT* networks (called Fast Ethernet) run at 100 Mbps, and *1000BaseT* networks (called Gigabit Ethernet) run at 1000 Mbps, or 1 Gbps. All three technologies—sometimes referred to collectively as *10/100/1000BaseT* or just plain Ethernet—use a *star bus* topology (discussed in the next section) and connect via a type of cable called unshielded twisted pair (UTP).

 NOTE Ethernet developers continue to refine the technology. *Fast Ethernet* (100BaseT) is still out there on many older devices. *Gigabit Ethernet* (1000BaseT) might be the most common desktop standard now, but 10-Gigabit Ethernet is common on server-to-server connections. 40/100-Gigabit Ethernet is slowly encroaching as well.

The Ethernet Star Bus

With all Ethernet networks, every individual host connects to a central box. You attach each system to this box via cables to special ports. The box takes care of all the tedious details required by the network to get frames sent to the correct systems. This layout (*or topology*), which looks something like a star, is called a *star bus* topology (see Figure 18-8). (The *bus* refers to the internal wiring in the box. The *star* refers to the wires leading from the box to the hosts. Star bus is thus a hybrid topology.)

The central box—the *switch*—provides a common point of connection for network devices. Switches can have a wide variety of ports. Most consumer-level switches have 4 or 8 ports, but business-level switches can have 32 or more ports.

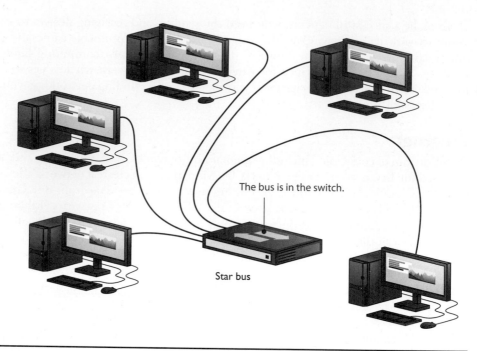

The bus is in the switch.

Star bus

Figure 18-8 Ethernet star bus

Early Ethernet networks used a *hub*. A switch is a far superior version of a hub and replaced hubs more than two decades ago. No clue why CompTIA continues to include hubs in the CompTIA A+ objectives. Figure 18-9 shows a typical consumer-level switch.

Figure 18-9
A switch

Hubs and switches look pretty much identical and they perform the same basic job: taking the signal from one host and then repeating the signal out to other hosts. Even though they look the same and do functionally the same job, they do the job differently. Basically, hubs were stupid *repeaters*: anything sent in one port automatically went out all the other connected ports. Switches are smart repeaters: they memorize the MAC addresses of all the connected devices and only send out repeated signals to the correct host. This makes switched networks much faster than hubbed networks.

A simple example demonstrates the difference between hubs and switches. Let's say you have a network of 32 machines, all using 100-Mbps NICs attached to a 100-Mbps hub or switch. We would say the network's *bandwidth* is 100 Mbps. If you put the 32 systems on a 32-port 100-Mbps hub, you would have 32 computers *sharing* the 100 Mbps of bandwidth. A switch addresses this problem by making each port its own separate network. Each system gets to use the full bandwidth. The bottom line? Once switches became affordable, hubs went away.

The connection between a computer and a switch is called a *segment*. With most cable types, Ethernet segments are limited to 100 meters or less. You cannot use a splitter to split a single segment into two or more connections with an Ethernet network that uses this star bus topology. Doing so prevents the switch from recognizing which host is sending or receiving a signal, and no hosts connected to a split segment will be able to communicate. Splitters negatively *affect signal quality.*

Cheap and centralized, Ethernet's star bus topology does not go down if a single cable breaks. True, the network would go down if the switch failed, but that is rare.

Unshielded Twisted Pair

Unshielded twisted pair (UTP) cabling is the specified cabling for 10/100/1000BaseT and is the predominant cabling system used today. Many types of twisted pair cabling are available, and the type used depends on the needs of the network. Twisted pair cabling consists of AWG 22–26 gauge wire twisted together into color-coded pairs. Each wire is individually insulated and encased as a group in a common jacket.

UTP cables come in categories that define the maximum speed at which data can be transferred (also called bandwidth). The major categories (Cats) are outlined in Table 18-1.

Cat 1	Standard telephone line.
Cat 3	Designed for 10-Mbps networks; a variant that used all four pairs of wires supported 100-Mbps speeds.
Cat 5	Designed for 100-Mbps networks.
Cat 5e	Enhanced to handle 1000-Mbps networks.
Cat 6	Supports 1000-Mbps networks at 100-meter segments; 10-Gbps networks up to 55-meter segments.
Cat 6a	Supports 10-Gbps networks at 100-meter segments.
Cat 6e	A nonstandard term used by a few manufacturers for Cat 6 or Cat 6a.
Cat 7	Supports 10-Gbps networks at 100-meter segments; shielding for individual wire pairs reduces crosstalk and noise problems. Cat 7 is *not* an ANSI/TIA standard.

Table 18-1   Cat Levels

The Cat level should be clearly marked on the cable, as Figure 18-10 shows.

The *Telecommunication Industry Association (TIA)* establishes the UTP categories, which fall under the ANSI/TIA 568 specification. The *American National Standards Institute (ANSI)* accredits TIA (and many other) standards so that they assure things

Figure 18-10
Cable markings
for Cat level

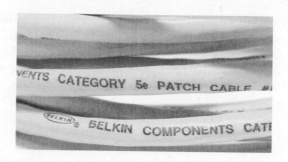

work across industry and, equally importantly, along with international standards. Currently, most installers use Cat 5e, Cat 6, or Cat 6a cable.

Shielded Twisted Pair

Shielded twisted pair (STP), as its name implies, consists of twisted pairs of wires surrounded by shielding to protect them from EMI, or electromagnetic interference. STP is pretty rare, primarily because there's so little need for STP's shielding; it only really matters in locations with excessive electronic noise, such as a shop floor area with lots of lights, electric motors, or other machinery that could cause problems for other cables.

Ethernet with Twisted Pair

The 10BaseT and 100BaseT standards require two pairs of wires: a pair for sending and a pair for receiving. 10BaseT ran on an ancient Cat version called Cat 3, but typically used at least Cat 5 cable. 100BaseT requires at least Cat 5 to run. 1000BaseT needs all four pairs of wires in Cat 5e and higher cables. These cables use a connector called an *RJ-45* connector. The *RJ (registered jack)* designation was invented by Ma Bell (the phone company, for you youngsters) years ago and is still used today.

NOTE There are Cat levels for connectors as well as cables. Don't even try to use a Cat 5e RJ-45 connector with a Cat 6 cable.

Currently only two types of RJ connectors are used for networking: RJ-11 and RJ-45 (see Figure 18-11). *RJ-11* connects your telephone to the telephone jack in the wall of your house. It supports up to two pairs of wires, though most phone lines use only one pair. The other pair is used to support a second phone line. RJ-11 connectors are primarily used for telephone-based Internet connections (see Chapter 21, "The Internet"). RJ-45 is the standard for UTP connectors. RJ-45 has connections for up to four pairs and is visibly much wider than RJ-11. Figure 18-12 shows the position of the #1 and #8 pins on an RJ-45 jack.

Figure 18-11
RJ-11 (top) and
RJ-45 (bottom)

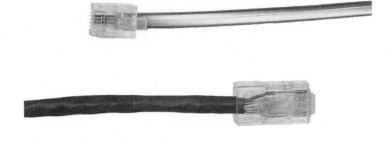

Figure 18-12
RJ-45 pin
numbers

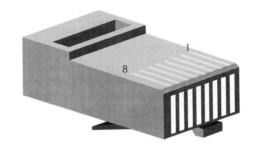

Plenum Versus PVC Cabling

Most workplace installations of network cable go up above the ceiling and then drop down through the walls to present a nice port in the wall. The space in the ceiling, under the floors, and in the walls through which cable runs is called the *plenum* space. The potential problem with this cabling running through the plenum space is that the protective sheathing for networking cables, called the jacket, is made from plastic, and if you get any plastic hot enough, it creates smoke and noxious fumes.

Standard network cables usually use *PVC (polyvinyl chloride)* for the jacket, but PVC produces noxious fumes when burned. Fumes from cables burning in the plenum space can quickly spread throughout the building, so you want to use a more fire-retardant cable in the plenum space. Plenum-grade cable is simply network cabling with a fire-retardant jacket and is required for cables that go in the plenum space. Plenum-grade cable costs about three to five times more than PVC, but you should use it whenever you install cable in a plenum space.

ANSI/TIA has two standards for connecting the RJ-45 connector to the UTP cable: *T568A* and *T568B*. Both are acceptable. You do not have to follow any standard as long as you use the same pairings on each end of the cable; however, you will make your life simpler if you choose a standard. Make sure that all of your cabling uses the same standard and you will save a great deal of work in the end. Most importantly, *keep records!*

Like all wires, the wires in UTP are numbered. A number does not appear on each wire, but rather each wire has a standardized color. Table 18-2 shows the official ANSI/TIA Standard Color Chart for UTP.

Pin	T568A	T568B	Pin	T568A	T568B
1	White/Green	White/Orange	5	White/Blue	White/Blue
2	Green	Orange	6	Orange	Green
3	White/Orange	White/Green	7	White/Brown	White/Brown
4	Blue	Blue	8	Brown	Brown

Table 18-2   UTP Cabling Color Chart

SIM   Check out the "568B Wiring" Challenge! sim for Chapter 18. It'll help you memorize the wiring standard for the CompTIA A+ 1001 exam. You find it here: http://totalsem.com/100x

Ethernet with Alternative Connections

UTP is very popular, but Ethernet, as well as other types of networks, can use alternative cabling that you need to be able to identify. Every CompTIA A+ certified tech needs to know about fiber optic cable and coaxial cable, so let's start there.

NOTE   You can hook two computers directly together using a special UTP cable called a *crossover cable*. A crossover cable is a standard UTP cable with one RJ-45 connector using the T568A standard and the other using the T568B standard. This reverses the signal between sending and receiving wires and thus does the job of a hub or switch. Crossover cables work great as a quick way to connect two computers directly for a quick and dirty network. You can purchase a crossover cable at any computer store.

Fiber Optic

Fiber optic cable is a very attractive way to transmit Ethernet network frames. First, because it uses light instead of electricity, fiber optic cable is immune to electrical problems such as lightning, short circuits, and static. Second, fiber optic signals travel much farther, 2000 meters or more (compared with 100 meters on UTP). Most fiber Ethernet networks use *62.5/125 multimode* fiber optic cable. All fiber Ethernet networks that use this type of cabling require two cables. Figure 18-13 shows three of the more common connectors used in fiber optic networks. The round connector on the left is called an *ST* connector. The square-shaped middle connecter is called an *SC* connector, and on the far right is an *LC* connector.

Figure 18-13
Typical fiber
optic cables with
ST, SC, and LC
connectors

Fiber optics are half-duplex, meaning data flows only one way—hence the need for two cables in a fiber installation. With the older ST and SC connectors, you needed two connectors on every fiber connection. Newer connectors like LC are designed to support two fiber cables in one connector, a real space saver.

Light can be sent down a fiber optic cable as regular light or as laser light. Each type of light requires totally different fiber optic cables. Most network technologies that use fiber optics use light-emitting diodes (LEDs) to send light signals. These use *multimode* fiber optic cabling. Multimode fiber transmits multiple light signals at the same time, each using a different reflection angle within the core of the cable. The multiple reflection angles tend to disperse over long distances, so multimode fiber optic cables are used for relatively short distances.

EXAM TIP   Know fiber connector types and the difference between multimode and single-mode fiber.

Network technologies that use laser light use *single-mode* fiber optic cabling. Using laser light and single-mode fiber optic cables allows for phenomenally high transfer rates over long distances. Except for long-distance links, single-mode is currently quite rare; if you see fiber optic cabling, you can be relatively sure it is multimode.

There are close to 100 different Ethernet fiber optic cabling standards, with names like 1000BaseSX and 10GBaseSR. The major difference is the speed of the network (there are also some important differences in the way systems interconnect, and so on). If you want to use fiber optic cabling, you need a fiber optic switch and fiber optic network cards.

Fiber networks follow the speed and distance limitations of their networking standard, so it's hard to pin down precise numbers on true limitations. Multimode overall is slower and has a shorter range than single-mode. A typical multimode network runs at 10, 100, or 1000 Mbps, though some can go to 10,000 Mbps. Distances for multimode runs generally top out at ~600 meters. With single-mode, speed and distance—depending on the standard—can blow multimode away. The record transmission speed way back in 2011, for example, was 100 *terabits* per second and that was over 100 *miles*!

EXAM TIP   There are a number of Ethernet standards that use fiber optic cable instead of UTP.

Coaxial

Early versions of Ethernet ran on *coaxial cable* instead of UTP. While the Ethernet standards using coax are long gone, coax lives on, primarily for cable modems and satellite connections. Coax cable consists of a center cable (core) surrounded by insulation. This in turn is covered with a *shield* of braided cable (see Figure 18-14). The center core actually carries the signal. The shield effectively eliminates outside interference. The entire cable is then surrounded by a protective insulating cover.

Figure 18-14

Typical coax

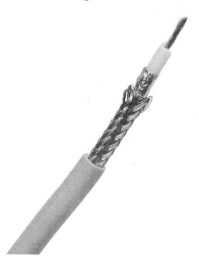

Coax cables are rated using an RG name. There are hundreds of RG ratings for coax, but the only two you need to know for the CompTIA A+ exam are *RG-59* and *RG-6*. Both standards are rated by impedance, which is measured in ohms. (*Impedance* is the effective resistance to the flow of an alternating current electrical signal through a cable.) Both RG-6 and RG-59 have a 75-ohm impedance. Both of these coax cables are used by your cable television, but RG-59 is thinner and doesn't carry data quite as far as RG-6. The RG rating is clearly marked on the cable.

NOTE   Although it's not in the objectives, expect to see more use of the next step up from RG-6, called RG6QS (quad shield) coaxial cable, over the next few years. The extra shielding reduces interference and enables stronger internal signals, useful for pushing more data through the cable. (Think multiple 4K television signals and you'll be on the money about what's driving the upgrade.)

Coax most commonly uses two different types of connectors. A *BNC* connector (see Figure 18-15) uses a quarter twist connector, and an *F-type connector* uses a screw connector. BNC is uncommon, but F-type is on the back of all cable modems and most televisions (see Figure 18-16).

Figure 18-15
BNC connector

Figure 18-16
F-type connector

NOTE BNC stands for different things, depending on who you ask. The two most common interpretations are *Bayonet Neill-Concelman* or *British Naval connector*. Just say "BNC" and network people will know what you mean.

Coaxial cable implementations can offer acceptable speeds, topping 100 Mbps in some cases. Using splitters to connect multiple hosts to a single cable, however, negatively effects signal quality, lowering the overall speed of the network.

Implementing Ethernet

Regardless of the cabling choice—UTP or fiber—Ethernet networks use a star bus topology. The illustration of a star used earlier in the chapter doesn't quite translate into real life, so let's turn briefly to look at common implementations of Ethernet.

The Typical LAN

A *local area network (LAN)* is a group of computers located physically close to each other—no more than a few hundred meters apart at most. A LAN might be in a single room, on a single floor, or in a single building. But I'm going to add that a LAN is almost always a group of computers that are able to "hear" each other when one of them sends a broadcast. A group of computers connected by one or more switches is a *broadcast domain* (see Figure 18-17), which means that all nodes receive broadcast frames from every other node.

Figure 18-17   Two broadcast domains—two separate LANs

 EXAM TIP   For the CompTIA A+ exams, remember that a LAN is a group of networked computers that are close to each other. Also, remember that a LAN is almost always a broadcast domain.

You can set up a LAN in a small office/home office (SOHO) environment in several ways. The most common way—using wireless technology called *Wi-Fi*—dispenses with wires altogether. We'll get there in detail in Chapter 20, "Wireless Networking."

Another option uses the existing electrical network in the building for connectivity. This option, called *Ethernet over Power*, requires specialized bridges that connect to power outlets. Figure 18-18 shows a typical Ethernet over Power bridge.

A *bridge* is a device that connects dissimilar network technologies that transmit the same signal. In this case the bridge connects UTP to power lines. There are many other places we see bridges: there are bridge devices to connect wireless to UTP, coax to UTP, and so forth.

Ethernet over Power has its place in the right situations and recent innovations have brought speeds up to almost matching Gigabit Ethernet. If you have a computer in a weird place where wireless won't work and traditional cables can't reach, try Ethernet over Power.

Figure 18-18
Ethernet over
Power bridge

Structured Cabling

If you want a functioning, dependable, real-world network, you need a solid understanding of a set of standards collectively called *structured cabling*. These standards, defined by the ANSI/TIA—yes, the same folks who tell you how to crimp an RJ-45 onto the end of a UTP cable—give professional cable installers detailed standards on every aspect of a cabled network, from the type of cabling to use to standards on running cable in walls, even the position of wall outlets.

The CompTIA A+ exams require you to understand the basic concepts involved in installing network cabling and to recognize the components used in a network. The CompTIA A+ exams do not, however, expect you to be as knowledgeable as a professional network designer or cable installer. Your goal should be to understand enough about real-world cabling systems to communicate knowledgeably with cable installers and to perform basic troubleshooting. Granted, by the end of this section, you'll know enough to try running your own cable (I certainly run my own cable), but consider that knowledge extra credit.

The idea of structured cabling is to create a safe, reliable cabling infrastructure for all of the devices that may need interconnection. Certainly this applies to computer networks, but also to telephone, video—anything that might need low-power, distributed cabling.

NOTE   A structured cabling system is useful for more than just computer networks. You'll find structured cabling defining telephone networks and video conferencing setups, for example.

You should understand three issues with structured cabling. We'll start with the basics of how cables connect switches and computers. You'll then look at the components of a network, such as how the cable runs through the walls and where it ends up. This section wraps up with an assessment of connections leading outside your network.

Cable Basics—A Star Is Born

Earlier in this chapter we developed the idea of an Ethernet LAN in its most basic configuration: a switch, some UTP cable, and a few computers—in other words, a typical physical star network (see Figure 18-19).

Figure 18-19
A switch connected by UTP cable to two computers

No law of physics prevents you from placing a switch in the middle of your office and running cables on the floor to all the computers in your network. This setup works, but it falls apart spectacularly when applied to a real-world environment. Three problems present themselves to the network tech. First, the exposed cables running along the floor are just waiting for someone to trip over them, giving that person a wonderful lawsuit opportunity. Simply moving and stepping on the cabling will, over time, cause a cable to fail due to wires breaking or RJ-45 connectors ripping off cable ends. Second, the presence of other electrical devices close to the cable can create interference that confuses the signals going through the wire. Third, this type of setup limits your ability to make any changes to the network. Before you can change anything, you have to figure out which cables in the huge rat's nest of cables connected to the switch go to which machines. Imagine *that* troubleshooting nightmare!

"Gosh," you're thinking (okay, I'm thinking it, but you should be, too), "there must be a better way to install a physical network." A better installation would provide safety, protecting the star from vacuum cleaners, clumsy coworkers, and electrical interference. It would have extra hardware to organize and protect the cabling. Finally, the new and improved star network installation would feature a cabling standard with the flexibility to enable the network to grow according to its needs and then to upgrade when the next great network technology comes along. That is the definition of structured cabling.

Structured Cable Network Components

Successful implementation of a basic structured cabling network requires three essential ingredients: a telecommunications room, horizontal cabling, and a work area. Let's zero in on one floor of a typical office. All the cabling runs from individual workstations to a central location, the *telecommunications room*. What equipment goes in there—a switch or a telephone system—is not the important thing. What matters is that all the cables concentrate in this one area.

All cables run horizontally (for the most part) from the telecommunications room to the workstations. This cabling is called, appropriately, *horizontal cabling*. A single piece of installed horizontal cabling is called a *run*. At the opposite end of the horizontal cabling from the telecommunications room is the work area. The *work area* is often simply an office or cubicle that potentially contains a workstation and a telephone. Figure 18-20 shows both the horizontal cabling and work areas.

Figure 18-20
Horizontal cabling and work areas

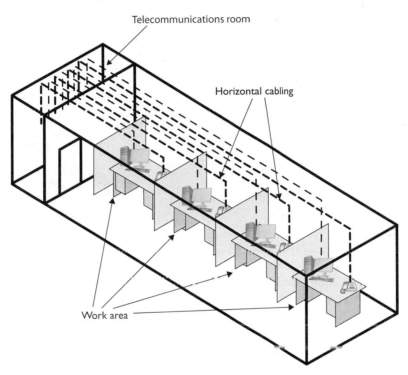

Each of the three parts of a basic star network—the telecommunications room, the horizontal cabling, and the work area(s)—must follow a series of strict standards designed to ensure that the cabling system is reliable and easy to manage. The cabling standards set by ANSI/TIA enable techs to make sensible decisions on equipment installed in the telecommunications room, so let's tackle horizontal cabling first, and then return to the telecommunications room. We'll finish up with the work area.

Horizontal Cabling A horizontal cabling run is the cabling that goes more or less horizontally from a work area to the telecommunications room. In most networks, this cable is a Cat 5e or better UTP, but when you move into structured cabling, the ANSI/TIA standards define a number of other aspects of the cable, such as the type of wires, number of pairs of wires, and fire ratings.

 EXAM TIP A single piece of cable that runs from a work area to a telecommunications room is called a *run*. In most networks, this cable is Cat 5e or better UTP.

Solid Core Versus Stranded Core   All UTP cables come in one of two types: solid core or stranded core. Each wire in *solid core* UTP uses a single solid wire. With *stranded core*, each wire is actually a bundle of tiny wire strands. Each of these cable types has its benefits and downsides. Solid core is a better conductor, but it is stiff and will break if handled too often or too roughly. Stranded core is not quite as good a conductor, but it will stand up to substantial handling without breaking. Figure 18-21 shows a close-up of solid and stranded core UTP.

Figure 18-21
Solid and
stranded core
UTP

ANSI/TIA specifies that horizontal cabling should always be solid core. Remember, this cabling is going into your walls and ceilings, safe from the harmful effects of shoes and vacuum cleaners. The ceilings and walls enable you to take advantage of the better conductivity of solid core without the risk of cable damage. Stranded cable also has an important function in a structured cabling network, but I need to discuss a few more parts of the network before I talk about where to use stranded UTP cable.

The Telecommunications Room

The telecommunications room is the heart of the basic star. This room is where all the horizontal runs from all the work areas come together. The concentration of all this gear in one place makes the telecommunications room potentially one of the messiest parts of the basic star. Even if you do a nice, neat job of organizing the cables when they are first installed, networks change over time. People move computers, new work areas are added, network topologies are added or improved, and so on. Unless you impose some type of organization, this conglomeration of equipment and cables decays into a nightmarish mess.

Fortunately, the ANSI/TIA structured cabling standards define the use of specialized components in the telecommunications room that make organizing a snap. In fact, it might be fair to say that there are too many options! To keep it simple, we're going to stay with the most common telecommunications room setup and then take a short peek at some other fairly common options.

Equipment Racks   The central component of every telecommunications room is one or more equipment racks. An *equipment rack* provides a safe, stable platform for all the different hardware components. All equipment racks are 19 inches wide, but they vary in height from two- to three-foot-high models that bolt onto a wall (see Figure 18-22) to the more popular floor-to-ceiling models (see Figure 18-23).

Figure 18-22
A short
equipment rack

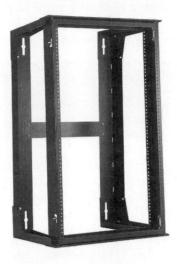

Figure 18-23
A floor-to-ceiling
rack

NOTE Equipment racks evolved out of the railroad signaling racks from the 19th century. The components in a rack today obviously differ a lot from railroad signaling, but the 19-inch width has remained the standard for well over 100 years.

You can mount almost any network hardware component into a rack. All manufacturers make rack-mounted switches that mount into a rack with a few screws. These switches are available with a wide assortment of ports and capabilities. There are even rack-mounted servers, complete with slide-out keyboards, and rack-mounted uninterruptible power supplies (UPSs) to power the equipment (see Figure 18-24).

Figure 18-24
A rack-mounted
UPS

All rack-mounted equipment uses a height measurement known simply as a *U*. A U is 1.75 inches. A device that fits in a 1.75-inch space is called a 1U; a device designed for a 3.5-inch space is a 2U; and a device that goes into a 7-inch space is called a 4U. Most rack-mounted devices are 1U, 2U, or 4U.

Patch Panels and Cables   Ideally, once you install horizontal cabling, you should never move it. As you know, UTP horizontal cabling has a solid core, making it pretty stiff. Solid core cables can handle some rearranging, but if you insert a wad of solid core cables directly into your switches, every time you move a cable to a different port on the switch, or move the switch itself, you will jostle the cable. You don't have to move a solid core cable many times before one of the solid copper wires breaks, and there goes a network connection!

Luckily for you, you can easily avoid this problem by using a patch panel. A *patch panel* is simply a box with a row of female connectors (ports) in the front and permanent connections in the back, to which you connect the horizontal cables (see Figure 18-25).

Figure 18-25
Typical patch
panels

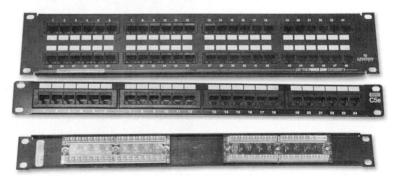

The most common type of patch panel today uses a special type of connector called a *110 block*, or sometimes a *110-punchdown block*. UTP cables connect to a 110 block using a *punchdown tool*. Figure 18-26 shows a typical punchdown tool, and Figure 18-27 shows the punchdown tool punching down individual strands.

The punchdown block has small metal-lined grooves for the individual wires. The punchdown tool has a blunt end that forces the wire into the groove. The metal in the groove slices the cladding enough to make contact.

Figure 18-26
Punchdown tool

Figure 18-27
Punching down
a 110 block

 EXAM TIP The CompTIA A+ exams expect you to know that a punchdown tool is used for securing UTP connections to a punchdown block. It's not until you go for CompTIA Network+ certification that you'll be expected to know how to use these tools.

Not only do patch panels prevent the horizontal cabling from being moved, but they are also your first line of defense in organizing the cables. All patch panels have space in the front for labels, and these labels are the network tech's best friend! Simply place a tiny label on the patch panel to identify each cable, and you will never have to experience that sinking feeling of standing in the telecommunications room of your nonfunctioning network, wondering which cable is which. If you want to be a purist, there is an official, and rather confusing, ANSI/TIA labeling methodology called ANSI/TIA 606, but a number of real-world network techs simply use their own internal codes (see Figure 18-28).

Figure 18-28
Typical patch
panels with
labels

Patch panels are available in a wide variety of configurations that include different types of ports and numbers of ports. You can get UTP, STP, or fiber ports, and some manufacturers combine several different types on the same patch panel. Panels are available with 8, 12, 24, 48, or even more ports.

UTP patch panels, like UTP cables, come with Cat ratings, which you should be sure to check. Don't blow a good Cat 6 cable installation by buying a cheap patch panel—get a Cat 6 patch panel! A higher-rated panel supports earlier standards, so you can use a Cat 6 or even Cat 6a rack with Cat 5e cabling. Most manufacturers proudly display the Cat level right on the patch panel (see Figure 18-29).

Figure 18-29
Cat level on
patch panel

Once you have installed the patch panel, you need to connect the ports to the switch through *patch cables*. Patch cables are short (typically two- to five-foot) UTP cables. Patch cables use stranded rather than solid cable, so they can tolerate much more handling. Even though you can make your own patch cables, most people buy premade ones. Buying patch cables enables you to use different-colored cables to facilitate organization (yellow for accounting, blue for sales, or whatever scheme works for you). Most prefabricated patch cables also come with a reinforced (booted) connector specially designed to handle multiple insertions and removals (see Figure 18-30).

Figure 18-30
Typical patch
cable

Rolling Your Own Patch Cables   Although most people prefer simply to purchase premade patch cables, making your own is fairly easy. To make your own, use stranded UTP cable that matches the Cat level of your horizontal cabling. Stranded cable also requires specific crimps, so don't use crimps designed for solid cable. Crimping is simple enough, although getting it right takes some practice.

Figure 18-31 shows the main tool of the crimping trade: an RJ-45 *crimper* with both a *wire stripper* and wire snips built in. Professional cable installers naturally have a wide variety of other tools as well.

Figure 18-31
Crimper with
built-in stripper
and snips

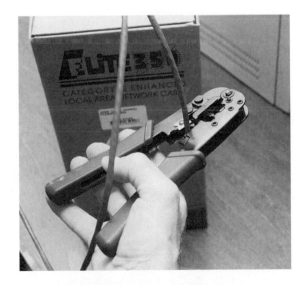

 EXAM TIP   The CompTIA A+ exams expect you to know that a cable tech uses a crimper or crimping tool to attach an RJ-45 to the end of a UTP cable.

Here are the steps for properly crimping an RJ-45 onto a UTP cable. If you have some crimps, cable, and a crimping tool handy, follow along!

1. Cut the cable square using RJ-45 crimpers or scissors.
2. Strip off one-half inch of plastic jacket from the end of the cable (see Figure 18-32).
3. Slowly and carefully insert each individual wire into the correct location according to either ANSI/TIA 568A or B (see Figure 18-33). Unravel as little as possible.
4. Insert the crimp into the crimper and press (see Figure 18-34). Don't worry about pressing too hard; the crimper has a stop to prevent you from using too much pressure.

Figure 18-35 shows a nicely crimped cable. Note how the plastic jacket goes into the crimp. (The extra strands you can see along with the wires are called *marker threads* or *ripcord*. The Kevlar strands strengthen the cable and enable installers to rip the sheath off easily.)

Figure 18-32
Properly stripped cable

Figure 18-33
Inserting the individual strands

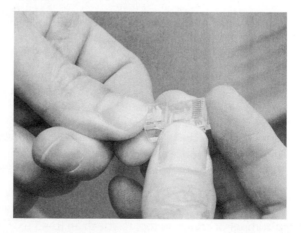

Figure 18-34
Crimping the cable

Figure 18-35
Properly crimped cable

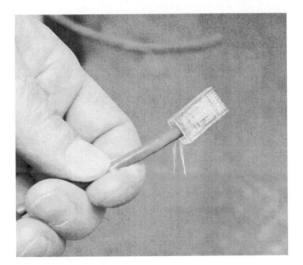

A good patch cable should include a boot. Figure 18-36 shows a boot being slid onto a newly crimped cable. Don't forget to slide each boot onto the patch cable *before* you crimp both ends!

After making a cable, you need to test it to make sure it's properly crimped. We use a handy *cable tester*, available in any good electronics store, to verify all the individual wires are properly connected and in the correct location (see Figure 18-37).

The Work Area

From a cabling standpoint, a work area is nothing more than a wall outlet that serves as the termination point for horizontal network cables: a convenient insertion point for a

Figure 18-36
Adding a boot

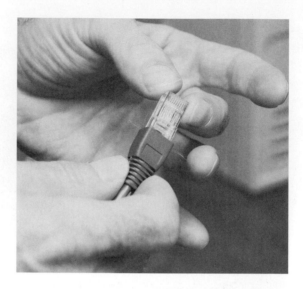

Figure 18-37
Typical tester

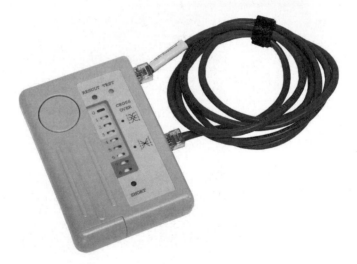

workstation and a telephone. (In practice, of course, the term "work area" includes the office or cubicle.) A wall outlet itself consists of one or two female jacks to accept the cable, a mounting bracket, and a faceplate. You connect the workstation to the wall outlet with a patch cable (see Figure 18-38).

The female RJ-45 jacks in these wall outlets also have Cat ratings. You must buy Cat-rated jacks for wall outlets to go along with the Cat rating of the cabling in your network. In fact, many network connector manufacturers use the same connectors, often 110 punchdowns, in the wall outlets that they use on the patch panels (see Figure 18-39). These modular outlets significantly increase the ease of installation.

The last step is connecting the workstation to the wall outlet. Here again, most folks use a patch cable. Its stranded cabling stands up to the abuse caused by moving equipment, not to mention the occasional kick.

Figure 18-38
Typical work area outlet

Figure 18-39
Punching down a modular jack

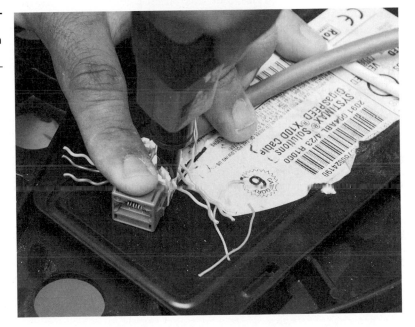

The work area may be the simplest part of the structured cabling system, but it is also the source of most network failures. When a user can't access the network and you suspect a broken cable, the first place to look is the work area.

Going Wide

A *wide area network (WAN)* is a widespread group of computers connected using long-distance technologies. You connect LANs into a WAN with a magical box called a *router* (see Figure 18-40). The best example of a WAN is the Internet.

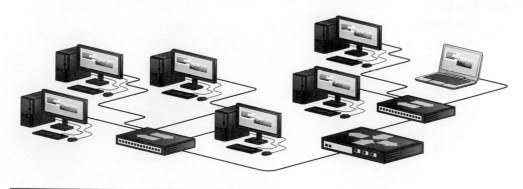

Figure 18-40 Two broadcast domains connected by a router—a WAN

You can connect multiple smaller networks into a bigger network, turning a group of LANs into one big WAN, but this raises a couple of issues with network traffic. A computer needs some form of powerful, flexible addressing to address a frame so that it goes to a computer within its own LAN or to a computer on another LAN on the same WAN. Broadcasting is also unacceptable, at least between LANs. If every computer saw every frame, the network traffic would quickly spin out of control! Plus, the addressing scheme needs to work so that routers can sort the frames and send them along to the proper LAN. This process, called *routing*, requires routers and a routing-capable protocol to function correctly.

Routers destroy any incoming broadcast frames, by design. No broadcast frame can ever go through a router. This makes broadcasting still quite common within a single broadcast domain, but never anywhere else.

To go beyond a LAN requires a network protocol—a way machines agree to communicate—that can handle routing. That protocol, for the vast majority of networks, is called TCP/IP, and Chapter 19 begins with the details. For now, review the end-of-chapter material and take some practice exams. See you in Chapter 19!

Chapter Review

Questions

1. How many bits are in a MAC address?

   A. 24

   B. 36

   C. 48

   D. 64

2. What is the minimum Cat level cable required for a 100BaseT network?

   A. Cat 1

   B. Cat 5

   C. Cat 5e

   D. Cat 6

3. Which of the following is an example of a hybrid topology?

   A. Bus

   B. Ring

   C. Star

   D. Star bus

4. A typical Cat 6 cable uses which connector?

   A. RJ-11

   B. RJ-45

   C. Plenum

   D. PVC

5. Why would you use STP over UTP cabling?

   A. Cheaper.

   B. Easier to install.

   C. Better to avoid interference.

   D. They're interchangeable terms.

6. What kind of frame gets received by all NICs in a LAN?

   A. Cat 7

   B. Broadcast

   C. WAN

   D. SC, ST, or LC

7. Microsoft Internet Explorer, Mozilla Firefox, Google Chrome, and Microsoft Edge are all examples of what?

   A. Web servers

   B. Print servers

   C. Web browsers

   D. Proxy servers

8. John's boss asks for a recommendation for connecting the company network to a small satellite building about 1 km from the main campus. The company owns the verdant land in between. Given such a scenario, what network technology implementation should John suggest?

   A. Ethernet over UTP

   B. Ethernet over STP

   C. Ethernet over multimode fiber

   D. Ethernet over single-mode fiber

9. Erin is stuck. She needs data from a friend's laptop to work on her desktop, but neither of them brought a thumb drive. She has any number of Ethernet cables at her disposal, but the last port on the switch is taken. What's her best option, given such a scenario?

   A. Connect the two computers directly using a patch cable.

   B. Connect the two computers directly using a crossover cable.

   C. Connect the two computers directly using an STP cable.

   D. Run to the store, buy a thumb drive, get back to the lab, and physically move the data.

10. Eddard hands Will a cable. Will hands it back and says, meaningfully, "That's a nice F-type connector you've got there." What kind of cable does Eddard have?

    A. Coaxial

    B. Fiber optic

    C. STP

    D. UTP

Answers

1. **C.** MAC addresses are 48-bit.

2. **B.** 100BaseT networks need Cat 5 or better UTP.

3. **D.** A star bus topology, like the one used with Ethernet networks, is a hybrid topology.

4. **B.** Cat 6 cables use an RJ-45 connector.

5. **C.** Shielded twisted pair cabling handles interference from other electronics much better than unshielded twisted pair.

6. **B.** All NICs in a LAN will receive broadcast frames.

7. **C.** All these programs are Web browsers.

8. **D.** John should suggest the only network technology implementation (listed here) that can cover those distances, Ethernet over single-mode fiber.

9. **B.** Erin should connect the computers directly using a crossover cable.

10. **A.** Eddard has a mighty fine coaxial cable in his hands.

Local Area Networking

In this chapter, you will learn how to
- Explain the basics of TCP/IP
- Install and configure wired networks
- Troubleshoot wired networks

Networks dominate the modern computing environment. A vast percentage of businesses have PCs connected in a small local network, and big businesses simply can't survive without connecting their many offices into a single bigger network.

Because networks are so common today, every good tech needs to know the basics of networking technology, operating systems, implementation, and troubleshooting. Accordingly, this chapter teaches you how to build and troubleshoot a basic network.

The first part of this chapter explores the TCP/IP protocol suite and how Windows uses it in a typical network. Every modern network uses TCP/IP for communicating among devices. You need to know this stuff.

Next, we'll go through the process of setting up a small network from start to finish. This includes details on planning a network, installing and configuring NICs, setting up switches, configuring TCP/IP—everything you need so that modern OSs can enable you to share folders, printers, libraries, and so on.

The chapter closes with troubleshooting a network. Modern operating systems come with plenty of tools to help you when the network stops functioning. I'll show you the tools and combine that with a troubleshooting process that helps you get a network up and running again.

NOTE This chapter only covers local area networks, such as a group of computers in a single office. We'll save connecting to the Internet for Chapter 21, "The Internet." But be ready! You need to understand everything in this chapter before you can take the next step and connect to the Internet.

1001/1002

TCP/IP

The *Ethernet* hardware protocol does a fine job of moving data from one machine to another, as you learned in Chapter 18, "Essentials of Networking." But Ethernet alone isn't enough to make a complete network; many other functions need to be handled. For example, an Ethernet frame holds a maximum of 1500 bytes. What if the data being moved is larger than 1500 bytes? Something has to chop up the data into chunks on one end of a connection and something else needs to reassemble those chunks on the other end so the data can be put to use.

Another issue arises if one of the machines on the network has its network card replaced. Up to this point, the only way to distinguish one machine from another was by the MAC address on the network card. To solve this, each machine must have a unique name, an identifier for the network, which is "above" the MAC address. Something needs to keep track of the MAC addresses on the network and the names of the machines so that frames and names can be correlated. If you replace a PC's network card, the network will, after some special queries, update the list to associate the name of the PC with the new network card's MAC address.

Network protocol software takes the incoming data received by the network card, keeps it organized, sends it to the application that needs it, and then takes outgoing data from the application and hands it to the NIC to be sent out over the network. All networks use some network protocol. Over the years there have been many network protocols, most combining multiple simple protocols into groups, called *protocol stacks* or *protocol suites*. This led to some crazily named network protocols, such as TCP/IP.

The *Transmission Control Protocol/Internet Protocol* (*TCP/IP*) is the primary protocol of most modern networks, including the Internet. For a computing device to access the Internet, it must have TCP/IP loaded and configured properly. Let's look at some aspects of the TCP/IP protocol suite.

Network Addressing with IPv4

Any network address must provide two pieces of information: it must uniquely identify the machine and it must locate that machine within the larger network. In a TCP/IP network, the *IP address* identifies the node and the network on which it resides. If you look at an IP address, it's not apparent which part of the address identifies the network and which part is the unique identifier of the computer.

IP Addresses

The IP address is the unique identification number for your system on the network. Most systems today rely on the *Internet Protocol version 4* (*IPv4*) addressing scheme. IPv4 addresses consist of four sets of eight binary numbers (octets), each set separated by a period. This is called *dotted-decimal notation*. So, instead of a computer being called SERVER1, it gets an address like so:

202.34.16.11

Written in binary form, the address would look like this:

11001010.00100010.00010000.00001011

To make the addresses more comprehensible to users, the TCP/IP folks decided to write the decimal equivalents:

00000000 = 0
00000001 = 1
00000010 = 2

. . .

11111111 = 255

Subnet Mask

Part of every IP address identifies the network (the *network ID*), and another part identifies the local computer (the *host ID*, or host) on the network. A NIC uses a value called the *subnet mask* to distinguish which part of the IP address identifies the network ID and which part of the address identifies the host. The subnet mask blocks out (or masks) the network portion of an IP address.

Let's look at a typical subnet mask: 255.255.255.0. When you compare the subnet mask to the IP address, any part that's all 255s is the network ID. Any part that's all zeros is the host ID. Look at the following example:

IP address: 192.168.4.33
Subnet mask: 255.255.255.0

Because the first thee octets are 255, the network ID is 192.168.4 and the host ID is 33.

Every computer on a single local area network (LAN) must have the same network ID and a unique host ID. That means every computer on the preceding network must have an IP address that starts with 192.168.4. Every computer on the network must have a unique IP address. If two computers have the same IP address, they won't be able to talk to each other, and other computers won't know where to send data. This is called an *IP conflict*.

You can never have an IP address that ends with a 0 or a 255, so for the preceding example, the LAN can have addresses starting at 192.168.4.1 and ending at 192.168.4.254: a total of 254 addresses.

Originally, subnets fell into "classes," such as A, B, or C, determined by the corresponding octet in the subnet mask. A Class C address, like the one just discussed, had a subnet mask of 255.255.255.0. A Class B address, in contrast, had a subnet mask of 255.255.0.0. The latter class left two full octets (16 bits) just for host numbers. That meant a single Class B network ID could have $2^{16} - 2$ unique host IDs = 65,534 addresses. For completeness, note that a Class A address subnet mask was 255.0.0.0.

Although it's still common to see subnet masks as one to three groups of "255," the class system is long gone. Because the subnet mask numbers are binary, you can make a subnet with any number of ones in the subnet mask.

The current system is called *Classless Inter-Domain Routing* (*CIDR*) and it works easily in binary, but a little less prettily when you show the numbers in the octets. A quick example should suffice to illustrate this point.

A subnet mask of 255.255.255.0 translates into binary as such:

11111111.11111111.11111111.00000000

With CIDR, network techs refer to the subnet mask by the number of ones it contains. The preceding subnet mask, for example, has 24 ones. Jill the tech would call this subnet a /24 (*whack twenty-four*). As you've seen already, a /24 network ID offers up to 254 host IDs.

If you want a network ID that enables more host IDs, buy one that has a subnet mask with fewer ones, like this one:

11111111.11111111.11110000.00000000

Count the ones. (There are 20.) The ones mask the network ID. That leaves 12 digits for the host IDs. Do the binary math: $2^{12} - 2 = 4094$ unique addresses in a single /20 network ID.

When you change the binary number—11110000—to an octet, you get the following:

255.255.240.0

It might look a little odd to a new tech, but that's a perfectly acceptable subnet mask. The binary behind the octets works.

From a practical standpoint, all you must know as a tech is how to set up a computer to accept an IP address and subnet mask combination that your network administrator tells you to use.

Interconnecting Networks

Figure 19-1 shows a typical LAN you might find in a home or a small office. Every device on this network has an IP address of, in this example, 192.168.4.*x*, where *x* must be a unique value between 1 and 254 (0 and 255 are reserved). Given that every IP address in this group has the same three values (192.168.4), those make up the *network ID* of 192.168.4 for the LAN. Note that every system in this LAN has a unique address, but each must start with 192.168.4. The subnet of 255.255.255.0 tells the system that the first three numbers must match (the 255s) and the last value can be any legal value (the 0).

IP addressing enables interconnecting of network IDs, making larger networks called *wide area networks* (*WANs*). Switches interconnect systems on a LAN—the switch filters and forwards by MAC address. Interconnecting LANs requires a device—a *router*—that filters and forwards by IP address. Figure 19-2 shows a typical router used in a small office.

Figure 19-1
A LAN showing
the network ID
and subnet mask

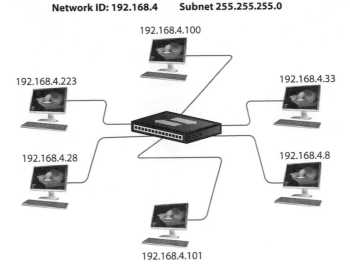

Network ID: 192.168.4   Subnet 255.255.255.0

192.168.4.100

192.168.4.223

192.168.4.33

192.168.4.28

192.168.4.8

192.168.4.101

Figure 19-2
Typical SOHO
router

A router will have at a minimum two connections to enable it to connect to two different LANs. Every LAN that connects to the Internet must have a router like the one shown in Figure 19-2. One port on the router connects to your LAN's switch and receives an IP address that's part of your network ID. The other port on the router connects to the next network, usually your Internet service provider (ISP), which in turn connects to millions of other routers and billions of other computers (see Figure 19-3). The IP address of the "LAN" side of your router (the port connected to your LAN) is the address your computer uses to send data to anything outside your network ID. This is called the *default gateway*.

Domain Name Service (DNS) Knowing that users could not remember lots of IP addresses, early Internet pioneers came up with a way to correlate those numbers with more human-friendly designations. The system they came up with is called the

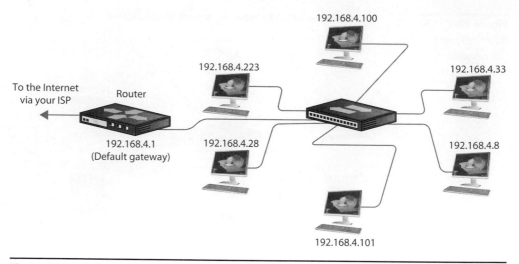

Figure 19-3 Default gateway

Domain Name Service (DNS). Special computers, called *DNS servers*, keep databases of IP addresses and their corresponding names. For example, let's say a machine with the IP address 209.34.45.163 hosts a Web site and we want it to be known as www .totalsem.com. When we set up the Web site, we would pay for a DNS server to register the DNS name www.totalsem.com to the IP address 209.34.45.163. So instead of typing "http://209.34.45.163" to access the Web page, you can type "www.totalsem.com." Your system will then query the DNS server to get www.totalsem.com's IP address and use that to find the right machine. Unless you want to type in IP addresses all the time, you'll need to use DNS servers (see Figure 19-4).

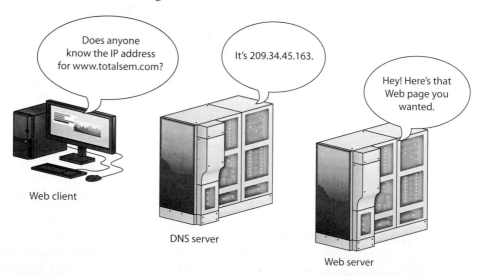

Figure 19-4 Domain name service

The Internet regulates domain names. If you want a domain name that others may access on the Internet, you must register your domain name and pay a small yearly fee. Originally, DNS names all ended with one of the following seven domain name qualifiers, called *top-level domains* (*TLDs*):

.com	General business	**.org**	Nonprofit organizations
.edu	Educational organizations	**.gov**	Government organizations
.mil	Military organizations	**.net**	Internet organizations
.int	International		

NOTE Today, Web servers host multiple Web sites using the same IP address. Accessing a single site via IP rather than name is increasingly difficult to do. For example, the address used in the previous example does not map to our Web site. Back off, hackers!

As more and more countries joined the Internet, a new level of domains was added to the original seven to indicate a DNS name from a country, such as .uk for the United Kingdom. It's common to see DNS names such as www.bbc.co.uk or www.louvre.fr. The *Internet Corporation for Assigned Names and Numbers* (*ICANN*) has added many more domains, including .name, .biz, .info, .tv, and others.

Entering the IP Information   When you're configuring a computer to connect to a network, the operating system must provide you an interface to enter the IP address, the subnet mask, the default gateway, and at least one DNS server. Let's review:

- **IP address**   Your computer's unique address on the network
- **Subnet mask**   Identifies your network ID
- **Default gateway**   IP address on the LAN side of your router
- **DNS server**   Tracks easy-to-remember DNS names for IP addresses

There are two ways to enter IP information on system: statically or dynamically. Figure 19-5 shows the IP settings dialog box. Here you can enter the information statically.

As you look at Figure 19-5, note the radio button for Obtain an IP address automatically. This is a common setting for which you don't need to enter any information. You can use this setting if your network uses *Dynamic Host Control Protocol* (*DHCP*). If you have DHCP (most networks do) and your computer is configured to obtain an IP address automatically, your computer boots up and will broadcast a DHCP request. The *DHCP server* provides your computer with all the IP information it needs to get on the network (see Figure 19-6).

You can also manually input an IP address, by the way, creating a *static IP address*. Static means it doesn't change until you or some other tech changes it manually.

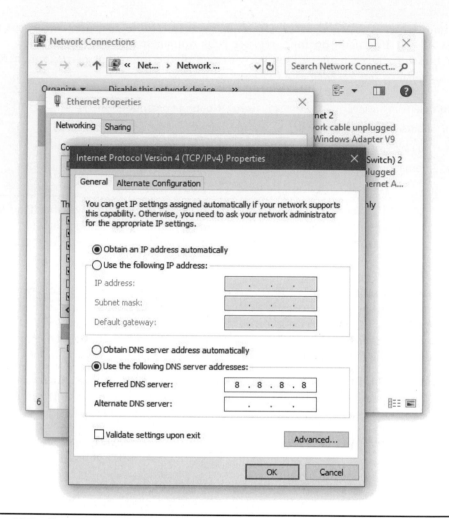

Figure 19-5   IP settings on a Windows 10 system

EXAM TIP   Network administrators set up DHCP servers to save IP addresses for specific functions, such as servers or printers. These are called *DHCP reservations*. Typically, any servers have a reserved IP address. A small network with network ID of 192.168.4.*x* will commonly reserve .1 for the default gateway and .2 through .9 for servers.

TCP/UDP

When moving data from one system to another, the TCP/IP protocol suite needs to know if the communication is connection-oriented or connectionless. When you want to be positive that the data moving between two systems gets there in good order, use a

Figure 19-6
A DHCP server
handing out an
IP address

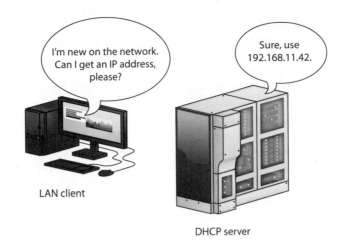

connection-oriented application. If it's not a big deal for data to miss a bit or two, then connectionless is the way to go. The connection-oriented protocol used with TCP/IP is called the *Transmission Control Protocol* (*TCP*). The connectionless one is called the *User Datagram Protocol* (*UDP*).

Let me be clear: you don't *choose* TCP or UDP. The people who developed the applications decide which protocol to use. When you fire up your Web browser, for example, you're using TCP because Web browsers use a protocol called HTTP. HTTP is built on TCP.

EXAM TIP Expect a question on the CompTIA A+ 1001 exam about TCP vs. UDP. Think connection-oriented vs. connectionless and you'll get the right answer.

Over 95 percent of all TCP/IP applications use TCP. TCP gets an application's data from one machine to another reliably and completely. As a result, TCP comes with communication rules that require both the sending and receiving machines to acknowledge the other's presence and readiness to send and receive data.

UDP is the "fire and forget" missile of the TCP/IP protocol suite. UDP doesn't possess any of the extras you see in TCP to make sure the data is received intact. UDP works best when you have a lot of data to send that doesn't need to be perfect or when the systems are so close to each other that the chances of a problem occurring are too small to bother worrying about. A few dropped frames on a Voice over IP (VoIP) call, for example, won't make much difference in the communication between two people. So there's a good reason to use UDP: it's smoking fast compared to TCP.

NOTE The CompTIA A+ exams expect you to know about other TCP/IP protocols for accomplishing Internet communications. They're all covered in Chapter 21.

TCP/IP Services

TCP/IP is a different type of protocol. Although it supports File and Printer Sharing, it adds unique sharing functions, lumped together under the umbrella term *TCP/IP services*. Most folks know the *Hypertext Transfer Protocol* (*HTTP*), the language of the World Wide Web. If you want to surf the Web, you must have TCP/IP. But TCP/IP supplies many other services beyond just HTTP. By using a service called *Secure Shell* (*SSH*), for example, you can access a remote system's terminal as though you were actually in front of that machine.

TCP/IP links any two hosts whether the two computers are on the same LAN or on some other network within the WAN. The LANs within the WAN are linked together with a variety of connections, ranging from basic dial-ups to dedicated high-speed (and expensive) data lines (see Figure 19-7). To move traffic between networks, you use routers (see Figure 19-8). Each host sends traffic to the router only when that data is destined for a remote network, cutting down on traffic across the more expensive WAN links. The host makes these decisions based on the destination IP address of each packet.

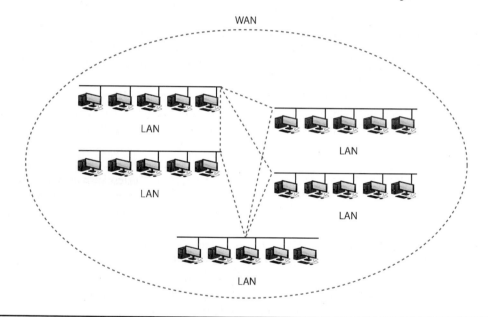

Figure 19-7   WAN concept

Figure 19-8
Typical router

TCP/IP Settings

TCP/IP has a number of unique settings that you must configure correctly to ensure proper network functionality. Unfortunately, these settings can be quite confusing, and there are several of them. Not all settings are used for every type of TCP/IP network, and it's not always obvious where you go to set them.

In Windows, you can configure network settings from the appropriate networking applet. Right-click on Network in File Explorer and select Properties, or open the Control Panel and select Network and Sharing Center. Click *Change adapter settings* on the left. In Windows 10, you can also access properties from Settings. Go to Start | Settings | Network & Internet | Status. Click *Change adapter options* under the *Change your network settings* field on the right to get to installed NICs.

The CompTIA A+ certification exams assume that someone else, such as a tech support person or some network guru, will tell you the correct TCP/IP settings for the network. You need to understand roughly what those settings do and to know where to enter them so the system works.

TCP/IP Tools

All modern operating systems come with handy tools to test and configure TCP/IP. Those you're most likely to use in the field are ping, ipconfig, ifconfig, nslookup, tracert, and traceroute. All of these programs are command-line utilities. Open a command prompt to run them.

ping The *ping* command provides a really great way to see if you can talk to another system. Here's how it works. Get to a command prompt or terminal and type **ping** followed by an IP address or by a DNS name, such as **ping www.totalsem.com**. Press the ENTER key and away it goes! Figure 19-9 shows the common syntax for ping.

The ping command has a few useful options beyond the basics. The first option to try in Windows is the –t switch. If you use the –t switch, ping continuously sends ping packets until you stop it with the break command (CTRL-C). That's the default behavior for ping in macOS and Linux; you press CTRL-C again to make it stop. The second option in Windows is the –l switch, which enables you to specify how big a ping packet to send. This helps in diagnosing specific problems with the routers between your computer and the computer you ping.

ipconfig/ifconfig Windows offers the command-line tool *ipconfig* for a quick glance at your network settings. From a command prompt, type **ipconfig/ all** to see all of your TCP/IP settings (see Figure 19-10). The *ifconfig* command in macOS and Linux provides the same level of detail with no switches applied.

When you have a static IP address, ipconfig does little beyond reporting your current IP settings, including your IP address, subnet mask, default gateway, DNS servers, and WINS servers. When using DHCP, however, ipconfig is also the primary tool for releasing and renewing your IP address. Just type **ipconfig /renew** to get a new IP address or **ipconfig /release** to give up the IP address you currently have.

```
Command Prompt                                             —    □    ✕

C:\Users\scott>ping /?

Usage: ping [-t] [-a] [-n count] [-l size] [-f] [-i TTL] [-v TOS]
            [-r count] [-s count] [[-j host-list] | [-k host-list]]
            [-w timeout] [-R] [-S srcaddr] [-c compartment] [-p]
            [-4] [-6] target_name

Options:
    -t             Ping the specified host until stopped.
                   To see statistics and continue - type Control-Break;
                   To stop - type Control-C.
    -a             Resolve addresses to hostnames.
    -n count       Number of echo requests to send.
    -l size        Send buffer size.
    -f             Set Don't Fragment flag in packet (IPv4-only).
    -i TTL         Time To Live.
    -v TOS         Type Of Service (IPv4-only. This setting has been deprecated
                   and has no effect on the type of service field in the IP
                   Header).
    -r count       Record route for count hops (IPv4-only).
    -s count       Timestamp for count hops (IPv4-only).
    -j host-list   Loose source route along host-list (IPv4-only).
    -k host-list   Strict source route along host-list (IPv4-only).
    -w timeout     Timeout in milliseconds to wait for each reply.
    -R             Use routing header to test reverse route also (IPv6-only).
                   Per RFC 5095 the use of this routing header has been
                   deprecated. Some systems may drop echo requests if
                   this header is used.
    -S srcaddr     Source address to use.
    -c compartment Routing compartment identifier.
    -p             Ping a Hyper-V Network Virtualization provider address.
    -4             Force using IPv4.
    -6             Force using IPv6.

C:\Users\scott>_
```

Figure 19-9   The ping command's syntax

nslookup   The *nslookup* command is a powerful command-line program that enables you to determine exactly what information the DNS server is giving you about a specific host name. Every modern OS makes nslookup available when you install TCP/IP. To run the program, type **nslookup** from the command prompt and press the ENTER key (see Figure 19-11). Note that this gives you a little information and that the prompt has changed. That's because you're running the application. Type **exit** and press ENTER to return to the command prompt.

NOTE   You can do some cool stuff with nslookup, and consequently some techs absolutely love the tool. Type **help** at the nslookup prompt and press ENTER to see a list of common commands and syntax.

Figure 19-10 An ipconfig/ all command in Windows 10

tracert/traceroute The *tracert* (Windows) and *traceroute* (macOS, Linux) utilities show the route that a packet takes to get to its destination. From a command line, type **tracert** or **traceroute** followed by a space and an IP address or URL. The output describes the route from your machine to the destination machine, including all devices the packet passes through and how long each hop between devices takes (see Figure 19-12).

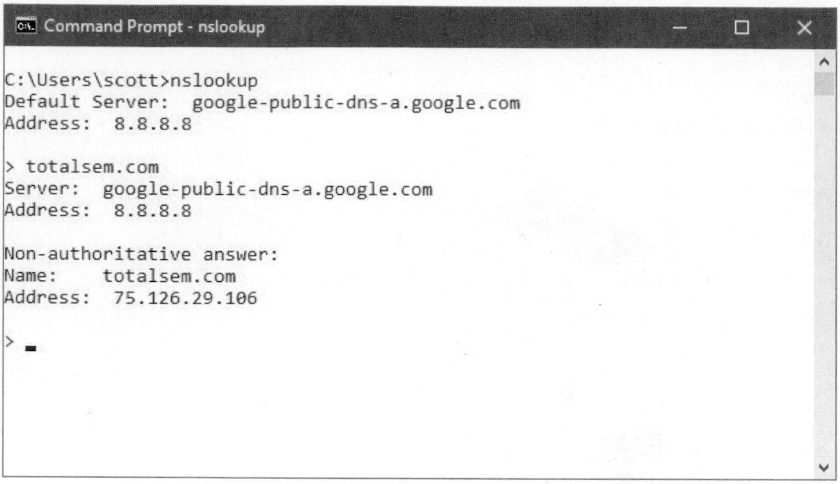

Figure 19-11 The nslookup command in action

The tracert/traceroute command can come in handy when you have to troubleshoot bottlenecks. When users complain of difficulty reaching a particular destination by using TCP/IP, you can run this utility to determine whether the problem exists on a machine or connection over which you have control, or if it is a problem on another machine or router. Similarly, if a destination is completely unreachable, tracert/traceroute can again determine whether the problem is on a machine or router over which you have control.

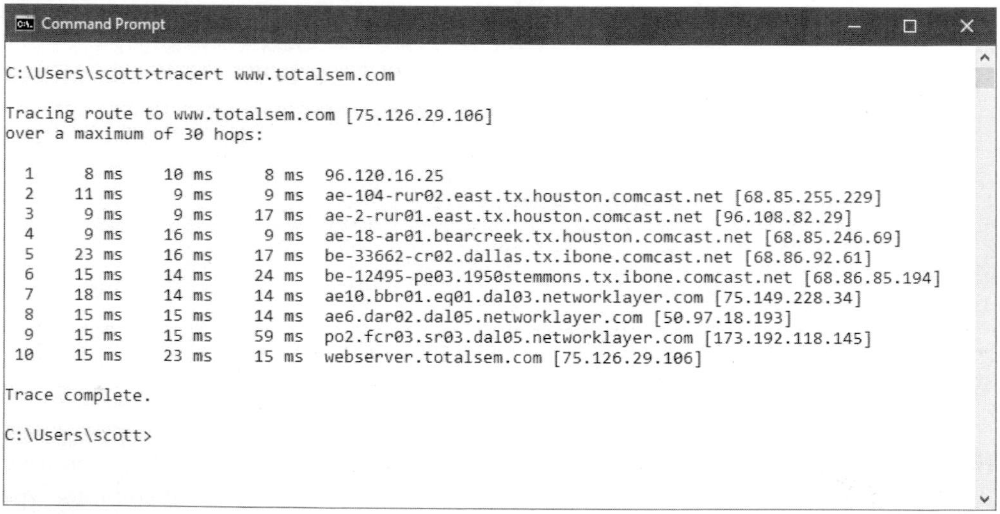

Figure 19-12 The tracert command in action

Try This!   Running tracert/traceroute

Ever wonder why your e-mail takes *years* to get to some people but arrives instantly for others? Or why some Web sites are slower to load than others? Part of the blame could lie with how many hops away your connection is from the target server. You can use tracert/traceroute to run a quick check of how many hops it takes to get to somewhere on a network, so try this!

1. Run tracert or traceroute on some known source, such as www.microsoft.com or www.totalsem.com. How many hops did it take? Did your tracert/traceroute time out or make it all the way to the server?

2. Try a tracert/traceroute to a local address. If you're in a university town, run a tracert or traceroute on the campus Web site, such as www.rice.edu for folks in Houston, or www.ucla.edu for those of you in Los Angeles. Did you get fewer hops with a local site?

Configuring TCP/IP

By default, TCP/IP is configured to receive an IP address automatically from a DHCP server on the network (and automatically assign a corresponding subnet mask). As far as the CompTIA A+ certification exams are concerned, Network+ techs and administrators give you the IP address, subnet mask, and default gateway information and you plug them into the PC. Occasionally, you might need to configure an *alternative IP address in Windows*, either for the computer or for something upstream, like the DNS server. Here's how to do it manually:

1. In Windows, open the Control Panel and go to the Network and Sharing Center applet. Click Change adapter settings. After that, double-click the Local Area Network icon.

2. Click the Properties button, highlight Internet Protocol Version 4 (TCP/IPv4), and click the Properties button.

3. In the Properties dialog box (see Figure 19-13), click the radio button next to Use the following IP address.

4. Enter the IP address in the appropriate fields.

5. Press the TAB key to skip down to the Subnet mask field. Note that the subnet mask is entered automatically, although you can type over this if you want to enter a different subnet mask.

6. Optionally, enter the IP address for a default gateway.

7. Optionally, enter the IP addresses of a Preferred DNS server and an Alternate DNS server. (The configuration in Figure 19-13 uses the Google DNS servers.)

8. Click the OK button to close the Properties dialog box.

9. Click the Close button to exit the Local Area Connection Status dialog box.

Figure 19-13

Setting up IP

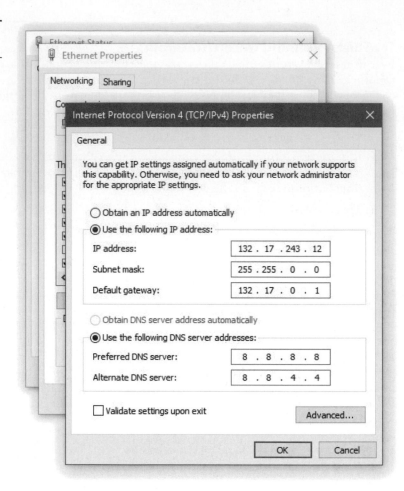

Automatic Private IP Addressing

Modern operating systems support a feature called *Automatic Private IP Addressing* (*APIPA*) in Windows or *zeroconf* in other operating systems that automatically assigns an IP address to the system when the client cannot obtain an IP address automatically. The Internet Assigned Numbers Authority (IANA), the nonprofit corporation responsible for assigning IP addresses and managing root servers, has set aside the range of addresses from 169.254.0.1 to 169.254.255.254 for this purpose.

If the computer system cannot contact a DHCP server, the computer randomly chooses an address in the form of 169.254.*x.y* (where *x.y* is the computer's identifier) and a 16-bit subnet mask (255.255.0.0) and broadcasts it on the network segment (subnet). If no other computer responds to the address, the system assigns this address to itself. When using APIPA/zeroconf, the system can communicate only with other computers on the same subnet that also use the 169.254.*x.y* range with a 16-bit mask. APIPA/zeroconf is enabled by default if your system is configured to obtain an IP address automatically.

NOTE A computer system on a network with an active DHCP server that has an IP address in this range usually indicates a problem connecting to the DHCP server.

Network Addressing with IPv6

When the early developers of the Internet set out to create an addressing or naming scheme for devices on the Internet, they faced several issues. Of course, they needed to determine how the numbers or names worked, and for that they developed the Internet Protocol and IP addresses. But beyond that, they had to determine how many computers might exist in the future, and then make the IP address space even bigger to give Internet naming longevity. But how many computers would exist in the future?

The 32-bit IPv4 standard offers only 4 billion addresses. That was plenty in the beginning, but seemed insufficient once the Internet went global.

The Internet Engineering Task Force (IETF) developed an IP addressing scheme called *Internet Protocol version 6* (*IPv6*) that is slowly replacing IPv4. IPv6 extends the 32-bit IP address space to 128 bits, allowing up to 2^{128} addresses! That should hold us for the foreseeable future! This number—close to 3.4×10^{38} addresses—is something like all the grains of sand on Earth or 1/8 of all the molecules in the atmosphere.

NOTE If you really want to know how many IP addresses IPv6 provides, here's your number: 340,282,366,920,938,463,463,374,607,431,768,211,456. Say that three times fast!

Although they achieve the same function—enabling computers on IP networks to send packets to each other—IPv6 and IPv4 differ a lot when it comes to implementation. This section provides you with a quick overview to get you up to speed with IPv6 and show you how it differs from IPv4.

IPv6 Address Notation

The familiar 32-bit IPv4 addresses are written as 197.169.94.82, using four octets. The 128-bit IPv6 addresses are written like this:

```
2001:0000:0000:3210:0800:200c:00cf:1234
```

IPv6 uses a colon as a separator, instead of the period used in IPv4's dotted-decimal format. Each group is a hexadecimal number between 0000 and ffff called, unofficially, a *field* or *hextet*.

EXAM TIP You'll see the hexadecimal letters in IPv6 written both uppercase and lowercase. It doesn't matter to the computer, but the people behind IPv6 insist (per RFC 5952) that notation should be lowercase. That's the convention used here. You might see the letters uppercase on the CompTIA Network+ exam. It's all the same, so don't get thrown off!

NOTE For those who don't play with hex regularly, one hexadecimal character (for example, F/f) represents 4 bits, so four hexadecimal characters make a 16-bit group. For some reason, the IPv6 developers didn't provide a name for the "group of four hexadecimal characters," so many techs and writers have taken to calling them fields or "hextets" to distinguish them from IPv4 "octets."

A complete IPv6 address always has eight groups of four hexadecimal characters. If this sounds like you're going to type in really long IP addresses, don't worry, IPv6 offers a number of ways to shorten the address in written form.

EXAM TIP IPv4 addresses use 32 bits, and IPv6 addresses use 128 bits. Be sure you can identify their address length differences and address conventions.

First, leading zeros can be dropped from any group, so 00cf becomes cf and 0000 becomes 0. Let's rewrite the previous IPv6 address using this shortening method:

```
2001:0:0:3210:800:200c:cf:1234
```

Second, you can remove one or more consecutive groups of all zeros, leaving the two colons together. For example, using the :: rule, you can write the previous IPv6 address as

```
2001::3210:800:200c:cf:1234
```

You can remove any number of consecutive groups of zeros to leave a double colon, but you can only use this trick *once* in an IPv6 address.

Take a look at this IPv6 address:

```
fe80:0000:0000:0000:00cf:0000:ba98:1234
```

Using the double-colon rule, you can reduce four groups of zeros; three of them follow the fedc and the fourth comes after 00cf. Because of the "only use once" stipulation, the best and shortest option is to convert the address to this:

```
fe80::cf:0:ba98:1234
```

You may not use a second :: to represent the fourth groups of zeros—only one :: is allowed per address! This rule exists for a good reason. If more than one :: was used, how could you tell how many groups of zeros were in each group? Answer: you couldn't.

Here's an example of a very special IPv6 address that takes full advantage of the double-colon rule, the IPv6 loopback address:

```
::1
```

Without using the double-colon nomenclature, this IPv6 address would look like this:

```
0000:0000:0000:0000:0000:0000:0000:0001
```

NOTE The unspecified address (all zeros) can never be used, and neither can an address that contains all ones (in binary) or all *f*s (in hex notation).

IPv6 uses the *"/x" prefix length* naming convention, similar to the CIDR naming convention in IPv4. Here's how to write an IP address and prefix length for a typical IPv6 host:

```
fe80::cf:0:ba98:1234/64
```

SIM Check out the excellent "IPv6 Address" Type! simulation in the Chapter 19 section of http://totalsem.com/100x. It's good for reinforcing your knowledge of IPv6 and getting practice with performance-based questions.

Where Do IPv6 Addresses Come From?

With IPv4, IP addresses come from one of two places: either you type in the IP address yourself (*static IP addressing*) or you use DHCP (also called *dynamic IP addressing*). With IPv6, addressing works very differently. Instead of one IP address, you will have multiple IPv6 addresses on a single network card.

When a computer running IPv6 first boots up, it gives itself a *link-local address*, IPv6's equivalent to IPv4's APIPA/zeroconf address. Although an APIPA/zeroconf address can indicate a loss of network connectivity or a problem with the DHCP server, computers running IPv6 always have a link-local address. The first 64 bits of a link-local address are always fe80::. That means every address always begins with fe80:0000:0000:0000. If your operating system supports IPv6 and IPv6 is enabled, you can see this address. Figure 19-14 shows the link-local address for a typical system running the ipconfig utility.

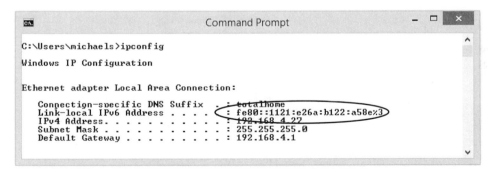

Figure 19-14   Link-local address in ipconfig

The second 64 bits of a link-local address, the *interface ID*, are generated in two ways. Every current operating system generates a 64-bit random number. Very old operating systems, such as Windows XP and Windows Server 2003, used the device's MAC address to create a 64-bit number called an *Extended Unique Identifier, 64-bit* (*EUI-64*).

The link-local address does all the hard work in IPv6, and, as long as you don't need an Internet connection, it's all you need. The old concepts of static and DHCP addressing don't really make much sense in IPv6 unless you have dedicated servers (even in IPv6, servers generally still have static IP addresses). Link-local addressing takes care of all your local network needs.

IPv6 Prefix Lengths

Systems use IPv6 *prefix lengths* to determine whether to send packets to a local MAC address or to the default gateway to send the packets out to the Internet. But you need to focus on two rules:

- The last 64 bits of an IPv6 address are generated by the NIC, leaving a maximum of 64 bits for the prefix. Therefore, no prefix is ever longer than /64.
- The five Regional Internet Registries (RIRs) pass out /48 prefixes to big ISPs and end users who need large allotments. ISPs and others will borrow another 16 bits for subnetting and then pass out /64 interface IDs to end users. Link-local addressing uses a prefix length of /64. Other types of IPv6 addresses get the subnet information automatically from their routers.

Global Unicast Addresses

To get on the Internet, a system needs a second IPv6 address called a *global unicast address*, often referred to as a "global address." The most common way to get a global address is to request it from the default gateway router, which must be configured to pass out global IPv6 addresses. When you plug a computer into a network, it sends out a very special packet called a *router solicitation* (*RS*) message, looking for a router (see Figure 19-15). The router hears this message and responds with a *router advertisement* (*RA*). This RA tells the computer its network ID and subnet (together called the *prefix*) and DNS server (if configured).

Figure 19-15
Getting a global
unicast address

NOTE A router solicitation message uses the address ff02::2. This address is read only by other computers running IPv6 in the network. This type of address is different from a broadcast address and is called a *multicast address*. In IPv6, there is no broadcast, only multicast!

Once the computer gets a prefix, it generates the rest of the address just like with the link-local address. The computer ends up with a legitimate, 128-bit public IPv6 address as well as a link-local address. Figure 19-16 shows the IPv6 information in macOS.

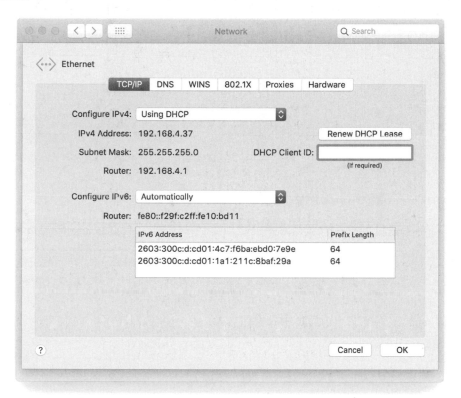

Figure 19-16 macOS system with a global IPv6 address

A global address is a true Internet address. If another computer is running IPv6 and also has a global address, it can access your system unless you have some form of firewall.

 EXAM TIP Computers using IPv6 need a global unicast address to access the Internet.

The addition of IPv6 makes programs such as ipconfig complex. Look at Figure 19-17, ipconfig information from a Windows 8.1 computer

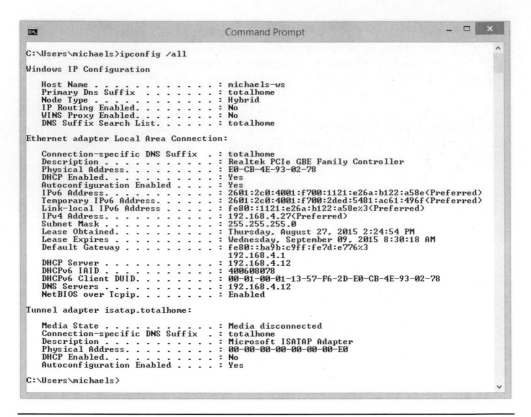

Figure 19-17 The ipconfig command with IPv6 and IPv4

Installing and Configuring a Wired Network

To have network connectivity, you need to have three things in place:

- **Connected NIC**   The physical hardware that connects the computer system to the network media.

- **Properly configured IP addressing**   Your device needs correct IP addressing for your network, either via DHCP or static.

- **Switch**   Everything connects to a switch in a wired network.

If you want to share resources on your PC with other network users, you also need to enable Microsoft's File and Printer Sharing. When you install a NIC, by default Windows installs upon setup the TCP/IP protocol, the Client for Microsoft Networks, and File and Printer Sharing for Microsoft Networks. macOS computers come fully set up for networking. Different Linux distros offer setup options similar to the Windows options.

Installing a NIC

The NIC is your computer system's link to the network, and installing one is the first step required to connect to a network. This used to be a big deal and might show up as such in a CompTIA A+ scenario question, but every modern desktop computer has a built-in Gigabit NIC. Windows will automatically install a driver for the NIC at installation.

Full-Duplex and Half-Duplex

All modern NICs run in *full-duplex* mode, meaning they can send and receive data at the same time. The vast majority of NICs and switches use a feature called *autosensing* to accommodate very old devices that might attach to the network and need to run in half-duplex mode. *Half-duplex* means that the device can send and receive, but not at the same time. If you need to adjust the duplex or the *speed* of the NIC manually, you can do so in the NIC's properties. Open the Network and Sharing Center in Control Panel and select *Change adapter settings*. In Network Connections, right-click on the NIC you want to change and select Properties. Click Configure to get to the NIC. Click the Advanced tab and scroll down in the Property section until you find Speed & Duplex. Adjust the Value on the right to match whatever ancient device is giving you problems (Figure 19-18).

Figure 19-18
Adjusting the Speed & Duplex settings of a NIC in Windows

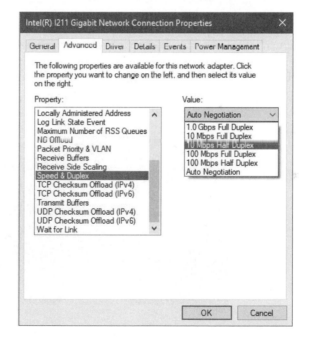

Link Lights

Network interfaces have some type of light-emitting diode (LED) *status indicator* that gives information about the state of the NIC's link to whatever is on the other end of the connection. Even though you know the lights are actually LEDs, get used to calling them *link lights*, because that's the term all network techs use. NICs can have between one and four different link lights, and the LEDs can be any color. These lights give you clues about what's happening with the link and are one of the first items to check whenever you think a system is disconnected from the network (see Figure 19-19).

Figure 19-19
Mmmm, pretty
lights!

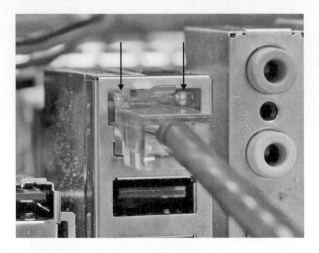

Switches also have link lights, enabling you to check the connectivity at both ends of the cable. If a PC can't access a network, always check the link lights first. Multispeed devices usually have a link light that tells you the speed of the connection. In Figure 19-20, the light for port 2 on the top photo is orange, for example, signifying that the other end of the cable is plugged into either a 10BaseT or 100BaseT NIC. The same port connected to a Gigabit NIC—that's the lower picture—displays a green LED.

Figure 19-20
Multispeed lights

A properly functioning link light is steady on when the NIC is connected to another device. No flickering, no on and off, just on. A link light that is off or flickering shows a connection problem.

Another light is the *activity light*. This little guy turns on when the card detects network traffic, so it makes an intermittent flickering when operating properly. The activity light is a lifesaver for detecting problems, because in the real world, the connection light sometimes lies to you. If the connection light says the connection is good, the next step is to try to copy a file or do something else to create network traffic. If the activity light does not flicker, you have a problem.

No standard governs how NIC manufacturers use their lights; as a result, LEDs in NICs come in an amazing array of colors and layouts. When you encounter a NIC, take a moment to try to figure out what each LED means. Although different NICs have different ways of arranging and using their LEDs, the functions are always the same: link, activity, and speed.

EXAM TIP Though no real standard exists for NIC LEDs, the CompTIA A+ exams will test you on some more-or-less *de facto* LED meanings. You should know that a solid green light means connectivity, a flashing green light means intermittent connectivity, no green light means no connectivity, and a flashing amber light means there are collisions on the network (which is sometimes okay). Also, know that the first things you should check when having connectivity issues are the NIC's LEDs.

Wake-on-LAN

A popular feature of most NICs is the ability to turn on or wake up a powered-down or sleeping PC. You'll learn more about power management in Chapter 23, "Portable Computing," but for now, know that *Wake-on-LAN* is handy when you want to wake up one or multiple computers that you aren't physically near. To wake up a PC with Wake-on-LAN, you'll need to use a second PC to send either a special pattern or a *magic packet* (a broadcast packet that essentially repeats the destination MAC address many times).

A powered-down or sleeping PC knows to look for this special pattern or packet, at least after configured to do so. Go to the Control Panel and open Network and Sharing Center. Click *Manage network connections* or *Change adapter settings* on the left. For all versions of Windows, right-click on the adapter and select Properties. Click the Configure button in the Properties dialog box and then select the Power Management tab (see Figure 19-21). To enable Wake-on-LAN, make sure the checkbox next to *Allow this device to wake the computer* is checked. Optionally, you can select *Only allow a magic packet to wake the computer*, which will instruct the NIC to ignore everything but magic packets.

Wake-on-LAN is very convenient, but it has one nasty downside. As noted in the Properties dialog box, Wake-on-LAN can wake up or turn on laptops using wireless connections, even when they aren't plugged in or are inside a carrying case. Don't let your laptop overheat or drain its battery—unless you know that you'll need it, turn off Wake-on-LAN on your laptop.

QoS

Quality of service (QoS) enables busy networks to prioritize traffic. While we'll look at QoS from the router's perspective in Chapter 21, individual systems play an important role in the QoS process by tagging their frames, enabling networking hardware to treat them according to rules defined by network administrators. Support for QoS tagging

Figure 19-21
Wake-on-LAN
settings on
the Power
Management tab

(or priority) should be enabled by default on most network adapters—but if you need to modify this setting, you can find the Packet Priority & VLAN option on the Advanced tab of your NIC's Properties dialog box (see Figure 19-22). (Windows 7 just calls the option Priority & VLAN.)

NOTE Your BIOS might also have settings for controlling Wake-on-LAN functions. Check your CMOS System Configuration tool to find out.

Configuring IP Addressing

This one's easy. All operating systems by default will be set for DHCP and acquire IP addressing settings automatically. This is true for both IPv4 and IPv6 configuration options. On the off-chance scenario where you need to configure a client to use a static IP address, you can readily do so.

Connecting to a Switch

Every wired computer connects to a switch, enabling communication with other computers on the network. Networks feature two types of switches, unmanaged and managed. An *unmanaged switch* is a smart, automatic device. Plug devices into it and they will communicate via MAC addresses with no configuration needed by techs. An unmanaged switch doesn't do much more than connecting devices.

Figure 19-22
Network adapter
Packet Priority &
VLAN setting

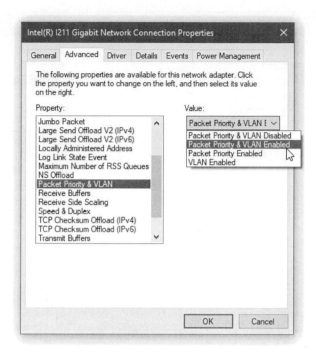

A *managed switch* offers a lot of extra features that modern networks use to provide added security and efficiency. Managed switches have an IP address that you can use to configure the options. Figure 19-23 shows a managed switch interface. Dealing with managed switches falls into the realm of CompTIA Network+ and CompTIA Security+ techs, but if you run into a scenario where you need to access such a switch, know that you'll access them via IP address and some network app.

NOTE I'm glossing over the complexity involved with managed switches. Some switches have a simple IP-based interface like the one pictured here. Others are managed via software over a network. There's a ton of variety out there.

Let me give you one great example of the power of managed switches: VLANs. You can use special managed switches to break up or *segment* a single physical network into two or more distinct networks. Each *virtual local area network* (*VLAN*) you create can talk with other computers within the same VLAN, but not to computers on another VLAN. Here's the cool part. You can have a single switch with, say, 24 computers connected. Normally, all 24 would be on the same network, right? But with a VLAN-capable switch, you can access the management console and assign physical ports to different VLANs. You could assign ports 1 through 12 to VLAN100 and ports 13 through 24 to VLAN200.

Figure 19-23   Managed switch interface

Computers connected to ports 12 and 13 wouldn't even know the other computer was there. I'll save the big discussion of VLANs and cool things you can do with managed switches for the CompTIA Network+ book in your near future.

Sharing and Security

Windows systems can share all kinds of *resources* across your network: files, folders, entire drives, printers, faxes, Internet connections, and much more. Conveniently for you, the scope of the CompTIA A+ certification exams is limited to sharing a system's files and folders, printers, multifunction devices, and Internet connections. You'll see how to share folders and printers now; multifunction devices are discussed in Chapter 26, "Printers and Multifunction Devices," and Internet connection sharing is discussed in Chapter 21.

Network Shares

When you share over a network, every OS uses specific network sharing permissions to allow, restrict access, or deny access to shared resources. These permissions do not have anything to do with file- or folder-level permissions like you find in Windows with NTFS (covered in Chapter 13, "Users, Groups, and Permissions"). But file- and folder-level permissions definitely affect share permissions. Here's the scoop.

On a non-NTFS volume like an optical media disc or a flash-media USB drive, you have three levels of permission when using the default Sharing Wizard: Read, Read/Write, and Owner, which are discussed later in this chapter. With Advanced Sharing, the three permission levels are called Read, Change, and Full Control.

If you share a folder on an NTFS drive, as you normally do these days, you must set *both* the network permissions and the NTFS permissions to let others access your shared resources. You use the network share to share the resource, but use NTFS to say what folks can do with that resource.

Some good news: This is no big deal! Just set the network permissions to give everyone Full Control, and then use the NTFS permissions to exercise more precise control over *who* accesses the shared resources and *how* they access them. Open the Security tab to set the NTFS permissions. We'll get into the details a little more in the "Network Organization" section, discussed next.

 EXAM TIP You need to understand the difference between share permissions and NTFS permissions. Share permissions only apply to network sharing. NTFS permissions affect both network and local access to shared resources.

Network Organization

Once a network is created, users need to be able to share resources in some organized fashion. Operating systems need a way to determine which users can access resources such as folders and printers and how those resources can be used. Microsoft designed Windows networks to work in one of three categories: workgroups, domains, or homegroups. (These are the Microsoft terms, but the concepts have been adopted by the entire computer industry and apply to macOS and other operating systems.) These three organizations differ in control, number of machines needed, compatibility, and security.

Let's start with the oldest and most common network organization: workgroups.

Workgroups

Workgroups are the most basic and simplistic of the three network organizations. They are also the default for almost every fresh installation of Windows.

By default, all computers on the network are assigned to a workgroup called WORKGROUP. You can see your workgroup name by opening the System applet in Control Panel, as shown in Figure 19-24.

There's nothing special about the name WORKGROUP, except that every computer on the network needs the same workgroup name to be able to share resources. If you want

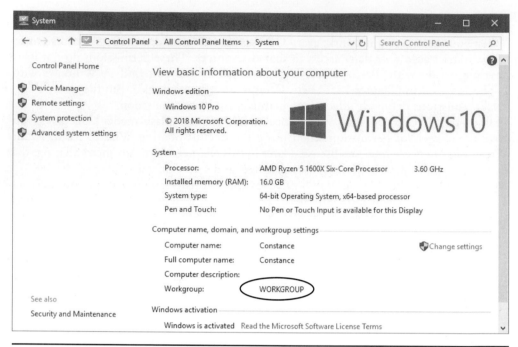

Figure 19-24 Default workgroup

to change your workgroup name, you need to use the System applet. In the *Computer name, domain, and workgroup settings* section on the right, click the Change settings link to open the System Properties dialog box. Then click the Change button to change your workgroup name (see Figure 19-25).

 NOTE If you change the workgroup name for one system, you need to change it for all other devices you want connected to that workgroup.

In macOS, you can change the workgroup name in System Preferences | Network. Click the Advanced button and then click WINS.

 NOTE Linux distros require a lot more manual configuration of both Windows machines and Linux machines to get them to play nicely on a Windows workgroup. A quick Internet search will show many step-by-step instructions for those of you interested.

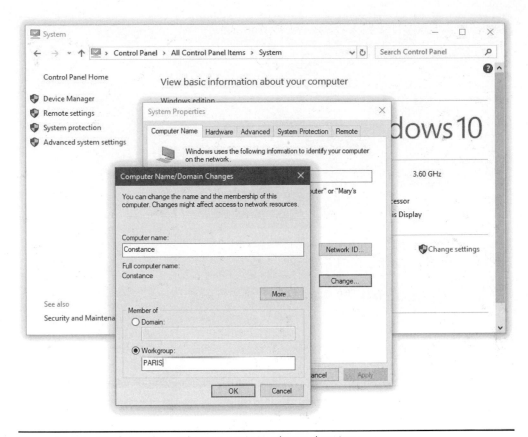

Figure 19-25 Changing the workgroup name in advanced settings

Workgroups lack centralized control over the network; all systems connected to the network are equals. This works well for smaller networks because there are fewer users, connections, and security concerns to think about. But what do you do when your network encompasses dozens or hundreds of users and systems? How can you control all of that?

User Names and Passwords   As you'll recall from Chapter 13, when you log on to a Windows computer, you need to enter a user name and password. Windows makes this easy by giving you a pretty logon interface, as shown in Figure 19-26. Entering a user name is *identification*; putting in a password that matches that user name in the OS provides *authentication*, the process that enables a system to give a user access to system resources.

NOTE   The distinction between identification and authentication is not important for the CompTIA A+ exams, though it becomes important for Network+ and Security+. Good to learn it now!

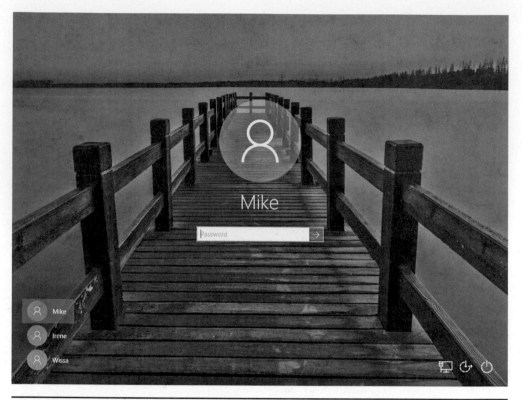

Figure 19-26 Windows logon screen

The user names and their passwords are stored in an encrypted format on your computer. User names have a number of jobs on your computer, but at this point the job most interesting to us is to give a user access to the computer. User names work well when you access your own computer, but these same user names and passwords are used to access shared resources on other computers in the network—and that's where we run into trouble. Let's watch a typical folder share take place on a network of Windows systems.

Sharing Folders with the Sharing Wizard

All personal computers can share folders and printers out of the box. Sharing a folder in Windows is easy, for example, because the Sharing Wizard is enabled by default. Just right-click on the folder and select Share with | Specific people (in Windows 7) or Give access to | Specific people (Windows 8/8.1/10) to get to the *Choose people to share with* dialog box (see Figure 19-27).

By default, you'll see every user account that's currently on this system. You may give an account Read or Read/Write permission, while the person who created the folder is assigned as Owner. The following list describes these permissions:

- **Read** You can see what's in the folder. You may open files in the folder, but you can't save anything back into the folder.

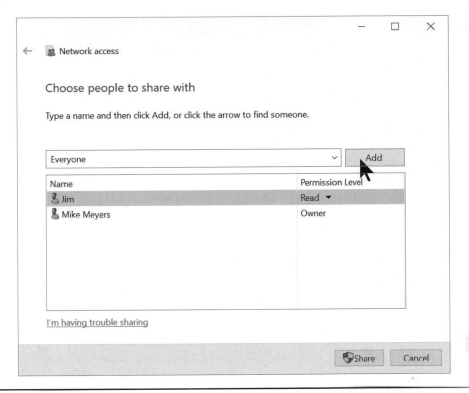

Figure 19-27 Folder sharing in Windows 10

- **Read/Write** Same as Read but you can save files into the folder.
- **Owner** Same as Read/Write plus you can set the permissions for other users on the folder.

NOTE You'll recall from Chapter 13 that all versions of Windows come with a far more powerful and much more complex form of permissions based on NTFS.

Sharing Folders with Advanced Sharing Advanced Sharing enables you to create network shares with more precise control over access to the contents (though in practice techs tend to set everything to Full Control and let NTFS handle authorization at the local level). To create a network share, right-click on the folder you want to share and select Properties. Select the Sharing tab—Figure 19-28 shows the Sharing tab for a folder called Music, where I save .mp3 and .aac files of some of my favorites.

Click Advanced Sharing to open the Advanced Sharing dialog box. Then click Share this folder to make it active (Figure 19-29). Here you can set the share name—by default it's the same as the folder name, but it can be unique. You can also limit simultaneous users and add comments, among other things. Click Permissions to get to the last step (Figure 19-30).

Figure 19-28
Sharing tab for
Music folder

Figure 19-29
Advanced
Sharing dialog
box, ready for
sharing

Figure 19-30
Permissions for the about-to-be-created network share

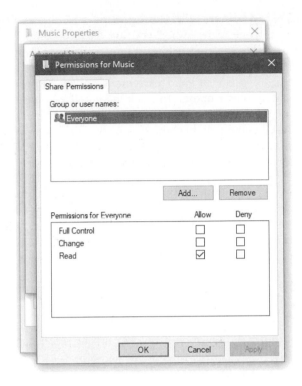

By default, the Everyone group is set to Read permissions, but you have options here. You can add or remove groups or user names. Click Add to open the Select Users or Groups dialog box where you can search for users/groups currently on the local computer. (That's important to note, as you'll see in the next section, "Accessing Shared Folders with Workgroups.") Also note the other options here.

You have three permission levels—Read, Change, and Full Control—and you can set those permissions to Allow or Deny. Just like you saw with NTFS permissions, Deny always trumps Allow. Advanced Sharing gives you control over what specific user accounts and groups can do with a network share. You could grant Full Control to everyone, for example, but then add a specific user—Bob in Accounting—and Deny Full Control to that user account. That would effectively let everyone but Bob access to the Music share, to add, rename, delete, and so on.

EXAM TIP Expect a question or two on the CompTIA A+ 1002 exam that requires you to compare *NTFS vs. share permissions*. NTFS applies superior local control over all resources on a computer. Share permissions only apply to network shares (whether created using the Sharing Wizard or Advanced Sharing). *Allow vs Deny* works similarly in both types of sharing, with Deny trumping Allow.

Accessing Shared Folders with Workgroups   So all this sharing seems to work quite nicely, except for one issue: When you log on to a computer, you access a user name and database on that computer. The account you access is stored on the local computer; how do you give someone from another computer access to that shared folder? You have to give that other person a valid user name and password. We use the nomenclature <computer name>\<user name> to track logons. If you log on to Computer A as Mike, we say you are logged on to ComputerA\Mike. This nomenclature comes in very handy when networked computers become part of the process.

Figure 19-31 shows Computers A and B. Assume there is a shared folder called Timmy on Computer A and the Mike account has Read/Write permission.

Figure 19-31
Computers A
and B

Computer A\Mike

Computer B\Fred

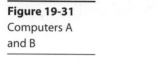

A person fires up Computer B, logging on as Fred. He opens his Network menu option and sees Computer A, but when he clicks on it he sees a network password prompt (see Figure 19-32).

The reason is that the person is logged on as ComputerB\Fred and he needs to be logged on as ComputerA\Mike to successfully access this folder. So the user needs to

Figure 19-32   Prompt for entering user name and password

know the password for ComputerA\Mike. This isn't a very pretty way to protect user names and passwords. So what can you do? You have three choices:

1. You can make people log on to shares as just shown.

2. You can create the same accounts (same user name and same password) on all the computers and give sharing permissions to all the users for all the shares.

3. You can use one account on all computers. Everyone logs on with the same account, and then all shares are by default assigned to the same account.

 EXAM TIP Moving and copying folders and files within network shares and between network shares and local computers doesn't affect the file attributes. If you copy a read-only file from a network share to your desktop, for example, it'll still be read-only. You can easily change this sort of file attribute by right-clicking the file and selecting Properties.

Domains

Workgroups work well in smaller networks (<30 computers), but for larger networks, or if you desire a network with more control and security, it's far better to use a Windows *domain*, a network organization that centralizes user accounts, passwords, and access to resources. Look at Figures 19-33 and 19-34. In a Windows workgroup, each computer has its own set of local user accounts. In a Windows domain, a computer running Windows Server is configured as a *domain controller*. A domain controller stores a set of *domain accounts*. A user logging on to any computer on the domain may use their one domain account to log on to the entire network.

 NOTE Even though a computer is on a domain, you can still log on using a local user account, though this is rarely needed. You'll only see this happen with troubleshooting scenarios, like when we rebuilt corrupted profiles in Chapter 16, "Troubleshooting Operating Systems." Otherwise, once you're a member of a domain, you'll log in with your domain account.

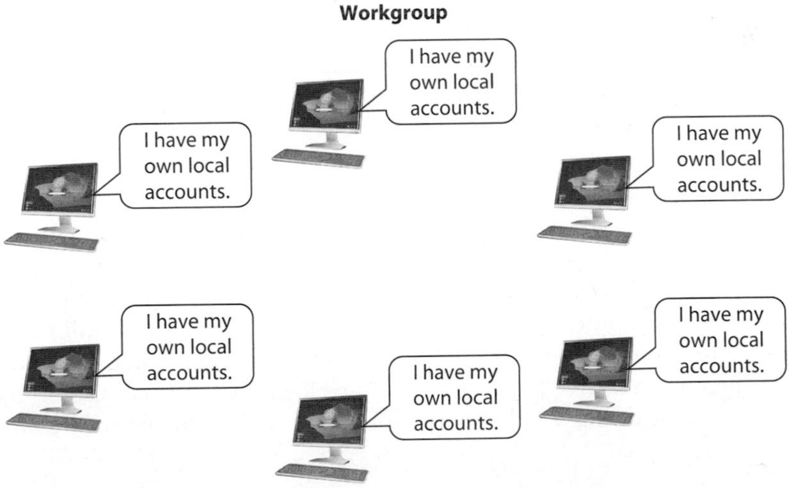

Figure 19-33
Workgroup

Workgroup

I have my own local accounts.

I have my own local accounts.

I have my own local accounts.

I have my own local accounts.

I have my own local accounts.

I have my own local accounts.

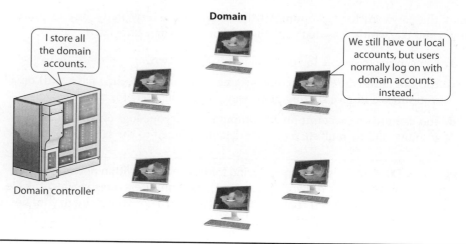

Figure 19-34 Domain

A Windows domain makes it easy for anyone with a domain account to log on to any computer in the domain with a single account, a process called *single sign-on*. Each user does not need a separate local account stored on every computer. User authentication through the single domain account enables access to all machines on the domain, thus the term single sign-on.

If you have a single computer storing all the domain user names and passwords, why not take it one step higher and store information about the domain, including printer information, computer names, location information—anything you might need to define the entire network. Modern versions of Windows use an *Active Directory* domain to accomplish these tasks.

To use a domain on a network of Windows machines, for example, you must have a computer running a version of Windows Server (see Figure 19-35). Windows Server is a completely different, much more powerful, and much more expensive version of Windows. You then need to promote the server to a domain controller. This creates the Active Directory.

 EXAM TIP Look for a comparison question on the CompTIA A+ 1002 exam on *workgroup vs. domain* network setup. The former takes no effort; the latter requires a Windows Server set up as a domain controller, so a lot more equipment and such is needed.

Once a server is set up as a domain controller, creating the Active Directory, each PC on the network needs to join the domain (which kicks you off the workgroup). When you log on to a computer that's a member of a domain, Windows will prompt you for a user name instead of showing you icons for all the users on the network (see Figure 19-36).

When using Active Directory, you don't log on to your computer. Instead, you log on directly to the domain. All user accounts are stored on the domain controller, as shown in

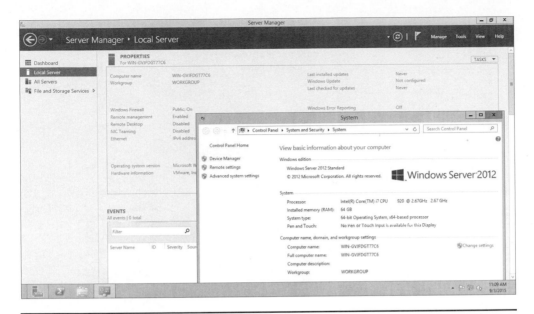

Figure 19-35 Windows Server

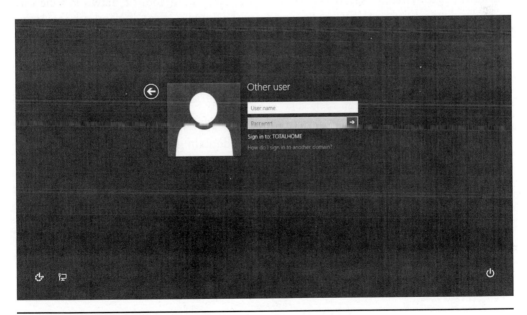

Figure 19-36 Domain logon screen

Figure 19-37. A lot of domains have names that look like Web addresses, like totalhome
.com or totalhome.local. Using the previous nomenclature, you can log on to a domain
using <domain>\<domain user name>. If the domain totalhome.local has a user account
called Mike, for example, you would use totalhome.local\Mike to log on.

Figure 19-37
Active Directory
network

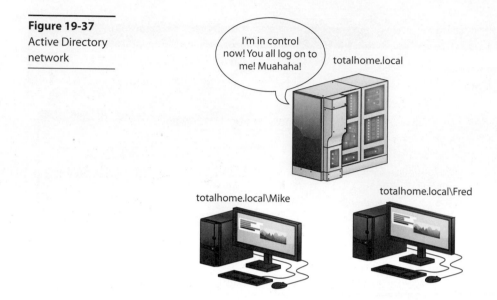

Domain Organization Active Directory stores everything about a network. One way to see the Active Directory is to log on directly to the domain controller and run the Active Directory Users and Computers utility—the tool that provides basic Active Directory functions (see Figure 19-38). Note the name of the domain (in this case totalhome. local) on the left side. The folders underneath the domain name show the domains' organization. Those really aren't folders. They're called organizational units (even though they look like folders), but we'll save that definition for a moment. Here are a few of the more noteworthy folders.

- **Builtin** (*sic*)   This is where all the built-in domain groups are stored, such as Domain Administrators and Users.

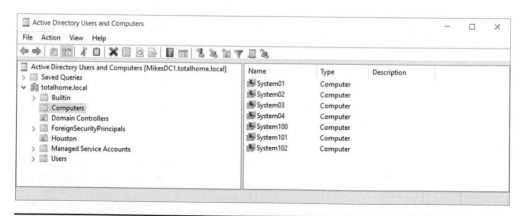

Figure 19-38   Active Directory Users and Computers

- **Computers**   Every system from servers to workstations are listed in this folder.
- **Domain Controllers**   It's always a good idea to have more than one domain controller in case one goes down. This folder lists all of them.
- **Users**   This area stores all the non-built-in users for the domain.

Domain Administration   Just as individual systems have an administer account, the domain also has domain administrators. The accounts are extremely powerful and enable you to join a computer to a domain. Certain domain jobs require domain admin rights. Here's how to deal with adding and removing computers and users from a domain.

To have a computer join a domain, use the System Properties dialog box like you did when changing a workgroup name. Access the System applet and click the *Change settings* link in the *Computer name, domain, and workgroup settings* section to open the System Properties dialog box. Then click the Network ID button on the Computer Name tab to reach the dialog box shown in Figure 19-39. Make sure you have access to a Domain account that can join the domain!

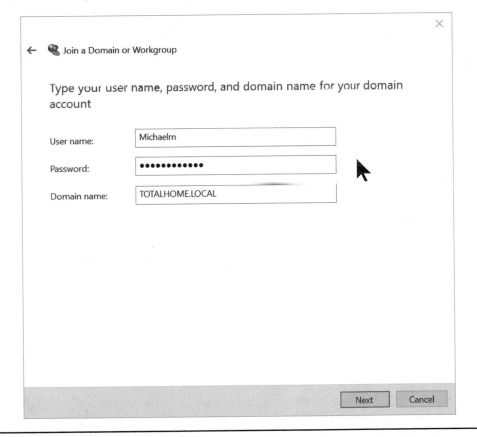

Figure 19-39   Joining a domain

Removing a system from a domain just means accessing the domain controller, going into Active Directory Users and Computers, right-clicking the computer in question to get to Properties. Select the Member Of tab, select the unwanted computer, and click the Remove button to remove the computer (see Figure 19-40).

Figure 19-40
Removing a
computer from
the domain

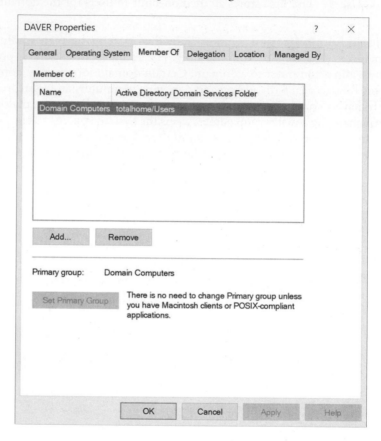

There's no way to promote a local user or group to a domain user or group. A domain admin must create a fresh new domain account on the domain controller using Active Directory Users and Computers. Right-click on Users and select New | User (Figure 19-41) to open the New Object - User dialog box. Figure 19-42 show the dialog with user account information filled in.

Domain administrators use the Active Directory Users and Computers to clean up account issues. To reset a password, right-click a user account and select Reset Password . . . to open the Reset Password dialog box (Figure 19-43). Type in a new password; confirm it; and click Okay. From the same dialog box, you can select the check box to *Unlock the user's account* if needed, such as in the case of accidental, multiple mistyped logon attempts. Finally, you can enable or disable a user account from the context menu by selecting—you guessed it—Enable Account or Disable Account.

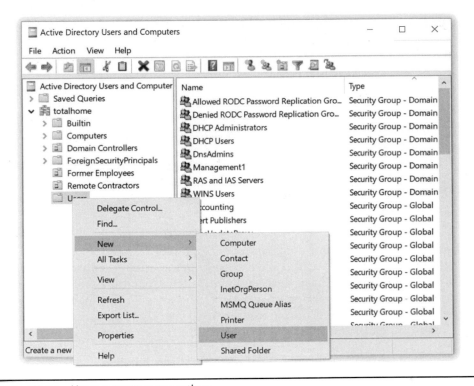

Figure 19-41 Users context menu options

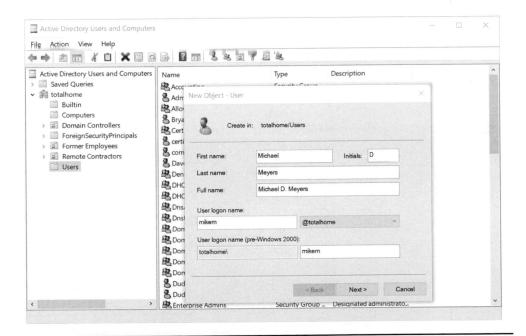

Figure 19-42 Adding a new domain account

Figure 19-43
Reset Password
dialog box

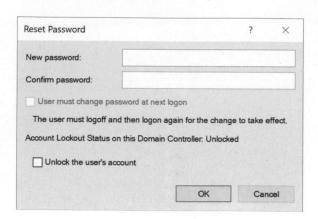

There's a lot of power in a domain account, allowing features you rarely see in a local account. For example, you can add a *logon script* that runs every time the user logs in that can create network shares, place an information box on the screen, run special applications (like anti-malware); pretty much anything you wish to do. Just add the path and name of the script file under the Profile tab (see Figure 19-44). (Note that CompTIA calls a logon script a *login* script. It's the same thing.)

Figure 19-44
Adding a logon
script to a
domain account

Another great feature built into Active Directory is the ability to pick where you want to store users *home folders* (such as Pictures, Downloads, Documents, etc.). This requires the use of roaming profiles rather than local profiles. Let me explain. Every time you log on to a computer that's new to your user account, Windows will set up a new home folder for your domain account on that local machine. It won't be populated with any of your stuff, though, because it's a new home folder.

This creates some frustration because users might want to have only one Documents folder, one Downloads folder, one Pictures folder . . . in other words, a single unified home folder. To accomplish this "oneness," administrators set up roaming profiles on the server. When a user logs on to the domain, the roaming profile applies and the user can access his or her files.

Additionally, administrators can specify the location of users' home folders, so that when users log on, they access home folders on a remote server rather than the local machine. This process, called *folder redirection*, helps administrators keep tighter control over network resources.

Just to be clear, administrators handle the processes involved in setting up roaming profiles and folder redirection (and many other cool Active Directory features). CompTIA A+ techs need to know that these features exist so they're not surprised in the field.

Active Directory enables extremely flexible organization of Active Directory users and computers via the use of *organizational units* (*OUs*), holding spaces, containers, buckets if you will, that enable you to organize users and computers by function, location, permission . . . Whatever makes sense for your organization, you can use OUs to manage those assets.

Figure 19-45 shows an example of a heavily modified Active Directory for the totalhome.local domain. Note the OUs for different locations, inactive accounts, and even printers.

EXAM TIP The domain controller authenticates a user when that user logs on to a domain computer. The domain controller is therefore also called an *authentication server*.

Homegroups

The problem with workgroups is that they provide almost no security and require lots of signing on to access resources. Domains provide single sign-on and lots of security, but require special servers and lots of administration. To address this, Microsoft introduced a feature in Windows 7 called *HomeGroup*.

EXAM TIP HomeGroup works in Windows 7/8/8.1 and in early versions of Windows 10. Microsoft dropped support for HomeGroup in Windows 10 in 2018. You will see HomeGroup as an active feature of Windows on the CompTIA 1002 exam. The CompTIA 1001 objective 1.6 lists "HomeGroup vs. Workgroup," so look out for trick questions.

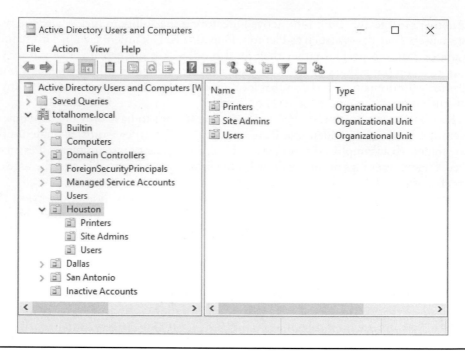

Figure 19-45 totalhome.local domain

HomeGroup uses the idea that people want to share data, not folders. Most people just want to share their music, not their My Music or Music folder. So homegroups skip folders completely and share your Windows libraries. A homegroup connects a group of computers using a common password—no special user names required. Each computer can be a member of only one homegroup at a time. Let's make a homegroup and see how this works.

 EXAM TIP Homegroups require the IPv6 protocol. Luckily, IPv6 is enabled by default.

To make a homegroup, open the HomeGroup Control Panel applet. Assuming you currently connect to a workgroup and haven't already created a homegroup, you'll see a dialog box like the one shown in Figure 19-46.

Click the *Create a homegroup* button to create a homegroup. You'll then see the Create a Homegroup dialog box shown in Figure 19-47.

Notice the five options: Pictures, Music, Videos, Documents, and Printers. The Documents checkbox is probably not checked, but go ahead and check it to share all five things. Click Next to see the homegroup's password (see Figure 19-48).

Figure 19-46
Default
HomeGroup
dialog box

Figure 19-47
Create a
Homegroup
dialog box

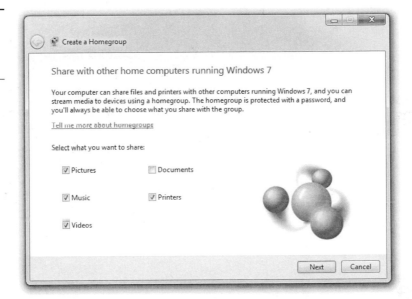

NOTE Interestingly, all homegroup data is encrypted between systems.

Perhaps you've heard that you shouldn't write down passwords? Well, this password is so long that you might *need* to write it down. The dialog box even gives you a way to print it out! Click Next one more time to see the dialog box shown in Figure 19-49. This is the dialog box you will now see every time you click the HomeGroup applet in the Control Panel.

Figure 19-48
The homegroup's password

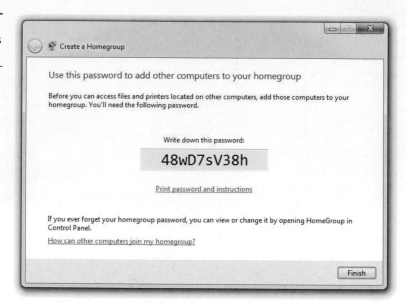

Figure 19-49
Homegroup configured

Let's look at this carefully. Notice the *How do I share additional libraries?* link below the checkboxes in the top section, Share libraries and printers. By default, homegroups share libraries, not individual folders. The Music, Pictures, and Videos libraries are shared by default. Documents are not. Although printers get their own checkbox, this setting remains the same as a normal printer share. It's just a handy place to add printer sharing, as even the most basic users like to share printers.

EXAM TIP   Remember that homegroups share libraries, not folders, by default.

Once you've created a homegroup, go to another computer on the network and open the HomeGroup Control Panel applet. Assuming all the factors stated earlier, you will see a dialog box like Figure 19-50.

Figure 19-50
HomeGroup
showing
an existing
homegroup

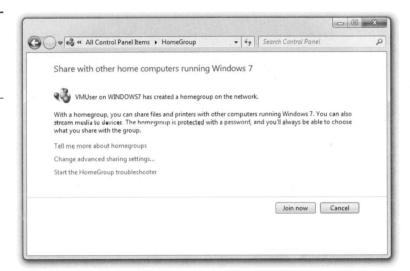

Click the Join now button, enter the password, choose which libraries you want to share with everyone else, and the new computer is in the homegroup!

Access the files shared through a homegroup by opening Windows Explorer or File Explorer, as shown in Figure 19-51. To see what others are sharing, select the corresponding computer name. You can then open those libraries to see the shared folders.

NOTE   Once you create a homegroup, you can access it from Windows Explorer/File Explorer.

Sharing more libraries is easy, and, if you'd like, you can even share individual folders. Just right-click on the library or folder and select Share with, as shown in Figure 19-52.

Figure 19-51
Using
homegroups

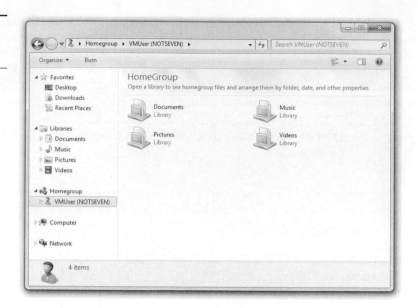

Notice you have four options: Nobody, Homegroup (Read), Homegroup (Read/Write), and Specific people. The Nobody option means the item is not shared.

 EXAM TIP Windows Explorer also adds a *Share with* toolbar button that works exactly like the menu shown in Figure 19-52.

Figure 19-52
The Share with
menu

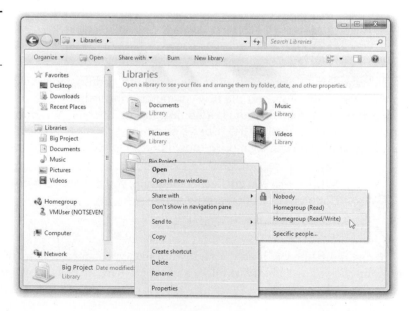

By sharing libraries with homegroups, Microsoft hides folders for most users, helping users share their stuff (documents, pictures, music, and videos) instead of folders. Homegroups fit a very specific world—smaller, non-domain home networks—but within that realm, they work wonderfully.

Sharing Printers

Sharing printers in Windows follows the same process as sharing files and folders. Assuming that the system has printer sharing services loaded, go to the Devices and Printers folder in the Control Panel and right-click on the printer you wish to share. Select Printer properties (not Printers), and then select the Sharing tab (see Figure 19-53). Click *Share this printer*, add a share name, click OK or Apply, and you're done.

Figure 19-53

Giving a name to a shared printer on Windows 8.1

NOTE To learn about accessing shared printers in Windows, check out Chapter 26 for more information.

One of the most pleasant aspects of configuring a system for networking under all versions of Microsoft Windows is the amazing amount of the process that is automated. For example, if Windows detects a NIC in a system, it automatically installs the NIC driver, a network protocol (TCP/IP), and Client for Microsoft Networks. So if you want to share a resource, everything you need is automatically installed. Note that although File and Printer Sharing is also automatically installed, you still must activate it by checking the appropriate checkbox in the Local Area Connection Properties dialog box.

Troubleshooting Networks

Once you go beyond a single PC and enter the realm of networked computers, your troubleshooting skills need to take a giant leap up in quality. The secret to finding the right answer to networking problems on the CompTIA A+ exams is to remember that the exams only ask about the skills to get a single computer back on the network. Focus your network troubleshooting answers to scenario questions on getting a single system up and running.

NOTE The troubleshooting issues discussed here apply only to a LAN, and do not cover issues related to troubleshooting Internet access. We'll cover Internet troubleshooting in Chapter 21, using the knowledge you've gained in this chapter and adding even more tools.

CompTIA likes to ask scenario questions that deal with "no connectivity" or "intermittent connectivity." There are two ways to look at connectivity issues, and CompTIA A+ exam objectives don't specify which type is covered on the exams. The first type of connectivity scenario (and probably the one CompTIA means) is when a computer loses physical connectivity. The second type is when you're on the network and can't access a specific resource (you can access other resources, just not the one you want right now). Let's consider both.

NOTE The CompTIA A+ 1001 objective 5.1 on their troubleshooting methodology applies to individual computers and components *and* to networking. You read about this way back in Chapter 1, "Safety and Professionalism," for the former. As you read through the next sections, think about the troubleshooting methodology and how it can apply in networking scenarios.

Repairing Physical Cabling

"The network's down!" is one of the most terrifying phrases a network tech will ever hear. Networks fail for many reasons, and the first thing to know is that good-quality, professionally installed cabling rarely goes bad, but you need to know what to do when it does. Let's take a moment now to discuss what to do when you think you've got a problem with your physical network.

Symptoms

Physical connectivity interruptions stand out in Windows. Windows displays a red X over the network icon in the notification area to show you're not connected (see Figure 19-54).

Figure 19-54
Windows 7 red X
error notification
icon

If you encounter this problem, first check the obvious. Run **ipconfig** from the command line. Do you see an APIPA/zeroconf address, like 169.254.15.22? That's a clear sign of a disconnect between the system and the DHCP server. Is the cable unplugged at the system? At the wall outlet? Then go for the less obvious: Is the NIC disabled in Device Manager? If these checks don't solve the problem, take a peek on the other side of the cable. If you're not connected to a running switch, you're going to get the disconnect errors.

TIP If you're in macOS or Linux, you can use the ifconfig or ip commands to get the same information that ipconfig gives you in Windows.

Intermittent connectivity is often the same issue but typically is harder to figure out. Either way, read the next section to see how to get serious about testing for these pesky connectivity problems.

EXAM TIP The CompTIA A+ 1001 exam objectives list *APIPA/link local address* as a common symptom of wired and wireless network problems, but that's only half true. Certainly, getting an APIPA address rather than an accurate network address points to a disconnect between the workstation and the DHCP server that could be caused by many factors. But every computer gets a link-local address these days. That's just the way IPv6 works.

For the exam, though, CompTIA equates link-local addresses with APIPA and will likely lump the two together in a troubleshooting scenario. You know better, but don't miss the exam question by overthinking.

Diagnosing Physical Problems

Look for errors that point to physical disconnection. A key clue that the computer may have a physical problem is that a user gets a "No server is found" error, or tries to use the operating system's network explorer utility (like Network in Windows) and doesn't see any systems besides his or her own.

Multiple systems failing to access the network often points to hardware problems. This is where knowledge of your network cabling helps. If all the systems connected to one switch suddenly no longer see the network, but all the other systems in your network still function, you not only have a probable hardware problem, but also have a suspect—the switch.

Check the Lights

If you suspect a hardware problem, first check the link lights on the NIC and switch. If they're not lit, you know the cable isn't connected somewhere. If you're not physically at the system in question (if you're on a tech call, for example), you can have the user check his or her connection status through the link lights or through software.

If the problem system clearly cannot connect, eliminate the possibility of a failed switch or other larger problem by checking to make sure other people can access the network, and that other systems can access the shared resource (server) that the problem system can't see. Inspect the cable running from the back of the computer to the outlet. Finally, if you can, plug the system into a known good outlet and see if it works. A veteran network tech keeps a long patch cable for just this purpose. If you get connectivity with the second outlet, you should begin to suspect the structured cable running from the first outlet to the switch. Assuming the cable is installed properly and has been working correctly before this event, a simple continuity test will confirm your suspicion in most cases.

Check the NIC

Be warned that a bad NIC can also generate a "can't see the network" problem. Use the utility provided by the OS to verify that the NIC works. If you've got a NIC with diagnostic software, run it—this software will check the NIC's circuitry. The NIC's female connector is a common failure point, so NICs that come with diagnostic software often include a special test called a *loopback test*. A loopback test sends data out of the NIC and checks to see if it comes back. Some NICs perform only an internal loopback, which tests the circuitry that sends and receives, but not the actual connecting pins. A true external loopback requires a *loopback plug* inserted into the NIC's port (see Figure 19-55). If a NIC is bad, replace it.

Figure 19-55
Loopback plug

NOTE Onboard NICs on laptops are especially notorious for breaking due to frequent plugging and unplugging. On some laptops, the NICs are easy to replace; others require a motherboard replacement. Or you can always use a USB-to-Ethernet adapter.

Cable Testing

The vast majority of network disconnection problems occur at the work area. If you've tested those connections, though, and the work area seems fine, it's time to consider deeper issues.

With the right equipment, diagnosing a bad horizontal cabling run is easy. Anyone with a network should own a midrange time-domain reflectometer (TDR) tester such as the Fluke MicroScanner. A TDR measures impedance in network cabling. If the tester measures any impedance, something is wrong with the cable. With a little practice, you can easily determine not only whether a cable is disconnected but also where the disconnection takes place. Sometimes patience is required, especially if the cable runs lack labels, but you will find the problem.

When you're testing a cable run, always include the patch cables as you test. This means unplugging the patch cable from the PC, attaching a tester, and then going to the telecommunications room. Here you'll want to unplug the patch cable from the switch and plug the tester into that patch cable, making a complete test, as shown in Figure 19-56.

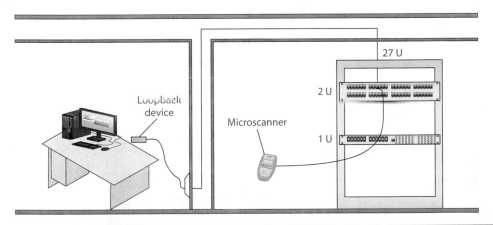

Figure 19-56 Cable tester in action

Testing in this manner gives you a complete test from the switch to the system. In general, a broken cable must be replaced. A bad patch cable is an easy fix, but what happens if the horizontal cable is to blame? In these cases, I get on the phone and call my local installer. If a cable is bad in one spot, the risk of it being bad in another is simply too great to try anything other than total replacement.

Toners

It would be nice to say that all cable installations are perfect and that over the years they won't tend to grow into horrific piles of spaghetti-like, unlabeled cables. In the real world, though, you might eventually find yourself having to locate or *trace* cables. Even in the best-planned networks, labels fall off ports and outlets, mystery cables appear behind walls, new cable runs are added, and mistakes are made counting rows and columns on patch panels. Sooner or later, most network techs will have to be able to pick out one particular cable or port from a stack.

When the time comes to trace cables, network techs turn to a device called a toner for help. *Toner* is the generic term for two separate devices that are used together: a tone generator and a tone probe. The *tone generator* connects to the cable using alligator clips, tiny hooks, or a network jack, and it sends an electrical signal along the wire at a certain frequency. The *tone probe* emits a sound when it is placed near a cable connected to the tone generator. These two devices are often referred to by the brand-name Fox and Hound, a popular model of toner made by the Triplett Corporation (see Figure 19-57).

Figure 19-57
Fox and Hound

 EXAM TIP　You'll see a tone probe referred to on the CompTIA A+ exam as a *tone generator and probe*.

To trace a cable, connect the tone generator to the known end of the cable in question, and then position the tone probe next to the other end of each of the cables that might be the right one. The tone probe makes a sound when it's placed next to the right cable. Some toners have one tone probe that works with multiple tone generators. Each generator emits a separate frequency, and the probe sounds a different tone for each one. Even good toners are relatively inexpensive ($75 or so); although inexpensive toners can cost less than $25, they don't tend to work well, so spending a little more is worthwhile. Just keep in mind that if you have to support a network, you'd do best to own a decent toner.

Fixing Common Problems

Let's go back and look at the second possible meaning for a loss in connectivity. It's very common to try to connect to a shared resource and either fail or find that a shared resource you've used time and again has suddenly disappeared. This applies (in this chapter, at least) to local resources—shares on the LAN, shared printers, e-mail server, and so on. Troubleshooting access to unavailable resources is part of a tech's bread-and-butter job.

Failing to Connect to a New Resource

When you can't connect to a resource on the first try, it often points to a configuration issue. In most cases, a quick double-check of the sharing system will reveal one of the following problems (and call for the associated solution):

- You don't have the right share name? Go check at the serving system.

- You don't have the required user name/password? Ask someone who might have this knowledge, or double-check that your account has access.

- You don't have permission to use/access/connect to the shared resource? Make sure you have the correct permissions.

- You're not on the right homegroup/domain/workgroup? Check your system and the sharing system to verify which workgroup/domain name to use. On a homegroup, make sure you've used the proper password.

- The folder or printer isn't shared? Share it!

- The folder or printer doesn't exist? Make sure the serving system still hosts the folder you want. Install the network printer if you haven't yet.

Failing to Connect to a Previously Used Resource

If you suddenly can't connect to a resource that you've used many times before, go with the easy answers first:

- Check that you can see the resource using Network.

- Check that the serving system is on.

- Check that the computer is physically connected to the serving system.

The net Command

Windows enables you to view a network quickly from the command line through the *net command*. This works great when you plug into a network for the first time and, naturally, don't know the names of the other computers on that network. To see the many options that net offers, type **net** at a command prompt and press ENTER. The view and use options offer excellent network tools.

You can think of net view as the command-line version of Network. When run, net view returns a list of Windows computers on the network:

```
C:\Users\Mike>net view
Server Name              Remark
-------------------------------------------------
\\SABERTOOTH
\\UBERBOX
\\SERVER1
The command completed successfully.
C:\Users\Mike>
```

Once you know the names of the computers, you type **net view** followed by the computer name. The net view command will show any shares on that machine and whether they are mapped drives:

```
C:\>net view server1
Shared resources at SERVER1
Share name  Type  Used as  Comment
-------------------------------------------------
FREDC       Disk
Research    Disk  W:
The command completed successfully.
```

The net use command is a command-line method for mapping network shares. For example, if you wanted to map the Research share shown in the previous example to the X: drive, you simply type

```
C:\>net use x: \\server1\research
```

This will map drive X: to the Research share on the SERVER1 computer. *Mapping a drive* means the drive will show up in File Explorer as a selectable resource, just like a local drive.

 NOTE The net command can give a quick snapshot of the Windows network settings, such as computer name, OS version, workgroup or domain name, and more. Type **net config workstation**. It's quick and easy!

The nbtstat Command

The nbtstat command is an old command-line utility that predates Windows. It stands for NetBIOS over TCP/IP Statistics. Many versions ago, Windows used NetBIOS for many aspects of LAN file sharing, and even though NetBIOS is long gone, bits of

NetBIOS hang on as a way for Windows to resolve host names on the network when a DNS server is not available.

While not as useful as it once was, *nbtstat* can still provide insight when troubleshooting naming issues in small workgroups. Here are a couple of usage examples; to see what your computer's NetBIOS name is, use the nbtstat –n command:

```
C:\Users\mmeyers>nbtstat -n

Local Area Connection:
Node IpAddress: [192.168.4.43] Scope Id: []

            NetBIOS Local Name Table

    Name               Type         Status
    ---------------------------------------------
    mmeyers ws      <00>  UNIQUE     Registered
    WORKGROUP       <00>  GROUP      Registered
    mmeyers-ws      <20>  UNIQUE     Registered

C:\Users\mmeyers>
```

You can also query a remote machine by IP to find out its NetBIOS name with nbtstat –A (note the uppercase "A"; use a lowercase "a" if you know the machine's NetBIOS name already):

```
C:\Users\mmeyers>nbtstat -A 192.168.4.52

Local Area Connection:
Node IpAddress: [192.168.4.43] Scope Id: []

        NetBIOS Remote Machine Name Table

    Name               Type         Status
    ---------------------------------------------
    UNITEDKINGDOM   <00>  UNIQUE     Registered
    UNITEDKINGDOM   <03>  UNIQUE     Registered
    UNITEDKINGDOM   <20>  UNIQUE     Registered
    .._MSBROWSE__.<01>  GROUP        Registered
    TOTALHOME       <00>  GROUP      Registered
    TOTALHOME       <1D>  UNIQUE     Registered
    TOTALHOME       <1E>  GROUP      Registered

    MAC Address = 00-00-00-00-00-00
```

Finally, you can see all the names that NetBIOS has in its local cache with nbtstat –c:

```
C:\Users\mmeyers>nbtstat -c

Local Area Connection:
Node IpAddress: [192.168.4.43] Scope Id: []

        NetBIOS Remote Cache Name Table

    Name           Type     Host Address    Life [sec]
    --------------------------------------------------------
    CLASS-SERVER  <00>  UNIQUE   192.168.4.50        447
    CLASS-SERVER  <20>  UNIQUE   192.168.4.50        447
```

```
TOTALHOME        <1B>   UNIQUE        192.168.4.12        450
UNITEDKINGDOM    <20>   UNIQUE        192.168.4.52        417
UNITEDKINGDOM    <00>   UNIQUE        192.168.4.52        417
WIN7-64          <20>   UNIQUE        192.168.4.220       450
```

Because the cache is temporary, you may find that it is empty if you haven't browsed your LAN or interacted with another machine recently.

Chapter Review

Questions

1. Steven's Windows system can't connect to the Internet, and he comes to you, his PC tech, for help. You figure out that it's a DHCP problem. What program should you run to troubleshoot his DHCP problem from the client side?

   A. ipconfig

   B. ifconfig

   C. config

   D. dhcp /review

2. What command would you use to view the path taken by an Ethernet packet?

   A. ping

   B. ipconfig

   C. tracert

   D. nslookup

3. Which of the following is the correct net syntax for discovering which network shares on a particular server are mapped on your computer?

   A. net view \\fileserver

   B. net \\fileserver

   C. net map \\fileserver

   D. net share \\fileserver

4. What small device enables you to test a NIC's circuitry?

   A. Loopback plug

   B. Port tester

   C. Multimeter

   D. Integrated network and logic probe

5. Which command can be used to display the cached NetBIOS names for a Windows system?

  A. nslookup

  B. dig --cache

  C. nbtstat –c

  D. nbtstat –a

6. You are down under your desk organizing some wires when you notice that the activity light on your NIC is blinking erratically. Is there a problem?

  A. Yes, the activity light should be on steadily when the computer is running.

  B. Yes, the activity light should be blinking steadily, not randomly.

  C. No, the light blinks when there is network traffic.

  D. No, the light blinks to show bus activity.

7. What is a common symptom of a bad network cable?

  A. Rapidly blinking link lights

  B. No link lights

  C. Solid on link lights

  D. Steady blinking link lights

8. What command-line utility would you run to show a list of network computers?

  A. net send

  B. show net_servers

  C. net use

  D. net view

9. What benefit does full-duplex offer?

  A. It enables NICs to send and receive signals at the same time.

  B. It enables NICs to send data twice as fast.

  C. It enables NICs to receive data twice as fast.

  D. It enables a switch to connect to both coaxial and fiber optic cables.

10. What do most techs call a toner or tone generator?

  A. TDR

  B. UTP

  C. UDP

  D. Fox and Hound

Answers

1. **A.** You should run ipconfig, or more specifically ipconfig /release and then ipconfig /renew to get a new IP address if a DHCP server is available for Steven's Windows system. This typically resolves most DHCP client-side problems. ifconfig is the program used by macOS and Linux systems for this task. Neither config nor dhcp is valid.

2. **C.** The tracert command in Windows traces the path a data packet takes to get to its destination. macOS and Linux use the traceroute utility for similar purposes.

3. **A.** To see the network shares mapped on your computer, use net view \\fileserver.

4. **A.** A loopback plug will test the NIC's Ethernet port and circuitry.

5. **C.** nslookup and dig only work with DNS, not NetBIOS. nbtstat –a is for querying a remote system's name, but nbtstat –c displays the cached names.

6. **C.** The lights should be blinking to show activity—this is normal.

7. **B.** If there are no link lights, you probably have a bad network cable.

8. **D.** Use the net view command to show a list of computers on the network.

9. **A.** Full-duplex technology enables NICs to send and receive signals at the same time.

10. **D.** Most techs refer to a toner or tone generator as a Fox and Hound, the name of a popular brand of tone generator.

Wireless Networking

In this chapter, you will learn how to
- Describe wireless networking components
- Analyze and explain wireless networking standards
- Install and configure wireless networks
- Troubleshoot wireless networks

Wireless networks have been popular for many years now, but unlike wired networks, so much of how wireless works continues to elude people. Part of the problem might be that a simple wireless network is so inexpensive and easy to configure that most users and techs never really get into the *hows* of wireless. The chance to get away from all the cables and mess and just *connect* has a phenomenal appeal. The lack of understanding, though, hurts techs when it comes time to troubleshoot wireless networks. Let's change all that and dive deeply into wireless networking.

Historical/Conceptual

Wireless Networking Components

Instead of a physical set of wires running between network nodes, wireless networks use either radio waves or beams of infrared light to communicate with each other. Various kinds of wireless networking solutions have come and gone in the past. The wireless radio wave networks you'll find yourself supporting these days are based on the *IEEE 802.11* wireless Ethernet standard—marketed as Wi-Fi—and on Bluetooth technology. Wireless networks using infrared light are limited to those that use the Infrared Data Association (IrDA) protocol. Finally, the cell phone companies have gotten into the mix and offer access to the Internet through cellular networks.

Wireless networking capabilities of one form or another are built into many modern computing devices. Infrared *transceiver* ports have been standard issue on portable computers and high-end printers for years, although they're absent from most of the latest PCs and portable computers. Figure 20-1 shows the infrared transceiver ports on an older laptop and personal digital assistant (PDA)—a precursor to the smartphone. Back in the day, these infrared capabilities were used to transfer data between nearby devices.

Figure 20-1
Infrared
transceiver ports
on a laptop and
PDA

Today an infrared interface on a device such as a smartphone is present primarily so the device can be used as a wireless remote control. In place of infrared as a data transfer mechanism, Wi-Fi and Bluetooth capabilities are now common as integrated components, and you can easily add them when they aren't. Figure 20-2 shows a PCIe Wi-Fi adapter. Built-in cellular networking is less common, found on some portable computers (and smartphones, of course). You can also add wireless network capabilities by using external USB wireless network adapters or *wireless NICs*, as shown in Figure 20-3.

Figure 20-2
Wireless PCIe
add-on card

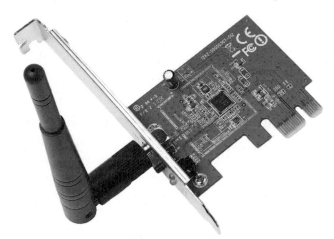

Wireless networking is not limited to PCs. Most smartphones and tablets have wireless capabilities built in or available as add-on options. Figure 20-4 shows a smartphone accessing the Internet over a Wi-Fi connection.

Figure 20-3
External USB
wireless NIC

Figure 20-4
Smartphone
with wireless
capability

NOTE   See Chapter 24, "Understanding Mobile Devices," for the scoop on mobile devices like smartphones and tablets.

1001

To extend the capabilities of a wireless Ethernet network, such as connecting to a wired network or sharing a high-speed Internet connection, you need a *wireless access point* (*WAP*). A WAP centrally connects wireless network nodes in the same way that a hub connects wired Ethernet PCs. Many WAPs also act as switches and Internet routers, such as the Linksys device shown in Figure 20-5.

Figure 20-5
Linksys device that acts as wireless access point, switch, and router

Like any other electronic devices, most WAPs draw their power from a wall outlet. More advanced WAPs, especially those used in corporate settings, can also use a feature called *Power over Ethernet (PoE)*. Using PoE, you only need to plug a single Ethernet cable into the WAP to provide it with both power and a network connection. The power and network connection are both supplied by a *PoE-capable switch*.

NOTE   Other devices can use PoE, even in places where there's no power. A *Power over Ethernet injector*, for example, can extend a PoE connection up to 100 meters. This is great for Ethernet devices such as security cameras.

Wireless communication via Bluetooth comes as a built-in option on newer computers and peripheral devices, or you can add it to an older PC via an external USB Bluetooth adapter. All macOS devices—desktop and portable—have Bluetooth. Most commonly these days, you'll see Bluetooth used to connect a portable speaker to a smartphone,

Figure 20-6
Bluetooth
keyboard and
tablet

for music on the go, and keyboards to tablets. Figure 20-6 shows a Bluetooth keyboard paired with a Bluetooth-enabled Apple iPad.

EXAM TIP Wireless access points are commonly known as WAPs, APs, or access points.

Wireless Networking Software

Wireless devices use the same networking protocols and client that their wired counterparts use, and they operate by using the *carrier sense multiple access/collision avoidance* (*CSMA/CA*) networking scheme. The *collision avoidance* aspect differs slightly from the *collision detection* standard used in wired Ethernet. A wireless node listens in on the wireless medium to see if another node is currently broadcasting data. If so, it waits a random amount of time before retrying. So far, this method is exactly the same as the method used by wired Ethernet networks. Because wireless nodes have a more difficult time detecting data collisions, however, they offer the option of using the *Request to Send/Clear to Send* (*RTS/CTS*) protocol. With this protocol enabled, a transmitting node sends an RTS frame to the receiving node after it determines the wireless medium is clear to use. The receiving node responds with a CTS frame, telling the sending node that it's okay to transmit. Then, once the data is sent, the transmitting node waits for an acknowledgment (ACK) from the receiving node before sending the next data packet. This option is very elegant, but keep in mind that using RTS/CTS introduces significant overhead to the process and can impede performance.

In terms of configuring wireless networking software, you need to do very little. Wireless network adapters are plug and play, so any modern version of Windows or macOS immediately recognizes one when it is installed, prompting you to load any needed hardware drivers. You will, however, need a utility to set parameters such as the network name.

Current versions of Windows and macOS (see Figure 20-7) include built-in tools for configuring these settings, but some wireless adapters also come with configuration tools provided by the wireless network adapter vendor. Using this utility, you can determine your link state and signal strength, configure your wireless networking *mode* (discussed next), and set options for security encryption, power saving, and so on.

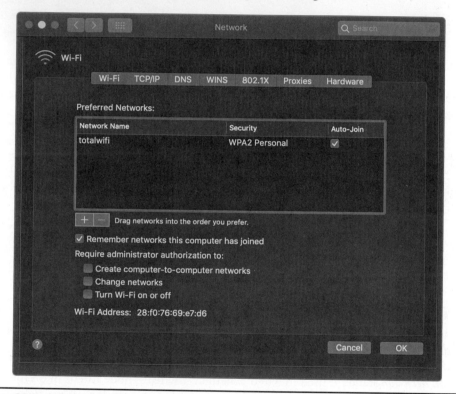

Figure 20-7   Wireless configuration utility

Wireless Network Modes

The simplest wireless network consists of two or more computers or devices communicating directly with each other without cabling or any other intermediary hardware. More complicated wireless networks use a WAP to centralize wireless communication and bridge wireless network segments to wired network segments. These two methods are called ad hoc mode and infrastructure mode.

Ad Hoc Mode

Ad hoc mode is sometimes called *peer-to-peer mode*, with each wireless node in direct contact with every other node in a decentralized free-for-all, as shown in Figure 20-8. Two or more wireless nodes communicating in ad hoc mode form what's called an *Independent Basic Service Set* (*IBSS*). Ad hoc mode networks are suited for small groups of computers (less than a dozen or so) that need to transfer files or share printers and for temporary networks such as study groups or business meetings.

Figure 20-8
Wireless ad hoc
mode network

 NOTE Starting in Windows 8.1, Microsoft has disabled default support for ad hoc networks. If you need to use them, you'll have to enable full support manually from the command line first.

Infrastructure Mode

Wireless networks running in *infrastructure mode* use one or more WAPs to connect the wireless network nodes to a wired network segment, as shown in Figure 20-9. A single WAP servicing a given area is called a *Basic Service Set* (*BSS*). This service area can be extended by adding more WAPs. This is called, appropriately, an *Extended Basic Service Set* (*EBSS*).

 EXAM TIP The CompTIA A+ 220-1001 exam will most likely ask you about the appropriate scenario for implementing an infrastructure vs. ad hoc Wi-Fi network. Infrastructure is the default, but ad hoc makes sense for limited impromptu networks. This is about the only time you'll hear about ad hoc networks today.

Figure 20-9
Wireless infrastructure mode network

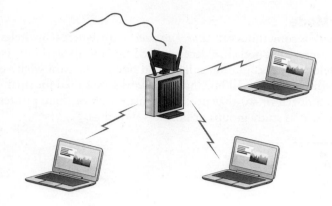

Wireless networks running in infrastructure mode require more planning and are more complicated to configure than ad hoc mode networks, but they also give you fine control over how the network operates. Infrastructure mode is better suited to networks that need to share dedicated resources such as Internet connections and centralized databases. Infrastructure networks are created to support small office/home office (SOHO) networks, and the access points in these environments are known as SOHO WAPs and SOHO routers.

EXAM TIP Many manufacturers produce devices for a type of hybrid wireless topology, where most of the nodes connect in a mesh network, but that also includes some wired machines as well. The key characteristic of a *wireless mesh network* (*WMN*) is that the nodes act like routers, forwarding traffic for other nodes, but without the wires.

In practice, a WMN tends to be more static than a traditional ad hoc network; that is, devices don't tend to come in and out rapidly. Plus, they'll have a mix of wired nodes as well. WMNs are currently in use in specific environments, such as interconnecting computers in deployed U.S. Army field units and Google Home devices.

1002

Wireless Networking Security

One of the major complaints against wireless networking is that it offers weak security, but the industry has made progress on this front in recent years. After all, data packets are floating through the air instead of safely wrapped up inside network cabling—what's to stop an unscrupulous person with the right equipment from grabbing those packets out of the air and reading that data? In the past, you could access a wireless network by walking into a WAP's coverage area, turning on a wireless device, and connecting. These days, it has grown hard to find accidentally open networks as hardware makers have trended toward using some type of security by default. Still, issues with these well-intentioned defaults are common, so it's still important to review the settings on new equipment.

Wireless networks use three methods to secure access to the network itself and secure the data being transferred: MAC address filtering, authentication, and data encryption. But before anyone encounters the on-network security, there are some measures we can take to reduce the likelihood our network will be targeted in the first place. Let's take a look at these practices first, followed by the methods for securing the network itself.

SSID

The *service set identifier (SSID)* parameter—also called the *network name*—defines the wireless network. Wireless devices *want* to be heard, and WAPs are usually configured to announce their presence by broadcasting the SSID to their maximum range. This is very handy when you have several wireless networks in the same area, but a default SSID also gives away important clues about the manufacturer (and maybe even model) of an access point.

Always change the default SSID to something unique and change the password right away. Configuring a unique SSID name and password is the very least that you should do to secure a wireless network. Older default SSID names and passwords are well known and widely available online. While newer models may come with unique SSIDs and passwords, the SSID may still leak information about your hardware—and the generated password may use rules that make it easy to break.

These defaults are intended to make setting up a wireless network as easy as possible but can cause problems in places with a lot of overlapping wireless networks. Keep in mind that each wireless access point in a network needs to be configured with the same unique SSID name. This SSID name is then included in the header of every data packet broadcast in the wireless network's coverage area. Data packets that lack the correct SSID name in the header are rejected. When it comes to picking a new unique SSID, it's still good to think about whether the name will make your network a more interesting target, or give away details that could help an attacker gain physical or remote access.

Another trick often seen in wireless networks is to tell the WAP not to broadcast the SSID. In theory, people not authorized to access the network will have a harder time knowing it's there, as it won't show up in the list of nearby networks on most devices.

In practice, even simple wireless scanning programs can discover the name of an "unknown" wireless network. Disabling the SSID broadcast just makes it harder for legitimate clients to connect. It doesn't stop bad actors at all—except on a CompTIA A+ exam question.

 EXAM TIP CompTIA lists changing the default SSID and disabling SSID broadcast on the WAP as steps for securing a new wireless network. These practices for managing your SSID *don't secure your network in practice.* You need to have robust security protocols configured.

Access Point Placement and Radio Power

When setting up a wireless network, keep the space in mind; you can limit risk by hiding the network from outsiders. When using an omni-directional antenna that sends and receives signals in all directions, for example, keep it near the center of the home or office. The closer you place it to a wall, the further away someone outside the home or office can be and still detect the wireless network.

Many wireless access points enable you to adjust the radio power levels of the antenna. Decrease the radio power until you can get reception at the furthest point *inside* the target network space, but not outside. This will take some trial and error.

EXAM TIP Don't forget to secure the WAP. Most WAPs have physical Ethernet ports in addition to their wireless capabilities. These ports are not password-protected or encrypted. Keep the WAP in a location where unscrupulous folks can't get to it.

MAC Address Filtering

Most WAPs support *MAC address filtering*, a method that enables you to limit access to your wireless network based on the physical, hard-wired address of the units' wireless NIC. MAC address filtering is a handy way of creating a type of "accepted users" list to limit access to your wireless network, but it works best when you have a small number of users. A table stored in the WAP lists the MAC addresses that are permitted to participate in the wireless network. Any data packets that don't contain the MAC address of a node listed in the table are rejected.

NOTE MAC filtering might sound airtight, but it isn't. An attacker can use special software to listen for the MAC addresses of nearby clients and *spoof* the address of an accepted client.

Wireless Security Protocols and Authentication Methods

Wireless security protocols provide authentication and encryption to lock down wireless networks. Wireless networks offer awesome connectivity options, but equally provide tempting targets. Wireless developers have worked very hard to provide techs the tools for protecting wireless clients and communication. Wireless authentication accomplishes the same thing wired authentication does, enabling the system to check a user's credentials and give or deny him or her access to the network. Encryption scrambles the signals on radio waves and makes communication among users secure.

This section looks at several generations of wireless security protocols, covering WEP, WPA, WPA2, and WPA3. We'll look at typical authentication methods, and finish with a simple consumer-oriented solution. (See "Infrastructure Mode" later in this chapter for the scoop on enterprise authentication installations.)

WEP   Early on, Wi-Fi developers introduced the *Wired Equivalent Privacy* (*WEP*) protocol to attempt to ensure that data is secured while in transit over the airwaves. WEP encryption uses a standard 40-bit encryption to scramble data packets. Many vendors also support 104-bit encryption. Note that some vendors advertise 128-bit encryption, but they use a 104-bit encryption key. Unfortunately, WEP encryption includes a flaw that makes it extremely vulnerable to attack. Although WEP is better than no encryption at all, WEP will not protect you from knowledgeable intruders.

It's worth knowing that all WEP traffic is encrypted with the same key, so one user's traffic isn't protected from other members of the network. For improved encryption which uses a different key for each client, see WPA or WPA2, both discussed next.

WPA   The *Wi-Fi Protected Access* (*WPA*) protocol addresses the weaknesses of WEP and acts as a security protocol upgrade to WEP. WPA uses the *Temporal Key Integrity Protocol* (*TKIP*), which provides a new encryption key for every sent packet. This protects WPA from many of the attacks that make WEP vulnerable, though TKIP has since been deprecated, as it has flaws of its own. WPA also offers security enhancements over WEP such as an encryption key integrity-checking feature and user authentication through the industry-standard *Extensible Authentication Protocol* (*EAP*). EAP provides a huge security improvement over WEP encryption. Even with these enhancements, WPA was intended only as an interim security solution until the IEEE 802.11i (wireless security standards committee) finalized and implemented the next generation of wireless security: WPA2.

WPA2   Today, Linux, macOS, and Windows support the full IEEE 802.11i standard, more commonly known as *Wi-Fi Protected Access 2* (*WPA2*), to lock down wireless networks. WPA2 uses the *Advanced Encryption Standard* (*AES*), among other improvements, to provide a secure wireless environment. If you haven't upgraded to WPA2, you should. All current WAPs and wireless clients support WPA2 and most routers have a "backward compatible" mode for the handful of client devices that still use first-generation WPA. This is necessary when using older network cards or WAPs—think early implementations of 802.11b wireless networking—because the old hardware in these products cannot support WPA2. Later iterations of these devices have upgrades to support AES and WPA2.

 EXAM TIP   Be sure you are familiar with WEP, WPA, WPA2, TKIP, and AES wireless encryption types.

WPA3   The eventual successor to WPA2 (WPA3, of course!) was announced in early 2018. Support for WPA3 is a work in progress for now (it's expected to land in Windows 10 in the first half of 2019), but it should become increasingly common in the wild over the next few years. WPA3 addresses some security and usability issues, including encryption to protect the data of users on open (public) networks.

 EXAM TIP   WPA3 didn't make it into the CompTIA A+ objectives this time around, so this chapter and the exam both treat WPA2 as the latest-and-greatest in Wi-Fi security. If you live in the real world and aren't a time-traveler from before 2019, follow these tips. Keep an eye on software and hardware support for WPA3, and recommend WPA3-compatible devices once they're available. Implement WPA3 networks when practical, and eventually disable WPA2 once all of the devices you need to support are WPA3-compatible.

WPS   While most techs can configure wireless networks blindfolded, the thought of passwords and encryption might intimidate the average user. Most people just plug in their wireless router and go on their merry way. Because everyone should secure their wireless network, the developers of Wi-Fi created *Wi-Fi Protected Setup* (*WPS*), a standard included on most WAPs and clients to make secure connections easier to configure.

WPS works in one of two ways. Some devices use a push button, such as the one shown in Figure 20-10, and others use a password or code.

Figure 20-10
WPS button on
an e2500 Router

Let's say you want to connect a WPS-capable wireless printer to a WPS-capable WAP. First, you would press the button on the printer for a short moment (usually two seconds). You then have a set time (usually two minutes) to press the button on the WAP. This should automatically configure a secure connection.

Some devices enable you to use a code. A WPS-capable WAP will have an eight-digit numeric code printed on the device. To access the WAP, just enter the code in the OS as you would a WPA/WPA2 password. Now you're on the network.

Sadly, WPS has a security flaw. A hacker can use a program to repeatedly guess the eight-digit code. Because of how the code is set up, it's very easy to guess. As long you have WPS enabled on your WAP, you are vulnerable. The only way to stop this hack is to shut down WPS. Check the WAP manufacturer's Web site for instructions on turning off WPS.

1001

Speed and Range Issues

Wireless networking data throughput speeds depend on several factors. Foremost is the standard that the wireless devices use. Depending on the standard used, wireless throughput speeds range from a measly 2 Mbps to a snappy 1+ Gbps. One of the other factors affecting speed is the distance between wireless nodes (or between wireless nodes and centralized access points). Wireless devices dynamically negotiate the top speed at which they can communicate without dropping too many data packets. Speed decreases as distance increases, so the maximum throughput speed is achieved only at extremely close range (less than 25 feet or so). At the outer reaches of a device's effective range, speed may decrease to around 1 Mbps before it drops out altogether.

Interference caused by solid objects and other wireless devices operating in the same frequency range—such as cordless phones or baby monitors—can reduce both speed and range. So-called *dead spots* occur when something capable of blocking the radio signal comes between the wireless network nodes. Large electrical appliances such as refrigerators block wireless network signals *very* effectively. Other culprits include electrical fuse boxes, metal plumbing, air conditioning units, and similar objects.

NOTE You can see the speed and signal strength on your wireless network by looking at the wireless NIC's status. In Windows, open the Network and Sharing Center, select Change adapter settings, then double-click your wireless NIC to view the status dialog box.

Wireless networking range is difficult to define, and you'll see most descriptions listed with qualifiers, such as "*around* 150 feet" and "*about* 300 feet." This is simply because, like throughput speed, range is greatly affected by outside factors. Interference from other wireless devices affects range, as does interference from solid objects. The maximum ranges listed in the next section are those presented by wireless manufacturers as the theoretical maximum ranges. In the real world, you'll experience these ranges only under the most ideal circumstances. True effective range is probably about half what you see listed.

You can increase range in a couple of ways. You can install multiple WAPs to permit "roaming" between one WAP's coverage area and another's—an EBSS, described earlier in this chapter. Or, you can install a replacement WAP with greater signal strength and range. If that is still not enough, signal boosters that can give you even more power are available, as are *wireless repeaters/extenders*, which can receive and rebroadcast your Wi-Fi signal.

EXAM TIP Look for basic troubleshooting questions on the CompTIA A+ certification exams dealing with factors that affect wireless connectivity, range, and speed.

Wireless Networking Standards

Most wireless networks use *radio frequency* (*RF*) technologies, in particular the 802.11 (Wi-Fi) standards. Other standards, such as infrared, Bluetooth, and cellular, hold a much smaller place in today's market, although cellular connections to the Internet surpass anything else, at least with smartphones. To help you gain a better understanding of wireless network technologies, this section provides a brief look at the standards they use.

NOTE Radio frequency is the part of the electromagnetic spectrum used for radio communication.

IEEE 802.11-Based Wireless Networking

The IEEE 802.11 wireless Ethernet standard, more commonly known as *Wi-Fi*, defines methods devices may use to communicate via *spread-spectrum* radio waves.

Spread-spectrum broadcasts data in small, discrete chunks over the frequencies available within a certain frequency range.

NOTE Wi-Fi and other wireless communication technologies use radio frequencies that fall in *industrial, scientific, and medical (ISM) radio bands.* This can lead to interference with other devices, such as microwave ovens and baby monitors.

The 802.11-based wireless technologies broadcast and receive on one of two radio bands: 2.4 GHz and 5 GHz. A band is a contiguous range of frequencies that is usually divided up into discrete slices called *channels.* Over the years, the original 802.11 standard has been extended to 802.11a, 802.11b, 802.11g, 802.11n, and 802.11ac variations used in Wi-Fi wireless networks. Each of these versions of 802.11 uses one of the two bands, with the exception of 802.11n, which uses one but may use both. Don't worry; I'll break this down for you in a moment.

NOTE Wi-Fi is by far the most widely adopted wireless local networking type today, while cellular is the big dog in wide area roaming networks. Not only do millions of private businesses and homes have wireless networks, but many public places such as coffee shops and libraries also offer Internet access through wireless networks.

Newer wireless devices typically provide backward compatibility with older wireless devices. If you are using an 802.11n WAP, all of your 802.11g devices can use it. An 802.11ac WAP is backward compatible with 802.11b, g, and n. The exception to this is 802.11a, which requires a 5-GHz radio, meaning only 802.11ac and dual-band 802.11n WAPs are backward compatible with 802.11a devices. The following paragraphs describe the important specifications of each of the popular 802.11-based wireless networking standards.

802.11a　Despite the "a" designation for this extension to the 802.11 standard, *802.11a* was actually on the market after 802.11b. The 802.11a standard differs from the other 802.11-based standards in significant ways. Foremost is that it operates in the 5-GHz frequency range. This means devices using this standard are less prone to interference from other devices that use the same frequency range. 802.11a also offers considerably greater throughput than 802.11 and 802.11b at speeds up to 54 Mbps, though its actual throughput is no more than 25 Mbps in normal traffic conditions. Although its theoretical range tops out at about 150 feet, its maximum range will be lower in a typical office environment. Despite the superior speed of 802.11a, it isn't as widely adopted as some of the following 802.11 versions.

802.11b　*802.11b* was the first standard to take off and become ubiquitous in wireless networking. The 802.11b standard supports data throughput of up to 11 Mbps (with actual throughput averaging 4 to 6 Mbps)—on par with older wired 10BaseT networks—and a maximum range of 300 feet under ideal conditions. In a typical office environment, its maximum range is lower. The main downside to using 802.11b is that it uses a very popular frequency. The 2.4-GHz ISM band is already crowded with baby monitors, garage door openers, microwaves, and wireless phones, so you're likely to run into interference from other wireless devices.

802.11g *802.11g* came out in 2003, taking the best of 802.11a and b and rolling them into a single standard. 802.11g offers data transfer speeds equivalent to 802.11a, up to 54 Mbps, with the wider 300-foot range of 802.11b. More important, 802.11g runs in the 2.4-GHz ISM band, so it is backward compatible with 802.11b, meaning that the same 802.11g WAP can service both 802.11b and 802.11g wireless nodes.

802.11n The *802.11n* standard brought several improvements to Wi-Fi networking, including faster speeds and new antenna technology implementations.

The 802.11n specification requires all but hand-held devices to use multiple antennas to implement a feature called *multiple in/multiple out* (*MIMO*), which enables the devices to make multiple simultaneous connections. With up to four antennas, 802.11n devices can achieve amazing speeds. The official standard supports throughput of up to 600 Mbps, although practical implementation drops that down substantially (to 100+ Mbps at 300+ feet).

 NOTE Because cellular telephones typically support both cellular networks and 802.11x Wi-Fi networks, many can be used to bridge the gap. Using internal utilities or apps, you can set up your phone as a Wi-Fi WAP that can pass signals to and from the Internet via the cellular connection. Turning your phone into a WAP is known as *creating a hotspot*; using it to bridge to the cellular network is called *tethering*. Check out Chapters 21 and 24 for the scoop on these techniques.

Many 802.11n WAPs employ *transmit beamforming*, a multiple-antenna technology that helps get rid of dead spots—or at least make them not so bad. The antennas adjust the signal once the WAP discovers a client to optimize the radio signal.

Like 802.11g, 802.11n WAPs can run in the 2.4-GHz ISM band, supporting earlier, slower 802.11b/g devices. 802.11n also supports the more powerful, so-called *dual-band* operation. To use dual-band, you need a more advanced (and more expensive) WAP that runs at both 5 GHz and 2.4 GHz simultaneously; some support 802.11a devices as well as 802.11b/g devices.

802.11ac *802.11ac* is a natural expansion of the 802.11n standard, incorporating even more streams, wider bandwidth, and higher speed. To avoid device density issues in the 2.4-GHz band, 802.11ac only uses the 5-GHz band. The latest versions of 802.11ac include a new version of MIMO called *Multiuser MIMO* (*MU-MIMO*). MU-MIMO gives a WAP the ability to broadcast to multiple users simultaneously. Like 802.11n, 802.11ac supports dual-band operation. Some WAPs even support tri-band operation, adding a second 5-GHz signal to support a lot more 5-GHz connections simultaneously at optimal speeds.

EXAM TIP   Two developments in late 2018 and early 2019 *won't* appear on the CompTIA A+ 1001 exam, but will have relevance for techs over the next few years. First, the next generation of Wi-Fi, called *802.11ax*, will roll out in 2019. Manufacturers produced a lot of preliminary devices in 2017 and 2018. The standard offers faster speeds than 802.11ac and initially uses the 2.4- and 5-GHz spectrums. 802.11ax is also known as *High Efficiency Wireless* (*HEW*).

Second, in October 2018 the Wi-Alliance announced new branding for 802.11n, 802.11ac, and 802.11ax. The new names are *Wi-Fi 4*, *Wi-Fi 5*, and *Wi-Fi 6*, respectively. Manufacturers are using these terms as the book goes to print, so expect to use them with clients.

Table 20-1 compares the important differences among the versions of 802.11*x*.

	802.11a	802.11b	802.11g	802.11n	802.11ac
Max. throughput	54 Mbps	11 Mbps	54 Mbps	100+ Mbps	1+ Gbps
Max. range	150 feet	300 feet	300 feet	300+ feet	300+ feet
Frequency	5 GHz	2.4 GHz	2.4 GHz	2.4 and 5 GHz	5 GHz
Security	SSID, MAC filtering, industry-standard WEP, WPA, WPA2	SSID, MAC filtering, industry-standard WEP, WPA, WPA2 (later hardware)	SSID, MAC filtering, industry-standard WEP, WPA, WPA2	SSID, MAC filtering, industry-standard WEP, WPA, WPA2	SSID, MAC filtering, industry-standard WEP, WPA, WPA2
Compatibility	802.11a	802.11b	802.11b, 802.11g	802.11b, 802.11g, 802.11n, (802.11a in some cases)	802.11a, 802.11b, 802.11g, 802.11n
Communication mode	Ad hoc or infrastructure	Ad hoc or infrastructure	Ad hoc or infrastructure	Ad hoc or infrastructure	Ad hoc or infrastructure
Description	Eight available channels. Less prone to interference than 802.11b and 802.11g.	Fourteen channels available in the 2.4-GHz band (only eleven of which can be used in the U.S. due to FCC regulations). Three non-overlapping channels.	Improved security enhancements. Fourteen channels available in the 2.4-GHz band (only eleven of which can be used in the U.S. due to FCC regulations). Three non-overlapping channels.	Same as 802.11g but adds the 5-GHz band that 802.11a uses. 802.11n can also make use of multiple antennas (MIMO) to increase its range and speed.	Expands on 802.11n by adding streams, bandwidth, and higher speed in the 5-GHz band. Uses MU-MIMO and beamforming antenna technology to optimize wireless connections.

Table 20-1   Comparison of 802.11 Standards

SIM Check out the "Wireless Technologies" Challenge! sim in the Chapter 20 section of https://totalsem.com/100x to reinforce the differences among 802.11a, 802.11b, 802.11g, 802.11n, and 802.11ac. This will help you with any performance-based questions CompTIA might throw your way.

Try This! 802.11ac Products

802.11ac is the standard for any new Wi-Fi rollout. You need to understand variations, so try this! Head out to a big box electronics retail store, like Microcenter, Fry's, or even Best Buy (or go online to Newegg). What variations of 802.11ac products do you see? Note the letters and numbers associated with the products. The base models—the least expensive—might say AC1200. Products listed as AC1900 might be twice as much.

The differences among the 802.11ac routers and WAPs boil down to the radio frequencies, the number of antennas used, and the number of radios employed within the device. The speed differences claimed are pretty astonishing. An AC1200 module offers 867 Mbps throughput on the 5-GHz band, for example, whereas an AC3100 module can crank 2167 Mbps throughput. Real-world experiences aren't so extreme.

Other Wireless Standards

While Wi-Fi dominates the wireless networking market, it isn't the only standard. A lot of smaller networks (we're talking two computers small) use infrared or Bluetooth to connect devices. Mobile devices, such as smartphones, wearables, and tablets, connect wirelessly via cellular networks. They often use other standards to connect with each other or to other technologies such as car stereos, GPS devices, smart televisions, flying drones, and an endless litany of wireless-enabled products.

Infrared Wireless Networking

Wireless networking using infrared technology is largely overlooked these days, probably because of the explosion of interest in newer, faster wireless and cellular standards. But it is still a viable method to transfer files on some older devices.

Communication through infrared devices is implemented via the *Infrared Data Association (IrDA)* protocol. All versions of Windows and pretty much the whole computing industry support the IrDA protocol stack as an industry standard.

NOTE Apple and Linux computers also support IrDA.

In speed and range, infrared isn't very impressive. Infrared devices are capable of transferring data up to 4 Mbps—not too shabby, but hardly stellar. The maximum distance between infrared devices is 1 meter. Infrared links are direct line-of-sight and are susceptible to interference. Anything that breaks the beam of light can disrupt an infra-red link: a badly placed can of Mountain Dew, a coworker passing between desks, or even bright sunlight hitting the infrared transceiver can cause interference.

Infrared is designed to make a point-to-point connection between two devices only in ad hoc mode. No infrastructure mode is available. You can, however, use an infrared access point device to enable Ethernet network communication using IrDA. Infrared devices operate at half-duplex, meaning that while one is talking, the other is listening—they can't talk and listen at the same time. IrDA has a mode that emulates full-duplex communication, but it's really half-duplex. The IrDA protocol offers exactly nothing in the way of encryption or authentication. Infrared's main security feature is the fact that you have to be literally within arm's reach to establish a link. Clearly, infrared is not the best solution for a dedicated network connection, but for a quick file transfer or print job without getting your hands dirty, it'll do in a pinch. Here are the specifications for infrared:

Max. throughput	Up to 4 Mbps
Max. range	1 meter (39 inches)
Security	None
Compatibility	IrDA
Communication mode	Point-to-point ad hoc

Bluetooth

Bluetooth wireless technology (named for tenth-century Danish king Harald Bluetooth) is designed to create small wireless networks preconfigured to do very specific jobs. Some great examples are wearable technology, audio devices such as headsets or automotive entertainment systems that connect to your smartphone, *personal area networks* (*PANs*) that link two computers for a quick-and-dirty wireless network, and input devices such as keyboards and mice. Bluetooth is *not* designed to be a full-function networking solution, nor is it meant to compete with Wi-Fi.

Bluetooth, like any technology, has been upgraded over the years to make it faster and more secure. The first generation (versions 1.1 and 1.2) supports speeds around 1 Mbps. The second generation (2.0 and 2.1) is backward compatible with its first-generation cousins and adds support for more speed by introducing Enhanced Data Rate (EDR), which pushes top speeds to around 3 Mbps. The third generation (3.0 + HS) tops out at 24 Mbps, but this is accomplished over an 802.11 connection after Bluetooth negotiation. The High Speed (+ HS) feature is optional. Instead of continuing to increase top speed, the fourth generation (4.0, 4.1, and 4.2), also called Bluetooth Smart, is largely focused on improving Bluetooth's suitability for use in networked "smart" devices/appliances by reducing cost and power consumption, improving speed and security, and introducing IP connectivity. The fifth generation (just *Bluetooth 5*) adds options to increase speed at the expense of range or by changing packet size. Bluetooth 5 adds better support for the Internet of Things (IoT) devices, like smart speakers, lights, and so on.

NOTE Chapter 21, "The Internet," details the Internet of Things. We'll get there!

The IEEE organization has made first-generation Bluetooth the basis for its 802.15 standard for wireless PANs. Bluetooth uses a broadcasting method that switches between any of the 79 frequencies available in the 2.45-GHz range. Bluetooth hops frequencies some 1600 times per second, making it highly resistant to interference.

Generally, the faster and further a device sends data, the more power it needs to do so, and the Bluetooth designers understood a long time ago that some devices (such as a Bluetooth headset) could save power by not sending data as quickly or as far as other Bluetooth devices may need. To address this, all Bluetooth devices are configured for one of three classes that define maximum power usage in milliwatts (mW) and maximum distance:

Class	Max Power Usage	Max Range
Class 1	100 mW	100 meters
Class 2	2.5 mW	10 meters
Class 3	1 mW	1 meter

Bluetooth personal networks are made to replace the snake's nest of cables that currently connects most PCs to their various peripheral devices—keyboard, mouse, printer, speakers, scanner, and the like—but you probably won't be swapping out your 802.11-based networking devices with Bluetooth-based replacements anytime soon. Despite this, Bluetooth's recent introduction of IP connectivity may bring more and more Bluetooth-related traffic to 802.11 devices in the future.

Having said that, Bluetooth-enabled wireless networking is comparable to other wireless technologies in a few ways:

- Like infrared, Bluetooth is acceptable for quick file transfers where a wired connection (or a faster wireless connection) is unavailable.
- Bluetooth's speed and range make it a good match for wireless print server solutions.

As mentioned earlier in the chapter, Bluetooth hardware comes either built into newer portable electronic gadgets such as smartphones or as an adapter added to an internal or external expansion bus. Bluetooth networking is enabled through ad hoc device-to-device connections, or in an infrastructure-like mode through Bluetooth access points. Bluetooth access points are very similar to 802.11-based access points, bridging wireless Bluetooth PAN segments to wired LAN segments.

Cellular

A *cellular wireless network* enables you to connect to the Internet through a network-aware smartphone, tablet, or other mobile device. Although the CompTIA exam objectives list cellular as a general wireless networking standard, it's not really used for local area networking. You'll find it much more common in connecting devices to the Internet. Some very old technology embraced add-on expansion cards for cellular that I'll discuss a little later in this chapter, just in case you get a random ancient question on the CompTIA A+ exams.

 NOTE Chapter 21 covers the cellular standards in detail.

1002

Installing and Configuring Wireless Networking

The mechanics of setting up a wireless network don't differ much from a wired network. Physically installing a wireless network adapter is the same as installing a wired NIC, whether it's an internal card, a laptop add-on wireless card, or an external USB device. Simply install the device and let plug and play handle the rest. Install the device's supplied driver when prompted and you're practically finished.

The trick is in configuring the wireless network so that only specific wireless nodes are able to use it, and securing the data that's being sent through the air.

Wi-Fi Configuration

As discussed earlier in the chapter, Wi-Fi networks support ad hoc and infrastructure operation modes. Which mode you choose depends on the number of wireless nodes you need to support, the type of data sharing they'll perform, and your management requirements.

Ad Hoc Mode

Ad hoc mode wireless networks don't need a WAP. The only requirements in an ad hoc mode wireless network are that each wireless node be configured with the same network name (SSID) and that no two nodes use the same IP address. Figure 20-11 shows a wireless network configuration utility with ad hoc mode selected.

The only other configuration steps to take are to make sure no two nodes are using the same IP address (this step is usually unnecessary if all nodes are using DHCP) and ensuring that the File and Printer Sharing service is running on all nodes.

Infrastructure Mode

Typically, infrastructure mode wireless networks employ one or more WAPs connected to a wired network segment, such as a corporate intranet, the Internet, or both. As with ad hoc mode wireless networks, infrastructure mode networks require that the same SSID be configured on all nodes, and additionally on all WAPs. Figure 20-12 shows an older version of Ubuntu's Wi-Fi configuration screen set to infrastructure mode.

Figure 20-11
Selecting ad
hoc mode
in a wireless
configuration
utility

Figure 20-12
Infrastructure
mode is set
in a wireless
configuration
utility.

Most consumer WAPs have an integrated Web server and are configured through a browser-based setup utility. Typically, you open a Web browser on a networked computer and enter the WAP's default IP address, such as 192.168.1.1, to bring up the configuration page. You will need to supply an administrative password, included with your WAP's documentation, to log in (see Figure 20-13). Most newer WAPs ask you to create an administrative password at installation. Setup screens vary from vendor to vendor and from model to model. Figure 20-14 shows the initial setup screen for a popular Linksys WAP/router.

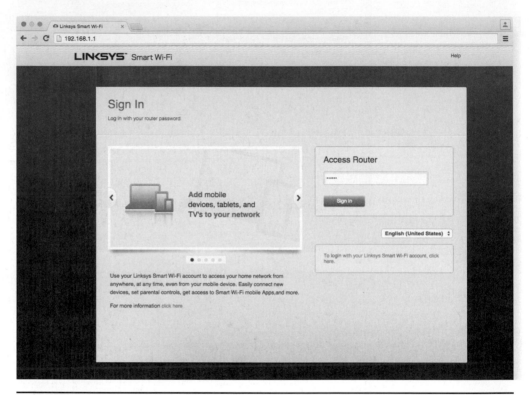

Figure 20-13   Security login for Linksys WAP

To make life easier, current WAPs come with a Web-based utility that autodetects the WAP and guides the user through setting up all of its features.

When you purchase a new WAP, there is a pretty good chance the vendor already has updated firmware for it. This is even more true if you've had your WAP for a while. Before configuring your WAP for your users to access it, you should check for updates. Refer to the section "Software Troubleshooting," later in the chapter, for more on updating WAP firmware.

Configure the SSID option where indicated. Remember that it's better to configure a unique SSID than it is to accept the well-known default one. The default may help an attacker identify your hardware and focus on any vulnerabilities it is known to have.

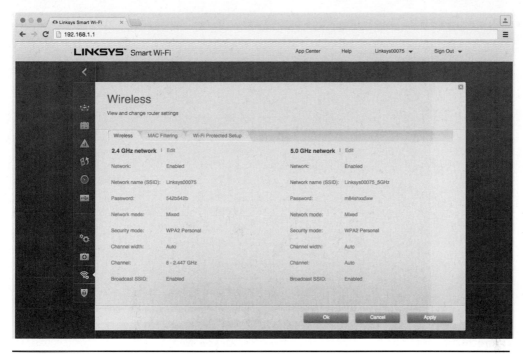

Figure 20-14 Linksys WAP setup screen

Avoid names that include an address, name, number, or other description that would help an attacker locate the physical device.

Channel selection is usually automatic, but you can reconfigure this option if you have particular needs in your organization (for example, if you have multiple wireless networks operating in the same area). Use a wireless analyzer to find the "quietest" channel where you intend to install the WAP and select that channel in the appropriate WAP setup/configuration screen. This provides the lowest chance of interference from other WAPs. Clients automatically search through all frequencies and channels when searching for broadcasted SSIDs.

To increase security even more, use MAC filtering. Figure 20-15 shows the MAC filtering configuration screen for a Linksys WAP. Simply click the Add MAC Address button and enter the MAC address of a wireless node that you wish to allow (or deny) access to your wireless network. Set up encryption by setting the security mode on the WAP and then generating a unique security key or password. Then configure all connected wireless nodes on the network with the same credentials. Figure 20-16 shows a basic WAP properties panel configured for WPA2 Personal wireless security.

EXAM TIP As noted earlier in the chapter, the WEP protocol provides security, but it's easily cracked. Use WPA3 or WPA2 or, if you have older equipment, settle for WPA until you can upgrade.

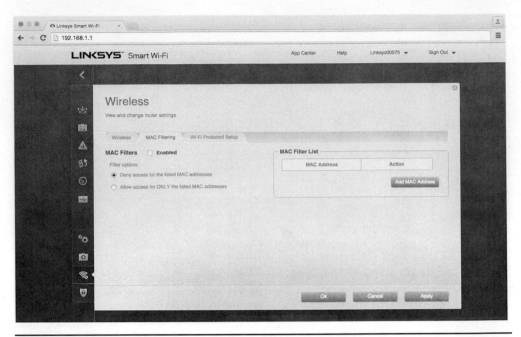

Figure 20-15 MAC filtering configuration screen for a Linksys WAP

Figure 20-16
Basic properties
panel for a
Linksys WAP

If you're dealing with older equipment and find yourself performing the unseemly task of setting up WEP, you should have the option of automatically generating a set of encryption keys or doing it manually; save yourself a headache and use the automatic method. Select an encryption level—the usual choices are either 64-bit or 128-bit—and then enter a unique *passphrase* and click the Generate button (or whatever the equivalent button is called on your WAP). Then select a default key and save the settings. The encryption level, key, and passphrase must match on the wireless client node or communication will fail. Many WAPs have the capability to export the WEP encryption key data onto a media storage device so you can easily import it on a client workstation, or you can manually configure encryption by using the Windows wireless configuration utility.

WPA and WPA2 encryption are configured in much the same way. While it may seem that there are many configuration options, there are effectively two ways to set up WPA/WPA2: Personal/Pre-shared Key (PSK) or Enterprise. WPA/WPA2 Personal is the most common for small and home networks (see Figure 20-17). Enterprise is much more complex, requires extra equipment, and is only used in the most serious and secure wireless networks. After selecting the Personal option, there may be "subselections" such as Mixed mode, which allows a WPA2-encrypted WAP to also support WPA. You may see

Figure 20-17
Encryption screen on client wireless network adapter configuration utility

Figure 20-18
Encryption
screen with
RADIUS option

RADIUS server:	192	168	10	25
RADIUS port:	1812
Shared key:	$%8]Q0[lzf>,te4DM:
Network mode:	Mixed
Security mode:	WPA2 Enterprise

the term PSK, Pre-Shared Key, or just Personal in the configuration options. If you have the option, choose WPA2 encryption for the WAP as well as the NICs in your network.

Settings such as WPA2 for the Enterprise assume you'll enable authentication by using something called a *RADIUS* server (see Figure 20-18). Larger businesses tend to need more security than a single network-wide password can offer. Their networks often require individual users to log in with their own credentials.

EXAM TIP We call using only a user name and password *single-factor authentication* because they're both something you *know*. More robust *multifactor authentication* systems may require something you *have* (like a security card), *are* (face and fingerprint scans), and more. Chapter 25, "Care and Feeding of Mobile Devices," takes a closer look at the role these factors play in authentication.

To accomplish this, the network uses authentication protocols like RADIUS and TACACS+ to authenticate each user with an authentication server. Remote Authentication Dial-In User Service (RADIUS) and Terminal Access Controller Access-Control System Plus (TACACS+) are protocols for authenticating network users and managing what resources they may access. RADIUS is partially encrypted and uses UDP; TACACS+ is fully encrypted and uses TCP.

EXAM TIP TACACS dates back to 1984, and it has mostly been replaced with the backward-incompatible TACACS+ (which came out in 1994). The CompTIA A+ objectives just say "TACACS," but I hope they'll only ask you about TACACS+. Just in case, be prepared to look for context clues if you see a detailed question about TACACS. The original TACACS has no encryption, uses TCP or UDP, and only handles authentication. TACACS+ is fully encrypted, uses only TCP, and can handle authentication, authorizing users to access specific resources, and keeping track of the resources used.

This way, businesses can allow only people with the proper credentials to connect to their Wi-Fi networks. For home use, select the Personal version of WPA3/WPA2/WPA.

Use the best encryption you can. If you have WPA3 or WPA2, use it. If not, use WPA. WEP is configured in much the same way, but it is a terrible choice for a general network. If you can't upgrade or replace any WEP-only devices, consider setting up a separate WEP network just for them.

NOTE   Always try WPA3-Personal or WPA2-Personal first, depending on what your WAP can handle. If you then have wireless computers that can't connect to your WAP, fall back to WPA2-Personal or WPA-Personal. Use Mixed mode so the newer clients can still take advantage of the extra security provided by WPA3 or WPA2 while older clients can use WPA-Personal.

With most home networks, you can simply leave the channel and frequency of the WAP at the factory defaults, but in an environment with overlapping Wi-Fi signals, you'll want to adjust one or both features. To adjust the channel, find the option in the WAP configuration screens and simply change it. Figure 20-19 shows the channel option in a Linksys WAP.

Figure 20-19
Changing the
channel

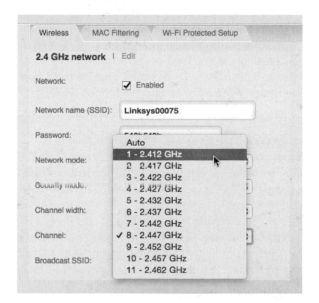

With dual-band 802.11n and 802.11ac WAPs, you can choose which band to put traffic on, either 2.4 GHz or 5 GHz. In an area with overlapping signals, most of the traffic (at least as of this writing) will be on the 2.4-GHz frequency. In addition to other wireless devices (such as cordless phones), microwaves also use the 2.4-GHz frequency and can cause a great deal of interference. You can avoid any kind of conflict with your 802.11ac devices by using the 5-GHz frequency exclusively. Figure 20-20 shows the configuration screen for a dual-band 802.11ac WAP.

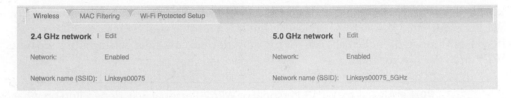

Wireless	MAC Filtering	Wi-Fi Protected Setup		
2.4 GHz network	Edit		**5.0 GHz network**	Edit
Network:	Enabled		Network:	Enabled
Network name (SSID):	Linksys00075		Network name (SSID):	Linksys00075_5GHz

Figure 20-20　Linksys router sporting dual bands

EXAM TIP　This chapter (and much of the 1002 exam) focuses on SOHO wireless deployment. Techs handle the WAP configuration at each WAP, using the built-in firmware, and that's fine for networks with no more than a few access points. Scaling up to cover an entire campus or enterprise building, on the other hand, makes that configuration impossibly time consuming.

Years ago, manufacturers developed wireless LAN controllers to centralize configuration of many dumb WAPs. An organization might have a thousand WAPs, but a single software interface for configuring all of them. These days, that configuration interface can be hosted on a local computer or, increasingly, via a cloud-based infrastructure. The latter uses *cloud-based network controllers*—that's the CompTIA term. You're also likely to see such networks referred to as *cloud-managed WLANs*.

Placing the Access Point(s)

The optimal location for an access point depends on the area you want to cover, whether you care if the signal bleeds out beyond the borders, and what interference exists from other wireless sources. You start by doing a site survey. A site survey can be as trivial as firing up a wireless-capable laptop and looking for existing SSIDs. Or it can be a complex job where you hire people with specialized equipment to come in and make lots of careful plans defining the best place to put WAPs and which wireless channels to use. To make sure the wireless signal goes where you want it to go and not where you don't, you need to use the right antenna. Let's see what types of antennas are available.

Omni-directional and Centered　For a typical network, you want blanket coverage and would place a WAP with an omni-directional antenna in the center of the area (see Figure 20-21). With an omni-directional antenna, the radio wave flows outward from the WAP. This has the advantage of ease of use—anything within the signal radius can potentially access the network. Most wireless networks use this combination, especially in the consumer space. The standard straight-wire antennas that provide most omni-directional function are called *dipole antennas*. Dipole antennas look like a stick, but inside they have two antenna arms or poles aligned on the antenna's axis, hence "dipole."

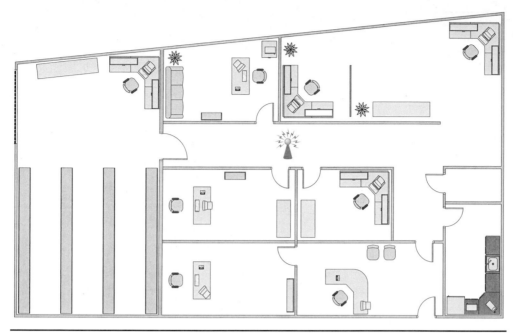

Figure 20-21   Room layout with WAP in the center

Gaining Gain   An antenna strengthens and focuses the radio frequency output from a WAP. The ratio of increase—what's called *gain*—is measured in decibels (dB). The gain from a typical WAP is 2 dB, enough to cover a reasonable area but not a very large room. To increase that signal requires a bigger antenna. Many WAPs have removable antennas that you can replace. To increase the signal in an omni-directional and centered setup, simply replace the factory antennas with one or more bigger antennas (see Figure 20-22). Get a big enough antenna and you can crank it all the way up to 11 dB!

Gain antennas cause the antenna to pick up weaker signals and have an amplifying effect on transmitted signals. They come in several common flavors. Increasing the size of a dipole will increase its gain evenly in all directions. Parabolic dish-type antennas and multi-element *Yagi* antennas increase gain in a specific direction and reduce gain in all the other directions. You'll know a Yagi antenna when you see one; it looks like the old television antennas that we used to use to receive over-the-air television signals, only much smaller. In general, the more elements a Yagi has, the higher the directional gain.

It's a Polarizing Issue   Antennas and the signals that they transmit have an electro-magnetic property called *polarization*. Without getting too deep into the weeds, think of polarization as the signal having the same alignment as the antenna. If the antenna on your WAP or computer is aligned up and down, your transmitted signal will have vertical alignment. Likewise, if you tilt your antenna over on its side, the signal will have

Figure 20-22
WAP with
replacement
antenna

horizontal polarization. Of course, you can also align your antenna somewhere between vertical and horizontal. You may have not thought about it before, but your laptop or notebook usually has vertical polarization because the antenna goes up the side of the lid, next to the screen. When the screen is open, it's generally open to a near vertical position.

 EXAM TIP To achieve a good compromise in supporting connections to clients with different antenna polarization, orient the WAP antennas on a 45-degree angle.

For the best connection between a client and a WAP, the wireless signals should have the same polarization. The worst connection strength between WAPs and clients happens when one has vertical antennas and the other has horizontal. While it is pretty easy to make sure the antenna on a desktop computer is optimally aligned, it is more challenging to dictate antenna orientation in laptops, notebooks, smartphones, and tablets. If your WAP has more than one antenna, consider orienting them differently to accommodate different client configurations. What is the right orientation? The best way to determine that is with testing; try one vertical and another horizontal and then sample the clients throughout the coverage area to check connection strength. Then try some other orientations until you achieve the strongest coverage.

EXAM TIP If you want to know whether your local café, bookstore, airport, or other public place has a Wi-Fi access point (a hotspot), you can use a *Wi-Fi* or *wireless locator*. The locator is usually the size of your car remote and lights up or otherwise signals you whenever you are in range of a Wi-Fi access point. Wi-Fi locators, also called *Wi-Fi analyzers*, can also be installed as an app on a Wi-Fi smartphone.

Bluetooth Configuration

As with other wireless networking solutions, Bluetooth devices are completely plug and play. Just connect the adapter and follow the prompts to install the appropriate drivers if your OS needs them. Once installed, you'll need to start the *pairing* process to enable the devices to create a secure connection—you wouldn't want every Bluetooth client in range to automatically connect with your smartphone! Figure 20-23 shows a Google Nexus phone receiving a pairing request from an iMac called "mediamac."

Figure 20-23
Goggle Nexus receiving a pairing request

Pairing takes a few steps. The first step, of course, is to enable Bluetooth. Some devices, such as Bluetooth headsets, always have Bluetooth enabled because it's their sole communication method. Others, like a Bluetooth adapter in your computer, may be enabled or disabled in the Network and Sharing Center.

Once enabled, the two devices must be placed into pairing mode. Some devices, like the stereo in my car, continuously listen for a pairing request, while others must be set to pairing (or discovery) mode. The devices in pairing mode will discover each other and agree on a compatible Bluetooth version, speed, and set of features.

The final step of the pairing process, the security component, requires you to confirm your intent to pair the devices. Depending on Bluetooth version and device capabilities, there are a number of different ways this could go; these range from the devices confirming the connection without user input to requiring the user to input a short code on one or both devices. If used, these codes are most often four or six digits, but older devices may differ. Refer to your device's documentation for specific details on its pairing process.

Done, right? Well, almost. There remains the final step: make sure everything works. Are you getting sound into your Bluetooth headset or speakers? Does the Bluetooth microphone work when making phone calls or recording notes on your smartphone app? Can you stream music from your smartphone to your car stereo? You get the idea. If something isn't working, it's time to check for two common problems: unsuccessful/incomplete pairing, and configuration issues.

The pairing process is quick and easy to repeat. You may have to delete the pairing from one of the devices first. After re-pairing, test again. If the pairing process never gets started, you have no Bluetooth connectivity. Make sure both devices are on, have Bluetooth enabled, and are in pairing mode. Check battery power in wireless devices and check configuration settings.

If the pairing appears successful but the connection test is not, look for configuration issues. Check microphone input settings and audio output settings. Use any vendor-provided testing and troubleshooting utilities. Keep at it until it works or until you confirm that one or both devices are bad or incompatible.

You'll need to do a little more than just pair devices to connect to a Bluetooth PAN. This connection is handled by your OS in most cases. Figure 20-24 shows the macOS network configuration for a Bluetooth PAN connected through a Nexus phone.

 NOTE A Bluetooth Internet connection is a rare sight out in the real world. Today, mobile devices use Wi-Fi or a cellular connection to access network and Internet resources.

Cellular Configuration

In the early days of cellular access to networks (notably the Internet), manufacturers developed add-on cellular cards to enable computers—especially portables—to get on the Web from anywhere. There was no single standard for configuring a cellular network card because the cards and software changed based on your service provider. The cell phone companies made installing their cards very simple.

With most cellular cards, you simply plugged the card into your computer, often via USB, and the setup program automatically launched. These cards almost always had all the required software and drivers built in, so there was no need for an optical disc or

Figure 20-24 macOS Bluetooth PAN connected

other installation media. Once you installed the necessary software, you launched the connection application.

Standalone cellular cards are out there (and with the rollout of 5G networks in 2019, I expect to see more). Much more common these days is to get a dedicated wireless hotspot, like you see in Figure 20-25. These devices connect to a valid (i.e., you paid

Figure 20-25
AT&T LTE hotspot

for it) cellular network. You configure a computing device to connect via Wi-Fi to the hotspot, and you're golden. Chapter 21 goes into much more detail about Wi-Fi hotspots and 5G.

Troubleshooting Wi-Fi

Wireless networks are a real boon when they work right, but they can also be one of the most vexing things to troubleshoot when they don't. Let's turn to some practical advice on how to detect and correct wireless hardware, software, and configuration problems.

As with any troubleshooting scenario, your first step in troubleshooting a wireless network is to break down your tasks into logical steps. First, of course, identify the problem, then figure out the scope of the problem. Ask yourself *who*, *what*, and *when*:

- Who is affected by the problem?
- What is the nature of their network problem?
- When did the problem start?

In the formal process of troubleshooting, answering these questions is step one, known as gathering information. The answers to these questions dictate at least the initial direction of your troubleshooting.

So, who's affected? If all machines on your network—wired and wireless—have lost connectivity, you have bigger problems than a few wireless machines that cannot access the network. Troubleshoot this situation the way you'd troubleshoot any network failure. Once you determine which wireless nodes are affected, it's easier to pinpoint whether the problem lies in one or more wireless clients or in one or more access points.

After you narrow down the number of affected machines, your next task is to figure out specifically what type of error the users are experiencing. If they can access some, but not all, network services, it's unlikely that the problem is limited to their wireless equipment. For example, if they can browse the Internet but can't access any shared resources on a server, they're probably experiencing a permissions-related issue rather than a wireless one.

The last bit of gathering information for this issue is to determine when the problem started. What has changed that might explain your loss of connectivity? Did you or somebody else change the wireless network configuration? For example, if the network worked fine two minutes ago, and then you changed the encryption key or level on the access point, and now nobody can see the network, you have your solution—or at least your culprit! Did your office experience a power outage, power sag, or power surge? Any of these might cause a WAP to fail. And that leads us to the next step of the formal troubleshooting process, establishing a theory, which was discussed back in Chapter 1, "Safety and Professionalism." For now, let's focus on the specifics of troubleshooting Wi-Fi issues.

Once you figure out the who, what, and when, you can start troubleshooting in earnest. Typically, your problem is going to center on your hardware, software, connectivity, or configuration.

Hardware Troubleshooting

Wireless networking hardware components are subject to the same kind of abuse and faulty installation as any other hardware component. Troubleshooting a suspected hardware problem should bring out the technician in you.

Open Windows Device Manager and look for an error or conflict with the wireless adapter. If you see a big exclamation point next to the device, you have a driver error. A downward-facing arrow next to the device indicates that it has been disabled. Enable it if possible or reinstall the device driver as needed.

If you don't see the device listed at all, perhaps it is not seated properly or plugged all the way in. These problems are easy to fix. Just remove and reinstall the device.

 NOTE As with all things computing, don't forget to do the standard PC troubleshooting thing and reboot the computer before you make any configuration or hardware changes!

Software Troubleshooting

Because you've already checked to confirm your hardware is using the correct drivers, what kind of software-related problems are left? Two things come immediately to mind: the wireless adapter configuration utility and the WAP's firmware version.

As I mentioned earlier, some wireless devices won't work correctly unless you install the vendor-provided drivers and configuration utility before plugging in the device. This is particularly true of wireless USB devices. If you didn't do this already, go into Device Manager and uninstall the device, then start again from scratch.

By the time you unpack your new WAP, there's a good chance its firmware is already out of date. Out-of-date firmware could manifest in many ways. Your WAP may enable clients to connect, but only at such slow speeds that they experience frequent timeout errors; you may find that, after a week, your clients can connect but have no Internet access until you reboot the WAP; Apple devices may have trouble connecting or running at advertised speeds. The important thing here is to be on the lookout for strange or erratic behavior.

Manufacturers regularly release firmware updates to fix issues just like these—and many more—so it's good to update the access point's firmware. For older WAPs, go to the manufacturer's Web site and follow the support links until you find the latest firmware version. You'll need your device's exact model number and hardware version, as well as the current firmware version—this is important, because installing the wrong firmware version on your device is a guaranteed way to render it useless! Modern WAPs have built-in administration pages to upload the newly downloaded firmware. Some can even check for firmware updates and install them. Because there are too many WAP variations to cover here, always look up and follow the manufacturer's instructions for updating the firmware to the letter.

NOTE When updating the firmware of any device, including your WAP, there's always a chance something could go wrong and render it unusable—and you may hear techs say such a device has been "bricked." Why? It's no more useful than a brick!

Connectivity Troubleshooting

Properly configured wireless clients should automatically and quickly connect to the desired SSID, assuming both the client and WAP support the correct bands. If this isn't taking place, it's time for some troubleshooting. Most wireless connectivity problems come down to either an incorrect configuration (such as an incorrect password) or low signal strength. Without a strong signal, even a properly configured wireless client isn't going to work. Wireless clients use a multi-bar graph (usually five bars) to give an idea of signal strength: zero bars indicates no wireless connectivity and five bars indicates maximum signal. Weak signals can result in slow overall data transfer and intermittent wireless connections.

Whether configuration or signal strength, the process to diagnose and repair uses the same methods you use for a wired network. First, if your wireless NIC has link lights, check to see whether it's passing data packets to and from the network. Second, check the wireless NIC's configuration utility. Figure 20-26 shows Windows 10 displaying the link state and signal strength.

Figure 20-26
Windows
10's wireless
configuration
utility

The link state defines the wireless NIC's connection status to a wireless network: connected or disconnected. If your link state indicates that your computer is currently disconnected, you may have a problem with your WAP. If your signal is too weak to receive (referred to on the CompTIA A+ exams as a "low RF signal"), you may be out of range of your access point, or there may be a device causing interference.

You can fix these problems in a number of ways. Because Wi-Fi signals bounce off of objects, you can try small adjustments to your antennas to see if the signal improves. You can swap out the standard antenna for one or more higher-gain antennas. You can relocate the PC or access point, or locate and move the device causing interference.

Other wireless devices that operate in the same frequency range as your wireless nodes can cause interference as well. Look for wireless telephones, intercoms, and so on as possible culprits. One fix for interference caused by other wireless devices is to change the channel your network uses. Another is to change the channel the offending device uses, if possible. If you can't change channels, try moving the interfering device to another area or replacing it with a different device.

Configuration Troubleshooting

With all due respect to the fine network techs in the field, the most common type of wireless networking problem is misconfigured hardware or software. That's right—the dreaded *user error*! Given the complexities of wireless networking, this isn't so surprising. All it takes is one slip of the typing finger to throw off your configuration completely. The things you're most likely to get wrong are the SSID and security configuration, though dual-band routers have introduced some additional complexity.

Verify SSID configuration (for any bands in use) on your access point first, and then check on the affected wireless nodes. With most wireless devices, you can use any characters in the SSID, including blank spaces. Be careful not to add blank characters where they don't belong, such as trailing blank spaces behind any other characters typed into the name field.

In some situations, clients that have always connected to a WAP with a particular SSID may no longer be able to connect. The client may or may not give an error message indicating "SSID not found." There are a couple possible explanations for this and they are easy to troubleshoot and fix. The simplest culprit is that the WAP is down—easy to find and easy to fix. On the opposite end of the spectrum is a change to the WAP. Changing the SSID of a WAP will prevent the client from connecting. The fix can be as simple as changing the SSID back or updating the client configuration. A client may not connect to a new WAP, even if it has the same SSID and connection configuration as the previous one. Simply delete the old connection profile from the client and create a new one.

If you're using MAC address filtering, make sure the MAC address of the client that's attempting to access the wireless network is on the list of accepted users. This is particularly important if you swap out NICs on a PC, or if you introduce a new device to your wireless network.

Check the security configuration to make sure that all wireless nodes and access points match. Mistyping an encryption key prevents the affected node from talking to the wireless network, even if your signal strength is 100 percent! Remember that many access points have the capability to export encryption keys onto a thumb drive or other removable media. It's then a simple matter to import the encryption key onto the PC by using the wireless NIC's configuration utility. Remember that the encryption level must match on access points and wireless nodes. If your WAP is configured for WPA2, all nodes must also use WPA2.

Chapter Review

Questions

1. Which of the following 802.11 standards functions only on the 5-GHz band?

   A. 802.11g

   B. 802.11n

   C. 802.11ac

   D. 802.11i

2. Which encryption protocol offers the best security?

   A. Hi-Encrypt

   B. WEP

   C. WPA

   D. WPA2

3. Which device enables you to extend the capabilities of a wireless network?

   A. WAP

   B. WEP

   C. WPA

   D. WPA2

4. In which mode do all the wireless devices connect directly to each other?

   A. Ad hoc mode

   B. Circular mode

   C. Infrastructure mode

   D. Mesh mode

5. What determines the name of a wireless network?

   A. EAP

   B. MAC address

    C. SSID

    D. WAP

6. What technology enables 802.11n networks to make multiple simultaneous connections and thus improve speed over previous Wi-Fi standards?

    A. Use of the 2.4-GHz frequency

    B. Use of the 5-GHz frequency

    C. MIMO

    D. WPA2

7. What's the top speed for data transfers using IrDA technology?

    A. 2 Mbps

    B. 4 Mbps

    C. 11 Mbps

    D. 54 Mbps

8. Bluetooth technology enables computers to link into what sort of network?

    A. Bluetooth area network (BAN)

    B. Personal area network (PAN)

    C. Local area network (LAN)

    D. Wide area network (WAN)

9. What is the name for the common omni-directional antennas found on wireless access points?

    A. Bipole antennas

    B. Dipole antennas

    C. Omni antennas

    D. RF antennas

10. Ralph has installed a wireless network in his house, placing the wireless access point in the kitchen, a centralized location. The Wi-Fi works fine in the living room and dining room but goes out almost completely in the bedroom. What's most likely the problem?

    A. Interference with some metal object

    B. Improper antenna setup

    C. Use of the default SSID

    D. The SSID overlapping with a neighbor's SSID

Answers

1. **C.** The 802.11ac standard functions exclusively on the 5-GHz band, while 802.11g functions on 2.4 GHz, 802.11n functions on both, and 802.11i is a security standard called WPA2.

2. **D.** WPA2 is the best of the encryption technologies listed.

3. **A.** A wireless access point (WAP) enables you to extend the capabilities of a wireless network.

4. **A.** In ad hoc mode networks, all the nodes connect directly to each other.

5. **C.** The SSID determines the name of a wireless network.

6. **C.** The multiple in/multiple out (MIMO) technology implementing multiple antennas enables 802.11n networks to run at much faster speeds than previous Wi-Fi networks.

7. **B.** Data transfers using the IrDA protocol top out at 4 Mbps.

8. **B.** Bluetooth creates personal area networks.

9. **B.** Standard omni-directional antennas are called dipole antennas.

10. **A.** Watch out for microwave ovens, refrigerators, and pipes in the walls. They can interfere with a Wi-Fi signal and create dead spots.

The Internet

In this chapter, you will learn how to

- Explain how the Internet works
- Connect to the Internet
- Use Internet application protocols
- Troubleshoot an Internet connection

Imagine coming home from a long day at work building and fixing computers, sitting down in front of your shiny new computer, double-clicking on the single icon that sits dead center on your monitor … and suddenly you're enveloped in an otherworldly scene, where 200-foot trees slope smoothly into snow-white beaches and rich blue ocean. Overhead, pterodactyls soar through the air while you talk to a small chap with pointy ears and a long robe about heading up the mountain in search of a giant monster …. A TV show from the Syfy channel? Spielberg's latest film offering? How about an interactive game played by millions of people all over the planet on a daily basis by connecting to the Internet? If you guessed the last one, you're right.

This chapter covers the skills you need as a tech to help people connect to the Internet. It starts with a brief section on how the Internet works, along with the concepts of connectivity, and then it goes into the specifics of hardware, protocols, and software that you use to make the Internet work for you (or for your client). Finally, you'll learn how to troubleshoot a bad Internet connection. Let's get started!

Historical/Conceptual

How the Internet Works

Thanks to the Internet, people can communicate with one another over vast distances, often in the blink of an eye. As a tech, you need to know how computers communicate with the larger world for two reasons. First, knowing the process and pieces involved in the communication enables you to troubleshoot effectively when that communication goes away. Second, you need to be able to communicate knowledgeably with a network technician who comes in to solve a more complex issue.

Internet Tiers

You probably know that the Internet is millions and millions of computers all joined together to form the largest network on earth, but not many folks know much about how these computers are organized. To keep everything running smoothly, the Internet is broken down into groups called *tiers*. The main tier, called *Tier 1*, consists of a small number of companies called *Tier 1 providers*. The Tier 1 providers own long-distance, high-speed fiber optic networks called *backbones*. These backbones span the major cities of the earth (not all Tier 1 backbones go to all cities) and interconnect at special locations called *network access points* (*NAPs*). Anyone wishing to connect to any of the Tier 1 providers must pay large sums of money. The Tier 1 providers do not charge each other to connect.

Tier 2 providers own smaller, regional networks and must pay the Tier 1 providers. Most of the famous companies that provide Internet access to the general public are Tier 2 providers. *Tier 3 providers* are even more regional and connect to Tier 2 providers.

The piece of equipment that makes this tiered Internet concept work is called a backbone router. *Backbone routers* connect to more than one other backbone router, creating a big, interwoven framework for communication. Figure 21-1 illustrates the decentralized and interwoven nature of the Internet. The key reason for interweaving the backbones of the Internet was to provide alternative pathways for data if one or more of the routers went down. If Jane in Houston sends a message to her friend Polly in New York City, for example, the shortest path between Jane and Polly in this hypothetical situation might be: Jane's message originates at Rice University in Houston, bounces to Emory University in Atlanta, flits through Virginia Commonwealth University in Richmond, and then zips into SUNY in New York City (see Figure 21-2). Polly happily reads the message and life is great. The Internet functions as planned.

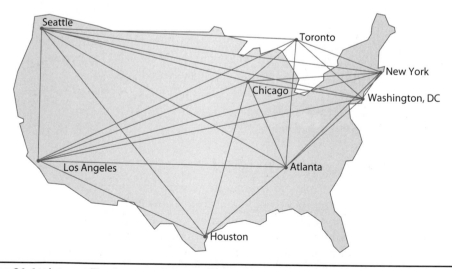

Figure 21-1 Internet Tier 1 connections

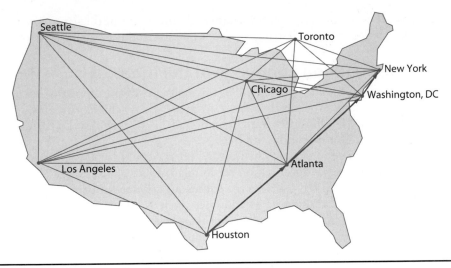

Figure 21-2   Message traveling from Houston to NYC

But what would happen if the entire southeastern United States were to experience a huge power outage and Internet backbones in every state from Virginia to Florida were to go down? Jane's message would fail to go through, so the Rice computers would resend Jane's message. Meanwhile, the routers would update their list of good routes and then attempt to reroute the message to functioning nodes—say, Rice to University of Chicago, to University of Toronto, and then to SUNY (see Figure 21-3). It's all in a day's work

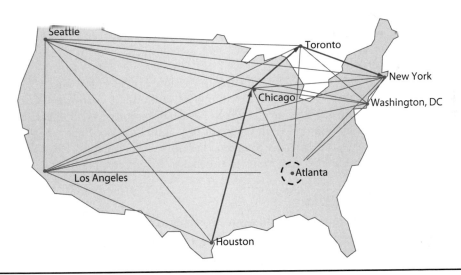

Figure 21-3   Rerouted message from Houston to NYC

for the highly redundant and adaptable Internet. At this point in the game, the Internet simply cannot go down fully—barring, of course, a catastrophe of Biblical proportions.

TCP/IP: The Common Language of the Internet

As you know from all the earlier chapters in this book, hardware alone doesn't cut it in the world of computing. You need software to make the machines run and create an interface for humans. The Internet is no exception. TCP/IP provides the basic software structure for communication on the Internet.

Because you spent a good deal of Chapter 19, "Local Area Networking," working with TCP/IP, you should have an appreciation for its adaptability and, perhaps more importantly, its extensibility. TCP/IP provides the addressing scheme for computers that communicate on the Internet through IPv4 addresses, such as 192.168.4.1 or 16.45.123.7. As a protocol, though, TCP/IP is much more than just an addressing system. TCP/IP provides the framework and common language for the Internet. And it offers a phenomenally wide-open structure for creative purposes. Programmers can write applications built to take advantage of the TCP/IP structure and features, creating what are called *TCP/IP services*. The cool thing about TCP/IP services is that they're limited only by the imagination of the programmers.

At this point, you have an enormous functioning network. All the backbone routers connect redundant, high-speed backbone lines, and TCP/IP enables communication and services for building applications that enable humans and machines to interface across vast distances. What's left? Oh, of course: How do you tap into this great network and partake of its goodness?

Internet Service Providers

Every Tier 1 and Tier 2 provider leases connections to the Internet to companies called *Internet service providers* (*ISPs*). ISPs essentially sit along the edges of the Tier 1 and Tier 2 Internet and tap into the flow. In turn, you can lease connections from an ISP to get on the Internet.

ISPs come in all sizes. Comcast, the cable television provider, has multiple, huge-capacity connections into the Internet, enabling its millions of customers to connect from their local machines and surf the Web. Contrast Comcast with Electric Power Board (EPB) of Chattanooga, an ISP in Chattanooga, Tennessee (see Figure 21-4), which bills itself as " . . . the fastest Internet available. Period." Unfortunately, EPB only offers its blazingly fast gigabit fiber connections to the lucky citizens of Chattanooga.

Connection Concepts

Connecting to an ISP requires two things to work perfectly: hardware for connectivity, such as a modem and a working cable line; and software, such as protocols to govern

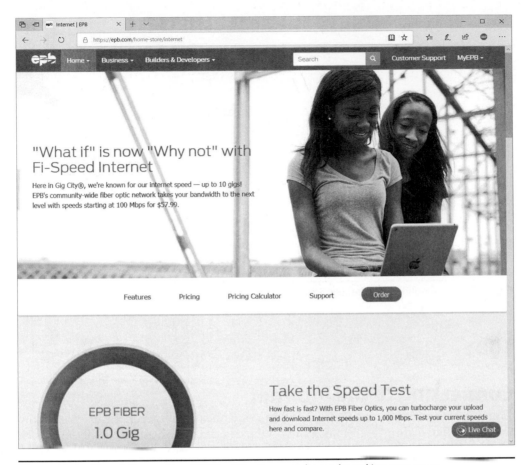

Figure 21-4 Electric Power Board (EPB) of Chattanooga home-based Internet page

the connections and the data flow (all configured in the OS) and applications to take advantage of the various TCP/IP services. Once you have a contract with an ISP to grant you access to the Internet, they will either send a technician to your house or mail you a package containing any hardware and software you might need. With most ISPs, a DHCP server will provide your computer with the proper TCP/IP information. As you know from Chapter 19, the router to which you connect at the ISP is often referred to as the *default gateway*. Once your computer is configured, you can connect to the ISP and get to the greater Internet. Figure 21-5 shows a standard computer-to-ISP-to-Internet connection. Note that various protocols and other software manage the connectivity between your computer and the default gateway.

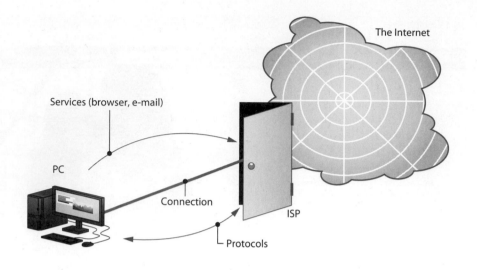

Figure 21-5   Simplified Internet connectivity

1001

Connecting to the Internet

Computers commonly connect to an ISP by using one of eight technologies that fit into four categories: dial-up, both analog and ISDN; dedicated, such as DSL, cable, and fiber; wireless, including Wi-Fi and cellular; and satellite. Analog dial-up is the slowest of the bunch and requires a telephone line and a special networking device called a modem. ISDN uses digital dial-up and has much greater speed. Dedicated connections (DSL, cable, and fiber) most often use a box that connects to a regular Ethernet NIC like you played with in Chapter 19. Wireless connections are a mixed bag, depending on the device and service you have. Some are built-in, while others use a box you attach to your LAN. Satellite is the odd one out here; it may use either a modem or a NIC, depending on the particular configuration you have, although most folks will use a NIC. Let's take a look at all these various connection options, and then finish this section by discussing basic router configuration and sharing an Internet connection with other computers.

Dial-Up

A dial-up connection to the Internet requires two pieces to work: hardware to dial the ISP, such as a modem or ISDN terminal adapter; and software to govern the connection, such as Microsoft's *Dial-up Networking* (*DUN*). Let's look at the hardware first, and then we'll explore software configuration.

Modems

At some point in the early days of computing, some bright guy or gal noticed a colleague talking on a telephone, glanced down at a computer, and then put two and two together: Why not use telephone lines for data communication? The basic problem with this idea is that traditional telephone lines use analog signals, while computers use digital signals (see Figure 21-6). Creating a dial-up network required equipment that could turn digital data into an analog signal to send it over the telephone line, and then turn it back into digital data when it reached the other end of the connection. A device called a modem solved this dilemma.

Figure 21-6

Analog signals used by a telephone line versus digital signals used by the computer

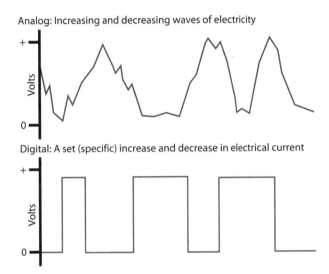

Analog: Increasing and decreasing waves of electricity

Digital: A set (specific) increase and decrease in electrical current

Modems enable computers to talk to each other via standard commercial telephone lines by converting analog signals to digital signals, and vice versa. The term *modem* is short for modulator/demodulator, a description of transforming the signals. Telephone wires transfer data via analog signals that continuously change voltages on a wire. Computers hate analog signals. Instead, they need digital signals, voltages that are either on or off, meaning the wire has voltage present or it does not. Computers, being binary by nature, use only two states of voltage: zero volts and positive volts. Modems take analog signals from telephone lines and turn them into digital signals that the computer can understand (see Figure 21-7). Modems also take digital signals from the computer and convert them into analog signals for the outgoing telephone line.

Phone lines have a speed based on a unit called a *baud*, which is one cycle per second. The fastest rate a phone line can achieve is 2400 baud. Modems can pack multiple bits of data into each baud; a 33.6 kilobits per second (Kbps) modem, for example, packs 14 bits into every baud: $2400 \times 14 = 33.6$ Kbps.

NOTE Modems connect to telephone cables with a four-wire connector and port. Telephone cable is CAT 1; the connectors and ports are RJ-11.

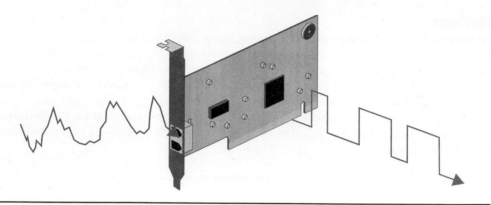

Figure 21-7   Modem converting analog signal to digital signal

Modem Connections   Internal modems connect to the computer very differently from how external modems connect. Almost all internal modems connect to a PCI or PCI Express (PCIe) expansion bus slot inside the computer (see Figure 21-8).

Figure 21-8
An internal
modem

Contemporary external modems connect to the computer through an available USB port (see Figure 21-9). USB offers simple plug and play and easy portability between machines, plus such modems require no external electrical source, getting all the power they need from the USB connection.

Dial-Up Networking

The software side of dial-up networks requires configuration within the OS to include information provided by your ISP. The ISP provides a dial-up telephone number or numbers, as well as your user name and initial password. In addition, the ISP will tell you about any special configuration options you need to specify in the software setup. The full configuration of dial-up networking is beyond the scope of this book, but you should at least know where to go to follow instructions from your ISP. Let's take a look at the Network and Sharing Center applet in Windows 7.

Figure 21-9

A USB modem

Configuring Dial-Up To start configuring a dial-up connection, open the Network and Sharing Center applet and click *Set up a new connection or network* (see Figure 21-10).

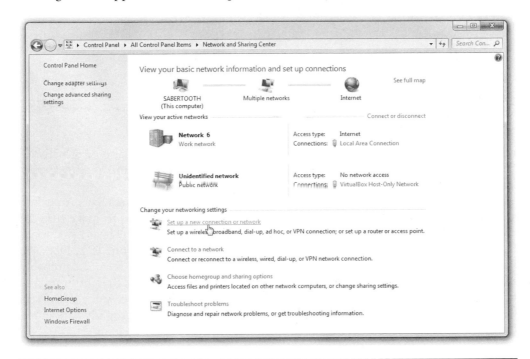

Figure 21-10   Setting up a new connection or network in Windows 7

Select Connect to the Internet and enter your dial-up information, as shown in Figure 21-11.

PPP   Dial-up links to the Internet have their own special hardware protocol called *Point-to-Point Protocol* (*PPP*). PPP is a streaming protocol developed especially for dial-up

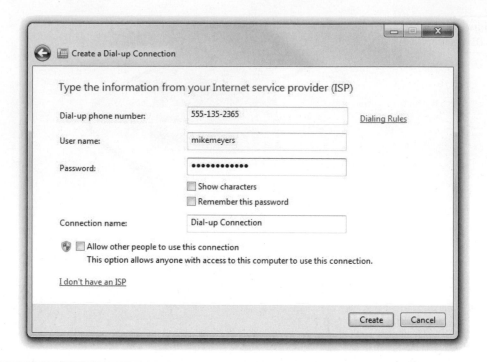

Figure 21-11　Creating a dial-up connection in Windows 7

Internet access. To Windows, a modem is nothing more than a special type of network adapter. You can configure a new dial-up connection in the Network and Sharing Center in current versions of Windows.

Most dial-up "I can't connect to the Internet"-type problems are user errors. Your first area of investigation is the modem itself. Use the modem's properties to make sure the volume is turned up. Have the user listen to the connection. Does she hear a dial tone? If she doesn't, make sure the modem's line is plugged into a good phone jack. Does she hear the modem dial and then hear someone saying, "Hello? Hello?" If so, she probably dialed the wrong number! Wrong password error messages are fairly straightforward—remember that the password may be correct but the user name may be wrong. If she still fails to connect, it's time to call the network folks to see what is not properly configured in your dial-up modem's Properties dialog box.

ISDN

A standard telephone connection comprises many pieces. First, the phone line runs from your phone out to a network interface box (the little box on the side of your house) and into a central switch belonging to the telephone company. (In some cases, intermediary steps are present.) Standard metropolitan areas have a large number of central offices, each with a central switch. Houston, Texas, for example, has nearly 100 offices in the general metro area. These central switches connect to each other through high-capacity *trunk lines*. Before 1970, the entire phone system was analog; over time, however, phone companies began to upgrade their trunk lines to digital systems. Today, the entire telephone system, with the exception of the line from your phone to the central office (and sometimes even that) is digital.

During this upgrade period, customers continued to demand higher throughput from their phone lines. The old telephone line was not expected to produce more than 28.8 Kbps (56-Kbps modems, which were a *big* surprise to the phone companies, didn't appear until 1995). Needless to say, the phone companies were very motivated to come up with a way to generate higher capacities. Their answer was actually fairly straightforward: make the entire phone system digital. By adding special equipment at the central office and the user's location, phone companies can now achieve a throughput of up to 64 Kbps per line over the same copper wires already used by telephone lines. This process of sending telephone transmission across fully digital lines end-to-end is called *integrated services digital network* (*ISDN*) service.

ISDN service consists of two types of channels: Bearer (B) channels and Delta (D) channels. B channels carry data and voice information at 64 Kbps. D channels carry setup and configuration information and data at 16 Kbps. Most ISDN providers allow the user to choose either one or two B channels. The more common setup is two B/one D, usually called a *basic rate interface* (*BRI*) setup. A BRI setup uses only one physical line, but each B channel sends 64 Kbps, doubling the throughput total to 128 Kbps. ISDN also connects much faster than modems, eliminating that long, annoying mating call you get with phone modems. The monthly cost per B channel is slightly more than a regular phone line, and usually a fairly steep initial fee is levied for the installation and equipment. The big limitation is that you usually need to be within about 18,000 feet of a central office to use ISDN.

 NOTE Another type of ISDN, called a primary rate interface (PRI), is composed of twenty-three 64-Kbps B channels and one 64-Kbps D channel, giving it a total throughput of 1.544 megabits per second (Mbps). PRI ISDN lines are also known as T1 lines.

The physical connections for ISDN bear some similarity to analog modems. An ISDN wall socket usually looks something like a standard RJ-45 network jack. The most common interface for your computer is a device called a *terminal adapter* (*TA*). TAs look much like regular modems, and like modems, they come in external and internal variants. You can even get TAs that connect directly to your LAN.

While 128 Kbps was a nice upgrade over an analog modem in the 1990s, today with the proliferation of faster connections such as DSL and cable, finding an ISDN line in the wild has become rare. You will find them in sites that need rock-solid security, like in military field command centers.

DSL

Digital subscriber line (*DSL*) connections to ISPs use a standard telephone line with special equipment on each end to create always-on Internet connections at speeds much greater than dial-up.

Service levels for DSL can vary widely. At the low end of the spectrum, speeds are generally in the single digits—less than 1 Mbps upload and around 3 Mbps download. Where available, more recent *x*DSL technologies can offer competitive broadband speeds measured in tens or hundreds of megabits per second.

DSL requires little setup from a user standpoint. A tech comes to the house to install the DSL receiver, often called a DSL modem (see Figure 21-12), and possibly hook up a wireless router. Even if you skip the tech and have the installation equipment mailed to you, all you have to do is plug a couple special filters in and call your ISP. These *DSL microfilters* remove the high-pitch screech of the DSL signal, enabling phones and fax machines to operate correctly. The receiver connects to the telephone line and the computer (see Figure 21-13). The tech (or the user, if knowledgeable) then configures the DSL modem and router (if there is one) with the settings provided by the ISP, and that's about it! Within moments, you're surfing the Web. You don't need a second telephone line. You don't need to wear a special propeller hat or anything. The only kicker is that your house has to be within a fairly short distance from a main phone service switching center (central office). This distance can depend on the DSL variant and can range from several hundred feet to around 18,000 feet.

Figure 21-12
A DSL receiver

Figure 21-13
DSL connection

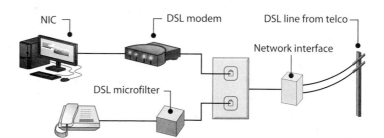

NOTE   The two most common forms of DSL you'll find are *asymmetric* (*ADSL*) and *symmetric* (*SDSL*). ADSL lines differ between slow upload speed (such as 384 Kbps, 768 Kbps, and 1 Mbps) and faster download speed (usually 3–15 Mbps). SDSL has the same upload and download speeds, but telecom companies charge a lot more for the privilege. DSL encompasses many such variations, so you'll often see it referred to as xDSL.

Cable

Cable offers a different approach to high-speed Internet access, using regular cable TV cables to serve up lightning-fast speeds. It offers faster service than most DSL connections, with upload speeds from 5 to 35+ Mbps and download speeds ranging anywhere from 15 to 1000+ Mbps. *Cable Internet* connections are theoretically available anywhere you can get cable TV.

NOTE   The term *modem* has been warped and changed beyond recognition in modern networking. Both DSL and cable—fully digital Internet connections—use the term *modem* to describe the box that takes the incoming signal from the Internet and translates it into something the computer can understand.

Cable Internet connections start with an RG-6 or RG-59 cable coming into your house. The cable connects to a cable modem that then connects to a small home router or your network interface card (NIC) via Ethernet. Figure 21-14 shows a typical cable setup using a router.

Figure 21-14
Cable connection

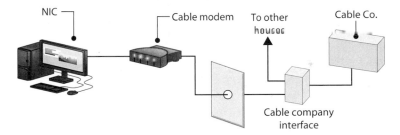

Fiber

In the past, high costs meant that only those with money to burn could enjoy the super-fast speeds of a fiber connection. Subsequently, DSL providers developed very popular fiber-to-the-node (FTTN) and fiber-to-the-premises (FTTP) services that provide Internet (and often Internet and telephone services over the same connection), making them head-to-head competitors with the cable companies. Entrants like Google Fiber and local municipalities have added momentum to the fiber rollout.

With FTTN, the fiber connection runs from the provider to a box somewhere in your neighborhood. This box connects to your home or office using normal coaxial or Ethernet cabling. FTTP runs from the provider straight to a home or office, using fiber the whole way. Once inside the home or office, you can use any standard cabling (or wireless) to connect your computers to the Internet.

One popular fiber-based service is AT&T Internet (formerly called U-verse), which generally offers download speeds from 10 to 100 Mbps and upload speeds from 1 to 20 Mbps for their FTTN service. AT&T Fiber is their FTTP service that gives you 100 Mbps to 1 Gbps for download and upload (see Figure 21-15). Verizon's Fios service is the most popular and widely available FTTP service in the United States, providing upload and download speeds ranging from 50 Mbps to 1 Gbps (if you can afford it, of course). Google Fiber, for its part, offers a 1-Gbps upload/download service.

Figure 21-15
An AT&T FTTP
terminal hidden
behind my
refrigerator

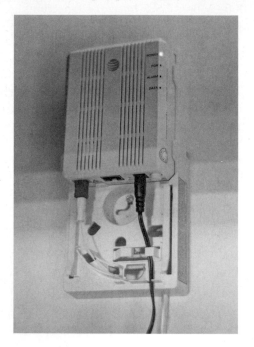

Wi-Fi

Wi-Fi (or 802.11 wireless) is so prevalent that it's the way many of us get to the Internet. Wireless access points (WAPs) designed to serve the public abound in coffee shops, airports, fast-food chains, and bars. Even some cities provide partial to full Wi-Fi coverage.

NOTE An 802.11 network that covers a single city is an excellent example of a *metropolitan area network* (*MAN*).

We covered 802.11 in detail in Chapter 20, "Wireless Networking," so there's no reason to repeat the process of connecting to a hotspot. Do remember that most open hotspots do not provide any level of encryption, meaning it's easy for a bad guy to monitor your connection and read everything you send or receive.

CAUTION Secure your public hotspot Web browsing using HTTPS-secured sites. It's surprisingly easy to do. Instead of typing www.facebook.com, for example, type in https://www.facebook.com or use a browser extension like the Electronic Frontier Foundation's HTTPS Everywhere.

Line-of-Sight Wireless

Wi-Fi works well as an Internet access option for densely populated areas, but Wi-Fi's short range makes it impractical in areas where it's not easy to place new access points. In certain circumstances, you can address the range issue by using high-powered, directional antennas and Ethernet bridge devices. These can give you a *line-of-sight wireless Internet connection* up to eight miles or more. These work great in places such as ski resorts, where you want to connect the restaurant halfway up the mountain to the main lodge, or lake cottages, where you want to connect a boathouse to the main house. To support higher bandwidths over these ranges, connections move up the radio spectrum. Wi-Fi operates at 2.4 or 5.0 GHz, as you'll recall from Chapter 20, but line-of-sight devices could use another band, such as 24-GHz.

Cellular

Who needs computers when you can get online with any number of mobile devices? Okay, there are plenty of things a phone or tablet can't do, but with the latest advances in cellular data services, your mobile Internet experience will feel a lot more like your home Internet experience than it ever has before.

EXAM TIP You can share a phone or tablet connection to a cellular network using a process called *tethering*. You'll need to turn on the service on your device, and then connect your phone to your computer, either wirelessly as a *mobile hotspot* or directly using a USB connection. Most carriers charge extra to enable tethering on your phone or tablet. Check with your carrier to see if your service plan supports tethering.

Cellular data services have gone through a number of names over the years, so many that trying to keep track of them and place them in any order is extremely challenging. In an attempt to make organization somewhat clearer, the cellular industry developed a string of marketing terms using the idea of generations: first-generation devices are called 1G, second-generation are 2G, followed by 3G, 4G, and 5G. On top of that, many technologies use G-names such as 2.5G to show they're not 2G but not quite 3G. You'll see these terms on your phones, primarily if you're not getting the best speed possible (see Figure 21-16). Marketing folks tend to bend and flex the definition of these

Figure 21-16
iPhone
connecting
over 4G

terms in advertisements, so you should always read more about the device and not just its generation.

The first generation (1G) of cell phone data services was analog and not at all designed to carry packetized data. It wasn't until the early 1990s that two fully digital technologies called the Global System for Mobile Communications (GSM) and code division multiple access (CDMA) came into wide acceptance. GSM evolved into GPRS and EDGE, while CDMA introduced EV-DO. GPRS and EDGE were 2.5G technologies, while EV-DO was true 3G. Standards, with names like UTMS, HSPA+, and HSDPA, have brought GSM-based networks into the world of 3G and 3.5G. These mobile data services provide modest real-world download speeds of a few (generally under 10) Mbps.

We're now well into the fourth generation. Devices and networks using *Long Term Evolution* (*LTE*) technology rolled out worldwide in the early 2010s and now dominate wireless services. As early as 2013, for example, LTE already had ~20 percent market share in the United States, and even higher in parts of Asia. The numbers have only grown since then. Marketed as and now generally accepted as a true *4G* technology, LTE networks feature theoretical speeds of up to 1 Gbps download and 100 Mbps upload (see Figure 21-17).

NOTE LTE has become synonymous with 4G these days. You'll often see the mashed-up term *4G LTE*, which I guess is an attempt by marketing folks to make sure they get all the buzzwords out there.

With excellent speed and the broad coverage of cell towers, LTE can readily replace wired network technology. To connect a computer to the Internet when in rural areas, for example, you don't need a physical connection, such as DSL, cable, or fiber, to an ISP. You can instead connect to a *mobile hotspot*—a device that connects via cellular and enables other devices to access the Internet—and be on your merry way. Hotspots can be dedicated devices, or simply a feature of a modern smartphone. (See Chapter 24, "Understanding Mobile Devices," for a deep dive into smartphone technologies.)

EXAM TIP Just like LANs and WANs, we also have WLANs and WWANs. A wireless wide area network (WWAN) works similarly to a wireless LAN (WLAN), but connects multiple networks similarly to a WAN.

Figure 21-17
Real-world LTE
speed test

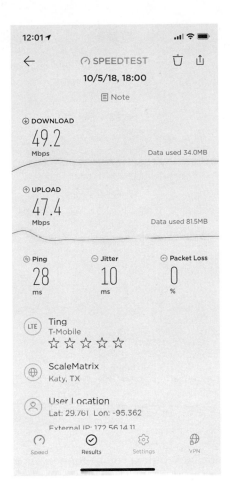

Using a hotspot to connect to the Internet is a form of *tethering*, in this case wireless tethering. You can directly connect via USB to cellular devices such as a smartphone and use that device's cellular connection to get on the Internet (see Figure 21-18). This latter use of the technology is wired tethering or USB tethering, though most drop the wired/USB part and just call it *tethering*.

The fifth-generation cellular networks—appropriately called *5G*—saw a big development push in 2018, followed by a rollout in 2019 and 2020. The IMT-2020 specifications call for speeds up to *20 Gbps*, blazingly fast!

Satellite

Satellite connections to the Internet get the data beamed to a satellite dish on your house or office; a receiver handles the flow of data, eventually sending it through an Ethernet cable to the NIC in your computer. I can already sense people's eyebrows raising.

Figure 21-18
Tethering

The early days of satellite required you to connect via a modem. You would upload at the slow 26- to 48-Kbps modem speed, but then get speedier downloads from the dish. It worked, so why complain? You really can move to that shack on the side of the Himalayas to write the great Tibetan novel and still have DSL-speed Internet connectivity. Sweet!

Satellite might be the most intriguing of all the technologies used to connect to the Internet today. As with satellite television, though, you need to make sure the satellite dish points toward the satellites (generally toward the south if you live in the northern hemisphere). Satellite starts with a dish, professionally installed with line-of-sight to the satellite. A coax cable runs from the dish to your satellite modem. The satellite modem has an RJ-45 connection, which you may then connect directly to your computer or to a router. Current offerings from HughesNet (the biggest player in the satellite market) feature up to 25 Mbps download and 3 Mbps upload speeds.

Getting your Internet from the stars has a few downsides. The first significant issue is the upfront cost of the dish and installation. Then there's the distance the signal must travel to the satellite, creating a delay called the *satellite latency*. This latency is usually unnoticeable for general Web use, but can make any real-time activity such as gaming or voice/video chat difficult in the best of circumstances. It can get worse when the signal degrades in foul weather such as rain and snow. Finally, most satellite operators implement various usage caps to keep the system from getting overloaded. These caps have names such as HughesNet's *fair access policy* and often come with not only blanket caps but more limitations during peak usage hours.

Connection to the Internet

So you went out and signed up for an Internet connection. Now it's time to get connected. You basically have two choices:

1. Connect a single computer to your Internet connection
2. Connect a network of computers to your Internet connection

Connecting a single computer to the Internet is easy. If you're using wireless, you connect to the wireless box using the provided information, although a good tech will always go through the proper steps described in Chapter 20 to protect the wireless network. If you choose to go wired, you run a cable from whatever type of box is provided to the computer.

If you want to connect multiple computers using wired connections, you'll need to grab a router. Several manufacturers offer robust, easy-to-configure routers that enable multiple computers to connect to a single Internet connection. These boxes require very little configuration and provide firewall protection between the primary computer and the Internet, which you'll learn more about in Chapter 27, "Securing Computers." All it takes to install one of these routers is simply to plug your computer into any of the LAN ports on the back, and then to plug the cable from your Internet connection into the port labeled Internet or WAN.

There are hundreds of perfectly fine choices for SOHO (small office/home office) routers (see Figure 21-19 for an example). Most have four Ethernet switch ports for wired connections, and one or more Wi-Fi radios for any wireless computers you may have. All SOHO routers use a technology called *Network Address Translation* (*NAT*) to perform a little network subterfuge: It presents an entire LAN of computers to the Internet as a single machine. It effectively hides all of your computers and makes them appear invisible to other computers on the Internet. All anyone on the Internet sees is your *public* IP address. This is the address your ISP gives you, while all the computers in your LAN use private addresses that are invisible to the world. NAT therefore acts as a firewall, protecting your internal network from probing or malicious users on the outside.

Figure 21-19
Common SOHO
router with Wi-Fi

EXAM TIP Many computers can share a smaller pool of routable IP addresses with dynamic NAT (DNAT). A NAT might have 10 routable IP addresses, for example, to serve 40 computers on the LAN. LAN traffic uses the internal, private IP addresses. When a computer requests information beyond the network, the NAT doles out a routable IP address from its pool for that communication. Dynamic NAT is also called Pooled NAT.

This works well enough—unless you're the unlucky 11th person to try to access the Internet from behind the company NAT—but has the obvious limitation of still needing many true, expensive, routable IP addresses.

Basic Router Configuration

SOHO routers require very little in the way of configuration and in many cases will work perfectly (if unsafely) right out of the box. In some cases, though, you may have to deal with a more complex network that requires changing the router's settings. The vast majority of these routers have built-in configuration Web pages that you access by typing the router's IP address into a browser. The address varies by manufacturer, so check the router's documentation. If you typed in the correct address, you should then receive a prompt for a user name and password, as in Figure 21-20. As with the IP address, the

Figure 21-20 Router asking for user name and password

default user name and password vary depending on the model/manufacturer. Once you enter the correct credentials, you will be greeted by the router's configuration pages (see Figure 21-21). From these pages, you can change any of the router's settings.

Figure 21-21   Configuration home page

Now we'll look at a few of the basic settings that CompTIA wants you to know. (We'll discuss more advanced settings in Chapter 27 that help keep your network and the computers on it secure while they use services available over the Internet.)

 EXAM TIP   A lot of networking devices designed for the residential space use a feature called *universal plug and play* (*UPnP*) to seek out, find, and connect to other UPnP devices. This feature enables seamless interconnectivity at the cost of somewhat lowered security.

Changing User Name and Password   All routers have a user name and password that gives you access to the configuration screen. One of the first changes you should make to your router after you have it working is to change the user name and password to something other than the default. This is especially important if you have open wireless turned on, which you'll recall from Chapter 20. If you leave the default user name and password, anyone who has access to your LAN can easily gain access to the router and change its settings. Fortunately, router manufacturers make it easy to change a router's login credentials, as shown in Figure 21-22.

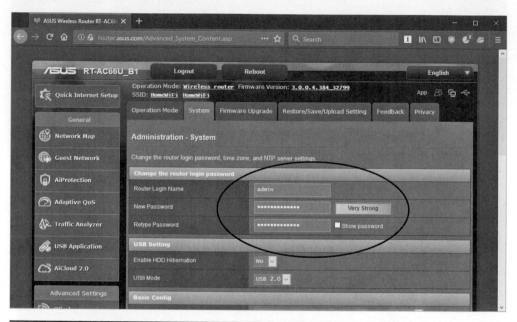

Figure 21-22 Changing the password

Setting Static IP Addresses With the user name and password taken care of, let's look at setting up the router to use a static IP address for the Internet or WAN connection. In most cases, when you plug in the router's Internet connection, it receives an IP address using DHCP just like any other computer. Of course, this means that your Internet IP address will change from time to time, which can be a bit of a downside. This does not affect most people, but for some home users and businesses, it can present a problem. To solve this problem, most ISPs enable you to order a static IP (for an extra monthly charge). Once your ISP has allocated you a static IP address, you must manually enter it into your router. You do this the same way as the previous change you've just looked at. My router has an Internet Setup configuration section where I can enter all the settings that my ISP has provided to me (see Figure 21-23). Remember, you must change your connection type from Automatic/DHCP to Static IP to enter the new addresses.

Updating Firmware

Routers are just like any other computer in that they run software—and software has bugs, vulnerabilities, and other issues that sometimes require updating. The router manufacturers call these "firmware updates" and make them available either through the router's administration interface or on their Web sites for easy download.

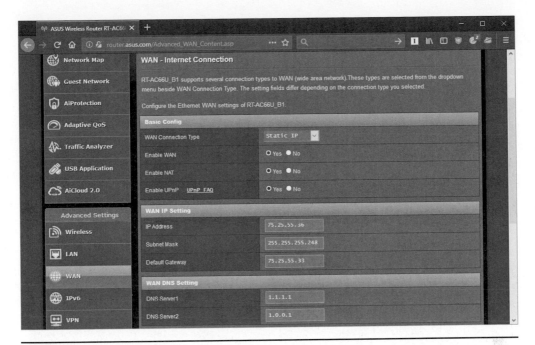

Figure 21-23 Entering a static IP address

NOTE While these methods are generally true of routers available commercially, routers provided by your ISP may update automatically.

If the firmware update is available directly through your router's administration interface, a firmware update may be a few clicks away. If not, download the latest firmware from the manufacturer's Web site to your computer. Then enter the router's configuration Web page and find the firmware update screen. On my router, it looks like Figure 21-24. From here, just follow the directions and click Upgrade (or your router's equivalent). A quick word of caution: Unlike a Windows update, a firmware update gone bad can *brick* your router. In other words, it can render the hardware inoperable and make it as useful as a brick sitting on your desk. This rarely happens, but you should keep it in mind when doing a firmware update.

Internet Application Protocols

Once you've established a connection to the Internet, you need applications to get anything done. If you want to surf the Web, you need an application called a *Web browser*, such as Mozilla Firefox, Google Chrome, or Microsoft Edge. If you want to make a VoIP phone call, you need an application like Skype or Google Voice. These applications in turn use very clearly designed application protocols. All Web browsers use the *Hypertext Transfer Protocol* (*HTTP*). All e-mail clients use Post Office Protocol 3 (POP3) or

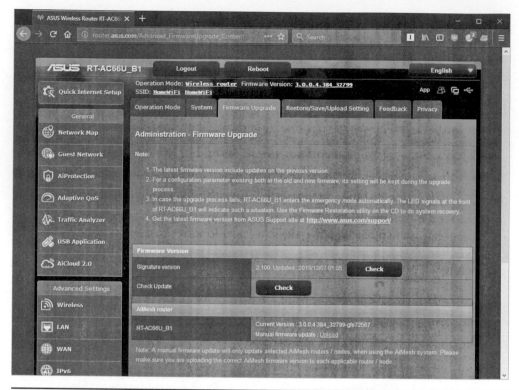

Figure 21-24 Firmware update page

Internet Message Access Protocol (IMAP) to receive e-mail. All e-mail applications use Simple Mail Transfer Protocol (SMTP) to send their e-mails. Every Internet protocol has its own rules and its own port numbers. Though there are tens of thousands of application protocols in existence, lucky for you, CompTIA only wants you to understand the following commonly used application protocols (except SFTP and SIP, which CompTIA doesn't list in the objectives but I've added for completeness):

- World Wide Web (HTTP and HTTPS)
- E-mail (POP3, IMAP, and SMTP)
- Telnet
- SSH
- FTP/SFTP
- Remote Desktop Protocol (RDP)
- VoIP (SIP)

In addition to the application protocols we see and use daily, there are hundreds, maybe thousands, of application protocols that run behind the scenes, taking care of important jobs to ensure that the application protocols we do see run well. You've encountered a number of these hidden application protocols back in Chapter 19. Take DNS. Without DNS, you couldn't type www.google.com in your Web browser and end up at the right address. DHCP is another great example. You don't see DHCP do its job, but without it, any computers relying on DHCP won't receive IP addresses.

Here's another one: Many people don't like to send credit card information, home phone numbers, or other personal information over the Web for fear this information might be intercepted by hackers. Fortunately, there are methods for encrypting this information, the most common being *Hypertext Transfer Protocol Secure* (*HTTPS*). Although HTTPS looks a lot like HTTP from the point of view of a Web browser, HTTPS uses port 443. It's easy to tell if a Web site is using HTTPS because the Web address starts with *https*, as shown in Figure 21-25, instead of just *http*. But you don't deal with HTTPS directly; it just works in your browser automatically.

Figure 21-25   A secure Web page

In order to differentiate the application protocols you see from the application protocols you don't see, I'm going to coin the term "utility protocol" to define any of the hidden application protocols. So, using your author's definition, HTTP is an application protocol and DNS is a utility protocol. All TCP/IP protocols use defined ports, require an application to run, and have special settings unique to that application. You'll look at several of these services and learn how to configure them. As a quick reference, Table 21-1 lists the names, functions, and port numbers of the application protocols CompTIA would like you to know (except, again, SFTP and VoIP [SIP]). Table 21-2 does the same for utility protocols.

Application Protocol	Function	Port Number
HTTP	Web pages	80
HTTPS	Secure Web pages	443
FTP	File transfer	20, 21
SFTP	Secure file transfer	22
IMAP	Incoming e-mail	143
POP3	Incoming e-mail	110
SMTP	Outgoing e-mail	25
Telnet	Terminal emulation	23
SSH	Encrypted terminal emulation	22
RDP	Remote Desktop	3389
SIP	Voice over IP	5060

Table 21-1 Application Protocol Port Numbers

Utility Protocol	Function	Protocol	Port Number
DNS	Allows the use of DNS naming	UDP	53
DHCP	Automatic IP addressing	UDP	67, 68
LDAP	Querying directories	TCP	389
SNMP	Remote management of network devices	UDP	161, 162
SMB	Windows naming/folder sharing; also CIFS	TCP	445
		UDP	137, 138, 139
AFP	macOS file services	TCP	548
SLP	Services discovery protocol	TCP/UDP	427
NetBIOS/NetBT	NetBIOS over TCP/IP	TCP	137, 139
		UDP	137, 138

Table 21-2 Utility Protocol Port Numbers

NOTE It's important to know what protocols and ports an application uses. Refer to Chapter 19 if you need a refresher on the TCP and UDP protocols. That's also where we discussed NetBIOS.

Let's look at the protocols listed in Tables 21-1 and 21-2, plus Virtual Private Networks and the protocols they use.

EXAM TIP Know all of the protocols and ports listed in Tables 21-1 and 21-2 for the 1001 exam.

1002

The World Wide Web

The Web provides a graphical face for the Internet. *Web servers* (servers running specialized software) provide Web sites that you access by using the HTTPS protocol on port 443 and HTTP on port 80 and thus get more-or-less useful information. Using a Web browser, such as Apple Safari, Microsoft Edge, Google Chrome, or Mozilla Firefox, you can click a link on a Web page and be instantly transported— not just to some Web server in your home town—to anywhere in the world. Figure 21-26 shows Firefox at the home page of my company's Web site, www.totalsem.com. Where is the server located? Does it matter? It could be in a closet in my office or in a huge data center in Northern Virginia. The great part about the Web is that you can get from here to there and access the information you need with few clicks or taps.

Setting up a Web browser takes almost no effort. As long as the Internet connection is working, Web browsers work automatically. This is not to say you can't make plenty of custom settings, but the default browser settings work almost every time. If you type in a Web address, such as that of the biggest data hoard on the planet—www.google .com—and it doesn't work, check the line and your network settings and you'll figure out where the problem is.

Configuring Internet Explorer

Web browsers are highly configurable. On most Web browsers, you can set the default font size, choose whether to display graphics, and adjust several other settings. Although all Web browsers support these settings, where you go to make these changes varies dramatically. If you are using legacy Internet Explorer (IE) that comes with Windows, you will find configuration tools in the Internet Options Control Panel applet or under the Tools menu in Internet Explorer (see Figure 21-27).

Figure 21-26   Mozilla Firefox showing a Web page

NOTE   Eagle-eyed readers may note that the window title in Figures 21-28 and 21-29 is Internet Properties, not Internet Options as in Figure 21-27. Don't ask me why, but the title is Internet Options if you open it from Internet Explorer, and it's Internet Properties if you open it from Control Panel. Don't get confused; they have the same settings!

I find it bizarre that CompTIA specifically lists *Internet Options* as an objective on the CompTIA A+ 1002 exam. It's just so . . . Microsofty. There are obviously more browsers than just Internet Explorer, so I'll begin by explaining the options available to you in Internet Explorer, and then show you some of the common options found in other browsers, too.

When you open the Internet Options applet, you'll see seven tabs along the top. The first tab is the General tab. These settings control the most basic features of Internet

Figure 21-27
Internet Options
applet

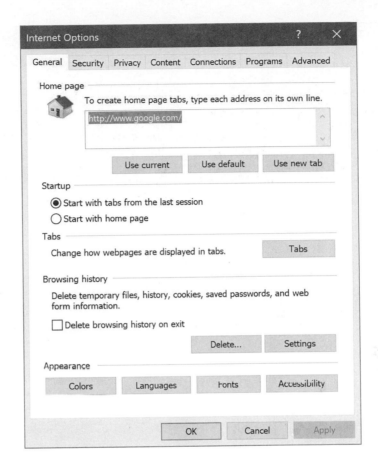

Explorer: the home page, tab management, your browsing history, searching, and other appearance controls. If you want to delete or change how Internet Explorer stores the Web sites you've visited, use this tab.

The Security tab enables you set how severely Internet Explorer safeguards your Web browsing (see Figure 21-28). Each setting can be adjusted for a particular zone, such as the Internet, your local intranet, trusted sites, and restricted sites. You can configure which Web sites fall into which zones. Once you've picked a zone to control, you can set Internet Explorer's security level. The High security level blocks more Web sites and disables some plug-ins, while Medium-high and Medium allow less-secure Web sites and features to display and operate.

The Privacy tab works a lot like the Security tab, except it controls privacy matters, such as cookies, location tracking, pop-ups, and whether browser extensions will run in private browsing mode. There is a slider that enables you to control what is blocked—everything is blocked on the highest setting; nothing is blocked on the lowest. Go here

Figure 21-28
The Security
tab in Internet
Options

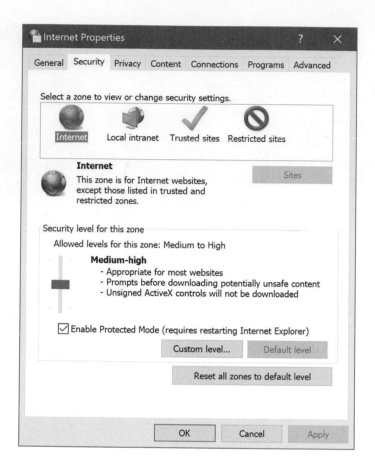

if you don't like the idea of Web sites tracking your browsing history (though cookies do other things, too, like authenticate users).

The Content tab controls what your browser will and will not display. This time, however, it enables you to gate access to insecure or objectionable sites—a practice called *content filtering*—using certificates and a *parental-control* tool called Family Safety, which lets system administrators restrict Web, game, and app usage (by rating system and exception lists) and even control when an account can log in. The Content tab also enables you to adjust the AutoComplete feature that fills in Web addresses for you, as well as control settings for RSS feeds and Web Slices (both methods for subscribing to a Web page's content updates).

The Connections tab enables you to do a lot of things. You can set up your connection to the Internet via broadband or dial-up; connect to a VPN; or adjust some LAN settings, which you probably won't need to deal with except perhaps to configure a proxy server connection. Because proxy servers are a little complicated and CompTIA wants you to know about them, let's quickly talk about uses for proxy servers.

Many corporations use a proxy server to filter employee Internet access, and when you're on their corporate network, you need to set your proxy settings within the Web browser (and any other Internet software you want to use). A *proxy server* is software that enables multiple connections to the Internet to go through one protected computer. Applications that want to access Internet resources send requests to the proxy server instead of trying to access the Internet directly, which both protects the client computers and enables the network administrator to monitor and restrict Internet access. Each application must therefore be configured to use the proxy server.

Moving on, the Programs tab in Internet Options contains settings for your default Web browser, any add-ons you use (like Java), and how other programs deal with HTML files and e-mail messages.

 EXAM TIP Given a specific scenario, be sure you know how to use the various Internet Options.

The Advanced tab does exactly what it sounds like: lists a bunch of advanced options that you can turn on and off with the check of a box (see Figure 21-29). The available options include accessibility, browsing, international, and, most importantly, security settings. From here, you can control how Internet Explorer checks Web site certificates, among many other settings. It also hosts a settings-reset button in case you need a fresh start.

Figure 21-29
The Advanced tab in Internet Options

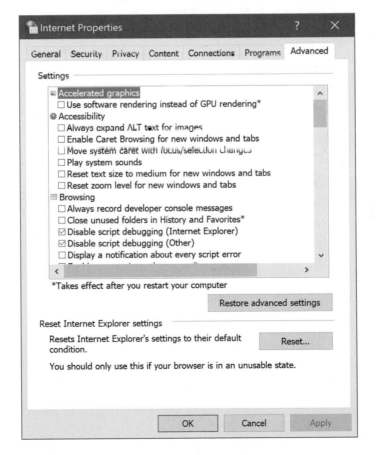

NOTE Windows comes with a great Control Panel applet called *Credential Manager* that manages all the saved logon information for Web sites (as well as connected applications and networks). You can use Credential Manager to delete passwords or other logon information.

Configuring Other Web Browsers

I want to stomp all over Internet Explorer and tell you how bad it is—but the truth of the matter is that, after a big push to get IE back on track in recent versions, Microsoft did the right thing to help the Web move beyond IE by focusing on its replacement, Microsoft Edge. Edge is a powerful, clean, modern Web browser that supports current Web standards. I use it a lot, though I can't say we date exclusively.

You'll probably want to download one of several other Web browsers that support current Web standards as well and offer different experiences than Edge. This gives you a quick fix if you run into a site that has a problem or if a nasty security vulnerability is discovered in your usual browser. Two of the big browser heavyweights that fit this description are Mozilla Firefox and Google Chrome.

You control their settings much like you do in Internet Explorer, though you won't find an applet tucked away in Control Panel. In Google Chrome, you can click the three-dot icon in the upper-right corner of the browser and select Settings. In Mozilla Firefox, the icon looks like a stack of horizontal lines, but it's also in the upper-right corner, and you're looking for the Options button.

In these menus, you'll find a lot of settings very similar to the ones you find in Internet Options. Firefox (see Figure 21-30) and Google Chrome (see Figure 21-31) settings are Web pages built into the browsers, but they still control the same features: home page, security, font size, cookies, and all your old favorites. Take some time to use these browsers and explore their settings. You'll be surprised how well your knowledge of one browser helps you set up another.

NOTE If you use a macOS computer, you'll most likely use yet another Web browser, *Safari*. Safari supports every modern Web standard and works great. You can also use Chrome or Firefox (but not Edge) on your macOS machine. Happy Web browsing!

E-mail

To set up and access e-mail, you have a lot of choices today. You can use the traditional ISP method that requires a dedicated e-mail application. Increasingly today, though, people use e-mail clients built into whatever device they use. Finally, you can use a Web-based e-mail client accessible from any device. The difficulty with this section is that all of this is blending somewhat with the advent of account-based access to devices, such as using your Microsoft account to log on to your Windows PC.

All e-mail addresses come in the *accountname@Internet domain* format. To add a new account, provide your name, e-mail address, and password. Assuming the corporate or organization server is set up correctly, that's all you have to do today.

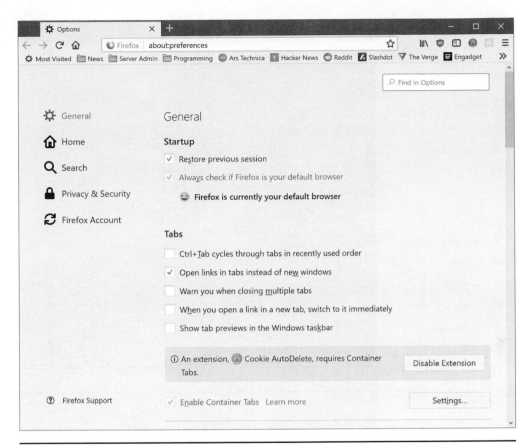

Figure 21-30 Mozilla Firefox Options

In the not so distant past, however, and still referenced on the CompTIA A+ exams, setting up an e-mail client had challenges. Not only did you have to have a valid e-mail address acquired from the provider and a password, you had to configure both the incoming and outgoing mail server information. You would add the names of the *Post Office Protocol version 3* (*POP3*) or *Internet Message Access Protocol version 4* (*IMAP4*) server and the *Simple Mail Transfer Protocol* (*SMTP*) server. The POP3 or IMAP server is the computer that handles incoming (to you) e-mail. Most mail happens through the latest version of IMAP, *IMAP4*. The SMTP server handles your outgoing e-mail.

 EXAM TIP   Make sure you know your port numbers for these e-mail protocols! POP3 uses port 110, IMAP uses port 143, and SMTP uses port 25. Also, you will almost certainly get one or two questions on which protocol handles incoming mail (POP3 or IMAP) and outgoing mail (SMTP).

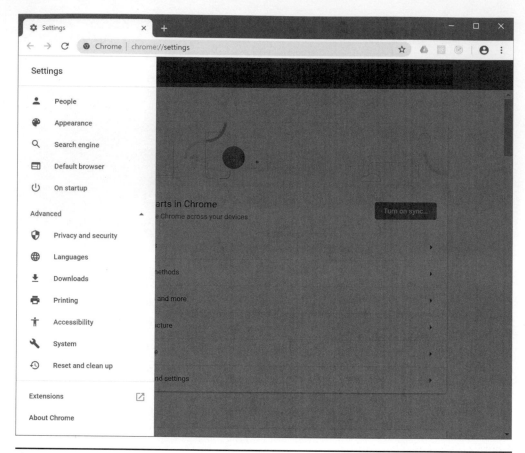

Figure 21-31 Google Chrome Settings

Integrated Solutions

All mobile devices have an integrated e-mail client, fully configured to work within the mobile ecosystem. Apple devices, such as the iPad, enable you to create and use an *iCloud* account that syncs across all your Apple devices. The iCloud e-mail setup process assumes you'll use iCloud for all that sending and receiving stuff and thus you have no other configuration to do. All the settings for IMAP, POP, SMTP, and so on happen behind the scenes. CompTIA calls this sort of lack of configuration *integrated commercial provider email configuration*. That's pretty accurate, if a little bland. You will see more of this in Chapter 24.

Web Mail

Most people use Web-based e-mail, such as Yahoo! Mail, Gmail from Google, or Exchange Online from Microsoft, to handle all of their e-mail needs (see Figure 21-32). Web-based mail offers the convenience of having access to your e-mail from any Internet-connected computer, smartphone, tablet, or other Internet-connected device. While desktop clients may offer more control over your messages and their content, Web-based e-mail has caught up in most respects. For example, Web services can provide superior spam-filtering experience by relying on feedback from a large user base to detect unwanted or dangerous messages.

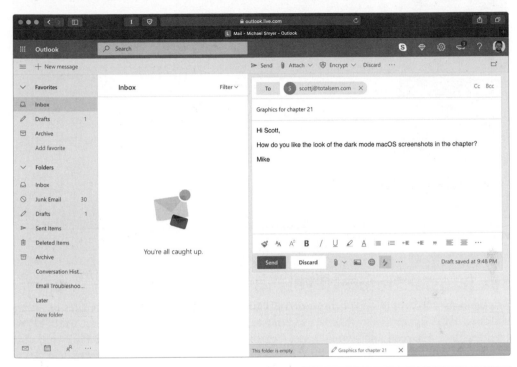

Figure 21-32 Web-based e-mail

EXAM TIP CompTIA A+ 1001 exam objective 1.6 mentions Google/Inbox as an example of Web mail. Inbox by Gmail was an alternative to Gmail for a couple of years, available on the Web and as an app for both Android and iOS devices. Google phased it out in early 2019, but it might show up as an option on the exam.

Unified Internet Accounts

When I log on to my Windows 10 desktop computer, I use my Microsoft account, a fully functional e-mail account hosted by Outlook. Doing so defines the default e-mail experience on that machine. When I access the Mail client, for example, it immediately accesses my Hotmail account (see Figure 21-33). There's no configuration from a user's or tech's perspective. The same is true when you log on to any Apple device, whether it's a mobile device or smartphone, or a macOS desktop machine. Microsoft calls this feature *Live sign in*.

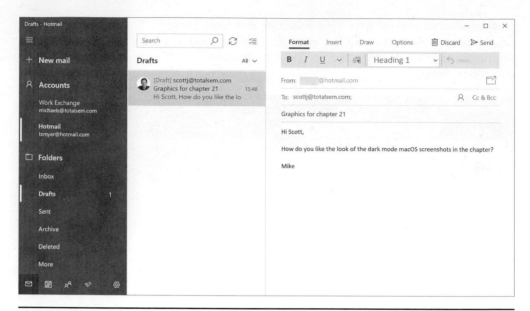

Figure 21-33   Windows 10 Mail

File Transfer Protocol (FTP)

File Transfer Protocol (*FTP*), using ports 20 and 21, is a great way to share files between systems. FTP server software exists for most operating systems, so you can use FTP to transfer data between any two systems regardless of the OS. To access an FTP site, you must use an FTP client such as FileZilla, although most Web browsers provide at least download support for FTP. Just type in the name of the FTP site. Figure 21-34 shows Firefox accessing a NASA FTP site.

Although you can use a Web browser, all FTP sites require you to log on. Your Web browser will assume that you want to log on as "anonymous." If you want to log on as a specific user, you have to add your user name to the URL. (Instead of typing **ftp://ftp .example.com**, you would type **ftp://mikem@ftp.example.com**.) An anonymous logon works fine for most public FTP sites. Many techs prefer to use third-party programs such as *FileZilla* or *Cyberduck* on macOS (see Figure 21-35) for FTP access because these third-party applications can store user name and password settings. This enables you to access the FTP site more easily later. Keep in mind that FTP was developed during a more trusting time, and that whatever user name and password you send over the network is sent in clear text. Don't use the same password for an FTP site that you use for your domain logon at the office!

Telnet and SSH

Telnet is a terminal emulation program for TCP/IP networks that uses port 23 and enables you to connect to a server or fancy router and run commands on that machine as if you were sitting in front of it. This way, you can remotely administer a server and

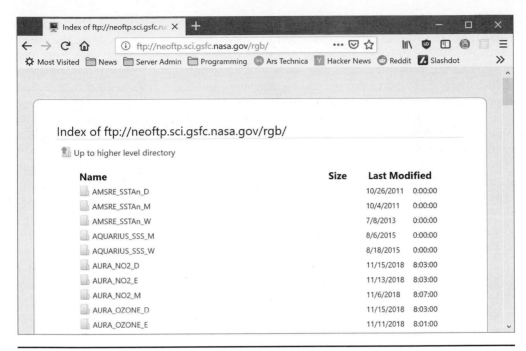

Figure 21-34 Accessing an FTP site in Firefox

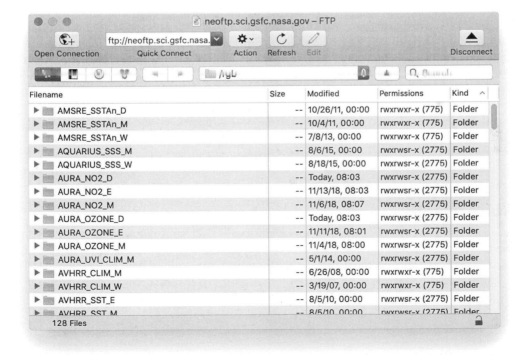

Figure 21-35 The Cyberduck FTP program running on macOS

communicate with other servers on your network. As you can imagine, this is rather risky. If *you* can remotely control a computer, what's to stop others from doing the same? Of course, Telnet does not allow just *anyone* to log on and wreak havoc with your network. You must enter a special user name and password to run Telnet. Unfortunately, Telnet shares FTP's bad habit of sending passwords and user names as clear text, so you should generally use it only within your own LAN.

If you need a remote terminal that works securely across the Internet, you need *Secure Shell* (*SSH*). In fact, today SSH has replaced Telnet in almost all places Telnet used to be popular. To the user, SSH works just like Telnet. Behind the scenes, SSH uses port 22, and the entire connection is encrypted, preventing any eavesdroppers from reading your data. SSH has one other trick up its sleeve: it can move files or any type of TCP/IP network traffic through its secure connection. In networking parlance, this is called *tunneling*, and it is the core of most secure versions of Internet technologies such as SFTP (discussed next) and VPN, which I will discuss in more depth later in the chapter.

EXAM TIP The CompTIA A+ 1002 exam tests your knowledge of a few networking tools, such as Telnet, but only enough to let you support a Network+ tech or network administrator. If you need to run Telnet or SSH, you will get the details from a network administrator. Implementation of Telnet and SSH falls well beyond CompTIA A+.

SFTP

Secure FTP is a network protocol for transferring files over an encrypted SSH connection. You can (and should!) use SFTP for the same things you'd use FTP for—but it is technically its own distinct protocol. The SFTP protocol was written as an extension of SSH, so you can find SFTP client and server support built into SSH software, such as the popular OpenSSH. In Figure 21-36, I'm using SFTP to transfer a Web server log.

Figure 21-36
OpenSSH

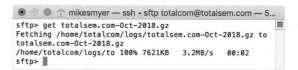

Voice over IP

You can use *Voice over IP* (*VoIP*) to make voice calls over your computer network. Why have two sets of wires, one for voice and one for data, going to every desk? Why not just use the extra capacity on the data network for your phone calls? That's exactly what VoIP does for you. VoIP works with every type of high-speed Internet connection, from DSL to cable to satellite.

VoIP doesn't refer to a single protocol but rather to a collection of protocols that make phone calls over the data network possible. The most common VoIP application protocol is Session Initiation Protocol (SIP), but some popular VoIP applications such as Skype are completely proprietary.

Vendors such as Skype, Cisco, Vonage, Arris, and Comcast offer popular VoIP solutions, and many corporations use VoIP for their internal phone networks. A key to remember when installing and troubleshooting VoIP is that low network latency is more important than high network speed. *Latency* is the amount of time a packet takes to get to its destination and is measured in milliseconds. The higher the latency, the more problems, such as noticeable delays during your VoIP call.

VoIP isn't confined to your computer, either. It can completely replace your old copper phone line. Two popular ways to set up a VoIP system are to either use dedicated *VoIP phones*, like the ones that Cisco makes, or use a dedicated VoIP box (see Figure 21-37) that can interface with your existing analog phones.

Figure 21-37
Arris VoIP
telephony
modem

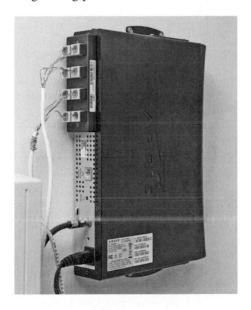

True VoIP phones have RJ-45 connections that plug directly into the network and offer advanced features such as HD-quality audio and video calling. Unfortunately, these phones require a complex and expensive network to function, which puts them out of reach of most home users.

For home users, it's much more common to use a VoIP phone adaptor to connect your old-school analog phones. These little boxes are very simple to set up: just connect it to your network, plug in a phone, and then check for a dial tone. With the VoIP service provided by cable companies, the adapter is often built right into the cable modem itself, making setup a breeze.

> **Try This!   Checking Latency with ping**
>
> Latency is the bane of any VoIP call because of all the problems it causes if it is too high. A quick way to check your current latency is to use the ever-handy ping, so try this!
>
> 1. Run ping on some known source, such as www.microsoft.com or www .totalsem.com.
>
> 2. When the ping finishes, take note of the average round-trip time at the bottom of the screen. This is your current latency to that site.

Remote Desktop

While folders and printers might be the primary things shared over a network, sometimes it would be convenient to be "transported" to another computer—to feel as if your hands were actually on its keyboard. There are plenty of programs that do exactly this, generically called remote desktops.

 NOTE   Because "remote desktop" is a generic term, you may find some programs with confusingly similar names. Microsoft and Apple both at one point made a program called *Remote Desktop* (the latter is a paid offering), though Microsoft's version is called *Remote Desktop Connection* in current versions of Windows. Then there's Microsoft's *Remote Desktop Connection for Mac*, which is just for enabling macOS machines to connect to a Windows remote desktop.

While some operating systems include a remote desktop client, many third-party remote desktop applications are also available. Most of these make use of either the *Remote Desktop Protocol* (*RDP*) or *Virtual Network Computing* (*VNC*). TightVNC, for example, is totally cross-platform, enabling you to run and control a Windows system remotely from your Mac or vice versa, for example. Figure 21-38 shows TightVNC in action.

 NOTE   All terminal emulation programs require separate server and client programs.

Windows offers an alternative to VNC: Remote Desktop Connection. *Remote Desktop Connection* provides control over a remote server with a fully graphical interface. Your desktop *becomes* the server desktop (see Figure 21-39).

Figure 21-38 TightVNC in action

Figure 21-39
Windows
Remote Desktop
Connection
dialog box

NOTE The name of the Remote Desktop Connection executable file is mstsc .exe. You can also open Remote Desktop Connection from a command-line interface or the Search bar by typing **mstsc** and pressing enter.

Wouldn't it be cool if, when called about a technical support issue, you could simply see what the client sees? When the client says that something doesn't work, it would be great if you could transfer yourself from your desk to your client's desk to see precisely what the client sees. This would dramatically cut down on the miscommunication that can make a tech's life so tedious. Windows Remote Assistance does just that. *Remote Assistance* enables you to give anyone control of your desktop or take control of anyone else's desktop. If a user has a problem, that user can request support (see Figure 21-40) directly from you. Upon receiving the support-request e-mail, you can then log on to the user's system and, with permission, take the driver's seat.

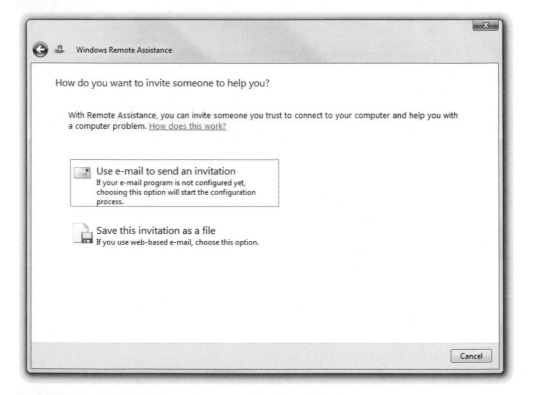

Figure 21-40 Creating a Remote Assistance request

With Remote Assistance, you can do anything you would do from the actual computer. You can troubleshoot some hardware configuration or driver problem. You can install drivers, roll back drivers, download new ones, and so forth. You're in command of the remote machine as long as the client allows you to be. The client sees everything you do, by the way, and can stop you cold if you get out of line or do something that makes the client nervous! Remote Assistance can help you teach someone how to use a particular application. You can log on to a user's computer and fire up Outlook, for example, and then walk through the steps to configure it while the user watches. The user can then take over the machine and walk through the steps while you watch, chatting with one another the whole time. Sweet!

Remote desktop applications provide everything you need to access one system from another. They are common, especially considering that Microsoft provides Remote Desktop for free. Whichever application you use, remember that you will always need both a server and a client program. The server goes on the system you want to access and the client goes on the system you use to access the server. With many solutions, the server and client software are integrated into a single product.

EXAM TIP While Apple sells a Remote Desktop product marketed to business customers that includes remote assistance features, macOS also has more modest *screen sharing* built in to the operating system. This built-in functionality, which can be enabled in System Preferences, should suffice for general remote access, collaboration, and light remote troubleshooting.

In Windows, you can turn Remote Assistance and Remote Desktop on and off and configure other settings. Go to the System applet in Control Panel and then select the *Remote settings* link on the left. Under the Remote tab in System Properties you will see checkboxes for both Remote Assistance and Remote Desktop, along with buttons to configure more detailed settings.

EXAM TIP Windows is also capable of running specific applications hosted on another machine. Think of it as Remote Desktop without the desktop—a single application run on one machine (a server) and appearing on another desktop (a client). You can set up your connection using the RemoteApp and Desktop Connections applet in Control Panel.

Virtual Private Networks

Remote connections have been around for a long time, long before the Internet existed. The biggest drawback about remote connections was the cost to connect. If you were on one side of the continent and had to connect to your LAN on the other side of the continent, the only connection option was a telephone. Or, if you needed to connect two LANs across the continent, you ended up paying outrageous monthly charges for a private connection. The introduction of the Internet gave people wishing to connect to their home networks a very cheap connection option, but with one problem: the whole Internet is open to the public. People wanted to stop using dial-up and expensive private connections and use the Internet instead, but they wanted to do it securely.

Those clever network engineers worked long and hard and came up with several solutions to this problem. Standards have been created that use encrypted tunnels between a computer (or a remote network) to create a private network through the Internet (see Figure 21-41), resulting in what is called a *Virtual Private Network* (*VPN*).

Figure 21-41
VPN connecting computers across the United States

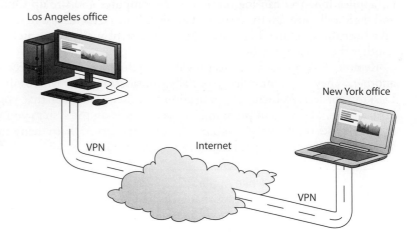

An encrypted tunnel requires endpoints—the ends of the tunnel where the data is encrypted and decrypted. In the SSH tunnel you've seen thus far, the client for the application sits on one end and the server sits on the other. VPNs do the same thing. Either some software running on a computer or, in some cases, a dedicated Internet appliance such as an *endpoint management server* must act as an endpoint for a VPN (see Figure 21-42).

Figure 21-42
Typical tunnel

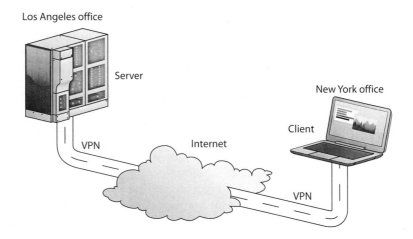

 NOTE An *Internet appliance* is a dedicated box that accomplishes a specific function or functions. You'll see these in many other uses in Chapter 27.

VPNs require a protocol that itself uses one of the many tunneling protocols available and adds the capability to ask for an IP address from a local DHCP server to give the tunnel an IP address that matches the subnet of the local LAN. The connection keeps the IP address to connect to the Internet, but the tunnel endpoints must act like NICs (see Figure 21-43). Let's look at one of the protocols, PPTP.

Figure 21-43
Endpoints must
have their own IP
addresses.

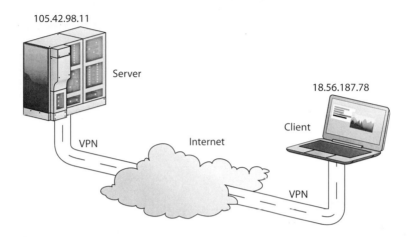

PPTP VPNs

So how do we make IP addresses appear out of thin air? Microsoft got the ball rolling with the *Point-to-Point Tunneling Protocol* (*PPTP*), an advanced version of PPP (used for dial-up Internet, as discussed earlier) that handles all of this right out of the box. The only trick is the endpoints. In Microsoft's view, a VPN is intended for individual clients (think employees on the road) to connect back to the office network, so Microsoft places the PPTP endpoints on the client and a special remote access server program called Routing and Remote Access Service (RRAS), available on Server versions of Windows (see Figure 21-44).

On the Windows client side, in Windows 7, type **VPN** into the Start Search bar and press ENTER. In Windows 8/8.1/10, type **VPN** at the Start screen and select *Manage virtual private networks* (*VPN*) *on 8/8.1* or *VPN settings* on 10. This presents you with a screen where you can enter all your VPN server information. Your network administrator will most likely provide this to you. The result is a virtual network card that, like any other NIC, gets an IP address from the DHCP server back at the office (see Figure 21-45).

EXAM TIP   A system connected to a VPN looks as though it's on the local network but often performs much slower than if the system were connected directly back at the office.

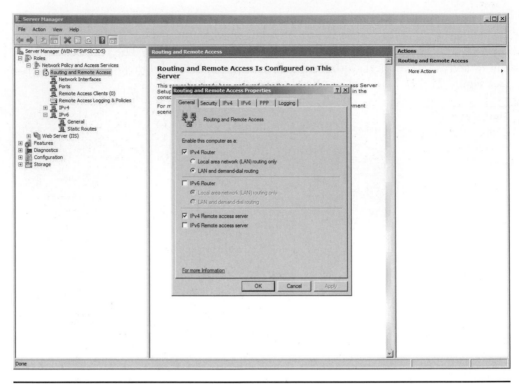

Figure 21-44 RRAS in action

When your computer connects to the RRAS server on the private network, PPTP creates a secure tunnel through the Internet back to the private LAN. Your client takes on an IP address for that network, as if your computer were plugged into the LAN back at the office. Even your Internet traffic will go through your office first. If you open your Web browser, your client will go across the Internet to the office LAN and then use the LAN's Internet connection! Because of this, Web browsing is very slow over a VPN.

File Sharing

The last extra Internet function to discuss is also probably the most controversial: *file sharing*. Modern file sharing started in the late 1990s and consisted of a whole bunch of computers running the same program, such as Napster or Kazaa. The *file-sharing* program enables each of the computers running that program to offer files to share, such as music and movies. Once all of the file-sharing programs are connected to the Internet, any of them can download any file offered by any other in the group.

File sharing through such *distributed* sharing software feels almost anonymous and free—and that's the problem. You can share *anything*, even copyright-protected music, movies, and more. The music industry (and later the film industry) came out swinging

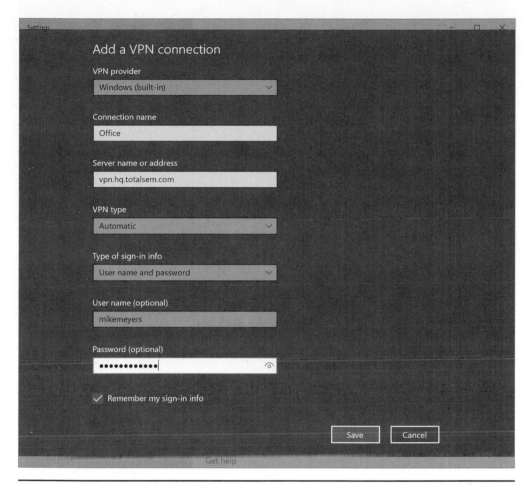

Figure 21-45 VPN connection in Windows

to try to stop file-sharing practices. The result has been a series of legal campaigns against sites and companies that facilitate file sharing, and to shut down individuals who share lots of files.

 EXAM TIP Look for questions on the CompTIA A+ 1001 exam on remote access scenarios that use *file share* technologies. The rest of us call it *file sharing*, but it means the same thing—using legal technologies to access both legal and illegal content.

Software developers and file sharers didn't back down, responding to the pressure by creating Internet protocols such as *BitTorrent* that can share files faster and more effi-ciently. BitTorrent is a peer-to-peer file sharing program, meaning that each computer that downloads a portion of a shared resource will by default also share that portion with everyone else trying to download the shared resource. The effect of this P2P model is that the more popular something is, the more quickly flows the download. You can download an episode of *Game of Thrones* in seconds, for example, but that ripped copy of *Gigli* might take days to acquire.

Figure 21-46 shows one of the more popular BitTorrent protocol programs, called Deluge. BitTorrent has many legitimate uses as well—it is extremely efficient for the distribution of large files and has become the method of choice for distributing Linux distributions, and it is even used to distribute Blizzard games (and patches for those games) like *World of Warcraft* and *Starcraft*! Still, BitTorrent users need the ability to discover valid trackers for the files they want to obtain, and sites listing these trackers have been a big target of continual legal action.

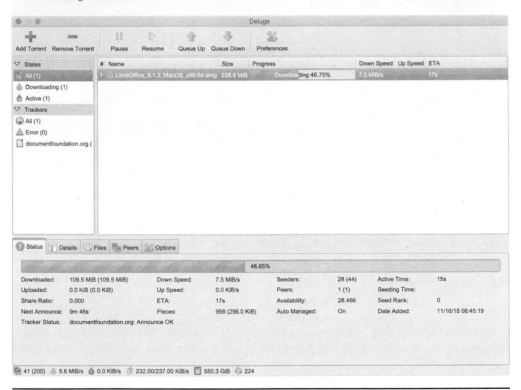

Figure 21-46   Deluge

For all of the legal maneuvering, the last several years suggest the evolving business models of content-creation companies have helped defuse the situation by providing consumers with better access to digital content. Before, the options for obtaining digital copies of most content online were almost always illegal. In the past few years, industry-sanctioned streaming services by Netflix, HBO, and Spotify (see Figure 21-47), among others, have provided legal avenues for consumers to get the content they want, when they want it, without buying physical media (or even dealing with the very real risk of downloading malware instead of a legitimate file).

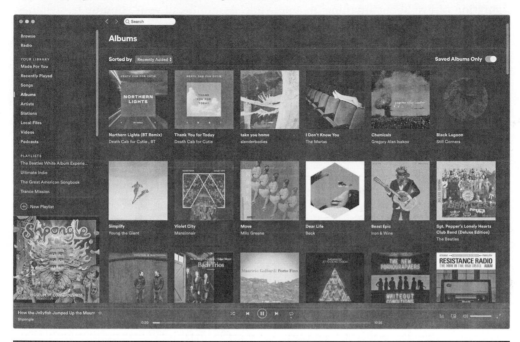

Figure 21-47   An eclectic collection of albums on Spotify

These example programs just scratch the surface of the many applications that use the Internet. One of the more amazing aspects of TCP/IP is that its basic design is around 40 years old. We use TCP/IP in ways completely outside the original concept of its designers, yet TCP/IP continues to show its power and flexibility. Pretty amazing!

Internet Utility Protocols

The CompTIA A+ 1002 objectives list five rather unique protocols. Personally, I doubt you'll ever deal directly with two of them, LDAP and SNMP. The third, SMB, is more common to LANs, not the Internet. And the fourth, AFP, is specific to macOS. The fifth, SLP, is most common in network-aware print devices. You should know a little bit about all five anyway.

LDAP

The *Lightweight Directory Access Protocol* (*LDAP*) enables operating systems and applications to access directories. If you've got a Windows Server system running Active Directory, for example, Windows uses LDAP to do anything with Active Directory. If you're sitting at a computer and add it to an Active Directory domain, Windows uses LDAP commands to update the Active Directory with the computer's information. You don't see LDAP, but it works hard to keep networks running smoothly.

SNMP

The *Simple Network Management Protocol* (*SNMP*) enables remote query and remote configuration of just about anything on a network. Assuming all your computers, switches, routers, and so on are SNMP-capable, you can use programs to query the network for an unimaginable amount of data. SNMP is a popular protocol to check on your network, but it's the sort of thing you probably won't need to use unless you're a Network+ tech.

SMB

The *Server Message Block* (*SMB*) protocol is Windows' network file and print sharing protocol. UNIX and Linux systems used a competing protocol, *Network File System* (*NFS*), but that use has declined. Today, every major OS uses SMB: Windows, macOS, and Linux (using SAMBA). SMB is the protocol of choice for LAN file servers.

 EXAM TIP Over the years, Microsoft has introduced several versions (what Microsoft calls dialects) of SMB, and one of the more widespread dialects is *Common Internet File System* (*CIFS*). CIFS is currently deprecated but still widely supported, making knowledge of it important for passing the CompTIA A+ 1002 exam.

AFP

Like Microsoft and SMB, Apple developed the *Apple Filing Protocol* (*AFP*) in the late 1980s to support file sharing between Macintosh computers on early LANs. Just like SMB, AFP survives to this day as a way for macOS machines to share files with Macs new and old. AFP is also the protocol used by macOS Time Machine for backing up macOS over the network due to its support for HFS+ file system particularities. Support for AFP beyond macOS is solid on Linux, but Windows lacks out-of-box support for the protocol.

SLP

Devices use the *Service Location Protocol* (*SLP*) to advertise available services over a local network and to discover those services. You see this most commonly with network-aware print devices, although some OSs use SLP with file shares as well. SLP uses both UDP and TCP port 427.

1001

The Internet of Things

More and more devices connect to the Internet to make our lives easier, more connected, and ridiculously cool. These devices run the gamut, from refrigerators to thermostats, light switches, security cameras, door locks, and digital assistants. We can access, configure, and command these devices over the Internet. Collectively they're known as the Internet of Things (IoT). Configuration options of these *smart devices* varies wildly among the many manufacturers and software developers, so I can't show you how every device works. Let's use three examples here so you get a sense of what you can do with IoT devices: thermostats, lights, and digital assistants. Then we'll look at some of the protocols that run home automation, the process of using IoT devices.

Home Automation: Thermostats

You can control a smart thermostat from any device connected to the Internet, such as your computer at the office or your smartphone on the commute home. Figure 21-48 shows a smart thermostat.

Figure 21-48

Honeywell Wi-Fi VisionPRO 8000 smart thermostat

Setting up such a device follows straightforward steps. You need to connect the device to a Wi-Fi network. You do this at the device. It will scan the area for networks; select the proper one and input the password/passphrase. You'll most likely need an account with the manufacturer. The Honeywell folks use software called *Total Connect Comfort*.

Once you've made the account, you need to associate the account with the device. This takes a couple of steps. To set up the thermostat listed here, for example, I had to type in the MAC address of the thermostat plus some other information. Once the Honeywell servers could access the device, then I had to change the temp settings to a specific number set by Honeywell so they could confirm I had physical control over the thermostat. Once that was done, success! I downloaded the Total Connect Comfort app to my iPad and logged in (see Figure 21-49). Now I have complete control over my heat/AC from anywhere via the Internet.

Home Automation: Lights

Who knew light bulbs could be so sexy? A lot of companies have created smart lighting options for home automation. You can access these IoT devices from anywhere to set things like when to turn on at night or turn off during the day. You can set up automation options so that lights will change warmth settings as the evening goes on. You might want bright blue-white lights during the early evening, for example, but increasingly warmer and dimmer lights (better for getting sleepy) as the night goes on.

Figure 21-49   Controlling my Honeywell IoT thermostat remotely

Figure 21-50 shows Apple HomeKit controlling the lighting at my developer Michael's apartment via smartphone. How cool is that?

Digital Assistants

```
Me: Alexa! Play songs by Jesse Cook.

Alexa: Shuffling songs by Jesse Cook on Amazon Music.

[Room fills with nuevo flamenco guitar awesomeness.]
```

The big four (Amazon, Apple, Google, and Microsoft) have produced amazing *voice-enabled smart speaker/digital assistants* to connect your home to the Internet in many ways. Amazon's Echo line, for example, enables you to connect a tiny device to your Amazon account and gain access to all music you've purchased, information from the Internet, and more, all by simply saying, "Alexa!" and giving the device further instructions (see Figure 21-51).

Figure 21-50
Controlling
lighting over the
Internet

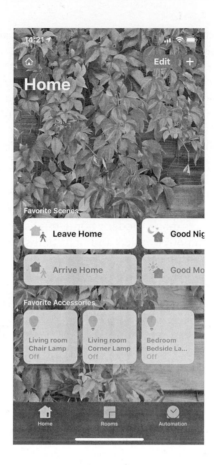

Figure 21-51
Echo Dot

Ask Apple's Siri about the weather tomorrow or about election results in another state. She'll answer with crisp accuracy. "Hey Google" garners a response from Google SmartHome devices in the same way. Microsoft reached into gamer land and produced Cortana (from the popular *Halo* game) as your digital assistant. Cortana will answer just as readily from Microsoft devices.

Setting up these personal assistants is straightforward. Connect the device to the local Wi-Fi and log on to the device from a Web browser to personalize. Once you associate the device with your manufacturer account, the device is good to go, making your life better.

Protocols: Z-Wave and Zigbee

Using wireless technology for home automation has many challenges. First are the huge number of IoT devices that a modern home might potentially use, from thermostats to washing machines to power outlets and light bulbs. Secondly, homes, unlike offices, are filled with small rooms, narrow staircases, and other obstacles that make regular radio-based wireless difficult. Yet demand for home automation is strong, and two competing technologies, Z-Wave and Zigbee, are in direct, head-to-head competition in wireless home automation. Z-Wave is a proprietary standard (with an open API for programmers), while Zigbee is a completely open standard. Both use a mesh networking topology to facilitate communication in homes, yet both also have hubs that act as the network interconnect.

Internet Troubleshooting

There isn't a person who's spent more than a few hours on a computer connected to the Internet who hasn't run into some form of connectivity problem. I love it when I get a call from someone saying, "The Internet is down!" as I always respond the same way: "No, the Internet is fine. It's the way you're trying to get to it that's down." Okay, so I don't make a lot of friends with that remark, but it's actually a really good reminder of why we run into problems on the Internet. Let's review the common symptoms CompTIA lists on their objectives for the CompTIA A+ 220-1001 exam and see what we can do to fix these all-too-common problems.

The dominant Internet setup for a SOHO environment consists of some box from your ISP: a cable or fiber modem, a DSL modem, etc. that connects via Ethernet cable to a home router. This router is usually 802.11 capable and includes four Ethernet ports. Some computers in the network connect through a wire and some connect wirelessly (see Figure 21-52). It's a pretty safe assumption that CompTIA has a setup like this in mind when talking about Internet troubleshooting, and we'll refer to this setup here as well.

One quick note before we dive in: Most Internet connection problems are network connection problems. In other words, everything you learned in Chapter 19 applies here. We're not going to rehash those repair problems in this chapter. The following issues are Internet-only problems, so don't let a bad cable fool you into thinking a bigger problem is taking place.

Figure 21-52
Typical SOHO
setup

No Connectivity

As you'll remember from Chapter 19, "no connectivity" has two meanings: a disconnected NIC or an inability to connect to a resource. Since Chapter 19 already covers wired connectivity issues and Chapter 20 covers wireless issues, let's look at lack of connectivity from a "you're on the Internet but you can't get to a Web site" point of view:

1. Can you get to other Web sites? If not, go back and triple-check your local connectivity.

2. Can you ping the site? Go to a command prompt and try pinging the URL as follows:

```
C:\>ping www.cheetos1.com
Ping request could not find host www.cheetos1.com.
Please check the name and try again.
C:\>
```

The ping is a failure, but we learn a lot from it. The ping shows that your computer can't get an IP address for that Web site. This points to a DNS failure, a very common problem. To fix a failure to access a DNS server, try these options:

- In Windows, go to a command prompt and type **ipconfig /flushdns**:

```
C:\>ipconfig /flushdns
Windows IP Configuration
Successfully flushed the DNS Resolver Cache.
C:\>
```

NOTE   While the commands are similar, ifconfig and iwconfig aren't suitable for flushing the DNS cache, if it exists, in macOS or Linux.

- In Windows 10, go to Network & Internet in the Settings app and click *Network troubleshooter* (see Figure 21-53).
- Try using another DNS server. There are lots of DNS servers out there that are open to the public. Try Google's famous 8.8.8.8 and 8.8.4.4 or Cloudflare's 1.1.1.1 and 1.0.0.1.

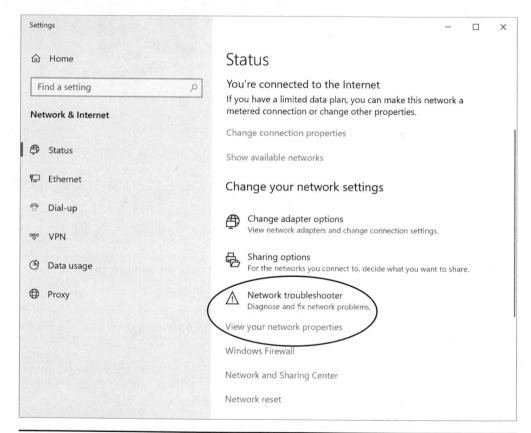

Figure 21-53   Diagnosing a network problem in Windows 10

If DNS is OK, make sure you're using the right URL. This is especially true when you're entering DNS names into applications such as e-mail clients.

EXAM TIP The CompTIA A+ 1001 exam will ask questions about unavailable resources, such as no access to the Internet or e-mail. Look at connectivity issues or configuration problems, such as DNS discussed here, for a correct answer.

Limited Connectivity

Limited connectivity points to a DHCP problem, assuming you're connected to a DHCP server. Run **ipconfig** and see if you have an APIPA address:

```
C:\>ipconfig
Windows IP Configuration
Ethernet adapter Local Area Connection:
        Connection-specific DNS Suffix  . :
        IP Address. . . . . . . . . . . : 169.254.0.16
        Subnet Mask . . . . . . . . . . : 255.255.0.0
        Default Gateway . . . . . . . . :
C:\>
```

Uh-oh! No DHCP server! If your router is your DHCP server, try restarting the router. If you know the Network ID for your network and the IP address for your default gateway (something you should know—it's your network!), try setting up your NIC statically.

Local Connectivity

Local connectivity means you can access network resources but not the Internet. First, this is a classic symptom of a downed DHCP server since all the systems in the local network will have APIPA/link local addresses. However, you might also have a problem with your router. You need to ping the default gateway; if that's successful, ping the other port (the WAN port) on your router. The only way to determine the IP address of the other port on your router is to access the router's configuration Web page and find it (see Figure 21-54). Every router is different—good luck!

You can learn a lot by looking at your WAN IP address. Take a look at Figure 21-55. At first glance, it looks the same as Figure 21-54, but notice that there is no IP address. Most ISPs don't provide static IP addresses—they simply give you the physical connection, and your router's WAN network card uses DHCP, just like most internal networks. If you're lucky, you can renew your DHCP address using some button on the router's configuration. If not, try resetting the cable/fiber/DSL modem. If that doesn't work, it's time to call your ISP.

Slow Transfer Speeds

No matter how fast the connection is, we all want our Internet to go faster. People tolerate a certain amount of waiting for a large program to download or an HD video to buffer, but your connection can sometimes slow down to unacceptable speeds.

Remember that your Internet connection has a maximum speed at which it can transfer. If you divide that connection between multiple programs trying to use the Internet,

Figure 21-54 Router's WAN IP address

all of your programs will connect very slowly. To see what's happening on your network, open a command prompt and type *netstat*, which shows all the connections between your computer and any other computer. Here's a very simplified example of netstat output:

```
C:\>netstat
Active Connections
  Proto  Local Address          Foreign Address           State
  TCP    10.12.14.47:57788      totalfs3:microsoft-ds     ESTABLISHED
  TCP    192.168.15.102:139     Sabertooth:20508          ESTABLISHED
  TCP    192.168.15.102:50283   Theater:netbios-ssn       ESTABLISHED
  TCP    192.168.15.102:60222   dts1.google.com:https     ESTABLISHED
  TCP    192.168.15.102:60456   www.serve2.le.com:http    ESTABLISHED
  TCP    192.168.15.102:60482   64.145.92.65:http         ESTABLISHED
  TCP    192.168.15.102:60483   12.162.15.1:57080         TIME_WAIT
C:\>
```

Figure 21-55 No WAN connection

If you look at the Foreign Address column, you'll see that most of the connections are Web pages (HTTP and HTTPS) or shared folders (microsoft-ds, netbios-ssn), but what is the connection to 12.162.15.1:57080? Not knowing every connection by heart, I looked it up on Google and found out that there was a background torrent program running on my machine. I found the program and shut it down.

When everyone on the network is getting slow Internet connectivity, it's time to check out the router. In all probability, you have too many people that need too much bandwidth—go buy more bandwidth!

When additional bandwidth isn't an acceptable solution, you'll need to make the most of what you have. Your router can use a feature called *Quality of Service (QoS)* to prioritize access to network resources. QoS enables you to ensure certain users, applications, or services are prioritized when there isn't enough bandwidth to go around by limiting the bandwidth for certain types of data based on application protocol, the IP address of a computer, and all sorts of other features. Figure 21-56 is a typical router's QoS page.

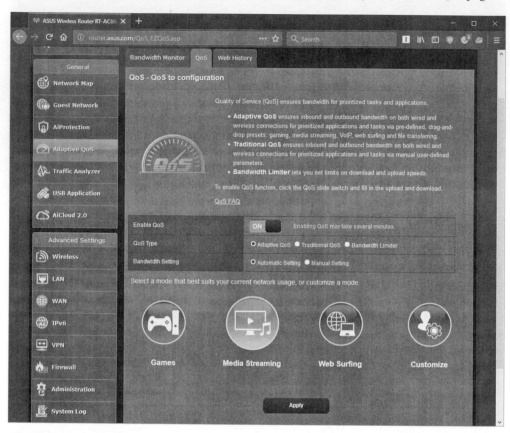

Figure 21-56 QoS

Beyond A+

The areas covered by the CompTIA A+ certification exams do a great job on the more common issues of dealing with the Internet, but one hot topic (although beyond the scope of the CompTIA A+ exams) is so common and important that you need to know it: online gaming.

Online Gaming

One of the more exciting and certainly more fun aspects of the Internet is online gaming. Competing online against one or more real people makes for some pleasant gaming. Enjoying classics such as Hearts and Backgammon with another human can be challenging and fun. Another popular genre of online gaming is the "first-person shooter." These games place you in a small world with up to 64 other players. A great example is Valve Software's *Counter-Strike: Global Offensive* (see Figure 21-57).

Figure 21-57 Counter-Strike: GO

No discussion of online gaming is complete without talking about the most amazing game type of all: the massively multiplayer online role-playing game (MMORPG). Imagine being an elfin wizard, joined by a band of friends, all going on adventures together in a world so large that it would take a real 24-hour day to journey across it! Imagine that in this same world, 2000 to 3000 other players, as well as thousands of game-controlled characters, are participating! Plenty of MMORPGs are out there, but the most popular today is still, surprisingly, *World of Warcraft* (see Figure 21-58).

Figure 21-58 My editor playing *World of Warcraft*

Note that each of these games employs TCP/IP to send information over ports reserved by the game.

Chapter Review

Questions

1. Of the following four Internet connection options, which typically offers the *slowest* connection speed?

    A. Cable

    B. Dial-up

    C. DSL

    D. Satellite

2. What port does POP3 use?

    A. 22

    B. 110

    C. 42

    D. 256

3. What advantage does dial-up have over DSL?

   A. Dial-up is faster than DSL.

   B. You can be farther than 18,000 feet from a main phone service switching center.

   C. You can get a second phone line to use just for dial-up.

   D. None. Dial-up has no advantages over DSL.

4. Which protocol can you use to send e-mail?

   A. IMAP

   B. POP3

   C. PPP

   D. SMTP

5. Which protocols can you use to receive e-mail? (Select two.)

   A. IMAP

   B. POP3

   C. PPP

   D. SMTP

6. What advantage does satellite have over cable for connecting to the Internet?

   A. Satellite is faster than cable.

   B. Cable degrades in stormy weather; satellite does not.

   C. Satellite requires you to be within 18,000 feet of a central switch.

   D. Cable is limited to areas with cable installed; satellite is not.

7. Which of the following represent invalid port to protocol matchups? (Select two.)

   A. 137, 138, 139, 445 = SMB

   B. 3398 = RDP

   C. 80 = HTTPS

   D. 22 = SSH

8. What option often enables you to diagnose TCP/IP errors such as connection problems?

   A. FTP

   B. ping

   C. QoS

   D. APIPA

9. Which of the following cellular data technologies is often considered 4G?

A. EDGE

B. UMTS

C. LTE

D. CDMA

10. Which of the following programs enable you to access and work on a remote computer from your local computer? (Select two.)

A. FTP

B. DNAT

C. Remote Desktop Connection

D. Telnet

Answers

1. **B.** Dial-up connections are robust but much slower than the other connection types.

2. **B.** Post Office Protocol 3 (POP3) uses port 110.

3. **B.** DSL has a fairly short limit of 18,000 feet from a main switch, leaving people in rural areas (in the United States, at least) out of luck. Dial-up just requires a phone line.

4. **D.** You can use Simple Mail Transfer Protocol (SMTP) to send e-mail messages.

5. **A, B.** You can use either Internet Message Access Protocol (IMAP) or POP3 to receive e-mail messages.

6. **D.** Clearly, satellite cuts you loose from the wires!

7. **B, C.** Remote Desktop Protocol (RDP) uses port 3389. Hypertext Transfer Protocol Secure (HTTPS) uses port 443; HTTP uses port 80.

8. **B.** You can often use the ping command to diagnose TCP/IP problems.

9. **C.** Long Term Evolution (LTE) is usually considered a 4G cellular data technology.

10. **C, D.** Both Remote Desktop Connection and Telnet enable you to access and work on a remote computer. The former is just prettier and more secure!

Virtualization

In this chapter, you will learn how to
- Explain why virtualization is so highly adopted
- Create and use a virtual machine
- Describe the service layers and architectures that make up cloud computing

The subject of this chapter, virtualization, can cause brains to lock up if approached cold, so let's start with a scenario. Mario has just launched his own company that hosts Web sites and his first client is Bayland Widgets Corporation. What does Mario need to produce a Web site? In a very basic sense, hosting a Web site requires four components:

- A computer
- An operating system
- Web-server software
- A network connection

Mr. Schwarz, the head of IT for Bayland Widgets, has pretty specific likes and dislikes about hardware and software to optimize the company's Web site. For a computer, he likes a Dell running Microsoft Windows Server OS. For Web-server software, he wants Microsoft Internet Information Services (IIS). So that makes up the first machine.

A second client walks through the door, the IT guy from Highland Gadgets Corporation, one of Bayland Widgets' competitors. Highland's software needs are very different from those of Bayland's. Mr. Barber—the IT guy—also likes Dell computers, but he prefers Linux for an OS, running Apache for the Web-server software.

So now Mario has two dedicated computers, running different operating systems and Web-server software, using two network connections, and sucking up electricity. This doesn't seem very efficient!

To add insult to injury, the two Dell machines have a ton of computing power left unused because the Web sites don't draw a lot of traffic yet. What a waste!

Modern IT addresses these problems through *virtualization*, where a single *host* computer running specialized software can create environments (saved in separate files) that replicate other computers. These environments are called *virtual machines* (*VMs*) or *guests*.

To solve the problems—inefficiency and waste—in this scenario, for example, Mario can install virtualization software onto a Dell computer running Windows Server and then install standalone copies of Windows and Linux running IIS and Apache, respectively. And the two Web servers would never interfere with each other because they are contained within individual files. This is the heart of virtualization.

This chapter delves into virtualization in detail, starting with the reasons why virtualization is important today. The next section goes into the practical implementations of virtualization. The chapter wraps up with a discussion of cloud computing, uses for virtualization that incorporate the Internet. Let's get started.

1001

Benefits of Virtualization

Virtualization offers tremendous benefits to companies. Here are the top four:

- Power saving
- Hardware consolidation
- System management and security
- Research

Power Saving

Before virtualization, each OS needed to be on a unique physical system. With virtualization, you can place multiple virtual servers or clients on a single physical system, reducing electrical power use substantially. Rather than one machine running a Windows file server, another Windows system acting as a DNS server, and a third machine running Linux for a DHCP server, why not use one physical computer to handle all three servers simultaneously as virtual machines (see Figure 22-1)?

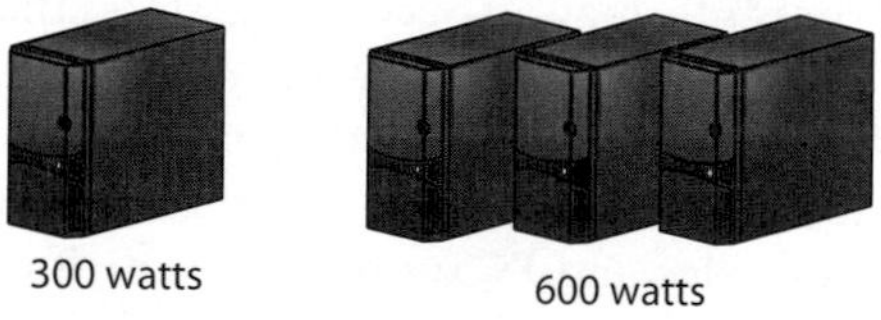

Figure 22-1
Virtualization
saves power.

300 watts

600 watts

Hardware Consolidation

Much in the way you can save power by consolidating multiple servers or clients into a single powerful server or client, you can also avoid purchasing expensive hardware that is rarely if ever run at full capacity during its useful lifetime. Complex desktop PCs can be replaced with simple but durable *thin clients*, which may not need hard drives, fans, or optical drives, because they only need enough power to access the server. For that matter, why buy multiple high-end servers, complete with multiple processors, RAID arrays, redundant power supplies, and so on, and only run each server using a fraction of its resources? With virtualization, you can easily build a single physical server machine and run a number of servers or clients on that one box.

System Management and Security

The most popular reason for virtualizing is probably the benefits we reap from easy-to-manage systems. We can take advantage of the fact that VMs are simply files: like any other files, they can be copied. New employees can be quickly set up with a department-specific virtual machine with all of the software they need already installed.

These management advantages turn out to be a nice security advantage, too. Let's say you have set up a new employee with a traditional physical system. If that system goes down—due to hacking, malware, or so on—you need to restore the system from a backup (which may or may not be easily at hand) or break out the OS installation media. With virtualization, the host machine, hypervisor, and any other VMs it runs are generally unaffected and uninfected; you merely need to shut down the virtual machine and reload an alternate (clean) copy of it. And because VMs are just files, these are easy to keep around.

 EXAM TIP I say *generally* because VMs connected to a network face the same risks—and pose the same risks to other networked devices—as any other networked computer. Networked VMs have *security requirements* similar to a physical system and should usually get whatever security treatment you'd give physical systems. VMs still need regular OS and software updates, firewalls, anti-malware software, accounts with strong passwords, and good general security hygiene.

Most virtual machines also let us make a *snapshot* or *checkpoint*, which saves the virtual machine's state at that moment, allowing us to quickly return to this state later. Snapshots are great for doing risky (or even not-so-risky) maintenance with a safety net, and the freedom they give you to install updates without worrying they'll render the OS unusable can make it easier to keep the system secure. These aren't, however, a long-term backup strategy—each snapshot may reduce performance and should be removed as soon as the danger has passed. Figure 22-2 shows VMware vSphere saving a snapshot.

 EXAM TIP Virtualized operating systems use the same security features as real operating systems. For each virtual machine user account, you'll need to keep track of user names, passwords, permissions, and so on, just like on a normal PC.

Research

Here's a great example that happens in my own company. I sell my popular Total Tester test banks: practice questions for you to test your skills on a broad number of certification topics. As with any distributed program, I tend to get a few support calls. Running a problem through the same OS helps my team solve it. In the pre-virtualization days,

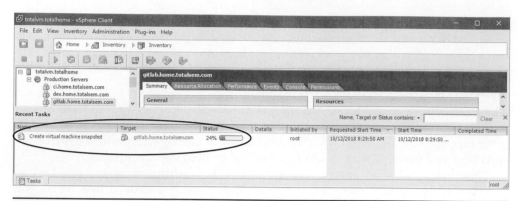

Figure 22-2 Saving a snapshot

I usually had seven to ten multiboot computers laying around my office just to keep active copies of specific Windows versions and other operating systems. Today, a single virtualization host enables us to support a huge number of OSs with one machine.

Implementing Virtualization

Let's turn now to specific implementations of virtualization in modern IT. Specifically, this section discusses the host system variations and how guest systems manifest. Figure 22-3 shows one such example: a Windows system using a program called Hyper-V to host two guest virtual machines: one running Ubuntu Linux and another running Windows 10.

Meet the Hypervisor

A normal operating system uses programming called a *supervisor* to handle very low-level interaction among hardware and software, such as task scheduling, allotment of time and resources, and so on. Figure 22-4 shows how the supervisor works between the OS and the hardware.

Because virtualization enables one machine—the host—to run multiple guest operating systems simultaneously, full virtualization requires an extra layer of sophisticated programming called a *hypervisor* to manage the vastly more complex interactions. Figure 22-5 shows a single hypervisor hosting three different guest virtual machines.

There are a number of companies that make hypervisors. One of the oldest, and arguably the one that put PC virtualization on the map, is VMware (www.vmware.com). VMware released VMware Workstation way back in 1999 for Windows and Linux systems. Since then VMware has grown dramatically, offering a broad cross-section of virtualization products (see Figure 22-6).

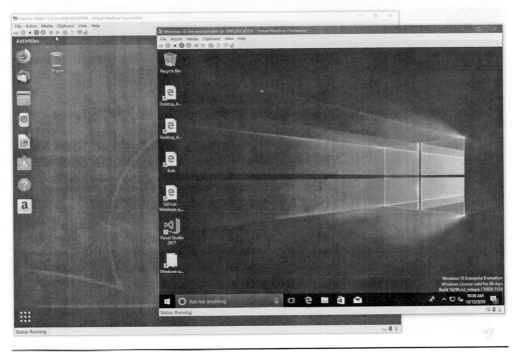

Figure 22-3   Hyper-V running Linux and Windows 10

Microsoft's Hyper-V comes with Windows Server as well as desktop Windows starting with Windows 8 Pro. While not as popular as VMware products, it has a large base of users that's growing all the time (see Figure 22-7)

Figure 22-4
Supervisor on a
generic single
system

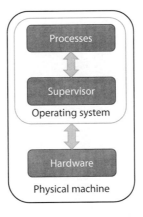

Figure 22-5
Hypervisor on a generic single system hosting three virtual machines

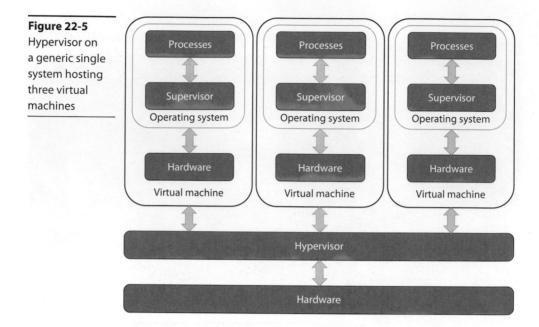

Another very popular hypervisor is Oracle VM VirtualBox (see Figure 22-8). VirtualBox is powerful and runs on Windows, macOS, and Linux.

If you run macOS, the most popular hypervisor choices are VMware Fusion and Parallels Desktop (see Figure 22-9). Both of these macOS hypervisors are quite powerful, but unlike Hyper-V or VirtualBox, they cost money.

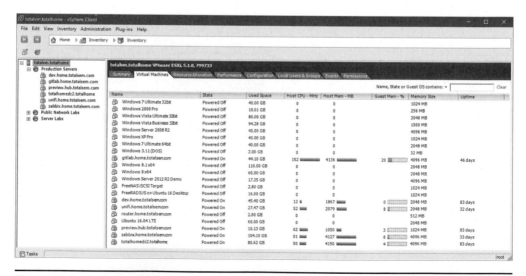

Figure 22-6   Author's busy VMware vSphere ESXi server

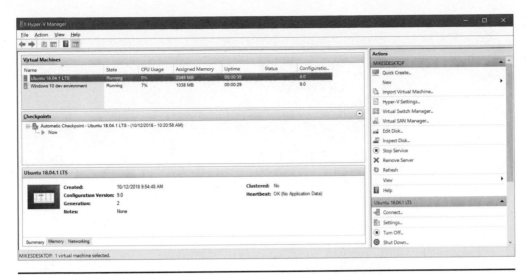

Figure 22-7 Hyper-V on a Windows 10 system

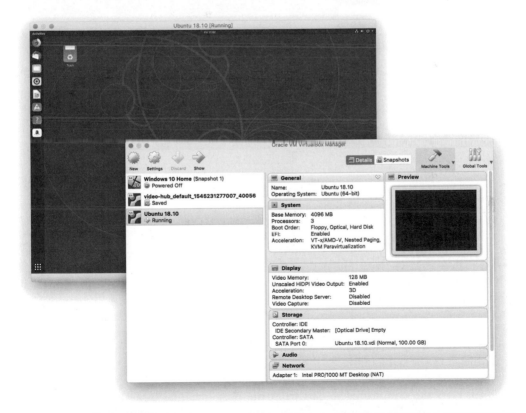

Figure 22-8 Oracle VM VirtualBox

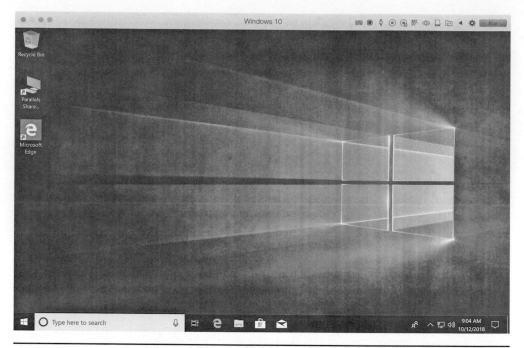

Figure 22-9   Parallels Desktop

This is in no way a complete list of all the hypervisors available out there. Many Linux users swear by KVM, for example, but the hypervisors introduced in this section are the ones you're most likely to see on desktop systems. Make sure you are aware of at least Microsoft's Hyper-V for the exam!

 NOTE   VMware makes a number of amazing virtualization products, but they can be pricey. Microsoft's Hyper-V, Linux's KVM, and Oracle's VirtualBox are all free.

Emulation Versus Virtualization

Virtualization takes the hardware of the host system and allocates some portion of its power to individual virtual machines. If you have an Intel system, a hypervisor creates a virtual machine that acts exactly like the host Intel system. It cannot act like any other type of computer. For example, you cannot make a virtual machine on an Intel system that acts like a Nintendo 3DS. Hypervisors simply pass the code from the virtual machine to the actual CPU.

Emulation is very different from virtualization. An *emulator* is software or hardware that converts the commands to and from the host machine into an entirely different platform. Figure 22-10 shows a Super Nintendo Entertainment System emulator, Snes9X, running a game called *Donkey Kong Country* on a Windows system.

Figure 22-10 Super Nintendo emulator running on Windows

  EXAM TIP While the CompTIA A+ 220-1001 exam objectives include *emulator requirements* as a part of virtualization, the concepts are not the same. For the sake of completeness, however, know that emulating another platform (using a PC to run Sony PlayStation 4 games, for example) requires hardware several times more powerful than the platform being emulated.

Client-Side Virtualization

This chapter will show you a few of the ways you can use virtualization, but before I go any further, let's take the basic pieces you've learned about virtualization and put them together in one of its simplest forms. *Client-side virtualization* is running a virtual machine on your local system (in contrast to VMs run elsewhere, which we'll look at later in the chapter) regardless of whether the VM file itself might be stored locally or on a central server accessed via the network.

The basic process for creating virtual machines is as follows:

1. Set up your system's hardware to support virtual machines and verify it can meet the resource requirements for running them.

2. Install a hypervisor on your system.

3. Create a new virtual machine that has the proper virtualized hardware requirements for the guest OS.

4. Start the new virtual machine and install the new guest OS exactly as you'd install it on a new physical machine.

Hardware Support and Resource Requirements

While any computer running Linux, Windows, or macOS will support a hypervisor, there are a few hardware requirements we need to address. First, every hypervisor will run better if you enable hardware virtualization support.

Every Intel-based CPU since the late 1980s is designed to support a supervisor for multitasking, but it's hard work for that same CPU to support multiple supervisors on multiple VMs. Both AMD and Intel added extra features to their CPUs more than a decade ago just to support hypervisors: Intel's *VT-x* and AMD's *AMD-V*. This is *hardware virtualization support*.

If your CPU and BIOS support hardware virtualization, you can turn it on or off inside the system setup utility. Figure 22-11 shows the virtualization setting in a typical system setup utility.

RAM Apart from hardware virtualization support, the second—and most important—concern is RAM. Each virtual machine needs just as much RAM as a physical one, so it's common practice to absolutely stuff your host machine with large amounts of RAM. The more virtual machines you run, the more RAM you need. Generally, there are two issues to keep in mind:

- Leave enough RAM for the hypervisor to run adequately.

- Add enough RAM so that every VM you run at the same time will run adequately.

It will take some research to figure out how much RAM you need. I have a VirtualBox hypervisor running on a Windows 8.1 (64-bit) host system. There are three VMs running at all times: Windows 7 running a test bank simulation tool, Ubuntu Linux (64-bit) running a Web server, and Windows 10 (64-bit) being used as a remote desktop server. All of these VMs are quite busy. I determined the following requirements by looking around the Internet (and guessing a little):

- 4 GB for the host OS and VirtualBox

- 1 GB for Windows 7

- 512 MB for Ubuntu

- 2.5 GB for Windows 10

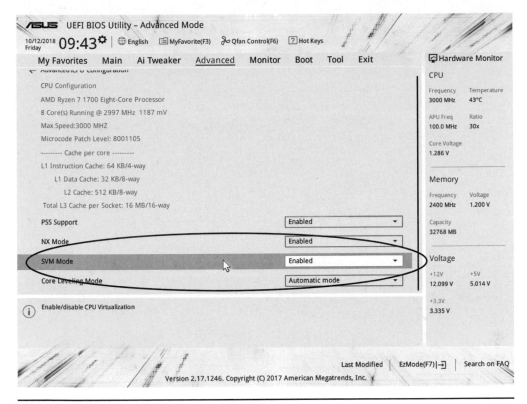

Figure 22-11 BIOS setting for CPU virtualization support

Not wanting to run short, I just dumped 32 GB of RAM into my system. So far it runs pretty well! Be careful here. It is difficult to get perfect answers for these situations. If you research this you may get a different answer.

NOTE As we discussed way back in Chapter 4, "RAM," different motherboards can support different quantities of RAM. If you plan to build a PC to run virtual machines, it pays to do your research. You don't want to get stuck with a board that maxes out at 16 GB of RAM.

VM Storage VM files can be huge because they include everything installed on the VM; depending on the OS and how the VM is used, the VM file could range from megabytes to hundreds of gigabytes. On top of that, every snapshot or checkpoint you make requires space. Figure 22-12 shows a newly minted Windows 10 VM taking about 10 GB of storage space.

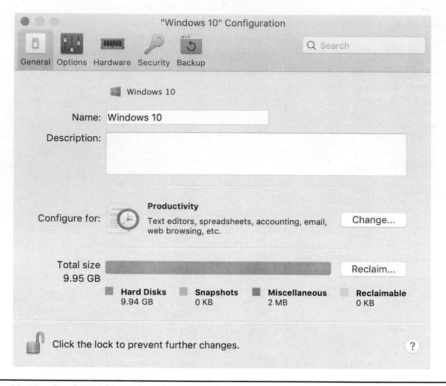

Figure 22-12   Single VM file taking about 10 GB

The particulars depend on your circumstances, but here are a few basic recommendations:

- Make sure you have plenty of storage space for all of the VMs you plan to have, and room to grow.

- Your VM files are precious. Plan ahead to protect them with good RAID arrays and regular backups to make sure they are available when you need them.

- If performance is critical for your VMs, plan to store them on a SATA or NVMe SSD.

Network Requirements

Probably one of the coolest features of VMs is the many different ways you can "virtually" network them. Don't just limit yourself to thinking, "Oh, can I get a VM to connect to the Internet?" Well, sure you can, but hypervisors do so much more. Every hypervisor has the capability to connect each of its virtual machines to a network in a number of different ways depending on your *network requirements*.

Internal Networking   Let's say you have a scenario where you have four VMs and you want them to see each other, but nothing else. No Internet connection: just four VMs that think they are the only computers in existence. Go into the settings for all four VMs and set their respective virtual NICs to an *internal network* (see Figure 22-13). In this case, every VM running on that one hypervisor will act as though it is connected to its own switch and nothing else.

Figure 22-13
Configuring a VM
for an internal
network in
VirtualBox

Internal networking is really handy when you want to play with some cool networking tool but don't want to do something potentially unsafe to anything but your little virtual test network. I often find fun utilities that do all kinds of things that you would *never* want to do on a real network (malware utilities, network scanners, and so on). By making a few VMs and connecting them via an internal network, I can play all I wish without fear of messing up a real network.

Bridged Networking   When most people think of networking a new VM, it's safe to say they are really thinking, "How do I get my new VM on the Internet?" You first connect to the Internet by connecting to a real network. There are plenty of scenarios where you might want a VM that connects to your real network, exactly as your host machine connects to the network. To do this, the VM's virtual NIC needs to piggyback (the proper word is *bridge*) the real NIC to get out to the network. A VM with a bridged network connection accesses the same network as the host system. It's a lot like the virtual machine has its own cable to connect it to the network. Bridged networking is a simple way to get a VM connected to the Internet (assuming the host machine has an Internet connection, of course).

EXAM TIP   A VM connected using bridged networking is subject to all the same security risks as a real computer on the Internet.

Here's a scenario where bridged networking is important. Let's say someone is trying to access my online videos, but is having trouble. I can make a VM that replicates a customer's OS and browser. In this case, I would set up the VM's NIC as a bridged network. This tells the real NIC to allow the *virtual NIC* to act as though it is a physical NIC on the same network. The virtual NIC can take Dynamic Host Configuration Protocol (DHCP) information just like a real NIC.

EXAM TIP On almost every hypervisor, when you create a new VM, it will by default use bridged networking unless you specifically reconfigure the VM's NIC to do otherwise.

Virtual Switches   Think about this for a moment: If you are going to make an internal network of four virtual machines, aren't they going to need to somehow connect together? In a real network, we connect computers together with a switch. The answer is actually kind of cool: hypervisors make *virtual switches*! Every hypervisor has its own way to set up these virtual switches. Most hypervisors, like VirtualBox, just do this automatically and you don't see anything. Figure 22-14 shows the VMware vSphere Client virtual switch configuration.

No Networking   The last and probably least network option is no network at all. Just because you make a VM doesn't mean you need any kind of network. I have a number of VMs that I keep around just to see what my test bank software does on various standalone systems. I don't need networking at all. I just plug in a thumb drive with whatever I'm installing and test.

EXAM TIP Know the purpose of hypervisors and virtual machines. Be sure you are familiar with client-side virtual machine resource, emulator, security, and network requirements.

Installing a Virtual Machine

The actual process of installing a hypervisor is usually no more complicated than installing any other type of software. Let's use Hyper-V as an example. If you have a Windows 8/8.1/10 system, you can enable Microsoft's Hyper-V by going to the Programs and Features Control Panel applet and selecting *Turn Windows features on or off*, which opens the Windows Features dialog box, as shown in Figure 22-15.

Once you've installed the hypervisor of choice, you'll have a virtual machine manager that acts as the primary place to create, start, stop, save, and delete guest virtual machines. Figure 22-16 shows the manager for VirtualBox.

Creating a Virtual Machine

So it's time to build a virtual machine. On pretty much any virtual machine manager, this is simply a matter of selecting New | Virtual Machine, which starts a wizard to ensure you're creating the right virtual machine for your guest OS. Most hypervisors will have

Figure 22-14
VMware
vSphere Client's
virtual switch
configuration

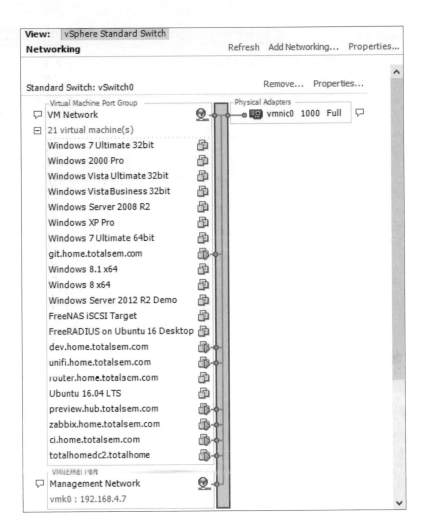

presets for a number of crucial settings to ensure your guest OS has the virtual hardware it needs to run. Figure 22-17 shows the VirtualBox wizard asking what OS I intend to install. By selecting the correct preset, I'll make sure my guest OS has the minimum virtual RAM, hard drive space, and so forth, that it needs. You also need to give the virtual machine a name. For this overview I'm going with Fedora Workstation.

NOTE Use descriptive names for virtual machines. This will spare you a lot of confusion when you have multiple VMs on a single host.

Next, we get to pick how much memory we want for our VM (see Figure 22-18). VirtualBox recommends at least 1 GB for Fedora, but I'm going with 2 GB to give my VM more RAM with which to work.

Figure 22-15

Installing
Hyper-V in
Windows

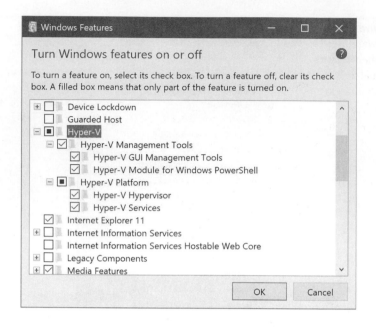

Figure 22-16 Oracle VM VirtualBox Manager (four VMs installed)

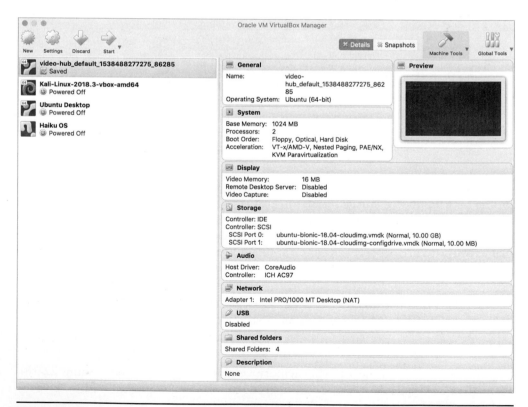

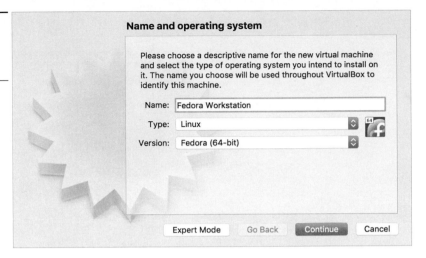

Figure 22-17
Creating a new
VM in Oracle
VirtualBox

Name and operating system

Please choose a descriptive name for the new virtual machine
and select the type of operating system you intend to install on
it. The name you choose will be used throughout VirtualBox to
identify this machine.

Name: Fedora Workstation

Type: Linux

Version: Fedora (64-bit)

Expert Mode   Go Back   Continue   Cancel

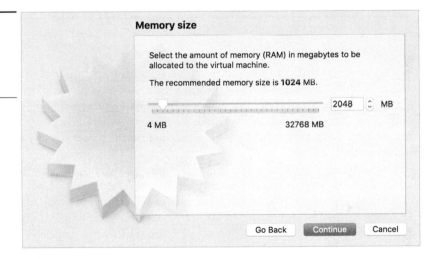

Figure 22-18
Selecting the
amount of
memory for
the VM

Memory size

Select the amount of memory (RAM) in megabytes to be
allocated to the virtual machine.

The recommended memory size is **1024** MB.

2048   MB

4 MB   32768 MB

Go Back   Continue   Cancel

Next, we need to create the virtual hard drive. The VirtualBox wizard asks several technical questions about hard disk file type and how it should allocate the space. I'm just going with the defaults, but it can be useful to change them in certain situations. Finally, on the last screen we get to set how big the virtual disk will be, the default being 8 GB. That's a bit small for me, so I've gone with 25 GB, as shown in Figure 22-19. With that, we've created a new virtual machine.

Installing the Operating System

Once you've created the new guest VM, it's time to install a guest operating system. Just because you're creating a virtual machine, don't think the operating system and

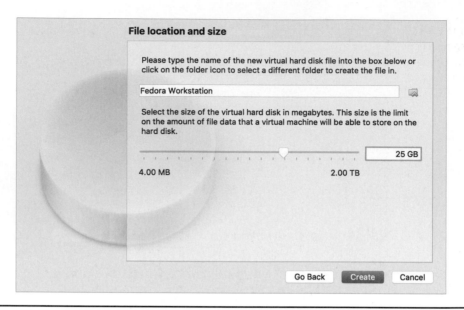

Figure 22-19   Setting the virtual drive size

applications aren't real. You need to install an operating system on that virtual machine. You can do this using some form of optical media, just as you would on a machine without virtualization. Would you like to use Microsoft Windows in your virtual machine? No problem, but know that every virtual machine on which you create and install Windows requires a separate, legal copy of Windows; this also goes for any licensed software installed in the VM.

Because virtual machines are so flexible on hardware, all good virtual machine managers enable you to use the host machine's optical drive, a USB thumb drive, or an ISO file. One of the most popular ways is to tell the new virtual machine to treat an ISO file as its own optical drive. In Figure 22-20, I'm installing Fedora Workstation on a VirtualBox virtual machine. I downloaded an ISO image from the Fedora Web site (https://getfedora.org), and as the figure shows, I've pointed the dialog box to that image. From here I click Start and install Fedora like any other installation.

After you've gone through all the configuration and OS installation screens, you can start using your virtual machine. You can start, stop, pause, add, or remove virtual hardware, treating the VM exactly as though it were a real machine. Figure 22-21 shows VirtualBox running the newly installed Fedora Workstation.

Congratulations! You've just installed a *virtual desktop*. (That's the CompTIA phrase. Most techs just call it a new VM.)

 NOTE   CompTIA uses the term virtual desktop in an odd way; we've used it the same way here, to describe a simple desktop environment on a virtual machine. In practice, a virtual desktop more commonly refers to the multiple desktop environments you can access in modern operating systems, such as clicking the Task View icon in Windows 10 and going to a second desktop.

Figure 22-20
Selecting the
installation
media

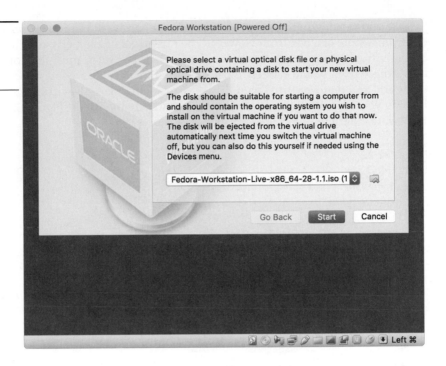

Figure 22-21   Fedora Workstation running in VirtualBox

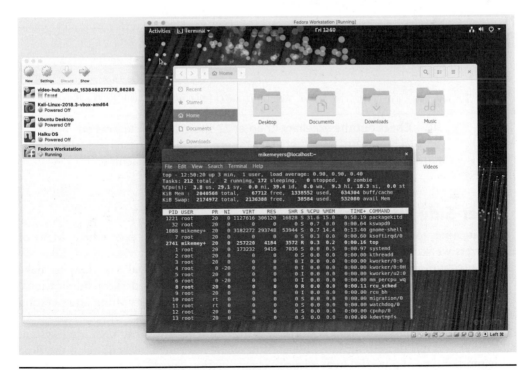

Like with a real system, you can add or remove hardware, but it won't take a trip to the electronics store or a box from Newegg. The real power of a hypervisor is in the flexibility of the virtual hardware. A hypervisor has to handle every input and output that the operating system would request of normal hardware. With a good hypervisor, you can easily add and remove virtual hard drives, virtual network cards, virtual RAM, and so on, helping you adapt your virtual desktop to meet changing needs. Figure 22-22 shows the Hardware Configuration screen from VirtualBox.

Figure 22-22
Configuring virtual hardware in VirtualBox

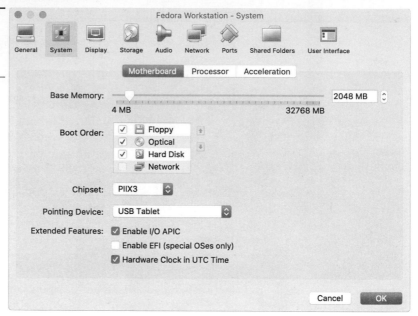

 SIM   Check out the excellent Chapter 22 Show! and Click! sims on "Virtual Hardware" over at http://totalsem.com/100x. These help reinforce terminology and typical steps for setting up a virtual machine.

Server-Side Virtualization

When it comes to servers, virtualization has pretty much taken over everywhere. Many of the servers we access, particularly Web and e-mail servers, are now virtualized. Like any popular technology, virtualization engrosses a lot of people continually working to make it better. VMWare Workstation and VirtualBox are very powerful desktop applications, but they still need to run on top of a single system that is already running an operating system—the host operating system.

What if you could improve performance by removing the host operating system altogether and install nothing but a hypervisor? Well, you can! This is done all the time with another type of powerful hypervisor/OS combination called a *bare-metal* hypervisor. We call it bare metal because there's no other software between it and the hardware—just bare metal. The industry also refers to this class of hypervisors as *Type-1*, and applications such as VMware Workstation as *Type-2* (see Figure 22-23).

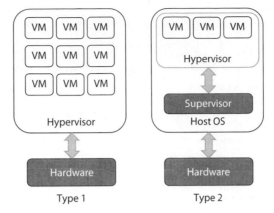

In 2001 VMware introduced a bare-metal hypervisor, originally called ESX, that shed the unnecessary overhead of an operating system. ESX has since been supplanted by ESXi in VMware's product lineup. ESXi is a free hypervisor that's powerful enough to replace the host operating system on a physical box, turning the physical machine into a system that does nothing but support virtual ones. ESXi, by itself, isn't much to look at; it's a tiny operating system/hypervisor that's often installed on something other than a hard drive. In fact, you won't manage a single VM at the ESXi server itself, as pretty much everything is done through a Web interface (see Figure 22-24).

A host running its hypervisor from flash memory can dedicate all of its available disk space to VM storage, or even cut out the disks altogether and keep its VMs on specialized devices that consolidate many drives into a single system and provide storage services to many hosts. This can improve performance and— because all of the drives are in the same place—makes maintaining, administering, and backing up the drives easier. Figure 22-25 shows how I loaded my copy of ESXi: via a small USB thumb drive. The server loads ESXi off the thumb drive when I power it up, and in short order a very rudimentary interface appears where I can input essential information, such as a master password and a static IP address.

Don't let ESXi's small size fool you. It's small because it only has one job: to host virtual machines. ESXi is an extremely powerful bare-metal hypervisor.

To understand the importance of virtualization fully, you need to get a handle on how it increases flexibility as the scale of an operation increases. Let's take a step back and talk about money. One of the really great things money does is give us common, easily divisible units we can exchange for the goods and services we need. When we don't have money, we have to trade goods and services to get it, and before we had money at all we had to trade goods and services for other goods and services.

Let's say I'm starving and all I have is a hammer, and you just so happen to have a chicken. I offer to build you something with my hammer, but all you really want is a hammer of your own. This might sound like a match made in heaven, but what if my

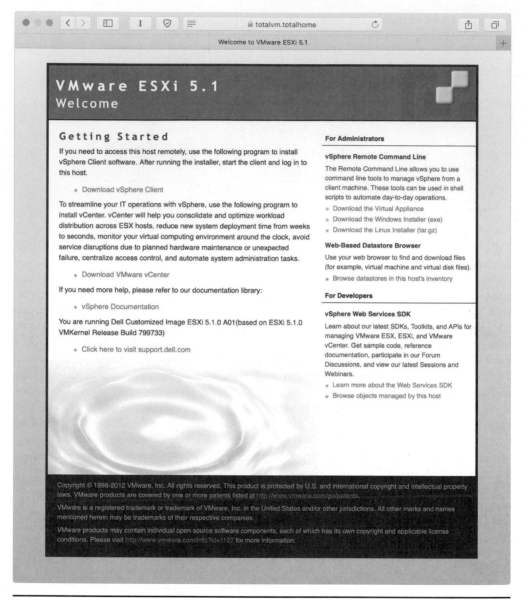

Figure 22-24 Web interface for ESXi

hammer is actually worth at least five chickens, and you just have one? I can't give you a fifth of a hammer, and once I trade the hammer for your chicken, I can't use it to build anything else. I have to choose between going without food and wasting most of my hammer's value. If only my hammer was money.

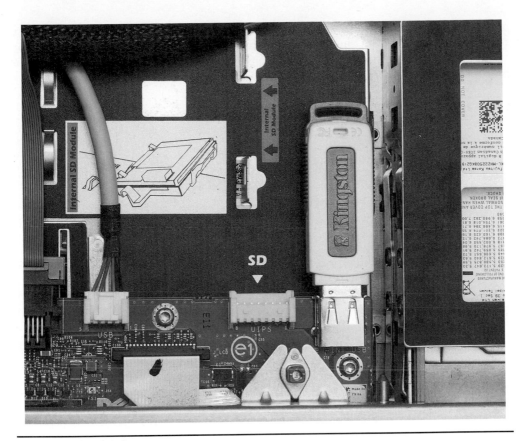

Figure 22-25 USB drive on server system

In the same vein, suppose Mario has only two physical servers; he basically has two really expensive hammers. If he uses one server to host an important site on his intranet, its full potential might go almost unused (especially since his intranet site will never land on the front page of reddit). But if Mario installs a hypervisor on each of these machines, he has taken a big step toward using his servers in a new, more productive way.

 NOTE For those who haven't hit it yet, reddit is an amazing gathering space for geeks on the Internet. Check out the CompTIA forum at www.reddit .com and say hello. It has lots of good information on CompTIA A+ and other certifications.

In this new model, Mario's servers become less like hammers and more like money. I still can't trade a fifth of my hammer for a chicken, but Mario can easily use a virtual machine to serve his intranet site and only allocate a fifth—or any other fraction—of the host's physical resources to this VM. As he adds hosts, he can treat them more and more like a pool of common, easily divisible units used to solve problems. Each new host adds resources to the pool, and as Mario adds more and more VMs that need different amounts of resources, he increases his options for distributing them across his hosts to minimize unused resources (see Figure 22-26).

Figure 22-26
No vacancy on these hosts

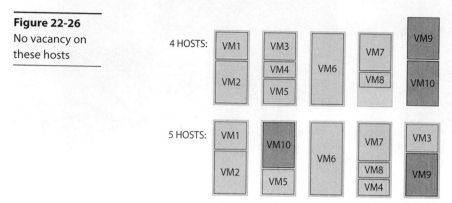

To the Cloud

While simple virtualization enabled Mario to optimize and reallocate his computing resources in response to his evolving needs (as described in the previous section), he can't exceed the capabilities of his local hardware. Luckily, he's no longer stuck with just the hardware he owns. Because his virtual machines are just files running on a hypervisor, he can run them in *the cloud* on networks of servers worldwide.

Let's reconsider a simple Web server, like in the Bayland Widgets scenario that started the chapter. In the not-so-long-ago days, if you wanted a Web site, you needed to build a system, install a Web server, get a commercial-grade Internet link, obtain and properly configure the box with a public IP address, set up firewalls, and provide real-time administration to that system. The cost for even a single system would be thousands of dollars upfront for installation and hundreds of dollars a month for upkeep (and heaven forbid your system ever went down).

As time passed we began to see hosting services that offered to do most of the work of setting up server infrastructure. You merely "hosted" some space on a single server that was also hosting other Web sites. This saved you from having to set up infrastructure, but it was still relatively expensive.

Around 2005/2006, a number of companies, Amazon being the best example, started offering a new kind of hosting service. Instead of using individual physical computers or directories on a shared host, Amazon discovered it could use large groups of virtualized servers combined with a powerful front end to enable customers to simply click and start the server they wanted. Cloud computing was born.

When we talk about the "cloud," we're talking not just about friendly file-storage services like Dropbox or Google Drive, but also about interfaces to a vast array of on-demand computing resources sold by Amazon (see Figure 22-27), Microsoft, and many other companies over the open Internet. The technology at the heart of these innovative services is virtualization.

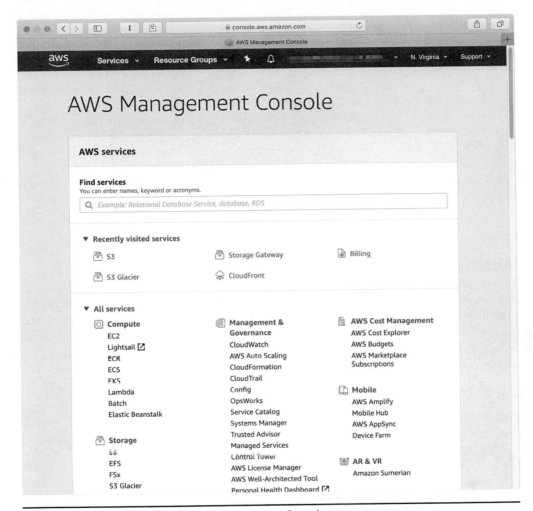

Figure 22-27 Amazon Web Services Management Console

The Service-Layer Cake

Service is the key to understanding the cloud. At the hardware level, we'd have trouble telling the difference between the cloud and the servers and networks that comprise the Internet as a whole. We use the servers and networks of the cloud through layers of software that add great value to the underlying hardware by making it simple to perform complex tasks or manage powerful hardware. As end users we generally interact with just the sweet software icing of the service-layer cake—Web applications like Dropbox, Gmail, and Facebook, which have been built atop it. The rest of the cake exists largely to support Web applications like these and their developers. Let's slice it open (see Figure 22-28) and start at the bottom.

Figure 22-28
A tasty three-layer cake

Infrastructure as a Service

Building on the ways virtualization allowed Mario to make the most efficient use of hardware in his local network, large-scale global *Infrastructure as a Service* (*IaaS*) providers use virtualization to minimize idle hardware, protect against data loss and downtime, and respond to spikes in demand. Mario can use big IaaS providers like Amazon Web Services (AWS) to launch new virtual servers using an operating system of his choice on demand (see Figure 22-29) for pennies an hour. The beauty of IaaS is that you no longer need to purchase expensive, heavy hardware. You are using Amazon's powerful infrastructure as a service.

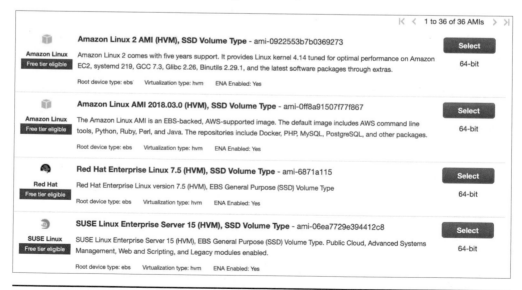

Figure 22-29   Creating an instance on AWS

A huge number of Web sites are really more easily understood if you use the term *Web applications*. If you want to access Mike Meyers' videos, you go to https://hub.totalsem.com.

This Web site is really an application that you use to watch videos, practice simulation questions, and so forth. This Web application is a great tool, but as more people access the application, we often need to add more capacity so you won't yell at us for a slow server. Luckily, our application is designed to run distributed across multiple servers. If we need more servers, we just add as many more virtual servers as we need. But even this is just scratching the surface. AWS provides many of the services needed to drive popular, complex Web applications—unlimited data storage (see Figure 22-30), database servers, caching, media hosting, and more—all billed by usage.

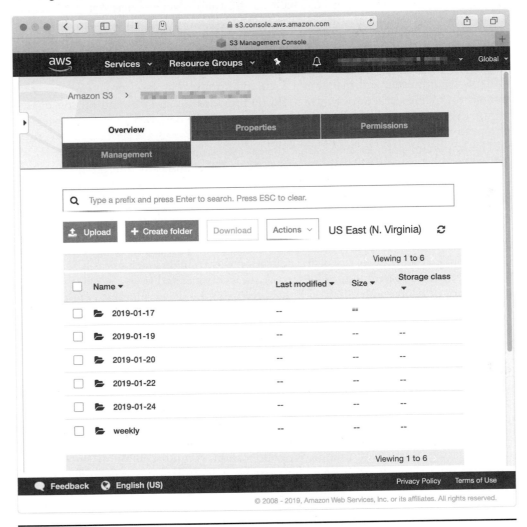

Figure 22-30 Amazon Simple Storage Service (S3)

The hitch is that, while we're no longer responsible for the hardware, we are still responsible for configuring and maintaining the operating system and software of any virtual machines we create. This can mean we have a lot of flexibility to tune it for our needs, but it also requires knowledge of the underlying OS and time to manage it. If you want someone to handle the infrastructure, the operating system, and everything else (except your application), you need to move up to Platform as a Service (PaaS).

Platform as a Service

Web applications are built by programmers. Programmers do one thing really well: they program. The problem for programmers is that a Web application needs a lot more than just a programmer. Developing a Web application requires people to manage the infrastructure: system administrators, database administrators, general network support, and so on. A Web application also needs more than just hardware and an operating system. It needs development tools, monitoring tools, database tools, and potentially hundreds of other tools and services. Getting a Web application up and running is a big job.

A *Platform as a Service* (*PaaS*) provider gives programmers all the tools they need to deploy, administer, and maintain a Web application. The PaaS provider starts with some form of infrastructure, which could be provided by an IaaS, and on top of that infrastructure the provider builds a platform: a complete deployment and management system to handle every aspect of a Web application.

The important point of PaaS is that the infrastructure underneath the PaaS is largely invisible to the developer. The PaaS provider is aware of their infrastructure, but the developer cannot control it directly, and doesn't need to think about its complexity. As far as the programmer is concerned, the PaaS is just a place to deploy and run his or her application.

Heroku, one of the earliest PaaS providers, creates a simple interface on top of the IaaS offerings of AWS, further reducing the complexity of developing and scaling Web applications. Heroku's management console (see Figure 22-31) enables developers to increase or decrease the capacity of an application with a single slider, or easily set up add-ons that add a database, monitor logs, track performance, and more. It could take days for a tech or developer unfamiliar with the software and services to install, configure, and integrate a set of these services with a running application; PaaS providers help cut this down to minutes or hours.

Software as a Service

Software as a Service (*SaaS*) sits at the top layer of the cake. SaaS shows up in a number of ways, but the best examples are the Web applications we just discussed. Some Web applications, such as Total Seminars Training Hub, charge for access. Other Web applications, like Google Maps, are offered for free. Users of these Web applications don't own this software; you don't get an installation DVD, nor is it something you can download once and keep using. If you want to use a Web application, you must get on the Internet and access the site. While this may seem like a disadvantage at first, the SaaS model provides access to necessary applications wherever you have an Internet connection, often without having to carry data with you or regularly update software. At the enterprise level, the subscription model of many SaaS providers makes it easier to budget and keep hundreds or thousands of computers up to date (see Figure 22-32).

The challenge to defining SaaS perfectly is an argument that almost anything you access on the Internet could be called SaaS. A decade ago we would've called the Google search

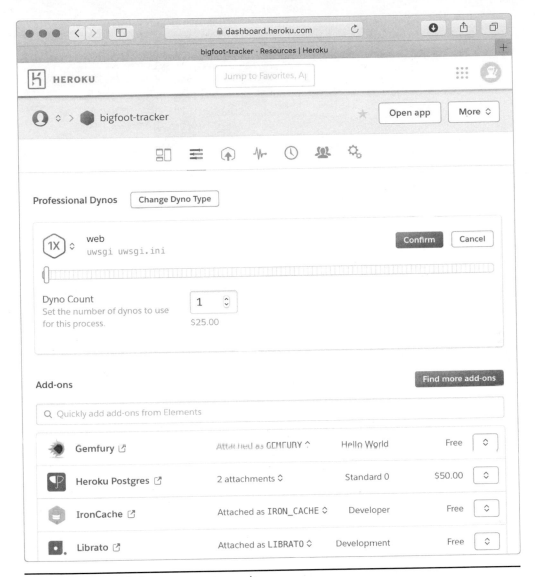

Figure 22-31   Heroku's management console

engine a Web site, but it provides a service (search) that you do not own and that you must access on the Internet. If you're on the Internet, you're arguably always using SaaS.

It isn't all icing, though. In exchange for the flexibility of using public, third-party SaaS, you often have to trade strict control of your data. Security might not be crucial when someone uses Google Drive to draft a blog post, but many companies are concerned about sensitive intellectual property or business secrets traveling through untrusted networks and being stored on servers they don't control.

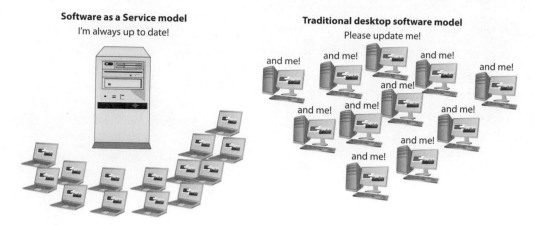

Figure 22-32 SaaS versus every desktop for themselves

 EXAM TIP Know the differences between basic cloud concepts such as SaaS, IaaS, and PaaS.

Ownership and Access

Security concerns like those just discussed don't mean organizations have to forfeit all of the advantages of cloud computing, but they do make their management think hard about the trade-offs between cost, control, customization, and privacy. Some organizations also have unique capacity, performance, or other needs no existing cloud provider can meet. Each organization makes its own decisions about these trade-offs, but the result is usually a cloud network that can be described as public, private, community, or hybrid.

Public Cloud

Most folks usually just interact with a *public cloud*, a term used to describe software, platforms, and infrastructure delivered through networks that the general public can use. When we talk about *the* cloud, this is what we mean. Out on the open, public Internet, cloud services and applications can collaborate in ways that make it easier to think of them collectively as *the cloud* than as many public clouds. The public doesn't *own* this cloud—the hardware is often owned by companies like Amazon, Google, and Microsoft—but there's nothing to stop a company like Netflix from building its Web application atop the IaaS offerings of all three of these companies at once.

The public cloud sees examples of all the *x*aaS varieties, which give specific names to these *cloud concepts*:

- Public IaaS
- Public PaaS
- Public SaaS

Private Cloud

If a business wants some of the flexibility of the cloud, needs complete ownership of its data, and can afford both, it can build an internal cloud the business actually owns—a *private cloud*. A security-minded company with enough resources could build an internal IaaS network in an onsite data center. Departments within the company could create and destroy virtual machines as needed, and develop SaaS to meet collaboration, planning, or task and time management needs all without sending the data over the open Internet. A company with these needs but without the space or knowledge to build and maintain a private cloud can also contract a third party to maintain or host it.

Again, there are private versions of each of the cloud concepts:

- Private IaaS
- Private PaaS
- Private SaaS

Community Cloud

While a community center is usually a public gathering place for those in the community it serves, a *community cloud* is more like a private cloud paid for and used by more than one organization. Community clouds aren't run by a city or state for citizens' use; the community in this case is a group of organizations with similar goals or needs. If you're a military contractor working on classified projects, wouldn't it be nice to share the burden of defending your cloud against sophisticated attackers sponsored by foreign states with other military and intelligence contractors?

Just like with the public and private cloud, there are community cloud versions of all the *x*aaS varieties:

- Community IaaS
- Community PaaS
- Community SaaS

Hybrid Cloud

Sometimes we *can* have our cake and eat it too. Not all data is crucial, and not every document is a secret. Needs that an organization can only meet in-house might be less important than keeping an application running when demand exceeds what it can handle onsite. We can build a *hybrid cloud* by connecting some combination of public, private, and community clouds, allowing communication between them. Using a hybrid cloud model can mean not having to maintain a private cloud powerful enough to meet peak demand—an application can grow into a public cloud instead of grind to a halt, a technique called *cloud bursting*. But a hybrid cloud isn't just about letting one Web application span two types of cloud—it's also about integrating services across them. Let's take a look at how Jimmy could use a hybrid cloud to expand his business.

 EXAM TIP   Know the differences between public, private, community, and hybrid cloud models.

Jimmy runs a national chain of sandwich shops and is looking into drone-delivered lunch. He'll need a new application in his private cloud to calculate routes and track drones, and that application will have to integrate with the existing order-tracking application in his private cloud. But then he'll also need to integrate it with a third-party weather application in the public cloud to avoid sending drones out in a blizzard, and a flight-plan application running in a community cloud to avoid other drones, helicopters, and aircraft (and vice versa). The sum of these integrated services and applications *is* the hybrid cloud that will power Jimmy's drone-delivered lunch. Like the other three clouds, the hybrid cloud sees examples of all the *x*aaS varieties, which give specific names to these cloud concepts:

- Hybrid IaaS
- Hybrid PaaS
- Hybrid SaaS

Why We Cloud

Cloud computing is the way things are done today. But let's take a moment to discuss some of the reasons we use the cloud instead of the old-style hammer of individual servers.

Virtualization

The cloud relies on virtualization. All of the power of virtualization discussed throughout this chapter applies to the cloud. Without virtualization's savings of power, resources, recovery, and security, the cloud simply could not happen.

Shared Resources

Real hardware can be virtualized, meaning made available as partial or full resources to a virtual machine. Hardware can be combined and then shared; these shared resources can be both internal and external and apply to one or many machines. Virtualization provides flexibility.

Rapid Elasticity

Let's say you start a new Web application. If you use an IaaS provider such as Amazon, you can start with a single server and get your new Web application out there. But what happens if your application gets really, really popular? No problem! Using AWS features, you can easily expand the number of servers, even spread them out geographically, with just a click of the switch. We call this ability *rapid elasticity*.

On-Demand

So what if you have a Web application that has wild swings in demand? A local university wants to sell football tickets online. When there isn't a game coming, their bandwidth demands are very low. But when a game is announced, the Web site is pounded with ticket requests. With cloud computing, it's easy to set up your application to add or reduce capacity based on demand with *on-demand*. The application adjusts according to the current demands.

Resource Pooling

Any time you can consolidate systems' physical and time resources, you are *resource pooling*. While a single server can pool the resources of a few physical servers, imagine the power of a company like Amazon. AWS server farms are massive, pooling resources that would normally take up millions of diverse physical servers spread all over the world!

Measured and Metered Service

Ah, the one downside to using the public cloud: you have to write a check to whoever is doing the work for you—and boy can these cloud providers get creative about how to charge you! In some cases you are charged based on the traffic that goes in and out of your Web application, and in other cases you pay for the time that every single one of your virtualized servers is running. Regardless of how costs are measured, this is called *measured service* because of how it differs from more traditional hosting with a fixed monthly or yearly fee. Some companies charge by the amount of processing resources used, such as CPU usage, a *metered service* rate. This enables very careful monetizing of resources used. You pay for what parts of the hardware you use, rather than a more general fee for all the hardware of a system.

Cloud-Based Applications

The earlier discussion about SaaS hinted at one of the most vital and compelling reasons to move to cloud-based computing: getting all the software we need without having to install or upgrade that software manually. For many organizations, the Microsoft Office productivity suite forms the backbone of production throughout the organization. The applications in the suite include Word, Excel, PowerPoint, and Access—the typical "office" apps. Microsoft has gradually increased the suite over various versions to include a lot of other apps that some—but not all—organizations rely on heavily, such as Outlook for e-mail and calendaring, Planner for project management, OneNote for sharing project notes throughout the organization, and many more. As a software manager for an organization, how do you decide what apps to install for each user? Scaling that up to 50 or 100 or more users, that planning and rollout (and upgrades) ends up as a major chore.

With Office 365, Microsoft changed the process in many ways. First, they moved to a subscription-based fee structure, where users or organizations pay a yearly fee for access to the full Office suite. Second, users (or managers) can install only necessary applications. Third, Microsoft updates the applications when necessary, and those updates happen to all the computers connected to the Internet. No manual updates are necessary. Fourth, Microsoft enabled cloud-based versions of the Office applications, so users can access the apps from any Internet-connected computing device, without installing anything locally. This *virtual application streaming* makes Office applications available for smartphones, tablets, laptops, and desktops. (CompTIA uses the term *cell phone* rather than *smartphone*, but they mean the latter when it comes to cloud-based applications.)

Microsoft made Outlook available in the cloud as well, making it arguably the most robust *off-site e-mail application* available. The fully featured calendaring system plus the received and sent e-mail messages are available from any Internet-connected computing device. This is more than traditional Web-based mail; Outlook online is the real deal.

Cloud-Based Virtual Desktops

Earlier in this chapter, we walked through the steps required to set up a virtual desktop inside a VM running on your local system. There's no reason you can't run that same virtual desktop VM in the cloud, and then access it remotely. A number of services have popped up that make it dead simple to create a *cloud-based virtual desktop* and pay monthly or even hourly for access. Interacting with them over the network adds a little lag, but you can do a few neat tricks with them.

Ever wish you had the processing power of a top-of-the-line desktop system and the convenience of a laptop? Any laptop with an Internet connection can spin up a virtual desktop with a few times more processing power. Too boring? What if I said you could use your puny laptop to play the latest computer games (*at max settings!*) by remotely accessing a beastly cloud gaming rig that has everything but the LED lights?

Cloud File Storage Services

Cloud file storage services, like Dropbox and Box, were early smash successes in getting people to move to the cloud for some of their storage needs. They include *synchronization apps* with their desktop versions, so that you can easily have the same version of every file in multiple places (desktop, laptop, online).

As part of Office 365, Microsoft includes cloud file storage services as well through SharePoint. This enables project groups to share files readily, enhancing the collaborative options in Office.

Chapter Review

Questions

1. Upgrading which component of a host machine would most likely enable you to run more virtual machines simultaneously?

   A. CPU

   B. Hard drive

   C. RAM

   D. Windows

2. What is the difference between a virtual machine (VM) and an emulator?

   A. A VM converts commands to and from a host machine to an entirely different platform, whereas an emulator creates an environment based on the host machine and does no converting.

   B. An emulator converts commands to and from a host machine to an entirely different platform, whereas a VM creates an environment based on the host machine and does no converting.

    C. An emulator requires a host OS, whereas a VM runs on bare-metal servers without an OS.

    D. A VM requires a host OS, whereas an emulator runs on bare-metal servers without an OS.

3. What feature lets you save a VM's state so you can quickly restore to that point? (Choose two.)

    A. Checkpoint

    B. Save

    C. Snapshot

    D. Zip

4. What do you need to install a legal copy of Windows 10 into a virtual machine using VirtualBox?

    A. A valid Windows 10 license

    B. Valid Windows 10 installation media

    C. A valid ESXi key

    D. A second NIC

5. Which of the following is an advantage of a virtual machine over a physical machine?

    A. Increased performance

    B. Hardware consolidation

    C. No backups needed

    D. Operating systems included

6. Janelle wants to start a new photo-sharing service for real pictures of Bigfoot, but doesn't own any servers. How can she quickly create a new server to run her service?

    A. Public cloud

    B. Private cloud

    C. Community cloud

    D. Hybrid cloud

7. After the unforeseen failure of her Bigfoot-picture-sharing service, bgFootr—which got hacked when she failed to stay on top of her security updates—Janelle has a great new idea for a new service to report Loch Ness Monster sightings. What service would help keep her from having to play system administrator?

    A. Software as a Service

    B. Infrastructure as a Service

    C. Platform as a Service

    D. Network as a Service

8. Powerful hypervisors like ESXi are often booted from _____.

   A. Floppy diskettes

   B. USB thumb drives

   C. Firmware

   D. Windows

9. When a virtual machine is not running, how is it stored?

   A. Firmware

   B. RAM drive

   C. Optical disc

   D. Files

10. BigTracks is a successful Bigfoot-tracking company using an internal service to manage all of its automated Bigfoot monitoring stations. A Bigfoot migration has caused a massive increase in the amount of audio and video sent back from their stations. In order to add short-term capacity, they can create new servers in the public cloud. What model of cloud computing does this describe?

   A. Public cloud

   B. Private cloud

   C. Community cloud

   D. Hybrid cloud

Answers

1. **C.** Adding more RAM will enable you to run more simultaneous VMs. Upgrading a hard drive could help, but it's not the best answer here.

2. **B.** An emulator converts from one platform to another, whereas a virtual machine mirrors the host machine.

3. **A, C.** The saved state of a VM is called a snapshot or checkpoint. Not to be confused with a true backup.

4. **A.** You need a valid Windows 10 license to run Windows legally.

5. **B.** A big benefit of virtualization is hardware consolidation.

6. **A.** Using the public cloud will enable Janelle to quickly create the servers she needs.

7. **C.** By switching to a PaaS, Janelle can concentrate on creating her service and leave the lower-level administration up to the PaaS provider.

8. **B.** A good hypervisor can be tiny, loading from something as small as a USB thumb drive.

9. **D.** VMs are just files, usually stored on a hard drive.

10. **D.** BigTracks is creating a hybrid cloud by connecting its internal private cloud to a public cloud to quickly expand capacity.

Portable Computing

In this chapter, you will learn how to

- Describe the many types of portable computing devices available
- Explain ways to expand portable computers
- Manage and maintain portable computers
- Upgrade and repair portable computers
- Troubleshoot portable computers

There are times when the walls close in, when you need a change of scenery to get that elusive spark that inspires greatness . . . or sometimes you just need to get away from your coworkers for a few hours because they're driving you nuts! For many occupations, that's difficult to do. You need access to your documents and spreadsheets; you can't function without e-mail or the Internet. In short, you need a computer to get your job done.

Portable computing devices combine mobility with accessibility to bring you the best of both worlds; portables enable you to take some or even all of your computing capabilities with you when you go. Featuring all the bells and whistles of a desktop system, many portables offer a seamless transition from desk to café table.

This chapter looks at the classic portable computer, essentially a desktop transformed into a mobile format. While classic portables usually run Windows, macOS, or some flavor of Linux, operating systems based on Linux—like Chrome OS—can also be found on portable computers.

Historical/Conceptual

Portable Computing Devices

All portable devices share certain features. For output, they use LCD screens, although these vary from 20-inch behemoths to diminutive 10-inch displays. Portable computing devices employ sound of varying quality, from bland mono playback to fairly nice faux-surround reproductions. All of them run on DC electricity stored in batteries when not plugged into an AC outlet.

NOTE Other portable devices, such as smartphones and tablets, run mobile operating systems—such as Apple iOS on the iPad and iPhone—designed to take advantage of small form factors and touchscreens. In practice (and on the CompTIA A+ exams), such mobile devices differ a lot from classic portable computers. While these devices get their own chapters later in the book, it is worth being aware that mobility has encouraged a lot of innovation in recent years and some of the resulting products do a really good job of blurring the line between these categories.

When asked about portable computing devices, most folks describe the traditional clamshell *notebook* computer, such as the one in Figure 23-1, with built-in LCD monitor, keyboard, and input device (a *touchpad*, in this case). The notebook is also called a portable or a *laptop*. All the terms are synonymous. A typical laptop functions as a fully standalone computer, but there are always trade-offs that come with portability. Common trade-offs are price, weight, size, battery life, computing power, input devices, ports, drives, support for hardware upgrades, storage capacity, durability, and the quality of any warranty/support programs. Finding the *right* portable is easier if you can figure out what it will be used for and narrow your search to only devices with essential features and exclude those with unacceptable trade-offs.

Figure 23-1
An older
notebook
computer

Taxonomy

The companies making mobile and portable devices experiment a lot, so the terms we use to describe these devices are always in flux. New device categories and their related marketing terms may flood the market and blur the lines between existing categories one year, only to fall out of use within a few years.

The CompTIA A+ objectives don't focus on these terms and categories, but it's still a good idea to keep up with them. Knowing how to categorize portable and mobile devices makes it easier to identify devices that are a good fit for specific uses. It also helps you apply the best troubleshooting procedures for a given device. These categories can be slippery, so don't think of them as mutually exclusive. Sometimes more than one of these terms apply to a single device.

A number of terms address the size or purpose of traditional clamshell laptops/notebooks, but it helps to understand that today's laptops (driven by the success of the MacBook Air) are a lot thinner, lighter, and more powerful than they were when many of these terms were coined (see Figure 23-2).

Figure 23-2
Older full-size laptop (left) versus the thin-slice aesthetic of the MacBook Air (right)

- A *desktop replacement* traditionally features a massive screen, a roomy keyboard, a dedicated graphics card, the latest high-end mobile processors, plenty of hard drive space, tons of ports, and maybe an optical drive (see the portable on the left in Figure 23-3). Think power first, portability second—it does everything most people want to do with a desktop and doesn't compromise on performance just to make the laptop a few pounds lighter or the battery last an extra hour.

Figure 23-3
Desktop replacement (left) next to a standard portable computer (right)

- *Gaming laptops*, which tend to have flashy designs, typically come loaded with the latest top-end processors, graphics cards, RAM, SSDs, and large, high-quality displays. They also tend to come with thoughtful touches like high-quality keyboards that are extensively customizable.

- A *Chromebook* is a portable computer running Google's Linux-based Chrome OS. Chromebooks offer an experience focused on Web applications by making use of virtually unlimited data storage in the cloud and Software as a Service (SaaS) applications available over the Web. Because they offload so much work, Chromebooks have a reputation for being cheap and light, but premium Chromebooks are increasingly common.

It's even more important to know how to categorize devices that play with the traditional clamshell format, because they often blur the line between portable and mobile devices.

- *2-in-1s* are touchscreen computers somewhere along the spectrum from laptop-and-tablet to tablet-and-laptop. We'll take a closer look at pure mobile tablets (such as the Apple iPad or various Android tablets) in Chapter 24, "Understanding Mobile Devices."

- *Convertibles* are laptops that can "convert" into something you can use like a tablet. Some have *removable screens*—where you separate the screen from the rest of the laptop—while others have special hinges that enable you to fold the entire device up and use it like a tablet. The latter are called *rotating screens*. If the screen is removable, you'll lose access to any ports or components in the base but effectively have a tablet computing device.

- A *hybrid* laptop/tablet is most often a device with a tablet form factor that is designed to integrate with a detachable keyboard (which may or may not come bundled with the device). Some of these keyboards may double as soft/pliable covers for the tablet (see Figure 23-4), while others are built more like a small traditional keyboard. You may also hear someone use the term *slate* to describe a hybrid or tablet designed for use with a special pen (an input device called a *stylus*).

Figure 23-4
Microsoft Surface
Pro 6 with its
keyboard cover
(Used with
permission from
Microsoft)

 NOTE Innovative portable form factors like those in the hybrid and convertible categories are often designed to be handled, rotated, flipped, and passed around. As a result, Windows now supports the automatic screen-rotation tricks we've seen on smartphones and tablets for years. Anyone who has used a device like this for long knows that occasionally you'll run into problems with the automatic screen-orientation sensor; see the "Troubleshooting Portable Computers" section later in the chapter for fixes.

1001

Input Devices

Portable computers come with a variety of input devices. Most have a fully functional keyboard and a device to control the mouse pointer.

Keyboard Quirks

Laptop keyboards differ somewhat from those of desktop computers, primarily because manufacturers have to cram all the keys onto a smaller form factor. They use the QWERTY format, but manufacturers make choices with key size and placement of the non-alphabet characters.

Almost every portable keyboard uses a *Function* (*FN*) *key* to enable some keys to perform an extra duty. You'll either hold the FN key to access the extra function, or you'll hold it to access the traditional function (the latter is more common with extra functions on the F1–F12 keys). On some systems, you can also configure this behavior.

Figure 23-5 compares a laptop keyboard with a standard desktop keyboard. You'll note that the former has no separate number pad on the right. To use the number pad, you press the FN key (lower left in this case) to transform the (7, 8, 9), (U, I, O), (J, K, L), and (M) keys into the (7, 8, 9), (4, 5, 6), (1, 2, 3), and (0) keys.

Figure 23-5   Keyboard comparison

Pointing Devices

Portables need a way to control your mouse pointer, but their smaller size requires manufacturers to come up with clever solutions. Beyond the built-in solutions, portables usually have USB ports and can use every type of pointing device you'd see on a desktop. Early portables used *trackballs*, often plugged in like a mouse and clipped to the side of the case. Other models with trackballs placed them in front of the keyboard at the edge of the case nearest the user, or behind the keyboard at the edge nearest the screen.

NOTE   The FN key also enables you to toggle other features specific to a portable, such as GPS tracking or the keyboard backlight, to save battery life.

The next wave to hit the laptop market was IBM's *TrackPoint* device, a joystick the size of a pencil eraser, situated in the center of the keyboard (see Figure 23-6). With the TrackPoint, you can move the pointer around without taking your fingers away from the "home" typing position. You use a forefinger to push the joystick around, and then click or right-click, using two buttons below the spacebar. This type of pointing device has since been licensed for use by other manufacturers, and it continues to appear on laptops today.

Figure 23-6
IBM TrackPoint

By far the most common laptop pointing device found today is the *touchpad* (see Figure 23-7)—a flat, touch-sensitive pad just in front of the keyboard. To operate a touchpad, you simply glide your finger across its surface to move the pointer, and tap the surface once or twice to single- or double-click. You can also click by using buttons just below the pad. Most people get the hang of this technique after just a few minutes of practice. The main advantage of the touchpad over previous laptop pointing devices is that it uses no moving parts—a fact that can really extend the life of a hard-working laptop.

Figure 23-7
Touchpad on
a laptop

EXAM TIP Use the Settings | Devices | Mouse dialog or the Mouse applet in Control Panel for *touchpad configuration*. You can change sensitivity and much more in either tool.

Some manufacturers today include a *multitouch* touchpad that enables you to perform *gestures*, or actions with multiple fingers, such as scrolling up and down or swiping to another screen or desktop. The *Multi-Touch trackpad* on Apple's laptops pioneered such great improvements to the laptop-pointing-device experience that the lack of a mouse is no longer a handicap on many laptops.

 EXAM TIP In the past it was common to accidentally "use" a touchpad with your palm while typing, so you may find some devices with a hardware switch or FN key combination for disabling the touchpad. More recent touchpads are usually capable of detecting and ignoring accidental input like this on their own.

Continuing the trend of mobile's influence on more traditional portables, a growing number of laptops now come equipped with a *touchscreen* like you would find on a smartphone or tablet, again relying heavily on gestures to enable users to fluidly perform complex actions. In some cases these are otherwise very traditional laptops that happen to include a touchscreen, but in other cases they are devices that are intended to be used as both a tablet *and* a laptop. We'll take a closer look at touchscreens when we discuss mobile devices in Chapter 24.

Webcams and Microphones

The ability to communicate with others through real-time video is such a common expectation of mobile and portable devices these days that most of these devices (including laptops) come equipped with some sort of front-facing video camera—a *webcam* in the case of laptops—and one or more built-in microphones. A single *microphone* may be suitable for picking up the user's voice, and additional microphones can help noise-cancellation routines improve the audio quality.

Even though most of us may just use the microphone in conjunction with the webcam, a growing number of programs support voice commands. Take Microsoft, for example, which promotes its *Cortana* functionality built into Windows 10. Any Windows 10 user on a system with a microphone, as long as they can live with letting Windows listen in on them, can perform voice searches and other actions from anywhere within earshot (mic-shot?) of their device.

The downside of these input devices becoming ubiquitous is the security risk they pose. It might be bad enough if a nefarious hacker or government agency (from any country . . .) managed to get malware into my computer to see everything I click or type, but the risks are amplified if they can also hear and see anything going on near the device. It's common enough for webcams to include a light that indicates when they're recording, but built-in microphones don't do the same. In some cases, vulnerabilities allow the recording indicator to be disabled anyway.

Display Types

Laptops come in a variety of sizes and at varying costs. One major contributor to the overall cost of a laptop is the size of the LCD screen. Most laptops offer a range between 10.1-inch to 17.3-inch screens (measured diagonally), while a few offer just over 20-inch screens.

In the past, 4:3 aspect ratio screens were common, but these days it's hard to find one on anything but special-purpose or ruggedized laptops; almost all regular laptops come in one of two widescreen format ratios. *Aspect ratio* is the comparison of the screen width to the screen height, as you'll recall from Chapter 17, "Display Technologies." While widescreens can have varying aspect ratios, *almost* all of the screens you find in present-day laptops will be 16:9 or 16:10. Very old laptop screens had a 4:3 aspect ratio.

 EXAM TIP   Laptop LCDs are the same in almost every way as desktop LCDs with a TFT screen, an inverter (if using a CCFL backlight), and a backlight (CCFL or LED). You know all about these screens from Chapter 17. Expect questions about laptop displays, but know that they're pretty much the same as desktop displays. The only major difference is that the LCD frame contains an antenna, and may contain a camera and microphone, but we'll discuss this later in the chapter.

Laptop screens typically come with one of two types of finish: *matte* or *high-gloss*. The matte finish was the industry standard for many years and offered a good trade-off between color richness and glare reduction. The better screens have a wide viewing angle and decent response time. The major drawback for matte-finished laptop screens is that they wash out a lot in bright light. Using such a laptop at an outdoor café, for example, is almost hopeless during daylight.

Manufacturers released high-gloss laptop screens more than a decade ago, and they rapidly took over many store shelves. The high-gloss finish offers sharper contrast, richer colors, and wider viewing angles when compared to the matte screens. The drawback to the high-gloss screens is that, contrary to what the manufacturers claim, they pick up lots of reflection from nearby objects, including the user! So, although they're usable outside during the day, you'll need to contend with increased reflection as well.

With the advent of LED backlighting for LCD panels, many manufacturers have switched back to an anti-glare screen, though they're not quite the matte screens of old. When the LED brightness is up high, these are lovely screens. (See the "Troubleshooting Portable Computers" section, later in this chapter, for issues specific to LED-backlit portables.)

As with other LCD technologies that you'll recall from Chapter 17, most LCD/LED screens use *twisted nematic* (*TN*) technology. Some laptop screens use *in-plane switching* (*IPS*) panels for the greater viewing angle and better color quality. You'll mostly find IPS panels on higher-grade portables.

What you will *not* find on portables are two other display technologies, plasma and organic light-emitting diode (OLED). Plasma displays demand a lot more electricity than LCDs demand and are completely inappropriate for portable devices. OLED screens sip energy when compared to LCDs, but they're still so expensive that you'll mostly find them on smartphones and tablets today. Chapter 24 discusses OLED screen technology.

 EXAM TIP The CompTIA A+ 1001 exam objectives refer to OLED displays for laptops. Several makers have experimented with OLED laptop screens recently, but most appear to have backed away from the technology for now. You may not see one in the wild, but know they exist for the exam!

Extending Portable Computers

In the dark ages of mobile computing, you had to shell out top dollar for any device that would operate unplugged, and what you purchased was what you got. Upgrade a laptop? Connect to external devices? You had few if any options, so you simply paid for a device that would be way behind the technology curve within a year and functionally obsolete within two.

Portable computers today offer a few ways to enhance their capabilities. Most feature external ports that enable you to add completely new functions, such as attaching a scanner, mobile printer, or both. You can take advantage of the latest wireless technology breakthrough simply by slipping a card into the appropriate slot on the laptop.

I'll first describe single-function ports, and then turn to networking options. Next, I'll cover card slots, and then finish with a discussion of general-purpose ports.

Single-Function Ports

All portable computers come with one or more single function ports. You'd have a hard time finding a portable computing device that doesn't have an audio port, for example. Laptops often provide a video port for hooking up an external monitor, though wireless screen sharing and screencasting are gaining popularity as an alternative.

Ports work the same way on portable computers as they do on desktop models. You plug in a device to a particular port and, as long as the operating system has the proper drivers, you will have a functioning device when you boot.

Audio

Portable computers have a standard 3.5-mm audio-out port and some have a similarly sized microphone-in port (see Figure 23-8), though built-in microphones are increasingly common. You can plug in headphones, regular PC speakers, or even a nice surround sound set to enable the laptop to play music just as well as a desktop computer can.

Figure 23-8
Standard audio ports

You can control the sound (both out and in) through the appropriate Control Panel applet in Windows, System Preferences in macOS, or some kind of switches on the laptop. The portable in Figure 23-9, for example, enables you to mute the speakers by pressing a special mute button above the keyboard. Other portables use a combination of the FN key and another key to toggle mute on and off, as well as to play, pause, fast-forward, and rewind audio (or any other media options). Most portables will have volume up/down controls in the same location.

Figure 23-9
The mute button on a laptop

Display

Most laptops support a second monitor via a digital port of some sort. There are many of these—you may find HDMI (including Mini-HDMI and Micro-HDMI), Display-Port (including USB Type-C and Thunderbolt), and DVI; on ancient or special-purpose portables, there's even a chance you may still find an analog VGA. With a second monitor attached, you can duplicate your screen to the new monitor, or extend your desktop across both displays, letting you move windows between them. Not all portables can do all variations, but they're more common than not.

Most portables use the FN key plus another key on the keyboard to cycle through display options. Figure 23-10 shows a typical keyboard with the FN key; note the other options you can access with the FN key, such as indicated on the F2 key. To engage the second monitor or to cycle through the modes, hold the FN key and press F2.

Figure 23-10
Laptop keyboard showing Function (FN) key that enables you to access additional key options, as on the F2 key

NOTE Although many laptops use the Function key method to cycle the monitor selections, that's not always the case. You might have to pop into the Display applet or System Preferences to click a checkbox. Just be assured that if the laptop has a video output port, you can cycle through monitor choices!

You can control what the external monitor shows by adjusting your operating system's display settings. In Windows 10, this is all contained in the Display area of the Settings app. Open the Settings app and navigate to System | Display; from there scroll down till you find the Multiple displays section (see Figure 23-11). You'll see a drop-down menu with several options. *Extend these displays* makes your desktop encompass both the laptop and the external monitor. *Duplicate these displays* places the same thing on both displays. You'd duplicate these displays for a presentation, for example, rather than for a work space.

 EXAM TIP The CompTIA A+ 1001 exam objectives refer to multiple monitors as *dual displays*.

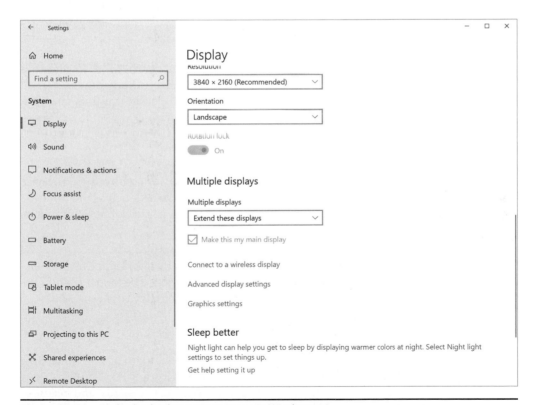

Figure 23-11 Multiple-display options menu in Windows 10

Smart Card Reader

It isn't really a port, but you'll find some portable computers—especially ones designed for and marketed to business users—with a very thin slot the width of a credit card on one side or the other. No, it isn't an expansion or memory card slot—it's a *smart card reader*. If you've seen a credit or debit card with a little metallic chip (see Figure 23-12), you've seen a smart card. While smart cards have tons of uses, what matters here is that you can log in to a portable device (if it has a built-in or USB smart card reader) using *your* smart card and a PIN number. We'll go into a little more detail on the use of smart cards for authentication in Chapter 27, "Securing Computers."

Figure 23-12
Smart card

Networking Options

It's a rare item to find a portable computer without at least one network connection option. Today's portables come with some combination of 802.11, Bluetooth, and wired Ethernet connections. Generally they work exactly as you've seen in previous chapters, but you may stumble into a few issues that are unique to portables. (Mobile devices—tablets, smartphones—get even more options, as you'll see in Chapter 24.)

802.11 Wireless

Most portables today have Wi-Fi built directly into the chipset for connecting the device to a wireless access point (WAP) and from there to a bigger network, such as the Internet. The 802.11g or 802.11n standard is common on older laptops; newer portable computers use 802.11ac.

 NOTE While the newest portables are shipping with 802.11ac, be aware that, especially as portables are getting powerful enough to live longer useful lives, you may see a few previous standards built into devices in the wild.

Bluetooth

While not quite as ubiquitous as 802.11, most portables use Bluetooth as well. Bluetooth is really handy on a laptop because, as you may recall from Chapter 20, "Wireless Networking," it enables you to add wireless peripherals such as mice, keyboards, and headsets, as well as communicate with smartphones, speakers, and other Bluetooth devices.

Hardware Switches

Portable computers that come with wireless technologies such as 802.11, mobile broadband, GPS, or Bluetooth have some form of on/off switch to toggle the antenna off or on so that you may use the laptop in areas where emissions aren't allowed (like a commercial aircraft). The switch may be hard wired, like the one shown in Figure 23-13, or it may be a toggle of the FN key plus another key on the keyboard. Also, if you're not using Wi-Fi or Bluetooth, turn them off to save electricity and lengthen the portable's battery life.

Figure 23-13
Wireless switch

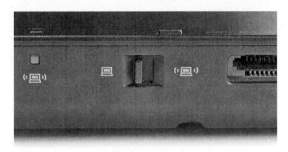

 EXAM TIP   Hardware switches or special Function key toggles enable you to switch features on and off, such as wireless networking, cellular networking, and Bluetooth. Toggle them off when in a scenario where battery life takes priority over networking.

Wired Ethernet

Most *full-size* laptops have an RJ-45 wired Ethernet connection like the one shown in Figure 23-14. These work exactly like any other Ethernet jack—they have link lights and connect via UTP cable. Be aware, however, that wired Ethernet is one of the things many smaller contemporary laptops and hybrids leave out.

There are two issues with RJ-45s on laptops. First, they do not have an on/off switch like the 802.11 and Bluetooth connections. You can turn them off just like you would turn off the NIC on a desktop: disable the NIC in Device Manager or turn the

Figure 23-14
Ethernet port
on laptop

NIC off in BIOS. The other issue is the relative weakness of the physical connection. If you ever plug a laptop into a wired network and the OS doesn't see a connection, check the RJ-45 port.

Portable-Specific Expansion Slots

The makers of portable computers have developed methods for you to add features to a portable via specialized connections known generically as *expansion slots*. For many years, the *Personal Computer Memory Card International Association* (*PCMCIA*) established standards involving portable computers, especially when it came to expansion cards and slots. Once a common feature on laptops, these specialized expansion slots are almost impossible to find due to the dominance of USB. The last standard was called ExpressCard.

ExpressCard comes in two widths: 34 mm and 54 mm, called *ExpressCard/34* and *ExpressCard/54*. Figure 23-15 shows both ExpressCard varieties. Both cards are 75 mm long and 5 mm thick.

Figure 23-15
34-mm and
54-mm
ExpressCards

You can enhance an older laptop that has an ExpressCard slot in a several ways. The most common are adding a *smart card reader*—so the portable can grab pictures off an SD card, for example—and a *cellular card*. The latter enables you to connect the laptop to the Internet via a valid cellular telephone subscription, like you would get from AT&T or Verizon. You can also find *wireless cards*, though the limits of ExpressCard technology tops these out at 802.11n, not the most current Wi-Fi options.

ExpressCards connect to either the Hi-Speed USB 2.0 bus or the PCI Express bus. These differ phenomenally in speed. The amazingly-slow-in-comparison USB version has a maximum throughput of 480 Mbps. The PCIe version, in contrast, roars in at 2.5 Gbps in unidirectional communication.

Table 23-1 shows the throughput and variations for ExpressCards.

Standard	Maximum Theoretical Throughput
ExpressCard using Hi-Speed USB 2.0 bus	480 Mbps
ExpressCard using PCIe bus	2.5 Gbps

Table 23-1 ExpressCard Speeds

Storage Card Slots

Many portable computers offer one or more flash memory card slots to enable you to add storage to the portable. These slots also enable the fast transfer of data from the card to the portable, and vice versa. They come in the standard varieties that you already know from Chapter 10, "Essential Peripherals," such as SD or microSD.

General-Purpose Ports

Portable computers rarely come with all of the hardware you want. Today's laptops usually include at least USB ports to give you the option to add more hardware. Some special-purpose laptops may still provide legacy general-purpose expansion ports (PS/2, RS-232 serial ports, eSATA, FireWire, and so on) for installing peripheral hardware, while other portables focus on more modern ports like Thunderbolt. If you're lucky, you will have a docking station so you don't have to plug in all of your peripheral devices one at a time.

USB, Thunderbolt, FireWire, and eSATA

Universal serial bus (USB), Thunderbolt, and FireWire (or more properly, IEEE 1394) enable users to connect a device while the computer is running—you won't have to reboot the system to install a new peripheral. With USB and FireWire, just plug the device in and go! Because portables don't have a desktop's multiple internal expansion capabilities, USB and Thunderbolt (and FireWire to a much lesser extent) are some of the more popular methods for attaching peripherals to laptops and other portables (see Figure 23-16).

Figure 23-16
Devices attached to USB on a portable PC

Docking Stations

Docking stations offer legacy and modern single- and multi-function ports (see Figure 23-17). The traditional docking station uses a proprietary connection, though the high speeds of USB 3.*x* and Thunderbolt 2 and 3 have made universal docks more common. A docking station makes an excellent companion to small portables with fewer ports.

Figure 23-17
Docking station

Port Replicators

A *port replicator* supplies one of the most critical aspects of docking stations, but in a smaller, more portable format: support for connectors that the laptop lacks. A modern USB Type-C port replicator, for example, will plug into a laptop's USB-C port and offer an array of other port types, such as VGA, HDMI, USB Type-A (2, 3, 3.1), RJ-45, and more. Port replicators work great with ultra-light, ultra-thin laptops to enhance the capabilities of the machine.

USB Adapters

When you don't need access to a number of ports at once, you can often find a USB adapter for whatever you need to connect. When it comes to drives or connectors that you need only occasionally, these adapters can enable you to use a much more portable device.

Two great examples of this are wired Ethernet and optical drives. I don't know about you, but I haven't spun up an optical disc in months, nor am I sure when I last opened my laptop within a few feet of a wired Ethernet connection. A USB to Ethernet (RJ-45) dongle and a USB optical drive can provide these features when and where I need them, leaving me a much smaller laptop to carry the rest of the time.

Another good use for USB adapters is updating connectivity support for older devices. A USB to Wi-Fi dongle or a USB Bluetooth adapter can let me update an old laptop to 802.11ac, or add Bluetooth to a laptop that didn't come with it built in.

 EXAM TIP The 1001 exam expects you to be familiar with USB to Ethernet adapters.

Managing and Maintaining Portable Computers

Most portables come from the factory fully assembled and configured. From a tech's standpoint, your most common work on managing and maintaining portables involves taking care of the batteries and extending the battery life through proper power management, keeping the machine clean, and avoiding excessive heat.

Everything you normally do to maintain a computer applies to portable computers. You need to keep current on OS updates and use stable, recent drivers. Use appropriate tools to monitor the health of your storage drives and clean up unwanted files. That said, let's look at issues specifically involving portables, with one caveat: because more compact or hybrid portables are often built like mobile devices, you may need to approach those devices by combining steps mentioned here with troubleshooting ideas from Chapter 25, "Care and Feeding of Mobile Devices."

Batteries

Manufacturers over the years have used a few types of batteries for portable computers: Nickel-Cadmium (Ni-Cd), Nickel-Metal Hydride (Ni-MH), and *Lithium-Ion* (*Li-Ion*). Today, only Li-Ion is used because that battery chemistry provides the highest energy density for the weight and has few problems with external factors.

Lithium-Ion

Li-Ion batteries are powerful, and last much longer than the Ni-MH and Ni-Cd ones we used in the 1990s. If Li-Ion batteries have a downside, it's that they will explode if overcharged or punctured, so all Li-Ion batteries have built-in circuitry to prevent accidental overcharging. Lithium batteries can only power systems designed to use them. They can't be used as replacement batteries to keep that retro laptop from 1998 going. Figure 23-18 shows a typical Li-Ion battery.

Figure 23-18
Li-Ion battery

 NOTE Strictly speaking, *lithium polymer* (*LiPo*) batteries are a variation of Li-Ion that places the heart of the battery—the electrolyte—into a solid polymer shape rather than an organic solvent. This enables the batteries to take on unusual forms beyond the simple cylinder or rectangle shapes. In practice, most of the batteries people call LiPo are actually traditional Li-Ion electrolyte packed in polymer bags instead of a rigid case. LiPo batteries haven't replaced Li-Ion in most portables, but they are used a lot in smaller electronics such as tablets, smartphones, portable media players, and in compact portable computers such as hybrids and Ultrabooks (a super-thin laptop form factor).

The Care and Feeding of Batteries

In general, keep in mind the following basics. First, always store batteries in a cool place. Although a freezer might seem like an excellent storage place, the moisture, extreme freezing cold, metal racks, and food make it a bad idea. Second, keep the battery charged, at least to 70–80 percent. Third, never drain a battery all the way down unless required to do so as part of a *battery calibration* (where you, in essence, reset the battery according to steps provided by the manufacturer). Rechargeable batteries have only a limited number of charge-discharge cycles before overall battery performance is reduced. Fourth, *never* handle a battery that has ruptured or broken; battery chemicals are very dangerous and flammable (check YouTube for videos of what happens when you puncture a Li-Ion or LiPo battery). Finally, always recycle old batteries.

Try This!   Recycling Old Portable Device Batteries

Got an old portable device battery lying around? Well, you need to get rid of it, and there are some pretty toxic chemicals in that battery, so you can't just throw it in the trash. Sooner or later, you'll probably need to deal with such a battery, so try this!

1. Do an online search to find the battery recycling center nearest to you. Electronics retailers are getting much better about accepting a wide array of e-waste, including batteries, though they often place quantity limits.

2. Sometimes, you can take old laptop batteries to an auto parts store that disposes of old car batteries—I know it sounds odd, but it's true! See if you can find one in your area that will do this.

3. Many cities offer a hazardous materials disposal or recycling service. Check to see if and how your local government will help you dispose of your old batteries.

Power Management

Many different parts are included in the typical laptop, and each part uses power. The problem with early laptops was that every one of these parts used power continuously, whether or not the system needed the device at that time. For example, the hard drive continued to spin even when it was not being accessed, the CPU ran at full speed even when the system was doing light work, and the LCD panel continued to display even when the user walked away from the machine.

Over the years, a lot of work has gone into improving the battery life of portable devices. Beyond engineering better batteries and ever-more-efficient components, the system firmware and OS of most modern portables collaborate with the firmware of individual components to manage their power use. To reduce power use, the computer can power off unused components until they are needed, enter a low-power mode when the device isn't in use, and throttle the performance of power-hungry components like the CPU to fit the current workload. This process of cooperation among the hardware, BIOS, and OS to reduce power use is known generically as *power management*.

Low-Power Modes

If you don't know what's going on under the hood, computers usually appear to be clearly off or on. In reality, most computers (both desktops and portables!) that appear to be off are using at least a little power, and may be in one of a few low-power modes. The CompTIA A+ 220-1002 exam focuses on configuring basic power options in the Windows Control Panel, but it's good to have a handle on low-power modes in general.

NOTE Low-power mode names can differ from OS to OS (and even from version to version), but the basic concepts are the same.

When the computer is off, turning it on will boot the OS from scratch. You can think of there being two kinds of true off mode:

- **Mechanical off mode** The system and all components, with the exception of the real-time clock (RTC), are off.
- **Soft power-off mode** The system is mostly off except for components necessary for the keyboard, LAN, or USB devices to wake the system.

Computers that appear to be off may actually be in a *sleep* (also called *standby* or *suspend*) mode: waking them will resume any programs, processes, and windows that were open when they entered the low-power mode. There are a number of fine-grained sleep modes, but the highlights are

- A device can wake quickly from normal sleep mode (sometimes called suspend to RAM) because it doesn't power down the RAM, enabling the system to save its place. If the device loses power unexpectedly, it can lose whatever was in RAM.
- Devices wake more slowly from a deeper sleep mode called *hibernate* (or suspend to disk) because they save everything in RAM to a hard drive (and restoring it all takes a moment) before powering down. On the up side, hibernation saves more power and won't lose its place if the device loses power.

Configuring Power Options

You configure power options via the system setup utility or through the operating system. OS settings override CMOS settings. Implementations differ, but certain settings apply generally, like the ability to enable or disable power management; configure which devices can wake the system; configure what the power button does; and configure what the system should do when power is restored after an outage.

Operating systems tend to use friendly terms like *Energy Options* or *Power Options*, but you might run into some more technical terms in a system configuration utility. If you can't find these settings under an obvious name, they might be named for the Intel-developed specifications that define them: *Advanced Power Management* (*APM*) or *Advanced Configuration and Power Interface* (*ACPI*). APM was introduced in 1992, and succeeded by ACPI in 1996.

Many CMOS versions present settings to determine wake-up events, such as directing the system to monitor a modem or a NIC (see Figure 23-19). You'll see this feature as

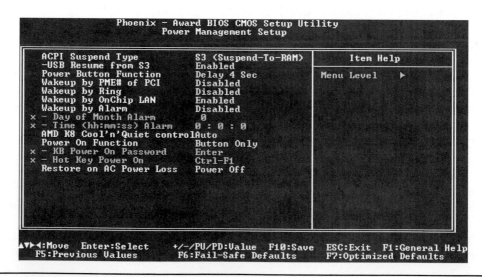

Figure 23-19 Setting a wake-up event in CMOS

Wake on LAN, or something similar. Figure 23-20 shows a system setup utility with an ACPI setup option.

In Windows, APM/ACPI settings can be found in the Power & sleep | Settings app in Windows 10 and the Control Panel applet Power Options. Windows offers *power plans* that enable better control over power use by customizing a Balanced, High performance, or Power saver power plan (see Figure 23-21).

NOTE While you can customize most laptops' power plans to your heart's content, on some models, such as Microsoft's Surface Pro line, you are restricted to just the default Balanced plan.

Figure 23-20 CMOS with ACPI setup option

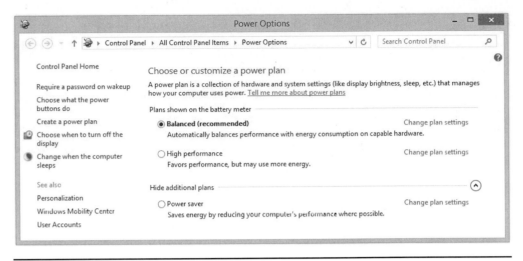

Figure 23-21 Windows 8 Balanced, High performance, and Power saver power plan options

You can customize a power plan for your laptop, for example, and configure it to turn off the display at a certain time interval while on battery versus plugged in, or configure it to put the computer to sleep (see Figure 23-22). To see the specific power plans, click *Additional power settings* or go directly to the Control Panel Power Options applet. There you can tweak a lot more, including choices like hibernation (see Figure 23-23).

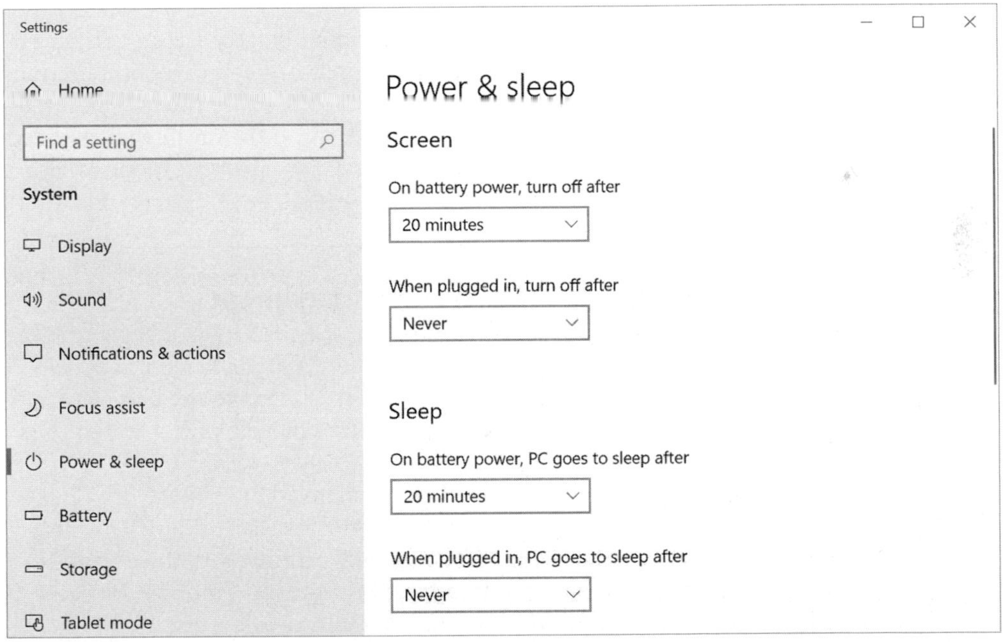

Figure 23-22 Customizing a laptop power plan in Windows 10

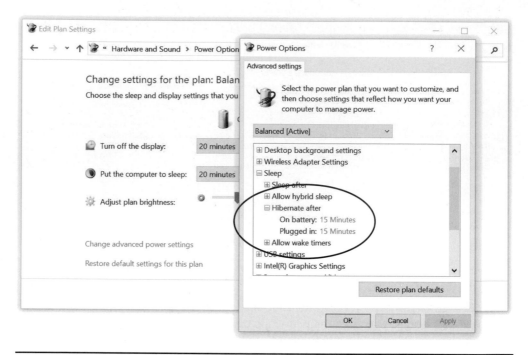

Figure 23-23   Windows 10 hibernation settings in the Power Options applet

Manual Control over Power Use

Most portables give you several manual options for reducing battery use in certain circumstances. We've already discussed using the on/off switch or keyboard combinations for disabling the Wi-Fi antenna or shutting off Bluetooth, but many modern portables borrow a feature from smartphones and tablets for disabling most or all their wireless components at once: *airplane mode*. Beyond its intended use, airplane mode is also a great way to disable power-sucking components quickly.

Try This!   Adjusting Your System's Power Management

Go into the Power Options applet on a Windows computer and look at the various settings. What is the current power plan for the computer? Check to see if it is running a Balanced or High performance power plan. If it is, change the power plan to Power saver and click *Change plan settings*. Familiarize yourself with some of the advanced power settings (click on the *Change advanced power settings* link).

Try changing the individual settings for each power scheme. For instance, set a new value for the *Turn off the display* setting—try making your display turn off after five minutes. Don't worry; you aren't going to hurt anything if you fiddle with these settings.

Note that Microsoft changed power settings for laptops in Windows 10 to be Balanced. You can still adjust advanced power settings and tweak everything.

Laptops with backlit keyboards will have some way you can disable this feature when it's not needed, usually with a keyboard combination. You can also reduce the output of the LCD backlight using a combination of FN and another key to eke out a few more precious minutes of computing time before you have to shut down. Figure 23-24 shows a close-up of the FN-activated keys for adjusting screen brightness.

Figure 23-24
Keys for
adjusting screen
brightness

One of the best ways to conserve battery is to plan ahead for times when you'll be unplugged. This can mean a lot of different things in practice, but they all boil down to thinking of ways to minimize the number of programs and hardware devices/radios you'll need to use while your laptop is running on battery power. When I travel, for example, and know that I'm going to need a certain set of files stored on my file server at the office, I put those files on my laptop before I leave, while it's still plugged into the AC. It's tempting to throw the files on a thumb drive so I don't have to break out my laptop at the office, or to let Dropbox do my syncing for me when I get to a Wi-Fi hotspot, but both USB and Wi-Fi use electricity.

Better than that, Windows enables me to designate the files and folders I need as *offline files*, storing a local, duplicate copy of the files and folders on my hard drive. When I connect my laptop to my office network, those offline files are automatically synced with the files and folders on the file server. Anything I changed on the laptop gets written to the server. Anything anyone changed in those folders on the server gets written to my laptop. If changes were made on both sides, a sync conflict pops up automatically, enabling me to resolve problems without fear of overwriting anything important.

To designate a folder and its contents as offline files, right-click the folder you want and select *Always available offline* from the context menu. The sync will occur and you're done. When you want to open the files offline, go to the Control Panel and open the Sync Center applet (see Figure 23-25). Click the *Manage offline files* link in the Tasks list to open the Offline Files dialog box (see Figure 23-26). Click the *View your offline files* button and you're in.

EXAM TIP Another option for extending battery life is to bring a spare battery. Some smaller portable devices have range-extending external rechargers that can also help.

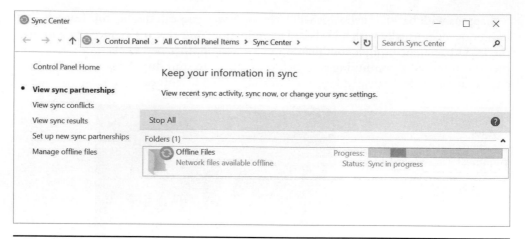

Figure 23-25   Sync Center applet

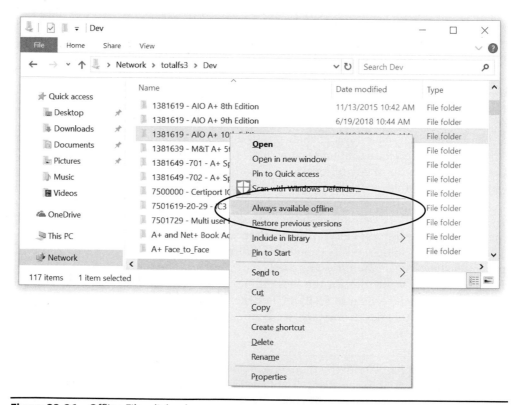

Figure 23-26   Offline Files dialog box

Cleaning

Most portable computers take substantially more abuse than a corresponding desktop model. Constant handling, travel, airport food on the run, and so on, can radically shorten the life of a portable if you don't take action. One of the most important things you should do is clean the device regularly. Use an appropriate screen cleaner (not a glass cleaner!) to remove fingerprints and dust from the fragile LCD panel. (Refer to Chapter 17 for specifics.)

We'll go into greater detail on environmental threats in Chapter 27, but if you've had the portable in a smoky or dusty environment where air quality alone can cause problems, try cleaning it with compressed air. Compressed air works great for blowing out dust and crumbs from the keyboard and for keeping any ports, slots, and sockets clear. Don't use water on your keyboard! Even a little moisture inside the portable can toast a component.

Heat

To manage and maintain a healthy portable computer, you need to deal with heat issues. Every portable has a stack of electronic components crammed into a very small space. Unlike their desktop brethren, portables don't have lots of freely moving air space that enables fans to cool everything down. Even with lots of low-power-consumption devices inside, portable computers crank out a good deal of heat. Excessive heat can cause system lockups and hardware failures, so you should handle the issue wisely.

The following steps have more traditional portables in mind; very compact portables are usually designed to handle heat more like mobile devices—Chapter 25 will approach heat issues with mobile device construction in mind. For more traditional portables, try this as a starter guide:

- Use power management, even if you're plugged into the AC outlet. This is especially important if you're working in a warm (more than 80 degrees Fahrenheit) room.

- Keep air space between the bottom of the laptop and the surface on which it rests. Putting a laptop on a soft surface, such as a pillow on your lap, creates a great heat-retention system—not a good thing! Always use a hard, flat surface.

- Don't use a keyboard protector for extended amounts of time.

- Listen to your fan, assuming the laptop has one. If it's often running very fast—you can tell by the whirring sound—examine your power management settings, environment, and running programs so you can change whatever is causing heat retention.

- Speaking of fans, be alert to a fan that suddenly goes silent. Fans do fail on laptops, causing overheating and failure.

Protecting the Machine

Although prices continue to drop for basic laptops, a fully loaded system is still pricey. To protect your investment, you'll want to adhere to certain best practices. You've already read tips in this chapter to deal with cleaning and heat, so let's look at the "portable" part of portable computers.

Tripping

Pay attention to where you run the power cord when you plug in a laptop. One of the primary causes of laptop destruction is people tripping over the power cord and knocking the laptop off of a desk. This is especially true if you plug in at a public place such as a café or airport. Remember, the life you save could be your portable's!

Storage

If you aren't going to use your portable for a while, storing it safely will go a long way toward keeping it operable when you do power it up again. A quality case is worth the extra few dollars—preferably one with ample padding. Not only will this protect your system on a daily basis when transporting it from home to office, but it will keep dust and pet hair away as well. Also, protect from battery leakage, at least on devices with removable batteries, by removing the battery if you plan to store the device for an extended time. Regardless of whether the battery is removable or built in, it's a good idea to store the battery partially charged and top it up occasionally to keep it from fully discharging.

Travel

If you travel with a laptop, guard against theft. If possible, use a case that doesn't look like a computer case. A well-padded backpack makes a great travel bag for a laptop and appears less tempting to would-be thieves, though some brands and styles of these are still quite obvious. Smaller portables can often hide in less obvious bags. Don't forget to pack any accessories you might need, like modular devices, spare batteries, and AC adapters. Make sure to remove any optical disks from their drives. Most importantly—back up any important data before you leave!

Make sure to have at least a little battery power available. Heightened security at airports means you might have to power on your system to prove it's really a computer and not a transport case for questionable materials. And never let your laptop out of your sight. If going through an x-ray machine, request a manual search. The x-ray won't harm your computer like a metal detector would, but if the laptop gets through the line at security before you do, someone else might walk away with it. If flying, stow your laptop under the seat in front of you where you can keep an eye on it.

If you travel to a foreign country, be very careful about the electricity. North America uses ~115-V power outlets, but most of the world uses ~230-V outlets. Most portable computers have *auto-switching power supplies*, meaning they detect the voltage at the outlet and adjust accordingly (but most people just call it a *charger*). An auto-switching power supply will have an input voltage range printed on it somewhere (see Figure 23-27).

Figure 23-27
Input and output
voltages on
laptop power
brick

Double-check the charger to make sure its supported range covers voltages used in any country you plan to visit. If it doesn't, you may need a full-blown electricity-converting device, either a step-down or step-up *transformer*. You should be able to find converters and transformers at electronics retailers, travel stores, and most other stores with a large electronics department.

Shipping

Much of the storage and travel advice can be applied to shipping. If possible, remove batteries and optical discs from their drives. Pack the portable well and disguise the container as best you can. Back up any data and verify the warranty coverage. Ship with a reputable carrier and always request a tracking number and, if possible, delivery signature. It's also worth the extra couple of bucks to pay for the shipping insurance. And when the clerk asks what's in the box, it's safer to say "electronics" rather than "a new 17-inch laptop computer."

Security

The fact is, if someone really wants to steal your laptop, they'll find a way. While we cover securing devices against physical theft in Chapter 27, there are some things you can do to make yourself, and your portable devices, less desirable targets. As you've already learned, disguise is a good idea.

Another physical deterrent is a laptop lock. Similar to a steel bicycle cable, there is a loop on one end and a lock on the other. The idea is to loop the cable around a solid object, such as a bed frame, and secure the lock to the small security hole on the side of the laptop (see Figure 23-28). Again, if someone really wants to steal your computer, they'll find a way. They'll dismantle the bed frame if they're desperate. The best protection is to be vigilant and not let the computer out of your sight.

An alternative to securing a laptop with a physical lock is to use a software tracking system that makes use of GPS. It won't keep your device from being taken, but tracking software can use the many sensors and networking capabilities of modern devices to help recover them. While functionality differs by application, common features include seeing the location of the stolen computer, capturing images or audio with its sensors, and wiping sensitive files from the device. Because this functionality is more common in mobile devices, we'll save the details for Chapter 25.

Figure 23-28
Cable lock

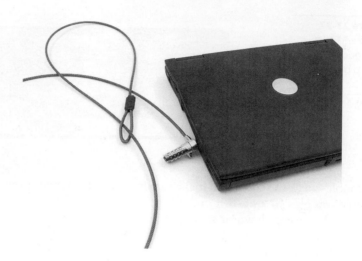

Upgrading and Repairing Laptop Computers

A competent tech can upgrade and repair portable computers to a degree, though true laptop techs are specialists. Upgrading the basics usually means breaking out the trusty screwdriver and avoiding electrostatic discharge (ESD). *Repairing* portables successfully, on the other hand, requires research, patience, organization, special tools, and documentation. Plus, you need a ridiculously steady hand. This section provides an overview of the upgrade and repair process. Keep in mind that the growing number of form factors and the shrinking size of portable devices mean there are many exceptions, especially for very compact portables; these devices may be trickier to take apart, and components may be soldered on or use less-common interfaces.

Disassembly Process

Disassembling a portable PC is usually pretty easy, if it was designed to be upgraded or serviced by casual users. Putting it back together in working condition is the hard part! You need to follow a four-step process to succeed in disassembly/reassembly.

First, *document and label every cable and screw location*. Laptops don't use standard connectors or screws. Often you'll run into many tiny screws of varying threads. If you try to put a screw into the wrong hole, you could end up stripping the screw, stripping the hole, or getting the screw wedged into the wrong place.

Second, *organize any parts you extract from the laptop*. Seriously, put a big white piece of construction paper on your work surface, lay each extracted piece out in logical fashion, and clearly mark where each component connects and what it connects to as well. You may even want to use a smartphone camera to take pictures or a webcam to record your workspace in case something goes missing.

Third, *refer to the manufacturer's resources*. I can't stress this point enough. Unlike desktops, portables have no standardization of internal structure. Everything in the portable is designed according to the manufacturer's best engineering efforts. Two portables from the same manufacturer might have a similar layout inside, but it's far more likely that every model differs a lot.

Finally, you need to *use the appropriate hand tools*. A portable, especially on the inside, will have a remarkable variety of tiny screws that you can't remove/reinsert without tiny-headed Phillips or Torx drivers. You'll need tiny pry bars—metal and plastic—to open components. Figure 23-29 shows an entry-level toolkit for a laptop tech that you can order from iFixit.com (more on this site in a moment). Their professional toolkit version has 70 tools, plus there's an expansion kit! Like I said at the beginning of this section, portable techs are specialists.

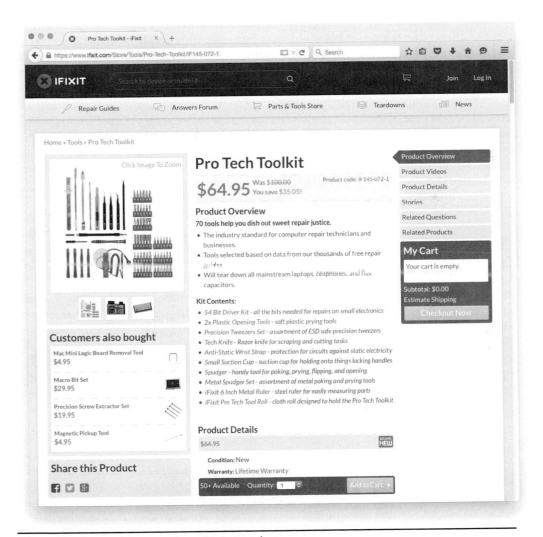

Figure 23-29   Bare-minimum laptop repair tools

EXAM TIP Know the four-step disassembly process for the CompTIA A+ 220-1001 exam:

- Document and label cable and screw locations.
- Organize parts.
- Refer to the manufacturer's resources.
- Use appropriate hand tools.

Now that you have the official line on the disassembly process, let's get one thing clear: a lot of manufacturers don't provide access to their resources to just any tech, but only to authorized repair centers. So what do you do when faced with an unfamiliar laptop that a client brought in for repair?

You have essentially two options. First, you can find a dedicated laptop tech and refer your client to that person. If the problem is exceptionally complicated and the portable in question is mission critical, that's often the best option. If you want to tackle the problem or it looks like something you should be able to do, then you go to third-party sources: YouTube and iFixit.com.

Every portable computer has a specific make and model. Open up a Web browser and go to YouTube. Type in precisely what you want to do, such as "Dell Inspiron 5567 keyboard replacement," and see what pops up (see Figure 23-30). You'll most likely get results back, especially if the laptop in question is a couple of years old. People all over the world have to deal with broken devices, so you're not alone.

Once you've found the appropriate video or something that's close enough to enable the repair attempt, watch it. If it's too difficult for your skill level or requires a set of expensive tools, then fall back to step one and go find a dedicated tech. Otherwise, figure out what tools and parts you need. Parts specific to a laptop (as in that Dell keyboard in the preceding example) will need to be purchased from the manufacturer. More generic parts, like hard drives, CPUs, and so on, can be purchased from Newegg (my favorite tech store) or some other online retailer.

For general tools, parts, and a lot of very detailed step-by-step instructions, I highly recommend iFixit.com. Billed as "the free repair guide for everything, written by everyone," iFixit is built by techs like you and me who conquer a problem, document the steps, and post the details (see Figure 23-31). This means the next tech along who runs into the same problem doesn't have to reinvent the wheel. Just go to iFixit.com. The proceeds from parts and tools they sell, by the way, go toward supporting the site.

Standard Upgrades

Every CompTIA A+ tech should know how to perform the two standard upgrades to portable computers: adding RAM and replacing a hard drive. Let's go through the steps.

Upgrading RAM

Stock factory portable computers almost always come with a minimal amount of RAM, so one of the first laptop upgrades you'll be called on to do is to add more RAM. Luckily, most laptops have upgradeable RAM slots. Older systems use 200-pin DDR and

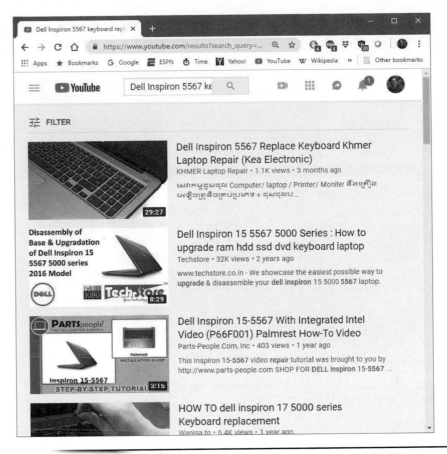

Figure 23-30   YouTube search result

DDR2 SO-DIMMs; while current systems primarily use 204-pin DDR3 SO-DIMMs (see Figure 23-32) or newer 260-pin DDR4 SO-DIMMs. You can refer back to Chapter 4, "RAM," to refresh your memory of these RAM technologies, but keep in mind that portable and desktop RAM may use different numbers of pins—even if the specification is the same.

EXAM TIP   Expect a question or two on the CompTIA A+ 1001 exam about scenarios where you should install (and configure) laptop memory—as in random access *memory* (i.e., RAM). The typical scenario is when your client runs applications that demand more memory than the current laptop has, so the computer uses the page file a lot to swap things in and out of active RAM. This results in sluggish performance. Adding RAM or replacing existing sticks with more RAM will dramatically improve performance.

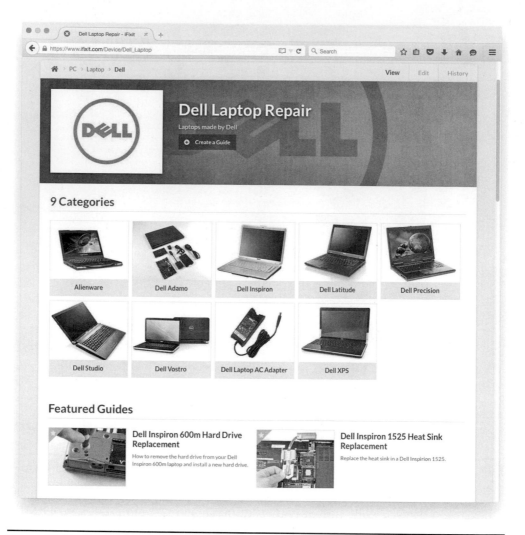

Figure 23-31 Some of the Dell laptop repair walkthroughs at iFixit.com

How to Add or Replace RAM   Upgrading the RAM in a portable PC requires a couple of steps. First, you need to get the correct RAM. Refer to the manufacturer's Web site or to the manual (if any) that came with the portable for the specific RAM needed. Once you know the type, you need to make sure you know the configuration of any existing RAM in the system. If you are planning to upgrade from 4 GB to 8 GB, you need to know if your portable already has one module at 4 GB, or two modules at 2 GB.

 CAUTION   Some portables may have both built-in and removable batteries.

Figure 23-32
204-pin SO-
DIMM stick
(front and back)

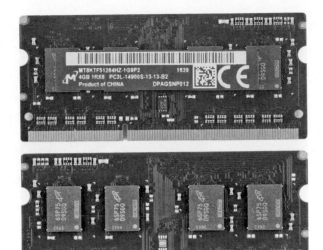

Second, every portable offers a unique challenge to the tech who wants to upgrade the RAM, because there's no standard location for RAM placement in portables. The RAM slots may not even be in the same spot. More often than not, you need to unscrew or pop open a panel on the underside of the portable (see Figure 23-33). Then you press out on the restraining clips and the RAM stick pops up (see Figure 23-34). Gently remove the old stick of RAM and insert the new one by reversing the steps.

Always remove all electrical power from the laptop before removing or inserting memory. Disconnect the AC cord from the wall outlet. Take out any removable batteries! Failure to disconnect from power can result in a fried laptop. In the case of systems with built-in batteries, consult the manufacturer's resources to evaluate the safety of working on the system and any additional steps or precautions you should take.

Figure 23-33
Removing
a RAM panel

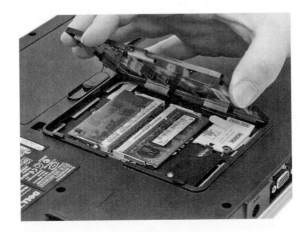

Figure 23-34
Releasing
the RAM

Shared Memory   Some laptops (and desktops) support *shared memory*. Shared memory reduces the cost of video cards by reducing the amount of memory on the video card itself. The video card uses regular system RAM to make up for the loss.

The obvious benefit of shared memory is a less expensive video card (and a less expensive laptop!) with performance comparable to its mega-memory alternative. The downside is that your overall system performance will suffer because a portion of the system RAM is no longer available to programs. (The term *shared* is a bit misleading because the video card takes control of a portion of RAM. The video portion of system RAM is *not* shared back and forth between the video card processor and the CPU.)

Some systems give you control over the amount of shared memory, while others simply allow you to turn shared memory on or off. The settings are found in CMOS setup on systems that support shared memory.

Adding more system RAM to a laptop with shared memory will improve laptop performance. Although it might appear to improve video performance, that doesn't tell the true story. It'll improve overall performance because the OS and CPU get more usable RAM. On some laptops, you can improve video performance as well, but that depends on the CMOS setup. If the shared memory is not set to maximum by default, increasing the overall memory and upping the portion reserved for video will improve video performance specifically.

Upgrading Mass Storage

You can replace a hard disk drive (HDD), solid-state drive (SSD), or solid-state hybrid drive (SSHD) in a portable fairly easily, especially if the laptop is only a few years old. SATA drives in the 2.5-inch drive format now rule in all laptops. Although much smaller than regular 3.5-inch hard drives, they use all the same features and configurations.

As you'd expect, the smaller size limits capacity. The largest 2.5-inch hard drives hold up to 5 TB of data, while 3.5-inch hard drives top out at more than 8 TB of data! Unfortunately, most laptops only have room for drives 7 mm or 9.5 mm thick, but the largest 2.5-inch drives are 15 mm thick. The largest 2.5-inch drives that will fit in a typical laptop top out at 2 TB.

 EXAM TIP 1.8-inch drives exist, though they have fallen out of favor as flash memory usurps their role in portable music players and other small portables. These days, they are quite rare. If you find one, it almost certainly will be in an older portable on the small end of the scale.

If you have an ancient laptop, it might have a PATA drive, which means you need to pay more attention to cabling and jumpers. Some PATA drive manufacturers may require you to set the drive to use a cable-select setting as opposed to master or slave, so check with the laptop maker for any special issues. Otherwise, no difference exists between 2.5-inch drives and their larger 3.5-inch brethren (see Figure 23-35).

Figure 23-35
The 2.5-inch and 3.5-inch drives are mostly the same.

 NOTE If you have a newer portable, chances are the computer uses one of the newer, smaller SSD formats—mSATA or M.2. You read about them in detail back in Chapter 8, but glance back to refresh your memory if necessary.

Most manufacturers make it fairly easy to replace or upgrade an mSATA or M.2 drive. Remove the bottom plate or dedicated drive bay covering from the computer. Remove the tiny retaining screw and pop the old drive out. Put the new drive in its place, insert the retaining screw, and reattach the covering. You're good to go, at least from the hardware side of things.

One of the best upgrades you can make on a laptop is to go from an HDD to an SSD. Obviously, you'll get a lot less storage capacity for the money, but the trade-offs can be worth it. First, the SSD will use a lot less electricity than an HDD, thus extending battery life. Second, any SSD is rip-roaringly faster than an HDD and performance across the board will be boosted. For a time, SSHDs, or hybrid drives, were a good compromise between the speed of an SSD and the size of a traditional HDD. These days, the inroads SSDs have made on price and capacity have made SSHDs a lukewarm choice. 2- and 4-TB SSDs are common, though still a bit pricey, while 500-GB SSDs are under $60.

Try This!   Comparing HDD with SSD Today

As I write this chapter, you can get roughly twice the storage capacity on an HDD for the same cost as an SSD. In other words, $60 spent on an SSD could give you ~512 GB of storage, whereas you could purchase a 1-TB, 2.5-inch HDD for the same $60. So do some comparison shopping. What's the price point now? Are the trade-offs worth it for you or for your clients to make the switch from HDD to SSD?

The process of replacing a hard drive mirrors that of replacing RAM. You find the hard drive hatch—either along one edge or in a compartment on the underside of the computer—and release the screws (see Figure 23-36). Remove the old drive and then slide the new drive into its place (see Figure 23-37). Reattach the hatch or cover and boot the computer. Grab a Windows DVD or bootable USB flash drive and prepare to reinstall.

Figure 23-36
Removing the drive compartment cover

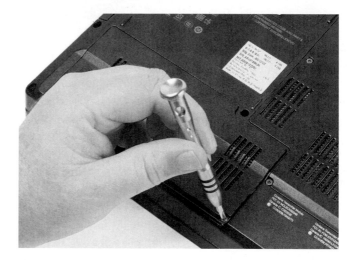

Hardware/Device Replacement

Once you get beyond upgrading RAM and replacing a hard drive on a portable, you take the plunge into the laptop-repair specialty. You can replace some components by lifting them out, detaching a ribbon cable, and then reversing the steps with the replacement part. Other parts require a full teardown of the laptop to the bare bones, which presents a much greater magnitude of difficulty. Because every portable differs, this section provides guidance, but not concrete steps, for replacement. Be aware, as mentioned earlier,

Figure 23-37
Inserting a
replacement
drive

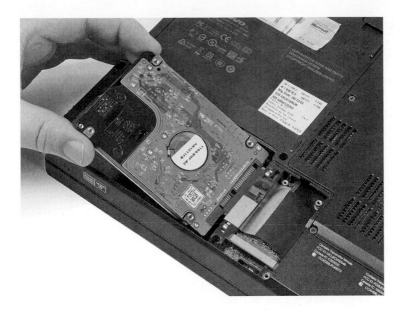

that some systems are trending toward more integrated parts; make sure the part you're replacing is actually replaceable in the specific system you're working on.

Components

Replaceable components require more work than the RAM or drive upgrades, but replacing them generally falls into the category of "doable." What I call *components* are the battery, keyboard, optical drive, internal speaker(s), frame, expansion cards, and CPU.

Battery If a battery's performance falls below an acceptable level, you can replace it with a battery from the manufacturer or from an aftermarket vendor. Although this should be a simple swap replacement (and usually is, at least if the battery isn't built in), you might encounter a situation where the real problem wasn't the battery *per se*, but an inadequate or malfunctioning charging system. The new battery might not give you any better performance than the old one. Try it.

Keyboard Getting a keyboard off a laptop computer often requires little pry bars, but also look for screws, clips, and so on. Keyboards connect via a tiny, short, and very delicate cable, often held down by tape. Replacing one is tricky, but doable.

Optical Drive Replacing an optical drive can present a challenge. If the drive is part of a modular system, just pop out the old drive and pop in a new one. If the drive is part of the internal chassis of the portable, on the other hand, you're looking at a full dissection. (See the upcoming "Integral Parts" section for tips on dismantling the portable.)

Speaker Replacing the internal speaker or speakers on a laptop can be simple or a total pain, depending on where the speakers connect. Some laptops have speakers mounted on the outside of the chassis. You pry off the covers, pull out the little speakers, disconnect the cable, and then reverse the process for replacement speakers. If the speakers are inside the chassis, on the other hand, you need to dismantle the portable to get to them. (See the "Integral Parts" section.)

Frame   All of the sophisticated electrified components that make our portables work are held together by a variety of plastic, metal, and rubber parts. Generally these frame parts are pretty durable, but over time—or in an accident—these components can warp, bend, crack, split, dent, and chip. Frame parts can be replaced, provided you can locate a suitable replacement part.

You'll need to know the device model to get started, and you may also need to hunt down the part number using manufacturer or third-party resources. Many device parts appear similar, and some parts will appear in many other portables. You may also find that the part you need is only available as a piece of a larger assembly or group of parts, in which case you may end up paying a silly sum to get the part you need.

Expansion Cards   Many portables have one or more true expansion slots for add-on cards. The more modular varieties will have a hatch on the bottom of the case that opens like the hatch that gives you access to the RAM slot(s). This enables you to change out an 802.11n wireless card, for example, for an 802.11ac card, thus greatly enhancing the Wi-Fi experience on this device. Similarly, you could change out a Bluetooth module for an upgraded version. Figure 23-38 shows a wide-open laptop with the expansion slot exposed.

Figure 23-38
Mini-PCIe
expansion slot on
laptop

   NOTE   Check with the portable manufacturer to get a Wi-Fi card that's compatible with the portable. Just because a card will fit in the slot does not, in this case, mean it will work.

Just like when installing RAM in a portable, you must avoid ESD and remove all electricity before you take out or put in an expansion card. Failure to remove the battery and the AC adapter (or follow any extra steps and precautions in the manufacturer's resources if the battery is built in) can and probably will result in a shorted-out laptop motherboard, and that just makes for a bad day.

The only other consideration with expansion cards applies specifically to wireless. Not only will you need to connect the card to the slot properly, but you must reattach the antenna connection and often a separate power cable. Pay attention when you remove the card as to the placement of these vital connections.

You'll find one of two types of expansion slot in a portable: Mini-PCIe and M.2. The older ones (think 2013 and earlier) use *Mini-PCIe*, while newer devices use *M.2*.

CPU Replacing a CPU on a modern portable takes a lot more work than replacing RAM or a Mini-PCIe expansion card, but follows the same general steps. Many CPUs mount facing the bottom of the portable, so that it vents away from your hands. When sitting properly on a flat surface, the heated air also goes to the back of the laptop and not toward the user. You access the CPU in this sort of system from the bottom of the portable.

As you can see in Figure 23-39, the CPU has an elaborate heat-sink and fan assembly that includes both the CPU and the chipset. Each of the pieces screws down in multiple places, plus the fan has a power connection. Aside from the tiny screws, there's no difference here in process between replacing a mobile CPU and replacing a desktop CPU that you learned way back in Chapter 3, "CPUs."

Figure 23-39
CPU heat-sink and fan assembly exposed

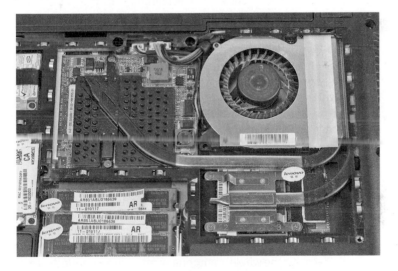

First, remove all power from the laptop, including the battery if possible; consult manufacturer or third-party resources for any extra steps or precautions for systems with built-in batteries. Remove the hatch to expose the CPU. Remove the heat-sink and fan assembly and lift out the CPU. Replace it with another CPU, apply thermal paste, and reattach the heat-sink and fan assembly. Reconnect the fan power connector and you're good to go.

Some laptops use passive cooling and may have the CPU pointed up rather than down. They have a heat sink beneath the keyboard that cools everything down. With that style laptop, you remove the keyboard and heat sink to expose the CPU.

Display and Its Components   A laptop screen presents unique challenges when faced with a replacement scenario. The display has the typical parts you'd expect in an LCD, such as the panel, backlight(s), and inverter (on older portables); plus, the display typically has other components along for the ride, such as the Wi-Fi antenna, a Webcam, and a microphone. Finally, a touchscreen display offers even more of a challenge. CompTIA expects you to know the process for replacing (the objectives say *installing*, but whatever) the screen as well as each component within the display. Here's the scoop.

EXAM TIP   The CompTIA A+ 1001 objectives mention both LCD and OLED display types for laptops when discussing possible scenarios where you'd install components within the display. As discussed in Chapter 17, OLED laptops did not exist (for consumers, at least) when the 1001/1002 exams went live in early 2019. That said, the process for replacing OLED screens and components within the screens should mirror the process with LCDs.

The process for replacing the screen (flat, touchscreen, digitizer), inverter, Wi-Fi antenna, Webcam, or microphone follows the same steps. You pry the plastic frame off the display, most commonly using a spudger or other tool from your iFixit toolkit, then remove any exposed screws. The screen will lift out, plus you'll need to detach the internal parts. I can't give you precise details, because one model differs from another, but the parts are usually secured with tiny screws or compression, or mild adhesive. Plus, you'll need to gently disconnect data cables for each component. If you're just replacing a defective Webcam or microphone, you won't need to disconnect other parts (most likely), but if you need to replace the screen or inverter, you'll have to remove everything.

Take pictures with your phone. Keep track of which connectors go where. Don't rush the process when dealing with so many tiny connectors and parts. Document the locations and types of screws. The extra work you do to record each step or layer will pay off with a properly repaired laptop. Trust me!

EXAM TIP   Expect a question or two on the CompTIA A+ 1001 exam on a typical scenario where replacement of the screen or components within the display needs to happen. These are obvious—cracked screen, failure of the digitizer/touchscreen, Wi-Fi antenna malfunction, and so on. (Note that the specific objective language on the antenna is *WiFi antenna connector/placement*, which refers to the wireless antenna wires—pun intended—that run along the top and sides of the display and connect with a tiny ribbon cable.)

Integral Parts

Some hardware replacements require you to get serious with the laptop, opening it fully to the outside, removing many delicate parts, and even stripping it down to the bare chassis. I leave these repairs to the professional laptop repair folks, simply because they have the specific tools and expertise to do the job efficiently. CompTIA expects you to understand the process, though, so I've outlined it here. This pertains to three components: DC jack, touchpad, and system board.

EXAM TIP   Although you might get a question on the CompTIA A+ 1001 exam about replacing the video card on a laptop, that's a rare thing to do. Only a handful of models from various manufacturers over the years had a discrete removeable/replaceable video card. Most commonly, the video processing components are part of the system board. Replacing the video card in that case means replacing the board.

Portables open in two different ways, depending on the manufacturer. You either peel away layers from the top down, through the keyboard, or from the bottom up, through the base. Either direction requires careful attention to detail, part connectivity, and locations. You'll need a system to keep track of the dozens of tiny screws.

Every one of the replacements here requires you to detach the screen from the main chassis of the portable. Aside from finding the connection points and removing the proper screws, you need to pay attention to the connection points for the data stream to the monitor and the antenna that's in the frame of the display, as mentioned earlier.

Once you have the portable stripped down, you replace whichever component you're in there to replace and then begin the process of building it back up into a coherent unit. Pay incredibly careful attention to getting data cables connected properly as you rebuild. I can't imagine a worse tech experience than replacing a touchpad and rebuilding a laptop only to have missed a connection and having to do it all over again.

 EXAM TIP   The DC jack requires extra-special love when you need to replace one. The part is soldered to the main board, so replacing it means you'll need to not only strip the laptop to the bare metal but also unsolder the old part and solder the new part. Then you'll rebuild the laptop and hope you got everything right. CompTIA cannot expect a CompTIA A+ technician to know how to do this stuff. Expect a question that explores whether it *can* be done. Rest assured, specialized techs can replace *any* component on a laptop, even the DC jack.

Troubleshooting Portable Computers

Many of the troubleshooting techniques you learned about for desktop systems can be applied to laptops. For example, take the proper precautions before and during disassembly. Use the proper hand tools, and document, label, and organize each plastic part and screw location for reassembly. Additionally, here are some laptop-specific procedures to try.

Power and Performance

Some of the most common portable device issues relate to how well they do (or don't!) run—so let's take a look at a few issues related to power, performance, and heat.

Laptop Won't Power On

- If a laptop won't power up—a *no power* scenario—verify AC power by plugging another electronic device into the wall outlet. If the other device receives power, the outlet is good.

- If the outlet is good, connect the laptop to the wall outlet and try to power on. If no LEDs light up, you may have a bad AC adapter. Swap it out with a known good power adapter.

- A faulty peripheral device might keep the laptop from powering up. Remove any peripherals such as USB, FireWire, or Thunderbolt devices.

Poor Performance

- The most common reason for slow performance is that running applications and processes are consuming high resources. All operating systems have a way to check this—such as the Task Manager in Windows or Activity Monitor in macOS—and look into problems with any you find. They may need to be closed or stopped, you may need to reboot, or the application may need an update.

- Extreme performance issues may lead to a frozen system. If they don't resolve on their own and you can't interact with the device, you may need to perform a hard reboot (which may result in the loss of any unsaved work). Usually, holding down the power button for 10 seconds is sufficient, though you may need to check the manufacturer's resources for the proper procedure. If the battery is removable, you may be able to reboot the device by pulling the battery out and replacing it.

NOTE Be aware, especially when working with hybrid devices, that you might find official or third-party resources discussing hard and soft resets. These are *not* the same as hard and soft reboots, so you should pay careful attention to the instructions and make sure you're performing the correct procedure. See Chapter 25 for more on hard and soft resets.

Battery Issues

- A *swollen battery* will probably go unnoticed at first, and the symptoms it creates may be hard to identify if you aren't aware it can happen. The cause is usually over-charging, perhaps due to a failure in the circuits that should prevent it, but the early symptoms might be a laptop that doesn't quite sit right on flat surfaces, a screen that doesn't fit flush when closed, problems with input devices like the touchpad or keyboard, and trouble removing or inserting a removable battery. Eventually, the device's case may be obviously deformed. While battery packs are designed to handle a little swelling, it increases the risk they'll puncture—and a punctured battery can be dangerous. Don't ignore these symptoms; open the case carefully to check the battery, and very carefully deliver it to an e-waste recycling or disposal site.

- If you have a laptop with a battery that won't charge up—a *battery not charging* problem—it could be one of two things: the battery might be cooked or the AC adapter isn't doing its job. To troubleshoot, replace the battery with a known good battery. If the new battery works, you've found the problem. Just replace the battery. Alternatively, remove the battery and run the laptop on AC only. If that works, you know the AC adapter is good. If it doesn't, replace the AC adapter.

- The reasons for very short battery life in a battery that charges properly are fairly benign. The battery has usually outlived its useful life and needs to be replaced, or some programs or hardware are drawing much more power than usual. Check wireless devices you usually keep disabled to make sure they aren't on. Follow recommendations in the preceding "Poor Performance" section to address problem programs.

Overheating

- Because overheating can be both a symptom and a cause of a variety of issues, you should be alert to any device that is hot to the touch, or is running hotter than usual. Note which parts of the device are hot—this can give you important clues. If the device feels dangerously hot, err on the side of protecting the device from heat damage instead of trying to diagnose the cause. Power the device down and remove the battery if possible. Set it on a cool, hard surface, out of direct sunlight, with the hottest part of the device exposed to air if possible.

- Likewise, look for possible signs a device is overheating—like inconsistent reboots, graphical glitches, system beeps—and rule out heat issues.

- Listen for fans. While some portables don't have any, complete silence may indicate a failed fan, and unusual noise may signal one on its way out.

- Know when to expect a hot device. Busy or charging devices create a lot of heat; follow the steps mentioned in the preceding "Poor Performance" and "Battery Issues" sections for identifying components that shouldn't be on, especially if they are hot to the touch, and finding runaway programs. If the device is charging, unplug it and see if the device cools. If you find nothing unexpected and the device is unusually hot, it may have an airflow problem. Check any fan vents for blockages, and open the device if necessary to check any fans and heat sinks for issues.

- If the entire device is hot, it was most likely left in direct sunlight or a hot environment. Cool the device down and see if the trouble goes away.

Components

Various hardware components can use help too. Such devices include the display, wireless networking, audio, and input devices.

Display Problems

- If the laptop is booting (you hear the beeps and the drives) but the screen doesn't come on properly—a *no display* problem—first make sure the display is turned on. Press the FN key and the key to activate the screen a number of times until the laptop display comes on. If that doesn't work, check the LCD cutoff switch—on many laptops, this is the small nub somewhere near the screen hinge that shuts the monitor off when you close the laptop—and make sure it isn't stuck in the down position. If the device is a convertible with a removable screen, make sure it is properly attached and that it is receiving power.

- If the laptop display is very dim—a *dim display* problem—you may have lost an inverter. (Note that this is only an issue with the older CCFL technology.) The clue here is that inverters never go quietly. They can make a nasty hum as they are about to die and an equally nasty popping noise when they actually fail. Failure often occurs when you plug in the laptop's AC adapter, as the inverters take power directly from the AC adapter. It's also possible that the backlights in the LCD panel have died, though this is much less common than a bad inverter.

- If the screen won't come on or is cracked, most laptops have a port for plugging in an external monitor, which you can use to log in to your laptop.

- If you plug a laptop into an external monitor and that monitor does not display, remember that you have both a hardware and an OS component to making dual displays successful. There's usually a combination of FN and another key to toggle among only portable, only external, and both displays. Plus, you have the Display Settings or Display applet in the Control Panel to mirror or extend the desktop to a second monitor.

- Many manufacturers have switched to LED displays on laptops, which has led to a phenomenon many techs thought long behind us: *flickering displays*. The LED backlights don't work quite the same as CCFL backlights, especially when you lower the brightness. This doesn't affect desktop LED displays, because they're usually so bright it doesn't matter. But portables need to be able to dim to save battery life. One technique for dimming LEDs is to have them turn on and off rapidly enough to keep the pixels lit, but slowly enough that there's a reduction in visible light and electricity use. With some of these panels, that flickering is not only noticeable, but headache and eyestrain inducing. There are two ways to fix a flickering LED display: crank up the brightness so that it goes away (and thus live with reduced battery life) or replace the laptop.

- If the screen orientation on a Windows portable doesn't change when the device is rotated, auto-rotation may be disabled. Likewise, if the orientation changes at the wrong time, you can lock rotation in Settings, or via the Display applet in the Control Panel. If the rotation needs to remain locked, the orientation can still be changed via Settings/Display, or possibly with FN key combinations.

Wireless Devices (Bluetooth, Wi-Fi, Mobile Broadband, NFC, or GPS) Don't Work or Work Intermittently

- If the wireless doesn't work at all, check along the front, rear, or side edges of the laptop for a physical switch that toggles the internal wireless adapter, Bluetooth adapter, or airplane mode on and off. Also check your notification area for an airplane icon.

 EXAM TIP Expect a couple of questions on the CompTIA A+ 1001 exam that explore scenarios where a client experiences *no wireless connectivity* or *no Bluetooth connectivity*.

- If a tech has recently replaced a component that required removal of the laptop display, dead wireless could mean simply a disconnected antenna. Most portables have the antenna built into the display panel, so check that connection.

- Try the special key combination for your laptop to toggle the wireless or Bluetooth adapter, or one for toggling airplane mode. You usually press the FN key in combination with another key.

- You might simply be out of range or, if the wireless works intermittently, right at the edge of the range. Physically walk the laptop over to the wireless router or access point to ensure there are no out-of-range issues. You might also be experiencing congestion, too many wireless devices operating in the same frequency range.

- With Bluetooth specifically, remember that the pairing process takes action or configuration on both devices to succeed. Turn on the Bluetooth device, actively seek it, and try again.

- If only the GPS is not functioning, privacy options may be preventing applications from accessing your GPS location information. Check the Location Settings applet in the Control Panel or the Privacy section of the Settings app to see whether the GPS device is enabled, and if location services are enabled both system wide and for the appropriate applications. Check System Preferences in macOS or a similar location in Linux for the same options.

- While we won't discuss near field communication (NFC) in depth until Chapter 24, some portable computers may have NFC support; if NFC isn't functioning, you may need to enable a setting to enable communication with nearby devices. In Windows, open the Proximity applet in the Control Panel (only present if you have NFC hardware) and make sure Proximity support is enabled.

Audio Problems

- If audio isn't working when it should be, check for a hardware mute or volume button or switch and verify through the notification area Volume icon that the audio output isn't muted. Verify proper output device configuration through the operating system, and verify the application is using the right output device.

- If the device has had repairs or upgrades lately, make sure the speakers are properly connected.

- If no sound is coming from the device speakers, try plugging in a pair of headphones or some external speakers. If these work fine, there's a chance the built-in speakers have been damaged. Depending on their location, it can be easy to get them wet.

- If headphones work fine with the device, the speakers may need replacing. First, make sure the device has been rebooted, double-check the audio output device settings, try changing and resetting the default output device, and try disabling and re-enabling the appropriate device.

Input Problems

- Before assuming an input problem is hardware related, confirm that the system is otherwise running smoothly. Input devices may appear not to work or work erratically if the system is freezing up. Refer to the previous "Power and Performance" section for troubleshooting a frozen system.

- If none of the keys work on your laptop, there's a good chance you've unseated the keypad connector. These connectors are quite fragile and are prone to unseating from any physical stress on the laptop. Check the manufacturer's disassembly procedures to locate and reseat the keypad.

- If you're getting numbers when you're expecting to get letters, the number lock (NUM LOCK) function key is turned on. Turn it off. Pay attention to the NUM LOCK *indicator lights*, if any, on a portable if you experience these sorts of problems.

- Laptop keyboards take far more abuse than the typical desktop keyboard, because of all those lunch meetings and café brainstorm sessions. Eating and drinking while over or around a keyboard just begs for problems. If you have a portable with sticking keys, look for the obvious debris in the keys. Use compressed air to clean them out. If you have serious goo and need to use a cleaning solution, disconnect the keyboard from the portable first. Make sure it's fully dried out before you reconnect it or you'll short it out.

- A laptop keyboard key that doesn't register presses or feels sticky may also have had its switch knocked out of place, especially if the key appears slightly raised or tilted. These switches can be delicate, so be careful if you want to avoid ordering replacements. Research what kind of switch your device's keyboard uses, and be aware that a single keyboard may use a few different kinds. Look up steps for detaching and reattaching keys on that specific device if possible, and otherwise find generic instructions for the clip type before proceeding.

- If the touchpad is having problems, a shot of compressed air does wonders for cleaning pet hair out of the touchpad sensors. You might get a cleaner shot if you remove the keyboard before using the compressed air. Remember to be gentle when lifting off the keyboard and make sure to follow the manufacturer's instructions.

- The touchpad driver might need to be reconfigured. Try the various options in the Control Panel | Mouse applet, or the equivalent location in System Preferences.

- If the touchscreen is unresponsive or erratic, a good first step is checking the screen for dirt, grease, or liquids, which can make the sensors go haywire; wipe it down with a dry microfiber cloth.

- Some touchscreens may appear to work improperly if they are registering an unintentional touch. Depending on the design of the device, it may be tempting to hold it in a way that leaves some part of your hand or arm too close to the edge of the screen; some devices will register this as a touch.

- Your device may have touchscreen diagnostics available through hardware troubleshooting menus accessible through the BIOS. Refer to the manufacturer's resources for how to access these diagnostics. If available, they are a quick way to identify whether you're looking at a hardware or software/configuration issue. The Mouse applet in the Control Panel or Settings enables you to calibrate or reset your touch support. macOS has a Trackpad applet in System Preferences. Attempt to reset and recalibrate the display.

 EXAM TIP The troubleshooting issue known as a *ghost cursor* can mean one of two things. First, the display shows a trail of ghost cursors behind your real cursor as you move it. This might point to an aging display or an improperly configured refresh rate. Second, the cursor moves erratically or drifts slowly in a steady direction (also known as *pointer drift*), whether you are touching the touchpad or not. If a reboot doesn't fix the pointer drift, the touchpad has probably been damaged in some way and needs to be replaced.

Chapter Review

Questions

1. Which of the following are good ideas when it comes to batteries? (Select two.)

    A. Keep the contacts clean by using alcohol and a soft cloth.

    B. Store them in the freezer if they will not be used for a long period of time.

    C. Toss them in the garbage when they wear out.

    D. Store them in a cool, dry place.

2. To replace a wireless antenna in a laptop, what must you do?

    A. Remove the keyboard.

    B. Remove the screen.

    C. Remove the expansion slot cover on the bottom of the laptop.

    D. This cannot be done.

3. ExpressCards connect to which buses? (Select two.)

    A. ACPI

    B. PCI

    C. PCIe

    D. USB

4. Clara's laptop has a DVI connector to which she has connected a projector. As she prepares to make her presentation, however, nothing comes on the projector screen. The laptop shows the presentation, and the projector appears to be functional, with a bright white bulb making a blank image on the screen. What's most likely the problem?

    A. She needs to plug in the projector.

    B. She's running the laptop on batteries. She needs to plug in the laptop to use the DVI connector.

    C. She needs to update her ExpressCard services to support projectors.

    D. She needs to press the Function key combination on her keyboard to cycle through monitor modes.

5. What is the primary benefit to adding more RAM to a laptop that uses shared memory? (Select the best answer.)

    A. Improved battery life.

    B. Improved system performance.

    C. Improved video performance.

    D. None. Adding more RAM is pointless with systems that use shared memory.

6. Which of the following display types will you commonly find on a portable PC today?

    A. CRT

    B. LCD

    C. OLED

    D. Plasma

7. Steve complains that his aging Windows laptop still isn't snappy enough after upgrading the RAM. What might improve system performance?

    A. Add more RAM.

    B. Replace the power supply.

    C. Replace the battery.

    D. Replace the HDD with an SSD.

8. Jim likes his laptop but complains that his wireless seems slow compared to all the new laptops. On further inspection, you determine his laptop runs 802.11n. What can be done to improve his network connection speed?

    A. Add more RAM.

    B. Replace the display with one with a better antenna.

    C. Replace the Mini-PCIe 802.11n card with an 802.11ac card.

    D. Get a new laptop, because this one can't be upgraded.

9. Edgar successfully replaced the display on a laptop (a toddler had taken a ballpoint pen to it), but the customer called back almost immediately complaining that his wireless didn't work. What could the problem be?

    A. The problems are unrelated, so it could be anything.

    B. Edgar inadvertently disconnected the antenna from the Mini-PCIe 802.11 card.

    C. Edgar replaced the display with one without an internal antenna.

    D. Edgar failed to reconnect the antenna in the new display.

10. Rafael gets a tech call from a user with a brand new laptop complaining that working on it was causing headaches. What could the problem be?

    A. The laptop uses a plasma display.

    B. The laptop uses a CRT display.

    C. The laptop uses an LED display in power saving mode.

    D. The laptop uses an LED display in full power mode.

Answers

1. **A, D.** Keeping a battery in the freezer is a good idea in theory, but not in practice. All batteries contain toxic chemicals and should *never* be treated like regular trash.

2. **B.** The antenna for laptop Wi-Fi connections is located in the screen portion of the laptop. To access the antenna, remove the screen (or at least the plastic frame parts).

3. **C, D.** ExpressCards connect to either the PCI Express bus or the USB bus.

4. **D.** Clara needs to press the Function key combination on her keyboard to cycle through monitor modes.

5. **B.** Improved overall system performance is the primary benefit to adding more RAM to a laptop that uses shared memory.

6. **B.** You'll only see LCD displays on portables today (though they may be marketed as LED displays).

7. **D.** Replacing the HDD with an SSD will speed up the system.

8. **C.** He can have the 802.11n NIC replaced with an 802.11ac NIC.

9. **D.** A disconnected antenna makes Wi-Fi unhappy.

10. **C.** Flicker is a side effect of dimming on some lower-end LED monitors.

Understanding Mobile Devices

In this chapter, you will learn how to
- Explain the features and capabilities of mobile devices
- Describe the major mobile operating systems
- Describe how to configure mobile devices

It's hard to imagine that most of the mobile devices we use today—in particular, the popular iPhone and Android devices—didn't even exist ten years ago. Mobile devices revolutionized the way we work and play. Devices such as smartphones, tablets, and even smart watches enable people to access unique tools and features from just about anywhere and accomplish essential tasks on the go.

As amazing as mobile devices are, it's not easy to find a definition of *mobile device* that everyone agrees on. If you ask folks who are comfortable with these devices, you'll get lots of descriptions of functions and capabilities as opposed to what they are. In essence, the following aspects make a device mobile (and even these will sometimes create debate):

- Lightweight, usually less than two pounds
- Small, designed to move with you (in your hand or pocket)
- Touch or stylus interface; no keyboard or mice
- Sealed unit lacking any user-replaceable parts
- Non-desktop OS; mobile devices use special mobile operating systems

The last one is important—it's the one easy way to differentiate something like a hybrid portable computer in a tablet form factor from a plain tablet mobile device. Your typical portable computer runs a desktop OS such as Windows, macOS, or some Linux distribution such as Ubuntu. A true mobile device will run Apple iOS or Google Android.

EXAM TIP The CompTIA A+ objectives mention both Microsoft Windows and Google Chrome OS as operating systems for phones and tablets. That's true, but unbelievably limited in market share (as in less than 1% combined). Just be prepared if Windows or Chrome OS is the only possible right answer for a mobile device OS question.

This chapter explores mobile devices in detail. We'll first look at the hardware features and capabilities of devices common in the mobile market. Next, the chapter examines mobile operating system software. The chapter finishes with the details of configuring the devices for personal use. We'll save mobile device troubleshooting and security for Chapter 25, "Care and Feeding of Mobile Devices." The CompTIA A+ certification exams are serious about mobile devices and we have a lot of ground to cover, so let's get started.

1001

Mobile Computing Devices

The specialized hardware of mobile devices defines to a large degree the capabilities of those devices. This first section examines the various form factors of mobile devices, then looks at specific hardware common to most devices.

Device Variants

Most modern mobile devices fall into one of a few categories, including smartphones, tablets, and wearable technology, which all have similar features and capabilities. There are a few other mobile device types, and they are best understood as devices purpose-built to be better at some task than a general-purpose device such as a smartphone or tablet; an e-reader is a good example. The CompTIA A+ 1001 exam objectives have a pretty long list of devices, so let's start with the most popular and go through them one at a time to understand what they do.

Smartphones

One of the earliest types of mobile device was the *personal digital assistant* (*PDA*), such as the Compaq iPaq from the late 1990s. PDAs had the basic features of today's mobile devices but lacked cellular connectivity, so you couldn't make a phone call. Many people, your author included, spent close to ten years carrying a mobile phone and a PDA, wondering when somebody would combine these two things. Starting around 2003–2005, companies began marketing PDAs that included cellular telephones (although cool features like using the PDA to access Internet data weren't well developed). Figure 24-1 shows an early PDA-with-a-phone, the once very popular RIM BlackBerry.

Figure 24-1
RIM BlackBerry
(courtesy of the
TotalSem Tech
Museum)

While these tools were powerful for their time, it wasn't until Apple introduced the iPhone (see Figure 24-2) in 2007 that we saw the elements that define a modern *smartphone*:

- A multi-touch interface as the primary input method for using the smartphone
- A well-standardized application programming interface (API) enabling developers to create new apps for the system
- Tight consolidation of cellular data to the device, enabling any application (Web browsers, e-mail clients, games, and so on) to exchange data over the Internet
- Synchronization and distribution tools that enable users to install new apps and synchronize or back up data

Figure 24-2
Early Apple
iPhone

Since then, smartphones have developed many more features and uses. They have come to play a big role in the trend toward ever-present connectivity and seamless data access across all of our devices. Because smartphones do so much more than simply make and receive phone calls—we surf the Web with them, stream music and video, send and receive e-mail, and even do work with them—the infrastructure and technologies that connect smartphones with a mesh of networked data and services must be fast, robust, and secure.

Most smartphones run one of the big two operating systems: Google Android or Apple iOS (see Figure 24-3). iOS runs exclusively on Apple hardware, such as the iPhone. Phones running Android come from a multitude of manufacturers. Smartphones typically have no user-replaceable or field-replaceable components, and have to be brought into specialized (and in some cases, authorized) service centers for repair.

Figure 24-3
Examples of the big two smartphone OSs: Android (left), iOS (right)

Tablets

Tablets are very similar to smartphones; they run the same OSs and apps, and use the same multi-touch screens. From a tech's perspective, they are like large smartphones (without the phone). While a typical smartphone screen is around 5 inches, tablets run around 7 to 12.9 inches (see Figure 24-4).

Unlike smartphones, tablets generally (there are a few exceptions) lack a cellular data connection, instead counting on 802.11 Wi-Fi to provide Internet connectivity. There are low-end tablets, usually running some variation of Android with limited hardware, and then there are the higher-end tablets, such as the Apple iPad. The differences between the low and high end of the cost spectrum are hardware quality, capabilities, and features.

Purpose-Built Mobile Devices

In the introduction I mentioned other purpose-built devices. Because these devices are laser-focused on being good at one of the many things we could use a general-purpose mobile device for, a few things tend to be true. First, general-purpose devices usually have

Figure 24-4
Typical tablet

apps for performing the same task. Second, the justification for purpose-built devices tends to get less obvious over time as general-purpose devices handle the task well enough that the convenience of a single device wins out. Standalone MP3 players are a good example of a purpose-built device that smartphones have already gobbled up.

CompTIA wants you to know about two of these devices: e-readers and GPS devices. Because GPS devices are tightly designed around the hardware components they are named after, we'll introduce them when we discuss GPS in the upcoming "Mobile Hardware Features" section. For now we'll look at e-readers, which are better seen as small tablets tailored for reading.

E-readers   To give the obvious definition, an *e-reader* is a device designed for reading electronic books (e-books). The stereotypical e-reader uses a low-power grayscale screen technology called e-paper, and a simple interface designed around obtaining e-books, navigating through them, and performing related tasks such as highlighting, bookmarking, sharing passages, and looking up definitions. Initially these interfaces used hardware buttons, but over time they have shifted to touchscreen interfaces, such as the one used by the Amazon Kindle Paperwhite in Figure 24-5.

Along the way, some e-reader product lines have grown to include full-fledged tablets. Both the Amazon Kindle and Barnes & Noble Nook product lines started with simple black-and-white devices; both now include tablets alongside the simple e-readers. While tablets are better at general computing and media use, purpose-built e-readers have features optimized for reading, such as long battery life measured in days or weeks, and screens designed for hours of comfortable reading in a wide range of lighting conditions (versus playing games or watching HD video). Both Kindle and Nook also have e-reader apps available for other platforms. Like standalone e-readers, these apps can connect to online bookstores, download e-books, and maintain a library of books for the user.

Wearable Technology Devices

The limitation of traditional mobile devices is that they're basically useless if they aren't in your hand. A few motivations drive most new wearables: collecting more information about our lives, and creating new interfaces that integrate data and technology with the natural flow of daily life. Wearable tech has been around for a few years, but with the

Figure 24-5
Kindle
Paperwhite
e-reader

recent advent of smart watches, such as the Apple Watch and Android Wear OS watches, it's evident that the major players in the mobile tech world have embraced wearable devices.

Wearable devices have a number of features that distinguish them from other mobile devices:

- Very small; almost always well under a pound, usually a few ounces
- Small interfaces; screens less than 2 inches, often much less
- Light OSs used to perform a small subset of functions of a typical mobile device OS
- Limited hardware, although accelerometers are very common (for step counting)
- Pairs with a host device (often a smartphone)

The CompTIA A+ 220-1001 exam objectives specifically list three type of wearable devices: smart watches, fitness monitors, and VR/AR headsets. Let's see what these are all about.

NOTE Wearable devices aren't designed to replace a smartphone, only augment it by handling some of the simpler functions. Some tasks are hard or impossible to perform on a wearable device. If you wonder why we don't group wearables such as fitness monitors with the purpose-built devices discussed earlier, the difference is the standalone nature of the purpose-built devices.

Smart Watches   A *smart watch* minimizes the effort of frequent smartphone tasks such as notifications, time, messages, weather, controlling music playback, and fitness tracking. Figure 24-6 shows a typical smart watch, the Apple Watch.

Figure 24-6
Apple Watch

Fitness Monitors   A growing number of *fitness monitors* or trackers aim to help you meet your fitness goals. Some of the most common fitness tracker features are counting your steps using accelerometers, registering your heart rate through sensors, using the *Global Positioning System* (*GPS*) network to track your exercise, and providing vibration tools to remind you to get moving. Fitness monitors come in two common forms: fobs that clip to your body, and more sophisticated fitness wristbands. Fobs usually do little more than count steps. Wristbands, like your author's well-worn Fitbit Surge (see Figure 24-7), provide a wealth of features, including GPS and heart-rate monitoring.

Figure 24-7
Mike's battered
Fitbit Surge

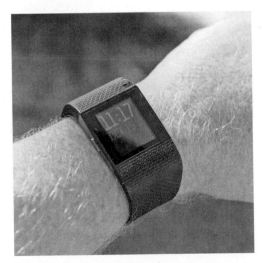

VR/AR Headsets Headsets offer a variety of wearable computing experiences. Like that opening vague statement? Here's the scoop. Headsets come in several varieties. The most common aren't computing devices, but speakers and a microphone designed for chatting via the computer (via Voice over IP or Skype, for example, as discussed in Chapter 21, "The Internet"). Figure 24-8 show a typical headset.

Figure 24-8
Typical cam chat setup

As computing devices, you'll find two very different headsets, one for *virtual reality* (*VR*) and the other for *augmented reality* (*AR*). We discussed *VR headsets* in Chapter 17, "Display Technologies," devices designed to take you into a three-dimensional world. Using high-end systems and VR software, you can explore some pretty amazing places from your game room or couch. Figure 24-9 shows a co-worker enjoying the latest VR headset technology in the Totalsem orbital HQ.

Figure 24-9
VR headset/ player (who doesn't realize how silly he looks)

Augmented reality offers what the words imply, additional elements added to what you can see with your eyes or hear with your ears. AR does not immerse you in something artificial, but can add astonishing details to your physical input devices (i.e., eyes and ears). Here's a very mundane, but cool example. The Sweden-based furniture/housewares retailer, IKEA, makes an app called IKEA Place that enables you to see—literally—how a piece of IKEA furniture will look in your physical space. Figure 24-10 shows my editor Scott's empty dining room, for example, with a potential dining room table and chairs displayed via AR on an iPhone.

Figure 24-10
IKEA AR app on
the loose

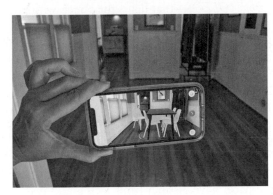

AR headsets up the game considerably, integrating information displays, cameras, and more into eyewear. One of the first AR headsets was *Google Glass*. It had a built-in camera and Bluetooth connectivity, enabling you to take video and photos from a first-person view. It also enabled you to connect to your smartphone via Bluetooth, so you could answer calls and see information from your phone in the lens of the glass. One of the big issues with Google Glass, as people later discovered, was privacy. Since it was quite simple for someone wearing Google Glass to film or photograph his or her surroundings, often without the knowledge of others, it created an uncomfortable invasion of personal space. In fact, some business establishments, such as restaurants, bars, and other public places, banned the use of Google Glass on their premises.

A new crop of AR headsets focuses more on specific hobbies or skill groups. The Garmin Varia Vision, Solos Smart Glasses, and Everysight Raptor AR headsets, for example, enable cyclists to track their speed, pedaling cadence, heart rate, distance traveled, calories burned, elevation, and a whole lot more. They sync with smartphones as well, so you can track your stats over time. Some connect to other cycling devices to track your surroundings, so you know when you're about to be run over by a car, for example.

Mobile Hardware Features

Much of the usefulness of mobile devices is driven by the many hardware features they include. This section explores the basics: screen technologies, cameras, microphones, digitizers, and GPS connectivity.

Screen Technologies

Mobile devices use a variety of screen types. Most tablets use some type of LCD panel, just like portable devices and desktop monitors. The less expensive ones use twisted nematic (TN); the better ones, like the Apple iPad, use an in-plane switching (IPS) panel for richer colors and better viewing angles. Refer back to Chapter 17 if you need to review the difference between these panel types. We'll take a look at the technology that turns these screens into touch interfaces in the upcoming "Digitizers" section.

Some smaller devices, like the better smartphones, use a related technology—*organic light-emitting diode* (*OLED*)—that lights the screen with an organic compound. Applying an electric current causes the organic layer to glow in the precise spots desired. Some devices use active matrix OLED (AMOLED), which adds a TFT layer for more control over the screen. OLEDs and AMOLEDs don't use backlights at all, which means: they *can* display true black, they're lighter, and they use less electricity than LCDs.

 EXAM TIP OLED screens use an organic compound exposed to electrical current for lighting; they don't have a traditional backlight.

Cameras

Many mobile devices have distinct front-facing and rear-facing cameras. These cameras enable chatting with Grandma over Facetime, tearful YouTube confessionals, and Instagram selfies! Devices with a camera can transmit video over cellular and IP-based networks (such as the Internet).

The most recent round of camera upgrades on mobile devices, particularly on smartphones, rival and sometimes beat dedicated point-and-shoot cameras (see Figure 24-11).

Figure 24-11
Author's camera
app on his
iPhone XS

Modern smartphone camera features include high dynamic range (HDR), light compensation, and other functions that enable the user to finely tune a photo or video. Additionally, these cameras offer a variety of options when taking photos and video; some cameras enable you to take "bursts" of shots (like ten in a single second) to make sure you capture faster-moving objects and action shots, as well as slow-motion video. When coupled with the multitude of apps available for mobile devices, you can edit photos and videos on-the-fly, adding light-filter effects, cleaning up shots, and even adding special effects.

Microphones

Almost all mobile devices incorporate at least one microphone. Smartphones certainly wouldn't be of much value without a microphone, and you wouldn't be very effective at communicating over Skype or FaceTime without them. Additionally, many people use mobile devices to dictate speech or record other sounds, so microphones serve many purposes on mobile devices.

As with the portable devices discussed in the previous chapter, mobile devices commonly have more than one microphone to enable noise-cancelling routines to work their magic. In contrast to those more traditional portables, you may need to take more care to avoid blocking any of the microphones on a mobile device.

Digitizers

When electrical engineers talk about a digitizer, they refer to a component that transforms analog signals into digital ones; that is to say, it digitizes them. That's not what we techs talk about when discussing digitizers on mobile devices. A *digitizer* refers to the component that provides the "touch" part of a touchscreen. When your finger contacts a touchscreen, the digitizer's fine grid of sensors under the glass detects your finger and signals the OS its location on the grid. As with modern trackpads, you can use one or more fingers to interact with most touchscreens.

EXAM TIP The CompTIA A+ 1001 exam objectives mention touchscreen configuration as something you do on a laptop or mobile device. While this might be a thing on laptops like the Microsoft Surface, it doesn't really apply to mobile devices at all.

Global Positioning System

One major feature of mobile devices is the ability to track the device's location through GPS, cellular, or Wi-Fi connections. Users rely on *location services* to conveniently find things near them, such as stores and restaurants, or to determine when their Uber driver will show up. This section will discuss some of what a mobile device such as a smartphone can do with GPS capability, followed by a look at standalone GPS devices, and privacy concerns associated with location tracking.

A great example of how smartphones can use GPS is the traffic and navigation app *Waze* (see Figure 24-12). Waze not only navigates, but its crowd-sourced data collection provides you with amazing real-time knowledge of the road ahead.

Another cool use of GPS is finding your phone when it's missing. The iPhone offers the Find My iPhone app (see Figure 24-13), for example. This feature is part of the iCloud service that comes free with any iOS device.

Standalone GPS Devices   Beyond these uses of GPS technology within smartphones, many purpose-built GPS devices exist. The one you're most likely familiar with is the common GPS-enabled navigational aids that attach to the dash or windshield of

Figure 24-12

Waze in action

an automobile. With just a little imagination, you can probably visualize variations on this theme for any other vehicle you need to navigate that didn't come GPS-equipped, such as a boat, airplane, or bicycle. You can also buy hand-held GPS devices for navigation away from a vehicle—and you'll also find customized versions of these designed for SCUBA diving, hiking, hunting, and so on.

While GPS-enabled smartphones suffice for day-to-day navigation in tame environments, these other types of GPS can have a mix of features that better suit them to their niche, such as preloaded special-purpose maps, other sensors or functions useful for the intended task, waterproofing, impact resistance, route memory, bookmarking, stored locations, low power use, simple replaceable batteries, and so on.

Figure 24-13
Find My
iPhone app

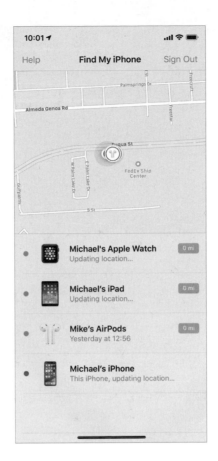

Location Tracking and Privacy Tracking your location is generally a good thing . . . when you want to be tracked. By default, mobile OSs track and in many cases record your location for an extended amount of time. This is called *geotracking*, and not everyone likes it. If you don't like this feature, turn it off. Figure 24-14 shows turning off Location on an Android phone.

 EXAM TIP Because mobile devices tap into the Internet or cellular phone networks, the devices have identifying numbers such as a MAC address. The cell phone companies and government agencies can use the ID or MAC address to pinpoint where you are at any given time. *Geotracking* has a lot of room for abuse of power.

Figure 24-14
Turning off
Location

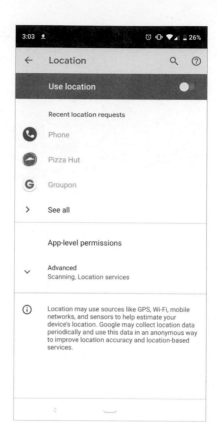

1002

Mobile Operating Systems

Most mobile devices run either Apple iOS or Google Android. This section discusses their development and implementation models, as well as some of their major features, including how their app stores work.

Development Models

Before we look at each mobile operating system in detail, let's step back to consider the big picture. The different underlying philosophies inspiring these operating systems—and guiding the companies that make them—help us understand why they do something one way instead of another. We'll start with a look at closed source and open source as development models. You may have heard these terms regarding how software is released and licensed (if not, Chapter 27, "Securing Computers," will discuss how these terms apply to licensing), but they also provide an interesting framework for looking at how products are developed and released. Then we'll discuss how these models apply to operating systems.

Closed Source

When it comes to development models, it may help to think of *closed source* as another way to refer to the traditional practice of making and selling a product without telling anyone how you made it. The traditional model makes intuitive sense, at least in our culture; how your product is made is a trade secret—something that gives you a competitive edge—and sharing it could inspire competitors to use your design, or potential customers to make it themselves.

Vendor-Specific and Proprietary We sometimes apply the terms *proprietary* or *vendor-specific* to a closed-source product or technology, most often when we're trying to highlight something that doesn't use common, open standards. The terms are related to closed source, but don't confuse them; they aren't interchangeable. These labels often imply that the product may not play nice (or be interoperable) with other products, may have connectors and cables that are hard to find or expensive, may not be friendly to users who want to tinker with or modify it, may be harder to repair, and may pose a host of other problems.

The concept behind and use of these terms is sometimes slippery. As you'll see later in the chapter, a device maker may use a common standard such as USB 3.0, but design its own connector. Even though the device maker is technically using part of the open USB 3.0 standard, we'll still call the device's ports and cables proprietary.

Open Source

In this broader sense, you can think of a product as *open source* if its maker releases the instructions for making it—it doesn't have to be software (though that's usually the context). When a company commits to open sourcing one or more products, it has to operate differently than companies using a closed-source model. Secrecy, for example, is necessarily a smaller part of its business; knowing that anyone could make its products, the company has to focus on other factors (such as price, service, support, convenience, quality, innovation, etc.) to stay competitive.

Just because a company releases these instructions to the public doesn't mean anyone else gets to own them. Much as artists and authors set terms that specify whether the rest of us can legally copy or modify their work, the owners or authors of the instructions for making a product will specify terms for how others are allowed to use them. Sometimes the owners or authors may just say they're releasing the instructions for personal use or educational purposes—you can study what they've done and make your own product, but you can't start selling copies. When it comes to open-source software, these terms commonly dictate whether companies who modify the software are obliged to publish their changes, and whether they're allowed to profit from how they use it.

Development Models and the Mobile OS

The development model is one of many choices that reflect underlying company philosophy and goals. A company that makes an open-source mobile operating system like Google Android has little control over how the OS will be used and who can modify it. A company that makes a closed-source operating system like Microsoft Windows but licenses the OS to device makers has more control—the company knows the OS won't be modified and can be picky about which devices to license it for. A company making a closed-source OS like Apple iOS for its own devices can tailor-fit the software to the hardware it will run on. A company that builds an OS others can use and modify as they see fit and a company that builds an OS hand-crafted exclusively for its own hardware obviously have very different underlying philosophies and goals.

The big thing to keep in mind with an open-source operating system like Android is that companies building devices that use the OS don't have to share the OS developer's underlying philosophy—they can have wildly varying goals and development models of their own. If the operating system's license allows it, each of the device makers could modify the OS before installing it on their own device—and never release those modifications. The modifications might just enable special hardware to work, but they could also install apps you don't want and can't remove, cause third-party apps coded without knowledge of the modifications to malfunction, or collect information about how you use the device.

To bring this all together, the point is that a manufacturer can put an open-source operating system on an otherwise closed-source device—don't assume a device is itself open source just because the mobile OS it uses is. In fact, vanishingly few of the devices with an open-source OS are best seen as open-source products.

Think back to the earlier discussion of an open-source development process and apply it to a smartphone. The most extreme interpretation of an open-source smartphone is that the maker has released all of the instructions and code someone else would need to manufacture an identical smartphone and all of the components inside it. A more likely (but still exceptional) scenario is that all of the software on the device when it leaves the factory is open sourced, including the operating system, drivers, and the firmware powering its components.

Apple iOS

Apple's closed-source mobile operating system, *iOS* (see Figure 24-15), runs on the iPhone and iPad. (The Apple iWatch runs a different OS, called watchOS. It is also closed source.) The Apple model of development is very involved: Apple tightly controls the development of the hardware, OS, developer tools, and app deployment platform. Apple's disciplined development model is visible in its strict development policies and controls for third-party developers, and this control contributes to the high level of security in iOS.

iOS apps are almost exclusively purchased, installed, and updated through Apple's *App Store*. An exception is providers of line-of-business apps specific to a particular organization. These internal development groups reside within an organization and can develop iOS apps, but deploy them only to devices that are under the organization's

Figure 24-15
iOS 12

control, skipping the public App Store. They still have to undergo a type of Apple partnering and enterprise licensing approval process.

Google Android

For simplicity, think of Android and iOS as opposites. *Android* (see Figure 24-16) is an open-source platform, based on yet another open platform, Linux, and is owned by Google. Because Android is open source, device manufacturers can (and do!) alter or customize it as they see fit; there are differences among the implementations from various vendors. Google writes the core Android code and occasionally releases new versions (naming each major update after a dessert or candy of some sort), at which point vendors customize it to add unique hardware features or provide a branded look and feel.

Android apps are available to purchase and download through various app stores, such as *Google Play* and the Amazon Appstore. Android app stores tend to be fairly open in contrast to the high standards and tight control Apple applies to its third-party app developers, and Android makes it easier to install arbitrary applications downloaded from a Web site.

Figure 24-16
Android 8 (Oreo)

NOTE Android-based devices may be more open than iOS ones on average, but it isn't a given. How open or closed an individual Android device is will depend greatly on how its manufacturer has modified the OS.

Mobile OS Features

Mobile operating systems come in a variety of flavors and sometimes have different features as well as different interfaces. But they also have a great deal in common, because consumers expect them to perform most of the tasks they are used to seeing in other mobile devices, regardless of operating system. Regardless of whether you are using an iPhone, an Android phone, or a smart watch, you still expect to be able to send texts, check your e-mail, and make video calls. Because of this, OS differences boil down to hardware and app support, look and feel, and philosophical differences that manifest in how the OS goes about a common task. We'll take a quick look at some of the features common to all mobile operating systems and point out differences along the way.

User Interfaces

All mobile OSs have a *graphical user interface* (*GUI*), meaning you interact with them by accessing icons on the screen. Current models do not offer any command-line interface. Each OS usually has either a major button or a row of icons that enables the user to navigate to the most prominent features of the device. They also all support touch *gestures*, such as *swiping* to navigate between screens or *pinching* to zoom in or out. Most mobile OSs have some type of menu system that enables the user to find different apps and data.

iOS offers some customization of the user interface. You can group apps together into folders, for example, and reposition most apps for your convenience. The iOS look and feel, however, will remain consistent.

Android offers a very different GUI experience by employing programs called *launchers* that enable users to customize their Android device extensively. Many companies make launchers, and different manufacturers ship devices preloaded with launchers they make or prefer. Samsung devices use the TouchWiz launcher, for example. I use the Nova launcher on my Android phone. The launcher enables you to change nearly every aspect of the GUI, including icon size, animations, gestures, and more.

Most mobile devices include an *accelerometer* and a *gyroscope*, one to measure movement in space and the other to maintain proper orientation of up and down. These extend the user interface to include how you move the device itself; a common use is changing the *screen orientation* when you rotate a device from vertical to horizontal, for example, to enhance watching videos on YouTube. See "Adding Apps," later in this chapter, for more uses of these technologies.

Wi-Fi Calling

While every mobile device that calls itself a phone must have support for cellular wireless, another feature that many mobile devices include is *Wi-Fi calling*, the capability to make regular phone calls over Wi-Fi networks. Wi-Fi calling is very useful if you often find yourself in a place with poor cellular coverage but good Wi-Fi. To use Wi-Fi calling, first both your phone and carrier need to support it, then you need to enable it in your phone settings (see Figure 24-17). Once Wi-Fi calling is enabled, the phone will use any Wi-Fi network it's connected to (assuming the performance is acceptable) for all phone calls.

Virtual Assistants

"Hey, Siri!"

"Yes, Mike?"

"What's the weather like today?"

"Always sunny where you are, Mike."

Okay, maybe they're not quite that cool, but the *virtual assistants* on the latest smartphones and tablets enable quick, vocal interaction to accomplish common goals. For example, one only has to ask Siri (Apple's virtual assistant) how to find the nearest restaurant or tourist attraction, and she (Siri's voice is female by default) will respond with the information sought. Virtual assistants can also be useful in performing Internet searches and, in some cases, even activating and using certain apps on the mobile device. This helps people who may have certain disabilities that may prevent them from tapping or typing on the device, by enabling them to use voice commands.

Figure 24-17
Option to enable
Wi-Fi calling on
an iPhone XS

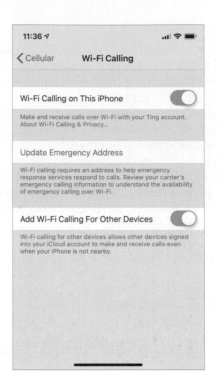

A virtual assistant is also useful if you must use your smartphone while driving (although *anything* that diverts your attention from the road is discouraged for safety reasons). You can speak to the smartphone's virtual assistant to place a call or get directions while driving, especially if the smartphone is paired with the car's Bluetooth system. The Windows 10 equivalent to Siri is called Cortana, and essentially serves the same functions and provides the same services and features. Google's virtual assistant, Google Assistant, is also available for iOS and any of Google's many platforms like Google Home and Android TV. In addition to the big three's virtual assistants, there are also apps you can download that provide other virtual assistant services, depending upon your platform.

Software Development Kits

Most mobile operating systems come with some sort of *software development kit* (*SDK*) or application development kit that you can use to create custom apps or add features to existing apps on the device. Figure 24-18 shows the development (programming) environment for the iOS SDK, *Xcode*, with the code for an iOS app open in the background window, and the same app code running in the iPhone 6 simulator on top.

Each mobile OS poses its own challenge to app developers. Apple's rigid development model makes it such that your app must pass a rigorous testing program before it is allowed into the App Store. Microsoft's development model, while not typically as rigid, is similar in nature. Google, on the other hand, allows anyone to create Android apps and distribute them to the masses without much interference.

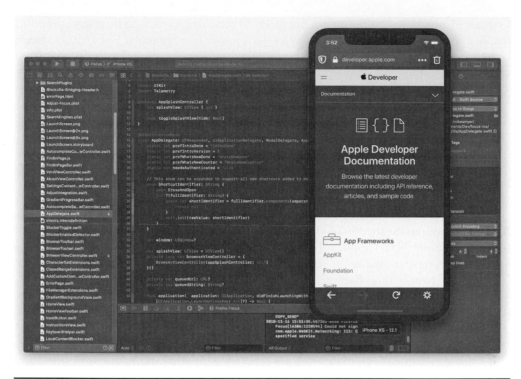

Figure 24-18   Xcode running an app written with the iOS SDK

Emergency Capabilities

One feature almost all currently marketed smartphones have built in is the *emergency notification* feature that enables them to receive broadcasts from national emergency broadcast systems, such as the Emergency Alert System (EAS) in the United States. This can be a very useful feature during severe weather, enabling you to receive warning text messages. In the event someone reports a child missing in your immediate area, it enables you to get AMBER Alerts. Many of these emergency broadcast system alerts also force your phone to emit a very loud sound or vibrate incessantly in order to get your attention.

EXAM TIP   A software development kit (SDK) is used to write apps. Don't confuse it with the *Android application package* (APK), which is a package file containing the assets compiled from an Android app's code, then used to install the app on an Android device.

While modern smartphones can place 911 calls effectively, the old 911 system relied on the Public Switched Telephone Network (PSTN) to trace a call and determine its location, in order to dispatch emergency responders to the correct address quickly. This was problematic with mobile devices, so legislation was passed (the Wireless

Communications and Public Safety Act of 1999) requiring carriers to be able to pinpoint the location of a mobile device, such as a smartphone. The *Enhanced 911* (*E911*) system uses GPS and cellular networks to triangulate the location of a phone by its distance from cell towers, its transmission delay time, and other factors.

Mobile Payment Service

As smartphones and other mobile devices have become so much more commonplace in our daily lives, we've become very reliant on them to store our personal and sensitive information such as passwords, credit card numbers, financial documents, receipts, and more. Over time, smartphone manufacturers, as well as merchants, realized that the next logical step was to enable you to pay for goods and services simply by scanning your smartphone or using an app.

The app connects to your bank information and automatically transfers the funds from your bank to the merchant. This feature is called *mobile payment service*. Near Field Communication (NFC) applications refine the process further: simply place your device on or near the special pad at the register in order to authorize payment to the merchant. (See "NFC," later in this chapter, for the scoop on these tiny networks.)

Additionally, smartphone manufacturers produce their own payment systems. The Apple payment system, called *Apple Pay*, was first implemented with the iPhone 6, and support has been integrated into the Apple Watch. Apple Pay supports major credit card payment terminals and point-of-sale systems, including those fielded by Visa, MasterCard, and American Express. Apple Pay can use contactless payment terminals with NFC and supports in-app payments for online purchases.

Airplane Mode

Airplane mode is simply a switch (either an actual hardware switch located on the mobile device or a software switch that can be located in the device's configuration settings) that turns off all cellular and wireless services, including Bluetooth (see Figure 24-19). The aptly named mode disables these communications so passengers can comply with restrictions protecting aircraft instruments from interference, though you can also use it as a shortcut for turning off communication functions.

Radio Firmware

Mobile devices use a wide variety of radio technologies to access the Internet, e-mail, and corporate infrastructures. Generally, mobile devices have two types of radios: 802.11 and Bluetooth. If the device can make calls, it also has some form of cellular radio.

PRL, PRI, and Baseband Updates   As mobile devices travel, they frequently have to pass through areas that don't have strong signals, or into areas that the carrier does not service. When a mobile device connects to different carriers' networks, we say it is *roaming*; roaming may result in additional service charges, depending upon the carriers involved.

Your phone's firmware will receive occasional automatic updates to its *Preferred Roaming List* (*PRL*) from the carrier; the PRL is a priority-ordered list of the other carrier networks and frequencies it should search for when it can't locate its home

Figure 24-19
Airplane mode
enabled on
iOS 12

carrier's network. Updates to this list are sent via your phone's cellular connection (called baseband updates, or over-the-air updates) or, in some cases, through firmware updates during normal operating system and firmware upgrades via synchronization.

CDMA devices may also receive *product release instruction* (*PRI*) updates, which modify a host of complex device settings. Don't worry about specifics, here—these settings can pertain to the intricacies of many functions such as GPS, cellular connectivity, and messaging—but instead focus on the fact that carriers use these product release instructions to ready the device for deployment on their networks, enable the network to route calls or messages to the device, and more. As such, PRI updates may be needed if the network is evolving during the lifetime of a device, the device needs to be moved to a new network, or the device has a new owner.

 EXAM TIP PRL and PRI updates are handled automatically during firmware/ OS updates. They are only for CDMA networks. No one but the nerdiest of nerds will ever see these updates.

IMEI, ICCID, and IMSI   There are three particular identifiers you will need to understand both for the exam and for real-life management of mobile devices. The *International Mobile Equipment Identity* (*IMEI*) number is a 15-digit number used to uniquely identify a mobile device. IMEI numbers are unique to devices using the *Global System for Mobile Communications* (*GSM*) family of technologies, including its present-day descendants: 4G LTE and LTE-Advanced. You can typically find this number printed inside the battery compartment of the mobile device, but you may not need to take the device apart: some operating systems enable you to view it inside the device configuration settings (see Figure 24-20).

Figure 24-20
IMEI settings
on an Android
phone

The IMEI number can be used to identify a specific device and even to block that device from accessing the carrier's network. If the device is lost or stolen, the user can notify her carrier, and the carrier can make sure the device can't be used on the network.

NOTE   Always write down your IMEI number when you get a new phone, as it can prove you are the actual owner if it ever is stolen or lost.

The ICCID number, which stands for Integrated Circuit Card Identifier, uniquely identifies a subscriber identity module (SIM). The SIM contains information unique to the subscriber (the owner of the phone), and is used to authenticate the subscriber to the network. SIMs can be moved from phone to phone, usually with no problems.

The third number is the *International Mobile Subscriber Identity* (*IMSI*) number. It is also included on the SIM, but represents the actual user associated with the SIM. This number is not normally accessible from the phone, but is usually available from the carrier, to ensure that stolen phones are not misused. The IMSI number can also be used to unlock a phone.

You might want to record these numbers for each managed device in the enterprise, whether for inventory purposes or so that you have them handy when you work with your *mobile device management* (*MDM*) software (look for more about managing many mobile devices with MDM software throughout Chapter 25). The MDM typically collects these identifiers along with other device information (such as the telephone number or MAC address) during the provisioning process and stores them in the mobile device inventory for you. Figure 24-21 shows how IMEI and ICCID numbers are listed for a newer Android device in the device settings.

Figure 24-21
IMEI and ICCID numbers

EXAM TIP Remember the differences between the IMEI and IMSI numbers for the CompTIA A+ 1001 exam. The IMEI number represents the device. The IMSI number is tied to the user's account with the carrier, and is included with the SIM.

VPN

As you'll recall from earlier chapters, VPNs establish secure connections between a remote client and the corporate infrastructure, or between two different sites, such as a branch office and the corporate office. VPNs are typically implemented using tunneling methods through an unsecure network, such as the Internet. In a client VPN setup, the host has client VPN software specially configured to match the corporate VPN server or concentrator configuration. This configuration includes encryption method and strength, as well as authentication methods.

A site-to-site VPN scenario uses VPN devices on both ends of the connection, configured to communicate only with each other, while the hosts on both ends use their respective VPN concentrators as a gateway. This arrangement is usually transparent to the users at both sites; hosts at the other site appear as if they are directly connected to the user's network.

VPNs can use a variety of technologies and protocols. The most popular ways to create a VPN are to use either a combination of the Layer 2 Tunneling Protocol (L2TP) and IPsec (see Figure 24-22), or Secure Sockets Layer (SSL)/Transport Layer Security (TLS). When using the L2TP/IPsec method, UDP port 1701 is used and must be opened on packet-filtering devices. In this form of VPN, users connect to the corporate network and can use all of their typical applications, such as their e-mail client, and can map shares and drives as they would if they were actually connected onsite to the corporate infrastructure.

An SSL/TLS-based VPN, on the other hand, uses the standard SSL/TLS port, TCP 443, and is typically used through a client's Web browser. SSL/TLS-based VPNs don't normally require any special software or configuration on the client itself, but they don't give the client the same direct access to resources on the corporate network. As such, users may have to access these network resources through the client browser via an access portal.

Configuring a Mobile Device

Mobile devices require some setup and configuration to function seamlessly in your life, though the industry is constantly refining and simplifying this process. Modern devices typically come preconfigured with everything but your user account and network credentials. Just because you don't have to do much to get up and running anymore doesn't mean you're out of the woods, though. You may well need to configure corporate e-mail accounts, device add-ons, apps, synchronization settings, and other advanced features.

You can add capabilities by enhancing hardware and installing productivity apps. You also need to set up network connectivity, add Bluetooth devices, configure e-mail account(s), and enable the devices to synchronize with a computer. Plus you have a lot of add-on options; let's take a look.

Figure 24-22
Configuring
a VPN

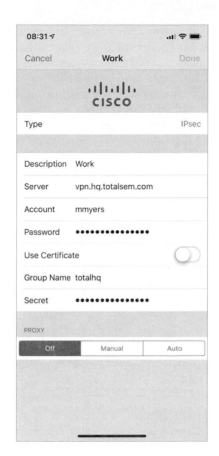

Enhancing Hardware

A mobile device is a computer, just like your desktop or laptop, with the same basic components doing the same basic things. The construction centers on a primary circuit board, the motherboard, onto which every other component is attached. The biggest of these components is often the *system on a chip* (*SoC*), a wonder of miniaturization combining a CPU, GPU, and sundry other support logic onto a single silicon die, saving a lot of space and power in the process. An interesting aside about the CPUs used in these devices is that they are rarely Intel x86 based; instead, you are much more likely to run across an ARM architecture chip when perusing the spec sheets of your new tablet. The iPad uses an Apple-designed ARM A-series chip, for example, and the ASUS Transformer features an NVIDIA-designed Tegra ARM SoC.

Mobile devices use storage, though you'll never see one using a traditional magnetic *hard disk drive* (*HDD*) with spinning platters. Mobile devices use flash media such as a *solid-state drive* (*SSD*) or microSD card because they are smaller, use less power, and are much, much faster than spinning HDDs. Plus they're cooler, just like you.

Mobile devices differ from their larger brethren in two very significant areas of importance to techs. First, none of them offer any user-replaceable parts. If something breaks, you send the device back to the manufacturer, visit a local manufacturer-supported retail outlet such as the Apple Store, or take it to a specialized repair shop. Second, you can't upgrade mobile devices at all. Even a laptop enables you to upgrade RAM or a mass storage drive, for example, but the mobile device you buy is exactly what you get. You want something better? Buy a new one.

That said, every mobile device enables you to attach some kind of peripheral or external storage device. But every device offers different expansion capabilities, so it's hard to generalize about them. The closest you can get is the audio jack—if you ignore e-readers and wearable devices. Most smartphones and tablets have a single 3.5-mm audio jack for plugging in earbuds or speakers (see Figure 24-23).

Figure 24-23
Earbuds
plugged into a
smartphone

Note this is quickly changing as Apple dropped the jack as of the iPhone 7, and many premium Android devices have started leaving the port off as well. Current iPhones and most iPads use the Lightning jack for physical external connections.

Apple Expansion Options

Apple devices offer the least expansion capability of all mobile devices, so even though they dominate the U.S. marketplace, there's not much to say about them. Most of the expansion on Apple devices is limited to proprietary cables and devices. The iPhone and iPad have historically used a single proprietary port for charging the device and connecting to the few external devices available. Figure 24-24 shows the typical use for the port: connecting to a USB AC adapter to charge.

Figure 24-24
USB charger
connected to
proprietary port

While the vast majority of Apple's iOS devices stick with the proprietary Lighting connector, Apple has switched to USB Type-C with current iPad Pros. Who knows what this means for the iPhone line, but it is nice to see Apple expanding their use of the industry standard. We'll return to USB Type-C along with a number of other connectors later in the chapter.

iPhones and iPads enable you to mirror the screen to a multimedia device such as a projector. This enables seamless presentations, for example, through the excellent Apple Keynote program (see Figure 24-25). The multimedia connection requires another adapter (see Figure 24-26).

Figure 24-25
Apple Keynote on an iPad and a projector

Figure 24-26
Apple Digital AV Adapter

Android Expansion Options

Devices that use Google Android come with a variety of connections and expansion capabilities. Many offer microSD slots for adding storage in the form of these tiny flash memory cards (see Figure 24-27).

Figure 24-27
microSD card
and slot

While most Android devices use standard USB Type-C or micro-USB ports for charging and expansion, you may occasionally see one with a full-sized or mini-USB port. Some older Android devices have a proprietary connector (usually still based on USB technology) for this purpose, but almost all of these are tablets. Figure 24-28 shows a proprietary connector for power.

Figure 24-28
ASUS proprietary
power connector

Finally, many tablets (but rarely smartphones) sport a connector for attaching the device to an external monitor, such as a big screen or projector. Figure 24-29 shows a Micro-HDMI port and connector.

Figure 24-29
Micro-HDMI port
and connector

Bluetooth

The last way that mobile devices expand their physical capabilities is wirelessly, most often using the Bluetooth standard (if you need a refresher on Bluetooth, refer back to

Chapter 20, "Wireless Networking"). Traditionally, extending a mobile device with Bluetooth has meant adding a headset, mouse (though not with Apple iOS products), keyboard, or speaker. Figure 24-30 shows a diminutive Apple keyboard for the iPad and the iPad resting in a stand to make typing a little easier than using the virtual keyboard. With Bluetooth-enabled wearable devices growing in popularity, it can be tricky to decide how self-sufficient one of these must be before it stops counting as a mobile enhancement and enters the realm of full-fledged mobile device.

Figure 24-30
Keyboard
associated
with iPad

 NOTE See the "Bluetooth" section toward the end of this chapter for the steps to set up a tablet with a Bluetooth keyboard.

Installing and Configuring Apps

Mobile devices come from the manufacturer with a certain number of vital apps installed for accessing e-mail, surfing the Web, taking notes, making entries in a calendar, and so on. Almost all mobile devices offer multimedia apps to enable you to listen to music, take pictures, watch YouTube videos, and view photos. You'll find instant messaging tools and, in the case of smartphones, telephone capabilities.

Beyond these essentials, you'll install most other apps through an app store. As you read about the app ecosystem for each mobile OS, consider how well the details of each ecosystem mesh with the development models discussed earlier in the chapter. Even though the rules of each app ecosystem usually reflect this development model, don't assume the apps on offer will follow suit—you'll find plenty of closed-source apps available on Android and open-source apps available for iOS.

iOS Apps

Apple iPhone and the iPad use the iOS operating system. Apple exerts more control over the user experience than any other manufacturer by insisting all iOS app developers follow strict guidelines.

Apple maintains strict control over what apps can be installed onto iOS devices, meaning that if you want to get an app for your iPhone or iPad, you can only get it from the Apple App Store (see Figure 24-31). Apple must approve any app before it goes into the App Store, and Apple reserves the right to refuse to distribute any app that fails to measure up.

Figure 24-31

App Store

To add an app, select the App Store icon from the home screen. You can explore featured apps in the Today tab or peruse by category. You can check out the popular games, or simply search for what you want (see Figure 24-32).

The first time you try to purchase an app through the App Store, you'll be prompted to set up an account. You can use an account that you created previously through the Apple iTunes music and video store or create a new Apple ID account. You can create a new Apple ID account with a few quick steps (see Figure 24-33) and a valid credit card.

Figure 24-32
Searching for
Monument
Valley 2

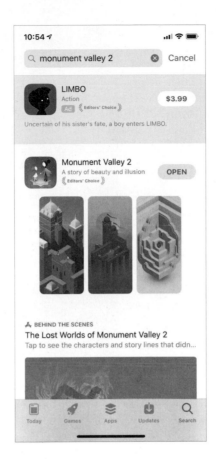

Another iCloud feature, the iCloud Key Chain, builds on the Key Chain feature in macOS to synchronize user information, passwords, payment information, and other credentials with all of your Apple devices. (See "Synchronization," a little later in the chapter.) Key Chain can seamlessly store many non-Apple credentials as well, such as logins for Facebook, Amazon, and other providers, and use them to auto-complete repetitive forms in both device apps and on Web sites. The real benefit is that you can authorize Apple to save this sensitive information, instead of authorizing each individual app or site to keep a copy.

Android Apps

Google Android powers many smartphones and a solid portion of tablets. Unlike Apple iOS, Google gives core Android away, enabling manufacturers to differentiate their Android devices from those of other manufacturers. A Samsung tablet, in other words, uses a version of Android that differs somewhat from the Android an ASUS tablet uses.

Figure 24-33
Creating an
Apple ID for
iCloud and App
Store purchases

Likewise, OnePlus developed a custom interface called OxygenOS to change the look and feel of Android on its devices.

Because of these modifications, few Android users ever use "stock" or unmodified Android. Despite the shared core OS, Android users familiar with devices from one manufacturer may get tripped up by the different interface on Android devices from a different maker. These differences make it important to combine knowledge of the Android version a smartphone or tablet runs with knowledge about the manufacturer and its modifications to Android. The manufacturer will typically assign a version number to each release of its modifications.

Android devices can usually get apps from more than one source. The most common is Android's default app store, Google Play (which offers well over 2 million apps)—but some manufacturers (such as Amazon, for its line of Fire devices) modify Android to change this.

Many manufacturers offer a store with apps developed or customized to work with their devices. These *vendor-specific* stores enable you to get apps that should work well with your Android smartphone or tablet.

You can also go to a third-party app store or market for apps developed "for Android" that probably will work with your device, but there's no guarantee that they'll work on all Android devices. This Wild West approach to apps makes the Android smartphone or tablet experience vastly different from the experience on iOS.

Network Connectivity

Mobile devices connect to the outside world through the cellular networks or through various 802.11 Wi-Fi standards. You learned specifics about the standards in Chapter 20, so I won't rehash them here. This section looks at standard configuration issues from the perspective of a mobile device.

When you want to connect to a Wi-Fi network, you need to enable Wi-Fi on your device and then actively connect to a network. If the network is properly configured with WPA, WPA2, or WPA3 encryption, then you also need to have the logon information to access the network. The most common way to connect is through the Settings app (see Figure 24-34).

Figure 24-34
Selecting the Settings icon

The Settings app enables you to do the vast majority of configuration necessary to a mobile device. To join a network, for example, tap the Wi-Fi (or Networks) option to see available networks (see Figure 24-35). Simply select the network you want to join and type in the passphrase or passcode. Give the mobile device a moment to get IP and DNS information from the DHCP server, and you're on the network.

Figure 24-35
Browsing
available
networks

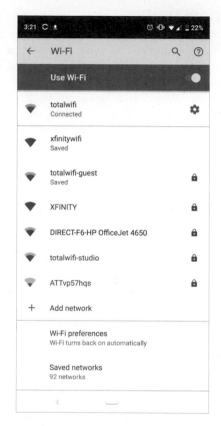

After you connect to a network successfully, all mobile devices store that network access information automatically, creating a *profile* for the network based on its SSID. This works just like with any other device that connects to a Wi-Fi network. If the SSID of a network changes after you've connected to that network, your mobile device will fail to connect to the rechristened network. You need to delete the profile and reconnect. Delete the profile through the Settings app by choosing the Wi-Fi network and selecting *Forget this network*.

 EXAM TIP You can use the Settings app to turn off Wi-Fi or to go into airplane mode to stop the device from sending any signals out.

Data

Many mobile devices can use the cellular data services discussed in Chapter 20 to access the Internet. This way you can use your smartphone, tablet, or other mobile devices to get e-mail or browse the Web pretty much anywhere.

By default, mobile devices that use cellular networks for Internet connectivity use *data roaming*, meaning they'll jump from cell tower to cell tower and from your provider to another provider without obvious notice. This is no big deal when you travel within your own country where competing providers have inexpensive roaming agreements.

Watch out for data roaming outside your country! If you travel to another country, your mobile device will happily and seamlessly connect via another cell provider if one is available. This can lead to some shockingly huge bills from your cell phone company when you get back from that cruise or international trip. If you're going outside your cell provider's coverage area, get a plan that specifics that you're traveling. It'll still be more expensive than your regular plan, but not nearly as crazy as an accidental roaming charge.

If you don't need to connect when out of country, turn data roaming off. You'll find the feature in the Settings app, as you might expect. You can also turn off cellular data entirely or only turn off cellular services selectively if your device can do more than one type. You would want to turn off cellular data, for example, if you don't have an unlimited data plan and are getting near your limits. There are also some security reasons to disable cellular connections while traveling, which we'll explore further in Chapter 25.

 EXAM TIP The CompTIA A I 1001 objectives include Google/Inbox as a type of commercial e-mail program. By the time you're reading this, though, Google has merged *Inbox by Gmail* into Gmail. Expect an exam question to include Google/Inbox as a correct answer.

E-mail

Every mobile device uses an e-mail service set up specifically from the mobile OS developer. Plus, you can configure devices to send and receive standard e-mail as well. Let's look at the integrated options first.

iOS, Android, and Windows Phone devices offer e-mail services from Apple, Google, and Microsoft, respectively. iOS devices integrate perfectly with iCloud, Apple's one-stop shop for e-mail, messaging, and online storage. Android devices assume a Gmail account, so they feature a Gmail (or Inbox by Gmail) option front and center. Windows devices integrate Exchange Online e-mail options. The 1001 exam describes these options with a whale of a phrase: *integrated commercial provider email configuration*. Yeah.

Aside from the integrated e-mail options, mobile devices enable you to set up standard corporate and ISP e-mail configurations as well. The process is similar to that of setting up e-mail accounts that you learned about in Chapter 21. Apple devices go through the Settings app, then the Passwords & Accounts (or Mail, Contacts, Calendars before iOS 12) option (see Figure 24-36). Tap the Add Account option to bring up the default e-mail options (see Figure 24-37). If you want to connect to a Microsoft Exchange Server–based e-mail account, tap the appropriate option here and type in your e-mail address, domain, user name, password, and description.

Figure 24-36
Passwords &
Accounts screen
on iPhone

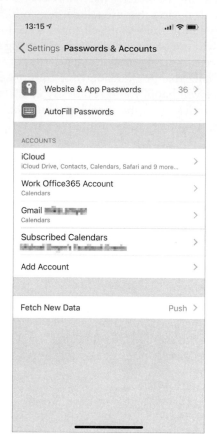

Neither POP3 nor IMAP4 is one of Apple's suggested options, so if you want to set up an account of either type, you'll need to tap the Other option on the initial Add Account screen. Eventually you'll get prompted to choose POP3 or IMAP and type in addresses for the sending (SMTP) and receiving servers.

Android-based devices assume you'll have a Gmail account as your primary account, so you'll find Gmail's distinctive app icon on the home screen (see Figure 24-38). This also can talk to other, non-Gmail e-mail services for setting up Exchange, POP3, or IMAP4 accounts; you configure it the same way as you would a desktop e-mail application, including putting in the port number and security type, such as SSL or TLS if the server lacks autoconfigure (see Figure 24-39).

Figure 24-37
Default e-mail
types on iPhone

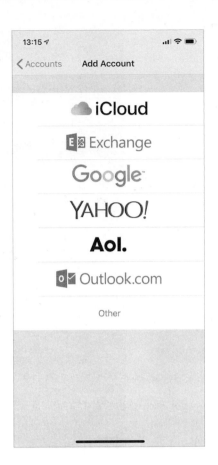

NOTE The latest versions of Android simply query the e-mail server to configure port numbers and security types automatically, just like modern desktop-based e-mail clients. Even though current devices automate this process, the CompTIA A+ 1001 objectives include port numbers, so you need to know them.

The 1001 exam will hit you pretty hard on e-mail settings, specifically on TCP port numbers for the various e-mail protocols. We've covered these in earlier chapters, but here's a quick cheat sheet and a few alternative numbers for real-world applications:

- POP3 uses TCP port 110.
- IMAP4 uses TCP port 143.
- SMTP uses TCP port 25.

Figure 24-38
Gmail app

Many servers block these default ports; plus, when you move to more secure versions of the protocols, you need to use other port numbers. I have no clue whether CompTIA will quiz on the secure ports for POP3, IMAP4, and SMTP, but here they are:

- Secure POP3 uses TCP port 995.
- Secure IMAP4 uses TCP port 993.
- Secure SMTP uses TCP port 465 or 587.

Finally, you may also have to configure other settings, such as *Secure/Multipurpose Internet Mail Extensions* (*S/MIME*) standard, used to configure digital signature settings for e-mail, and contacts from the corporate address book, depending on how the corporate e-mail server is set up.

Figure 24-39
Setting up a
secure IMAP
account

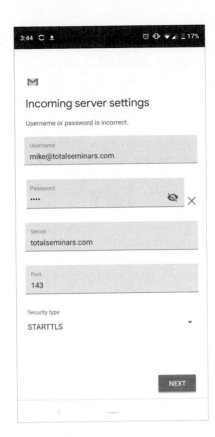

 EXAM TIP Be familiar with integrated commercial provider e-mail
configuration settings for Gmail (or Inbox by Gmail), Yahoo, Outlook.com,
and iCloud. Know the corporate and ISP e-mail configuration settings for
POP3, IMAP4, port and SSL settings, Exchange, and S/MIME.

Synchronization

From the first day mobile devices came into existence there was a problem: synchronizing
data. People don't want their contacts on their mobile devices to be different than the
contacts on their desktop—or online contacts. People don't want to edit e-mail on their
mobile device and then have to go online to make the same changes. People only want
one calendar. If you have a mobile device, you're going to want a method for all these different sets of data to synchronize so you only have one set of contacts, one e-mail inbox,
one calendar, and so forth.

To keep files and data up to date, smartphones and tablets can *synchronize*, or *sync*, with
cloud-based servers over the Internet or with local machines. These files and data include

personal documents, Internet bookmarks, calendar appointments, social media data, e-books, and even location data. Older devices, such as BlackBerry and Palm Pilot, had a specialized sync program you installed on your computer to sync contacts, calendars, and so on. Today's devices sync through the cloud or optionally use a dedicated program.

Various mobile devices sync differently, depending upon the device vendor and software required. iOS devices use Apple iCloud to sync iPhones, iPads, and Macs via the cloud. Android devices can use Google's many services to sync certain configuration settings, apps, photos, texts, and so on. In some cases individual apps will synchronize directly; for example, a podcast app might synchronize data such as subscribed shows. Older versions of iOS needed to sync to a laptop or desktop computer via Apple's iTunes application. While this is still fully supported, most users will just let iCloud handle everything in the background.

 EXAM TIP Synchronization enables mobile devices to keep up to date with a lot of essential information. You should know the types of data typically synced, including contacts, programs (apps), e-mail, pictures, music, videos, calendar information, bookmarks, documents, location data, social media data, e-books, and passwords. It's a lot. You can do this!

Synchronize to the Automobile

Automobile makers know you will talk on the phone while driving. While inherently dangerous—a good conversation can distract you from surroundings, including other 3000-pound death machines—everyone does it. Modern automobiles come equipped with voice communication systems, hands-free calling that uses your smartphone via Bluetooth (see Figure 24-40). *Synchronizing to the automobile* enables voice-activated contact calling, among other things, and often hooks up with a car's navigation system to help you get from point A to point B.

Figure 24-40
Calling via an iPhone using a car's built-in entertainment system

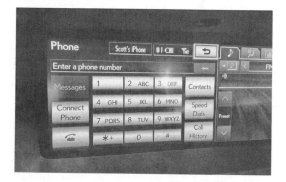

Exchange ActiveSync

Exchange ActiveSync (EAS) is a Microsoft protocol used to synchronize Microsoft Exchange e-mail, contacts, and calendars that has become widely used across a range of mobile OS platforms and hardware vendors, including Apple and Android devices.

It was originally developed as a synchronization protocol for Microsoft Exchange corporate users, but has evolved over time to include more device control and management features. EAS not only has the capability to set up and configure network connectivity and secure e-mail options for clients that connect to Microsoft Exchange corporate servers, but also has the capability to control a much wider range of functions. Some of these functions include the ability to set password policies, remotely wipe or lock a mobile device, and control some device settings.

Synchronization Methods

In the old days, mobile devices were synchronized to a desktop (uphill, both ways, in the snow!), using a specific type of synchronization software provided with the device. Also, the type of data was typically limited to contact information, but we liked it because it was all we had. Now, there are newfangled ways you can sync device contacts, media files, and even apps. You can also get updates and patches from the device manufacturer by syncing your device.

With faster cellular and Wi-Fi networking technologies, you can skip the desktop and sync even large amounts of data to the cloud. Each phone vendor has its own cloud technology that can tie to your user account and store personal data from your mobile device. Apple has iCloud, Microsoft has OneDrive, and Google has Google Drive, as do some of the individual manufacturers that make Android devices.

There are also independent cloud providers that enable you to store your personal data, and even share it with others. Dropbox is a prime example of this type of provider, although there are many others. Most cloud storage services require you to set up security measures to protect your data, such as requiring a user name and password for authentication. Some cloud providers also allow you to encrypt data stored in their cloud.

Synchronizing your data to a personal computer (or laptop) has both advantages and disadvantages. Some advantages of syncing to a personal computer are that you can be in full control of storing and protecting your own data, encrypted any way you choose, and can also move it to portable storage in case you need a backup of it later. A disadvantage is that you must be able to connect to your computer—a small problem if you can't bring it with you.

Syncing to the cloud also has its advantages and disadvantages. If you have a good cellular or wireless signal, you can sync from anywhere. You do have to be careful of syncing over insecure public wireless networks, however, since there is a possibility that your data could be intercepted and read over these insecure networks. Another disadvantage of syncing to the cloud is that once your data is in the cloud, you no longer fully control it. You are at the mercy of the security mechanisms and privacy policies of your provider. You have to accept whatever security mechanisms they use, such as encryption strength (or lack thereof), and you have to abide by their privacy policies, which may allow them to turn your data over to other companies for marketing, or even to law enforcement. Additionally, some cloud providers may limit the type and amount of data you are allowed to store in their cloud. These restrictions are typically in place to prevent software, movie, and music piracy.

These are all considerations you'll have to think carefully about when choosing whether to sync to the desktop, the cloud, or both.

 EXAM TIP The 1001 objectives add a curious phrase in the discussion of synchronization, "mutual authentication for multiple services (SSO)." It's hard to tell precisely what CompTIA expects here, but a properly coded application on a modern mobile device can enable you to log in with one of the other accounts you're probably already logged into, such as Google, Apple ID, Facebook, Twitter, etc. The process for using your active authenticated session with one of these common services to sign you into other services is called *single sign-on* (*SSO*).

Synchronization Issues

The most common synchronization issue is a connectivity, device, or remote infrastructure problem that leaves data partially synced. A partial sync could result in incompletely downloaded e-mail or even duplicate messages as the device tries over and over to successfully sync, repeatedly downloading the same e-mail messages. A device may attempt to sync to download an OS patch or update and may fail. The most likely culprit is connectivity issues with Wi-Fi or cellular connections, and the problem can usually be resolved by moving the device to an area with a stronger signal. This doesn't prevent upstream connectivity issues, which may also have to be examined.

There are other problems that prevent synchronization, including authentication issues, OS version issues, or incorrect configuration settings. If a device won't sync even after getting it to a stronger, more stable connection, these are some of the things you should examine. Another problem may be the remote end of the connection. This may be the enterprise e-mail server, or even the entry point into the enterprise network. Failure to properly authenticate or meet the requirements of the entry device may prevent a device from synchronizing.

Another issue you may want to examine when you have synchronization trouble is that multiple sources may be trying to sync the same data. A device can synchronize from an enterprise app store, for example, as well as the vendor app store; personal e-mail services, such as Gmail and Yahoo Mail; and even from third-party providers of "whatever-as-a-service" and cloud storage. This could be as simple as a configuration change you had to make for one service preventing another from working—or the sources might be independently trying to sync different data to the same location. In the enterprise environment, it's the mobile device management team's job to put together a management and technical strategy that will ensure minimal conflict between different synchronization sources.

iTunes and iCloud

Apple iPhones and iPads can sync through Apple iTunes installed on a Mac or PC. Everything, such as music, videos, contacts, pictures, e-mail, programs, and so on, can be stored locally. You can choose to back up all the apps on your iPhone or iPad to iTunes as well. This single source for backup makes it easy to recover if something catastrophic happens to your Apple device. If you replace an Apple device, for example, you can simply sync the new device to copy all of your files, contact information, and apps over.

 EXAM TIP Apple iTunes will run on just about any macOS or Windows machine. To install the latest iTunes for Windows (64-bit), Apple suggests a Windows 7 (64-bit) or later PC with a 1-GHz Intel or AMD CPU supporting SSE2, and 512-MB RAM. You can play music with a 1-GHz CPU and a 16-bit sound card, for example, but for complex media, such as HD video, you need a 2.4-GHz CPU with two or more cores. For a Mac, the basic software requirements are OS X version 10.10.5 or later. For more information, visit www.apple.com.

With iCloud, you can have all your iPhone or iPad data backed up online and thus accessible anywhere. This includes: any media purchased through iTunes, calendars, contacts, reminders, and so forth.

Android and Gmail

Android-based mobile devices don't have a central desktop application accomplishing what iTunes does for Apple devices. Rather, they sync over the Internet. The options for what you can sync depend on what Google services you use and your installed apps, but some common options include app data, contacts, calendars, e-mail, any media purchased through Google Play, files in Google Drive or Google Pictures, and more. For any other type of data or media, you can still treat the Android device like a thumb drive—you drag and drop files from or to the appropriate folder on the smartphone or tablet.

Mobile Device Communication and Ports

Mobile devices wouldn't be nearly as useful if they didn't have ways to interconnect with the outside world. This section looks at the many technologies and connections mobile devices use to get data flowing to the Internet and other devices.

Micro-USB/Mini-USB

If you have an Android device made before 2017, it's very likely it has either a micro- or mini-USB port to charge, connect to laptops or desktops, and sync between those devices. *Micro-USB* or *mini-USB* connectors were standard on most Android devices. That's not to say that you won't be able to find devices using proprietary connectors; Google provides the OS to multiple device manufacturers, and some manufacturers do maintain a proprietary connector.

Lightning Connector

With the iPhone 5, Apple introduced its most recent proprietary connector, known as the *Lightning* connector. It replaced the older 30-pin dock connector that Apple used on previous iPhones and iPads. The Lightning connector is an 8-pin connector (see Figure 24-41), and can be inserted without regard to proper orientation; in other words, it's not "keyed" to insert a specific way (such as right-side up or upside down, as traditional USB connectors are) into the device.

Figure 24-41
Lightning
connector

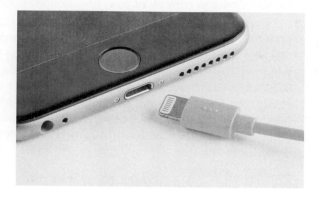

The proprietary nature of the Lightning cable means it's more expensive than a normal USB cable. It is licensed to other manufacturers through the *made for iPhone* (*MFi*) program, but to prevent widespread production of fake Lightning connectors by unlicensed manufacturers, it contains a small chip that identifies it as a true Lightning connector, and cables without that chip typically won't work or will only have limited use.

 EXAM TIP   The Apple Lightning standard is the poster child for *proprietary vendor-specific ports and connectors*. Only iOS devices use Lightning for communication and power. Android devices typically use industry-standard, vendor-neutral ports and connectors.

USB Type-C

USB Type-C (see Figure 24-42), the newest iteration of USB connectors, is quickly becoming the *de facto* standard port on Android devices today, which is awesome because

Figure 24-42
USB Type-C
connector

you can use one charger for your laptop and phone. In fact, Apple even embraced Type-C in its latest iPad Pros due to its compatibility with a huge number of peripherals and its higher power handling that provides faster charging.

Like the Lightning connector, the USB Type-C connector is not keyed, allowing it to be inserted right-side up or upside down. It can (but doesn't have to) support USB 3.1 technology with very fast data transfer rates of up to 10 Gbps. Don't assume Type-C is synonymous with a specific version of USB—some devices using a Type-C connector are using it with USB 2.0.

EXAM TIP You will likely see micro- and mini-USB, USB Type-C, and Lightning mobile device connection types on the exams. Know their characteristics and differences.

Bluetooth

While we discussed Bluetooth at some length, including configuring and pairing, in Chapter 20, let's review an outline of how the process will work on a mobile device. You can pair a Bluetooth device with a mobile device using a simple process that begins with enabling Bluetooth on the mobile device (if it isn't already enabled). Steps vary, but you can accomplish this in the quick settings menu or the full device settings menu. Next, power on the Bluetooth device (or ensure Bluetooth is enabled if the device is already on). Return to the mobile device to discover and select the Bluetooth device for pairing, and then enter the appropriate personal identification number (PIN) code (see Figure 24-43). To add a keyboard, for example, the smartphone or tablet will display a set of characters for you to type on the keyboard. Once you type in the PIN code, the devices connect.

Figure 24-43
Prompting
for PIN

EXAM TIP Not all Bluetooth pairings require a PIN code, but there's always some kind of pairing action to perform on both devices.

Always remember to test the connectivity between a mobile device and a newly added Bluetooth accessory. If you've added a keyboard, open a note-taking app and start typing to make sure it works.

 EXAM TIP Most mobile devices have Bluetooth discovery disabled by default to conserve battery life. An active search for devices to pair with uses electricity, as does completed pairing, so use Bluetooth only when you need to use it and be prepared for the battery hit.

NFC

Near Field Communication (*NFC*) uses chips embedded in mobile devices that create electromagnetic fields when these devices are close to each other. The typical range for NFC communications is anywhere from a very few centimeters to only a few inches. The devices must be very close to or touching each other, and can be used to exchange contact information, small files, and even payment transactions through stored credit cards using systems like Apple Pay and Google Pay. This technology is seeing widespread adoption in newer mobile devices, as well as the infrastructures and applications that support them. *Tap pay devices* are increasingly common, using NFC and your phone so your credit cards stay in your wallet or purse.

Magnetic Readers and Chip Readers

Merchants can attach a magnetic reader or a chip reader to a smartphone to enable very quick credit card transactions via the cellular network (see Figure 24-44). This technology has empowered vendors small and large to free themselves from static cash registers, enabling commerce to happen literally anywhere two people want to exchange goods and services for money. Every merchant at the Texas Renaissance Festival this year,

Figure 24-44
Magnetic credit
card reader
attached to
smartphone

for example, had credit card readers attached to smartphones to take the Totalsem crew's money when they dressed up and went there to play (see Figure 24-45). Cheers!

Figure 24-45
Totalsem crew
at the Texas
Renaissance
Festival

Infrared

Now largely replaced by other, faster technologies, such as Bluetooth and 802.11 wireless, infrared (IR) was previously used to transfer data between mobile devices, such as laptops and some older PDAs. Infrared was used to create the first real personal area networks (PANs). Infrared uses the wireless Infrared Data Association (IrDA) standard, and at one time was widely used to connect devices such as wireless remotes, printers, wireless mice, digitizers, and other serial devices. IrDA requires *line of sight*, meaning that devices have to be directly facing each other, requires very short distances (sometimes inches) between devices, and has very slow data rates.

NOTE If you find an infrared window on a modern mobile device, it's almost certainly an *infrared blaster* capable of emitting (but not receiving) infrared signals so the device can function as a remote control. The IR blaster still requires line of sight, but should function at greater distances.

Hotspots and Tethering

A *mobile hotspot* is a small device that shares access to cellular technologies such as 3G, 4G, and 4G LTE via Wi-Fi. Most of these devices can be purchased from wireless providers such as Verizon, Sprint, AT&T, T-Mobile, or other carriers, and are usually specific to their type of broadband network. A mobile hotspot is basically a wireless router that routes traffic between Wi-Fi devices and broadband technologies, providing wireless access for up to five to ten devices at a time.

Depending upon the carrier, many cellular phones, as well as tablets, can act as portable hotspots. You'll recall this from Chapter 21. When used in this manner, it's called *tethering* to the cell phone. While some devices configured as hotspots can use your existing data plan with your carrier, some carriers separate out and limit the amount of data that can be used for tethering.

To configure a device as a hotspot, you typically enable its cellular data connection and turn on an additional hotspot setting that causes the device to broadcast a Wi-Fi network. Now the mobile device serves as a router between the cellular network and the traditional Wi-Fi network it is broadcasting. Then any devices that you wish to tether to the hotspot simply see the device as a wireless router. You can also configure a password so that not just anyone can connect to the hotspot. Figure 24-46 shows a screenshot of an Android phone serving as a portable hotspot.

Figure 24-46
An Android phone acting as a portable hotspot

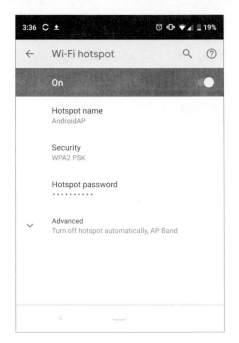

Accessories

Mobile device accessories come in a wide variety of types, packing a huge range of features. Some of the most common accessories that people want for their mobile device, particularly smartphones and tablets, include devices that wirelessly connect to them, typically using Bluetooth technologies. It's not unusual to find Bluetooth headsets and high-quality *external speakers* for users to listen to music and chat with friends.

Game controllers, including gamepads and other accessories that plug into tablets via a USB port or connect via Bluetooth, are also common, effectively turning tablets into full-scale gaming platforms. Additionally, there are specialized tablets that are outfitted with game controllers built in and used specifically as gaming platforms. The NVIDIA SHIELD is a specialized Android device used as a gaming platform, and it can perform the same functions as other Android tablets.

One feature that Android and some Microsoft mobile devices offer is the ability to use removable external storage, such as *miniSD* or *microSD memory cards*, effectively upgrading the storage capacity of the device. This is something Apple hasn't quite embraced with its devices.

There are also accessories no mobile device user should be without, including *extra battery packs* (if your mobile device supports battery removal and replacement; many don't) or a phone or device charger. To recharge mobile devices, *device chargers* either plug into a wall outlet and the mobile device, or plug into a computer and the mobile device.

Some chargers don't require connection to the device at all; they simply require you to lay the device on top of a special pad that recharges the battery wirelessly. Specifics differ a little depending on whether the device was designed for wireless charging or the capability is being added with an aftermarket kit—but in either case the pad creates an electromagnetic field for transmitting power to an antenna in the device. Despite being a wireless technology, the range is measured in centimeters and charging works best when the mobile device is on the pad.

The marketplace has settled on the *Qi* (pronounced "chee") standard from the Wireless Power Consortium (WPC) as the wireless charging standard of choice. Apple's 2017 decision to adopt the Qi standard and become a member of that consortium sealed the fate of early rival standards.

 EXAM TIP   Removable batteries can usually be directly charged with a *battery charger* (that is, after all, the best way to take advantage of having a spare battery). Insert the battery, plug in the charger, and charge away.

Some devices also have specialized accessories, including *docking stations* (typically for tablets; much like the docks discussed for portables in Chapter 23, "Portable Computing") produced by the device manufacturer, and even *credit card readers*, allowing small businesses to take credit card payments from their mobile device. It's not unusual to see a food truck use a portable credit card reader plugged into the headphone port on an iPad, for example.

Another important accessory is a case for the device. These include an almost unimaginable variety of designer cases, as well as hardened cases designed to withstand falls and other impacts. There also screen protectors—*protective covers*—that range from flimsy plastic all the way to hardened glass that can protect a mobile device screen from scratches and impact. You can find cases made of plastic, leather, rubber, wood, metal, and unicorn horn. Some of these cases are even waterproof, allowing the more adventurous folks to take their phones with them while they are diving in oceans or river-rafting.

We've covered only a few of the hundreds of accessories that are available for mobile devices. Many accessories also come with apps to help control or get the most out of the accessory.

Chapter Review

Questions

1. Which of the following is used in mobile devices to convert analog video and sound to digital video and sound?

    A. Calibrator

    B. SDK

    C. Virtual assistant

    D. Digitizer

2. John has a high-resolution image on his iPad of his 2-year-old son and the family dog. The image initially displays smaller than the screen, so he wants to zoom in to get the details of his son's expression. What gesture can he use to accomplish this task?

    A. Click the mouse in the middle of the picture to select it, then use the scroll wheel on the mouse to zoom in.

    B. Tap the picture with his index finger on his son's face.

    C. Long-press on the image and select zoom from the pop-up menu.

    D. Touch his son's face on the screen with his thumb and finger, then pinch outward to scroll in.

3. Which mobile device screen technology uses no backlight?

    A. BYOD

    B. LCD

    C. LED

    D. OLED

4. What can a government use to determine your location at a specific time as long as you're using your mobile device?

    A. Multifactor authentication

    B. Geotracking

    C. Google Earth

    D. Authenticator applications

5. What are the steps involved in pairing a Bluetooth keyboard with a tablet?

    A. Enable Bluetooth on the tablet; turn on the Bluetooth device; find the device with the tablet; enter a PIN code or other pairing sequence.

    B. Turn on the Bluetooth device; find the device with the tablet; enter a PIN code or other pairing sequence.

   C. Search for a Bluetooth device from the tablet; select **pair** from the options to enable the device.

   D. Enable Bluetooth on the tablet; turn on the Bluetooth device; find the device with the tablet; select **pair** from the options to enable the device.

6. Which of the following is a 15-digit number used to uniquely identify a mobile device that connects to a cellular network?

   A. IMEI

   B. GSM

   C. ICCID

   D. IMSI

7. Mary returned from a cruise to the Bahamas and got a bill from her cell phone company (Sprint) that was over $1000. What could have happened?

   A. Mary connected to the Internet with her smartphone using the cruise ship company's Wi-Fi.

   B. Mary's smartphone connected to the Internet in the Bahamas via a cell provider that wasn't Sprint.

   C. Mary used her smartphone to do Internet gambling and Sprint frowns on that activity.

   D. Bills after international trips are always reported in the currency of the country visited. When translated from Bahamian dollars to U.S. dollars, the amount is the same she normally pays.

8. Leonard just purchased a very expensive comic book and paid for it using the stored credit card information on his smartphone. What technology did he use to make the transaction?

   A. Swipe lock

   B. Wi-Fi calling

   C. NFC

   D. BitLocker To Go

9. What information do you need to connect an Android-based tablet to an IMAP account?

   A. POP3 server DNS name

   B. User name and password

   C. User name, password, sending and receiving server addresses

   D. Exchange server name, user name, and password

10. Which mobile OS enables developers to customize the user experience without restrictions?

   A. Android

   B. Blackberry

   C. iOS

   D. Windows Phone

Answers

1. **D.** Digitizers are used in mobile devices to convert analog video and sound to digital video and sound, or to interpret analog signals associated with touch movement on a screen into digital equivalents.

2. **D.** John should touch his son's face on the screen with his thumb and finger, then pinch outward to zoom in.

3. **D.** OLED technology does not use a backlight.

4. **B.** Geotracking can locate you and your GPS-equipped mobile device.

5. **A.** To pair a Bluetooth keyboard with a tablet, enable Bluetooth on the tablet, turn on the Bluetooth device, find the Bluetooth device in the tablet's settings screen, then enter a PIN code or finalize the pairing.

6. **A.** The International Mobile Equipment Identity (IMEI) number is a 15-digit number used to uniquely identify a mobile device, typically a smartphone or other device that connects to a cellular network.

7. **B.** Mary's smartphone connected to the Internet in the Bahamas via a cell provider that wasn't Sprint.

8. **C.** Leonard likely purchased his comic book using Near Field Communication (NFC) technology, which can be used for payment transactions through stored credit card information in mobile applications.

9. **C.** To connect an Android-based tablet to an IMAP account, you'll need a user name and password and the sending and receiving server addresses.

10. **A.** Google Android is open source, enabling developers to create custom versions for their devices.

Care and Feeding of Mobile Devices

In this chapter, you will learn how to
- Troubleshoot common mobile device and application issues
- Explain basic mobile device security
- Describe typical mobile OS and application security issues

Mobile devices are packed with tightly integrated hardware, aren't designed to be upgraded by their users, and come with mobile-oriented operating systems. Because of these major differences, the troubleshooting and security practices for mobile devices differ a lot from those for desktop computers, and somewhat from those for other portable devices. This chapter explores general troubleshooting of mobile devices and their apps first, then covers security features and capabilities of devices common in the mobile market. The chapter finishes by jumping into preventing, detecting, and addressing security issues with mobile operating systems and applications. CompTIA loves those performance-based scenario questions, so get ready for some real-world issues when it comes to security and application troubleshooting.

1001/1002

Troubleshooting Mobile Device Issues

The CompTIA A+ exam objectives divide mobile device problems into two groups: general issues with mobile device hardware and software, and security issues (1002 exam) with the mobile OS and apps. In this section we're going to cover tools for troubleshooting general hardware, OS, and app issues, and apply these tools to common problems. These common problems happen across all varieties, types, and manufacturers of mobile devices. This chapter includes references to Apple iOS, Google Android, and also Microsoft Windows (Phone). Although Windows Phone has disappeared from the marketplace, it shows up on the exam and in legacy devices. It's important to know it's out there just in case you have to deal with *that* tech call.

NOTE Few mobile devices have components you can service in the field. In the event of a hardware problem, send the device to a service center for repair. Companies like iFixit (www.ifixit.com) are making some components field-replaceable, but usually only for skilled techs.

Troubleshooting Tools

Because mobile device hardware typically can't be repaired or replaced by a user or field tech, mobile device troubleshooting focuses on ruling out software issues. The few things you can try are common to almost all mobile devices, and it's best to start with ones that inconvenience the user least. Sometimes these tools will fix the problem, but other times they'll just restore normal functionality until the problem recurs, or help you rule out causes.

Just because you'll troubleshoot a mobile device a little differently doesn't mean you should throw out what you already know. Reflect on the troubleshooting methodology covered in Chapter 1, "Safety and Professionalism," and use the troubleshooting tools you learn about here to help you work through that process. If the troubleshooting process doesn't fix the problem or identify a cause you can resolve in-house, the next step is to take the device to an authorized service center.

Keep in mind that the steps you'll need to take to perform any of these operations will depend on the specific device, its operating system, and the OS version. Be prepared to consult manufacturer and OS resources for exact steps. Let's dive in.

NOTE Most of these tools either are guaranteed to erase data and customizations or have some risk of doing so under the right circumstances. Remember to communicate with the device's user what steps you'll be taking, including what kinds of data loss it can entail, and give the user a chance to back up his or her data.

Try This! Practice on the Real Deal

If you have access to a smartphone or tablet, practice getting to the tools used for troubleshooting mobile devices. You're going to read about a bunch of places to adjust things such as screen brightness, close or uninstall apps, and much more. Access the device's Settings and explore. Just don't do anything specifically to any device without proper permissions.

Check and Adjust Configuration/Settings

Modern mobile operating systems have tons of configurable settings, as do many of the apps users install on them. Always be on the look-out for "problems" that sound a lot like a simple configuration issue, and investigate these early if they seem likely. It won't cost you much (except time) to check relevant settings, but it might save you from having to perform later steps that require backing up and restoring user data.

If the issue isn't likely related to configuration, save your time and revisit configuration after you've tried rebooting the device, which we'll discuss in the upcoming "Soft Reset" section; you don't want to waste tons of time toggling settings if a reboot could fix the problem. If you find a setting that doesn't seem right and want to see if a change resolves the issue, make sure to keep track of what you changed and what the previous setting was!

Close Running Apps

All of the mobile operating systems provide at least one way to close running applications—the most common is to swipe the app in a particular direction from the device's list of *recent apps*. If you come at this with a traditional mindset shaped by how desktop operating systems work, there's a chance you'll misunderstand when and why we close mobile apps, so let's consider a much-simplified version of what goes on under the hood.

On a traditional computer, you open an application when you need it, and it will run until it completes its work, crashes, or you close it. Because mobile devices have more limited computing resources and battery power, you don't want open applications eating up big chunks of resources and burning power while they aren't in focus or the device isn't even being used. To address this problem, modern mobile OS versions manage running apps to optimize performance and battery life.

The catch is that the way they manage apps makes the term "running" a little slippery. While your current app may be running in the traditional sense, the various processes that power your recent out-of-focus apps may keep running if they have work to do, be cached until you return to the app, or get killed if the OS needs its resources for other apps. For the most part the OS will do a good job of managing well-designed apps, but you may still need to close an app if it has frozen, begins to malfunction, or you suspect it is causing the device to misbehave.

 NOTE When closing an app, keep in mind that the user may lose unsaved data when you close it, and (depending on the app) that their device may lose certain functionality they expect it to have until the app is restarted.

Some apps may (intentionally or accidentally) leave background processes running even after the GUI has closed. In Android, the Application Manager will let you *force stop* an app, also killing its background processes (Figure 25-1). You can likewise control background tasks in Windows Phone through application or battery settings. In iOS, a swipe will generally do the job.

Soft Reset

To maintain mobile devices, it's important to understand the terminology surrounding resets, especially if you're coming at this from a desktop-oriented mindset. On a desktop, you typically initiate a soft reboot from within the operating system, or trigger it by pressing a button dedicated to restarting the system; the hallmark of a soft reboot is that the machine never powers all the way down. In contrast, you can perform a hard reboot by holding down the system's power button for several seconds until it turns completely off; you don't want to reboot this way if you can avoid it, but you'll need to if the system is frozen.

Figure 25-1
Force stop in
Android

On mobile devices, the term *soft reset* describes restarting the device, whether you do it from within the OS or with hardware buttons on the device. If the device still won't restart, confirm the soft reset procedure in the manufacturer resources; if you know you're performing it correctly, you can force a device with a removable battery to power down by removing the back cover and the battery.

Much like a reboot on a traditional computer, you can fix all kinds of strange behavior on a mobile device with a soft reset. I'm listening to Spotify on my Android device as I write this section, for example, and when I got started this morning the playback was stopping every few songs; I performed a soft reset and now it's working fine. Unfortunately, the soft reset is the easy reset to remember correctly; we'll continue this discussion in the "Reset to Factory Default" section coming up in a moment.

Uninstall/Reinstall Apps

Uninstalling and reinstalling apps can be an important troubleshooting process. You can uninstall apps through either the app store they were installed with or the device's *application manager*; you can also, of course, reinstall them via the app store. If the user started having trouble shortly after installing a new app, uninstalling it to see if the problem goes away is an obvious way to rule out a potential cause. If they've been successfully using the app, make sure to jot down important settings and back up their data if possible before you uninstall it.

The problems you can fix or troubleshoot by uninstalling and reinstalling aren't always as obvious as this. If a user has had an app for a long time and it only recently started acting up, it's possible the app's developers released a bad update; after a bad update, the app might not work at all, or it might work fine if you uninstall and reinstall it. Sometimes this can be a no-win situation for a tech—what if the only fix to a user's problem is removing an app they use daily until its developers fix a problem?

Reset to Factory Default

This other reset—known by many names such as *hard reset*, *factory reset*, or *reset to factory default*—will clear all user data and setting changes, returning the device (well, its software) to the state it was in when it left the factory. Take extra care not to confuse a hard reset with a hard reboot; if you're reading documentation or a how-to page that uses the terms reboot and reset interchangeably, pay close attention to what the author intends you to do—and consider finding a less-ambiguous resource.

Because the hard reset removes all of a user's data and settings changes, it's the most disruptive option here—typically one you won't perform until after backing up the user's data (which we'll discuss later in the chapter). The big exception is when you're intentionally performing a factory reset in order to clear user data off a device before it is sold, recycled, or assigned to a new user.

Despite the inconvenience, resetting a device to factory defaults is an important troubleshooting step on the way to determining whether it should be sent to a service center. If a factory reset fixes the device's issues but they return some time after restoring a backup of user data and programs, return to earlier steps for tracking down the troublemaking app.

Touchscreen and Display Issues

Modern mobile devices are almost all screen, and some provide little beyond a touchscreen and a power button for interacting with the device. While display issues tend to be urgent for most devices, the touchscreen's integral role in controlling a modern mobile device makes it all the more so. We already touched on some important steps for troubleshooting a touchscreen in the "Input Problems" section at the end of Chapter 23, "Portable Computing," so be prepared to integrate those steps with the more mobile-centric issues discussed here.

Dim Display

Mobile devices have a *brightness control* that can be set to auto mode or controlled manually. These settings don't always work perfectly, and sometimes apps that need special control over brightness settings can cause the device's display to be too dark or bright for the user's comfort.

A dim display might be a sign that there's a problem with the panel, but first you need to check the display settings. Turn off any auto-adjustment setting and manually change the display brightness from the dimmest to brightest setting and observe whether it covers an appropriate range of output. If it doesn't, there may be a problem with the display panel; if it does, there may be something keeping the auto-adjustment from working right.

The auto-adjustment is affected by how much light a sensor or camera on the front of the device can detect. Make sure the sensor isn't covered with dirt or some other obstruction. If the display is too bright in a dim room, check the surroundings for bright light that isn't close enough to illuminate the area, but that the sensor might pick up if pointed in the right direction.

Be on the lookout for apps that tinker with the display's brightness. These apps may use distinct brightness settings, or they may modify system-wide brightness. Reading apps, like Amazon Kindle, are one example. See if a soft reset returns the display to normal operation, and then investigate whether using these apps causes the brightness issue to return. Every once in a while, Kindle on my Android tablet will interfere with the system's *auto-brightness*, causing all sorts of strange brightness changes until I restart the tablet by performing a soft reset. The solution in this case may be as simple as teaching the user to reset their device when an app like this has caused a problem.

Touchscreen Responsiveness

When a user tries to interact with a mobile device but finds the touchscreen nonresponsive or gets an inaccurate touchscreen response, there are a few simple things to rule out first: dirt, accidental touches, and performance issues. With those out of the way, we'll turn to more catastrophic causes.

Accidental Touch   The simplest issue to resolve is an accidental touch. Sometimes a user will hold a device in such a way that its touchscreen detects some part of their arm or hand as an intentional touch, and it may not react at all when they try to manipulate it intentionally. Oversensitive sensors or bad design might exacerbate this, but the fix is always the same: show the user how the sensors pick up an accidental touch, and teach them how to hold the device to avoid them.

Dirty Screen   Another simple issue to resolve is a dirty screen. Sometimes simply wiping the touchscreen down with a dry microfiber cloth to get rid of fingerprints, dust, dirt, grease, and other foreign objects will fix a responsiveness problem (see Figure 25-2).

Figure 25-2
Cleaning a
smartphone

Performance Problems   Much like a mouse cursor may slow, freeze, or move erratically when a traditional computer is having performance issues, a touchscreen may appear not to work at all or have severe accuracy and response problems if the mobile device is performing poorly. Be patient with the device, and look for signs it is struggling to keep up. Is it displaying the right time? If it has an animated lock screen or wallpaper, are the animations playing smoothly?

If the device appears to have network connectivity, are weather or stock widgets on the lock screen updating? Is it slow to respond when you press unrelated hardware buttons? If the device can receive them, see if it responds normally when you call or text it. If the problem seems to be performance related, perform a soft reset and see if the touchscreen starts working.

A lot of users add a screen protector to their mobile devices to give a little extra help in case of a drop. A poorly installed screen protector can cause touchscreens not to work properly. Check the guidelines from the manufacturer and remove and replace a subpar screen protector.

Calibration and Diagnostics

If a soft reset doesn't get the touchscreen working, look online for information about whether the device has a hidden *diagnostics menu* or *service menu*. You might reach this menu by inputting a series of digits into the device's dialer, or by holding specific buttons while the device is booting up during a soft reset. If the device has a touchscreen diagnostic here, it should help you decide whether the touchscreen itself is in good working order. Some Android and Windows Phone devices may also have a setting in either the primary OS settings menu or a hidden device menu for calibrating the touchscreen.

Physical Damage

While we covered the previous issues when we discussed portable devices in Chapter 23, smaller mobile and wearable devices have a greater risk of some problems that are rarer with larger portables. Everyone knows a quick dip in a toilet, margarita glass, or swimming pool can kill a mobile device, but sometimes getting one wet or dropping it on a hard surface can cause trouble short of complete death. A smartphone in your pocket when you get caught in the rain, or on a table when you spill a drink, could end up with liquid in all sorts of nooks and crannies.

Although some mobile devices can handle a little bit of moisture, most can't handle immersion at all. Dropping a smartphone in a toilet makes for a very bad day. Without removable batteries, there's not much you can do to save a liquid-soaked mobile device.

If you rule out the simplest explanations and fixes in this section and the touchscreen is still not responding properly, it's time to inspect the device for evidence it has been dropped or gotten wet. There's always the old-fashioned way—ask the user. Just be aware that it may be hard to get someone to admit their touchscreen stopped working after they sprayed milk through their nose because they tried to read XKCD while eating breakfast.

 TIP   For a good dose of tech-oriented humor, check out the comics at http://xkcd.org. Geeky fun at its finest!

Even if the glass isn't broken, drops or impacts can break internal connections. Moisture can cause internal shorts, and lingering liquid could cause sensors to behave in really strange ways. Most mobile devices will contain a few *liquid contact indicator* (*LCI*) stickers that change color when exposed to water, as shown in Figure 25-3. While these are really so the carrier or manufacturer can refuse to cover water damage under warranty, look up their locations online and then check them on the device. There's often one on the battery or in the battery compartment, if it's accessible; it'll usually be white if it hasn't gotten wet.

Figure 25-3
Pristine LCI
sticker (top)
and LCI sticker
absorbing a drop
of water (bottom)

Apps Not Loading

A mobile device app may not load or install correctly for a few reasons. First, the app may not be compatible with some combination of the mobile device's hardware, operating system version, or vendor/carrier customizations to the OS. With Android devices, for example, different manufacturers can tweak the OS to suit their own needs, which may cause compatibility issues with other vendors' apps.

NOTE This section details reasons an app may always fail to load or install correctly. Remember, an app may fail to install or load correctly before you perform a soft reset, but do so fine afterward. Perform a soft reset and then try loading or reinstalling the app.

Another reason an app may not load is that the device doesn't meet the app's hardware requirements. These might be more traditional requirements such as amount of available RAM, storage space, and processor type, but the app might also require a sensor or radio your device lacks, or require capabilities your device's camera doesn't support. It's always a good idea to review an app's requirements before installing it (or when you run into trouble).

Both iOS and Android devices track errors with applications. You'll need third-party tools to access *app log errors*—or what I assume are *logs of app errors* (thanks, CompTIA!). Something to keep in mind if a senior tech or app programmer (in the case of custom apps for an organization) needs help with troubleshooting.

Overheating

Just as with the portable devices discussed in Chapter 23, overheating can cause permanent damage to a mobile device; most of the recommendations given there still apply. That said, our relationship with mobile devices is a little different. They are usually on, spend more time in our hands and pockets, and we take them places we wouldn't dream of taking a larger portable. A mobile device is more likely to get left on the car seat on a hot summer day, or be nestled close to our body in well-insulated winter clothing.

Focus on overheating as a combination of the heat a mobile device produces itself, heat added to it by external sources like the sun or a lamp, and how well its environment dissipates or retains heat. Since we handle these devices more often, we have a lot of chances to notice what's normal and what isn't; when a device is hot, combine these three factors and see how well they explain the device's temperature. The process of looking for a good explanation can help you catch performance problems before they drain the battery, prevent heat damage to components, or identify problems with the battery or power systems before they become dangerous.

Charging, large data transfers, frozen apps, recording HD video, and other intensive tasks can all make a mobile device much hotter than normal; avoid letting the device do intense work in hot or well-insulated spaces. If you can avoid it, don't bring mobile devices into very hot environments; if you can't, minimize risk by turning the device off altogether. If the device is hot to the touch in a cool environment, you can put it into airplane mode, close all running programs, and see if it cools down. If it doesn't, turn it off until it cools and then try again.

Your biggest concerns are a device that overheats for no obvious reason, or gets hot enough that it could burn someone. These problems are usually caused by some sort of hardware issue, possibly a defective battery or other power circuit within the device. There's really not much you can do; turn it off to protect the device from further damage and take it to a service center.

The dangers of not addressing an overheating mobile device—even one that is overheating for otherwise benign reasons—are, at best, an eventual device failure and requisite data loss. At worst, a severely overheating device can become a safety risk with the potential to burn or shock a user and, especially if the battery ruptures, cause a fire or explosion.

Slow Performance

Mobile devices can suffer from performance issues just like regular desktop computers and laptops, and often for the same reasons. Performance issues can be caused by storage space being almost filled up on a mobile device, making it unable to save data or install apps efficiently. Performance can also suffer when there are too many apps running at the same time, eating up RAM.

Usually, the mobile device's OS has configuration settings that enable you to stop apps or view their resource usage, including memory and storage space. If storage space is an issue, you may have to uninstall some apps, or reinstall them so that they are stored on removable storage devices, such as microSD or miniSD memory cards.

A device with performance issues will often be running hot, and this heat can be a big clue. Use the recommendations in the previous section to evaluate whether the device or the environment is the source of this heat. A hot, sluggish device could be using *thermal throttling* to protect the device's CPU from heat damage by reducing its power; in this case, performance should pick up as it cools.

One of the first troubleshooting steps you can take in resolving performance issues is to perform a soft reset of the device; this clears running apps—perhaps even ones that are frozen or malfunctioning—from RAM. As far as troubleshooting tools go, you can use the device settings or third-party apps to measure the device's performance. Sometimes those apps can help point the way to what's causing the performance problems. If you ultimately determine that a hardware issue is causing performance problems, you should take the device to an authorized repair facility.

Battery Life

Just like the portable devices discussed in Chapter 23, modern mobile devices use Lithium-Ion (Li-Ion) batteries. While it's usually not too hard to make use of a more traditional portable computer while it's charging, the ergonomics of mobile devices can make it miserable to use one while it's charging—so it's even more important to make sure your device has power when you need it. Our purpose here is to look at how you can manage any battery to get the most out of it, but first we need to talk about the cornerstone of good battery management.

Meeting User Power Needs

Mobile devices are rated in terms of how long their battery should power a device during "normal" use, how long the device can go between battery charges, and the levels of power that both the battery provides and requires in order to charge. Make sure you and your users have mobile devices that have a chance to last long enough to perform normal activities for an adequate amount of time.

The numbers advertised by a device's maker are a good start, but be suspicious of these figures. Mobile device review sites will benchmark the performance of more popular mobile devices and tell you how long they survived while performing some battery-sucking tasks like playing HD video. Know how long a given user's device will need to last on a charge, and try to make sure they get a device that can last at least 20 percent longer, to account for how the battery's capacity will dwindle over its lifetime.

If there's no existing device that can meet the user's needs most of the time, make sure they either have a device with a removable battery and a spare or have a portable external battery recharger. You can plug a mobile device into a *portable battery recharger* (sometimes called *external battery*, *power pack*, or *portable charger*) to recharge when there's no available outlet.

Managing Battery Life

There are two ways to think about battery life: how long it will last on each charge, and how long the battery can meet your needs before you have to replace it. Luckily, you can optimize both of these at the same time. When you waste battery life on device features you aren't using, not only will your device need to recharge sooner than necessary, but the extra recharge cycles will also shorten the useful life of your battery. Let's take a look at the biggest battery drains while keeping in mind that these are generalizations: check your device's battery usage monitor to see what is consuming most of its power.

Display While it depends somewhat on how big your device's screen is and what kind of display it uses, the fastest way to drain most modern mobile devices is leaving the screen on. Keep the display off when you can, and use the lowest acceptable brightness setting. Because the screens look so much more vibrant at full brightness, there's a good chance this will be their default setting. The battery savings from using the lowest setting may be enticing, but the best compromise is usually to configure the device to control brightness automatically. Figure 25-4 displays the battery usage for an Android smartphone. Notice how much of the battery is being drained by the screen alone!

Figure 25-4

Battery usage for a smartphone

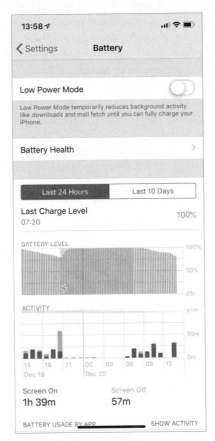

There are more options for optimizing how much power your display uses, though some of these differ by device or manufacturer. You can usually adjust how long the screen will stay on without input, and whether it will turn on when you receive a notification. Some devices have *power-saving modes* and may even be able to save power by displaying grayscale instead of full color. OLED displays use less power to display darker colors; if your device uses an OLED panel, you can also reduce power consumption by using black wallpapers and configuring apps to use a dark theme if the option is available.

Wireless Communication   To paint with a very broad brush, another big battery drain is the process of communicating without wires. It's good to keep in mind that every form of wireless communication your mobile device is capable of (such as cellular voice, cellular data, Wi-Fi, Bluetooth, NFC, etc.) corresponds to a radio inside the device. In order to use that type of communication, the radio needs to be on and drawing power. If you aren't actively using that mode of communication but the radio is on, you're wasting power. Each communication technology draws varying amounts of energy under different circumstances, but here are two helpful guidelines: searching for signals is power intensive, and your device's apps will do more work in the background when connections are available.

Especially when traveling outside of populated areas, a mobile device can use lots of power talking with distant towers and base stations; this constant search can significantly drain battery power. You may be able to control this power drain through configuration changes that limit device roaming or searching for new wireless networks, but another approach is disabling these communications technologies until you need them or are back in an area with good coverage. You don't want to get stuck in the snow on a rural highway only to discover that your phone has almost completely drained its battery searching for cellular signals.

Even when the device maintains a strong connection, it constantly uses power to transmit and receive data. Having the connection available is often worth this slow drain, but beware that some of your apps will lightly sip power while disconnected and burn through much more doing background work when a connection is present. The easy way to rein this in is to disable communication, but the operating system (and sometimes the app itself) will have settings for controlling when an app can send and receive data in the background, and what connections it can use.

Location   While you can apply the same guidelines for managing GPS or location services, some small differences make it worth discussing separately. When location services are on, the device's apps can query the location of the device. Depending on how you've configured the device, it may approximate your location using low-power (less-accurate) methods like nearby cellular and Wi-Fi networks, higher-accuracy (higher-power) methods like GPS, or combine both of these. This could be for apps that require location data in the background, or for active apps, such as mapping software, that use the GPS receiver. The power drain here can vary widely between an app occasionally checking low-accuracy location in the background, and one constantly requesting high-quality updates.

The simplest solution is to keep location services off when they aren't required, but you may be able to find a happy medium by setting per-app restrictions. When an app requires location data (common examples are apps for navigating, mapping, geocaching, or finding nearby users, restaurants, garage sales, or movie theaters) but location is disabled, the device will usually prompt you to turn it on.

Because apps for which location data is less critical may happily use a stale location, the best combination of trade-offs will ultimately depend on how you use your device and what apps you have running. If you regularly use the device to take location-tagged pictures cataloging graffiti or potholes, you may want the highest quality location data available at all times, regardless of the battery drain. Another tip is to review configuration settings for apps that use location services and disable the ones that don't need to have immediate location data.

EXAM TIP Be familiar with the factors that can reduce battery power and battery life.

Swollen Battery

As we discussed in Chapter 23, one of the more insidious problems you'll see in mobile devices is a swollen battery. The main cause is overcharging, usually when the circuits designed to prevent overcharging fail. Non-OEM chargers or batteries, especially if they aren't rated for the correct voltage and wattage, represent an additional risk, as does overheating. Sometimes the battery is just bad.

 CAUTION You should never try to repair a battery under any circumstances, let alone when it's swollen, as it can cause bodily harm and damage to equipment.

Prevention may be the best cure. Don't let batteries overheat, especially while charging. Prefer OEM chargers and batteries. Check the manufacturer's documentation for specific actions to take or avoid. Regardless, prevention can't always work, and swollen batteries may rupture, leak, and catch fire. It's important to be aware it can happen, vigilant for signs it is occurring, and careful when disposing swollen batteries.

Look for subtle clues, like changes in how the device's frame and screen come together, how it sits on a flat surface, how the back cover sits on the device, weird creaking or popping, inexplicable heat, etc. If the device has a removable cover, it's pretty simple to check the battery. If it doesn't, you may need to find a service center or a mobile technician comfortable taking the device apart to check.

When you encounter a swollen battery, dispose of it according to the recommendations in the "Try This! Recycling Old Portable Device Batteries" section of Chapter 23 and replace it with a known good battery, preferably from the original device vendor.

 EXAM TIP You need to be proactive with toxic waste handling, like disposing of or recycling mobile device batteries. Cell phones, tablets, wearable devices . . . take them to a proper recycling facility when you're done with them. Putting them in the trash pollutes and is bad for all of us.

Frozen System

While a mobile device can freeze up just like a desktop system (and for the same reasons), the difference between operating systems and inputs means there aren't as many ways to successfully deal with a frozen mobile device. The immediate goal is getting the device back to a usable state. If the device isn't responding, you'll need to perform a soft reset, and without access to the OS you'll have to follow the manufacturer's steps for performing a soft reset—probably either by holding the power button for a few seconds or removing the battery.

 NOTE When a device seems to be frozen, there's also a chance the touchscreen just isn't responding. Check if the device responds normally to hardware button presses or enabled voice and gesture commands before assuming it is frozen.

If the device is still at least partially responsive, you can try to close an offending process from your list of recent apps. Even if you get the app to close, you may find the device unstable again as soon as you reopen the app. It's often best to save yourself wasted time: close the offending app, save any work in other open apps, and perform a soft reset.

When the device is usable again, there may be more steps to take. If you know the device froze when you opened a newly installed or updated app, you may need to uninstall it and consider waiting for an update or looking for a replacement. Sometimes operating system issues can cause device freezes, especially right after a device update, so look for follow-up OS patches correcting these types of issues. If the device randomly (and with increased frequency) freezes up, whenever using apps performing similar tasks (any app that uses the GPS or camera, for example), then your device likely has a hardware issue and needs service.

There's also a chance you'll find that the device is still unusable after the soft reset, in which case you'll need to look for the manufacturer's documentation on how to boot the device into any special modes that enable you to either remove an offending app, repair the OS installation, or reset the device to factory default. If this process also fails to render the device stable, you'll need to send it to a service center.

Cannot Broadcast to an External Monitor

Back in Chapter 24, "Understanding Mobile Devices," we saw that some mobile devices have video output that enables you to broadcast the display onto an external monitor or projector. When done correctly, this is usually an almost automatic process: plug some adapter into your mobile device, plug that adapter into your external monitor's VGA, DVI, DP, or HDMI port, and it all just works.

Well, that's the theory. In reality, broadcasting your mobile device's screen to an external monitor is fraught with problems. While these vary by type of device, here are a few tried and true things to check when your device cannot broadcast to an external monitor:

- Is your source correct on the external monitor? All monitors, TVs, and projectors have lots of inputs. Is the external monitor pointing at the right source?

- Do you have the right adapter for your device? Apple alone has come out with five different types of video adapters in the last few years—and don't even get me started on the many adapters for Android! Make sure you have an adapter that is known to work for your device.

- Does your adapter need its own power source?

- For HDMI: Did the HDMI recognize your device and your external monitor? Depending on the make and model, you may need to reset one or both devices to give the HDMI time to see connections and set itself up.

No Sound from Speakers

Sound issues are also common on mobile devices. The most obvious (and probably most common) is that the volume was turned down or muted through software configuration or an app. This is easy to fix, but sometimes you have to go through many configuration settings for both the device and apps to figure out which one is controlling the volume at the moment or which one may actually be muting the speakers. A device may have separate settings for media, call volume, notifications, and more—and sometimes it's easy to change the wrong one.

Some mobile devices also have hardware volume controls on them, so check them. If that doesn't work, then start going into the configuration settings for the device and apps. If none of these steps works, then you may have a hardware issue: the speakers have been damaged or come disconnected inside the device. As with all other hardware issues, you'll likely have to take the device to a service center for repair.

Connectivity and Data Usage Issues

General network connectivity issues—the kind that can affect all devices—have been covered elsewhere within the book. For mobile devices in particular, you should be aware of some additional network connectivity issues that you will likely encounter at some point. We'll discuss these in respect to cellular signals, but the first issue applies to Wi-Fi and Bluetooth network connections as well. For the most part you can't directly fix these connection issues, but you'll inevitably find a connection issue is responsible for some problem, or at least need to rule it out on the way to the ultimate cause.

One of the most prominent connection issues plaguing mobile devices is weak signal. The signal might be weak because you're deep inside a building, nestled between skyscrapers, crossing the no-man's-land between cell towers in sparsely populated areas, or any of a wide array of similar situations. The primary symptoms of a weak signal are dropped connections, delays, slow transmission speeds, and frequent indications that the device is searching for a signal.

There isn't much you can do to troubleshoot a weak signal except monitor it. There are cellular signal boosters you can purchase, but these are of dubious value in some situations. They are most effective when the user is stationary in a location far from the cell tower, and usually aren't useful while the user is on the move.

 NOTE In addition to signal issues, performance problems on the device itself can cause the symptoms of slow data connectivity. We've covered these already, but they include high utilization of resources such as CPU, RAM, and network bandwidth, and a device's struggle to maintain a solid network connection.

Even if your signal is good, you may still run into connectivity problems—and they may be tricky to spot if you aren't aware of them. The first of these is an *overloaded network*, which is common during large public gatherings (such as a sporting event) or a widespread emergency that causes a surge in network use. Your device might have full bars but be unable to place calls, send texts, or transfer data. Another explanation for connectivity problems despite a strong signal are restrictions and limits the carrier enforces. You may experience slow data speeds while roaming just because the carrier of the network you are roaming on limits data rates for nonsubscribers. Exceeding the *data usage limits* that your carrier sets can also lead to slow data speeds.

CompTIA calls this last problem *data transmission over limit*. Typically a user will be notified via e-mail or text message, but they may not notice. What happens when a user crosses this line is up to the carrier and the terms set forth in the user's plan. Some carriers stop cellular data usage beyond the preset limits, charge additional data to the user at a much higher cost, or throttle the speed of the connection. Each causes its own complications, but the options are the same: pay to raise data limits, or monitor data use and disable cellular data usage in the configuration settings of the device (see Figure 25-5) as needed.

Figure 25-5
Option to disable
cellular data
in iOS

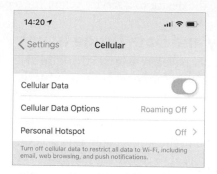

While the abstract side of data usage limits is important, the essential part is that you think about how these various scenarios could manifest on real devices. If you have a corporate plan, knowing the data limits and what happens when they're exceeded will give you a big leg up. What should you suspect when a user turns up at the end of the month with a device that suddenly has terrible call quality in Skype while using cellular data, but works fine over Wi-Fi? Or a traveling employee says she keeps getting calls from colleagues asking why she hasn't weighed in on an important e-mail discussion that hasn't turned up on her device, despite a good connection? A quick check to see whether the user is over the plan limit could spare both of you hours of troubleshooting.

GPS and Location Services Problems

Sometimes the location services on mobile devices will be better at finding where you aren't than where you are. Some inaccuracy can be explained by the hardware a device has available; a Wi-Fi-only tablet with no GPS can get only a general location.

Symptoms of location issues can vary depending on what apps are trying to use location services. Photos might end up tagged with the wrong location, or the coffee shop you picked because it was closest might actually be further away than your device suggests. A navigation app might have trouble identifying your location at all, or it might be sure it knows where you are even when you know you're blocks away. Other symptoms can include prompts and error or informational messages from the OS or apps that rely on location data (see Figure 25-6).

Troubleshooting location problems begins with simple actions such as making sure that your GPS, cellular data, and Wi-Fi are turned on and functioning properly, as sometimes these services can be inadvertently turned off by the user or by an app, and

Figure 25-6
GPS prompt

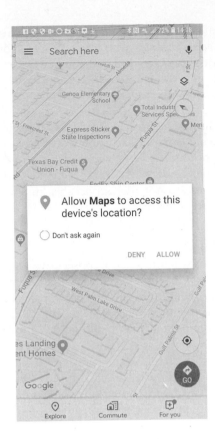

have to be periodically reactivated. Typically, a warning message will indicate that GPS or data services are turned off, so this is easy to identify and fix. Specific apps may have trouble if they are configured not to access or use location services. This is usually a matter of going into the app configuration or location settings and allowing the app to make use of those services.

EXAM TIP If you run into GPS error questions on the exam, remember that all apps will tell you if GPS is turned off and usually ask you if want to turn on GPS. Otherwise, before digging deeper, first consider simple issues such as whether you are in a place where you can get a good GPS signal.

Once you've checked the obvious software reasons for location trouble, it's a good idea to think about the physical environment before you go on a wild-goose chase. GPS won't work underground, will probably be spotty indoors unless you're near a window, and can really struggle in dense urban areas with tall buildings. Don't be spooked into a long search for subtle GPS problems if your device occasionally has trouble deciding which downtown street you're strolling along.

When you're sure there are frequent location problems unexplained by the environment, it's time to dig deeper. Along with the OS issues discussed previously, incorrect OS configuration settings for GPS, cellular, and Wi-Fi services may prevent location services from functioning properly. These configuration items should be checked when multiple apps are having location issues.

If the issues persist, there's a good chance the problem is in the actual GPS or network hardware inside the device, or the OS code that interfaces with it. Look online to see if other device owners report similar trouble on the same device software versions. If you don't see other reports of trouble, the device likely needs a trip to the service center. Although mobile devices may have removable network or GPS modules in them, most of these components are not user serviceable and have to be replaced or repaired by authorized service technicians.

System Lockout

System lockout occurs when too many consecutive login attempts fail, the purpose being to protect the device from brute-force attacks. Some mobile login methods offer enough security to keep someone from unlocking your device if you leave it unattended for a moment, but are not secure enough that someone who stole or found the device couldn't try combinations until one worked, especially if smudges on the screen help narrow the combinations down.

Differing lockout mechanisms may prevent further login attempts for some period of time, require to you log in with the full account credentials the device is registered to, or even wipe your user data as a precaution. Options like this can be configured on the device itself, or centrally through the organization's *mobile device management* (*MDM*) software. If your organization uses lockout, you should advise users not to exceed a certain number of login attempts, and to keep their devices away from toddlers and other miscreants who might trigger the mechanism.

For company-owned devices, the company should probably securely store PINs and maintain current backups of all its mobile devices. For devices owned by individual users, you have to hope that they have backed up their data as well.

In any event, if the device is centrally controlled through MDM software, the organization has the ability to remotely unlock the device. If it's not centrally controlled, then the user may have to plug the device in to a computer and use an application provided by the manufacturer to access the device with a passcode. In the end, if the user can't unlock the device, the only solution may be to restore the device from a backup, if available, or perform a reset to factory default.

Encryption Problems

Methods to secure e-mail messages from anyone but the intended recipient generally fall well outside the accepted parameters of the CompTIA A+ certification, but the exams expect you to troubleshoot mobile devices that are *unable to decrypt e-mail*. To understand the issue, we'd need to dive into a number of topics you won't see until you take the CompTIA Security+ exam. Instead, let's focus on the basics.

For an e-mail message to be secure, it must be *encrypted*—scrambled according to some kind of standard, such as *Pretty Good Privacy* (*PGP*) or *Secure/Multipurpose Internet Mail Extensions* (*S/MIME*). For the recipient to read the e-mail message, he or she needs to have software that can unscramble or *decrypt* the message. To ensure the sender and recipient alone can access the contents of the e-mail message, both people need specific keys that enable encryption and decryption. A *key* is a string of bits used by a computer program to encrypt or decrypt data.

In practice, there are a few reasons a mobile device won't be able to decrypt an e-mail. The simplest of these is that the e-mail client or application doesn't support the encryption standard used to encrypt the message; the fix may be a plugin or an entirely new client. Once you confirm that the e-mail client or app supports this encryption method, follow any steps for configuring the client to use it. Finally, the e-mail client will need access to keys for decrypting the message. With some standards, keys may always be exchanged manually; someone will need to contact the sender to exchange keys. In other cases, keys may be exchanged automatically in at least some circumstances (if you're part of the same organization, for example).

Securing Mobile Devices

Just like any computer we use to input or access sensitive data and network resources, we need to secure our mobile devices. Whether the device is company-owned or personal, we still need to protect ourselves from the needless inconvenience of easily prevented damage, theft, or malware infections, as well as from the chance of important data being lost completely or falling into the wrong hands.

BYOD Versus Corporate-Owned Devices

The *Bring Your Own Device* (*BYOD*) war was briefly fought and lost by organizations hoping to continue the long-held tradition that IT assets belonged to (and were strictly controlled by) the company, not the individual. As mobile devices proliferated, however, IT folks realized the genie was out of the bottle; they couldn't control these new technologies completely. Some companies enforce a policy prohibiting the use of personal devices to access corporate data and resources, particularly in high-security environments. Companies at the other end of the spectrum allow (and even encourage) the use of personal devices to save corporate IT dollars and keep employees happy.

Most organizations fall in the middle of the spectrum and have a mixed environment with both corporate-owned and employee-owned mobile devices. Some organizations institute a cost-sharing program, subsidizing an employee's personally owned device with a monthly phone stipend or discount agreement with mobile device and telecommunications vendors. Regardless of how comfortable an organization is with BYOD, there are important questions to answer.

One question is how much control the corporation has versus the individual. If corporate data is processed or stored on the device, the organization should have some degree of control over it. On the other hand, if the device also belongs to the employee, then the employee should have some control. Another question is who pays for the device and its use. If the organization allows the user to use her own device for company work, does the organization help pay for the monthly bill or compensate the user for its use? Again, this issue is best solved via formal policy and procedures. Yet another important question in a BYOD environment is how to handle employee privacy. If policy allows the organization some degree of control over the device, what degree of privacy does the user maintain on her own device? Can the organization see private data, or have the ability to remotely access a user's personal device and control its use?

The proliferation of mobile devices in the workplace has led to the development of *mobile device management (MDM) policies* that often combine a specialized app on the devices and specialized infrastructure to deal with those devices. These policies also inform *corporate versus end-user device configuration options*; in other words, who should make configuration decisions on things such as e-mail, wireless access, and so forth. As you might imagine, MDM policies are a big deal at the big organization level (the enterprise) because of the scale and complexity of the issues. A CompTIA A+ technician comes in to facilitate the installation of the MDM app, for example, or to help fix key infrastructure problems (like an overloaded WAP because all 25 members of a department bought iWatches at the same time).

Profile Security Requirements

A *profile* is a collection of configuration and security settings that an administrator has created in order to apply those settings to particular categories of users or devices. A profile can be created in several different ways, including through the MDM software, or in a program such as the Apple Configurator, for example. Profiles are typically text-based files, usually in an eXtensible Markup Language (XML) format, and are pushed out to the different devices that require them. Profiles should be developed based on the needs of the organization. You can develop a profile specific to certain platforms, operating systems, or devices, so that a particular type of device will get certain settings.

You can also develop profiles that are specific to different user categories or management groupings (such as mobile sales representatives, middle managers, senior managers, and executives). Your senior organizational executives might have a specific profile applied to their devices granting them additional permissions and access to special apps or connections.

You might also apply group-specific profiles to external users, such as consultants or business partners. These users may require limited access to organizational resources using their own mobile device, their organization's mobile devices, or even mobile devices temporarily issued by your organization. A group-specific profile applied to these external users may give them particular network configuration and security settings so that they can access a business extranet, for example, or use specific VPN settings. They may also require access to particular enterprise or business-to-business (B2B) apps hosted on your organization's servers. In any case, both device- and user-specific profiles can be very helpful in managing larger groups of users, delivering uniform security and configuration settings to their devices based on different mission or business requirements.

Depending on your organizational needs, you could conceivably apply several different profiles to a device at once, based on platform, user group, and so forth.

When multiple profiles are applied, there's a chance some settings will conflict. For example, some restrictive settings for a device profile may not be consistent with some less-restrictive ones in a group or user profile. When both are applied to the device, the different configuration settings may conflict and overwrite each other. The solution is to pay special attention to profile precedence and configure the MDM server to resolve conflicts using criteria such as user group membership or security requirements.

You should also develop profiles that apply to corporate-owned versus employee-owned devices. A profile applied to a device in a BYOD environment may be considerably different than one applied to a company-owned device. This would be based on policy settings affecting privacy, acceptable use of the device, and so on. Figure 25-7 shows how you can conceptually apply different profiles to different device and user groups.

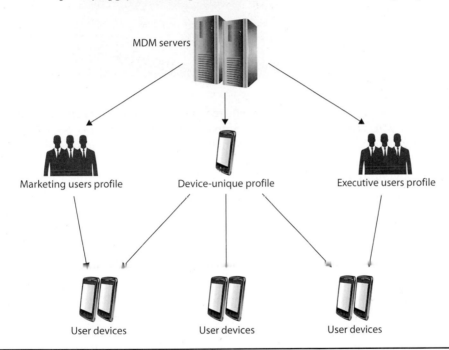

Figure 25-7   Applying profiles to different device and user groups

Preventing Physical Damage

For something shaped a lot like a bar of soap and sometimes almost as slippery, mobile phones can cost a lot of money. That means you need to take steps to prevent damage. The first step you should take to protect your slippery investment is a case, *protective cover*, or sleeve for the mobile device. It doesn't help the HD camcorder in your new iPad if you get a scratch across the lens! You'll get a scratched, blurry movie even though the camcorder is capable of much, much more. Apple makes very nice covers for iPhones and iPads, plus you can get many third-party covers and sleeves (see Figure 25-8).

Figure 25-8
Putting an Apple
Smart cover on
an iPad

Depending on the amount of money you're willing to spend, you can get a cover that helps protect your screen from scratches, impacts, and small amounts of water. Like to scuba with your Android device? Get a specialty waterproof case and go post your deep thoughts to Facebook from 40 feet underwater.

Do the obvious to protect your devices. Don't get them anywhere near liquids. Don't run your smartphone through the wash in your trousers. Don't even think about placing heavy objects on that ~$600 tablet! Use common sense.

Combating Malware

Malware on mobile devices is an interesting issue. Tight controls on the OS and apps make traditional malware infections almost impossible on iOS and Windows Phone devices. When malware strikes, the OS maker supplies periodic *patching/OS updates*, automatic updates and operating system patches. Android lacks some safeguards that we see in iOS and Windows Phone. To plug the gap, there are third-party antivirus and anti-malware single-user (user-level) and enterprise-level solutions available. Figure 25-9 shows an example of user-level antivirus software for an Android device.

In an ideal world, your mobile anti-malware software will cover all threats and work on all the devices used in your corporate network. In a heterogeneous real-world infrastructure, because there may be a variety of mobile devices from different vendors using different operating systems, a one-size-fits-all anti-malware solution probably won't work. Multiple solutions may be necessary for the different devices present on a network, or different modules covering specific types of device may be available from the vendor to integrate with an enterprise-level anti-malware solution.

In any case, the most important part of an enterprise-level anti-malware solution is delivering timely updates to the devices on a routine basis. Network access-control solutions can ensure a device is checked for the latest anti-malware signatures and updated as necessary when it attempts to connect to the network. In the case of user-managed

Figure 25-9
Antivirus app
for Android

devices, you may need policy, network access-control, and other technical solutions to ensure users are updating their own devices in a timely manner.

Dealing with Loss

The best way to make sure you're ready to survive losing a mobile device is to assume it's inevitable. Say it to yourself: every mobile device will get lost at least once. I hope most of your users will prove you wrong, but the odds are good we'll all misplace every device we own at least once. Most of us will be lucky and find it right where we left it, but it could just as easily go the other way.

When you start with the assumption that your device will end up at the mercy, kindness, or ignorance of strangers at least once, it's obvious: you should protect your data from access by putting a good *passcode lock* or *screen lock* on the device. Most mobile devices enable you to set a passcode lock or screen lock through Settings (see Figure 25-10). Do it right now! There are many types of these locks; the most common require you to input a password, PIN, pattern, fingerprint, or successful facial recognition to unlock the mobile device so you can use it. Modern iOS and Android use *full device encryption* to protect the built-in storage, so even a "finder" who dismantles the device to access the drive will not get your documents.

NOTE Chapter 27, "Securing Computers," goes into much depth on malware, including the types of malware as well as the most common sources and symptoms of malware infections.

Figure 25-10
Passcode option
in Settings

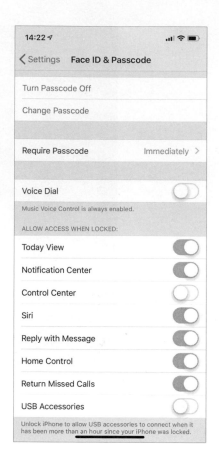

As we discussed in the "System Lockout" section earlier, mobile devices may also have a preset restriction on the number of login attempts that can fail before system lockout occurs. This system lockout slows down someone trying to guess the passcode of a found mobile device while you use locator services or applications to recover or remotely wipe it.

 EXAM TIP For the purposes of the CompTIA A+ 1002 exam, know that *fingerprint lock, face lock, swipe lock,* and passcode lock are screen lock methods used to secure mobile devices.

Apple and Google offer locator services for discovering the whereabouts of a misplaced mobile device. Using Apple's iCloud as an example, log in to your iCloud account and click the Find My iPhone button (despite the name, it also works for iPads). As soon as the device in question accesses the Internet (and thus receives an IP address and posts its MAC address), iCloud will pinpoint the location within a few yards (see Figure 25-11). Very slick!

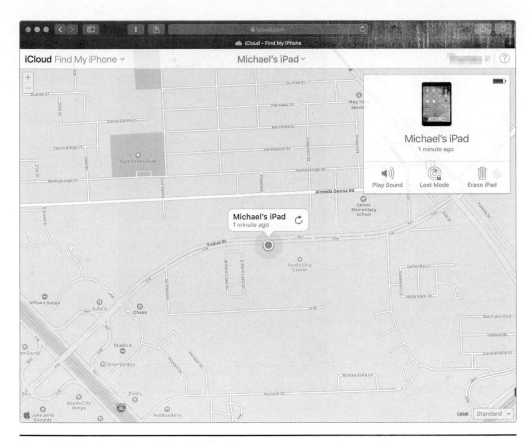

Figure 25-11   Locating a device in iCloud

Recovering from Theft

If your mobile device gets stolen and contains sensitive information, then you have a couple of options for dealing with it. Locator services help, but if you have credit card information or other risky data on your mobile device, you need to act quickly.

First, make sure you keep your data backed up. You should have everything synced to a local machine and, if possible, backed up to one of the remote backup applications—like Microsoft's OneDrive cloud service—to put your data beyond the reach of even a disaster that takes out your house. With Windows Phone, for example, go into Settings and select Backup. This screen lets you select what items on your phone get backed up (see Figure 25-12).

For Apple devices, you back up and restore with one of several services, such as iCloud, iTunes, or use the Apple Configurator to handle a fleet of iOS devices. Android devices use the Google Sync feature to back up and restore.

Second, you can *remotely wipe* your mobile device. Apple, for example, makes it supremely easy through your Apple account. Log in, locate, and nuke your device (see

Figure 25-12
Selecting items
to get backed up

Figure 25-13). You may never get the device back, but at least the bad guys won't have your data. It's equally simple with Android devices. Log in and follow the same process—locate and nuke.

Figure 25-13
Erase iPad

Securing Your Data

Every security scenario we've discussed so far (remote wipe excepted) was designed to secure the device itself. Let's turn to how we can protect our actual data.

Multifactor Authentication

The terms multifactor and single-factor authentication make the difference obvious enough: the number of factors used to authenticate the user. What the terms don't make obvious is what exactly an *authentication factor* is, and why one of the most popular authentication schemes—a user name and password—is a kind of single-factor authentication. Let's start with the factors. First, there is the *knowledge* factor: something the user knows, such as a user name, password, date of birth, Social Security number, etc. The second factor is *ownership* or *possession*: something the user has in her possession, such as a smart card or token. A third factor is *inherence*: something the user either is or something they do. An example of an inherence factor is a biometric identifier, such as a fingerprint or retinal pattern. You commonly hear these three factors referred to as something the user knows, something the user has, and something the user is.

Other authentication factors exist, but are not as commonly considered in security authentication. For example, there's the *location* factor: somewhere you are. This can be used if the individual's location can be pinpointed via GPS or some other method. The individual may be required to be at a certain location in order to log in to the system, for example. Yet another is the *temporal* factor. As the name implies, schemes using the temporal factor may require logon at a certain time of day, or even within so many seconds or minutes of another event. Token methods of authentication also use time factors, as the PIN displayed on a token is only good for a finite amount of time.

Armed with the factors, let's consider authenticating with a single factor. The most common schemes require a user name and password; both are something you know, so the scheme uses a single factor. You can also think of a traditional door lock as *single-factor authentication*, the key it requires is something the user has—a possession factor.

During the initial push to move beyond single-factor authentication, the term *two-factor authentication* grew common—and you'll still hear people use this term. Over the years, however, authentication methods using more than two factors have grown increasingly common, so it has become more correct to say multifactor authentication. *Multifactor authentication* can use a variety of methods, as long as it uses more than one.

Just because the term sounds fancy and might make us think of complex systems at secret government installations, don't assume multifactor authentication hasn't played a role in everyday life for decades. For example, when you use a bank's ATM, you're using multifactor authentication: something you possess (the ATM card) and something you know (the correct PIN).

 EXAM TIP Don't confuse the user name and password combination with multifactor authentication. Only one factor is being used here, the knowledge factor, making this a form of single-factor authentication.

Biometric Authentication

Combined with other authentication factors, biometric elements can provide a very secure multifactor authentication mechanism. An example of *biometric authentication* is presenting a smartcard to a proximity badge reader and then placing your finger on a fingerprint reader to access a secure area.

Mobile devices use biometrics, too. Laptops have included fingerprint readers for a few years already, and they are common in other mobile devices such as smartphones. A prime example is Apple's Touch ID; starting with the iPhone 5s, the iPhone can unlock with a fingerprint. Current iOS devices use facial recognition to identify and authenticate users. Check out Figure 25-14.

Figure 25-14
Face ID options

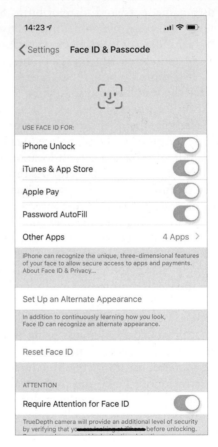

Authenticator Applications

Access to third-party or corporate networks often requires strong authentication methods. Access to a corporate VPN, for example, may require a specific app, approved and published by the organization, configured with the correct security settings. Generic apps have the ability to use multiple sets of credentials to access different Web sites, networks, or network-based services (for example, corporate e-mail, VPN access, and so forth). There are also apps that can act as tokens or issue temporary session PINs for multifactor authentication. The key to these apps is configuration; settings vary per app, but might include network configuration, authentication or encryption settings, and properly registering a given service with the authenticator app.

Trusted Sources Versus Untrusted Sources

For the most part, getting software from *trusted sources*—legitimate app stores run by the major vendors, such as Apple, Google, Microsoft, and Amazon—is both easy and secure. Different vendors have their own requirements (including security) that developers must meet in order to get an app into the vendor's store. Most differences stem from the development and support model used by the vendor.

Apple strictly controls all aspects of the device and the apps available in the App Store (though organizations have some freedom to distribute apps developed in-house to their own devices). For example, Apple has exact requirements for how developers must create an app sold via the App Store. Android, on the other hand, has much less central control. One way Android's relaxed controls manifest is the ability to install apps from *untrusted sources*.

The operating system flavors developed by different Android device makers can change which sources are and aren't trusted. What may run on devices sold by one vendor isn't necessarily guaranteed to run on another vendor's device, even though they all use variations of the Android operating system. A prime example is Amazon's line of Fire devices (including products like Fire TV, Fire Tablet, and Kindle Fire), which can only get apps from the Amazon Appstore. Additionally, even apps from the Google Play store aren't subject to guidelines as strict as the ones Apple uses. That doesn't mean they are necessarily less secure, but it does make security issues more likely.

The security weakness third-party app stores create is essentially apps from *unapproved* or *unofficial* sources. There are definitely legitimate app sources outside of Google Play, such as device manufacturers, communications carriers, and in-house corporate development sources. Some sources are not so legitimate, and are usually unapproved by the vendors, manufacturers, and corporate customers. You may also need to modify your mobile OS to run some apps you obtain through unofficial channels. See "Unauthorized Root Access," later in the chapter, for more details.

When getting apps from questionable sources, risks include apps that contain malware or steal personal data and transmit it to a third party. Additionally, some apps require replacing the operating system with one that's not approved by the vendor; this not only invalidates the warranty on most devices, but could cause the device to be unstable and not operate properly.

Firewalls

While we'll discuss them in greater depth in Chapter 27, for now it's enough to know that software firewalls on individual hosts protect them from network-based threats. It isn't completely clear what CompTIA expects you to know about firewalling mobile devices. Generally, mobile devices don't use a firewall, because they don't have lots of services listening on open ports (like a traditional computer would). But, because they aren't listening, you can think of them as having a de facto firewall. The cellular and Wi-Fi networks mobile devices use also employ firewalls to protect all networked devices.

Depending on the OS, you may be able to find and install more traditional software firewall packages. One example of a software firewall for Android is shown in Figure 25-15. Android software firewall packages include basic rule elements for constructing rules to filter specific traffic coming into the host. Many of these packages also include solutions for anti-malware and basic intrusion detection.

Figure 25-15

An Android
firewall app

Some of these software firewall solutions are standalone and must be configured and managed by the user, whereas some are enterprise-level solutions and can be centrally configured, updated, and managed by the systems administrator. Keep in mind that software firewall packages work at a very basic level and can't possibly contain every single network threat. Still, they serve as a second line of defense for the host, and are part of any good, layered, defense-in-depth security design.

Mobile OS and Application Security Issues

Security is a complicated, ever-evolving topic. We've already discussed aspects of mobile device security at various points in the chapter, but there are some additional security issues the user and organization need to be aware of and take steps to prevent. We'll begin with a discussion of tools you can use to troubleshoot mobile OS and application security issues broadly, and then turn to some of the common risks, symptoms, and clues related to mobile security issues.

Troubleshooting Tools

While the foundation of good security is staying informed of new threats and being vigilant about the patches, configuration updates, policy changes, anti-malware updates, and user re-education required to address these new threats, this foundation is just about not giving attackers an easy win. Beyond this, we have to cope with security issues that require constant vigilance: novel threats, avoiding insecure applications, and irresolvable vulnerabilities.

Though your greatest assets are your own curiosity, instincts, and persistence, you can augment these with a variety of technical tools for troubleshooting mobile security issues. Let's look at some of these tools, grouped in terms of the issues they are most useful for addressing: network attacks and app security.

Network Attacks

Device makers originally designed mobile devices to be gregarious by nature—they are more useful this way—but network attacks can exploit such openness. We'll consider specific issues a little later in the "Unintended Connections" section, and focus now on tools for identifying and mitigating risks: device security settings, user training, Wi-Fi analyzers, and cell tower analyzers.

Device Security Settings Because network attacks generally prey on devices that are overeager to connect, the first step to mitigating these threats is to make sure your devices won't automatically connect to any open Wi-Fi network or nearby Bluetooth device. You can apply these settings manually on each device, but you can also use an MDM (remember, that's a mobile device manager), or similar software made for managing more than one device, such as Apple Configurator.

User Training It won't help (much) to configure your devices to avoid automatic connections if your users still select any open Wi-Fi network or agree to any pairing request without considering the consequences. Similarly, your network will be at risk if your users don't recognize any of the warning signs that their connection to your organization's secure Wi-Fi network has been intercepted by an evil-twin wireless access point (WAP). Teach them what is normal, and train them to stop and report anything that seems out of place.

Wi-Fi Analyzer In addition to using a *Wi-Fi analyzer* for tasks such as figuring out what channel a network should use, optimizing WAP placement, or finding dead spots, you can use one to map out nearby networks (see Figure 25-16). Most of these are probably genuine networks in neighboring buildings or offices, but there's always a chance someone will set up a WAP for the wrong reasons.

Cell Tower Analyzer Like a Wi-Fi analyzer, a *cell tower analyzer* helps identify nearby cellular signals, estimate their distance and direction (see Figure 25-17), measure their signal strength, and collect other information such as the technologies they are using, network names, and more. A simple use might be to confirm signal quality for a user having trouble connecting, or to map out access in the building. There's also a chance you'll spot an illegitimate tower operating nearby—and your organization might be the target.

Figure 25-16
A Wi-Fi analyzer
app on Android
showing several
SSIDs in the area

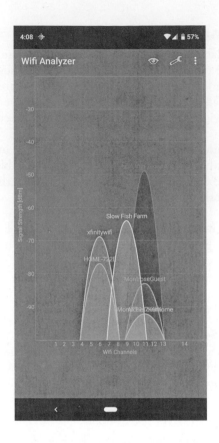

App Security

One of the important things to understand about malware is that the "best" malware accomplishes its objective without anyone detecting it. Almost anyone could figure out that malware is to blame for a device that runs like it's full of molasses and constantly redirects your searches or Web requests to sites that announce that you've won a round-trip to Mars. Because the most dangerous malware is subtle, you need to use tools to help you catch the easy stuff, freeing your attention to see subtle signs something is amiss.

Anti-Malware and App Scanners   Mobile anti-malware apps, much like their desktop counterparts, use signatures and lists to scan a device in order to identify, block, remove, or warn about known malware. An *app scanner*, by contrast, looks through the permissions requested by your installed apps to assess the risk they pose to security and privacy. You may find some separate apps for performing each of these tasks, or combined apps that can do both. You won't find these apps available for iOS, but many of the same features are available through the Settings app.

App scanners typically run before an app is installed or updated, and can give you information such as what network connectivity the app requires, what permissions it needs, and what access the app has to certain hardware and functions on your device.

Figure 25-17
My Android-based cell tower analyzer estimating the location of a cell tower

App scanners can also tell you what type of data access the app has to your personal information, such as contacts and media files (see Figure 25-18).

App scanners may sound a little less useful at first, but think of every installed app as posing a few different risks. First, there's the direct risk that the app is designed to spy on you or steal your data. Next, there's the risk that the app maker will lose control of your personal information once it leaves your device. Finally, there's the risk that a vulnerability in the app will allow an attacker to use it against you.

Some users are savvy enough to avoid directly installing malware. But how many of those users know enough to assess the risk that an attacker in the future will be able to exploit a vulnerability in an app they're installing today?

Backup and Restore   Maintaining a current backup of your device is one measure you need to take in case all else fails. Different tools used to perform backups and restore data include MDM software, iTunes, and the various synchronization tools for Android and Microsoft devices; another option is to back up the data to the manufacturer's user cloud storage, such as Microsoft OneDrive or Apple iCloud.

Some malware can put down deep roots and be hard to expunge. A recent full backup predating the infestation can give you the confidence to focus on making sure you get rid of the malware, rather than focusing on being sure you don't lose important data.

Figure 25-18
Combined anti-
malware and
app scanner

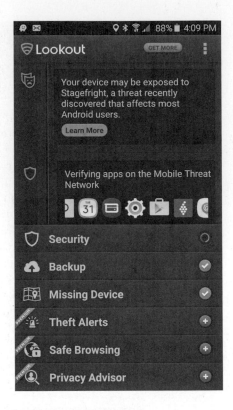

App Troubleshooting Tools We've already looked at tools for troubleshooting general mobile device and app issues: force stop, uninstalling and reinstalling apps, and a factory reset. You can also use these tools to pinpoint and address app security issues.

Whenever you see clues or symptoms of malware or another app security issue, remember that one way you can isolate the cause is to stop apps until you identify the cause. When you know what is causing the symptoms, uninstall it. If the app is reputable and the symptoms could be nonmalicious, reinstall it to see if this fixes the problem. If these steps don't resolve the behavior, use a factory reset to cleanse the device.

Risks, Symptoms, and Clues

The value of your curiosity, intuition, and persistence begins to show in a big way when we look at the risks, symptoms, and clues that malware or some other security problem is present. When you read about a potential risk here, don't assume you'll only see it by itself. Because malware and other attacks can be creative, complex, and multifaceted, view the scenarios discussed below as risks to understand and manage, symptoms of malware or an attack, or merely clues of an attack underway.

Much like you shouldn't assume you'll see these things as isolated incidents, you shouldn't assume when you encounter one or more of them that malware or an attack is necessarily present. In fact, we've already discussed many of the issues in this section as they relate to other kinds of mobile device problems.

Unexpected Resource Use

If you think about it, malware is just software or a program that uses your device for work or tasks you don't want it to do. Like any program working hard, malware can cause resource issues. Because resource issues can also be relatively benign problems fixed by a soft reset, it's easy to shrug them off. Be suspicious, especially if you see patterns and can't find an obvious explanation; the first clues of an ongoing attempt to spy on your company may well be an uptick in data outbound from affected cellular devices.

Power Drain and High Resource Utilization   A hot phone, high resource use, and excessive power drain can be common signs that an app is frozen or malfunctioning, but they might also be symptoms that your device is doing precisely what a malware developer intends. The device might be hot, sluggish, or low on battery because it's a live recording device uploading everything it records in real time, or because it's copying files available on the network to a remote location.

Slow Data Speeds   Likewise, slow data speeds can be signs of a network issue, signal-quality problem, frozen apps, regular syncing of large files—or a sign the device is busy uploading or downloading something without your knowledge. Slow data speeds may also clue you in to one or more devices that are attempting to use an illegitimate WAP or cell tower that has a lower capacity than its official counterpart.

Data Transmission Over Limit   As discussed earlier, a data transmission limit is a line in the sand that indicates when a device has used more data than its plan or carrier allots for it. Perhaps the user drove across the country while listening to Spotify, or perhaps the device is uploading stolen data from the device and other networked locations.

Unintended Connections

A major security issue is unintended network (such as cellular, Wi-Fi, and Bluetooth) connections. Unintended cellular network connections aren't common since these are preprogrammed into the phone by the carrier and periodically updated, but there is a technique called *tower spoofing* that involves setting up equipment to spoof a carrier's tower and infrastructure and cause a cellular device to use it instead of the normal tower equipment. It requires overpowering the nearest legitimate cell signal, causing the cellular device to lock onto it instead. Equipment used in tower spoofing can also eavesdrop on any conversation, even if it is encrypted. In some cases, the equipment can fool the device into turning off encryption completely—and sophisticated attacks can even install malware on the device.

Just as hackers have been using this technique for a few years, law enforcement officials have been reportedly using it as well. Since 2010, there have been numerous court cases highlighted in the media questioning the admissibility of evidence obtained from cell signal interception. Media reports say various federal, state, and local law enforcement agencies use a device called a "Stingray" to intercept a suspect's cell traffic using tower spoofing equipment and techniques. There's even an aircraft-mounted version, known as a "Dirtbox."

NOTE Though much of the news coverage on tower spoofing focuses on U.S. law enforcement agencies using the Stingray, you could just as easily encounter malicious cellular or Wi-Fi networks run (for a variety of reasons) by individuals, businesses, organized crime, and governments anywhere in the world.

Unintended Wi-Fi connections and *unintended Bluetooth pairings* can enable malicious people to access, steal, or modify data. Configure your mobile device not to connect to unknown Wi-Fi networks or automatically pair with other Bluetooth devices. This will require you to manually connect to known and trusted Wi-Fi networks, and manually pair with Bluetooth devices—but it's worth it. If the device is centrally managed, MDM software can enforce these protections via profile settings.

Signal Drop and Weak Signal

Earlier, we looked at dropped and weak signals in terms of their impact on battery life, power management, and running apps. Sometimes these signal issues go unnoticed or are only a minor inconvenience. When it comes to cellular signals, they can also be one of the few clues you'll get that your device is interacting with a spoofed cell tower.

If you or your users are in an area where the signal quality should be (and usually is) excellent, be curious—especially if you have multiple reports of difficulty. Check with the relevant cellular providers to see if they have any known tower issues in the area. Fire up a cell tower analyzer and compare nearby signals with what you've seen in the past, or with third-party resources online.

If users are suddenly reporting that Wi-Fi quality is low in an area where it was high, or you notice your device sees a network with a strong signal and the correct SSID in what used to be a dead spot, check it out. There may be a rogue WAP on the loose.

Unauthorized Data Access

Securing data stored on a mobile device is hard. The building's security guards might stop a courier from walking out with a desktop under his arm, but they probably won't notice an extra phone in his pocket. Even if they do, he might just confidently claim he has to carry an extra phone for work and go on his way. If I accidentally leave my phone behind at lunch, there's a chance I won't notice until I head to my car that evening. Device locks and remote wipe can usually prevent unauthorized users from accessing data on a mobile device—as long as you wipe the device before it is compromised.

Data can leak out other ways, though, such as removable memory storage cards, and settings in the device's OS or applications. Removable memory cards should be encrypted if they contain sensitive data, so an unauthorized person can't access data if they are removed from the device. Security and privacy settings on the device can help protect personal data, and the same settings can be configured in different apps that need to access personal data.

One of the more obvious risks to every networked app with access to data is the possibility that it will leak some of that data (whether intentionally or not). In some cases, it can be hard to figure out where the leak is. If an attacker used tax returns you stuck in Dropbox to obtain a loan in your name, where and when did the data go? You had local copies on your phone, laptop, and desktop, plus what was available if your Dropbox credentials were compromised, and any copies that transited over the network. Perhaps the attacker stole them directly from the company that did your taxes.

The point is that leaked files are a risk, a potential symptom of an ongoing security issue, and a possible clue to what that issue might be. A full audit of the many ways an important file could've leaked out of a networked environment is beyond what can be expected of a CompTIA A+ tech, but he or she may well get the first chance to escalate the issue, or write it off as a compromised login and make the user change passwords.

 EXAM TIP Portable and mobile devices present amazing opportunities for your personal information to become much less personal and a lot more public. The CompTIA A+ 1002 exam calls this "leaked personal files/data," but it could just as easily be translated as "your phone password wasn't strong and you left the phone in a kiosk at the ski resort." (Not that this has ever happened to me.)

Unauthorized Account Access

Unauthorized account access is a big deal not only for the mobile device itself, but also for all organizational networks it can connect to. If someone steals the account credentials or is able to access a mobile device configured to remember the credentials, then they have an entry point into an organizational network. As discussed earlier, you should plan based on the assumption every device will be lost.

To keep VPN and e-mail connections secure, the device should not store user names and passwords for connecting automatically. This way, lost or stolen devices can't be used to access these services (at least not without also stealing credentials) because they still require authentication. Unauthorized account access can lead to a malicious person stealing or accessing data not only on the device, but also on the larger network.

When a device is lost, act with an abundance of caution. Treat the previously described precaution as something to protect you until the device is reported missing. Once you know it is missing, change the user's credentials. Keep in mind that compromised account credentials could also be a clue that one of the user's devices itself has been compromised, and may be an ongoing threat to the organization.

Unauthorized Root Access

To help secure the device, mobile operating systems all restrict the actions (such as installing apps or changing settings) that a user can normally perform. There are ways around these restrictions, though the name of each method differs by OS, depending on how the OS restricts what the user can do. In order to remove these restrictions, a user has to either *jailbreak* (iOS) or *root* (Android) the device; let's take a look at each.

 EXAM TIP Know jailbreak and root and the OS associated with each, but keep in mind that it's common to see both of these terms used in relation to removing access restrictions from any given device.

Jailbreaking means the user installs a program on the iOS device that changes settings Apple didn't intend for users to change. Jailbreaking allows a user to install blocked software, such as apps that don't come from the App Store or apps that don't meet Apple's legal and quality requirements. Jailbreaking also enables a user to unlock functionality on the device.

Rooting an Android device is a similar procedure to grant the user full administrative access to the lower-level functionality of the device. As in the case of jailbreaking, this is also done to install software or enable functions that could not otherwise be used on the device. Although none of the popular device vendors condone rooting, they have little recourse beyond voiding the warranty if the user owns the device.

The important thing to keep in mind with all of these methods is that they give the user more power at the expense of disabling protections that limit the damage malicious apps can do to the device. There are some things you just can't use a device for without removing these restrictions, but the benefit should always be weighed against the risk, especially when it comes to deciding whether to allow jailbroken/rooted devices on your network.

 NOTE Organizational networks may use an MDM to detect and block devices that have used one of these methods to remove restrictions.

The manufacturer or service provider may prevent a device from connecting to their services if they detect the change. There are also immediate risks: a failed attempt could brick the device, or perhaps just render it unusable until you restore it completely from a backup (removing the jailbreaking/rooting software in the process).

Unauthorized Location Tracking

We discussed the benefits of GPS and location tracking earlier, but there are also risks involved. Configuration settings in the OS and apps may allow a user's location to be sent to third parties, sometimes without explicit consent or knowledge. The best way to prevent this is to turn off the GPS function or location services unless they are needed. Another way is to configure the device and apps that use geotracking to prevent unauthorized tracking, if the device allows it. Some apps—or specific features—simply won't work until geotracking is enabled (see Figure 25-19).

Keep in mind that the GPS functionality in a mobile device is not the only way to track its location; cellular networks and Wi-Fi are also used to track device location, although not as precisely as GPS. Some of the network attacks in the "Unintended Connections" section can also be used to locate or track a device.

An organization can track when its employees enter or exit a predefined area using a process called *geofencing*, though the employees may rebel against this form of workplace surveillance. Disgruntled employees might just leave their devices unattended and walk out of the building. Or they might seek legal advice and consider bringing litigation

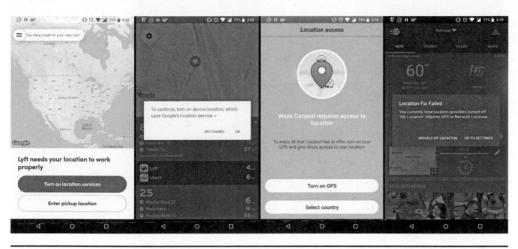

Figure 25-19 Four Android apps prompting the user to enable location services

against the organization for invasion of privacy. Before implementing a geofencing program, it's a good idea to talk through the expected benefits, legal consequences, and impact on employee satisfaction.

Unauthorized Camera and Microphone Activation

App features, malware, and unauthorized network connections can potentially be used to activate (or disable!) some features on a mobile device. Any built-in cameras and microphones are of particular concern, because they enable an attacker to move beyond sensitive data on the device and effectively spy on anyone near it.

NOTE Some of the most sophisticated attacks using methods discussed in the earlier "Unintended Connections" section can reportedly cause a device to appear to power down, while still leaving its microphone active. Attacks of this quality may be unavoidable until carriers and device makers secure their networks and devices against them, but you can still be on the lookout for strange behavior.

The ways to prevent these exploits are by restricting camera and microphone permissions in apps or operating systems (when they allow it), taking steps previously described to prevent unauthorized network connections, and using anti-malware solutions on the device. Even when you're looking at a popular app by a trustworthy developer, such as the iOS apps with camera permissions in Figure 25-20, keep in mind that any vulnerabilities in a networked app with camera and microphone permissions could allow an attacker to listen in.

Figure 25-20
Apps with
permission
to access my
iPhone's camera

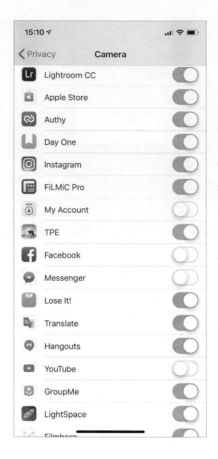

Chapter Review

Questions

1. After five minutes of struggling with a painfully sluggish device, you finally manage to close the offending application. What's the best next step?

    A. Reopen the application and hope it doesn't freeze again.

    B. Uninstall the application and look for a replacement.

    C. Perform a soft reset and see if the app runs smoothly afterward.

    D. Close all open applications and attempt to reopen the application to see if it freezes again.

2. Which of the following would be a legitimate reason a mobile device is running slowly?

    A. Incorrect calibration

    B. RAM too slow

    C. Lack of storage space

    D. Incorrect version of application

3. Joyce notices her GPS map app gives the error "GPS coordinates not available." What should she try first?

    A. Run another GPS app.

    B. Stop and start GPS on the mobile device.

    C. Move to a place where she can get a good GPS signal.

    D. Update the mobile device's firmware.

4. You've lost your iPhone. What would you use to try to find it?

    A. iTunes

    B. iFind

    C. Location Services

    D. iCloud

5. Fred wants to play *World of Warcraft* on his desktop system. He logs in and then the game asks for a code that is generated by an authenticator app on his Android phone. This is an example of:

    A. Multifactor authentication

    B. Factor authorization

    C. Multifactor authorization

    D. Factor authentication

6. Jailbreaking an iPhone gives access to:

    A. The administrator account

    B. The root account

    C. The /bin folder

    D. The system BIOS

7. A great way to protect data on a removable media card is to:

    A. Encrypt it

    B. Lock it

    C. Remove it when unneeded

    D. Format it

8. Which mobile operating system requires a third-party software firewall?

   A. Android

   B. macOS

   C. Windows Mobile

   D. iOS

9. Users bringing personally owned mobile devices into an enterprise environment is called:

   A. Importing

   B. CYMK

   C. Providing

   D. BYOD

10. What do app scanners do?

    A. Scan QR codes and barcodes for hidden codes

    B. Analyze the traffic into and out of an application for suspicious behavior

    C. Analyze the permissions used by installed applications to highlight security risks

    D. Analyze Wi-Fi signals to identify evil-twin WAPs

Answers

1. **C.** After five minutes of struggling with a painfully sluggish device, definitely perform a soft reset and see if the app runs smoothly afterward.

2. **C.** Lack of storage space would be a legitimate reason a mobile device is running slowly.

3. **C.** Joyce needs to move to a place where she can get a good GPS signal.

4. **D.** Apple's iPhone uses the Find My iPhone feature of iCloud.

5. **A.** Using both a password and a security code is an example of multifactor authentication.

6. **B.** Jailbreaking is unique to iOS to provide access to the root account.

7. **A.** A great way to protect data on a removable media card is to encrypt it.

8. **A.** Only Android requires a third-party software firewall.

9. **D.** Users bringing personally owned mobile device into an enterprise environment is known as Bring Your Own Device (BYOD).

10. **C.** App scanners analyze the permissions used by installed applications to highlight security risks.

Printers and Multifunction Devices

In this chapter, you will learn how to
- Describe current printer and multifunction device technologies
- Explain the laser printing process
- Install and configure a printer or multifunction device
- Recognize and fix basic printer and multifunction device problems

Despite all the talk about the "paperless office," paper documents continue to be a vital part of the typical office. Some computers are used exclusively for the purpose of producing paper documents. Many people simply still prefer dealing with a hard copy, even as portable devices have proliferated. Developers cater to this preference by using metaphors such as *page*, *workbook*, and *binder* in their applications.

In the past, your average office had an array of electronic and mechanical devices dedicated to performing a single task with paper documents. Think printers, copiers, scanners, and fax machines. Back in the 1990s, the *multifunction device* (*MFD*), also known as a *multifunction printer* (*MFP*), tried to consolidate multiple functions (often printing and scanning) into a single device. At first these devices weren't terribly great at any of their functions, but today's mature multifunction devices get their many jobs done well.

The CompTIA A+ certification strongly stresses the area of printing and expects a high degree of technical knowledge of the function, components, maintenance, and repair of all types of printers and multifunction devices.

This chapter examines the common varieties of printers and scanners, then looks at specifics of how a laser printer works. The chapter continues with the steps for installing a multifunction device in a typical personal computer and concludes with troubleshooting issues.

1001

Printer and Multifunction Device Components and Technologies

The multifunction devices your average person encounters in daily life probably sit on a desk, shelf, or countertop, and they tend to be fairly similar in appearance. Because of this, when most of us think about MFDs, we tend to picture small desktop *all-in-one* devices (which can usually be used as a printer, scanner, copier, and fax machine) connected to a nearby computer (see Figure 26-1 for an example).

Figure 26-1
All-in-one
printer/scanner/
fax machine/
copier/iPhone
dock

The reality is that these desktop devices, descendants of the desktop printer and scanner, are just the low end of the market. As you head upmarket, multifunction printers look more like the descendants of copy machines and even small printing presses. Despite how different these high-end devices may look, they still share a core set of components—a printer and scanner of some sort—with the all-in-ones you're probably familiar with. As you go upmarket, the greatest improvements tend to be in speed/capacity, durability, and document handling/finishing features such as sorting, stapling, binding, and so on.

Because MFDs are so varied, we'll look at some of the individual components and technologies you may find inside them separately—be prepared to encounter these components as both standalone devices and included with other components in an MFD. I've added 3-D printers to this section; you won't find these as anything but standalone devices, not MFDs.

Printers

No other piece of your computer system is available in a wider range of styles, configurations, and feature sets than a printer, or at such a wide price variation. What a printer can and can't do is largely determined by the type of printer technology it uses—that is, how it gets the image onto the paper. Modern printers can be categorized into several types: impact, inkjet, dye-sublimation, thermal, laser, 3-D, and virtual.

Impact Printers

Printers that create an image on paper by physically striking an ink ribbon against the paper's surface are known as *impact printers*. Although *daisy-wheel* printers (essentially an electric typewriter attached to the computer instead of directly to a keyboard) have largely disappeared, their cousins, *dot-matrix printers*, still soldier on in many offices. Although dot-matrix printers don't deliver what most home users want—high quality and flexibility at a low cost—they're still widely found in businesses for two reasons: dot-matrix printers have a large installed base in businesses, and they can be used for multipart forms because they actually strike the paper. Impact printers tend to be relatively slow and noisy, but when speed, flexibility, and print quality are not critical, they provide acceptable results. Computers that print multipart forms, such as *point of sale* (*POS*) machines, use special *impact paper* that can print receipts in duplicate, triplicate, or more. These POS machines represent the major market for new impact printers, although many older dot-matrix printers remain in use.

Dot-matrix printers use a grid, or matrix, of tiny pins, also known as *printwires*, to strike an inked printer ribbon and produce images on paper (see Figure 26-2). The case that holds the printwires is called a *printhead*. Using either 9 or 24 pins, dot-matrix printers treat each page as a picture broken up into a dot-based raster image. The 9-pin dot-matrix printers are generically called *draft quality*, while the 24-pin printers are known as *letter quality* or *near-letter quality* (*NLQ*). The BIOS for the printer (either built into the printer or a printer driver) interprets the raster image in the same way a monitor does, "painting" the image as individual dots. Naturally, the more pins, the higher the resolution. Figure 26-3 illustrates the components common to dot-matrix printers. Many dot matrix printers use continuous-feed paper with holes on its sides that are engaged by metal sprockets to pull the paper through—this is known as *tractor-feed paper* because the sprockets are reminiscent of the wheels on a tractor.

Figure 26-2
An Epson FX-880+ dot-matrix printer (photo courtesy of Epson America, Inc.)

 EXAM TIP Printers can also use *duplex assemblies*, which enable the printer to automatically print on both sides of the paper. Some printers include this feature built in, while others require a piece of additional hardware that flips the paper for the printer.

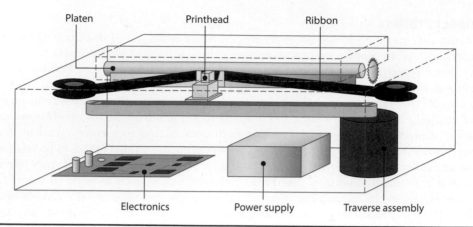

Figure 26-3   Inside a dot-matrix printer

Inkjet Printers

Inkjet printers (also called *ink-dispersion printers*) like the one in Figure 26-4 are relatively simple devices. An inkjet printer uses a *printhead* connected to a *carriage* that contains the ink. A belt and motor move the carriage back and forth so the ink can cover the whole page. A *roller* grabs paper from a paper tray (usually under or inside the printer) or feeder (usually on the back of the printer) and advances it through the printer (see Figure 26-5).

Figure 26-4
Typical inkjet
printer

The ink is ejected through tiny tubes. Most inkjet printers use heat to move the ink, while a few use a mechanical method. The heat-method printers use tiny resistors or electroconductive plates at the end of each tube that literally boil the ink; this creates a tiny air bubble that ejects a droplet of ink onto the paper, thus creating a portion of the image (see Figure 26-6).

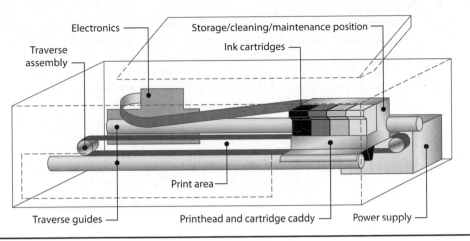

Figure 26-5 Inside an inkjet printer

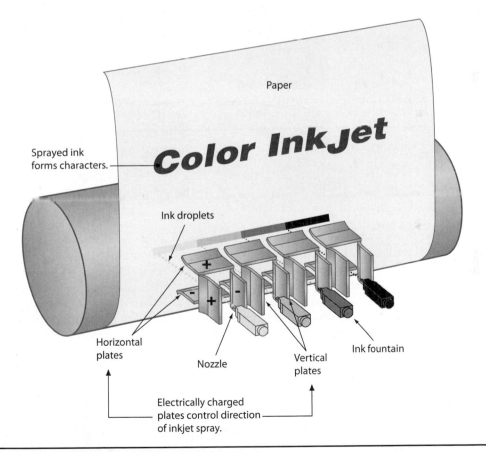

Figure 26-6 Detail of the inkjet printhead

The ink is stored in special small containers called *ink cartridges*. Older inkjet printers had two cartridges: one for black ink and another for colored ink. The color cartridge had separate compartments for cyan (blue), magenta (red), and yellow ink, to print colors by using a method known as CMYK (you'll read more about CMYK later in this chapter). If your color cartridge ran out of one of the colors, you had to purchase a whole new color cartridge or deal with a messy refill kit.

Printer manufacturers began to separate the ink colors into three separate cartridges so that printers came with four cartridges: one for each color and a fourth for black (see Figure 26-7). This not only was more cost-effective for the user, but it also resulted in higher-quality printouts. Today you can find color inkjet printers with six, eight, or more color cartridges. In addition to the basic CMYK inks, the additional cartridges provide for green, blue, gray, light cyan, dark cyan, and more. Typically, printers using more ink cartridges produce higher-quality printed images—and cost more.

Figure 26-7
Inkjet ink
cartridges

In recent years, manufacturers such as Epson and Canon have introduced ink-jet printers with refillable ink tanks, radically changing the economics of printing. Rather than selling printers inexpensively and raking in money on throw-away ink cartridges, consumers and businesses can print in glorious color without the hassle (or guilt). The printers, such as the Epson EcoTank line, cost a lot more than previous models (think $400–$600 rather than $60–$120), but come with a couple of years' worth of ink fresh out of the box. Let the color flow.

The two key features of an inkjet printer are the *print resolution*—how densely the printer lays down ink on the page—and the print speed. Resolution is measured in horizontal and vertical *dots per inch* (*dpi*), such as 2400 × 600 dpi. Higher numbers mean that the ink dots on the page are closer together, so your printed documents will look better. Resolution is most important when you're printing complex images such as full-color photos, or when you're printing for duplication and you care that your printouts look good. Print speed is measured in *pages per minute* (*ppm*), and this specification is normally indicated right on the printer's box. Most printers have one (faster) speed for monochrome printing—that is, using only black ink—and another for full-color printing.

Another feature of inkjet printers is that they can support a staggering array of print media. Using an inkjet printer, you can print on a variety of matte or glossy photo papers, iron-on transfers, and other specialty media; some printers can print directly onto specially coated optical discs, or even fabric. Imagine running a T-shirt through your printer with your own custom slogan (how about "I'm CompTIA A+ Certified!"). The inks have improved over the years, too, now delivering better quality and longevity than ever. Where older inks would smudge if the paper got wet or start to fade after a short time, modern inks are smudge proof and of archival quality—for example, some inks by Epson are projected to last up to 200 years.

For best results with all this variety of media available, you need to make sure the print settings match the paper/media type. In Windows 10, for example, go to Settings | Devices | Printers & scanners. Select the printer installed, click Manage, and go to Printer preferences. There you can change the media type to match.

EXAM TIP   Print resolution is measured in dots per inch (dpi) and print speed is measured in pages per minute (ppm).

Try This!   Pages per Minute Versus Price

Printer speed is a key determinant of a printer's price, and this is an easy assertion to prove, so try this!

1. Open a browser and head over to the Web site for HP (www.hp.com), Canon (www.canon.com), Epson (www.epson.com), Brother (www.brother .com), or Samsung (www.samsung.com). These five companies make most of the printers on the market today.

2. Pick a printer technology and check the price, from the cheapest to the most expensive. Then look for printers that have the same resolution but different ppm rates.

3. Check the prices and see how the ppm rate affects the price of two otherwise identical printers.

Dye-Sublimation Printers

The term *sublimation* means to cause something to change from a solid form into a vapor and then back into a solid. This is exactly the process behind *dye-sublimation printing*, sometimes called *thermal dye transfer* printing. *Dye-sublimation printers* are used mainly for photo printing, high-end desktop publishing, medical and scientific imaging, and other applications for which fine detail and rich color are more important than cost and speed. Smaller, specialized printers called snapshot printers use dye-sublimation specifically for printing photos at a reduced cost compared to their full-sized counterparts.

The dye-sublimation printing technique is an example of the so-called CMYK (**c**yan, **m**agenta, **y**ellow, blac**k**) method of color printing. It uses a roll of heat-sensitive plastic film embedded with page-sized sections of cyan (blue), magenta (red), and yellow dye; many also have a section of black dye. A printhead containing thousands of heating elements, capable of precise temperature control, moves across the film, vaporizing the dyes and causing them to soak into specially coated paper underneath before cooling and reverting to a solid form. This process requires one pass per page for each color. Some printers also use a final finishing pass that applies a protective laminate coating to the page. Figure 26-8 shows how a dye-sublimation printer works.

Figure 26-8
The dye-sublimation printing process

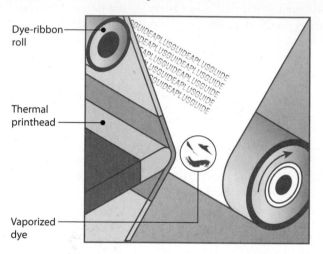

Dye-ribbon roll

Thermal printhead

Vaporized dye

Documents printed through the dye-sublimation process display *continuous-tone* images, meaning that the printed image is not constructed of pixel dots but a continuous blend of overlaid differing dye colors. This is in contrast to other print technologies' *dithered* images, which use closely packed, single-color dots to simulate blended colors. Dye-sublimation printers produce high-quality color output that rivals professional photo-lab processing.

Thermal Printers

Thermal printers use a heated printhead to create a high-quality image on special or plain paper. You'll see two kinds of thermal printers in use. The first is the *direct thermal* printer, and the other is the *thermal wax transfer* printer. Direct thermal printers use a heating element to burn dots into the surface of special heat-sensitive *thermal paper*. If you remember the first generation of fax machines, you're already familiar with this type of printer. Many retail businesses still use it as a receipt printer, using large rolls of thermal paper housed in a *feed assembly* that automatically draws the paper past the heating element; some receipt printers can even cut the paper off the roll for you.

Thermal wax printers work similarly to dye-sublimation printers, except that instead of using rolls of dye-embedded film, the film is coated with colored wax. The thermal printhead passes over the ribbon and melts the wax onto the paper. Thermal wax printers don't require special papers like dye-sublimation printers do, so they're more flexible and somewhat cheaper to use, but their output isn't quite as good.

Laser Printers

Using a process called *electro-photographic imaging*, *laser printers* produce high-quality and high-speed output of both text and graphics. Figure 26-9 shows a typical laser printer. Laser printers rely on the photoconductive properties of certain organic compounds. *Photoconductive* means that particles of these compounds, when exposed to light (that's the "photo" part), will *conduct* electricity. Laser printers usually use lasers as a light source because of their precision. Some lower-cost printers use LED arrays instead.

Figure 26-9
Typical laser
printer

The first laser printers created only monochrome images; you can also buy a color laser printer, but most laser printers produced today are still monochrome. Although a color laser printer can produce complex full-color images such as photographs, they really shine for printing what's known as *spot color*—for example, eye-catching headings, lines, charts, or other graphical elements that dress up an otherwise plain printed presentation.

Hidden Costs

Some printers use consumables—such as ink—at a much faster rate than others, prompting the industry to rank printers in terms of their cost per page. Using an inexpensive printer (laser or inkjet) costs around 4 cents per page, while an expensive printer can cost more than 20 cents per page—a huge difference if you do any volume of printing.

This hidden cost is particularly pernicious in the sub-$100 inkjet printers on the market. Their low prices often entice buyers, who then discover that the cost of consumables is outrageous—these days, a single set of color and black inkjet cartridges can cost as much as the printer itself, if not more!

The CompTIA A+ certification exams take a keen interest in the particulars of the laser printing process—or specifically, the *imaging process*—so it pays to know your way around a laser printer (see Figure 26-10). Let's take a look at the many components of laser printers and their functions.

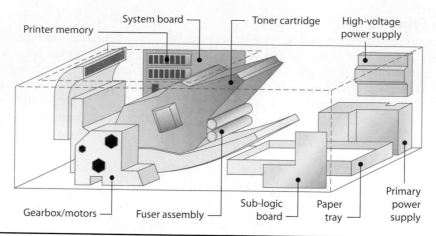

Printer memory — System board — Toner cartridge — High-voltage power supply

Gearbox/motors — Fuser assembly — Sub-logic board — Paper tray — Primary power supply

Figure 26-10   Components inside a laser printer

Toner Cartridge   The *toner cartridge* in a laser printer is so named because of its most obvious activity: supplying the toner that creates the image on the page (see Figure 26-11). To reduce maintenance costs, however, many other laser printer parts, especially those that suffer the most wear and tear, have been incorporated into the toner cartridge. Although this makes replacement of individual parts nearly impossible, it greatly reduces the need for replacement; those parts that are most likely to break are replaced every time you replace the toner cartridge.

Figure 26-11
Laser printer's
toner cartridge

NOTE Color laser printers have four toner cartridges: black, cyan, magenta, and yellow.

Imaging Drum The *imaging drum* (also called the *photosensitive drum*) is an aluminum cylinder coated with particles of photosensitive compounds. The drum itself is grounded to the power supply, but the coating is not. When light hits these particles, whatever electrical charge they may have "drains" out through the grounded cylinder.

Erase Lamp The *erase lamp* exposes the entire surface of the imaging drum to light, making the photosensitive coating conductive. Any electrical charge present in the particles bleeds away into the grounded drum, leaving the surface particles electrically neutral.

Primary Corona/Charge Roller The *primary corona* wire (or *primary charge roller*, in newer laser printers), located close to the photosensitive drum, never touches the drum. When the primary corona or primary charge roller is charged with an extremely high voltage, an electric field (or corona) forms, enabling voltage to pass to the drum and charge the photosensitive particles on its surface. The primary grid regulates the transfer of voltage, ensuring that the surface of the drum receives a uniform negative voltage of between ~600 and ~1000 volts.

Laser The *laser* acts as the writing mechanism of the printer. Any particle on the drum struck by the laser becomes conductive and its charge is drained away into the grounded core of the drum. The entire surface of the drum has a uniform negative charge of between ~600 and ~1000 volts following its charging by the primary corona wire or charge roller. When particles are struck by the laser, they are discharged and left with a ~100-volt negative charge. Using the laser, we can "write" an image onto the drum. Note that the laser writes a positive image to the drum.

Toner The *toner* in a laser printer is a fine powder made up of plastic particles bonded to pigment particles. The toner cylinder charges the toner with a negative charge of between ~200 and ~500 volts. Because that charge falls between the original uniform negative charge of the photosensitive drum (~600 to ~1000 volts) and the charge of the particles on the drum's surface hit by the laser (~100 volts), particles of toner are attracted to the areas of the photosensitive drum that have been hit by the laser (that is, areas that have a relatively positive charge with reference to the toner particles).

EXAM TIP The black toner used in laser printers is typically carbon mixed into polyester resin, while color toner trades carbon for other pigments.

Transfer Corona/Transfer Roller To transfer the image from the photosensitive drum to the paper, the paper must be given a charge that will attract the toner particles off of the drum and onto the paper. In older printers, the *transfer corona*, a thin wire, applied a positive charge to the paper, drawing the negatively charged toner particles to the paper. Newer printers accomplish the same feat using a *transfer roller* that draws the toner onto the paper. The paper, with its positive charge, is also attracted to the negatively charged drum. To prevent the paper from wrapping around the drum, a *static charge eliminator* removes the charge from the paper.

In most laser printers, the transfer corona/roller is outside the toner cartridge, especially in large, commercial-grade machines. The transfer corona/roller is prone to a build-up of dirt, toner, and debris through electrostatic attraction, and it must be cleaned. It is also quite fragile—usually finer than a human hair. Most printers with an exposed transfer corona/roller provide a special tool to clean it, but you can also—very delicately—use a cotton swab soaked in denatured alcohol (don't use rubbing alcohol because it contains emollients). As always, never service any printer without first turning it off and unplugging it from its power source.

Fuser Assembly The *fuser assembly* is almost always separate from the toner cartridge. It is usually quite easy to locate, as it is close to the bottom of the toner cartridge and usually has two rollers to fuse the toner. Sometimes the fuser is somewhat enclosed and difficult to recognize because the rollers are hidden from view. To help you determine the location of the fuser, think about the path of the paper and the fact that fusing is the final step of printing.

The toner is merely resting on top of the paper after the static charge eliminator has removed the paper's static charge. The toner must be melted to the paper to make the image permanent. Two rollers, a pressure roller and a heated roller, are used to fuse the toner to the paper. The pressure roller presses against the bottom of the page, and the heated roller presses down on the top of the page, melting the toner into the paper. The heated roller has a nonstick coating such as Teflon to prevent the toner from sticking to it.

Power Supplies All of the devices described in this chapter have power supplies, but when dealing with laser printers, techs should take extra caution. The corona in a laser printer requires extremely high voltage from the power supply, making a laser printer power supply one of the most dangerous devices in computing! Turn off and unplug the printer as a safety precaution before performing any maintenance.

Turning Gears A laser printer has many mechanical functions. First, the paper must be grabbed by the *pickup roller* and passed over the *separation pad*, which uses friction to separate a single sheet from any others that were picked up. Next, the photosensitive roller must be turned and the laser, or a mirror, must be moved back and forth. The toner must be evenly distributed, and the fuser assembly must squish the toner into the paper. Finally, the paper must be kicked out of the printer and the assembly must be cleaned to prepare for the next page.

More sophisticated laser printers enable duplex printing, meaning they can print on both sides of the paper. This is another mechanical function with a dedicated *duplexing assembly* for reversing the paper.

 EXAM TIP Be sure you are familiar with laser printer components, including the imaging drum, fuser assembly, transfer roller, pickup rollers, separation pads, and duplexing assembly. The CompTIA A+ 1001 exam objectives refer to the *separate pads*; don't get tripped up if you see it worded this way.

All of these functions are served by complex gear systems. In most laser printers, these gear systems are packed together in discrete units generically called *gear packs* or *gearboxes*. Most laser printers have two or three gearboxes that you can remove relatively easily in the rare case one of them fails. Most gearboxes also have their own motor or solenoid to move the gears.

All of these mechanical features can wear out or break and require service or replacement. See the "Troubleshooting Printers" section, later in this chapter, for more details.

System Board   Every laser printer contains at least one electronic board. On this board is the main processor, the printer's ROM, and the RAM used to store the image before it is printed. Many printers divide these functions among two or three boards dispersed around the printer (also known as sub-logic boards, as seen back in Figure 26-10). An older printer may also have an extra ROM chip and/or a special slot where you can install an extra ROM chip, usually for special functions such as PostScript.

On some printer models, you can upgrade the contents of these ROM chips (the *firmware*) by performing a process called *flashing* the ROM. Flashing is a lot like upgrading the system BIOS, which you learned about in Chapter 5, "Firmware." Upgrading the firmware can help fix bugs, add new features, or update the fonts in the printer.

Of particular importance is the printer's RAM. When the printer doesn't have enough RAM to store the image before it prints, you get a memory overflow problem. Also, some printers store other information in the RAM, including fonts or special commands. Adding RAM is usually a simple job—just snapping in a SIMM or DIMM stick or two—but getting the *right* RAM is important. Call or check the printer manufacturer's Web site to see what type of RAM you need. Although most printer companies will happily sell you their expensive RAM, most printers can use generic DRAM like the kind you use in a computer.

Ozone Filter   The coronas inside laser printers generate ozone (O_3). Although not harmful to humans in small amounts, even tiny concentrations of ozone will cause damage to printer components. To counter this problem, most laser printers have a special ozone filter that needs to be vacuumed or replaced periodically.

Sensors and Switches   Every laser printer has a large number of sensors and switches spread throughout the machine. The sensors are used to detect a broad range of conditions such as paper jams, empty paper trays, or low toner levels. Many of these sensors are really tiny switches that detect open doors and so on. Most of the time these sensors/switches work reliably, yet occasionally they become dirty or broken, sending a false signal to the printer. Simple inspection is usually sufficient to determine if a problem is real or just the result of a faulty sensor/switch.

3-D Printers

3-D printers (Figure 26-12) use melted material to create prints of three-dimensional objects. The most common 3-D printers use *plastic filament* on spools (see Figure 26-13). Some 3-D printers enable you to print with multiple colors.

Figure 26-12
3-D printer

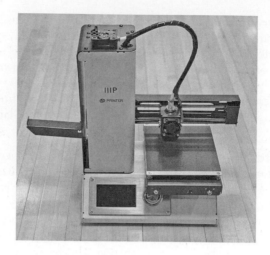

Figure 26-13
3-D printer
plastic filament

3-D printers take a 3-D illustration and build it in tiny layers or slices, one by one. Simple printers can create relatively simple shapes, such as blocks, pyramids, and so on. Better printers can create more exciting shapes, such as the stylized replacement game pieces for the popular board game Settlers of Catan pictured in Figure 26-14. Even better 3-D printers can make elaborate structures, with lots of holes and gaps within the layers.

Installation of 3-D printers requires more than the typical printer installation. The connections (USB) and drivers are typical, but 3-D printers also need manual connection of the plastic filament(s) to the print device. You'll also need specialized software designed to print in 3-D. Most manufacturers' 3-D printing software enables you to use standard 3-D drawings, such as STL, OBJ, and CAD files. Figure 26-15 shows the Ultimaker Cura software pushing a print job to a 3-D printer. Sweet!

Figure 26-14
3-D-printed
game pieces
(photo courtesy
of Donny Jansen)

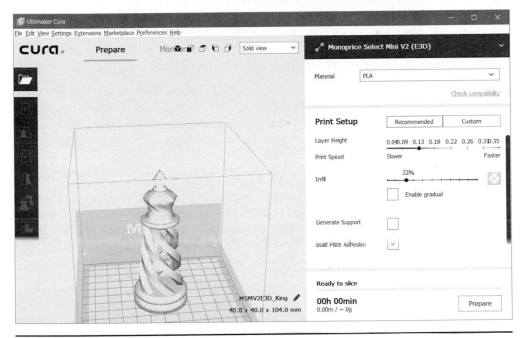

Figure 26-15   Managing a new 3-D print job

Virtual Printers

The most quizzical printer of all, the *virtual printer*, doesn't look like much, but it's actually still pretty similar to physical or "real" printing. When you print to a virtual printer, your system goes through all the steps to prepare a document for printing, and sends it off to a virtual printer—a program that converts the output from your computer into a specific format and saves the result to a portable file that looks like the printed page would have. You can print this file later if you like, or maybe send it to someone else to print, but you can also just keep it in digital format. Virtual printers provide a nice way to save anything you can print, and they're particularly good for saving reference copies of information found on the Web. CompTIA wants you to know specifically about a few of these options, so we'll discuss them in a little more depth.

 EXAM TIP The CompTIA A+ 1001 exam objectives include *Print to file*, which produces a file that can be later printed without access to the program that created it, but you usually won't want to use it as a virtual printer. Print to file is a legacy option you'll often see as a checkbox on your print screen, but it may not work well with USB printers (and even if it works, the resulting file will be difficult to work with). Be aware that this option exists, but use one of the other options described here instead.

Print to PDF   One of the most popular virtual printing options is the ability to *print to PDF*, a feature every operating system supports out of the box these days. Windows didn't join the party until Windows 10, however, so be aware that you'll need to install a virtual PDF printer on older versions of Windows. You can get these through official Adobe software, but there are also some third-party options.

Print to XPS   We'll talk a little about what exactly XPS is in the next section, but Windows versions since Vista include the Microsoft XPS Document Writer as a printer, which you can use to create a .xps file that can be opened by the included XPS Viewer program. Support in other operating systems varies, but most of them have third-party software available for working with XPS files.

Print to Image   This option lets you save a regular image file, such as BMP, GIF, JPG, PNG, TIFF, and more. Image formats tend to have some problems when being used for documents—text won't scale as well and can't be easily searched/selected/copied, for example—but they are very portable, and can often be viewed with software included in any operating system and on many types of devices. You will generally need to find and install third-party virtual printer software in order to print to the image format you desire on a given operating system.

Cloud and Remote Printing   Blurring the line between traditional and virtual printing, a variety of applications, such as Google Cloud Print, will install a virtual printer on your system that wraps up your document and sends it out over the Internet or other network to a cloud server, which eventually ends up routing it to a real printer for printing—all without needing to have a driver installed for it.

Printer Languages

Now that you've learned about the different types of print devices and techniques, it's time to take a look at how they communicate with the computer. How do you tell a printer to make a letter *A* or to print a picture of your pet iguana? Printers are designed to accept predefined printer languages that handle both characters and graphics. Your software must use the proper language when communicating with your printer, in order to output paper documents. Following are the more common printer languages.

ASCII   You might think of the *American Standard Code for Information Interchange* (*ASCII*) language as nothing more than a standard set of characters, the basic alphabet in upper- and lowercase with a few strange symbols thrown in. ASCII actually contains a variety of control codes for transferring data, some of which can be used to control printers. For example, ASCII code 10 (or 0A in hex) means "Line Feed," and ASCII code 12 (0C) means "Form Feed." These commands have been standard since before the creation of IBM computers, and all printers respond to them. If they did not, the PRT SCR (print screen) key would not work with every printer. Being highly standardized has advantages, but the control codes are extremely limited. Printing high-end graphics and a wide variety of fonts requires more advanced languages.

PostScript   Adobe Systems developed the *PostScript* page description language in the early 1980s as a device-independent printer language capable of high-resolution graphics and scalable fonts. PostScript interpreters are embedded in the printing device. Because PostScript is understood by printers at a hardware level, the majority of the image processing is done by the printer and not the computer's CPU, so PostScript printers print faster. PostScript defines the page as a single raster image; this makes PostScript files extremely portable—they can be created on one machine or platform and reliably printed out on another machine or platform (including, for example, high-end typesetters).

HP Printer Command Language (PCL)   HP developed its *Printer Command Language* (*PCL*) as a more advanced printer language to supersede simple ASCII codes. PCL features a set of printer commands greatly expanded from ASCII. HP designed PCL with text-based output in mind; it does not support advanced graphical functions. The most recent version of PCL, PCL6, features scalable fonts and additional line-drawing commands. Unlike PostScript, however, PCL is not a true page description language; it uses a series of commands to define the characters on the page. Those commands must be supported by each individual printer model, making PCL files less portable than PostScript files.

 EXAM TIP   The CompTIA A+ Acronyms list identifies PCL as Printer *Control* Language. *Control* or *Command* is rather irrelevant at this point in time. HP refers to PCL as simply PCL in all its documentation.

Windows GDI and XPS   Windows uses the *graphical device interface* (*GDI*) component of the operating system to handle print functions. Although you can use an external printer language such as PostScript, most users simply install printer drivers and let Windows do all the work. The GDI uses the CPU rather than the printer to process a print job and then sends the completed job to the printer. When you print a letter with a TrueType font in Windows, for example, the GDI processes the print job and then sends bitmapped images of each page to the printer. The printer sees a page of TrueType text, therefore, as a picture, not as text. As long as the printer has a capable enough raster image processor (explained later in this chapter) and plenty of RAM, you don't need to worry about the printer language in most situations. We'll revisit printing in Windows in more detail later in this chapter.

Windows Vista also introduced a new printing subsystem called the *XML Paper Specification* (*XPS*) *print path* in 2006. In 2009, the ECMA-388 standard formally named XPS the *Open XML Paper Specification* (*OpenXPS*), although Microsoft and others continue to use only *XPS* in documentation and screen elements. XPS provides several improvements over GDI, including enhanced color management (which works with Windows Color System, introduced in the "Optimizing Print Performance" section later in the chapter) and better print layout fidelity. The XPS print path requires a driver that supports XPS. Additionally, some printers natively support XPS, eliminating the requirement that the output be converted to a device-specific printer control language before printing.

Scanners

You can use a scanner to make digital copies of existing paper photos, documents, drawings, and more. Better scanners give you the option of copying directly from a photographic negative or slide, providing images of stunning visual quality—assuming the original photo was halfway decent, of course! In this section, you'll look at how scanners work and then turn to what you need to know to select the correct scanner for you or your clients.

How Scanners Work

All *flatbed scanners*, the most common variety of scanner, work the same way. You place a photo or other object face down on the glass (called the platen), close the lid, and then use software to initiate the scan. The scanner runs a bright light along the length of the platen once or more to capture the image. Figure 26-16 shows an open scanner.

Figure 26-16
Scanner open
with photograph
face down

NOTE Many serious flatbed scanners and multifunction devices will have an automatic document feeder (ADF) to remove most of the manual labor from this process. Check out the upcoming "Automatic Document Feeder" section for more.

The scanning software that controls the hardware can manifest in a variety of ways. Nearly every manufacturer has some sort of drivers and other software to create an interface between your computer and the scanner. When you push the front button on the Epson Perfection scanner, for example, the Epson software loads, ready to start scanning (see Figure 26-17).

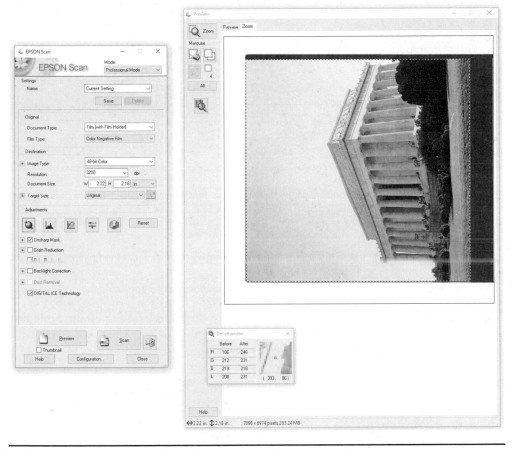

Figure 26-17 Epson software

You can also open your favorite image-editing software first and choose to acquire a file from a scanner. Figure 26-18 shows the process of acquiring an image from a scanner in the popular free image-editing software, GNU Image Manipulation Program (otherwise known as GIMP). As in most such software, you choose File | Create and then select Scanner. In this case, the scanner uses the traditional TWAIN drivers. *TWAIN* stands for *Technology Without an Interesting Name*—I'm not making this up!—and has been the default driver type for scanners for a long time.

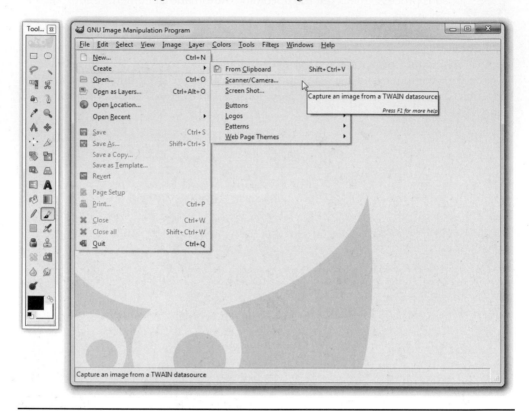

Figure 26-18   Acquiring an image in GNU Image Manipulation Program (GIMP)

At this point, the drivers and other software controlling the scanner pop up, providing an interface with the scanner (as shown back in Figure 26-17). Here you can set the resolution of the image as well as many other options.

NOTE   In addition to loading pictures into your computer, many scanners offer a feature called optical character recognition (OCR), a way to scan a document and have the computer turn the picture into text that you can manipulate by using a word processing program.

How to Choose a Scanner

You must consider four primary variables when choosing a scanner: resolution, color depth, grayscale depth, and scan speed. You can and will adjust the first three during the scanning process, although probably only down from their maximum. The scan speed relates to all four of the other variables, and the maximum speed is hard-coded into the scanner.

Configurable Variables Scanners convert the scanned image into a grid of pixels (often referred to as dots). The maximum number of pixels determines how well you can capture an image and how the image will look when scaled up in size. Most folks use the term resolution to define the grid size. As you might imagine, the higher-resolution images capture more fine detail.

Older scanners can create images of only 600 × 600 dots per inch (dpi), while newer models commonly achieve four times that density, and high-end machines do much more. Manufacturers cite *two* sets of numbers for a scanner's resolution: the resolution it achieves mechanically—called the *optical resolution*—and the enhanced resolution it can achieve with assistance from some onboard software.

The enhanced resolution numbers are useless. I recommend at least 2400 × 2400 dpi optical resolution or better, although you can get by with a lower resolution for purely Web-destined images.

The *color depth* of a scan defines the number of bits of information the scanner can use to describe each individual pixel. This number determines color, shade, hue, and so forth, so color depth makes a dramatic difference in how easily you can adjust the color and tone in your photo editor. With binary numbers, each extra bit of information *doubles* the color detail in the scan. The most common color depth options you will run across in scanners today are 24-bit and 48-bit. A 24-bit scan, for example, can save up to 256 shades for each of the red, green, and blue subpixels that make up an individual pixel. This gives you a total of 16,777,216 color variations in the scanned image, which explains why some scanners refer to this as "millions of colors" in their settings. A 48-bit scan, in contrast, can save up to 65,536 shades per subpixel, giving you a scan that holds a massive 281,474,976,710,656 color variations. All this extra color does come with a downside: images scanned at 48 bits are twice the size of 24-bit scans and can easily be hundreds of megabytes per file!

These days, 48-bit scanners are common enough that you shouldn't have to settle for less, even on a budget. Figures 26-19, 26-20, and 26-21 show pretty clearly the difference resolution makes when scanning.

Figure 26-19 Earring scanned at 72 dpi and 24-bit color

Figure 26-20 Same earring, scanned at 300 dpi and 24-bit color

Figure 26-21 Same earring, scanned at 1200 dpi and 24-bit color

Scanners differ a lot in *grayscale depth*, a number that defines how many shades of gray the scanner can save per pixel. This matters if you work with black-and-white images in any significant way, because grayscale depth may be advertised with a much lower number than color depth. Current consumer-level scanners come in 8-bit, 12-bit, and 16-bit grayscale varieties. You might recognize these three numbers from the previous color depth discussion, because grayscale images only need a third the information it takes to represent the red, green, and blue values that make up a color image. I recommend 16-bit.

Scanning Speed   Scanners have a maximum scanning speed defined by the manufacturer. The time required to complete a scan is also affected by the parameters you set; the time increases as you increase the amount of detail captured. A typical low-end scanner, for example, takes upward of 30 seconds to scan a 4 × 6 photo at 300 dpi. A faster scanner, in contrast, can crank out the same scan in 10 seconds.

Raise the resolution of the scan to 600 dpi at 48-bit resolution, and that faster scanner can take a full minute to complete the scan. Adjust your scanning settings to optimize for your project. Don't always go for the highest possible scan if you don't need the resolution and color depth.

Scanning Tips

As a general rule, you should obtain the highest quality scan you can manage, and then play with the size and image quality when it's time to print it or share it over the Web. The amount of RAM in your system—and to a lesser extent, the processor speed—dictates how big a file you can handle.

 TIP   If you're set to do some heavy scanning—like archiving all those old family photos—check out Wayne Fulton's Web site, www.scantips.com. The site has a simple, direct interface, and a treasure trove of excellent information on scanners and scanning. I've used his knowledge for years now and recommend it highly.

If you travel a lot, you'll want to make sure to use the locking mechanism for the scanner light assembly. Just be sure to unlock before you try to use it or you'll get a light that's stuck in one position. That won't make for very good scans!

Copy and Fax Components

The scanning and printing capabilities of a multifunction device enable manufacturers to add copy-machine features easily. To copy a document or photo, you essentially scan a document or photo and then print it, but all with a single press of the Copy button.

Faxing generally requires separate functions in the machine, such as a document feed and a connection to a traditional, analog phone line. Assuming you have those and an account with the local telecom company, the process of faxing is pretty simple. You put a document in the feeder, plug in the fax number, and press the Send button (or whatever the manufacturer labels it).

Automatic Document Feeders

An MFD uses an *automatic document feeder* (*ADF*) to grab pages to copy, scan, or fax. An ADF is typically on top of the MFD and you place a stack of pages in the tray (see Figure 26-22). Different machines require documents face up or face down; they'll typically have some marking to show which way to feed the pages (see Figure 26-23).

Figure 26-22
Typical automatic document feed loaded with pages to copy

Figure 26-23
Wonderfully descriptive markings on MFD telling user to load pages face up in ADF

Connectivity

Most printers, scanners, and multifunction devices connect to a computer via a USB port, but Wi-Fi or Ethernet network connections are also very popular. You'll need to know how to support networked connections as well as the plug-and-play USB ones.

USB Connections

New printers and multifunction devices use USB connections that you can plug into any USB port on your computer. USB printers may not come with a USB cable, so you need to purchase one when you purchase a printer. (It's quite a disappointment to come home with your new printer only to find you can't connect it because it didn't come with a USB cable.) Most printers use the standard USB type A connector on one end and the smaller USB type B connector on the other end, although some use two type A connectors. Whichever configuration your USB printer has, just plug in the USB cable—it's that easy!

Network Connections

Connecting a printer or multifunction device to a network isn't just for offices anymore. More and more homes and home offices are enjoying the benefits of network printing. It used to be that you would physically connect the printer to a single computer and then share the printer on the network. The downside to this was that the computer connected to the printer had to be left on for others to use the printer.

Today, the typical *network printer* comes with its own built-in 802.11(a, b, g, n, ac) Wi-Fi adapter to enable wireless printing over infrastructure or ad hoc network connections, though you should avoid ad hoc connections for security reasons when possible (see Chapter 20, "Wireless Networking," for more on setting up an ad hoc wireless network).

Other printers include an onboard network adapter that uses a standard RJ-45 Ethernet cable to connect the printer directly to the network by way of a router. The printer can typically be assigned a static IP address, or it can acquire one dynamically from a DHCP server. (Don't know what a router, IP address, or DHCP server is? Take a look back at Chapter 18, "Essentials of Networking," and Chapter 19, "Local Area Networking.") Once connected to the network, the printer acts independently of any single computer. Alternatively, some printers offer a Bluetooth interface for networking.

NOTE Since printers tend to have longer lives than most other computing devices, be aware that printers with a built-in wireless print connection may be using older Wi-Fi or Bluetooth standards than you're used to encountering.

Even if a printer does not come with built-in Ethernet, Wi-Fi, or Bluetooth, you can purchase a standalone network device known as a *print server* to connect your printer to the network—but beware that you may not be able to use all features of an MFD connected to a print server. These print servers, which can be Ethernet or Wi-Fi, enable one or several printers to attach via USB cable (or even parallel port, if you still have a printer that old). You may not need to go to the store to find a print server, though—check your router, first, to see if it has an *integrated print server*. If it does, you may be able to plug your printer into a USB port on the router. So take that ancient ImageWriter dot-matrix printer and network it—I dare you!

EXAM TIP You'll find print servers outside network devices. In fact, your Windows system is capable of operating as a print server. Anytime you plug a printer into a computer and share the printer over the network, the sharing system can be referred to as a print server.

Other Connections

Plenty of other connection types are available for printers. We've focused mainly on USB and networked connections. Be aware that you may run into old printers using a parallel port, a serial port, or SCSI. Although this is unlikely, know that it's a possibility. You might also see standalone scanners using Thunderbolt.

The Laser Printing Process

The *imaging process* with a laser printer breaks down into seven steps, and the CompTIA A+ 1001 exam expects you to know them all. As a tech, you should be familiar with these phases, as this can help you troubleshoot printing problems. If an odd line is printed down the middle of every page, for example, you know there's a problem with the photosensitive drum or cleaning mechanism and the toner cartridge needs to be replaced.

The seven steps to the laser printing process may be performed in a different order, depending on the printer, but it usually goes like this:

1. Processing
2. Charging
3. Exposing
4. Developing
5. Transferring
6. Fusing
7. Cleaning

Processing

When you click the Print button in an application, several things happen. First, the CPU processes your request and sends a print job to an area of memory called the print spooler. The *print spooler* enables you to queue up multiple print jobs that the printer will handle sequentially. Next, Windows sends the first print job to the printer. That's your first potential bottleneck—if it's a big job, the OS has to dole out a piece at a time and you'll see the little printer icon in the notification area at the bottom right of your screen. Once the printer icon goes away, you know the print queue is empty—all jobs have gone to the printer.

Once the printer receives some or all of a print job, the hardware of the printer takes over and processes the image. That's your second potential bottleneck, and it has multiple components.

Raster Images

Impact printers transfer data to the printer one character or one line at a time, whereas laser printers transfer entire pages at a time to the printer. A laser printer generates a *raster image* (a pattern of dots) of the page, representing what the final product should look like. It uses a device (the laser imaging unit) to "paint" a raster image on the photosensitive drum. Because a laser printer has to paint the entire surface of the photosensitive drum before it can begin to transfer the image to paper, it processes the image one page at a time.

A laser printer uses a chip called the *raster image processor* (*RIP*) to translate the raster image into commands to the laser. The RIP takes the digital information about fonts and graphics and converts it to a rasterized image made up of dots that can then be printed. An inkjet printer also has a RIP, but it's part of the software driver instead of onboard hardware circuitry. The RIP needs memory (RAM) to store the data that it must process.

A laser printer must have enough memory to process an entire page. Some pages printed at high resolution and containing very complex designs (lots of fonts, complex formatting, high-resolution graphics, and so on) require more memory. Insufficient memory will usually be indicated by a memory overflow ("MEM OVERFLOW") error. If you get a memory overflow or *low memory error*, try reducing the resolution, printing smaller graphics, reducing the complexity, or turning off RET (see the following section for the last option). Of course, the best solution to a memory overflow error is simply to add more RAM to the laser printer.

Do not assume that every error with the word *memory* in it can be fixed simply by adding more RAM to the printer. Just as adding more RAM chips will not solve every conventional computer memory problem, adding more RAM will not solve every laser printer memory problem. The message "21 ERROR" on an HP LaserJet, for example, indicates that "the printer is unable to process very complex data fast enough for the print engine." This means that the data is simply too complex for the RIP to handle. Adding more memory would *not* solve this problem; it would only make your wallet lighter. The only answer in this case is to reduce the complexity of the page image.

Resolution

Laser printers can print at different resolutions, just as monitors can display different resolutions. The maximum resolution a laser printer can handle is determined by its physical characteristics. Laser printer resolution is expressed in dots per inch (dpi), such as 2400 × 600 dpi or 1200 × 1200 dpi. The first number, the horizontal resolution, is determined by how fine a focus can be achieved by the laser. The second number is determined by the smallest increment by which the drum can be turned.

Higher resolutions produce higher-quality output, but keep in mind that higher resolutions also require more memory. In some instances, complex images can be printed only at lower resolutions because of their high memory demands. Even printing at 300 × 300 dpi, laser printers produce far better quality than dot-matrix printers because of *resolution enhancement technology* (*RET*).

RET enables the printer to insert smaller dots among the characters, smoothing out the jagged curves that are typical of printers that do not use RET (see Figure 26-24). Using RET enables laser printers to output high-quality print jobs, but it also requires a portion of the printer's RAM. If you get a MEM OVERFLOW error, disabling RET will sometimes free up enough memory to complete the print job.

Figure 26-24
RET fills in gaps with smaller dots to smooth out jagged characters.

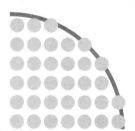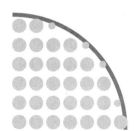

Charging

Now we turn to the physical side of the printing process. To make the drum receptive to new images, it must be charged (see Figure 26-25). Using the primary corona wire or primary charge roller, a uniform negative charge is applied to the entire surface of the drum (usually between ~600 and ~1000 volts).

Figure 26-25
Charging the drum with a uniform negative charge

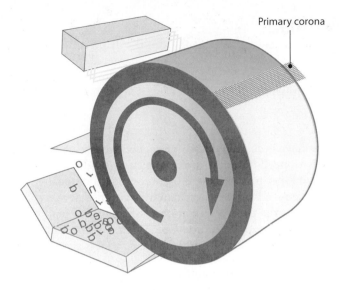

Exposing

A laser is used to create a positive image on the surface of the drum. Every particle on the drum hit by the laser releases most of its negative charge into the drum.

Developing

Those particles with a lesser negative charge are positively charged relative to the toner particles and attract them, creating a developed image (see Figure 26-26).

Figure 26-26
Writing the image and applying the toner

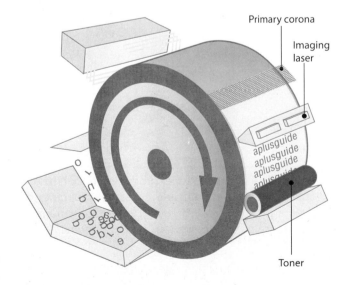

Transferring

The printer must transfer the image from the drum onto the paper. The transfer corona or transfer roller gives the paper a positive charge; then the negatively charged toner particles leap from the drum to the paper. At this point, the particles are merely resting on the paper and must still be permanently fused to the paper.

Fusing

The particles have been attracted to the paper because of the paper's positive charge, but if the process stopped here, the toner particles would fall off the page as soon as you lift it. Because the toner particles are mostly composed of plastic, they can be melted to the page. Two rollers—a heated roller coated in a nonstick material and a pressure roller—melt the toner to the paper, permanently affixing it. Finally, a static charge eliminator removes the paper's positive charge (see Figure 26-27). Once the page is complete, the printer ejects the printed copy and the process begins again with the physical and electrical cleaning of the printer.

Figure 26-27
Transferring the image to the paper and fusing the final image

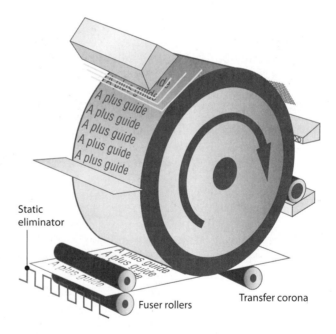

Static eliminator

Fuser rollers

Transfer corona

 CAUTION The heated roller produces enough heat to melt some types of plastic media, particularly overhead transparency materials. This could damage your laser printer (and void your warranty), so make sure you print on transparencies designed for laser printers!

Cleaning

The printing process ends with the physical and electrical cleaning of the photosensitive drum (see Figure 26-28). Before printing another new page, the drum must be returned to a clean, fresh condition. All residual toner left over from printing the previous page must be removed, usually by scraping the surface of the drum with a rubber cleaning blade. If residual particles remain on the drum, they will appear as random black spots and streaks on the next page. The physical cleaning mechanism either deposits the residual toner in a debris cavity or recycles it by returning it to the toner supply in the toner cartridge. The physical cleaning must be done carefully—a damaged drum will cause a mark to be printed on every page until it is replaced.

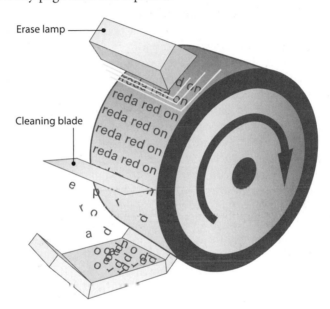

Figure 26-28
Cleaning and erasing the drum

The printer must also be electrically cleaned. One or more erase lamps bombard the surface of the drum with the appropriate wavelengths of light, causing the surface particles to discharge into the grounded drum. After the cleaning process, the drum should be completely free of toner and have a neutral charge.

NOTE Color laser printers use four different colors of toner (cyan, magenta, yellow, and black) to create their printouts. Most models send each page through four different passes, adding one color at each pass to create the needed results, while others place all the colors onto a special transfer belt and then transfer them to the page in one pass. In some cases, the printer uses four separate toner cartridges and four lasers for the four toner colors, and in others the printer simply lays down one color after the other on the same drum, cleaning after each of four passes per page.

Installing a Multifunction Device

Installing a multifunction device differs a lot from installing single-function devices. In the consumer space, the process is messy because of the complexity of the devices. Here's the scoop.

First, most multifunction devices today connect via USB and wirelessly, so you need to consider connectivity. Second, you need to install drivers for each of the various functions of the MFD. Initially, that seems fine, because you can use the driver disc/download that came with the MFD and can install everything for the OS you choose.

That default process can rapidly turn into a mess, though, because of several factors. The drivers are often outdated. Updating specific drivers takes time and clicking. Worse, manufacturers often add absurdly bad applications to "support" specific functions of MFDs, such as special photo organization tools that bog down the system and function far worse than readily available tools like Lightroom from Adobe (not free, but reasonably priced).

Third, you're dealing with a very complex machine that can break in interesting ways. Maintenance and troubleshooting take on new dimensions by the sheer number of options to consider, from ink levels to scanner mechanics to dogged-out phone lines. Although none of these fall into the category of installation, you can minimize the problems by practicing a more compartmentalized installation.

Rather than focus on the multifunction aspect of MFDs, you will often fare better for you and your customers if you think about each function as a separate action. Pull the machine apart in essence, for example, and install a printer, a scanner, a copy machine, and a fax machine. Share these individual parts as needed on a network. Update drivers for each component separately. Conceptualize each function as a separate device to simplify troubleshooting. This way, if your print output goes south, for example, think about the printer aspects of the MFD. You don't have to worry about the scanner, copy, or fax aspects of the machine.

The next sections cover installation of single-function devices, though the bulk of information is on printers. That's both what the CompTIA A+ exams cover and what you'll have to deal with as a tech for the most part.

Setting Up Printers in Windows

You need to take a moment to understand how Windows handles printing, and then you'll see how to install, configure, and troubleshoot printers.

 EXAM TIP The CompTIA A+ exams test you on installing and troubleshooting printers, so read these sections carefully!

To Windows, a printer is not a physical device; it is a *program* that controls one or more physical printers. The *physical* printer is called a print device by Windows (although I continue to use the term "printer" for most purposes, just like almost every tech on the planet). Printer drivers and a spooler are still present, but in Windows, they are integrated into the printer itself (see Figure 26-29). This arrangement gives Windows amazing flexibility. For example, one printer can support multiple print devices, enabling a system to act as a print server. If one print device goes down, the printer automatically redirects the output to a working print device.

Figure 26-29
Printer driver
and spooler in
Windows

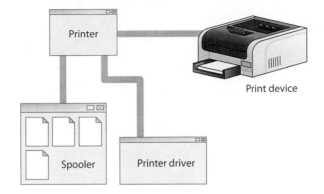

The general installation, configuration, and troubleshooting issues are basically identical in all modern versions of Windows. Here's a review of a typical Windows printer installation. I'll mention the minor differences among Windows 7, 8/8.1, and 10 as I go along. Setting up a printer is so easy it's almost scary. Most printers are plug and play, so installing a printer is reduced to simply plugging it in and loading the driver if needed. With USB printers, Windows won't even wait for you to do anything—Windows immediately detects and installs a printer once you connect it. If the system does not detect the printer in Windows 7/8/8.1, open the Devices and Printers applet in the Control Panel. As you might guess, you install a new printer by clicking the Add a printer icon/button. This starts the Add Printer Wizard.

Although you can use the Control Panel applet in Windows 10, most users will opt for the simpler Settings | Devices | Printers & scanners for setting up a printer (see Figure 26-30). Click the *Add a printer or scanner* option to find a connectable printer.

Standard Users and Printers

A standard user—that is, not an administrator—can install a printer just fine in Windows. The user can also use one of the built-in printer drivers and print fine.

Windows will balk, however, when the user tries to install software and drivers from optical disc or downloaded from the Internet. For those options, you need administrative rights. CompTIA calls this an error in the 1001 objectives, as "unable to install printer."

If you're stuck in that position, such as rolling out corporate laptops to company employees who will want to install printers at home, you can work around the problem. Microsoft suggests changing the Group Policy Driver Installation policy to allow non-administrators to install drivers for printers.

You should be able to find detailed instructions on this if need be at https://technet.microsoft.com. We'll discuss Group Policy editing in Chapter 27, "Securing Computers."

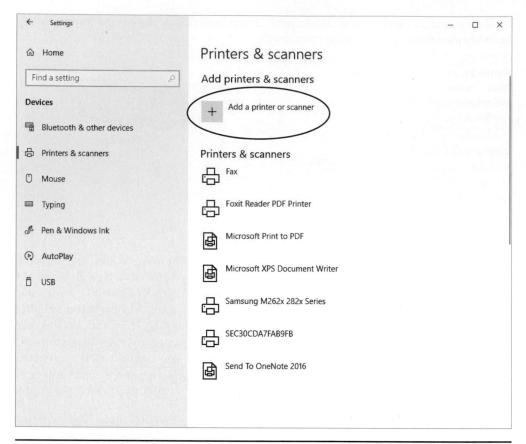

Figure 26-30 Printers & scanners in Settings

The Add Printer Wizard enables you to install a local printer or a network printer. This distinction is actually a little misleading. Windows divides printer installation into two scenarios: a printer connected directly to a computer (your local system or another one on a network), or a standalone printer directly connected to a switch or router. While you might expect the local and network installation options to divide these scenarios nicely, they don't. Let's take a quick look at both local and network installations so you know when to use each.

Installing a Local Printer

At first glance, you might think the local printer installation option is used to install your standard USB printer, but don't forget that Windows will automatically detect and install USB printers (or any other plug-and-play printer). So what do you use it for? This option is most commonly used to install standalone network printers using an IP address. Using current versions of Windows and a modern printer, you shouldn't need to use the IP address to install a standalone network printer, but it can be a helpful alternative if Windows refuses to detect it any other way.

If you need to install a standalone network printer, use its hostname or IP address. In Windows 7, click *Add a local printer*. In the *Create a new port* drop-down box, select Standard TCP/IP Port. Click Next. Type the IP address here. Windows 8/8.1/10 is even simpler: If Windows doesn't automatically detect your new printer, click *The printer that I want isn't listed* and select *Add a printer using TCP/IP address or hostname*. In Windows 10, both the Settings app and the Control Panel app give you the same choices.

Whether you use a USB port or a TCP/IP port, you'll need to select the proper driver manually (see Figure 26-31). Windows includes a lot of printer drivers, but you can also use the handy Have Disk option to use the disc that came with the printer. If you use the driver included on the disc, Windows will require administrator privileges to proceed; otherwise, you won't be able to finish the installation. The Windows Update button enables you to grab the latest printer drivers via the Internet.

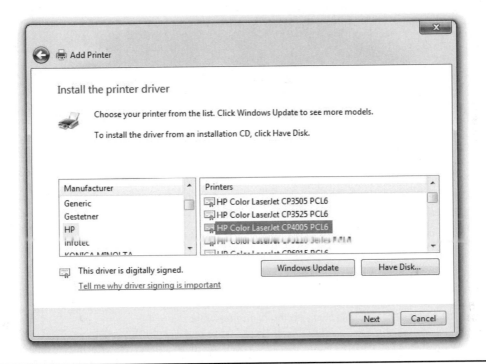

Figure 26-31 Selecting drivers

After clicking the Next button, you'll be asked if the new local printer should be the default printer and whether you want to share it with other computers on the network. And before you ask, yes, you can share a standalone network printer connected to your computer via a TCP/IP port using File and Printer Sharing, though the printer would be disabled for other users any time you turned off your computer. You'll be asked to print a test page to make sure everything works. Then you're done!

EXAM TIP Windows-based printer sharing isn't the only game in town. Apple's *AirPrint* functionality can be used in conjunction with its *Bonjour Print Service* (installed separately, or along with iTunes) to share a printer connected to a Windows system with AirPrint-compatible macOS and Apple iOS devices.

Installing a Network Printer

Setting up network printers in a typical SOHO LAN doesn't require much more effort than setting up local printers. When you try to install a network printer, the Settings app or Add Printer Wizard will scan for any available printers on your local network. More often than not, the printer you are looking for will pop up in a list (see Figure 26-32). When you select that printer and click Add device or Next, Windows will search for drivers. If you need to, you can pick from a list of available drivers or use the disc that came with the printer. Either way, you're already done.

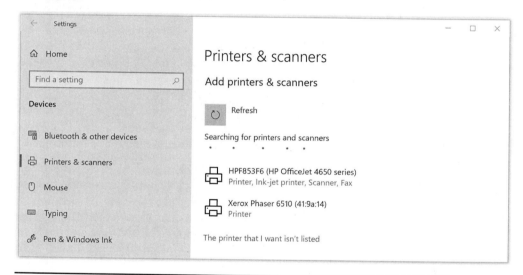

Figure 26-32 List of available shared printers on a network

If Windows fails to find your printer, you'll need to configure the network printer manually. Every version of Windows includes multiple methods of doing this. These methods change depending on whether you are connected to a domain or a workgroup.

NOTE Remember printer sharing from Chapter 19? Here's the other side of the operation. Keep in mind that after you install a shared printer onto your computer, you can actually share it with others. Windows considers it *your* printer, so you can do what you want with it, including sharing it again.

If you are on a workgroup, you can browse for a printer on your network, connect to a specific printer (using its name or URL), or use a TCP/IP address or hostname, as you see in Figure 26-33. In a domain, most of these options remain the same, except that instead of browsing the workgroup, you can search and browse the domain using several search parameters, including printer features, printer location, and more. Once you've found your printer, you might be prompted for drivers. Provide them using the usual methods described earlier and then you are finished!

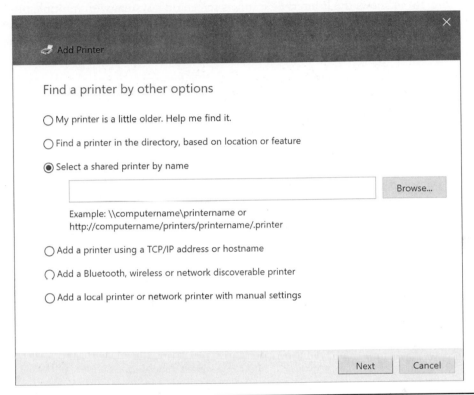

Figure 26-33 Options for finding network printers

 NOTE If you are a member of a Windows homegroup and printer sharing is enabled, all printers connected to the homegroup are shared with you automatically. This applies only to Windows 7/8/8.1. While early versions of Windows 10 supported HomeGroup, current versions do not.

Remember that Windows doesn't always see your network's printers exactly how they are physically arranged. Imagine you have a network with three computers. Andy's computer has a printer connected via USB, whereas Beth's computer and Carol's computer have no printers. There is, however, a second printer connected directly to their router via Ethernet. Beth has configured her system to connect directly to the network printer using an IP address. As such, she can actually share that printer with the rest of her network, even though it's not attached to her computer—Windows doesn't care where it is.

The process for sharing a local printer and a network printer is identical because Windows considers both printers to be installed on your computer and under your control. So now Andy and Beth both share printers. When Carol goes looking for shared printers to use, the network printer attached to the router will look like Beth's printer, as if it were directly connected to Beth's machine.

Figure 26-34 shows the Printers & scanners screen on a system with multiple printers installed. Note the text *Default* below the printer's name; this shows that the device is the default printer. If you have multiple printers, you can change the default printer by right-clicking the printer's icon and selecting Set as default printer.

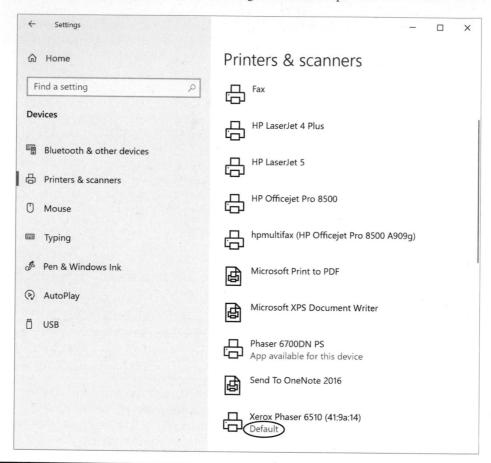

Figure 26-34   Installed default printer in Printers & scanners in Settings

In addition to the regular driver installation outlined previously, some installations use printer emulation. *Printer emulation* simply means using a substitute printer driver for a printer, as opposed to using one made exclusively for that printer. You'll run into printer emulation in two circumstances. First, some new printers do not come with their own drivers. They instead emulate a well-known printer (such as an HP LaserJet 4) and run perfectly well on that printer driver. Second, you may see emulation in the "I don't have the right driver!" scenario. I keep about three different HP LaserJet and Epson inkjet printers installed on my computer because I know that with these printer drivers, I can print to almost any printer. Some printers may require you to set them into an *emulation mode* to handle a driver other than their native one.

1002

As you might imagine, setting up printers and MFDs in an enterprise environment differs from the process in a SOHO environment. Here's a scenario. Bayland Widgets Corporation has 30 users who share access to two high-end color laser printers, two very fast black-and-white laser printers, one MFD (mainly used for scanning and copying purposes, but it also prints), and a trio of very nice inkjet printers. The printers and MFD are located in various places for convenience and managed by a single print server.

To make things a lot simpler than going to each client machine and installing these networked printers, Tony the Admin deploys the printers and MFD using Windows group policy to map the correct printers for all 30 workstations (plus several laptops as well). As users log in each morning, the group policy maps the MFD and the closest color laser printer to all of the workstations and laptops. It only maps the high-quality inkjet printers to the marketing department workstations, however, and the fast black-and-white laser printers to accounting. This all happens automatically with the correct drivers loaded as necessary.

EXAM TIP Expect a question or two on the CompTIA A+ 1002 exam giving you a scenario where you need to choose *printer sharing vs. network printer mapping*. The big difference is scale. Sharing a printer or MFD in a SOHO LAN is pretty easy. It's also easy to install a shared network printer. Once you scale up, though, management of many workstations and printers/MFDs becomes a pain unless you map via a group policy that applies to a lot of computers or users.

Note that you could also automate printer mapping via an Active Directory domain *logon script*, as discussed back in Chapter 19. Be careful on the exam if logon script is an option and group policy is not.

We'll hit group policy in Chapter 27. But deploying or mapping printers and multifunction devices in this way enables much faster rollout, updates, replacements, and so on.

EXAM TIP In addition to the Devices and Printers applet, Windows also includes the Print Management console. This tool enables you to view and modify all the printers and drivers on your system or connected to your network. You can also manage any Windows print servers connected to the network. Many of Print Management's advanced features go beyond the scope of the CompTIA A+ exams, but know that it centralizes (and in a few cases, enhances) the standard printer controls in Windows. You can find Print Management in Control Panel | Administrative Tools | Print Management.

Configuring Print Settings

Once your printer is installed, a good first stop is the Printing preferences menu, accessible by right-clicking the desired printer in the Devices and Printers applet in the Control Panel. This is where you'll be able to control how your printer will print your documents. Be aware that these settings can vary depending on features available on your printer or multifunction device, but let's take a look at some of the ones you're most likely to find.

Layout

The settings you're most likely to change from time to time are probably the layout settings, which control how the printer determines what to print where.

- The *duplex* setting lets you specify whether and how to use each side of a printed page. Simple duplexing will just use the front and back of each sheet sequentially, but you may find more advanced options for laying out booklets.

- The *orientation* setting lets you specify whether to print in *landscape* or *portrait* mode.

- The *multiple page* setting will let you print multiple document pages on each physical page.

- The *scaling* setting, not to be confused with the multiple page setting, is usually for fitting a large document to a single page, or scaling a small document up to the size of a full page.

- *Reverse* or *invert* options let you print the mirror image of your document, which is useful for printing on transfer paper and other special-use cases.

Paper

Many of the settings you'll find are for telling your printer what kind of paper it will be using, and (especially if the printer has multiple paper trays) where to find it.

- Set the *paper size* to one of several common paper sizes, or define a custom one.

- Specify the *paper type*, which may involve setting thickness, coating, and special formats such as envelopes and labels.

- A *paper source* setting will let you select any available paper trays, and possibly *manual feed*, in which case the printer will wait for you to feed it each sheet individually. This is useful if you need to feed in one-off items or paper that won't fit in the tray.

Quality

There are usually a number of different settings that have bearing on quality, but be aware that the name or description of some settings that affect quality may discuss ink or toner use (and may as such be located with other ink/toner-related settings).

- The most obvious of these, *resolution*, specifies what dpi the document should be printed at.
- Some printers may let you choose some mode or quality presets that optimize printing for graphics or text, or choose to manually configure your own advanced settings.
- Some printers may have settings that reduce ink or toner used, for economic and environmental reasons.

Other Common Settings

Some print devices offer options useful in specific, but limited, occasions.

- The *apply a watermark* setting will let you choose from presets or define your own. A watermark is a lightly printed mark across every page. Use a watermark to designate a draft copy of a document, for example, rather than a final copy.
- *Header/footer* settings can be used to add information about when a document was printed and who printed it.
- A *collate* option lets you specify the order in which multiple copies of a multi-page document are printed. If the option is unchecked and you print ten copies, each page will be printed ten times before the printer moves on. If the option is checked, the printer will print the full document before starting over.

Optimizing Print Performance

Although a quality printer is the first step toward quality output, your output relies on factors other than the printer itself. If you've ever tweaked a photograph until it looked perfect on your screen only to discover the final printout was darker than you hoped, you made an important discovery. What you see on the screen may not match what comes out of the printer unless both devices are properly calibrated.

 EXAM TIP *Calibration* is a general term for a manual or automatic process that corrects differences between how a device or component currently works and how it *should* work. All kinds of devices need calibration, but the 1001 objectives focus on calibrating inkjet and laser printers. This section describes one kind of calibration—but keep an eye out for additional calibration steps in the "Inkjet Printer Maintenance" and "Laser Printer Maintenance" sections later in this chapter.

Color calibration uses hardware to generate an International Color Consortium (ICC) color profile, a file that defines the color characteristics of a hardware device. The operating system then uses this profile to correct any color shifts in your monitor. With a calibrated monitor, you know any color shifts in your photograph are really in the photo, not an artifact of your monitor.

NOTE Two of the best monitor calibration hardware manufacturers are Datacolor Spyder—that's the one I use most—and X-Rite ColorMunki Display. Get one. You'll be much happier with your print outcome! Here are the main URLs: www.datacolor.com and www.xrite.com.

Where these ICC color profiles really start to get interesting is that they can be created for printers as well. Just like with a monitor, they let the computer know the unique color quirks of a specific printer on a specific paper. When your printer and monitor have been properly calibrated and the profiles installed, your prints and monitor display should match. Color profiles are sometimes included on the installation media with a printer, but you can create or purchase custom profiles as well. Windows includes *Windows Color System* (*WCS*) to help build color profiles for use across devices. WCS is based on a newer component Microsoft calls the *color infrastructure and translation engine* (*CITE*).

Managing Public/Shared/Networked Devices

While we've looked at a few of the ways you can share a printer or multifunction device over a network, there's more to know about sharing these devices than just how to set them up. A few big issues are network security and data privacy.

Network Security

The ease of access that makes wired or wireless network printers and multifunction devices so useful is also a big risk; at best it means they're vulnerable to attacks over the LAN, and at worst it means they may be open to attack from the entire Internet. While hardening a network printer or MFD is beyond the scope of this book, it's important to be aware of the risks these devices present. There are the obvious immediate risks to the data and documents flowing through the device, but because security is often overlooked on these devices, they are also common starting points for an attack on the broader network.

Data Privacy

If you think about it, a lot of sensitive information can pass through a printer or MFD in most organizations, especially in places like schools and hospitals where privacy is strictly regulated. When all of this information passes through the printer or MFD, it's important to make sure it isn't leaking out. Unfortunately, it's common for modern devices to contain a hard drive or other storage media used to cache copies of documents the device prints, scans, copies, or faxes. Depending on the device, you may be able to disable this feature, schedule regular deletion of the cache, or manually clear the cache regularly to limit the amount of damage a compromise could cause. It's also important to clear this information before disposing of the device.

 EXAM TIP The CompTIA A+ 1001 objectives refer to this as *hard drive caching,* so be prepared to see this phrasing on the exam.

Disabling features like this wouldn't be much good if anyone who could use the device could also change the settings, so enterprise models often allow for *user authentication* on the device. This can address a number of the risks these devices present by limiting use to authenticated users, and restricting the features each user can access to only what they need.

Just because the data on your device is secure doesn't mean documents rolling off of it are free from prying eyes. User authentication can also help out by letting users send documents to the printer, but waiting to print them until the user authenticates at the device. It can also minimize some of the risk to unsupervised documents by restricting the ability of less-trusted users to scan/copy/e-mail a document from the device, limiting the ease with which they could steal a copy of an unattended document and leave the original.

Troubleshooting Printers

Once set up, printers tend to run with few issues, assuming that you install the proper drivers and keep the printer well maintained. But printer errors do occasionally develop. Take a look at the most common print problems, as well as problems that crop up with specific printer types.

 NOTE Every printer is different. Read the documentation included with your printer to learn how you can perform the tasks listed in this section.

Troubleshooting General Issues

Printers of all stripes share some common problems, such as print jobs that don't print, strangely sized prints, and misalignment. Other issues include disposing of consumables, sharing multiple printers, and crashing on power-up. Let's take a look at these general troubleshooting issues, but start with a recap of the tools of the trade.

 EXAM TIP Don't forget to check the obvious. Many printers include tiny displays that can clue you in to what's wrong. Most brands use a series of *error codes* that indicate the problem. Use the manual or the manufacturer's Web site to translate the error code into meaningful information.

Tools of the Trade

Before you jump in and start to work on a printer that's giving you fits, you'll need some tools. You can use the standard computer tech tools in your toolkit, plus a couple of printer-specific devices. Here are some that will come in handy:

- A multimeter for troubleshooting electrical problems such as faulty wall outlets
- Various cleaning solutions, such as denatured alcohol
- An extension magnet for grabbing loose screws in tight spaces and cleaning up iron-based toner
- An optical disc or USB thumb drive with test patterns for checking print quality
- Your trusty screwdrivers—both a Phillips-head and flat-head, because if you bring just one kind, it's a sure bet that you'll need the other

Print Job Never Prints

If you click Print but the *printer will not print*, first check all the obvious explanations. Is the printer on? Is it connected? Is it online? Is there an error message on its display? Does it have paper? Is your computer online?

If the printer is on, the display might have a useful message. It'll usually let you know if the printer is out of paper, has a paper jam that needs to be resolved, or has had a *memory full/low memory error*. If so, refill the paper, resolve the jam, or try reprinting the job at a lower quality, accordingly.

If you can't connect to the printer, check all cables, ports, and power involved. If everything is plugged in and ready to go, check the printer's display for any indication that it has *no connectivity* (you may need to navigate its menu system to view its connectivity status). If the printer was previously connected, turn it off for a moment, and then turn it back on and see if it successfully connects. If it doesn't, the menu system will typically have an option to manually configure network settings. Try resetting or manually configuring them.

If the printer does have connectivity, double-check the appropriate printer applet for your version of Windows. If you don't see the printer you are looking for, you'll need to reinstall it.

If you attempt to use a printer shared by another computer but Windows pops up with an "Access Denied" error, you might not have permission to use the printer. Go to the host system and check the Security tab of the Printer Properties dialog box. Make sure your user account is allowed to use the printer.

Assuming the printer is in good order, it's time to look at the spooler. You can see the spooler status either by double-clicking the printer's icon in the appropriate printer Control Panel applet or by double-clicking the tiny printer icon in the notification area if it's present. If you're having a problem, the printer icon will almost always be there. Figure 26-35 shows the print spooler open.

A *backed-up print queue* can easily overflow or become corrupt due to a lack of disk space, too many print jobs, or one of a thousand other factors. The status window shows all of the pending print jobs and enables you to delete, start, or pause jobs. I usually just delete the affected print job(s) and try again.

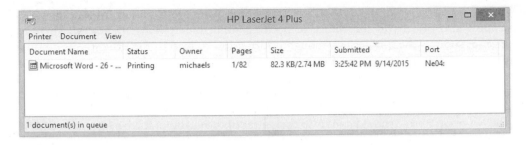

Figure 26-35   Print spooler

Print spoolers are handy. If the printer goes down, you can just leave the print jobs in the spooler until the printer comes back online. If you have a printer that isn't coming on anytime soon, you can simply delete the print job in the spooler window and try another printer.

If you have problems with the print spooler, you can get around them by changing your print spool settings. Go into the Printers/Devices and Printers applet, right-click the icon of the printer in question, and choose Printer properties. In the resulting Properties dialog box (see Figure 26-36), choose the *Print directly to the printer* radio button on

Figure 26-36
Print spool
settings

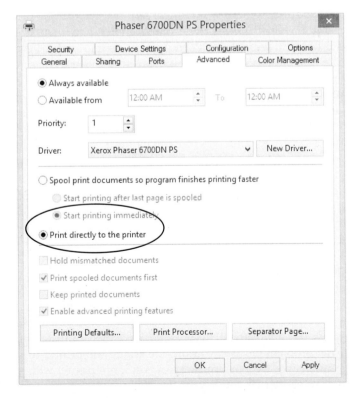

the Advanced tab and click OK; then try sending your print job again. Note that this window also offers you the choice of printing immediately—that is, starting to print pages as soon as the spooler has enough information to feed to the printer—or holding off on printing until the entire job is spooled.

If that isn't enough, try restarting the print spooler service. Open the Start menu and right-click on Computer. Select Manage—you'll need administrator privileges to continue. In the column on the left, double-click Services and Applications, and then click Services. The Services console should appear in the center of the Computer Management window. Scroll down and find the service named Print Spooler. Right-click on the service and simply click Restart, if available; otherwise, select Stop, wait for it to stop, right-click on the service again, and select Start. You should be able to print using the print spooler again.

Another possible cause for a stalled print job is that the printer is simply waiting for the correct paper! Laser printers in particular have settings that tell them what size paper is in their standard paper tray or trays. If the application sending a print job specifies a different paper size—for example, it wants to print a standard No. 10 envelope, or perhaps a legal sheet, but the standard paper tray holds only 8.5 × 11 letter paper—the printer usually pauses and holds up the queue until someone switches out the tray or manually feeds the type of paper that this print job requires. You can usually override this pause, even without having the specified paper, by pressing the OK or GO button on the printer.

The printer's default paper tray and paper size options will differ greatly depending on the printer type and model. To find these settings, go into the printer's Properties dialog box from the Printers/Devices and Printers applet, and then select the Device Settings tab. This list of settings includes Form To Tray Assignment, where you can specify which tray (in the case of a printer with multiple paper trays) holds which size paper.

Strange Sizes

A print job that comes out an unexpected size usually points to a user mistake in setting up the print job. All applications have a Print command and a Page Setup interface. The Page Setup interface enables you to define a number of print options, which vary from application to application. Figure 26-37 shows the Page Setup options for Microsoft Word. Make sure the page is set up properly before you blame the printer for a problem.

If you know the page is set up correctly, recheck the printer drivers. If necessary, uninstall and reinstall the printer drivers. If the problem persists, you may have a serious problem with the printer's print engine, but that comes up as a likely answer only when you continually get the same strangely sized printouts using a variety of applications.

Misaligned or Garbage Prints

Misaligned or garbage printouts (CompTIA calls this *garbled characters on paper*) often point to a corrupted or incorrect driver, but it's worth trying to reboot the printer before jumping to conclusions. If that doesn't help, make sure you're using the right driver (it's hard to mess this up, but not impossible) and then uninstall and reinstall the printer driver. If the problem persists, you may be asking the printer to do something it cannot do. For example, you may be printing to a PostScript printer with a PCL driver. Check the printer type to verify that you haven't installed the wrong type of driver for that printer!

Figure 26-37
Page Setup
options for
Microsoft Word

If none of these help, it's also worth making sure there isn't a data cable or power issue. Swap out the data cable for one you know is good. Move the printer to another outlet (with no power strip or surge protector). If the printer supports more than one type of connection, try a different one.

Dealing with Consumables

All printers tend to generate a lot of trash in the form of *consumables*. Impact printers use paper and ribbons, inkjet printers use paper and ink cartridges, and laser printers use paper and toner cartridges. In today's environmentally sensitive world, many laws regulate the proper disposal of most printer components. Be sure to check with the local sanitation department or disposal services company before throwing away any component. Of course, you should never throw away toner cartridges—certain companies will *pay* for used cartridges!

 NOTE When in doubt about how to dispose of any computer component, check with the manufacturer for a *material safety data sheet* (*MSDS*). These standardized forms provide detailed information about not only the potential environmental hazards associated with different components but also proper disposal methods. For example, surf to https://epson.com/support/sds to find the latest MSDS for all Epson products. This isn't just a printer issue—you can find an MSDS for most computer components.

Color Prints in Wrong Color

If you print in color, sooner or later something is going to come out in the *wrong* color. A good first step is printing out the appropriate diagnostic/test page—this should help separate problems with the printer from problems with what or how you're printing.

Some pretty simple things can cause a color mismatch, so let's check those first. If you print a document with color and it comes out in black and white, double-check both the app you used to print and your print settings to make sure they aren't configured to use grayscale. Double-check the color ink/toner levels.

If something you expected to come out black comes out an odd tone, your printer may be low on black ink/toner. Colors that *appear* black may be a *rich black* with other colors mixed in—if there isn't enough black in the mix, you might end up with something unexpected.

If your printer's color registration is out of whack, you might see a sliver of unexpected color (usually cyan, magenta, or yellow) to either side of larger elements. This can be less obvious with text—it may just look blurry, discolored, or appear to have an unexpected shadow. If so, run your printer's registration or alignment routine.

Check the print settings on your system and the printer itself to see if it's configured to adjust any colors. If so, it may be misconfigured. If your printer has a color calibration routine, run it to see if the issue improves. It's also possible your system is using the wrong color profile for either the printer or the monitor. In the first case, your printer might be *right*, and your *monitor* might be wrong. Make sure your system isn't using an incorrect color profile for either device. If the profiles are correct and you have the right tools to color calibrate either device, go ahead and do so.

Some reasons for color problems are a lot less fun. If your printer has separate cartridges or tanks for different colors, it's possible someone installed the wrong color in one of the slots/tanks. If it's an inkjet, *someone* will need to spend a good bit of time cleaning the incorrect ink out of the tubing and printheads. If the right colors are in the right slots, a gunked-up printhead may be keeping the printer from laying down the right amount of a color—but the solution will still be cleaning.

EXAM TIP   MSDSs contain important information regarding hazardous materials such as safe use procedures and emergency response instructions. An MSDS is typically posted anywhere a hazardous chemical is used.

Crashes on Power-Up

Both laser printers and computers require more power during their initial power-up (the POST on a computer and the warm-up on a laser printer) than once they are running. HP recommends a *reverse power-up*. Turn on the laser printer first and allow it to finish its warm-up before turning on the computer. This avoids having two devices drawing their peak loads simultaneously.

Display Screen Malfunction

The small menu display screens included on many modern printers and multifunction devices can, like any other display screen, have a number of issues. The display might freeze or get stuck on a specific screen; it might not come on at all; it might light up but never show an image (CompTIA calls this *no image on printer* display); it might only display a single color, have artifacts such as lines showing on the display, or even just slowly fade from decades of steady use. Unfortunately, there's not a lot you can do about these problems. Turning the device off and back on is a good start, and some manufacturers recommend completely unplugging it for a few minutes. If the screen is still misbehaving but the device is otherwise functional and the problem didn't appear immediately after a firmware update, it's time to take the device to a service center.

Troubleshooting Impact Printers

Impact printers require regular maintenance but will run forever as long as you're diligent. Keep the platen (the roller or plate on which the pins impact) and the printhead clean with denatured alcohol. Be sure to lubricate gears and pulleys according to the manufacturer's specifications. Never lubricate the printhead, however, because the lubricant will smear and stain the paper. Don't forget to replace the ink ribbon every so often.

Most impact printers use paper continuously fed from a roll or ream, so changing or replacing the paper is a little more involved than adding sheets to the tray. First you'll need to swap out the rolls or move the new ream into position, and then you'll need to feed the new paper. If there is already paper in the printer, you'll need to finish feeding it out first. Like with other printers, paper quality, debris, and improperly fed paper can all lead to jams, which you'll typically clear by feeding the paper one way or the other.

For all of these processes, look up the printer's documentation; if you don't follow the instructions, there's a chance you'll damage the printer. There's often a manual feeding wheel or roller, or you may just need to pull the paper firmly from one side of the printer; both of these can break the feeding system if performed improperly.

Bad-Looking Text

White bars going through the text point to a dirty or damaged printhead. Try cleaning the printhead with a little denatured alcohol. If the problem persists, replace the printhead. Printheads for most printers are readily available from the manufacturer or from companies that rebuild them. If the characters look chopped off at the top or bottom, the printhead probably needs to be adjusted. Refer to the manufacturer's instructions for proper adjustment. If the characters have simply degraded or grown faint over time and your printer is used frequently, the printhead may be wearing out; replace it.

Bad-Looking Page

If the page is covered with dots and small smudges—the "pepper look"—the platen is dirty. Clean the platen with denatured alcohol. If the image is faded, and you know the ribbon is good, try adjusting the printhead closer to the platen. If the image is okay on one side of the paper but fades as you move to the other, the platen is out of adjustment. Platens are generally difficult to adjust, so your best plan is to take it to the manufacturer's local warranty/repair center.

Troubleshooting Thermal Printers

Compared to other printer styles, thermal printers are simple to troubleshoot and maintain. With direct thermal printers, you only need to worry about three things: the heating element, the rollers, and the paper. With thermal wax printers, you also need to care for the wax ribbon.

To clean the heating element, turn off the thermal printer and open it according to the manufacturer's instructions. Use denatured alcohol and a lint-free cloth to wipe off the heating element. You might need to use a little pressure to get it completely clean. Clean the rollers with a cloth or compressed air. You want to keep them free of debris so they can properly grip the paper. Replacing the paper is as easy as sliding off the old roll and replacing it with a new one. Remember to feed the paper through the heating element, because otherwise you won't print anything. Replacing the ribbon is similar to replacing the roll of paper; make sure to feed it past the heating element, or the printer won't work properly. Your printer's manufacturer should include any special instructions for installing a new ribbon.

Troubleshooting Inkjet Printers

Inkjet printers are reliable devices that require little maintenance as long as they are used within their design parameters (high-use machines will require more intensive maintenance). Because of the low price of these printers, manufacturers know that people don't want to spend a lot of money keeping them running. If you perform even the most basic maintenance tasks, they will soldier on for years without a whimper. Inkjets generally have built-in maintenance programs that you should run from time to time to keep your inkjet in good operating order.

Inkjet Printer Maintenance

Inkjet printers don't get nearly as dirty as laser printers, and most manufacturers do not recommend periodic cleaning. Unless your manufacturer explicitly tells you to do so, don't vacuum an inkjet. Inkjets generally do not have maintenance kits, but most inkjet printers come with extensive maintenance software (see Figure 26-38). Usually, the

Figure 26-38 Inkjet printer maintenance screen

hardest part of using this software is finding it in the first place. Look for an option in Printing Preferences, a selection on the Start menu, or an option on the printer's management Web page. Don't worry—it's there!

When you first set up an inkjet printer, it normally instructs you to perform a routine (sometimes referred to as *calibration*) to align the printheads properly. Specifics differ, but the printer will usually print at least one *test page* and either ask you to place it in the scanner (if it has one) or use the menu to indicate which sets of numbered lines align best.

If this isn't done, the print quality will show poor color *registration*—a fancy way of saying the different color layers that make up your print aren't aligned properly. The good news is that you can perform this procedure at any time. If a printer is moved or dropped or it's just been working away untended for a while, it's often worth running the alignment/registration routine. Some printers will even do this automatically from time to time.

Inkjet cartridges are usually easy to replace, but the exact process can vary widely from printer to printer. Refer to the documentation, but typically you'll open a compartment on the printer and see one or more cartridges attached to the printhead. If the printhead isn't accessible, don't try to force it out; printheads often move to the center of the printer for easy access, in which case you'll need the printer to be on before you replace cartridges.

Cartridges may simply slide into place, but the printer may also have clips to lock them in. Check the clips or slots on the printhead for an indicator of which cartridge goes where. Follow the manufacturer's instructions for removing the cartridge you need to change, then remove the new cartridge from its packaging. Look for a piece of tape or other protective covering over its nozzles or contacts; you'll need to remove that before inserting it. Make sure you follow the insertion process carefully, as an improperly seated cartridge may catch on other components when the printhead moves. Once you insert the new cartridges and close the compartment, the printhead should move back into place.

Inkjet Printer Problems

Did I say that you never should clean an inkjet? Well, that may be true for the printer itself, but there is one part of your printer that will benefit from an occasional cleaning: the inkjet's printer head nozzles. The nozzles are the tiny pipes that squirt the ink onto the paper. A common problem with inkjet printers is the tendency for the ink inside the nozzles to dry out when not used even for a relatively short time, blocking any ink from exiting. If your printer is telling Windows that it's printing and feeding paper through, but either nothing is coming out (usually the case if you're just printing black text) or only certain colors are printing, the culprit is almost certainly dried ink clogging the nozzles.

 NOTE All inkjet inks are water-based, and water works better than denatured alcohol to clean them up.

Every inkjet printer has a different procedure for cleaning the printhead nozzles. On older inkjets, you usually have to press buttons on the printer to start a maintenance program. On more modern inkjets, you can access the head-cleaning maintenance program from Windows.

 NOTE Cleaning the heads on an inkjet printer is sometimes necessary, but I don't recommend that you do it on a regular basis as preventive maintenance. The head-cleaning process uses up a lot of that very expensive inkjet ink—so do this only when a printing problem seems to indicate clogged or dirty printheads!

Definitely use inkjet printers regularly—that's good maintenance. Keeping the ink flowing through the printheads prevents them from drying up and clogging. If you don't have anything "real" to print for a week, run a test page.

Another problem that sometimes arises is the dreaded multi-sheet paper grab. This is often not actually your printer's fault—humidity can cause sheets of paper to cling to each other—but sometimes the culprit is an overheated printer, so if you've been cranking out a lot of documents without stopping, try giving the printer a bit of a coffee break. Also, fan the sheets of the paper stack before inserting it into the paper tray.

Finally, check to see if excess ink overflow is a problem. In the area where the printheads park, look for a small tank or tray that catches excess ink from the cleaning process. If the printer has one, check to see how full it is. If this tray overflows onto the main board or even the power supply, it will kill your printer. If you discover that the tray is about to overflow, you can remove excess ink by inserting a twisted paper towel into the tank to soak up some of the ink. It is advisable to wear latex or vinyl gloves while doing this. Clean up any spilled ink with a paper towel dampened with distilled water.

Troubleshooting Laser Printers

Quite a few problems can arise with laser printers, but before getting into those details, you need to review some recommended procedures for *avoiding* those problems.

 CAUTION Before you service a laser printer, always, *always* turn it off and unplug it! Don't expose yourself to the very dangerous high voltages found inside these machines.

Laser Printer Maintenance

Unlike computer maintenance, laser printer maintenance follows a fairly well-established procedure. Of course, you'll need to replace the toner cartridge every so often, but keeping your laser printer healthy requires following these maintenance steps.

Keep It Clean   Laser printers are quite robust as a rule. A good cleaning every time you replace the toner cartridge will help that printer last for many years. I know of many examples of original HP LaserJet I printers continuing to run perfectly after a dozen or more years of operation. The secret is that they were kept immaculately clean.

Your laser printer gets dirty in two ways: Excess toner, over time, will slowly coat the entire printer. Paper dust, sometimes called *paper dander*, tends to build up where the paper is bent around rollers or where pickup rollers grab paper. Unlike (black) toner, paper dust is easy to see and is usually a good indicator that a printer needs to be cleaned. Usually, a thorough cleaning using a can of compressed air to blow out the printer is the best cleaning you can do. It's best to do this outdoors, or you may end up looking like one of those chimney sweeps from *Mary Poppins*! If you must clean a printer indoors, use a special low-static vacuum—often called a toner vac—designed especially for electronic components, like some of the great products from Metro Vacuum.

Every laser printer has its own unique cleaning method, but the cleaning instructions tend to skip one little area. Every laser printer has a number of rubber guide rollers through which the paper is run during the print process. These little rollers tend to pick up dirt and paper dust over time, making them slip and jam paper. They are easily cleaned with a small amount of 90 percent or better denatured alcohol on a fibrous cleaning towel. The alcohol will remove the debris and any dead rubber. If the paper won't feed, you can give the rollers and separator pads a textured surface that will restore their feeding properties by rubbing them with a little denatured alcohol on a nonmetallic scouring pad.

 CAUTION The photosensitive drum, usually (but not always) contained in the toner cartridge, can be wiped clean if it becomes dirty, but be very careful if you do so! If the drum becomes scratched, the scratch will appear on every page printed from that point on. The only repair in the event of a scratch is to replace the toner cartridge or photosensitive drum.

If you're ready to get specific, get the printer's service manual. They are a key source for information on how to keep a printer clean and running. Sadly, not all printer manufacturers provide these, but most do. While you're at it, see if the manufacturer has a Quick Reference Guide; these can be very handy for most printer problems!

Periodic Maintenance Although keeping the printer clean is critical to its health and well-being, every laser printer has certain components that you need to replace periodically. Your ultimate source for determining the parts that need to be replaced (and when to replace them) is the printer manufacturer. Following the manufacturer's maintenance guidelines will help to ensure years of trouble-free, dependable printing from your laser printer.

Many manufacturers provide kits that contain components that you should replace on a regular schedule. These *maintenance kits* include sets of replacement parts, such as a fuser, as well as one or more rollers or pads. Typically, you need to reset the page counter after installing a maintenance kit so the printer can remind you to perform maintenance again after a certain number of pages have been printed.

Some ozone filters can be cleaned with a vacuum and some can only be replaced—follow the manufacturer's recommendation. You can clean the fuser assembly with 90 percent or better denatured alcohol. Check the heat roller (the Teflon-coated one with the light bulb inside) for pits and scratches. If you see surface damage on the rollers, replace the fuser unit.

Most printers will give you an error code when the fuser is damaged or overheating and needs to be replaced; others will produce the error code at a preset copy count as a preventive maintenance measure. Again, follow the manufacturer's recommendations.

 NOTE Failure of the thermal fuse (used to keep the fuser from overheating) can necessitate replacing the fuser assembly. Some machines contain more than one thermal fuse. As always, follow the manufacturer's recommendations. Many manufacturers have kits that alert you with an alarm code to replace the fuser unit and key rollers and guides at predetermined page counts.

The transfer corona can be cleaned with a 90 percent denatured alcohol solution on a cotton swab. If the wire is broken, you can replace it; many just snap in or are held in by a couple of screws. Paper guides can also be cleaned with alcohol on a fibrous towel.

CAUTION The fuser assembly operates at 200 to 300 degrees Fahrenheit, so always allow time for this component to cool down before you attempt to clean it.

As with inkjet printers, some laser printers also have calibration routines to ensure the quality of color prints. *Registration* routines ensure that each color prints in the correct location, and *color calibration* ensures that the printer lays down the right amount of each color. Some devices will perform these automatically from time to time. If not, the printer's manual or menu panel should recommend when to run these routines and walk you through the process.

Laser Printer Problems

Laser printer problems usually result in poor output. One of the most important tests you can do on any printer, not just a laser printer, is called a *diagnostic print page* or an *engine test page*. You do this by either holding down the On Line button as the printer is started or using the printer's maintenance software. If the print quality is poor, check for a calibration routine on your device, and see if this resolves the issue.

Faded Prints or Blank Pages If a laser printer is spitting out *faded prints* or even *printing blank pages*, that usually means the printer is running out of toner. If the printer does have toner and nothing prints, print a diagnostic/test page. If that is also blank, remove the toner cartridge and look at the imaging drum inside. If the image is still there, you know the transfer corona or the high-voltage power supply has failed. Check the printer's maintenance guide to see how to focus on the bad part and replace it.

Dirty or Smudged Printouts If the fusing mechanism in a laser printer gets dirty, it will leave a light dusting of toner all over the paper, particularly on the back of the page. When you see toner speckles on your printouts, you should get the printer cleaned.

If the printout looks smudged or readily rubs off on your fingers, the fuser isn't properly fusing the toner to the paper (CompTIA says *toner not fused to the paper*). Depending on the paper used, the fuser needs to reach a certain temperature to fuse the toner. If the toner won't fuse to the paper, try using a lighter-weight paper. You might also need to replace the fuser.

Ghosting Ghost images sometimes appear at regular intervals on the printed page. This happens when the imaging drum has not fully discharged and is picking up toner from a previous image or when a previous image has used up so much toner that either the supply of charged toner is insufficient or the toner has not been adequately charged. Sometimes it can also be caused by a worn-out cleaning blade that isn't removing the toner from the drum.

Light Ghosting Versus Dark Ghosting A variety of problems can cause both light and dark ghosting, but the most common source of light ghosting is "developer starvation." If you ask a laser printer to print an extremely dark or complex image, it can use up so much toner that the toner cartridge will not be able to charge enough toner to print the next image. The proper solution is to use less toner. You can fix ghosting problems in the following ways:

- Lower the resolution of the page (print at 300 dpi instead of 600 dpi).
- Use a different pattern.
- Avoid 50 percent grayscale and "dot-on/dot-off patterns."
- Change the layout so that grayscale patterns do not follow black areas.
- Make dark patterns lighter and light patterns darker.
- Print in landscape orientation.
- Adjust print density and RET settings.
- Print a completely blank page immediately prior to the page with the ghosting image, as part of the same print job.

In addition to these possibilities, low temperature and low humidity can aggravate ghosting problems. Check your user's manual for environmental recommendations. Dark ghosting can sometimes be caused by a damaged drum. It may be fixed by replacing the toner cartridge. Light ghosting would *not* be solved in this way. Switching other components will not usually affect ghosting problems because they are a side effect of the entire printing process.

White Vertical Lines on Page   White vertical lines usually occur when the toner is clogged, preventing the proper dispersion of toner on the drum. Try shaking the toner cartridge to dislodge the clog. If that doesn't work, replace the toner cartridge.

Blotchy Print   Blotches are commonly a result of uneven dispersion of toner, especially if the toner is low. Shake the toner from side to side and then try to print. Also be sure that the printer is sitting level. Finally, make sure the paper is not wet in spots. If the blotches are in a regular order, check the fusing rollers and the photosensitive drum for any foreign objects.

Spotty Print   If spots appear at regular intervals, the drum may be damaged or some toner may be stuck to the fuser rollers. Try wiping off the fuser rollers. Check the drum for damage. If the drum is damaged, get a new toner cartridge.

Embossed Effect   If your prints are getting an embossed effect (like putting a penny under a piece of paper and rubbing it with a lead pencil), there is almost certainly a foreign object on a roller. Use 90 percent denatured alcohol or regular water with a soft cloth to try to remove it. If the foreign object is on the photosensitive drum, you're going to have to use a new toner cartridge. An embossed effect can also be caused by the contrast control being set too high. The contrast control is actually a knob on the inside of the unit (sometimes accessible from the outside, on older models). Check your manual for the specific location.

Incomplete Characters   You can sometimes correct incompletely printed characters on laser-printed transparencies by adjusting the print density. Be extremely careful to use only materials approved for use in laser printers.

Creased Paper   Laser printers have up to four rollers. In addition to the heat and pressure rollers of the fuser assembly, other rollers move the paper from the source tray to the output tray. These rollers crease the paper to avoid curling that would cause paper jams in the printer. If the creases are noticeable, try using a different paper type. Cotton bond paper is usually more susceptible to noticeable creasing than other bonds. You might also try sending the output to the face-up tray, which avoids one roller. There is no hardware solution to this problem; it is simply a side effect of the process.

Paper Jams   Every printer jams now and then. If you get a jam, always refer first to the manufacturer's jam removal procedure. It is simply too easy to damage a printer by pulling on the jammed paper! If the printer reports a jam but there's no paper inside, you almost certainly have a problem with one of the many jam sensors or paper feed sensors inside the printer, and you'll need to take it to a repair center.

Pulling Multiple Sheets   If the printer grabs multiple sheets at a time, first try opening a new ream of paper and loading that in the printer. If that works, you have a humidity problem. If the new paper angle doesn't work, check the separation pad on the printer. The separation pad is a small piece of cork or rubber that separates the sheets as they are pulled from the paper feed tray. A worn separation pad looks shiny and, well, worn! Most separation pads are easy to replace.

Paper Not Feeding   If your printer has paper in the tray but you try to print and notice *paper not feeding*, you might need to clean (or even replace) your printer's pick-up rollers. First, rule out some simple alternatives. Make sure the printer is configured to use the same tray you're expecting it to use. Check the paper: make sure the tray isn't over-filled and confirm the paper there is well aligned, positioned correctly in the tray, and not ripped or bent. See if the weight or coating are different than what you normally use and whether the print settings specify the correct kind of paper. If the paper is different than what you normally use, test whether it'll pick up the normal paper just fine. If the tray has adjustable guides, make sure they aren't holding the paper too tightly.

Warped, Overprinted, or Poorly Formed Characters   Poorly formed characters can indicate either a problem with the paper (or other media) or a problem with the hardware.

Incorrect media cause a number of these types of problems. Avoid paper that is too rough or too smooth. Paper that is too rough interferes with the fusing of characters and their initial definition. If the paper is too smooth (like some coated papers, for example), it may feed improperly, causing distorted or overwritten characters. Even though you can purchase laser printer–specific paper, all laser printers print acceptably on standard photocopy paper. Try to keep the paper from becoming too wet. Don't open a ream of paper until it is time to load it into the printer. Always fan the paper before loading it into the printer, especially if the paper has been left out of the package for more than just a few days.

The durability of a well-maintained laser printer makes hardware a much rarer source of character printing problems, but you should be aware of the possibility. Fortunately, it is fairly easy to check the hardware. Most laser printers have a self-test function—often combined with a diagnostic printout, but sometimes as a separate process. This self-test shows whether the laser printer can properly develop an image without actually having to send print commands from the computer. The self-test is quite handy to verify the question "Is it the printer or is it the computer?" Run the self-test to check for connectivity and configuration problems.

Possible solutions include replacing the toner cartridge, especially if you hear popping noises; checking the cabling; and replacing the data cable, especially if it has bends or crimps or if objects are resting on the cable. If you have a front menu panel, turn off advanced functions and high-speed settings to determine whether the advanced functions are either not working properly or not supported by your current software configuration (check your manuals for configuration information). If these solutions do not work, the problem may not be user serviceable. Contact an authorized service center.

Troubleshooting 3-D Printers

Creating objects by melting and reforming plastic has a lot of potential for a big mess. Common issues include unwanted strings connecting open spaces (called *stringing* or *oozing*), overheating to melt part of the final product, and *layers shifting* so that they don't align properly. All filaments differ in quality, just to make an already complex process more problematic. Using poor-quality filament might save money up front, but can lead to *clogged extruders* in short order.

Although 3-D printers have been around for a decade or so, the technology still has growing pains. Troubleshooting 3-D printers is way outside the scope of the CompTIA A+ exams, primarily because the processes and such vary tremendously among the many models of printers. For the most part, check the manufacturer's Web site for help. Try one of the many excellent enthusiast sites out there for help guides, such as www.fabbaloo.com. Good luck!

Chapter Review

Questions

1. What mechanism is used by most inkjet printers to push ink onto the paper?

    A. Electrostatic discharge

    B. Gravity

    C. Air pressure

    D. Electroconductive plates

2. With a laser printer, what creates the image on the photosensitive drum?

   A. Primary corona

   B. Laser imaging unit

   C. Transfer corona

   D. Toner

3. What is the proper order of the laser printing process?

   A. Process, clean, charge, expose, develop, transfer, and fuse

   B. Process, charge, expose, develop, transfer, fuse, and clean

   C. Clean, expose, develop, transfer, process, fuse, and charge

   D. Clean, charge, expose, process, develop, fuse, and transfer

4. On a dot-matrix printer, what physically strikes the ribbon to form an image?

   A. Electromagnets

   B. Printwires

   C. Character wheel

   D. Print hammers

5. Which of these items are considered to be dot-matrix printer consumables? (Select all that apply.)

   A. Drive motor

   B. Paper

   C. Flywheel

   D. Ribbon

6. What part must be vacuumed or replaced periodically to prevent damage caused by the action of the corona?

   A. The rubber rollers

   B. The ozone filter

   C. The transfer filter

   D. The cleaning blade

7. Which one of the following port types do most printers support?

   A. PS/2

   B. USB

   C. Infrared

   D. RS-232

8. A standalone printer prints a test page just fine, but it makes gobbledygook out of your term paper. What's probably wrong?

   A. Out of toner

   B. Fuser error

   C. Printer interface

   D. Faulty software configuration

9. What printing process uses heat-sensitive plastic film embedded with various color dyes?

   A. Dye-sublimation

   B. Inkjet

   C. Ink-dispersion

   D. Dye-dispersion

10. Which tool would help you determine why a print job didn't print?

   A. Printer driver

   B. Printer setup

   C. Print spooler

   D. System setup

Answers

1. **D.** Most inkjet printers use electroconductive plates to push the ink onto the paper.

2. **B.** The laser imaging unit creates an image on the photosensitive drum.

3. **B.** Process, charge, expose, develop, transfer, fuse, and clean is the proper process.

4. **B.** Printwires physically strike the ribbon in dot-matrix printers.

5. **B, D.** Both paper and ribbons are considered dot-matrix printer consumables.

6. **B.** The ozone filter should be periodically vacuumed or changed.

7. **B.** You'll find almost all non-networked printers hooked up to USB ports.

8. **D.** The application (software) that is trying to print is probably configured incorrectly.

9. **A.** Dye-sublimation printers use heat-sensitive plastic film embedded with various color dyes.

10. **C.** The print spooler can help you determine why a print job didn't print.

Securing Computers

In this chapter, you will learn how to
- Explain the threats to your computers and data
- Describe key security concepts and technologies
- Explain how to protect computers from network threats

Your PC is under siege. Through your PC, malicious people can gain valuable information about you and your habits. They can steal your files. They can run programs that log your keystrokes and thus gain account names and passwords, credit card information, and more. They can run software that takes over much of your computer processing time and use it to send spam or steal from others. The threat is real and immediate. Worse, they're doing these things to your clients as I write these words. You need to secure your computer and your users' computers from these attacks.

But what does computer security mean? Is it an anti-malware program? Is it big, complex passwords? Sure, it's both of these things, but what about the fact that your laptop can be stolen easily or that improper ventilation can cause hard drives and other components to die?

To secure computers, you need both a sound strategy and proper tactics. For strategic reasons, you need to understand the threat from unauthorized access to local machines as well as the big threats posed to networked computers. Part of the big picture is knowing what policies, software, and hardware to put in place to stop those threats. From a tactical in-the-trenches perspective, you need to master the details to know how to implement and maintain the proper tools. Not only do you need to install anti-malware programs in your users' computers, for example, but you also need to update those programs regularly to keep up with the constant barrage of new malware.

1002

Analyzing Threats

Threats to your data and PC come from two directions: accidents and malicious people. All sorts of things can go wrong with your computer, from users getting access to folders they shouldn't see to a virus striking and deleting folders. Files can be deleted, renamed, or simply lost (what Nancy Drew might call "The Case of the Disappearing Files"). Hard drives can die, and optical discs get scratched and rendered unreadable. Accidents happen, and even well-meaning people can make mistakes.

Unfortunately, a lot of people out there intend to do you harm. Combine that intent with a talent for computers, and you have a dangerous combination. Let's look at the following issues:

- Unauthorized access
- Social engineering
- Denial of Service
- Data destruction, whether accidental or deliberate
- Administrative access
- Catastrophic hardware failures
- Physical theft
- Malware
- Environmental threats

Unauthorized Access

Unauthorized access occurs when a person accesses resources without permission. "Resources" in this case means data, applications, and hardware. A user can alter or delete data; access sensitive information, such as financial data, personnel files, or e-mail messages; or use a computer for purposes the owner did not intend.

Not all unauthorized access is malicious—often this problem arises when users who are poking around in a computer out of curiosity or boredom discover they can access resources in a fashion the primary user did not have in mind. Unauthorized access becomes malicious when people knowingly and intentionally take advantage of weaknesses in your security to gain information, use resources, or destroy data!

One way to gain unauthorized access is intrusion. You might imagine someone kicking in a door and hacking into a computer, but more often than not it's someone sitting at a home computer, trying various passwords over the Internet. Not quite as glamorous, but it'll do.

Dumpster diving is the generic term for searching refuse for information. This is also a form of intrusion. The amount of sensitive information that makes it into any organization's trash bin boggles the mind! Years ago, I worked with an IT security guru who gave me and a few other IT people a tour of our office's trash. In one 20-minute tour of the personal wastebaskets of one office area, we had enough information to access the network easily, as well as to seriously embarrass more than a few people. When it comes to getting information, the trash is the place to look!

Shoulder surfing is another technique for gaining unauthorized access. Shoulder surfing is simply observing someone's screen or keyboard to get information, often passwords. As the name implies, it usually requires the bad guy looking over your shoulder to see what you are doing.

Social Engineering

Although you're more likely to lose data through accidents, the acts of malicious users get the headlines. Most of these attacks come under the heading of *social engineering*—the process of using or manipulating people inside the organization to gain access to its network or facilities—which covers the many ways humans can use other humans to gain unauthorized information. This information may be a network login, a credit card number, company customer data—almost anything you might imagine that one person or organization may not want outsiders to access.

Social engineering attacks aren't hacking—at least in the classic sense of the word—but the goals are the same. Let's look at a few of the more classic types of social engineering attacks.

NOTE Social engineering attacks are often used together, so if you discover one of them being used against your organization, it's a good idea to look for others.

Infiltration

Hackers can use impersonation to enter your building physically disguised as cleaning personnel, repair technicians, messengers, and so on. They then snoop around desks, looking for whatever they can find. They might talk with people inside the organization, gathering names, office numbers, department names—little things in and of themselves, but powerful tools when combined later with other social engineering attacks.

Dressing the part of a legitimate user—with fake badge and everything—enables malicious people to gain access to locations and thus potentially your data. Following someone through the door, for example, as if you belong, is called *tailgating*. Tailgating is a common form of infiltration.

To combat tailgating, facilities often install a *mantrap* at the entrance to sensitive areas, or sometimes at the entrance to the whole building. A mantrap is a small room with a set of two doors, one to the outside, unsecured area and one to the inner, secure area. When walking through the mantrap, the outer door must be closed before the inner door can be opened. In addition to the double doors, the user must present some form of authentication. For additional security, a mantrap is often controlled by a *security guard* who keeps an *entry control roster*. This document keeps a record of all comings and goings from the building.

Telephone Scams

Telephone scams are probably the most common social engineering attack. In this case, the attacker makes a phone call to someone in the organization to gain information. The attacker attempts to come across as someone inside the organization and uses this to get the desired information. Probably the most famous of these scams is the "I forgot my user name and password" scam. In this gambit, the attacker first learns the account name of a legitimate person in the organization, usually using the infiltration method. The attacker then calls someone in the organization, usually the help desk, in an attempt to gather information, in this case a password.

> **Hacker:** "Hi, this is John Anderson in accounting. I forgot my password. Can you reset it, please?"
> **Help Desk:** "Sure, what's your user name?"
> **Hacker:** "j_w_anderson."
> **Help Desk:** "OK, I reset it to e34rd3."

Telephone scams certainly aren't limited to attempts to get network access. There are documented telephone scams against organizations aimed at getting cash, blackmail material, or other valuables.

Phishing

Phishing is the act of trying to get people to give their user names, passwords, or other security information by pretending to be someone else electronically. A classic example is when a bad guy sends you an e-mail that's supposed to be from your local credit card company asking you to send them your user name and password. Phishing is by far the most common form of social engineering done today.

Phishing refers to a fairly random act of badness. The attacker targets anyone silly enough to take the bait. *Spear phishing* is the term used for targeted attacks, like when a bad guy goes after a specific celebrity. The dangerous thing about spear phishing is that the bait can be carefully tailored using details from the target's life.

Denial of Service

A *denial of service (DoS)* attack uses various methods to overwhelm a system, such as a Web server, to make it essentially nonfunctional. DoS attacks were relatively common in the early days of the Web. These days you'll see *distributed denial of service (DDoS)* attacks that use many machines simultaneously to assault a system.

Data Destruction

Often an extension of unauthorized access, data destruction means more than just intentionally or accidentally erasing or corrupting data. It's easy to imagine some evil hacker accessing your network and deleting all your important files, but authorized users may also access certain data and then use that data beyond what they are authorized to do. A good example is the person who legitimately accesses a Microsoft Access product database to modify the product descriptions, only to discover that she can change the prices of the products, too.

This type of threat is particularly dangerous when users are not clearly informed about the extent to which they are authorized to make changes. A fellow tech once told me about a user who managed to mangle an important database when someone gave him incorrect access. When confronted, the user said: "If I wasn't allowed to change it, the system wouldn't let me do it!" Many users believe that systems are configured in a paternalistic way that wouldn't allow them to do anything inappropriate. As a result, users often assume they're authorized to make any changes they believe are necessary when working on a piece of data they know they're authorized to access.

Administrative Access

Every operating system enables you to create user accounts and grant those accounts a certain level of access to files and folders in that computer. As an administrator, supervisor, or root user, you have full control over just about every aspect of the computer. This increased control means these accounts can do vastly more damage when compromised, amplifying the danger of several other threats. The idea is to minimize both the number of accounts with full control and the time they spend logged in.

Even if a user absolutely needs this access, uses strong passwords, and practices good physical security, malware installed by a convincing spear phishing attack could leverage that control to access files, install software, and change settings a typical account couldn't touch.

System Crash/Hardware Failure

As with any technology, computers can and will fail—usually when you can least afford for it to happen. Hard drives crash, the power fails . . . it's all part of the joy of working in the computing business. You need to create redundancy in areas prone to failure (such as installing backup power in case of electrical failure) and perform those all-important data backups. Chapter 14, "Maintaining and Optimizing Operating Systems," goes into detail about using backups and other issues involved in creating a stable and reliable system.

Physical Theft

A fellow network geek once challenged me to try to bring down his newly installed network. He had just installed a powerful and expensive firewall router and was convinced that I couldn't get to a test server he added to his network just for me to try to access. After a few attempts to hack in over the Internet, I saw that I wasn't going to get anywhere that way.

So I jumped in my car and drove to his office, having first outfitted myself in a techy-looking jumpsuit and an ancient ID badge I just happened to have in my sock drawer. I smiled sweetly at the receptionist and walked right by my friend's office (I noticed he was smugly monitoring incoming IP traffic by using some neato packet-sniffing program) to his new server.

I quickly pulled the wires out of the back of his precious server, picked it up, and walked out the door. The receptionist was too busy trying to figure out why her e-mail wasn't working to notice me as I whisked by her carrying the 65-pound server box. I stopped in the hall and called him from my cell phone.

> **Me (cheerily):** "Dude, I got all your data!"
> **Him (not cheerily):** "You rebooted my server! How did you do it?"
> **Me (smiling):** "I didn't reboot it—go over and look at it!"

Him (really mad now): "YOU <EXPLETIVE> THIEF! YOU STOLE MY SERVER!"

Me (cordially): "Why, yes. Yes, I did. Give me two days to hack your password in the comfort of my home, and I'll see everything! Bye!"

I immediately walked back in and handed him the test server. It was fun. The moral here is simple: Never forget that the best network software security measures can be rendered useless if you fail to protect your systems physically!

NOTE Physical security for your systems extends beyond the confines of the office as well. The very thing that makes laptops portable also makes them tempting targets for thieves. One of the simplest ways to protect your laptop is to use a simple *cable lock*. The idea is to loop the cable around a solid object, such as a bed frame, and secure the lock to the small security hole on the side of the laptop.

Malware

Networks are without a doubt the fastest and most efficient vehicles for transferring computer viruses among systems. News reports focus attention on the many malicious software attacks from the Internet, but a huge number of such attacks still come from users who bring in programs on optical discs and USB drives. The "Network Security" section of this chapter describes the various methods of virus infection and other malware and what you need to do to prevent such attacks from damaging your networked systems.

Environmental Threats

Your computer is surrounded by a host of dangers all just waiting to wreak havoc: bad electricity from the power company, a host of chemicals stored near your computer, dust, heat, cold, wet . . . it's a jungle out there!

EXAM TIP Expect questions on environmental threats on the CompTIA A+ 220-1002 exam.

Power

We've covered power issues extensively back in Chapter 7, "Power Supplies." Don't ever fail to appreciate the importance of surge suppressors and uninterruptible power supplies (UPSs) to protect your electronics from surges, brownouts, and blackouts. Also remember that network devices need power protection as well. Figure 27-1 shows a typical UPS protecting a network rack.

How's the Air in There?

Proper environmental controls help secure servers and workstations from the environmental impact of excessive heat, dust, and humidity. Such *environmental controls* include air conditioning, proper ventilation, air filtration, and monitors for temperature and humidity.

Figure 27-1
UPS on rack

A CompTIA A+ technician maintains an awareness of temperature, humidity level, and ventilation, so that he or she can tell very quickly when levels or settings are out of whack.

A computer works best in an environment where the air is clean, dry, and room temperature. CompTIA doesn't expect you to become an environmental engineer, but it does expect you to explain and deal with how dirty or humid or hot air can affect a computer. We've covered all of these topics to some extent throughout the book, so let's just do a quick overview with security in mind.

Dirty Air   Dust and debris aren't good for any electronic components. Your typical office air conditioning does a pretty good job of eliminating the worst offenders, but not all computers are in nice offices. No matter where the computers reside, you need to monitor your systems for dirt. The best way to do this is observation as part of your regular work. Dust and debris will show up all over the systems, but the best place to look are the fans. Fans will collect dust and dirt quickly (see Figure 27-2).

Figure 27-2
Dirty fan

All electronic components get dirty over time. To clean them, you need to use either compressed air or a nonstatic vacuum. So which one do you use? The rule is simple: If you don't mind dust blowing all over the place, use compressed air. If you don't want dust blowing all over the place, use a vacuum.

Equipment closets filled with racks of servers need proper airflow to keep things cool and to control dusty air. Make sure that the room is ventilated and air-conditioned (see Figure 27-3) and that the air filters are changed regularly.

Figure 27-3
Air-conditioning
vent in a small
server closet

If things are really bad, you can enclose a system in a dust shield. Dust shields come complete with their own filters to keep a computer clean and happy even in the worst of environments.

 EXAM TIP   Always use proper ventilation, air filters, and enclosures. To protect against airborne particles, consider wearing a protective mask.

Temperature and Humidity   Most computers are designed to operate at room temperature, which is somewhere in the area of 22°C (72°F) with the relative humidity in the 30–40 percent range. Colder and dryer is better for computers (but not for people), so the real challenge is when the temperature and the humidity go higher.

A modern office will usually have good air conditioning and heating, so your job as a tech is to make sure that things don't happen to prevent your air conditioning from doing its job. That means you're pretty much always on ventilation patrol. Watch for the following to make sure air is flowing:

- Make sure ducts are always clear of obstructions.
- Make sure ducts are adjusted (not too hot or too cold).
- Don't let equipment get closed off from proper ventilation.

Hazardous Materials

Offices are filled with chemicals and substances that pose health risks. Some of these are immediate—they can burst into flames or damage your skin, lungs, and eyes. Others may cause cancer or other health conditions through regular exposure over many years. The 1002 objectives want you to know about *compliance to government regulations* that apply to working with these substances.

Regulations may sound intimidating, but the goal here is simple: people who work with or around dangerous substances deserve to know what the risks are, what precautions they should take, and what to do if there's an accident. You'll need to consult and comply with local regulations, but you should at least be familiar with the material safety data sheet (MSDS)—a document that details the risks, precautions, and clean-up/disposal procedures—for any substances you work with regularly, and know how to find the MSDS if something you aren't familiar with spills.

 NOTE Most U.S. cities have one or more environmental services centers that you can use to recycle electronic components. For your city, try a Google (or other search engine) search on the term "environmental services" and you'll almost certainly find a convenient place for e-waste disposal.

Security Concepts and Technologies

Once you've assessed the threats to your computers and networks, you need to take steps to protect those valuable resources. Depending on the complexity of your organization, this can be a small job encompassing some basic security concepts and procedures, or it can be exceedingly complex. The security needs for a three-person desktop publishing firm, for example, would differ wildly from those of a defense contractor supplying top-secret toys to the Pentagon.

From a CompTIA A+ certified technician's perspective, you need to understand the big picture (that's the strategic side), knowing the concepts and available technologies for security. At the implementation level (that's the tactical side), you're expected to know where to find such things as security policies in Windows. A CompTIA Network+ or CompTIA Security+ tech will give you the specific options to implement. (The exception to this level of knowledge comes in dealing with malicious software such as viruses, but we'll tackle that subject in the second half of the chapter.) So let's look at four concept and technology areas: access control, data classification and compliance, licensing, and incident response.

Access Control

Controlling access is the key. If you can control access to the data, programs, and other computing resources, you've secured your systems. *Access control* is composed of inter-linked areas that a good security-minded tech should think about: physical security, authentication, users and groups, and security policies. Much of this you know from previous chapters, but this section should help tie it all together as a security topic.

Secure Physical Area

The first order of security is limiting access to your physical hardware. The security market is huge, but the options basically boil down to doors, locks, alarms, and keeping a close eye on things. The first step is understanding that all of these pieces can (and will) fail or be beaten; great security involves arranging and layering many pieces so that they can enhance each other's strengths and compensate for each other's weaknesses.

Think back to the mantraps you saw earlier in the chapter. A low-tech solution like a traditional door lock is just a speed-bump to someone with a lock-pick and a moment alone with the lock. Mantraps are great because they combine simple measures like doors, *door locks*, *security guards*, and an entry control roster in a way that is much harder to beat than one or two locked doors.

Traditional door locks aren't terrible, but keys are easy to copy and the cost of frequently re-keying locks adds up fast. An organization ready to move beyond the basics can step up to a keyless lock system driven by employee *ID badges*—especially ones with authentication tools such as *radio frequency identification* (*RFID*) or smart cards (see "Authentication," later in this chapter)—to control building and room access. Figure 27-4 shows a typical badge.

Figure 27-4
Typical employee
badge/smart
card

Lock Down Systems

Once an attacker has physical access to the building, protecting your hardware gets a lot harder. There are some options here, but don't plan on them doing much more than slow someone down by a few minutes and make it obvious to anyone watching that they're up to no good:

- Lock the doors to your workspaces. A fast, reliable keyless lock system can make it painless to lock them even when the user steps out for a moment.

- *Cable locks* can keep someone from quickly walking off with the hardware.

- *USB locks* make it harder to plug in a USB drive to load malware for stealing data.
- RJ-45 locks limit an intruder's ability to gain access to the wired network.
- *Server locks* limit access to a server's ports and drives. There are also locking rack doors to limit access to the front or back of an entire server rack.

These devices are meaningless if an intruder can walk in like they belong, sit down at an unattended, logged-in computer, and get to work. Don't leave a logged-in PC unattended, even if it's just a Standard or Guest user. May the gods help you if you walk away from a server still logged in as an administrator. You're tempting fate.

If you must step away for a moment, manually lock the computer (or screen) with a hotkey or the primary OS menu. On a Windows system, just press WINDOWS-L on the keyboard to lock it. It's also a good idea to set up a screensaver with a short wait time and configure it to show the logon screen on resume.

EXAM TIP If you're in charge of multiple-user security best practices, having a *screensaver required* on each workstation—configured to show the logon screen on resume—can help a lot with users who might forget to lock their systems when taking a break or going to lunch. Both Windows and macOS enable you to take this a step further and set automatic *timeout* and a *screen lock*, where the screen goes blank after a few minutes and a password is required for logon.

Protect Sensitive Information

Locking unattended systems is a great habit, but it won't help much if the intruder manages to watch the user enter their password or read it off a sticky note on the monitor. Don't write down passwords and leave them in plain sight. Teach users to follow the strong password guidelines set forth in Chapter 13, "Users, Groups, and Permissions." Be aware of the risk of shoulder surfing. Ideally, the office layout should make it impossible for someone to watch the user without their knowledge.

If users need to work with sensitive information anywhere someone unauthorized could see the screen, they may need a privacy filter (also called a privacy screen)—a framed sheet or film that you apply to the front of your monitor. Privacy filters reduce the viewing angle, making it impossible to see the screen unless you're directly in front of it (see Figure 27-5). Lock up paper copies of critical, personal, or sensitive documents out of sight and shred any you don't need immediately.

MAC Address Filtering

It's far from bulletproof, but if an attacker does gain physical access to your site, you may be able to throw up another hurdle to limit their ability to access your network with any of their own devices. Both wired and wireless networks can use *MAC filtering* or *port security* to enable you to *blacklist* or *whitelist* devices based on their MAC address.

Use a *blacklist* to block specific computers, adding their MAC addresses to the ranks of the undesired. You can use a *whitelist* to pre-specify the only MAC addresses allowed access. I say this isn't bulletproof because a savvy attacker *can* spoof an address (they'll

Figure 27-5   Privacy filter

have a much easier time sniffing a valid Wi-Fi MAC address than a wired one, though) from another device accessing the network.

Keeping devices you don't control out of your network is a big win! If the attacker can't gain access to your network with one of their own devices (which they have probably preloaded with tools for attacking your systems or network), they'll have to resort to breaking into one of your devices to do the heavy lifting.

Authentication

Security requires properly implemented *authentication*, which means in essence how the computer determines who can or should access it and, once accessed, what that user can do. A computer can authenticate users through software or hardware, or a combination of both.

You can categorize ways to authenticate into three broad areas: knowledge factors, ownership factors, and inherence factors. You read about *multifactor authentication* in detail in Chapter 25, "Care and Feeding of Mobile Devices," when talking about mobile device security. It works the same way when securing a desktop computer, a laptop, a server, or a building. There's no reason to rehash it here. The only thing to add is that many organizations use *two-factor authentication*. An example is a key fob that generates a numeric key. A user authenticates by entering his or her user name and password (something the user knows) and enters the key (something the user has) when prompted.

 EXAM TIP   The 1002 exam will quiz you on multifactor and two-factor authentication. This applies to all computing devices.

Software Authentication: Proper Passwords   It's still rather shocking to me to power up a friend's computer and go straight to his or her desktop, or with my married-with-kids friends, to click one of the parents' user account icons and not be prompted for a password. This is just wrong! I'm always tempted to assign passwords right then and there—and not tell them the passwords, of course—so they'll see the error of their ways when they try to log on next. I don't do it but always try to explain gently the importance of good passwords.

 EXAM TIP Oddly, the 1002 exam lists *recovery console* as a viable security tool, but that only applied to Windows XP, not the OSs on the current exam. Look for recovery console as a false answer.

You know about passwords from Chapter 13, so I won't belabor the point here. Suffice it to say that you must require that your users have proper passwords, and ensure they are set to expire on a regular basis. Don't let them write passwords down or tape them to the underside of their mouse pads either!

It's not just access to Windows that you need to think about. There's always the temptation for people to do other mean things, such as change CMOS settings, open up the case, and even steal hard drives. Any of these actions renders the computer inoperable to the casual user until a tech can undo the damage or replace components. All modern CMOS setup utilities come with a number of tools to protect your computer, such as drive lock, intrusion detection, and of course system access BIOS/UEFI passwords such as the one shown in Figure 27-6. Refer to Chapter 5, "Firmware," to refresh yourself on what you can do at a BIOS level to protect your computer.

Figure 27-6
BIOS/UEFI
access password
request

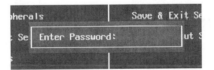

Hardware Authentication   Gates, doors, and computers can make use of *badge readers*, *smart card readers*, and *biometric scanners* to authenticate users with more authority than mere passwords. *Smart cards* are credit card–sized cards with circuitry that can identify the bearer of the card. Smart cards are relatively common for tasks such as authenticating users for mass transit systems but are fairly uncommon in computers. Figure 27-7 shows a smart card and keyboard combination.

Figure 27-7
Keyboard-
mounted smart
card reader
being used for
a commercial
application
(photo courtesy
of Cherry Corp.)

Security tokens are devices that store some unique information that the user carries on their person. They may be digital certificates, passwords, or biometric data. They may also store an RSA token. *RSA tokens* are random-number generators that are used with user names and passwords to ensure extra security. Most security *hardware tokens* come in the form of *key fobs*, as shown in Figure 27-8.

Figure 27-8
RSA key fob
(photo courtesy
of EMC Corp.)

You can also get many types of security tokens as software. Anyone who plays *World of Warcraft* knows that there's an entire illegal industry known as "gold farmers" who like to hack accounts and steal all the hard-earned loot your character collects. It's a terrible feeling to log in to the game only to find your character cleaned out (see Figure 27-9).

Figure 27-9 I've been robbed! My fine armor is gone, my bags are empty, and my bank account only has a few copper pieces!

To counter this problem, Blizzard Entertainment, the folks who own *World of Warcraft*, provide free security tokens. Most folks think "hardware" in the form of key fobs when they hear the words "security tokens," but you can also download a *software token*—Blizzard offers one of many software token apps for your smartphone, as shown in Figure 27-10.

Figure 27-10
Blizzard
Entertainment
software security
token for iPhone

People can guess or discover passwords, but it's a lot harder to forge someone's fingerprints. The keyboard in Figure 27-11 authenticates users on a local machine by using a fingerprint lock.

Figure 27-11   Microsoft keyboard with fingerprint accessibility

NOTE How's this for full disclosure? Microsoft does not claim that the keyboard in Figure 27-11 offers any security at all. In fact, the documentation specifically claims that the fingerprint reader is an accessibility tool, not a security device. Because it enables a person to log on to a local machine, though, I think it falls into the category of authentication devices.

Other devices that will do the trick are key fobs and retinal scanners. Devices that require some sort of physical, flesh-and-blood authentication are called *biometric devices* or *biometric locks*.

Clever manufacturers have developed key fobs and smart cards that use RFID to transmit authentication information so users don't have to insert something into a computer or card reader. The Privaris plusID combines, for example, a biometric fingerprint fob with an RFID tag that makes security as easy as opening a garage door remotely!

Retinal scanners loom large in media as a form of biometric security, where you place your eye up to a scanning device. While retinal scanners do exist, I have been in hundreds of high-security facilities and have only seen one retinal scanner in operation in almost 30 years as a tech. Figure 27-12 shows about the only image of a retinal scanner in operation you'll ever encounter.

Figure 27-12   Retinal scanner in *Half-Life 2*

Current smartphones and tablets use full facial recognition for identification and authentication, although they also use passcodes for when the recognition fails. Figure 27-13 shows a user logging in to an Apple iPhone via facial recognition. (Note the open lock. Hard to show the process in action because it happens so fast!)

Figure 27-13
Unlocking an
iPhone via facial
recognition

Users and Groups

Windows uses user accounts and groups as the bedrock of access control. A user account is assigned to a group, such as Users, Power Users, or Administrators, and by association gets certain permissions on the computer. Using NTFS enables the highest level of control over data resources.

Assigning users to groups is a great first step in controlling a local machine, but this feature really shines in a networked environment. Let's take a look.

NOTE   The file system on a hard drive matters a lot when it comes to security. On modern systems, the file system on the boot drive has support for an *access control list (ACL)*, a rich form of user and groups permissions. But this security only extends to drives/cards formatted with modern file systems such as NTFS, HFS+, and ext3/4. If you copy a file to a drive/card formatted with exFAT or the older FAT32, such as many cameras and USB flash drives use, the OS will strip all permissions and the file will be available for anyone to read!

Access to user accounts should be restricted to the assigned individuals, and those who configure the permissions to those accounts must follow the *principle of least privilege*: Accounts should have permission to access only the resources they need and no more. Tight control of user accounts is critical to preventing unauthorized access. Disabling unused accounts is an important part of this strategy, but good user account management goes far deeper than that.

Groups are a great way to achieve increased complexity without increasing the administrative burden on network administrators, because all operating systems combine permissions. When a user is a member of more than one group, which permissions does that user have with respect to any particular resource? In all operating systems, the permissions of the groups are *combined*, and the result is what you call the *effective permissions* the user has to access a resource. As an example, if Rita is a member of the

Sales group, which has List Folder Contents permission to a folder, and she is also a member of the Managers group, which has Read and Execute permissions to the same folder, Rita will have both List Folder Contents *and* Read and Execute permissions to that folder.

 EXAM TIP You can use directory permissions to limit access to sensitive information on a shared file server, protect user-specific files from snooping by other users on a multiuser system, and protect the system's own software from being compromised by any scripts or programs the user runs. The job doesn't end here, though! Anyone with physical access to a drive can ignore your controls. Use full-disk *data encryption* to protect data *at rest* (data in storage, not in use or moving around the network).

Watch out for *default user accounts and groups*—they can become secret backdoors to your network! All network operating systems have a default Everyone group that can be used to sneak into shared resources easily. This Everyone group, as its name implies, literally includes anyone who connects to that resource. Windows gives full control to the Everyone group by default, for example, so make sure you know to lock this down! The other scary one is the Guest account. The Guest account is the only way to access a system without a user name and password. Unless you have a compelling reason to provide guest access, you should always make sure the Guest account is disabled.

All of the default groups—Everyone, Guest, Users—define broad groups of users. Never use them unless you intend to permit all of those folks access to a resource. If you use one of the default groups, remember to configure them with the proper permissions to prevent users from doing things you don't want them to do with a shared resource!

Security Policies

Although permissions control how users access shared resources, there are other functions you should control that are outside the scope of resources. For example, do you want users to be able to access a command prompt on their Windows system? Do you want users to be able to install software? Would you like to control what systems a user can log on to or at what time of day a user can log on? All network operating systems provide you with some capability to control these and literally hundreds of other security parameters, under what Windows calls *policies*. I like to think of policies as permissions for activities, as opposed to true permissions, which control access to resources.

A policy is usually applied to a user account, a computer, or a group. Let's use the example of a network composed of Windows systems with a Windows Server. Every Windows client has its own local policies program, which enables policies to be placed on that system only. Figure 27-14 shows the tool you use to set local policies on an individual system, called *Local Security Policy*, being used to deny the Guest account the capability to log on locally.

Local policies work great for individual systems, but they can be a pain to configure if you want to apply the same settings to more than one PC on your network. If you want to

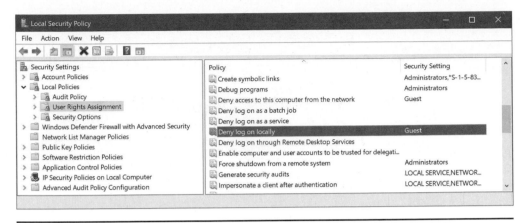

Figure 27-14 Local Security Policy

apply policy settings *en masse*, you need to step up to features of domain-based Windows Active Directory, like you read about in Chapter 19, "Local Area Networking." You can use *organizational units* (*OUs*) that organize users and devices logically into a folder-like hierarchy, and then exercise deity-like (Microsoft prefers the term granular) control to apply a different *group policy* to the network clients in each unit. Let me explain group policy a little more.

EXAM TIP Group policy changes may not immediately apply to all systems. Windows will fetch the group policy when the system boots or someone logs in. It will also refresh the policy from time to time while running, though some policy changes won't apply without a reboot anyways. You can run **gpupdate /force** from the command line to update group policy for a specific computer immediately.

Want to set the default wallpaper for every PC in your domain? Group policy can do that. Want to make certain tools inaccessible to everyone but authorized users? Group policy can do that, too. Want to control access to the Internet, redirect home folders, run scripts, deploy software, or just remind folks that unauthorized access to the network will get them nowhere fast? Group policy is the answer. Figure 27-15 shows group policy; I'm about to change the default title on every instance of Internet Explorer on every computer in my domain!

That's just one simple example of the settings you can configure by using group policy. You can apply literally hundreds of tweaks through group policy, from the great to the small, but don't worry too much about familiarizing yourself with each and every one. Group policy settings are a big topic on most of the Microsoft certification tracks, but for the purposes of the CompTIA A+ exams, you simply have to be comfortable with the concept behind group policy.

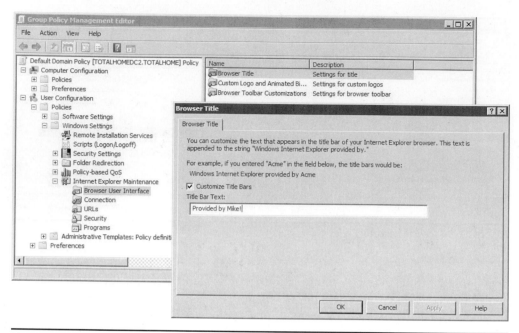

Figure 27-15 Using group policy to make IE title say "Provided by Mike!"

Although I could never list every possible policy you can enable on a Windows system, here's a list of some commonly used ones:

- **Prevent Registry Edits**   If you try to edit the Registry, you get a failure message.
- **Prevent Access to the Command Prompt**   Keeps users from getting to the command prompt by turning off the Run command and the Command Prompt shortcut.
- **Log On Locally**   Defines who may log on to the system locally.
- **Shut Down System**   Defines who may shut down the system.
- **Minimum Password Length**   Forces a minimum password length.
- **Account Lockout Threshold**   Sets the maximum number of logon attempts a person can make before being locked out of the account.
- **Disable Windows Installer**   Prevents users from installing software.
- **Printer Browsing**   Enables users to browse for printers on the network, as opposed to using only assigned printers.

Although the CompTIA A+ exams don't expect you to know how to implement policies on any type of network, you are expected to understand that policies exist, especially on Windows networks, and that they can do amazing things to control what users can do on their systems. If you ever try to get to a command prompt on a Windows system only to discover the Run command is dimmed, blame it on a policy, not the computer!

 EXAM TIP Account management security policy best practices dictate that you should implement restrictive user permissions, login time restrictions, account lockout based on failed attempts, and disable the operating system's built-in AutoRun or AutoPlay features. Finally, you should always change default system user names and passwords where possible.

Data Classification and Compliance

Larger organizations, such as government entities, benefit greatly from organizing their data according to its sensitivity—what's called *data classification*—and making certain that computer hardware and software stay as uniform as possible. In addition, many government and internal regulations apply fairly rigorously to these organizations.

Data classification systems vary by the organization, but a common scheme classifies documents as public, internal use only, highly confidential, top secret, and so on. Using a classification scheme enables employees such as techs to know very quickly what to do with documents, the drives containing documents, and more. Your strategy for recycling a computer system left from a migrated user, for example, will differ a lot if the data on the drive was classified as internal use only or top secret.

Compliance means, in a nutshell, that members of an organization or company must abide by or comply with all of the rules that apply to the organization or company. Statutes with funny names such as Sarbanes-Oxley impose certain behaviors or prohibitions on what people can and cannot do in the workplace.

 EXAM TIP The CompTIA A+ 1002 objectives use specific language for compliance. People must *follow all policies and security best practices*. Follow the rules and stay on top of new threats, in other words.

From a technician's point of view, the most common compliance issue revolves around software, such as what sort of software users can be allowed to install on their computers or, conversely, why you have to tell a user that he can't install the latest application that may help him do the job more effectively because that software isn't on the approved list. This can lead to some uncomfortable confrontations, but it's part of a tech's job.

Unapproved or non-compliant software added by users can be a serious vulnerability. These non-compliant systems are clearly violations of security best practices and should be fixed.

The concepts behind compliance in IT are not, as some might imagine at first blush, to stop you from being able to work effectively. Rather, they're designed to stop users with insufficient technical skill or knowledge from installing malicious programs or applications that will destabilize their systems. This keeps technical support calls down and enables techs to focus on more serious problems.

> ### Regulated Data Terms Spelled Out
>
> The CompTIA A+ 1002 exam calls out a few different kinds of *regulated data* by acronym alone. Let's look at each:
>
> - **Personally identifiable information (PII)** is a big umbrella for any data that can lead back to a specific individual.
> - **Protected health information (PHI)** is basically any PII that involves a person's health status, medical records, and healthcare services they have received. (The CompTIA Acronyms list spells out PHI as *personal* health information, but *protected* is the correct term.)
> - **Payment Card Industry (PCI)** is a common shorthand for the Payment Card Industry Data Security Standard (PCI DSS), a rigorous set of rules for systems that accept, transmit, process, or store credit/debit card payments.
> - The **General Data Protection Regulation (GDPR)** is a fairly new law that defines a broad set of rights and protections for the personal information of citizens living in countries in the European Union.
>
> Consult your superiors about your organization's policies for working with regulated data.

Licensing

Software licensing has many twists that can easily lead a user or a tech out of compliance. Like other creative acts, programmers are granted copyright to the software they create. The copyright owner then decides how he or she or it (the corporation) will license that software for others to use. The licensing can be commercial or non-commercial, personal or enterprise. The software can be closed source or open source. Each of these options has variations as well, so this gets complex. Let's start at the top and work through the variations.

Commercial Licensing

When software is released under a commercial license, you have a legal obligation to pay money for access to it—but a lot of variations apply. Traditionally, you bought a copy of a program and could use it forever, sell it to someone else, or give it away. You bought copies for each user with a personal license, or multiple users with an enterprise license.

Today, the picture is muddier. You can buy the use of Microsoft Office, for example, as long as you pay a monthly or yearly fee. The personal license enables you to share the software with several other people or accounts and use it on several of your personal machines.

The *End User License Agreement* (*EULA*) you agree to abide by when you open or install new software obligates you to abide by the use and sharing guidelines stipulated by the software copyright holder. You agree to the EULA for Microsoft Office, in other words, and you don't try to make illegal copies or share beyond what Microsoft says is okay.

Various forms of *digital rights management* (*DRM*) enforce how you use commercial software. Many programs require activation over the Internet, for example, or a special account with the copyright holder. To use Adobe software, such as Photoshop, you need an account with Adobe.com.

Non-Commercial Licensing

For moral or philosophical reasons, some developers want their software to be free for some or all purposes. When Linus Torvalds created the Linux operating system, for example, he made it freely available for people. GIMP image-editing software likewise is available to download and use for free.

Non-commercial licensing has variations. Many non-commercial programs are only "free" for personal use. If you want to use the excellent TeamViewer remote access program at your office, for example, you need to buy a commercial license. But if you want to log in to your home machine from your personal laptop, you can use TeamViewer for free.

Open Source Versus Closed Source

Another huge variation in software use and licensing is what you can do with the source code of an application. *Open source software* licenses generally allow you to take the original code and modify it. Some open source licenses require you to make the modified code available for free download; others don't require that at all. *Closed source software* licenses stipulate that you can't modify the source code or make it part of some other software suite.

Although CompTIA A+ 1002 exam objectives list *open source vs. commercial license*, that distinction does not exist in the real world. There are plenty of open source programs with commercial licensing fees, like server versions of Linux. Many "free" programs are likewise closed source.

The key for a tech is to know the specific licenses paid for by her company and ensure that the company abides by those licenses. Using pirated software or exceeding the use limits set by a EULA, or using private-license programs in a commercial enterprise, is *theft*, no matter how easy it is to do in practice.

Incident Response

Organizations need policies and procedures in place to deal with negative events that affect their networks and systems—an incidence response. The larger the organization, the more detailed the incidence response, both from the team involved to the planning and steps in every contingency. This is a gigantic topic that we devote a lot of time to in more advanced certifications, such as CompTIA Security+. From a CompTIA A+ tech's standpoint, you need to understand your role and what you should (and definitely should *not*) do when an incident happens. This section explores the first response actions, identifying and reporting the incident, and chain-of-custody issues.

First Response

If you're part of the incident response team, your *first response* duties will be spelled out in detail in the incident response plan. Most likely, your team's first action when something bad happens is to secure the area. Then, determine the scope of the incident (single system, whole group of users, and so on) and explore the seriousness and impact on the company.

Securing the area can mean physical lockdown (no one in or out) or other lockdown (no network traffic in or out of the affected section). Determining the scope of the incident can be accomplished by questioning users, reviewing log files, and so on. Your network and security people will handle the possible impact scenarios the organization will face.

Identify and Report

You need to identify clearly and report any security issues so a network administrator or technician can take steps resolve them. You can set up auditing within Windows so that the OS reports problems to you. *Event Viewer* enables you to read the logs created by auditing. You can then do your work and report those problems. Let's take a look.

Auditing　The Security section of Event Viewer doesn't show much by default. To unlock the full potential of Event Viewer, you need to set up auditing. *Auditing* in the security sense means to tell Windows to create an entry in the Security Log when certain events happen, such as when a user logs on (called *event auditing*) or tries to access a certain file or folder (called *object access auditing*). Figure 27-16 shows Event Viewer tracking logon and logoff events.

The CompTIA A+ certification exams don't test you on creating a brilliant auditing policy for your office—that's what network administrators do. You simply need to know what auditing does and how to turn it on or off so you can provide support for the network administrators in the field. To turn on auditing at a local level, go to Local Security Policy in Administrative Tools. Select Local Policies and then click Audit Policy. Double-click one of the policy options and select one or both of the checkboxes in the Properties dialog box that opens. Figure 27-17 shows the Audit object access Properties dialog box.

NOTE　Event Viewer stores log files in %SystemRoot%\System32\Config.

Incident Reporting　Once you've gathered data about a particular system or you've dealt with a computer or network problem, you need to complete the mission by telling your supervisor. This is called *incident reporting*, and it involves *use of documentation/documentation changes*. Many companies have pre-made forms that you simply fill out and submit. Other places are less formal. Regardless, you need to do this!

Incident reporting does a couple of things for you. First, it provides a record of work you've accomplished. Second, it provides a piece of information that, when combined with other information you might or might not know, reveals a pattern or bigger problem to someone higher up the chain. A seemingly innocuous security audit report, for example, might match other such events in numerous places in the building at the same time and thus show the cause was conscious, coordinated action rather than a glitch.

Evidence Handling and Chain of Custody

As a tech, you'll need to deal with people who use company computers in prohibited ways. In most cases, you're not paid to be the police and should not get involved.

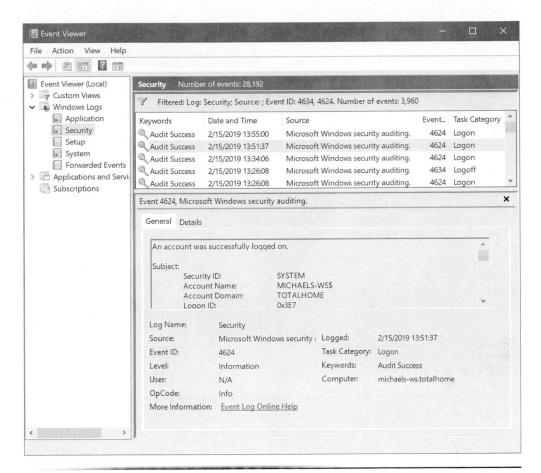

Figure 27-16 Event Viewer displaying security alerts

There are times, however, where something bad—really bad—takes place on one of the systems you support, and if you're the first tech person there, everyone is going to turn to you for action.

EXAM TIP Look for evidence-handling questions on the CompTIA A+ 220-1002 exam.

A technician should ignore personal information in and around a person's computer. As mentioned back in Chapter 1, "Safety and Professionalism," you should treat anything said to you and anything you see as a personal confidence, not to be repeated to customers, coworkers, or bosses. Here's Mike's Rule of Confidentiality: "Unless it's a felony or an imminent physical danger, you didn't see nothin'." This includes any

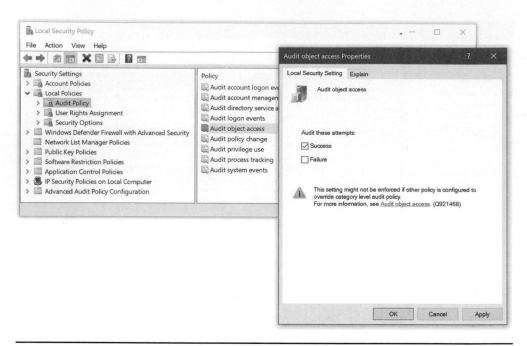

Figure 27-17 Audit object access Properties dialog box, with Local Security Policy open in the background

confidential customer materials. Try not to look at anything that isn't directly related to your job. Sometimes that's impossible, but limit your exposure. If you're waiting on a printout at a printer and suddenly there's a bunch of printed pages coming out of the printer with employee payroll information, set it to the side and pretend you never saw it.

But what about the scary stuff? Obvious espionage? Child pornography? People passing out personal information? Hacking? In these cases, you've just become the first line of defense and you need to act accordingly. Let's address the objectives as listed by CompTIA for the 220-1002 exam.

Identify the Action or Content as Prohibited   Use common sense, but keep in mind that most organizations have an Acceptable Use Policy that employees must sign. The *Acceptable Use Policy (AUP)* defines what actions employees may or may not perform on company equipment. Remember that these polices aren't just for obvious issues such as using a computer for personal use. These policies cover computers, phones, printers, and even the network itself. This policy will define the handling of passwords, e-mail, and many other issues.

Report Through Proper Channels   In most cases, you'll report any prohibited actions or content directly to your supervisor. There's also a chance your company will have a security officer or *incident response leader* who you'll contact instead. Do not speak to the person making the infraction unless your supervisor approves that contact.

Data/Device Preservation   You might end up in a situation serious enough that a computer or other device becomes evidence. In these cases, the location of the system and who has touched it may come into question, so you need to establish a *chain of custody*: a documented history of who has been in possession of the system. This is all about the *tracking of evidence/documenting process*. You should have a legal expert to guide you, but the following are fairly common rules:

1. Isolate the system. Shut down the system and store it in a place where no one else can access it.

2. Document when you took control of the system and the actions you took: shutting it down, unplugging it, moving it, and so on. Don't worry about too much detail, but you must track its location.

3. If another person takes control of the system, document the transfer of custody.

Network Security

Networks are under threat from the outside as well, so this section looks at issues involving Internet-borne attacks, firewalls, and wireless networking. This content is the security bread and butter for a CompTIA A+ technician, so you need to understand the concepts and procedures and be able to implement them properly.

Malicious Software

The beauty of the Internet is the ease of accessing resources just about anywhere on the globe, all from the comfort of your favorite chair. This connection, however, runs both ways, and people from all over the world can potentially access your computer from the comfort of their evil lairs. The Internet is awash with malicious software that is, even at this moment, trying to infect your systems.

The term *malware* defines any program or code that's designed to do something on a system or network that you don't want done. Malware comes in quite a variety of guises, such as viruses, worms, ransomware, spyware, Trojan horses, keyloggers, and rootkits. Let's examine all these forms of malware, look at what they do to infected systems, and then examine how these nasties get onto your machines in the first place.

Forms of Malware

Malware has been pestering PC users since the 1980s and has evolved into many forms over the years. From the classic boot sector viruses of the '90s to the modern threats of CryptoLocker and drive-by downloads, malware is an ever-changing threat to your users and data. To better understand these threats, you need to understand the different forms that malware can take.

Virus   A *virus* is a program that has two jobs: to replicate and to activate. *Replication* means it makes copies of itself, by injecting itself as extra code added to the end of executable programs, or by hiding out in a drive's boot sector. *Activation* is when a virus does something like corrupting data or stealing private information. A virus only replicates to other drives, such as thumb drives or optical media. It does not self-replicate across networks. A virus needs human action to spread.

Worm   A *worm* functions similarly to a virus, except it does not need to attach itself to other programs to replicate. It can replicate on its own through networks, or even hardware like Thunderbolt accessories. If the infected computer is on a network, a worm will start scanning the network for other vulnerable systems to infect.

Trojan Horse   A *Trojan horse* is a piece of malware that appears or pretends to do one thing while, at the same time, it does something evil. A Trojan horse may be a game, like poker, or ironically, a fake security program. The sky is the limit. Once installed, a Trojan horse can have a hold on the system as tenacious as any virus or worm; a key difference is that installed Trojan horses do not replicate.

Keylogger   *Keylogger* malware does pretty much what you might imagine, recording the user's keystrokes and making that information available to the programmer. You'll find keylogging functions as part of other malware as well. Keyloggers are not solely evil; a lot of parental control tools use keyloggers.

Rootkit   For malware to succeed, it often needs to come up with some method to hide itself. As awareness of malware has grown, anti-malware programs make it harder to find new locations on a computer to hide malware. A *rootkit* is a program that takes advantage of very low-level operating system functions to hide itself from all but the most aggressive of anti-malware tools. Worse, a rootkit, by definition, gains privileged access to the computer. Rootkits can strike operating systems, hypervisors, and even firmware (including hard drives and accessories . . . yikes!).

The most infamous rootkit appeared a while back as an antipiracy attempt by Sony on its music CDs. Unfortunately for the media giant, the rootkit software installed when you played a music CD and opened a backdoor that could be used maliciously.

Behavior

Knowing what form the malware takes is all well and good, but what really matters is how "mal" the malware will be when it's running rampant on a system. To get things started, let's dive into an old favorite: spyware.

Spyware   *Spyware*—malicious software, generally installed without your knowledge—can use your computer's resources to run distributed computing applications, capture keystrokes to steal passwords, or worse. Classic spyware often sneaks onto systems by being bundled with legitimate software—software that functions correctly and provides some form of benefit to the user. What kind of benefit? Way back in 2005, Movieland (otherwise known as Movieland.com and Popcorn.net) released a "handy" movie download service. They didn't tell users, of course, that everyone who installed the software was "automatically enrolled" in a three-day trial. If you didn't cancel the "trial," a pop-up window filled your screen demanding you pay them for the service that you never signed up for. The best part, however, was that you couldn't uninstall the application completely. The uninstaller redirected users to a Web page demanding money again. (Movieland was shut down in 2007.)

For another classic example, look at Figure 27-18: the dialog box asks the user if she trusts the Gator Corporation (a well-known spyware producer from ages ago). Because everyone eventually knew not to trust Gator, they would click No, and the company faded away.

Figure 27-18
Gator
Corporation's
acknowledgment
warning

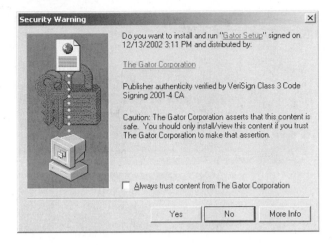

If Movieland was a problem back in 2005, what are the big spyware applications today? Unfortunately, I can't tell you—not because it's a secret, but because we don't know about them yet. You'll probably only run into spyware these days on the CompTIA A+ 1002 exam.

Ransomware As bad as spyware can be, at least you still have access to your data. *Ransomware*, on the other hand, encrypts all the data it can gain access to on a system. To top it off, many versions of ransomware can even encrypt data on mapped network drives!

Once it has locked up all your data, the ransomware application pops up a message asking for money (often bitcoins) to decrypt your data. Also, to encourage a faster payment, this ransom is presented with a timer that, when it reaches 0, triggers deletion of the encryption keys, leaving you with a drive full of scrambled data.

 EXAM TIP Know the various types of malware, including viruses, worms, Trojan horses, rootkits, spyware, and ransomware.

A Bot on the Net Full of Zombies Another type of malware I want to talk about is the botnet ("bot" as in robot, get it!). A *botnet*, as "net" in its name implies, isn't a single type of malware, but a network of infected computers (*zombies*) under the control of a single person or group, with sizes easily growing into the millions of zombies for the largest networks.

With that many machines under their control, botnet operators have command of massive computing and network resources. One of the most common uses of botnets is sending spam. If you've ever wondered how spammers pay for all that bandwidth, they don't! They use the bandwidth of millions of zombie machines spread all around the world, from grandma's e-mail machine to hacked Web servers.

Spam is but one use of a botnet. The criminals who run these networks also use all that collective power to attack companies and governments and demand a ransom to call off the attack.

Attack Methods and Sources

As bad as all this malware is, it doesn't seep onto a computer via osmosis; it needs what security people call an *attack vector*—the route the malware takes to get into and infect the system. As a good CompTIA A+ tech, you need to know where the vulnerabilities lie so you can make sure your computers are protected.

As with everything else in computing, there are multiple ways to try and get malware into a system, everything from the first floppy boot sector virus all the way up to modern Internet worms and drive-by downloads.

Zero-Day Attacks   A *zero-day attack* is an attack on a vulnerability that wasn't already known to the software developers. It gets the name because the developer of the flawed software has had zero days to fix the vulnerability. Microsoft, Apple, and other software developers regularly post patches to fix flaws as they're discovered.

Spoofing   *Spoofing* is the process of pretending to be someone or something you are not by placing false information into your packets. Any data sent on a network can be spoofed. Here are a few quick examples of commonly spoofed data:

- Source MAC address and IP address, to make you think a packet came from somewhere else

- E-mail address, to make you think an e-mail came from somewhere else

- Web address, to make you think you are on a Web page you are not on

- User name, to make you think a certain user is contacting you when in reality it's someone completely different

Generally, spoofing isn't so much a threat as it is a tool to make threats. If you spoof my e-mail address, for example, that by itself isn't a threat. If you use my e-mail address to pretend to be me, however, and to ask my employees to send in their user names and passwords for network login? That's clearly a threat. (And also a waste of time; my employees would *never* trust me with their user names and passwords.)

Man-in-the-Middle   In a *man-in-the-middle* (*MITM*) attack, an attacker taps into communications between two systems, covertly intercepting traffic thought to be only between those systems, reading or in some cases even changing the data and then sending the data on. A classic man-in-the-middle attack would be a person using special software on a wireless network to make all the clients think his laptop is a wireless access point. He could then listen in on that wireless network, gathering up all the conversations and gaining access to passwords, shared keys, or other sensitive information.

Session Hijacking   Somewhat similarly to man-in-the-middle attacks, *session hijacking* tries to intercept a valid computer session to get authentication information.

Unlike man-in-the-middle attacks, session hijacking only tries to grab authentication information, not necessarily listening in like a man-in-the-middle attack.

Brute Force   CompTIA describes brute force as a threat, but it's more of a method that threat agents use. Brute force is a method where a threat agent guesses many or all possible values for some data. Most of the time the term *brute force* refers to an attempt to crack a password, but the concept also applies to other attacks. You can brute force a search for open ports, network IDs, user names, and so on. Pretty much any attempt to guess the contents of some kind of data field that isn't obvious (or is hidden) is considered a brute force attack.

CompTIA's list of threats also includes two tools attackers use to brute force passwords: dictionaries and rainbow tables. A dictionary attack is a form of brute force attack that essentially guesses every word in a dictionary. Don't just think of Webster's dictionary—a *dictionary* used to attack passwords might contain every password ever leaked online.

Before we can talk about rainbow tables, we need to look closer at password leaks. One (terrible!) way to authenticate users is to save a copy of their password in a database and check it every time they log in. Hackers *love* to steal these databases because they can go try the user name and password on popular services, and use the passwords to improve the dictionaries they use to guess passwords.

In response to this threat, authentication systems only save a special value (called a *hash*) computed from the password; each time the user logs in, the system re-computes this special value and compares it with the saved copy. If an attacker steals one of these databases, they only get a bunch of user names and hashes. Hashes are special because the computation that creates them is irreversible; the only way to figure out what password produced a given hash is to guess a password, perform the same computation, and see if the hashes match.

Attackers fought back by pre-computing large lookup tables—known as *hash tables*— of passwords and the corresponding hash. When they find a large database of hashed passwords, they can just look up the corresponding password in their hash table. Hash tables for passwords more than a few characters long eat tons of storage space, so they're turned into *rainbow tables* to save space (at the expense of a little speed and accuracy.) *Rainbow tables* use complicated math to condense dictionary tables with hashed entries dramatically. They're binary files, not text files, and can store amazing amounts of information in a relatively small size. Rainbow tables generally fall into the realm of CompTIA Security+ or even higher-level certifications, but the phrase has become common enough that CompTIA A+ techs need to know what it means.

 EXAM TIP   For the exam, know that rainbow tables are used to reverse password hashes. In the real world, rainbow tables are only a real threat to older/legacy systems. Well-designed modern authentication systems add other values (a process called *salting*) to the password before hashing and storing it. Rainbow tables are useless for reversing properly salted hashes.

Pop-Ups and Drive-By Downloads   *Pop-ups* are those surprise browser windows that appear automatically when you visit a Web site, proving themselves irritating and unwanted.

Getting rid of pop-ups is actually rather tricky. You've probably noticed that most of these pop-up browser windows don't look like browser windows at all. They have no menu bar, button bar, or address window, yet they are separate browser windows. HTML coding permits Web site and advertising designers to remove the usual navigation aids from a browser window so all you're left with is the content. In fact, as I'll describe in a minute, some pop-up browser windows are deliberately designed to mimic similar pop-up alerts from the Windows OS. They might even have buttons similar to Windows' own exit buttons, but you might find that when you click them, you wind up with more pop-up windows instead! What to do?

The first thing you need to know when dealing with pop-ups is how to close them without actually having to risk clicking them. As I said, most pop-ups have removed all navigation aids, and many are also configured to appear on your monitor screen in a position that places the browser window's exit button—the little × button in the upper-right corner—outside of your visible screen area. Some even pop up behind the active browser window and wait there in the background. Most annoying! To remedy this, use alternate means to close the pop-up browser window. For instance, you can right-click the browser window's taskbar icon to generate a pop-up menu of your own. Select Close, and the window should go away. You can also press ALT-TAB to bring the browser window in question to the forefront and then press ALT-F4 to close it.

Most Web browsers have features to prevent pop-up ads in the first place, but I've found that these features often miss the types of annoyances and threats that greet modern Web users. To combat these new problems, extensions such as uBlock Origin and Ghostery control a variety of Internet annoyances, including pop-up windows, cookies, and trackers, and are more configurable—you can specify what you want to allow on any particular domain address—but that much control is too confusing for most novice-level users.

Another popular spyware method is to use pop-up browser windows crudely disguised as Windows' own system warnings (see Figure 27-19). When clicked, these may trigger a flood of other browser windows, or may even start a file download. Those unwanted, unknown, or unplanned file downloads are called *drive-by downloads*.

The lesson here is simple: *Don't click*, at least not without researching the suspicious-looking program first. If you visit a Web site that prompts you to install a third-party application or plug-in that you've never heard of, *don't install it*. Well-known and reputable plug-ins, such as Adobe Flash, are safe(ish), but be suspicious of any others. Don't click *anywhere* inside of a pop-up browser window, even if it looks just like a Windows alert window or command-line prompt—as I just mentioned, it's probably fake and the Close button is likely a hyperlink. Instead, use other means to close the window, such as pressing ALT-F4 or right-clicking the browser window's icon on the taskbar and selecting Close.

You can also install spyware detection and removal software on your system and run it regularly. Let's look at how to do that.

Some spyware makers are reputable enough to include a routine for uninstalling their software. Gator, for instance, made it fairly easy to get rid of their programs; you just used the Windows Add/Remove Programs or Programs and Features applet in the

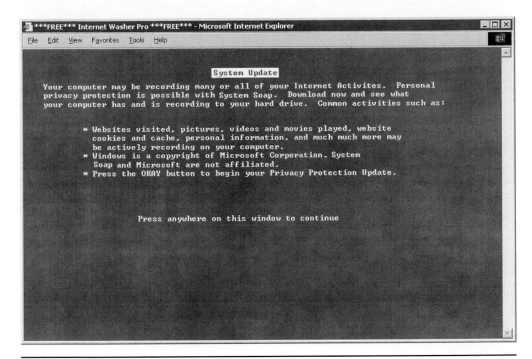

Figure 27-19 A spyware pop-up browser window, disguised as an old-school Windows alert

Control Panel. Others, however, aren't quite so cooperative. In fact, because spyware is so, well, sneaky, it's entirely possible that your system already has some installed that you don't even know about.

Windows comes with Windows Defender (simply called Virus & threat protection in Windows 10, as shown in Figure 27-20), a fine tool for catching most spyware, but it's not perfect. You can also supplement Windows Defender with a second spyware removal program. My personal favorite is Malwarebytes.

These applications work exactly as advertised. They detect and delete spyware of all sorts—hidden files and folders, cookies, Registry keys and values, you name it. Malwarebytes is free for personal use. Figure 27-21 shows Malwarebytes in action.

Try This!   Malwarebytes

If you haven't done this already, do it now. Go to www.malwarebytes.com and download the latest copy of Malwarebytes. Install it on your computer and run it. Did it find any malware that slipped in past your defenses?

Spam   E-mail that arrives in your Inbox from a source that's not a friend, family member, or colleague, and that you didn't ask for, can create huge problems for you and

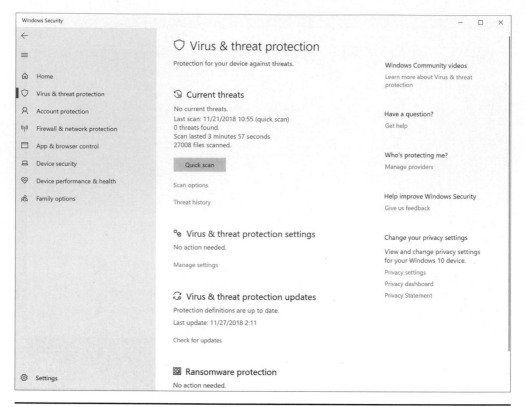

Figure 27-20   Windows 10 Virus & threat protection

your computer. This unsolicited e-mail, called *spam*, accounts for a huge percentage of traffic on the Internet. Spam comes in many flavors, from legitimate businesses trying to sell you real products to scammers who just want to take your money. Hoaxes, pornography, and get-rich-quick schemes pour into the Inboxes of most e-mail users. They waste your time and can easily offend.

You can use several options to cope with the flood of spam. The first option is defense. Never post your e-mail address on the Internet. Spammers crawl the Web looking for e-mail addresses posted out in the open.

Filters and e-mail filtering software can block spam at your mail server and at your computer. Gmail has powerful blocking schemes, for example, that drop the average spam received by its subscribers by a large percentage, usually more than 90 percent. You can set most e-mail programs to block e-mail from specific people—good to use if someone is harassing you—or to specific people. You can block by subject line or keywords.

A lot of spam contains malware or points to dangerous Web sites. Never click on any link or open an e-mail from someone you don't know! You might just save your computer.

Spam is also notorious for phishing scams. As discussed earlier in the chapter, phishing works by sending you an e-mail message that looks legitimate, like a bill or account

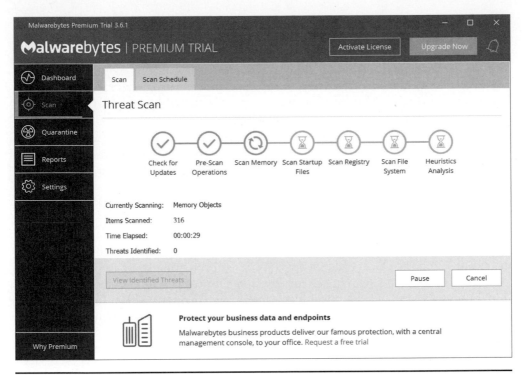

Figure 27-21 Malwarebytes

information, hoping you will enter important personal information. If you receive an e-mail purporting to be from Amazon.com, eBay.com, or some other site (like your bank), don't click on it! Hover the cursor over the link. Chances are, it's not what it pretends to be. Like Admiral Ackbar said in *Return of the Jedi*, "It's a trap!"

Malware Signs and Symptoms

If your PC has been infected by malware, you'll bump into some strange things before you can even run an anti-malware scan. Like a medical condition, malware causes unusual symptoms that should stand out from your everyday computer use. You need to become a PC physician and understand what each of these symptoms means.

Malware's biggest strength is its flexibility: it can look like anything. In fact, a lot of malware attacks can feel like normal PC "wonkiness"—momentary slowdowns, random one-time crashes, and so on. Knowing when a weird application crash is actually a malware attack is half the battle.

Slow performance in a PC can mean you're running too many applications at once, or that you've been hit with malware. Applications can crash at random, even if you don't have too many loaded. How do you tell the difference? In this case, it's the frequency. If it's happening a lot, even when all of your applications are closed, you've got a problem. This goes for frequent lockups, too—whether it seems to be *PC- or OS-based lockups*. If Windows starts misbehaving (more than usual), run your anti-malware application right away.

Malware, however, doesn't always jump out at you with big system crashes. Some malware tries to rename system files, change file permissions, or hide files completely. You might start getting e-mail messages from colleagues or friends questioning a message "you" sent to them that seemed spammy. (CompTIA terms this *responses from users regarding email.*) You might get *automated replies from unknown sent e-mail* that you know you didn't send. Most of these issues are easily caught by a regular anti-malware scan, so as long as you remain vigilant, you'll be okay.

 EXAM TIP While it's not necessarily a malware attack, watch out for *hijacked e-mail* accounts belonging either to you or to someone you know. Hackers can hit both e-mail clients and Webmail users. If you start receiving some fishy (or phishy) e-mail messages, change your Webmail user name and password and scan your PC for malware.

Some malware even fights back, defending itself from your many attempts to remove it. If your Windows Update feature stops working, preventing you from patching your PC, you've got malware. (CompTIA speak: *OS updates failure.*) If other tools and utilities throw up an "Access Denied" road block, you've got malware. If you lose all Internet connectivity, either the malware is stopping you or the process of removing the malware broke your connection. (CompTIA calls these *Internet connectivity issues,* which seems very polite.) In this case, you might need to reconfigure your Internet connection: reinstall your NIC and its drivers, reboot your router, and so on.

Even your browser and anti-malware applications can turn against you. If you type in one Web address and end up at a different site than you anticipated, a malware infection might have overwritten your *hosts* file. The hosts file overrules any DNS settings and can redirect your browser to whatever site the malware adds to the file. Most browser redirections point you to phishing scams or Web sites full of free downloads (that are, of course, covered in even more malware). In fact, some free anti-malware applications are actually malware—what techs call *rogue anti-malware* programs. You can avoid these rogue applications by sticking to the recommended lists of anti-malware software found online at reputable tech sites, like Ars Technica, Tom's Hardware, Anandtech, and others.

 EXAM TIP The 1002 exam objectives list *system/application log errors* as a symptom. Some malware definitely leaves traces of what it's up to in these logs, and they can provide a wealth of information for discovering what the malware was up to. You might catch it destabilizing programs, disabling services that protect your system, or triggering warnings about resource use. Patterns might even distinctly identify the malware. That said, you or your users will almost certainly notice some other symptom before you go trawling these logs for anything fishy.

Watch for security alerts in Windows, either from Windows' built-in security tools or from your third-party anti-malware program. Windows built-in tools alert you via the Action Center or the Windows Defender Security Center (Windows 10), which you learned about back in Chapter 16, "Troubleshooting Operating Systems." Figure 27-22 shows the older Action Center. You don't configure much here; it just tells you whether or not you are protected. The Action Center or Security Center will pop up a notification in the notification area whenever Windows detects a problem.

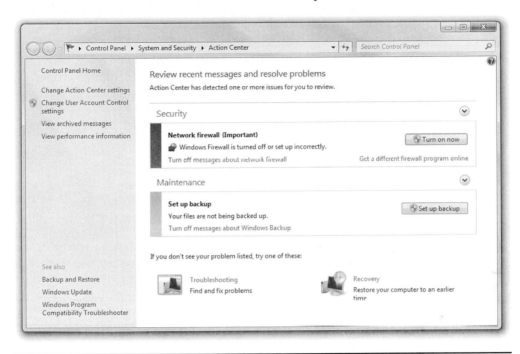

Figure 27-22   Windows 7 Action Center

Malware Prevention and Recovery

The only way to permanently protect your PC from malware is to disconnect it from the Internet and never permit any potentially infected software to touch your precious computer. Because neither scenario is likely these days, you need to use specialized anti-malware programs to help stave off the inevitable assaults. Even with the best anti-malware tools, there are times when malware still manages to strike your computer. When you discover infected systems, you need to know how to stop the spread of the malware to other computers, how to fix infected computers, and how to remediate (restore) the system as close to its original state as possible.

Dealing with Malware

You can deal with malware in several ways: anti-malware programs, training and awareness, patch/update management, and remediation.

At the very least, every computer should run an anti-malware program. If possible, add an appliance that runs anti-malware programs against incoming data from your network. Also remember that an anti-malware program is only as good as its updates—keep everyone's definition file (explained a bit later) up to date with, literally, nightly updates! Users must be trained to look for suspicious ads, programs, and pop-ups, and understand that they must not click these things. The more you teach users about malware, the more aware they'll be of potential threats. Your organization should have policies and procedures in place so everyone knows what to do if they encounter malware. Finally, a good tech maintains proper incident response records to see if any pattern to attacks emerges. He or she can then adjust policies and procedures to mitigate these attacks.

 EXAM TIP One of the most important malware mitigation procedures is to keep systems under your control patched and up to date through proper *patch management*. Microsoft, Apple, and the Linux maintainers do a very good job of putting out bug fixes and patches as soon as problems occur. If your systems aren't set up to update automatically, then perform manual updates regularly.

Anti-Malware Programs

An *anti-malware program* such as a classic *antivirus program* protects your PC in two ways. It can be both sword and shield, working in an active seek-and-destroy mode and in a passive sentry mode. When ordered to seek and destroy, the program scans the computer's boot sector and files for viruses and, if it finds any, presents you with the available options for removing or disabling them. Antivirus programs can also operate as *virus shields* that passively monitor a computer's activity, checking for viruses only when certain events occur, such as a program execution or file download.

 NOTE The term *antivirus* (and antispyware, or anti-anything) is becoming obsolete. Viruses are only a small component of the many types of malware. Many people continue to use the term as a synonym for anti-malware.

Antivirus programs use different techniques to combat different types of viruses. They detect boot sector viruses simply by comparing the drive's boot sector to a standard boot sector. This works because most boot sectors are basically the same. Some antivirus programs make a backup copy of the boot sector. If they detect a virus, the programs use that backup copy to replace the infected boot sector. Executable viruses are a little more difficult to find because they can be on any file in the drive. To detect executable viruses, the antivirus program uses a library of signatures. A *signature* is the code pattern of a known virus. The antivirus program compares an executable file to its library of signatures. There have been instances where a perfectly clean program coincidentally held a virus signature. Usually the antivirus program's creator provides a patch to prevent further alarms.

 EXAM TIP Be prepared for a question on the CompTIA A+ 1002 exam about *rogue antivirus* software. This can mean one of two things. First, the software might be a Trojan Horse, as we discussed earlier—a security program that looks like it's doing good for you but actually infects your computer. Or, second, it could be horribly invasive anti-malware software that protects your computer at the cost of making it not run well. You're more likely to see the first definition on the exam.

Now that you understand the types of viruses and how antivirus programs try to protect against them, let's review a few terms that are often used to describe virus traits.

 SIM Check out the excellent Challenge! sim, "Fixing Viruses," in the Chapter 27 sims over at http://totalsem.com/100x.

Polymorphic/Polymorphs A *polymorphic virus*, often shortened to simply a *polymorph*, attempts to change its signature to prevent detection by antivirus programs, usually by continually scrambling a bit of useless code. Fortunately, the scrambling code itself can be identified and used as the signature—once the antivirus makers become aware of the virus. One technique used to combat unknown polymorphs is to have the antivirus program create a checksum on every file in the drive. A *checksum* in this context is a number generated by the software based on the contents of the file rather than the name, date, or size of that file. The algorithms for creating these checksums vary among different antivirus programs (they are also usually kept secret to help prevent virus makers from coming up with ways to beat them). Every time a program is run, the antivirus program calculates a new checksum and compares it with the earlier calculation. If the checksums are different, it is a sure sign of a virus.

Stealth The term "stealth" is more of a concept than an actual virus function. Most *stealth virus* programs are boot sector viruses that use various methods to hide from antivirus software. The AntiEXE stealth virus hooks on to a little-known but often-used software interrupt, for example, running only when that interrupt runs. Others make copies of innocent-looking files.

User Education

A powerful tool to prevent malware attacks and to reduce the impact of malware attacks when they happen is to educate your end users. Teach users to be cautious of incoming e-mail they don't clearly recognize and to never click on an attachment or URL in an e-mail unless they are 100 percent certain of the source.

Explain the dangers of going to questionable Web sites to your users and teach them how to react when they see questionable actions take place. All Web browsers have built-in attack site warnings like the one shown in Figure 27-23.

Nobody wants their systems infected with malware. Users are motivated and happy when you give them the skills necessary to protect themselves. The bottom line is that educated and aware users will make your life a lot easier.

Malware Prevention Tips

The secret to preventing damage from a malicious software attack is to keep from getting malware on your system in the first place. One way to do this is with a variation on traditional DNS—secure DNS (the 1002 objectives use a single word: *SecureDNS*). Secure DNS can describe software or a remote DNS provider that implements some additional filtering to block your devices from visiting all kinds of malicious Web sites.

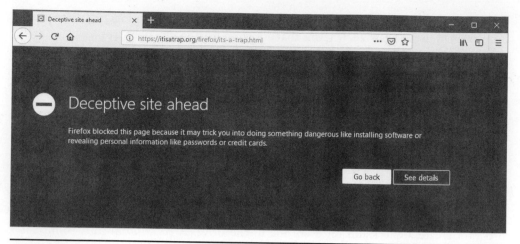

Figure 27-23   Attack site warning

If you can't keep the malware from reaching your system, a good next step is catching it on the way in the door. As discussed earlier, for example, all good antivirus/anti-malware programs include a virus shield that scans e-mail, downloads, running programs, and so on automatically (see Figure 27-24).

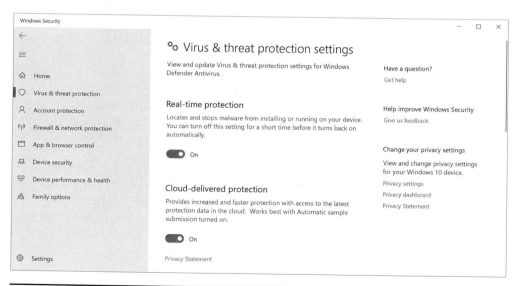

Figure 27-24   A Windows 10 virus shield in action

Use your antivirus shield. It is also a good idea to scan PCs daily for possible virus attacks. All antivirus programs include terminate-and-stay-resident programs (TSRs) that run every time the PC is booted. Last but not least, know the source of any software before you load it. Only install apps from trusted sources, such as the manufacturer's Web site, or well-known app stores like Valve's Steam service. Avoid untrusted software sources, like free registry cleaners from some .support domain, at all costs.

Keep your antivirus and anti-malware programs updated. New viruses and other malware appear daily, and your programs need to know about them. The list of virus signatures your antivirus program can recognize, for example, is called the *definition file*, and you must keep that definition file up to date so your antivirus software has the latest signatures. Fortunately, most antivirus programs update themselves automatically. Further, you should periodically update the core anti-malware software programming—called the *engine*—to employ the latest refinements the developers have included.

Boot Media Anti-Malware Tools

If you run anti-malware software and your computer still gets infected, especially after a reboot, you need a more serious anti-malware tool. Many anti-malware companies provide bootable CDs or USB flash drives (or show you how to make one) that enable you to boot from a known-clean OS and run the same anti-malware software, but this time not corrupted by the malware on your system.

Try This! Scoring Excellent Anti-Malware Programs

You can download many excellent anti-malware programs for free, either for extended trial periods or for indefinite use. Since you need these programs to keep your systems happy, try this! Download one or more anti-malware programs, such as the following:

- **Malwarebytes (www.malwarebytes.com)** Malwarebytes rocks the house in terms of dealing with malicious software. There's a free version that scans your computer for malware and quarantines it, and a Premium version that crushes online threats instantly, automatically. Malwarebytes is my first choice in dealing with malware on a client's computer.

- **Adaware (www.adaware.com)** Adaware is an excellent anti-malware program. Adaware Antivirus offers free antivirus and spyware protection and will root out all sorts of files and programs that can cause your computer to run slowly (or worse). Adaware Antivirus Pro is available at a cost and offers advanced protection with a two-way firewall, threat blocking algorithms, and phishing protection.

- **Spybot (www.safer-networking.org)** Spybot from Safer Networking Ltd. is another superb anti-malware/antispyware program. Many folks use both Adaware and Spybot—though sometimes the two programs detect each other as spyware! You can also purchase Spybot Home or Spybot Pro, both of which offer additional protection and features.

Malware Recovery Tips

When the inevitable happens and either your computer or one of your user's computers gets infected by malware such as a computer virus, you need to follow certain steps to stop the problem from spreading and get the computer back up safely into service. The 1002 exam outlines the following multistep process as the *best practice procedures for malware removal*:

1. Identify and research malware symptoms.

2. Quarantine the infected systems.

3. Disable System Restore (in Windows).

4. Remediate the infected systems.

    A. Update the anti-malware software.

    B. Scan and use removal techniques (Safe Mode, Preinstallation Environment).

5. Schedule scans and run updates.

6. Enable System Restore and create a restore point (in Windows).

7. Educate the end user.

 EXAM TIP In addition to this malware removal process, the 1002 objectives also mention *Backup/restore* as another way to make sure your system is malware-free—just restore a full system backup (in Windows, you can take or restore one with the Backup and Restore utility). There are hurdles to using this approach.

    You must have space to store one or more full backups, plan far enough ahead to have one or more recent backup available, know at least one is malware-free, and be prepared to either back up user files/data separately or lose any created/modified since the last backup. You won't always have this option, but a good way to get started is backing up user files and data *separately* and taking a full backup of the system itself once you have all of the software you need installed and configured.

Recognize and Quarantine The first step is to identify and recognize that a potential malware outbreak has occurred. If you're monitoring network traffic and one computer starts spewing e-mail, that's a good indicator of malware. Or users might complain that a computer that was running snappily the day before seems very sluggish.

    Many networks employ software such as the open source PacketFence that automatically monitors network traffic and can cut a machine off the network if that machine starts sending suspicious packets. You can also quarantine a computer manually by disconnecting the network cable. Once you're sure the machine isn't capable of infecting others, you're ready to find the virus or other malware and get rid of it.

    At this point, you should disable System Restore. If you make any changes going forward, you don't want the virus to be included in any saved restore points. To turn off System Restore in Windows, open the Control Panel and then the System applet. Click the System protection link. In the Protection Settings section, select a drive and click Configure. In the System Protection dialog box that opens, select Turn off system protection. Repeat the procedure for each hard drive on the system.

Search and Destroy   Once you've isolated the infected computer (or computers), you need to get to a safe boot environment and run anti-malware software. You can first try Windows Safe Mode in Windows 7 or the Windows Recovery Environment in Windows 8/8.1/10, because they don't require anything but a reboot. If that doesn't work, or you suspect a boot sector virus, you need to turn to an external bootable source, such as a bootable optical disc or USB flash drive.

Get into the habit of keeping around a bootable anti-malware flash drive or optical media. If you suspect a virus or other malware, use the boot media, even if your anti-malware program claims to have eliminated the problem. Turn off the PC and reboot it from the anti-malware disc or flash drive (you might have to change CMOS settings to boot to optical or USB media). This will put you in a clean boot environment that you know is free from any boot sector viruses. If you only support fairly recent computers, you will likely be booting to a USB flash drive, so you can put a boot environment on a thumb drive for even faster start-up speeds.

You have several options for creating the bootable optical disc or flash drive. First, some antivirus software comes in a bootable version. Second, you can download a copy of Linux that offers a live CD or DVD option such as Ubuntu. With a live disc, you boot to the disc and install a complete working copy of the operating system into RAM, never touching or accessing the hard drive, to give you full Internet-ready access so you can reach the many online anti-malware sites you'll need for access to anti-malware tools.

Finally, you can download and burn a copy of the Ultimate Boot CD. It comes stocked with several antivirus and anti-malware programs, so you won't need any other tool. Find it at www.ultimatebootcd.com. The only downside is that the anti-malware engines will quickly be out of date, as will their malware libraries.

Once you get to a boot environment, update your anti-malware software and then run its most comprehensive scan. Then check all removable media that were exposed to the system, and any other machine that might have received data from the system or that is networked to the cleaned machine. A virus or other malicious program can often lie dormant for months before anyone knows of its presence.

E-mail is still a common source of viruses, and opening infected e-mails is a common way to get infected. Viewing an e-mail in a preview window opens the e-mail message and exposes your computer to some viruses. Download files only from sites you know to be safe and avoid the less reputable corners of the Internet, the most likely places to pick up computer infections.

 EXAM TIP   CompTIA considers the process of removing a virus part of the remediation step. Since you can't remediate a PC until after a virus is gone, I've laid out the steps as you see here.

Remediate Malware infections can do a lot of damage to a system, especially to sensitive files needed to load Windows, so you might need to remediate formerly infected systems after cleaning off the drive or drives. *Remediation* simply means that you fix things the virus or other malware harmed. This can mean replacing corrupted Windows Registry files or even startup files.

If you can't start Windows after the malware scan is finished, you need to boot to the Windows Preinstallation Environment and use the Windows Recovery Environment/ System Recovery Options.

With the Windows Recovery Environment (covered in detail in Chapter 16), you have access to more repair tools, such as Startup Repair, System Restore, System Image Recovery, Refresh, and Command Prompt (see Figure 27-25). Run the appropriate option for the situation and you should have the machine properly remediated in a jiffy.

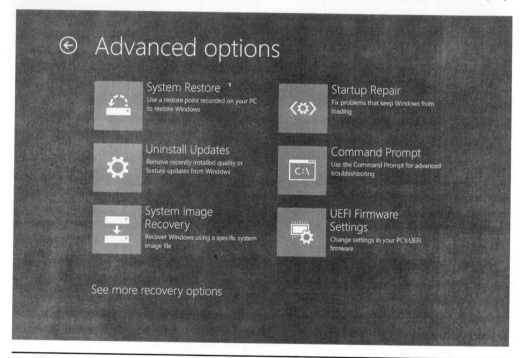

Figure 27-25 System Recovery Options

 TIP Remember to re-enable System Restore and create a new restore point once the system has been repaired.

Educate End Users The best way to keep from having to deal with malware is education. It's your job as the IT person to talk to your users, especially the ones whose systems you've just spent an hour ridding of nasties, about how to avoid these programs.

Show them samples of dangerous e-mails they should not open, Web sites to avoid, and the types of programs they should not install and use on the network. Any user who understands the risks of questionable actions on their computers will usually do the right thing and stay away from malware.

Finally, have your users run antivirus and antispyware programs regularly. Schedule them while interfacing with the user so you know it will happen.

Firewalls

Much as anti-malware programs are essential tools in the fight against malicious programs on the Internet, *firewalls* are devices or software that protect an internal network from unauthorized access to and from the Internet at large. Firewalls use a number of methods to protect networks, such as hiding IP addresses and blocking TCP/IP ports.

A typical network uses one of two types of firewalls: *hardware firewalls*, often built into routers, and *software firewalls* that run on your computers. Both types of firewall protect your computer and your network. You also run them at the same time. Let's look at both a typical SOHO router's firewall features and your computer's software firewall to see how they protect your network and your computers.

Hardware Firewall Settings

Most SOHO networks use a hardware firewall, often as a feature built into a router like the ASUS model shown in Figure 27-26. A hardware firewall protects a LAN from outside threats by filtering the packets before they reach your internal machines, which you learned about back in Chapter 21, "The Internet." Routers, however, have a few other tricks up their sleeves. From the router's browser-based settings screen (see Figure 27-27), you can configure a hardware firewall. Let's walk through a few of the available settings.

Figure 27-26
ASUS router as a
firewall

Figure 27-27 Default Web interface

A hardware firewall watches for and stops many common threats—all you have to do is turn it on. Hardware firewalls use *Stateful Packet Inspection* (*SPI*) to inspect each incoming packet individually (see Figure 27-28). SPI also blocks any incoming traffic that isn't in response to your outgoing traffic. You can even disable ports entirely, blocking all traffic in or out. But what if you want to allow outside users access to a Web server on the LAN? Because Network Address Translation (NAT) hides the true IP address of that system (as described in Chapter 21), you'll need a way to allow incoming traffic past the router/firewall and a way to redirect that traffic to the right PC.

Port forwarding enables you to open a port in the firewall and direct incoming traffic on that port to a specific IP address on your LAN. In the case of the Web server referenced

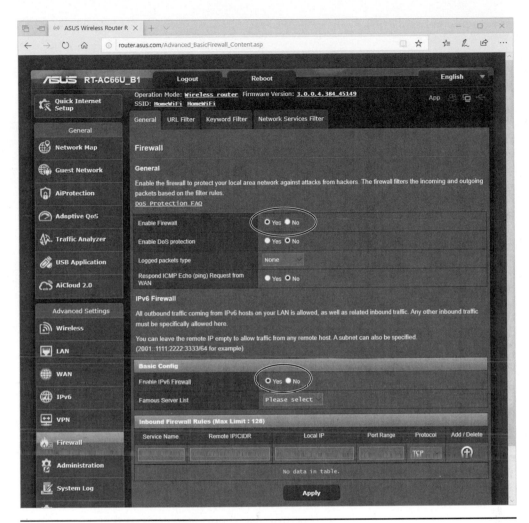

Figure 27-28 SPI firewall settings with firewalls enabled

in the previous paragraph, you would open port 80 (for HTTP packets) and instruct the router to send all incoming traffic to the server machine. Figure 27-29 shows port forwarding configured to send all HTTP packets to an internal Web server.

Port forwarding isn't the only way to open ports on a firewall. *Port triggering* enables you to open an incoming connection to one computer automatically based on a specific outgoing connection. The *trigger port* defines the outgoing connection, and the *destination port* defines the incoming connection. If you set the trigger port to 3434 and the destination port to 1234, for example, any outgoing traffic on port 3434 will trigger the router to open port 1234 and send any received data back to the system that sent the

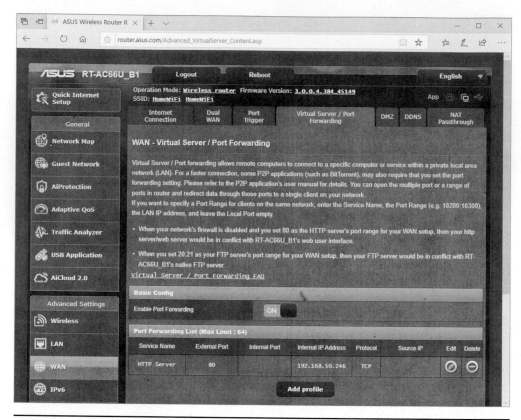

Figure 27-29 Port forwarding

original outgoing traffic. Figure 27-30 shows a router set up with port triggering for an Internet Relay Chat (IRC) server.

If you want to go beyond port forwarding and port triggering and open every port on a machine, you need a demilitarized zone (DMZ). A DMZ puts systems with the specified IP addresses outside the protection of the firewall, opening all ports and enabling all incoming traffic (see Figure 27-31). If you think this sounds incredibly dangerous, you are right! Any PC inside the DMZ will be completely exposed to outside attacks. Don't use it!

Software Firewalls

While a hardware firewall does a lot to protect you from outside intruders, you should also use a software firewall, such as the firewalls built into each version of Windows, called (appropriately) Windows Defender Firewall or Windows Defender Firewall with Advanced Security. (Earlier versions of Windows just called the tool(s) *Windows Firewall.* That's how you'll see it on the 1002 exam as well.) Windows Defender Firewall (see Figure 27-32) handles the heavy lifting of port blocking, security logging, and more.

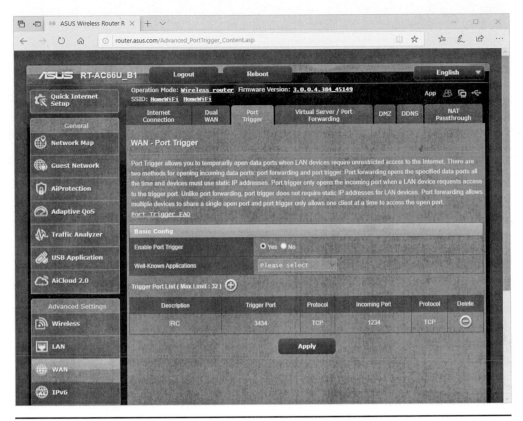

Figure 27-30 Port triggering

You can access Windows Defender Firewall by opening the Windows Defender Firewall applet in the Control Panel. Configuring Windows Firewall involves turning it on or off, and choosing which programs and services can pass through the firewall, known as *exceptions*. If you wanted to run a *Minecraft* server (a game that requires an Internet connection), for example, it would need to be on the list of exceptions for your firewall—most programs you install add themselves to this list automatically, otherwise Windows Defender Firewall prompts you the first time you run it and asks if you want to add the program as an exception.

EXAM TIP To turn Windows Defender Firewall off (which I don't recommend doing), open the Windows Defender Firewall applet, select *Turn Windows Defender Firewall on or off*, then select *Turn off Windows Defender Firewall (not recommended)* for each network type you use.

When Microsoft first introduced Windows Firewall, way back in Windows XP, its biggest shortcoming was that it failed to consider that a single PC, especially a portable,

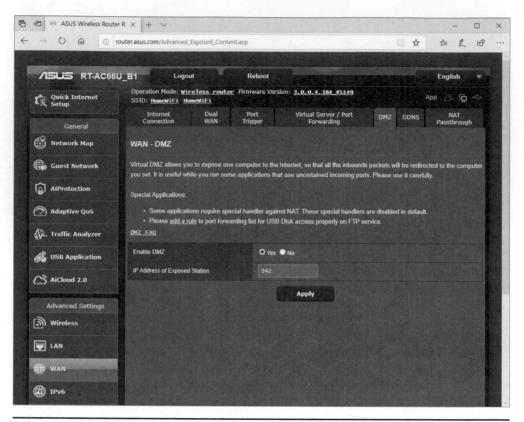

Figure 27-31 DMZ set up on a SOHO router

might connect to multiple networks. You don't necessarily want the same firewall settings used for both public and private networks. Microsoft developed a way for you to separate trustworthy networks (like the one in your house or at the office) from non-trustworthy networks (like a public Wi-Fi Internet connection at the airport) by including three network types: Domain, Private, and Guest or Public.

- A *Domain* network is a Windows network controlled by a Windows domain controller that runs Active Directory Domain Services. In this case, the domain controller itself tells your machine what it can and cannot share. You don't need to do anything when your computer joins a domain.

- A *Private* network enables you to share resources, discover other devices, and allow other devices to discover your computer safely.

- A *Guest or Public* network prevents your computer from sharing and disables all discovery protocols.

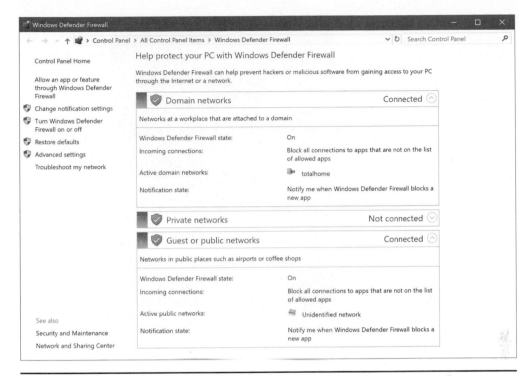

Figure 27-32 Windows 10 Firewall settings

When your computer connects to a network for the first time, Windows will prompt you to choose the network type. Windows 7 spelled them out: Home, Work, or Guest or Public location. Windows 10 asks if you want to allow other devices on the network to discover your PC (see Figure 27-33). It will mark the network Private if you answer yes; Public if you answer no. In either case, Windows uses your answer to decide whether to share files and resources or lock them down tight.

When your computer joins a domain, Windows automatically sets your network location to Domain (unless your domain controller chooses something different, which is unlikely).

When running on a Private (Home or Work) network, Windows enables Network Discovery and File and Printer Sharing as exceptions. When running on a Guest or Public network, Windows disables these exceptions.

EXAM TIP The Network Discovery setting dictates whether a computer can find other computers or devices on a network, and vice versa. Even with Network Discovery activated, several firewall settings can overrule certain connections.

Figure 27-33
Windows 10
network options,
public or private?

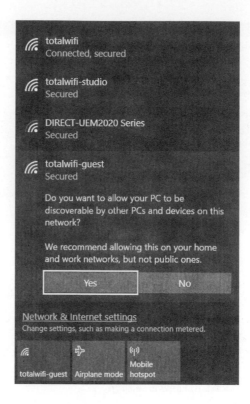

That's the end of the story if your Windows machine never changes networks, but what about machines (mainly laptops) that hop from one network to another (see Figure 27-34)? In that case, you need different firewall settings for each network the system might encounter.

Figure 27-34
Many machines
need more than
one network
setting.

To support this, Windows asks you if it should trust a new network when you first connect. Windows even includes three different firewall settings: one for Domains, one for Private networks (Home or Work), and one for Guest or Public networks.

EXAM TIP Expect a scenario question on home vs. work vs. public network options on the CompTIA A+ 1002 exam. Just remember that you trust home and work networks, but don't trust public ones.

Once you've picked a network type, you might want to customize the firewall settings further. If you click the Advanced settings option in the Windows Defender Firewall applet, you'll discover a much deeper level of firewall configuration. In fact, it's an entirely different tool called *Windows Defender Firewall with Advanced Security* (see Figure 27-35). You can also access it directly through the Administrative Tools in Control Panel.

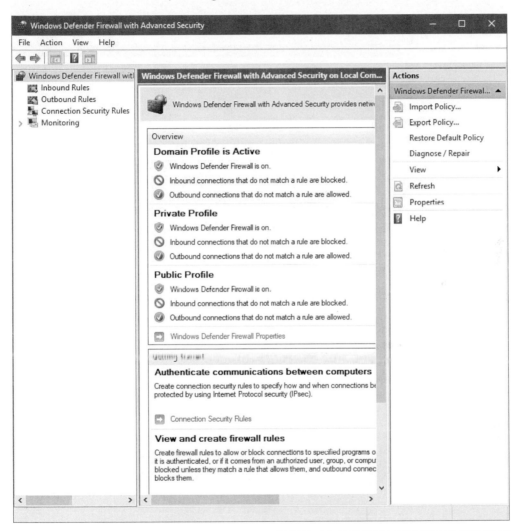

Figure 27-35   Windows Defender Firewall with Advanced Security

From the Windows Firewall with Advanced Security snap-in, you have much more control over how Windows treats exceptions. In the standard Windows Firewall applet, you can only choose a program and make it an exception, giving it permission to pass through the firewall. But programs both send and receive network data, and the basic applet doesn't give you much control over the "inbound" and "outbound" aspect of firewalls. The Windows Firewall with Advanced Security snap-in takes the exceptions concept and expands it to include custom rules for both inbound and outbound data. Figure 27-36 shows the outbound rules for a typical Windows system.

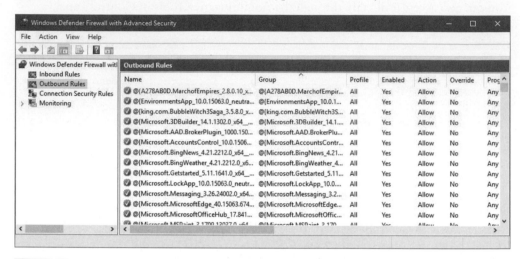

Figure 27-36   Outbound Rules list

A rule always includes at least the following:

- The name of the program
- Group: an organizational group that helps sort all the rules
- The associated profile (All, Domain, Public, Private)
- Enabled/disabled status
- Remote and local address
- Remote and local port number

You can add, remove, and customize any rule to your liking. It quickly gets complicated, so unless you need to set a lot of custom rules, stick to the standard Windows Firewall applet.

Internet Appliances

The discussion of firewalls barely scratches the surface of tools used to secure a large network. While enterprise networking is generally beyond the scope of an A+ tech's duties, the CompTIA 1002 objectives cover two devices critical to modern network security—IDS and IPS—plus the concept of unified threat management. Let's take a look.

An *intrusion detection system* (*IDS*) is an Internet application that inspects packets, looking for active intrusions. An IDS functions inside the network, watching for threats that a firewall might miss, such as viruses, illegal logon attempts, and other well-known attacks. Plus, because it inspects traffic inside the network, the IDS can discover internal threats, like the activity of a vulnerability scanner smuggled in on a flash drive by a disgruntled worker planning an attack on an internal database server.

An IDS always has some way to let the network administrators know if an attack is taking place: at the very least the attack is logged, but some IDSs offer a pop-up message, an e-mail, or even a text message to an administrator's phone. An IDS can also respond to detected intrusions with action. The IDS can't stop the attack directly, but can request assistance from other devices—like a firewall—that can.

An *intrusion prevention system* (*IPS*) is very similar to an IDS, but an IPS sits directly in the flow of network traffic. This active monitoring has a trio of consequences. First, an IPS can stop an attack while it is happening. There's no need to request help from any other devices. Second, the network bandwidth and latency take a hit. Third, if the IPS goes down, the network link might go down too. Depending on the IPS, it can block incoming packets on-the-fly based on IP address, port number, or application type. An IPS might go even further, literally fixing certain packets on-the-fly.

All these network Internet appliances, no matter how advanced and aware they become, are still singular tools in the box used to protect networks. That is why modern dedicated firewall/Internet appliances are built around providing *unified threat management* (*UTM*). UTM takes the traditional firewall and packages it with many other security services such as IPS, VPN, load balancing, antivirus, and many other features depending on the make and model. The UTM approach to building network gear helps build robust security deep into the network, protecting what really matters: our data.

Authentication and Encryption

You know that the first step in securing data is authentication, through a user name and password. But when you throw in networking, you're suddenly not just a single user sitting in front of a computer and typing. You're accessing a remote resource and sending login information over the Internet. What's to stop someone from intercepting your user name and password?

Firewalls do a great job of controlling traffic coming into a network from the Internet and going out of a network to the Internet, but they do nothing to stop interceptor hackers who monitor traffic on the public Internet looking for vulnerabilities. Worse, once a packet is on the Internet itself, anyone with the right equipment can intercept and inspect it. Inspected packets are a cornucopia of passwords, account names, and other tidbits that hackers can use to intrude into your network. Because we can't stop hackers from inspecting these packets, we must turn to *encryption* to make them unreadable.

Network encryption occurs at many levels and is in no way limited to Internet-based activities. Not only are there many levels of network encryption, but each encryption level also provides multiple standards and options, making encryption one of the most complicated of all networking issues. You need to understand where encryption comes into play, what options are available, and what you can use to protect your network.

Network Authentication

Have you ever considered the process that takes place each time a person types in a user name and password to access a network, rather than just a local machine? What happens when this *network* authentication is requested? If you're thinking that information is sent to a server of some sort to be authenticated, you're right—but do you know how the user name and password get to the serving system? That's where encryption becomes important in authentication.

In a local network, authentication and encryption are usually handled by the OS. In today's increasingly interconnected and diverse networking environment, there is a motivation to enable different operating systems to authenticate any client system from any other OS. Modern operating systems such as Windows and macOS use standard authentication encryptions such as MIT's *Kerberos*, enabling multiple brands of servers to authenticate multiple brands of clients. These LAN authentication methods are usually transparent and work quite nicely, even in mixed networks.

Data Encryption

Encryption methods don't stop at the authentication level. There are a number of ways to encrypt network *data* as well. The encryption method is dictated to a large degree by what method the communicating systems will connect with. Many networks consist of multiple networks linked together by some sort of private connection, usually some kind of WAN connection such as old T1s or Metro Ethernet. Microsoft's encryption method of choice for this type of network is called *IPsec* (derived from *IP security*). IPsec provides transparent encryption between the server and the client.

A virtual private network (VPN) can also use IPsec, but VPNs typically use other encryption methods. Speaking of VPNs, if you're on an untrusted network, you can also protect your network traffic by tunneling it all through a VPN connection. Security-conscious organizations may even require all of their portable devices access the Internet through a VPN connection to one of their home offices.

Application Encryption

When it comes to encryption, even TCP/IP applications can get into the swing of things. The most famous of all application encryptions is the *Secure Sockets Layer* (*SSL*) security protocol, which was used to secure Web sites. Everyone uses *Transport Layer Security* (*TLS*) in *HTTPS* (HTTP over TLS) protocol these days. (SSL has been replaced by TLS, in other words.) These protocols make it possible to secure the Web sites people use to make purchases over the Internet. You can identify HTTPS Web sites by the *https://* (rather than http://) included in the URL (see Figure 27-37).

TIP Many security appliances include a context-based set of rules called Data Loss Prevention (DLP) to help companies avoid accidental leakage of data. DLP works by scanning packets flowing out of the network, stopping the flow when something triggers.

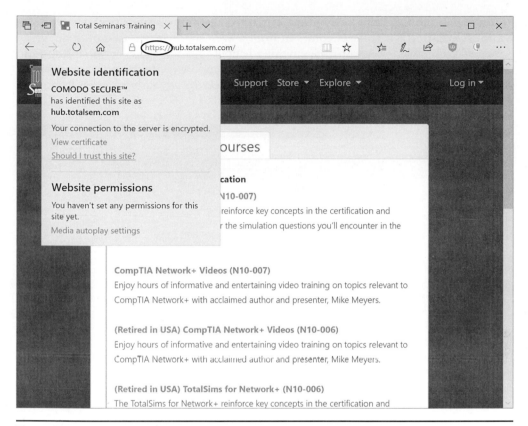

Figure 27-37   A secure Web site

To make a secure connection, your Web browser and the Web server must encrypt their data. That means there must be a way for both the Web server and your browser to encrypt and decrypt each other's data. To do this, the server sends a public key to your Web browser so the browser knows how to decrypt the incoming data. These public keys are sent in the form of a *digital certificate*. This certificate is signed by a trusted *certificate authority* (*CA*) that guarantees that the public key you are about to get is actually from the Web server and not from some evil person trying to pretend to be the Web server. A number of companies issue digital certificates, such as Symantec (formerly VeriSign), Comodo, and many others.

NOTE   HTTPS originally meant HTTP over SSL, so the "S" in HTTPS made grammatical sense. Most Web sites use the more robust TLS to encrypt connections. The Internet people just quietly switched TLS for SSL, but didn't make a new acronym such as "HTTPT."

Your Web browser has a built-in list of trusted certificate authorities, referred to as *trusted root CAs*. If a certificate comes in from a Web site that uses one of these highly respected companies, you won't see anything happen in your browser; you'll just go to the secure Web page, where a small lock icon will appear in the browser status bar or address bar. Figure 27-38 shows the list of trusted certificate authorities built into the Firefox Web browser.

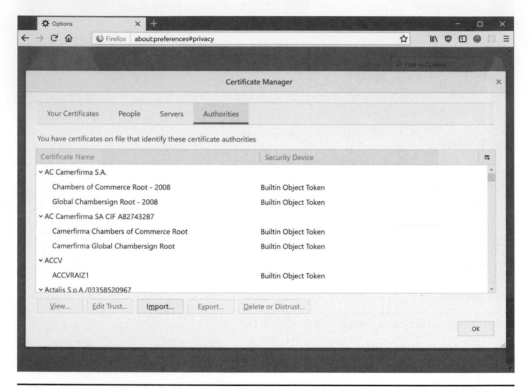

Figure 27-38 Trusted authorities

If you receive a certificate that your browser thinks is fishy, such as one that is expired or one for which the browser does not have a trusted root CA, the browser will warn you and usually give you some way to make an exception for the certificate, as shown in Figure 27-39.

We all have to make our own decisions here, but you should usually heed the browser's warning and advice. Most invalid certificates are invalid for boring reasons, like the site owner forgetting to update it on time. But the invalid certificate could just as easily indicate that the site or your connection to it is compromised! Only add an exception if you *know* it's safe. You might, for example, need to add an exception to access a site on your organization's intranet.

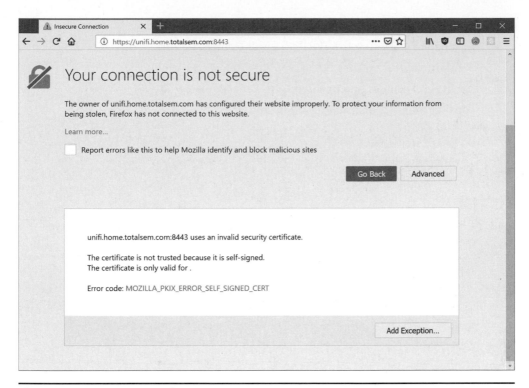

Figure 27-39   Incoming certificate

Wireless Issues

Wireless networks add a whole level of additional security headaches for techs to face, as you know from Chapter 20, "Wireless Networking." Here are a few points to consider:

- Set up wireless encryption, at least WPA but preferably the more secure WPA2, and configure clients to use it.
- Disable DHCP and require your wireless clients to use a static IP address.
- If you need to use DHCP, only allot enough DHCP addresses to meet the needs of your network, to avoid unused wireless connections.
- Change the WAP's SSID from the default.
- Filter by MAC address to allow only known clients on the network.
- Change the default user name and password. Even if the defaults are generated and look secure, knowledge of how they were generated might make them easier to guess.

- Update the firmware as needed.
- If available, make sure the WAP's firewall settings are turned on.
- Configure SOHO router NAT/DNAT settings.
- Use SOHO router content filtering/parental controls.
- Consider physical security of SOHO router.

Chapter Review

Questions

1. What is the process for using or manipulating people to gain access to network resources?

    A. Cracking

    B. Hacking

    C. Network engineering

    D. Social engineering

2. Which of the following might offer good hardware authentication?

    A. Strong passwords

    B. Encrypted passwords

    C. NTFS

    D. Smart cards

3. Which of the following tools would enable you to stop a user from logging on to a local machine but still enable him to log on to the domain?

    A. AD Policy Filter

    B. Group policy auditing

    C. Local Security Policy

    D. User Settings

4. Which hardware firewall feature enables incoming traffic on a specific port to reach an IP address on the LAN?

    A. Port forwarding

    B. NAT

    C. DMZ

    D. Multifactor authentication

5. Zander downloaded a game off the Internet and installed it, but as soon as he started to play, he got a Blue Screen of Death. Upon rebooting, he discovered that his Documents folder had been erased. What happened?

   A. He installed spyware.

   B. He installed a Trojan horse.

   C. He broke the Group Policy.

   D. He broke the Local Security Policy.

6. Which of these choices would provide better security for Mary's Wi-Fi router?

   A. SecureDNS

   B. WEP

   C. WPA

   D. WPA2

7. What tool would you use to enable auditing on a local level?

   A. AD Policy

   B. Group policy

   C. Local Security Policy

   D. User Settings

8. John dressed up in a fake security guard uniform matching the ones used by a company and then walked into the company's headquarters with some legitimate employees in an attempt to gain access to company resources. What kind of attack is this?

   A. Administrative access

   B. Data destruction

   C. Spoofing

   D. Tailgating

9. The first day on the job, Jill received a spreadsheet that listed approved software for users and clear instructions not to allow any unapproved software. What kind of policy must she follow?

   A. Classification

   B. Compliance

   C. Group

   D. Security

10. Edna wants to put a policy in place at her company to prevent or at least limit viruses. What policies would offer the best solution?

   A. Install antivirus software on every computer. Teach users how to run it.

   B. Install antivirus software on every computer. Set up the software to scan regularly.

   C. Install antivirus software on every computer. Set up the software to update the definitions and engine automatically. Set up the software to scan regularly.

   D. Install antivirus software on every computer. Set up the software to update the definitions and engine automatically. Set up the software to scan regularly. Educate the users about sites and downloads to avoid.

Answers

1. **D.** Social engineering is the process of using or manipulating people to gain access to network resources.

2. **D.** Smart cards are an example of hardware authentication devices.

3. **C.** You can use Local Security Policy to stop someone from logging on to a local machine.

4. **A.** To open a port on your hardware firewall and send incoming traffic to a specific PC, use port forwarding.

5. **B.** Zander clearly installed a Trojan horse, a virus masquerading as a game.

6. **D.** Mary should set up WPA2 on her Wi-Fi router.

7. **C.** You can enable local auditing through Local Security Policy.

8. **D.** John just practiced tailgating on the unsuspecting company.

9. **B.** Jill needs to enforce compliance to help keep the tech support calls at a minimum and the uptime for users at a maximum.

10. **D.** The best policy includes updating the software engine and definitions, scanning PCs regularly, and educating users.

Operational Procedures

In this chapter, you will learn how to

- Compare best practices associated with types of documentation
- Implement basic change management properly
- Implement basic disaster prevention and recovery

The term *operational procedures* encompasses a lot for any organization, from best practices for safety (Chapter 1, "Safety and Professionalism") to dealing with environmental factors (Chapter 27, "Securing Computers"); from company polices for handling prohibited content or activities (also Chapter 27) to proper communication techniques and professionalism all techs should employ (again, Chapter 1). The CompTIA A+ 1002 exam even throws in basics of scripting (Chapter 15, "Working with the Command-Line Interface") and remote access technologies (Chapter 21, "The Internet") (though those feel like a reach to me).

This chapter explores another aspect of operational procedures, namely business practices that enable *continuity*, a fancy way of saying that an organization should keep working more or less the same in the face of both mundane day-to-day change and sudden disasters. We'll focus here on three categories of business continuity and operational procedures: documentation, change management, and disaster prevention and recovery.

1002

Documentation Best Practices

Organizations need documentation to provide continuity and structure. Documentation can take many forms, but the three categories of concern to a new tech are network documentation, company policies, and inventory management.

Network Documentation

Network documentation provides a road map for current and future techs who need to make changes or repairs over time. For the most part, CompTIA Network+ techs and system administrators handle the oversight of the network, but CompTIA A+ techs do a lot of the implementation of fixes. You need to know how to read network topology diagrams, understand where to find and the scope of the company knowledge base or company articles, and provide incident documentation when you run into problems.

Network Topology Diagrams

A *network topology diagram* provides a map for how everything connects in an organization's network. These diagrams include switches, routers, WAPs, servers, and workstations (see Figure 28-1). More complex diagrams describe connection types and speeds, and the technologies in use (listing a WAP as an 802.11ac AC2600, for example). Many organizations rely on the Cisco icon set as a universal visual aid for creating these diagrams (see Figure 28-2).

Figure 28-1
Typical network topology diagram

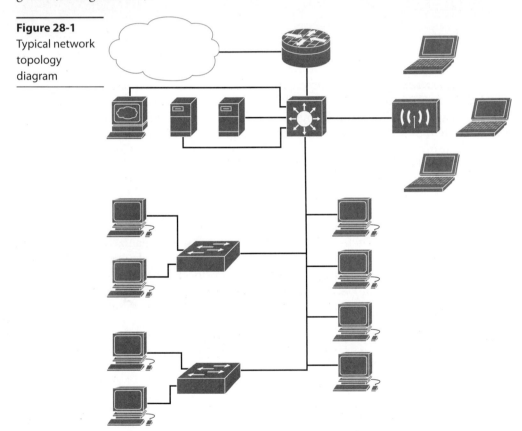

Knowledge Base/Company Articles

Organizations use documentation to enable cooperation among employees and coordination among departments. From a tech's perspective, documentation helps in troubleshooting various issues. Creating and maintaining a company *knowledge base*—a set of documents that tell the tale of equipment used, problems encountered, and solutions to

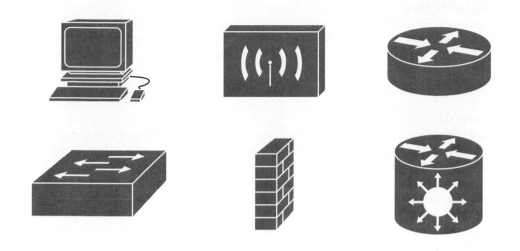

Figure 28-2 A sampling of Cisco network diagram icons

those problems—provides an essential tool for current and future techs. These company-specific articles illuminate very specific details about company tech, including links to manufacturer sites and information.

Incident Documentation

Tracking specific problems through *incident documentation* helps current and future techs deal with problematic hardware and individuals. If you have five identical color laser printers in five departments, for example, and one starts jamming regularly after 10,000 pages, documenting the problem—the incident—and the solution will point very clearly to the potential problems with the other four printers when they reach that same usage level.

Company Policies

Organizations adopt goals and rules for employees that enhance the company profits and compliance with government regulations. These *company policies* include regulatory compliance policies, acceptable use polices, and password policies, among other things.

Regulatory Compliance

Part of a government's job is to ensure safe work environments and minimize exploitation of workers. To this end, governments develop rules and regulations that specify how organizations are *supposed* to manage their workplaces, workers, and materials. Properly run organizations enforce *regulatory compliance*—following the laws and regulations—to maintain a healthy workforce.

Acceptable Use

An *acceptable use policy* (*AUP*) describes what employees can and cannot do with company property. Such policies include things like using a company laptop only for company business, for example. Or, an AUP could bar company employees from accessing illegal Web sites from the organization's computers. AUPs are often very detailed and specific documents that employees must agree to and sign as a step in the employment process.

Passwords

We've touched on password policies in Chapter 13, "Users, Groups, and Permissions," so here I'll just add that organizations will have detailed password policies in place that can touch on almost any aspect of how members of the organization create, use, and manage accounts and credentials. Here's a teeny tiny sample of what you might find in a thorough *password policy*: how long and complex passwords should be, how to compose them, when to use multifactor authentication, whether passwords should expire (and if so, how often), whether to set a BIOS password, and even what you should do if your manager demands to know one of your passwords!

Inventory Management

Techs help organizations institute *inventory management* practices to protect company assets. These include barcodes and asset tags on items, among other things.

Barcodes

Many inventory items have simple stickers or printed labels with *barcodes*—unique symbols/numbers that track specific items. Figure 28-3 shows a typical barcode. A barcode acts as a fingerprint for an item, binary code that can be readily scanned. One drawback to barcodes is that they're read-only. You can't add data or information to them at all.

Figure 28-3
Barcode on an SSD encoding its serial number

Asset Tags

Asset tags can use the *radio frequency identification* (*RFID*) wireless networking protocol to keep track of inventory (see Figure 28-4). The asset tag includes an RFID tag (consisting

Figure 28-4
RFID tag

of a microchip and antenna) that an RFID scanner or reader can electronically read and identify even without line of sight to the item. Most RFID tags are passive, meaning that the tag receives all the power it needs from the scanner's signal! An active RFID tag, on the other hand, uses a battery or external power source to send out and receive signals. Both types of RFID enable inventory management. Unlike barcodes, the information stored in an RFID tag can be updated with new details.

Managing Change Management

CompTIA A+ techs get a front-row seat on infrastructure management. You see what works, what doesn't, and what needs to change. The old laser printers in the accounting department, for example, can't keep up with user needs and you're spending way too much time each week keeping them running. And you're tired of users yelling at you. Change is needed.

Change isn't only grass-roots driven, but often comes from the top. Every seasoned tech can tell you about the pain of major operating system upgrades; of the ridiculous amount of work required to upgrade some critical application or introduce a new, absolutely necessary application.

Every organization has formal and informal change management processes. You can't just buy a new laser printer, for example, without considering the cost and impact. You can't upgrade the operating systems for 100 users without thorough testing and analysis of the OS. Let's look at change management processes and implementation procedures.

Change Management Processes

A *change management* process enables organizations to implement changes to IT infrastructure in a safe and cost-effective manner. There's no single guide to change management, though most organizations follow common-sense guidelines. Here's an outline of the best practices CompTIA recommends:

- Consult documented business processes.
- Determine the purpose of the change.

- Analyze the scope of the change.
- Analyze risk involved in making (or not making) the change.
- Plan for the change.
- Educate end users about the need, benefit, and cost of the change.
- Create a dedicated team to manage the change.
- Have a backout plan in place in case the change creates negative consequences.
- Document everything thoroughly.

Implementing Change (Scenario)

Any organization with a change management process is going to have their own specific method to enact changes that should manifest as clearly documented business processes. One of your first jobs as a tech is to consult these documents so that—when change comes your way (either from you or from on high)—you'll already understand the processes. When it's time for a change, start by reviewing these documented business practices to avoid being embarrassed for missing some important step.

Here's a typical scenario to use for examples of managing change. Jamie at Bayland Widgets Corp. wants to upgrade 16 systems in the design lab from Windows 7 to Windows 10. Users are clamoring for the newer OS.

Purpose of the Change

No organization is ever going to give you new equipment or allow you to make upgrades without knowing why they are needed. To propose a change, you'll almost certainly need to document the *purpose of the change*. In Jamie's scenario, users have demanded the latest OS from Microsoft to better serve customers who have (all) jumped to Windows 10. The purpose of the change, therefore, is improved performance and support for clients.

Scope of the Change

Usually included as part of the purpose of the change, the *scope of the change* defines who and what this change will affect. This includes an inventory of all systems involved, the number of people involved in making the change, how long the change will take, and often the estimated cost of the change.

The design lab, as mentioned, has 16 computing devices that will be affected. (The overall budget will be determined by which edition of Windows 10 will be installed: Home, Pro, or Enterprise.)

Risk Analysis

All changes to infrastructure come with risk. A proper change management request will certainly require a *risk analysis*, a detailed assessment of possible problems that could result from the change. What if the upgrade fails? Has the new application been tested on a sample system? Will the new computers have adequate firewalls? Don't panic (well, not too much), as any risk analysis will almost certainly be passed off to a security person in your organization—but that person might have great interest in your opinions and concerns!

Plan for the Change

What needs to be done before the change starts? What needs to be purchased? Where will new, uninstalled equipment be stored? On which days will you implement this change? During what time period? Who will cover your other duties while you're otherwise engaged? Anything that needs to be ready before Jamie starts is covered in the *plan for the change*.

End-User Acceptance

Part of successful change management is educating the end users in both the need for the change and how to adapt to changed systems. *End-user acceptance* is vital for successful change. More than anything else this means training. Do the users know how to use the new features on your super printer? What new features in this OS upgrade do end user need to learn? Are the end users versed in the new application (and know not to use the old one)?

Change Board

So Jamie has all this documentation. Who does she show this to for approval to make this change? That's the job of the change board. The *change board* consists of techs and representatives from management, IT security, and administration who meet on a regular basis (quarterly is common). They review the change documentation and either approve or deny the change. More often than not they ask for more information or details, making a "proposal–rejection–fix–back to change board" cycle that repeats itself until everyone is satisfied.

Backout Plan

What if this change is a failure? This happens more than you think. There must a *backout plan* that defines the steps needed to return the infrastructure to its pre-change environment. OS rollbacks, uninstallation, or return to old equipment are all possible parts of a good backout plan.

Jamie at Bayland Widgets Corp. wants to upgrade 16 systems in the design lab. She's gotten approval from management to upgrade from Windows 7 to Windows 10 and subsequently implemented the upgrade. After a few days, several users have complained that an important CAD application BWC uses is having issues, like software freezes.

Jamie looks at the backout plan documentation that lays out the steps for undoing the upgrades. She follows through with the undo process, making notes about the steps, then awaits further instructions for how to get the design lab computers upgraded without failures.

Change Documentation

Every step of a change needs documentation. A *change documentation* package created by a CompTIA A+ tech will include almost all of the preceding steps plus receipts, overtime records, an inventory of changed systems, lists of new users created, signed end-user acceptance forms, and so on.

Disaster Prevention and Recovery

Disaster prevention and recovery is a gigantic topic, near and dear to the hearts of network and security techs and administrators in every organization. From a CompTIA A+ perspective, it means three things: maintaining proper power, backup and recovery procedures, and account recovery.

Power Protection

Computing devices need adequate and regular electricity. As you'll recall from Chapter 7, power companies supply alternating current (AC) to businesses and residences. That AC doesn't always flow at a consistent rate; it can experience dips, drops, or surges. Using a *surge suppressor*—to protect against power spikes—and an *uninterruptible power supply* (*UPS*)—to protect against power dips and blackouts—can mean the difference between a properly functioning computing component and a fried paperweight. Figure 28-5 shows a typical UPS.

Figure 28-5
Personal UPS

Companies can and should secure all electronic components with a surge protector or UPS. This includes personal computers—the obvious choice—and switches, WAPs, and routers. Every server should run on its own UPS to protect the valuable contents of drives (like you saw in Figure 27-1 in the previous chapter).

Backup and Recovery Procedures

Techs help users and the organization maintain data using well-known and reliable backup procedures. When things go *south*, techs implement recovery procedures to get users back up and running as quickly as possible.

Backup Options

Specific backup technologies and processes are covered in detail in Chapter 14, "Maintaining and Optimizing Operating Systems." This section focuses on broader questions like what to back up, where to put it, and how long to keep older backups. There aren't perfect answers to these questions for everyone—the answers depend on a ton of factors, including how you work, what kind of data you work with, how critical the data is, how fast it changes, what kind of problems you need to recover from, how quickly you need to be back up and running, and how much money you can throw at the problem.

All of the choices involve trade-offs between the risk of data loss on one hand and convenience, cost, and effort on the other. A few things are true no matter how you do it:

- Lots of copies keep stuff safe. They also cost more and increase the odds of a data leak.

- Much as investors limit risk by diversifying their investment portfolio, you can reduce the risk of data loss by taking separate backups with more than one backup program, keeping copies in different regions, and storing them on a mix of different hardware.

- Storing backups off-site reduces the risk of complete loss, but it also increases the time it takes to recover unless you also keep a local copy.

- Automatic backups take a little more work to set up, but they beat the socks off manual backups once you've got everything ironed out. Manual backups are better than *nothing*, but people *will* forget to do them.

Another big question is how much data you can afford to store. Storage is cheap, but the cost of storing many copies of frequent backups still adds up fast. Different backup methods and software use many strategies—such as compression, deduplication, incremental backups that only record changes since the previous backup, and so on—to cut down on the amount of data stored.

It's also common to discard all but one backup for a given period of time as the backups age. You might keep hourly backups for the most recent day, but only keep one per day for the rest of the week, one a week for the rest of the month, one a month for the rest of the year, and then keep a single backup per year thereafter. You have to be careful with incremental backups, though: restoring a specific incremental backup requires an *unbroken* chain of incremental backups from the last full backup.

Here's a scenario for a CompTIA A+ tech handling backup options. Chris at Bayland Widgets is responsible for maintaining the data for the accounting department, which consists of four Windows 10 workstations and a file server with critical accounting data. It's not a huge department, but one that's *absolutely essential* for company operations. Chris needs to get it right. Let's look at file-level backups, critical application backups, and image-level backups.

File Level   *File-level backups* are a simple way to make sure important files and directories get backed up. Anyone can perform the most basic file-level backup without special software: just manually select a file or folder and copy it to an external drive, like a USB thumb drive (see Figure 28-6), or cloud-based account, like Dropbox. From a user standpoint, this means each of the accountants would save copies of their personal files elsewhere. In such a scenario, Chris would make sure the accountants have access to an external drive or install and configure Dropbox on their machines.

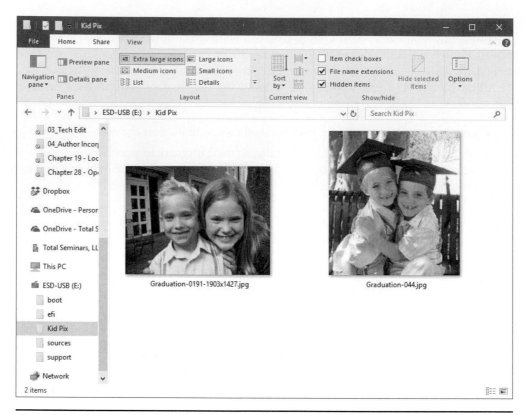

Figure 28-6 Using a thumb drive to store favorite kid pix

Manual backups are fine, but the cold, hard truth is that Bayland Widgets is a lot more likely to survive a disaster or freak accident if they have a backup script or program that automatically runs on a schedule (such as every night or once an hour), configured to save everything important. In this case, Chris would need to set up and schedule the appropriate script(s) or application(s), configure them to capture critical files, and confirm the backups run as scheduled.

Both Windows and macOS feature automatic, local, file-level backups through File History and Time Machine, respectively, as you will recall from Chapter 14. These work best with an external mass storage drive plugged into a USB port. These are better than manual backups and fine for recovering non-critical files that get accidentally deleted or overwritten, but a backup strategy for protecting your organization's critical data will require third-party backup software and off-site backup storage.

Critical Applications When it comes to applications, assess the essential backup or recovery option. First, recognize the critical *applications* (for individual users, and for the organization as a whole). It's a good idea to keep a list.

Second, determine the critical *data*. It's easy to spend days learning enough about how an application is structured and what gets saved where, figuring out how to completely back up every last user setting—but it might all change with the next update. The less you try to save, the easier it will be to get it right and keep it working.

Some software is still deployed on optical media, but so much of it today relies on Internet downloads that backing up the application installer makes less and less sense. You'll certainly back up the data created with the application, and you might be able to back up customized settings. Sometimes these are so entwined that backing up the whole application is the only way to get it right.

Recovery of critical applications means—at the least—clearly documenting the steps for reinstalling, including:

- License keys
- Where to download the application installer (or find a copy of the installation media for an old-style physical installation)
- Any essential installation options
- Any account information or credentials that may be required for access

This documentation assists the current tech and any future techs that need to help out.

If you really want to back up an installed application with a file-level backup, you'll need to know the location of the application files, Registry settings, temp file locations, startup files, and configuration settings. The only way this works—in Windows, at least—is through third-party applications. You might be able to find a third-party application that has built-in support for backing up all of the known locations where popular applications save data, but otherwise you'll have to explicitly configure your backup software to save them all.

NOTE There's no guarantee data or settings backed up from one version of an application will work with another version. You can try—but don't be surprised if you have to jump through hoops to restore this data, such as installing the *exact* same version of the application that was installed when the backup was created, restoring the data, and then updating the application.

Many critical applications have some sort of backup functions built in. The accounting department uses Sage 50 software, for example, to handle the numbers for Bayland Widgets. Figure 28-7 shows the backup options in Sage.

The key is that some of these applications are backing up to cloud storage, while others (including Sage 50 in this example) are really just *exporting a local copy* of the application data. Chris's responsibility here is to make sure the accountants know how and when to use Sage 50 to export a backup of the application data *and* make sure that the exported application data actually gets included in the regularly scheduled backup of each user's files or system.

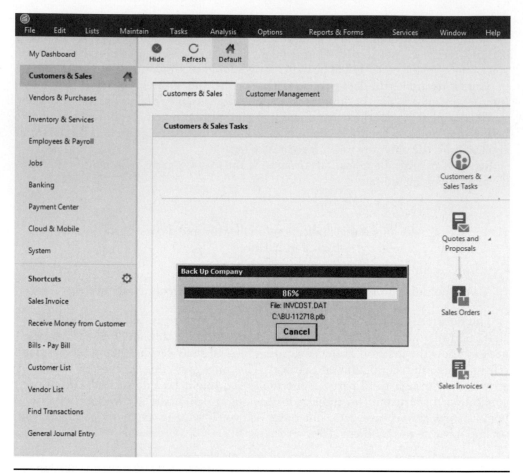

Figure 28-7   Backing up the accounting database in Sage 50

Image Level   *Image-level backup* means not messing around with files or folders, but backing up a complete volume—including the OS, boot files, all installed applications, and all the data. To decide which scenarios are a good fit for image backups, it'll help to know a bit about how they work:

- You can restore an image to a blank drive, pop it in a new system, and boot it right up—as long as the imaged system is compatible with the new hardware. Restoring from an image can get a system back up and running fast.

- Images are big. They contain gigabytes of OS and program files that could easily be recovered by reinstalling the OS and applications on a fresh system.

- Because you don't specify which files to copy, image-level backups are easy for techs and users.

- You won't always want to restore a full image. Maybe the image contains malware or corrupt drivers. Or you need to move the user to a new OS. Or they just want to recover a few files that turned up corrupted. You'll have to mount the full image, if your backup software lets you, and go ferret out whatever the user needs.

In any image-level backup scenario, Chris would need to schedule backups, of course, using a built-in tool (though Microsoft deprecated the Windows tool in Windows 10) or a third-party application (see Figure 28-8). If the software supports incremental images, this schedule should specify how often to take an incremental backup and how often to take a full one. Remember that restoring an incremental backup will require an unbroken chain of incremental backups all the way back to the last full image!

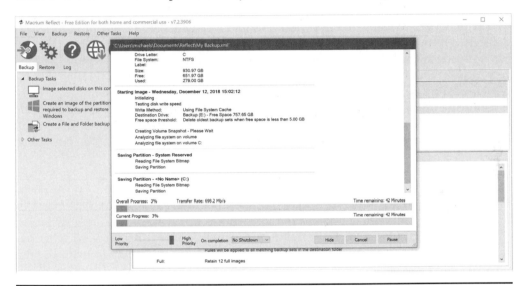

Figure 28-8   Macrium Reflect – Free Edition

Cloud Storage Versus Local Storage

Increasingly, storing backups on Internet servers—*cloud storage*—is replacing local backups as the preferred option. This movement leaves a lot of problems in its wake. Let's explore the good parts of cloud storage and compare to the benefits of local storage.

First off, cloud backups are available everywhere. You need to be on the Internet, of course, but this is a great option for file backups. iPhone users, for example, have Apple iCloud accounts, which automatically back up their photos and videos. The basic account costs nothing (thanks, Apple!) and more advanced/robust storage options cost a nominal fee. Cloud storage secures data against lost or damaged phones or devices. Your stuff is safe. (Android users have similar options, of course.)

On the downside, cloud storage can be tedious for very large backups (such as image backups). Even with modern 10+ MBps upload speeds, it can take a while to upload a full storage drive. Seriously. As an example, with a sustained 10-MBps speed, it would take over a day to upload a 1-TB drive.

This may not be a big deal for your parent's photo collection, but it *is* such a big deal that you can throw stacks of cash at Amazon to have a few of their finest rumble up to your doorstep in an AWS Snowmobile—a semi-truck hauling a shipping container stuffed to the gills with *over 100,000 terabytes* of data storage capacity—if you're looking to transfer massive data sets in or out of *the cloud*. If you *really* mean business, they'll even throw in a security escort vehicle.

Local storage provides the opposite experience. First off, you don't need the Internet (or even space to park a semi-truck), only local media. Mass storage drives are inexpensive and easily implemented, so local storage works great for both image backups and file backups.

The drawback to relying on *local* storage is that it provides zero protection from *local* disasters. I'm in Houston, Texas, home of semi-regular hurricanes. So far my company has not been swiped by one, but the danger is always there, May to November of each year. Relying on local backups for our intellectual property would mean running the risk of losing everything each hurricane season.

Consequently, we do both types of backups, as do many organizations. It's a little more complicated, but using both cloud and local storage options—the former for critical data, the latter for typical daily backups—means our stuff is secure. This is a good thing!

Backup Testing

Expect a question or two on the CompTIA A+ 1002 exam about *backup testing* or *verifying a backup*. The rule is: *always verify your backups*. You could easily invest a dozen years of time and money taking daily backups and following best practices like storing encrypted copies in multiple physical locations and cloud accounts, only to discover—when disaster strikes—that you can't successfully recover the files or disk images they contain. Backup strategies that don't involve verifying your backups are just fancy make-believe. You might as well leave your failed hard drives under your pillow for the tooth fairy.

Unfortunately, verifying backups isn't as simple as it sounds. The *gold standard* is being able to restore whatever you backed up—whether files or disk images—and end up with *exactly* what you *think* you have. Reality is tricky, though. Imagine, as soon as you take a backup, you compare the backup with the files on disk to make sure they're identical. If files on your disk are corrupt, verifying the backup just guarantees that you've meticulously copied the corrupt files.

Backup tools worth your time and money *will* provide a way to verify that a backup hasn't changed since it was saved, but this is *no* substitute for periodically verifying that you can restore *and actually use* backups of any critical system images, applications, files, and data.

In practice, this means: If your backup software can verify backups, do so regularly. No matter what your backup software does, you should regularly test them. Full images should restore and boot, and all critical applications should run. It's hard to check everything, but critical files restored from a file backup should open correctly in appropriate software. Critical applications should be carefully tested to make sure essential settings, configuration, and data are working.

Account Recovery

What do you do when you can't remember a user name or password? *Account recovery* provides options for getting access to your old password or resetting the account to a temporary password; users will change to a permanent password upon first login.

In a domain environment, the domain administrator will handle any password or account recovery settings. Techs and users don't need much more than access to that domain admin person.

In a local environment, or a workgroup, the tech needs to be more proactive. You can run third-party software to erase a password and allow a user to log in and create a new password.

Instead of trying to recover a forgotten password, be proactive and create a password reset disc. In Windows 10, for example, go to Control Panel | User Accounts and select *Create a password reset disc* from the options on the left (see Figure 28-9). Note that this only works with local accounts. If you're logged in with a Microsoft account, you can't create a local disc. Write your Microsoft user account and password down on a 3×5 card and put it in a safe. Trust me. You don't want to lose these credentials.

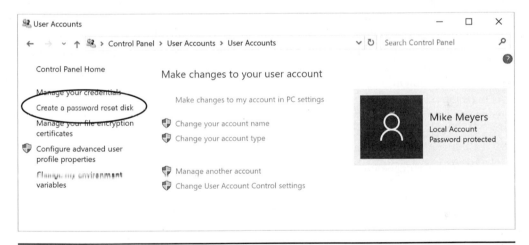

Figure 28-9 Users with local accounts should create a password reset disc.

Beyond A+

Whew! You've just finished a 1500+ page book that covers everything you need to know to take and pass the CompTIA A+ 1001/1002 exams. Congratulations! What's next?

First, go back to the Introduction and review the study chart and guidelines. Review, review, review! Take the practice exams and look for exam sources online to get even more scoop on the types of questions you'll see.

Second, schedule your exams if you haven't already done so (pressure and diamonds and all that). Having that endpoint in sight helps focus.

Go back to my original question once you've taken and passed both A+ exams. What's next? The two logical steps are to start studying for CompTIA Network+ and CompTIA Security+. These complete CompTIA's Core curriculum and round out tech skills needed for today's interconnected and security-heightened world. There are a lot of great writers and videographers out there who have excellent materials on Net+ and Sec+ (including me), so you won't find it hard to get study materials.

Good luck, my friend, and keep in touch!

Mike Myers

Chapter Review

Questions

1. Henry gets a help desk call from Arthur in Accounting who reports that his keyboard is not working. This seems like a familiar problem, one that another tech mentioned a short time back. Where should Henry look to find information on the problem?

   A. Change documentation

   B. Incident documentation

   C. Inventory management documentation

   D. Risk management documentation

2. Annie wants to mark several Mac laptops issued to salespeople so that she can set up a scanner at the office door to track each time the laptops enter and leave the building. What will help her accomplish this goal?

   A. Add a barcode sticker to each laptop.

   B. Add an RFID tag to each laptop.

   C. Submit a change document to the change board.

   D. It can't be done, because the laptops run macOS.

3. Joan has proposed upgrading the inkjet printers in the marketing department with color laser printers. The purpose of the change is to reduce the cost per page printed, because toner is less expensive than ink and the duty cycle of laser printers is longer than that of inkjet printers. The marketing department currently has three inkjet printers. What's her logical next step?

   A. She should complete the scope of change part of the change document to factor in the price of the printers.

   B. She should perform a risk analysis to determine any potentially negative consequences.

  C. She should download the documentation on the new printers and begin the education process for the marketing department on how to use them.

  D. She should contact the change board with her initial proposal.

4. Once the change board has reviewed and approved Joan's plan for the new printers, what's her next step?

  A. Create a backout plan in case the quality of print with the laser printers isn't sufficient for the marketing materials.

  B. Test the backup plan.

  C. Finalize the change documentation.

  D. Implement the change plan.

5. What broad term describes the process of creating a road map for current and future techs to make changes or repairs over time for an organization?

  A. Change documentation

  B. Change management

  C. Management documentation

  D. Network documentation

6. What broad term describes the process of enabling organizations to implement changes to IT infrastructure in a safe and cost-effective manner?

  A. Change documentation

  B. Change management

  C. Management documentation

  D. Network documentation

7. As part of the change management process, educating users on new systems is an important component in which of the following?

  A. Backout plan

  B. Accessibility training

  C. End-user acceptance

  D. Risk analysis

8. Which device protects computing devices from power dips and blackouts?

  A. GPS

  B. Surge suppressor

  C. Surge protector

  D. UPS

9. Which of the following should Eddi in sales use to protect her folder of client information from natural disasters?

   A. Local file-level backup

   B. Cloud-based file-level backup

   C. Local image backup

   D. Cloud-based local image backup

10. What does creating a password recovery disc do for you in a Windows 10 system?

   A. Enables you to log in without using a password

   B. Enables you to share your password with a remote user

   C. Provides account recovery in case you forget your password

   D. Provides a changeable password for added security

Answers

1. **B.** Henry should check the incident documentation to see if there's a history of problems with the computer at that workstation.

2. **B.** Annie should add a radio frequency identification (RFID) tag to each laptop and install a scanner at the door to track when the laptops are taken out of the office and returned.

3. **A.** Joan hasn't finished the scope of change yet, so she should include the price of the printers.

4. **A.** Once the change board has approved the change plan, Joan should make sure to have a good backout plan in place in case something unforeseen and negative happens.

5. **D.** The term network documentation describes the road map for current and future techs to make changes or repairs over time for the organization.

6. **B.** The term change management describes the process organizations use to implement changes to IT infrastructure in a safe and cost-effective manner.

7. **C.** Training users in new or updated systems leads to end-user acceptance of the changes.

8. **D.** An uninterruptible power supply (UPS) protects computing devices from power dips and blackouts.

9. **B.** Eddi should use a cloud-based file-level backup to protect her folder from natural disasters.

10. **C.** A password recovery disc provides account recovery in case of a forgotten password.

Mapping to the CompTIA A+ Objectives

220-1001 Exam Objectives

Competency	Chapter(s)
1.0 Mobile Devices	
1.1 Given a scenario, install and configure laptop hardware and components	
• Hardware/device replacement	23
• Keyboard	23
• Hard drive	23
• SSD vs. hybrid vs. magnetic disk	23
• 1.8in vs. 2.5in	23
• Memory	23
• Smart card reader	23
• Optical drive	23
• Wireless card/Bluetooth module	23
• Cellular card	23
• Video card	23
• Mini PCIe	23
• Screen	23
• DC jack	23
• Battery	23
• Touchpad	23
• Plastics/frames	23
• Speaker	23
• System board	23
• CPU	23

Competency (220-1001)	Chapter(s)
1.5 Given a scenario, connect and configure accessories and ports of other mobile devices	
• Connection types	
• Wired	24
• Micro-USB/Mini-USB/USB-C	24
• Lightning	24
• Tethering	24
• Proprietary vendor-specific ports (communication/power)	24
• Wireless	24
• NFC	24
• Bluetooth	24
• IR	24
• Hotspot	24
• Accessories	24
• Headsets	24
• Speakers	24
• Game pads	24
• Extra battery packs/battery chargers	24
• Protective covers/waterproofing	24
• Credit card readers	24
• Memory/MicroSD	24
1.6 Given a scenario, configure basic mobile device network connectivity and application support	
• Wireless/cellular data network (enable/disable)	24
• Hotspot	24
• Tethering	24
• Airplane mode	24
• Bluetooth	24
• Enable Bluetooth	24
• Enable pairing	24
• Find a device for pairing	24
• Enter the appropriate pin code	24
• Test connectivity	24
• Corporate and ISP email configuration	24
• POP3	24
• IMAP	24

Competency (220-1001)	Chapter(s)
• 802.11ac	20
• Frequencies	20
• 2.4Ghz	20
• 5Ghz	20
• Channels	20
• 1–11	20
• Bluetooth	20
• NFC	24
• RFID	28
• Zigbee	21
• Z-Wave	21
• 3G	21
• 4G	21
• 5G	21
• LTE	21
2.5 Summarize the properties and purposes of services provided by networked hosts	
• Server roles	
• Web server	18, 21
• File server	18
• Print server	18, 26
• DHCP server	19
• DNS server	19
• Proxy server	21
• Mail server	18, 24
• Authentication server	19
• syslog	16
• Internet appliance	
• UTM	27
• IDS	27
• IPS	27
• End-point management server	21
• Legacy/embedded systems	18
2.6 Explain common network configuration concepts	
• IP addressing	19
• Static	19
• Dynamic	19

Competency (220-1001)	Chapter(s)
• Cable tester	18, 19
• Loopback plug	19
• Punchdown tool	18
• WiFi analyzer	20
3.0 Hardware	
3.1 Explain basic cable types, features, and their purposes	
• Network cables	18
• Ethernet	18
• Cat 5	18
• Cat 5e	18
• Cat 6	18
• Plenum	18
• Shielded twisted pair	18
• Unshielded twisted pair	18
• 568A/B	18
• Fiber	18
• Coaxial	18
• Speed and transmission limitations	18
• Video cables	17
• VGA	17
• HDMI	17
• MINI-HDMI	17
• DisplayPort	17
• DVI	17
• DVI-DDVI-I	17
• Multipurpose cables	
• Lightning	24
• Thunderbolt	10
• USB	10
• USB-C	10, 24
• USB 2.0	10
• USB 3.0	10
• Peripheral cables	10
• Serial	10

Competency (220-1001)	Chapter(s)
• Liquid	3
• Thermal paste	3
• Expansion cards	
• Video cards	6, 17
• Onboard	6, 17
• Add-on card	6, 17
• Sound cards	6, 10
• Network interface card	6, 18–21
• USB expansion card	6, 10
• eSATA card	6, 8

3.6 *Explain the purposes and uses of various peripheral types*

• Printer	26
• ADF/flatbed scanner	26
• Barcode scanner/QR scanner	10
• Monitors	17
• VR headset	17, 24
• Optical	10
• DVD drive	10
• Mouse	10
• Keyboard	10
• Touchpad	10, 23
• Signature pad	10
• Game controllers	10
• Camera/webcam	10
• Microphone	10
• Speakers	10
• Headset	10, 24
• Projector	17
• Lumens/brightness	17
• External storage drives	8
• KVM	10
• Magnetic reader/chip reader	24
• NFC/tap pay device	24
• Smart card reader	10

Competency (220-1001)	Chapter(s)
5.4 Given a scenario, troubleshoot video, projector, and display issues	
• Common symptoms	
• VGA mode	17
• No image on screen	17
• Overheat shutdown	17
• Dead pixels	17
• Artifacts	17
• Incorrect color patterns	17
• Dim image	17
• Flickering image	17
• Distorted image	17
• Distorted geometry	17
• Burn-in	17
• Oversized images and icons	17
• Multiple failed jobs in logs	17
5.5 Given a scenario, troubleshoot common mobile device issues while adhering to the appropriate procedures	
• Common symptoms	23, 25
• No display	23
• Dim display	23
• Flickering display	23
• Sticking keys	23
• Intermittent wireless	23
• Battery not charging	23
• Ghost cursor/pointer drift	23
• No power	23
• Num lock indicator lights	23
• No wireless connectivity	23
• No Bluetooth connectivity	23
• Cannot display to external monitor	23
• Touchscreen non-responsive	25
• Apps not loading	25
• Slow performance	25
• Unable to decrypt email	25
• Extremely short battery life	25
• Overheating	25

Competency (220-1001)	Chapter(s)
• Local resources	19
• Shares	19
• Printers	19
• Email	19
• No connectivity	19, 21
• APIPA/link local address	19, 21
• Intermittent connectivity	19
• IP conflict	19
• Slow transfer speeds	21
• Low RF signal	20
• SSID not found	20

220-1002 Exam Objectives

Competency	Chapter(s)
1.0 Operating Systems	
1.1 Compare and contrast common operating system types and their purposes	
• 32-bit vs. 64-bit	2, 3
• RAM limitations	3, 4
• Software compatibility	3, 14
• Workstation operating systems	2
• Microsoft Windows	2
• Apple Macintosh OS	2
• Linux	2
• Cell phone/tablet operating systems	2
• Microsoft Windows	24
• Android	24
• iOS	24
• Chrome OS	23
• Vendor-specific limitations	
• End-of-life	11
• Update limitations	11
• Compatibility concerns between operating systems	11

Competency (220-1002)	Chapter(s)
• Extended	9
• Logical	9
• GPT	9
• File system types/formatting	
• ExFAT	9
• FAT32	9
• NTFS	9
• CDFS	10
• NFS	21
• ext3, ext4	9
• HFS	9
• Swap partition	9
• Quick format vs. full format	9
• Load alternate third-party drivers when necessary	11
• Workgroup vs. Domain setup	11
• Time/date/region/language settings	11
• Driver installation, software, and Windows updates	11, 14
• Factory recovery partition	9
• Properly formatted boot drive with the correct partitions/format	11
• Prerequisites/hardware compatibility	11
• Application compatibility	11
• OS compatibility/upgrade path	11
1.4 Given a scenario, use appropriate Microsoft command line tools	
• Navigation	15
• dir	15
• cd	15
• ..	15
• ipconfig	19
• ping	19
• tracert	19
• netstat	21
• nslookup	19
• shutdown	15
• dism	11
• sfc	15
• chkdsk	15

Competency (220-1002)	Chapter(s)
• Task Manager	12, 14, 16
• Applications	12
• Processes	12, 16
• Performance	12
• Networking	12
• Users	12
• Disk Management	8, 9
• Drive status	9
• Mounting	9
• Initializing	9
• Extending partitions	9
• Splitting partitions	9
• Shrink partitions	9
• Assigning/changing drive letters	9
• Adding drives	9
• Adding arrays	9
• Storage spaces	9
• System utilities	
• Regedit	12
• Command	15
• Services.msc	12
• MMC	14
• MSTSC	21
• Notepad	15
• Explorer	2, 13, 15, 19
• Msinfo32	14
• DxDiag	17
• Disk Defragmenter	9, 14
• System Restore	14, 16
• Windows Update	14
1.6 Given a scenario, use Microsoft Windows Control Panel utilities	
• Internet Options	21
• Connections	21
• Security	21
• General	21
• Privacy	21

Competency (220-1002)	Chapter(s)
4.4 Explain common safety procedures	
• Equipment grounding	7
• Proper component handling and storage	1
• Antistatic bags	1
• ESD straps	1
• ESD mats	1
• Self-grounding	1
• Toxic waste handling	
• Batteries	1, 23, 25
• Toner	1, 26
• CRT	1, 17
• Cell phones	25
• Tablets	25
• Personal safety	1
• Disconnect power before repairing PC	1
• Remove jewelry	1
• Lifting techniques	1
• Weight limitations	1
• Electrical fire safety	1
• Cable management	1, 18
• Safety goggles	1
• Air filter mask	1
• Compliance with government regulations	1, 28
4.5 Explain environmental impacts and appropriate controls	
• MSDS documentation for handling and disposal	27
• Temperature, humidity level awareness, and proper ventilation	27
• Power surges, brownouts, and blackouts	7
• Battery backup	7
• Surge suppressor	7
• Protection from airborne particles	27
• Enclosures	27
• Air filters/mask	27
• Dust and debris	26, 27
• Compressed air	26, 27
• Vacuums	26, 27
• Compliance to government regulations	27, 28

Competency (220-1002)	Chapter(s)
4.6 Explain the processes for addressing prohibited content/activity, and privacy, licensing, and policy concepts	
• Incident response	27
• First response	27
• Identify	27
• Report through proper channels	27
• Data/device preservation	27
• Use of documentation/documentation changes	27, 28
• Chain of custody	27
• Tracking of evidence/documenting process	27
• Licensing/DRM/EULA	27
• Open-source vs. commercial license	27
• Personal license vs. enterprise licenses	27
• Regulated data	27
• PII	27
• PCI	27
• GDPR	27
• PHI	27
• Follow all policies and security best practices	27
4.7 Given a scenario, use proper communication techniques and professionalism	
• Use proper language and avoid jargon, acronyms, and slang, when applicable	1
• Maintain a positive attitude/project confidence	1
• Actively listen (taking notes) and avoid interrupting the customer	1
• Be culturally sensitive	1
• Use appropriate professional titles, when applicable	1
• Be on time (if late, contact the customer)	1
• Avoid distractions	1
• Personal calls	1
• Texting/social media sites	1
• Talking to coworkers while interacting with customers	1
• Personal interruptions	1
• Dealing with difficult customers or situations	1
• Do not argue with customers and/or be defensive	1
• Avoid dismissing customer problems	1
• Avoid being judgmental	1

Competency (220-1002)	Chapter(s)
• Clarify customer statements (ask open-ended questions to narrow the scope of the problem, restate the issue, or question to verify understanding)	1
• Do not disclose experiences via social media outlets	1
• Set and meet expectations/timeline and communicate status with the customer	1
• Offer different repair/replacement options, if applicable	1
• Provide proper documentation on the services provided	1
• Follow up with customer/user at a later date to verify satisfaction	1
• Deal appropriately with customers' confidential and private materials	1
• Located on a computer, desktop, printer, etc.	1
4.8 Identify the basics of scripting	
• Script file types	15
• .bat	15
• .ps1	15
• .vbs	15
• .sh	15
• .py	15
• .js	15
• Environment variables	15
• Comment syntax	15
• Basic script constructs	15
• Basic loops	15
• Variables	15
• Basic data types	15
• Integers	15
• Strings	15
4.9 Given a scenario, use remote access technologies	
• RDP	21
• Telnet	21
• SSH	21
• Third-party tools	21
• Screen share feature	21
• File share	21
• Security considerations of each access method	21

About the Online Content

This book comes complete with:

- A video from author Mike Meyers introducing the CompTIA A+ certification exam
- TotalTester Online practice exam software with practice exam questions for both exam 220-1001 and 220-1002, as well as a pre-assessment to get you started
- More than 25 sample TotalSim interactive simulations from Total Seminars
- More than an hour of video training episodes from Mike Meyers' CompTIA A+ Certification Video Training series
- A link to a collection of Mike's favorite tools and utilities for PC troubleshooting

System Requirements

The current and previous major versions of the following desktop browsers are recommended and supported: Chrome, Microsoft Edge, Firefox, and Safari. These browsers update frequently, and sometimes an update may cause compatibility issues with the Total Tester Online or other content hosted on the Training Hub. If you run into a problem using one of these browsers, please try using another until the problem is resolved.

Your Total Seminars Training Hub Account

To get access to the online content, you will need to create an account on the Total Seminars Training Hub. Registration is free, and you will be able to track all your online content using your account. You may also opt in if you wish to receive marketing information from McGraw-Hill Education or Total Seminars, but this is not required for you to gain access to the online content.

Privacy Notice

McGraw-Hill Education values your privacy. Please be sure to read the Privacy Notice available during registration to see how the information you have provided will be used. You may view our Corporate Customer Privacy Policy by visiting the McGraw-Hill Education Privacy Center. Visit the **mheducation.com** site and click on **Privacy** at the bottom of the page.

Single User License Terms and Conditions

Online access to the digital content included with this book is governed by the McGraw-Hill Education License Agreement outlined next. By using this digital content you agree to the terms of that license.

Access   To register and activate your Total Seminars Training Hub account, simply follow these easy steps.

1. Go to **hub.totalsem.com/mheclaim**.

2. To Register and create a new Training Hub account, enter your email address, name, and password. No further personal information (such as credit card number) is required to create an account.

 NOTE   If you already have a Total Seminars Training Hub account, select **Log in** and enter your email and password. Otherwise, follow the remaining steps.

3. Enter your Product Key: `rxvk-94kw-qhxf`

4. Click to accept the user license terms.

5. Click **Register and Claim** to create your account. You will be taken to the Training Hub and have access to the content for this book.

Duration of License   Access to your online content through the Total Seminars Training Hub will expire one year from the date the publisher declares the book out of print.

Your purchase of this McGraw-Hill Education product, including its access code, through a retail store is subject to the refund policy of that store.

The Content is a copyrighted work of McGraw-Hill Education, and McGraw-Hill Education reserves all rights in and to the Content. The Work is © 2019 by McGraw-Hill Education, LLC.

Restrictions on Transfer   The user is receiving only a limited right to use the Content for the user's own internal and personal use, dependent on purchase and continued ownership of this book. The user may not reproduce, forward, modify, create derivative works based upon, transmit, distribute, disseminate, sell, publish, or sublicense the Content or in any way commingle the Content with other third-party content without McGraw-Hill Education's consent.

Limited Warranty   The McGraw-Hill Education Content is provided on an "as is" basis. Neither McGraw-Hill Education nor its licensors make any guarantees or warranties of any kind, either express or implied, including, but not limited to, implied warranties of merchantability or fitness for a particular purpose or use as to any McGraw-Hill Education Content or the information therein or any warranties as to the accuracy, completeness, correctness, or results to be obtained from, accessing or using the McGraw-Hill Education Content, or any material referenced in such Content or any information entered into licensee's product by users or other persons and/or any material available on or that can be accessed through the licensee's product (including via any hyperlink or otherwise) or as to non-infringement of third-party rights. Any warranties of any kind, whether express or implied, are disclaimed. Any material or data obtained through use of the McGraw-Hill Education Content is at your own discretion and risk and user understands that it will be solely responsible for any resulting damage to its computer system or loss of data.

Neither McGraw-Hill Education nor its licensors shall be liable to any subscriber or to any user or anyone else for any inaccuracy, delay, interruption in service, error or omission, regardless of cause, or for any damage resulting therefrom.

In no event will McGraw-Hill Education or its licensors be liable for any indirect, special or consequential damages, including but not limited to, lost time, lost money, lost profits or good will, whether in contract, tort, strict liability or otherwise, and whether or not such damages are foreseen or unforeseen with respect to any use of the McGraw-Hill Education Content.

TotalTester Online

TotalTester Online provides you with a simulation of the A+ exams 220-1001 and 220-1002. Exams can be taken in Practice Mode or Exam Mode. Practice Mode provides an assistance window with hints, references to the book, explanations of the correct and incorrect answers, and the option to check your answer as you take the test. Exam Mode provides a simulation of the actual exam. The number of questions, the types of questions, and the time allowed are intended to be an accurate representation of the exam environment. The option to customize your quiz allows you to create custom exams from selected domains or chapters, and you can further customize the number of questions and time allowed.

To take a test, follow the instructions provided in the previous section to register and activate your Total Seminars Training Hub account. When you register you will be taken to the Total Seminars Training Hub. From the Training Hub Home page, click the Study dropdown menu at the top of the page, click CompTIA A+ Certification, and then click A+ (220-100x) TotalTester (or, alternatively, find the exam on the list of Your Topics on the Home page). Select the TotalTester Online item on the right and then click the Tester! icon. You can then select the option to customize your quiz and begin testing yourself in Practice Mode or Exam Mode. All exams provide an overall grade and a grade broken down by domain.

Pre-Assessment Test

In addition to the exam questions, the TotalTester also includes a pre-assessment test that covers topics from both exams to help you assess your understanding of the topics before reading the book. To launch the pre-assessment test, click A+ (220-100x) TotalTester, select the Assessment item on the right, and click the Tester! icon. The A+ pre-assessment test has 50 questions and runs in Exam mode. When you complete the test, you can review the questions with answers and detailed explanations by clicking See Detailed Results.

Other Online Book Resources

The sections below detail the other resources available with your book. You can access these items by selecting the Resources tab or by selecting CompTIA A+ Certification from the Study dropdown menu at the top of the page or from the list of Your Topics on the Home page. The tabs at the top and the menu on the right side of the screen outline all of the available resources.

TotalSims for A+

 From your Total Seminars Training Hub account, select TotalSims for A+ (220-100x) from the list of Your Topics on the Home page. Click the TotalSims tab. The simulations are organized by chapter, and there are over 25 free simulations available for reviewing topics referenced in the book, with an option to purchase access to the full TotalSims for A+ (220-100x) with over 200 simulations.

Mike's Video Training

Over an hour of training videos, starring Mike Meyers, are available for free. Select CompTIA A+ Videos (220-100x) from the list of Your Topics on the Home page. Click the TotalVideos tab. Along with over an hour of free videos, you'll find an option to purchase Mike's complete video training series.

Playing the Mike Meyers Introduction Video

You can watch the video introduction to the CompTIA A+ exam from Mike online. Select CompTIA A+ Certification from the list of Your Topics on the Home page. Click the Resources tab, and then select the Mike Meyers A+ Intro.

Mike's Cool Tools

Mike loves freeware/open source networking tools! Access the utilities mentioned in the text by selecting CompTIA A+ Certification from the list of Your Topics on the Home page. Click the Resources tab, and then select Mike's Cool Tools.

Technical Support

For questions regarding the Total Tester software or operation of the Training Hub, visit **www.totalsem.com** or e-mail **support@totalsem.com**. For questions regarding book content, e-mail **hep_customer-service@mheducation.com**. For customers outside the United States, e-mail **international_cs@mheducation.com**.

10BaseT   Ethernet cabling system designed to run at 10 Mbps on twisted pair cabling.

100BaseT   Ethernet cabling system designed to run at 100 Mbps on twisted pair cabling. Also called Fast Ethernet.

1000BaseT   Ethernet cabling system designed to run at 1000 Mbps on twisted pair cabling. Also called Gigabit Ethernet.

10-Gigabit Ethernet (10GbE)   Ethernet standard that supports speeds of up to 10 Gbps and is common on server-to-server connections. Requires Cat 6 or better twisted pair or fiber optic cabling.

110 block   The most common connection used with structured cabling, connecting horizontal cable runs with patch panels.

1.5 Gbps   SATA drive variety with maximum throughput of 150 MBps. *See* SATA.

2.1 speaker system   Speaker setup consisting of two stereo speakers combined with a subwoofer.

2-In-1   Portable devices that attempt to serve as both a laptop and a tablet.

3 Gbps   SATA drive variety with maximum throughput of 300 MBps. *See* SATA.

3-D graphics   Video technology that attempts to create images with the same depth and texture as objects seen in the real world.

3-D printer   Device that creates (or "prints") three-dimensional objects, typically by melting material (such as plastic filament) and reassembling it in layers.

3G   Third-generation cellular data technologies (such as EV-DO, UTMS, HSPA+, and HSDPA) with real-world speeds under 10 Mbps.

40-pin ribbon cable   PATA cable used to attach EIDE devices (such as hard drives) or ATAPI devices (such as optical drives) to a system. *See* PATA.

4G   The fourth generation of cellular data technologies. Most popularly implemented as Long Term Evolution (LTE), a wireless data standard with theoretical download speeds of 1 Gbps and upload speeds of 100 Mbps.

5.1 speaker system   Speaker setup consisting of four satellite speakers plus a center speaker and a subwoofer.

5G   The fifth generation of cellular data technologies. Technologies in this wave are still cutting their teeth, with development just getting underway in 2019.

6 Gbps   SATA drive variety with maximum throughput of 600 MBps. *See* SATA.

64-bit processing   A type of processing that can run a compatible 64-bit operating system, such as Windows 7, 8, 8.1, or 10, and 64-bit applications. 64-bit PCs have a 64-bit-wide address bus, enabling them to use more than 4 GB of RAM.

7.1 speaker system   Speaker setup consisting of six satellite speakers (two front, two side, two rear) plus a center speaker and a subwoofer.

802.11a   Wireless networking standard that operates in the 5-GHz band with a theoretical maximum throughput of 54 Mbps.

802.11ac   Wireless networking standard that operates in the 5-GHz band and uses multiple in/multiple out (MIMO) and multi-user MIMO (MU-MIMO) to achieve a theoretical maximum throughput of 1+ Gbps.

802.11b   Wireless networking standard that operates in the 2.4-GHz band with a theoretical maximum throughput of 11 Mbps.

802.11g   Wireless networking standard that operates in the 2.4-GHz band with a theoretical maximum throughput of 54 Mbps and is backward compatible with 802.11b.

802.11n   Wireless networking standard that can operate in both the 2.4-GHz and 5-GHz bands and uses multiple in/multiple out (MIMO) to achieve a theoretical maximum throughput of 100+ Mbps.

AC (alternating current)   Type of electricity in which the flow of electrons alternates direction, back and forth, in a circuit.

accelerated processing unit (APU)   AMD product that consolidates the GPU and CPU into a single chip.

accelerometer   Feature in smartphones and tablets that rotates the screen when the device is physically rotated.

access control   Security concept using physical security, authentication, users and groups, and security policies.

access control list (ACL)   A clearly defined list of permissions that specifies what actions an authenticated user may perform on a shared resource.

account recovery   A process enabling users to regain account access, typically by resetting a lost or forgotten password.

ACPI (Advanced Configuration and Power Interface)   Power management specification that far surpasses its predecessor, APM, by providing support for hot-swappable devices and better control of power modes.

Action Center   A one-page aggregation of event messages, warnings, and maintenance messages in Windows 7.

activation (software)   Process of confirming that an installed copy of a Microsoft product (most commonly Windows or a Microsoft Office application) is legitimate. Usually done at the end of software installation.

activation (virus)   *See* virus.

active matrix   Type of liquid crystal display (LCD) that replaced the passive matrix technology used in most portable computer displays. Also called TFT (thin film transistor).

active partition   On a hard drive, primary partition that contains an operating system.

active PFC (power factor correction)   Circuitry built into PC power supplies to reduce harmonics.

actively listen   Part of respectful communication involving listening and taking notes without interrupting.

activity light   An LED on a NIC, hub, or switch that blinks rapidly to show data transfers over the network.

ad hoc mode   Decentralized wireless network mode, otherwise known as peer-to-peer mode, where each wireless node is in meshed contact with every other node.

address bus   Set of wires leading from the CPU to the memory controller chip (traditionally the northbridge) that enables the CPU to address RAM. Also used by the CPU for I/O addressing. On current CPUs with built-in memory controllers, the address bus refers to the internal electronic channel from the microprocessor to RAM, along which the addresses of memory storage locations are transmitted. Like a post office box, each memory location has a distinct number or address; the address bus provides the means by which the microprocessor can access every location in memory.

address space   Total amount of memory addresses that an address bus can contain.

administrative shares   Administrator tool to give local admins access to hard drives and system root folders.

Administrative Tools   Group of Control Panel applets, including Computer Management, Event Viewer, Performance Monitor, and Task Scheduler.

administrator account   User account, created when the OS is first installed, that is allowed complete, unfettered access to the system without restriction.

administrator password   Credentials for the system administrator account.

Administrators group   List of members with complete administrator privileges.

ADSL (asymmetric digital subscriber line)   Fully digital, dedicated connection to the telephone system that provides average download speeds of 3–15 Mbps and upload speeds of 384 Kbps to 15 Mbps. *Asymmetric* identifies that upload and download speeds are different, with download usually being significantly faster than upload.

Advanced Encryption Standard (AES)   A block cipher created in the late 1990s that uses a 128-bit block size and a 128-, 192-, or 256-bit key size. Practically uncrackable.

Advanced Host Controller Interface (AHCI)   An efficient way for motherboards to work with SATA host bus adapters. Using AHCI unlocks some of the advanced features of SATA, such as hot-swapping and native command queuing (NCQ).

Advanced Startup Options menu   Windows 7 menu that can be reached during the boot process that offers advanced OS startup options, such as to boot to Safe Mode or boot into Last Known Good Configuration.

adware   Type of malicious program that downloads ads to a user's computer, generating undesirable network traffic.

Aero   The Windows 7 desktop environment. Often used as a shorthand for one of its more obvious aesthetic effects: a window transparency feature called Aero Glass.

AGP (Accelerated Graphics Port)   A 32/64-bit expansion slot designed by Intel specifically for video that ran at 66 MHz and yielded a throughput of at least 254 Mbps. Later versions (2×, 4×, 8×) gave substantially higher throughput.

air filter mask   A mask designed to keep users from inhaling particulate matter, as when cutting drywall.

airplane mode   Mode for mobile devices that disables all wireless and cellular communication for use on airplanes.

algorithm   Set of rules for solving a problem in a given number of steps.

ALU (arithmetic logic unit)   CPU logic circuits that perform basic arithmetic (add, subtract, multiply, and divide).

AMD (Advanced Micro Devices)   CPU and chipset manufacturer that competes with Intel. Produces FX, A-Series, Ryzen, and Opteron CPUs and APUs. Also produces video card processors under its ATI brand.

amperage   *See* current.

amperes (amps or A)   Unit of measure for amperage, or electrical current.

analog   Device that uses a physical quantity, such as length or voltage, to represent the value of a number. By contrast, digital storage relies on a coding system of numeric units.

AnandTech (anandtech.com)   Computer hardware, technology, and Internet news and information site.

Android   Smartphone and tablet OS created by Google.

Android application package (APK)   Installation software for Android apps.

ANSI/TIA   The Telecommunication Industry Association (TIA) establishes the UTP categories under the ANSI/TIA 568 specification. The American National Standards

Institute (ANSI) accredits TIA standards to ensure compatibility of industry and international standards. *See also* UTP.

anti-aliasing   In computer imaging, blending effect that smooths sharp contrasts between two regions—e.g., jagged lines or different colors. Reduces jagged edges of text or objects. In voice signal processing, process of removing or smoothing out spurious frequencies from waveforms produced by converting digital signals back to analog.

anti-malware program   Software designed to identify and block or remove malware. Typically powered by frequently updated definition files containing the signatures of known malware.

antistatic bag   Bag made of antistatic plastic into which electronics are placed for temporary or long-term storage. Used to protect components from electrostatic discharge.

antistatic mat   Special surface on which to lay electronics. These mats come with a grounding connection designed to equalize electrical potential between a workbench and one or more electronic devices. Used to prevent electrostatic discharge.

antistatic wrist strap   Special device worn around the wrist with a grounding connection designed to equalize electrical potential between a technician and an electronic device. Used to prevent electrostatic discharge.

antivirus program   Software designed to combat viruses by either seeking out and destroying them or passively guarding against them.

AOL   You've got mail!

API (application programming interface)   A library of related commands available for programmers to use. OpenGL and DirectX, for example, are two well-known 3-D graphics APIs that make it easier to build 3-D games.

APIPA (Automatic Private IP Addressing)   Feature of Windows that automatically assigns an IP address to the system when the client cannot obtain an IP address automatically.

APM (Advanced Power Management)   BIOS routines (developed by Intel in 1992 and upgraded over time) that enable the CPU to turn on and off selected peripherals. In 1996, APM was supplanted by Advanced Configuration and Power Interface (ACPI).

app   A program for a tablet or smartphone. Also, a program written for the Windows 8 Metro interface.

App history   Tab added to Task Manager in Windows 8 to collect stats such as CPU time and network usage on programs that have run recently.

app scanner   Program that scans apps installed on a device to highlight risks posed by apps and what actions they have permission to take.

App Store   Apple's mobile software storefront, where you can purchase apps for your smartphone, tablet, or other Apple products.

Apple Filing Protocol (AFP)   Enables sharing between Macs. Also used by macOS Time Machine for backing up macOS over the network. Uses TCP port 548.

Apple Pay   Apple's technology and service for making secure credit card payments in stores and apps via the iPhone and Apple Watch.

applet   Generic term for a program in the Windows Control Panel.

application   A program that enables you to perform a specific task on a computer, such as write a document or play a game.

application manager   Mobile device interface for removing and managing apps running on the device.

application programming interface   *See* API.

Applications   Tab in Task Manager that lists running applications.

Apps & Features   Area of the Windows 10 Settings app that enables users to add and remove programs and Windows features.

apt-get   Linux command for installing or updating a program using the advanced packaging tool.

augmented reality (AR)   Using some form of hardware (such as a smartphone or an AR headset) to enhance the wearer's experience of the world by adding an interface layer. The interface layer presents information such as the time or navigation instructions and may also support interaction.

AR headset   A non-immersive headset (such as a set of glasses) that places an interface between the wearer and the world. *See also* augmented reality.

ARM   Energy-efficient processor design frequently used in mobile devices.

ARP (Address Resolution Protocol)   Protocol in the TCP/IP suite used with the command-line utility of the same name (arp) to determine the MAC address that corresponds to a particular IP address.

Ars Technica (arstechnica.com)   Internet technology news site.

ASCII (American Standard Code for Information Interchange)   Industry-standard 8-bit characters used to define text characters, consisting of 96 upper- and lowercase letters, plus 32 nonprinting control characters, each of which is numbered. These numbers were designed to achieve uniformity among computer devices for printing and the exchange of simple text documents.

aspect ratio   Ratio of width to height of a display. Wide-screen displays such as modern TVs, desktop computer monitors, portable computer displays, and even smartphones commonly use 16:9 or 16:10, but you can find devices with many other aspect ratios.

assertive communication Means of communication that is not pushy or bossy but is also not soft. Useful in dealing with upset customers as it both defuses their anger and gives them confidence that you know what you're doing.

asset tag Inventory tracking tags (which may be simple barcodes or use wireless networking protocols such as RFID) that help an organization track items such as equipment.

AT (Advanced Technology) Model name of the second-generation, 80286-based IBM computer. Many aspects of the AT, such as the BIOS, CMOS, and expansion bus, became de facto standards in the PC industry. Though now obsolete, this physical organization of the components on the motherboard is called the AT form factor.

ATA (AT Attachment) A series of hard drive standards defining both the older parallel ATA (PATA) and modern serial ATA (SATA) drives. *See also* PATA *and* SATA.

ATAPI (ATA Packet Interface) Series of standards that enables mass storage devices other than hard drives to use the IDE/ATA controllers. Popular with optical drives. *See also* EIDE.

attack vector The route or methods used by a given attack (including malware).

attributes Values in a file that determine the hidden, read-only, system, and archive status of the file.

ATX (Advanced Technology Extended) Popular motherboard form factor that generally replaced the AT form factor.

audio editing workstation A computer workstation for editing audio needs a fast multicore CPU, lots of RAM, and a large monitor. It also needs large, fast hard drives and a high-quality audio interface, and may make use of specialized input devices for mixing audio.

audio interface High-end external sound device used by audio engineers and recording artists.

audio jack Very popular connector used to transmit two audio signals; perfect for stereo sound. Confusingly, you can find the diameter described as both 1/8 inch and 3.5 mm.

augmented reality *See* AR.

AUP (Acceptable Use Policy) Defines what actions employees may or may not perform on company equipment, including computers, phones, printers, and even the network itself. This policy defines the handling of passwords, e-mail, and many other issues.

authentication The process of identifying and granting access to some user trying to access a system.

authentication factor A thing that can be used to identify an individual, such as something they know (password), something they have (smartcard), or something they are (fingerprint).

authorization   The process that defines what resources an authenticated user may access and what he or she may do with those resources.

auto-brightness   Feature on modern mobile devices that attempts to use a camera or other light sensor to adjust screen brightness based on how light or dark it is.

autodetection   Process through which new disks are automatically recognized by the BIOS.

automatic document feeder (ADF)   A tray (usually on top) of a scanner or multifunction device that holds a document and enables the device to grab and scan each page automatically for easier scanning, copying, or faxing of long documents.

AutoPlay   A Windows feature that opens a dialog box when removable media is inserted into the computer, providing options based on what Windows finds on the drive, including starting the Autorun application.

Autorun   A feature that enables Windows to look for and read a file called autorun.inf immediately after a removable media device (optical disc or thumb drive) is inserted and automatically run whatever program the file lists.

autorun.inf   File included on some media. Lists which program or installation routine Autorun should run.

backlight   A component used in LCDs to illuminate an image. In older LCDs this was a CCFL; current LCDs use LEDs. *See also* CCFL, *direct LED backlighting, and* edge LED backlighting.

backout plan   In case a change doesn't go as planned, a set of steps necessary to undo the change and restore the infrastructure to its previous state.

backside bus   On older CPUs, a set of wires that connected the CPU to Level 2 cache. First appeared in the Intel Pentium Pro. *See also* frontside bus *and* external data bus.

Backup and Restore   Windows 7's backup utility. It offers two options: create a backup or restore from a backup. Windows 10 still supports restoring these backups, which it calls Backup and Restore (Windows 7). *See also* File History.

backup testing   The process of ensuring that file or system backups have produced backups from which you can restore usable systems and files.

bandwidth   The capacity of a network to transmit a given amount of data during a given period.

bank   Total number of DIMMs that can be accessed simultaneously by the chipset. The "width" of the external data bus divided by the "width" of the DIMM sticks. Specific DIMM slots must be populated to activate dual-, triple-, or quad-channel memory.

barcode   A scannable, read-only binary code often used to mark items for inventory tracking.

bash   Default command shell on macOS and most Linux distributions. *See* shell.

basic disk   Hard drive partitioned in the "classic" way with a master boot record (MBR) and partition table. *See also* dynamic disks.

battery charger   Plugs into a power source and directly charges a device battery. Most convenient with a spare battery, since it requires removing the battery to charge it.

baud   One analog cycle on a telephone line. In the early days of telephone data transmission, the baud rate was often analogous to bits per second. Due to advanced modulation of baud cycles as well as data compression, this is no longer true.

bcdedit   Command-line tool that enables you to view the BCD store, which lists the Windows boot options.

BD-R (Blu-ray Disc-Recordable)   Blu-ray Disc format that enables writing data to blank discs.

BD-RE (Blu-ray Disc-REwritable)   Blu-ray Disc equivalent of the rewritable DVD, allows writing and rewriting several times on the same BD. *See* Blu-ray Disc.

BD-ROM (Blu-ray Disc-Read Only Media)   Blu-ray Disc equivalent of a DVD-ROM or CD-ROM. *See* Blu-ray Disc.

beep codes   Series of audible tones produced by a motherboard during the POST. These tones identify whether the POST has completed successfully or whether some piece of system hardware is not working properly. Consult the manual for your particular motherboard for a specific list of beep codes.

binary numbers   Number system with a base of 2, unlike the number systems most of us use that have bases of 10 (decimal numbers), 12 (measurement in feet and inches), and 60 (time). Binary numbers are preferred for computers for precision and economy. An electronic circuit that can detect the difference between two states (on–off, 0–1) is easier and more inexpensive to build than one that could detect the differences among ten states (0–9).

biometric authentication   Authentication process using biometric data such as voice, fingerprints, or retinal scans.

biometric device   Hardware device used to support authentication; works by scanning and remembering a unique aspect of a user's various body parts (e.g., retina, iris, face, or fingerprint) by using some form of sensing device such as a retinal scanner.

BIOS (basic input/output services) (basic input/output system)   Classically, software routines burned onto the system ROM of a PC. More commonly seen as firmware that directly controls a particular piece of hardware. This firmware handles startup operations and low-level control of hardware such as disk drives, the keyboard, and monitor.

bit   Single binary digit. Also, any device that can be in an on or off state.

bit depth   Indicates the number of signal characteristics a device can capture or produce, or the number recorded in a file. Greater bit depths mean more characteristics can be captured, stored, and reproduced. Often used to describe the quality of audio or video signals.

BitLocker Drive Encryption   Drive encryption software offered in high-end versions of Windows. BitLocker requires a special chip to validate hardware status and to ensure that the computer hasn't been hacked.

BitTorrent   Peer-to-peer file-sharing program.

Bluetooth   Wireless technology designed to create small wireless networks preconfigured to do specific jobs, but not meant to replace full-function networks or Wi-Fi.

Blu-ray Disc (BD)   Optical disc format that stores up to 100 GB of data, designed as a replacement media for DVD. Competed with HD DVD.

BNC   Uncommon coax connector secured with a quarter twist.

boot   To initiate an automatic routine that clears the memory, loads the operating system, and prepares the computer for use. Term is derived from "pull yourself up by your bootstraps." Necessary because RAM doesn't retain program instructions when power is turned off.

Boot Camp   Apple tool used to install and boot to versions of Windows on a macOS computer.

Boot Configuration Data (BCD) file   File that contains information about the various operating systems installed on the system as well as instructions for how to actually load (bootstrap) them.

boot method   Media a computer uses to initiate the booting process. Includes optical media, removable drives, or a networked location. *For the related CMOS setting, see* boot sequence.

boot options   Settings in the system setup program that define which devices the system will attempt to boot from (and in what order).

boot sector   First sector on a storage drive. The boot-up software in ROM tells the computer to load whatever program is found there. If a system disk is read, the program in the boot record directs the computer to the root directory to load the operating system.

boot sequence   List containing information telling the bootstrap loader in which order to check the available storage devices for an OS. Configurable in CMOS setup.

bootable disk   Any storage device with a self-starting operating system.

bootmgr   Windows Boot Manager. Manages the boot process using information from the Boot Configuration Data (BCD) file.

bootrec   A Windows Recovery Environment troubleshooting and repair tool that repairs the master boot record, boot sector, or BCD store. It replaces the fixboot and fixmbr Recovery Console commands used in Windows XP and earlier operating systems.

bootstrap loader   Segment of code in a system's BIOS that scans for an operating system, looks specifically for a valid boot sector, and, when one is found, hands control over to the boot sector; then the bootstrap loader removes itself from memory.

botnet   Network of computers infected with malware that can be controlled to do the bidding of the malware developers, or anyone who pays them. A common use is carrying out distributed denial of service (DDoS) attacks.

bridge   A device that connects dissimilar network technologies that transmit the same signal.

brightness control   Mobile device feature controlling screen brightness. Can be set to automatically adjust to ambient light or be manually changed.

broadband   Commonly understood as a reference to high-speed, always-on communication links that can move large files much more quickly than a regular phone line.

broadcast   A network transmission addressed for every node on the network.

broadcast domain   Group of computers connected by one or more switches—that is, a group of computers that receive broadcast frames from each other.

browser   Program specifically designed to retrieve, interpret, and display Web pages.

brute force   Simple attack that attempts to guess credentials or identify vulnerabilities by trying many possibilities.

BSoD (Blue Screen of Death)   Infamous error screen that appears when Windows encounters an unrecoverable error.

buffered/registered RAM   Usually seen in motherboards supporting more than four sticks of RAM; used to address interference issues caused by the additional sticks. It accomplishes this with a small register installed on some memory modules to act as a buffer between the DIMM and the memory controller.

bug   Programming error that causes a program or a computer system to perform erratically, produce incorrect results, or crash. The term was coined when a real bug was found in one of the circuits of one of the first ENIAC computers.

burn   Process of writing data to a writable optical disc, such as a DVD-R.

burn-in failure   Critical failure usually associated with manufacturing defects.

bus   Series of wires connecting two or more separate electronic devices, enabling those devices to communicate. Also, a network topology where computers all connect to a main line called a bus cable.

BYOD (bring your own device)   An arrangement in some companies' IT departments where employees are permitted to use their own phones or other mobile devices instead of company-issued ones. Also, a feature of some wireless carriers where you can buy an unsubsidized device and use it to get cheaper wireless rates.

byte   Unit of 8 bits; fundamental data unit of personal computers. Storing the equivalent of one character, the byte is also the basic unit of measurement for computer storage.

cable Internet   Fast Internet connection from a cable TV provider via RG-6 or RG-59 cable and a cable modem.

cable lock   Simple anti-theft device for securing a laptop to a nearby object.

cable tester   Device for verifying that the connectors and wires in a cable (such as UTP) are in good order.

cache (disk)   Special area of RAM that stores the data most frequently accessed from the hard drive. Cache memory can optimize the use of your systems.

cache (L1, L2, L3, etc.)   Special section of fast memory, usually built into the CPU, used by the onboard logic to store information most frequently accessed by the CPU.

CAD/CAM design workstation   *See* graphics workstation.

calibration   Process of matching the print output of a printer to the visual output of a monitor.

camcorder   Portable device for recording audio and video. While camcorders originally recorded to tape (first analog, and later digital), most modern digital camcorders record to flash media.

camera   Device that captures visible light to preserve images in analog (film) or digital format. *See* digital camera.

CAPTCHA (Completely Automated Public Turing Test to tell Computers and Humans Apart)   Authentication challenge using images, videos, sounds, or other media to be identified by a user. Computers have a much more difficult time discerning the content of these tests than humans, making the challenge useful in determining if a human or a computer is attempting access.

card reader   Device with which you can read data from one of several types of flash memory.

Cat 5   Category 5 wire; an ANSI/TIA standard for UTP wiring that can operate at up to 100 Mbps.

Cat 5e   Category 5e wire; ANSI/TIA standard for UTP wiring that can operate at up to 1 Gbps.

Cat 6   Category 6 wire; ANSI/TIA standard for UTP wiring that can operate at up to 10 Gbps.

Cat 6a   Category 6a wire; augmented Cat 6 UTP wiring that supports 10-Gbps networks at the full 100-meter distance between a node and a switch.

Cat 7   Supports 10-Gbps networks at 100-meter segments; shielding for individual wire pairs reduces crosstalk and noise problems. Cat 7 is not an ANSI/TIA standard.

catastrophic failure   A failure in which a component or whole system will not boot; usually related to a manufacturing defect of a component. Could also be caused by overheating and physical damage to computer components.

CCFL (cold cathode fluorescent lamp) Light technology used in older LCDs and flatbed scanners. CCFLs use relatively little power for the amount of light they provide.

cd Command-line utility for changing the focus of the command prompt from one directory to another. Shorthand for "change directory."

CD (compact disc) Originally designed as the replacement for vinyl records, but (along with other optical media) is also useful for long-term storage of music and data.

CD quality Audio quality that has a sample rate of 44.4 KHz and a bit rate of 128 bits.

CDDA (CD-Digital Audio) Special format used for early CD-ROMs and all audio CDs; divides data into variable-length tracks. A good format to use for audio tracks but terrible for data because of lack of error checking.

CDFS (Compact Disc File System) Generic name for ISO-9660. File structure, rules, and conventions used when organizing and storing files and data on a CD.

CD-R (CD-recordable) CD technology that accepts a single "burn" but cannot be erased after that one burn.

CD-ROM (compact disc/read-only memory) Read-only compact storage disc for audio or video data. CD-ROMs are read by using CD-ROM drives and optical drives with backward compatibility, such as DVD and Blu-ray Disc drives.

CD-RW (CD-rewritable) CD technology that accepts multiple reads/writes like a hard drive.

Celeron Lower-cost brand of Intel CPUs.

cell tower analyzer Program, app, or device to scan and analyze the properties of nearby cellular signals. Can be used to diagnose signal quality issues or identify security threats such as tower spoofing.

cellular card A cellular modem on an expansion card designed for older laptop expansion slots. Current add-on cellular modems are typically attached via USB (and called USB modems by cellular service providers).

cellular wireless networks Networks that enable cell phones, smartphones, and other mobile devices to connect to the Internet.

certificate authority (CA) Trusted entity that signs digital certificates to guarantee that the certificate was signed by the Web site in question (and not forged).

certification License that demonstrates competency in some specialized skill.

Certified Cisco Network Associate (CCNA) One of the certifications demonstrating a knowledge of Cisco networking products.

CFS (Central File System) Method to unify all storage devices within a network or organization to facilitate a single management point and to provide user access to any file or data within the organization.

CFS (Command File System or Common File System) This term is found in the Acronyms list of the CompTIA A+ learning objectives, and nowhere else. After diligent research, your intrepid author has not found a satisfactory reference to this alleged technology and believes that your ability to recognize that CFS can stand for Command File System or Common File System will be sufficient knowledge to pass any exam questions about this topic on the corresponding test. —Mike Meyers

chain of custody A documented history of who has been in possession of a system.

change Modify configuration or status of a system, such as updating an NTFS permission or modifying a password.

change board A group of representatives from around the organization who review and approve change proposals.

change documentation Collected documentation for all aspects of a change process, including plans leading up to the change as well as receipts, overtime documents, an inventory of changed systems, a list of created users, and signed end-user acceptance forms.

change management A well-defined process composed of many planning and execution steps that enables organizations to change their IT infrastructure in a safe, cost-effective manner.

channel Used in a common method for numbering boot devices; the first boot device is channel 1, the second is channel 2, and so on.

charms In Windows 8 and 8.1, tools located in the hidden Charms bar, such as a search function, a sharing tool, a settings tool, and more.

Charms bar The location in Windows 8 and 8.1 of the charms tools. Accessed by moving the cursor to the upper-right corner of the screen.

chassis intrusion detection Feature offered in some chassis that trips a switch when the chassis is opened.

checkpoint Also known as a *snapshot*. Saves changes to a virtual machine's state. Checkpoints are great for performing maintenance with a safety net, but they aren't a complete backup, and many snapshots can slow a VM down. Get rid of them when the danger has passed.

checksum Value generated from some data, like a file, and saved for comparing to other checksums later. Can be used to identify identical data, such as files on a user's system that match known viruses. Checksums can also be used to monitor whether a program is changing itself over time, which is a strong warning sign that it may be malware that evolves to avoid detection.

chipset Electronic chips, specially designed to work together, that handle all of the low-level functions of a PC. In the original PC, the chipset consisted of close to 30 different chips. For most of the 1990s and 2000s, chipsets usually consisted of one, two, or three separate chips embedded into a motherboard. Today's CPUs have controllers built in, such as the memory and display controllers. Almost all chipsets are now a single chip.

chkdsk (checkdisk)   Hard drive error detection and, to a certain extent, correction utility in Windows, launched from the command-line interface. Originally a DOS command (chkdsk.exe); also the executable for the graphical Error checking tool.

chmod   Linux command used to change permissions.

chown   Linux command used to change the owner and the group to which a file or folder is associated.

Chrome OS   Google's Linux-based operating system designed to connect users via the Internet into Google applications, such as Gmail, Google Docs, and more. Chrome OS comes preinstalled on purpose-built hardware such as the Chromebook portable computers.

Chromebook   Strictly, any portable computer running Google's Chrome OS. Chromebooks offer an experience focused on Web applications by making use of virtually unlimited data storage in the cloud and software as a service (SaaS) applications available over the Web. Because they offload so much work, Chromebooks have a reputation for being cheap and light, but premium Chromebooks are increasingly common.

CIFS (Common Internet File System)   A dialect of the Server Message Block (SMB) protocol. Currently deprecated but still widely supported.

Classless Inter-Domain Routing (CIDR)   Current system for creating and notating IPv4 subnets; replaced the older, less flexible three-class system.

clean installation   Installing an operating system on a fresh drive, following a reformat of that drive. Often it's the only way to correct a problem with a system when many of the crucial operating system files have become corrupted.

client   Computer program that uses the services of another computer program. Also, software that extracts information from a server; your auto-dial phone is a client, and the phone company is its server. Also, a machine that accesses shared resources on a server.

client/server   Relationship in which client software obtains services from a server on behalf of a person.

client-side virtualization   Using a hypervisor installed on a client machine to run a virtual machine. The VM may be created and stored on the client machine or accessed over the network.

clock cycle   Single charge to the clock wire (CLK) of a CPU, informing the CPU that another piece of information is waiting to be processed.

clock speed   The maximum number of clock cycles that a CPU can handle in a given period of time, measured in MHz or GHz. In modern CPUs, the internal speed is a multiple of the external speed. *See also* clock-multiplying CPU.

clock wire (CLK)   A special wire that, when charged, tells the CPU that another piece of information is waiting to be processed.

clock-multiplying CPU   CPU that takes the incoming clock signal and multiples it inside the CPU to let the internal circuitry of the CPU run faster.

closed source   Describes a product for which the plans, schematics, recipes, or other information used to create it are solely controlled by its creator or distributor. Most commonly applied to software.

closed source software   Software for which the source code is kept secret.

cloud computing   A model for enabling and accessing computing storage and other shared (or not shared) resources on-demand. The "cloud" is based on servicing models that include IaaS, PaaS, and SaaS, or hybrid mixtures of these services.

cloud file storage services   Internet-based shared file storage spaces that enable users to save, edit, share, and collaborate on stored files, as well as synchronize files among multiple devices and users.

CLRTC   *See* CMOS clear.

cluster   To overcome some limitations in addressing inherent in each file system, Windows file systems organize data into groups called clusters. Cluster size varies by file system and partition size.

CMOS (complementary metal-oxide semiconductor)   Originally, computer systems had a standalone CMOS chip—a tiny bit RAM hooked up to a small battery that enabled it to hold system settings for the BIOS firmware even with the computer off. This has long since been incorporated into the chipset. CMOS is often informally used to refer to the CMOS setup program or system setup utility.

CMOS battery   A coin cell lithium-ion battery that maintains power to the CMOS memory chip when the computer is otherwise unpowered. The usual battery size is CR2032.

CMOS clear   A jumper setting or button on the motherboard that, when set, will revert CMOS settings to the factory defaults.

CMOS setup program   Program enabling you to access and update CMOS data. Also referred to as the system setup utility, BIOS setup utility, UEFI/BIOS setup, and similar names.

CNR (communications and networking riser)   Proprietary slot used on some motherboards to provide a connection for modems, sound cards, and NICs that is free from sound interference.

coaxial cable   Cabling in which an internal conductor is surrounded by another, outer conductor, thus sharing the same axis.

code   Set of symbols representing characters (e.g., ASCII code) or instructions in a computer program (a programmer writes source code, which must be translated into executable or machine code for the computer to use).

code names   Names that keep track of different variations within CPU models.

codec (compressor/decompressor)   Software that compresses or decompresses media streams.

color depth (display)   The number of bits (the bit depth) necessary to represent the number of colors in a graphics mode. Common color bit depths are 16-bit and 32-bit, representing 65,536 colors and 16.7 million colors (plus an 8-bit alpha channel for transparency levels), respectively.

color depth (scanner)   Term to define a scanner's ability to produce color, hue, and shade.

color space   The portion of all possible colors that a device (such as an LCD display or camera) is able to display or save.

COM port(s)   Serial communications ports once common on computers. COMx is used to designate a uniquely numbered COM port such as COM1, COM2, etc.

command   A request, typed from a terminal or embedded in a file, to perform an operation or to execute a particular program.

command mode   One of two modes (along with insert mode) used in vi. Enables inputting commands such as copy or paste. *See* vi.

command prompt   Text prompt for entering commands.

command-line interface (CLI)   Text user interface. Users input text commands and receive text output. CLI commands, which are more flexible and often faster (or use fewer resources) than a graphical equivalent, are also easy to compose into scripts for performing frequent tasks.

comment   Annotation text included in scripts, programs, and configuration files, which may be used to describe what the code or setting does and how or why it does it. Most scripting, programming, and configuration languages specify how to mark comment text.

community cloud   Cloud network that serves a community or group with shared needs and interests, such as hospitals or defense contractors.

CompactFlash (CF)   The oldest, most complex, and physically largest of all removable flash media cards.

compatibility modes   Feature of Windows to enable software written for previous versions of Windows to operate in newer operating systems.

compliance   Concept that members of an organization must abide by the rules created by and applying to that organization (including government regulations). For a technician, this often defines what software can or cannot be installed on an organization's computers.

component failure   Occurs when a system device fails due to a manufacturing or some other type of defect.

Component Services   Programming tools in Windows for the sharing of data objects between programs.

compression   Process of squeezing data to eliminate redundancies, allowing files to use less space when stored or transmitted.

CompTIA A+ 220-1001   The first half of the CompTIA A+ certification for computer technicians. The 1001 exam focuses primarily on understanding terminology and technology, how to do fundamental tasks such as upgrading RAM, and basic network and mobile device support.

CompTIA A+ 220-1002   The second half of the CompTIA A+ certification for computer technicians. The 1002 exam focuses primarily on software, security, and troubleshooting.

CompTIA A+ certification   Industry-wide, vendor-neutral computer certification program that demonstrates competency as a computer technician.

CompTIA Network+ certification   Industry-wide, vendor-neutral certification for network technicians, covering network hardware, installation, and troubleshooting.

computer   An electronic device that can perform calculations.

Computer   Commonly used interface for Windows Explorer that displays hard drives and devices with removable storage.

Computer Management   Applet in Windows' Administrative Tools that contains several useful snap-ins, such as Device Manager and Disk Management.

computing process   Four parts of a computer's operation: input, processing, output, and storage.

Computing Technology Industry Association (CompTIA)   Nonprofit IT trade association that administers the CompTIA A+ and CompTIA Network+ exams, and many other vendor-neutral IT certification exams.

conditionals   Functions that enable a script or program to perform different actions under different conditions. For example, a backup script might "run" every hour, but only create a new backup *if* the system is idle and *if* it has been at least a day since the last backup was created.

connector   Small receptacle used to attach a cable to a device or system. Common types of connector include USB, PS/2, RJ-45, VGA, HDMI, DVI, HD15, DisplayPort, and Thunderbolt.

consumables   Materials used up by printers, including paper, ink, ribbons, and toner cartridges.

container file File containing two or more separate, compressed tracks, typically an audio track and a moving-picture track. Also known as a *wrapper*.

content filtering Gating access to insecure or objectionable sites using certificates or parental control tools.

context menu Small menu brought up by right-clicking on objects in Windows.

contrast ratio Difference in intensity between the lightest and the darkest spot that a device can display (in the case of a monitor) or capture (in the case of a camera or scanner).

control construct Loops and conditional statements (such as the "if" statement) are examples of control constructs, which enable programmers to control the conditions under which certain sections of code will run.

Control Panel Collection of Windows applets, or small programs, that can be used to configure various pieces of hardware and software in a system.

controller card Card adapter that connects devices, such as a drive, to the main computer bus/motherboard.

convertible A subset of 2-in-1 portables that use a hinge or latch mechanism to convert between laptop and tablet modes.

copy command Command-line tool used to make a copy of a file and paste it in another location.

Core Name used for the family of Intel CPUs that succeeded the Pentium 4, such as the Core i3, Core i5, and Core i7.

counter Used to track data about a particular object when using Performance Monitor.

cp Copy command in Linux.

CPU (central processing unit) "Brain" of the computer. Microprocessor that handles primary calculations for the computer. CPUs are known by names such as Core i7 and Opteron.

CRC (cyclic redundancy check) Very accurate mathematical method used to check for errors in long streams of transmitted data. Before data is sent, the main computer uses the data to calculate a CRC value from the data's contents. If the receiver calculates from the received data a different CRC value, the data was corrupted during transmission and is re-sent. Ethernet packets use the CRC algorithm in the FCS portion of the frame.

Credential Manager A Windows Control Panel applet which manages saved logon information for Web sites, applications, and networks.

credit card reader Device that can be attached to mobile phones and tablets to take credit card payments.

crimper A specialized tool for connecting twisted pair wires to an RJ-45 connector. Also called a *crimping tool*.

cron   Tool used by many Linux distributions for automatically running tasks based on a schedule.

crossover cable   A standard UTP cable with one RJ-45 connector using the T568A standard and the other using the T568B standard. This reverses the signal between sending and receiving wires and thus simulates the connection to a switch.

CRT (cathode ray tube)   Tube of a monitor in which rays of electrons are beamed onto a phosphorescent screen to produce images. Also, a shorthand way to describe a monitor that uses CRT rather than LCD technology.

CSMA/CA (carrier sense multiple access/collision avoidance)   Networking scheme used by wireless devices to transmit data while avoiding data collisions, which wireless nodes have difficulty detecting.

CSMA/CD (carrier sense multiple access/collision detection)   Networking scheme used by Ethernet devices to transmit data and resend data after detection of data collisions.

current   Amount of electrons moving past a certain point on a wire, measured in units called amperes. Also called amperage.

DAC (discretionary access control)   Authorization method based on the idea that there is an owner of a resource who may at his or her discretion assign access to that resource. DAC is considered much more flexible than mandatory access control (MAC).

data classification   System of organizing data according to its sensitivity. Common classifications include public, highly confidential, and top secret.

Data Collector Sets   Windows log repository that accepts log entries from other Windows computers.

data roaming   A feature of cellular data systems that enables the signal to jump from cell tower to cell tower and from your provider to another provider without obvious notice.

data storage   Saving a permanent copy of your work so that you can come back to it later.

data structure   Scheme that directs how an OS stores and retrieves data on and off a drive. Used interchangeably with the term file system. *See also* file system.

data usage limit   Restrictions on how much data a user may consume. Once the user exceeds the limit, data may be blocked entirely or bandwidth may be throttled.

DB connectors   D-shaped connectors once used for a variety of connections in the PC and networking world. Can be male (with prongs) or female (with holes) and have a varying number of pins or sockets. Also called D-sub, D-subminiature, or D-shell connectors. They are still reasonably common, but rarely used.

DB-9   A two-row DB connector (male) used to connect the computer's serial port to a serial-communication device such as a modem or a console port on a managed switch.

DC (direct current)   Type of electricity in which the flow of electrons is in a complete circle in one direction.

dd   Linux command for copying entire block volumes.

DDOS (distributed denial of service)   An attack on a computer or network device in which multiple computers send data and requests to the device in an attempt to overwhelm it so that it cannot perform normal operations.

DDR SDRAM (double data rate SDRAM)   Type of DRAM that makes two processes for every clock cycle. *See also* DRAM.

DDR2 SDRAM   Type of SDRAM that sends 4 bits of data in every clock cycle. *See also* DDR SDRAM.

DDR3 SDRAM   Type of SDRAM that transfers data at twice the rate of DDR2 SDRAM.

DDR3L   Low-voltage version of DDR3. Provides cost savings in large deployments, such as a data center.

DDR3U   Ultra-low-voltage version of DDR3.

DDR4 SDRAM   Type of SDRAM that offers higher density and lower voltages than DDR3, and can handle faster data transfer rates. Maximum theoretical capacity of DDR4 DIMMs is up to 512 GB.

DE (desktop environment)   Name for the various user interfaces found in Linux distributions.

debug   To detect, trace, and eliminate errors in computer programs.

decibel   Unit of measurement typically associated with sound. The higher the number of decibels, the louder the sound.

decrypt   To pass decryption keys and encrypted data through the appropriate decryption algorithm in order to retrieve the original unencrypted data. *See* encryption.

dedicated server   Machine that is not used for any client functions, only server functions.

default gateway   In a TCP/IP network, the nearest router to a particular host. This router's IP address is part of the necessary TCP/IP configuration for communicating with multiple networks using IP.

default user accounts/groups   Users or groups that are enabled by default. Some, such as the guest account, represent a security risk.

definition file   Files that enable anti-malware programs to identify viruses on your system and clean them. These files should be updated often. Also called signature files.

defragmentation (defrag)   Procedure in which all the files on a hard disk drive are rewritten on disk so that all parts of each file reside in contiguous clusters. The result is an improvement in disk speed during retrieval operations.

degaussing   Data destruction procedure used to reduce or remove the electromagnetic fields that store data on magnetic hard drives.

del (erase)   Command-line tool used to delete/erase files.

Desktop   User's primary interface to the Windows operating system.

destination port   In port triggering, the port that the router opens to receive a response after the router sends outbound traffic on the trigger port. *See* trigger port.

Details   Tab added to Task Manager in Windows 8 to collect much of the detail from the older Processes tab, including executable names, PIDs, status, executing user, a description, and present resource use. Many more columns can be enabled as well.

device charger   Plugs into a power source and charges a device through one of its ports, such as USB or Lightning. Convenient for charging while the device stays on.

device driver   Program used by the operating system to control communications between the computer and peripherals.

Device Manager   Utility that enables techs to examine and configure all the hardware and drivers in a Windows PC.

DFS (distributed file system)   A storage environment where shared files are accessed from storage devices within multiple servers, clients, and peer hosts.

DHCP (Dynamic Host Configuration Protocol)   Protocol that enables client hosts to request and receive TCP/IP settings automatically from an appropriately configured server. Uses UDP ports 67 and 68.

diagnostics menu   Hidden mobile device menu that contains tests and diagnostics for verifying the functionality of various device hardware.

dictionary attack   Type of brute force attack using a dictionary to guess things like usernames and passwords. Don't think Webster's—these dictionaries may be full of usernames and passwords that have leaked or been used as defaults over the years.

digital camera   Camera that simulates film technology electronically.

digital certificate   Form in which a public key is sent from a Web server to a Web browser so that the browser can decrypt the data sent by the server.

digital rights management (DRM)   Code schemes for enforcing what users can and can't do with commercial software or digital media files.

digitizer (peripheral)   Device enabling users to paint, ink, pencil, or otherwise draw with a computer. Also known as a pen tablet.

digitizer (screen)   The touchscreen overlay technology that converts finger and stylus contact into input data for the device to use.

DIMM (dual inline memory module) 32- or 64-bit type of DRAM packaging with the distinction that each side of each tab inserted into the system performs a separate function. DIMMs come in a variety of sizes, with 184-, 240-, and 288-pin being the most common on desktop computers.

dipole antennas Standard straight-wire antennas that provide the most omnidirectional function.

dir Command-line tool used to display the entire contents of the current working directory.

direct LED backlighting Matrix of LEDs that illuminates a display from directly behind the display panel.

directory Another name for a folder.

DirectX Set of APIs enabling programs to control multimedia, such as sound, video, and graphics. Used in Windows 7 to draw the Aero desktop.

discretionary access control *See* DAC.

Disk Cleanup Utility built into Windows that can help users clean up their hard drives by removing temporary Internet files, deleting unused program files, and more.

Disk Defragmenter A program that maintains performance by rearranging chunks of data on a storage device to ensure chunks that comprise a file are stored contiguously. Renamed to Optimize Drives in Windows 8 and up.

disk duplexing Type of disk mirroring using two separate controllers rather than one; marginally faster than traditional mirroring because one controller does not write each piece of data twice.

disk initialization A process that places special information on every hard drive installed in a Windows system.

Disk Management Snap-in available with the Microsoft Management Console that enables techs to configure the various disks installed in a system; available in Computer Management in Administrative Tool.

disk mirroring Process by which data is written simultaneously to two or more disk drives. Read and write speed is decreased, but redundancy in case of catastrophe is increased.

disk quota Application allowing network administrators to limit hard drive space usage.

disk striping Process by which data is spread among multiple (at least two) drives. Increases speed for both reads and writes of data. Considered RAID level 0 because it does not provide fault tolerance.

disk striping with parity   Method for providing fault tolerance by writing data across multiple drives and then including an additional drive, called a parity drive, that stores information to rebuild the data contained on the other drives. Requires at least three physical disks: two for the data and a third for the parity drive. This provides data redundancy at RAID levels 5, 10, and 0+1 with different options.

disk thrashing   Hard drive that is constantly being accessed due to lack of available system memory. When system memory runs low, a Windows system will utilize hard disk space as "virtual" memory, thus causing an unusual amount of hard drive access.

Disk Utility   macOS tool that checks for hard drive errors.

diskpart   A fully functioning command-line partitioning tool.

dism (Deployment Image Servicing and Management)   A command-line tool bundled with Windows 10 to support image deployment. Also known as dism.exe.

display adapter   Handles all the communication between the CPU and the monitor. Also known as a *video card*.

Display applet   Tool in Windows 7/8/8.1 used to adjust display settings, including resolution, refresh rate, driver information, and color depth.

Display Settings   Windows 10 utility that enables a user to change color schemes, font sizes, and other aspects of what appears on the computer monitor.

DisplayPort   Digital video connector used by some Apple Mac desktop models and some PCs, notably from Dell. Designed by VESA as a royalty-free connector to replace VGA and DVI.

distended capacitors   Failed capacitors on a motherboard, which tend to bulge out at the top. This was especially a problem during the mid-2000s, when capacitor manufacturers released huge batches of bad capacitors.

distribution (distro)   A specific variant of Linux.

DLP (Data Loss Prevention)   System or set of rules designed to stop leakage of sensitive information. Usually applied to Internet appliances to monitor outgoing network traffic.

DLP (Digital Light Processing)   Display technology that reflects and directs light onto a display surface using micromechanically operated mirrors.

DLT (digital linear tape)   High-speed, magnetic tape storage technology used to archive and retrieve data from faster, online media such as hard disks.

DMA (direct memory access)   Technique that some PC hardware devices use to transfer data to and from the memory without using the CPU.

DMA controller   Resides between the RAM and the devices and handles DMA requests.

DMZ (demilitarized zone)   A lightly protected or unprotected subnet network positioned between an outer firewall and an organization's highly protected internal network. DMZs are used mainly to host public address servers (such as Web servers).

DNS (Domain Name Service)   TCP/IP name resolution system that translates a host name into an IP address. Uses UDP port 53.

DNS domain   Specific branch of the DNS name space. Top-level domains (TLDs) include .com, .gov, and .edu.

Dock   A bar at the bottom of the macOS desktop where application icons can be placed for easy access.

docking station   Device that provides a portable computer extra features such as an optical drive, in addition to legacy and modern ports. Similar to a port replicator. Also, a charging station for mobile devices.

document findings, actions, and outcomes   Recording each troubleshooting job: what the problem was, how it was fixed, and other helpful information. (Step 6 of 6 in the CompTIA troubleshooting methodology.)

Documents folder   Windows folder for storing user-created files.

Dolby Digital   Technology for sound reductions and channeling methods used for digital audio.

domain   Groupings of users, computers, or networks. In Microsoft networking, a domain is a group of computers and users that share a common account database and a common security policy. On the Internet, a domain is a group of computers that share a common element in their hierarchical name. Other types of domains exist—e.g., broadcast domain, etc.

domain controller   A computer running Windows Server that stores a set of domain accounts.

domain-based network   Network that eliminates the need for logging on to multiple servers by using domain controllers to hold the security database for all systems.

DoS (denial of service)   An attack on a computer resource that prevents it from performing its normal operations, usually by overwhelming it with large numbers of requests in an effort to monopolize its resources.

DOS (Disk Operating System)   First popular operating system available for PCs. A text-based, single-tasking operating system that was not completely replaced until the introduction of Windows 95.

dot-matrix printer   Printer that creates each character from an array of dots. Pins striking a ribbon against the paper, one pin for each dot position, form the dots. May be a serial printer (printing one character at a time) or a line printer.

double-sided RAM   RAM stick with RAM chips soldered to both sides of the stick. May only be used with motherboards designed to accept double-sided RAM. Very common.

dpi (dots per inch)   Measure of printer resolution that counts the dots the device can produce per linear (horizontal) inch.

DRAM (dynamic random access memory or dynamic RAM)   Memory used to store data in most personal computers. DRAM stores each bit in a "cell" composed of a transistor and a capacitor. Because the capacitor in a DRAM cell can only hold a charge for a few milliseconds, DRAM must be continually refreshed, or rewritten, to retain its data.

drive cloning   Taking a PC and making a duplicate of the hard drive, including all data, software, and configuration files, and transferring it to another PC. *See* image deployment.

drive letter   A letter designating a specific drive or partition.

drive-by download   Undesired file downloads generated by turpid Web sites and ads.

driver signing   Digital signature for drivers used by Windows to protect against potentially bad drivers.

DSL (digital subscriber line)   High-speed Internet connection technology that uses a regular telephone line for connectivity. DSL comes in several varieties, including asymmetric (ADSL) and symmetric (SDSL), and many speeds. Typical home-user DSL connections are ADSL, with faster download speeds than upload speeds.

D-subminiature   *See* DB connectors.

DTS (Digital Theatre Systems)   Technology for sound reductions and channeling methods, similar to Dolby Digital.

dual boot   Refers to a computer with two operating systems installed, enabling users to choose which operating system to load on boot. Can also refer to kicking a device a second time just in case the first time didn't work.

dual-channel architecture   Using two sticks of RAM (either RDRAM or DDR SDRAM) to increase throughput. *See also* triple-channel architecture *and* quad-channel architecture.

dual-channel memory   Form of DDR, DDR2, and DDR3 memory access used by many motherboards that requires two identical sticks of DDR, DDR2, or DDR3 RAM.

dual-core   CPUs that have two execution units on the same physical chip but share caches and RAM.

dual-voltage   Type of power supply that works with either 110- or 220-volt outlets.

dumpster diving   To go through someone's trash in search of information.

DUN (Dial-up Networking)   Software used by Windows to govern the dial-up connection between the modem and the ISP.

duplexing   Similar to mirroring in that data is written to and read from two physical drives, for fault tolerance. Separate controllers are used for each drive, both for additional fault tolerance and for additional speed. Considered RAID level 1. Also called *disk duplexing* or *drive duplexing*.

duplexing assembly   Mechanical feature of some printers that can automatically flip the paper to print on both sides.

DVD (digital versatile disc)   Optical disc format that provides for 4–17 GB of video or data storage.

DVD-ROM   DVD equivalent of the standard CD-ROM.

DVD-RW/DVD+RW   Incompatible rewritable DVD media formats.

DVD-video   DVD format used exclusively to store digital video; capable of storing over 2 hours of high-quality video on a single DVD.

DVI (digital visual interface)   Special video connector designed for digital-to-digital connections; most commonly seen on PC video cards and LCD monitors. Some versions also support analog signals with a special adapter.

dxdiag (DirectX Diagnostics Tool)   Diagnostic tool for getting information about and testing a computer's DirectX version.

dye-sublimation printer   Printer that uses a roll of heat-sensitive plastic film embedded with dyes, which are vaporized and then solidified onto specially coated paper to create a high-quality image.

dynamic disks   Special feature of Windows that enables users to span a single volume across two or more drives. Dynamic disks do not have partitions; they have volumes. Dynamic disks can be striped, mirrored, and striped or mirrored with parity.

dynamic range   Gamut of color or intensity of light that can be displayed or detected by a device.

ECC (error correction code)   Special software, embedded on hard drives, that constantly scans the drives for bad blocks.

ECC RAM/DRAM (error correction code RAM/DRAM)   RAM that uses special chips to detect and fix memory errors. Commonly used in high-end servers where data integrity is crucial.

edge LED backlighting   Columns or rows of LEDs placed along the sides or top of a display panel to illuminate the display.

effective permissions   User's combined permissions granted by multiple groups.

EFS (encrypting file system)   Storage organization and management service, such as NTFS, that has the capability of applying a cipher process to the stored data.

EIDE (Enhanced IDE)   Marketing concept of hard drive–maker Western Digital, encompassing four improvements for IDE drives, including drives larger than 528 MB, four devices, increase in drive throughput, and non–hard drive devices. *See also* ATAPI.

electric potential   The voltage differential between any two objects, one of which is frequently ground or earth, resulting in a degree of attraction for the electrons to move from one of the objects to the other. A large difference between a person and a doorknob, for example, can lead to a shocking experience when the two touch. *See* electrostatic discharge.

electromagnetic interference (EMI)   Electrical interference from one device to another, resulting in poor performance of the device being interfered with. Examples: Static on your TV while running a blow dryer, or placing two monitors too close together and getting a "shaky" screen.

electromagnetic pulse (EMP)   Potentially damaging burst of electromagnetic energy caused by events such as electrostatic discharge (ESD), lightning, nuclear detonations, and so on.

electrostatic discharge (ESD)   Uncontrolled rush of electrons from one object to another. A real menace to PCs, as it can cause permanent damage to semiconductors.

eliciting answers   Communication strategy designed to help techs understand a user's problems better. Works by listening to a user's description of a problem and then asking cogent questions.

e-mail (electronic mail)   Messages, usually text, sent from one person to another via computer. Can also be sent automatically to a group of addresses (mailing list).

emergency notification   Feature built into smartphones enabling them to receive messages from emergency broadcast systems, such as the Emergency Alert System (EAS) in the United States.

emergency repair disk (ERD)   Saves critical boot files and partition information and is the main tool for fixing boot problems in older versions of Windows. Newer versions of Windows call this a system repair disc (Windows 7) or recovery drive (Windows 8/8.1 and 10).

emulator   Software or hardware that converts the commands to and from the host machine into an entirely different platform.

encrypted   Data that has been passed through an encryption algorithm, rendering it unreadable without the decryption keys. *See* encryption.

encryption   Making data unreadable by those who do not possess a key or password.

end process   Option in Task Manager to halt a program or background process. Other supporting processes continue to run after ending a process they support.

end process tree   Option in Task Manager to halt a program or background process and all of its supporting processes.

end-user acceptance   Change management step that entails educating and training users about what has changed and how to use any new systems, devices, or features.

Enhanced 911 (E911) Improves 911 service for cellular phones by using GPS and cellular network triangulation to locate the device and dispatch emergency responders.

entry control roster Document for recording who enters and leaves a building.

environment variables System data such as the date and time, currently logged-in users, running operating system version, and more. Scripts and programs on a system often use these variables to tailor their behavior to the system's capabilities and configuration.

environmental control Practice of protecting computing equipment from environmental damage by taking measures such as air conditioning, proper ventilation, air filtration, temperature monitoring, and humidity monitoring.

equipment rack A metal structure used in equipment rooms to secure network hardware devices and patch panels. Most racks are 19 inches wide. Devices designed to fit in such a rack use a height measurement called *units*, or simply *U*.

erase *See* del.

erase lamp Component inside laser printers that uses light to make the coating of the photosensitive drum conductive.

e-reader Mobile electronic device used for reading e-books.

Error checking Windows graphical tool that scans and fixes hard drive problems. Often referred to by the name of the executable, chkdsk, or Check Disk. The macOS equivalent is the Disk Utility, and Linux offers a command-line tool called fsck.

eSATA Serial ATA-based connector for external hard drives and optical drives.

escalate Process used when person assigned to repair a problem is not able to get the job done, such as sending the problem to someone with more expertise.

ESD mat *See* antistatic mat.

ESD strap *See* antistatic wrist strap.

establish a plan of action to resolve the problem and implement the solution
After establishing and testing a theory about a particular problem, techs solve the problem. (Step 4 of 6 in the CompTIA troubleshooting methodology.)

establish a theory of probable cause (question the obvious) After identifying a problem, techs question the obvious to determine what might be the source of the problem. (Step 2 of 6 in the CompTIA troubleshooting methodology.)

Ethernet Name coined by Xerox for the first standard of network cabling and protocols that define everything necessary to get data from one computer to another. Since its inception, Ethernet has gone through hundreds of improvements and even forms the basis of wireless networking signals.

Ethernet over Power Uses a building's existing electrical network for Ethernet. Requires specialized bridges between the Ethernet network and power outlets.

Ethic of Reciprocity   Golden Rule: Do unto others as you would have them do unto you.

EULA (End User License Agreement)   Agreement that accompanies a piece of software, to which the user must agree before using the software. Outlines the terms of use for the software and also lists any actions on the part of the user that violate the agreement.

event auditing   Feature of Event Viewer's Security section that creates an entry in the Security Log when certain events happen, such as a user logging on.

Event Viewer   Utility made available in Windows as an MMC snap-in that enables users to monitor and audit various system events, including network bandwidth usage and CPU utilization.

exFAT   A Microsoft-proprietary file system that breaks the 4-GB file-size barrier, supporting files up to 16 exabytes (EB) and a theoretical partition limit of 64 zettabytes (ZB). Envisioned for use with flash media devices with a capacity exceeding 2 TB.

expansion bus   Set of wires going to the CPU, governed by the expansion bus crystal, directly connected to expansion slots of varying types (PCI, AGP, PCIe, and so on).

expansion bus crystal   Controls the speed of the expansion bus.

expansion slots   Connectors on a motherboard that enable users to add optional components to a system. *See also* AGP, PCI, *and* PCIe.

ExpressCard   The high-performance serial version of the PC Card that replaced PC Card slots on laptop PCs over the past decade. ExpressCard comes in two widths: 34 mm and 54 mm, called *ExpressCard/34* and *ExpressCard/54*.

ext4 (Fourth Extended File System)   File system used by most Linux distributions.

extended partition   Type of nonbootable hard disk partition. May only have one extended partition per disk. Purpose is to divide a large disk into smaller partitions, each with a separate drive letter.

Extensible Authentication Protocol (EAP)   Authentication wrapper that EAP-compliant applications can use to accept one of many types of authentication. While EAP is a general-purpose authentication wrapper, its only substantial use is in wireless networks.

extension   *See* file extension.

external data bus (EDB)   Primary data highway of all computers. Everything in your computer is tied either directly or indirectly to the external data bus. *See also* frontside bus *and* backside bus.

external enclosure   Casing that encloses an external hard drive.

external speaker   Portable device that can substantially improve on the audio output of a mobile device or portable computer. Typically connects via Bluetooth or a regular headphone jack.

extra battery pack   For devices with removable batteries, an extra battery that can be swapped in as needed.

face lock   Technology that enables use of facial features to unlock a mobile device or personal computer.

factory recovery partition   *See* recovery partition.

factory reset   Returns a device's software to how it left the factory by removing all user-installed data, programs, and customizations.

FAT (file allocation table)   Hidden table that records how files on a hard disk are stored in distinct clusters; the only way DOS knows where to access files. The address of the first cluster of a file is stored in the directory file. The FAT entry for the first cluster is the address of the second cluster used to store that file. In the entry for the second cluster for that file is the address for the third cluster, and so on until the final cluster, which gets a special end-of-file marker. There are two FATs, mirror images of each other, in case one is destroyed or damaged. Also refers to the 16-bit file allocation table when used by Windows 2000 and later NT-based operating systems.

FAT32   File allocation table that uses 32 bits to address and index clusters. Commonly used with USB flash-media drives and versions of Windows prior to XP.

fdisk   Disk-partitioning utility used in DOS and Windows 9*x* systems.

fiber optic cable   High-speed cable for transmitting data, made of high-purity glass sealed within an opaque tube. Much faster than conventional copper wire such as coaxial cable. Most common connectors include ST, SC, and LC.

file   A named collection of any form of data that is stored beyond the time of execution of a single job. A file may contain program instructions or data, which may be numerical, textual, or graphical information.

file association   Windows term for the proper program to open a particular file; for example, the file association for opening .MP3 files might be MusicBee.

File Explorer   A tool in Windows 8/8.1/10 that enables users to browse files and folders. Previously known as Windows Explorer in Windows 7 and earlier versions.

file extension   Two, three, four, five, or more letters that follow a filename and identify the type of file (file format). Common file extensions are .zip, .exe, .doc, .java, and .xhtml

file format   How information is encoded in a file. Two primary types are binary (pictures) and ASCII (text), but within those are many formats, such as BMP and GIF for pictures. Commonly represented by a suffix (the file extension) at the end of the filename; for example, .txt for a text file or .exe for an executable.

File History   Control Panel applet introduced in Windows 8 for backing up personal files and folders.

file permission   Specifies what degree of access the system should grant a user or group to a particular file.

file server   Computer designated to store software, courseware, administrative tools, and other data on a LAN or WAN. It "serves" this information to other computers via the network when users enter their personal access codes.

file system   Scheme that directs how an OS stores and retrieves data on and off a drive; FAT32 and NTFS are both file systems. Used interchangeably with the term "data structure." *See also* data structure.

file-level backup   Manually or automatically copying individual files or folders to one or more backup locations.

filename   Name assigned to a file when the file is first written on a disk. Every file on a disk within the same folder must have a unique name. Filenames can contain any character (including spaces), except the following: \ / : * ? " < > |

Finder   macOS's file and folder browser.

fingerprint lock   Type of biometric device that enables a user to unlock a mobile device using a fingerprint.

firewall   Device that restricts traffic between a local network and the Internet.

FireWire (IEEE 1394)   Interconnection standard to send wide-band signals over a serialized, physically thin connector system. Serial bus developed by Apple and Texas Instruments; enables connection of 63 devices at speeds up to 800 Mbps. Mostly supplanted by Thunderbolt.

firmware   Embedded programs or code stored on a ROM chip. Generally OS-independent, thus allowing devices to operate in a wide variety of circumstances without direct OS support. The system BIOS is firmware.

firmware update   Process by which the BIOS of a motherboard can be updated to reflect patched bugs and added features. Performed, usually, through CMOS, though some motherboard manufacturers provide a Windows program for performing a firmware update.

fitness monitors   Devices that encourage physical fitness by counting steps using accelerometers, registering heart rate through sensors, using GPS to track exercise, and offering vibration tools to remind the user to get moving. Fitness trackers fit into one of two type: fobs that clip to the body and more sophisticated fitness bands and watches.

flash ROM   ROM technology that can be electrically reprogrammed while still in the PC. Overwhelmingly the most common storage medium of BIOS in computers today, as it can be upgraded without a need to open the computer on most systems.

flatbed scanner   Most popular form of consumer scanner; runs a bright light along the length of the tray to capture an image.

FlexATX   Motherboard form factor. Motherboards built in accordance with the FlexATX form factor are very small (much smaller than microATX motherboards).

folder permission   Specifies what degree of access the system should grant a user or group to a particular folder.

force stop   Terminate an Android app and all associated background processes. More extreme than simply closing the app, which may leave background processes running.

form factor   Standard for the physical organization of motherboard components and motherboard size. Most common form factors are ATX, microATX, and Mini-ITX.

format   Command-line tool used to format a storage device.

formatting   The process of preparing a partition to store files by creating a file system to organize the blocks and creating a root directory.

FPU (floating point unit)   Formal term for math coprocessor (also called a numeric processor) circuitry inside a CPU. A math coprocessor calculates by using a floating point numerical system (which allows for decimals). Before the Intel 80486, FPUs were separate chips from the CPU.

fragmentation   Occurs when files and directories get jumbled on a fixed disk and are no longer contiguous. Can significantly slow down hard drive access times and can be repaired by using the defrag utility included with each version of Windows. *See also* defragmentation.

frame   A data unit transferred across a network. Frames consist of several parts, such as the sending and receiving MAC addresses, the data being sent, and the frame check sequence.

freeware   Software that is distributed for free, with no license fee.

frequency   Measure of a sound's tone, either high or low.

frontside bus   On older PC architectures, the wires that connect the CPU to its external memory controller.

front-view projector   Shoots the image out the front and counts on you to put a screen in front at the proper distance.

FRU (field replaceable unit)   Any part of a PC that is considered to be replaceable "in the field," i.e., a customer location. There is no official list of FRUs—it is usually a matter of policy by the repair center.

fsck   Linux command-line tool that checks for hard drive errors.

FTP (File Transfer Protocol)   Rules that enable two computers to talk to one another during a file transfer. Protocol used when you transfer a file from one computer to another across the Internet. FTP uses port numbers 20 and 21.

F-type connector   Common coax connector secured with a screw connector.

full device encryption   Enhances mobile device security by encrypting the device's internal storage.

full format   Format process that tests every sector to mark out the unusable ones in the file allocation table (FAT). *See* formatting.

full-duplex   Any device that can send and receive data simultaneously.

Full-Speed USB   USB standard that runs at 12 Mbps. Also known as *USB 1.1.*

fully qualified domain name (FQDN)   A complete, bottom-to-top label of a DNS host going from the specific host to the top-level domain that holds it and all of the intervening domain layers, each layer being separated by a dot. FQDNs are entered into browser bars and other utilities in formats like *mail.totalseminars.com.*

Function (FN) key   Special key on many laptops that enables some keys to perform a third duty.

fuser assembly   Mechanism in laser printers that uses two rollers to fuse toner to paper during the print process.

gain   Ratio of increase of radio frequency output provided by an antenna, measured in decibels (dB).

game controller   An input device specifically designed for playing computer games. Typically has an array of buttons and triggers that control movement and actions on screen.

gamepad   A type of game controller that usually consists of one or more thumbsticks, a directional pad, multiple face buttons, and two or more triggers.

gaming laptop   Variant of the desktop-replacement laptop designed to play resource-hungry games on the go, often at a high price.

gaming PC   A powerful desktop system designed to play the latest resource-hungry games using high-performance processors, RAM, and graphics cards. Typical peripherals are fast, high-quality monitors, rich sound systems, and input devices such as mice and keyboards tailored to high-performance gaming.

GDDR5   Fifth generation of graphical DDR RAM found on high-performance video cards.

GDI (graphical device interface)   Component of Windows that utilizes the CPU rather than the printer to process a print job as a bitmapped image of each page.

gearbox   Separate units or packages, also called gear packs, that combine multiple gears for performing mechanical functions in a printer. Most laser printers have two or three gearboxes that can be replaced individually if one fails.

General Data Protection Regulation (GDPR)   European Union law that defines a broad set of rights and protections of personal information for citizens of the EU.

general protection fault (GPF)   Error code usually seen when separate active programs conflict on resources or data. Can cause an application to crash.

geofencing   Using mobile device features to detect when the device enters or exits a defined area.

geotracking   Feature in cellular phones that enables the cell phone companies and government agencies to use the ID or MAC address to pinpoint where a phone is at any given time.

gestures   Specific motions the user performs on a touchscreen, such as pinching or swiping, that have a special meaning to the app being used.

getting answers   *See* eliciting answers.

giga   Prefix for the quantity 1,073,741,824 (2^{30}) or for 1 billion. One gigabyte would be 1,073,741,824 bytes, except with hard drive labeling, where it means 1 billion bytes. One gigahertz is 1 billion hertz.

Global Positioning System (GPS)   Technology that enables a mobile device to determine where you are on a map.

global user account   Login information and associated settings maintained at a location accessible by any computer, irrespective of location or local account configuration.

globally unique identifier (GUID) partition table (GPT)   Partitioning scheme that enables you to create more than four primary partitions without needing to use dynamic disks.

Google Play   Google's app and media store for Android devices.

gpresult   Windows command for listing group policies applied to a user.

GPU (graphics processing unit)   Specialized processor that helps the CPU by taking over all of the 3-D rendering duties.

gpupdate   Windows command for making immediate group policy changes in an individual system.

graphics workstation   A computer workstation for graphics design that requires a fast, multicore CPU, maximum RAM, and serious storage space to work with massive graphics files. It also needs a high-quality graphics card and monitor.

grayscale depth   Number that defines how many shades of gray the scanner can save per dot.

grep   Linux command to search through text files or command outputs to find specific information or to filter out unneeded information.

group   Collection of user accounts that share the same access capabilities.

group policy   Means of easily controlling the settings of multiple network clients with policies such as setting minimum password length or preventing Registry edits.

GSM (Global System for Mobile Communications)   Wireless data standard for mobile devices.

guest   An operating system running inside a virtual machine.

guest account   Very limited built-in account type for Windows; a member of the Guests group.

Guests group   User group that enables someone without an account to use a system. *See* group.

GUI (graphical user interface)   Interface that enables user to interact with computer graphically, by using a mouse or other pointing device to manipulate icons that represent programs or documents, instead of using only text as in early interfaces. Pronounced "gooey."

gyroscope   Device that can detect the position of the tablet or phone in 3-D space.

HAL (hardware abstraction layer)   Part of the Windows OS that separates system-specific device drivers from the rest of the operating system.

half-duplex   Transmission mode where a device can either send or receive, but not do both at once.

hang   Occurs when a computer or program stops responding to keyboard commands or other input; a computer or program in such a state is said to be "hung."

hang time   Number of seconds a too-often-hung computer is airborne after you have thrown it out a second-story window.

hard drive   *See* HDD.

hard reset   For mobile devices, another term for a factory reset. Don't confuse this with a hard reboot. *See* factory reset.

hardware   Physical computer equipment such as electrical, electronic, magnetic, and mechanical devices. Anything in the computer world that you can hold in your hand. A hard drive is hardware; Microsoft Word is not.

hardware firewall   Firewall implemented within networking hardware such as a router. *See* firewall.

hardware protocol   Defines many aspects of a network, from the packet type to the cabling and connectors used.

hardware token   Dedicated device that contains information used as an authentication factor when logging on to a secure site.

hardware virtualization support   Processor features that speed up and simplify virtualization. Required for some hypervisors to function.

hash   A special value computed from some other value using an irreversible computation. Has many uses in computing, and plays a key role in modern authentication systems.

Instead of saving user passwords directly in a database (which would make them a huge target for attackers), well-designed authentication systems compute and save only a (salted) hash of each password. When the user attempts to log in, the system hashes the provided password to see if it matches the saved hash. *See also* salted hash.

HBA (host bus adapter)   Connects SATA devices to the expansion bus. Also known as *SATA controller*.

HDBaseT   Wired video transmission system to carry uncompressed HD video over Cat 5a or Cat 6 network cables.

HDD (hard disk drive)   Data-recording system using solid disks of magnetic material turning at high speeds to store and retrieve programs and data in a computer.

HDMI (High Definition Multimedia Interface)   Single multimedia connection that includes both high-definition video and audio. Used to connect a computer to LCDs, projectors, and VR headsets.

headphones   Audio output device that sits on top of or in a user's ears.

heat dope   *See* thermal compound.

heat sink   A specially designed hunk of metal such as aluminum or copper that conducts heat away from a CPU or other heat-producing component and out into fins that transfer the heat to circulating air. When used to cool a CPU, a heat sink is typically paired with a fan assembly to improve its performance.

heating element   Printing component of direct thermal printers. Burns dots into the surface of heat-sensitive thermal paper.

hex (hexadecimal)   Base-16 numbering system using ten digits (0 through 9) and six letters (A through F). In the computer world, shorthand way to write binary numbers by substituting one hex digit for a four-digit binary number (e.g., hex 9 = binary 1001).

hibernate   Power management setting in which all data from RAM is written to the hard drive before the system goes into sleep mode. Upon waking up, all information is retrieved from the hard drive and returned to RAM. Also called *suspend to disk*.

hidden attribute   File attribute that, when used, does not allow the dir command to show a file.

hierarchical directory tree   Method by which Windows organizes files into a series of folders, called directories, under the root directory. *See also* root directory.

Hierarchical File System Plus (HFS+)   Classic file system used by older Macs. Still required for Time Machine drives. Replaced in new Macs and existing compatible systems with Apple File System (AFS).

High Dynamic Range (HDR)   Video technology that increases the bandwidth of display colors and light intensity above standard dynamic range.

high gloss   Laptop screen finish that offers sharper contrast, richer colors, and wider viewing angles than a matte finish, but is also much more reflective.

high-level formatting   Format that sets up a file system on a drive.

Hi-Speed USB   USB standard that runs at 480 Mbps. Also referred to as USB 2.0.

home screen   The default "desktop" of a mobile device.

home server PC   A computer built to store files on a small office/home office (SOHO) network.

HomeGroup   A Windows feature that connects a group of computers using a common password—no special user names required. Each computer can be a member of only one homegroup at a time. Homegroups enable simple sharing of documents and printers between computers. Homegroups are available in Windows 7, 8, 8.1, and 10.

honesty   Telling the truth—a very important thing for a tech to do.

horizontal cabling   Cabling that connects the equipment room to the work areas.

host (networking)   On a TCP/IP network, a single device that has an IP address—any device (usually a computer) that can be the source or destination of a data packet. In the mainframe world, computer that is made available for use by multiple people simultaneously. Also, in virtualization, a computer running one or more virtual operating systems.

host (virtualization)   The system running (or hosting) a virtual machine.

host ID   The address of a TCP/IP device such as a computer, printer, camera, or other device.

hostname   Windows command for displaying the name of a computer.

hotspot   *See* mobile hotspot.

hot-swappable   Any hardware that may be attached to or removed from a PC without interrupting the PC's normal processing.

hot-swapping   Replacing a bad drive in a RAID array without needing to reboot or power down.

HTML (Hypertext Markup Language)   ASCII-based, script-like language for creating hypertext documents such as those on the World Wide Web.

HTPC   A home theater PC designed to attach to a TV or projector for movie and TV viewing.

HTTP (Hypertext Transfer Protocol)   Extremely fast protocol used for network file transfers in the WWW environment. Uses port 80.

HTTPS (HTTP over Secure Sockets Layer)   Secure form of HTTP used commonly for Internet business transactions or any time when a secure connection is required. Uses port 443. *See also* HTTP.

hub   Electronic device that sits at the center of a star bus topology network, providing a common point for the connection of network devices. Hubs repeat all information out to all ports and have been replaced by switches, although the term "hub" is still commonly used.

hybrid (networking)   A network topology that combines features from multiple other topologies, such as the star bus topology.

hybrid (portable device)   Portable devices that stuff portable-computer power in mobile device–style form factors, such as a tablet.

hybrid cloud   A combination of cloud resources from more than one other cloud type, such as community, private, or public.

hybrid hard drive (HHD)   Storage drive that combines the flash memory used in solid-state drives with the spinning platters used in magnetic hard drives; a compromise between the speed and power efficiency of SSDs and the capacity of HDDs.

Hyper-Threading   Intel CPU feature (generically called *simultaneous multithreading*) that enables a CPU to run more than one thread at once.

hypervisor   Software that enables a single computer to run multiple operating systems simultaneously.

I/O (input/output)   General term for reading and writing data to a computer. "Input" includes data entered from a keyboard, identified by a pointing device (such as a mouse), or loaded from a disk. "Output" includes writing information to a disk, viewing it on a monitor, or printing it to a printer.

IaaS (Infrastructure as a Service)   Cloud-hosted provider of virtualized servers and networks.

iCloud   Apple cloud-based storage. iCloud enables a user to back up all iPhone or iPad data, and makes that data accessible from anywhere. This includes any media purchased through iTunes as well as calendars, contacts, reminders, and so forth.

icon   Small image or graphic, most commonly found on a system's desktop, that launches a program when selected.

ID badge   Small card or document for confirming the identity of its holder and what access they should be granted. May use built-in authentication tools such as RFID or smart card to function as a "something you have" authentication factor.

IDE (integrated drive electronics)   PC specification for small- to medium-sized hard drives in which the controlling electronics for the drive are part of the drive itself, speeding up transfer rates and leaving only a simple adapter (or "paddle"). IDE only supported two drives per system of no more than 504 MB each, and has been completely supplanted by Enhanced IDE. EIDE supports four drives of over 8 GB each and more than doubles the transfer rate. The more common name for PATA drives. Also known as *intelligent drive electronics. See* PATA.

identify the problem   To question the user and find out what has been changed recently or is no longer working properly. (Step 1 of 6 in the CompTIA troubleshooting methodology.)

IEC-320   Connects the cable supplying AC power from a wall outlet into the power supply.

IEEE (Institute of Electronic and Electrical Engineers)   Leading standards-setting group in the United States.

IEEE 1394   IEEE standard governing FireWire communication. *See also* FireWire.

IEEE 1394a   FireWire standard that runs at 400 Mbps.

IEEE 1394b   FireWire standard that runs at 800 Mbps.

IEEE 802.11   Wireless Ethernet standard more commonly known as Wi-Fi.

ifconfig   Linux command for finding out a computer's IP address information.

image deployment   Operating system installation that uses a complete image of a hard drive as an installation media. Helpful when installing an operating system on a large number of identical PCs.

image file   Bit-by-bit image of data to be burned on CD or DVD—from one file to an entire disc—stored as a single file on a hard drive. Particularly handy when copying from CD to CD or DVD to DVD.

image-level backup   Backing up a complete volume including any OS, boot files, applications, and data it contains.

imaging drum   Aluminum cylinder in a laser printer that is coated with particles of photosensitive compounds. When light hits these particles, whatever electrical charge they may have "drains" out through the grounded cylinder. After the particles are selectively charged by the laser, they attract the toner particles, forming the image that will be transferred. Often built into the toner cartridge. Also known as *photosensitive drum*.

imaging process   Seven-step process in laser printing. While it can vary by printer, the steps are typically: processing, charging, exposing, developing, transferring, fusing, and cleaning.

IMAP4 (Internet Message Access Protocol version 4)   An alternative to POP3 that retrieves e-mail from an e-mail server; IMAP uses TCP port 143.

IMC (integrated memory controller)   Memory controller circuitry built into the CPU that enables faster control over things like the large L3 cache shared among multiple cores.

IMEI (International Mobile Equipment Identity) A 15-digit number used to uniquely identify a mobile device, typically a smartphone or other device that connects to a cellular network.

impact printer Uses pins and inked ribbons to print text or images on a piece of paper. Impact printers can make use of a few special types of paper. Tractor-feed paper has holes so that printers with sprockets can continuously print massive stacks of the stuff. Special multi-part impact paper can be used to print receipts in duplicate, triplicate, or more.

impedance Amount of resistance to an electrical signal on a wire. Relative measure of the amount of data a cable can handle.

impersonation Backing up a complete volume including any OS, boot files, applications, and data it contains.

IMSI (International Mobile Subscriber Identity) A unique number that represents the actual user associated with a particular SIM card. The IMSI is usually available from the carrier, to ensure that stolen phones are not misused. The IMSI number can be used to unlock a phone as well.

incident report Record of the details of an accident, including what happened and where it happened.

incident reporting Process of reporting gathered data about a system or problem to supervisors. Creates a record of work accomplished, and may help identify patterns. Often documented on an incident report form.

incident response leader In some organizations, a person other than a supervisor responsible for receiving and responding to all incident reports.

information technology (IT) Field of computers, their operation, and their maintenance.

infrastructure mode Wireless networking mode that uses one or more WAPs to connect the wireless network nodes to a wired network segment.

inheritance NTFS feature that passes on the same permissions in any subfolders/files resident in the original folder.

ink cartridge Small container of ink for inkjet printers.

inkjet printer Uses liquid ink, sprayed through a series of tiny jets, to print text or images on a piece of paper (which is typically fed into the printer from a paper tray under the printer, or an angled feeder on the back of the printer).

in-place upgrade *See* upgrade installation.

input *See* I/O.

insert mode One of two modes (along with command mode) used in vi. Enables typing input to the document. *See* vi.

installation media   A disc (typically a CD-ROM or DVD) or drive (such as a USB flash drive) that holds all the necessary device drivers.

instruction set   All of the machine-language commands that a particular CPU is designed to understand.

integer   A whole number. Integers and floating point numbers are handled differently in programs and by CPUs.

integrated GPU   GPU integrated with the motherboard or processor, in contrast to GPUs on separate graphics cards. This typically lowers power consumption, saves space, reduces heat, and may speed up communication with the GPU.

integrity   Always doing the right thing.

interface   Means by which a user interacts with a piece of software.

interpolation   Video capture and display technology that calculates the color value and light intensity between pixels to fill in information that is not directly captured or saved.

interrupt/interruption   Suspension of a process, such as the execution of a computer program, caused by an event external to the computer and performed in such a way that the process can be resumed. Events of this kind include sensors monitoring laboratory equipment or a user pressing an interrupt key.

intrusion detection system (IDS)   Application that inspects packets, looking for active intrusions. Functions inside the network, looking for threats a firewall might miss, such as viruses, illegal logon attempts, and other well-known attacks. May also discover threats from inside the network, such as a vulnerability scanner run by a rogue employee.

intrusion prevention system (IPS)   Application similar to an intrusion detection system (IDS), except that it sits directly in the flow of network traffic. This enables it to stop ongoing attacks itself, but may also slow down the network and be a single point of failure.

inventory management   A process for protecting devices and equipment by tagging them with barcodes or asset tags, and keeping track of these tagged devices.

inverter   Device used to convert DC current into AC. Commonly used in older laptops and flatbed scanners with CCFLs.

iOS   The operating system of Apple mobile devices such as smartphones and tablets.

IP address   Numeric address of a computer connected to the Internet. An IPv4 address is made up of four octets of 8-bit binary numbers translated into their shorthand numeric values. An IPv6 address is 128 bits long. The IP address can be broken down into a network ID and a host ID. Also called *Internet address*.

ipconfig   Command-line utility for Windows servers and workstations that displays the current TCP/IP configuration of the machine. Similar to ifconfig.

IPS (in-plane switching)   Display technology that replaces the older twisted nematic (TN) panels for more accurate colors and a wider viewing angle.

IPsec (Internet Protocol security)   Microsoft's encryption method of choice for networks consisting of multiple networks linked by a private connection, providing transparent encryption between the server and the client.

IPv4 (Internet Protocol version 4)   Internet standard protocol that provides a common layer over dissimilar networks; used to move packets among host computers and through gateways if necessary. Part of the TCP/IP protocol suite. Uses the dotted-decimal format—*x.x.x.x*. Each *x* represents an 8-bit binary number, or 0–255. Here's an example: 192.168.4.1.

IPv6 (Internet Protocol version 6)   Protocol in which addresses consist of eight sets of four hexadecimal numbers, each number being a value between 0000 and ffff, using a colon to separate the numbers. Here's an example: fedc:ba98:7654:3210:0800:200c:0 0cf:1234.

IrDA (Infrared Data Association) protocol   Protocol that enables communication through infrared devices, with speeds of up to 4 Mbps.

IRQ (interrupt request)   Signal from a hardware device, such as a modem or a mouse, indicating that it needs the CPU's attention. In PCs, IRQs are sent along specific IRQ channels associated with a particular device. IRQ conflicts were a common problem in the past when adding expansion boards, but the plug-and-play specification has removed this headache in most cases.

ISA (Industry Standard Architecture)   Design found in the original IBM PC for the slots that allowed additional hardware to be connected to the computer's motherboard. An 8-bit, 8.33-MHz expansion bus was designed by IBM for its AT computer and released to the public domain. An improved 16-bit bus was also released to the public domain. Replaced by PCI in the mid-1990s.

ISDN (integrated services digital network)   The process of sending telephone transmission across fully digital lines end-to-end, replacing the analog telephone system. ISDN is superior to POTS telephone lines because it supports a transfer rate of up to 128 Kbps for sending information from computer to computer. It also allows data and voice to share a common phone line. DSL reduced demand for ISDN substantially.

ISO file   Complete copy (or image) of a storage media device, typically used for optical discs. ISO image files typically have a file extension of .iso.

ISO-9660   CD format to support PC file systems on CD media, often referred to by the more generic term CD File System (CDFS).

ISP (Internet service provider)   Company that provides access to the Internet, usually for money.

ITX   A family of motherboard form factors. Mini-ITX is the largest and the most popular of the ITX form factors but is still quite small.

iwconfig   Linux command for viewing and changing wireless settings.

jack (physical connection)   Part of a connector into which a plug is inserted. Also referred to as a port.

jailbreaking   Process for circumventing the security restrictions present on an iOS device.

joule   Unit of energy describing (in this book) how much energy a surge suppressor can handle before it fails.

joystick   A type of game controller. Commonly used for flight-simulator games.

jumper   Pair of small pins that can be shorted with a shunt to configure many aspects of PCs. Often used in configurations that are rarely changed, such as master/slave settings on IDE drives.

Keep my files   Windows Recovery Environment option in Windows 10 that rebuilds the OS, but preserves user files, settings, and Microsoft Store applications (while deleting all other applications on the system).

Kerberos   Authentication encryption developed by MIT to enable multiple brands of servers to authenticate multiple brands of clients.

kernel   Core portion of program that resides in memory and performs the most essential operating system tasks.

kernel panic   The Linux equivalent of a Blue Screen of Death (BSoD). An error from which the OS can't recover without a reboot. *See* BSoD.

key fob   Generically, just about anything attached to a key ring that isn't a key. Some security tools, such as hardware security tokens and RFID authentication devices, are commonly designed as key fobs.

keyboard   Input device. Three common types of keyboards exist: those that use a mini-DIN (PS/2) connection, those that use a USB connection, and those that use wireless technology.

Keychain   macOS password management and storage service that saves passwords for computer and non-computer environments. Also, the *iCloud Keychain* adds synchronization among any macOS and iOS devices connected to the Internet for a user account.

keylogger   Software, usually malware, that copies, saves, and sometimes uploads all keystrokes and other inputs on a computer. Keyloggers are used gather information such as passwords, sites visited, and other activities performed on a computer.

Knowledge Base   Large collection of documents and FAQs that is maintained by Microsoft. Found on Microsoft's Web site, the Knowledge Base is an excellent place to search for assistance on most operating system problems.

kill   In UNIX shells (such as Bash) and in PowerShell, this command terminates the indicated process.

KVM (keyboard, video, mouse) switch   Hardware device that enables multiple computers to be viewed and controlled by a single mouse, keyboard, and screen.

lamp   Light source in a projector.

LAN (local area network)   Group of computers connected via cabling, radio, or infrared that use this connectivity to share resources such as printers and mass storage.

laptop   Traditional clamshell portable computing device with built-in LCD monitor, keyboard, and trackpad.

laser   Single-wavelength, in-phase light source that is sometimes strapped to the head of sharks by bad guys. Note to henchmen: Lasers should never be used with sea bass, no matter how ill-tempered they might be.

laser printer   Electro-photographic printer in which a laser is used as the light source.

Last Known Good Configuration   Option on the Advanced Startup Options menu that enables your system to revert to a previous configuration to troubleshoot and repair any major system problems.

latency   Amount of delay before a device may respond to a request; most commonly used in reference to RAM.

launchd   macOS tool for automatically running tasks based on a schedule.

launcher   An Android app that serves as the device's desktop, often with more extensive customization features than launchers provided by Google or the device maker.

LBA (logical block addressing)   Addressing scheme that presents storage chunks on a storage device to the OS as a sequence of blocks beginning with LBA0. This saves the OS from having to deal directly with the details of how storage space is arranged on a hard drive or SSD.

LC   Type of fiber optic connector. *See* fiber optic cable.

LCD (liquid crystal display)   Type of display commonly used on portable computers. LCDs have also replaced CRTs as the display of choice for desktop computer users. LCDs use liquid crystals and electricity to produce images on the screen.

LED (light-emitting diode)   Solid-state device that vibrates at luminous frequencies when current is applied.

Level 1 (L1) cache   First RAM cache accessed by the CPU, which stores only the absolute most accessed programming and data used by currently running threads. Always the smallest and fastest cache on the CPU.

Level 2 (L2) cache   Second RAM cache accessed by the CPU. Much larger and often slower than the L1 cache, and accessed only if the requested program/data is not in the L1 cache.

Level 3 (L3) cache   Third RAM cache accessed by the CPU. Much larger and slower than the L1 and L2 caches, and accessed only if the requested program/data is not in the L2 cache.

LGA (land grid array)   Arrangement of a large number of pins extending from the CPU socket to corresponding contact points on the bottom of the CPU.

Library   Feature in Windows 7 and later that aggregates folders from multiple locations and places them in a single, easy-to-find spot in Windows Explorer or File Explorer. Default libraries in Windows include Documents, Music, Pictures, and Videos.

Lightning   An 8-pin connector, proprietary to Apple, that can be inserted without regard to orientation. Used to connect mobile devices to a power or data source.

Lightweight Directory Access Protocol (LDAP)   Protocol used by many operating systems and applications to access directories.

Li-Ion (Lithium-Ion)   Battery commonly used in portable computing devices. Li-Ion batteries don't suffer from the memory effects of Nickel-Cadmium (Ni-Cd) batteries and provide much more power for a greater length of time.

line of sight   An unobstructed view between two devices. Required for IR communications.

link light   An LED on NICs, hubs, and switches that lights up to show good connection between the devices.

link-local address   IPv6 address a computer gives itself when it first boots. IPv6's equivalent to IPv4's APIPA address.

Linux   Open-source UNIX-clone operating system.

liquid contact indicator (LCI)   Small sticker that permanently changes color after getting wet, often from white to red. Installed at various locations inside mobile and portable devices.

liquid cooling   A method of cooling a PC that works by running some liquid—usually water—through a metal block that sits on top of the CPU, absorbing heat. The liquid gets heated by the block, runs out of the block and into something that cools the liquid, and is then pumped through the block again.

lithium polymer (LiPo)   Technically, a variant of Li-Ion batteries that use a solid, polymer electrolyte. In practice, this term is commonly applied to traditional Li-Ion batteries packed in polymer bags.

local area network   *See* LAN.

Local Security Policy   Windows tool used to set local security policies on an individual system.

local user account   List of user names and their associated passwords with access to a system, contained in an encrypted database.

Local Users and Groups   Tool enabling creation and changing of group memberships and accounts for users.

location data   Information provided by a mobile device's GPS; used for mapping functions as well as for location-aware services, such as finding nearby restaurants or receiving coupons for nearby shops.

location services   Mobile device feature that can detect the device's location, enabling apps to request and use this information to provide location-aware services, such as finding nearby restaurants.

log files   Files created in Windows to track the progress of certain processes.

logical drives   Sections of an extended partition on a hard drive that are formatted and (usually) assigned a drive letter, each of which is presented to the user as if it were a separate drive.

logon screen   First screen of the Windows interface, used to log on to the computer system.

LoJack   Security feature included in some BIOS/UEFI that enables a user to track the location of a stolen PC, install a key logger, or remotely shut down the stolen computer.

Long Term Evolution (LTE)   Fourth-generation cellular network technology supporting theoretical download speeds up to 1 Gbps and upload speeds up to 100 Mbps. Marketed as and now generally accepted as a true 4G technology.

loop   Control construct used in a script or program to repeat a sequence of instructions when certain conditions are met. For example, a script could use a loop to a set of instructions for resizing an image once for every image file in a directory.

loopback plug   Device used during loopback tests to check the female connector on a NIC.

loopback test   Special test to confirm a NIC can send and receive data. A full external loopback test requires a loopback plug inserted into the NIC's port.

Low-Speed USB   USB standard that runs at 1.5 Mbps. Also called USB 1.1.

ls   UNIX equivalent of the dir command, which displays the contents of a directory.

lumens   The amount of light given off by a light source from a certain angle that is perceived by the human eye. Unit of measure for amount of brightness on a projector or other light source.

M.2   Type of space-efficient expansion slot common in recent portable computers. Formerly known as Next Generation Form Factor (NGFF). Also found on some desktop motherboards. While M.2 is a general expansion slot supporting devices such as Wi-Fi cards, it's often used to install an NVMe SSD.

Mac   Also *Macintosh*. Common name for Apple Computers' flagship operating system; runs on Intel-based hardware. CompTIA refers to the operating system as *Mac*. Apple calls the current operating system *macOS*.

MAC (mandatory access control)   Authorization method in which the system grants access to resources based on security labels and clearance levels. Less flexible than discretionary access control (DAC), which lets users assign access levels to resources they own. MAC may be used in organizations with very high security needs.

MAC (media access control) address   Unique 48-bit address assigned to each network card. IEEE assigns blocks of possible addresses to various NIC manufacturers to help ensure that the address is always unique. The Data Link layer of the OSI model uses MAC addresses to locate machines.

MAC address filtering   Method of limiting wireless network access based on the physical, hard-wired address of the wireless NIC of a computing device.

machine language   Binary instruction code that is understood by the CPU.

macOS   Operating system from Apple that powers their desktop and portable computers. Based on UNIX; macOS runs on Intel/IBM-based hardware, just like Microsoft Windows. Before 2016, it was known as OS X. *See also* Mac *and* OS X.

magnetic hard drives   Storage devices that read and write data encoded magnetically onto spinning aluminum platters.

mail server   Networked host or server that provides e-mail service.

maintenance   Periodic jobs that should be done to keep an operating system running well.

maintenance kit   Set of commonly replaced printer components provided by many manufacturers.

malware   Broadly, software designed to use your computer or device against your wishes. Includes adware, spyware, viruses, ransomware, etc. May be part of seemingly legitimate software or installed by exploiting a vulnerability in the device.

mandatory access control   *See* MAC (mandatory access control).

man-in-the-middle (MITM)   Attacker serves as an intermediary between two systems, enabling the attacker to observe, redirect, or even alter messages passing in either direction.

mantrap   Small room with a set of doors; one to the unsecured area and one to a secured area. Only one door can open at a time, and individuals must authenticate to continue. Combats tailgating.

mass storage Hard drives, optical discs, removable media drives, etc.

matte Laptop screen finish that offers a good balance between richness of colors and reflections, but washes out in bright light.

MBR (master boot record) Tiny bit of code that takes control of the boot process from the system BIOS.

MCC (memory controller chip) Chip that handles memory requests from the CPU. Although once a special chip, it has been integrated into the chipset or CPU on modern computers.

md (mkdir) Command-line tool used to create directories.

MDM (mobile device management) A formalized structure that enables an organization to account for all the different types of devices used to process, store, transmit, and receive organizational data.

measured service Billing model cloud service providers use to charge for services in small increments based on the computing resources the customer consumes.

media access control *See* MAC (media access control) address.

mega- Prefix that stands for the binary quantity 1,048,576 (2^{20}) or the decimal quantity of 1,000,000. One megabyte is 1,048,576 bytes. One megahertz, however, is a million hertz. Sometimes shortened to *Meg*, as in "a 286 has an address space of 16 Megs."

memory Device or medium for temporary storage of programs and data during program execution. Synonymous with storage, although it most frequently refers to the internal storage of a computer that can be directly addressed by operating instructions. A computer's temporary storage capacity is measured in kilobytes (KB), megabytes (MB), or gigabytes (GB) of RAM (random-access memory). Long-term data storage on hard drives and solid-state drives is also measured in megabytes, gigabytes, and terabytes.

memory addressing Taking memory address from system RAM and using it to address non-system RAM or ROM so the CPU can access it.

mesh topology Network topology where each computer has a dedicated line to every other computer, most often used in wireless networks.

metered service Fee charged by cloud service providers on the basis of how much of a resource was used. Fees may be based on things like access time, bandwidth used, bytes uploaded or downloaded, CPU usage, and other resource usage metrics.

Metro UI The original name for the Windows 8 user interface. Due to legal concerns, it was rebranded the "Modern UI."

MFA (multifactor authentication) Authentication schema requiring more than one unique authentication factor. The factors are knowledge, possession, inherence, location, and temporal. For example, a password (knowledge factor) and a fingerprint (inherence factor) is a basic form of multifactor authentication.

MFD (multifunction device)   Single device that consolidates functions from more than one document-handling device, such as a printer, copier, scanner, or fax machine.

MFT (master file table)   Enhanced file allocation table used by NTFS. *See also* FAT.

micro Secure Digital (microSD)   The smallest form factor of the SD flash memory standard. Often used in mobile devices.

microATX (μATX)   Variation of the ATX form factor, which uses the ATX power supply. MicroATX motherboards are generally smaller than their ATX counterparts but retain all the same functionality.

microphone   An input device for recording audio.

microprocessor   "Brain" of a computer. Primary computer chip that determines relative speed and capabilities of the computer. Also called the central processing unit (CPU).

micro-USB   USB connector commonly found on a variety of devices including Android phones. Slowly being replaced by USB Type-C connectors (especially in Android phones).

MIDI (Musical Instrument Digital Interface)   Interface between a computer and a device for simulating musical instruments. Rather than sending large sound samples, a computer can simply send "instructions" to the instrument describing pitch, tone, and duration of a sound. MIDI files are therefore very efficient. Because a MIDI file is made up of a set of instructions rather than a copy of the sound, modifying each component of the file is easy. Additionally, it is possible to program many channels, or "voices," of music to be played simultaneously, creating symphonic sound.

MIDI-enabled device   External device that enables you to input digital sound information in the MIDI format; for example, a MIDI keyboard (the piano kind).

migration   Moving users from one operating system or hard drive to another.

MIMO (multiple in/multiple out)   Feature of 802.11n devices that enables the simultaneous connection of up to four antennas, greatly increasing throughput. 802.11ac also uses MU-MIMO, which gives a WAP the capability to broadcast to multiple users simultaneously.

mini connector   One type of power connector from a PC power supply unit. Supplies 5 and 12 volts to peripherals.

mini Secure Digital (miniSD)   The medium-sized form factor of the SD flash memory standard. *See also* Secure Digital.

mini-DIN   Small connection most commonly used for keyboards and mice. Many modern systems implement USB in place of mini-DIN connections. Also called *PS/2*.

Mini-ITX   The largest and the most popular of the three ITX form factors. At a miniscule 6.7 by 6.7 inches, Mini-ITX competes with microATX and proprietary small form factor (SFF) motherboards.

Mini-PCI Specialized form of PCI designed for use in laptops.

Mini-PCIe Specialized form of PCIe designed for use in laptops.

mini-USB Smaller USB connector often found on digital cameras.

mirror set A type of mirrored volume created with RAID 1. *See also* mirroring.

mirror space Storage Space that mirrors files across two or more drives, like RAID 1 or RAID 10. *See* Storage Spaces.

mirrored volume Volume that is mirrored on another volume. *See also* mirroring.

mirroring Reading and writing data at the same time to two drives for fault tolerance purposes. Considered RAID level 1. Also called *drive mirroring*.

Mission Control A feature of macOS that enables switching between open applications, windows, and more.

mkdir *See* md.

MMC (Microsoft Management Console) A shell program in Windows that holds individual utilities called snap-ins, designed for administration and troubleshooting. The MMC enables an administrator to customize management tools by picking and choosing from a list of snap-ins. Available snap-ins include Device Manager, Local Users and Groups, and Computer Management.

mobile device Small, highly portable computing devices with tightly integrated components designed to be worn or carried by the user. Includes smartphones, tablets, and wearable devices.

mobile device management (MDM) policies Technical controls that govern how mobile devices are used as tools in the workplace. *See* MDM.

mobile hotspot A mobile device that broadcasts a small Wi-Fi network to share its mobile data network connection with nearby Wi-Fi devices. Often these are standalone devices, though many cellular phones and data-connected tablets can be set up to act as hotspots.

mobile payment service Smartphone feature that can use a connected bank account to automatically transfer payments to merchants. May work in conjunction with Near Field Communication (NFC).

modem (modulator/demodulator) Device that converts a digital bit stream into an analog signal (modulation) and converts incoming analog signals back into digital signals (demodulation). An analog communications channel is typically a telephone line, and analog signals are typically sounds.

module Small circuit board that DRAM chips are attached to. Also known as *stick*.

Molex connector Computer power connector used by optical drives, hard drives, and case fans. Keyed to prevent it from being inserted into a power port improperly.

monaural   Describes recording tracks from one source (microphone) as opposed to stereo, which uses two sources.

monitor   Screen that displays data from a PC. Typically a flat-panel display, such as an LCD.

motherboard   Flat piece of circuit board that resides inside your computer case and has a number of connectors on it. Every device in a PC connects directly or indirectly to the motherboard, including CPU, RAM, hard drives, optical drives, keyboard, mouse, and video cards.

motherboard book   Valuable resource when installing a new motherboard. Normally lists all the specifications about a motherboard, including the type of memory and type of CPU usable with the motherboard.

mount point   Drive that functions like a folder mounted into another drive.

mouse   Input device that enables users to manipulate a cursor on the screen to select items.

move   Command-line tool used to move a file from one location to another.

MP3   Short for MPEG Audio Layer 3, a type of compression used specifically for turning high-quality digital audio files into much smaller, yet similar-sounding, files.

MPEG-2   Moving Pictures Experts Group standard of video and audio compression offering resolutions up to 1280 × 720 at 60 frames per second.

MPEG-4   Moving Pictures Experts Group standard of video and audio compression offering improved compression over MPEG-2.

mSATA   Standardized smaller SATA form factor for use in portable devices.

msconfig (System Configuration utility)   Executable file that runs the Windows System Configuration utility, which enables users to configure a Windows 7 system's boot files and critical system files. Often used for the name of the utility, as in "just run msconfig." This functionality moved to Task Manager in Windows 8.

MSDS (Material Safety Data Sheet)   Standardized form that provides detailed information about potential environmental hazards and proper disposal methods associated with various computing components.

msinfo32 (System Information tool)   Provides information about hardware resources, components, and the software environment. Also known as System Information.

multiboot installation   OS installation in which multiple operating systems are installed on a single machine.

multicore processing   Using two or more execution cores on one CPU die to divide up work independently of the OS.

multifactor authentication   *See* MFA.

multifunction device (MFD)   *See* MFD.

multimeter   Device used to measure voltage, amperage, and resistance.

multimode   Type of fiber optic cabling capable of transmitting multiple light signals at the same time using different reflection angles within the cable core. Signals tend to degrade over distance, limiting multimode cable to short distances. *See* fiber optic cable.

multiple Desktops   A GUI feature that enables a computer to have more than one Desktop, each with its own icons and background. macOS supports multiple Desktops with Spaces. Most Linux distros use multiple Desktops, often called workspaces. Microsoft introduced the feature with Windows 10.

multi-rail   A power supply configuration; the current is split into multiple pathways, each with a maximum capacity and its own over-current protection (OCP) circuitry.

multitasking   Process of running multiple programs or tasks on the same computer at the same time.

multitouch   Input method on many smartphones and tablets that enables you to perform gestures (actions with multiple fingers) to do all sorts of fun things, such as using two fingers to scroll or swipe to another screen or desktop.

Multiuser MIMO (MU-MIMO)   New version of MIMO included in 802.11ac that enables a WAP to broadcast to multiple users simultaneously.

music CD-R   CD using a special format for home recorders. Music CD-R makers pay a small royalty to avoid illegal music duplication.

mv   The move command in Linux and macOS.

NAT (Network Address Translation)   A means of translating a system's IP address into another IP address before sending it out to a larger network. NAT manifests itself by a NAT program that runs on a system or a router. A network using NAT provides the systems on the network with private IP addresses. The system running the NAT software has two interfaces: one connected to the network and the other connected to the larger network.

   The NAT program takes packets from the client systems bound for the larger network and translates their internal private IP addresses to its own public IP address, enabling many systems to share a single IP address.

native command queuing (NCQ)   Disk-optimization feature for SATA drives enabling faster read and write speeds.

native resolution   Resolution on an LCD monitor that matches the physical pixels on the screen.

navigation pane   Windows 7's name for the Folders list in Windows Explorer.

nbtstat   Old command-line utility predating Windows. Provides information on NetBIOS. While not as useful as it once was, it can still help troubleshoot small workgroups.

net   Command-line utility in Windows that enables users to view and change a whole *host* of network settings and information.

net use   This subcommand of the Windows net command enables a user to connect, disconnect, and view information about existing connections to network resources.

net user   This subcommand of the Windows net command enables a user to create, delete, and change user accounts.

NetBIOS (Network Basic Input/Output System)   Protocol that operates at the Session layer of the OSI seven-layer model. This protocol creates and manages connections based on the names of the computers involved. Uses TCP ports 137 and 139, and UDP ports 137 and 138.

NetBoot   Tool that makes it easy to install, upgrade, and manage macOS on many remote systems at once, over a network.

netstat   Command-line tool in Windows and Linux to identify inbound and outbound TCP/IP connections with the host.

network   Collection of two or more computers interconnected by telephone lines, coaxial cables, satellite links, radio, and/or some other communication technique. Group of computers that are connected and that communicate with one another for a common purpose.

Network   Interface in File Explorer or Windows Explorer; displays networked computers and other devices, such as network printers.

network attached storage (NAS)   A device that attaches to a network for the sole purpose of storing and sharing files.

network connection   A method for connecting two or more computers together. *See also* network.

network documentation   A road map to an organization's network configuration and topology for techs who need to change or repair the network.

Network File System (NFS)   Network file and print sharing protocol for UNIX and Linux systems that competed with Server Message Block (SMB). Usage has declined as SMB won out.

network ID   Logical number that identifies the network on which a device or machine exists. This number exists in TCP/IP and other network protocol suites.

network printer   Printer that connects directly to a network.

network protocol   Software that takes the incoming data received by the network card, keeps it organized, sends it to the application that needs it, and then takes outgoing data from the application and hands it to the NIC to be sent out over the network.

network technology   A practical application of a topology and other critical standards to provide a method to get data from one computer to another on a network. It defines many aspects of a network, from the topology, to the frame type, to the cabling and connectors used.

network topology diagram   A map of how everything in an organization's network (including switches, routers, WAPs, services, and workstations) connects. May indicate connection types, speed, technologies, and so on.

Networking   Task Manager tab in Windows 7 (merged into the Performance tab in Windows 8), which shows activity on current network connections.

NFC (Near Field Communication)   Mobile technology that enables short-range wireless communication between mobile devices. Now used for mobile payment technology such as Apple Pay and Google Pay.

NIC (network interface card or controller)   Expansion card or motherboard interface that enables a PC to connect to a network via a network cable. A *wireless NIC* enables connection via radio waves rather than a physical cable.

Ni-Cd (Nickel-Cadmium)   Battery used in the first portable PCs. Heavy and inefficient, these batteries also suffered from a memory effect that could drastically shorten the overall life of the battery. *See also* Ni-MH *and* Li-Ion.

Ni-MH (Nickel-Metal Hydride)   Battery used in early portable PCs. Ni-MH batteries had fewer issues with the memory effect than Ni-Cd batteries. Ni-MH batteries in computing devices have been replaced by Lithium-Ion batteries. *See also* Ni-Cd *and* Li-Ion.

nit   Value used to measure the brightness of an LCD display. A typical LCD display has a brightness of between 100 and 400 nits.

NLQ (near-letter quality)   Designation for dot-matrix printers that use 24-pin printheads.

NLX   Second form factor for slimline systems. Replaced the earlier LPX form factor. (CompTIA lists NLX as New Low-profile Extended.)

NMI (non-maskable interrupt)   Interrupt code sent to the processor that cannot be ignored. Typically manifested as a BSoD in Windows.

nonvolatile   Describes storage that retains data even if power is removed; typically refers to a ROM or flash ROM chip, but also could be applied to hard drives, optical media, and other storage devices.

northbridge   In older chipsets, a chip that connects a CPU to memory, the PCI bus, Level 2 cache, and high-speed graphics. Communicates with the CPU through the frontside bus. Newer CPUs feature an integrated northbridge.

notebook   *See* laptop.

notification area   Contains icons representing background processes, the system clock, and volume control. Located by default at the right edge of the Windows taskbar. Many users call this area the system tray.

nslookup   Command-line program in Windows used to determine exactly what information the DNS server is providing about a specific host name.

NTFS (New Technology File System)   Robust and secure file system introduced by Microsoft with Windows NT. NTFS provides an amazing array of configuration options for user access and security. Users can be granted access to data on a file-by-file basis. NTFS enables object-level security, long filename support, compression, and encryption.

NTFS permissions   Restrictions that determine the amount of access given to a particular user on a system using NTFS.

NVIDIA Corporation   One of the foremost manufacturers of graphics cards and chipsets.

NVMe (Non-Volatile Memory Express)   SSD technology that supports a communication connection between the operating system and the SSD directly through a PCIe bus lane, reducing latency and taking full advantage of the speeds of high-end SSDs. NVMe SSDs come in a few formats, such as an add-on expansion card, though most commonly in M.2 format. NVMe drives are a lot more expensive currently than other SSDs, but offer much higher speeds. NVMe drives use SATAe.

NX bit   Technology that enables the CPU to protect certain sections of memory. This feature, coupled with implementation by the operating system, stops malicious attacks from getting to essential operating system files. Microsoft calls the feature Data Execution Prevention (DEP), turned on by default in every OS.

object   System component that is given a set of characteristics and can be managed by the operating system as a single entity.

object access auditing   Feature of Event Viewer's Security section that creates an entry in the Security Log when certain objects are accessed, such as a file or folder.

ODBC Data Source Administrator   Windows programming tool for configuring the Open Database Connectivity (ODBC) coding standard. Data Source Administrator enables you to create and manage entries called Data Source Names (DSNs) that point ODBC to a database. DSNs are used by ODBC-aware applications to query ODBC to find their databases.

offline files   Windows feature that enables storing a local, duplicate copy of files and folders on a hard drive. When the laptop connects to a network, Windows automatically syncs those offline files with the files and folders on a file server or other PC.

ohm(s)   Electronic measurement of a cable's impedance.

OLED (organic light-emitting diode)   Display technology where an organic compound provides the light for the screen, thus eliminating the need for a backlight or inverter. Used in high-end TVs and small devices such as smart watches, smartphones, and VR headsets.

on-demand   Self-service characteristic of cloud computing. Describes the customer's ability to set up, modify, and delete cloud resources (such as servers, storage, or databases) as needed.

open source   Describes a product for which the plans, schematics, recipes, or other information used to create it are released by its creator or distributor. Most commonly applied to software.

open source software   Software for which the source code is published instead of kept secret. Typically released under an open source license that specifies terms for those who wish to use the software or modify its source.

OpenGL   One of two popular APIs used today for video cards. Originally written for UNIX systems but now ported to Windows and Apple systems. *See also* DirectX.

optical disc/media   Types of data discs (such as DVDs, CDs, BDs, etc.) that are read by a laser.

optical drive   Drive used to read/write to optical discs, such as CDs or DVDs.

optical mouse   Pointing device that uses light rather than electronic sensors to determine movement and direction the mouse is being moved.

optical resolution   Resolution a scanner can achieve mechanically. Most scanners use software to enhance this ability.

optimization   Changes made to a system to improve its performance.

option ROM   Alternative way of telling the system how to talk to a piece of hardware. Option ROM stores BIOS for the card in a chip on the card itself.

OS (operating system)   Series of programs and code that creates an interface so users can interact with a system's hardware; for example, Windows, macOS, and Linux.

OS X   Operating system on older Apple Macintosh computers. Based on a UNIX core, early versions of OS X ran on Motorola-based hardware; later versions ran on Intel-based hardware. The X is pronounced "ten" rather than "ex." Renamed *macOS* in 2016.

output   *See* I/O.

overclocking   To run a CPU or video processor faster than its rated speed.

overloaded network   A network that, often due to a large public event, emergency, or network equipment failure, is unable to keep up with user demand. Users may have good signal quality but be unable to access data, text, or voice services.

owner   In both NTFS and UNIX permissions, the owner is usually the user that created a given file or folder, although both systems support changing ownership to another user.

Ownership permission   Special NTFS permissions granted to the account that owns a file or folder. Owners can do anything they want to the files and folders they own, including changing their permissions.

P1 power connector   Provides power to ATX motherboards; 20-pin with original ATX motherboards, 24-pin on current units.

P4 power connector   Provides additional 12-volt power to assist the 20/24-pin P1 motherboard power connector.

PaaS (Platform as a Service)   Cloud-based virtual server(s) combined with a platform that gives programmers tools needed to deploy, administer, and maintain a Web application.

packet   Basic component of communication over a network. Group of bits of fixed maximum size and well-defined format that is switched and transmitted as a single entity through a network. Contains source and destination addresses, data, and control information. Packets are included within (and are not the same thing as) a frame.

page fault   Minor memory-addressing error.

page file   *See* virtual memory.

PAN (personal area network)   Small wireless network created with Bluetooth technology and intended to link computers and other peripheral devices.

parallel execution   When a multicore CPU processes more than one thread.

parallel port   Connection for the synchronous flow of data along parallel lines to a device, usually a very old printer.

parity   Early method of error detection where a small group of bits being transferred is compared to a single parity bit set to make the total bits odd or even. The receiving device reads the parity bit and determines if the data is valid, based on the oddness or evenness of the parity bit.

parity RAM   Earliest form of error-detecting RAM; stored an extra bit (called the parity bit) to verify the data.

parity space   Storage Space that adds resiliency similar to RAID 5 or RAID 6. *See* Storage Spaces.

partition   Section of the storage area of a hard disk. Created during initial preparation of the hard disk, before the disk is formatted.

partition boot sector   Stores information for booting from the partition, such as the location of OS boot files.

partition boot sector Sector of a partition that stores information important to its partition, such as the location of the OS boot files. Responsible for loading the OS on a partition.

partition table Table located in the boot sector of a hard drive that lists every partition on the disk that contains a valid operating system.

partitioning Electronically subdividing a physical drive into one or more units called partitions (or volumes).

passcode lock Mobile device security feature that requires you to type in a series of letters, numbers, or motion patterns to unlock the mobile device each time you press the power button.

passwd Linux command for changing a user's password.

password Key used to verify a user's identity on a secure computer or network.

password reset disc External storage media such as an optical disc or USB flash drive with which users can recover a lost password without losing access to any encrypted, or password-protected, data. The password reset disc must be created proactively; if a user loses a password and did not already make a reset disc, it will be of no help to create one after the loss.

PATA (parallel ATA) Implementation that integrates the controller on the disk drive itself. *See also* ATA, IDE, *and* SATA.

patch Small piece of software released by a software manufacturer to correct a flaw or problem with a particular piece of software. Also called an update.

patch cables Short (typically two- to five-foot) UTP cables that connect patch panels to a switch or router.

patch management Process of keeping software updated in a safe, timely fashion.

patch panel A panel containing a row of female connectors (ports) that terminate the horizontal cabling in the equipment room. Patch panels facilitate cabling organization and provide protection to horizontal cabling.

path Route the operating system must follow to find an executable program stored in a subfolder.

PC tech Someone with computer skills who works on computers.

PCI DSS (Payment Card Industry Data Security Standard) A standard that sets common rules for systems that accept, process, transmit, or store credit/debit card payments. Often referred to as just *PCI*.

PCI (Peripheral Component Interconnect) Design architecture for the expansion bus on the computer motherboard that enabled system components to be added to the computer. Used parallel communication. Local bus standard, meaning that devices added to a computer through this port used the processor at the motherboard's full speed (up to 33 MHz) rather than at the slower 8-MHz speed of the regular bus. Moved data 32 or 64 bits at a time rather than the 8 or 16 bits the older ISA buses supported.

PCIe (PCI Express) Serialized successor to PCI and AGP that uses the concept of individual data paths called lanes. May use any number of lanes, although a single lane (×1) and 16 lanes (×16) are the most common on motherboards.

PCIe 6/8-pin power connector Connector on some power supplies for powering a dedicated graphics card.

PCI-X (PCI Extended) Enhanced version of PCI, 64 bits wide. Was typically seen in servers and high-end systems.

PCL (printer command language) Printer language created by Hewlett-Packard to supersede simple ASCII codes and used on a broad cross section of printers. Identified as printer *control* language in CompTIA A+ exam objectives.

PCM (pulse code modulation) Sound format developed in the 1960s to carry telephone calls over the first digital lines.

PCMCIA (Personal Computer Memory Card International Association) Consortium of computer manufacturers who devised the PC Card standard for credit card–sized adapter cards that add functionality in older notebook computers and other computer devices. PCMCIA shut down in 2009.

Pearson VUE Company that administers the CompTIA A+ exams.

peer-to-peer mode *See* ad hoc mode.

peer-to-peer network Network in which each machine can act as both a client and a server.

Pentium Name given to the fifth and later generations of Intel microprocessors; original had a 32-bit address bus, 64-bit external data bus, and dual pipelining. Also used for subsequent generations of Intel processors—the Pentium Pro, Pentium II, Pentium III, and Pentium 4. Currently used as a budget label for Intel CPUs.

Performance Tab in Task Manager that tracks PC performance, including CPU usage, available physical memory, size of the disk cache, and other details about memory and processes.

Performance Monitor Windows tool for tracking system resources over time.

Performance Options Tool that enables users to configure CPU, RAM, and virtual memory settings.

peripheral Any device that connects to the system unit.

permission propagation Describes what happens to permissions on an object, such as a file or folder, when you move or copy it.

personal computer (PC)   A general computing device that runs Microsoft Windows and can be used for various tasks.

personal digital assistant (PDA)   One of the earliest mobile devices. Lacked cellular connections and touch interfaces, but still shared basic features with current mobile devices.

personal safety   Keeping yourself away from harm.

Personalization applet   In Windows 8.1 and earlier, this Control Panel applet handles user preferences such as the background picture, colors of various interface elements, and so on.

Personalization Settings   Handles user preferences such as the background picture for both the desktop and lock screen, colors of interface elements, themes, which elements show on the Start screen, and so on. Replaced the Personalization applet in Windows 10.

personally identifiable information (PII)   Any data that can lead back to a specific individual.

PGA (pin grid array)   Arrangement of a large number of pins extending from the bottom of the CPU package into corresponding holes in the CPU socket.

Phillips-head screwdriver   Most important part of a PC tech's toolkit.

phishing   The act of trying to get people to give their user names, passwords, or other security information by pretending to be someone else electronically.

photosensitive drum   *See* imaging drum.

pickup roller   Begins the printing process by grabbing paper to be printed and passing it over the separation pad.

pin 1   Designator used to ensure proper alignment of hard drive connectors.

pinch   Multi-touch gesture that enables you to make an image bigger or smaller.

ping   Command-line utility used to send a "ping" message to another computer, which can be used to verify another system is on the network, spot potential DNS issues, identify latency problems, and so on.

pinned apps   Windows method of attaching programs to the taskbar. A pinned app gets a permanent icon displayed on the taskbar. Known as *pinned programs* in Windows 7.

Pinwheel of Death   *See* Spinning Pinwheel of Death.

pipe   Command-line operator that uses the | symbol to "pipe" output from one command to another, instead of printing it to the screen.

pipeline   Processing methodology where multiple calculations take place simultaneously by being broken into a series of steps. Often used in CPUs and video processors.

pixel (picture element)   In computer graphics, smallest element of a display space that can be independently assigned color or intensity.

pixels per inch (PPI)   Density of pixels on a display or a light sensor; the higher the density, the greater the resolution.

PKI (public key infrastructure)   Authentication schema where public keys are exchanged between all parties using digital certificates, enabling secure communication over public networks.

plastic filament   Raw material that a typical 3-D printer melts and then extrudes to create physical pieces and parts.

Platform Controller Hub (PCH)   Intel's name for the chip that collects functions once performed by multiple chips known as the chipset. *See also* chipset.

Play store   *See* Google Play.

plenum   Space in the ceiling, walls, and floor where special plenum-grade (fire-retardant) network cables can be run out of sight.

plug   Hardware connection with some sort of projection that connects to a port.

plug and play (PnP)   Combination of smart PCs, smart devices, and smart operating systems that automatically configure all necessary system resources and ports when you install a new peripheral device.

Point-to-Point Tunneling Protocol (PPTP)   Advanced version of the Point-to-Point Protocol (PPP; used for dial-up Internet) that has improved VPN support.

polarization   Describes the alignment (such as vertical or horizontal) of antennas and the signals they transmit. Because of polarization, a Wi-Fi client and WAP will have the best connection when their antennas are oriented.

policies   Control permission to perform a given action, such as accessing a command prompt, installing software, or logging on at a certain time of day. Contrast with true permissions, which control access to specific resources.

polygons   Multisided shapes used in 3-D rendering of objects. In computers, video cards draw large numbers of triangles and connect them to form polygons.

polymorphic virus   Virus that attempts to change its signature to prevent detection by antivirus programs, usually by continually scrambling a bit of useless code. Often shortened to *polymorph*.

POP3 (Post Office Protocol 3)   One of the two protocols that receive e-mail from SMTP servers. POP3 uses TCP port 110. While historically most e-mail clients used this protocol, the IMAP4 e-mail protocol is now more common.

pop-up   Irritating browser window that appears automatically when you visit a Web site.

port (networking)   In networking, the number used to identify the requested service (such as SMTP or FTP) when connecting to a TCP/IP host. Examples include application protocol ports such as 80 (HTTP), 443, (HTTPS), 21 (FTP), 23 (Telnet), 25 (SMTP), 110 (POP3), 143 (IMAP), and 3389 (RDP).

port (physical connection)   Part of a connector into which a plug is inserted. Physical ports are also referred to as jacks.

port forwarding   Preventing the passage of any IP packets through any ports other than the ones prescribed by the system administrator.

port replicator   Device that plugs into a USB port or other specialized port and offers common PC ports, such as VGA, HDMI, USB, network, and so on. Plugging a laptop into a port replicator can instantly connect the computer to nonportable components such as a printer, scanner, monitor, or full-sized keyboard. Port replicators are typically used at home or in the office with the nonportable equipment already connected.

port triggering   Router function that enables a computer to open an incoming connection to one computer automatically based on a specific outgoing connection.

portable battery recharger   Device containing a rechargeable battery that can be used to charge other devices, typically over USB, when no outlets are available.

positional audio   Range of commands for a sound card to place a sound anywhere in 3-D space.

POST (power-on self test)   Basic diagnostic routine completed by a system at the beginning of the boot process to make sure a display adapter and the system's memory are installed; it then searches for an operating system. If it finds one, it hands over control of the machine to the OS.

POST card   Device installed into a motherboard expansion slot that assists in troubleshooting boot problems by providing a two-digit code indicating the stop of the boot process where the problem is occurring.

PostScript   Language defined by Adobe Systems, Inc., for describing how to create an image on a page. The description is independent of the resolution of the device that will actually create the image. It includes a technology for defining the shape of a font and creating a raster image at many different resolutions and sizes.

potential   The amount of electrical energy stored in an object.

power conditioning   Ensuring and adjusting incoming AC wall power to as close to standard as possible. Most UPS devices provide power conditioning.

power good wire   Used to wake up the CPU after the power supply has tested for proper voltage.

power management   Cooperation between hardware, BIOS, and OS to reduce power consumption.

Power Options   Windows Control Panel applet that enables better control over power use by customizing a Balanced, Power saver, or High-performance power plan.

Power over Ethernet (PoE)   Technology that provides power and data transmission through a single network cable.

power plan   Preconfigured profiles (such as Balanced, High performance, and Power saver) in the Power Options applet that modify a Windows system's behavior to adjust power consumption.

power supply fan   Small fan located in a system power supply that draws warm air from inside the power supply and exhausts it to the outside.

power supply unit (PSU)   Provides the electrical power for a PC. Converts standard AC power into various voltages of DC electricity in a PC.

Power Users group   After Administrator/Administrators, the second most powerful account and group type in Windows. Power users have differing capabilities in different versions of Windows.

power-saving modes   Special power modes that limit or modify device functionality in order to prolong battery life. May take steps such as disabling communications, reducing processor speed, limiting programs, and dimming the screen.

PowerShell   *See* Windows PowerShell.

ppm (pages per minute)   Speed of a printer.

PPP (Point-to-Point Protocol)   Enables a computer to connect to the Internet through a dial-in connection and enjoy most of the benefits of a direct connection.

preboot execution environment (PXE)   Technology that enables a PC to boot without any local storage by retrieving an OS from a server over a network.

Pretty Good Privacy (PGP)   Standard for sending and receiving e-mail encrypted to obscure its message from anyone without the key to decrypt it. *See* encryption.

primary charge roller   Replaces the primary corona wire in newer laser printers. The roller, which is very close to the photosensitive drum, is given a very high charge, forming an electric field (corona) and passing a charge to the photosensitive drum.

primary corona wire   Charges the photosensitive particles on the imaging drum. Replaced by the primary charge roller in newer laser printers. *See* primary charge roller.

primary partition   Partition on a Windows hard drive that can store a bootable operating system.

principle of least privilege   Accounts should have permission to access only the resources they need and no more.

print resolution   How densely an inkjet printer lays down ink on the page, measured in dots per inch (dpi). Affects quality of a print image.

print server   Server, computer, or standalone network device that shares access to a printer over a network.

print spooler   Area of memory that queues up print jobs that the printer will handle sequentially.

print to PDF   Using a virtual printer that produces a PDF file you can save, instead of sending the document to a physical printer.

printed circuit board (PCB)   Copper etched onto a nonconductive material and then coated with some sort of epoxy for strength.

printer   Output device that can print text or illustrations on paper. Microsoft uses the term to refer to the software that controls the physical print device.

printhead   Case that holds the printwires in a dot-matrix printer.

printwires   Grid of tiny pins in a dot-matrix printer that strike an inked printer ribbon to produce images on paper.

private cloud   Cloud network built and maintained by or explicitly for a specific company or organization. Often on-site, but may be provided by a third party. While a public cloud network often requires more expertise and costs more, especially up front, it also enables greater customization and security.

PRL (Preferred Roaming List)   A list that is occasionally and automatically updated to a phone's firmware by the carrier so that the phone will be configured with a particular carrier's networks and frequencies, in a priority order, that it should search for when it can't locate its home carrier network.

Processes   Tab in Task Manager that lists all running processes on a system. Frequently a handy tool for ending buggy or unresponsive processes.

processing (computing)   The second step of the computing process, where the CPU completes the tasks that the user's input has given it.

processing (printing)   The first step of the laser printing process, in which the printer translates incoming print commands into pages rendered for printing.

product key   Code used during installation to verify legitimacy of the software.

product release instruction (PRI)   Carrier-made updates that modify many complex settings for CDMA devices to ready them for deployment on the carrier's network.

profile (color)   A list of settings that a calibration device creates when calibrating monitors and printers.

profile (MDM)   A collection of mobile device management (MDM) configuration and security settings that an administrator has created in order to apply those settings to particular categories of users or devices.

profile (network)   Collection of information necessary to automatically connect to a network, stored by the network's SSID. Enables mobile and portable devices to easily use many networks.

profile (user)   A user profile describes a Windows user account's customized environment, including Desktop preferences, color schemes, shortcuts, and so on.

program/programming   Series of binary electronic commands sent to a CPU to get work done.

Programs and Features   Windows Control Panel applet; enables uninstalling or changing program options and altering Windows features.

projector   Device for projecting video images from PCs or other video sources, usually for audience presentations.

prompt   A character or message provided by an operating system or program to indicate that it is ready to accept input.

proprietary   Technology unique to a particular vendor.

proprietary crash screen   A screen, differing between operating systems, that indicates an NMI. *See also* BSoD *and* Spinning Pinwheel of Death.

protected health information (PHI)   Personally identifiable information that relates to a person's health status, medical records, and healthcare services they have received.

protective cover   A case or sleeve that protects a mobile device from physical damage.

protocol   Agreement that governs the procedures used to exchange information between cooperating entities. Usually includes how much information is to be sent, how often it is to be sent, how to recover from transmission errors, and who is to receive the information.

proxy server   Software that enables multiple connections to the Internet to go through one protected computer. Common security feature in the corporate world. Applications that want to access Internet resources send requests to the proxy server instead of trying to access the Internet directly, which both protects the client computers and enables the network administrator to monitor and restrict Internet access.

ps   Linux command for listing all processes running on the computer.

public cloud   Cloud network built and maintained by a large company for use by any individual or company who wants to create an account and start paying for services.

Public folder   Folder that all users can access and share with all other users on the system or network.

punchdown tool   A specialized tool for connecting UTP wires to a punchdown block.

PVC (polyvinyl chloride)   Material used to make the plastic protective sheathing around many basic network cables. Produces noxious fumes when burned.

pwd   Linux command that displays the user's current path.

Qi   Standardized wireless charging technology.

QR scanner   An application or device capable of scanning and interpreting QR codes.

quad-channel architecture   Feature similar to dual-channel RAM, but making use of four sticks of RAM instead of two.

Quality of Service (QoS)   Router feature used to prioritize access to network resources. Ensures certain users, applications, or services are prioritized when there isn't enough bandwidth to go around by limiting the bandwidth for certain types of data based on application protocol, the IP address of a computer, and all sorts of other features.

queue   Area where objects wait their turn to be processed. Example: the print queue, where print jobs wait until it is their turn to be printed.

quick format   High-level formatting that creates just the file allocation table and a blank root directory. *See* formatting.

radio frequency (RF)   The part of the electromagnetic spectrum used for radio communication.

radio frequency identification (RFID)   Wireless technology that uses small tags containing small amounts of digital information, and readers capable of accessing it. Passive RFID tags operate by harvesting some of the power a scanner or reader emits, enabling a vast array of applications. Common uses such as tracking inventory, identifying lost pets, contactless payments, authentication, and wireless door locks are just scratching the surface. *See also* asset tag, ID badge, key fob, *and* smart card.

RAID (redundant array of independent [or inexpensive] disks)   Method for creating a fault-tolerant storage system. RAID uses multiple hard drives in various configurations to offer differing levels of speed/data redundancy.

RAID 0   Uses byte-level striping and provides no fault tolerance.

RAID 0+1   A RAID 0 configuration created by combining two RAID 1s. Provides both speed and redundancy, but requires at least four disks.

RAID 1   Uses mirroring or duplexing for increased data redundancy.

RAID 5   Uses block-level and parity data striping. Requires three or more drives.

RAID 5 volume (dynamic disks)   A software-based RAID 5 volume made up of three or more dynamic disks with equal-sized unallocated space. Created with Windows Disk Management.

RAID 6   Disk striping with extra parity. Like RAID 5, but with more parity data. Requires four or more drives, but you can lose up to two drives at once and your data is still protected.

RAID 10   The opposite of RAID 0+1, two mirrored RAID 0 configurations. Provides both speed and redundancy, and also requires four disks.

rails   Separate DC voltage paths within an ATX power supply.

rainbow table   Compressed file that contains a mapping of hashed passwords (or other account information) to the corresponding unhashed, plaintext password. Rainbow tables are useful for reversing unsalted hashes in older/legacy authentication systems, but are useless for reversing properly salted hashes used by well-designed, modern authentication systems.

RAM (random access memory)   Memory that can be accessed at random—that is, memory that you can write to or read from without touching the preceding address. This term is often used to mean a computer's main memory.

ransomware   A nasty form of malware that encrypts data or drives on the infected system and demands payment, often within a limited timeframe, in exchange for the keys to decrypt the data.

rapid elasticity   Characteristic of cloud computing that enables cloud consumers to add or remove capacity quickly. Because cloud servers are powered by virtual machines, customers can start or shut down new instances of VMs or move the VMs to more powerful hardware.

raster image   Pattern of dots representing what the printed page should look like. *See also* RIP.

rd (rmdir)   Command-line tool used to remove directories.

read-only attribute   File attribute that does not allow a file to be altered or modified. Helpful when protecting system files that should not be edited.

ReadyBoost   Windows feature enabling the use of flash media devices—removable USB thumb drives or memory cards—as dedicated virtual memory.

real-time clock (RTC)   Device within the CMOS memory chip that provides date and time information to the computer and operating system.

rearview projector   Display using a projector that illuminates a semi-transparent screen from the back. Once popular for televisions, but virtually unheard of for PCs.

recent apps   Interface for viewing a list of recently used apps on a mobile device.

reciprocity   *See* Ethic of Reciprocity.

recovery partition   Small hidden partition on a system's primary hard drive with a factory-fresh OS image to recover and reinstall from.

Recycle Bin   Location to which files are moved when they are deleted from a modern Windows system. To permanently remove files from a system, they must be emptied from the Recycle Bin.

refresh rate   Time required for a monitor to redraw the whole screen.

Refresh your PC   Windows Recovery Environment option in Windows 8/8.1 that rebuilds the OS, but preserves all user files and settings and any applications purchased from the Windows Store. Note well: Refresh deletes every other application on a system. Renamed *Keep my files* in Windows 10.

reg   Command-line tool for editing the Registry. *See* Registry *and* Registry Editor.

regedit   *See* Registry Editor.

regedit.exe   Program used to edit the Windows Registry.

register   Storage area inside the CPU used by the onboard logic to perform calculations. CPUs have many registers to perform different functions.

registered RAM   *See* buffered/registered RAM.

registration (printing)   Describes how accurately the printer lays down each color layer that makes up a page or image. Poor registration can result in muddled colors or a fringe of pure color around a shape or image. Printers usually have a routine (which may mention calibration, alignment, or registration) for detecting and fixing alignment issues.

registration (product)   Usually optional process that identifies the legal owner/user of the product to the supplier.

Registry   Complex binary file used to store configuration data about a particular Windows system. To edit the Registry, users can use the applets found in the Control Panel or use regedit.

Registry Editor   Program used to edit the Windows Registry.

remediation   Repairing damage caused by a virus.

remnant   Potentially recoverable data on a hard drive that remains despite formatting or deleting.

Remote Assistance   Feature of Windows that enables users to give anyone control of his or her desktop over the Internet.

remote desktop   Generically, the process of using one system to access the desktop or graphical user interface (GUI) of a remote system.

Remote Desktop Connection   Windows tool used to form a remote desktop connection and graphically access the GUI of a remote system.

Remote Desktop Protocol (RDP)   Protocol used for Microsoft's Remote Desktop tool. Uses port 3389.

remote network installation   A common method of OS installation where the source files are placed in a shared directory on a network server. Then, whenever a tech needs to install a new OS, he or she can boot the computer, connect to the source location on the network, and start the installation from there.

remotely wipe The ability to remotely delete user data from a mobile device that has been lost or stolen.

removable media Any storage on a computer that can be easily removed. For example, optical discs, flash drives, or memory cards.

Remove everything Windows Recovery Environment option in Windows 10 that deletes all apps, programs, user files, and user settings—resulting in a fresh installation of Windows. Use as a last resort when troubleshooting (and back up data first).

replication When a virus makes copies of itself, often by injecting itself into other executables. *See* malware *and* virus.

reset to factory default Another term for a factory reset.

Reset your PC Windows Recovery Environment option in Windows 8/8.1 that nukes the system—deleting all apps, programs, user files, and user settings—and presents a fresh installation of Windows. Use Reset as the last resort when troubleshooting a PC. And back up data first, if possible. Renamed to *Remove everything* in Windows 10.

resistance Difficulty in making electricity flow through a material, measured in ohms.

resistor Any material or device that impedes the flow of electrons. Antistatic wrist straps and mats use tiny resistors to prevent a static charge from racing through the device.

resolution Measurement for monitors and printers expressed in horizontal and vertical dots or pixels. Higher resolutions provide sharper details and thus display better-looking images.

Resource Monitor Windows utility that displays detailed performance information about a computer's CPU, memory, disk, and network activity.

resource pooling Consolidating resources from many systems into a smaller number of more powerful systems, reducing power, maintenance, and hardware costs.

resources Data and services such as files, folders, drives, printers, connections, and so on.

respect What all techs should show their customers.

response rate The amount of time it takes for all the sub-pixels on an LCD panel to change from one state to another. This change is measured in one of two ways: black-to-white (BtW) measures how long it takes the pixels to go from pure black to pure white and back again, and gray-to-gray (GtG) measures how long it takes the pixels to go from one gray state to another.

restore point A snapshot of a computer's configuration at a specific point in time, created by the System Restore utility and used to restore a malfunctioning system. *See also* System Restore.

RET (resolution enhancement technology) Technology that uses small dots to smooth out jagged edges that are typical of printers without RET, producing a higher-quality print job.

retinal scanner Biometric security device that authenticates an individual by comparing retinal scans. Rarer in the real world than in media such as movies or video games.

RFI (radio frequency interference) Another form of electrical interference caused by radio wave–emitting devices, such as cell phones, wireless network cards, and microwave ovens.

RG-59 Coaxial cable used for cable television, cable modems, and broadcast TV; thinner than RG-6, which makes it suitable for shorter patch cables.

RG-6 Coaxial cabling used for cable television. It has a 75-ohm impedance and uses an F-type connector.

RIP (raster image processor) Component in a printer that translates the raster image into commands for the printer.

riser card Special adapter card, usually inserted into a special slot on a motherboard, that changes the orientation of expansion cards relative to the motherboard. Riser cards are used extensively in slimline computers to keep total depth and height of the system to a minimum. Sometimes called a daughterboard.

risk analysis A detailed assessment of any problems that could result from a change.

RJ (registered jack) connector UTP cable connector, used for both telephone and network connections. RJ-11 is a connector for four-wire UTP; usually found in telephone connections. RJ-45 is a connector for eight-wire UTP; usually found in network connections.

RJ-11 *See* RJ (registered jack) connector.

RJ-45 *See* RJ (registered jack) connector.

rm Linux command for deleting files.

rmdir *See* rd (rmdir).

roaming When a mobile device connects to a network not owned by its home carrier.

robocopy Powerful command-line utility for copying files and directories, even over a network.

rogue anti-malware Free applications that claim to be anti-malware, but which are actually themselves malware.

ROM (read-only memory) Generic term for nonvolatile memory that can be read from but not written to. This means that code and data stored in ROM cannot be corrupted by accidental erasure. Additionally, ROM retains its data when power is removed, which makes it the perfect medium for storing BIOS data or information such as scientific constants.

root directory   Directory that contains all other directories.

root keys   Five main categories in the Windows Registry:

HKEY_CLASSES_ROOT
HKEY_CURRENT_USER
HKEY_LOCAL_MACHINE
HKEY_USERS
HKEY_CURRENT_CONFIG

rooting   Process for circumventing the security restrictions and gaining access to the root user account on an Android device.

rootkit   Program that takes advantage of very low-level functionality to gain privileged system access and hide itself from all but the most aggressive anti-malware tools. Can strike operating systems, hypervisors, and even device firmware.

router   Device connecting separate networks; forwards a packet from one network to another based on the network address for the protocol being used. For example, an IP router looks only at the IP network number. Routers operate at Layer 3 (Network) of the OSI seven-layer model.

RS-232   Standard port recommended by the Electronics Industry Association (EIA) for serial devices.

RSA token   Random-number generator used along with a user name and password to enhance security.

run   A single piece of installed horizontal cabling.

Run as administrator   Method of running a Windows program with elevated privileges, disabling protections that normally limit a program's ability to damage the system.

SaaS (Software as a Service)   Cloud-based service to store, distribute, and update programs and applications. The SaaS model provides access to necessary applications wherever you have an Internet connection, often without having to carry data with you or regularly update software. At the enterprise level, the subscription model of many SaaS providers makes it easier to budget and keep hundreds or thousands of computers up to date.

Safe Mode   Important diagnostic boot mode for Windows that runs only very basic drivers and turns off virtual memory.

safety goggles   Protective glasses that keep stuff out of your eyes.

salted hash   *See* salting.

salting   The process of protecting password hashes from being easily reversed with a rainbow table by adding additional values to each password before hashing and storing it.

sampling   Capturing sound waves in electronic format.

SAS (Serial Attached SCSI)   Fast, robust storage interface based on the SCSI command set. Also supports SATA drives. Used mainly in servers and storage arrays.

SATA (serial ATA)   Serialized version of the ATA standard that offers many advantages over PATA (parallel ATA) technology, including thinner cabling, keyed connectors, and lower power requirements.

SATA 3.2   Another term for SATAe. *See* SATA Express.

SATA Express (SATAe)   Version of SATA that ties capable drives directly into the PCI Express bus on motherboards. Each lane of PCIe 3.0 is capable of handling up to 8 Gbps of data throughput. A SATAe drive grabbing two lanes, therefore, could move a whopping 16 Gbps through the bus.

SATA power connector   15-pin, L-shaped connector used by SATA devices that support the hot-swappable feature.

satellite latency   Small signal delay caused by the distance traveled by satellite signals.

satellites   Two or more standard stereo speakers to be combined with a subwoofer for a speaker system (i.e., 2.1, 5.1, 7.1, etc.).

SC   Type of fiber optic connector. *See* fiber optic cable.

Scalable Link Interface (SLI)   Technology for connecting two or more NVIDIA GPUs together in a system. AMD competes with CrossFire technology.

scan code   Unique code corresponding to each key on the keyboard, sent from the keyboard controller to the CPU.

scope of the change   Defines who and what the change will affect. May include an inventory of systems to change, people involved, time required, and estimated cost.

screen lock   Mobile device feature that locks the screen until some form of authentication challenge is passed.

screen orientation   Describes whether a mobile device screen is in portrait or landscape mode, and the device settings that govern when the orientation may change. When the screen orientation setting is in automatic mode, the user interface (UI) will switch between portrait and landscape modes based on the device's orientation in physical space.

script   Set of text instructions that tells a computer a series of commands to execute in a repeatable fashion.

scripting language   Set of commands, syntax, variables, and format for scripts to be used in a specific computer environment. For example, *bash* is a scripting language often used in the Bash shell, which is common on UNIX environments.

SCSI (small computer system interface)   Long-lived storage drive technology once common in the server market. Has been through many iterations. Today, the SCSI command set lives on in Serial Attached SCSI (SAS) hard drives. *See also* SAS.

SCSI ID   Unique identifier used by SCSI devices. No two SCSI devices may have the same SCSI ID.

SD (Secure Digital)   Very popular format for flash media cards; also supports I/O devices. In addition to full-sized SD cards, the format also includes two smaller form factors: miniSD and microSD.

SDK (software development kit)   Software that is used to create custom apps or add features to existing apps on a mobile device.

SDRAM (synchronous DRAM)   DRAM that is synchronous, or tied to the system clock. This type of RAM is used in all modern systems.

Search box   Location on the Windows 10 Taskbar where users can input text and see suggestions (for settings, programs, files, and popular Web searches) that may be related.

sector   Magnetically preset storage areas on traditional magnetic hard drives. On older hard drives, a sector held 512 bytes of data; modern drives use 4096-byte *Advanced Format* (*AF*) sectors.

Secure Boot   UEFI feature that secures the boot process by requiring properly signed software. This includes boot software and software that supports specific, essential components.

Security tab   File/folder administrative preferences found in the Properties dialog in both File Explorer and Windows Explorer. These preferences govern user and group access to a particular file or folder.

security token   Devices that store some unique information that a user carries with them. May contain digital certificates, passwords, biometric data, or RSA tokens.

segment   The connection between a computer and a switch.

self-grounding   A less-than-ideal method for ridding yourself of static electricity by touching a metal object such as a computer case. Alternately, sending yourself to your own room as a form of punishment.

separation pad   Printer part that uses friction to separate a single sheet from any others the pickup roller grabbed.

Serial Attached SCSI   *See* SAS.

serial port   Common connector on older PC. Connects input devices (such as a mouse) or communications devices (such as a modem). Also referred to as a COM port.

server   Computer that shares its resources, such as printers and files, with other computers on a network. Example: network file system server that shares its disk space with a workstation that does not have a disk drive of its own.

Server Message Block (SMB)   Windows' network file and print sharing protocol, though every major OS now supports it. Protocol of choice for LAN file servers. Uses TCP port 445 and UDP ports 137, 138, and 139.

service   A process that runs in the background of a PC but displays no icons anywhere. You can view a list of services in the Windows Task Manager. Also, a program stored in a ROM chip.

Service Location Protocol (SLP)   Protocol for advertising and discovering available services over a network. Most common with print devices. Uses TCP/UDP port 427.

service menu   Hidden device menu containing tools for technicians servicing the device. May contain diagnostics, reports, or interfaces for changing otherwise inaccessible settings.

service pack   Collection of software patches released at one time by a software manufacturer.

Services   Tab in Windows Task Manager that lists all running services on a system. *See also* service.

session hijacking   Intercepting a valid computer session to get authentication information from it, enabling the attacker to use whatever resources the authentication grants access for as long as the authentication information or session is valid.

Settings app   Since its introduction in Windows 8, it has grown to combine a huge number of otherwise disparate utilities, apps, and tools traditionally spread out all over your computer into one fairly unified, handy Windows app.

sfc (System File Checker)   Command-prompt program (sfc.exe) that scans, detects, and restores Windows system files, folders, and paths.

SFTP (Secure FTP)   Secure version of the File Transfer Protocol (FTP). *See also* FTP.

shared memory   Means of reducing the amount of memory needed on a video card by borrowing from the regular system RAM, which reduces costs but also decreases performance.

share-level security   Security system in which each resource has a password assigned to it; access to the resource is based on knowing the password.

shell   Tool that interprets command-line input, also known as the command-line interpreter.

shoulder surfing   Looking for credentials or other sensitive information by watching someone use a computer or device, often over their shoulder.

shunt   Tiny connector of metal enclosed in plastic that creates an electrical connection between two posts of a jumper.

shutdown   Windows and Linux command-line tool for shutting down the computer.

SID (security identifier)   Unique identifier for every PC that most techs change when cloning.

side-by-side apps   Feature introduced in Windows 8 for quickly pinning an app to the left or right half of a screen.

signature (malware)   Code pattern of a known virus or malware that antivirus/anti-malware software uses to detect malware.

signed driver   A driver designed specifically to work with Windows that has been tested and certified by Microsoft to work stably with Windows.

SIMM (single in-line memory module)   An early DRAM package format that came in two common sizes: 30-pin and 72-pin.

simple space   Storage Space that just pools storage space, like JBOD. *See* Storage Spaces.

simple volume   Volume created when setting up dynamic disks. Acts like a primary partition on a dynamic disk.

single-factor authentication   A less-secure authentication process using only one of the authentication factors. *See also* MFA.

single-mode fiber optic cabling   Type of fiber optic cabling that uses laser light to transmit at very high rates over long distances. Still fairly rare. *See* fiber optic cable.

single rail   Power supply configuration where all power is supplied along a single pathway.

single sign-on (SSO)   Process that uses an account or credentials for a popular service (such as a Google Account) to sign on or authenticate with other services.

single-sided RAM   Has chips on only one side, as opposed to double-sided RAM.

sleep mode   Power management setting in which all data from RAM is preserved by powering down much of the computer but maintaining power to RAM, or by writing the contents of RAM to the mass storage drive before the system goes into a reduced-power mode. Upon waking up, the information is retrieved from the HDD or SSD and returned to RAM if necessary; the system continues where it left off.

slot covers   Metal plates that cover up unused expansion slots on the back of a PC. Useful in maintaining proper airflow through a computer case.

S.M.A.R.T. (Self-Monitoring, Analysis, and Reporting Technology)   Monitoring system built into hard drives that tracks errors and error conditions within the drive.

smart card   Hardware authentication involving a credit card–sized card with circuitry that can be used to identify the bearer of that card.

smart card reader   Device that scans the smart card chip, such as those in ID badges. Common applications include enhancing the security of doors or laptops.

smart watch   A watch incorporating features of and communicating with a mobile device.

smartphone   A cell phone enhanced to do things formerly reserved for fully grown computers, such as Web browsing, document viewing, and media consumption.

S/MIME (Secure/Multipurpose Internet Mail Extensions)   Technology used to configure digital signature settings for e-mail, and contacts from a corporate address book, depending on how the corporate e-mail server is set up.

SMTP (Simple Mail Transport Protocol)   Main protocol used to send electronic mail on the Internet. Uses port 25.

snap-ins   Utilities that can be used with the Microsoft Management Console.

snapshot   Virtualization feature that enables you to save an extra copy of the virtual machine as it is exactly at the moment the snapshot is taken.

SNMP (Simple Network Management Protocol)   A set of standards for communication with devices connected to a TCP/IP network. Examples of these devices include routers, hubs, and switches. Uses ports 161 and 162.

social engineering   Using or manipulating people inside the networking environment to gain access to that network from the outside.

SO-DIMM (small-outline DIMM)   Memory used in portable PCs because of its small size.

soft power   Characteristic of ATX motherboards, which can use software to turn the PC on and off. The physical manifestation of soft power is the power switch. Instead of the thick power cord used in AT systems, an ATX power switch is little more than a pair of small wires leading to the motherboard.

soft reset   The equivalent of a reboot or restart for a mobile device. An important troubleshooting step because it clears running programs from memory and restarts the operating system. Some portable devices that closely resemble mobile devices may also use soft resets.

software   Single group of programs designed to do a particular job; always stored on mass storage devices.

software firewall   Firewall implemented in software running on servers or workstations. *See* firewall.

software token   Programming (usually running on a general computing device such as a smartphone or portable computer) that enables the device to serve as an authentication factor when logging into a secure resource.

solid core   A cable that uses a single solid (not hollow or stranded) wire to transmit signals.

sound card   Expansion card that can produce audible tones when connected to a set of speakers.

southbridge   In older chipsets, a chip that handled all the inputs and outputs to the many devices in the PC.

Spaces   macOS feature enabling multiple desktops.

spam   Unsolicited e-mails from both legitimate businesses and scammers that account for a huge percentage of traffic on the Internet.

spanned volume   Volume that uses space on multiple dynamic disks.

SPD (serial presence detect)   Information stored on a RAM chip that describes the speed, capacity, and other aspects of the RAM chip.

S/PDIF (Sony/Philips Digital Interface Format)   High-quality digital audio connector. Users can connect their computers directly to a 5.1 speaker system or receiver with a single cable. S/PDIF comes in both a coaxial version and an optical version.

speaker   Device that outputs sound by using magnetically driven diaphragm.

spear phishing   Dangerous targeted phishing attack on a group or individual that carefully uses details from the target's life to increase the odds they'll take the bait.

spindle speed   Fixed speed in revolutions per minute (RPM) at which a given HDD's platters spin. The two most common speeds are 5400 and 7200 RPM; higher-performance drives (far less common) run at 10,000 and 15,000 RPM. Also called rotational speed.

Spinning Pinwheel of Death (SpoD)   A spinning rainbow wheel that serves as the macOS indicator that an application isn't responding and may be busy or frozen.

spoofing   Pretending to be someone or something else by placing false information into packets. Commonly spoofed data include a source MAC address or IP address, e-mail address, Web address, or user name. Generally a useful tool for enhancing or advancing other attacks, such as social engineering or spear fishing.

Spotify   Internet streaming music service.

sprite   Bitmapped graphic, such as a BMP file, used by early 3-D games to create the 3-D world.

spyware   Software that runs in the background of a user's PC, sending information about browsing habits back to the company that installed it onto the system.

SRAM (static RAM)   Very high-speed RAM built into CPUs that reduces wait states by preloading as many instructions as possible and keeping copies of already run instructions and data in case the CPU needs to work on them again.

sRGB   Color space standard that corresponds to Standard Dynamic Range (SDR).

SSD (solid-state drive)   Data storage device that uses flash memory to store data.

SSH (Secure Shell)   Terminal emulation program similar to Telnet, except that the entire connection is encrypted. Uses port 22.

SSID (service set identifier)   Parameter used to define a wireless network; otherwise known as the network name.

SSL (Secure Sockets Layer)   Security protocol used by a browser to connect to secure Web sites. Replaced by Transport Layer Security (TLS).

ST   Type of fiber optic connector. *See* fiber optic cable.

Standard Dynamic Range (SDR)   8-bit color standard that defines 256 colors or light intensities.

standard user account   User account in Windows that has limited access to a system. Part of the Users group. Accounts of this type cannot alter system files, cannot install new programs, and cannot edit some settings by using the Control Panel without supplying an administrator password.

standby   *See* sleep mode.

standoffs   Small mechanical separators that screw into a computer case. A motherboard is then placed on top of the standoffs, and small screws are used to secure it to the standoffs.

star bus topology   A hybrid network topology where the computers all connect to a central bus—a switch—and have a layout resembling a star.

Start button   Clickable element on the Windows taskbar that enables access to the Start menu.

Start menu   Menu that can be accessed by clicking the Start button on the Windows taskbar. Enables you to see all programs loaded on the system and to start them.

Start screen   Windows 10 version of the Start menu, which functions as a combination of the traditional Start menu and Windows 8/8.1 Modern UI.

Startup   Tab added to Task Manager in Windows 8 that allows a user to control which programs start with Windows and see what impact they are having on load time.

Startup Repair   A one-stop, do-it-all troubleshooting option that performs a number of boot repairs automatically.

Stateful Packet Inspection (SPI)   Used by hardware firewalls to inspect each incoming packet individually for purposes such as blocking traffic that isn't in response to outgoing requests.

static charge eliminator   Laser printer component that removes the static charge from paper to prevent the paper from wrapping around the imaging drum.

static IP address   Manually set IP address that will not change.

stealth virus   Virus that uses various methods to hide from antivirus software.

stereo   Describes recording tracks from two sources (microphones) as opposed to monaural, which uses one source.

stick   Generic name for a single physical SIMM or DIMM.

storage pool   One or more physical drives grouped into a single Storage Space.

Storage Spaces   In Windows 8 and later, a software RAID solution that enables users to group multiple drives into a single storage pool.

STP (shielded twisted pair)   Cabling for networks, composed of pairs of wires twisted around each other at specific intervals. Twists serve to reduce interference (also called crosstalk)—the more twists, the less interference. Cable has metallic shielding to protect the wires from external interference.

stranded core   A cable that uses a bundle of tiny wire filaments to transmit signals. Stranded core is not quite as good a conductor as solid core, but it will stand up to substantial handling without breaking.

streaming media   Broadcast of data that is played on your computer and immediately discarded.

string   In programming and scripting, a non-numeric sequence of alphanumeric data.

stripe set   Two or more drives in a group that are used for a striped volume.

striped volume   RAID 0 volumes. Data is spread across two drives for increased speed.

strong password   Password containing at least eight characters, including letters, numbers, and punctuation symbols.

structured cabling   ANSI/TIA standards that define methods of organizing the cables in a network for ease of repair and replacement.

su   Older Linux command for gaining root access.

subfolder   A folder located inside another folder.

subnet mask   Value used in TCP/IP settings to divide the IP address of a host into its component parts: network ID and host ID.

sub-pixels   Tiny liquid crystal molecules arranged in rows and columns between polarizing filters used in LCDs.

subwoofer   Powerful speaker capable of producing extremely low-frequency sounds.

sudo   Linux command for gaining root access.

Super I/O chip   Chip specially designed to control low-speed, legacy devices such as the keyboard, mouse, and serial and parallel ports.

SuperSpeed USB   A fast form of USB, with speeds up to 5 Gbps. Also called USB 3.0.

SuperSpeed USB 10 Gbps   Updated form of SuperSpeed USB providing speeds up to 10 Gbps. Also called USB 3.1.

surge suppressor   Inexpensive device that protects your computer from voltage spikes.

suspend   *See* sleep mode.

SVGA (super video graphics array)   Video display mode of 800 × 600. Native SVGA displays are rare these days, but Windows might go into SVGA mode if the video driver is corrupt.

swap file   *See* virtual memory.

swap partition   Special partition found on Linux and UNIX systems that behaves like RAM when your system needs more RAM than is installed.

swipe   Gesture for mobile devices where you hold your finger on the screen and slide it across the screen, either right to left or top to bottom, depending on the type of application.

swipe lock   Mobile device feature that uses a swipe gesture to unlock the mobile device.

switch   Device that filters and forwards traffic based on some criteria. A bridge and a router are both examples of switches. In the command-line interface, a switch is a function that modifies the behavior of a command.

swollen battery   A Li-Ion battery that has begun to swell as it fails, often due to manufacturing defects, heat, or overcharging. May also deform the device containing it. It is an explosion and fire risk if it ruptures, so dispose of it quickly and safely.

SXGA   Video display mode of 1280 × 1024.

sync   The process of keeping files on mobile devices up to date with the versions on desktop computers or over the Internet via cloud-based services.

Sync Center   Windows Control Panel applet where network files marked as *Always available offline* may be viewed.

synchronize   *See* sync.

syntax (command)   The proper way to write a command-line command so that it functions and does what it's supposed to do.

system BIOS   Primary set of BIOS stored on a flash ROM chip on the motherboard. Defines the BIOS for all the assumed hardware on the motherboard, such as keyboard controller, basic video, and RAM.

system bus speed   Speed at which the CPU and the rest of the PC operates; set by the system crystal.

System Configuration utility (msconfig)   *See* msconfig.

system crystal   Crystal that provides the speed signals for the CPU and the rest of the system.

system disk   *See* bootable disk.

system fan   Any fan controlled by the motherboard but not directly attached to the CPU.

System File Checker   *See* sfc.

System Information tool (msinfo32)   *See* msinfo32.

system lockout   Protects against attempts to brute-force a lock screen or login system by locking the user out until they perform some more thorough authentication process. Occurs when too many consecutive login attempts fail.

System Monitor   GNOME 3 utility that can evaluate and monitor system resources, such as CPU usage and memory usage.

system on a chip (SoC)   Single silicon die containing a CPU, GPU, and other important support logic.

System Preferences   macOS tool containing many administrative functions.

System Protection   Tab in Windows System Properties dialog box that enables you to configure how and when the system will create restore points and provides easy access to existing restore points via System Restore.

system resources   In classic terms, the I/O addresses, IRQs, DMA channels, and memory addresses. Also refers to other computer essentials such as hard drive space, system RAM, and processor speed.

System Restore   Utility in Windows that enables you to return your PC to a recent working configuration when something goes wrong. System Restore enables you to select a restore point and then returns the computer's system settings to the way they were at that restore point—all without affecting your personal files or e-mail.

system ROM   Flash ROM chip that stores the system BIOS.

system setup utility   *See* CMOS setup program.

System Tools   Windows 7 menu containing tools such as System Information and Disk Defragmenter, accessed by selecting Start | All Programs | Accessories | System Tools.

system tray   Contains icons representing background processes and the system clock. Located by default at the right edge of the Windows taskbar. Accurately called the notification area.

system unit   Main component of the PC, in which the CPU, RAM, optical drive, and hard drive reside. All other devices—the keyboard, mouse, and monitor—connect to the system unit.

system/application log errors Errors and warnings in the system/application logs may indicate the presence of a malware infestation and the scope of its effects.

%SystemRoot% The path where the operating system is installed.

T568A Wiring standard for Ethernet cable.

T568B Wiring standard for Ethernet cable.

tablet A mobile device consisting of a large touchscreen, enabling the user to browse the Web, view media, and even play games.

tailgating Form of infiltration and social engineering that involves following someone else through a door as if you belong in the building.

Take Ownership Special permission allowing users to seize control of a file or folder and potentially prevent others from accessing the file/folder.

tap Touchscreen gesture where you press a spot on the screen to start an app or interact with a running app.

Task Manager Windows utility that shows all running programs, including hidden ones, and is accessed by pressing CTRL-SHIFT-ESC. You can use the Task Manager to shut down an unresponsive application that refuses to close normally.

Task Scheduler Windows 7 utility enabling users to set tasks to run automatically at certain times.

Taskbar Contains the Start button, Search box (Windows 10), pinned apps, running apps, and the notification area. Located by default at the bottom of the desktop.

taskkill Windows command-line tool for killing running processes.

tasklist Windows command-line tool for listing and managing processes.

TCP/IP (Transmission Control Protocol/Internet Protocol) Communication protocols developed by the U.S. Department of Defense to enable dissimilar computers to share information over a network. TCP/IP is the primary protocol of most modern networks, including the Internet.

TCP/IP services Services such as HTTP or SSH that run atop TCP/IP.

TDR (time-domain reflectometer) Device for testing network cabling by measuring impedance (which is similar to resistance); any impedance means a bad cable.

tech toolkit Tools a PC tech should never be without, including a Phillips-head screwdriver, a pair of plastic tweezers, a flat-head screwdriver, a hemostat, a star-headed Torx wrench, a parts retriever, and a nut driver or two.

telecommunications room Area where all the cabling from individual computers in a network converges.

telephone scams   Social engineering attack in which the attacker makes a phone call to someone in an organization to gain information.

Telnet   Terminal emulation program for TCP/IP networks that allows one machine to control another as if the user were sitting in front of it. Uses port 23.

tera-   Prefix that usually stands for the binary number 1,099,511,627,776 (2^{40}). When used for mass storage, it's often shorthand for 1 trillion bytes.

terminal   Dumb device connected to a mainframe or computer network that acts as a point for entry or retrieval of information.

Terminal   A command-line tool available in macOS and various Linux distros.

terminal emulation   Software that enables a computer to communicate with another computer or network as if the computer were a specific type of hardware terminal.

test the theory to determine cause   Attempt to resolve the issue by either confirming the theory and learning what needs to be done to fix the problem, or by not confirming the theory and forming a new one or escalating. (Step 3 of 6 in the CompTIA troubleshooting methodology.)

tethering   The act of using a cellular network–connected mobile device as a mobile hotspot.

texture   Small picture that is tiled over and over again on walls, floors, and other surfaces to create the 3-D world.

TFT (thin film transistor)   Type of LCD screen. *See also* active matrix.

theory of probable cause   One possible reason why something is not working; a guess.

thermal compound   *See* thermal paste.

thermal paper   Special heat-sensitive paper for use in thermal printers.

thermal paste   Paste-like material with very high heat-transfer properties. Applied between the CPU and the cooling device, it ensures the best possible dispersal of heat from the CPU. Also called heat dope or thermal compound.

thermal printer   Printer that uses heated printheads to create high-quality images on special or plain paper. Common in retail receipt printers, which use large rolls of thermal paper housed in a feed assembly that automatically draws the thermal receipt paper over the heating element.

thick client   CompTIA's name for a standard desktop computer. Runs a modern operating system and general productivity applications to accomplish the vast majority of tasks needed by office and home users. It does not need a network connection to run and it meets the recommended requirements for its OS.

thin client   A system designed to store only very basic applications with an absolute minimum amount of hardware required by the operating system. Relies on resources from servers and thus needs a network connection. Meets minimum requirements for selected OS.

thin provisioning   Creating a Storage Space that reports a size greater than the actual capacity installed in the computer, with the ability to later add more physical capacity up to the reported size.

thread   Smallest logical division of a single program.

throttling   Power reduction/thermal control capability allowing CPUs to slow down during low activity or high heat build-up situations. Intel's version is known as SpeedStep, AMD's as PowerNow!.

throw   Size of the image a projector displays at a certain distance from the screen. Alternately, what you do with a computer that you just can't seem to get working.

Thunderbolt   An open standards connector interface that is primarily used to connect peripherals to devices, including mobile devices, if they have a corresponding port.

tiers   Levels of Internet providers, ranging from the Tier 1 backbones to Tier 3 regional networks.

tiles   The building blocks of Windows 8's Modern UI, as potentially "smart" app shortcuts, capable of displaying dynamic and changing information without even opening the app.

timbre   Qualities that differentiate the same note played on different instruments.

Time Machine   macOS backup tool that enables you to create full system backups, called local snapshots, and to recover some or all files in the event of a crash; it also enables you to restore deleted files and recover previous versions of files.

TKIP (Temporal Key Integrity Protocol)   Deprecated encryption standard used in WPA that provided a new encryption key for every sent packet.

TN (twisted nematic)   Older technology for LCD monitors. TN monitors produce a decent display for a modest price, but they have limited viewing angles and can't accurately reproduce all the color information sent by the video card.

tone generator   *See* toner (networking).

tone probe   *See* toner (networking).

toner (networking)   Generic term for two devices used together—a tone generator and a tone probe (locator)—to trace cables by sending an electrical signal along a wire at a particular frequency. The tone probe then emits a sound when it distinguishes that frequency.

toner (printing)   A fine powder made up of plastic particles bonded to pigment particles, used to create the text and images on a page printed with a laser printer.

toner cartridge   Object used to store the toner in a laser printer. *See also* laser printer *and* toner (printing).

topology   The way computers connect to each other in a network.

touch interface   The primary user interface on modern mobile devices where keys are replaced with tactile interaction.

touchpad   Flat, touch-sensitive pad that serves as a pointing device for most laptops.

touchscreen   Monitor with a type of sensing device (a digitizer) across its face that detects the location and duration of contact, usually by a finger or stylus.

tower spoofing   Broadcasting a rogue cellular signal that imitates a legitimate cell tower in order to trick cellular devices into connecting.

traceroute   macOS and Linux command-line utility for following the path a packet takes between hosts. The Windows version is named tracert.

tracert   Windows command-line utility used to follow the path a packet takes between two hosts. Called traceroute in macOS and Linux.

traces   Small electrical connections embedded in a circuit board.

trackball   Pointing device used in early portable computers, distinguished by a ball that is rolled with the fingers.

TrackPoint   IBM's pencil eraser–sized joystick used in place of a mouse on laptops.

transfer belt   A component that enables color laser printers to transfer all color layers to the paper in a single pass (as opposed to a separate pass to print each color layer).

transfer corona   Thin wire, usually protected by other thin wires, that applies a positive charge to the paper during the laser printing process, drawing the negatively charged toner particles off of the drum and onto the paper. Newer printers accomplish the same feat using a *transfer roller* that draws the toner onto the paper.

transfer rate   Rate of data transferred between two devices, especially over the expansion bus.

transfer roller   In more recent laser printers, replaces the transfer corona, but performs the same task: applying a positive charge to the paper to draw toner from the imaging drum to the paper.

Transmission Control Protocol (TCP)   Connection-oriented protocol used with TCP/IP. *See* UDP *and* TCP/IP.

transmit beamforming   Multiple-antenna technology that adjusts signal when clients are discovered to optimize quality and minimize dead spots. Used in many 802.11n WAPs.

Transport Layer Security (TLS)   Encryption protocol used to securely connect between servers and clients, such as when your Web browser securely connects to Amazon's servers to make a purchase. Replaces SSL.

trigger port   In port triggering, outbound traffic on this port will cause the router to open the destination port and wait for a response.

triple-channel architecture   A chipset feature similar to dual-channel RAM, but making use of three matched sticks of RAM instead of two.

Trojan horse   Program that does something other than what the user who runs the program thinks it will do. Used to disguise malicious code.

troubleshooting methodology   Steps a technician uses to solve a problem. CompTIA A+ defines six steps: identify the problem; establish a theory of probable cause (question the obvious); test the theory to determine cause; establish a plan of action to resolve the problem and implement a solution; verify full system functionality and, if applicable, implement preventive measures; and document findings, actions, and outcomes.

Trusted Platform Module (TPM)   A hardware platform for the acceleration of cryptographic functions and the secure storage of associated information. BitLocker, for example, requires a TPM chip on the motherboard to validate on boot that the computer has not changed.

trusted root CA   A highly respected certificate authority (CA) that has been placed on the lists of trusted authorities built into Web browsers.

trusted source   Legitimate app stores run by the major OS vendors such as Apple, Google, Microsoft, and Amazon.

tunneling   Creating an encrypted link between two programs on two separate computers.

TV tuner   Typically an add-on device that allows users to watch television on a computer.

TWAIN (Technology Without an Interesting Name)   Programming interface that enables a graphics application, such as a desktop publishing program, to activate a scanner, frame grabber, or other image-capturing device. Default driver type for scanners.

two-factor authentication   Authentication process that provides additional security by requiring two different authentication factors. *See also* MFA.

U (units)   The unique height measurement used with equipment racks; 1 U equals 1.75 inches. A 1U device fits in a 1.75-inch space, a 2U device fits in a 3.5-inch space, and a 4U device fits in a 7-inch space.

UAC (User Account Control)   Windows feature implemented to stop unauthorized changes to Windows. UAC enables standard accounts to do common tasks and provides a permissions dialog box when standard and administrator accounts do certain things that could potentially harm the computer (such as attempt to install a program).

UDF (universal data format)   Replaced the ISO-9660 formats, enabling any operating system and optical drive to read UDF formatted disks.

UEFI (Unified Extensible Firmware Interface)   Modern 32- or 64-bit firmware programming interface. Replaced the original 16-bit PC BIOS. UEFI supports large capacity storage drives, additional features, and a more direct booting process.

Ultrabook   Thin, powerful laptop powered by Intel processors and built according to the Intel design specification. Competes directly with the Apple Mac Air.

unattended installation   A type of OS installation where special scripts perform all the OS setup duties without human intervention.

unauthorized access   Anytime a person accesses resources in an unauthorized way. This access may or may not be malicious.

unbuffered RAM   RAM without a register to act as a buffer between the DIMM and memory controller; in other words, normal, consumer-grade RAM.

UNC (Universal Naming Convention)   Describes any shared resource in a network using the convention \\<*server name*>\<*name of shared resource*>.

Unicode   16-bit code that covers every character of the most common languages, plus several thousand symbols.

unified threat management (UTM)   Providing robust network security by integrating traditional firewalls with many other security services such as IPS, VPN, load balancing, anti-malware, and more.

unsigned driver   Driver that has not gone through the Windows Hardware Certification Program to ensure compatibility. Rarely seen on modern Windows machines, as only the last of the 32-bit Windows versions support unsigned drivers.

untrusted source   Stores or sites where apps can be obtained outside of the legitimate trusted sources run by major vendors. *See* trusted source.

UPC (Universal Product Code)   Barcode used to track inventory.

update   *See* patch.

upgrade installation   Installation of Windows on top of an earlier installed version, thus inheriting all previous hardware and software settings.

UPS (uninterruptible power supply)   Device that supplies continuous clean power to a computer system the whole time the computer is on. Protects against power outages and sags (and corresponding data loss).

URL (uniform resource locator)   An address that defines the location of a resource on the Internet. URLs are used most often in conjunction with HTML and the World Wide Web.

USB (Universal Serial Bus) General-purpose serial interconnect for keyboards, printers, joysticks, and many other devices. Enables hot-swapping of devices.

USB host controller Integrated circuit normally built into the chipset that acts as the interface between the system and every USB device that connects to it.

USB hub Device that extends a single USB connection to two or more USB ports, almost always directly from one of the USB ports connected to the root hub.

USB root hub Part of the host controller that makes the physical connection to the USB ports.

USB thumb drive Flash memory device that has a standard USB connector.

USB Type-C (connector) Reversible USB-type cable that supports up to USB 3.1 with a top speed of 10 Gbps. Quickly becoming the *de facto* standard port on Android devices. Thunderbolt-enabled USB Type-C ports can reach top speeds of 40 Gbps. *See also* Thunderbolt.

user account Container that identifies a user to an application, operating system, or network. Includes name, password, user name, groups to which the user belongs, and other information based on the user and the OS being used. Usually defines the rights and roles a user plays on a system.

User Accounts applet Applet in Control Panel that enables you to make changes to local user accounts, and (after Windows 7) gives you access to the Settings charm (or app in Windows 10) when you opt to add a new account.

User Datagram Protocol (UDP) Connectionless protocol used with TCP/IP. *See* TCP *and* TCP/IP.

user interface Visual representation of the computer on the monitor that makes sense to the people using the computer, through which the user can interact with the computer. This can be a graphical user interface (GUI) like Windows 10 or a command-line interface like Windows PowerShell.

user password Credentials assigned to a login account that does not have administrative capabilities.

user profiles Settings that correspond to a specific user account and may follow users regardless of the computers where they log on. These settings enable the user to have customized environment and security settings.

Users Tab in Task Manager that shows other logged-in users and enables you to log off other users if you have the proper permissions. Starting in Windows 8, also includes information on resources consumed by programs the user is running.

Users folder Windows default location for content specific to each user account on a computer. It is divided into several folders such as Documents, Pictures, Music, and Videos.

Users group   List of local users not allowed, among other things, to edit the Registry or access critical system files. They can create groups, but can only manage the groups they create.

USMT (User State Migration Tool)   Advanced application for file and settings transfer of many users. Only usable within a Windows Server Active Directory domain.

Utilities   macOS folder that contains tools for performing services on a Mac beyond what's included in System Preferences, including Activity Monitor and Terminal.

UTP (unshielded twisted pair)   Popular type of cabling for telephone and networks, composed of pairs of wires twisted around each other at specific intervals. The twists serve to reduce interference (also called crosstalk). The more twists, the less interference. Unlike its cousin, STP, UTP cable has no metallic shielding to protect the wires from external interference. 1000BaseT uses UTP, as do many other networking technologies. UTP is available in a variety of grades, called categories, as follows:

Cat 1 UTP   Regular analog phone lines—not used for data communications.
Cat 2 UTP   Supports speeds up to 4 Mbps.
Cat 3 UTP   Supports speeds up to 16 Mbps.
Cat 4 UTP   Supports speeds up to 20 Mbps.
Cat 5 UTP   Supports speeds up to 100 Mbps.
Cat 5e UTP   Supports speeds up to 1000 Mbps.
Cat 6 UTP   Supports speeds up to 10 Gbps.
Cat 6a UTP   Supports speeds up to 10 Gbps.
Cat 7 UTP   Supports 10-Gbps networks at 100-meter segments; shielding for individual wire pairs reduces crosstalk and noise problems. Cat 7 is not an ANSI/TIA standard.

variables   In scripting and programming, named labels for some portion of in-memory data. The actions taken by the script or program may change or replace the data in the variable.

vendor specific   Generically, a proprietary product or technology that doesn't use common, open standards. Vendor-specific products or features may not be completely or even partially compatible with products from other vendors. Also applies to stores that only sell products from one manufacturer, like the Apple store.

verify full system functionality and, if applicable, implement preventive measures   Making sure that a problem has been resolved and will not return. (Step 5 of 6 in the CompTIA troubleshooting methodology.)

vertical alignment (VA)   Display technology used in mid-range LCD panels. VA refers to how the liquid crystal matrix is arranged within the panel.

vertices   Used in the second generation of 3-D rendering; have a defined X, Y, and Z position in a 3-D world.

VESA mount A screen or display bracket that follows the industry standard—established by the Video Electronics Standards Association (VESA)—which specifies size, location, and type of mounting points.

VGA connector A 15-pin, three-row, D-type VGA monitor connector. Goes by many other names, such as D-shell, D-subminiature connector, DB-15, DE15, and HD15. The oldest and least-capable monitor connection type.

vi Linux and macOS command-line tool for editing text files.

video capture Computer jargon for the recording of video information, such as TV shows or movies.

video card Expansion card that works with the CPU to produce the images displayed on your computer's display.

video display *See* monitor.

video editing workstation A computer workstation for editing video. Combines the hardware requirements of graphics and audio editing workstations. Typically makes use of two or more high-quality color-calibrated monitors for both editing and viewing video at native resolution. The high-speed, high-capacity storage required to edit enormous video files is commonly provided by RAID arrays.

viewing angle Width (measured from the center to the side of a display) range within which the image can be fully seen.

virtual application streaming Cloud-based versions of local applications. Virtual application streaming enables access to programs using almost any device that can browse the Internet.

virtual assistant Voice-activated technology that responds to user requests for information. Virtual assistants can be used to search the Internet, make reminders, do calculations, and launch apps.

virtual desktop A traditional desktop OS installed in a VM. A local system could run its own VM containing a virtual desktop, or just connect to a virtual desktop running on a remote server.

virtual machine (VM) A complete environment for a guest operating system to function as though that operating system were installed on its own computer.

virtual machine manager (VMM) *See* hypervisor.

virtual memory Portion of the hard drive set aside by an OS to act like RAM when the system needs more RAM than is installed. A file containing this data is typically called a *page file* in Windows and a *swap file* in UNIX platforms like Linux and macOS.

Virtual Network Computing (VNC) Protocol enabling remote desktop connections. *See* remote desktop.

virtual NIC   Software network interface for a virtual machine. For access to a broader network than the host system is connected to, the virtual NIC needs to be bridged to the host's physical NIC. This enables the virtual NIC to receive an address from DHCP, just like a physical NIC.

virtual printer   Software that presents itself as a printer, but does something else rather than just print the document, such as saving it to a given file type.

virtual reality   *See* VR.

virtual switch   A non-physical version of a hardware switch, made by a hypervisor to network virtual machines.

virtualization workstation   A computer workstation for simultaneous work in multiple virtual machines. Requires enough power for the host OS, plus any virtual machines, including their operating systems and software. In practice, this means a powerful 64-bit CPU with many cores and maximum RAM.

virus   A virus is a program that has two jobs: to replicate and to activate. *Replication* means it copies itself. *Activation* is when a virus damages a system or data. A virus can't self-replicate across networks; it needs human action to spread to other drives. *See also* definition file.

virus shield   Passive monitoring of a computer's activity, checking for viruses only when certain events occur, such as a program execution or file download.

VMM (virtual machine manager)   *See* hypervisor.

VoIP (Voice over Internet Protocol)   Collection of protocols that makes voice calls over a data network possible.

VoIP phone   Device that looks like a regular landline phone but uses VoIP to communicate over a computer network.

volatile   Memory that must have constant electricity to retain data. Alternatively, any programmer six hours before deadline after a nonstop, 48-hour coding session, running on nothing but caffeine and sugar.

volts (V)   Measurement of the pressure of the electrons passing through a wire, or voltage.

volume   *See* partition.

voucher   Means of getting a discount on the CompTIA A+ exams.

VPN (Virtual Private Network)   Encrypted connection over the Internet between a computer or remote network and a private network.

VR (virtual reality)   Computer-generated 3-D video and audio paired with special hardware (usually including a VR headset and sensors to detect movement) to create an immersive simulation a user navigates by moving around in physical space.

VR headset Immersive headset or eyewear that enables its wearer to interact with simulated reality. *See also* VR.

wait state Occurs when the CPU has to wait for RAM to provide code. Also known as *pipeline stall*.

WAN (wide area network) A widespread group of computers connected using long-distance technologies.

WAP (wireless access point) Device that centrally connects wireless network nodes.

wattage (watts or W) Measurement of the amps and volts needed for a particular device to function.

WAV File format for audio faithfully recorded using the pulse code modulation (PCM) format; produces large file sizes.

Web browser Program designed to retrieve, interpret, and display Web pages.

Web server A computer that stores and shares the files that make up Web sites.

webcam PC camera most commonly used for Internet video communication.

Welcome screen Logon screen for Windows. Enables users to select their particular user account by clicking on their user picture.

WEP (Wired Equivalent Privacy) Wireless security protocol that uses a standard 40-bit encryption to scramble data packets. Does not provide complete end-to-end encryption and is vulnerable to attack.

wide area network *See* WAN.

Wi-Fi Common name for the IEEE 802.11 wireless Ethernet standard.

Wi-Fi analyzer Program, app, or device used to scan and analyze the properties of nearby Wi-Fi signals. Can be used to identify dead spots, avoid interference from other networks, or identify security threats such as illegitimate wireless access points (WAPs), and more.

Wi-Fi calling Mobile device feature that enables users to make voice calls over a Wi-Fi network, rather than a cellular network.

Wi-Fi Protected Setup (WPS) A standard included on many WAPs and clients to make secure connections easier to configure. WPS should be turned off, however, because it has a significant security flaw.

wildcard Character—usually an asterisk (*) or question mark (?)—used during a search to represent search criteria. For instance, searching for ***.docx** will return a list of all files with a .docx extension, regardless of the filename. The * is the wildcard in that search. Wildcards can be used in command-line commands to act on more than one file at a time.

Windows 7   Operating system developed by Microsoft. Version of Windows; comes in many different editions for home and office use, but does not have a Server edition. Succeeded by Windows 8/8.1.

Windows 8/8.1   Operating systems developed by Microsoft. Versions of Windows noted for the Metro interface. Used for desktop and portable PCs and for mobile devices. Succeeded by Windows 10.

Windows 10   Operating system developed by Microsoft that powers most desktop and portable computers in use today.

Windows Easy Transfer   Windows 7/8/8.1 method of transferring user data and personalization settings to a new PC. It is not available in Windows 10.

Windows Explorer   Windows 7 utility that enables you to manipulate files and folders stored on the drives in your computer. Rebranded as File Explorer in Windows 8, 8.1, and 10.

Windows Hardware Certification Program   Microsoft's rigorous testing program for hardware manufacturers, which hardware devices must pass before their drivers can be digitally signed.

Windows logo key   Key on a keyboard bearing the Windows logo that traditionally brings up the Start menu, but is also used in some keyboard shortcuts.

Windows Memory Diagnostic   Windows tool that can automatically scan a computer's RAM when a problem is encountered.

Windows PowerShell   Command-line tool included with Windows. Offers a number of powerful scripting tools for automating changes both on local machines and over networks.

Windows Preinstallation Environment (WinPE)   The installation program for Windows.

Windows Recovery Environment   *See* WinRE (Windows Recovery Environment).

Windows Update   Microsoft application used to keep Windows operating systems up to date with the latest patches or enhancements.

Windows Vista   Operating system developed by Microsoft. Version of Windows; came in many different editions for home and office use, but did not have a Server edition. Succeeded by Windows 7. No longer supported.

Windows XP   Version of Windows that replaced both the entire Windows 9*x* line and Windows 2000; does not have a Server version. No longer supported by Microsoft. Succeeded by Windows Vista.

Windows XP Mode   A Windows XP virtual machine that ships with Professional, Enterprise, and Ultimate editions of Windows 7 to enable users to run programs that don't work on Windows 7.

WinRE (Windows Recovery Environment) A special set of tools in the Windows setup that enables you to access troubleshooting and repair features.

wireless locator Small device with signal lights to indicate the presence of Wi-Fi signals.

wireless mesh network (WMN) A hybrid wireless topology in which most nodes connect in a mesh network while also including some wired machines. Nodes act like routers; they forward traffic for other nodes, but without wires.

wireless repeater/extender Device that receives and rebroadcasts a Wi-Fi signal to increase coverage.

work area In a basic structured cabling network, often simply an office or cubicle that potentially contains a PC attached to the network.

workgroup A simple, decentralized network that Windows PCs are configured to use by default.

working directory The current directory used by command-line commands unless they explicitly specify a target file or directory. The prompt usually indicates the working directory.

worm Similar to a virus, except it does not need to attach itself to other programs to replicate. It can replicate on its own through networks, or even hardware like Thunderbolt accessories.

WPA (Wi-Fi Protected Access) Wireless security protocol that uses encryption key integrity-checking/TKIP and EAP and is designed to improve on WEP's weaknesses. Supplanted by WPA2.

WPA2 (Wi-Fi Protected Access 2) Wireless security protocol, also known as IEEE 802.11i. Uses the Advanced Encryption Standard (AES) and replaces WPA.

wrapper *See* container file.

WUXGA Video display mode of 1920 × 1200.

WWW (World Wide Web) System of Internet servers that supports documents formatted in HTML and related protocols. Can be accessed by applications that use HTTP and HTTPS, such as Web browsers.

www.comptia.org CompTIA's Web site.

WXGA Video display mode. Most often of 1366 × 768, though a variety of similar resolutions are also known as WXGA.

x64 Describes 64-bit operating systems and software.

x86 Describes 32-bit operating systems and software.

xcopy   Command-line tool used to copy multiple directories at once, which the copy command could not do.

xD (Extreme Digital) Picture Card   Very small flash media card format.

Xeon   Line of Intel CPUs designed for servers.

XGA (extended graphics array)   Video display mode of 1024 × 768.

XML Paper Specification (XPS) print path   Printing subsystem in Windows. Has enhanced color management and good print layout fidelity.

Yagi   Multi-element antennas that increase signal gain in a specific direction. Resembles older television antennas, but smaller.

zero-day attack   Attack targeting a previously unknown bug or vulnerability that software or hardware developers have had zero days to fix.

ZIF (zero insertion force) socket   Socket for CPUs that enables insertion of a chip without the need to apply pressure. Intel promoted this socket with its overdrive upgrades. The chip drops effortlessly into the socket's holes, and a small lever locks it in.

Zigbee   Completely open wireless networking protocol designed to address home automation challenges.

zombie   Computer infected with malware that has turned it into a botnet member.

Z-Wave   Proprietary wireless networking protocol (with an open API for programmers) designed to address home automation challenges.

INDEX

Numbers

A

G

N

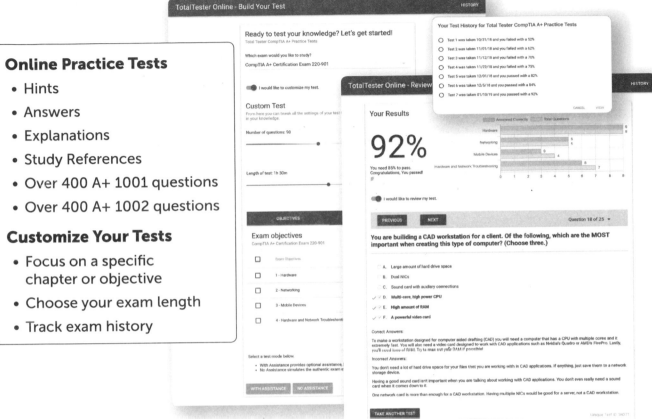
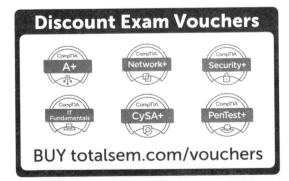